Finance Act Handbook 2016

While every care has been taken to ensure the accuracy of this work, no responsibility for loss or damage occasioned to any person acting or refraining from action as a result of any statement in it can be accepted by the authors, editors or publishers.

Finance Act Handbook 2016

Contributors

Alistair Bambridge, ACA, CTA, EA
Hilary Barclay
Graham Batty, BSc, ACA,
CTA, ATT (Fellow)
Laura Charkin
Richard Cherrett
Fiona Cole
Mike Dalton
Bill Dodwell
Mark Downey
Jason Dunlop
John Endacott
Anne Fairpo, CTA (Fellow) ATT
Matthew Findley
Paul Freeman
Jessica Ganagasegaran
Andrew Goodall
Phil Greatrex, FCA, ATII
Mark Groom
Kendra Hann
Philip Hare
John Hayward
Andrew Hubbard BMus, PhD,
CAT (Fellow), ATT (Fellow)
Zigurds Kronbergs, BSc, ARCS,
MA, ACA, FCCA

Anton Lane, CTA
Greg Limb
John Lindsay, BA, FCA, FTII
Luigi Lungarella, BA (Hons), CTA,
AIIT, ATT, AFTA
Pete Miller, CTA (Fellow)
Rory Mullan
David O'Keeffe, FCA, CTA
Stephen Pevsner
Melanie Reed
Craig Rowlands
Kathryn Sewell
Sara Stewart
Heather Thompson
Helen Thompson, ACA
Alec Ure
Richard Wallington, MA, Barrister
Neil Warren, CTA (Fellow),
ATT, FMAAT
David Whiscombe, FTII
Jeremy White, LLB, FIIT,
CTA, Barrister
Martin Wilson, MA, FCA
Stephen Woodhouse, LLB Partner
Tracey Wright

Members of the LexisNexis Group worldwide

United Kingdom	RELX (UK) Limited trading as LexisNexis, 1–3 Strand, London WC2N 5JR and 9–10 St Andrew Square, Edinburgh EH2 2AF
Australia	Reed International Books Australia Pty Ltd trading as LexisNexis, Chatswood, New South Wales
Austria	LexisNexis Verlag ARD Orac GmbH & Co KG, Vienna
Benelux	LexisNexis Benelux, Amsterdam
Canada	LexisNexis Canada, Markham, Ontario
China	LexisNexis China, Beijing and Shanghai
France	LexisNexis SA, Paris
Germany	LexisNexis GmbH, Dusseldorf
Hong Kong	LexisNexis Hong Kong, Hong Kong
India	LexisNexis India, New Delhi
Italy	Giuffrè Editore, Milan
Japan	LexisNexis Japan, Tokyo
Malaysia	Malayan Law Journal Sdn Bhd, Kuala Lumpur
New Zealand	LexisNexis NZ Ltd, Wellington
Singapore	LexisNexis Singapore, Singapore
South Africa	LexisNexis South Africa, Durban
USA	LexisNexis, Dayton, Ohio

© 2016 RELX (UK) Limited

Published by LexisNexis

This is a Tolley title

A CIP Catalogue record for this book is available from the British Library.

ISBN 9781405799997 (LNB)

Typeset by Letterpart Limited, Caterham on the Hill, Surrey CR3 5XL

Printed and bound by CPI Group (UK) Ltd, Croydon, CR0 4YY

Visit LexisNexis at www.lexisnexis.co.uk

FINANCE ACT 2016
FOREWORD

The much delayed Finance Act finally became law on 15 September 2016. It follows the trend since 2010 of adding another 600 pages or so to the statute book and adds several important concepts to UK tax law. As is now common, the Act contains many provisions which took effect from 1 or 6 April 2016.

Perhaps the most important change for individual taxpayers is the adoption from April 2016 of the personal savings allowance – £1,000 for basic rate taxpayers and £500 for higher rate taxpayers. The mechanics of the allowance are complex, especially when the nil rate savings band and the dividend allowance are added in. In practice most complexity arises for those with income close to the top of the basic rate or higher rate bands.

For those on average incomes, the savings allowance may give a modest tax cut. Pensioners are the most obvious group to benefit – but they could face the challenge of having to notify HMRC of their savings income to ensure that tax is collected on income exceeding the allowance.

The Act includes a handy table for Scottish (and, in future, Welsh) taxpayers, which makes it clear how their income is taxed: the UK rates (and allowances) continue to apply to dividends and savings income.

The dividend allowance is part of a package where dividends in excess of the allowance are liable to higher tax rates, which vary according to the income band. The government's objective is to narrow the difference between self-employed individuals and those who provide their services through the medium of a company. The effect is felt by a wider group, with higher/additional rate taxpayers with dividends of no more than £5,000 receiving a tax cut.

The dividend tax changes also bring additional anti-avoidance, intended to minimise the opportunity to convert income into capital. There is a new TAAR which counters "phoenixism" – the opportunity for an individual to wind up one company and receiving capital payments, whilst starting a new one conducting the same activity. The TAAR converts capital to income where there is a main purpose of avoiding tax. HMRC have provided some guidance, but clearances won't be considered.

Schedule 2 brings new rules for income from sporting testimonials. Testimonials were originally intended as a type of retirement payment for amateur players but are viewed as less relevant in today's professional world. Fortunately a limited income tax exemption of up to £100,000 is retained for income received from 6 April 2017, which may benefit those in less well-paid sports/levels.

The Act shows different approaches to two types of investment. Those investing new money in unquoted trading companies may benefit from an effective capital gains tax rate of 10% on gains of up to £10 million, realised after April 2017. However, those investing in "buy-to-let" residential property face progressive restrictions on the deduction of finance costs. The government's intention is that finance costs should be deductible at basic rate only, with the measure phased in over three years from 2017. The mechanism could push some investors into higher or additional tax rates, though, and some may find that tax charges exceed their economic return. The 3% stamp duty land tax surcharge for additional properties also makes an unwelcome appearance.

The UK is the first country to implement Action 2 of the G20/OECD's Base Erosion and Profit Shifting (BEPS) project. This action is intended to counter tax advantages from "hybrid mismatches" where differing treatment of instruments or entities in two countries could lead to tax deductions without equivalent taxable income, or two deductions for the same economic cost. The UK measures take effect from 1 January 2017 by removing tax relief for the tax deduction. The measure applies to branches as well as to companies; it is thought that late amendments at the report stage should protect trading branches. The UK's measure goes considerably further than the anti-hybrid rules in the EU's Anti-Tax Avoidance Directive and is thought to raise hundreds of millions of pounds.

A measure of broader effect is the new apprenticeship levy which applies from April 2017 to businesses with pay bills in excess of £3 million. There is considerable complexity is applying the measure to some groups. This is expected to bring in almost £3 billion annually although those which train apprentices may benefit from grants.

I would like to congratulate the publishers in preparing this book so quickly and the authors of the commentary in the speed of their analysis, which I hope will aid those charged with considering the many changes introduced by this Act.

Bill Dodwell
Deloitte LLP
September 2016

CONTENTS

Page

Contents

Contents

RELEVANT DATES AND ABBREVIATIONS

Budget Statement	16 March 2016
Finance Bill	24 March 2016
Royal Assent	15 September 2016

AIA	=	annual investment allowance
AIF	=	alternative investment fund
ALDA 1979	=	Alcoholic Liquor Duties Act 1979
APN	=	accelerated payment notice
ATED	=	annual tax on enveloped dwellings
ATT	=	Association of Taxation Technicians
BCE	=	benefit crystallisation event
BEPS	=	Base Erosion and Profit Shifting
BGDA 1981	=	Betting and Gaming Duties Act 1981
BPRA	=	business premises renovation allowances
CA 2006	=	Companies Act 2006
CAA 2001	=	Capital Allowances Act 2001
CBCR	=	country-by-country reporting
CEMA 1979	=	Customs and Excise Management Act 1979
CFC	=	controlled foreign companies
CGT	=	capital gains tax
Ch	=	Chapter (of a part of an Act)
CHP	=	combined heat and power
CIOT	=	Chartered Institute of Taxation
CITR	=	Community Investment Tax Relief
CPI	=	Consumer Prices Index
CPS	=	carbon price support
CRCA 2005	=	Commissioners for Revenue and Customs Act 2005
CRS	=	Common Reporting Standard
CSOP	=	company share option plan
CTA 2009	=	Corporation Tax Act 2009
CTA 2010	=	Corporation Tax Act 2010
DECC	=	Department of Energy & Climate Change
DOTAS	=	disclosure of tax avoidance schemes
DPT	=	diverted profits tax
ECA	–	enhanced capital allowances
ECJ	–	European Court of Justice
EEA	=	European Economic Area
EES	=	exploration expenditure supplement
EIS	=	Enterprise Investment Scheme
EMI	=	enterprise management incentive
ER	=	entrepreneurs' relief
EU	=	European Union
EU ETS	=	EU Emissions Trading Scheme
FA	=	Finance Act
FATCA	=	US Foreign Account Tax Compliance Act
FCA	=	Financial Conduct Authority
FISMA 2000	=	Financial Services and Markets Act 2000
FPE	=	foreign permanent establishment
FSMA 2000	=	Financial Services and Markets Act 2000
FTT	=	First-tier Tribunal
FWMA 2010	=	Flood and Water Management Act 2010
FYAs	=	first-year allowances
GAAP	=	generally accepted accounting practice
GAAR	=	general anti-abuse rule
GADs	=	Gift Aid Declarations
GBER	=	General Block Exemption Regulation
HMRC	=	Her Majesty's Revenue and Customs

ICTA 1988	=	Income and Corporation Taxes Act 1988
IFS	=	Institute for Fiscal Studies
IHT	=	inheritance tax
IHTA 1984	=	Inheritance Tax Act 1984
IPT	=	insurance premium tax
ITA 2007	=	Income Tax Act 2007
ITEPA 2003	=	Income Tax (Earnings and Pensions) Act 2003
ITTOIA 2005	=	Income Tax (Trading and Other Income) Act 2005
LAP	=	longer applicable period
LLPs	=	limited liability partnerships
LOI	=	loss on ignition
NRCGT	=	non-resident capital gains tax
OECD	=	Organisation for Economic Co-operation and Development
OEIC	=	open-ended investment company
OTA 1975	=	Oil Taxation Act 1975
OTA 1983	=	Oil Taxation Act 1983
OTS	=	Office of Tax Simplification
OWR	=	overseas workday relief
PA 2014	=	Pensions Act 2014
para	=	paragraph (of a Schedule to an Act)
PAYE	=	pay as you earn
PCC	=	protected cell company
PCLS	=	pension commencement lump sum
PCTA 1968	=	Provisional Collection of Taxes Act 1968
PIP	=	personal independence payment
PPN	=	partner payment notice
PPR	=	principal private residence
PRA	=	Prudential Regulation Authority
PRT	=	petroleum revenue tax
QROPS	=	qualifying recognised overseas pension scheme
R&D	=	research and development
reg	=	regulation (of an SI)
REIT	=	real estate investment trust
RFES	=	ring fence expenditure supplement
RHIs	=	Renewable Heat Incentives
RNUKS	=	relevant non-UK scheme
ROCs	=	Renewable Obligations Certificates
RPI	=	Retail Prices Index
RRQP	=	restricted relief qualifying policy
RTI	=	Real Time Information
s	=	section (of an Act)
SAP	=	shorter applicable period
SAYE	=	save as you earn
Sch	=	Schedule (to an Act)
SDI	=	single-dwelling interest
SDLT	=	stamp duty land tax
SDRT	=	stamp duty reserve tax
SEIS	=	seed enterprise investment scheme
SI	=	Statutory Instrument (since 1948)
SIP	=	share incentive plan
SITR	=	social investment tax relief
ss	=	sections (of an Act)
SSCBA 1992	=	Social Security Contributions and Benefits Act 1992
SSCB(NI)A 1992	=	Social Security Contributions and Benefits (Northern Ireland) Act 1992
STC	=	Simon's Tax Cases
sub-para	=	sub-paragraph
sub-s	=	subsection
SWTI	=	Simon's Weekly Tax Intelligence
TAAR	=	targeted anti-avoidance rule

TCGA 1992	=	Taxation of Chargeable Gains Act 1992
TIOPA 2010	=	Taxation (International and Other Provisions) Act 2010
TMA 1970	=	Taxes Management Act 1970
TPA 2014	=	Taxation of Pensions Act 2014
TPDA 1979	=	Tobacco Products Duty Act 1979
UCITS	=	undertaking for collective investment in transferable securities
UK	=	United Kingdom
US GAAP	=	US generally accepted accounting practice
UT	=	Upper Tribunal
VATA 1994	=	Value Added Tax Act 1994
VCT	=	Venture Capital Trust
VED	=	vehicle excise duty
VERA 1994	=	Vehicle Excise and Registration Act 1994

ABOUT THE AUTHORS

Alistair Bambridge, ACA, CTA, EA
Alistair Bambridge is the founder and an active partner of Bambridge Accountants, an award winning firm specialising in the creative industries and US expats. He is also the author of the annual US Tax Return Guide for Expats.

Alistair Bambridge has written the commentary for FA 2016 ss 54, 55, 165 and Schs 8 and 22.

Hilary Barclay
Hilary Barclay is Senior Counsel in the Tax group at Macfarlanes. She advises on a broad range of corporate tax matters including M&A, corporate reorganisations, group tax advice, transfer pricing and financing transactions. Hilary is a member of the International Fiscal Association and the City of London Law Society's Revenue Law Committee.

Hilary Barclay has written the commentary for FA 2016 s 180, 181, 182 and Sch 24.

Graham Batty, BSc, ACA, CTA, ATT (Fellow)
Graham Batty is an associate director at RSM where he specialises in advising charities and other not for profit organisations on direct tax matters. Graham has been a member of the HMRC Charity Tax Forum, a group of charity sector representatives, HMRC and Treasury senior staff that assists the Government with the practical development and application of charity tax policy since shortly after its inception. He is Deputy President of the Association of Taxation Technicians and chairman of the Chartered Institute of Taxation's charity tax working group.

Graham Batty has written the commentary for FA 2016 ss 173.

Laura Charkin
Laura Charkin is a partner in the tax department of King & Wood Mallesons' London office. She specialises in fund taxation and is an integral member of the firm's market leading Private Funds team, with a wide experience of structuring private equity, venture capital, debt, real estate and infrastructure funds and funds of funds. She also advises on executive incentivisation arrangements, investment structures, and the structuring of investment management platforms. Laura is a member of the EVCA International Tax & Tax Reporting Group and also the AIMA working groups on FATCA and carried interest taxation. She regularly gives internal and external seminars on fund taxation and FATCA. Laura is a chartered tax adviser and member of the Chartered Institute of Taxation.

Laura Charkin, Jessica Ganagasegaran and Stephen Pevsner have written the commentary for FA 2016 ss 36, 37, 38 and 89.

Richard Cherrett
Richard Cherrett is a Senior Manager in Deloitte's International Markets Group, and a member of the ICAEW. Richard advises large corporates principally on cross-border and financial instrument-related tax issues.

Richard Cherrett has written the commentary for FA 2016 Sch 10.

Fiona Cole

Fiona Cole is a Senior Manager within KPMG's Stamp Taxes Group. Fiona who previous worked at HMRC Stamp Office, has over 20 years of stamp taxes experience. She advises an extensive range of clients on all aspects of stamp taxes with particular focus on the financial services sector.

Fiona Cole has written the commentary for FA 2016 s 133 and Sch 16.

Mike Dalton

Mike Dalton is Director and Head of Stamp Taxes at Grant Thornton UK LLP. Mike is a Chartered Accountant and Chartered Tax Adviser and an active member of the Stamp Taxes Practitioners' Group. He is a member of Grant Thornton's Real Estate team and provides a wide range of clients with both stamp taxes and property tax advice.

Mike Dalton and Jason Dunlop have co-authored the commentary for FA 2016 ss 127–132.

Bill Dodwell

Bill Dodwell is Head of Tax Policy at Deloitte UK. He is responsible for consultations with HM Treasury, HMRC, the OECD and the EU.

Bill is 2016–17 President of the Chartered Institute of Taxation and he chaired the CIOT's Technical Committee from 2010–16. Bill regularly speaks to the UK media on taxation matters and tweets as @ukbudget.

Bill Dodwell has written the Foreword to the book.

Mark Downey

Mark Downey has written the commentary for FA 2016 ss 67 and 183.

Jason Dunlop

Jason Dunlop is a Tax Manager in the Real Estate Practice at Grant Thornton UK LLP and is a dedicated member of Grant Thornton's Stamp Taxes team. Jason is a Chartered Tax Adviser and has extensive experience advising corporate and non-corporate clients (UK and non-UK) on their real estate tax affairs.

Jason Dunlop and Mike Dalton have co-authored the commentary for FA 2016 ss 127–132.

John Endacott

John Endacott is Head of the Tax at PKF Francis Clark with particular responsibility for family businesses and professional partnerships, property and international tax services. He has considerable expertise in business structuring advice and long term planning with a particular focus on capital gains tax (entrepreneurs' relief, Enterprise Investment Scheme and investor's relief) and inheritance tax business property relief and agricultural property relief.

John Endacott has written the commentary for FA 2016 ss 83 and 90–92.

Anne Fairpo, CTA (Fellow) ATT

Anne Fairpo is a barrister who has substantial and diverse experience of tax matters gained both within law and accounting practices. Anne was called to the bar in 2009 after 15 years as a solicitor; her experience and expertise covers UK and international corporate tax planning and disputes, acting for a range of clients from small owner-managed businesses to listed multinationals, with a particular interest on technology-focussed businesses.

Anne Fairpo has written the commentary for FA 2016 40, 42 and 43.

Matthew Findley

Matthew Findley is an Employee Benefits and Executive Compensation partner based in the London office of Norton Rose Fulbright. He advises companies in relation to the design, implementation and operation of share plans and employee incentive arrangements both in the UK and internationally.

Matthew's experience extends to both executive plans and all-employee arrangements as well as dealing with employee benefits in the context of mergers and acquisitions, IPOs and demergers. He also has considerable experience relating to the corporate governance and investor relations issues associated with executive incentives and remuneration planning generally.

Matthew is recommended in both Chambers and Partners and Legal 500 and has been described as "an expert on global share plans", with clients remarking that he "is very knowledgeable and always provides advice that is considered, as opposed to off-the-cuff". He is also recognised for his responsive and comprehensive client service. Matthew has also been quoted in both UK Houses of Parliament on employee share ownership and is regularly quoted in both the international and trade press on employee incentive matters.

Matthew sits on the Tax Committee of the Share Plan Lawyers Group and the UK and Channel Islands Chapter Committee of the Global Equity Organisation. In 2015, Matthew was named in the Tax Journal's "40 under 40" guide to the 40 leading tax professionals based in the UK under the age of 40, who have demonstrated outstanding achievement in their careers to date.

Matthew Findley has written the commentary for FA 2016 s 16 and Sch 3.

Paul Freeman

Paul Freeman is a Senior Manager within KPMG's Banking Tax team, where he provides advice to banking groups on a range of corporate and international tax issues. In addition to those areas of the tax code specific to the banking sector, Paul particularly specialises in the taxation of financial instruments.

Paul is a member of both the ICAEW (winning the Institute's Spicer and Pegler Prize in his professional examinations) and the Chartered Institute of Taxation.

Paul Freeman has written the commentary for FA 2016 ss 56 and 57.

Jessica Ganagasegaran

Jessica Ganagasegaran is an associate in King & Wood Mallesons' UK tax group. She advises on a broad range of corporate and individual tax matters and her experience includes advising on UK and international M&A transactions, real estate transactions, including advising on property structures, and also various issues relating to employment taxation, including employee incentive schemes. Jessica is a chartered tax adviser.

Jessica Ganagasegaran, Laura Charkin and Stephen Pevsner have written the commentary for FA 2016 ss 36, 37, 38 and 89.

Andrew Goodall

Andrew Goodall is a freelance tax writer providing news, analysis and technical updates on UK taxes. He is a regular contributor to Tax Analysts. His work has been published by several LexisNexis titles including Tolley's Tax Digest, Tolley's Tax Guide, Simon's Taxes, Tax Adviser, Taxation and Tax Journal. Other publishers include ACCA and Civil Service World. Andrew is a non-practising member of the Chartered Institute of Taxation.

Andrew Goodall has written the commentary for FA 2016 ss 1–6, 10, 12, 13, 17, 24, 25, 27, 28, 39, 41, 167–169, 178, 184–189 and Schs 1, 2, 6, 23 and 25.

Phil Greatrex, FCA, ATII

Phil Greatrex qualified as a chartered accountant with a Big 4 practice in 1980 but has been a senior partner in his own practice, CW Energy, since 1990, providing advice to a wide range of clients, mainly in the oil and gas sector.

Phil is the consulting editor for the Oil and Gas Tax section of Halsbury's Laws of England. He has been a member and secretary of the Brindex tax committee since the late 1980s and has also been an active member of the UKOITC industry tax committee for a number of years. In these capacities he has extensive experience of dealing with Treasury and HMRC personnel on lobbying for tax changes.

Phil Greatrex has written the commentary for FA 2016 ss 58–63 and 140.

Mark Groom

Mark Groom is an employment tax partner in Deloitte's Compensation and Benefits group. He is also Vice Chairman of the Employment Taxes sub-committee of the Chartered Institute of Taxation. Mark specialises in pay and incentives, employment status and intermediaries, and benefits and expenses consulting and compliance including KYC, SAO, and HMRC investigations. He is a regular speaker at seminars and contributor to articles on employment tax matters and to HMRC consultations.

Mark Groom has written the commentary for FA 2016 ss 98–121.

Kendra Hann

Kendra Hann is the UK indirect tax leader responsible for managing Deloitte's UK indirect tax practice. This includes VAT, customs and excise duties, IPT and environmental taxes. She has worked in indirect tax since 1989 in the tax authority, business and the profession. Kendra specialises in advising multinational clients on their global indirect tax issues.

Kendra is a member of the Chartered Institute of Taxation and also represents Deloitte on a number of HM Treasury and HM Revenue & Customs working parties.

Kendra Hann has written the commentary for FA 2016 144–148 and 152–155.

Philip Hare

Philip Hare is a chartered accountant and chartered tax adviser. He has specialised in the venture capital tax reliefs (Venture Capital Trusts, Enterprise Investment Scheme and Seed Enterprise Investment Scheme) since their inception. He is the founder of Philip Hare & Associates, which advises companies, investment fund managers and investors on compliance with those schemes. Philip and his team have been awarded Best EIS Tax Advisor by the EIS Association nine times since 2006, including for 2015.

Philip Hare has written the commentary for FA 2016 ss 28–31.

John Hayward

John Hayward is a part-time self-employed pensions author. He has written for Pensions World and Tax Journal and is a member of the latter's Editorial Board. He has contributed to Butterworth's Tax Planning Service, Robin Ellison's Pensions Law and Practice, Simon's Taxes, Tolley's Finance and Law for the Older Client, Finance Act Handbook 2004 to 2015 and the ICAEW's TAXline. His specialist topics include small self-administered pension schemes and taxation aspects of all pension schemes.

John Hayward has written the commentary for FA 2016 ss 19–23 and Sch 5.

Andrew Hubbard BMus, PhD, CAT (Fellow), ATT (Fellow)

Andrew Hubbard is the editor-in-chief of Taxation magazine and consultant editor of Tolley's Tax Guide. He is a long-term contributor to Tolley's Tax Planning and Finance Act Handbook. In 2006 he won the tax writer of the year award at the Taxation Awards and is a former president of both the Chartered Institute of Taxation and the Association of Taxation Technicians. He is a partner in the Nottingham office of RSM specialising in tax dispute resolution and the taxation of entrepreneurial businesses. Andre originally trained as a musician before joining the Inland Revenue as an Inspector of Taxes.

Andrew Hubbard has written the commentary for FA 2016 ss 26, 32, 45, 46, 76–82, 176 and 177.

Zigurds Kronbergs, BSc, ARCS, MA, ACA, FCCA

Zigurds Kronbergs is an experienced writer on UK, European and international tax, and is a regular contributor to several publications, including Finance Act Handbook. A specialist in tax for over 30 years, he is also European Tax Coordinator for Moore Stephens Europe Ltd and the correspondent on Latvia for the IBFD.

Zigurds Kronbergs has written the Introduction to FA 2016.

Anton Lane, CTA

Anton Lane established Edge Tax LLP following a career at the Big 4 specialising in tax investigations. Edge Tax LLP is a bespoke tax practice specialising in the disclosure of tax irregularities to HMRC and tax risk management. Anton is the author of two Tolley's Tax Digests: Practicalities of Tax Investigations and Practical guidance: Anti avoidance legislation, offshore structures and the offshore disclosure facility. Anton is also responsible for producing many articles on the area of tax disclosures and anti-avoidance legislation.

Anton Lane has written the commentary for FA 2016 ss 159, 160, 162, 164, 166, 170–172 and Sch 18.

Greg Limb

Greg Limb is head of private client tax at KPMG and has over 25 years of practical tax experience, specialising in advising individuals, Family Offices (both UK and International), entrepreneurs, shareholders and Private Equity executives on their personal tax issues.

Greg Limb has written the commentary for FA 2016 s 87 and Sch 14.

John Lindsay, BA, FCA, FTII

John Lindsay is a consultant in the tax department of Linklaters LLP. He advises on all corporate taxes with a focus on the taxation of capital markets and securitisation transactions. John is a contributor to Simon's Taxes, Simon's Tax Planning and Tolley's Tax Planning and is also a co-author of the Taxation of Companies and Company Reconstructions (Sweet & Maxwell, 2009). He is a member of both the CIOT Technical Committee and the CIOT Corporate Tax Sub-committee and is also a member of a number of HMRC working groups.

John Lindsay has written the commentary for FA 2016 ss 50, 51, 65, 75 and Sch 7.

Luigi Lungarella, BA (Hons), CTA, AIIT, ATT, AFTA

Luigi Lungarella is a graduate in Economics, a Chartered Tax Adviser, a UK Taxation Technician and an Associate of the Federation of Tax Advisers. Luigi is an indirect tax director for PKF Littlejohn in Canary Wharf, and prior to that he was an indirect tax consultant for Arthur Andersen, KPMG and Dawnay Day.

Luigi Lungarella has written the commentary for FA 2016 ss 141, 142, 143 and 149.

Pete Miller, CTA (Fellow)

Pete Miller is Partner of The Miller Partnership and speaks and writes regularly on tax issues. Pete has worked in tax for over 28 years, starting as an Inspector of Taxes in 1988, before posts in Policy Division and Technical Division. He then worked for eleven years in Big 4 firms.

Pete formed The Miller Partnership in April 2011 to offer expert advice to other advisers on all business tax issues. His specialist areas include transactions in securities rules, reorganisations, reconstructions, HMRC clearances, disguised remuneration, Patent Box relief and taxation of intangible assets.

Pete is a member of the Editorial Boards of Taxation, Tax Journal and Simon's Taxes and a Consulting Editor to TolleyGuidance, and is General Editor of Whiteman & Sherry on Capital Gains Tax. He is co-author of Taxation of Company Reorganisations (4th edition, Bloomsbury Professional, June 2012) and author of Tolley's Tax Digests on Disguised Remuneration, the Substantial Shareholdings Exemption, the Patent Box and Transactions in Securities.

Pete Miller has written the commentary for FA 2016 ss 33–35, 52, 53, 64, 84–86, 156–158, Schs 9 and 13.

Rory Mullan

Rory Mullan is a barrister and chartered tax adviser. He was called to the Bar in 2000 and practices from Old Square Tax Chambers, Lincoln's Inn where he advises individuals, trusts and companies on a wide range of taxation matters. Rory also represents taxpayers in disputes before the Tax Tribunals and Courts. He has written extensively on tax related matters.

Rory Mullan has written the commentary for FA 2016 s 161.

David O'Keeffe, FCA, CTA

David O'Keeffe is an independent specialist adviser on the taxation of innovation, advising companies and other advisers on R&D tax relief, Patent Box and Intangible Asset taxation.

David has been involved with the UK's R&D tax relief regimes since the initial consultations on the introduction of the SME relief. In that time, he has developed an enviable level of knowledge of R&D tax relief both from a technical and a practical perspective. David established KPMG's specialist R&D tax relief team and was a founder member of KPMG International's Global R&D Tax Incentives Group, and he was a member of the Steering Group with direct responsibility for the EMEA region. Formerly a Tax Partner with KPMG LLP (UK), he retired in 2011 to establish Aiglon Consulting.

David O'Keeffe has written the commentary for FA 2016 ss 47 and 48.

Stephen Pevsner

Stephen Pevsner is a partner in King & Wood Mallesons' UK tax group. His practice covers the broad range of corporate and individual tax, with particular emphasis on UK and international M&A transactions, private fund formation, corporate reorganisations, structured finance, investment funds and new business set-ups. His work includes private fund and M&A structuring, fund executive and management incentive arrangements, advising on the implications for structures and documentation for developments such as FATCA and AIFMD, acting on new business set-ups – in particular, the establishment of investment management and advisory businesses, public equity transactions and advising on the full range of finance and structured finance transactions for private and public companies.

Stephen Pevsner, Laura Charkin and Jessica Ganagasegara have written the commentary for FA 2016 ss 36–39 and 89.

Melanie Reed

Melanie Reed is a partner and the head of corporate tax at RSM and is a Chartered Tax Advisor. She specialises in the provision of compliance and advisory services to the large corporate market. She has considerable experience in quarterly reporting, interim reporting and group reporting to overseas parents. Melanie has worked with many organisations on advisory projects, ranging from complex property acquisitions and disposals to tax efficient structuring (both within the UK and internationally).

Melanie Reed has written the commentary for FA 2016 s 68.

Craig Rowlands

Craig Rowlands is a tax senior manager at KPMG, specialising in advising individuals on transactions and shareholder tax issues.

Craig Rowlands has written the commentary for FA 2016 s 87 and Sch 14.

Kathryn Sewell

Kathryn Sewell is a Senior Manager in Deloitte UK's Energy and Resource indirect tax team. She has advised on indirect taxes in the UK and Australia for over eight years and specialises in advising power and utility companies on UK VAT, CCL and other indirect taxes. She regularly liaises with HMRC Policy and industry bodies on indirect taxes including in recent years in relation to The Energy Market Reform, contracts for difference and the domestic reverse charge for gas and power.

Kathryn Sewell has written the commentary for FA 2016 ss 144–148 and 152–155.

Sara Stewart

Sara Stewart is counsel at Vinson & Elkins RLLP. Sara's practice covers all direct taxes, stamp duties and value added tax, with a strong focus on corporate tax. She has extensive experience of corporate transactions.

Sara Stewart has written the commentary for FA 2016 ss 137–139.

Heather Thompson

Heather Thompson is a lawyer who has worked in tax based legal practice for over 25 years. She is qualified to practice law in England and Wales, and Scotland.

Heather Thompson has written the commentary for FA 2016 ss 134–136.

Helen Thompson, ACA

Helen Thompson is a Partner in Deloitte UK's indirect tax practice, specialising in environmental taxes and VAT, and leads Deloitte UK's Energy and Resources indirect tax group. She chaired the Chartered Institute of Taxation's Environmental Taxes Working Group from 2007 to 2010. Helen has extensive experience in advising businesses on their environmental tax obligations and liabilities and has provided specialist environmental due diligence services in relation to major acquisitions.

Helen Thompson has written the commentary for FA 2016 ss 144–148 and 152–155.

Alec Ure

Alec Ure is the principal associate of Alec Ure & Associates, Pensions and Taxation Specialists. He has more than 40 years of pensions experience. He became a self-employed consultant and author in 2003 and is a leading writer of books and articles on pensions. He had previously worked for Bacon & Woodrow, where he was senior consultant in their legal department, and Gissings' Technical Team. Alec advises on many aspects of pensions and taxation issues, and provides UK and offshore pension documentation. Previously, he worked for HMRC, 15 years being spent in the Pension Schemes Office (now HMRC PSS) in a senior role, involving tax and pension enquiries and dedicated work on documentation and pension provision and planning.

Alec Ure has written the commentary for FA 2016 s 19 and Sch 4.

Richard Wallington, MA, Barrister

Richard Wallington is an editor of Williams on Wills and Mellows' Taxation for Executors and Trustees.

Richard Wallington has written the commentary for FA 2016 ss 93–97.

Neil Warren, CTA (Fellow), ATT, FMAAT
Neil Warren is an independent VAT consultant and author and a past winner of the Taxation Awards Tax Writer of the Year. He writes extensively on VAT for most of the leading tax publications in the UK. He also acts as a technical expert on VAT for a number of publishers and is a member of the Association of Taxation Technicians' VAT Technical Committee. He worked for Customs and Excise for 13 years until 1997.

Neil Warren has written the commentary for FA 2016 ss 122–126.

David Whiscombe, FTII
David Whiscombe has worked in tax since 1976 when he joined the former Inland Revenue department as a Direct Entrant Inspector. Since 1991 he has headed the tax practice at BKL Chartered Accountants, including the specialist tax consultancy division BKL Tax. A non-practising barrister, he writes and speaks widely on tax.

David Whiscombe has written the commentary for FA 2016 ss 71–74.

Jeremy White, LLB, FIIT, CTA, Barrister
Jeremy White is a barrister practising in Pump Court Tax Chambers at 16 Bedford Row, London specialising in tax advice and advocacy. He is the consultant editor of Tolley's Customs and Excise Duties Handbook and Halsbury's Laws of England Customs and Excise volumes.

Jeremy White has written the commentary for FA 2016 ss 150, 151, 174, 175 and 179.

Martin Wilson, MA, FCA
Martin Wilson is Chairman of the Capital Allowances Partnership Limited, specialists in all aspects of capital allowances and related reliefs. He is the author of numerous published works on the subject, including Bloomsbury's Capital Allowances: Transactions & Planning, and the capital allowances content of Lexis®PSL, Tolley's Tax Guidance, Tolley's Tax Planning and Simon's Tax Planning.

Martin Wilson has written the commentary for FA 2016 ss 69 and 70.

Stephen Woodhouse, LLB Partner
Stephen Woodhouse is a partner in Pett, Franklin having previously been a partner at Deloitte. He has been an employment tax specialist with a particular focus on remuneration design and structuring for over 25 years. During that time he has been a regular contributor to the tax press across a range of subjects and advised clients across a range of sectors on tax structuring.

Stephen Woodhouse has written the commentary for FA 2016 s 88.

Tracey Wright
Tracey Wright is a partner in the tax team at Osborne Clarke LLP. She undertakes a full range of transactional and advisory tax work. She also has many years' experience of advising on employment tax matters and has a particular focus on the tax treatment of contingent workers.

Tracey Wright has written the commentary for FA 2016 ss 7–11, 14, 15 and 18.

FINANCE ACT 2016

INTRODUCTION

This Finance Act, the second of the new Parliament, which is the first since 1997 in which the Conservative Party has had an overall majority, shows no sign of breaking the precedent of the modern era in being another gigantesque production of 658 pages (including the table of contents), containing 191 sections and 25 Schedules, one of the longest ever. The set of measures taking up by far the greatest proportion of the Act in terms of pages is Pt 10 on "Tax Evasion and Avoidance" which occupies 133 pages (20.2%). If one adds to that the BEPS-inspired s 66 and Sch 10 ("Hybrid and Other Mismatches"), which itself alone takes up 70 pages and the further legislation on carried interest and disguised management fees (23 pages), one can see the way the wind is blowing. How far all these pages will stifle the behaviour they are aimed at is another matter.

PART 1
INCOME TAX

Charge and principal rates etc

Section 1 reimposes income tax for the year 2016/17 and sets the basic, higher and additional rates at the same levels as in 2015/16. They are 20% (the basic rate), 40% (the higher rate) and 45% (the additional rate). Whereas no amendment is made to the starting rate for savings under ITA 2007 s 7, amendments are made to the dividend rates (see under s 5) and a new savings nil-rate is introduced (see under s 4).

The basic, higher and additional rates charged by this section apply in England, Wales and Northern Ireland, but do not apply in Scotland. However, by resolution of the Scottish Parliament, the Scottish rate of income tax is 10p in the £, so that the basic, higher and additional rates applicable to Scottish taxpayers are also 20%, 40% and 45% in 2016/17.

With effect from a date yet to be appointed, these rates will cease to apply automatically in Wales also, by virtue of [prospective] ITA 2007 s 6B.

Section 2 provides that the basic-rate limit for 2017/18 shall be £33,500, instead of £32,400 as hitherto provided by F(No 2)A 2015 s 6(b), which amends FA 2015 s 4(1)(b), which in turn amends ITA 2007 s 10(5). The basic-rate limit for 2016/17 remains £32,000.

Section 3 increases the amount of the personal allowance for the year 2017/18. As provided by F(No 2)A 2015 s 5(b), which amends FA 2015 s 5(1)(b), which in turn amends ITA 2007 s 35, the personal allowance in that year was to be £11,200. This amount is now set at £11,500. The personal allowance for 2016/17, as provided by F(No 2)A 2015 s 5(a), which amends FA 2015 s 5(1)(a), which in turn amends ITA 2007 s 35, remains at £11,000.

Rate structure

Section 4 introduces the savings allowance and the savings nil-rate for savings income, with effect from 2016/17, and makes consequential amendments. Subsection (3) amends ITA 2007 s 7 to set a savings nil-rate, to be 0%, for savings income. Subsection (5) inserts new ITA 2007 ss 12A and 12B, which provide how and when the savings nil-rate is to apply to savings income.

New ITA 2007 s 12A applies in respect of an individual where two conditions are fulfilled. The first is that the individual has Step 3 income greater than the starting-rate limit for savings. That limit is £5,000 in 2016/17 (ITA 2007 s 12(3), as amended by FA 2014 s 3(2)). The second is that, when the individual's Step 3 income is divided into the part that is no more than the starting-rate limit (that being the lowest part of the individual's income) and the remainder, some of that remainder consists of savings income. The effect is that the savings nil-rate may only apply where the individual's savings income exceeds the starting-rate limit, since the starting rate for savings has priority over the savings nil-rate.

Where this is so, the new savings nil-rate applies to so much of that income as exceeds the starting-rate limit for savings and consists of savings income. If this excess is equal to or less than the amount of the individual's savings allowance (as determined in new ITA 2007 s 12B), the whole of the excess is chargeable at the savings nil-rate. If the excess is greater than the savings allowance (suppose it is £A), the savings nil-rate applies to the lowest £A of the excess and the highest applicable other rate(s) to the rest.

New ITA 2007 s 12B determines the amount of an individual's savings allowance. If the individual has any income that is "additional-rate income", the savings allowance is nil. If the individual has any income that is "higher-rate income" but no additional-rate income, the savings allowance is £500. If the individual has neither additional-rate income nor higher-rate income, the savings allowance is £1,000.

Additional-rate income is any income that is chargeable at the additional rate of income tax or at the dividend additional rate, but also includes (a) income that would have been charged at the additional rate but for application of the savings nil-rate; and (b) income that would have been charged at the dividend additional rate but for application of the dividend nil-rate, as well as certain income of Scottish and (from 2017–18) of Welsh taxpayers.

Similarly, higher-rate income is any income that is chargeable at the higher rate of income tax or the dividend upper rate, but also includes (a) income that would have been charged at the higher rate but for application of the savings nil-rate; and (b) income that would have been charged at the dividend upper rate but for application of the dividend nil-rate, as well as certain income of Scottish and (from 2017–18) of Welsh taxpayers.

Section 5 amends the tax treatment of dividend income by abolishing the dividend tax credit, replacing it by a "dividend nil-rate" on as much as £5,000 of an individual's dividend income, and amends the dividend ordinary rate, the dividend additional rate and the dividend trust rate. With effect from 2016/17, there is a new dividend nil-rate of 0%, the dividend ordinary rate is reduced from 10% to 7.5% and the dividend additional rate is increased from 37.5% to 38.1%, as is the dividend trust rate. The dividend upper rate remains 32.5%.

Subsection (5) inserts new ITA 2007 s 13A, which provides how the dividend nil-rate is to operate. Where at least some of an individual's income would otherwise be chargeable at the dividend ordinary, upper or additional rates, up to £5,000 of that income is now to be charged at the dividend nil-rate. Any amount in excess of £5,000 is to be charged at the rate that would apply if the dividend nil-rate did not exist.

Consequential amendments are made.

Schedule 1, introduced by sub-s (11), abolishes the dividend tax credit and makes consequential amendments. It consists of 73 paragraphs. Paragraph 1(1) omits ITTOIA 2005 ss 397–398, 400, 414 and 421. ITTOIA 2005 s 397 entitles UK residents and eligible non-UK residents receiving a qualifying distribution from a UK-resident company to a tax credit of one-ninth of the amount of the distribution. ITTOIA 2005 ss 397A, 397AA and 397BA grant entitlement to a tax credit in respect of relevant distributions made by a non-UK-resident company. ITTOIA 2005 s 398 increases an individual's taxable income by the amount of the tax credit. ITTOIA 2005 s 400 treats recipients of a "non-qualifying distribution" as having paid income tax at the ordinary dividend rate; ITTOIA 2005 s 414 treats recipients of UK stock dividends as having paid income tax at the ordinary dividend rate; and ITTOIA 2005 s 421 treats participators of a close company whose loan from that company has been released or written off as having paid income tax at the ordinary dividend rate on the amount charged to them in respect of the release or write-off. Paragraph 1(2) omits CTA 2010 s 1109, which entitles a UK-resident company in receipt of a qualifying distribution as entitled to a tax credit.

Paragraphs 2–27 make consequential amendments to other provisions of ITTOIA 2005. In particular, para 11 amends ITTOIA 2005 s 399, which has hitherto treated persons in receipt of qualifying distributions who are not entitled to a tax credit under ITTOIA 2005 ss 397 or 397A as having paid income tax on the distribution at the dividend ordinary rate. As amended, it is now to apply to non-UK residents in receipt of a distribution from a UK company, who are to be treated as having paid income tax at the dividend ordinary rate on the distribution. That income tax is not to be repayable. Paragraph 12 amends ITTOIA 2005 s 401, which has hitherto provided relief for recipients of a qualifying distribution linked to an earlier non-qualifying distribution on which they incurred an extra liability. The distributions in question were a non-qualifying distribution that consisted of the issue of share capital or security followed by a qualifying distribution consisting of a repayment of that share capital or of the principal of that security. As amended, the section now introduces the concept of a "CD distribution", which is a distribution that is only a distribution by virtue of CTA 2010 s 1000(1) paragraphs C or D. Paragraph C defines as a distribution the issue of redeemable share capital in respect of shares in or securities

Finance Act 2016

of the company otherwise than for new consideration. Paragraph D defines as a distribution a security issued by a company in respect of shares in or securities of the company otherwise than for new consideration. Such distributions have been "non-qualifying distributions" as defined by exception by CTA 2010 s 1136 (which is to be omitted). The concept of a CD distribution now replaces the previous concept of a non-qualifying distribution. Recipients of a CD distribution liable to income tax on that distribution are to have their liability to income tax on a subsequent non-CD distribution consisting of the repayment of that share capital or of the principal of that security reduced by the lower of the income tax to which the person is liable on the one distribution and on the other.

Paragraphs 28–50 make consequential amendments to CTA 2010. In particular, para 46 omits CTA 2010 s 1126, which defines "franked investment income", the concept of which becomes redundant upon the abolition of tax credits, and para 47 omits CTA 2010 s 1136, which defines "qualifying distribution", similarly redundant.

Paragraphs 48–72 make consequential amendments to TMA 1970, TA 1988, FA 1988, FA 1989, FA 1993, FA 1994, F(No 2)A 1997, FA 1998, ITEPA 2003, ITTOIA 2005, ITA 2007, FA 2008, CTA 2009, FA 2009, CTA 2010, TIOPA 2010, FA 2011, FA 2012, FA 2013, FA 2015, the Commonwealth Development Corporation Act 1999 and FISMA 2000.

Paragraph 73 provides for commencement. The general rule is that the amendments made by Sch 1 are to have effect for dividends and other distributions made or treated as made in 2016/17 or at any later time.

Section 6 reorganises the structure of income tax rates to take account of the devolution of further taxing powers to the Scottish Parliament and the prospective devolution of similar powers to the Welsh Assembly. It creates "main rates" and "default rates" of income tax and redesignates the rates applicable to savings income as the savings basic, higher and additional rates. The power to set the savings rates and the dividend rates has not been devolved to Scotland and Wales and there are currently no plans to do so in the near future. These provisions also provide a mechanism for the UK Government's commitment to the so-called EVEL (English Votes for English Laws) procedure.

New ITA 2007 s 9A inserted by sub-s (2), sets out in a table the various rates of income tax that are to apply to different types of taxpayer. UK-resident Individuals who are neither Scottish taxpayers nor Welsh taxpayers are to be charged (UK wide) savings rates on savings Income, (UK-wide) dividend rates on dividend income and "main rates" on other income. Scottish taxpayers are also to be charged savings rates on savings income, dividend rates on dividend income but Scottish rates on their other income. Welsh taxpayers will be charged savings rates on savings income, dividend rates on dividend income but main rates on their other income unless and until ITA 2007 s 11B, which provides for Welsh rates of income tax, is brought into effect. Individuals who are not UK-resident will be charged savings rates on savings income, dividend rates on dividend income but "default rates" on their other income. Finally, taxpayers who are not individuals will be charged the default basic rate on savings income, the dividend ordinary rate on dividend income and the default basic rate on other income. There is an exception for trustees, who may be charged at the trust rate or the dividend trust rate.

New ITA 2007 ss 6C and 7A, inserted by sub-ss (3) and (4) respectively, provide for Parliament to determine the default and savings basic, higher and additional rates for a tax year. New ITA 2007 s 11C, inserted by sub-s (9), provides that an individual who is not UK-resident is to be charged to income tax on his or her income at the default basic, higher and additional rates, to the extent that the individual's income is not instead subject to the savings rates, the starting rate for savings, the savings nil-rate, the dividend rates or any other provision of the Income Tax Acts. New ITA 2007 s 11D, also inserted by sub-s (9) provides for the savings basic, higher and additional rates to be charged on an individual's savings income that would otherwise be charged at the basic rate, higher rate or additional rate, or the default basic, higher or additional rates, but after any charge at the starting rate for savings or the savings nil-rate.

Consequential amendments are made to other provisions of ITA 2007 and TCGA 1992. Section 6 is to have effect from a date to be appointed under the Scotland Act 2016 s 13(14), which is expected to be 6 April 2017 and in respect of 2017/18 and later years.

Employment income: taxable benefits

Section 7 makes amendments to the charge to tax on certain benefits-in-kind, in order to clarify that the charge will apply regardless of whether the terms on which the benefits are provided constitute a fair bargain between the employer and employee and to ensure that the benefit is still treated as earnings from the employment even where the cash equivalent is nil. The benefits in question are those under ITEPA 2003 s 97 on living accommodation, ITEPA 2003 s 114 on cars, vans and related benefits, and ITEPA 2003 s 173 on beneficial loans. On the other hand, ITEPA 2003 s 117 is substituted so as to make it explicit that the charge to tax does not apply where the employer carries on a vehicle-hire business and the vehicle hired to the employee is of the same kind made available to the public, is hired in the course of that business and to the employee acting as an ordinary member of the public. The amendments have effect with effect from the tax year 2016/17.

Section 8 makes amendments, effective from 2019/20, to the amount of the "appropriate percentage" set by ITEPA 2003 ss 139–142 for calculating the taxable amount of car and van benefit, adding to the amendments made by FA 2015 s 7 in respect of 2017/18 and FA 2015 s 8 for 2018/19 and subsequent years, FA 2014 s 23 in respect of 2016/17 and by FA 2013 s 23 in respect of 2015/16. As a result of these and previous amendments, the appropriate percentage in 2016/17 for cars with CO_2 emissions is 7% for emissions of 50 g/km and lower, rising to 9% in 2017/18 and 13% in 2018/19; 11% for cars with emissions greater than 50 g/km but no greater than 75 g/km, rising to 13% in 2017/18 and 16% in 2018/19; 15% for cars with emissions greater than 75 g/km but less than 95 g/km, rising to 17% in 2017/18 and 19% in 2018/19. From 95 g/km, the relevant percentage then increases by one percentage point at 5 g/km intervals, reaching a maximum 37% for cars with emissions of 200 g/km or more in 2016/17, 190 g/km or more in 2017/18 and 180 g/km or more in 2018/19. For the tax year 2019/20 and later years, ITEPA 2003 s 139 is now amended to provide that the appropriate percentage is to be 16% for cars with emissions of 50 g/km and lower; 19% for cars with emissions greater than 50 g/km but no greater than 75 g/km; 22% for cars with emissions greater than 75 g/km but less than 95 g/km; and thereafter the relevant percentage increases by one percentage point at 5 g/km intervals, reaching a maximum 37% for cars with emissions of 165g/km and more.

Amendments are also made to the appropriate percentages for cars that do not have an emissions figure, as provided by ITEPA 2003 s 140 and for cars first registered before 1 January 1998, as provided by ITEPA 2003 s 142. The rates applicable in 2016/17, 2017/18, 2018/19 and 2019/20 and subsequent years under ITEPA 2003 s 140 are now as shown in Table 1 below.

Table 1: Appropriate percentage for cars without a CO_2 emissions figure

Cylinder capacity of car in cc	Appropriate percentage			
	2016/17	2017/18	2018/19	2019/20 onwards
1400 or less	16%	18%	20%	23%
More than 1400 but not more than 2000	27%	29%	31%	34%
More than 2000	37%	37%	37%	37%

The rates applicable under ITEPA 2003 s 142 for cars first registered before 1 January 1998 are now as shown in Table 2 below. They are identical to those under ITEPA 2003 s 140.

Table 2: Appropriate percentage for cars first registered before 1 January 1998

Cylinder capacity of car in cc	Appropriate percentage			
	2016/17	2017/18	2018/19	2019/20 onwards
1400 or less	16%	18%	20%	23%
More than 1400 but not more than 2000	27%	29%	31%	34%
More than 2000	37%	37%	37%	37%

Section 9 amends ITEPA 2003 s 140(3)(a), which defines the appropriate percentage for cars for cars that cannot in any circumstances emit CO_2 by being driven (such as electric cars) with effect for the years 2017/18 and 2018/19. The rates applicable from 2016/17 and subsequent years are now 7% in 2016/17, 9% in 2017/18, 13% in 2018/19 and (by virtue of s 8(7)) 16% in 2019/20 and subsequent years.

Section 10 has the effect, from 2016/17 onwards, of retaining the diesel supplement of three percentage points, by which every appropriate percentage, except 35%, 36% and 37% is increased where the car in question is a diesel car. FA 2014 s 24 has hitherto provided for repeal of the diesel supplement with effect from the 2016/17 tax year.

Section 11 again amends the provisions of ITEPA 2003 s 155 relating to zero-emission vans. Whereas FA 2015 s 10 provided for a progressive increase in the benefit charge for private use, other than restricted private use, of a zero-emission van from 20% of the full van-benefit charge of £3,150 beginning in 2015/16 rising to 40% in 2016/17, 60% in 2017/18, 80% in 2018/19, 90% in 2019/20 and 100% in 2020/21 and subsequent years, the new amendments provide for a slower tempo of increase. Accordingly, the 20% charge (£630) is to be retained in 2016/17 and 2017/18, only then rising to 40% (£1,260) in 2018/19, 60% (£1,890) in 2019/20, 80% (£2,520) in 2020/21, 90% (£2,835) in 2021/22 and 100% (£3,150) in 2022/23 and subsequent years.

Section 12 introduces **Sch 2**, which introduces a charge to income tax on sporting testimonial income received by employed sportspersons where the sportsperson concerned has neither a contractual right nor customary expectation of testimonial income, with a strictly limited exemption, to replace an extra-statutory exemption. Schedule 2 consists of four paragraphs.

Schedule 2 para 1 inserts new ITEPA 2003 s 226E into ITEPA 2003 Pt 3 Ch 12 ("Other amounts treated as earnings"). New ITEPA 2003 s 226E is the main charging section. It provides that a "sporting testimonial payment" made to an individual who is or has been employed as a professional sportsperson is to be treated as the individual's earnings from the employment of former employment to which the sporting testimonial is most closely linked. A "sporting testimonial" is defined as a single event or activity or a series of events or activities each having the same "controller" having as its or their purpose or one of its or their purposes to raise money for the sportsperson's benefit solely or mainly to recognise the sportsperson's service as a professional. The "controller" in relation to these provisions is a person who controls the disbursement of any money raised. An activity consisting solely of inviting and collecting donations is only a sporting testimonial if it is one of a series of events with the same controller. Single such events or activities are not to be regarded as sporting testimonials for this purpose if they meet certain conditions. A "sporting testimonial payment" is a payment made by or on behalf the controller of a sporting testimonial out of money raised for or for the benefit of the sportsperson and made to that person, a member of the sportsperson's family or household etc and would not otherwise constitute earnings from an employment.

Schedule 2 para 2 inserts new ITEPA 2003 s 306B into ITEPA 2003 Pt 4 Ch 8 ("Exemptions: special kinds of employees"), which is the exemption provision. No liability is to arise in respect of the first £100,000 of sporting testimonial payments within new ITEPA 2003 s 226E provided that the controller of the relevant activity or event or series is an independent person and the sportsperson has not already benefited from another exemption under this section; nor must payments be made out of funds from events or activities that took place over a year previously. Any balance remaining of the £100,000 remaining unused may be carried forward to the following year(s) where the testimonial events or activities take place over two or more tax years.

Schedule 2 para 3 inserts new CTA 2010 s 996A into CTA 2010 Pt 22 Ch 9 ("Other miscellaneous provisions"), which enables companies acting as controllers of a sporting testimonial event or activity making payments out of the proceeds to claim a deduction in respect of that payment where a deduction for those payments would not otherwise be available. The amount of the deduction in any accounting period is the sum of (a) that part of the payment paid to or for the benefit of the sportsperson; (b) income tax or employee's NICs deducted at source from the payment; and (c) any employer's NICs relating to that payment. The deduction is to be made from the company's total profits for the accounting period in which the payment is made and any qualifying previous periods. A claim for the deduction must be made within two years of the end of the accounting period in which the payment is made; the amount of the deduction may not exceed the company's taxable total profits.

Schedule 2 para 4 provides that Sch 2 has effect in relation to payments made out of money raised by a testimonial made public after 24 November 2015, but those payments must be made out of money raised by relevant events or activities taking place after 5 April 2017.

Section 13 continues the work on simplifying the taxation of expenses payments and benefits begun last year in FA 2015. It inserts new ITEPA 2003 ss 323A–323C in ITEPA 2003 Pt 4 Ch 11 ("Miscellaneous exemptions"). The new sections provide an exemption for trivial benefits provided by employers. New ITEPA 2003 s 323A provides that no liability to income tax is to arise in respect of benefits provided to or on behalf of an employee or a member of the employee's family or household where all of four (or in the event that the employer is a close company and the employee is a director or other office-holder of that company all of five) conditions (A–D or E) are met.

Condition A is that the benefit not be cash or a cash voucher. Condition B is that the "benefit cost" (as defined) of the benefit not exceed £50. Condition C is that the benefit not be provided in connection with salary-sacrifice arrangements or any other contractual obligations. Condition D is that the benefit not be provided in recognition or anticipation of particular services performed by the employee in the course of the employment. Condition E, which need be met only in the context of close companies is that the benefit cost of the benefit provided to the employee (or where provided to a member of the employee's family or household, the benefit cost allocated to the employee under new ITEPA 2003 s 323B) not exceed the employee's "available exempt amount".

New ITEPA 2003 s 323B provides for calculation of the "available exempt amount". This is the "annual exempt amount" (set at £300) less the sum of (a) the benefit cost of eligible benefits provided earlier in the tax year and (b) amounts allocated to the employee in respect of benefits provided to a member of the employee's family or household who is not also an employee of the employer. New s 323B(4) explains what amounts are allocated to an employee in these circumstances. New ITEPA 2003 s 323C confers power on HM Treasury to amend new ITEPA 2003 ss 323A and 323B by regulations. Section 13 has effect as from the tax year 2016/17.

Section 14 is intended to ensure that neither workers engaged through employment intermediaries nor their employers may benefit from relief for home-to-work travel expenses. ITEPA 2003 s 338 provides that an employee may claim a deduction from earnings for travel expenses attributable to necessary attendance at any place in performing the duties of the employment. Travel that is ordinary commuting or substantially ordinary commuting is excluded. Ordinary commuting is travel between the employee's home and a permanent workplace or between a place that is not a workplace and a permanent workplace. ITEPA 2003 s 339 defines "workplace" and "permanent workplace".

New ITEPA 2003 s 339A, inserted by s 14(1), applies where a worker personally provides services to a "client" and those services are provided under arrangements involving an employment intermediary and not under a contract directly between the client or a connected person and the worker. In these circumstances, each engagement the worker undertakes is to be regarded for the purposes of ITEPA 2003 ss 338 and 339 as a separate employment, so that travel between the engagements is excluded from relief under ITEPA 2003 s 338. However, the new rule does not apply where the worker provides the services in a way that is not subject to (or the right of) supervision, direction or control by any person, except where the worker's services are supplied through an intermediary so that ITEPA 2003 Pt 2 Ch 8 applies, the conditions in ITEPA 2003 ss 51, 52 or 53 (as modified) are met, and the employment intermediary is not a managed service company. Broadly speaking, ITEPA 2003 ss 51–53 set out the conditions under which payments made by the intermediary to the worker are treated as earnings from an employment where the intermediary (for these purposes, the employment intermediary) is a company, a partnership and an individual, respectively. Where the client or other relevant person provides the employment intermediary with a fraudulent document purporting to show that the exception applies and tax that should have been deducted is accordingly not deducted under PAYE, the worker is to be treated as having an employment with the client or relevant person, who must then account for the unpaid tax under PAYE regulations.

New ITEPA 2003 s 688B is inserted into ITEPA 2003 Pt 11 Ch 3 ("PAYE: Special types of payer/payee") by s 14(3), and provides for those regulations to be made. Section 14(4) inserts those regulations as Ch 3B (regs 97ZG–97M) of the PAYE Regulations (SI 2003/2682).

Section 15 amends ITEPA 2003 s 684(2) Item 1ZA to include mention of ITEPA 2003 Pt 3 Ch 4, so that regulations may be made to enable tax in respect of benefits-in-kind in the form of vouchers and credit-tokens to be collected under PAYE.

Employment income: other provision

Section 16 introduces Sch 3, which makes minor amendments relating to employee share schemes. Schedule 3 consists of nine paragraphs.

Schedule 3 para 1 amends ITEPA 2003 s 534 so that the disqualifying events there specified in relation to a company operating an enterprise management incentive (EMI) scheme do not apply where the company concerned is subject to an employee-ownership trust. The amendment is retroactive to 1 October 2014.

Schedule 3 para 2 amends ITEPA 2003 Sch 2 so as to provide that a share incentive plan ceases to be a qualifying share incentive plan ("Schedule 2 SIP") on the occurrence of a disqualifying event. It inserts new ITEPA 2003 Sch 2 Pt 10A, consisting of a single paragraph (para 85A). A disqualifying event occurs, with some exceptions, when an alteration is made in the share capital of a company any of whose shares are subject to the plan trust or in the rights attaching to any shares of such a company. These amendments are to have effect in relation to disqualifying events occurring after 14 September 2016.

Schedule 3 paras 3–5 alter the notification requirements for share incentive plans, SAYE option schemes and CSOP schemes, respectively. Schedule 2 para 3 amends ITEPA 2003 Sch 2 para 81A, which applies to share incentive plans (SIPs). For a SIP to be a Schedule 2 SIP, notice of it must be given to HMRC. Where that notice is given after 6 July in the tax year following that in which the first award date falls, the SIP obtains the status of a Sch 2 SIP from the beginning of that following year only and not from the beginning of the preceding tax year. The amendment now made enables that postponement to be overridden where the company can satisfy HMRC or a tribunal that it had a reasonable excuse for failing to give notice by the 6 July deadline. HMRC has 45 days within which to consider a company's submission that it has a reasonable excuse and notify the company of its decision. Failure to do so on HMRC's part is to be treated as a decision that there is no reasonable excuse. Under ITEPA 2003 Sch 2 para 81K as now amended, the company may appeal against a negative decision by HMRC. Schedule 2 para 4 makes parallel amendments to ITEPA 2003 Sch 3 paras 40A (notice to be given to HMRC of a SAYE option scheme) and 40K (appeals). Schedule 2 para 5 makes the analogous amendments to ITEPA 2003 Sch 4 paras 28A (notice to be given to HMRC of a CSOP scheme) and 28K (appeals). These amendments apply to notices under ITEPA 2003 Schs 2, 3 or 4 given after 5 April 2016.

Schedule 3 para 6 amends ITEPA 2003 Sch 3 para 28(1), which provides that the price at which shares may be acquired by exercising an option under an SAYE option scheme must be stated at the time when the option is granted and must not be manifestly less than 80% of the market value at that time of shares of the same class. ITEPA 2003 Sch 3 para 28(2) allows the scheme organiser and HMRC to agree to substitute an earlier time for the time at which the option is granted. The amendments now made omit ITEPA 2003 Sch 3 para 28(2) and provide instead in ITEPA 2003 Sch 3 para 28(1) that an earlier time may now be determined in accordance with guidance to be issued by HMRC.

ITEPA 2003 Sch 4 para 22(1) similarly provides that the price at which shares may be acquired by exercising an option under a CSOP scheme must not be manifestly less than the market value at the time the option is granted of shares of the same class. ITEPA 2003 Sch 4 para 22(2) similarly allows the scheme organiser and HMRC to agree to substitute an earlier time for the time at which the option is granted. The amendments now made by **Sch 3 para 7** omit ITEPA 2003 Sch 4 para 22(2) and provide instead in ITEPA 2003 Sch 4 para 22(1) that an earlier time may now be determined in accordance with guidance to be issued by HMRC. The amendments made by Sch 3 paras 6 and 7 have effect from 15 September 2016.

Schedule 3 para 8 amends ITEPA 2003 Sch 5 para 39. ITEPA 2003 Sch 5 Pt 6, of which it is a part, provides that the benefits of an enterprise management incentive (EMI) scheme may be preserved in certain circumstances when a company reorganisation takes place by the issue of replacement options. One of the definitions of a company reorganisation for these purposes is given in ITEPA 2003 Sch 5 para 39(1)(c), namely where a company becomes bound or entitled under Companies Act 2006 ss 979–982 in relation to a takeover offer to buy out a minority shareholder. The amendment now made extends the definition to include Companies Act 2006 ss 983–985, which refer to so-called tag-along schemes, under which minority shareholders have the right to have their share options acquired by the offeror and exchanged for share options in the offeror. This amendment is given retroactive effect back to 17 July 2013.

Schedule 3 para 9 omits TCGA 1992 Sch 7D Pt 4 (paras 14 and 16). TCGA 1992 Sch 7D para 14 provides that where a disqualifying event occurs in relation to a qualifying option (both an original option and a replacement option) under the EMI scheme, shares acquired by the exercise of that option are qualifying shares only if the option is exercised within 40 days of the event. TCGA 1992 Sch 7D para 16 provides that where there is a rights issue in respect of EMI qualifying shares by virtue of which there is a reorganisation, the identification rules under TCGA 1992 ss 127–130 are not to apply. Those rules, it will be remembered, deem the new holding to have been acquired at the same time as the old holding. The omission of TCGA 1992 Sch 7D Pt 4 therefore has the effect of dispensing with the 40-day rule and reinstating the identification rule in TCGA 1992 s 127. These amendments have no effect in relation to disqualifying events occurring before 6 April 2016 or rights issues taking place before that date.

Section 17 amends ITEPA 2003 ss 227and 418 and is addressed to the treatment of restricted stock units. ITEPA 2003 s 418 forms part of ITEPA 2003 Pt 7, which provides for the special charge to income tax on income from employment-related securities. ITEPA 2003 s 418(1) has hitherto provided that ITEPA 2003 Pt 3 Ch 1 (the general charge to tax on earnings) and Ch 10 (taxable benefits: residual liability to charge) may also apply in relation to securities and interests in securities, but not to securities options. The amendment now made to ITEPA 2003 s 418(1) makes it clear that ITEPA 2003 Pt 3 Chs 1 and 10 are not to have effect to the acquisition of employment-related securities options within ITEPA 2003 Pt 7 Ch 5 (securities options) or to chargeable events under ITEPA 2003 s 477. The effect of this and a consequential amendment made to ITEPA 2003 s 227 is to make it clear that the charge to tax on the acquisition of shares under a restricted stock unit (RSU) will be made under ITEPA 2003 Pt 7 (the employment-related securities rules).

Section 18 makes amendments to and in relation to ITEPA 2003 Pt 7A (ss 554A–554Z21), which was inserted by FA 2011 s 26 and Sch 2, and under which there is a charge to income tax in certain cases where remuneration is provided to an employee by the agency of a third party. Broadly speaking, the charge to tax applies where (a) a "relevant arrangement" exists to which an employee, former employee or prospective employee ("A") of another person ("B") or any person linked with A is a party and a "relevant step" (as defined in ITEPA 2003 ss 554B–554D) is taken by a "relevant third person" in connection with that arrangement, and (b) it is reasonable to suppose that the relevant arrangement insofar as it relates to A or any person linked with A is wholly or partly concerned with the provision of "rewards or recognition or loans" in connection with A's prospective, current or former employment with B.

ITEPA 2007 s 554Z2 contains the basic rule imposing a charge to tax. It provides that where a non-excluded "relevant step" is taken, the value of the relevant step is to be regarded as employment income of A in respect of A's employment with B. Section 18(2) inserts new ITEPA 2003 s 554Z2(1A) to deal with the situation where the value of a relevant step would otherwise count as the employment income of more than one person. Where that would be the case, the value is to be apportioned between each of those persons on a just and reasonable basis and references to the value of the relevant step in relation to A are to be taken as references to the value accordingly apportioned to A. Section 18(3) amends ITEPA 2003 s 554Z8. The latter section provides for a reduction in the value of the relevant step within ITEPA 2003 s 554C (the payment of a sum of money or the transfer of an asset) where the relevant step is taken in return for consideration consisting of the transfer of an asset from A to the person making the payment or the transfer, provided that there is no connection with a tax-avoidance arrangement. ITEPA 2003 s 554Z8 also applies in relation to a relevant step within ITEPA 2003 s 554C or ITEPA 2003 s 554D (making an asset available without transferring it) where the relevant step does not involve money and the consideration is money consideration. The amendment now made to ITEPA 2003 s 554Z8(5) makes it clear that the reduction in value of the relevant step in those circumstances is not to apply where there is any direct or indirect connection between the payment of the money consideration and a tax-avoidance arrangement.

Amendments are also made to FA 2011 Sch 2 para 59, which contains transitional provisions relating to the introduction of ITEPA 2007 Pt 7A to prevent a double charge to tax where a relevant step within ITEPA 2003 s 554B was taken before 6 April 2011 (when these provisions took effect) and followed by a relevant step within ITEPA 2003 ss 554C or 554D after they came into effect.

Pensions

Section 19 and **Sch 4** (introduced by s 19(10)) provide for the reduction of the lifetime allowance for pension savings from £1,250,000 to £1,000,000 and transitional provisions to protect existing pension savers from the full effect of the reduction.

FA 2004 s 218, as variously amended, has hitherto provided that the standard lifetime allowance (SLA) shall be £1.25 million but may be increased by Treasury order. As amended by s 19(2), it now provides that the SLA for the tax years 2016/17 and 2017/18 is to be £1 million and that for any later tax year, it shall remain at that amount unless the CPI for September in any prior tax year later than 2016/17 is higher than it was for the previous September. In that case, the SLA for the year following the prior tax year shall be the SLA for the prior tax year increased by the percentage increase in the index, rounding up to the nearest multiple of £100. Further amendments provide that where an individual's lifetime-allowance enhancement factor is provided for under any of FA 2004 ss 220 (pension credits), 222 (non-resident's money-purchase arrangements), 223 (non-resident's other arrangements) or 224 (transfers from recognised overseas pension schemes) and the time mentioned in the definition of SLA falls within the tax year 2014/15 or 2015/16, the allowance to be multiplied by the lifetime-allowance enhancement factor is to be £1.25 million if that is greater than SLA. Where, also, benefit-crystallisation event 7 (the payment of certain lump-sum death benefits) occurs after 5 April 2016 in respect of an individual's death occurring between 6 April 2014 and 5 April 2016, the SLA at the time of the event is to be taken as £1.25 million. Where benefit-crystallisation event 5C (designation within the relevant two-year period of relevant uncrystallised funds as available for payment to dependants or nominees) occurs after 5 April 2015 on the designation of sums or assets held for the purposes of an arrangement and the member died in either of the tax years 2012/13 or 2013/14, the SLA at the time of crystallisation is to be £1.5 million. Where, on the other hand, benefit-crystallisation event 5D (the occasion of a person's becoming entitled after 5 April 2015 but before the end of the relevant two-year period to a dependants' or nominees' annuity purchased using relevant unused uncrystallised funds) occurs and the member died in the period beginning on 3 December 2014 and ending on 5 April 2016, the SLA is to be £1.25 million.

Schedule 4, introduced by s 19(10), consists of six Parts. Part 1 (paras 1–8) introduces a new protection scheme, "Fixed Protection 2016"; Pt 2 (paras 9–13) introduces another protection scheme, "Individual Protection 2016"; P–t 3 (paras 14–20) deals with reference numbers; Pt 4 (paras 21–27) deals with information requirements; Pt 5 (para 28) provides for amendments relating to the protection of pre-April 2006 rights; and Pt 6 (paras 29–31) provides for interpretation and regulations.

Schedule 4 Pt 1 provides for a transitional protection scheme, "Fixed Protection 2016" for individuals adversely affected by the reduction in the SLA to £1 million. Schedule 4 paras 1 and 2 provide that where the required conditions are met, such individuals will have an SLA that is the greater of the normal SLA and £1.25 million. The required conditions are that at any particular time after 5 April 2016, (a) the individual is a member of one or more registered pension schemes or relieved non-UK pension schemes; (b) the individual is not covered by any of primary protection under FA 2004 Sch 36 para 7, enhanced protection under FA 2004 Sch 36 para 12 on 6 April 2016; Fixed Protection 2012 under FA 2011 Sch 18 para 14, Fixed Protection 2014 under FA 2013 Sch 2 para 1 or Individual Protection 2014 under FA 2014 Sch 6 para 1(2); (c) a protection-cessation event has not occurred after 5 April 2016; and (d) the individual has a "reference number" under Sch 4 Part 3. Sch 4 para 3 defines the protection-cessation events, which are any of (a) benefit accrual under a registered pension scheme; (b) an impermissible transfer into a registered pension scheme; (c) a non-permitted transfer of sums or assets in respect of accrued rights; (d) an arrangement relating to the individual under a registered pension scheme in non-permitted circumstances. Sch 4 para 4 defines what is meant by "benefit accrual"; Sch 4 para 5 defines what is meant by an "impermissible transfer"; Sch 4 para 6 defines what is a "permitted transfer" and Sch 4 para 7 defines what are "permitted circumstances"; Sch 4 para 8 provides how protection-cessation events are to be interpreted in relation to relieved members of relieved non-UK pension schemes.

Schedule 4 Pt 2 introduces another protection scheme – Individual Protection 2016. Schedule 4 para 9 provides that Individual Protection 2016 is to apply at any particular time after 5 April 2016 to an individual who is a member of a registered pension scheme or is a "relieved member" of a "relieved non-UK pension scheme" (as defined in FA 2004 Sch 34), has pension rights ("the relevant amount", as defined in

Sch 4 para 9(4), (7)) greater than £1 million in total; is not entitled to a lifetime-allowance enhancement factor under primary protection under FA 2004 Sch 36 para 7; and has a reference number under Sch 4 Pt 3.

Where Individual Protection 2016 applies to an individual, the individual's SLA is to be the greater of the individual's pension rights and the normal SLA in the particular tax year, but not so as to exceed £1.25 million. This enhanced SLA is not to apply where the individual is entitled to enhanced protection under FA 2004 Sch 36 para 12; Fixed Protection 2012 under FA 2011 Sch 18 para 14; Fixed Protection 2014 under FA 2013 Sch 22 para 1; Individual Protection 2014 under FA 2014 Sch 6 para 1(2)) or Fixed Protection 2016 under Sch 4 para 1(2). Schedule 4 para 9(4) provides that the pension rights ("the relevant amount") relevant to Schedule 4 Part 2 are the sum of amounts A–D as defined in Sch 4 paras 10–13. Schedule 4 para 9(6)–(8) reduces the pension rights to be taken into account where the individual's rights under a pension scheme become subject to a pension debit due to a transfer of rights following a divorce.

Schedule 4 para 10 provides for the calculation of Amount A, which represents the value of pensions already being paid to the individual on 6 April 2016 in respect of pension rights already accrued at 6 April 2006, both where there has been a "benefit-crystallisation event" (as defined in FA 2004 s 216) in the period 6 April 2006 to 5 April 2016 and where there has not. Schedule 4 para 11 provides for the calculation of Amount B, which represents the aggregate value of all benefit-crystallisation events that have occurred after 5 April 2006 and before 6 April 2016. Schedule 4 para 12 provides for the calculation of Amount C, which represents the value of any uncrystallised pension rights that the individual has under registered pension schemes as at 5 April 2016. Schedule 4 para 13 provides for the calculation of Amount D, which represents the value of any uncrystallised pension rights that the individual has under relieved non-UK pension schemes as at 5 April 2016.

Schedule 4 Pt 3 deals with reference numbers. Schedule 4 para 14 provides that a reference number is a number issued by or on behalf of HMRC to the individual and not withdrawn. Such numbers are not to be issued unless a valid application is made after 5 April 2016 to HMRC in respect of the individual for Fixed or Individual Protection 2016. Schedule 4 para 15 provides for the circumstances under which a reference number may be withdrawn, and Sch 4 para 16 for appeals against non-issue or withdrawal of reference numbers. Schedule 4 para 17 provides that an individual who has received a reference number, whose application for a reference number is pending or whose appeal against the non-issue or withdrawal of a reference number is in progress, must notify HMRC of any protection-cessation event within 90 days of its occurrence. Schedule 4 para 18 imposes a similar notification requirement on individuals who receive a discharge notice in relation to a pension debit, but they have 60 days from the date of the notice to inform HMRC of the amount and the transfer day. Schedule 4 para 19 authorises the personal representatives of a deceased pension-scheme member to apply for protection under this Schedule on the member's behalf. Schedule 4 para 20 makes a minor consequential amendment.

Schedule 4 Pt 4 (paras 21–27) requires individuals issued with reference numbers to preserve relevant records for a minimum of six years and amends existing regulations relating to the provision of information so that they extend to the 2016 protection schemes.

Schedule 4 para 28 amends FA 2004 Schs 29 and 34 to ensure that individuals with primary protection or enhanced protection receive the correct amount of tax-free lump sum in certain circumstances where they would otherwise not.

Schedule 4 paras 29 and **30** are interpretation paragraphs and Sch 4 para 31 provides for regulations to be made.

Section 20 addresses the question of bridging pensions, which are pensions paid in certain circumstances to individuals who have retired but not yet reached state pension age. Pension rules as set out in FA 2004 Sch 28 Pt 1 contain a rule (FA 2004 Sch 28 para 2(4)(c)) allowing for pensions to be reduced in certain circumstances, such as when a bridging pension ceases to be paid. In order to align this legislation with the Pensions Act 2014, which introduced a single-tier state pension beginning from 6 April 2016, the rule in FA 2004 Sch 28 para 2(4)(c) is now omitted, and the power to reduce will now be exercised by regulations issued under FA 2004 Sch 28 para 2(4)(h). Other consequential amendments are made.

Section 21 addresses the question of dependants' scheme pensions. Under FA 2004 Sch 28 para 16A, where a scheme member, having reached the age of 75, dies after 5 April 2006 while having dependants and being entitled or prospectively entitled to a scheme pension. In these circumstances, where a dependants' scheme pension is payable, the amount of that pension is tested under FA 2004 Sch 28 para 16B in the first year after the member's death against the so-called initial member pension limit. Any pension in excess of that limit is regarded as not a dependants' scheme pension and is thus taxable as an unauthorised payment. In subsequent years, the dependants' pension is tested against the "current member pension limit" under FA 2004 Sch 28 para 16C, with the same consequences for any excess. Section 21(3) inserts new FA 2004 Sch 28 paras 16AA–16AE. New FA 2004 Sch 28 para 16AA provides that the tests in FA 2004 Sch 28 paras 16B and 16C do not have to be carried out if the only benefit-crystallisation event that has occurred in relation to the deceased member is event 5B (unused funds under a money-purchase arrangement at age 75) or the member had enhanced protection under FA 2004 Sch 36 para 12. New FA 2004 Sch 28 para 16AB provides that the tests in FA 2004 Sch 28 paras 16B and 16C do not have to be carried out if at all times in any 12-month period, the payable annual rate of the dependants' pension is under a certain limit. That limit is the higher of the "general limit" set by new FA 2004 Sch 28 para 16AC and the "personal limit"; set by new FA 2004 Sch 28 para 16AD. New FA 2004 Sch 28 para 16AE provides for indexation of these two limits.

Amendments made by s 21(4) to FA 2004 Sch 28 para 16B allow for uprating of the value of tax-free lump sums taken by the member before his or her death when calculating the initial member pension limit. Section 21(5) makes similar amendments to FA 2004 Sch 28 para 16C for uprating when calculating the current member pension limit.

Subject to the exceptions in s 21(7), (8), the amendments made by s 21 have effect from 6 April 2016.

Section 22 introduces **Sch 5**, which makes amendments to the provisions for pension flexibility operative from 6 April 2015, and consists of 11 paragraphs.

Schedule 5 paras 1–4 omit FA 2004 s 205A, which imposes a 45% tax charge on a serious ill-health lump sum paid to a scheme member who has reached the age of 75, extend the funds from which a serious ill-health lump sum may be paid and, by amending ITEPA 2003 s 636A(3A), replace the 45% charge with a charge at the member's marginal rate of income tax under ITEPA 2003 s 579A. These amendments have effect for lump sums paid after 15 September 2016.

Schedule 5 para 5 amends FA 2004 Sch 29 para 18(1A) to remove the requirement that a charity lump-sum death benefit may be paid only in respect of members who have reached the age of 75 before they die, with effect for lump sums paid after 15 September 2016.

Schedule 5 para 6 addresses dependants' flexi-access drawdown funds. The meaning of "dependant" in FA 2004 Sch 28 para 15 is extended to include children of the member who are 23 and over and not physically or mentally impaired, so that children over 22 may continue to have access to dependants' drawdown pensions, dependants' short-term annuities, dependants' income withdrawal, dependants' drawdown pension funds and dependants' flexi-access drawdown funds.

Schedule 5 paras 7–9 deal with trivial commutation lump-sums. FA 2004 Sch 29 para 7(1)(aa) is amended so that a trivial commutation lump-sum is no longer limited to defined-benefits arrangements but may also be commuted from money-purchase arrangements (so-called in-payment money-purchase in-house scheme pensions). ITEPA 2003 s 636B, which deals with the taxation of trivial commutation lump-sums, is amended to provide that the taxable sum is reduced by 25% of the value of any uncrystallised rights extinguished by the lump-sum. These amendments have effect for lump-sums paid after 15 September 2016.

Schedule 5 para 10 addresses uncrystallised-funds lump-sum death benefits under FA 2004 Sch 29 para 15. Where a money-purchase arrangement is a cash-balance arrangement, and there is a dependant entitled to be paid a lump-sum on the death of a member, the employer is now to be enabled to make up any shortfall and the amount contributed is to be treated as relevant uncrystallised funds. The amendment has effect for contributions made after 15 September 2016.

Schedule 5 para 11 amends IHTA 1984 s 152 so that where an annuity is payable on death to a nominee, as well as to a dependant, widow(er) or surviving civil partner, some or all of the cost of which could instead have been paid to a personal representative, that amount is not to be treated as part of the deceased's chargeable estate, with effect from 6 April 2015 for deaths occurring on or after that date.

Section 23 inserts new ITEPA 2003 s 642A, to exempt from income tax pensions, annuities or other payments out of the Netherlands fund for the victims of oppression in 1940–45, paid under the *Wet uitkeringen vervolgingsslachtoffers 1940–45*. The exemption has effect from the tax year 2016/17.

Trading and other income

Section 24 amends the simplified home-expenses provisions in ITTOIA 2005 Pt 2 Ch 5A (ss 94B–94I). It amends ITTOIA 2005 ss 94H and 94I to allow the lump-sum deductions for use of the home for the purposes of the business to be claimed by a partnership in respect of the use of a partner's home, with effect from the tax year 2016/17.

Section 25 amends the averaging rules for farmers and related occupations in ITTOIA 2005 Pt 2 Ch 16 (ss 221–225). It introduces the option to average profits over a five years rather than two, as hitherto, and removes the marginal relief in year 2 for farmers and creative artists. Section 25(3) inserts new ITTOIA 2005 s 222A, which allows a person carrying on a qualifying trade, profession or vocation to make an averaging claim in respect of the profits of five consecutive tax years, provided that (a) the average of the relevant profits of the first four tax years involved is less than 75% of the profit of the fifth year involved, or vice versa ("the volatility condition") or (b) the relevant profits of at least one year (but not of all the years) are nil. The five-year option is to be open to farmers, market gardeners and intensive rearers of livestock or fish for human consumption but not to creative artists. However, with respect to all qualifying trades etc, the marginal adjustment where profits of one year are more than 70% but less than 75% of the other year's is abolished. Consequential amendments are made. The amendments made by s 25 have effect from the tax year 2016/17.

Section 26 amends the legislation introduced only last year by F(No 2) 2015 that had the effect of restricting relief for finance costs relating to a residential property business to a sum equivalent to the basic rate of income tax on the relievable amount. It replaces the existing ITTOIA 2005 ss 274A and 274B (inserted by F(No 2)A 2015 s 24(2)) by new ITTOIA 2005 ss 274A, 274AA, 274B and 274C.

New ITTOIA 2005 s 274A is limited to establishing the grounds for entitlement to a reduction for financing costs. It provides that an individual is entitled to relief under that section if he or she has one or more "relievable amounts", each of which must be in respect of a different property business. An individual has a relievable amount for a tax year in respect of a property business if he or she has one or more of (a) a "current-year amount"; (b) a "current-year estate amount"; and/or (c) a "brought-forward amount", and the relievable amount is the total of those amounts.

A current-year amount exists for a tax year where an amount (A) has been disallowed under ITTOIA 2005 s 272A in calculating the profits of a property business for that year; the individual is liable to income tax on N% of those profits (N must be greater than 0 and no greater than 100); and that liability is not in respect of estate income under ITTOIA 2005 Pt 5 Ch 6 (Beneficiaries' income from estates in administration), in which case the current-year amount is equal to N% of A. A current-year estate amount exists for a tax year where an amount (A) has been disallowed under ITTOIA 2005 s 272A in calculating the profits of a property business in a deceased person's estate whether for that year or an earlier year; the deceased person's personal representatives are liable to income tax on N% of those profits (N must be greater than 0 and no greater than 100); the individual is liable for income tax on estate income treated as arising in the current year from an interest in the estate; and the basic amount (as defined in ITTOIA 2005 s 656(4)) of that estate income consists of or includes an amount representing E% of the personal representatives' N% of the profits of the business, in which case the current-year estate amount is E% of N% of A. A brought-forward amount exists where there is an unrelieved excess from a previous year representing the excess of the relievable amount in that previous year over the actual amount of relief that could be given.

New ITTOIA 2005 s 274AA contains the calculation of the reduction available. The actual amount ("AA") on which relief may be given is normally the lower of (a) the relievable amount and (b) the sum of (1) the smaller of the "adjusted profits" of the property business of the year (the profits after any deduction under ITA 2007 s 118 for losses brought forward) and the share of the adjusted profits on which the individual is liable to income tax other than as estate income and (2) so much of the relievable amount as consists of current-year estate income. This amount is referred to as L. In most cases, L = AA. However, if the total (S) of the Ls for each property business is greater than the individual's adjusted total income (ATI) for the year, the actual amount, AA, for any one property business (and therefore relievable amount) is given by (ATI/S) x L. The amount of the relief in respect of a relievable amount is

AA x BR, where BR is the basic rate of income tax. An individual's ATI is the net income of the year (Step 2 in the calculation in ITA 2007 s 23), reduced by savings income and dividend income and personal allowances deducted at Step 3 in the calculation in ITA 2007 s 23.

New ITTOIA 2005 s 274B establishes the grounds for entitlement to a reduction on the part of trustees of an accumulated or discretionary trust. It provides that the trustees are entitled to relief under that section if they have one or more relievable amounts, each of which must be in respect of a different property business. The trustees have a relievable amount for a tax year in respect of a property business if they have a current-year amount or a brought-forward amount or both, and the relievable amount is the total of those amounts.

A current-year amount exists for a tax year for the trustees where an amount (A) has been disallowed under ITTOIA 2005 s 272A in calculating the profits of a property business for that year; the trustees are liable to income tax on N% of those profits (N must be greater than 0 and no greater than 100); and n% of those profits is accumulated or discretionary income, in which case the current-year amount is equal to N% of A. A brought-forward amount exists where there is an unrelieved excess from a previous year representing the excess of the relievable amount in that previous year over L as defined in new ITTOIA 2005 s 274C.

New ITTOIA 2005 s 274C contains the calculation of the reduction available for such trustees. The amount of the relief is given by L x BR, where BR is the basic rate of income tax and L is given by the lower of (a) the relievable amount and (b) the smaller of the "adjusted profits" of the property business of the year (the profits after any deduction under ITA 2007 s 118 for losses brought forward) and the share of the adjusted profits on which the trustees are liable to income tax and which is accumulated or discretionary income.

Where L is less than the relievable amount, the difference is the brought-forward amount for the following year.

Section 27 enables HM Treasury to make regulations to retain the tax-free status of an ISA after the death of the account holder, whereas this currently lapses with the holder's death. New ITTOIA 2005 s 694A, inserted by s 27(1), provides that for the purposes of the ISA exemption (ITTOIA 2005 Pt 6 Ch 3), the income of an individual from plan investments is to include the income of any person from "administration-period investments" under the plan and the income of any person from the estate of a deceased person, where all or part of the income of the deceased's personal representatives is income from "administration-period investments" under the plan. The meaning of "individual" in ITTOIA 2005 s 694(3)(a), (4) and ITTOIA 2005 s 695(1) is extended to include personal representatives and any other person on whose directions the plan managers agree to act. The meaning of "investor" in ITTOIA 2005 ss 699 and 701 is extended to include persons entitled to an exemption under regulations made under new ITTOIA 2005 s 694A. The meaning of "administration period investments" is defined and provision is made for regulations to amend TCGA 1992 s 62 in certain cases where an asset is acquired by a legatee.

Reliefs: enterprise investment scheme, venture capital trusts etc

Sections 28 to 30 make amendments to the EIS, SEIS and VCT schemes. **Section 28** amends ITA 2007 s 192(1) (excluded activities for the EIS and SEIS) and ITA 2007 s 303(1) (excluded activities for VCTs) so as in both cases to add also (a) the non-subsidised generation or export of electricity or the non-subsidised making available of electricity-generating capacity; (b) the non-subsidised generation of heat; (c) the non-subsidised generation of any form of energy not already excluded; and (d) the non-subsidised production of gas or fuel to the list of excluded activities. These activities where subsidised were already excluded. Consequential amendments are made. The amendments made by s 28 have effect for shares or relevant holdings issued after 5 April 2016.

Section 29 changes the definitions of certain periods in the EIS and VCT legislation pertaining to determinations of the maximum age limit for a company or its definition as a knowledge-intensive company.

In the definition of the permitted maximum-age requirement for the EIS scheme under ITA 2007 s 175A (inserted by F(No 2)A 2015 s 25 and Sch 5 para 12), the period over which the average turnover amount is measured (for the purposes of Condition B) is altered. Hitherto, that period was the five years ending with the later of (a) the date immediately before the beginning of the last accounts-filing period and (b) 12 months before the issue date. The new reference period is the five years ending with the date immediately before the beginning of the last accounts-filing period or, where the last accounts-filing period ends more than 12 months before the issue date, the five-year period ending 12 months before the issue date. Exactly the same amendments are made with relation to the permitted maximum-age condition for the VCT scheme in ITA 2007 s 280C (inserted by F(No 2)A 2015 s 26 and Sch 6 para 5) and the permitted company-age condition for the VCT scheme in ITA 2007 s 294A (inserted by F(No 2)A 2015 s 26 and Sch 6 para 11) except that references to the issue date are replaced by references to the investment date.

In the definition of "knowledge-intensive company" for the EIS scheme under ITA 2007 s 252A (inserted by F(No 2)A 2015 Sch 5 para 19), the period over which the operating-costs conditions must be met – "the relevant three preceding years" – has hitherto meant the three consecutive years the last of which ends on the later of (a) the date immediately before the beginning of the last accounts-filing period and (b) 12 months before the issue date of the relevant shares. The new reference period is the three consecutive years the last of which ends on the date immediately before the beginning of the last accounts-filing period or, where the last accounts-filing period ends more than 12 months before the issue date of the relevant shares, the three consecutive years ending 12 months before the issue date of the relevant shares. Exactly the same amendments are made with relation to the definition of "knowledge-intensive company" for the VCT scheme in ITA 2007 s 331A (inserted by F(No 2)A 2015 s 26 and Sch 6 para 20), except that references to the issue date of the relevant shares are replaced by references to the applicable time.

Subject to s 30, the amendments made by s 29 are deemed always to have had effect.

Section 30 allows a company receiving EIS or VCT investments to elect that the amendments made by s 29 not have effect. Specifically, the company concerned may (a) elect that the amendments made by s 29(1) to the definition of the relevant five-year period for the EIS scheme not apply in relation to shares issued by the company in the "material period"; (b) elect that the amendments made by s 29(2) to the definition of a knowledge-intensive company for the EIS scheme not apply on the date of issue of any shares issued by the company in the "material period"; (c) elect that the amendments made by s 29(3) to the definition of the relevant five-year period in respect of the permitted maximum-age condition for the VCT scheme not apply in relation to investments made in the company in the "material period"; (d) elect that the amendments made by s 29(4) to the definition of the relevant five-year period in respect of the permitted company-age requirement for the VCT scheme not apply in relation to any holding of shares or securities issued by the company in the "material period"; or (e) elect that the amendments made by s 29(5) to the definition of a knowledge-intensive company for the VCT scheme not apply at any applicable time within the "material period".

In all of these elections, the "material period" is the period from 18 November 2015 to 5 April 2016. To be valid, the election must be made in writing, signed by a director of the company, be referred to in any compliance statement with reference to the EIS scheme made by the company under ITA 2007 s 204(2) with respect to shares issued in the material period (where applicable) and provided in copy form to any company to which it has issued shares or securities in the material period (where applicable). The election is irrevocable.

Section 31 adds a further condition to those listed in ITA 2007 s 274 that must be satisfied in relation to a company in order for HMRC to approve the company for the purposes of the VCT scheme. The new condition, the "non-qualifying investments condition", is that the company must not have made nor will it make at any time in the "relevant period" an investment that is neither included in the company's qualifying holdings when made nor an investment falling within ITA 2007 s 274(3A). That subsection was inserted by F(No 2)A 2015 s 26 and Sch 6 para 3, and refers to certain short-term and easily realisable investments. The exclusion is clarified by amending ITA 2007 s 274(3A) and inserting a new ITA 2007 s 274(3ZA). These amendments and other consequential amendments made by s 30 have effect for investments made after 5 April 2016.

Reliefs: peer-to-peer lending

Section 32 inserts new ITA 2007 Pt 8 Ch 1A (containing ITA 2007 ss 412A–412J), to provide income-tax relief for losses incurred by taxpayers on irrecoverable "peer-to-peer" loans. Peer-to-peer loans are loans made by would-be lenders to would-be borrowers via a linking platform and are a fast-growing alternative to seeking conventional loan finance from a credit institution.

New ITA 2007 s 412A is the basic relieving section. It provides that where a person has made a peer-to-peer (abbreviated here to P2P) loan and any outstanding loan has become irrecoverable at any time after 5 April 2015, that person (here called "the lender") shall be entitled to relief under that section. For amounts becoming irrecoverable after 5 April 2016, relief under new ITA 2007 s 412A is automatic. For earlier write-offs, relief under new ITA 2007 s 412A must be claimed. The relief is to be given by deducting the outstanding irrecoverable amount (called in these notes "the lost loan") in calculating the lender's net income for the tax year in which the loan became irrecoverable (at Step 2 of the calculation in ITA 2007s 23) but the deduction may be made only from interest receivable by the lender on other P2P loans (a) made by the lender via the same platform ("the operator" in the legislation) or (b) in certain circumstances only, P2P loans made by other persons but assigned to the lender through the same operator. Those circumstances are that either the lender is a person satisfying Condition A or the borrower is a person satisfying Condition B (see below). The deduction may be made only to the extent that there is sufficient income from which to make it (the limitation in ITA 2007 s 25(4), (5)). However, there is an opportunity under new ITA 2007 s 412B for sideways relief and under new ITA 2007 s 412C for carry-forward relief.

Relief under new ITA 2007 s 412A is only available where the loan is of money and made on genuine commercial terms and not as part of a tax-avoidance scheme (a scheme to obtain a "tax advantage" as defined by FA 2013 s 208 for the purposes of the GAAR). A peer-to-peer loan is one that meets two of three conditions, i.e. Condition C and one of Conditions A and B. Condition C is that the lender would be liable for income tax on the loan interest (assuming that interest were paid). Condition A is that the lender is either (a) an individual; (b) a partnership of no more than three persons at least one of whom is not a body corporate; or (c) an unincorporated body of persons that is not a partnership and at least one of whom is not a body corporate. Alternatively, Condition B is met where the borrower (the recipient of the loan) is such a person as prescribed in Condition A and the loan is a personal loan (one not used wholly or predominantly for the purposes of a business or intended business of the recipient) or a loan of no more than £25,000 (a "small loan").

New ITA 2007 s 412B provides for sideways relief for lost loans. Where a lender is entitled to relief under new ITA 2007 s 412A, but there is insufficient or no income from which to make the deduction, the lender may claim for all or part of the amount not deductible under new ITA 2007 s 412A to be deducted in the same tax year against the lender's other interest income from other P2P loans made via other operators. There is no entitlement to deduct against other income generally, even interest from loans that are not P2P loans. As under new ITA 2007 s 412A, the sideways deduction may also be made against income from P2P loans made by other persons but assigned to the lender through the same operator. Here too, a further condition for assigned loans is that either the lender is a person satisfying Condition A or the borrower is a person satisfying Condition B (see above) and that the loan is a personal loan or a small loan. As under new ITA 2007 s 412A, the deduction is subject to the limitation in ITA 2007 s 25(4), (5).

New ITA 2007 s 412C provides for carry-forward relief for lost loans. Where a lender is entitled to relief under new ITA 2007 s 412A, but there is insufficient or no income from which to make the deduction under that section or the sideways deduction under new ITA 2007 s 412B, the lender may claim to carry the outstanding amount forward for up to four tax years. The amount thus brought forward may be deducted against (a) interest from the loan itself; (b) interest from any other P2P loan made by the lender through any operator; or (c) interest from P2P loans made by other persons and assigned to the lender through any operator, provided in the case of (c) that either the lender is a person satisfying Condition A or the borrower is a person satisfying Condition B (see below) and the loan is a personal loan or a small loan. New ITA 2007 s 412D provides that amounts brought forward must first be deducted against lending income in the first following tax year; any remaining balance against lending income of the second following tax year, and so on.

New ITA 2007 s 412E provides that where any lost loan for which a deduction has been made is subsequently wholly or partly recovered, the amount recovered is to be treated as interest on that loan paid to the lender in the tax year in which it was recovered. New ITA 2007 s 412F deals with assigned loans. Where the right to recover the principal of a loan is assigned to a person through an operator, the assignee makes a payment for the assignment and does not further assign the right, the assignee is to be treated as if he had made the loan via that operator. The deduction in respect of an assigned loan may not exceed the amount paid by the assignee less any amounts previously recovered by the assignee. New ITA 2007 s 412G provides that loans or payments or assignments made by or to a nominee or bare trustee of a person are to be treated as made by or to that person.

New ITA 2007 s 412H puts a limitation on the amount of relief that may be claimed under these provisions where relief in respect of the same loan has already been received under different provisions. The amount of the lost loan cannot exceed the amount of the principal that has actually become irrecoverable less any other relief in respect of that loan obtained by *any person* under other provisions. New ITA 2007 s 412I is an interpretation section. New ITA 2007 s 412J defines "operator". Broadly speaking, an operator is a person authorised by the Financial Conduct Authority under FISMA 2000 to act as a P2P platform or who has obtained equivalent authorisation by another country within the European Economic Area.

Transactions in securities

Sections 33 and 34 make important changes to the anti-avoidance legislation relating to transactions in securities (ITA 2007 Pt 13 Ch 1). The changes follow consultation and will affect both the targeted transactions and the procedure taken to counteract them.

Section 33 addresses the types of transaction at which the legislation aims. In ITA 2007 s 684, which defines the persons liable to counteraction, the class of persons targeted is widened to include not just the person who entered into the transaction but also any person who receives a tax advantage from the transaction. The focus of the section is shifted from the purpose of the person entering into the transaction to the purposes of the transaction itself. Two further types of transaction are added to the types of targeted transaction mentioned in ITA 2007 s 684(2), namely a repayment of share capital or share premium and a distribution in respect of securities in a winding-up.

ITA 2007 s 685 describes the conditions (A and B) in relation to the targeted transactions one of which must be met for the legislation to apply. Following the amendments to ITA 2007 s 684, the conditions are amended to refer to any relevant party to the transactions, and the "relevant consideration" received for the transactions, where it represents assets available for distribution by way of dividend, may now be assets so available in companies controlled by the company concerned and not just assets of the company concerned itself. The provision in ITA 2007 s 685(6) that references to assets do not include assets representing a return of capital subscribed for securities *despite* the fact that they are available for distribution by way of dividend in the law of the country of incorporation is amended to state that those references do not include assets representing a return of capital subscribed for securities *merely because* they are available for distribution by way of dividend in the law of the country of incorporation.

ITA 2007 s 686 defines the circumstances ("the excluded circumstances") which, if present, will prevent the application of the legislation to the transactions in question. Broadly speaking, for the section to apply, there must be at least a 75% ("fundamental") change of ownership. The focus of the test is now turned towards the position of the original shareholders after the transaction(s). The test of a fundamental change of ownership is where after the transaction(s) the original shareholder(s), together with any associate(s) do not directly or indirectly hold more than 25% of the company's ordinary share capital or shares carrying an entitlement to more than 25% of the distributions that the company may make or shares carrying more than 25% of the total voting rights in the company.

In ITA 2007 s 687, which defines the income tax advantage against which the legislation is aimed, the disregard of the excess of the relevant consideration over the maximum amount that could have been paid to the person concerned is broadened to include occasions where distributions could have been paid to an associate of that person. The time at which those distributions could have been paid is now to be a time when Condition A or B is met, and not when the relevant consideration is received. A definition of "associate" is inserted into ITA 2007 s 713.

These amendments are to have effect in relation to transactions occurring after 5 April 2016 or to a series of transactions any one or more of which occurs after that date. The previous wording thus applies to tax advantages that are obtained after 5 April 2016 but arise as a consequence of transactions on or before that date. Where a clearance has been given on an application under ITA 2007 s 701 made before 6 April 2016 but the transaction or any one or more of the transactions occurs after 5 April 2016 and the new wording renders the persons liable to counteraction, the clearance previously given is to be considered void.

Section 34 alters the procedure for counteracting a tax advantage under this legislation. Hitherto, the procedure has been that HMRC would issue a preliminary notice under ITA 2007 s 695 that there was reason to believe that a counteraction notice should be served, upon which the taxpayer concerned had 30 days under ITA 2007 s 696 within which to make a statutory declaration if he believed to the contrary. Where HMRC still saw reason to take further action, the matter would be referred to the tribunal under ITA 2007 s 697. A new ITA 2007 s 695 is now substituted, under which HMRC will now instead notify the taxpayer that it intends to open an enquiry into the transaction(s) concerned, which it must do within six years of the end of the tax year to which the advantage relates. ITA 2007 ss 696 and 697 are omitted. Instead, ITA 2007 s 698 is amended to provide that where HMRC, on concluding its enquiry, determines that the legislation does apply will serve a counteraction notice specifying the adjustments that must be made to counter the advantage. Assessments to tax in accordance with a counteraction notice may now be made at any time, regardless of the normal time limits for assessments, removing the six-year time limit hitherto provided in ITA 2007 s 698(5). Where, however, the result of the enquiry is that HMRC comes to the opinion that no counteraction is required, it must issue a no-counteraction notice under new ITA 2007 s 698A. The taxpayer may also apply to the tribunal for a direction requiring the issue of either a counteraction notice or a non-counteraction notice. The amendments made by s 34 have effect for transactions occurring after 5 April 2016 or to a series of transactions any one or more of which occurs after that date.

Section 35 introduces a new targeted anti-avoidance rule into ITTOIA 2005 aimed at distributions in a winding-up. The new rule is best seen as related to the changes in the transactions in securities legislation introduced by ss 33 and 34. Two new sections, ITTOIA 2005 ss 396B and 404A are inserted.

New ITTOIA 2005 s 396B provides that a distribution made to an individual in respect of share capital when a UK-resident company is wound up is to be a distribution (chargeable to income tax) when four conditions (A–D) are met and the distribution is not an excluded distribution. A distribution is excluded if or to the extent that its amount is such as would not result in the accrual of a chargeable gain or it is a distribution of irredeemable shares.

Condition A is that the individual has an interest of at least 5% in the company immediately before the winding-up. Condition B is that the company is a close company when it is wound up or was a close company at any time within the two years preceding the start of the winding-up.

Condition C is that any time in the two years following the date of the distribution, the individual receiving the distribution either (a) carries on a trade or activity same as or similar to that carried on by the company or an effective 51% subsidiary of the company; (b) is a partner in a partnership carrying on such a trade or activity; (c) is, or a person connected with the individual is, a participator in a company in which the individual has at least a 5% interest and which at that time carries on such a trade or activity or is connected with a company carrying on such a trade or activity; or (d) the individual is involved with the carrying-on of such a trade or activity by a person connected to the individual.

Condition D is the tax-avoidance condition, namely that it is reasonable to assume that the purpose or one of the main purposes of the winding-up is the avoidance or reduction of a charge to tax or the winding-up forms part of arrangements with that as their main purpose or as one of their main purposes.

Terms such as "effective 51% subsidiary" as well as what constitutes an interest of at least 5%, are defined.

New ITA 2007 s 404A contains the identical provisions in respect of distributions made by a company that is not UK-resident. References here to a close company are references to a company that would be close if it were UK-resident.

The amendments made by s 35 have effect for distributions made after 5 April 2016.

Disguised fees and carried interest

Sections 36 to 38 amend and expand the code on the taxation of disguised management fees first introduced by FA 2015 s 21(1) as ITA 2007 Pt 13 Ch 5E (ITA 2007 ss 809EZA–809EZH) and amended by F(No 2)A 2015 s 41. In relation to carried interest, the capital-gains charge first introduced by F(No 2)A 2015 s 40 as TCGA 1992 Pt 3 Ch 5 on carried interest treated as a capital gain is now supplemented by a charge to income tax on carried interest taking the form of income.

Section 36 amends the main charge to tax on disguised investment-management fees in ITA 2007 s 809EZA. The charge on disguised management fees takes the form of deeming the individual to be carrying on a trade of which the disguised fees are the profits. ITA 2007 s 809EZA(2) is now amended to make it clear that the disguised fees may arise not only in the year in which the individual actually performs the services but also in respect of past or future performance of those services. The meaning of a collective investment scheme for these purposes is extended to include arrangements permitting an external investor to participate in investments acquired by the scheme without participating in the scheme itself and arrangements under which sums arise in respect of management services in respect of the collective investment scheme but do not arise from the scheme itself. These amendments have effect for sums arising after 5 April 2016.

Section 37 introduces new ITA 2007 Pt 13 Ch 5F (consisting of 26 sections, ITA 2007 ss 809FZA–809FZZ) charging income tax on "income-based carried interest". A consequential amendment to ITA 2007 s 809EZB(1)(c) amends the exclusion of carried interest from the meaning of "management fee" so as to exclude only carried interest that is not income-based carried interest.

Within new ITA 2007 Pt 13 Ch 5F, new ITA 2007 s 809FZA is the overview section. It is made clear that nothing in the Chapter is to affect the liability to tax of the investment scheme or external investors in the scheme.

New ITA 2007 s 809FZB contains the general rule determining to what extent carried interest is income-based carried interest and thus chargeable to income tax under these provisions rather than to capital gains tax under TCGA 1992 Pt 3 Ch 5. The extent to which an amount of carried interest is to be income-based carried interest is now to depend on the average holding period (AHP), from 0% for an AHP of 40 months or more to 100% for an AHP of less than 36 months. This mathematical test replaces the case-law based test with reference to the badges of trade that has hitherto been used to identify the income element.

New ITA 2007 s 809FZC defines the AHP as the average length of time over which "relevant investments" have been held for the purposes of the scheme from which the carried interest arises. "Relevant investments" are those made for the purposes of the scheme and by reference to which the carried interest is calculated. The AHP is to be calculated by reference to the time the carried interest arises, in three steps. Step 1 is for each relevant investment to multiply the value invested at the time the investment was made by the length of time for which the investment was held before its disposal or has been held up to the time the carried interest arises. Step 2 is to add together all the amounts calculated under Step 1. Step 3 is to divide the total reached in Step 2 by the total value invested in all relevant investments. Intermediate holdings or intermediate holding structures are to be disregarded in this respect. The following 13 sections (ss 809FZD–809FZP) all have some bearing on the calculation of the average holding period.

New ITA 2007 s 809FZD deals with disposals. A disposal takes place not only where there is a disposal for CGT purposes of the actual investment or of that part of it held for the purposes of the scheme, but also where there is a disposal of an intermediate holding or intermediate holding structure by or through which the investment is held. There is a deemed disposal where arrangements have the result the scheme closes its position in substance on the investment or the scheme ceases to be exposed to risks and rewards in respect of the investment, and it is reasonable to suppose that the arrangements were designed to have that effect. FIFO is the identification rule to be used. New ITA 2007 s 809FZE provides for the treatment of part-disposals. The part disposed of and the part not disposed of are to be treated as two separate investments made at the same time. Their value is the appropriate proportion of the value first invested by reference to their value compared to the whole at the time of the disposal.

New ITA 2007 s 809FZF provides that the making and disposal of an unwanted short-term investment are to be disregarded if that investment is "excludable". Broadly speaking, an unwanted short-term investment is an investment that is made in order to secure a wanted investment but is in itself not an investment that the scheme wishes to hold and which it always intends to dispose of in the relatively short term. That term is defined differently in respect of different investments, e.g. the short term for land is 12 months, whereas the short term for unlisted securities is 6 months. An unwanted short-term investment is excludable if it is an investment in land, unlisted securities, a direct loan where the other investments are an unlisted company's shares or securities or the making of a direct loan that is a "qualifying loan" as defined in new ITA 2007 s 809FZR. The disregard of these investments is to cease when at any time it becomes reasonable to suppose that when the fund ceases to invest, 25% or more of the scheme's capital will have been invested in unwanted short-term investments.

New ITA 2007 s 809FZG sets out the treatment of derivative contracts. For the purposes of calculating the AHP, the value of an option contract is the cost of acquiring it; the value of a futures contract is the price specified in the contract for the subject matter; and in the case of a contract for differences, it is the notional principal of the contract. Events that are to constitute the disposal of a derivative are specified. A substantial variation in the terms of a derivative is to be treated as a disposal and a new acquisition. New ITA 2007 s 809FZH deals with the treatment of forex hedging contracts used as hedges against a relevant investment. Such contracts are not to be treated as scheme investments and entering into them is not to be regarded as a part-disposal of the related investment. However, if the hedging relationship is terminated but the contract subsists, the termination is to be treated as a scheme investment. Similarly, where an interest-rate contract is held as a hedge against a scheme investment, the interest-rate contract is not to be treated as a scheme investment and entering into one is not to be regarded as a part-disposal of the related investment. Here also, if the hedging relationship is terminated but the contract subsists, the termination is to be treated as a scheme investment.

New ITA 2007 s 809FZJ provides for the treatment of controlling interests that the scheme may have in a trading company or the holding company of a trading group. In these circumstances, any scheme investment in the company made after the acquisition of the controlling interest is to be treated as made at the time of that acquisition and any disposal of an investment in the company made after the acquisition of the controlling interest is to be treated as not having been made until there is a disposal that results in a diminution to under 40% of the scheme's interest in the company. New ITA 2007 s 809FZK provides for special rules where the investment scheme takes the form of a venture capital fund (as specially defined). Any venture-capital investment in a company in which the fund has a "relevant interest" made after the acquisition of the relevant interest is to be treated as made at the time of that acquisition and any disposal of a venture-capital investment in the company made after the acquisition of the controlling interest is to be treated as not having been made until (a) there is a disposal that has the effect that the fund has disposed of more than 80% of the greatest amount invested at any one time in the company or (b) the "scheme-director condition" ceases to be met. A "relevant interest" for these purposes is an interest of at least 5% in the company or a situation in which the value of venture-capital investments in the company held for the purposes of the scheme is more than £1million. The "scheme-director condition" is met where the scheme (either alone or acting with other investment schemes) is entitled to appoint a director of the company or of the company that controls the company and the director concerned is able to exercise specified rights.

New ITA 2007 s 809FZL sets out similar rules for situations where the investment scheme takes the form of a "significant equity-stake fund". This is a fund that is not a venture capital fund but of which it is reasonable to suppose that, at the time it begins to make investments, over the investment life of the fund more than 50% of the value of the investments it makes will be represented by "significant equity stakes" and more than 50% of that value will be invested in investments that are held for 40 months or more. A "significant equity stake" is an investment made in a company that is unlisted and likely to remain so and one that has the effect of creating an interest of 20% or more in the company, and one in respect of which the scheme-director condition (see new ITA 2007 s 809FZK) is met. Where such a fund has a significant equity stake in a trading company or the holding company of a trading group, any investment in the company made for the purposes of the fund after the acquisition of the significant equity stake is to be treated as made at the time of that acquisition and any disposal of an investment in the company made after the acquisition of the significant equity stake is to be treated as not having been made until there is a disposal that results in a diminution to under 15% of the fund's interest in the company or the scheme-director condition ceases to be met.

New ITA 2007 s 809FZM also provides similar rules, in this case in situations where the investment scheme takes the form of a "controlling equity-stake fund". This is a fund that is not a venture capital fund or a significant equity-stake fund but of which it is reasonable to suppose that, at the time it begins to make investments, over the investing life of the fund more than 50% of the value of the investments will be in controlling interests in trading companies or the holding companies of trading groups and more than 50% of that value will be invested in investments that are held for 40 months or more. Where such a fund has a 25% interest in a trading company or the holding company of a trading group, any investment in the company made for the purposes of the fund after the acquisition of the 25% interest is to be treated as made at the time of that acquisition and any disposal of an investment in the company made after the acquisition of the 25% interest is to be treated as not having been made until there is a disposal that results in a diminution to under 25% of the fund's interest in the company.

New ITA 2007 s 809FZN provides special rules to apply to real-estate funds having a major interest in land. A real-estate fund for this purpose is an investment scheme that is not a venture capital fund, a significant equity-stake fund nor a controlling equity-stake fund but of which it is reasonable to suppose that, at the time it begins to make investments, over the investing life of the fund more than 50% of the value of the investments will be in land and more than 50% of that value will be invested in investments that are held for 40 months or more. Where such a fund has a major interest in any land, any investment in that land made for the purposes of the fund after the acquisition of the major interest is to be treated as made at the time of that acquisition and any disposal of an investment in the land made after the acquisition of the major interest is to be treated as not having been made until there is a disposal that has the effect that the fund has disposed of more than 50% of the greatest amount invested at any one time in the land for the purposes of the fund. Where such a fund acquires a major interest in any land adjacent to other land in which it already has a major interest, the acquisition is treated as if it were an investment in the original land and thereafter the adjacent land is to be regarded as part of the original land.

New ITA 2007 s 809FZO provides special rules for a fund of funds. This is a fund of which it is reasonable to suppose that, at the time it begins to make investments, over the investing life of the fund substantially all of the total value of fund investments will be in collective investment schemes of which the scheme holds less than 50% by value; more than 50% of that value will be invested in investments that are held for 40 months or more, and more than 75% of the amount invested in the scheme will come from external investors. The disregard of intermediate holdings and holding structures under new ITA 2007 s 809FZC is not to apply where an investment is made for the purposes of a fund of funds in a collective investment scheme, but as an investment in the collective investment scheme itself. There is an exception to the rule where it is reasonable to suppose that the investment was made so as to reduce the proportion of income-based carried interest arising to any person. Where, as a result of the rule, a fund of funds thereby has a "significant investment" in the underlying collective investment scheme, any qualifying investment in the underlying scheme made for the purposes of the fund after the acquisition of the significant investment is to be treated as made at the time of that acquisition and any disposal of a qualifying investment in the underlying scheme made after the acquisition of the significant investment is to be treated as not having been made until there is a disposal that has the effect that (a) the fund of funds has disposed of at least 50% of the greatest amount invested at any one time in the underlying scheme for the purposes of the fund or (b) the investment of the fund of funds in the underlying scheme has diminished to the point that it is worth less than the greater of £1 million and 5% of the total value of the investments made in the underlying scheme before the disposal for the purposes of the fund of funds. A significant investment for these purposes is one of at least £1 million in the scheme or of at least 5% of the total raised or to be raised from external investors in the scheme. A definition is provided of what constitutes a qualifying investment.

New ITA 2007 s 809FZP provides similar rules for secondary funds. This is a fund of which it is reasonable to suppose that, at the time it begins to make investments, over the investing life of the fund substantially all of the total value of fund investments will be in the acquisition of investments in, or the acquisition of portfolios of investments from, unconnected collective investment schemes; more than 50% of that value will be invested in investments that are held for 40 months or more, and more than 75% of the amount invested in the scheme will come from external investors. As with a fund of funds, the disregard of intermediate holdings and holding structures under new ITA 2007 s 809FZC is not to apply to an investment acquired for the purposes of a secondary fund in a collective investment scheme, but as an investment in the collective investment scheme itself. There is an exception to the rule where it is reasonable to suppose that the investment was made so as to reduce the proportion of income-based carried interest arising to any person. Where, as a result of the rule, a secondary fund thereby has a "significant investment" in the underlying collective investment scheme, any qualifying investment in the underlying scheme acquired for the purposes of the secondary fund after the acquisition of the significant investment is to be treated as made at the time of that acquisition and any disposal of a qualifying investment in the underlying scheme made after the acquisition of the significant investment is to be treated as not having been made until there is a disposal that has the effect that (a) the secondary fund has disposed of at least 50% of the greatest amount invested at any one time in the underlying scheme for the purposes of the fund or (b) the investment of the secondary fund in the underlying scheme has diminished to the point that it is worth less than the greater of £1 million and 5% of the total value of the investments made in the underlying scheme before the disposal for the purposes of the secondary fund. A significant investment (the Bill has "significant interest" but presumably "significant investment" is meant) for these purposes is one of at least £1 million in the scheme or of at least 5% of the total raised or to be raised from external investors in the scheme. A definition is provided of what constitutes a qualifying investment.

New ITA 2007 s 809FZQ provides that carried interest arising from a direct-lending fund is entirely income-based carried interest, subject to the exception contained in new ITA 2007 s 809FZR. A direct-lending fund is an investment scheme that is not a venture capital fund, a significant equity-stake fund, a controlling equity-stake fund or a real-estate fund but of which it is reasonable to suppose that, at the time it ceases to make investments, a majority by value of the investments will have been direct loans it has made. A direct loan in this sense consists of advancing money at interest or for any other return calculated by reference to the time value of money. Direct loans made by other persons and acquired by the fund within 120 days of the date on which the money was first advanced are to be regarded as made by the fund.

Where a direct-lending fund meets the requirements of new ITA 2007 s 809FZR, the extent to which carried interest arising from the fund is income-based will be determined by the general rule in new ITA 2007 s 809FZB and not by the 100% attribution rule in new ITA 2007 s 809FZQ. The exception applies where the direct-lending fund is a limited partnership, the carried interest falls within ITA 2007 s 809EZD(2) or (3) (sums paid to an individual out of profits on the investments or on a particular investment but only after all or substantially all the investments have been repaid and any preferred return has been paid to external participants), and where it is reasonable to suppose that, at the time the fund ceases to make investments, at least 75% by value of the direct loans made by the fund will have been "qualifying loans". A definition is provided of what constitutes a qualifying loan.

New ITA 2007 ss 809FZS and 809FZT provide for some carried interest to be conditionally exempt from income tax in the early years of an investment scheme. Where carried interest is conditionally exempt under new ITA 2007 s 809FZS, it is to be regarded as not income-based to *any* extent. Conditional exemption will be conferred on carried interest where four conditions (A–D) are all met. Condition A is that the carried interest arises to the individual in the four years beginning with the day on which the scheme starts to invest or in the ten years beginning with that day if the carried interest is calculated on the "realisation model". Condition B is that the carried interest would otherwise be income-based to any extent. Condition C is that it is reasonable to suppose that if the carried interest were to arise to the individual at a later time in the fund's life (broadly, four or ten years after the carried interest begins to arise or within four years of the time the fund is expected to cease investing) it would not be income-based to any extent (because it related entirely to long-term investments). Condition D is that the individual makes a claim for conditional exemption. Under new ITA 2007 s 809FZT, conditional exemption is lost on the earliest of a number of events: (a) the winding-up of the scheme; (b) the end of the four-year period beginning immediately after the scheme ceases to invest; (c) the end of the four-year period from the day the carried interest arises (ten years if the realisation model is used); (d) the end of the four-year period beginning with the end of the period by reference to which the carried interest is determined; and (e) the time at which Condition C in new ITA 2007 s 809FZS ceases to be met. The "realisation model" is the approach to carried interest described in ITA 2007 s 809EZD and referenced in new ITA 2007 s 809FZR. Where carried interest ceases to be conditionally exempt, it is to be treated as having been income-based carried interest at the time that it arose to the extent that it would have been income-based had it arisen at the time it ceased to be conditionally exempt. Any capital gains tax that the individual has paid in respect of carried interest that now becomes income-based carried interest may be set off against the individual's liability to income tax arising from the change of status to income-based.

New ITA 2007 s 809FZU provides that carried interest arising from employment-related securities as defined by ITEPA 2003 s 421B(8) is not to be subject to these provisions. New ITA 2007 s 809FZV deals with "loan to own" investments. Where an investment scheme acquires impaired debt at a discount in order to obtain ownership of the assets on which the debt is secured or owned by the company that is the debtor, the assets and the debt are to be treated as a single investment for a value equal to the amount paid for the debt, provided that the assets are acquired within three months of the acquisition of the debt. New ITA 2007 s 809FZW contains the anti-avoidance proviso. No account is to be taken in determining the average holding period or whether an investment scheme is a venture capital fund, significant equity-stake fund, controlling equity-stake fund, real-estate fund, fund of funds or secondary fund of any arrangements the main purposes of which or one of the main purposes of which is to reduce the proportion of carried interest that is income-based. Furthermore, no regard is to be had in determining to what extent carried interest is income-based of any arrangements the main purposes of which or one of the main purposes of which is to secure that the charge to income tax on disguised investment-management fees under ITA 2007 s 809EZA does not apply in relation to some or all of the carried interest.

New ITA 2007 s 809FZX enables the Treasury to make regulations and new ITA 2007 s 809FZY defines what is meant by "reasonable to suppose" in these provisions. New ITA 2007 s 809FZZ is an interpretation section.

The amendments made by s 37, including the insertion of new ITA 2007 Pt 13 Ch 5F, are to have effect in relation to amounts of carried interest arising after 5 April 2016.

Section 38 amends the treatment of disguised investment-management fees under ITA 2007 s 809EZA to deal with the special situation of investment managers newly resident in the UK who receive those fees in respect of services they carried out while still non-resident. It does so by inserting new ITA 2007 s 809EZA(2A)–(2C).

The new rule applies to an investment manager who is UK-resident in a tax year in which disguised fees consisting of income-based carried interest arise to him or her from one or more investment schemes; that tax year is the first, second, third or fourth tax year of UK residence beginning immediately after a period of at least five consecutive tax years of non-residence; and the fees arise to the individual in respect of services carried out during the period of non-residence.

If some of those services, while being performed while the individual was non-resident, were nevertheless performed in the UK and some were performed outside the UK, the individual will be treated as carrying on two separate deemed trades: one that consists of performing the services that were performed in the UK and the other that consists of performing the services that were performed outside the UK ("the deemed non-UK trade"). Consequently, if the individual remains non-domiciled, he or she will be able to claim the remittance basis on the deemed non-UK trade. The amendments made by s 38 have effect for carried interest arising after 5 April 2016.

Deduction at source

Section 39 introduces **Sch 6**, which abolishes the requirement on deposit-takers to deduct income tax at source from most kinds of interest income. Schedule 6 consists of five Parts. Part 1 (para 1) abolishes the duty to deduct tax at source on most investments; Pt 2 (para 2) removes the duty to deduct tax from certain payments of yearly interest; Pt 3 (paras 3–25) makes consequential amendments to ITA 2007 and other statutes; Pt 4 (paras 26 and 27) concerns deduction at source from UK public-revenue dividends; and Pt 5 (para 28) provides for commencement.

Schedule 6 para 1 omits ITA 2007 s 851, which imposes on deposit-takers or building societies to deduct basic-rate tax at source from payments of interest on "relevant investments". Schedule 6 para 2 amends the wording of ITA 2007 s 856 so that deposit-takers are relieved of the duty imposed on them by ITA 2007 s 854 to deduct tax at source from certain payments of yearly interest where the underlying investment is a "relevant investment".

Schedule 6 Part 3 (paras 3–25) makes consequential amendments to ITA 2007 (paras 3–18) and other statutes (paras 19–25).

Schedule 6 para 26 makes a minor amendment to ITA 2007 s 876 (exemption from duty to deduct tax from public-revenue dividends), referring to ITA 2007 s 891 for a definition of "public-revenue dividend". Schedule 6 para 27 adds securities issued or treated as issued under the National Loans Act 1939 and the National Loans Act 1968 to the class of securities the interest on which is to be paid gross, so a direction to that effect under ITA 2007 s 894 is no longer needed.

Schedule 6 para 28 provides for commencement. Generally, the amendments have effect for interest, distributions, benefits, alternative-finance returns etc paid, conferred or credited after 5 April 2016.

Section 40 clarifies the duty under ITA 2007 s 906 to deduct income tax at source from royalty payments to persons whose usual place of abode is abroad and amends the definition of "intellectual property" for these purposes. Section 40(2) amends ITA 2007 s 906 so that it now provides that the duty to deduct income tax at the basic rate applies where either of two conditions – A or B – is met. Condition A is that the payment is a royalty or payment of any other kind for the use of or the right to use, intellectual property the owner of which has a usual place of abode outside the UK, where the payment is charged to income tax or corporation tax. This is largely a rephrase of the existing provision, except that there is no longer a requirement for the payments to be made periodically. Condition B is that the payment is of sums payable periodically in respect of intellectual property; that the person entitled to those sums has assigned the intellectual property and has his usual place of abode outside the UK; and that the payment is charged to income tax or corporation tax. This condition replaces the references in the existing legislation to the assignor as 'the seller'. The existing exemption for certain works or articles exported from the UK is retained. Section 40(3) substitutes a new ITA 2007 s 907, which defines what is meant by "intellectual property", replacing the existing definition of a "relevant intellectual-property right". The new definition is closely based on the definition of "intellectual property" in Art 12(2) of the OECD Model Tax Convention. The existing exemptions in ITA 2007 s 907 are retained, but an anti-avoidance proviso is added to the effect that no regard is had to when determining whether the duty to deduct under ITA 2007 s 906 applies to any arrangements the main purpose or one of the main purposes of which is to avoid that duty. The amendments made by s 40 have effect for payments made after 27 June 2016, with transitional provisions to prevent forestalling of the anti-avoidance rule.

Section 41 is a targeted anti-avoidance rule designed to counter the artificial use of double tax treaties to avoid the duty to deduct tax at source from the payment of certain royalties. It inserts new ITA 2007 s 917A into ITA 2007 Pt 15 Ch 8 (Special provisions in relation to royalties). New ITA 2007 s 917A provides that where an "intellectual-property royalty payment" is paid between connected persons and made under "DTA tax-avoidance arrangements", the duty imposed under ITA 2007 Pt 15 Chs 6 or 7 to deduct tax from the royalty payment is to apply regardless of the provisions of the treaties concerned. An "intellectual-property royalty payment" is defined by direct reference back to ITA 2007 s 906 as amended by s 40(?) (i.e. as a royalty or payment of any other kind for the use of, or the right to use, intellectual property or as a payment of sums payable periodically in respect of intellectual property). A "DTA tax-avoidance arrangement" is an arrangement of which it is reasonable to conclude that its main purposes or one of its main purposes is to obtain a tax advantage by virtue of a double tax treaty where obtaining that tax advantage is contrary to the object and purpose of the treaty provision(s) concerned. Persons are connected for these purposes if the participation condition in TIOPA 2010 s 148, as modified, is met between them. The amendments made by s 41 are to have effect in respect of payments made after 16 March 2016. However, for payments made after that date and on or before 15 September 2016, the definition of "intellectual-property royalty payment" is to be read as that appearing in the Bill as first published, which is to say as: a royalty or other sum in respect of the use of a patent; a royalty, or sum payable periodically, in respect of a "relevant intellectual property right" as defined in ITA 2007 s 907 before its substitution by s 40(3); or a qualifying annual payment within ITA 2007 s 899(3)(a)(ii). For payments made after 27 June 2016 and on or before 15 September 2016, the definition of "intellectual-property royalty payment" is also to include payments mentioned in ITA 2007 s 906 as amended by s 40(2).

Section 42 extends the scope of the charge to UK income tax on receipts from intellectual property arising from payments made by a non-resident in respect of a trade carried on by that non-resident through a permanent establishment in the UK. The mechanism for doing so is the insertion (by s 42(2)) of new ITTOIA 2005 s 577A.

ITTOIA 2005 s 577 provides that the charge to income tax under ITTOIA 2005 Pt 5 on miscellaneous income (including receipts from intellectual property), which is, broadly, the old Sch D Case VI charge, applies to income arising to a UK resident whether or not it derives from a source in the UK but that it applies to the income of a non-resident only to the extent that it does derive from a source in the UK. Section 42(1) amends ITTOIA 2005 s 577 to make reference to new ITTOIA 2005 s 577A, which is to define the territorial scope of receipts from intellectual property.

New ITTOIA 2005 s 577A provides that references in ITTOIA 2005 s 577 to income having its source in the UK are to include income arising as a result of the payment by a person not resident in the UK of a royalty or other sum in respect of intellectual property made in connection with a trade that the payer carries on through a permanent establishment in the UK. Where the trade is only partly carried on by the non-resident payer, a just and reasonable apportionment of the payment is to be made. In order to counter avoidance, no regard is to be had in determining whether income has its source in the UK of any arrangements the main purpose or one of the main purposes of which is to avoid the new rule. "Permanent establishment" and "intellectual property" are defined. The amendments made by s 42 are to have effect for royalties and other relevant sums paid after 27 June 2016, with transitional provisions to prevent forestalling of the anti-avoidance rule and the rule in new ITA 2007 s 917A against abuse of double tax treaties inserted by s 41 and to counter arrangements aiming to exploit the EU Interest and Royalties Directive.

Section 43 is to be seen in conjunction with s 42. It amends the provisions in FA 2015 Pt 3 on diverted profits tax so as to include within the charge to that tax amounts equal to royalties and other payments in respect of intellectual property made in connection with a trade carried on in the UK which would have been subject to deduction of tax at source had the "avoided" permanent establishment been an actual permanent establishment in the UK.

FA 2015 s 79 (as amended by F(No 2)A 2015 Sch 3 para 12) provides that the rate of diverted profits tax on diverted banking surcharge profits or notional banking surcharge profits is to be 33% rather than 25%. Section 43(2) amends FA 2015 s 79 to ensure that any royalty etc payments included in "notional PE profits" as redefined in FA 2015 s 88(5) as amended by s 43(3) are excluded from the 33% charge but remain chargeable at 25%.

FA 2015 s 88 defines "notional PE profits" variously brought into charge to diverted profits tax under FA 2015 ss 89–91. Section 43(3) amends FA 2015 s 88(5) so that "notional PE profits" are now to include a second element, namely an amount equal to the total royalties or other sums paid by the foreign company in question in connection with the trade carried on via the medium of the avoided permanent establishment in a way that avoids deduction of tax under ITA 2007 s 906. New FA 2015 s 88(5A), inserted by s 43(3), provides that, in this connection, avoidance of the duty to deduct tax under ITA 2007 s 906 means that that section does not apply but would have applied had the avoided permanent establishment been an actual UK permanent establishment through which the foreign company carried on the trade.

FA 2015 s 100 provides that in certain prescribed circumstances, a credit for a just and reasonable proportion of UK corporation tax or a similar foreign tax that a company pays may be set off against a liability to diverted profits tax that the company has in respect of the same profits or against another company's liability to diverted profits tax calculated by reference to all or part of those profits. Section 43(5) amends FA 2015 s 100 to exclude the set-off of such a credit against so much of a liability to diverted profits tax as arises from the inclusion of the royalties referred to in FA 2015 s 88(5)(b) as amended by s 43(3). New FA 2015 s 100(4A), (4B), inserted by s 43(6), prevent a double charge to tax under FA 2015 s 91(4) or (5) (mismatch condition: profits calculated by reference to the relevant alternative provision) on an amount represented by a single royalty or other sum within FA 2015 s 88(5)(b) by virtue of its inclusion in notional PE profits and the relevant taxable income of a connected company. New FA 2015 s 100(4C)-(4E), also inserted by s 43(6), provide for a credit to be given on a just and reasonable basis where relief would have been due under ITTOIA 2005 s 758 (EU Interest and Royalties Directive) or under a double tax treaty on a royalty or other payment within FA 2015 s 88(5)(b).

The amendments made by s 43 are to have effect for accounting periods ending after 27 June 2016, with transitional provisions to prevent forestalling.

Section 44 empowers HM Treasury to make regulations amending ITEPA 2005 Part 10 Chapters 1–5 so as either to exempt supplementary welfare payments (as defined) made in Northern Ireland from income tax or to make them chargeable on a different basis. Regulations made before 6 April 2017 and relating to the tax year 2016/17 may have retroactive effect from 6 April 2016.

PART 2
CORPORATION TAX

Charge and rates

Section 45 reimposes the charge to corporation tax for the financial year 2017. **Section 46** provides that the main rate of corporation tax for the financial year 2020 is to be 17%, and not 18% as hitherto provided by F(No 2)A 2015 s 7(2). The main rate of corporation tax for the financial year 2016 is 20% (FA 2015 s 6).

Section 47 abolishes vaccine research relief, first introduced in 2003 and limited to large companies by FA 2012 s 20 and Sch 3. It is now abolished altogether by the omission of CTA 2009 Pt 13 Ch 7 and consequential amendments. The amendments made by s 47 are to have effect in relation to expenditure incurred after 31 March 2017.

Section 48 amends the formula in CTA 2009 s 1114 for calculating a company's total R&D aid relevant to the State-Aid cap on such aid of € 7.5 million per project. The factor (N x CT), where N is the "notional relief" under CTA 2009 s 1118 and CT the main rate of corporation tax is replaced by N and the definition of N itself amended. N is now to refer to the "notional R&D expenditure credit", and is defined as the total amount of R&D expenditure credit that the claimant company could have claimed under CTA 2009 Pt 3 Ch 6A (Trade profits: R&D expenditure credits) in respect of an R&D project if it had been a large company throughout the accounting period concerned. This replaces the previous reference to large-company relief under CTA 2009 Pt 13 Ch 5, which has been replaced by the R&D expenditure credit since 1 April 2016. The amendments made by s 48 have effect for expenditure incurred after 31 March 2016.

Loan relationships

Section 49 introduces Sch 7, which makes changes to the loan-relationships and derivative-contracts legislation in CTA 2009 Pts 5 and 6. The changes address three areas: non-market loans, transfer-pricing rules and exchange gains and losses. Schedule 7 consists of 12 paragraphs.

Schedule 7 para 1 is introductory. Schedule 7 para 2 inserts new CTA 2009 s 446A into CTA 2009 Pt 5 Ch 15 (loan relationships: tax avoidance). Recent changes in accounting standards have created the possibility of a loan-relationship debit for interest-free and other loans not at market rates without a matching credit, especially where the lender is non-resident. New CTA 2009 s 446A is intended to eliminate that possibility.

It applies where the amount initially recognised in a company's accounts in respect of a debtor relationship is less than the transaction price (the amount borrowed) and the corresponding discount is not brought into account, or not wholly brought into account by the creditor. Where the creditor is a company, it must meet the "non-qualifying territory condition" for the new section to apply. The "non-qualifying territory condition" is met where the creditor company is resident or effectively managed in a non-qualifying territory for any part of the accounting period. TIOPA 2010 s 173 has effect for defining what is a non-qualifying territory. Where new CTA 2009 s 446A applies, the debits that the debtor company may bring into account may not include any amounts relating to the extent of the discount not recognised by the creditor.

Schedule 7 paras 3 and 4 address transfer-pricing rules. The intention is to ensure that to the extent that debits have been restricted as a result of transfer-pricing adjustments, the corresponding amount of credits need not be brought into account. CTA 2009 s 446 is amended so as to provide that no credits are to be brought into account to the extent that they correspond to amounts not previously brought into account as debits as a result of transfer-pricing adjustments. The analogous amendment is made to the corresponding provision in the derivative-contracts legislation, CTA 2009 s 693.

Schedule 7 paras 5–11 deal with exchange gains and losses. CTA 2009 s 447 provides that where an exchange gain or loss arises in respect of a liability representing a non-arm's length debtor relationship, and as a result of transfer-pricing adjustments, the company's profits and losses are calculated as if all or part of the loan had not been made, a corresponding element of the exchange gain or loss must be disregarded when determining the debits and credits to be brought into account. CTA 2009 s 447 is now amended to provide that where the debtor relationship is to any extent matched, the amounts of exchange gain or loss to be left out of account are to be limited to the smaller of the amount that would otherwise be left out of account and the exchange gain or loss arising on the unmatched element of the debtor relationship.

A similar amendment restricting the exclusion of exchange gains and losses to that corresponding to the unmatched element of the debtor relationship is made to CTA 2009 s 448 (equity notes where holder associated with issuer) In the case of CTA 2009 s 449 (creditor relationship: no corresponding debtor relationship), the amendment refers to the unmatched element of the creditor relationship. The amendment made to CTA 2009 s 451, which provides the exception to CTA 2009 s 449, is identically worded to that made to CTA 2009 s 447, except for the substitution of "creditor relationship" for "debtor relationship".

Under TIOPA 2010 s 192(1), a company that has guaranteed a loan relationship may claim to stand in the shoes of the borrower (the issuing company in respect of a security). CTA 2007 s 452 provides for the treatment of exchange gains and losses in connection with a loan relationship in respect of which a claim under TIOPA 2010 s 192(1) has been made or is deemed to have been made. Amendments now made to CTA 2007 s 452 to prevent double counting. The total amount of credits that may be brought into account in respect of exchange gains from the debtor relationship or relationships may not now exceed the exchange gains (or the appropriate proportion of those gains) left out of account by the issuing company under CTA 2009 s 447 in respect of the loan relationship (and not by reference to the creditor relationship, as hitherto). Similarly, the total amount of debits that may be brought into account in respect of exchange losses from the debtor relationship or relationships may not now exceed the exchange losses (or the appropriate proportion of those losses) left out of account by the issuing company under CTA 2009 s 447 in respect of the loan relationship.

New CTA 2009 s 475B, inserted by s 45(6), defines if and if so, to what extent, a loan relationship is matched for these purposes.

With respect to derivative contracts, the amendments are limited to a single section – CTA 2009 s 694. That section has hitherto provided that where a company that is a party to a derivative contract has exchange gains or losses from that contract and, as a result of the transfer-pricing rules, its profits and losses are to be calculated for tax purposes as if it were not a party to the contract, those gains or losses are to be left out of account in determining the credits and debits to be brought into account in respect of the contract. This exclusion is now amended where the contract is matched to any extent to limit it to the gains or losses corresponding to the unmatched element of the contract. Similarly, where the company's profits and losses are as a result of transfer-pricing adjustments to be calculated for tax purposes as if the contract were on arm's length terms, the rule has been that in determining the credits and debits to be brought into account, the exchange gains and losses to be taken into account are those that would have arisen on the hypothetical arm's length contract. That rule is now to apply only to the extent that the contract is unmatched. A definition of when and to what extent a contract is matched is inserted as new CTA 2009 s 694(11).

Schedule 7 para 12 provides that the amendments made by Sch 7 are to have effect in relation to accounting periods beginning after 31 March 2016. Periods straddling 1 April 2016 are to be treated as two separate periods.

Section 50 changes the rate of tax charged under CTA 2010 s 455(2) on a close company making a loan to a participator etc from 25% of the amount of the loan to that percentage of the amount that corresponds to the dividend upper rate. Similarly, the rate of tax charged on a close company conferring a benefit arising from a tax-avoidance arrangement on a participator etc from 25% of the value of the benefit to that percentage of the value that corresponds to the dividend upper rate. In 2016/17, the dividend upper rate is 32.5%. The amendments made by s 50 have effect for loans advanced or benefits conferred after 5 April 2016.

Section 51 is a relieving provision. It excludes loans or advances made to a trustee of a charitable trust and applied solely for the purposes of the charity from the tax charge under CTA 2010 s 455 on loans to participators etc, with effect for loans made after 24 November 2015.

Intangible fixed assets

Sections 52 and **53** are intended to counter schemes that purport to bring pre-FA 2002 intangible assets into the CTA 2009 Pt 8 régime without an effective change of ownership and at a value other than market value by using vehicles such as partnerships and limited-liability partnerships.

Section 52 amends CTA 2009 s 882. That section provides that assets may be included in the CTA 2009 Pt 8 régime where they are acquired (and not necessarily created) after 31 March 2002 where they are acquired from a non-related party and also from a related party provided that the acquisition falls within one of three cases. As regards assets created before 1 April 2002, only acquisitions within Case B, which involves an intermediary acquiring the asset from a non-related party, would fit the bill. The amendments (which insert new CTA 2009 s 882(5A)–(5D)) provide that persons are also to be regarded as related parties if the participation condition of TIOPA 2010 s 148 is met as between them. References to a person are to include a firm for the purposes of CTA 2009 s 1259 (which prescribes how the profits of a partnership including a partner within the charge to corporation tax are to be allocated to the corporate partner). New CTA 2009 s 882(5A)–(5D) are also to apply to CTA 2009 ss 894 (preserved-status condition) and 895 (assets acquired in connection with disposals of pre-FA 2002 assets).

Section 53 amends the market-value rule in CTA 2009 s 845, by inserting new CTA 2009 s 845(4A)–(4E). The rule in CTA 2009 s 845 is that any transfer of an intangible asset between a company and a related party is to be treated as made at market value, provided that the asset remains in the CTA 2009 Pt 8 régime. The same amendments are made to this section as are made to CTA 2009 s 882, namely that persons are also to be regarded as related parties if the participation condition of TIOPA 2010 s 148 is met as between them and that references to a person are to include a firm for the purposes of CTA 2009 s 1259. Additionally, however, where a gain by a firm on the disposal of an intangible asset is a gain to be taken into account for the purposes of CTA 2009 s 1259 and for those purposes references to a company in CTA 2009 s 845 are to be taken as references to a firm, that gain is to be treated as a "chargeable realisation gain" for the purposes of CTA 2009 s 741, which means that the underlying asset is an asset to which the CTA 2009 Pt 8 régime, and hence the market-value rule, applies. The amendment made by s 53 has effect, subject to transitional provisions, for transfers taking place after 24 November 2015.

Creative-industry reliefs

Section 54 introduces Sch 8, which provides tax relief for the production of orchestral concerts, the so-called orchestra tax relief. The provisions are closely modelled on those for TV tax relief and video games tax relief in CTA 2009 Pts 15A and 15B respectively and particularly so on theatre tax relief in CTA 2009 Part 15C.

Schedule 8 consists of three Parts. Part 1 (para 1) inserts new CTA 2009 Pt 15D providing for orchestra tax relief. Part 2 (paras 2–15) makes consequential amendments. Part 3 (paras 16–18) provides for commencement.

New CTA 2009 Pt 15D consists of six Chapters. Chapter 1 (Introduction) contains CTA 2009 ss 1217P–1217PB; Chapter 2 (Taxation of activities of production company) contains CTA 2009 ss 1217Q–1217QG); Chapter 3 (Orchestra tax relief) contains CTA 2009 ss 1217R–1217RM), Ch 4 (Losses of separate orchestral trade) contains CTA 2009 ss 1217S–1217SC); Ch 5 (Provisional entitlement to relief) contains CTA 2009 ss 1217T–1217RA; and Ch 6 (Interpretation) contains only one section (CTA 2009 s 1217U).

New CTA 2009 s 1217P is an overview section. It provides that a relief from corporation tax, to be known as "orchestra tax relief", may be given to a production company in relation to its "orchestral concert" or series of orchestral concerts in a separate trade.

New CTA 2009 s 1217PA defines what is meant by an "orchestral concert", which is a concert by an orchestra, ensemble, group or band consisting wholly or mainly of instrumentalists who are the primary focus of the concert. However, concerts are not orchestral concerts if their mainly intended to advertise or promote goods or services, they consist of or contain a competition or contest, or where the production company's main object in relation to the concert is to make a recording. New CTA 2009 s 1217PB defines what is meant by a "production company". This is a company, acting otherwise than in partnership, that (a) is responsible from start to finish for putting on the concert, hiring the performers etc; (b) is actively engaged in decision making in relation to the concert; (c) makes an effective creative, technical and artistic contribution to the concert; and (d) directly negotiates for, contracts for and pays for rights, gods and services relating to the concert. There can be no more than one production company in respect of a concert or concert series for the purposes of the relief.

New CTA 2009 s 1217Q provides that where a production company qualifies for relief in relation to a concert, its activities in producing that concert are to be treated as a trade (the "separate orchestral trade") separate from any other trades or activities it may carry on. Where the concert is one of a series, the company may elect under new CTA 2009 s 1217QA to have the production activities related to the series as a single separate trade.

New CTA 2009 s 1217QA contains the conditions for the concert series election. This must be made in writing before the date of the first concert in the series, specifying the concerts in the series and which (if any) are not to be "qualifying orchestral concerts". The election is irrevocable.

New CTA 2009 s 1217QB provides for the calculation of the profits or losses of the separate orchestral trade. For the first period of account, the costs of production incurred to date are to be brought into account as debits and the proportion of the estimated total income treated as earned at the end of that period is to be brought into account as a credit. That proportion for any period is given by (C/T) x I, where C is the total to date of production costs incurred, T is the estimated total production cost and I is the estimated total income. For subsequent periods, debits are the difference between the costs of production to date and the corresponding amount for the previous period; the credit is the difference between the proportion of estimated total income treated as earned at the end of that period and the corresponding amount for the previous period.

New CTA 2009 s 1217QC provides that income from the production includes receipts from ticket sales or sales of rights; royalties or other payments for use of the concert or concert series; payments for rights to produce merchandise; and the company's receipts by way of a profit-share agreement. Receipts that would otherwise be capital receipts are nevertheless to be treated as revenue receipts.

New CTA 2009 s 1217QD defines production costs. These are expenditure incurred by the company on activities involved in developing and staging the concert or concert series or on activities with a view to exploiting the concert or concert series. Expenditure that would otherwise be regarded as capital expenditure solely because it is incurred on the creation of an asset is to be treated as revenue expenditure.

New CTA 2009 s 1217QE provides for when costs are taken to be incurred. New CTA 2009 s 1217QF provides that production costs are incurred before the start of the separate orchestral trade, may be treated as incurred immediately after the company begins to carry on that trade.

New CTA 2009 s 1217QG provides that estimates must be made as at the balance-sheet date on a just and reasonable basis, taking into consideration all relevant circumstances.

New CTA 2009 s 1217R introduces new CTA 2009 Pt 15D Ch 3, which provides for the relief. New CTA 2009 s 1217RA provides that for a company to qualify for orchestral tax relief in respect of a concert not included in a concert series election: (a) the concert must be a "qualifying orchestral concert"; (b) it must be the production company in relation to that concert; (c) the company must intend that the concert be performed live before the paying public or for educational purposes; and (d) the "EEA-expenditure condition" must be met in relation to the concert. A "qualifying orchestral concert" is an orchestral concert involving at least 12 instrumentalists (so chamber-music concerts given by quartets etc do not qualify) in which none of the musical instruments or only a minority, are electronically or directly amplified. Similar conditions apply in respect of a concert series, in which all or a high proportion of concerts must be qualifying orchestral concerts and the production company must intend that all or a high proportion of the concerts be performed live before the paying public or for educational purposes.

New CTA 2009 s 1217RB contains the EEA-expenditure condition, which is that at least 25% of the "core expenditure" incurred on the production of the concert or concert series by the company is EEA expenditure, i.e. expenditure on goods or services provided from within the European Economic Area. New CTA 2009 s 1217RC defines "core expenditure".

New CTA 2009 s 1217RD provides that the relief is to take the form of an additional deduction that the company may claim in respect of any accounting period. Upon the making of the claim, the company becomes entitled to make the additional deduction in calculating its profit or loss from the separate orchestral trade. New CTA 2009 s 1217RE sets the amount of the additional deduction. For the first period of account, the amount of the additional deduction, E, is the smaller of (a) so much of the "qualifying expenditure" incurred to date as is EEA expenditure and (b) 80% of the total amount of qualifying expenditure incurred to date. In subsequent periods of account, the additional expenditure is given by E − P, where P is the total amount of additional deductions given to date. New CTA 2009 s 1217RF defines "qualifying expenditure" as core expenditure that falls to be taken into account in calculating the profit or loss from the separate orchestral trade and is not otherwise relievable.

Under new CTA 2009 s 1217RG, a company may claim an "orchestra tax credit" instead of an additional deduction in an accounting period in which it has a "surrenderable loss". A company making such a claim may surrender the whole or part of that loss in return for the payment of an orchestra tax credit of 25% of the amount surrendered. New CTA 2009 s 1217RH provides that a company's surrenderable loss in any accounting period is the smaller of its "available loss" for that period in the separate orchestral trade and its "available qualifying expenditure" for that period. The available loss is given by L + RUL, where L is the company's loss for that period in the separate orchestral trade and RUL is the amount of any "relevant unused loss". The relevant unused loss is so much of the available loss for the previous accounting period as has neither been surrendered under new CTA 2009 s 1217RG or brought forward under CTA 2010 s 45 and set off against profits of the separate orchestral trade. As for the available qualifying expenditure, in the first period of account this is simply E, as defined in new CTA 2009 s 1217RE; in any subsequent period, it is E - S, where S is the total amount previously surrendered under new CTA 2009 s 1217RG. The mechanism for payment of the orchestra tax credit is contained in new CTA 2009 s 1217RI. Where a company claims payment of the credit, HMRC must make the payment, but the credit together with any interest on tax overpaid under TA 1988 s 826 may be used to discharge all or part of the company's liability to corporation tax. If there is an ongoing enquiry into the company's tax return for the accounting period in question, no payment of the credit may be made until the enquiry is completed; nor will HMRC make any payment of the credit where the company has any outstanding liabilities under PAYE, in respect of NICs or in respect of withholding tax on visiting performers under ITA 2007 s 966. A payment of orchestra tax credit is not income of the company for any tax purpose.

New CTA 2009 s 1217RJ imposes the EU State Aid limit of € 50 million as the maximum that any undertaking (as defined in the General Block Exemption Regulation, No 651/2014/EU) may receive in orchestra tax credits in any year. New CTA 2009 s 1217RK provides that production costs that remain unpaid four months after the end of a period of account are to be disregarded when determining the amount of costs incurred in that period.

New CTA 2009 s 1217RL is the standard anti-avoidance override. It provides that a company shall not qualify for orchestra tax relief in relation to the production of a concert or concert series if there any tax-avoidance arrangements in place relating to the production. Furthermore, new CTA 2009 s 1217RM provides that transactions are to be ignored insofar as they are attributable to arrangements, other than tax-avoidance arrangements, that are not entered into for genuine commercial reasons.

New CTA 2009 s 1217S introduces new CTA 2009 Pt 15D Ch 4, which provides for the treatment of losses incurred in the separate orchestral trade. It defines the term "completion period" as the accounting period in which the company ceases to carry on the separate orchestral trade. New CTA 2009 s 1217SA provides that the only form of relief for a loss in the separate orchestral trade in any accounting period other than the completion period (such a period is referred to in new CTA 2007 s 1217T as an "interim accounting period") is to carry it forward under CTA 2010 s 45. New CTA 2009 s 1217SB deals with losses in the completion period, both losses brought forward and losses actually incurred in the completion period. As regards losses brought forward, the element of those losses not attributable to orchestra tax relief (i.e. what the losses would have been if there had been no additional deduction) may be treated as if incurred in the completion period. As for such losses, actual or deemed, loss relief under CTA 2010 s 37 (profits of the same accounting period or the immediately preceding year) and available for group relief under CTA 2010 Pt 5 is also restricted to that element not attributable to orchestra tax relief. Terminal loss relief is provided under new CTA 2010 s 1217SC. A terminal loss for these purposes is a loss at the end of the completion period which the company would have been able to carry forward had it not ceased to carry on the separate orchestral trade. Two avenues for obtaining relief are available for this terminal loss. The first avenue is open where the company is carrying on another separate orchestral trade when it ceases to carry on the other. The company may then claim to transfer all or part of the terminal loss to the other separate orchestral trade, in which it is treated as brought forward under CTA 2010 s 45 to the first accounting period beginning after the cessation. The second avenue is open where the company is part of a group and there are one or more other companies carrying on a separate orchestral trade at the time of the cessation. In such a case, the company with the terminal loss may elect to surrender all or part of that loss to the other group company. When it does so, the loss is treated by the transferee company as a loss brought forward under CTA 2010 s 45 to the first accounting period beginning after the cessation.

It will be seen that losses from a separate orchestral trade are strictly ring-fenced, and at no time are they available for set off against profits from a non-orchestral trade.

New CTA 2007 Pt 15D Ch 5, containing CTA 2007 ss 1217T and 1217TA, provide for claims to and clawback of provisional relief. New CTA 2007 s 1217T provides that a company is not entitled to orchestra tax relief in any interim accounting period unless in its company tax return for that period it has specified the amount of planned core expenditure on the production of the concert or concert series which is EEA expenditure and that amount is sufficient to indicate that the EEA expenditure condition (at least 25% EEA expenditure) will be met. If these requirements are met, the company is treated as provisionally entitled to relief. Under new CTA 2007 s 1217TA, if at any subsequent time, it appears that the EEA expenditure condition will not after all be met when the company ceases the separate orchestral trade, the provisional relief is lost, and the company must amend its company tax returns accordingly. Once a company has ceased the separate orchestral trade, a final statement of EEA expenditure must accompany the company tax return for the period of cessation. Where the final statement shows that the EEA expenditure condition has not been met, the company also loses entitlement to terminal loss relief under new CTA 2007 s 1217SC and the necessary adjustments must be made to the company's tax returns for the periods in question.

New CTA 2009 s 1217U contains definitions and cross-references to definitions.

Schedule 8 Pt 2 makes consequential amendments. One such amendment is the insertion by Sch 8 para 9 of new CTA 2009 s 808D. This provides that an intangible fixed asset held by an orchestral-concert production company may not be included in the CTA 2009 Pt 8 régime so far as it represents expenditure on a concert or concert series treated as expenditure on a separate orchestral trade. Also noteworthy is the insertion by Sch 8 para 14 of CTA 2010 Pt 8B of new CTA 2010 Pt 8B Ch 14A, consisting of new CTA 2010 ss 357UJ–357UQ. These provide for the operation of orchestra tax relief for a company that is a Northern Ireland company. CTA 2010 Pt 8B will have effect from an appointed day, when the Northern Ireland Assembly may set a special Northern Ireland rate of corporation tax.

Schedule 8 Pt 3 provides for commencement. The power to make regulations under Sch 8 is to come into force on 15 September 2016. The remainder of the amendments, except those made by Sch 8 paras 13–15, have effect for accounting periods beginning after 31 March 2016, with provision for straddling periods. Schedule 8 paras 13–15, which relate to the Northern Ireland rate of corporation tax, are to have effect from the appointed day for CTA 2010 Pt 8B, again with provision for straddling periods.

Section 55 makes minor consequential amendments overlooked when CTA 2009 s 1218 was renumbered CTA 2009 s 1218B following the introduction of the TV and video games tax reliefs.

Banking companies

Sections 56 and **57** make amendments to the special tax provisions for banks in CTA 2010 Pt 7A, which restricts the relief that banking companies may claim for certain losses, the provisions in CTA 2009 ss 133A–133N, which deny banking companies a deduction for tax purposes in respect of payments they make to customers as compensation for certain instances of misconduct, and to FA 2011 Sch 19 (the bank levy).

Section 56 amends various provisions defining which banking companies fall within the scope of, or are excluded from, these restrictive measures. It first amends CTA 2009 s 133F, which defines which companies are excluded from the disallowance for compensation payments. The amendment adds to the definition companies that would otherwise have been excluded but for a single line of business, which does not include accepting deposits and, when considered in isolation, would not cause the company to be both an IFPRU 730k investment firm and a full-scope IFPRU investment firm. The amendments are deemed always to have had effect. Section 56 secondly amends CTA 2009 s 133M to ensure that the same exclusions will apply also to corporate partners in a partnership from inception. The third set of amendments affect CTA 2010 Part 7A. CTA 2010 s 269BA, the parallel section to CTA 2009 s133F, is amended in analogous fashion. CTA 2010 s 269DO (the interpretation section) is amended to provide that a line of business is not to be regarded as involving the acceptance of deposits if the activity of accepting deposits is ancillary to asset-management activities that the company carries on and the company would not carry on that activity but for the fact that it carries on asset-management activities. The third set of amendments are made to FA 2011 Sch 19. The same type of exclusion as has been added to the other sets of provisions is inserted in FA 2011 Sch 19 para 73 (which provides for entities to be excluded from the levy). However, the bank-levy amendments (s 52(10)–(12)) are to have effect from 15 September 2016 only.

Section 57 further restricts the proportion of a banking company's annual taxable profit that may be offset by losses brought forward to 25% (the proportion is currently 50%). The amendments are to have effect for accounting periods beginning after 31 March 2016, with provision for straddling periods.

Oil and gas

In a further attempt to ease the pressure on oil and gas companies, **s 58** halves the rate of the supplementary charge on a company's adjusted ring-fence profits from 20% to 10%, with effect for accounting periods beginning after 31 December 2015. Where periods straddle 1 January 2016, they will be split into two; the 20% rate will apply to the new period that ends on 31 December 2015 and the 10% rate to the new period that begins on 1 January 2016. The rate of the supplementary charge was 32% before 1 January 2015.

Section 59 amends the disqualifying conditions for the oil and gas investment allowance (CTA 2010 Pt 8 Ch 6A). CTA 2010 s 332CA provides that expenditure incurred after 31 March 2015 on oil-related activities but in respect of an area that is only subsequently determined to be an oil field by a company that is a licensee in that field is to be treated for the purposes of the investment allowance as incurred on the oil field at the time that it is determined. The disqualifying conditions in CTA 2010 s 332D are, broadly, intended to prevent the giving of investment allowance where previous expenditure on an asset that has been acquired either qualified for investment allowance itself or, with reference to equity in an oil field transferred to the claimant company, would have done so had that section been in force at the time that previous expenditure was incurred. The disqualifying conditions are now amended to override the rule in CTA 2010 s 332CA so that, for the purposes of those conditions, expenditure it taken to be incurred when it is actually incurred. The amendments made by s 59 have effect for determining whether expenditure incurred or treated under CTA 2010 s 332CA as incurred after 15 March 2016 qualifies for investment allowance.

Section 60 amends CTA 2010 s 332F so as to give power to the Treasury to expand the meaning of "relevant income" for the activation of investment allowance. Any expenditure that is "relievable expenditure" generates investment allowance under CTA 2010 s 332C. However, that investment allowance is "held" (i.e. unactivated) until the company has production income ("relevant income") from a qualifying oil field and hence ring-fence profits against which (as adjusted) the investment allowance may be set under CTA 2010 s 332E. CTA 2010 s 332F contains the rules for calculating how much of a company's investment allowance may be activated in an accounting period in which it is a licensee in a qualifying oil field and there is no change in the company's equity share during that period. The meaning of "relevant income" is now extended to include income that is not production income but is of another nature and prescribed as relevant income under regulations The intention behind this is primarily to allow tariff income also to activate the investment allowance. The amendments made by s 60 are to have effect from 15 September 2016 but regulations made under this section may have retroactive effect.

Section 61 amends the disqualifying conditions for the oil and gas onshore allowance under CTA 2010 Pt 8 Ch 8. Like the investment allowance, the onshore allowance maybe set against the supplementary charge on adjusted ring-fence profits, but is generated by "relievable capital expenditure" in relation to a qualifying onshore site. In contrast to the corresponding provisions relating to the investment allowance, however, the conditions disqualifying otherwise relievable expenditure from generating onshore allowance (CTA 2010 s 356CA) are purely quantitative and make no reference to previous expenditure on an asset. This discrepancy is now remedied. New CTA 2010 s 356CAA, inserted by s 61(3), disqualifies expenditure in three cases.

The first disqualifying condition concerns expenditure on the acquisition of an asset previous expenditure on the acquisition, bringing into existence or enhancing the value of which has generated onshore allowance under CTA 2010 s 356C for any company. The second disqualifying condition concerns expenditure on the acquisition of an asset (a) that is either all or part of the equity in a qualifying onshore site or is acquired in connection with a transfer to the company concerned of all or part of such equity; (b) on the acquisition, bringing into existence or enhancing the value of which capital expenditure was incurred by any company; and (c) in respect of which any of that expenditure related to that qualifying site and would have qualified for onshore allowance had CTA 2010 s 356C been fully in force at that time. The third disqualifying condition relates to a situation where an election under CTA 2010 s 356CB has been or could be made. Under CTA 2010 s 356CB, a company may elect for capital expenditure not related to an established site nevertheless to be included in expenditure generating an onshore allowance. The third disqualifying condition specifies that capital expenditure on the acquisition of an asset will not be relievable where (a) it would otherwise be relievable by virtue of the election under CTA 2010 s 356CB and (b) previous expenditure on the acquisition, bringing into existence or enhancing the value of which has either become relievable by virtue of an election under CTA 2010 s 356CB or would be so relievable were such an election now to be made. The amendments made by s 61 have effect for determining whether expenditure incurred or treated under CTA 2010 s 356CB as incurred after 15 March 2016 on the acquisition of an asset qualifies for onshore allowance.

Sections 62 and **63** make amendments to yet another allowance against the supplementary charge, namely the cluster-area allowance under CTA 2010 Pt 8 Ch 9. **Section 62** makes amendments to the disqualifying conditions for cluster-area allowance. Those disqualifying conditions are contained in CTA 2010 s 356JFA and mirror those in CTA 2010 s 332D in relation to the investment allowance. The amendments add leasing to the types of previous expenditure on an asset which qualified for cluster-area allowance under CTA 2010 s 356JF which will cause capital expenditure subsequently incurred on the acquisition of that asset whether incurred by the same company or by another company not to be relievable expenditure. **Section 63** relates to the activation of cluster-area allowance. As with the investment allowance, until the company has production income ("relevant income") from a cluster area and hence ring-fence profits against which (as adjusted) the cluster-area allowance may be set under CTA 2010 s 356JG. CTA 2010 s 356JH contains the rules for calculating how much of a company's cluster-area allowance may be activated in an accounting period in which it is a licensee in a qualifying area and there is no change in the company's equity share during that period. As with the amendments made in relation to the investment allowance, the meaning of "relevant income" is now extended to include income that is not production income but is of another nature and prescribed as relevant income under regulations. The amendments made by s 63 are to have effect from 15 September 2016 but regulations made under this section may have retroactive effect.

Exploitation of patents etc

Section 64 and **Sch 9**, which together run to 27 pages of legislation, amend the patent-box régime of CTA 2010 Pt 8A, in order to comply with the new harmonised international structure for preferential tax treatment of intellectual property as part of the OECD's BEPS (Base Erosion and Profit Shifting) action plan. The new rules will apply to all companies and all relevant intellectual property (IP) for accounting periods beginning after 30 June 2021. "New entrants", i.e. companies in relation to which the first accounting period to which their first election or most recent election for the patent box has effect begins after 30 June 2016, or who elect to be new entrants, will be subject to the new rules *ab initio.*

CTA 2010 s 357A(1) provides for a qualifying company to elect for its "relevant IP profits" to be chargeable at a lower rate of corporation tax (i.e. for the patent-box régime to apply). CTA 2010 Pt 8A Chs 3 and 4 (CTA 2010 ss 357C–357CQ and ss 357D–357DC, respectively) provide for the calculation of "relevant IP profits" under two different methods: the proportional-split method (Ch 3) and the streaming method (Ch 4). The amendments made to CTA 2010 s 357A by s 64(2) provide that new CTA 2010 Pt 8A Ch 2A, inserted by s 64(3), is to apply to determine relevant IP profits or losses for new entrants immediately and to all other companies in relation to accounting periods beginning after 30 June 2021. The existing CTA 2010 Pt 8A Chs 3 and 4, on the other hand, together with new CTA 2010 Pt 8A Ch 2B, also inserted by s 64(3), are to have effect in various cases in relation to accounting periods beginning before 1 July 2021 and to companies other than new entrants. "New entrant" is defined.

Section 64(3) inserts new CTA 2010 Pt 8A Ch 2A, which consists of new CTA 2010 ss 357BF–357BNA.

New CTA 2010 s 357BF prescribes the steps to be taken in determining the "relevant IP profits" eligible for the reduced 10% rate of corporation tax. This is broadly similar to the existing streaming method calculation in CTA 2010 s 357DA. Either seven or eight steps are involved.

Step 1 is to take the company's credits (broadly, income) in calculating the profits of its trade for the accounting period concerned, other than any "finance income" (see new CTA 2010 s 357BG), and divided them into two streams – that which contains relevant IP income ("the relevant IP income stream") and that which does not ("the standard income stream").

Step 2 is to divide the relevant IP income stream into one of three sub-streams ("relevant IP income sub-streams"), representing income from one particular "qualifying IP right" (e.g. a patent) – this is an "individual IP-right sub-stream"; income from a particular kind of IP item – this is a "product sub-stream"; or a particular kind of IP process – this is a "process sub-stream".

Step 3 is to take the company's debits (broadly, expenditure) in calculating the profits of its trade for the accounting period concerned, other than any "excluded debits" (see new CTA 2010 s 357BI) and allocate them on a just and reasonable basis among the standard income stream on the one hand and each of the relevant IP income sub-streams on the other.

Step 4 is to deduct from each relevant IP income sub-stream two amounts: (1) the debits allocated to that sub-stream under Step 3 and (2) the "routine return figure" for the sub-stream (see new CTA 2010 s 357BJ). However, certain items defined in new CTA 2010 s 357BIA are not to be deducted at this Step.

Step 5 consists of deducting from each relevant IP income sub-stream that still records a positive amount the relevant "marketing-assets return figure" (see CTA 2010 s 357BK).

Step 6 is to multiply the amount of each relevant IP income sub-stream, reduced as above, by the "R&D fraction" for the sub-stream (see CTA 2010 s 357BL).

Step 7 is to aggregate all the relevant IP income sub-streams resulting from Step 6.

Step 8 applies only if the company has made an election under CTA 2010 s 357BM for certain profits arising before the grant of an IP right to be treated as relevant IP profits. In such a case, any amount found under CTA 2010 s 357BM(3) is added to the amount produced by Step 7.

Where the amount produced after all the necessary steps have been taken is positive, that amount is the relevant IP profits of the trade for the accounting period concerned. Where that amount is negative, it constitutes the relevant IP losses for that period.

New CTA 2010 s 357BF also defines what is meant by a "an IP item" and an "IP process"; when two or more IP items or IP processes may be treated as of the same kind, and when income may properly be attributed to a product sub-stream or process sub-stream.

New CTA 2010 s 357BG defines "finance income", which is excluded from being relevant IP income.

New CTA 2010 s 357BH defines "relevant IP income" as falling within one of five heads, corresponding to the existing heads under CTA 2010 s 357CC. Head 1 is sales income; Head 2 is licence fees, including royalties; Head 3 is the proceeds of the sale or disposal of IP rights or exclusive licences; Head 4 is damages for infringement; and Head 5 is other compensation.

New CTA 2010 s 357BHA defines a "notional royalty", along the lines of the existing definition in CTA 2010 s 357CD. This is the "appropriate percentage" of income that the company derives from exploitation of a qualifying IP right that is a UK or European patent or an equivalent EEA right and that it would need to pay to another person to exploit the right if it were not already entitled to do so. Under new CTA 2010 s 357BHA, as under the existing CTA 2010 s 357CD, the company may elect to treat this notional royalty as if were relevant IP income.

New CTA 2010 s 357BHB defines "excluded income", which may not be taken into account in calculating the notional royalty under new CTA 2010 s 357BHA. It consists of oil and gas ring-fence income and income from non-exclusive licences, and matches the existing definition in CTA 2010 s 357CE.

New CTA 2010 s 357BHC provides for the inclusion in relevant IP income of a just and reasonable proportion of "mixed income" and income paid under a "mixed agreement". It follows the existing provisions of CTA 2010 s 357CF. This income is, broadly, income under Head 1 of new CTA 2010 s 357BH, the sale of qualifying items (qualifying IP rights) and non-qualifying items sold together as a single unit or income paid under an agreement covering qualifying or non-qualifying items.

New CTA 2010 s 357BI defines "excluded debits", which are debits that may not be taken into account as deductions under Step 3 in calculating the relevant IP profits of the trade for an accounting period under new CTA 2010 s 357BF, and matches the existing CTA 2010 s 357CG(3). Excluded debits are debits in respect of loan relationships (broadly, interest payable) or derivative contracts and additional deductions for expenditure on research and development (under CTA 2009 Pt 13), television programmes (under CTA 2009 Pt 15A), video games (under CTA 2009 Pt 15B) and theatrical productions (under CTA 2009 Pt 15C).

New CTA 2010 s 357BIA provides for certain amounts not to be deducted from sub-streams at Step 4 in new CTA 2010 s 357BF. It applies where arrangements are in place between the company and a person that has assigned a qualifying IP right to the company or grants or transfers an exclusive licence in respect of a qualifying IP right to the company, and the company makes an "income-related payment" to that person. An "income-related payment" is one made by reference to the amount of income that has accrued to the company from the right or licence or a payment that the company is obliged to make by reason of that amount of income. In these circumstances, where the income-related payment is allocated to an IP income sub-stream at Step 3, the payment is not to be deducted from the sub-stream at Step 4 unless it will not affect the R&D fraction for the sub-stream (see Step 6).

New CTA 2010 s 357BJ defines what is meant by the "routine return figure", which falls to be deducted in Step 4 (see under new CTA 2010 s 357BF) in respect of each sub-stream when calculating relevant IP profits. It broadly matches existing CTA 2010 s 375DA(4), but is adapted for the new concept of sub-streams. The routine return figure for each sub-stream is defined as 10% of the "routine deductions" made by the company in calculating the profits of the trade and allocated to that sub-stream at Step 3. It is intended to represent the return that could be expected from the business if the company were not able to exploit its qualifying IP rights and other intangible assets. What is meant by "routine deductions" is defined in new CTA 2010 s 357BJA and matches the existing definitions in CTA 2010 s 357CJ. These are deductions falling within any of six Heads, namely (1) capital allowances; (2) costs of premises; (3) personnel costs; (4) plant and machinery costs; (5) professional services and (6) miscellaneous services. What is included in these Heads is further defined. New CTA 2010 s 357BJB, which matches the existing CTA 2010 s 357CK, defines what deductions are not routine deductions. Such deductions are deductions falling within any of six Heads, being (1) loan relationships and derivative contracts; (2) R&D expenses; (3) capital allowances for research and development or patents; (4) R&D-related employee share acquisitions; (5) television-production expenditure; and (6) video-games development expenditure. What is included in these Heads is further defined.

Step 5 in new CTA 2010 s 357BF requires a deduction to be made in respect of the "marketing-assets return figure". That figure is defined in new CTA 2010 s 357BK (a modified version of the existing CTA 2010 s 357CN) as the difference for each sub-stream between the notional marketing royalty (NMR) and the actual marketing royalty (AMR) in relation to the sub-stream for the accounting period concerned. Where, however, AMR exceeds NMR or the difference is less than 10 per cent of the relevant IP income sub-stream after Step 4 in new CTA 2010 s 357BF, the marketing-assets return figure for that sub-stream is deemed to be nil.

New CTA 2010 s 357BKA (a modified version of the existing CTA 2010 s 357CO) prescribes how NMR is to be ascertained. Broadly, NMR is the arm's length proportion of the income allocated to the sub-stream in question at Step 2 in new CTA 2010 s 357BF that the company would pay a third party for the right to exploit the "relevant marketing assets" on the assumption that it would otherwise have no such right. Relevant marketing assets in relation to a relevant IP income sub-stream are those marketing assets that are used to generate relevant IP income, and marketing assets are, broadly, anything in respect of which a passing-off action could be brought under the Trade Marks Act 1994 or an equivalent foreign asset or any signs or indications of the geographical origin of goods or services or relating to customers or potential customers. New CTA 2010 s 357BKB (a modified version of the existing CTA 2010 s 357CP) defines AMR (the actual marketing royalty) for a relevant IP income sub-stream as the aggregate of sums paid by the company for acquiring relevant marketing assets or the right to exploit them which have been allocated to that sub-stream at Step 3 under new CTA 2010 s 357BF).

Step 6 in new CTA 2010 s 357BF requires the amount of each relevant IP income sub-stream following Step 5 to be multiplied by the "R&D fraction". New CTA 2010 ss 357BL–357BLH contain the rules for calculating this fraction. Broadly speaking, the R&D fraction is what the OECD refers to as the "nexus fraction" or "nexus ratio" in Chapter 4 of its 2015 publication *Countering harmful tax practices more effectively, taking into account transparency and substance*. It is these sections that represent the material departure from the existing patent-box rules. New CTA 2010 s 357BL is introductory.

New CTA 2010 s 357BLA contains the basic formula for the R&D fraction. The R&D fraction is either 1 or, if less: $((D + S1) \times 1.3/D + S1 + S2 + A)$, where D is the company's "qualifying expenditure on relevant R&D undertaken in-house" (see new CTA 2010 s 357BLB), S1 is the company's qualifying expenditure on relevant R&D

subcontracted to unconnected persons (see new CTA 2010 s 357BLC); S2 is the company's qualifying expenditure on relevant R&D subcontracted to connected persons (see new CTA 2010 s 357BLD) and A is the company's qualifying expenditure on the acquisition of relevant qualifying IP rights (see new CTA 2010 s 357BLE). The R&D fraction may be increased in the exceptional circumstances outlined in new CTA 2010 s 357BLH.

New CTA 2010 s 357BLB defines the company's qualifying expenditure on relevant R&D undertaken in-house as expenditure incurred in "the relevant period" on staffing costs, software and consumable items; qualifying expenditure incurred on externally provided workers or incurred on relevant payments to the subjects of clinical trials, all of which must be attributable to relevant research and development undertaken by the company itself. Where the company has elected under CTA 2009 s 18A to exempt the profits of its foreign permanent establishments from UK tax, the R&D expenditure that would otherwise be regarded as undertaken in-house is instead to be taken as subcontracted to a connected person, to the extent that it was brought into account in determining the amount of those exempt profits. Definitions are provided of "relevant research and development", in part by reference to CTA 2009 ss 1123–1140.

New CTA 2010 s 357BLC defines the company's qualifying expenditure on relevant R&D subcontracted to unconnected persons. This is the expenditure incurred in the "relevant period" in making payments to an unconnected subcontractor in respect of relevant research and development contracted out to that subcontractor. Where the company has elected under CTA 2009 s 18A to exempt the profits of its foreign permanent establishments from UK tax, the R&D expenditure that would otherwise be regarded as subcontracted to unconnected persons is instead to be taken as subcontracted to a connected person, to the extent that it was brought into account in determining the amount of those exempt profits.

New CTA 2010 s 357BLD defines the company's qualifying expenditure on relevant R&D subcontracted to connected persons. This is the sum of the expenditure incurred in the "relevant period" in making payments to a connected subcontractor in respect of relevant research and development contracted out to that subcontractor and the amounts deemed to be incurred in this way under new CTA 2010 ss 357BLB and 357BLC as a result of the exemption of foreign permanent-establishment profits.

New CTA 2010 s 357BLE defines the company's qualifying expenditure on the acquisition of relevant qualifying IP rights as the expenditure incurred in "the relevant period" by the company in making payments in respect of (a) the assignment to the company of a relevant qualifying IP right; (b) the grant or transfer to the company of an exclusive licence in respect of such a right; or (c) the disclosure to the company of any item or process in respect of which the company applies for and is granted such a right.

A "relevant qualifying IP right" is in turn defined as the qualifying IP right to which the income in the sub-stream concerned is attributable (where the sub-stream is an individual IP right sub-stream); a qualifying IP right granted in respect of an item to which income in the sub-stream is attributable or which is incorporated in an item to which income in the sub-stream is attributable (where the sub-stream is a product sub-stream); or a qualifying IP right granted in respect of a process to which income in the sub-stream is attributable or which is incorporated in a process to which income in the sub-stream is attributable (where the sub-stream is a process sub-stream).

New CTA 2010 s 357BLF defines what is meant by the "relevant period" for new CTA 2010 ss 357BLB–357BLE.

New CTA 2010 s 357BLG prescribes what a company may do in respect of an accounting period beginning before 1 July 2021 in which the company is a new entrant and has insufficient information about its expenditure in the period from 1 July 2013 to 30 June 2016 to enable it to calculate the R&D fraction for a particular sub-stream.

New CTA 2010 s 357BLH prescribes how and in what exceptional circumstances a company may elect to increase the R&D fraction for a particular sub-stream.

Step 8 in new CTA 2010 s 357BF allows for the addition of amounts in respect of profits arising before a right is granted. Under new CTA 2010 s 357BM, which matches existing CTA 2010 s 357CQ, a company may elect to include such amounts in calculating its relevant IP profits, and that section prescribes how they are to be calculated.

New CTA 2010 ss 357BN-367DND provide smaller companies with a number of simplifying options. New CTA 2010 s 357BN provides that these options are available where (a) the company carries on only one trade in the accounting period concerned;

(b) new CTA 2010 s 357BF applies for determining the relevant IP profits of the trade for that accounting period; and (c) the "qualifying residual profit" of the trade for that period does not exceed the greater of £1 million and the "relevant maximum" for the period. The "qualifying residual profit" is the amount that would arise by aggregating the amount for each relevant IP income sub-stream after making the deductions in Step 4 in new CTA 2010 s 357BF, disregarding any negative amounts in respect of any sub-stream, if no election is made under new CTA 2010 s 357BN. The "relevant maximum" is £3 million, but is reduced pro rata where the company has "related 51% group companies" or where the accounting period is shorter than 12 months. Where these conditions are satisfied, the company may make any one of three elections – a "notional-royalty election" (for which see new CTA 2010 s 357BNA), a small-claims figure election" (for which see new CTA 2010 s 357BNB), or a "global-streaming election" (for which see new CTA 2010 s 357BNC). None of the elections is available if the qualifying residual profit of the trade exceeds £1 million and in any previous accounting period beginning in the four years preceding the beginning of the present accounting period, the company determined its relevant IP profits under new CTA 2010 s 357BF but did not make any of the three elections. The small-claims figure election is not available if the qualifying residual profit of the trade exceeds £1 million and in any previous accounting period beginning in the four years preceding the beginning of the present accounting period, the company used the current patent-box rules under CTA 2010 s 357C or the streaming option under CTA 2010 s 357DA to calculate its relevant IP profits but did not opt for small-claims treatment under CTA 2010 s 357CL under the existing rules.

New CTA 2010 s 357BNA provides for the effects of making the notional-royalty election. This enables the notional-royalty element of relevant IP profits to be calculated by fixing the appropriate percentage in new CTA 2010 s 357BHA as 75% and dispensing with the remainder of the steps outlined in that section.

New CTA 2010 s 357BNB provides for the effects of making the small-claims figure election, which broadly matches existing CTA 2010 s 357CL". When this election is made, Step 5 in new CTA 2010 s 357BF has effect by requiring the deduction of the "small-claims figure" instead of the marketing-assets return figure. Where 75% of the qualifying residual profit of the trade for the accounting period concerned is lower than the "small-claims threshold"), the small-claims figure for the sub-stream is 25% of the amount of the sub-stream following Step 4 in new CTA 2010 s 357BF. In the opposite case, the small-claims figure for the sub-stream is given by the expression (A - (A/QRP) x SCT), where A is the amount of the sub-stream after Step 4, QRP is the qualifying residual profit of the trade and SCT is the small-claims threshold. The small-claims threshold is £1 million, but is reduced pro rata where the company has related 51% group companies, or where the accounting period is shorter than 12 months.

New CTA 2010 s 357BNC provides for the effects of making the global-streaming election. Broadly speaking, for the purposes of determining the relevant IP profits of the trade under new CTA 2010 s 357BF, Step 7 is omitted, and in that section and other relevant sections, this option merges into one global stream all the relevant IP income instead of subdividing it into sub-streams.

New CTA 2010 Pt 8A Ch 2B, which contains new CTA 2010 ss 357BO–357BQ, and is inserted by s 63(3), applies in relation to accounting periods beginning before 1 July 2021 to companies that are not new entrants but acquire new IP rights. It sits alongside the existing CA 2010 Pt 8A Chs 3 and 4, which apply in the transitional period to companies that have existing IP rights and do not acquire new rights.

New CTA 2010 s 357BO is introductory. It explains that new CTA 2010 Pt 8A Ch 2B applies to relevant IP income that is properly attributable to a "new qualifying IP right" and has effect to modify the calculation of relevant IP profits in new CTA 2010 s 357BF, and prohibits the making of a global-streaming election under new CTA 2010 s 357BN(2)(c). New CTA 2010 s 357BP defines a new qualifying IP right as a qualifying IP right (a) which was granted or issued to the company in response to an application filed after 30 June 2016; or (b) which was assigned to the company after 30 June 2016; or (c) an exclusive licence in respect of which was granted to the company after 30 June 2016. Where the right or licence was granted or assigned to the company by a connected person neither liable to UK corporation tax nor to an equivalent foreign tax designated by regulations, and the main purpose or one of the main purposes of the assignment or grant was to avoid a foreign tax, that date is 1 January 2016. The regulations in question must be made no later than 31 December 2016. Any qualifying IP right that is not a new qualifying IP right is an "old qualifying IP right". New CTA 2010 s 357BQ sets out how the calculation of relevant IP profits under new CTA 2010 s 357BF is to be modified in these circumstances.

New CTA 2010 s 357GCA, inserted by s 63(5), provides for the treatment under the existing patent-box régime of qualifying IP rights acquired as part of the transfer of a trade. It applies where a transferor company ceases to carry on a trade involving the exploitation of a qualifying IP right and transfers the right or grants or transfers an exclusive licence in respect of that right to a transferee company that begins to carry on that trade. The effect is, broadly speaking, that the transferee steps into the shoes of the transferor. Thus, the transferee is not to be a new entrant and the relevant qualifying IP right is to be treated as an old qualifying IP right in the hands of the transferee if it was such in the hands of the transferor. Various types of research and development and acquisition expenditure incurred by the transferor are to be treated as incurred by the transferee.

Schedule 9, inserted by s 64(6), contains consequential amendments to CTA 2010 Pt 8A Chs 3 (in Sch 9 paras 2–11) and 4 (in Sch 9, paras 12–14), as they apply in respect of accounting periods beginning before 1 July 2021 to companies that are not new entrants where none of the amounts of relevant IP income brought into account in calculating the profits of the trade is properly attributable to a new qualifying IP right. Further consequential amendments are made in Sch 9 paras 15 and 16 to CTA 2010 Pt 8A Ch 5 (which provides for relevant IP losses), in Sch 9 paras 17 and 18 to CTA 2010 Pt 8A Ch 6 (anti-avoidance provisions) and in Sch 9 paras 19–23. These largely arise as a consequence of the new election for "new-entrant status" in CTA 2010 s 357A(11)(b), to clarify that the election to which the amended provisions apply is the election under CTA 2010 s 357A(1) for entry into the patent-box régime itself. Finally, Sch 9 para 24 inserts new terms into the index of defined expressions in CTA 2010 Sch 4.

The amendments made by s 64 and Sch 9 have effect for accounting periods beginning after 30 June 2016, with provision for straddling periods.

Miscellaneous

Section 65 amends CTA 2010 s 624 to permit HM Treasury to make regulations concerning the application of the Taxes Acts as a whole to securitisation companies; currently, the power to make regulations is limited to the application of corporation tax to those companies.

Section 66 introduces **Sch 10**, which is anti-avoidance legislation designed to counter avoidance through "hybrid and other mismatches", resulting in either deductions for various payments without corresponding taxable income or in double deductions. These extensive provisions, inserted as TIOPA 2010 Pt 6A, supersede the existing anti-arbitrage provisions in TIOPA 2010 Pt 6.

Schedule 10 consists of three Parts. Part 1 (para 1) inserts the main provisions; Pt 2 (paras 2–17) makes consequential amendments; Pt 3 (paras 18–25) provides for commencement.

New TIOPA 2010 Pt 6A ("the legislation"), inserted by para 1, consists of 14 Chapters. Chapter 1 (new TIOPA 2010 s 259A) provides an introduction; Ch 2 (new TIOPA 2010 ss 259B–259BF) contains key definitions; Chs 3–11 provide for the counteraction of mismatches arising from financial instruments (Ch 3, new TIOPA 2010 ss 259C–259CE); "hybrid transfer arrangements" (Ch 4, new TIOPA 2010 ss 259D–259DG); "hybrid payer deductions" (Ch 5, new TIOPA 2010 ss 259E–259ED); transfers by permanent establishments (Ch 6, new TIOPA 2010 ss 259F–259FB); "hybrid payee deductions" (Ch 7, new TIOPA 2010 ss 259G–259GE); "multinational payee deductions" (Ch 8, new TIOPA 2010 ss 259H–259HC); "hybrid-entity double deductions" (Ch 9, new TIOPA 2010 ss 259I–259IC); "dual-territory double-deduction cases" (Ch 10, new TIOPA 2010 ss 259J–259JD) and "imported mismatches" (Ch 11, new TIOPA 2010 ss 259K–259KC). Chapter 12 (new TIOPA 2010 ss 259L–259LA) provides for adjustments in the light of subsequent events. Chapter 13 (new TIOPA 2010 s 259M) contains anti-avoidance provisions. Chapter 14 (new TIOPA 2010 ss 259N–259NF) provides for interpretation.

New TIOPA 2010 s 259A gives an overview of the legislation. The mismatches at which the legislation is aimed are of two kinds: a deduction/non-inclusion mismatch and a double-deduction mismatch. A deduction/non-inclusion mismatch arises where an amount is deductible from one person's income but no corresponding amount of "ordinary income" arises to another person or where an amount of "ordinary income" does arise but is "undertaxed". A double-deduction mismatch, on the other hand, arises where an amount is deductible from the income of more than one person or an amount is deductible from a person's income in relation to more than one tax. The counteractions are to take the form of adjustments to a person's treatment for the purposes of corporation tax. Since Chs 3–10 require some or all of new TIOPA 2010

Pt 6A to be disregarded when determining whether a mismatch arises, a priority for application of the various Chapters arises, which is their numerical sequence, except that Ch 4 has priority over Ch 3.

New TIOPA 2010 s 259B provides that references to "tax" in the legislation are references to income tax, corporation tax on income, diverted profits tax, the CFC charge, foreign tax and a foreign CFC charge. "Foreign tax" in this connection means a foreign tax on income corresponding to UK income tax or a tax on income corresponding to UK corporation tax on income.

New TIOPA 2010 s 259BA provides that references in the legislation to equivalent provisions of a foreign territory are provisions of which it reasonable to suppose that they are based on the OECD's Final BEPS report (i.e. the *Final Report on neutralising the effects of hybrid-mismatch arrangements*, published in October 2015) and any replacement or supplementary publications and have effect for similar purposes to the legislation.

New TIOPA 2010 s 259BB defines terms such as "payment", "quasi-payment", "payer" and "payee". A "payment" involves the transfer of money or money's worth directly or indirectly from one person ("the payer") to one or more other persons, which would, were it not for the legislation or equivalent foreign legislation, result in a relevant deduction from the payer's income in computing the payer's taxable profits. A "quasi-payment" takes place when, were it not for the legislation or equivalent foreign legislation, a relevant deduction may be made from the payer's income and it is reasonable to expect an amount of "ordinary income" would arise to one or more other persons as a consequence. In the case of a quasi-payment, "payee" includes an entity that is not a distinct and separate person from the payer under UK law but is such a separate and distinct person under the law of the payee's jurisdiction in circumstances in which it would be reasonable to expect an amount of "ordinary income" to arise to that entity. A "payment period" is the taxable period in which the relevant deduction may be made from the payer's income.

New TIOPA 2010 s 259BC defines "ordinary income" as income brought into account before any deductions when calculating taxable income or profits, other than for the purposes of the UK or foreign CFC charge. Amounts of income are not to be ordinary income to the extent that they are subject to an exclusion, reduction, relief or credit applying specifically to some or all of that income or that arises in connection with the payment or quasi-payment.

New TIOPA 2010 s 259BD applies where an amount of income arises to a CFC or foreign CFC but is not that company's ordinary income or, in the case of a payment or quasi-payment linked to financial instruments or hybrid transfer arrangements, would otherwise be ordinary income but is undertaxed. It prescribes a series of steps to determine whether and to what extent that income is to be regarded as ordinary income in relation to the UK or foreign CFC charge.

New TIOPA 2010 s 259BE defines the terms "hybrid entity", "investor" and "investor jurisdiction". A hybrid entity is one that is regarded as being a person for tax purposes under the law of any territory and either (a) some or all of its income or profits are treated under the law of any territory as the income or profits of another person or (b) the entity is not regarded in one territory as a distinct and separate person from an entity or entities that are so regarded in another territory. An "investor" in a hybrid entity is either a person who is treated as having the income or profits of the entity or an entity that is regarded as a separate and distinct person to the hybrid entity in one territory but not in another. Any territory in which the investor is within the charge to tax is an "investor jurisdiction".

New TIOPA 2010 s 259BF defines "permanent establishment" by reference to CTA 2010 s 1119 or a similar concept in foreign law, whether or not based on Art 5 of the OECD Model Convention.

New TIOPA 2010 s 259C gives an overview of new TIOPA 2010 Pt 6A Ch 3 (new TIOPA 2010 ss 259C–259CE). The Chapter is aimed at "hybrid or otherwise impermissible deduction/non-inclusion mismatches" in connection with financial instruments. It has effect by altering the corporation tax treatment of a payer or payee within the charge to UK corporation tax.

New TIOPA 2010 s 259CA provides that the Chapter is to apply where all of four conditions (Conditions A–D) are met. Condition A is that a payment or quasi-payment is made in connection with a financial instrument. Condition B is that either the payer is within the charge to UK corporation tax for the payment period or that a payee is within that charge for an accounting period falling wholly or partly within that payment period. Condition C is that it is reasonable to suppose that there would otherwise (i.e. in the absence of Ch 3 and Chs 5–10 and any equivalent foreign provision) be a hybrid or otherwise impermissible deduction/non-inclusion mismatch in relation to the payment or quasi-payment. Condition D is that either (a) the payer and payee are "related" (as defined in new TIOPA 2010 s 259NC) at any time beginning with the making of any arrangement by the payer or payee in connection with the financial instrument and ending on the last day of the payment period; (b) the financial instrument or any connected arrangement is a "structured arrangement"; or (c) in the event of a quasi-payment, the payer is also a payee. "Structured arrangement" is defined.

New TIOPA 2010 s 259CB defines and quantifies a "hybrid or otherwise impermissible deduction/non-inclusion mismatch". This is taken to be present where either of two situations applies. The first is where the relevant deduction exceeds the sum of the amounts of ordinary income arising to each payee for a "permitted taxable period" by reason of the payment or quasi-payment and all or part of that excess arises by reason of the terms or other features of the financial instrument. To the extent that the excess arises by reason of a "relevant debt-relief provision" (as defined in new TIOPA 2010 s 259CC(3)), it is to be taken not to arise by reason of the terms or other features of the financial instrument. When, however, an excess is taken to arise for the reasons referred to, and what the "relevant assumptions" involved are, are defined. One of the assumptions is that where the payee is not within the charge to tax in any territory because it neither is resident nor has it a permanent establishment there, it is to be assumed that the payee is a company resident for tax purposes, and carrying on a business in connection with which the payment or quasi-payment is made, in the UK. The second situation is where there are one or more amounts of income that arise to a payee for a "permitted taxable period" by reason of the payment or quasi-payment and those amounts are "undertaxed" by reason of the terms or other features of the financial instrument. A "permitted taxable period" in relation to an amount of ordinary income arising as a result of a payment or quasi-payment is defined in new TIOPA 2010 s 259CC(2) as one that begins within 12 months of the end of the payment period. It may begin later, however, where a claim has been made for the period to be a permitted period and it is just and reasonable for the ordinary income to arise in that period rather than in an earlier period. New TIOPA 2010 s 259CC(4) provides that an amount of ordinary income is "undertaxed" if the highest rate at which tax is charged on that income as part of the payee's taxable profits is less than the payee's marginal rate of tax for that period, taking into account on a just and reasonable basis any credit for underlying tax. In the first situation, the amount of the mismatch is equal to the excess of the relevant deduction over the ordinary income. In the second situation, it is the sum of the amount for each undertaxed amount of the fraction $((UTA \times (FMR - R))/FMR$, where UTA is the undertaxed amount, FMR is the payee's full marginal rate and R is the highest rate at which tax is charged on the undertaxed amount as part of the payee's taxable profits. It is possible for both situations to apply at the same time, in which case the total mismatch is the sum of the mismatches calculated for the two situations separately.

New TIOPA 2010 s 259CC contains definitions of "permitted taxable period", "relevant debt-relief provision", "full marginal rate", "credit for underlying tax" and when ordinary income is "undertaxed".

New TIOPA 2010 s 259CD provides for counteraction where the payer is within the charge to UK corporation tax for the payment period. The counteraction is effected by reducing the relevant deduction by the amount of the mismatch. New TIOPA 2010 s 259CE provides for counteraction where it is the payee who is within the charge to UK corporation tax for an accounting period wholly or partly falling within the payment period. Where it is reasonable to suppose that neither new TIOPA 2010 s 259CD nor an equivalent foreign provision applies in relation to the payer, or where a foreign provision does apply, it does not fully counteract the mismatch, then an amount referred to as the "relevant amount" is treated as arising to the payee or payees. Where there is no counteraction in relation to the payer, the relevant amount is the amount of the mismatch, as calculated under new TIOPA 2010 s 259CD. Where there is partial counteraction abroad, the relevant amount is the smaller of (a) the excess of the mismatch over the amount by which it is reasonable to suppose the relevant deduction is reduced by the foreign provision and (b) the amount that the payer is still able to deduct in the foreign jurisdiction. The relevant amount is to be treated as income arising to the payee for the "counteraction period". Where there is more than one payee, it is the payee's share (as defined) of the relevant amount that is to be treated as arising to a payee. The "counteraction period" is either the payee's accounting period that coincides with the payment period or the payee's first accounting period that falls wholly or partly within the payment period.

New TIOPA 2010 s 259D gives an overview of new TIOPA 2010 Pt 6A Ch 4 (new TIOPA 2010 ss 259D–259DG). The Chapter is aimed at "hybrid-transfer deduction/non-inclusion mismatches" arising from hybrid transfer arrangements. It has effect by altering the corporation tax treatment of a payer or payee within the charge to UK corporation tax.

New TIOPA 2010 s 259DA provides that the Chapter is to apply where all of five conditions (Conditions A–E) are met. Condition A is that there is a "hybrid transfer arrangement" in relation to an "underlying instrument" (see new TIOPA 2010 s 259DB). Condition B is that a payment or quasi-payment is made in connection with the "hybrid transfer arrangement" or the underlying instrument. Condition C is either that the payer is within the charge to UK corporation tax for the payment period or a payee is within that charge for an accounting period falling wholly or partly within the payment period. Condition D is that it is reasonable to suppose that there would otherwise (i.e. in the absence of new TIOPA 2010 Pt 6A and any equivalent foreign provision) be a "hybrid-transfer deduction/non-inclusion mismatch" in relation to the payment or quasi-payment. Condition E is similar to Condition D in new TIOPA 2010 s 259CA, and is that either (a) the payer and payee are "related" (as defined in new TIOPA 2010 s 259NC) at any time beginning with the making of the hybrid transfer arrangement and ending on the last day of the payment period; (b) the hybrid transfer arrangement is a "structured arrangement"; or (c) in the event of a quasi-payment, the payer is also a payee. "Structured arrangement" is defined.

New TIOPA 2010 s 259DB defines terms such as "hybrid transfer arrangement" and "underlying instrument". A hybrid transfer arrangement is a repo, a stock-lending arrangement, or any other arrangement, providing for or relating to a financial instrument (the underlying instrument) and in respect of which the "dual-treatment condition" is met or under which a "substitute payment" could be made. The dual-treatment condition is, broadly, that for the purposes of a tax in relation to one person the arrangement is regarded as equivalent to the lending of money at interest and for another person in relation to a tax the arrangement would not be so treated. A substitute payment is broadly a payment or benefit representative of the underlying return which is paid or given to a person other than the one to whom the underlying return arises.

New TIOPA 2010 s 259DC defines and quantifies a "hybrid-transfer deduction/non-inclusion mismatch" and is worded similarly to new TIOPA 2010 s 259CB. This is taken to be present where either of two situations applies. The first situation is where the relevant deduction exceeds the sum of the amounts of ordinary income arising to each payee for a "permitted taxable period" by reason of the payment or quasi-payment and all or part of that excess arises either because (a) the dual-treatment condition is met in relation to a hybrid transfer arrangement in connection with which the payment or quasi-payment is made or (b) the payment or quasi-payment is a substitute payment (called here a "subsection (8) reason"). When an excess is taken to arise by such reason, and what the "relevant assumptions" involved are, are defined. Those assumptions are that (a) where the payee is not within the charge to tax in the payee jurisdiction because it benefits from an exclusion, immunity, exemption or relief, that exclusion etc does not apply; (b) where the ordinary income of the payee for the purposes of a tax charged in the payee jurisdiction does not include an amount of income because the payment or quasi-payment is not made in connection with a business that the payee carries on in that jurisdiction, that the payment or quasi-payment is nevertheless to be treated as made in connection with such a business; and (c) that where the payee is not within the charge to tax in any territory because it neither is resident nor has it a permanent establishment there, it is to be assumed that the payee is a company resident for tax purposes and carrying on a business in connection with which the payment or quasi-payment is made in the UK. The second situation is where there are one or more amounts of ordinary income that arise to a payee for a "permitted taxable period" by reason of the payment or quasi-payment and those amounts are undertaxed for a subsection (8) reason. A "permitted taxable period" in relation to an amount of ordinary income arising as a result of a payment or quasi-payment is defined in new TIOPA 2010 s 259DD(2) exactly as in new TIOPA 2010 s 259CC, as is the meaning of "undertaxed" as defined for these purposes by new TIOPA 2010 s 259DD(3). Similarly, in the first situation, the amount of the mismatch is equal to the excess of the relevant deduction over the ordinary income. In the second situation, it is the sum of the amount for each undertaxed amount of the same fraction $((UTA \times (FMR - R))/FMR$. It is possible for both situations to apply at the same time, in which case the total mismatch is the sum of the mismatches calculated for the two situations separately.

New TIOPA 2010 s 259DD contains definitions of "permitted taxable period", "full marginal rate", "credit for underlying tax" and when ordinary income is "undertaxed".

New TIOPA 2010 s 259DE provides for the financial-trader exclusion, under which related parts of the excess and of any undertaxed amounts referred to in new TIOPA 2010 s 259DC are disregarded. It applies with respect to substitute payments, where three conditions, A to C, are met. Condition A is that the excess or part of it arises or an amount is undertaxed because the payment or quasi-payment (a) is a substitute payment; (b) is treated for the purposes of tax on one person as representative of the underlying return and (c) is brought into account under CTA 2009 Pt 3 by another person (i.e. the financial trader) in calculating the profits of a trade (trading income) or an equivalent foreign provision. Condition B is that the financial trader also brings any "associated payments" (as defined) into account. Condition C is that were the underlying return to arise and be paid directly to the payee or payees of the substitute payment, neither new TIOPA 2010 Pt 6A Ch 3 nor any equivalent foreign provision would apply and the hybrid transfer arrangement is not a structured arrangement.

New TIOPA 2010 s 259DF follows new TIOPA 2010 s 259CD and provides for counteraction where the payer is within the charge to UK corporation tax for the payment period. The counteraction is effected by reducing the relevant deduction by the amount of the mismatch. New TIOPA 2010 s 259DG follows new TIOPA 2010 s 259CE and provides for counteraction where it is the payee who is within the charge to UK corporation tax for an accounting period wholly or partly falling within the payment period. Where it is reasonable to suppose that neither new TIOPA 2010 s 259DF nor an equivalent foreign provision applies in relation to the payer, or where a foreign provision does apply, it does not fully counteract the mismatch, then an amount referred to as the "relevant amount" is treated as arising to the payee or payees. Where there is no counteraction in relation to the payer, the relevant amount is the amount of the mismatch, as calculated under new TIOPA 2010 s 259DC. Where there is partial counteraction abroad, the relevant amount is the smaller of (a) the excess of the mismatch over the amount by which it is reasonable to suppose the relevant deduction is reduced by the foreign provision and (b) the amount that the payer is still able to deduct in the foreign jurisdiction. The relevant amount is to be treated as income arising to the payee for the "counteraction period". Where there is more than one payee, it is the payee's share (as defined) of the relevant amount that is to be treated as arising to a payee. The "counteraction period" is either the payee's accounting period that coincides with the payment period or the payee's first accounting period that falls wholly or partly within the payment period.

New TIOPA 2010 s 259E gives an overview of new TIOPA 2010 Pt 6A Ch 5 (new TIOPA 2010 ss 259E–259ED). The Chapter is aimed at "hybrid-payer deduction/non-inclusion mismatches" arising from payments or quasi-payments by a hybrid payer. It has effect by altering the corporation tax treatment of a payer or payee within the charge to UK corporation tax.

New TIOPA 2010 s 259EA provides that the Chapter is to apply where all of five conditions (Conditions A–E) are met. Condition A is that a payment or quasi-payment is made in connection with an arrangement. Condition B is that the payer is a hybrid entity. Condition C is that either the payer is within the charge to UK corporation tax for the payment period or a payee is within that charge for an accounting period falling wholly or partly within the payment period. Condition D is that it is reasonable to suppose that there would otherwise (i.e. in the absence of new TIOPA 2010 Pt 6A Chs 5 and 6–10 and any equivalent foreign provision) be a "hybrid-payer deduction/non-inclusion mismatch" in relation to the payment or quasi-payment. Condition E mirrors Condition E in new TIOPA 2010 s 259DA. It is that either (a) the payer and payee are in the same "control group" (see new TIOPA 2010 s 259NB) at any time beginning with the making of the arrangement and ending on the last day of the payment period; (b) the arrangement is a "structured arrangement"; or (c) in the event of a quasi-payment, the hybrid payer is also a payee. "Structured arrangement" is defined.

New TIOPA 2010 s 259EB defines and quantifies the "hybrid-payer deduction/non-inclusion mismatch". This is taken to be present where the relevant deduction exceeds the amounts of ordinary income arising to each payee by reason of the payment or quasi-payment for a "permitted taxable period" and all or part of the excess arises by reason of the fact that the hybrid payer is a hybrid entity (for which see new TIOPA 2010 s 259BE). When an excess is taken to arise by such reason, and what the "relevant assumptions" involved are, are defined. Those assumptions are that (a) where the payee is not within the charge to tax in the payee jurisdiction because it benefits from an exclusion, immunity, exemption or relief, that exclusion etc does not apply and (b) where the ordinary income of the payee for the purposes of a tax charged in the payee jurisdiction does not include an amount of income because the payment or quasi-payment is not made in connection with a business that the payee carries on in that jurisdiction, that the payment or quasi-payment is nevertheless to be treated as made in connection with such a business. A "permitted taxable period" in relation to an amount of ordinary income arising as a result of the payment or quasi-payment is defined exactly as in new TIOPA 2010 s 259CC. The amount of the mismatch is the amount of the excess.

New TIOPA 2010 s 259EC provides for counteraction where the hybrid payer is within the charge to UK corporation tax for the payment period. To the extent that the relevant deduction does not exceed the amount of the mismatch, that amount ("the restricted deduction") may not be deducted from any of the hybrid payer's income for the payment period that is not "dual-inclusion income" for that period. Dual-inclusion income of a payer for an accounting period is an amount arising to the payer in connection with the arrangement that is both ordinary income for that period for the purposes of UK corporation tax and ordinary income of an investor in the payer for a "permitted taxable period" for the purposes of tax in the investor jurisdiction. So much of this restricted deduction that may not be deducted from the payer's income as a result may be carried forward to subsequent accounting periods to be deducted for the purposes of UK corporation tax from dual-inclusion income (and not from any other income) to the extent that it cannot be deducted from the payer's income for any earlier period. "Permitted taxable period" as regards an investor is defined as beginning within 12 months of the end of the accounting period in which there is dual-inclusion income that is ordinary income for the purposes of UK corporation tax. It may begin later, however, where a claim has been made for the period to be a permitted period in relation to the amount of ordinary income and it is just and reasonable for the ordinary income to arise in that period rather than in an earlier period.

New TIOPA 2010 s 259ED follows new TIOPA 2010 s 259CE and provides for counteraction where it is the payee who is within the charge to UK corporation tax for an accounting period wholly or partly falling within the payment period. Where it is reasonable to suppose that neither new TIOPA 2010 s 259EC nor an equivalent foreign provision applies in relation to the payer, or where a foreign provision does apply, it does not fully counteract the mismatch, then an amount referred to as the "relevant amount" is treated as arising to the payee or payees. Where there is no counteraction in relation to the payer, the relevant amount is the amount of the mismatch, as calculated under new TIOPA 2010 s 259EB. Where there is partial counteraction abroad, the relevant amount is the smaller of (a) the excess of the mismatch over the amount by which it is reasonable to suppose the amount of the relevant deduction is prevented by a foreign provision equivalent to new TIOPA 2010 s 259EC from being deducted from the hybrid payer's income for the payment period other than dual-inclusion income and (b) the amount of the relevant deduction that may still be deducted by the hybrid payer in the foreign jurisdiction. The relevant amount as reduced by any dual-inclusion income is to be treated as income arising to the payee for the "counteraction period". Where there is more than one payee, it is the payee's share (as defined) of the relevant amount (less the relevant proportion (as defined) of dual-inclusion income) that is to be treated as arising to a payee. The "counteraction period" is either the payee's accounting period that coincides with the payment period or the payee's first accounting period that falls wholly or partly within the payment period. A "permitted taxable period" for an investor is a period beginning within 12 months of the end of the payment period. It may begin later, however, where a claim has been made for the period to be a permitted period and it is just and reasonable for the ordinary income to arise in that period rather than in an earlier period.

New TIOPA 2010 s 259F gives an overview of new TIOPA 2010 Pt 6A Ch 6 (new TIOPA 2010 ss 259F–259FB). The Chapter is aimed at "deduction/non-inclusion mismatches" relating to transfers of money or money's worth by the UK permanent establishment of a multinational company to the company in its parent jurisdiction. It has effect by altering the corporation tax treatment of that multinational company.

New TIOPA 2010 s 259FA provides that the Chapter is to apply where all of three conditions (Conditions A–C) are met. Condition A is that the company is a "multi-national company", i.e. a company resident outside the UK in its parent jurisdiction for the purposes of tax in that jurisdiction and within the charge to UK corporation tax by reason of carrying on a business through a permanent establishment in the UK. Condition B is that there would otherwise (i.e. in the absence of new TIOPA 2010 Pt 6A Chs 6 and 7–10 and any equivalent foreign provision) be an amount ("the PE deduction") that may in substance be deducted from the company's income in computing its taxable profits for the purposes of UK corporation tax for an accounting period "the relevant PE period" and it is in respect of a transfer of money or money's worth from the company in the UK to the company in its parent jurisdiction that the deduction is actually made or is in substance treated as made. Condition C is that it is reasonable to suppose that were it not for new TIOPA 2010 Pt 6A Chs 6 and 7–10 and any equivalent foreign provision, either (a) the circumstances giving rise to the PE deduction will not result (for the purposes of a tax charged in the parent jurisdiction in an increase in the company's taxable profits for any 'permitted taxable period' or will not result in a reduction of a loss made by the company for any such period; or (b) that those circumstances will result in such an increase or such a reduction for one or more "permitted taxable periods" but that the PE deduction exceeds the aggregate effect on taxable profits of those increases in profits or reductions in losses for a "permitted taxable period". Where it is reasonable to suppose that there is no increase in taxable profits or no reduction in losses (i.e. the first arm of Condition C), the whole of the PE deduction is the "excessive PE deduction" for the purposes of counteraction. Where, on the other hand, it is reasonable to suppose that the PE deduction exceeds the aggregate effect on taxable profits (i.e. the second arm of Condition C), it is that excess that is the "excessive PE deduction". A "permitted taxable period" for the company for tax charged in the parent jurisdiction is one that begins within 12 months of the end of the relevant PE period. It may begin later, however, where a claim has been made for the period to be a permitted period and it is just and reasonable for the circumstances giving rise to the PE deduction to affect the profits or loss made for that period rather than for an earlier period.

New TIOPA 2010 s 259FB provides for counteraction of the excessive PE deduction (as defined in new TIOPA 2010 s 259FA). The counteraction is effected by providing that the excessive PE deduction for the relevant PE period may only be deducted from the company's dual-inclusion income for that period. In this section, "dual-inclusion income" for an accounting period is an amount that is both the company's ordinary income for the purposes of UK corporation tax for that period and the company's ordinary income for a "permitted taxable period" for the purposes of tax in the parent jurisdiction. So much of the excessive PE deduction that may not be deducted from the company's income for the relevant PE period as a result may be carried forward to subsequent accounting periods of the company to be deducted for the purposes of UK corporation tax from the company's dual-inclusion income (and not from any other income) to the extent that it cannot be deducted from the company's income for any earlier period. A "permitted taxable period" in relation to the parent jurisdiction is one that begins within 12 months of the end of the accounting period in which there is dual-inclusion income that is the company's ordinary income for the purposes of UK corporation tax. It may begin later, however, where a claim has been made for the period to be a permitted period in relation to the amount of ordinary income and it is just and reasonable for the ordinary income to arise in that period rather than in an earlier period.

New TIOPA 2010 s 259G gives an overview of new TIOPA 2010 Pt 6A Ch 7 (new TIOPA 2010 ss 259G–259GE). The Chapter is aimed at "hybrid-payee deduction/non-inclusion mismatches" relating to payments or quasi-payments to a hybrid payee. It has effect by altering the corporation tax treatment of the payer; treating income chargeable to corporation tax as arising to the investor if the investor is within the charge to UK corporation tax; or treating income chargeable to corporation tax as arising to a payee that is a hybrid entity in the form of a limited-liability partnership.

New TIOPA 2010 s 259GA provides that the Chapter is to apply where all of five conditions (Conditions A–E) are met. Condition A is that a payment or quasi-payment is made in connection with an arrangement. Condition B is that a payee is a hybrid entity (a "hybrid payee"). Condition C is that the payer is within the charge to UK corporation tax for the payment period, or an investor in a hybrid payee is within the charge to UK corporation tax for an accounting period falling wholly or partly within the payment period; or a hybrid payee is a limited-liability partnership. Condition D is that it is reasonable to suppose that there would otherwise (i.e. in the absence of new TIOPA 2010 Pt 6A Chs 7 and 8–10 and any equivalent foreign provision) be a "hybrid-payee deduction/non-inclusion mismatch" in relation to the payment or quasi-payment. Condition E is that (a) the payer and a hybrid payee or an investor in a hybrid payee are in the same "control group" (see new TIOPA 2010 s 259NB) at any time beginning with the making of the arrangement and ending on the last day of the payment period; or (b) the arrangement is a "structured arrangement"; or (c) in the event of a quasi-payment, the payer is also a hybrid payee. "Structured arrangement" is defined.

New TIOPA 2010 s 259GB defines and quantifies the "hybrid-payee deduction/non-inclusion mismatch". This is taken to be present where the relevant deduction exceeds the amounts of ordinary income arising by reason of the payment or quasi-payment to each payee for a "permitted taxable period" and all or part of the excess arises by reason of the fact that one or more of the payees is a hybrid entity (for which see new TIOPA 2010 s 259BE). A "relevant amount" of the excess is taken to arise by such reason, where it would not otherwise have arisen, where three conditions are satisfied. These are that (a) a payee is a hybrid entity; (b) ordinary income arising to the payee by reason of the payment or quasi-payment escapes tax either because there is no territory where that payee is resident for tax purposes or because there is no territory in which the income is treated as taxable by virtue of the payee's having a permanent establishment there; and (c) no income arising to the payee by reason of the payment or quasi-payment is included in chargeable profits for the purposes of the UK or a foreign CFC charge. The "relevant amount" of the excess is the smaller of (a) the whole of the excess and (b) the amount of ordinary income that it is reasonable to suppose would arise to the payee by reason of the payment or quasi-payment for the purposes of UK corporation tax if the payee were a company and the payment or quasi-payment were made in connection with a trade the payee carried on in the UK through a UK permanent establishment. For these purposes, a "permitted taxable period" in relation to an amount of ordinary income arising by reason of the payment or quasi-payment is defined exactly as in new TIOPA 2010 s 259CC. The amount of the mismatch is the amount of the excess.

New TIOPA 2010 s 259GC provides for counteraction where the payer is within the charge to UK corporation tax for the payment period. The counteraction is effected by reducing the relevant deduction from the payer's income by the amount of the mismatch.

New TIOPA 2010 s 259GD provides for counteraction where the investor is within the charge to UK corporation tax for an accounting period falling wholly or partly within the payment period. Where it is reasonable to suppose that neither new TIOPA 2010 s 259GC nor an equivalent foreign provision applies in relation to the payer, or where such a foreign provision does apply, it does not fully counteract the mismatch, then an amount referred to as the "relevant amount" is treated as arising to the investor. Where there is no counteraction in relation to the payer, the relevant amount is the amount of the mismatch, as calculated under new TIOPA 2010 s 259GB. Where there is partial counteraction abroad, the relevant amount is the smaller of (a) the excess of the mismatch over the amount by which it is reasonable to suppose the relevant deduction is reduced by the foreign provision and (b) the amount that the payer is still able to deduct in the foreign jurisdiction. The relevant amount is to be treated as income arising to the investor for the "counteraction period". Where there is more than one investor in the hybrid payee, it is the investor's share (as defined) of the appropriate proportion (as defined) of the relevant amount that is to be treated as arising to the investor. The "counteraction period" is either the investor's accounting period that coincides with the payment period or the investor's first accounting period that falls wholly or partly within the payment period.

New TIOPA 2010 s 259GE provides for counteraction where a hybrid payee is a limited-liability partnership (LLP). Where it is reasonable to suppose on the one hand that none of new TIOPA 2010 s 259GC (counteraction where the payer is within the charge to corporation tax), new TIOPA 2010 s 259GD (counteraction where the investor is within the charge to corporation tax) or any equivalent foreign provision applies, or on the other hand that one or more of those provisions does apply but does not fully counteract the mismatch, an amount referred to as the "relevant amount" is treated as income arising to the hybrid payee. If there is no counteraction, the "relevant amount" is the amount of the mismatch as quantified under new TIOPA 2010 s 259GB. If there is counteraction to some extent, the "relevant amount" is the amount by which the smaller of (a) the difference between the amount of the mismatch and the amount by which it is reasonable to suppose the relevant deduction is reduced and (b) the amount of the relevant deduction that may still be deducted exceeds the sum of any amounts of income treated as arising under new TIOPA 2010 s 259GD or any equivalent foreign provision. Where there is only one hybrid payee, the relevant amount is to be treated as income arising to the hybrid payee on the last day of the payment period. Where there is more than one hybrid payee, it is the hybrid payee's share (as defined) of the relevant amount that is to be treated as arising to the hybrid payee on the last day of the payment period. The hybrid payee's share is determined by apportioning the relevant amount between all the hybrid payees on a just and reasonable basis.

New TIOPA 2010 s 259H gives an overview of new TIOPA 2010 Pt 6A Ch 8 (new TIOPA 2010 ss 259H–259HC). The Chapter is aimed at "multinational-payee deduction/non-inclusion mismatches" relating to payments or quasi-payments to a multinational-company payee within the charge to UK corporation tax. It has effect by altering the corporation tax treatment of the payer.

New TIOPA 2010 s 259HA provides that the Chapter is to apply where all of five conditions (Conditions A–E) are met. Condition A is that a payment or quasi-payment is made in connection with an arrangement. Condition B is that a payee is a multinational company. Here, the definition of "multinational company" is subtly different from that in Chapter 6. For the purposes of this Chapter, a company is a multinational company if it is resident in its parent jurisdiction for the purposes of tax in that jurisdiction and it is regarded as carrying on a business in another territory ("the PE jurisdiction") through a permanent establishment in that territory whether it is so regarded under the law of the parent jurisdiction, the PE jurisdiction or any other territory. By contrast with Chapter 6, there is no requirement for the company to be within the charge to tax in the PE jurisdiction because it carries on a business through its permanent establishment there. Condition C is that either the payee is within the charge to UK corporation tax for the payment period or the multinational company is within the charge to UK corporation tax for an accounting period falling wholly or partly within the payment period. Condition D is that it is reasonable to suppose that there would otherwise (i.e. in the absence of new TIOPA 2010 Pt 6A Chs 8 and 9–10 and any equivalent foreign provision) be a "multinational-payee deduction/non-inclusion mismatch" in relation to the payment or quasi-payment. Condition E parallels Condition E in new TIOPA 2010 s 259EA. It is that either (a) the payer and the multinational company are in the same "control group" (see new TIOPA 2010 s 259NA) at any time beginning with the making of the arrangement and ending on the last day of the payment period; (b) the arrangement is a "structured arrangement"; or (c) in the event of a quasi-payment, the payer is also a payee. "Structured arrangement" is defined

New TIOPA 2010 s 259HB defines and quantifies the "multinational-payee deduction/non-inclusion mismatch". This is taken to be present where the relevant deduction exceeds the amounts of ordinary income arising to each payee for a "permitted taxable period" and all or part of the excess arises by reason of the fact that one or more of the payees is a multinational company. A "permitted taxable period" in relation to an amount of ordinary income is defined exactly as for new TIOPA 2010 s 259CB. The amount of the mismatch is the amount of the excess.

New TIOPA 2010 s 259HC provides for counteraction where the payer is within the charge to UK corporation tax for the payment period. The counteraction is effected by reducing the relevant deduction from the payer's income by the amount of the mismatch.

New TIOPA 2010 s 259HD provides for counteraction where the UK is the parent jurisdiction and the multinational company is within the charge to UK corporation tax. It applies where the payee is a multinational company and (a) the UK is the parent jurisdiction; (b) the payee is within the charge to UK corporation tax for an accounting period falling wholly or partly within the payment period; and (c) it is reasonable to suppose that neither new TIOPA 2010 s 259HC nor an equivalent foreign provision applies or where such a foreign provision does apply, it does not fully counteract the mismatch. In such a case, an amount referred to as the "relevant amount" is to be treated as income arising to the payee for the counteraction period. Where there is no counteraction in relation to the payer, the relevant amount is the amount of the mismatch, as calculated under new TIOPA 2010 s 259HB. Where there is partial counteraction abroad, the relevant amount is the smaller of (a) the excess of the mismatch over the amount by which it is reasonable to suppose the relevant deduction is reduced by the foreign provision and (b) the amount that the payer is still able to deduct in the foreign jurisdiction. Where there is only one payee that is a multinational company, the relevant amount is to be treated as income arising to the payee for the "counteraction period". Where there is more than one payee that is a multinational company, it is the payee's share (as defined) of the relevant amount that is to be treated as arising to the payee. The "counteraction period" is either the payee's accounting period that coincides with the payment period or the payee's first accounting period that falls wholly or partly within the payment period.

New TIOPA 2010 s 259I gives an overview of new TIOPA 2010 Pt 6A Ch 9 (new TIOPA 2010 ss 259I–259IC). The Chapter is aimed at "hybrid-entity double-deduction mismatches" that it is reasonable to suppose would otherwise arise by reason that a particular person is a hybrid entity.

New TIOPA 2010 s 259IA provides that the Chapter is to apply where all of three conditions (Conditions A–C) are met. Condition A is that there is an amount that it would otherwise (i.e. in the absence of Chs 9 and 10 and any equivalent foreign provision) be reasonable to suppose (a) could be deducted from the income of a hybrid entity in calculating its taxable profits for a certain taxable period ("the hybrid-entity deduction period") and (b) could also be deducted from the income of an investor in the hybrid entity under the law of the investor jurisdiction in calculating that investor's taxable profits in another period ("the investor deduction period"). This amount is referred to as the "hybrid-entity double-deduction amount". Condition B is that the investor is within the charge to UK corporation tax for the investor deduction period or that the hybrid entity is within the charge to UK corporation tax for the hybrid-entity deduction period. Condition C is that either (a) the hybrid entity and any investor in it are "related" (for which see new TIOPA 2010 s 259HB) at any time in the investor deduction period or the hybrid-entity deduction period or (b) an arrangement to which the hybrid entity or any investor in it is a party is a "structured arrangement". "Structured arrangement" is defined.

New TIOPA 2010 s 259IB provides for counteraction where the investor is within the charge to UK corporation tax for the investor deduction period. In that event, the counteraction is effected by providing that the hybrid-entity double-deduction amount may only be deducted from the investor's dual-inclusion income for the investor deduction period. So much of the hybrid-entity double-deduction amount that may not be deducted from the investor's income for the investor deduction period as a result may be carried forward to subsequent accounting periods of the investor to be deducted for the purposes of UK corporation tax from the investor's dual-inclusion income (and not from any other income) to the extent that it cannot be deducted from the investor's income for any earlier period. However, if HMRC is satisfied that the investor will have no dual-inclusion income for an accounting period after the investor deduction period nor for any subsequent period, any of the hybrid-entity double-deduction amount that the investor has not been able to deduct from dual-inclusion income up to the end of the last investor deduction period (referred to as the "stranded amount") may instead be deducted from the investor's total taxable profits. If there is then still a balance of the stranded amount so far not deductible, it may be carried forward to subsequent accounting periods. Where it is reasonable to suppose that all or part of the hybrid-entity double-deduction amount has been deducted under foreign law from the income other than dual-inclusion income of any person for a taxable period, this amount, "the illegitimate overseas deduction" is to be taken as already having been deducted when determining how much of the hybrid-entity double-deduction amount may be deducted by the investor for an accounting period in which the taxable period in which the illegitimate overseas deduction has been made ends, and in any subsequent period.

New TIOPA 2010 s 259IC provides for counteraction where the hybrid entity is within the charge to UK corporation tax for the hybrid-entity deduction period. It applies where this is the case and both (a) it is reasonable to suppose that neither new TIOPA 2010 s 259IB nor an equivalent foreign provision applies as against the investor fully to counteract the mismatch or where such a foreign provision does apply, it does not fully counteract the mismatch; and (c) "the secondary-counteraction condition" is met. This is met where either (a) the hybrid entity and any investor in it are in the same "control group" (for which see new TIOPA 2010 s 259NA) at any time in the hybrid-entity deduction period or the investor deduction period or (b) there is a "structured arrangement" to which the hybrid entity or any investor in it is a party. "Structured arrangement" is defined.

Where these conditions are met, an amount referred to as the "restricted deduction" may only be deducted from the hybrid entity's dual-inclusion income and from no other of its income. For the purposes of this section, "dual-inclusion income" is an amount that is both the hybrid entity's ordinary income for the purposes of UK corporation tax and the hybrid entity's ordinary income for the purposes of tax in an investor jurisdiction. Where there is no counteraction against the investor, the "restricted deduction" is the full amount of the hybrid-entity double-deduction. Where there has been partial counteraction, the restricted deduction is the excess of the hybrid-entity double-deduction amount over the amount that it is reasonable to suppose the foreign provision equivalent to new TIOPA 2010 s 259IB prevents from being deducted from income for the investor deduction period other than the hybrid entity's dual-inclusion income for the hybrid-entity deduction period. So much of this restricted deduction that may not be deducted from the hybrid entity's income for the hybrid-entity deduction period as a result may be carried forward to subsequent accounting periods of the hybrid entity to be deducted for the purposes of UK corporation tax from dual-inclusion income (and not from any other income) to the extent that it cannot be deducted from the hybrid entity's income for any earlier period. However, if HMRC is satisfied that the hybrid entity will have no dual-inclusion income for an accounting period after the hybrid-entity deduction period nor for any subsequent period, any of the restricted deduction that the hybrid entity has not been able to deduct from dual-inclusion income up to the end of the last hybrid-entity deduction period (referred to as the "stranded deduction") may instead be deducted from the hybrid entity's total taxable profits. If there is then still a balance of the stranded deduction so far not deductible, it may be carried forward to subsequent accounting periods. Where it is reasonable to suppose that all or part of the hybrid-entity double-deduction amount has in substance been deducted under foreign law from the income (other than dual-inclusion income of the hybrid entity for an accounting period) of any person for a taxable period, this amount, "the illegitimate overseas deduction", is to be taken as already having been deducted when determining how much of the hybrid-entity double-deduction amount may be deducted by the hybrid entity for an accounting period in which the taxable period in which the illegitimate overseas deduction has been made ends, and in any subsequent period.

New TIOPA 2010 s 259J gives an overview of new TIOPA 2010 Pt 6A Ch 10 (new TIOPA 2010 ss 259J–259JD). The Chapter is aimed at double-deduction mismatches that it is reasonable to suppose would otherwise arise because the company in question is a dual-resident company or a "relevant multinational company".

New TIOPA 2010 s 259JA provides that the Chapter is to apply where both of two conditions (Conditions A and B) are met. Condition A is that there is a company that is a dual-resident company or a "relevant multinational company". A dual-resident company for these purposes is a company that is both UK-resident and within the charge to tax in a foreign jurisdiction by virtue of its incorporation, place of management or some other reason. A company is a "relevant multinational company" if it is within the charge to tax in a territory ("the PE jurisdiction") by virtue of carrying on business there through a permanent establishment and the UK is either the PE jurisdiction or the territory ("the parent jurisdiction") where the company is resident for tax purposes. Condition B is that it is reasonable to suppose that, disregarding new TIOPA 2010 Pt 6A Ch 10 and any equivalent foreign provision, by virtue of the company's being a dual-resident company or a relevant multinational company, there is an amount (referred to as "the dual-territory double-deduction amount") that could be deducted both from the company's income for the purposes of UK corporation tax for an accounting period ("the deduction period") and from the company's income for the purposes of a foreign tax for a taxable period ("the foreign deduction period").

New TIOPA 2010 s 259JB provides for counteraction where the mismatch arises because the company is a dual-resident company. The counteraction has effect by prohibiting deduction of the dual-territory double-deduction amount from any of the company's income other than dual-inclusion income. Dual-inclusion Income for the purposes of this section is income that is both the company's ordinary income for an accounting period for the purposes of UK corporation tax and its ordinary income for a "permitted taxable period" for the purposes of a foreign tax. A "permitted taxable period" of the dual-resident company for these purposes is one beginning within 12 months of the end of the accounting period of the company for which the dual-inclusion income is its ordinary income for the purposes of UK corporation tax. It may begin later, however, where a claim has been made for the period to be a permitted period in relation to the amount of ordinary income and it is just and reasonable for the ordinary income to arise in that period rather than in an earlier period.

So much of the dual-territory double-deduction amount that may not be deducted from the company's income for the deduction period as a result of these provisions may be carried forward to the company's subsequent accounting periods to be deducted for the purposes of UK corporation tax from its dual-inclusion income (and not from any other income) to the extent that it cannot be deducted from the company's income for any earlier period. However, if HMRC is satisfied that the company has ceased to be a dual-resident company, any of the dual-territory double-deduction amount that the company has not been able to deduct from dual-inclusion income to date (referred to as the "stranded deduction") may instead be deducted from the hybrid entity's total taxable profits of the accounting period in which it ceased to be a dual-resident company. If there is then still a balance of the stranded deduction so far not deductible, it may be carried forward to subsequent accounting periods. Where it is reasonable to suppose that all or part of the dual-territory double-deduction amount has in substance been deducted under foreign law from the income (other than the company's dual-inclusion income for an accounting period) of any person for a taxable period, this amount, "the illegitimate overseas deduction" is to be taken as already having been deducted when determining how much of the dual-territory double-deduction amount may be deducted by the company for an accounting period in which the taxable period in which the illegitimate overseas deduction has been made ends, and in any subsequent period.

New TIOPA 2010 s 259JC provides for counteraction where the mismatch arises because the company is a relevant multinational company and the UK is its parent jurisdiction. It applies where some or all of the dual-territory double-deduction amount is in substance deducted for the purposes of foreign tax from the income (other than the company's dual-inclusion income) from the income of any person for any taxable period. The amount so deducted in substance is referred to as "the impermissible overseas deduction". Dual-inclusion income of the company for the purposes of this section is defined as income that is both its ordinary income for the purposes of UK corporation tax for an accounting period and its ordinary income for the purposes of a foreign tax for a 'permitted taxable period'. Here, a "permitted taxable period" of the dual-resident company is one beginning within 12 months of the end of the accounting period of the company for which the dual-inclusion income is its ordinary income for the purposes of UK corporation tax. It may begin later, however, where a claim has been made for the period to be a permitted period in relation to the amount of ordinary income and it is just and reasonable for the ordinary income to arise in that period rather than in an earlier period.

Where all this is the case, the counteraction has effect by reducing the dual-territory double-deduction amount that the company may deduct from its income for the deduction period for the purposes of UK corporation tax by, as may be expected, the amount of the impermissible overseas deduction, making such just and reasonable adjustments as may be necessary for this purpose.

New TIOPA 2010 s 259JD provides for counteraction where the mismatch arises because the company is a relevant multinational company and there is no counter-action in its parent jurisdiction. It applies where the UK is the PE jurisdiction and it is reasonable to suppose that there is no provision in the parent jurisdiction that is equivalent to new TIOPA 2010 s 259JC. The counteraction has effect by prohibiting deduction of the dual-territory double-deduction amount from any of the company's income for the deduction period for the purposes of UK corporation tax other than its dual-inclusion income for that period. Dual-inclusion income for the purposes of this section is income that is both the company's ordinary income for an accounting period for the purposes of UK corporation tax and its ordinary income for a "permitted taxable period" for the purposes of a foreign tax. A "permitted taxable period" of the dual-resident company for these purposes is defined identically to the definition in new TIOPA 2010 s 259JC. That is to say, it is one beginning within 12 months of the end of the accounting period of the company for which the dual-inclusion income is its ordinary income for the purposes of UK corporation tax. It may begin later, however, where a claim has been made for the period to be a permitted period in relation to the amount of ordinary income and it is just and reasonable for the ordinary income to arise in that period rather than in an earlier period.

So much of the dual-territory double-deduction amount as may not be deducted from the company's income for the deduction period as a result may be carried forward to the company's subsequent accounting periods to be deducted for the purposes of UK corporation tax from its dual-inclusion income (and not from any other income) to the extent that it cannot be deducted from the company's income for any earlier period. However, if HMRC is satisfied that the company has ceased to be a relevant multinational company, any remaining amount of the dual-territory double-deduction amount that the company has not been able to deduct from dual-inclusion income to date (referred to as the "stranded deduction") may instead be deducted from the company's total taxable profits of the accounting period in which it ceased to be a relevant multinational company. If there is then still a balance of the stranded deduction so far not deductible, it may be carried forward to subsequent accounting periods. Where it is reasonable to suppose that all or part of the dual-territory double-deduction amount has in substance been deducted under foreign law from the income (other than dual-inclusion income of the company for an accounting period) of any person for any taxable period, this amount, "the illegitimate overseas deduction", is to be taken as already having been deducted when determining how much of the dual-territory double-deduction amount may be deducted by the company for an accounting period in which the taxable period in which the illegitimate overseas deduction has been made ends, and in any subsequent period.

New TIOPA 2010 s 259K gives an overview of new TIOPA 2010 Pt 6A Ch 11 (new TIOPA 2010 ss 259K–259KC). The Chapter seeks to deny a deduction in connection with a payment or quasi-payment made in connection with "imported mismatch arrangements" where the payer is within the charge to UK corporation tax for the payment period.

New TIOPA 2010 s 259KA provides that the Chapter is to apply where all of seven conditions (Conditions A to G) are met. Condition A is that a payment or quasi-payment (referred to as "the imported mismatch payment") is made in connection with an arrangement (referred to as "the imported mismatch arrangement"). Condition B is that the payer of the imported mismatch payment is within the charge to UK corporation tax for the payment period. Condition C is that the imported mismatch arrangement is one of a series of arrangements entered into in connection with another arrangement referred to as "the overarching arrangement". Condition D is that under one of the series of arrangements, but not the imported mismatch arrangement, a payment or quasi-payment ("the mismatch payment") is made which it is reasonable to suppose involves another hybrid mismatch, i.e. a mismatch under one of new TIOPA 2010 ss 259CB, 259DC, 259EB, 259GB, 259HB or a double-deduction amount that is either a hybrid-entity double-deduction amount (under new TIOPA 2010 s 259IA) or a "dual-territory double deduction" under new TIOPA 2010 s 259KB, i.e. an amount that a company may deduct for the purposes of tax in two separate jurisdictions. Alternatively, Condition D is also met if an "excessive PE deduction" (under new TIOPA 2010 s 259KB) arises as a consequence of another arrangement in the series. Whichever is the mismatch concerned is referred to as "the relevant mismatch". Condition E is that it is reasonable to suppose that none of new TIOPA 2010 Pt 6A Chs 3–5 or 7–10 or any equivalent foreign provision either applies or will apply by way of counteraction in relation to the tax treatment of any person in respect of the mismatch payment (where the first arm of Condition D applies) or (where the second arm of Condition D applies) it is reasonable to suppose that neither new TIOPA 2010 Pt 6A Ch 6 nor any equivalent foreign provision either applies or will apply by way of counteraction in relation to the tax treatment of the company to which the excessive PE deduction arises. Condition F applies in one of two situations. The first is where the first arm of Condition D applies and it is reasonable to suppose that such a provision (i.e. either one of new TIOPA 2010 Pt 6A Chs 3–5 or 7–10 or any equivalent foreign provision) *would* apply in relation to the tax treatment of a person ("P") if (a) P were the payer of the mismatch payment; or (b) P were a payee of the mismatch payment; or (c) where the relevant mismatch payment is a hybrid-payee deduction/non-inclusion mismatch (see new TIOPA 2010 Pt 6A Ch 7) or a hybrid-entity double-deduction amount (see new TIOPA 2010 Pt 6A Ch 9), P were an investor in the hybrid entity concerned. The second situation in which Condition F applies is where the relevant mismatch is an excessive PE deduction. Finally, Condition G applies where (a) the first arm of Condition D applies and P is in the same "control group" (for which see new TIOPA 2010 s 259NB) as the payer or payee in relation to the mismatch payment at any time in the period beginning with the making of the overarching arrangement and ending on the last day of the payment period for the imported mismatch payment; or where (b) in the case of an excessive PE deduction (the second arm of Condition D), P is in the same control group as the company to which the excessive PE deduction arises at any time in that period; or where (c) the imported mismatch arrangement or the overarching arrangement is a "structured arrangement". "Structured arrangement" is defined.

New TIOPA 2010 s 259KB defines "dual-territory double deduction", "excessive PE deduction" and "PE jurisdiction". A "dual-territory double deduction" is an amount that a company may deduct for tax purposes under the law of two separate jurisdictions. A "PE jurisdiction" is the jurisdiction in which a company is chargeable to tax because it has a permanent establishment there. A "PE deduction" is an amount in respect of a transfer of money or money's worth from the company in the PE jurisdiction to the company in its parent jurisdiction (the jurisdiction in which it is resident for tax purposes) which is actually made or is in substance treated as made for tax purposes and which may in substance be deducted from the company's income when calculating its taxable profits for a taxable period for the purposes of tax in its PE jurisdiction. An "excessive PE deduction" arises where that deduction exceeds the sum of two amounts. The first such amount is the total of any increases in the company's taxable profits for a "permitted taxable period" in its parent jurisdiction which result from the circumstances giving rise to the PE deduction. The second such amount consists of any amounts that go to reducing a loss made by the company for a "permitted taxable period" in its parent jurisdiction as a result of those circumstances. A "permitted taxable period" of the company is one that begins within 12 months of the end of the taxable period in which the PE deduction may in substance be made in the PE jurisdiction. It may begin later, however, where a claim has been made for the period to be a permitted period and it is just and reasonable for the circumstances giving rise to the PE deduction to affect the profits or loss of that period rather than those of an earlier period.

New TIOPA 2010 s 259KC provides for counteraction. The basic rule is that for the purposes of UK corporation tax, the relevant deduction in relation to the imported mismatch payment which the payer (P in new TIOPA 2010 s 259KA) may deduct from his income for the payment period is to be reduced by the amount of the relevant mismatch. Where, however, in addition to the imported mismatch payment there are or will be one or more "relevant payments" in relation to the relevant mismatch, the rule is that the relevant deduction is to be reduced by P's share of the relevant mismatch. Except where the relevant mismatch is an excessive PE deduction, P's share of that mismatch is to be determined by the extent to which the imported mismatch payment directly or indirectly funds the mismatch in comparison with each relevant payment. Where the relevant mismatch is an excessive PE deduction, P's share is to be determined by reference to the extent that the imported mismatch payment and relevant payments fund the transfer of money or money's worth made from the PE jurisdiction to the parent jurisdiction to which reference is made in new TIOPA 2010 s 259KB or the extent to which they would have funded the deemed transfer. "Relevant payment" is defined.

New TIOPA 2010 s 259L provides that where a reasonable supposition such as is mentioned in every Chapter of these provisions is made and later proves to be mistaken or otherwise ceases to be reasonable, all just and reasonable adjustments as are consequently necessary are to be made, by way of an assessment, modified assessment, adjustment or disallowance of a claim, or otherwise. However, these adjustments cannot be made outside the normal time limits.

New TIOPA 2010 s 259LA provides for a deduction from taxable total profits to be made when ordinary income arises late. It will be recalled that under any of new TIOPA 2010 ss 259CD (hybrid or otherwise impermissible deduction/non-inclusion mismatches), 259DF (hybrid-transfer deduction/non-inclusion mismatches), 259GC (hybrid-payee deduction/non-inclusion mismatches) and 259HC (multinational-payee deduction/non-inclusion mismatches), the payer's relevant deduction is reduced because it was reasonable to suppose that the relevant deduction exceeded or would exceed the amounts of ordinary income arising in a permitted taxable period to a payee from the payment or quasi-payment. Where this is the case, and an amount ("the late income") of ordinary income later arises (that is, in a taxable period, referred to as "the late period", which is not a permitted taxable period) to a payee, an amount equal to the late income may be deducted in calculating the payer's taxable total profits for the accounting period in which the late period ends.

Further conditions must be met for this to be so, however. Those conditions are that (a) no provision of new TIOPA 2010 Pt 6A, other than the one under which the relevant deduction was reduced, nor any equivalent provision, may or will apply to the tax treatment of any person in respect of the payment or quasi-payment; (b) the late income must arise to a payee for the late period by reason of the payment or quasi-payment but not as a consequence of new TIOPA 2010 Pt 6A or of any equivalent foreign provision. So much of the late income that may not be deducted in calculating the payer's income for the late period as a result may be carried forward to subsequent accounting periods of the payer from total taxable profits. Total deductions under this section may not exceed the amount by which the relevant deduction was originally reduced.

New TIOPA 2010 s 259M provides for counteraction of any tax advantage that avoidance arrangements attempt to obtain for any person, provided that the person in question is within the charge to UK corporation tax at the time he would obtain the tax advantage or would be within the charge to UK corporation tax at that time were it not for the arrangements. The tax advantage targeted is the avoidance to any extent of these provisions (new TIOPA 2010 Pt 6A) or equivalent foreign provisions of restrictions on the deductible amount or of the treatment of certain amounts as income. The counteraction takes the form of any just and reasonable adjustments as may be necessary. However, if the arrangements in question are intended to obtain a tax advantage that can reasonably be regarded as consistent with the principles and policy advantages of these provisions, notably by reference to the OECD Final Report, the counteraction is not to be brought about.

New TIOPA 2010 Pt 6A Ch 14 provides for interpretation. New TIOPA 2010 s 259N defines "financial instrument". New TIOPA 2010 s 259NA defines a "relevant investment fund". New TIOPA 2010 s 259NB defines "control group". Two persons are to be regarded as being in the same control group (a) throughout any period for which their accounts are consolidated or would be were it not for an exemption; (b) at any time at which the "participation condition" is met with respect to them; or (c) at any time at which the "50% investment condition" is met with respect to them. The participation condition is met as between two parties at a time when within the next six months one of the parties directly or indirectly participates in the management, control or capital of the other or the same person(s) directly or indirectly participate(s) in the management, control or capital of the other. The 50% investment condition is met in relation to two parties if one has a 50% investment in the other or a third person has a 50% investment in both. New TIOPA 2010 s 259NC provides that persons are "related" if they are in the same control group or the 25% investment condition is met in relation to them. The 25% investment condition is as the 50% investment condition with the relevant percentage change. New TIOPA 2010 s 259ND defines "50% investment" and "25% investment".

New TIOPA 2010 s 259NE provides that where a person is a member of a partnership, references to income, profits or amounts are references to that person's share of the partnership's income, profits or amounts. New TIOPA 2010 s 259NF defines other terms.

Schedule 10 Pt 2 (paras 2–17) makes consequential amendments to FA 1988, CTA 2009, CTA 2010 and other provisions of TIOPA 2010. In particular, Sch 10 para 15 omits the anti-arbitrage provisions of TIOPA 2010 Part 6 (TIOPA 2010 ss 231–259) in their entirety. **Schedule 10 Pt 3** (paras 18–26) provides for commencement. The Chapters countering deduction/non-inclusion mismatches from payments and quasi-payments (new TIOPA 2010 Pt 6A, Chs 3–5, 7–8) and new TIOPA 2010 Pt 6A, Ch 11, which counters imported mismatch payments, are to have effect for payments made after 31 December 2016 and quasi-payments the payment period for which begins after that date. New TIOPA 2010 Pt 6A Ch 6, which counters deduction/non-inclusion mismatches arising from transfers from permanent establishments is to have effect in relation to excessive PE deductions the relevant PE period for which begins after 31 December 2016. New TIOPA 2010 Pt 6A Chs 9 and 10, which counter double-deduction mismatches, is to have effect for accounting periods beginning after 31 December 2016.

Section 67 makes three amendments to the revised code for the tax treatment of insurance companies carrying on life-assurance and other long-term business in FA 2012 Pt 2, following consultation with the industry. FA 2012 s 73, which prescribes the six steps for calculating profits under the I - E basis, is amended so that at Step 4, the company's non-trading deficits (if any) from loan relationships and derivative contracts cannot be used to reduce any I - E receipt arising under FA 2012 s 93(5)(a) from the minimum-profits test. The amendment now made to FA 2012 s 88 allows an excess of BLAGAB debits over credits arising from the intangible fixed-assets régime under CTA 2009 Pt 8 to be set off as a management expense in the period in which it is incurred rather than in the following period. Finally, FA 2012 s 126, which restricts the BLAGAB trade loss in any accounting period by reference to non-trading deficits from loan relationships and derivative contracts, is amended so that non-trading deficits arising from derivative contracts are no longer to restrict the trade loss in this way. The amendments made by s 67 are to have effect for accounting periods beginning after 14 September 2016.

Section 68 amends the legislation in CTA 2010 Pt 20 (CTA 2010 ss 887–894) and ITA 2007 Pt 13 Ch 6 (ITA 2007 ss 809ZA–809ZF), which contain anti-avoidance provisions relating to leased plant and machinery, in response to avoidance schemes notified to HMRC that generate non-taxable consideration provided for assuming tax-deductible leasing obligations. The amendments are embodied in new CTA 2010 s 894A and its corollary for income tax, ITA 2007 s 809ZG. Where four conditions are satisfied, a payment for taking over a lease as lessee is to be treated for the purposes of corporation tax or income tax, as the case may be, as income received by the new lessee in the period of account or tax year in which that person takes over the obligations. The conditions are that (a) under an arrangement, a company or person ("A") within the charge to corporation tax or income tax takes over the obligations of another person as lessee under a lease of plant or machinery; (b) A or a connected person consequently becomes entitled to make income deductions; (c) as consideration for that agreement, a payment is payable to A or a connected person; and (d) that payment would not or not fully otherwise be chargeable to tax on or brought into account by A or a connected person s as income or be treated as a disposal receipt or proceeds from a balancing event or disposal event of A or a connected person under CAA 2001. This rule is to have priority over all other rules, except for the GAAR. The amendments made by s 68 have effect in relation to agreements made after 24 November 2015.

PART 3
INCOME TAX AND CORPORATION TAX

Capital allowances

Section 69 has effect to change the period over which 100% first-year allowances may be claimed under CAA 2001 s 45K for qualifying capital expenditure on plant or machinery in designated assisted areas. Hitherto, the expenditure had to be incurred within a period of eight years beginning with 1 April 2012. The qualifying period is now to be eight years beginning with the day on which the area is or is treated as designated.

Section 70 makes amendments to the capital-allowance anti-avoidance legislation relating to sale and lease-back etc of plant and machinery in CAA 2001 Pt 2 Ch 17. It has been drafted to counter avoidance schemes disclosed to HMRC which seek artificially to reduce the disposal value taken into account to below the full value attributable to disposals. CAA 2001, which sets the conditions for CAA 2001 Pt 2 Ch 17 to apply is amended to put it beyond doubt that the Chapter may have effect to adjust the transferor's allowances as well as those of the transferee. A definition of "disposal value", as the value brought into account by the transferor as a result of the targeted transactions, is inserted as CAA 2001 s 213(4). CAA 2001 s 215, which defines which provisions are to apply to restrict capital allowances obtainable by the transferee where the transaction has an avoidance purpose, is amended to refer also to the imposition of balancing charges on the transferor; to include avoiding liability for the whole or part of a balancing charge as an example of the tax advantage targeted by the section; and to introduce new CAA 2001 s 218ZB as the relevant counteracting provision where the tax advantage relates to the disposal value of the plant or machinery under the relevant transaction. New CAA 2001 s 218ZB, inserted by s 70(9), provides that where the circumstances fall within CAA 2001 s 215 and a payment is made that would not otherwise be taken into account in full or at all in determining the transferor's disposal value, that disposal value is to be adjusted in a just and reasonable way so as to include an amount of that payment sufficient to cancel the tax advantage. The amendments made by s 70 have effect for transactions taking place after 24 November 2015.

Trade and property-business profits

Section 71 is intended to bring fully into charge to tax trading profits received in non-monetary form. According to the Government, the aim of this legislation is to confirm existing law and practice on non-monetary receipts dating back to *Gold Coast Selection Trust Ltd v Humphrey* (1948) 30 TC 209, HL. It inserts new ITTOIA 2005 s 28A and new CTA 2009 s 49A. Both new sections apply where a transaction involving the receipt of money's worth is entered into in the course of a trade. They ensure that, where it would not otherwise be the case, a value of the money's worth equal to the amount that would have been brought into account as a receipt in calculating the profits of the trade had the transaction involved money is now to be brought into account in respect of the non-monetary transaction. The amendments made by s 71 have effect for transactions entered into after 15 March 2016.

Section 72 repeals the deduction available for capital expenditure on the replacement or alteration of trade tools under ITTOIA 2005 s 68 and CTA 2009 s 68 by omitting those sections with effect for expenditure incurred after 31 March or 5 April 2016, and by making consequential amendments to the cash-basis accounting rules of ITTOIA 2005 s 56A. The same relief available to property businesses is repealed by omitting the reference to the respective s 68 in ITTOIA 2005 s 272 and CTA 2009 s 210. The Government considers that these reliefs, which predate capital allowances, are redundant.

Property-business deductions

Sections 73 and **74** replace the 10% wear-and-tear allowance for furniture supplied by landlords as part of a property business by a targeted relief, to be known as "replacement domestic-items relief") for capital expenditure on the provision of furnishings, appliances and kitchenware.

Section 73, which inserts new ITTOIA 2005 s 311A and new CTA 2009 s 250A and makes consequential amendments, introduces the new relief. New ITTOIA 2005 s 311A (which applies for income tax) and new CTA 2009 s 250A (which applies for corporation tax) are identically worded *mutatis mutandis*, and provide that the relief is to apply where four conditions (Conditions A to D) are met. Condition A is that there is a person (called here "the landlord") who carries on a property business consisting of or including a dwelling-house. Condition B is that the landlord incurs expenditure on a "domestic item" for use in the dwelling-house as a replacement for an old domestic item so used, after which the old item is withdrawn from use in the dwelling-house. "Domestic item" is defined as "an item for domestic use", including furniture, furnishings, household appliances and kitchenware, but excluding fixtures. Condition C is that a deduction for the expenditure is disallowed under ITTOIA 2005 s 33 (or CTA 2009 s 53) on the grounds that it is capital expenditure (i.e. it is of a capital nature) but would not otherwise be disallowed under the "wholly and exclusively" rule in ITTOIA 2005 s 34 (or CTA 2009 s 54). Condition D is that no capital allowance could be claimed for the expenditure under CAA 2001. Where these conditions are met, the landlord may claim a deduction for the expenditure in calculating the profits of the property business, with two exclusions. The first exclusion concerns dwelling-houses that are used in the commercial letting of furnished holiday accommodation; the second exclusion concerns persons claiming rent-a-room relief for the purposes of income tax under ITTOIA 2005 ss 793 or 797 (there being no such relief for corporation tax). The amount of the deduction is limited, however, to the replacement cost. Thus, where the new item is the same or substantially the same as the old item, a deduction is allowed for the full cost of the new item. Where, on the other hand, it is not the same or substantially the same, the deduction is equal to the amount that would have been incurred on one that was the same or substantially the same. The wording would appear to leave the door open for a deduction greater than cost if the new item is inferior to and cheaper than the old item. Incidental expenditure on the disposal of the old item or on the acquisition of the new item may be included in the deduction. The amendments made by s 73 have effect for expenditure incurred after 31 March 2016 (for the purposes of corporation tax) or after 5 April 2016 (for the purposes of income tax).

Section 74 omits the provisions granting the wear-and-tear allowance in ITTOIA 2005 (namely, ITTOIA 2005 ss 308A–308C) and CTA 2009 (namely, CTA 2009 ss 248A–248C) with effect for income tax from the tax year 2016/17 and for corporation tax for accounting periods beginning after 31 March 2016, with provision for straddling periods.

Transfer pricing

Section 75 amends the definition of the OECD's transfer-pricing guidelines that apply for the interpretation of the transfer-pricing rules in TIOPA 2010 Pt 4 to include the OECD's BEPS Final Report ("Aligning Transfer-Pricing Outcomes with Value Creation, Actions 8–10, Final Report", published on 5 October 2015), with effect for accounting periods beginning after 31 March 2016.

Transactions in UK land

Sections 76-82 introduce a new charge to tax on the profits of persons not resident in the UK derived from a trade of dealing in or developing land situated in the UK. The charge is to both corporation tax and income tax, as appropriate. Sections 76, 77, 80 and 81 relate to corporation tax, whereas ss 78, 79 and 82 relate to income tax.

Section 76 deals with the necessary extension of the scope of corporation tax. Currently, CTA 2009 s 5 provides that a company that is not resident in the UK is chargeable to corporation tax only if it carries on a trade in the UK through a permanent establishment there. Section 76(2) amends CTA 2009 s 5 so that a charge to corporation tax will also arise where the non-resident company carries on a trade of "dealing in or developing UK land" and it will be so chargeable on all the profits of that trade wherever they may arise.

Section 76(5) inserts new CTA 2009 s 5A, intended to counter arrangements to avoid the new charge. Where a company enters into arrangements the main purpose or one of the main purposes of which is to obtain a tax advantage in relation to the new charge, that advantage is to be counteracted by making adjustments. Obtaining the tax advantage includes doing so by using the provisions of a double tax treaty in a manner that is "contrary to [their] object and purpose".

New CTA 2009 s 5B, also inserted by s 76(5), defines what is comprised in a trade of dealing in or developing UK land, namely dealing in UK land or developing it with a view to its disposal and any activities from which profits, gains or losses arise which are treated under CTA 2010 Pt 8ZB (inserted by s 77) as profits or losses of that trade. "Land" includes buildings and structures, estates, interests or rights over land

and land under the sea or otherwise covered by water. "Disposal" is to be interpreted in accordance with new CTA 2010 s 356OQ, which forms part of new CTA 2010 Pt 8ZB.

Section 76(6) amends CTA 2009 s 3 to prevent a double charge to tax by excluding from the charge to income tax a non-resident company's profits from a trade of dealing in or developing UK land.

Section 76(7) amends CTA 2009 s 18A to exclude the profits and losses of a trade of dealing in or developing UK land from those profits and losses of a company's foreign permanent establishments that it may elect to exempt from its total taxable profits. Other amendments, to CTA 2009 s 189 and CTA 2010 s 107, ensure that post-cessation receipts from a trade carried on wholly outside the UK will nonetheless be chargeable to corporation tax if that trade is one of dealing or developing UK land and include losses from a trade of dealing in or developing UK land in those losses that a non-resident company may not surrender under group relief.

Section 77 contains the substantive provisions charging corporation tax on certain profits or gains realised on disposals concerned with land in the UK, in the form of new CTA 2010 Pt 8ZB, inserted by s 77(1). The new provisions repeal and replace CTA 2010 Pt 18, which is the rewritten TA 1988 ss 776–778.

New CTA 2010 Pt 8ZB consists of CTA 2010 ss 356OA–356OT. New CTA 2010 s 356OA is an overview section. New CTA 2010 s 356OB defines the conditions for a profit or gain from a disposal of land in the UK to be treated under new CTA 2010 s 356OC as profits of a trade carried on by the company in question ("the chargeable company"). This is the case where certain persons realise such a profit or gain and any one of four conditions, A to D, is met. The persons in question are (a) the person acquiring, holding or developing the land; (b) a person associated (as defined) with a person in (a) at a "relevant time"; or (c) a person who is a party to or concerned in a certain type of arrangement enabling a profit or gain to be realised. The "relevant time" is any time in the period starting at the time when the activities of the "project" begin and ending six months after the disposal. The "project" means all activities carried out for dealing in or developing the land or for any of the purposes mentioned in Conditions A to D.

Condition A is that the main purpose or one of the main purposes of acquiring the land was to realise a profit or gain from its disposal. Condition B is that the main purpose or one of the main purposes of acquiring property deriving its value from the land was to realise a profit or gain from the disposal of the land. Condition C is that the land was held as trading stock. Condition D is that the main purpose or one of the main purposes of developing the land was to realise a profit or gain from disposing of the land when developed.

New CTA 2010 s 356OC provides that when the conditions in new CTA 2010 s 356OB are met, the profit or gain in question is to be treated for the purposes of corporation tax as profits of a trade carried on by "the chargeable company", as defined in new CTA 2010 s 356OG. Where the chargeable company is non-resident, that trade is the company's trade of dealing in or developing UK land, except to the extent that the profit or gain would otherwise be treated as the income of any person for the purposes of corporation tax or income tax. It does not matter if the gains are capital in nature.

New CTA 2010 s 356OD defines the conditions for a profit or gain from a disposal of property deriving at that time at least 50% of its value from land in the UK by a person to be treated under new CTA 2010 s 356OE as profits of a trade carried on by "the chargeable company". The conditions are that the person is a party to or concerned in an arrangement concerning some or all of the land concerned ("the project land") and that the arrangement is one the main purpose or one of the main purposes of which is to deal in or develop the land and realise a profit or gain from a disposal of property deriving all or part of its value from that land.

New CTA 2010 s 356OE provides that when the conditions in new CTA 2010 s 356OD are met, the "relevant amount" is to be treated for the purposes of corporation tax as profits of a trade carried on by "the chargeable company". As in new CTA 2010 s 356OC, where the chargeable company is non-resident, that trade is the company's trade of dealing in or developing UK land, except to the extent that the amount would otherwise be treated as the income of any person for the purposes of corporation tax or income tax. The "relevant amount" is so much of the profit or gain referred to in new CTA 2010 s 356OD(1) as is justly and reasonably apportionable to the "relevant UK assets". These latter are in turn defined as any land in the UK from which the property referred to in new CTA 2010 s 356OD(1) derives any of its value at the time of the disposal. It does not matter if the gains are capital in nature.

New CTA 2010 s 356OF provides that references to profits or gains are also to be taken as references to losses.

New CTA 2010 s 356OG defines "the chargeable company", i.e. the person to whom the profits are attributed. It provides that the general rule is that the chargeable company is the company, denoted as "C", that realises the profit or gain referred to in new CTA 2010 ss 356OB or 356OD. However, where all or part of the profit or gain accruing to C is derived from value provided directly or indirectly by another person (as defined in new CTA 2010 s 356OO), being a company, denoted "B", B is to be the chargeable company. This is so whether or not the value is put at C's disposal. Another exception to the general rule is where all or part of the profit or gain accruing to C is derived from an opportunity of realising a profit or gain provided directly or indirectly by yet another person, being a company, denoted "D", it is D that is to be the chargeable company. However, these exceptions do not apply to a profit or gain arising from "fragmented activities" as defined in new CTA 2010 s 356OH.

New CTA 2010 s 356OH is intended to counter the fragmentation of profits between associated parties so as to place some or all of those profits outside the charge to UK corporation tax. It provides that where there is a person, "R", who is associated with the company, "C", that makes a disposal of any land in the UK in respect of which any of the Conditions A to D referred to in new CTA 2010 s 356OB is met at a "relevant time" (defined exactly as in new CTA 2010 s 356OB) and R has made a "relevant contribution" to either the development of the land or any other activities directed towards realising a profit or gain from the disposal of the land. Any contribution that R makes is a "relevant contribution", unless the resulting profit that R expects to make is "insignificant" by comparison with the size of the project. "Associated" is defined by reference to CTA 2010 ss 1122 and 1123 and to new CTA 2010 s 356OT (related persons).

Where new CTA 2010 s 356OH applies, the profit or gain attributed to C from the disposal is taken to be what it would have been if R were not a distinct person and everything done by or in relation to R had in fact been done by or in relation to C. Where R pays an amount to C to cover the cost of the extra corporation tax payable by C as a result, that amount is not to be taken into account in calculating R's or C's profits (i.e. no deduction for R and no taxable receipt for C) nor regarded as a distribution.

New CTA 2010 ss 356OI and 356OJ prescribe how the profit or gain is to be calculated. New CTA 2010 s 356OI provides that the calculation is to follow the normal rules for trading income under CTA 2009 Pt 3, modified as appropriate. New CTA 2010 s 356OJ provides that any necessary apportionments are to be carried out on a just and reasonable basis.

New CTA 2010 s 356OK is the now customary targeted anti-avoidance rule. It provides that where any arrangements have been entered into to obtain a tax advantage in relation to the new charge (e.g. by reducing the chargeable amount or avoiding it altogether), whether or not those arrangements involve using the provisions of double tax treaties contrary to their object and purpose, the advantage is to be counteracted by the making of adjustments.

New CTA 2010 s 356OL exempts from the new charge profits or gains from the disposal of developed land (as per Condition D in new CTA 2010 s 356OB(7)) that can fairly be attributed to a period before the intention to develop the land was formed. A similar exemption is granted in respect of profits or gains from the disposal of property as referred to in new CTA 2010 s 356OE(5) which can fairly be attributed to a period before the person concerned was a party to, or concerned in, the arrangement in question.

New CTA 2010 s 356OM provides that where it is necessary to determine the extent to which the value of any property or right is derived from any other property or right, value may be traced back through any number of companies, partnerships or trusts, attributing property to shareholders, partners, beneficiaries or other participants as appropriate.

In determining whether the new charge applies under either new CTA 2010 s 356OC or new CTA 2010 s 356OE, new CTA 2010 s 356ON provides that account is to be taken of any method, however indirect, by which property or rights are transferred or by which their value is enhanced or diminished. A non-exhaustive list of methods is provided in new CTA 2010 s 356ON(3).

New CTA 2010 s 356OO defines what is meant by "other persons" in the context of a body of partners in a partnership, of trustees of settled property or of personal representatives. New CTA 2010 s 356OP defines "arrangement". New CTA 2010 s 356OQ defines "disposal" of any property so as to include any event in which there is an effective disposal of property by one or more transactions or by any arrangement, and defines a "part-disposal" for these purposes. New CTA 2010 s 356OR defines what is meant by "land" and "property deriving its value from land". New CTA 2010 s 356OS provides that references to a person's realising a gain include realising it for another person. New CTA 2010 s 356OT defines the circumstances in which persons are considered to be related, by reference to accounting consolidation, participation in management and control, or investment.

Section 78 establishes the new charge as regards income tax. ITTOIA 2005 s 6 currently provides that the profits of a non-resident's trade are chargeable to income tax only if they arise from a trade carried on wholly or partly in the UK. Section 78(1)(a) inserts new ITTOIA 2005 s 6(1)(a), which provides that profits of a trade of dealing in or developing UK land arising to a person not resident in the UK are to be chargeable to income tax under ITTOIA 2005 Pt 2 Ch 2 (trade profits) wherever the trade is carried on. Section 78(2) inserts new ITTOIA 2005 s 6A, which mirrors new CTA 2009 s 5A (inserted by s 76(5)). It is likewise intended to counter arrangements to avoid the new charge. It provides that where a person enters into arrangements the main purpose or one of the main purposes of which is to obtain a tax advantage in relation to the new charge, that advantage is to be counteracted by making adjustments. Obtaining the tax advantage includes doing so by using the provisions of a double tax treaty in a manner that is "contrary to [their] object and purpose".

New ITTOIA 2005 s 6B, also inserted by s 78(2), mirrors new CTA 2009 s 5B. It defines what is comprised in a trade of dealing in or developing UK land, namely dealing in UK land or developing it with a view to its disposal and any activities from which profits arise which are treated under ITA 2007 Pt 9A (inserted by s 79) as profits of that trade. "Land" includes buildings and structures, estates, interests or rights over land and land under the sea or otherwise covered by water. "Disposal" is to be interpreted in accordance with new ITA 2007 s 517R, which forms part of new ITA 2007 Pt 9A.

Section 79 contains the substantive provisions charging income tax on certain profits or gains realised on disposals concerned with land in the UK, in the form of new ITA 2007 Pt 9A, inserted by s 79(1). The new provisions repeal and replace ITA 2007 Pt 13 Ch 3, which is the rewritten TA 1988 ss 776–778.

New ITA 2007 Part 9A consists of ITA 2007 ss 517A–517U, patterned closely on the equivalent corporation tax provisions (see s 76). New ITA 2007 s 517A is an overview section. New ITA 2007 s 517B defines the conditions for a profit or gain from a disposal of land in the UK to be treated under new ITA 2007 s 517C as profits of a trade carried on by the person in question ("the chargeable person"). This is the case where certain persons realise such a profit or gain and any one of four conditions, A to D, is met. The persons in question are (a) the person acquiring, holding or developing the land; (b) a person associated (as defined) with a person in (a) at a "relevant time"; or (c) a person who is a party to or concerned in a certain type of arrangement enabling a profit or gain to be realised. The "relevant time" is any time in the period starting at the time when the activities of the "project" begin and ending six months after the disposal. The "project" means all activities carried out for dealing in or developing the land or for any of the purposes mentioned in Conditions A to D. What constitutes an "associated" person is defined by reference to ITA 2007 ss 993 and 994 and by reference to new ITA 2007 s 517U.

Condition A is that the main purpose or one of the main purposes of acquiring the land was to realise a profit or gain from its disposal. Condition B is that the main purpose or one of the main purposes of acquiring property deriving its value from the land was to realise a profit or gain from the disposal of the land. Condition C is that the land was held as trading stock. Condition D is that the main purpose or one of the main purposes of developing the land was to realise a profit or gain from disposing of the land when developed.

New ITA 2007 s 517C provides that when the conditions in new ITA 2007 s 517B are met, the profit or gain in question is to be treated for the purposes of income tax as profits of a trade carried on by "the chargeable person", as defined in new ITA 2007 s 517G. Where the chargeable person is non-resident, that trade is that person's trade of dealing in or developing UK land, except to the extent that the profit or gain would otherwise be treated as the income of any person for the purposes of corporation tax or income tax. It does not matter if the gains are capital in nature.

New ITA 2007 s 517D defines the conditions for a profit or gain from a disposal of property deriving at that time at least 50% of its value from land in the UK by a person to be treated under new ITA 2007 s 517E as profits of a trade carried on by "the chargeable person". The conditions are that the person is a party to or concerned in an arrangement concerning some or all of the land concerned ("the project land") and that the arrangement is one the main purpose or one of the main purposes of which is to deal in or develop the land and realise a profit or gain from a disposal of property deriving all or part of its value from that land.

New ITA 2007 s 517E provides that when the conditions in new ITA 2007 s 517D are met, the "relevant amount" is to be treated for the purposes of income tax as profits of a trade carried on by "the chargeable person". As in new ITA 2007 s 517C, where the chargeable person is non-resident, that trade is the chargeable person's trade of dealing in or developing UK land, except to the extent that the amount would otherwise be treated as the income of any person for the purposes of corporation tax or income tax. The "relevant amount" is so much of the profit or gain referred to in new ITA 2007 s 517D(1) as is justly and reasonably apportionable to the "relevant UK assets". These latter are in turn defined as any land in the UK from which the property referred to in new ITA 2007 s 517D(1) derives any of its value at the time of the disposal. It does not matter if the gains are capital in nature.

New ITA 2007 s 517F provides that references to profits or gains are also to be taken as references to losses.

New ITA 2010 s 517G defines "the chargeable person", i.e. the person to whom the profits are attributed. It provides that the general rule is that the chargeable person is the person, denoted as "P", that realises the profit or gain referred to in new ITA 2007 ss 517B or 517D. However, where all or part of the profit or gain accruing to P is derived from value provided directly or indirectly by another person (as defined in new ITA 2007 s 517P), denoted "B", B is to be the chargeable person. This is so whether or not the value is put at P's disposal. Another exception to the general rule is where all or part of the profit or gain accruing to P is derived from an opportunity of realising a profit or gain provided directly or indirectly by yet another person, denoted "D", it is D that is to be the chargeable company. However, these exceptions do not apply to a profit or gain arising from "fragmented activities" as defined in new ITA 2007 s 517H.

New ITA 2007 s 517H is intended to counter the fragmentation of profits between associated parties so as to place some or all of those profits outside the charge to UK tax. It provides that where there is a person, "R", who is associated with the person, "P", that makes a disposal of any land in the UK in respect of which any of the Conditions A to D referred to in new ITA 2007 s 517B is met at a "relevant time" (defined exactly as in new ITA 2007 s 517B) and R has made a "relevant contribution" to either the development of the land or any other activities directed towards realising a profit or gain from the disposal of the land. Any contribution that R makes is a "relevant contribution", unless the resulting profit that R expects to make is "insignificant" by comparison with the size of the project. "Associated" is again defined by reference to ITA 2010 ss 993 and 994 and to new ITA 2007 s 517U (related persons).

Where new ITA 2007 s 517H applies, the profit or gain attributed to P from the disposal is taken to be what it would have been if R were not a distinct person and everything done by or in relation to R had in fact been done by or in relation to P. Where R pays an amount to P to cover the cost of the extra income tax payable by P as a result, that amount is not to be taken into account in calculating R's or P's profits (i.e. no deduction for R and no taxable receipt for P) nor regarded as a distribution.

New ITA 2010 ss 517I and 517J prescribe how the profit or gain is to be calculated. New ITA 2007 s 517I provides that the calculation is to follow the normal rules for trading income under ITTOIA 2005 Pt 2, modified as appropriate. New ITA 2007 s 517J provides that any necessary apportionments are to be carried out on a just and reasonable basis.

New ITA 2007 s 517K is the now customary targeted anti-avoidance rule. It provides that where any arrangements have been entered into to obtain a tax advantage in relation to the new charge (e.g. by reducing the chargeable amount or avoiding it altogether), whether or not those arrangements involve using the provisions of double tax treaties contrary to their object and purpose, the advantage is to be counteracted by the making of adjustments.

New ITA 2007 s 517L exempts from the new charge profits or gains from the disposal of developed land (as per Condition D in new ITA 2007 s 517B(7)) that can fairly be attributed to a period before the intention to develop the land was formed. A similar exemption is granted in respect of profits or gains from the disposal of property as referred to in new ITA 2007 s 517E(5) which can fairly be attributed to a period before the person concerned was a party to, or concerned in, the arrangement in question.

New ITA 2007 s 517M has no equivalent in the corporation-tax provisions. It provides that no liability to income tax is to arise under these provisions in respect of a gain where it accrues to an individual and is exempt from capital gains tax under TCGA 1992 ss 222–226 as being attributable to an only or main residence or where it would have been so exempt but for the exclusion in TCGA 1992 s 224(3) in respect of gains from residences acquired partly with a view to making a gain.

New ITA 2007 s 517N provides that where it is necessary to determine the extent to which the value of any property or right is derived from any other property or right, value may be traced back through any number of companies, partnerships, trusts or other entities or arrangements, attributing property to shareholders, partners, beneficiaries or other participants as appropriate.

In determining whether the new charge applies under either new ITA 2007 s 517C or new ITA 2007 s 517E, new ITA 2007 s 517O provides that account is to be taken of any method, however indirect, by which property or rights are transferred or by which their value is enhanced or diminished. A non-exhaustive list of methods is provided in new ITA 2007 s 517O(3).

New ITA 2007 s 517P defines what is meant by "other persons" in the context of a body of partners in a partnership, of trustees of settled property or of personal representatives. New ITA 2007 s 517Q defines "arrangement". New ITA 2007 s 517R defines "disposal" of any property so as to include any event in which there is an effective disposal of property by one or more transactions or by any arrangement, and defines a "part-disposal" for these purposes. New ITA 2007 s 517S defines what is meant by "land" and "property deriving its value from land". New ITA 2007 s 517T provides that references to a person's realising a gain include realising it for another person. New ITA 2007 s 517U defines the circumstances in which persons are considered to be related, by reference to accounting consolidation, participation in management and control, or investment.

Section 80 returns to corporation tax and provides for the treatment of pre-trading expenditure. It applies in circumstances where a company that was previously carrying on a trade of dealing in or developing UK land through a permanent establishment in the UK immediately before a time ("T") when it becomes liable to the new charge by virtue of new CTA 2009 s 5(2)(a) (i.e. it begins to carry on that trade otherwise than through a UK permanent establishment while remaining non-resident). Where this is the case, the company may deduct expenditure incurred before time T as pre-trading expenditure under CTA 2009 s 61 as if it had begun to carry on the trade at time T. This is subject to the proviso that no deduction would otherwise be allowed for that expenditure but would be so allowed had the company not been within the charge to corporation tax in respect of that trade immediately before time T, and that no relief has been obtained for that expenditure in any foreign jurisdiction.

Section 81 contains the commencement provisions for the new charge to corporation tax. The amendments made by ss 76, 77 and 80 are to have effect in relation to disposals made after 4 July 2016. The anti-avoidance provisions of new CTA 2009 s 5A and new CTA 2010 s 356OK are not to apply to arrangements entered into before 16 March 2016. However, where a company obtains a tax advantage in relation to the new charge from a disposal made by any person after 15 March 2016 and before 5 July 2016 of land or property deriving all or part of its value from land to a person associated with the person making the disposal, that advantage is to be counteracted by making adjustments.

Section 82 makes the equivalent provisions for income tax. The amendments made by ss 78 and 79 are to have effect in relation to disposals made after 4 July 2016. The anti-avoidance provisions of new ITA 2007 s 6A and new ITA 2007 s 517K are not to apply to arrangements entered into before 16 March 2016. However, where a person obtains a tax advantage in relation to the new charge from a disposal made by any person after 15 March 2016 and before 5 July 2016 of land or property deriving all or part of its value from land to a person associated with the person making the disposal, that advantage is to be counteracted by making adjustments.

PART 4
CAPITAL GAINS TAX

Rate

Section 83 and **Schs 11** and **12** reduce the "basic" rate of capital gains tax for most purposes to 18% (for so-called upper-rate gains) and to 10% for capital gains that are not upper-rate gains. Upper-rate gains are "residential property gains" (as defined in new TCGA 1992 s 4BB, inserted by s 83(14)); NRCGT gains (as defined in TCGA 1992 s 14D) and "carried-interest gains" (as defined in the provisions inserted by s 83(12)). However, the corresponding rates for trustees and personal representatives are to be 28% for upper-rate gains and 20% for gains that are not upper-rate gains. Where any part of an individual's income is chargeable at the higher rate or the dividend upper rate, the rate of capital gains tax is to remain 28% on upper-rate gains but is reduced to 20% on gains that are not upper-rate gains. Where the individual has no income chargeable at the higher rate or the dividend upper rate but the amount chargeable to capital gains tax exceeds the unused part of the individual's basic-rate band, the tax rate on the excess is to be 20%, subject to provisions in new TCGA 1992 s 4BA, inserted by s 83(14). Where, however, the individual has "special-rate gains" (gains charged at the special 10% rate of entrepreneurs' relief and the new investors' relief (introduced by s 87 and Sch 14)) and an excess of gains over the unused part of the basic-rate band (this excess is referred to as "the higher-rate excess"), the unused part of the basic-rate band is reduced by the amount of the special-rate gains.

"Carried-interest gains" (as defined in new TCGA 1992 s 4(12), (13), inserted by s 83(12)) are gains treated as accruing to an individual under TCGA 1992 s 103KA (inserted by F(No 2)A 2015 s 40) from arrangements involving a partnership and also gains accruing to an individual under arrangements not involving a partnership but in respect of investment-management services that the individual directly or indirectly performs for an investment scheme. However, where the carried interest is in the nature of a repayment or return of all or part of a co-investment, the resulting gain is not to be a carried-interest gain for these purposes. Further definitions are contained in new TCGA 1992 s 4(13).

New TCGA 1992 s 4BA (inserted by s 83(14)) provides a mechanism for individuals who have spare capacity in their basic-rate band or dividend basic-rate band (i.e. no income tax chargeable at the higher rate or the dividend upper rate) and an amount of chargeable gains that exceeds the unused part of the basic-rate band and includes upper-rate gains to allocate their chargeable gains in the most beneficial way. In such a case, the individual may choose to subject any of his or her "available gains" (the total amount of gains on which the individual is chargeable to capital gains tax for the year less any special-rate gains) as are upper-rate gains to the 18% rate and those that are not upper-rate gains to the 10% rate. However, the total amount of gains that may be used in this way may not exceed the unused part of the basic-rate band less the total of special-rate gains. Any gains not used in this way are charged at 28% if they are upper-rate gains and at 20% if they are not upper-rate gains.

New TCGA 1992 s 4BB defines what is a "residential-property gain". As provided in new TCGA 1992 s 4(2A), such a gain is an upper-rate gain. A residential-property gain (or loss) is a gain (or loss) accruing on the disposal of a "residential-property interest" other than on a disposal that is a "non-resident CGT disposal" as defined in TCGA 1992 s 14B, i.e. a disposal by an individual who is not UK-resident in the tax year concerned or to whom the gain accrues in the overseas part of a split tax year. Two types of disposal of a residential-property interest are distinguished: the disposal of a UK residential-property interest and the disposal of a non-UK residential-property interest, defined in new TCGA 1992 Schs B1 and BA1 (the latter inserted by Sch 11), respectively. A residential-property gain (or loss) is to be computed as prescribed by new TCGA 1992 s 57C and new TCGA 1992 Sch 4ZZC, both inserted by Sch 12. The amendments made by s 83 and Schs 11 and 12 are to have effect for gains accruing after 5 April 2016.

Schedule 11, inserted by s 83(15), consists of five paragraphs. Schedule 11 para 1 is introductory. Schedule 11 para 2 makes a consequential amendment. Schedule 11 para 3 omits TCGA 1992 s 14C, which has hitherto introduced TCGA 1992 Sch B1, but is now superseded by new TCGA 1992 s 4BB, inserted by s 83(14). Schedule 11 para 4 has the effect of changing the date from which the "relevant ownership period" for the purposes of identifying a disposal of a UK residential-property interest starts. Hitherto, that period has started on the later of 6 April 2015 and the day on which the person disposing of the interest acquired it. It is now to start on the later of the day on which the person disposing of the interest acquired it and 31 March 1982 (except for the purpose of determining whether a disposal is a non-resident CGT disposal, in which case the earlier rule remains in force). Schedule 11 para 5 inserts new TCGA 1992 Sch BA1, which defines what type of disposal is the disposal of a non-UK residential-property interest.

New TCGA 1992 Sch BA1 itself consists of five paragraphs. New TCGA 1992 Sch BA1 para 1 provides that a disposal of an "interest in non-UK land" is a "disposal of a non-UK residential-property interest" where either of two conditions is met. The first condition is that (a) the land has at any time in the relevant ownership period (starting as under the new definition and ending on the day before the disposal occurs) consisted of or included a dwelling or (b) the interest in non-UK land subsists for the benefit of land such as mentioned in (a). The alternative condition is that the interest in non-UK land subsists under a "contract for an off-plan purchase" (as defined). Where the disponer has acquired the interest disposed of as a result of acquisitions at different times, the day on which the disponer is taken as having acquired the interest disposed of is the day of the earliest such acquisition.

New TCGA 1992 Sch BA1 para 2 defines what is an "interest in non-UK land". It is an estate, interest, right or power in or over land outside the UK or the benefit of an obligation, restriction or condition affecting the value of any such interest, right etc, but it excludes security interests (as defined) and licences to use or occupy land. New TCGA 1992 Sch BA1 para 3 provides that the grant of an option binding the grantor to sell an interest in non-UK land is to be treated as a disposal of that interest. New TCGA 1992 Sch BA1 para 4 defines what is meant by a "dwelling" and new TCGA 1992 Sch BA1 para 5 makes it clear that "land" includes a building.

Schedule 12, inserted by s 83(16), inserts new TCGA 1992 s 57C and new TCGA 1992 Sch 4ZZC, which provide how a gain or loss from disposals of residential-property interests are to be computed. Schedule 12 consists of five paragraphs. Schedule 12 para 1 is introductory. Schedule 12 para 2 amends TCGA 1992 s 57A, which concerns the interaction of high-value ATED-related disposals and non-resident CGT disposals. As amended, the section now also provides that where the result of applying TCGA 1992 Sch 4ZZA is that no ATED-related gain or loss accrues on a disposal, that is not to prevent the application of that Schedule where new TCGA 1992 Sch 4ZZC Pt 3 (RPI disposals involving relevant high-value disposals) applies. Schedule 12 para 3 inserts new TCGA 1992 Pt II Ch 7, containing new TCGA 1992 s 57C, which introduces new TCGA 1992 Sch 4ZZC, which is to apply to the computation of gains and losses on disposals of residential-property interests that are not non-resident CGT disposals. Schedule 12 para 4 makes a consequential amendment. Schedule 12 para 5 inserts new TCGA 1992 Sch 4ZZC.

New TCGA 1992 Sch 4ZZC is divided into three Parts. Part 1 (paras 1 and 2), provides for introduction and interpretation. Part 2 (paras 3–6) deals with RPI disposals not involving relevant high-value disposals. Part 3 (paras 7–20) deals with RPI disposals that do involve relevant high-value disposals. A relevant high-value disposal, it should be recalled, is defined in TCGA 1992 s 2C and is the only type of disposal that may give rise to an ATED-related gain. New TCGA 1992 Sch 4ZZC is patterned on TCGA 1992 Sch 4ZZA, which provides for the computation of gains and losses accruing on relevant high-value disposals.

New TCGA 1992 Sch 4ZZC para 1 defines the term "RPI disposal" used throughout the Schedule as meaning the disposal of a residential-property interest that is not a non-resident CGT disposal and provides that the purpose of the Schedule is to determine whether a residential-property gain or loss accrues on an RPI disposal and the amount of any such gain or loss and to determine whether any gain or loss that is not a residential-property gain or loss accrues on such a disposal and the amount of any such gain or loss. New TCGA 1992 Sch 4ZZC para 2 provides that a relevant high-value disposal is comprised in an RPI disposal if the RPI disposal is treated for the purposes of TCGA 1992 s 2C and Sch 4ZZA as two or more disposals, of which one is the relevant high-value disposal. It also defines "charge-able interest" (by reference to the ATED rules in FA 2013 Part 3) and "dwelling".

New TCGA 1992 Sch 4ZZC para 3 explains that Pt 3 of new TCGA 1992 Sch 4ZZC is to apply where a person makes an RPI disposal of an interest in land or of part of such an interest and the disposal is not a relevant high-value disposal or a disposal in which a relevant high-value disposal is comprised.

New TCGA 1992 Sch 4ZZC para 4 provides for the computation of the residential-property gain or loss in the circumstances described in new TCGA 1992 Sch 4ZZC para 3. The computation is a two- or three-step process. In Step 1, the gain or loss accruing to the disponer is to be determined, taking no regard of new TCGA 1992 s 57C or of new TCGA 1992 Sch 4ZZC itself. Step 2 then consists of applying the "relevant fraction" to the gain or loss computed in Step 1 to arrive at the residential-property gain or loss. The relevant fraction is given by RD/TD, where RD is the number of days in the relevant ownership period (abbreviated from now on in these notes to "ROP") on which the subject matter of the interest (or part thereof) disposed of consisted wholly or partly of a dwelling and TD is the total number of days in the ROP. If there has been mixed use of the land on the same day or days, there is a third step, which requires the result of Step 2 to be reduced by a just and reasonable appropriate fraction reflecting that mixed use.

New TCGA 1992 Sch 4ZZC para 5 provides for the computation of the gain or loss that is not a residential-property gain or loss. The computation consists of two steps. If there is a gain under Step 1 under new TCGA 1992 Sch 4ZZC para 4, then the amount of that gain after deducting the residential-property gain is, reasonably enough, the gain that is not a residential-property gain. Similarly, where there is a loss in Step 1 of para 4, the amount of that loss remaining after deducting the residential-property loss is the loss that is not a residential-property loss. New TCGA 1992 Sch 4ZZC para 6 provides how new TCGA 1992 Sch 4ZZC Pt 2 is to apply to disposals of contracts for an off-plan purchase.

New TCGA 1992 Sch 4ZZC Pt 3 provides for the more complex business of computing gains or losses on RPI disposals that involve relevant high-value disposals. New TCGA 1992 Sch 4ZZC para 7 is introductory. It provides that this Part applies to disposals by a person other than an "excluded person" (as defined in TCGA 1992 s 2B(2)) which are RPI disposals of an interest in land (or part thereof) and are either relevant high-value disposals or have relevant high-value disposals comprised in them. New TCGA 1992 Sch 4ZZC para 8 defines certain shorthand terms used in what follows. "Asset" means the chargeable interest or that part of a chargeable interest that is the subject matter of the relevant high-value disposal. The "disposed-of interest" ("interest disposed of" would have been more elegant) is the asset. A "residential-property chargeable day" is a day on which the subject matter of the disposed-of interest consists wholly or partly of a dwelling but is not an "ATED-related day" (as defined in TCGA 1992 Sch 4ZZA(3)).

In order to understand what follows, reference back must be made to TCGA 1992 Sch 4ZZA, as amended by FA 2015, in particular to the concepts of Cases 1, 2 and 3 and the election under TCGA 1992 Sch 4ZZA para 5. "Case 3" in TCGA 1992 Sch 4ZZA para 2 refers to the situation where the disposed-of interest was held by the disponer on 5 April 2016 and no "relevant single-dwelling interest" was subject to ATED on one or more days in the period ending on 31 March 2016 during which the disponer held the disposed-of interest. Case 2 is where the disponer held the disposed-of interest on 5 April 2015, no "relevant single-dwelling interest" was subject to ATED on one or more days in the period ending on 31 March 2015 during which the disponer held the disposed-of interest, and Case 3 does not apply. Case 1 is where the disponer held the disposed-of interest on 5 April 2013 and neither Case 2 nor Case 3 applies. A "single-dwelling interest" is defined in FA 2013 s 108 as a chargeable interest exclusively in or over land consisting on any day of a single dwelling. A "relevant single-dwelling interest" is the single-dwelling interest or each of those interests involved in satisfying the conditions (Condition B, to be precise) prescribed by TCGA 1992 s 2C for there to be a relevant high-value disposal. An election under TCGA 1992 Sch 4ZZA para 5 has the effect of disapplying the method for calculating the ATED-related gain or loss accruing on the relevant high value disposal and the gain or loss accruing on that disposal which is not ATED-related prescribed in TCGA 1992 Sch 4ZZA paras 3–4 and replacing it by the calculation in TCGA 1992 Sch 4ZZA para 6, which also applies where none of Cases 1, 2 or 3 applies. The election is effectively an election to opt out of the rebasing involved in the computations under TCGA 1992 Sch 4ZZA paras 3 and 4.

New TCGA 1992 Sch 4ZZC para 9 sets out the two-step process for computing the residential-property gain or loss accruing on a disposal of land (an RPI disposal) involving one or more relevant high-value disposals. Step 1 is to compute the residential-property gain for each of the disposals according to the methods prescribed in new TCGA 1992 Sch 4ZZC paras 10–15 and step 2 is simply to add those amounts together to produce the residential-property gain or loss. If there is only one relevant high-value disposal involved, Step 2 will be superfluous.

New TCGA 1992 Sch 4ZZC para 10 prescribes the computation of the residential-property gain or loss where the relevant high-value disposal is not within any of Cases 1, 2 or 3 or where the election under TCGA 1992 Sch 4ZZA para 5 has been made. The computation involves two steps. Step 1 is to determine the amount of the gain or loss accruing to the disponer, taking no regard of new TCGA 1992 s 57C or of new TCGA 1992 Sch 4ZZC itself. Step 2 is to take the result of Step 1 and multiply it by the fraction SD/TD, where SD is the number of residential-property chargeable days (for which see new TCGA 1992 Sch 4ZZC para 8) in the ROP and TD is the total number of days in the ROP, which begins as usual on the later of the disponer's acquisition of the interest and 31 March 1982 and ends on the day before the day on which the relevant high-value disposal takes place. The result of Step 2 is the residential-property gain or loss.

New TCGA 1992 Sch 4ZZC para 11 introduces the computation of the residential-property gain or loss where the relevant high-value disposal is within any of Cases 1, 2 or 3 and where the election under TCGA 1992 Sch 4ZZA para 5 has not been made. The computation in these circumstances is a little more complex, as it involves rebasing, and comprises three steps, as prescribed by new TCGA 1992 Sch 4ZZC para 12. Step 1 is to determine the amount equal to the SD/TD fraction of the "notional pre-ATED gain or loss". New TCGA 1992 Sch 4ZZC para 13 defines the terms. SD and TD represent the same days as those referred to in Step 2 in new TCGA 1992 Sch 4ZZC para 13, but the ROP depends on which of the three Cases is in point. If Case 1 applies, the ROP ends on 5 April 2013. If Case 2 applies, the ROP ends on 5 April 2015, and if Case 3 applies, it ends on 5 April 2016. The "notional pre-ATED gain or loss" is the gain or loss that would have accrued on 5 April of the relevant year (i.e. 2013, 2015 or 2016, as the case may be) if a disposal at market value had been made on that date of the disposed-of interest. Step 2 is to determine the amount equal to the SD/TD fraction of the "notional post-ATED gain or loss". As defined in new TCGA 1992 Sch 4ZZC para 14, the "notional post-ATED gain or loss" is the gain or loss that would have accrued on the relevant high-value disposal had the disponer acquired the disposed-of interest at its market value on 5 April of the relevant year (i.e. 2013, 2015 or 2016, as the case may be). SD and TD are as previously, but the ROP to which they relate is the one beginning on 6 April of 2013, 2015 or 2016, as the case may be, and ending on the day before the relevant high-value disposal takes place. New TCGA 1992 Sch 4ZZC para 15 provides how the notional post-ATED gain is to computed if a wasting asset or capital allowances are involved. Step 3 is to add the amount obtained at Step 1 to that obtained at Step 2. The result is the residential-property gain (or loss) on the relevant high-value disposal.

New TCGA 1992 Sch 4ZZC para 16 prescribes how the gain or loss that is neither ATED-related nor a residential-property gain or loss ("the balancing gain or loss") on the RPI disposal is to be computed. Here, a two-step process is involved. Step 1 is to determine the balancing gain or loss on each relevant high-value disposal comprised in the RPI disposal and in Step 2 simply add these together. If there is only one relevant high-value disposal involved, Step 2 will again be superfluous. New TCGA 1992 Sch 4ZZC paras 17 and 18 prescribe how the computation in Step 1 is to be carried out. New TCGA 1992 Sch 4ZZC para 17 applies where none of Cases 1, 2 or 3 applies or where the election under TCGA 1992 Sch 4ZZA para 5 has been made. In that event, the number of "balancing days" in the ROP must first be identified. Balancing days are days that are neither residential-property chargeable days (for which see new TCGA 1992 Sch 4ZZC para 8) nor ATED chargeable days (as defined in TCGA 1992 Sch 4ZZA para 3). The balancing gain or loss is then equal to the "balancing fraction" of the gain or loss determined without regard to new TCGA 1992 s 57C or to new TCGA 1992 Sch 4ZZC itself. The balancing fraction is BD/TD, where BD is the number of balancing days in the ROP and TD the total number of days in the ROP. Here, as in new TCGA 1992 Sch 4ZZC para 10, the ROP begins on the later of 31 March 1982 and the disponer's acquisition of the disposed-of interest and ends on the day before the day of the relevant high-value disposal. New TCGA 1992 Sch 4ZZC para 18 applies, on the other hand, where any of Cases 1, 2 or 3 applies and where the election under TCGA 1992 Sch 4ZZA para 5 has not been made. The amount of the balancing gain or loss on a relevant high-value disposal in these circumstances is the sum of the amount of the balancing gain or loss belonging to the notional pre-ATED gain or loss and the amount of the balancing gain or loss belonging to the notional post-ATED gain or loss. The balancing gain or loss belonging to the notional pre-ATED gain or loss is expressed to be the balancing fraction of the notional pre-ATED gain or loss; similarly, the balancing gain or loss belonging to the notional post-ATED gain or loss is expressed to be the balancing fraction of the notional post-ATED gain or loss. The balancing fraction is again BD/TD, but the ROP by reference to which those days are counted will vary according to whether the pre-ATED gain or loss or the post-ATED gain or loss is in point and which of Case 1, 2 or 3 is in point. The pre-ATED ROP begins in each case on the later of 31 March 1982 and the disponer's acquisition of the disposed-of interest and ends on 5 April 2013 if Case 1 applies; on 5 April 2015 if Case 2 applies; and on 5 April 2016 if Case 3 applies. The post-ATED ROP begins on 6 April 2013 if Case 1 applies; on 5 April 2015 if Case 2 applies; and on 5 April 2016 if Case 3 applies and in each case ends on the day before the day of the relevant high-value disposal.

New TCGA 1992 Sch 4ZZC para 19 provides that where some of the disposals involved in the disposal of land are not relevant high-value disposals and hence not ATED-related disposals, those other disposals are nevertheless to be treated as if they were relevant high-value disposals for the purposes of computing gains or losses under new TCGA 1992 Sch 4ZZC, and that any mixed use on the same day is to be apportioned on a just and reasonable basis. Where there is a disposal of a contract to purchase a dwelling off-plan, the land is to be treated as consisting of or including a dwelling throughout the disponer's period of ownership (new TCGA 1992 Sch 4ZZC para 20).

Entrepreneurs' relief

Sections 84–86 are examples of where anti-avoidance measures taken in one year prove to be too broad and remediating legislation needs to be enacted the following year in order to restore the relief for certain transactions where there was no instance of abuse but in respect of which relief was nevertheless withdrawn. The anti-avoidance legislation in question is FA 2015 ss 41–43. Section 84 remedies the unintended effects of FA 2015 s 41, whereas s 85 does likewise for FA 2015 s 42 and s 86 does so for FA 2015 s 43.

Section 84 amends TCGA 1992 s 169K in several substantive ways. TCGA 1992 s 169K provides the conditions under which a gain accruing on a disposal (of personal assets) associated with a material disposal of business assets may also qualify for entrepreneurs' relief along with the gain on the material disposal itself. Whereas previously, the material disposal had to meet one of Conditions A1, A2 or A3 and also two further conditions, B and C, it must now meet one of Conditions A1, A1A, A2 or A3 and *three* further conditions, B, C and D.

Section 84(3) inserts a new alternative condition to the existing conditions that need to be met for an associated disposal also to qualify for relief. This new condition, Condition A1A, is met where the material disposal made by the individual is one of the whole of his or her interest in the assets of a partnership, that interest is one of less than 5% but that individual has held an interest of at least 5% in those assets for at least three consecutive years within the eight years preceding the date of the disposal. The effect of inserting Condition A1A is that the minimum-size (5%) requirement is now lifted, provided that an interest of at least that extent subsisted for the time specified in the past and that what is now disposed of is the entire interest.

Both Condition A1 and Condition A1A require, as does Condition B, there to be no "partnership-purchase arrangements" to be in place. Broadly speaking, these are arrangements under which the individual or a person connected with that individual is entitled to acquire or increase that person's interest in the partnership. The existing definition of "partnership-purchase arrangements" in TCGA 1992 s 169K(6) is omitted and replaced by slightly different definitions tailor-made to the appropriate condition or conditions.

First, as regards Conditions A1 and A1A, the material disposal itself is not to be a partnership-purchase arrangement. Second, for the purposes of Condition B, "partnership-purchase arrangements" are not to include arrangements in connection with a material disposal in respect of which Condition A1 or A1A is met.

Conditions A2 and A3 both require, as does Condition B, there to be no "share-purchase arrangements" in place. The definition of "share-purchase arrangements" is now amended for the purpose of these conditions to exclude the material disposal itself.

Condition B, which is itself slightly amended, now requires the associated disposal to be made as part of the individual's withdrawal from participation in the business carried on by the partnership or company, as the case may be, provided that, at the time of the associated disposal, no "partnership-purchase arrangements" are in place in the case of withdrawal from the business of a partnership and no "share-purchase arrangements" are in place in the case of withdrawal from the business of a company. The definition of "share-purchase arrangements" is amended to exclude arrangements in connection with a material disposal in relation to which either Condition A2 or A3 is met.

As regards both the amended definitions of "share-purchase arrangements" and "partnership-purchase arrangements", they are now made subject to the rule in new TCGA 1992 s 169K(6A), inserted by s 84(11). This provides that, where there is a material disposal and the associated disposal mentioned in Condition B, arrangements are not to be share-purchase arrangements or partnership-purchase arrangements if they were made before both those disposals and without regard to either of them.

The new Condition D that must be met by the associated disposal is inserted by s 84(9) and requires the associated disposal mentioned in Condition B to be of an asset that the individual has owned for at least the three years ending on the date of the disposal.

The amendments made by s 84 have two different commencement dates. The addition of Condition D has effect for disposals of assets acquired after 12 June 2016, whereas the other amendments have retroactive effect for disposals taking place after 17 March 2015.

Section 85 addresses the question of disposals of goodwill and mitigates the impact of the changes made by FA 2015 s 42. TCGA 1992 s 169LA, inserted by FA 2015 s 42, broadly excludes disposals of goodwill from qualifying for entrepreneurs' relief where the disposal is made directly or indirectly to a close company ("C") to which the disponer ("P") is a related party at the time of the disposal and where P is not a "retiring partner". The scope of the section is now limited to instances where P and any "relevant connected person" either (a) together own 5% or more of the ordinary share capital of C or of a company which is a fellow group member of the group to which C belongs or (b) together hold 5% or more of the voting rights in C or in a company which is a fellow group member of the group to which C belongs. A "relevant connected person" is either a company connected with P or trustees connected with P. There is a further exclusion. Where the section may now otherwise apply because 5% or more of the share capital of C is held, entrepreneurs' relief may nevertheless be due where three conditions are met. The first is that P and any relevant connected person dispose of the whole of their holding of C's ordinary share capital to another company, "A", within 28 days of the qualifying business disposal (the disposal involving the disposal of goodwill). The second condition is that, where A is a close company, immediately before the end of that 28-day period, P and any relevant connected person together hold less than 5% of the ordinary share capital of A or of a company which is a fellow group member of the group to which A belongs. The third condition also applies where A is a close company and is that P and any relevant connected person must together hold less than 5% of the voting rights in A or in a company which is a fellow group member of the group to which A belongs. The amendments made by s 85 have retroactive effect for disposals taking place after 2 December 2014.

Section 86 introduces **Sch 13**, which amends the definitions of "trading company" and "trading group" for the purposes of entrepreneurs' relief. They are together intended to mitigate the effects of the changes made by FA 2015 s 43, which excluded the activities of joint-venture companies or of partnerships of which the company is a partner from being considered as activities of that company for the purposes of those definitions.

Schedule 13 consists of six paragraphs. Schedule 13 para 1 is introductory. Schedule 13 paras 2 and 3 make consequential amendments. In particular, Sch 13 para 3 provides that the definitions of "trading company" and "trading group" previously contained in TCGA 1992 s 169S(4A), which was inserted by FA 2015 s 43 with effect from 18 March 2015, are never to have had effect. Instead, Sch 13 para 4 inserts new TCGA 1992 s 169SA, which introduces new TCGA 1992 Sch 7ZA, which is inserted by Sch 13 para 5, and contains the new definitions of "trading company" and "trading group". These replace the amended definitions in TCGA 1992 s 169S(4A)

New TCGA 1992 Sch 7ZA comprises four Parts. Part 1 (paras 1 and 2) contains the basic definition of "trading company" and "trading group". Part 2 (paras 3–12) modifies those definitions in relation to joint-venture companies. Part 3 (paras 13–23) modifies the definition of "trading activities" in relation to partnerships. Part 4 (paras 24–26) supplies interpretation.

New TCGA 1992 Sch 7ZA paras 1 and 2 define two different meanings of "trading company" and "trading group". For the specific purposes of Conditions A, B, C and D in TCGA 1992 s 169I, which defines what constitutes a material disposal of business assets and of TCGA 1992 s 169J, which defines what constitutes a disposal of trust business assets, these terms are to have the same meaning as in TCGA 1992 s 165A (including TCGA 1992 s 165A(7) and (12)), as modified by new TCGA 1992 Sch 7ZA Pt 2. The definition of "trading activities" in TCGA 1992 s 165A(4) and (9) is to be modified by reference to TCGA 1992 Sch 7ZA Part 3.

For all other provisions relating to entrepreneurs' relief, they are to have the same meaning as in TCGA 1992 s 165A, but disregarding TCGA 1992 s 165A(7) and (12). This is the current definition for all purposes of entrepreneurs' relief, except that the exclusions relating to joint-venture companies and partnerships of which the company is a partner are omitted.

New TCGA 1992 Sch 7ZA Pt 2 provides the conditions under which the activities of a joint-venture company may be attributed to the company the shares or securities of or in which are the subject of the disposal. Where there is a disposal of shares or securities or of interests in such shares or securities of a company ("A"), new TCGA 1992 Sch 7ZA para 3 provides that the activities of a joint-venture company may be attributed to a company for the purposes of TCGA 1992 s 165A(7) and (12) only where the individual claiming the relief ("P") passes two tests. These are the "shareholding test" and the "voting-rights test".

New TCGA 1992 Sch 7ZA para 4 defines the meaning of "investing company", which occurs in the tests. An "investing company" in relation to P and the joint-venture company in question is one in which P holds shares directly and which itself directly or indirectly holds shares in the joint-venture company.

New TCGA 1992 Sch 7ZA paras 5–8 contain the shareholding test. In essence, this is that the sum of the percentage of the ordinary share capital of the joint-venture company directly owned by P and indirectly owned by P via one or more investing companies is at least 5% throughout the "relevant period" (defined in new TCGA 1992 Sch 7ZA para 25). New TCGA 1992 Sch 7ZA paras 6 and 7 provide that P's indirect holding via any one investing company at any time is given by $R \times S \times 100$, where R is the fraction of the investing company's ordinary share capital owned by P at that time and S is the fraction of the joint-venture company's ordinary share capital directly or indirectly held by the investing company at that time. New TCGA 1992 Sch 7ZA para 8 prescribes how the fraction of the joint-venture company's ordinary share capital owned indirectly by the investing company is to be calculated and on what assumptions.

New TCGA 1992 Sch 7ZA paras 9–12 contain the voting-rights test. As with the shareholding test, this is in essence that the sum of the percentage of the voting rights in the joint-venture company directly held by P and P's "indirect voting-rights percentage" is at least 5% throughout the "relevant period" (defined in new TCGA 1992 Sch 7ZA para 25). New TCGA 1992 Sch 7ZA paras 10 and 11 provide that P's indirect voting-rights percentage (held through one or more investing companies) at any time is given by $T \times U \times 100$, where T is the fraction of the voting rights in the investment company held by P at that time and U is the fraction of the voting rights in the joint-venture company directly or indirectly held by the investing company at that time. New TCGA 1992 Sch 7ZA para 12 prescribes how the fraction of the voting rights in the joint-venture company indirectly held by the investing company is to be calculated and on what assumptions.

New TCGA 1992 Sch 7ZA Pt 3 provides, by way of negatives, the conditions under which activities carried on by a company as a member of a partnership may be treated as trading activities of the company. Where there is a disposal of shares or securities or of interests in such shares or securities of a company ("A"), new TCGA 1992 Sch 7ZA para 13 provides that the activities carried on by a company as a member of a partnership shall not be treated as trading activities of the company for the purposes of TCGA 1992 s 165A(4) and (9) where the individual claiming the relief ("P") fails either or both of two tests. These are the "profits and assets test" and the "voting-rights test" in relation to the partnership. It also provides that activities carried on by a company as a member of a partnership are also to be treated as not being trading activities of the company where the company is not a member of the partnership throughout the relevant period, as defined in new TCGA 1992 Sch 7ZA para 25.

New TCGA 1992 Sch 7ZA para 14 defines the meaning of "direct-interest company" and "relevant corporate partner", which occur in the tests. A "direct-interest company" is one in which P holds shares directly. A relevant corporate partner in relation to P and a partnership is a company (a) in which P's direct-interest company directly or indirectly owns ordinary share capital; (b) is a member of the same group of companies of which the direct-interest company is a member; and (c) is a member of the partnership in question.

New TCGA 1992 Sch 7ZA paras 15–20 contain the profits and assets test. P meets that test if, throughout the "relevant period" (defined in new TCGA 1992 Sch 7ZA para 25), the sum of the following percentages is at least 5%: P's direct interest in the partnership's assets; P's indirect interest in the partnership's assets via direct-interest companies that are partners in the partnership; and P's indirect interest in the partnership's assets via direct-interest companies and relevant corporate partners in the partnership. New TCGA 1992 Sch 7ZA paras 16 and 17 provide that P's share in the partnership through any one direct-interest company that is itself a partner in the partnership (the second element of the sum in new TCGA 1992 Sch 7ZA para 15) at any time is given by $R \times V \times 100$, where R is the fraction of the direct-interest company's ordinary share capital owned by P and V is the smaller of (a) the fraction of the partnership's profits in which the direct-interest company has an interest at that time and (b) the fraction of the partnership's assets in which the direct-interest company has an interest at that time. New TCGA 1992 Sch 7ZA paras 18 and 19 provide that P's share in the partnership through a particular direct-interest company and a particular relevant corporate partner in the partnership is given by R x V x W x 100, where R is as above, but V is the smaller of: (a) the fraction of the partnership's profits in which the corporate partner has an interest at that time and (b) the fraction of the partnership's assets in which the corporate partner has an interest at that time, and W is the fraction of the corporate partner's ordinary share capital directly or indirectly owned by the direct-interest company at that time. New TCGA 1992 Sch 7ZA para 20 prescribes how the fraction of a company's ordinary share capital that is owned indirectly by the direct-interest company is to be calculated and on what assumptions.

New TCGA 1992 Sch 7ZA paras 21–23 contain the voting rights test. P meets this test if, throughout the "relevant period" (defined in new TCGA 1992 Sch 7ZA para 25), the sum of P's "direct voting-rights percentage" and P's "indirect voting-rights percentage" is at least 5%. The "direct voting-rights percentage" is simply the percentage of the voting rights that P holds in each direct-interest company that is a member of the partnership and the "indirect voting-rights percentage" is found by calculating the percentage represented by P's indirect holding of voting rights in each relevant corporate partner in the partnership through each direct-interest company. New TCGA 1992 Sch 7ZA para 22 provide that P's indirect holding of voting rights in a particular relevant corporate partner in the partnership through a particular direct-interest company is given by T x X x 100, where T is the fraction of the voting rights in the direct-interest company that P holds at any one time and X is the fraction of the voting rights in the relevant corporate partner that the direct-interest company directly or indirectly holds at that time. New TCGA 1992 Sch 7ZA para 23 prescribes how the fraction of the voting rights in a company held indirectly by a direct-interest company is to be calculated and on what assumptions.

New TCGA 1992 Sch 7ZA para 24 defines "P" both in relation to a material disposal of business assets and in relation to a disposal of trust business assets. New TCGA 1992 Sch 7ZA para 25 defines "relevant period", which differs according to whether it is Conditions A and C in TCGA 1992 s 169I (material disposal of business assets), Conditions B and D in that section, or TCGA 1992 s 169J (disposal of trust business assets) that is under consideration. New TCGA 1992 Sch 7ZA para 26 provides other interpretations.

Schedule 13 para 6 provides that, except for the negation of TCGA 1992 s 169S(4A), the amendments made by Sch 13 are to have retroactive effect for disposals made after 17 March 2015, but only for the purposes of determining what is a trading company or trading group at times after that date. It also ensures that Sch 13 is to have no effect on the trading or non-trading status of a company at any time before 18 March 2015.

Investors' relief

Section 87 and **Sch 14**, which it introduces, provide for a new relief against capital gains tax, to be known as "investors' relief", for disposals of qualifying shares held by external investors in unlisted companies.

Schedule 14 consists of three paragraphs. Schedule 14 para 1 makes consequential amendments to headings. Schedule 14 para 2 inserts new TCGA 1992 Pt 5 Ch 5 (new TCGA 1992 ss 169VA–169VY), entitled "Investors' relief".

New TCGA 1992 s 169VA is an overview section, and makes it clear that investors' relief is to take the form of a lower rate of capital gains tax in respect of disposals of certain ordinary shares in unlisted companies and of interests in such shares.

New TCGA 1992 s 169VB provides what shares will, may and will not be qualifying shares for the purposes of the relief where there is a disposal of all or part of a holding of shares in a company. Qualifying shares must meet a number of conditions, including the following. They must be ordinary shares; the investor (the person making the disposal) must have subscribed for them (as defined in new TCGA 1992 s 169VU); the shares must be issued no earlier than 17 March 2016; the investor must have held them continuously; the company must be an unlisted company when the shares are issued; the company must be a trading company or the holding company of a trading group (as defined in new TCGA 1992 s 169VV) throughout the share-holding period; neither the investor nor a connected person may be a "relevant employee" (as defined in new TCGA 1992 s 169VW) of the company at any time in that period; and the shares must have been held for a period of at least three years at the date of the disposal, but the three-year period is to run from 6 April 2016. Qualifying shares may become disqualified if the investor receives value (for which see new TCGA 1992 Sch 7ZB, inserted by Sch 13 para 3). Shares that meet all the conditions except for the minimum three-year holding period are to be "potentially qualifying shares". "Excluded shares" are shares that are neither qualifying shares nor potentially qualifying shares.

New TCGA 1992 s 169VC provides for the relief. Where a "qualifying person" makes a disposal of a holding or part-holding of shares wholly or partly consisting of qualifying shares, then, upon a claim for relief, the rate of capital gains tax in respect of the chargeable gain (as reduced by allowable losses) on those qualifying shares is to be 10%. A "qualifying person" is either an individual or a trustee. New TCGA 1992 s 169VD provides for the calculation of the part of the gain qualifying for relief where not all the shares in the disposal are qualifying shares. There is also a lifetime cap on the relief, set by new TCGA 1992 ss 169VKand 169VL. These provisions are also qualified by new TCGA 1992 ss 169VH and 169VI, which impose extra conditions on certain disposals by trustees.

New TCGA 1992 s 169VD provides that where only some of the shares in the holding are qualifying shares, the part of the chargeable gain on the disposal that qualifies for the relief is to be Q/T times the entire chargeable gain, where Q is the number of qualifying shares in the disposal and T the total number of shares disposed of. Qualifying shares are to be treated as disposed of in priority to other shares.

New TCGA 1992 ss 169VE–169VG have effect for identifying shares where there have been previous disposals out of the holding. Where previous disposals have been the subject of claims for investors' relief, the identification rules in new TCGA 1992 s 169VF apply. Where there has been no previous claim for investors' relief, new TCGA 1992 s 169VG applies to identify the shares included in the current disposal.

Broadly speaking, new TCGA 1992 s 169VF provides that in any previous disposal that was the subject of a claim for investors' relief, qualifying shares are deemed to have been disposed of first, followed by excluded shares and then by potentially qualifying shares. Where it is necessary to identify potentially qualifying shares, a LIFO basis is to be used.

New TCGA 1992 s 169VG has effect where there has been no claim for investors' relief on a previous disposal. In that case, broadly speaking, the deemed order of disposal is excluded shares first, potentially qualifying shares second and qualifying shares last. Where it is necessary to identify potentially qualifying shares, a LIFO basis is to be used.

New TCGA 1992 ss 169VH and 169VI provide rules for disposals of qualifying shares by trustees of a settlement. New TCGA 1992 s 169VH provides that a disposal by trustees is not to be eligible for relief unless at least one of the beneficiaries of the settlement is an individual who is an "eligible beneficiary". An "eligible beneficiary" is an individual who has an interest in possession (other than for a fixed term) in the qualifying shares immediately before the disposal, has held that interest for an uninterrupted period of at least three years up to that point, and was at no time in that period a "relevant employee" of the company that issued the shares. Furthermore, the individual must, before the claim for relief is made, have elected to be an eligible beneficiary, by informing the trustees that he or she wishes to be so treated. The election may be withdrawn at any time before the trustees make the claim.

New TCGA 1992 s 169VI provides for the division of the gain among two or more eligible beneficiaries in proportion to their beneficial interest.

New TCGA 1992 s 169VJ allows for disposals of an interest in a "relevant holding" of qualifying shares also to qualify for relief. A "relevant holding" is either (a) a number of shares of the same class and acquired in the same capacity jointly by two or more persons including the qualifying person or (b) a number of shares of the same class and acquired in the same capacity by the qualifying person alone.

New TCGA 1992 ss 169VK and 169VL impose a lifetime cap of £10 million on the total of chargeable gains realised by or on behalf of an individual which may benefit from the relief. The cap includes gains made by trustees in respect of which the individual was an eligible beneficiary.

New TCGA 1992 s 169VM prescribes how to make claims for relief and who should make them. Where an individual makes the disposal, it is that individual who must make the claim. Where it is trustees who make the disposal, it is they and the eligible beneficiary or beneficiaries who must make the claim jointly. The last date for making the claim is the first anniversary of the 31 January immediately following the tax year in which the disposal occurs. The very first such time limit therefore expires on 31 January 2022, since the first qualifying disposals cannot be made before 6 April 2019 (the tax year 2019/20).

New TCGA 1992 ss 169VN–169VT deal with the situation where qualifying shares have been the subject of a reorganisation, share exchange or reconstruction. New TCGA 1992 ss 169VN–169VO provide for the consequences where no consideration was given for the new shares on a reorganisation; new TCGA 1992 ss 169VP–169VT apply where consideration was given on the reorganisation; new TCGA 1992 s 169VQ applies on a share exchange; new TCGA 1992 ss 169VR applies where there has been a scheme of reconstruction. New TCGA 1992 s 169VS modifies the meaning of "qualifying share" on a disposal following a reorganisation or reconstruction and new TCGA 1992 s 169VT provides for an election to disapply the normal treatment of reorganisations and share exchanges.

New TCGA 1992 ss 169VN and 169VO apply where there is a reorganisation within the meaning of TCGA 1992 s 126 and the investor neither gives nor becomes liable to give any consideration for the new holding. In essence, they provide that the proportion of qualifying, potentially qualifying and excluded shares in the new holding is to be the same as their proportion in the original holding, and where the investor had subscribed for and held shares comprised in the original holding for a continuous period, the investor is treated as having subscribed for and held the corresponding new shares for the same period.

New TCGA 1992 s 169VP addresses the situation where the investor gives consideration for the new holding. Shares in the new holding for which consideration was given are to be treated as having been issued when they were actually issued and not when the corresponding original shares were issued. Where some of the new shares are shares for which consideration was not given, their treatment is to follow that prescribed in new TCGA 1992 ss 169VN and 169VO.

New TCGA 1992 s 169VQ provides that where there is an exchange of shares in one company for shares in another within TCGA 1992 s 135, the two companies are to be treated as if they were the same company and the exchange is to be treated as if it were a reorganisation. The same treatment is to be accorded under new TCGA 1992 s 169VR to an exchange of shares on a scheme of reconstruction within TCGA 1992 s 136.

New TCGA 1992 s 169VS applies when there is a disposal of shares out of the new holding following a reconstruction, reorganisation or exchange of shares. As regards qualifying shares, the conditions regarding the necessity for the company to be a trading company or the holding company of a trading group and the prohibition on the investor's (or a connected person's) being a "relevant employee" of the company must be met both in the period ending with the exchange of shares by the original shares and in the period from the exchange to the disposal by the new shares.

As is well known, where there has been a reorganisation (under TCGA 1992 s 126) or an exchange of shares within TCGA 1992 ss 135 or 136, TCGA 1992 s 127 has effect to treat the original shares and the new holding as if they were the same asset for the purposes of capital gains tax. New TCGA 1992 s 169VT offers the investor to elect to disapply TCGA 1992 s 127, and claim investors' relief as if the reorganisation or exchange had involved a disposal of the original shares. The election must be made by the investor or the trustees and eligible beneficiary/ies no later than the first anniversary of the 31 January following the tax year in which the reorganisation or exchange takes place.

New TCGA 1992 s 169VU defines what is meant by "subscribing" for shares for the purposes of investors' relief and new TCGA 1992 s 169VV defines "trading company" and "the holding company of a trading group" (by reference back to TCGA 1992 s 165A). New TCGA 1992 s 169VW defines who is a "relevant employee". Essentially, any individual who has been an officer or employee of the issuing company or of a connected company at any time during the period in which the individual held the shares is a "relevant employee". In the case of a disposal by trustees, the relevant period is the three years immediately preceding the disposal during which the eligible beneficiary held a qualifying interest in possession. However, an exception is made for "unremunerated directors" (as defined in new TCGA 1992 s 169VW and further in new TCGA 1992 s 169VX).

New TCGA 1992 s 169VY contains general definitions.

Schedule 14 para 3 inserts new TCGA 1992 Sch 7ZB, which has effect to disqualify qualifying or potentially qualifying shares where the investor receives "value", in ways similar to the equivalent receipt of value provisions for the purposes of the EIS (ITA 2007 ss 213–223).

New TCGA 1992 Sch 7ZB comprises six paragraphs. New TCGA 1992 Sch 7ZB para 1 provides that where an investor holds qualifying shares or potentially qualifying shares and receives value other than insignificant value from the company in which those shares are held at any time in the four-year period beginning one year before the issue of the shares and ending immediately before the third anniversary of their issue.

New TCGA 1992 Sch 7ZB para 2 provides what constitutes a receipt of value. The provisions of this paragraph mirror almost exactly those of ITA 2007 s 216 (receipt of value for the purposes of the EIS), as modified by ITA 2007 s 168(2) (payments received by a director that do not establish a connection). New TCGA 1992 Sch 7ZB para 3 provides what the amount of value received is for each occasion of receipt specified in new TCGA 1992 Sch 7ZB para 2, and in that respect it mirrors exactly the equivalent provisions of ITA 2007 s 217 (amounts of value received for the purposes of the EIS). It also provides that receipts of insignificant value are not to be ignored if, taken together, they are not insignificant. An amount of value is insignificant if it does not exceed £1,000, unless arrangements are in place within the year preceding the issue of the shares for the investor to receive value, in which case no amount of value received is to be considered insignificant. These provisions exactly match those of ITA 2007 s 215. New TCGA 1992 Sch 7ZB para 4 is the equivalent for investors' relief of the EIS provisions for receipt of replacement value in ITA 2007 s 222 and matches those provisions almost to the letter. Essentially, where the investor or other person who received the value provides replacement value to the supplier of the original value under the conditions specified, the receipt of the original value is not to be regarded as disqualifying the shares in question. New TCGA 1992 Sch 7ZB para 5 matches ITA 2007 s 223 and provides that any replacement value received by the original supplier may be counted once only in overriding the disqualification that would otherwise result from the receipt of the original value. New TCGA 1992 Sch 7ZB para 6 provides for interpretation.

Employee shareholder shares

Section 88 imposes a lifetime cap of £100,000 on the exempt gains a person may make on the disposal of employee-shareholder shares but also provides for several reliefs to be available on a reorganisation, where hitherto there have been none. Employee-shareholder shares are shares acquired by an employee in consideration for entering into an employee-shareholder agreement, under which the employee surrenders certain employment rights. TCGA 1992 s 236B, which provides for the relief from capital gains tax, is now amended to provide that where an employee disposes of exempt employee-shareholder shares ("EES shares") acquired under an agreement entered into after 16 March 2016, any gain accruing to the employee is to be exempt only to the extent that it and any other exempt gains on previous disposals of such shares do not exceed £100,000. The cap is thus not retroactively imposed on shares acquired under agreements predating 17 March 2016. Section 88 also amends TCGA 1992 s 58, which deals with transfers between spouses and civil partners, to modify the impact of the rule excluding the no-gain no-loss transfer where the disposal is of EES shares. The effect of the amendments is that where the transferor of the EES shares has exhausted his or her lifetime allowance, the no-gain, no-loss rule of TCGA 1992 s 58 shall apply to the transfer. Where the transferor's gain would be less than the unused balance of his or her lifetime allowance, TCGA 1992 s 58 is not to apply and the transfer will be treated as made at market value. Where, however, the transferor's gain would be greater than the unused balance of the lifetime allowance, the transfer is to be treated as made for such a consideration as would use up the unused balance of the lifetime allowance.

TCGA 1992 s 127 provides that where there is a qualifying reorganisation, there is no disposal for the purposes of capital gains tax, and the new shares "step into the shoes" of the old shares. TCGA 1992 s 236F has hitherto provided quite simply that the relief provided by TCGA 1992 s 127 does not apply to EES shares on the occasion of a reorganisation or other company reconstruction, so that when a reorganisation or reconstruction takes place, there is a disposal of the shares. However, if that disposal is the first disposal of the EES shares, such a gain is exempt by virtue of TCGA 1992 s 236B(1), except to the extent that the £100,000 cap is exceeded.

Section 88(5) now amends TCGA 1992 s 236F by inserting new TCGA 1992 s 236F(1A)–(1K), with the intention of providing that in certain circumstances, the disposal is to be regarded as one where there is no gain and no loss.

The new rules provide that where an EES share ("the original EES share") or shares held by a person is or are involved in a reorganisation, as a result of which there is a disposal of the share(s), the shareholder is to be treated as if the disposal had taken place for a consideration – the "relevant amount") – determined by reference to the "notional gain", which is the gain that would accrue to the shareholder if the consideration for the disposal were for the market value of the share(s) at the time of the reorganisation. Where the whole of the notional gain would be a chargeable gain by virtue of new TCGA 1992 s 236B(1A) (because the lifetime cap has already been exceeded), the relevant amount (the deemed consideration) is the amount that would produce no gain and no loss. Where, on the other hand, only part of the notional gain would be a chargeable gain (because it would carry the shareholder over the cap limit), the deemed consideration is to be the maximum amount (which may not exceed the market value of the original EES share(s)) that would ensure no chargeable gain would accrue to the shareholder. Where no part of the notional gain would be a chargeable gain (because taken together with previous gains, the total still falls within the lifetime cap), the deemed consideration is the market value.

Where, on the other hand, no notional gain would accrue to the shareholder on the disposal of the original EES share(s), the deemed consideration is the amount that would produce no gain and no loss.

The amendments made by s 88 have effect for disposals made after 16 March 2016.

Section 89 also relates to employee-shareholder shares. It amends TCGA 1992s 236B so as to remove exemption from gains on a disposal where the proceeds of that disposal constitute either disguised management fees under ITA 2007 Pt 13 Ch 5E or carried interest under ITA 2007 s 809EZC.

Sections 90 and **91** concern disposals of UK residential property by non-residents. **Section 90** makes corrections to the calculation of gains and losses on relevant high-value disposals. The first amendment corrects a reference in TCGA 1992 Sch 4ZZA para 2(1) to para 6 of that Schedule to one to para 6A. This ensures that the override of the computations under TCGA 1992 Sch 4ZZA paras 3 and 4 of the ATED-related and non-ATED-related gains has effect as originally intended. The second amendment is to TCGA 1992 Sch 4ZZB para 17. This paragraph applies to compute the balancing gain or loss on a relevant high-value disposal of assets held at 5 April 2015 in respect of which no election has been made under either TCGA 1992 Sch 4ZZB para 2(1)(b) for the retrospective basis of computation to apply or under TCGA 1992 Sch 4ZZA para 5 to avoid rebasing and rebasing in 2016 is not required. The effect of the amendment is to ensure that the "notional pre-April 2013 gain or loss" is taken into account in every circumstance where the disposed-of interest was held on 5 April 2013. The amendments made by s 90 have effect for disposals made after 25 November 2015.

Section 91 introduces two circumstances in which an NRCGT return need not be made in respect of non-resident CGT disposals. It inserts new TMA 1970 s 12ZBA, which provides that an NRCGT return need not, but may be, made in two circumstances. The first circumstance is where the disposal is made after 5 April 2015 and neither a gain nor a loss accrues to the disponer as a result of any of the no-gain no-loss provisions. The second circumstance is where the disposal takes the form of the arm's length grant for no premium of a lease after 5 April 2015 to a person who is not connected to the grantor. The penalty for late returns under FA 2009 Sch 55 para 1 is not to apply to an elective return under new TMA 1970 s 12ZBA.

Section 92 adds capital gains tax to the taxes that may be collected on a provisional basis under PCTA 1968 s 1. This measure is preparatory to the intended extension of payments on account of capital gains tax to UK-resident persons.

PART 5
INHERITANCE TAX ETC

Section 93 introduces **Sch 15**, which amends the provisions on the extended nil-rate band of inheritance tax in respect of the transfers of a family home, introduced by F(No 2)A 2015. The amendments are intended to confer further relief where a person "downsizes" or ceases to own a home altogether and assets of an equivalent value are passed on death to a direct descendant. Whatever the merits or otherwise of the intention, the amendments add yet more complexity to an already complex set of provisions.

Schedule 15 consists of 12 paragraphs. Schedule 15 para 1 is introductory. Schedule 15 paras 2–4 make consequential amendments. Noteworthy is the amendment made by Sch 15 para 3(3) to IHTA 1984 s 8E(7), which provides for the computation of the residence nil-rate amount where not all of the residential interest passes to lineal descendants. In the case where the person's residence nil-rate amount is calculated to be greater than the value transferred, the person's residence nil-rate amount is now to be adjusted down to the value transferred and the amount available for carry-forward is to be one of two amounts, depending on whether the estate at death is less or greater than the taper threshold. Where it is no greater than the taper threshold, which is currently £2,000,000, the amount available for carry-forward is to be the difference between the value transferred and the person's "default allowance" (the sum of the residential enhancement in the year of death and any transferred residence nil-rate amount ("the brought-forward allowance"). Where the estate at death is greater than the taper threshold, the amount available for carry-forward is to be the difference between the value transferred and the person's "adjusted allowance".

Schedule 15 para 5 inserts new IHTA 1984 ss 8FA–8FE. New IHTA 1984 s 8FA applies to determine entitlement to the "downsizing addition" where there is a low-value residential interest in the deceased's (the person's) estate at death. Entitlement is conditional on meeting all of six conditions, A to F. Condition A is that either (a) the person's qualifying residential interest (QRI) or the proportion that is closely inherited is less than the maximum nil-rate amount or (b) none of the QRI is closely inherited and either so much of the value transferred (VT) as is attributable to the QRI is less than the person's default allowance where the estate is less than or equal to the taper threshold or is less than the person's adjusted allowance where the estate at death is greater than the taper threshold. Condition B is that not all of the value transferred is attributable to the QRI. Condition C is that the person has a "qualifying former residential interest" (as defined in new IHTA 1984 s 8H(4A)–(4F) and new IHTA 1984 s 8HA, inserted by Sch 15 para 7(5)). Condition D is that the value of the qualifying former residential interest (QFRI) is greater than the QRI comprised in the value transferred (hence the "downsizing"). Condition E is that at least some of the remaining estate (the estate other than the QRI) is closely inherited. Condition F is simply that a claim be made for the downsizing addition. Where these conditions are all met, the amount of the downsizing addition is to be "the lost relievable amount" (as defined in new IHTA 1984 s 8FE), but this can be no more than that part of the remainder of the estate that is closely inherited.

New IHTA 1984 s 8FB provides the conditions for entitlement to the downsizing addition where there is no residential-property interest in the estate at death. There are five such conditions, G to K. Condition G is that the estate at death does not include a residential-property interest. Condition H is that the value transferred is greater than nil. Condition I is that the person has a QFRI. Condition J is that at least some of the estate is closely inherited, and Condition K is simply that a claim be made for the downsizing addition. Where these conditions are all met, the amount of the downsizing addition is to be "the lost relievable amount" (as defined in new IHTA 1984 s 8FE), but her too this can be no more than that part of the remainder of the estate that is closely inherited.

New IHTA 1984 s 8FC provides that where all or some of the QRI is closely inherited, so that IHTA 1984 s 8E applies to determine the residence nil-rate amount, the effect is to add the amount of the downsizing addition to the residence nil-rate amount that would otherwise be due. New IHTA 1984 s 8FD explains how the downsizing addition is to be given effect where there is either no QRI in the estate at death or none of the QRI is closely inherited, so that IHTA 1984 s 8F would normally have effect. In these circumstances, new IHTA 1984 s 8FD(3)–(6) displace the rules in IHTA 1984 s 8F. The effect is that the person's residence nil-rate amount is equated to the downsizing addition. Unless the value of the estate is no greater than the taper threshold and the downsizing addition is less than the person's default allowance, there is no carry-forward amount. Where these two conditions are satisfied, however, the carry-forward amount is the difference between the downsizing addition and the default allowance.

New IHTA 1984 s 8FE prescribes the calculation of the "lost relievable amount". This is effectively the amount of the residence nil-rate amount that has been forfeited by downsizing or disposal of a residence. Where new IHTA 1984 s 8FA applies (so there is a QRI at death some or all of which is closely inherited), the lost relievable amount is calculated by a four-step process. Step 1 is to determine the percentage of the person's "former allowance" represented by the value of the QFRI, subject to a maximum of 100. Step 2 is to determine the percentage of the person's "allowance on death" represented by the QRI, subject again to a maximum of 100. Step 3 is to deduct the result of Step 2 from the result of Step 1; the result, P%, may not be less than zero. Step 4 is to determine P% of the person's allowance on death, which is the lost relievable amount. The person's "former allowance" is the sum of (a) the residential enhancement at the time the disposal of the QFRI was completed; (b) any brought-forward allowance the person would have had if the person had died at the time of the disposal; and (c) any excess of the brought-forward allowance at the time of the person's actual death over the hypothetical brought-forward allowance referred to in (b). The amount in (c) is adjusted if the estate on death exceeds the taper threshold, so that the person has an adjusted allowance to replace the default allowance. If the disposal of the QFRI takes place before 6 April 2017, the residential enhancement is taken to be £100,000 and the brought-forward allowance to be zero. The person's allowance on death is simply the default allowance if the estate at death is no greater than the taper threshold and is the adjusted allowance (default allowance minus half of the excess of the estate over the taper threshold) if the estate is greater than the taper threshold. Where, however, new IHTA 1984 s 8FB applies, as none of any QRI at death is closely inherited, the lost relievable amount is simply that percentage of the person's allowance on death as is equal to the percentage of the person's former allowance represented by the person's QFRI.

Schedule 15 para 6 makes consequential amendments. Schedule 15 para 7 amends IHTA 1984 s 8H, which defines "qualifying residential interest" (QRI), to cover situations in which the deceased had more than one interest in a former residence. Where a person disposes of a residential-property interest after 7 July 2015, that person's personal representatives may after the person's death nominate the dwelling-house concerned or one such dwelling-house as the one qualifying for the downsizing addition, thereby creating the QFRI. The nominated dwelling-house must have been occupied by the person before its disposal. If the person had before death disposed of a residential property interest in the nominated dwelling-house after 7 July 2015 and after it had first become that person's residence (a "post-occupation time") and that is the only such disposal at a post-occupation time, the interest disposed of is to be a QFRI in relation to that person. The same is true if the person disposes of two or more residential property interests in the nominated dwelling-house at the same post-occupation time or at different times on the same day. If, on the other hand, the person disposes of residential property interests in the nominated dwelling-house on two or more days at post-occupation times and the personal representatives nominate only one of those days, the interest(s) disposed of on the nominated day are the QFRI in relation to the person. Disposals by way of a gift with reservation are not to be treated as disposals for this purpose but the making of a potentially exempt transfer when the property ceases to be subject to a reservation are to be treated as a disposal.

Schedule 15 para 8 inserts new IHTA 1984 s 8HA, which deals with interests in possession in property consisting of or including an interest in a dwelling-house. Broadly speaking, where a person ("P") has an interest in possession in property which consists of or includes an interest in a dwelling-house until the trustees dispose of the interest in the dwelling-house to a person other than P, P is regarded as having made a disposal of the interest in the dwelling-house, so that it may become a QFRI. On the other hand, if P disposes of the interest in possession or it comes to end during P's lifetime, either event is to be treated as a disposal by P of P's interest in the dwelling-house. Definitions of the type of interest P may have – essentially those that would form part of P's estate under IHTA 1984 s 5 – are included. Schedule 15 paras 9–11 make consequential amendments.

Schedule 15 para 12 amends IHTA 1984 s 8M, which provides for calculation of the residence nil-rate amount where the transfer of value on death involves a conditionally exempt transfer including some or all of the QRI. Hitherto, IHTA 1984 s 8M has provided that an "exempt percentage" (X/QRI x 100) of the QRI is to be treated as not being closely inherited, where X is the portion of the value transferred by the conditionally exempt transfer that is attributable to the QRI. The amendments made to the section now stipulate what the residence nil-rate amount and the amount (if any) available for carry-forward are to be if the person has an entitlement to a downsizing addition.

Section 94 inserts new IHTA 1984 s 12A to ensure that where a person dies having failed to exercise rights over the flexible drawdown pension funds there specified, the omission is not to constitute a deemed disposition on death and thus give rise to a potential charge to inheritance tax. In the case of the drawdown pension funds specified, the amendments have effect in relation to deaths after 5 April 2011 and are deemed to have come into force on 6 April 2011. In the case of the flexi-access drawdown funds specified, the amendments have effect in relation to deaths after 5 April 2015 and are deemed to have come into force on 6 April 2015.

Section 95 puts existing extra-statutory concession F20 on a statutory footing, as new IHTA 1984 s 153ZA and new Sch 5A, and extends its scope. The effect is to provide a tax exemption (by way of a tax credit) for one-off late financial compensation and ex gratia payments for claims by victims of persecution in the "Second World War era". New IHTA 1984 s 153ZA provides that where a person, P, dies, after having received a "qualifying payment", or before his personal representatives receive a qualifying payment, the tax chargeable on the value transferred on P's death is to be reduced by an amount equal to the smaller of the "relevant percentage" of the qualifying payment and the amount of tax that would otherwise be chargeable on the value transferred. The "relevant percentage" is 40% (or whatever other rate of IHT may apply above the nil-rate band in the future). A payment is a qualifying payment if it is either (A) a payment specified in new IHTA 1984 Sch 5A Pt 1 and is made to a person or to that person's personal representatives by virtue of that person's being a victim of National-Socialist persecution or the spouse or civil partner of such a victim; (B) a payment specified in new IHTA 1984 Sch 5A Pt 2; or (C) a payment of a kind specified in Treasury regulations and made to persons (or to their personal representatives) who were prisoners of war or civilian internees during the Second World War or the spouses or civil partners of such persons.

New IHTA 1984 Sch 5A, inserted by s 95(2), consists of two Parts. Part 1 specifies nine foreign funds compensation payments of a fixed amount from which are qualifying payments where made to the persons specified in Condition A in s 95(1). Part 2 specifies a single, UK fund, the Far Eastern Prisoners of War Ex Gratia Scheme, payments from which are qualifying payments where made to the persons specified in Condition C in s 95(1). The amendments made by s 95 have effect in relation to deaths occurring after 31 December 2014.

Section 96 transfers the responsibility for approving certain national institutions referred to in IHTA 1984 Sch 3 back to HM Treasury. Gifts to bodies listed in that Schedule qualify for various IHT reliefs. Although the approval function was originally awarded to the Treasury, FA 1985 s 95 transferred it to HMRC. Museums and art galleries maintained by local authorities and universities are also specified in IHTA 1984 Sch 3. The amendment now made by s 95(4) adds museums and galleries formerly, but no longer, maintained by those institutions to the list. The transfer of the approval function does not have effect for approvals made before 15 September 2016.

Section 97 makes technical amendments and corrects anomalies in connection with estate duty (to the extent that it still applies) and its interaction with IHT. The amendments address two particular issues. One concerns the charge to estate duty when an object of national, scientific, historic or artistic interest with an outstanding estate-duty exemption is lost. The amendments made by s 96 provide that estate duty is to be charged on the value of the object at the time of the loss at the rate that would have been applicable on the last death on which the objects passed on the principal value of the estate concerned. Hitherto, no charge to tax has arisen on such an occasion. The amendments have effect from 15 September 2016. The second issue concerns claims under IHTA 1984 Sch 6 for conditional exemption from IHT for such objects with an estate-duty exemption on the death of their owner. The amendments now made to IHTA 1984 Sch 6 ensure that on a subsequent chargeable event in relation to the object, HMRC may levy estate duty or IHT as it elects. These particular amendments have effect for chargeable events subsequent to a conditionally exempt transfer made after 16 March 2016.

PART 6
APPRENTICESHIP LEVY

Part 6, consisting of ss 98–121, introduce the new tax called apprenticeship levy, to be charged on large employers in order to fund new apprenticeships.

Basic provisions

Section 98 introduces the tax and places the responsibility for is collection and management on HMRC.

Section 99 provides that, subject to specific exceptions, the apprenticeship levy is to be charged on a person who has a "pay bill" for a tax year and where 0.5% ("the relevant percentage") of that bill exceeds the "levy allowance" for that year. The levy allowance is normally to be £15,000 in any tax year. The levy will therefore normally be charged where the pay bill exceeds £3 million. The amount of the levy will be N - A, where N is 0.5% of the pay bill for the tax year and A is the amount of the levy allowance.

Section 100 defines what is and what comprises a pay bill. A person has a pay bill if that person is the secondary contributor in relation to payments of earnings to or for the benefit of one or more employed earners and therefore incurs liability to pay secondary Class 1 national insurance contributions. The amount of the pay bill for the tax year is the total amount of earnings in respect of which the liability to pay secondary Class 1 national insurance contributions is incurred. Liability to pay secondary Class 1 national insurance contributions is deemed to be incurred as if the secondary earnings threshold were nil.

Sections 101 and **102** specify instances where a person's levy allowance may be nil. **Section 101** provides that where two or more companies that are not charities are connected at the beginning of a tax year and each of them would otherwise be entitled to a levy allowance for that year, they form a "company unit" for that tax year. The members of such a company unit must choose between themselves how much of the single levy allowance (including zero) each is to claim, provided that the total comes to £15,000. Once the choice has been made, it cannot afterwards be altered, except to correct a mistake whereby the total claimed exceeds or falls short of £15,000. Where members of a company unit have together claimed more than £15,000, and take no remedial action to correct their claims after prompting from HMRC, HMRC is required to correct each member's claim by multiplying it by (15,000/T), where T is the total claimed by all the members. Where a member has not made a return, its allowance is to be zero.

Where the total amount of apprenticeship levy paid by the members of a company unit in respect of a tax year or any period in a tax year is less than the total due and payable by them, and either the members have made no returns for any period in the tax year concerned or those returns contain insufficient information for HMRC to determine how the £15,000 allowance is to be used by the members, then following failure on the members' part to take the appropriate remedial action, HMRC is required to allocate the levy allowance equally between them in the amount (£15,000/N), where N is the number of members of the company unit.

"Connected" is defined by reference to NICA 2014 Sch 1 Pt 1. "Company" is defined by reference to CTA 2010 s 1121(1). **Section 102** makes the similar provision with regard to two or more connected charities. With regard to charities, "connected" is defined in s 118.

Anti-avoidance

Section 103 is designed to counteract avoidance arrangements, which are defined as arrangements the main purpose or one of the main purposes of which is to secure benefits or further benefits from an entitlement to a levy allowance for a tax year or otherwise to obtain an advantage in relation to the apprenticeship levy. Two situations are envisaged. The first is where as the result of avoidance arrangements, a person incurs a liability to pay secondary Class 1 contributions in one particular tax year (i.e. because the earnings are paid in that year) rather than in another. If this would otherwise result in an advantage in relation to the levy, the arrangement is to be ignored and the levy is to be charged as if the liability had been incurred and hence the earnings had been paid in the year in which it was actually incurred and the earnings actually paid. The second situation is where, as a result of the arrangements, a person would be in a position to use or make greater use of a levy allowance than in their absence or would otherwise obtain an advantage in relation to the levy. If that is the case, entitlement to the levy allowance is to be withdrawn.

Section 104 adds apprenticeship levy to existing anti-avoidance provisions relating to the disclosure of tax-avoidance schemes (FA 2004 s 318); taxes subject to the GAAR (FA 2013 s 206); follower notices and accelerated payments (FA 2014 Pt 4); and promoters of tax-avoidance schemes (FA 2014 Pt 5).

Payment, collection and recovery

Section 105 allows HMRC to make regulations concerning the assessment, payment, collection and recover of the apprenticeship levy. **Section 106** clarifies that regulations under s 105 may make provision for the recovery of apprenticeship levy from third parties, in the manner that secondary Class 1 contributions may be recovered from third parties. **Section 107** clarifies that regulations under s 105 may require information concerning payments of apprenticeship levy to be reported within the real-time information system.

Section 108 provides that, as a general rule, assessments for apprenticeship levy may not be issued more than four years after the end of the tax year to which they relate. Where loss of apprenticeship levy has been caused by a person's carelessness, the time limit for assessment is to be extended to six years. Where the loss has been brought about deliberately, arises from arrangements in respect of which there has been a failure to comply with reporting obligations under DOTAS or a failure to notify HMRC of a promoter reference number, the time limit is to be extended to 20 years. As regards assessments to recover amounts of apprenticeship levy repaid in error, these may be made at any time before the end of the tax year following that in which the repayment was made.

Section 109 prohibits the making of deductions in respect of apprenticeship levy from any payment of earnings or the recovery of all or part of its cost from any person who is or has been a relevant earner or the making of any arrangements to do anything so prohibited.

Section 110 provides that the provisions of TMA 1970 ss 60 (issue of demand notes and receipts), 61 (distraint by collectors in Northern Ireland) and 65–68 (court proceedings) are to apply also to apprenticeship levy, as is FA 2008 Pt 7 Ch 5 (payment and enforcement).

Information and penalties

Section 111 gives HMRC the power to make regulations requiring records relating to apprenticeship levy to be kept and preserved for a specified period. **Section 112** extends HMRC's information and inspection powers under FA 2008 Sch 36 to matters concerning apprenticeship levy.

Section 113 adds apprenticeship levy returns to those in respect of which penalties may be charged under FA 2007 Sch 24 for errors and to those failure to make which is liable to a penalty under FA 2009 Sch 55, and adds the failure to pay apprenticeship levy on time to the defaults in respect of which a penalty may be charged under FA 2009 Sch 56.

Appeals

Section 114 provides for appeals to be made against assessments of apprenticeship levy or other amounts under regulations made under s 105. Appeals must be made within 30 days of the date on which the notice of assessment is given, and TMA 1970 Part 5 concerning appeals is to apply as it applies to an appeal against assessments to income tax.

General

Section 115 adds apprenticeship levy to the taxes in respect of which dishonest conduct by a tax agent may be sanctioned under FA 2012 Sch 38. **Section 116** adds apprenticeship levy to the taxes that may be provisionally collected under PCTA 1968 s 1 following a resolution of the House of Commons. **Section 117** binds the Crown.

Sections 118 and **119** define when two charities are considered to be connected with one another. **Section 120** provides for general interpretation and **s 121** provides for further regulation-making powers.

PART 7
VAT

Section 122 is intended to allow non-departmental public bodies and similar arm's length bodies to be able to recover VAT when they enter into cost-sharing arrangements. It inserts new VATA 1994 s 33E, which enables HM Treasury to direct HMRC to refund the VAT chargeable to specified persons on the making of a claim in a manner to be prescribed by HMRC. The VAT in question is that chargeable on the supply of goods or services to the specified person, the intra-EU acquisition of goods by that specified person and the importation of goods from outside the European Union by that person, all for non-business purposes.

Sections 123 and **124** are linked provisions intended to give HMRC greater powers for tackling online fraud. **Section 123** amends VATA 1994 s 48, which deals with VAT representatives. Under new VATA 1994 s 48(1ZA), HMRC is given the power to direct that a non-established taxable person shall appoint a UK-established representative who registered in a special register. A taxable person who has not been given such a direction may also be required to appoint a UK-established representative. HMRC is given the power to refuse to register a prospective representative or to cancel an existing representative's registration. Other amendments update references to the EU mutual-assistance provisions and define a UK-established person as one who is established, or has a fixed establishment in the UK, or, in the case of an individual, one who has his or her usual place of residence or permanent address in the UK.

Section 124 establishes joint and several liability for unpaid VAT for operators of online marketplaces in respect of goods sold to UK customers via that marketplace. It inserts new VATA 1994 ss 77B–77D and makes consequential amendments.

New VATA 1994 s 77B is to apply where a person who is not established in the UK makes taxable supplies of goods through an "online marketplace" but fails to comply with any requirement imposed on him in respect of VAT In those circumstances,

HMRC may serve a notice ("the liability notice") on the "operator" of the online marketplace requiring that either (a) the operator take steps to prevent the person from offering goods for sale via that marketplace for the period specified in the notice or (b) the operator become jointly and severally liable to HMRC for the VAT payable by that person in respect of all taxable supplies made by him via the marketplace in the period specified in the notice. The terms "online marketplace" and "operator" are defined. For these purposes "established in the United Kingdom" is defined by reference to Art 10 of EU Implementing Regulation (EU) No 282/2011.

New VATA 1994 s 77C provides for assessments to be made where joint and several liability on the operator is invoked under new VATA 1994 s 77B. An assessment in respect of a particular month must be made no later than (a) two years after the end of that month or (b) one year after evidence comes to HMRC which is sufficient in its opinion to justify making the assessment. Such as assessment may be followed by a further assessment within one year of the time when further evidence sufficient for that purpose becomes available, but no later than four years after the end of the month in question. These assessments are open to appeal in the normal way.

New VATA 1994 s 77D allows interest to be charged on amounts of VAT remaining outstanding more than 30 days after the issue of assessments under new VATA 1994 s 77C by way of separate assessments. The interest is to be recoverable as if it were VAT.

Section 125 amends FA 2010 Sch 6 para 2 to add the High Court of the Isle of Man to the courts recognised under that Schedule as having jurisdiction, so that charities established in the Isle of Man may benefit from the VAT reliefs available to UK-established charities.

Section 126 provides for supplies of "women's sanitary products" to be zero-rated, by the insertion of new VATA 1994 Sch 8 Group 19. What products are envisaged are defined in the Note to the Group. These products are currently liable at the 5% reduced rate. The zero-rating is to have effect from a day to be appointed but this may not be after the later of 1 April 2017 and the earliest date consistent with the UK's obligations to the European Union.

PART 8
SDLT AND ATED

Stamp duty land tax

Section 127 abolishes the slab system for charging stamp duty land tax (SDLT) on non-residential and mixed property in favour of a progressive scale, following the similar measure in respect of residential property contained in SDLTA 2015. The new Table B substituted in FA 2003 s 55 by s 127(3)(c) charges SDLT on land transactions involving land that is not residential property at 0% on the first £150,000; 2% on the next £100,000 and at 5% on any balance over £250,000. The SDLT charge on leases of commercial or mixed property (transactions where the chargeable consideration consists of or includes rent), which has always charged tax at progressive rate bands (albeit only two), is also amended to add a 5% rate band for so much of the consideration as consists of a rent with a net present value exceeding £5 million. FA 2003 Sch 5 para 9A, which restricted the 0% band where part of the chargeable consideration did not involve rent, is omitted. The amendments made by s 127 have effect for land transactions the effective date of which is after 16 March 2016. However, the purchase may elect not to have the amendments apply where contracts were exchanged before 17 March 2016, but substantial performance or completion did not take place until on or after that date. Section 127 has no effect in Scotland, where land and buildings transaction tax (LBTT) applies instead of SDLT. SDLT will also cease to apply in Wales from a day to be appointed under the Wales Act 2014.

Section 128 imposes higher rates of SDLT on individuals purchasing second or additional dwellings (whether for their own occupation or use or to let) and on any purchases by persons other than individuals. The chargeable consideration can be as little as £40,000 for the higher rates to come into play. Section 128(2) amends FA 2003 s 55 to provide that new FA 2003 Sch 4ZA is to apply to determine the amount of tax chargeable in respect of certain transactions involving major interests in dwellings. Section 128(3) inserts new FA 2003 Sch 4ZA.

New FA 2003 Sch 4ZA consists of 19 paragraphs, divided into three Parts. Part 1 (para 1) sets out the higher rates; Pt 2 (paras 2–7) provides for the nature of the transactions that are to subject to the higher rates; and Pt 3 (paras 8–19) contains supplementary provisions.

New FA 2003 Sch 4ZA para 1 provides that for a chargeable transaction that is a "higher-rates transaction", the rates of SDLT in respect of transactions involving solely residential property are to be three percentage points higher for each band, i.e. the lowest rate, that charged on the first £125,000 of chargeable consideration is to be 3% (instead of 0%) and the highest rate, that charged on the balance of chargeable consideration above £1.5 million is to be 15% (instead of 12%).

New FA 2003 Sch 4ZA para 2 sets out how a "higher-rates transaction" is to be identified. In the case of a single purchaser, it will be such a transaction if it falls within any of new FA 2003 Sch 4ZA paras 3–7. Where there are two or more purchasers, a transaction will be a higher-rates transaction if, considering each purchaser separately, it falls into any of those paragraphs with respect to any one of the purchasers. The grant of a leasehold interest of a term not exceeding seven years at the date of the grant is not to be a "major interest" for these purposes.

New FA 2003 Sch 4ZA paras 3 and 4 provide for when a single-dwelling transaction is to be regarded as a higher-rates transaction. Where the purchaser is an individual, a transaction is a higher-rates transaction where the main subject-matter is a major interest in a single dwelling, and four further conditions (A–D) are met. Condition A is that the chargeable consideration is not less than £40,000. Condition B is that where on the effective date of the transaction the purchased dwelling is subject to a lease on which the main subject-matter is reversionary, the unexpired term of that lease may not exceed 21 years. Condition C is that at the end of that effective date, the purchaser has a major interest in a dwelling other than the purchased dwelling; that major interest has a market value of at least £40,000 and where the purchased dwelling is subject to a lease on which the main subject-matter is reversionary, the unexpired term of that lease does not exceed 21 years. Condition D is that the dwelling is not a replacement for the purchaser's only or main residence. What constitutes a replacement property is defined. Broadly speaking, there are two instances where this is or may be so. In the first instance, the purchaser must intend the purchased dwelling to be his or her only or main residence to replace a dwelling the major interest in which was disposed of by the purchaser, or the purchaser's spouse or civil partner, in the three immediately preceding years and which was occupied at any time within those three years as the purchaser's only or main residence. The second instance is where the purchaser intends purchased dwelling to be his or her only or main residence to replace a dwelling the major interest in which will be disposed of by the purchaser, or the purchaser's spouse or civil partner, in the three immediately following years and which will be occupied at any time within those three years as the purchaser's only or main residence. However, for land transactions whose effective date is before 26 November 2018, the three-year period is waived and the former disposal can take place at any time before the purchase of the replacement property.

Where the purchaser is not an individual, new FA 2003 Sch 4ZA para 4 provides that a transaction is a higher-rates transaction where the main subject-matter is a major interest in a single dwelling and Conditions A and B in new FA 2003 Sch 4ZA para 3 applicable to individuals are met.

New FA 2003 Sch 4ZA paras 5–7 cover multiple-dwelling transactions. Under new FA 2003 Sch 4ZA para 5, a transaction is a higher-rates transaction where the purchaser is an individual, the main subject-matter is a major interest in two or more dwellings and three further conditions, Conditions A, B and C, are met in respect of at least two of the dwellings. Condition A is that the proportion of the chargeable consideration justly and reasonably attributable to the purchased dwelling is at least £40,000. Condition B is that where on the effective date of the transaction the purchased dwelling is subject to a lease on which the main subject-matter is reversionary, the unexpired term of that lease may not exceed 21 years. Condition C is that the purchased dwelling is not subsidiary to another of the purchased dwellings. A dwelling ("A") is subsidiary to another dwelling ("B") if (a) dwelling A is situated within the grounds of, or within the same building as, dwelling B; and (b) the amount of the chargeable consideration justly and reasonably attributable to dwelling B is no less than two-thirds of the chargeable consideration justly and reasonably attributable to the following taken together: dwellings A and B and each of the other purchased dwellings situated within the grounds of or within the same building as dwelling B.

Under new FA 2003 Sch 4ZA para 6, a transaction is a higher-rates transaction where (a) the purchaser is an individual; (b) the main subject matter is a major interest in two or more dwellings; (c) only one of the purchased dwellings meets Conditions A, B and C in new FA 2003 Sch 4ZA para 5; (d) that purchased dwelling is not a replacement for the purchaser's only or main dwelling; and (e) that at the end of the effective date of the transaction, the purchaser has a major interest in a dwelling other than the purchased dwelling; that major interest has a market value of at least £40,000 and where the purchased dwelling is subject to a lease on which the main subject-matter is reversionary, the unexpired term of that lease does not exceed 21 years. Where the purchaser is not an individual, new FA 2003 Sch 4ZA para 7 provides that a multiple-dwellings transaction is a higher-rates transaction where the main subject-matter is a major interest in two or more dwellings and at least one of the purchased dwellings meets Conditions A and B in new FA 2003 Sch 4ZA para 5.

New FA 2003 Sch 4ZA para 8 provides for a land-transaction return in respect of an earlier higher-rates transaction to be amended where it ceases to be one because the original only or main residence is sold within the three-year period thereby meeting the condition for the property purchased in the earlier transaction to be a replacement property. The amended return may be made no later than the later of (a) the end of the three months following the second transaction and (b) the end of the 12 months following the filing date for the original return.

New FA 2003 Sch 4ZA para 9 provides for the case where one spouse or civil partner is not a party to a land transaction that the other spouse or civil partner with whom he or she is living enters into. In these circumstances, the transaction is still a higher-rates transaction if it would have been such had the non-purchasing spouse or civil partner been the purchaser.

New FA 2003 Sch 4ZA paras 10–13 deal with purchases by the trustees of settlements and bare trusts. Under FA 2003 Sch 4ZA para 10, in the two instances specified, it is the beneficiary of the settlement or bare trust who is to be treated as the purchaser and not the trustee. The first instance is where the beneficiary will be entitled to occupy the dwelling(s) for life or to the income from the dwelling(s). The second is where the main subject-matter of the transaction consists of a lease (a term of years absolute) and the purchaser is acting as a trustee of a bare trust. New FA 2003 Sch 4ZA para 11 specifies two instances of existing ownership where the beneficiary and not the trustee is to be treated as holding the major interest in the dwelling concerned and to be making the disposal of that interest when the trustee disposes of it. The first instance is where part of the trust property consists of a major interest in a dwelling and a beneficiary is entitled to occupy the dwelling for life or to the income from the dwelling. The second instance is a bare trust part of the trust property of which consists of a lease. An exception is made under new FA 2003 Sch 4ZA para 12 where the beneficiary under new FA 2003 Sch 4ZA paras 10 or 11 is a minor child. In that case, it is the child's parent or the parent's spouse or civil partner who is regarded as stepping into the shoes of the child. New FA 2003 Sch 4ZA para 13 provides that where the purchaser or one of the purchasers is an individual acting as trustee of a settlement but no beneficiary is entitled in the way described in new FA 2003 Sch 4ZA para 10. In that case, the purchase is treated as if it were a purchase by a person other than an individual.

New FA 2003 Sch 4ZA para 14 deals with purchases by members of a partnership acting independently of that partnership. Where a purchaser in a transaction involving a major interest in a dwelling or dwellings is a member of a partnership but does not enter into the transaction for the purposes of the partnership, any major interest in any other building owned by the partnership for the purposes of trade is not to be treated as held by the purchaser when applying the tests in new FA 2003 Sch 4ZA paras 3 or 6.

New FA 2003 Sch 4ZA para 15 provides for alternative finance arrangements. Where a chargeable transaction is the first transaction under an alternative finance arrangement between a person and a financial institution, it is the person and not the institution that is to be treated as the purchaser in the transaction.

New FA 2003 Sch 4ZA para 16 provides for special treatment where a person inherits a major interest no greater than 50% in a dwelling jointly with one or more other persons. In such a case, the person is not to be treated as having a major interest in that dwelling for the tests in new FA 2003 Sch 4ZA paras 3 or 6 at any time within the three years immediately following the date of the inheritance, until and unless that person's interest comes to exceed 50%.

New FA 2003 Sch 4ZA para 17 provides that where the dwelling concerned is located outside England, Wales or Northern Ireland, key terms such as "major interest", "land transaction" etc are to be taken as the equivalent right, event or interest under the law of the relevant jurisdiction. New FA 2003 Sch 4ZA para 18 defines what is meant by a "dwelling". New FA 2003 Sch 4ZA para 19 provides for HM Treasury to make regulations.

Subject to transitional provisions, the amendments made by s 128 have effect for land transactions the effective date of which is after 31 March 2016.

Sections 129 to **131** introduce reliefs from the higher (15%) rate of SDLT.

Section 129 provides an additional relief where land is purchased for commercial use. The existing reliefs are contained in FA 2003 Sch 4A para 5, which specifies four qualifying instances for the exclusive purposes of which the interest in the property may be purchased. Three new qualifying instances are now added. The first is where the interest is acquired for use as business premises for the purposes of a qualifying property-rental business (other than one giving rise to income wholly or mainly consisting of excluded rents). The second new instance is use for the purposes of a "relievable trade". The third new instance is development or redevelopment and exploitation as a source of non-excluded rents or other receipts in the course of a qualifying property-rental business; use as business premises for such a business; or use for the purposes of a relievable trade. A "relievable trade" is a trade that is run on a commercial basis and with a view to profit. A qualifying property-rental business is as defined for the purposes of ATED in FA 2013 s 133. The amendments made by s 129 have effect in relation to land transactions whose effective date falls after 31 March 2016.

Section 130 introduces a relief from the higher rate of SDLT for a type of equity-release scheme known as a regulated home-reversion plan. Under new FA 2003 Sch 4A para 5CA, inserted by s 130(2), relief applies to a chargeable transaction if the purchaser is an "authorised plan provider" who acquires the subject-matter of the transaction under a regulated home-reversion plan into which the purchaser enters as a plan provider. This is a plan under which an individual or individuals sell(s) all or part of the individual's or individuals' home to the plan provider in return for an annuity or lump sum and a life tenancy. "Authorised plan provider" is defined by reference to Article 63B(1) of the Financial Services and Markets (Regulated Activities) Order 2001. New FA 2003 Sch 4A para 5IA, inserted by s 130(3), provides for withdrawal of the new relief if within three years of the chargeable transaction, the purchaser comes to hold the interest for a purpose other than for the regulated home-reversion plan. The amendments made by s 130 have effect in relation to land transactions whose effective date falls after 31 March 2016.

Section 131 introduces two new reliefs from the higher rate of SDLT for purchases of properties occupied by certain employees. FA 2003 Sch 4A para 5D has hitherto provided relief for the purchase by a purchaser for the purposes of his "relievable trade" of dwellings to be occupied as living accommodation by one or more qualifying employees or partners. The definition of "relievable trade" is as under s 129. References to a relievable trade are now replaced by references to a relievable business, which is analogously defined as a trade or property-rental business run on a commercial basis and with a view to profit. The second new relief is set out in new FA 2003 Sch 4A para 5EA, inserted by s 131(4). This provides that relief shall be available where the interest purchased is in or over a flat that is one of at least three flats in the same premises and is acquired by a tenants' management company and intended for occupation by a caretaker. New FA 2003 Sch 4A para 5JA, inserted by s 131(5), provides for withdrawal of the new relief if within three years of the chargeable transaction, the purchaser comes to hold the interest for a purpose other than making the flat available as accommodation for a caretaker of the premises. The amendments made by s 131 have effect in relation to land transactions whose effective date falls after 31 March 2016.

Section 132 makes minor corrective amendments to FA 2003 s 55.

Section 133 introduces Sch 16, which provides relief from SDLT for the initial transfer of properties into a Property Authorised Investment Fund (PAIF) or Co-ownership Authorised Contractual Scheme (COACS) and changes the treatment of a COACS for the purposes of SDLT.

Schedule 16 consists of four Parts. Part 1, which comprises para 1, deals with the SDLT treatment of a COACS. Part 2 (paras 2–4) provides "seeding relief" for PAIFs and COACSs). Part 3 (paras 5–14) makes consequential amendments, whereas Part 4 (para 15) provides for commencement.

Schedule 16 para 1 inserts new FA 2003 s 102A, which provides that for the purposes of SDLT, a COACS is to be treated as if it were a company and the rights (units) of the scheme participants were shares in that company. The one exception is with regard to FA 2003 Sch 7, which provides for SDLT group relief. This aligns the treatment of a COACS with that of a unit-trust scheme. Hitherto, a COACS has been treated as transparent for SDLT purposes so that the unitholders are regarded as the beneficial owners of the underlying properties. The terms "umbrella COACS" and "sub-scheme" (of an umbrella COACS) are defined. Each sub-scheme is to be treated as if it were a separate COACS, and not the umbrella COACS as a whole.

Schedule 16 para 2 is introductory. Schedule 16 para 3 inserts new FA 2003 s 65A, which introduces new FA 2003 Sch 7A to provide "seeding relief" for PAIFs and COACSs. It provides that any claim to seeding relief must be made in a land-transaction return or amended land-transaction return, and prescribes what is to be contained in the notice accompanying such a return. Schedule 16 para 4 inserts new FA 2003 Sch 7A.

New FA 2003 Sch 7A consists of three Parts. Part 1 (paras 1–9) provides the relief for PAIFs. Part 2 (paras 10–19) provides the relief for COACSs and Part 3 (paras 20–21) provides for interpretation.

New FA 2003 Sch 7A para 1 provides that a land transaction shall be exempt from SDLT if four conditions, A to D, are all met, by means of "PAIF seeding relief". Condition A is that the purchaser is a PAIF. Condition B is that the main subject-matter of the transaction is a major interest in land. Condition C is that the only consideration for the transaction is the issue of units in the PAIF to the vendor. Condition D is that the effective date of the transaction falls within the "seeding period".

New FA 2003 Sch 7A para 2 defines a PAIF as an open-ended investment company to which the Authorised Investment Funds (Tax) Regulations, SI 2006/964, Pt 4A applies. These funds may be exempt from corporation tax on their property-investment business under those Regulations. A PAIF may also take the form of a collective investment scheme that is a company incorporated in another EEA state. New FA 2003 Sch 7A para 3 defines the "seeding period". This the period beginning with the first property-seeding date and ending with the date of the first external investment into the PAIF, but may not be longer than 18 months. The PAIF may elect to bring the seeding period to an end sooner than it would otherwise end.

New FA 2003 Sch 7A para 4 prescribes three instances in which PAIF seeding relief is not to be available even where Conditions A to D in new FA 2003 Sch 7A para 1 are met. The first instance in which it is not to be available is where there are arrangements in existence for the vendor to make a disposal of units in the PAIF such as would cause a withdrawal of relief in the circumstances outlined in new FA 2003 Sch 7A para 7. The second instance where relief is not to be available is where the transaction is not carried out for bona fide commercial reasons or forms part of tax-avoidance arrangements. The third instance in which relief is not available is where there are no arrangements in place requiring the vendor to notify the appropriate officer of the PAIF of certain matters.

New FA 2003 Sch 7A paras 5–8 outline four events on the occurrence of which relief once given may be withdrawn. New FA 2003 Sch 7A para 5 provides that relief is to be withdrawn or partially withdrawn where the PAIF ceases to be a PAIF at any subsequent time within the seeding period or the three immediately following years ("the control period") or in connection with arrangements made before the end of the control period. However, for relief to be withdrawn, the PAIF still holds the chargeable interest that gave rise to the seeding relief or a chargeable interest derived from that interest. Withdrawal is to give rise to a charge to tax on the amount that would have been chargeable in the absence of the relief. If some part of the chargeable interest is no longer held, there will be a partial withdrawal, of an appropriate proportion of the relief.

New FA 2003 Sch 7A para 6 provides that relief is to be withdrawn or partially withdrawn where the PAIF fails to meet the "portfolio test" at the end of the seeding period. The portfolio test is met if either the "residential portfolio test" or the "non-residential portfolio test" is met; it is impossible for both of them to be met at one and the same time. The "residential portfolio test" is that the total chargeable consideration for all the "seeded interests" held by the PAIF is at least £100 million and at least 100 of the seeded interests are interests in or over residential property. A "seeded interest" is a chargeable interest acquired by the PAIF in a transaction for which PAIF seeding relief was granted (whether or not subsequently withdrawn). The non-residential portfolio test is that the PAIF holds at least 10 seeded interests, that the total chargeable consideration for all the seeded interests held by the PAIF is at least £100 million and that no more than 10% of the chargeable consideration can be in respect of interests in or over residential property. Failure to meet the portfolio test gives rise to a charge to tax on what the chargeable amount would have been in the absence of the relief. Relief is also withdrawn if the portfolio test is met at the end of the seeding period but fails to be met at any time in the control period or after the control period if failure is due to arrangements made before the end of the control period. Again, relief is only withdrawn if the PAIF still holds the chargeable interest that gave rise to the seeding relief or a chargeable interest derived from that interest.

If some part of the chargeable interest is no longer held, there will be a partial withdrawal, of an appropriate proportion of the relief.

New FA 2003 Sch 7A para 7 provides for relief to be withdrawn or partially withdrawn where a person (V) makes a "relevant disposal" of one or more units in a PAIF and there is a "relevant seeding transaction" in respect of that disposal. The disposal may be made at any time within the seeding period or the control period or at any subsequent time if due to arrangements made before the end of the control period. A "relevant seeding transaction" is a seeding transaction (a transaction in respect of which PAIF seeding relief was available, whether or not subsequently withdrawn) the effective date of which predates or is the same day as the date of the disposal, in which the PAIF is or was the purchaser and in which the vendor is either V or a member of V's group where V is a company. A "relevant disposal" is a disposal where one quantity, A, is greater than another quantity, B. B is the value of V's investment in the PAIF immediately after the disposal and A is one of two amounts. A is the smaller of the value of V's investment in the PAIF immediately before the disposal and the total of the chargeable consideration for all relevant seeding transactions. Where the two are equal, A is the total of the chargeable consideration for all relevant seeding transactions. The value of V's investment in the PAIF at any time is the market value of all the units V holds in the fund; where V is a company, units held by other group members as a result of transactions where they were the vendors and the PAIF was the purchaser are to be taken into account also. The amount of tax that is to be charged in respect of each seeding transaction is $(A - B/CCRST) \times T$ where CCRST is the total of the chargeable consideration for all relevant seeding transactions and T is the tax that would have been payable in respect of the relevant seeding transaction in the absence of PAIF seeding relief.

New FA 2003 Sch 7A paras 8 and 9 provide for relief to be withdrawn or partially withdrawn where a "non-qualifying individual" comes to occupy a dwelling held in the PAIF. Specifically, new FA 2003 Sch 7A para 8 has effect where PAIF seeding relief has been allowed in respect of a transaction ("the relevant transaction") of which the main subject-matter was a chargeable interest in or over land involving a dwelling, and a "non-qualifying individual" is permitted to occupy the dwelling at any time on or after the effective date of the transaction. A "non-qualifying individual" is defined in new FA 2003 Sch 7A para 9. The definition is modelled on but is not identical to the definition of the same term in FA 2013 s 136 for the purposes of ATED. Here, a "non-qualifying individual" can be any of a number of individuals, namely: (a) a "major participant" (a person with an interest of at least 50% in the fund's profits or income or distributable profits or income or in the assets of the fund distributable on a winding-up) in the PAIF; (b) an individual connected with a major participant; (c) an individual connected with the PAIF; (d) a "relevant settlor"); (e) the spouse or civil partner of any of the foregoing; (f) a relative of an individual within (b), (c) or (d), or the spouse or civil partner of such a relative; (g) a relative of the spouse or civil partner referred to in (f); or (g) the spouse or civil partner of such a relative. Various terms relevant to these categories are defined. If a non-qualifying individual is first permitted to occupy the dwelling after the end of the control period, relief is only to be withdrawn or partially withdrawn if the PAIF fails at that time to meet the "genuine diversity of ownership condition" set out in the Authorised Investment Funds (Tax) Regulations, SI 2006/964, reg 9A. A PAIF meets this condition at any time when it meets three other conditions, A–C. Broadly speaking, these all relate to the requirement that units in the fund should be intended, available for and marketed to a sufficiently wide and diverse category of investor. Again, relief is only withdrawn if the PAIF still holds the chargeable interest that gave rise to the seeding relief or a chargeable interest derived from that interest. If some part of the chargeable interest is no longer held, there will be a partial withdrawal, of an appropriate proportion of the relief. The withdrawal of the relief gives rise to a charge to tax on what the chargeable amount would have been in the absence of the relief.

New FA 2003 Sch 7A Pt 2 (paras 10–19) provide for COACS seeding relief, which mirrors PAIF seeding relief. Consequently, the conditions for the relief as prescribed in new FA 2003 Sch 7A para 10 are exactly those for PAIF seeding relief in new FA 2003 Sch 7A para 10, with the substitution of the one fund for the other. The definition of "seeding period" in new FA 2003 Sch 7A para 11 follows exactly the corresponding definition for PAIF seeding relief in new FA 2003 Sch 7A para 3. New FA 2003 Sch 7A para 12 prescribes the same three instances in which COACS seeding relief is not to be available even where Conditions A to D in new FA 2003 Sch 7A para 10 are met as new FA 2003 Sch 7A para 4 prescribes in respect of PAIF seeding relief, mutatis mutandis. The same holds good for the withdrawal of relief under new FA 2003 Sch 7A para 13 in the event that the COACS ceases to be a COACS, for which see new FA 2003 Sch 7A para 5.

New FA 2003 Sch 7A paras 14 and 15, however, prescribe and additional test, namely that the scheme should meet the "genuine diversity of ownership condition" at the end of the seeding period, at any time in the control period or after the control period if failure is due to arrangements made before the end of the control period. The definition of this test in FA 2003 Sch 7A para 15 is closely modelled on the same condition as set out in the Authorised Investment Funds (Tax) Regulations, SI 2006/964, reg 9A, to which reference is also made in new FA 2003 Sch 7A para 8. The COACS also meets the genuine diversity of ownership condition at any time when there is a "feeder fund" in relation to the scheme and the feeder fund meets Conditions A to C. Should the genuine diversity of ownership condition not be met, the relief is to be withdrawn or partially withdrawn but only to the extent that the scheme still holds the chargeable interest that gave rise to the seeding relief or a chargeable interest derived from that interest. Withdrawal is to give rise to a charge to tax on the amount that would have been chargeable in the absence of the relief. If some part of the chargeable interest is no longer held, there will be a partial withdrawal, of an appropriate proportion of the relief. The operator of the COACS may apply to HMRC for a clearance that the scheme meets the genuine diversity of ownership condition.

Under new FA 2003 Sch 7A para 16 COACS seeding relief will be withdrawn or partially withdrawn when the portfolio test is not met at any of the specified times. The provisions of this paragraph are identical, reading references to the PAIF as references to the COACS, as those of new FA 2003 Sch 7A para 6. New FA 2003 Sch 7A para 17 provides that COACS seeding relief will be withdrawn or partially withdrawn where a person (V) makes a "relevant disposal" of one or more units in a COACS and there is a "relevant seeding transaction" in respect of that disposal. Again, the provisions of this paragraph are identical, reading references to the PAIF as references to the COACS, as those of new FA 2003 Sch 7A para 7. The same is also true of new FA 2003 Sch 7A paras 18 and 19, which provide for COACS seeding relief to be withdrawn or partially withdrawn when a "non-qualifying individual" comes to occupy a dwelling held in the COACS, which exactly mirror the corresponding provisions for PAIF seeding relief in new FA 2003 Sch 7A paras 8 and 9, except that, in new FA 2003 Sch 7A para 19, in the definition of "non-qualifying individual", category (c) encompasses an individual who is connected with the operator or depositary of the scheme.

New FA 2003 Sch 7A para 20 defines what constitutes a feeder fund for a PAIF on the one hand and for a COACS on the other, and defines "units" for the purposes of the two types of investment vehicle. New FA 2003 Sch 7A para 21 contains interpretations of other terms.

Schedule 16 paras 5–14 make consequential amendments. Schedule 16 para 15 provides that, subject to transitional provisions, the amendments made by Sch 16 Pts 2 and 3 are to have effect for land transactions the effective date of which falls after 14 September 2016.

Annual tax on enveloped dwellings

Section 134 provides relief from ATED is to be available for any day in which a single-dwelling interest is held by an "authorised plan provider" who has entered into a regulated home-reversion plan relating to the single-dwelling interest and on which the "occupation condition" is met. This relief is complementary to the corresponding relief from SDLT provided in s 130 and is contained in new FA 2013 s 144A. The occupation condition varies according to whether or not the "qualifying termination event" has occurred. This event is to be interpreted in accordance with the Financial Services and Markets (Regulated Activities) Order 2001, reg 63B. If the qualifying termination event has occurred, the occupation condition is that the single-dwelling interest is being held with the intention of selling it without delay except as far as commercial considerations justify and that no non-qualifying individual is permitted to occupy the dwelling or any part of it. If the qualifying termination event has not yet occurred, the occupation condition is that a person who was originally entitled to occupy the dwelling or any part of it under the plan is still entitled to do so. Consequential amendments are also made. The amendments made by s 134 have effect for chargeable periods beginning after 31 March 2016.

Section 135 introduces two new reliefs from ATED where a property is occupied by certain employees. These match the corresponding reliefs from the higher rate of SDLT introduced by s 131.

As with the SDLT relief, FA 2013 s 145 has hitherto provided relief for any day on which a single-dwelling interest is held for the purposes of making the dwelling available for use as living accommodation by one or more qualifying employees or partners where the person entitled to the interest is carrying on a "qualifying trade". A "qualifying trade" is one that is carried on on a commercial basis and with a view to profit. The relief is also now to be available in respect of a "qualifying property-rental business", which is defined by reference to FA 2013 s 133(3), i.e. as a property-rental business run on a commercial basis and with a view to profit. The second new relief is set out in new FA 2013 s 147A, inserted by s 135(7). This provides that relief shall be available on a day when (a) a tenants' management company holds a single-dwelling interest in relation to a flat for the purposes of making it available as "caretaker accommodation"; (b) the flat is located in premises that also contain at least two other flats; (c) the tenants of at least two of the other flats are members of the management company; (d) the management company owns the freehold of the premises; and (e) the management company is not carrying on a trade or a property-rental business. "Caretaker accommodation" means the accommodation is available as living accommodation. Consequential amendments are made. The amendments made by s 135 have effect for chargeable periods beginning after 31 March 2016.

Section 136 makes a consequential amendment to FA 2013 s 157, which deals with alternative property-finance arrangements, to delete references to land in Scotland, which are now obsolete following the replacement in Scotland of SDLT by LBTT. However, to ensure that ATED continues to apply in the same way for qualifying alternative property-finance arrangements in Scotland, s 136 inserts new FA 2013 s 157A. This applies where two conditions, A and B, are met. Condition A is that under arrangements between a lessee and a financial institution, the institution purchases a major interest in land ("the first transaction"); grants a lease or sub-lease to the lessee out of that interest ("the second transaction"); and the lessee has a right to require that the institution transfer the major interest purchased under the first transaction to him. Condition B is that the land in which the major interest is purchased in the first transaction lies in Scotland and involves one or more dwellings or parts of a dwelling. Where the lessee is a company, ATED is to be charged as long as the arrangements are in effect as if the interest held by the financial institution were held by the company and the lease or sub-lease granted under the second transaction had not been granted. Provision is made for situations where the company as lessee is a member of a partnership and where the lessee is a collective investment scheme. The amendments made by s 136 have effect for chargeable periods beginning after 31 March 2016.

PART 9
OTHER TAXES AND DUTIES

Stamp duty and stamp duty reserve tax

Section 137 is an anti-avoidance provision denying share-for-share relief from stamp duty under FA 1986 s 77 on the acquisition of the target company's share capital where arrangements are in place at the time of the exchange for control of the acquiring company to change. An extra condition (in the form of new FA 1986 s 77(3)(i)) is added for relief under that section to be available, namely that there must be no "disqualifying arrangements" in place at the time the instrument transferring shares is executed. New FA 1986 s 77A, inserted by s 137(5), defines "disqualifying arrangements" as arrangements in respect of which it is reasonable to assume that their purpose or one of their purposes is to secure that a particular person or two or more particular persons together obtain(s) control of the acquiring company. However, two types of arrangement are excluded from this definition. These are the share-for-share arrangements themselves (unless they are part of a wider scheme or arrangement including disqualifying arrangements) and any "relevant merger arrangements", as defined. The amendments made by s 137 are to have effect for instruments executed after 28 June 2016.

Section 138 makes amendments to the stamp duty charge under FA 1986 s 67 on transfers to depositaries and under FA 1986 s 70 on transfers to clearance services. FA 1986 s 67 is amended to provide that duty on a non-bearer instrument transferring securities to a depositary-receipt issuer or the issuer's nominee, executed under an option to buy or sell the securities and subject to a further condition is to be charged at 1.5% on the higher of (a) the consideration for the sale to which the instrument gives effect and (b) the value of the securities at the date of execution. New FA 1986 s 67(2A), inserted by s 138(2)(b), explains that the further condition referred to is that either the instrument is also executed pursuant to a term of the option providing for the securities to be transferred to the depositary-receipt issuer or under a direction given by or on behalf of the purchaser under the option for the securities to be so transferred. Exactly the same amendments are made to FA 1986 s 70, which imposes the 1.5% duty on instruments transferring securities to a clearance service. The amendments made by s 138 have effect for instruments in relation to options granted after 24 November 2015 and exercised after 22 March 2016.

Section 139 makes similar amendments to the charge to stamp duty reserve tax (SDRT) under FA 1986 s 93 on transfers of securities to a depositary-receipt issuer and under FA 1986 s 96 on transfers to clearance services. Thus FA 1986 s 93 is amended to provide that SDRT on a transfer for consideration of securities to a depositary-receipt issuer or the issuer's nominee, pursuant to an option to buy or sell the securities and subject to a further condition is to be charged at 1.5% on the higher of (a) the consideration and (b) the value of the securities. New FA 1986 s 93(4A), inserted by s 138(2)(b), explains that the further condition referred to is that either the transfer is also carried out pursuant to a term of the option providing for the securities to be transferred to the depositary-receipt issuer or under a direction given by or on behalf of the purchaser under the option for the securities to be so transferred. Exactly the same amendments are made to FA 1986 s 96, which imposes 1.5% SDRT on transfers of securities to a clearance service. The amendments made by s 139 have effect for transfers in relation to options granted after 24 November 2015 and exercised after 22 March 2016.

Petroleum revenue tax

Section 140 reduces the rate of petroleum revenue tax (PRT) charged under OTA 1975 s 1 from 35% to 0%, with effect for chargeable periods ending after 31 December 2015. The amendments also remove the cap under OTA 1975 Sch 2 para 17 on interest on repayments of PRT on the grounds that it is now redundant and removes the duty under FA 1982 Sch 19 para 2 to pay PRT in instalments for the chargeable period ending on 31 December 2015.

Insurance premium tax

Section 141 increases the standard rate of insurance premium tax (IPT) from 9.5%–10%, for premiums regarded as received after 30 September 2016, with transitional provisions for the period to 1 February 2017 for insurers using the special accounting scheme under FA 1994 s 68. The transitional provisions do not apply where additional premiums are received after 30 September 2016 in respect of risks not covered by the insurance contract before 1 October 2016. Consequential amendments are made to the anti-forestalling provisions in FA 1994 ss 67A–67C.

Landfill tax

Section 142 increases the standard rate of landfill tax from £84.40 per tonne to £86.10 and the £2.65 reduced rate to £2.70, with effect for disposals made or treated as made after 31 March 2017. **Section 143** further increases the standard rate to £88.95 per tonne and the £2.70 reduced rate to £2.80, with effect for disposals made or treated as made after 31 March 2018.

Climate change levy

Section 144 abolishes the exemption from climate change levy (CCL) for supplies of electricity from renewable sources where the electricity is *supplied* after 31 March 2018. F(No 2)A 2015 s 45 has already removed the exemption for electricity *generated* from renewable sources after 31 July 2015. Consequential amendments are to come into effect from a day to be appointed. **Section 145** increases all the rates of CCL by approximately 1.6% for supplies treated as taking place after 31 March 2017, in line with changes in the RPI. **Section 146** further increases the rates of CCL by approximately 2.5% over the 2017 rates supplies treated as taking place after 31 March 2018. **Section 147** makes substantial increases in CCL rates for supplies treated as taking place after 31 March 2019. The relationship between the rates is also to be rebalanced, so that the ratio between electricity and gas is to be adjusted from 2.9:1–2.5:1. Thus, whereas the rate for electricity is to increase by 45.3%, the rate for gas is to increase by 67.0%. **Section 148** reduces the reduced rate of CCL for eligible supplies of electricity from 10% of the standard rate to 7% of the standard rate and for other reduced-rate supplies from 35% of the standard rate to 22%. These amendments are to have effect for supplies treated as taking place after 31 March 2019.

Air passenger duty

Section 149 increases the rates of air passenger duty for Band B flights. The reduced rate is increased from £71 to £73 and the standard rate from £142–£146. The amendments have effect for flights beginning after 31 March 2016.

Vehicle excise duty

Section 150 amends VERA 1994 Sch 1 so as to change the rates of vehicle excise duty for vehicles first registered before 1 March 2001 with an engine capacity exceeding 1549 cc; the graduated rates of duty applying general to light passenger vehicles first registered after 28 February 2001; the rates for light goods vehicles first registered after 28 February 2001; and the rates for motorcycles weighing no more than 450 kg unladen. The amendments have effect for licences issued after 31 March 2016.

Section 151 places the 40-year rolling exemption for classic vehicles, so that from 1 April each year, vehicles constructed more than 40 years before the start of the calendar year concerned are to be automatically exempt from duty. The amendments made by s 150 are to have effect from 1 April 2017.

Other excise duties

Section 152 puts into effect the annual uprating of gaming-duty bands in FA 1997 s 11(2), to have effect for accounting periods beginning after 31 March 2016.

Section 153 introduces **Sch 17**, which imposes special rates of fuel duty on aqua methanol, an alternative road fuel. Schedule 17 consists of three Parts. Part 1 (paras 1–11) contains the main charging provisions; Part 2 (paras 12 and 13) make consequential amendments; Part 3 (para 14) provides for commencement.

Schedule 17 para 1 is introductory. Schedule 17 para 2 inserts new HODA 1979 s 2AC, which defines aqua methanol, and Sch 17 para 3 makes a consequential amendment. Schedule 17 para 4 inserts new HODA 1979 ss 6AG and 6AH. New HODA 1979 s 6AG provides that a duty of excise is to be charged on the allocation for chargeable use of aqua methanol to be used as fuel or as an additive or extender to fuel. The rate of duty is to be £0.079 per litre for its direct use as fuel. New HODA 1979 s 6AH provides HM Treasury with the power to make regulations to provide that specified references in HODA 1979 to hydrocarbon oil are to be taken as referring also to aqua methanol. Schedule 17 para 5 makes consequential amendments. Schedule 17 para 6 inserts new HODA 1979 ss 20AAC and 20AAD. New HODA 1979 s 20AAC prohibits the mixing of aqua methanol on which duty has been paid with any other "relevant" substance, being biodiesel, bioethanol, bioblend, bioethanol blend or hydrocarbon oil. To do so intentionally is to commit a criminal offence. Where, notwithstanding the prohibition in new HODA 1979 s 20AAC, such mixing takes place, new HODA 1979 s 20AAD provides that the mixture is to be charged to duty at the general rate applicable to heavy oil. Schedule 17 paras 7–13 make minor and consequential amendments. Schedule 17 para 14 provides that, except for the power to make regulations (which is to come into effect on 15 September 2016), the amendments made by Sch 17 are to come into force on 14 November 2016.

Section 154 amends TPDA 1979 Sch 1 to increase the rates of duty on tobacco and tobacco products by RPI + 2%, with effect from 18:00 hrs on 16 March 2016.

Section 155 increases the rates of duty charged under ALDA 1979 on sparkling cider and perry of a strength exceeding 5.5% and on wine and made-wine at or below 22% abv (alcohol by volume). Other rates remain unchanged. The amendments made by s 155 are to be treated as having come into force on 21 March 2016.

PART 10
TAX AVOIDANCE AND EVASION

General anti-abuse rule

Section 156 inserts new FA 2013 ss 209A–209F. These empower HMRC to issue a provisional counteraction notice to a taxpayer and make the necessary adjustments where an officer of HMRC reasonably believes the taxpayer has entered into arrangements that are abusive within the meaning of the GAAR. The taxpayer concerned may appeal against the adjustments made as a result of the notice

New FA 2013 s 209A provides that adjustments made by an officer of HMRC under a provisional counteraction notice are to be treated as effecting a valid counteraction of the tax advantage as provided by FA 2013 s 209 for all purposes, where a number of conditions are met. These are that the adjustments were specified in the notice given to the person concerned; the notice has not been cancelled; the adjustments are made in respect of a tax advantage that would otherwise arise from tax arrangements that are abusive; and would have effected a valid counteraction of that advantage were it not for the fact that the matter has not been referred to the GAAR Advisory Panel. A provisional counteraction notice (abbreviated to "PCN" in these notes) must (a) specify the adjustments that the officer reasonably believes may be required under FA 2013 s 209 to counteract the tax advantage that would otherwise arise to the person concerned from tax arrangements; (b) specify the arrangements and the tax advantage concerned; (c) inform the person of the right to appeal against the adjustments once made; (d) state that if such an appeal is made, no steps may be taken in relation to that appeal unless and until HMRC gives the person one of the notices referred to in new FA 2013 s 209F(2); and (e) state that the adjustments will be cancelled if HMRC fails to take at least one of the actions specified in new FA 2013 s 209B within the required time. The notice may be given before or at the same time as the adjustments are made.

New FA 2013 s 209B specifies the actions that HMRC must take within the 12 months following the date of issue of a PCN when the taxpayer appeals against the making of the adjustments. Those actions are any of the following: (a) an officer of HMRC notifies the taxpayer that the adjustments are cancelled; (b) an officer of HMRC gives the taxpayer written notice that the PCN has been withdrawn but without cancelling the adjustments, provided that the officer has the authority to do so; (c) a designated HMRC officer gives the taxpayer a notice under FA 2013 Sch 43 para 3 initiating the process of referral to the Advisory Panel. The proposed adjustments specified in that notice may be the same or smaller than the adjustments specified in the PCN; (d) a designated HMRC officer gives the taxpayer a pooling notice or a "notice of binding" under new FA 2013 Sch 43A (inserted by s 157(2)), which binds the tax arrangements concerned to "lead arrangements" to which the arrangements in question are equivalent. The proposed adjustments specified in that notice may be the same or smaller than the adjustments specified in the PCN; or (e) a designated HMRC officer gives the taxpayer a notice of generic referral to the Advisory Panel of those and other equivalent tax arrangements under new FA 2013 Sch 43B para 1 (inserted by s 157(3)). The proposed adjustments specified in that notice may be the same or smaller than the adjustments specified in the PCN. If none of these actions is taken, the notified adjustments are to be treated as cancelled at the end of the 12-month period. The giving of any of the four abovementioned notices under FA 2013 Sch 43, new FA 2013 Sch 43A or new FA 2013 Sch 43B may in fact precede the giving of the PCN as well as follow it. Where the giving of such a notice follows the giving of the PCN, however, and that notice specifies smaller adjustments than the PCN, HMRC must modify the adjustments made under the PCN accordingly.

New FA 2013 s 209C prescribes the procedures and consequences where a designated HMRC officer has given the taxpayer a notice under FA 2013 Sch 43 para 3 of proposed referral to the Advisory Panel and HMRC then decides not to proceed with the referral. In that case, the adjustments under the PCN are to be treated as cancelled from the date of the designated HMRC officer's decision not to proceed. However, the notice that HMRC gives to the taxpayer under new FA 2013 Sch 43 para 6(3) (inserted by s 157(11)) ("the para 6(3) notice") of its decision not to proceed may specify that the adjustments are not to be cancelled because HMRC believes it would have been authorised to make them under some other provision of the Taxes Acts. Where the matter is referred to the Advisory Panel, and the designated HMRC officer, having received the Panel's opinion, decides not to proceed under the GAAR, the notice he then gives to the taxpayer under FA 2013 Sch 43 para 12 may also specify that the adjustments are nevertheless not to be treated as cancelled, on the same grounds as those referred to in the para 6(3) notice.

New FA 2013 s 209D makes analogous provision to new FA 2013 s 209C for the case where HMRC has given the taxpayer a pooling notice or a notice of binding under new FA 2013 Sch 43A. Where, having received the opinion of the Advisory Panel, the designated HMRC officer decides not to proceed under the GAAR, the notice he then gives to the taxpayer under new FA 2013 Sch 43A para 5(2) or 6(2) may also specify that the adjustments are nevertheless not to be treated as cancelled, on the same grounds as those referred to in the para 6(3) notice.

New FA 2013 s 209E makes analogous provision to new FA 2013 s 209C for the case where HMRC has given the taxpayer a notice of generic referral under new FA 2013 Sch 43B para 1. Where the notice is subsequently withdrawn, the adjustments made under the PCN are to be treated as cancelled unless the notice of withdrawal specifies that the adjustments are nevertheless not to be treated as cancelled, on the same grounds as those referred to in the para 6(3) notice. Similarly, a notice under new FA 2013 Sch 43B para 9(2) not to proceed under the GAAR after consideration of the Advisory Panel's opinion may also specify that the adjustments are nevertheless not to be treated as cancelled, on the same grounds.

New FA 2013 s 209F provides for appeals to be made against the adjustments specified in the PCN. After the initial notice of appeal from the taxpayer, no steps are to be taken (unless to withdraw the appeal) unless and until HMRC gives the taxpayer any of the following notices: a notice under new FA 2013 s 209B(4)(b) withdrawing the PCN but not cancelling the adjustments; a notice under new FA 2013 Sch 43 para 6(3) not to proceed under the GAAR but not cancelling the adjustments; or notices to proceed with counteraction under the GAAR under FA 2013 Sch 43 para 12, FA 2013 Sch 43A para 5(2) or 6(2) or new FA 2013 Sch 43B para 9. The taxpayer then has 30 days within which to specify the grounds of appeal.

The amendments made by s 156 are to have effect in relation to tax arrangements entered into at any time.

Section 157 introduces binding arrangements under the GAAR, so that an opinion from the GAAR Advisory Panel in respect of certain arrangements may enable counteraction to be taken against other equivalent arrangements relating to other taxpayers without the need to refer all those arrangements separately to the Advisory Panel. It inserts new FA 2013 Schs 43A and 43B and makes consequential amendments. New FA 2013 Sch 43A (entitled "Procedural requirements: pooling notices and notices of binding") consists of 13 paragraphs and new FA 2013 Sch 43B (entitled "Procedural requirements: generic referral of tax arrangements") consists of 10 paragraphs.

New FA 2013 Sch 43A para 1 provides when equivalent arrangements may be bound to "lead arrangements". HMRC must first have given a taxpayer ("the lead taxpayer") a notice under FA 2013 Sch 43 para 3 that it considers that a tax advantage has arisen to the taxpayer under abusive arrangements ("the lead arrangements") and that advantage ought to be counteracted under FA 2013 s 209. One further condition must also be met. That condition is that the 45 days within which the original taxpayer may make representations has expired, but that HMRC has neither yet given the taxpayer a notice of final decision under FA 2013 Sch 43 para 12 or a notice of final decision under new FA 2013 Sch 43B para 8 concerning generic arrangements. In these circumstances, if a designated HMRC officer considers that a tax advantage has also arisen to another person ("R") from abusive arrangements equivalent to the lead arrangements and that this advantage ought also to be counteracted under FA 2013 s 209, the officer may as soon as reasonably practicable give R a "pooling notice" in relation to R's arrangements, placing them in a pool with the lead arrangements. All arrangements placed in a pool with the lead arrangements are regarded as contained in one and the same pool, including the lead arrangements themselves. Arrangements are not to leave the pool unless there is express provision for them to do so in new FA 2013 Sch 43A, even if the lead arrangements are no longer in the pool. A pooling notice may not be given to R if R has already been given a notice under FA 2013 Sch 43 para 3 of proposed counteraction of those arrangements. What a notice of binding must contain is set out in new FA 2013 Sch 43A para 1(7).

Once HMRC gives a person a "counteraction notice" in relation to any arrangements ("the counteracted arrangements") that have been placed in a pool, new FA 2013 Sch 43A para 2 provides that a designated HMRC officer may give another person ("R") a "notice of binding" in relation to R's arrangements if that officer considers that a tax advantage has arisen to R from abusive arrangements equivalent to the counteracted arrangements and that this advantage ought also to be counteracted under FA 2013 s 209. HMRC may not give R a notice of binding if it has already given R a pooling notice under new FA 2013 Sch 43A para 1 or a notice of proposed counteraction under FA 2013 Sch 43 para 3. A "counteraction notice" is a notice of final decision to counteract under either FA 2013 Sch 43 para 12 or new FA 2013 Sch 43B para 8 (see also under new FA 2013 Sch 43A para 1).

New FA 2013 Sch 43 para 3 provides that HMRC must take the decision whether or not to give R a pooling notice or notice of binding, and then give that notice where appropriate as soon as is reasonably practicable after it has become aware of the relevant facts. What a pooling notice and a notice of binding must contain is set out in new FA 2013 Sch 43A para 3(2). A pooling notice or notice of binding may also set out steps that R may take to avoid the proposed counteraction.

New FA 2013 Sch 43A para 4 provides that if a person to whom HMRC has given a pooling notice or notice of binding takes the "relevant corrective action" before the beginning of the "closed period" defined in new FA 2013 s 209(9) (inserted by s 157(4)), that person is to be treated as nevertheless not having received a pooling notice or notice of binding when it comes to a notice of final decision to counteract or to the provisions on generic referral under new FA 2013 Sch 43B, and the arrangements in question thereby leave the pool. The "relevant corrective action" consists of two steps. The first is for the person to amend a return or claim so as to counteract the advantage or (where the person has made a "tax appeal", as defined in new FA 2013 Sch 43 para 1A, inserted by s 156(7), claiming the advantage in question) to enter into a written agreement with HMRC to relinquish the advantage. The second step is for that person to notify HMRC that he has taken the first step and of any additional amount of tax that has or will become due as a result.

New FA 2013 Sch 43A para 5 provides that where the "lead taxpayer" (the person to whom a notice under FA 2013 Sch 43 para 3 has been given in respect of the lead arrangements) takes the required corrective action under new FA 2013 Sch 43 para 4A (action that will avert referral to the GAAR Advisory Panel), which is inserted by s 157(8), within 75 days of being given that notice, the lead arrangements are to be treated as ceasing to be in the pool.

New FA 2013 Sch 43A para 6 provides for the issue of a "pooled-arrangements opinion notice" and a "bound-arrangements opinion notice". HMRC must give a person a pooled-arrangements opinion notice where it previously gave that person a pooling notice and subsequently receives an opinion notice or notices from the GAAR Advisory Panel (referred to as "the Panel" from now on) under FA 2013 Sch 43 para 11(2) about another set of arrangements ("the referred arrangements") in the pool. HMRC may not give more than one pooled-arrangements opinion notice to a person in respect of the same arrangements. HMRC must give a person a bound-arrangements opinion notice at the same time as it gives that person a notice of binding.

New FA 2013 Sch 43A para 7 provides for the contents of both of these notices and confers on the person concerned the right to make representations within 30 days. There are two possible grounds for the representations: (a) that no tax advantage has arisen to that person from the arrangements in question; or (b) as to why the arrangements in question are or may be materially different from the referred arrangements (in the case of a pooled-arrangements opinion notice) or the counter-acted arrangements (in the case of a bound-arrangements opinion notice).

New FA 2013 Sch 43A para 8 explains the procedure when any tax arrangements have been placed in a pool by a pooling notice given to a person under new FA 2013 Sch 43A para 1 and a designated officer has given a notice of final decision under FA 2013 Sch 43 para 12 to a person in relation to any other arrangements in the pool ("the referred arrangements"). The officer must then, having considered the Panel's opinion on the referred arrangements and any representations made under new FA 2013 Sch 43A para 7 in relation to the pooled arrangements, notify the person concerned in writing whether or not the tax advantage in question is to be counteracted under the GAAR.

New FA 2013 Sch 43A para 9 explains the procedure where HMRC has given a notice of binding under new FA 2013 Sch 43A para 2 to a person and the 30-day period within which that person may make representations in respect of the bound-arrangements opinion notice has expired. In these circumstances, a desig-nated HMRC officer must then, having considered the Panel's opinion on the counteracted arrangements and any representations the person has made in relation to the arrangements specified in the notice of binding, notify that person in writing whether or not the tax advantage specified in the notice of binding is to be counteracted under the GAAR.

Where a notice under new FA 2013 Sch 43A paras 8(2) or 9(2) states that a tax advantage is to be counteracted, new FA 2013 Sch 43A para 10 requires that notice to specify the adjustments needed to give effect to the counteraction and any steps the person concerned may be required to take in that connection.

New FA 2013 Sch 43A para 11 provides that for the purposes of new FA 2013 Sch 43A para 1, arrangements are to be regarded as equivalent to one another when they are substantially the same having regard to their substantive results, the means of achieving them and the characteristics suggestive of their being abusive.

New FA 2013 Sch 43A para 12 provides that a designated HMRC officer may give a notice or do anything else under new FA 2013 Sch 43A where the officer considers that a tax advantage *might* have arisen as well as that it has arisen.

New FA 2013 Sch 43A para 13 confers on HM Treasury the power to amend the Schedule by regulations.

New FA 2013 Sch 43B, inserted by s 157(3), provides for generic referrals of equivalent arrangements to the Panel. New FA 2013 Sch 43B paras 1 provides that a designated HMRC officer may give each person involved a written notice ("the para 1 notice") of a proposal to make a generic referral of tax arrangements to the Advisory Panel where that officer considers that there are at least two cases where a tax advantage that ought to be counteracted under the GAAR has arisen to different persons under abusive tax arrangements that are equivalent to one another. Such a notice may not, however, be given unless HMRC has already given a notice of binding under new FA 2013 Sch 43A para 1(4) in respect of at least one of those sets of arrangements or in respect of arrangements equivalent to those arrangements. What a para 1 notice must contain is set out in new FA 2013 Sch 43B para 1(45), and the persons to whom the designated officer gives the notices of proposal are referred to as "the notified taxpayers". HMRC may make only one determination in relation to any one pool.

Under new FA 2013 Sch 43B para 2, the person concerned then has 30 days within which to propose to HMRC that he is willing for the arrangements to be considered by the Panel and should not proceed with the proposal to make a generic referral. A designated office must then consider this proposal.

New FA 2013 Sch 43B para 3 provides the mechanism for making a generic referral. If, after a designated HMRC officer has given notices of proposal to the notified taxpayers and none of them has made a proposal under new FA 2013 Sch 43B para 2 for his arrangements to be considered by the Panel within the permitted 30-day period, the officer must make a generic referral to the Panel in respect of the notified taxpayers and the specified arrangements. Where at least one of the taxpayers has made a proposal under new FA 2013 Sch 43B para 2, the officer must decide after the end of the 30-day period whether to give a notice of proposed counteraction under FA 2013 Sch 43 para 3 in respect of one set of arrangements in the relevant pool or make the generic referral.

New FA 2013 Sch 43B para 4 specifies what information the designated HMRC officer must provide to the Panel when making the general referral. Under new FA 2013 Sch 43B para 5, the officer must also notify each of the notified taxpayers of the generic referral and provide them with a copy of the statement made to the Panel with the generic referral.

New FA 2013 Sch 43B para 6 provides that on receiving a generic referral, the Panel Chair must convene a three-member sub-panel and produce one or more opinion notices on the matter, in the same way as FA 2013 Sch 43 paras 10 and 11 already provides for single referrals.

Under new FA 2013 Sch 43B para 7, having received an opinion notice or notices from the Panel, the designated HMRC officer must give each of the notified taxpayers a copy of that notice or those notices and explain how the taxpayers may make representations. Those representations must be made within 30 days on one of three possible grounds: (a) that no tax advantage has arisen from the specified arrangements; (b) that the taxpayer has already received a pooled-arrangements opinion notice or a bound-arrangements opinion notice under new FA 2013 Sch 43A para 6 in respect of the same arrangements; or (c) that the statement made by HMRC to the Panel was materially inaccurate.

New FA 2013 Sch 43B para 8 provides that, having received an opinion notice or notices from the Panel, the designated HMRC officer must consider in respect of each notified taxpayer that opinion and any representations that the taxpayer makes, and then notify the taxpayer in writing whether or not the taxpayer's specified advantage is to be counteracted under the GAAR. Where the notice states that a tax advantage is to be counteracted, that notice must specify the adjustments needed to give effect to the counteraction and any steps the taxpayer concerned may be required to take in that connection.

New FA 2013 Sch 43B para 9 provides that a designated HMRC officer may give a notice or do anything else under the Schedule where the officer considers that a tax advantage *might* have arisen as well as that it has arisen. New FA 2013 Sch 43B para 10 gives HM Treasury the power to amend the Schedule by regulations.

Section 157(4)–(29) make consequential amendments. In particular, s 157(11) inserts new FA 2013 Sch 43 para 6(3) requiring the designated HMRC officer to notify the taxpayer in writing as soon as is reasonably practicable whether or not the matter is to be referred to the Panel.

The amendments made by s 157 are to have effect for arrangements entered into at any time.

Section 158 introduces a new tax-geared penalty payable by taxpayers whose tax advantages it has successfully counteracted under the GAAR. Under new FA 2013 s 212A, inserted by s 158(2), the amount of the penalty is to be 60% of the value of the counteracted advantage.

Further details concerning the penalty are contained in new FA 2013 Sch 43C, inserted by s 158(3). New FA 2013 Sch 43C has 11 paragraphs.

New FA 2013 Sch 43C para 1 is introductory. New FA 2013 Sch 43C para 2 sets out the basic rule that the value of the counteracted tax advantage is the additional amount of tax due or payable as a result of the counteraction. This includes amounts of tax erroneously repaid and amounts that would have been repayable in the absence of the counteraction. Group relief and any relief under CTA 2010 s 458 on the repayment or release of a close-company loan are to be ignored. Consequential relieving adjustments made under FA 2013 s 210 are to be regarded as part of the counteraction in question.

New FA 2013 Sch 43C para 3 modifies the basic rule where the tax advantage includes a loss. Broadly speaking, where the whole of the wrongly recorded loss was used to reduce the amount of tax due or payable, the value of the advantage is the additional amount of tax due and payable. Where only part of the loss was so used, 10% of the unused loss must be added to the additional amount of tax due and payable when calculating the value. New FA 2013 Sch 43C para 4 prescribes how to value a tax advantage involving a deferment of tax.

New FA 2013 Sch 43C para 5 provides for HMRC to assess the penalty, which must then be paid within 30 days of the issue of the assessment. A penalty assessment must be made no later than the end of the appeal period for the assessment that gave effect to the counteraction or, where there was no such assessment, no later than the latest date on which the counteraction becomes final. Assessments to the penalty are to be treated as if they were assessments to tax. New FA 2013 Sch 43C para 6 allows for the issue of a supplementary penalty assessment where there has been an underestimate of the value of the counteracted advantage and for adjustment of the original penalty assessment where there has been an overestimate. New FA 2013 Sch 43C para 7 allows for a penalty assessment to be revised where a consequential adjustment is made by HMRC under FA 2013 s 210(7). New FA 2013 Sch 43C para 8 provides for aggregation of two or more penalties imposed on the same person, one of which is the GAAR penalty under new FA 2013 s 212A.

New FA 2013 Sch 43C para 9 provides for appeals against the penalty. Taxpayers may appeal within 30 days of the issue of the assessment against the imposition of a penalty or the amount assessed. The first of those grounds may be invoked only where the taxpayer disputes that the arrangements were abusive or that there was any tax advantage to be counteracted. The appellant is not to be required to pay the penalty before the appeal is determined. New FA 2013 Sch 43C para 10 gives HMRC the discretion to mitigate or entirely remit a penalty. New FA 2013 Sch 43C para 11 provides for interpretation.

Section 158(4) inserts new FA 2013 s 209(8)–(10). These subsections provide that where a matter has been referred to the Panel under FA 2013 Sch 43 paras 5 or 6, the taxpayer may not make any GAAR-related adjustments (as defined) in relation to his tax affairs during the "closed period". This runs from the 31st day after the end of the 45-day representation period to the day immediately before the day on which HMRC gives the taxpayer the notice of final decision under FA 2013 Sch 43 para 12. Where, on the other hand, HMRC has issued a pooling notice or notice of binding to a person under new FA 2013 Sch 43A, the closed period runs from the 31st day after the date of issue of the notice to either (a) the day immediately before the day on which HMRC gives the taxpayer the notice of final decision under new FA 2013 Sch 43A paras 8(2) or 9(2) or under new FA 2013 Sch 43B para 8(2) stating whether or not the tax advantage is to be counteracted (in the case of a pooling notice); or (b) with the 30th day of the date of issue of the notice of binding (in the case of a notice of binding).

Section 158(5)–(9) make amendments to FA 2013 Sch 43 (the GAAR procedural requirements). Section 158(6) inserts new FA 2013 Sch 43 para 1A, which provides a definition of "tax appeal" for the purposes of the GAAR legislation (FA 2013 Pt 5). These are appeals against assessments or notices under matters not involving the GAAR. Section 158(7) makes a consequential amendment. Section 158(8) inserts new FA 2013 Sch 43 para 4A, allowing the taxpayer to take corrective action in order to avoid a referral to the Panel. It follows the equivalent provisions in new FA 2013 Sch 43A para 4. It provides that where the taxpayer takes the "relevant corrective action" before the closed period begins, the matter will not be referred to the Panel.

As with the equivalent provision, the "relevant corrective action" consists of two steps. The first is for the person to amend a return or claim to counteract the advantage or (where the taxpayer has made a tax appeal claiming the advantage in question) to enter into a written agreement with HMRC to relinquish the advantage. The second step is for that person to notify HMRC that he has taken the first step and of any additional amount of tax that has or will become due as a result.

Section 158(10)–(14) make consequential amendments to other legislation. Section 158(15) provides that the amendments made by s 158 are to have effect in relation to arrangements entered into after 14 September 2016.

Section 159 introduces **Sch 18**, which provides for warnings and escalating sanctions for persons who persistently engage in tax-avoidance schemes that HMRC defeats.

Schedule 18 consists of seven Parts. Part 1 (para 1) is introductory. Part 2 (paras 2–16) provides for the issue of warning notices and defines basic concepts. Part 3 (paras 17 and 18) provides for the giving of information notices and the naming of persistent defaulters. Part 4 (paras 19–29) provides for the restriction of reliefs. Part 5 (paras 30–44) provides for penalties to be charged. Part 6 (paras 45–53) applies the provisions to corporate groups, associated persons and partnerships, whereas Pt 7 (paras 54–65) contains definitions, supplementary provisions and makes consequential amendments.

Schedule 18 para 1 gives an overview of Sch 18. Schedule 18 para 2 places a duty on HMRC to give a written "warning notice" to a person who incurs a "relevant defeat" (defined in Sch 18 para 11) in relation to any arrangements within 90 days of the day on which the relevant defeat is incurred. The notice must set out when the "warning period" (defined in Sch 18 para 3) begins and ends, specify the relevant defeat to which the notice relates and explain the effect of the provisions in Sch 18. A warning notice under Sch 18 para 49 given to partnerships must also explain the related information provisions in Sch 18 para 51.

Schedule 18 para 3 defines the warning period as the five years beginning with the day after the issue of the warning notice. However, should the person incur another relevant defeat while the warning period is still running, the period is extended to end five years after the latest relevant defeat. Schedule 18 para 4 sets out the taxes in respect of which Sch 18 has effect. These are income tax, corporation tax (including amounts chargeable as if they were corporation tax), capital gains tax, petroleum revenue tax, diverted profits tax, apprenticeship levy, inheritance tax, stamp duty land tax, ATED, VAT and national insurance contributions. Schedule 18 para 5 defines what is meant by a tax advantage in relation to VAT. The definition is taken verbatim from that in VATA 1994 Sch 11A para 2, except for eschewing the use of the masculine singular pronoun. The same is true of Sch 18 para 6 (which takes its definition of "non-deductible tax" in relation to VAT from VATA 1994 Sch 11A para 2A). Schedule 18 para 7 defines "tax advantage" in relation to other taxes. Schedule 18 para 8 defines "DOTAS arrangements" for the purposes of Sch 18 and Sch 18 para 9 defines "disclosable VAT arrangements". Schedule 18 para 10 defines what "failure to comply" means in relation to DOTAS arrangements or disclosable VAT arrangements.

Schedule 18 para 11 defines what is meant by a "relevant defeat". This is a defeat incurred by a person ("P") in relation to arrangements when any one of five conditions, A–E, is met and is deemed to be incurred when the relevant condition is first met. Schedule 18 para 12 provides Condition A, which is where HMRC has given a notice of final decision to P under FA 2013 Sch 43 para 12, FA 2013 Sch 43A paras 8 or 9 (pooled arrangements; inserted by s 157) or FA 2013 Sch 43B para 8 (generic referrals; also inserted by s 157) stating that it will counteract a tax advantage under the GAAR, that tax advantage has been counteracted and the counteraction is final (i.e. the adjustments and any amounts arising from the adjustments can no longer be varied on appeal or otherwise). Schedule 18 para 13 provides Condition B, which applies where Condition A does not apply and where HMRC has given P (or a partnership in relation to which P is a relevant partner) a follower notice under FA 2014 Pt 4 Ch 2 in respect of which the necessary corrective action has been taken or where the advantage has otherwise been counteracted in a way that is now final. Schedule 18 para 14 provides Condition C, which can only apply if neither Condition A nor Condition B applies. This condition is that the arrangements are DOTAS arrangements, P has relied on the arrangements in his tax affairs, but those arrangements have been counteracted and the counteraction is final. Schedule 18 para 15 provides Condition D, which replicates Condition C, but in relation to disclosable VAT arrangements. Schedule 18 para 16 provides Condition E, which is met where P is a party under disclosable VAT arrangements under which another person supplies goods or services to P in such a way that P might expect to obtain a tax advantage but the tax advantage has been counteracted as against S and the counteraction is final.

Schedule 18 para 17 provides that where HMRC has given a person a warning notice, that person must provide HMRC with a written "information notice" for each "reporting period" within the warning period. The first "reporting period" is the period beginning with the first day of the warning period and ends with a day that HMRC is to specify. Thereafter, warning periods are periods of 12 months beginning immediately after the end of the previous warning period, except that the last reporting period is to end at the same time as the warning period. The information notice must state whether or not the person has made a claim or election or delivered a return based on a "relevant tax advantage" or failed to comply with an obligation on the basis of DOTAS arrangements or disclosable VAT arrangements to which the person is a party, or become a party to arrangements relating to the VAT position of a third-party supplier expected to confer a "relevant tax advantage" on the person. A "relevant tax advantage" is an advantage that enables or might be expected to enable the person to obtain a tax advantage under DOTAS arrangements or disclosable VAT arrangements. Where the person has done any of those things, the information notice must state whether it is that person's view that the expected tax advantage does indeed arise, and if so, how the arrangements enable that person to obtain the advantage and also quantify that advantage. Failure to give an information notice within 30 days of the end of the reporting period or to comply with any other obligation imposed by Sch 18 para 17 may cause HMRC to extend the warning period to end five years after the day by which the person should have given the notice or complied with the obligation or five years after the person gave a defective notice, as the case may be.

Schedule 18 para 18 enables HMRC to publish information of a prescribed nature about persons who have incurred a relevant defeat in relation to arrangements that they have used in a warning period and to whom at least two warning notices in respect of other defeats for arrangements used in the same warning period. Such information must be published for the first time no later than 12 months after the most recent warning notice and may not continue for longer than 12 months. Before publication commences, HMRC must inform the person concerned and allow that person enough time to make representations why the information should not be published.

Schedule 18 para 19 places a duty on HMRC to give a written "restriction of relief notice" to a person who has incurred a relevant defeat in relation to arrangements used in a warning period and to whom HMRC have given at least two warning notices in respect of other relevant defeats for arrangements used in the same warning period. A further condition is that the defeats must themselves meet three conditions. Those are that each defeat arises by virtue of Conditions A, B or C (for which see Sch 18 paras 12–14), that each relates to the misuse of a relief and that the counteraction was effected by means of a "particular avoidance-related rule" (defined in Sch 18 para 25) or involved the misuse of a loss relief. Such a notice must explain the effect of the restrictions and specify the "restricted period" (the period during which the restrictions apply).

Schedule 18 para 20 explains what is involved in a restriction of relief under Sch 18 para 19. Principally, the person concerned may not make any claim for relief during the entire period. Certain relies in relation to charities, registered pension schemes and double taxation arrangements are excluded from the restriction. Neither may the person: (a) surrender group relief; (b) claim a deduction in respect of trade losses brought forward for either income tax or corporation tax; (c) claim a deduction in respect of property-business losses brought forward for either income tax or corporation tax; (d) claim relief for annual payments under ITA 2007 ss 448 or 449; (e) deduct management expenses relating to an investment business under CTA 2009 s 1219; (f) claim a deduction for allowable losses for the purposes of capital gains tax; (g) claim a deduction for ring-fenced ATED-related allowable losses when calculating the total amount of ATED-related gains; (h) claim a deduction for allowable losses when calculating the total amount of chargeable NRCGT gains; or (i) claim a deduction for the deemed payments by trustees of an exempt unauthorised unit trust under SI 2013/2819 reg 18.

Schedule 18 para 21 provides that the restricted period is the period of three years beginning with the day on which HMRC gives the person the restriction of relief notice. Where the person incurs a further defeat of a specified kind during the currency of the restricted period, the restricted period is extended to end three years after the further relevant defeat is sustained. The defeats triggering an extension of the restricted period are also those involving the misuse of a relief and sustained by virtue of Conditions A, B or C. If the further defeat is sustained after the end of the restricted period but during the currency of the warning period, a new restricted period begins.

Schedule 18 para 22 provides that a relevant defeat is to be disregarded (i.e. is deemed not to have been incurred and the related warning notice is deemed never to have been given) if the person concerned satisfies HMRC or on appeal the Tribunal, that he had a reasonable excuse for the matters to which the defeat relates. If HMRC deems there are exceptional circumstances involved, Sch 18 para 23 allows HMRC to mitigate the restriction and allow the person concerned partial or full access to a particular relief.

Schedule 18 para 24 allows a person to appeal against a restriction of relief notice or a notice extending the restricted period within 30 days of the issue of the notice.

Schedule 18 para 25 defines what is meant by an "avoidance-related rule" (see Sch 18 para 19). This is a rule belonging to one of two categories. Category 1 is a rule that refers, broadly speaking, to the obtaining of a tax advantage as the main purpose or one of the main purposes of a transaction etc or to the avoidance of tax or the obtaining of a tax advantage as being the sole or main benefit or one of the main benefits to be or that may be expected from a transaction etc. Category 2 is a rule directing that a person may be treated differently for tax purposes depending on whether or not purposes to which the rule refers are commercial purposes. Schedule 18 para 26 defines "relief" for the purposes of Sch 18 and Sch 18 para 27 provides that a claim for relief includes any election or similar action substantially amounting to a claim for relief. Schedule 18 para 28 provides that for the purposes of Sch 18 Pt 4 (restriction of relief), "tax" does not include VAT. Schedule 18 para 29 gives HM Treasury the power to amend certain paragraphs by regulations.

Schedule 18 Pt 5 (paras 30–44) deals with the imposition of penalties. Schedule 18 para 30 provides that a person who incurs a relevant defeat in relation to arrangements used in a warning period is to be liable to a penalty. The amount of the penalty varies according to the number of prior warning notices the person has received. The penalty is 20% of the value of the counteracted advantage if the person had not received a warning notice in relation to the defeated arrangements before incurring the relevant defeat. It is 40% if the person had received one prior warning notice (i.e. the relevant defeat is the second incurred in the warning period) and 60% if the person had received two or more prior warning notices. Schedule 18 para 31 provides for the case where a person simultaneously incurs two or more relevant defeats in relation to different arrangements. In that case, the penalty amount is calculated on the premise that the defeat with the lowest value of the counteracted advantage was incurred last, the next lowest second last and so on.

Schedule 18 paras 32–37 contain the rules for calculating the amount of the counteracted advantage. These rules not surprisingly closely match the same valuation rules relating to the GAAR penalty under s 157.

Thus, as in new FA 2013 Sch 43C para 2, the basic rule for taxes other than VAT as stated in Sch 18 para 32 is that the value where the defeat is incurred by virtue of Conditions A, B or C (see Sch 18 paras 12–14), is the additional amount of tax due or payable. This includes amounts of tax erroneously repaid and amounts that would have been repayable in the absence of the counteraction. Schedule 18 para 33, matching new FA 2013 Sch 43C para 3, modifies the basic rule where the tax advantage includes a loss. Broadly speaking, where the whole of the wrongly recorded loss was used to reduce the amount of direct tax due or payable, the value of the counteracted advantage is the additional amount of tax due and payable. Where only part of the loss was so used, 10% of the unused loss must be added to the additional amount of tax due and payable when calculating the value. Similarly, Sch 18 para 34 matches new FA 2013 Sch 43C para 4 in prescribing how to value a tax advantage involving a deferment of tax. Schedule 18 para 35 defines what is meant by "the counteracted advantage" in Sch 18 paras 33 and 34. Schedule 18 para 36 addresses the calculation of the value of the counteracted advantage where the relevant defeat is incurred by virtue of Conditions D or E, which both involve disclosable VAT arrangements. This paragraph has no equivalent in new Sch 43C. Broadly speaking, the value of the counteracted advantage is calculated by adding the tax advantages that would have been obtained but for the counteraction by means of: (a) reducing the amount of VAT otherwise due and payable in a prescribed accounting period; (b) obtaining a VAT credit where otherwise there would have been none; (c) obtaining a greater VAT credit than would otherwise have been obtained;

and (d) reducing the non-deductible tax that would otherwise have been incurred. Schedule 18 para 37 contains the parallel valuation rule for delayed VAT to the rule for deferred tax in Sch 18 para 34.

Schedule 18 para 38 provides for HMRC to assess the penalty, which must then be paid within 30 days of the issue of the assessment. A penalty assessment must be made no later than 12 months after the date of the relevant defeat. Assessments to the penalty are to be treated as if they were assessments to tax. Schedule 18 para 39 allows for the issue of a supplementary penalty assessment where there has been an underestimate of the value of the counteracted advantage and for adjustment of the original penalty assessment where there has been an overestimate. Schedule 18 para 40 provides for the reduction of the penalty under Sch 18 where any other penalty or surcharge is incurred by the person concerned and is or are calculated by reference to the same tax liability, but this does not include the GAAR penalty under new FA 2013 s 212A or the follower-notice penalty under FA 2014 Pt 4.

Schedule 18 para 41 provides for appeals against the penalty. Taxpayers may appeal within 30 days of the issue of the assessment against the amount assessed. The appellant is not to be required to pay the penalty before the appeal is determined. Schedule 18 para 42 removes liability to a penalty if the person concerned satisfies HMRC or on appeal the Tribunal that he had a reasonable excuse for the "relevant failure" to which the relevant defeat relates. **Schedule 18 para 43** defines "relevant failure". Under Sch 18 para 44 HMRC has the discretion to mitigate or entirely remit a penalty or to stay or compound any proceedings for a penalty.

Schedule 18 Pt 6 (paras 45–53) apply the penalty provisions to corporate groups, associated persons and partnerships. Schedule 18 para 45 provides that in the case of a VAT group, successive representative members are treated as if they were the same person. Schedule 18 para 46 provides that where HMRC gives a warning notice to a company that is a member of a group, it must give the notice to every member of the group. Any warning notice previously given to a current group member is to be treated as given to each current group member. References to a warning period must be interpreted accordingly. However, where a company incurs a relevant defeat, HMRC is not to give it a restriction of relief notice unless the defeat is incurred in what would have been that company's warning period if it were not a member of the group. Similarly, a company that incurs a relevant defeat is not to be liable to a penalty under Sch 18 para 30 unless the defeat is incurred in what would have been that company's warning period if it were not a member of the group. "Group" for these purposes is defined.

Schedule 18 para 47 provides that where a person ("P") has incurred a relevant defeat, any other person who is associated with P at the time when HMRC gives P a warning notice in respect of that defeat is also to be treated as having incurred that defeat, thereby invoking HMRC's duty under Sch 18 para 2 to give those persons a warning notice also. However, this is not to apply where P and the associated person(s) is or are members of the same group of companies. Schedule 18 para 48 defines when two persons are to be regarded as associated for this purpose.

Schedule 18 paras 49–53 apply these provisions to partnerships. Schedule 18 paras 49 and 50 provide that when a partnership has made a partnership return on the basis that a tax advantage arises to a partner from any arrangements, and the partner concerned incurs a relevant defeat in relation to the advantage and the arrangements by virtue of Condition A (as defined in Sch 18 para 12, i.e. a counteraction notice), Condition B (as defined in Sch 18 para 13, i.e. following a follower notice) or Condition C (as defined in Sch 18 para 14, i.e. the arrangements are DOTAS arrangements) each person who was a "relevant partner" in that partnership at any time during the period covered by the return is also to be regarded as having incurred that relevant defeat. Schedule 18 para 51 provides that in the circumstances outlined in Sch 18 paras 49 and 50, a partner nominated by HMRC must provide it with a "partnership information notice" in respect of each "sub-period" in the period of five years beginning immediately after the day of the relevant defeat, unless the partnership is dissolved during that period. Should a new relevant defeat occur, a new five-year reporting period begins. The partnership information notice must state whether any other partnership return claiming a tax advantage based on DOTAS arrangements has or ought to have been made in the sub-period concerned and whether or not there has been any failure to deliver a return. Schedule 18 para 52 provides that in the circumstances described, an emendation under TMA 1970 s 12ABA of a partnership return as the result of a full and unprompted disclosure is not to be regarded as a relevant defeat. Schedule 18 para 53 defines terms and provides interpretation for the partnership paragraphs.

Schedule 18 para 54 defines "adjustments". Schedule 18 para 55 defines the time when defeated arrangements are regarded as being used. Schedule 18 para 56 lists what documents are to be treated as returns in the case of inheritance tax, and provides that "assessment" includes a determination. Schedule 18 para 57 adapts the provisions of Sch 18 to national insurance contributions. Schedule 18 para 58 provides for general interpretation. Schedule 18 paras 59–62 make consequential amendments.

Schedule 18 para 63 provides that, subject to the transitional provisions contained in Sch 18 paras 64 and 65, Sch 18 is to have effect in relation to relevant defeats incurred after 15 September 2016.

Section 160 makes changes to the POTAS (promoters of tax avoidance schemes) legislation in FA 2014 Pt 5. In particular, it introduces a new threshold condition identifying persons who are promoters to whom a conduct notice may be given. It inserts new FA 2014 ss 237A–237D, 241A and 241B and Sch 34A.

New FA 2014 s 237A, inserted by s 160(2), provides that where an authorised officer becomes aware at any time ("the relevant time") that a person who is carrying a business as a promoter meets any of three conditions, the officer must determine whether the promoter's meeting that condition is significant so as to merit the issue of a conduct notice to that promoter. The conditions are: (a) that in the period of three years immediately before the relevant time, taxpayers have incurred three or more relevant defeats in relation to arrangements promoted by him; (b) taxpayers have incurred at least two relevant defeats in relation to arrangements promoted by him at times when a "single-defeat notice" under new FA 2014 s 241A (inserted by s 160(3)) had effect in relation to the promoter; or (c) taxpayers have incurred at least one relevant defeat in relation to arrangements promoted by him at times when a "double-defeat notice" under new FA 2014 s 241A had effect in relation to the promoter. The authorised officer may only determine that the conditions in (b) or (c) have been met while the defeat notice in question still has effect or within 90 days of its ceasing to have effect. An authorised officer must make a determination concerning significance concerning both issues where the officer becomes aware at any time that a person meets one of these conditions and another person who is at that time a promoter meets that condition by virtue of his being a member of a body corporate or partnership, as provide in new FA 2014 Sch 34A Pt 4 (inserted by s 160(6)).

These new threshold conditions are not to apply if the promoter is already subject to a conduct notice or a monitoring notice, nor where the officer is already considering whether to give the relevant promoter a conduct notice under FA 2014 s 237, but in making that decision, the officer is required to take into account that the relevant promoter meets the new threshold condition in new FA 2014 s 237A. Where the officer considers that the relevant promoter's meeting any of the conditions is significant, the officer must issue the conduct notice, unless it would be inappropriate to do so when regard is had to the likely extent of the impact of the promoter's activities on the collection of tax.

New FA 2014 s 237A(15) introduces new FA 2014 Sch 34A, which makes provisions concerning relevant defeats.

New FA 2014 s 237B, also inserted by s 160(2), applies where a promoter has been subject to a conduct notice issued under new FA 2014 s 237A which was provisional and has now ceased to have effect, except in certain specified circumstances. If the authorised officer determines that the promoter had failed to comply with one or more conditions in the conduct notice, and three more conditions are satisfied, the officer must issue the promoter with a conduct notice under this section ("the section 237B notice"). The further conditions are that (a) the first conduct notice relied on a "Case 3 relevant defeat" (as defined in new FA 2014 Sch 34C, with the substitution of "100% of the tested arrangements" for references there to "75% of the tested arrangements"); (b) during the time after the conduct notice ceased to have effect, one or more relevant defeats have occurred by virtue of Cases 1 or 2 (as also defined in new FA 2014 Sch 34C) in relation to the promoter and to any arrangements to which the Case 3 relevant defeat also relates; and (c) had the relevant defeat(s) occurred while the conduct notice was still current, the conduct notice would have ceased to be provisional. The authorised officer does not have to issue the section 237B notice if the promoter is already subject to a conduct notice or a monitoring notice, nor where it would be inappropriate to do so when regard is had to the likely extent of the impact of the promoter's activities on the collection of tax.

New FA 2014 s 237C, also inserted by s 160(2), applies to define when a conduct notice given under new FA 2014 s 237A is provisional. Such a notice is provisional at all times where it relies on a Case 3 relevant defeat (as modified by new FA 2014 s 237B), unless an authorised officer notifies the promoter that the notice is no longer provisional, which the officer must do if either of two conditions is met. The first condition is that only one of the three relevant defeats by reference to which the conduct notice under new FA 2014 s 237A was given would not have been a relevant defeat if Case 3 had required 100% and not 75% of the tested arrangements to have been defeated and a "full relevant defeat" occurs in relation to the promoter. The alternative condition is that two or all three of the relevant defeats by reference to which the conduct notice under new FA 2014 s 237A was given would not have been a relevant defeat if Case 3 had required 100% and not 75% of the tested arrangements to have been defeated and the same number of full relevant defeats occur in relation to the promoter. A "full relevant defeat" occurs in relation to a promoter if it occurs to him otherwise than by virtue of Case 3 (as defined in new FA 2014 Sch 34C) or circumstances arise which would be a Case 3 relevant defeat if it had been the requirement for 100% of the tested arrangements to be defeated.

New FA 2014 s 237D, also inserted by s 160(2), provides that a conduct notice ceases to have effect where a court or tribunal upholds a tax advantage that has been asserted in connection with any of the related arrangements to which the relevant defeat relates, and the court's determination is final.

New FA 2014 s 241A, inserted by s 160(3), provides for the issue of defeat notices to a promoter. HMRC may give a promoter a defeat notice (a "single-defeat notice") within 90 days of when the officer concerned becomes aware that one and only one relevant defeat has occurred in relation to the promoter in the three years immediately preceding the date of the issue of the notice. HMRC may also give a promoter a double-defeat notice within 90 days of when the officer concerned becomes aware that two but no more than two relevant defeats have occurred in relation to the promoter in the three years immediately preceding the date of the issue of the notice. If a single-defeat notice ceases to have effect because the defeat to which it relates is overturned by a court, HMRC may give the promoter a new single-defeat notice if a further relevant defeat occurs in relation to the promoter when the original single-defeat notice was still in force. A defeat notice must contain specified information, including the dates of the "look-forward period" for the notice. This is the period during which the notice is valid and is normally the period of five years beginning on the day after the notice is issued. However, in the case of a new single-defeat notice following a judicial ruling, the look-forward period ends five years after the day on which the further relevant defeat occurs. A defeat notice will cease to have effect before the end of the look-forward period if the asserted tax advantage that was defeated is later upheld by a court.

New FA 2014 s 241B, also inserted by s 160(3), provides for when and how a relevant defeat may be overturned and for the consequences for the defeat notice at issue. A relevant defeat is overturned where the notice relates to a Case 3 relevant defeat that could not have been specified if instead of the 75% of tested arrangements referred to in new FA 2014 Sch 34A para 9, 100% of the tested arrangements would have had to have been defeated, and there is a final ruling of a court or tribunal upholding a corresponding tax advantage in relation to any of the "related arrangements" to which the relevant defeat relates. Where one of the relevant defeats in respect of a double-defeat notice is overturned, the notice is to be treated as if it had always been a single-defeat notice. If both relevant defeats are overturned on the same day, the notice ceases to have effect there and then.

New FA 2014 Sch 34A, inserted by s 160(5), makes provisions concerning relevant defeats. It consists of five Parts. Part 1 (para 1) is introductory. Part 2 (paras 2–16) defines and categorises relevant defeats. Part 3 (paras 17–19) provides for the attribution of relevant defeats to associated persons. Part 4 (paras 20–23) provides a mechanism for persons associated by membership of partnerships or bodies corporate to meet the defeat conditions in new FA 2014 s 237A. Part 5 (paras 24–31) contains definitions and supplementary provisions.

New FA 2014 Sch 34A para 1 is introductory. New FA 2014 Sch 34A para 2 defines "related arrangements". Separate arrangements are related to one another if and only if they are substantially the same. Specific circumstances in which the arrangements are always to be treated as related if they would otherwise not be, are described. New FA 2014 Sch 34A para 3 defines promoted arrangements as relevant arrangements of which a person is a promoter including, for this purpose only, arrangements to obtain a VAT advantage. New FA 2014 Sch 34A para 4 provides that a defeat of arrangements promoted by a promoter which are "stand-alone", i.e. not related to any other arrangements promoted by that promoter, is to be a "relevant defeat" in relation to that promoter. Arrangements are defeated for all purposes of new FA 2014 Sch 34A Part 2 if any of Conditions A to F (set out in new FA 2014

Finance Act 2016

Sch 34A paras 11–16) is met in relation to those arrangements. New FA 2014 Sch 34A paras 5–9, on the other hand, define a "relevant defeat" in relation to a promoter in respect of related arrangements.

New FA 2014 Sch 34A para 5 provides that if one of three Cases, Cases 1, 2 or 3 (set out in new FA 2014 Sch 34A paras 7–9), applies with respect to arrangements promoted by a promoter which are related to other arrangements promoted by that promoter, a "relevant defeat" occurs in relation to the promoter and each of the related arrangements. New FA 2014 Sch 34A para 6 places a limit on relevant defeats of the same or related arrangements. It provides that once a relevant defeat has occurred in respect of particular arrangements, there can be no further relevant defeats of those or related arrangements.

New FA 2014 Sch 34A para 7 defines a Case 1 relevant defeat as one where any of the related arrangements has been counteracted under any of Conditions A to E (set out in new FA 2014 Sch 34A paras 11–15) and the decision to make the relevant counteraction has been upheld by a final judicial ruling.

New FA 2014 Sch 34A para 8 defines a Case 2 relevant defeat as one where any of the related arrangements has been counteracted under Condition F (set out in new FA 2014 Sch 34A para 16).

New FA 2014 Sch 34A para 9 defines a Case 3 relevant defeat as one where at least 75% of the "tested arrangements" have been defeated and no final judicial ruling in respect of any of the related arrangements has upheld a corresponding tax advantage asserted in connection with any of the related arrangements. "Tested arrangements" are those arrangements out of a set of related arrangements to which either of the following circumstances apply: (a) where HMRC has given a GAAR counteraction notice in relation to the arrangements and all or part of the asserted advantage; or (b) HMRC has taken other action on the basis that the expected tax advantage from those arrangements does not arise.

New FA 2014 Sch 34A para 10 defines what constitutes a "defeat" for arrangements (see under new FA 2014 Sch 34A para 4).

New FA 2014 Sch 34A para 11 defines Condition A, which is that a tax advantage has been wholly or partly counteracted under the GAAR, under the procedure set out in FA 2013 Sch 43, new FA 2013 Sch 43A or new FA 2013 Sch 43B, and the counteraction is final.

New FA 2014 Sch 34A para 12 defines Condition B, which is that, following a follower notice under FA 2014 s 204, the person concerned has taken compliant action under FA 2014 s 208, the denied tax advantage has been wholly or partly counteracted and the counteraction is final.

New FA 2014 Sch 34A para 13 defines Condition C, which is that the arrangements are DOTAS arrangements, the relevant tax advantage under which has been counteracted and the counteraction is final.

New FA 2014 Sch 34A para 14 defines Condition D, which is that the arrangements are disclosable VAT arrangements to which a taxable person is a party, the relevant tax advantage has been counteracted and the counteraction is final.

New FA 2014 Sch 34A para 15 defines Condition E, which is that the arrangements are disclosable VAT arrangements to which a taxable person is a party and involve a third-party supplier, the arrangements have been counteracted and the counteraction is final.

New FA 2014 Sch 34A para 16 defines Condition F, which is that the obtaining of the expected tax advantage relies on the non-application of a particular avoidance-related rule, and a final judicial ruling has held that the rule does apply.

New FA 2014 Sch 34A para 17 considers a situation where (a) an event occurs to bring about a relevant defeat in relation to particular arrangements and a person ("Q") or that would have brought about such a defeat had Q not ceased to exist; (b) at the time of the event there is a person ("P") acting as a promoter; and (c) either of two conditions, 1 or 2, is met in relation to P and Q. Condition 1 is that P is not an individual; at a time when Q was promoting the defeated arrangements, P was a "relevant body" controlled by Q or Q was a "relevant body" controlled by P; and at the time of the event, P was a "relevant body" controlled by Q or Q was a "relevant body" controlled by P or P and Q were "relevant bodies" controlled by a third person. Condition 2 is that P and Q are "relevant bodies"; at a time when Q was promoting the defeated arrangements, a third person controlled Q; and the same person controls P at the time of the event. "Relevant body" is defined in new FA 2014 Sch 34A para 19. Where this is the case, the event is to be treated as a relevant defeat in relation to P and the defeated arrangements, regardless of whether or not this is also a relevant defeat in relation to Q, or whether P existed at a time when Q was promoting the arrangements.

New FA 2014 Sch 34A para 18 provides for situations where defeat notices are deemed to have been given to certain persons in the event of third-party defeats. This is a situation where (a) an authorised officer (called here "the first authorised officer") becomes aware that a relevant defeat has occurred in relation to a promoter ("P"); (b) more than three years previously, one or two third-party defeats have occurred; and (c) two further conditions are met.

In the event of a single previous third-party defeat, the further conditions that must be met are referred to as Conditions A1 and B1. Condition A1 has three legs, all of which must apply. The first is that a conduct notice or a single or double-defeat notice has been given to a third party in relation to a third-party defeat. The second is that at the time of the third-party defeat, an authorised officer would have had the power under new FA 2014 Sch 34A para 17 to give P a defeat notice in respect of the third-party defeat had the officer been aware that the third-party defeat was a relevant defeat for P. The third leg is that, as far as the first authorised officer is aware, the conditions for giving P a defeat notice in respect of the third-party defeat have never been met.

Condition B1 is that had an authorised officer given P a defeat notice in respect of the third-party defeat at the time, that defeat notice would still have had effect at the time when the first authorised officer becomes aware that the relevant defeat has occurred.

In the event that there have been two third-party defeats, the further conditions that must be met are referred to as Conditions A2 and B2. Condition A2, like Condition A1, also has three legs. First, a conduct notice or a single or double-defeat notice must have been given to a third party in relation to each or both of the third-party defeats. Second, it must be the case that at the time of the second third-party defeat, an authorised officer would have had the power under new FA 2014 Sch 34A para 17 to give P a double-defeat notice in respect of the third-party defeats had the officer been aware that either of the third-party defeats was a relevant defeat for P. Third, it must be the case that as far as the first authorised officer is aware, the conditions for giving P a defeat notice in respect of those third-party defeats or either of them have never been met.

Condition B2 is that had an authorised officer given P a defeat notice in respect of the two third-party defeats at the time of the second defeat, that defeat notice would still have had effect at the time when the first authorised officer becomes aware that the relevant defeat has occurred.

New FA 2014 Sch 34A para 19 defines a "relevant body" as being a body corporate or partnership, and defines what is meant by "control".

New FA 2014 Sch 34A Part 4 defines when a relevant body, as defined in new FA 2014 Sch 34A Pt 3 may be treated as meeting a so-called "section 237A condition" so that a conduct notice may be given to it.

New FA 2014 Sch 34A para 20 deals with persons under the control of others. It provides that a relevant body is to be treated as meeting a s 237A condition at the time when an authorised officer becomes aware that a person who is carrying a business as a promoter meets any of three conditions specified in that section (this time is referred to as "the section 237A(2) relevant time") if: (a) that person ("C") other than an individual meets that condition at a time when C is carrying on business as a promoter or the relevant body was carrying on business as a promoter at a time when it was controlled by C and (b) C controls the relevant body at the s 237A(2) relevant time. It is not to matter whether the relevant body existed at the time when C met the s 237A condition.

New FA 2014 Sch 34A para 21 deals with controlling persons. It provides that a person other than an individual is to be treated as meeting a s 237A condition at the s 237A(2) relevant time if: (a) a relevant body met the condition at a time when it was under that person's control and (b) at that time, either that relevant body or another relevant body also under the control of that person at that time was carrying on business as a promoter. It is not to matter whether either or neither relevant body existed at the s 237A(2) relevant time.

New FA 2014 Sch 34A para 22 deals with persons under common control. It provides that a relevant body is to be treated as meeting a s 237A condition at the s 237A(2) relevant time if: (a) another relevant body met the condition at a time when it was under the control of a person ("C"); (b) at that time, a relevant body also under the control of that person at that time was carrying on business as a promoter; and (c) the first relevant body was controlled by C at the s 237A(2) relevant time.

New FA 2014 Sch 34A para 23 provides for interpretation of new FA 2014 Sch 34A Pt 4.

New FA 2014 Sch 34A Pt 5 contains definitions and consequential amendments. New FA 2014 Sch 34A para 24 defines "adjustments". New FA 2014 Sch 34A para 25 defines "avoidance-related rule". This definition repeats verbatim the definition of the same term in Sch 18 para 25. New FA 2014 Sch 34A paras 26 and 28 define "DOTAS arrangements". New FA 2014 Sch 34A paras 27 and 28 define "disclosable VAT arrangements". New FA 2014 Sch 34A para 29 defines when a counteraction is to be regarded as final. New FA 2014 Sch 34A para 30 modifies the meaning of "assessment" and "return" to accommodate similar terms in relation to inheritance tax, SDRT, VAT and petroleum revenue tax. New FA 2014 Sch 34A para 31 gives HM Treasury the power to amend new FA 2014 Sch 34A by regulations.

Section 160(6)–(19) make consequential amendments. Section 159(20)–(22) make transitional provisions to ensure that certain defeats are to be ignored if they relate to judicial rulings made before 16 September 2016.

Section 161 introduces **Sch 19**, which introduces a statutory requirement on all qualifying large businesses to publish a tax strategy in relation to their taxation in the UK. Failure to do so fully and persistent non-cooperative behaviour may lead to the imposition of penalties. Section 160 is to have effect as regards the publication of a tax strategy in relation only to financial years beginning after 14 September 2016. Similarly, HMRC may not give a warning notice to a relevant entity before the beginning of its first financial year beginning after that date.

Schedule 19 consists of four Parts. Part 1 (paras 1–15) is interpretative. Part 2 (paras 16–34) provides for the duty to publish a tax strategy. Part 3 (paras 35–53) imposes penalties for persistent non-cooperative behaviour, whereas Part 4 (paras 54 and 55) contains supplementary provisions.

Schedule 19 para 1 is introductory. Schedule 19 para 2 defines a "relevant body" to which the provisions of Sch 19 may apply. Such a body is a UK company or any other body corporate, but does not include a limited-liability partnership. A relevant body incorporated abroad is a "relevant foreign body". Schedule 19 para 3 defines "UK company", excluding open-ended investment companies and investment trusts. Schedule 19 para 4 defines the term "UK permanent establishment". Schedule 19 para 5 defines "qualifying company", which is a company to which the provisions of Sch 19 apply. A company is a qualifying company in any financial year if at the end of the previous financial year, it was not a member of a UK group or UK sub-group and either its turnover was more than £200 million or its balance-sheet total was more than £2,000 million (= £2 "billion"), or both. A company is also a qualifying company if at the end of the previous financial year, it was a member of a foreign group that met the "qualification test" for a group and it was not a member of that foreign group's UK sub-group. A UK permanent establishment of a foreign relevant body is to be treated as if it were a UK company and if the foreign relevant body is a member of a UK group or UK sub-group, as a member of that group or sub-group.

Schedule 19 para 6 defines a "group" as two or more relevant bodies that together constitute an "MNE Group" or a "group other than an "MNE Group". A "UK group" is a group whose "head" is a relevant body incorporated in the UK. A "foreign group" is a group whose "head" is a foreign relevant body. Schedule 19 para 7 defines "MNE Group" by reference to the OECD Model Legislation in the OECD Country-by-Country Reporting Implementation Package. Schedule 19 para 8 defines a "group other than an "MNE Group". Membership of a group is defined by reference to 51% subsidiaries. Schedule 19 para 9 defines the "head" of a group as whichever relevant body in a group is not a 51% subsidiary of another relevant body in that group.

Schedule 19 para 10 defines a "qualifying group". In the case of an MNE Group, the group is a qualifying group if, at the end of the previous financial year, it was subject to a mandatory country-by-country reporting requirement under FA 2015 s 122 or it would have been subject such a requirement if its head had been resident in the UK. In the case of a group other than an MNE Group, the group is a qualifying group if, at the end of the previous financial year, its group turnover was more than £200 million or its group balance-sheet total was more than £2,000 million, or both. Schedule 19 para 11 defines a "UK sub-group" as two or more relevant bodies that would be a UK group were they not members of a larger group whose head is a foreign relevant body. The "head" of a UK sub-group is defined analogously to the definition of head of a group in Sch 19 para 9.

Schedule 19 para 12 defines a "UK partnership" as a partnership within the Partnership Act 1890, the Limited Partnerships Act 1907, or a limited-liability partnership incorporated in the UK. It is a "qualifying partnership" if, at the end of the previous financial year, its turnover was more than £200 million or its balance-sheet total was more than £2,000 million, or both. Schedule 19 para 13 defines "financial year"; Sch 19 para 14 defines "turnover" and "balance-sheet total". Schedule 19 para 15 defines the UK taxes in relation to the provisions of Sch 19 as income tax (including amounts under PAYE regulations), corporation tax (including amounts chargeable as if they were corporation tax), petroleum revenue tax, diverted profits tax, insurance premium tax, stamp duty land tax, ATED, SDRT, VAT, customs duties, excise duties and national insurance contributions.

Schedule 19 para 16 provides that the head of a qualifying UK group must prepare and publish a tax strategy for the group in every financial year in which the group is a qualifying group. It must publish the strategy before the end of the current financial year and, if the group was a qualifying group also in the previous financial year, no more than 15 months after its previous group tax strategy was published. The strategy must be published on the internet by any of the UK members of the group and be accessible to the public free of charge.

Schedule 19 para 17 prescribes the contents of the group tax strategy as published. The strategy must set out the group's approach to risk management and governance arrangements in relation to UK taxation; the attitude of the group towards tax planning as regards UK taxation; the group's acceptable level of risk in relation to UK taxation; and the approach of the group towards its dealings with HMRC. HM Treasury may make regulations requiring the group tax strategy to include a country-by-country report.

Schedule 19 para 18 provides that the head of a UK group is to be liable to a penalty of £7,500 in the event of a failure to publish the group tax strategy for the financial year or a failure to keep the strategy accessible free of charge on the internet for the prescribed period. If the failure to publish has not been remedied by the end of six months after the original due date, there is a further penalty of £7,500 and further subsequent penalties of £7,500 per month while the failure continues.

Schedule 19 para 19 imposes a like duty to publish a tax strategy on behalf of a UK sub-group on the head of that sub-group, within the same timeframe and under the same accessibility conditions. As regards the contents of the strategy, Sch 19 para 20 applies the provisions of Sch 19 para 17, as appropriately modified. Exactly the same penalties as imposed under Sch 19 para 18 on the head of a UK group are imposed by Sch 19 para 21 on the head of a UK sub-group in respect of the like failures.

Schedule 19 para 22 imposes a like duty on a qualifying UK company to publish its tax strategy on the same terms as Sch 19 para 16 imposes on a qualifying UK group. The contents of that strategy as prescribed by Sch 19 para 23 match those required of a UK group under Sch 19 para 17. The penalties under Sch 19 para 24 for non-compliance match those imposed for non-compliance on a UK group under Sch 19 para 18 and on a UK sub-group under Sch 19 para 21. Schedule 19 para 25 requires a qualifying UK partnership to publish a partnership tax strategy under the same terms.

Schedule 19 paras 26–33 contain general provisions relating to penalties under Sch 19 Pt 2. Schedule 19 para 26 defines "failure", "liability to a penalty" and "penalty". Schedule 19 para 27 allows HMRC to extend the time limit for failure to do anything required before a penalty may be imposed. Schedule 19 para 28 allows for a reasonable excuse as a defence against the imposition of a penalty. Schedule 19 para 29 provides for HMRC to assess a penalty for failure. A penalty assessment must be made no later than six months after the failure first comes to the attention of HMRC and no later than six years after the end of the financial year in which the tax strategy to which the failure relates was due to be published. Assessments to the penalty are to be treated as if they were assessments to tax. Schedule 19 para 30 provides for appeals against the penalty. Persons may appeal within 30 days of the issue of the assessment stating the grounds. Schedule 19 para 31 provides that the penalty must be paid no later than 30 days after the issue of the assessment. If the assessment is under appeal, the last date for payment of the penalty is 30 days after the appeal is determined or withdrawn. A penalty is enforceable as if it were corporation tax charged in an assessment and due and payable. Under Sch 19 para 32, HM Treasury may alter the prescribed amount of a penalty by regulations. Schedule 19 para 33 applies relevant provisions of TMA 1970 and Sch 34 defines "tax strategy".

Schedule 19 Pt 3 (paras 35–53) imposes sanctions on large businesses that are "persistently uncooperative". Schedule 19 para 35 defines which large groups fall within the compass of this Part. These are UK groups that have "persistently engaged in uncooperative behaviour" (as defined in Sch 19 paras 36–38), where all or some of that behaviour has resulted in two or more unresolved significant "tax issues" (as defined in Sch 19 para 39), and where there is a reasonable likelihood that there will be further instances of uncooperative behaviour by the group resulting in further significant tax issues. Schedule 19 para 36 defines engaging in uncooperative behaviour by reference to two conditions – the "behaviour condition" and the "arrangements condition", the meeting of either or both of which constitutes such behaviour where it has been engaged in by a member of the group or two or more members taken together. Where one member or two or more members taken together have persistently engaged in such behaviour, the UK group is taken to have done so. Doing something persistently includes doing it on a sufficient number of occasions for it to be clear that it represents a pattern of behaviour. Schedule 19 para 37 defines the "behaviour condition", which is that a member or two or more members taken together behaved in a manner that has delayed or otherwise hindered HMRC in its function of determining the group's or a member's liability to UK taxation. A non-exclusive list of factors indicating such behaviour is given in Sch 19 para 37(2). The "arrangements condition" is defined in Sch 19 para 38 as met where a member of the UK group is a party to a tax-avoidance scheme, a counteraction notice in respect of which has been given under FA 2013 Sch 43 para 12, new FA 2013 Sch 43A paras 5 or 6, or new FA 2013 Sch 43B para 9. A notifiable scheme under the DOTAS rules of FA 2004 Pt 7 is also a tax-avoidance scheme for this purpose, as is a disclosable VAT scheme under VATA 1994 Sch 11A. Schedule 19 para 39 provides that a "significant tax issue" arises where there is a disagreement between HMRC and a member of the group affecting the member's or the group's liability to UK taxation; the issue has been or could be referred to a court or tribunal, and the difference between HMRC's view and the group's or member's view of the liability is or is likely to be not less than £2 million. Schedule 19 para 40 provides that things done by a relevant body that was formerly a member of the group when it was a member are to be taken into account but things done by a current member before it was a member are to be disregarded.

Schedule 19 para 41 provides for a designated HMRC officer to give the head of a UK group a warning notice if the officer considers that the group is a qualifying group falling within Sch 19 Part 3. A warning notice expires 15 months after its issue unless withdrawn earlier. Schedule 19 para 42 provides that where the head of the group has previously received a warning notice that is still current and more than 12 months but less than 15 months have elapsed since the issue of the notice, a designated HMRC officer may issue a "special measures notice" to the head of the UK group. The officer must consider any representations made by a member of the group within 12 months of the issue of the warning notice when deciding whether to give a special measures notice. Schedule 19 para 43 provides that a special measures notice expires 27 months after its issue or last confirmation unless withdrawn earlier. Schedule 19 para 44 provides that where the head of the group has previously received a special measures notice that is still current and more than 24 months but less than 27 months have elapsed since the issue of the notice, a designated HMRC officer may issue a "confirmation notice" to the head of the UK group. The officer must consider any representations made by a member of the group within 24 months of the issue of the special measures notice or the latest confirmation notice when deciding whether to give a confirmation notice. A confirmation notice expires 27 months after its issue unless withdrawn earlier. Schedule 19 para 45 provides for additional circumstances when a confirmation notice may be given. These are where the warning notice or a special measures notice has expired but, within six months of the expiry date, the group has again engaged in uncooperative behaviour and it is reasonably likely that HMRC would have given the head of the group a special measures notice or a confirmation notice if it had engaged in that behaviour before the expiry of the earlier notice. In that case, a designated HMRC officer must inform the head of the group no later than seven months after the expiry of the earlier notice that the issue of a special measures notice is being contemplated. The officer must consider any representations made by a member of the group within eight months of the expiry of the original notice when deciding whether to give a special measures notice on this occasion. If the decision is to give the notice, this must be done no later than nine months after the expiry of the original notice. Schedule 19 para 46 provides for the circumstances in which notices are treated as having been given when the composition of a group changes.

Schedule 19 para 47 provides that for the purposes of the error-penalty legislation in FA 2007 Sch 24, an inaccuracy in a document given to HMRC is to be regarded as being due to a failure to take reasonable care if the person concerned gave the document to HMRC at a time when the person was a member of a group subject to a special measures notice and the inaccuracy relates to a tax-avoidance scheme the person entered into while the group was under notice or is attributable to an interpretation of UK tax law that is speculative. Schedule 19 para 48 makes a consequential amendment.

Schedule 19 para 49 enables HMRC to "name and shame" a UK group under a confirmed special measures notice by publishing prescribed information about it. Before proceeding, however, HMRC must notify the head of the group that it is considering doing so and allow the head of the group a reasonable opportunity to make representations.

Schedule 19 para 50 provides for a large UK sub-group to fall within Sch 19 Pt 3 where the sub-group has persistently engaged in uncooperative behaviour, where all or some of that behaviour has resulted in two or more unresolved significant tax issues, and where there is a reasonable likelihood that there will be further instances of uncooperative behaviour by the sub-group resulting in further significant tax issues. Schedule 19 Pt 3 then applies, with some modifications, as it would apply to a UK group. Schedule 19 para 51 does likewise for large companies that are not members of a group, where the company has persistently engaged in uncooperative behaviour, where all or some of that behaviour has resulted in two or more unresolved significant tax issues, and where there is a reasonable likelihood that there will be further instances of uncooperative behaviour by the company resulting in further significant tax issues. Schedule 19 Pt 3 then applies, with some modifications, as it would apply to a UK group. In particular, references to the head of a group are to be taken as references to the company. Schedule 19 para 52 does likewise for a large partnership, where the partnership has persistently engaged in uncooperative behaviour, where all or some of that behaviour has resulted in two or more unresolved significant tax issues, and where there is a reasonable likelihood that there will be further instances of uncooperative behaviour by the partnership resulting in further significant tax issues. Schedule 19 Pt 3 then applies, with some modifications, as it would apply to a UK group. In particular, references to the head of a group are to be taken as references to the representative partner of the partnership, references to a UK group are to be taken as references to a UK partnership and references to a member of a UK group are to be taken as references to a partner in the partnership, acting as such.

Schedule 19 para 53 defines "designated HMRC officer". Schedule 19 para 54 makes a consequential amendment relating to regulatory powers. Schedule 19 para 55 provides that regulations under Sch 19 are to be made by statutory instrument subject to annulment. The Schedule ends with an unnumbered destination table of definitions.

Offshore activities

Sections 162–165 introduce new civil penalties for persons who deliberately enable offshore tax evasion or other forms of non-compliance and new "naming and shaming" powers in respect to these enablers. The new provisions are to come into force from an appointed day.

Section 162 introduces Sch 20, which imposes the civil penalty for enablers of offshore tax evasion or non-compliance. Schedule 20 consists of three Parts. Part 1 (paras 1–17) establishes liability to the penalty. Part 2 (paras 18–21) applies the information powers of FA 2008 Sch 36. Part 3 (paras 22 and 23) provides for publication of details concerning persons liable to the penalty.

Schedule 20 para 1 provides that a penalty is to be payable by a person ("P") who has enabled another person ("Q") to carry out offshore tax evasion or non-compliance, in circumstances where two conditions, A and B, are met, and in relation to income tax, capital gains tax or inheritance tax (and not corporation tax, for example). A person carries out "offshore tax evasion or non-compliance" where that person commits a "relevant offence" or engages in conduct that makes him liable to a "relevant civil penalty" if the applicable conditions are met. A person is regarded as having enabled another to carry out offshore tax evasion or non-compliance if he has encouraged, assisted or otherwise facilitated that other person in carrying out offshore tax evasion or non-compliance. A "relevant offence" is any of the following: (a) cheating the public revenue; (b) fraudulent evasion of income tax under TMA 1970 s 106A; or (c) offences under TMA 1970 ss 106B-106D in relation to returns under TMA 1970 ss 7 or 8, all involving offshore activity. A "relevant civil penalty" is any of: (a) a penalty for errors in a document under FA 2007 Sch 24 para 1 involving an offshore matter or offshore transfer; (b) a penalty for failure to notify etc under FA 2008 Sch 41 para 1 involving offshore activity; (c) a penalty for failure to make a return for 12 months under FA 2009 Sch 55 involving offshore activity; or (d) a penalty in connection with relevant offshore-asset moves under FA 2015 Sch 21.

The first further condition that has to be met for the penalty to be imposed, Condition A, is that P knew when he carried out his actions that they enabled or were likely to enable Q to carry out offshore tax evasion or non-compliance (abbreviated in these notes from now on to "OTENC"). Condition B is that, where the OTENC consists of the commission of a relevant offence, Q has been convicted of the offence and the conviction is final; or where the OTENC consists of conduct that makes Q liable to a relevant penalty, that Q has been found liable to such a penalty, the penalty has been assessed and the penalty is final or that Q and HMRC have contracted that HMRC will take no further steps to assess the penalty or enforce it.

Schedule 20 para 2 defines conduct "involving offshore activity". This is conduct involving an offshore matter, an offshore transfer or a relevant offshore-asset move. Conduct involves an offshore matter where it results in a potential loss of revenue in relation to income arising from a source outside the UK; assets situated or held outside the UK; activities carried out wholly or mainly outside the UK; or anything having effect as if it were income, assets or activities of the kind described. Where inheritance tax is concerned, regard is had to where the assets are held or situated immediately after the transfer of value in question. Conduct involves an offshore transfer if it does not involve an offshore matter but is deliberate and results in a potential loss of revenue and the condition in FA 2007 Sch 24 para 4AA is satisfied. Finally, conduct involves a relevant offshore-asset move if while Q is the beneficial owner of the asset, either it ceases to be held or situated in a specified territory and becomes held or situated in a non-specified territory (within the meaning of FA 2015 Sch 21 para 4); the person holding the asset ceases to be resident in a specified territory and becomes resident in a non-specified territory; or there is a change in the arrangements for the ownership of the asset, while Q remains the beneficial owner of the asset after the move.

Schedule 20 para 3 sets the amount of the penalty at the higher of 100% of the potential lost revenue and £3,000. However, where P has enabled Q to engage in conduct making Q liable to a penalty for a relevant offshore-asset move, the amount of the penalty is to be the higher of 50% of the potential lost revenue in respect of the conduct that incurred the original penalty and £3,000. Schedule 20 para 4 defines the amount of potential lost revenue where P is liable to the penalty for enabling Q to commit a relevant offence as the same amount as it would be for the corresponding civil penalty, and defines the corresponding civil penalty in each case. Schedule 20 para 5 defines the amount of potential lost revenue where P is liable to the penalty for enabling Q to engage in conduct making Q liable to a relevant civil penalty. This is, broadly, the amount of potential lost revenue for the purposes of that relevant civil penalty. Where potential lost revenue is attributable to both Q's OTENC and other tax evasion or non-compliance by Q, Sch 20 para 6 provides that the amount attributable to the OTENC is to be a just and reasonable proportion of the whole.

Schedule 20 para 7 allows for reduction of the penalty where P makes a disclosure to HMRC that HMRC regards as of assistance in assessing P's liability to the penalty or assists HMRC in an investigation that leads to Q's being charged with a relevant offence or Q's being found liable to a relevant penalty, according to the quality of the disclosure or assistance. However, in the case of unprompted disclosure or assistance, the penalty may not be reduced below the greater of 10% of the potential lost revenue and £1,000; in the case of prompted disclosure or assistance, the penalty may not be reduced below the greater of 30% of the potential lost revenue and £3,000. Schedule 20 para 8 explains how P may make a disclosure or provide assistance and what is prompted and unprompted. Schedule 20 para 9 allows HMRC to reduce the amount of the penalty because of special circumstances.

Schedule 20 para 10 provides for HMRC to assess the penalty, which must then be paid within 30 days of the issue of the assessment. Assessments to the penalty are to be treated as if they were assessments to tax. HMRC may issue of a supplementary penalty assessment where the original assessment was based on an underestimate of the liability to tax and for adjustment of the original penalty assessment where there has been an overestimate. Schedule 20 para 11 provides that a penalty assessment may be made no later than two years after the fact that Conditions A and B referred to in Sch 20 para 1 were met first comes to the attention of HMRC. Schedule 20 para 12 provides for appeals against the penalty. Persons may appeal against either the decision that the person concerned is liable to the penalty or the amount of the penalty. Schedule 20 para 13 provides that the appeal is to be treated in the same way as an appeal against an assessment to the tax concerned. However, the penalty is not thereby to become payable before the appeal is determined.

Schedule 20 para 14 prescribes what decision the tribunal may come to on the appeal. Schedule 20 para 15 prevents double jeopardy where the person on whom the penalty would otherwise be charged where that person has been convicted of an offence or been assessed to any other penalty in respect of the same conduct. Schedule 20 para 16 applies relevant provisions of TMA 1970, and Sch 20 para 17 provides that references to an assessment are to be taken to include references to a determination where inheritance tax is involved.

Schedule 20 Part 2 applies the information powers given in FA 2008 Schs 36–20, with appropriate modifications. Schedule 20 para 18 provides that the information and inspection powers conferred by FA 2008 Sch 36 are to apply for the purpose of checking a person's position as regards liability for a penalty under Sch 20 as they apply for checking a person's tax position generally, but with the modifications expressed in Sch 20 paras 19–21. Specific exclusions are made in Sch 20 para 20, and refer to FA 2008 Sch 36 paras 24–27 (exceptions for auditors and tax advisers) and FA 2008 Sch 36 paras 50 and 51 (tax-related penalties).

Schedule 20 Pt 3 enables information of a prescribed nature concerning persons assessed to a penalty under Sch 20 to be published. Schedule 20 para 22 provides that the persons information about whom may be published are those who have been assessed to one or more penalties under Sch 20, the combined potential lost revenue involved in which exceeds £25,000. Also liable are persons who have incurred five or more penalties under Sch 20 in any five-year period. Before proceeding to publish, HMRC must inform the person concerned and allow that person the opportunity to make representations. The information may not be published before the penalty or the latest of the penalties becomes final and the date of first publication cannot be later than 12 months after that date. There are restrictions on publication where the penalty has been reduced due to disclosure or assistance. Schedule 20 para 23 permits HM Treasury to vary the monetary threshold for publication by regulations.

Section 163 introduces **Sch 21**, which amends the existing penalty provisions in FA 2007 Sch 24 (errors in returns etc), FA 2008 Sch 41 (failure to notify) and FA 2009 Sch 55 (failure to make a return etc) to increase penalties in relation to offshore matters or transfers resulting from deliberate behaviour. Schedule 21, which is to come into force on a day or days to be appointed, consists of 12 paragraphs. Schedule 21 paras 1–4 amend FA 2007 Sch 24; Sch 21 paras 5–8 amend FA 2008 Sch 41 and Sch 21 paras 9–12 amend FA 2009 Sch 55.

Schedule 21 para 1 is introductory. Schedule 21 para 2 amends FA 2007 Sch 24 para 9, which provides reductions in the penalties under that Schedule in return for disclosure. Currently, while the extent of the reductions differs as between prompted and unprompted disclosure, it is neutral as to whether the disclosure concerns a domestic matter or an offshore matter. The rate reductions are shown in tables under FA 2007 Sch 24 para 10. FA 2007 Sch 24 para 9 as now amended provides that FA 2007 Sch 24 para 10 is to provide, inter alia, for reductions in penalties (under FA 2007 Sch 24 para 1) where a person discloses an inaccuracy involving a domestic matter, whereas there is no change in the scope of reductions in penalties provided by FA 2007 Sch 24 para 10 as regards reductions in penalties (under FA 2007 Sch 24 para 1A) for disclosing a supply of false information or withholding of information or reductions in penalties (under FA 2007 Sch 24 para 2) for disclosing a failure to disclose an underassessment. New FA 2007 Sch 24 para 10A, inserted by Sch 21 para 4, is now to provide for reductions in penalties where a person discloses an inaccuracy involving an offshore matter or an offshore transfer. New FA 2007 Sch 24 para 9(1B)(d), inserted by Sch 21 para 2(4), adds a further method of disclosure qualifying for a penalty reduction, namely "providing HMRC with additional information". New FA 2007 Sch 24 paras 9(1C)-(1E) provide that HM Treasury is to make regulations setting out what is meant by "additional information" for this purpose. Whether an inaccuracy involves an offshore matter, an offshore transfer or a domestic matter is to be determined by FA 2007 Sch 24 para 4A(4)–(5).

Schedule 21 para 3 inserts a new Table in FA 2007 Sch 24 para 10(2), which now contains only the standard penalty rates and the relevant reductions applicable to domestic matters, but these are unchanged. Schedule 21 para 4 inserts new FA 2007 Sch 24 para 10A, the Table in which displays the maximum reductions for prompted and unprompted disclosure relating to offshore matters or offshore transfers. Compared to existing maximum reductions and prospective maximum reductions enacted by FA 2015 Sch 20 para 5 (but yet to be brought into effect), the new maximum reductions for both prompted and unprompted disclosure are reduced for all standard rates of 70% and above.

Schedule 21 para 5 is introductory. Schedule 21 para 6 amends FA 2008 Sch 41 para 12 to provide that, henceforth, FA 2008 Sch 41 para 13 will provide for reductions in penalties (under FA 2008 Sch 41 para 1) for disclosure of a relevant failure involving a domestic matter whereas it will still provide also for reductions in penalties (under FA 2008 Sch 41 paras 2–4) for disclosure of a relevant act or failure. New FA 2008 Sch 41 para 13A, inserted by Sch 21 para 8, is now to provide for reductions in penalties where a person discloses a relevant failure involving an offshore matter or an offshore transfer. New FA 2008 Sch 41 para 12(2B)(d), inserted by Sch 21 para 6(4), adds a further method of disclosure qualifying for a penalty reduction, namely "providing HMRC with additional information". New FA 2008 Sch 41 paras 13(2C)–(2E) provide that HM Treasury is to make regulations setting out what is meant by "additional information" for this purpose. Whether an inaccuracy involves an offshore matter, an offshore transfer or a domestic matter is to be determined by FA 2008 Sch 41 para 6A(4)–(5).

Schedule 21 para 7 inserts a new Table in FA 2007 Sch 24 para 10(2), which now contains only the standard penalty rates and the relevant reductions applicable to domestic matters, but these are unchanged. Schedule 21 para 8 inserts new FA 2008 Sch 41 para 13A, the Table in which displays the maximum reductions for prompted and unprompted disclosure relating to offshore matters or offshore transfers. Compared to existing maximum reductions and prospective maximum reductions enacted by FA 2015 Sch 20 para 9 (but yet to be brought into effect), the new maximum reductions for both prompted and unprompted disclosure are reduced for all standard rates of 70% and above.

Schedule 21 para 9 is introductory. Schedule 21 para 10 amends FA 2009 Sch 55 para 14 to provide that, henceforth, FA 2009 Sch 55 para 15 will provide for reductions in penalties (under FA 2009 Sch 55 para 6(3) or (4)) for disclosure of relevant information involving a domestic matter whereas it will still provide also for reductions in penalties (under FA 2009 Sch 55 paras 11(3) or (4)) for disclosure of relevant information. New FA 2009 Sch 55 para 15A, inserted by Sch 21 para 12, is now to provide for reductions in penalties where a person discloses relevant information involving an offshore matter or an offshore transfer. New FA 2009 Sch 55 para 14(2B)(d), inserted by Sch 21 para 10(5), adds a further method of disclosure qualifying for a penalty reduction, namely "providing HMRC with additional information". New FA 2009 Sch 55 paras 14(2C)–(2E) provide that HM Treasury is to make regulations setting out what is meant by "additional information" for this purpose. Whether relevant information involves an offshore matter, an offshore transfer or a domestic matter is to be determined by FA 2009 Sch 55 para 6A(4)–(5).

Schedule 21 para 11 inserts a new Table in FA 2009 Sch 55 para 15(2), which now contains only the standard penalty rates and the relevant reductions applicable to domestic matters, but these are unchanged. Schedule 21 para 12 inserts new FA 2009 Sch 55 para 15A, the Table in which displays the maximum reductions for prompted and unprompted disclosure relating to offshore matters or offshore transfers. Compared to existing maximum reductions and prospective maximum reductions enacted by FA 2015 Sch 20 para 14 (but yet to be brought into effect), the new maximum reductions for both prompted and unprompted disclosure are reduced for all standard rates.

Section 164 amends FA 2009 s 94, which enables prescribed information about deliberate tax defaulters, in order to ensure that where there is an inaccuracy in a taxpayer's document or failure to notify involving offshore matters or offshore transfers, only full, unprompted disclosure will prohibit publication. The amendments also provide for the publication of details relating to certain persons who have benefited from the inaccuracy or failure. New FA 2009 s 94(4A)–(4D) provide that where a body corporate or a partnership has incurred a penalty under FA 2007 Sch 24 para 1 in respect of deliberate inaccuracy involving an offshore matter or an offshore transfer or a penalty under FA 2008 Sch 41 para 1 in respect of a deliberate failure involving an offshore matter or an offshore transfer, HMRC may also publish information concerning any individual who controls the body corporate and has obtained a tax advantage as a result of the inaccuracy or failure. Likewise, where one or more trustees of a settlement have incurred a penalty under FA 2007 Sch 24 para 1 in respect of deliberate inaccuracy involving an offshore matter or an offshore transfer or a penalty under FA 2008 Sch 41 para 1 in respect of a deliberate failure involving an offshore matter or an offshore transfer, HMRC may also publish information concerning those trustees who are individuals and have obtained a tax advantage as a result of the inaccuracy or failure. Section 163(5) amends FA 2009 s 94 to provide that in respect of penalties under FA 2007 Sch 24 para 10A or penalties under FA 2008 Sch 41 para 13A, only unprompted disclosure of a quality sufficient to merit the greatest reduction possible is to prevent publication of the person's details. The amendments made by s 164 are to come into force on a day to be appointed.

Section 165 introduces **Sch 22**, which is to come into force on a day to be appointed. It provides for the imposition of asset-based penalties on certain taxpayers already subject to a penalty for deliberate offshore inaccuracies and failures. Schedule 22 consists of five Parts. Schedule 22 Pt 1 (paras 1–6) establishes liability for the penalty. Schedule 22 Pt 2 (paras 7–9) determines the amount of the penalty, Sch 22 Pt 3 (paras 10–14) provides for the identification and valuation of assets; Sch 22 Pt 4 (paras 15–18) provides for procedure. Schedule 22 Pt 5 (paras 19–21) contains general provisions.

Schedule 22 para 1 provides that an asset-based penalty is to be payable by a person on whom one or more "standard offshore tax penalties" have been imposed in relation to a tax year and in respect of which the potential lost revenue has reached a threshold amount. A "standard offshore tax penalty" (abbreviated in these notes from now on to "SOTP") may be (a) a penalty under FA 2007 Sch 24 para 1 (inaccuracy in a document) imposed in respect of a deliberate inaccuracy involving an offshore matter or offshore transfer and in respect of which the tax involved is (or includes) asset-based income tax, capital gains tax or inheritance tax; (b) a penalty under FA 2008 Sch 41 para 1 (failure to notify) imposed in respect of a deliberate failure involving an offshore matter or offshore transfer and in respect of which the tax involved is (or includes) asset-based income tax, capital gains tax or inheritance tax; or (c) a penalty under FA 2009 Sch 55 para 6 (failure to make a return more than 12 months after the filing date) imposed in respect of deliberate withholding of information involving an offshore matter or offshore transfer and in respect of which the tax involved is (or includes) asset-based income tax, capital gains tax or inheritance tax. "Asset-based income tax" is income tax charged under any of the provisions listed in Column 1 of the Table in Sch 22 para 13.

Schedule 22 para 3 defines the tax year to which an SOTP is to be regarded as relating. Schedule 22 para 4 defines the "potential lost-revenue threshold" as reached where the offshore potential lost revenue ("offshore PLR") exceeds £25,000 in relation to any tax year. Schedule 22 para 5 defines the offshore PLR for a tax year as the sum of (a) the potential lost revenue in the case of an SOTP under FA 2007 Sch 24 or FA 2008 Sch 41 and (b) the liability to tax in the case of an SOTP under FA 2009 Sch 55, by reference to which all the SOTPs imposed on the person concerned are assessed for the tax year in question. Rules are provided for identifying the element of a combined penalty (where a part of the potential lost revenue is also attributable to penalties other than an SOTP). Schedule 22 para 6 places a restriction on the imposition on the same person of multiple asset-based penalties in relation to the same asset. Where an SOTP has been imposed on a person and the potential lost revenue threshold is met in relation to more than one tax year in the same "investigation period", that person is to pay no more than one asset-based penalty in the investigation period in relation to any given asset. That single penalty is to be charged by reference to the tax year in the "investigation period" with the highest offshore PLR. An "investigation period" is the period starting with the day on which Sch 22 comes into force and ending on the last day of the last tax year before notice is given to the person concerned of an asset-based penalty in relation to a given asset and subsequent periods beginning with the day after the previous period ended and ending on the last day of the last tax year before notice is given to the person concerned of an asset-based penalty in relation to the same asset.

Schedule 22 para 7 provides that the standard amount of the asset-based penalty is to be the lower of 10% of the value of the asset and 10 times the offshore PLR. Schedule 22 para 8 provides for reduction of the penalty for disclosure and cooperation. HMRC *must* reduce the standard amount of the asset-based penalty where the person concerned does all of the following: (a) makes a disclosure of the inaccuracy or failure relating to the SOTP; (b) provides HMRC with a reasonable valuation of the asset; and (c) provides HMRC with information or access to records that it requires from the person for the purposes of valuing the asset. The amount of the reduction will depend on the quality of the person's cooperation. The maximum amount of the reduction is to be set out in regulations to be made by HM Treasury. Schedule 22 para 9 provides for HMRC to make a special reduction in the penalty if there are special circumstances.

Schedule 22 Pt 3 (paras 10–14) deal with valuation. Schedule 22 para 10 provides that an asset-based penalty may relate to more than one asset. Where the "principal tax at stake" is capital gains tax, Sch 22 para 11 is to apply for identification and valuation; where it is inheritance tax, Sch 22 para 12 is to apply, whereas if asset-based income tax is the principal tax at stake, Sch 22 para 13 is to apply. Where more than one tax is involved in the SOTP(s), the principal tax at stake is the one giving rise to the highest offshore PLR value. Schedule 22 para 11 applies in the case of capital gains tax. The asset concerned is the one whose disposal or deemed disposal gave rise to the capital gains tax to which the SOTP relates. Its value is to be taken as the value of the consideration to be used in the calculation of the chargeable gain under TCGA 1992, except that in the case of part-disposal, the asset-based penalty is to be calculated by reference to the full market value of the asset immediately before the disposal. Schedule 22 para 12 applies in the case of inheritance tax. The asset concerned is the property whose disposition gave rise to the inheritance tax to which the SOTP relates. The value to be used for the penalty is the value HMRC takes for assessing the liability to inheritance tax. Schedule 22 para 13 applies in the case of asset-based income tax. The Table in Sch 22 para 13(2) identifies the asset by reference to the provision under which the income tax is charged. Broadly speaking, if a disposal or part-disposal of the asset takes place during the tax year, it is its market value immediately before the disposal that is taken; if the person still holds the asset at the end of the tax year, the relevant value is its market value on the last day of the tax year. Schedule 22 para 14 prescribes how to value jointly held assets.

Schedule 22 para 15 provides for HMRC to assess the penalty, which must then be paid within 30 days of the issue of the assessment. Assessments to the penalty are normally to be treated as if they were assessments to tax. An asset-based penalty assessment may be made no later than the time limit for making the assessment for the SOTP to which the asset-based penalty relates. Schedule 22 para 16 provides for appeals against the penalty as to the amount. Schedule 22 para 17 provides that the appeal is to be treated in the same way as an appeal against an assessment to the tax concerned. However, the penalty is not thereby to become payable before the appeal is determined. Schedule 22 para 18 prescribes what decision the tribunal may come to on the appeal.

Schedule 22 para 19 provides definitions of some terms. Schedule 22 para 20 makes consequential amendments and Sch 22 para 21 provides that TMA 1970 s 97A is not to apply to an asset-based penalty under Sch 22.

Section 166 introduces a new criminal offence of failing to disclose offshore income and gains. It inserts new TMA 1970 ss 106B–106H.

New TMA 1970 s 106B provides for an offence in relation to giving notice of chargeability to tax. A person who is required under TMA 1970 s 7 to give notice of being chargeable to income tax and/or capital gains tax for a year of assessment and fails to do so by the end of the notification period commits an offence if the tax in question is chargeable wholly or partly by reference to offshore income, assets or activities and the total amount of income tax and capital gains tax chargeable for the year of assessment and attributable to the offshore income, assets or activities exceeds "the threshold amount". Reasonable excuse is to be a defence against a charge under new TMA 1970 s 106B but not the lack of intent.

New TMA 1970 s 106C provides for an offence in relation to delivering a return. A person who is required under TMA 1970 s 8 to make and deliver a return for a year of assessment and fails to do so by the end of the withdrawal period commits an offence if an accurate return would have disclosed liability to income tax and/or capital gains tax chargeable for the year of assessment by reference to offshore income, assets or activities and the total amount of income tax and capital gains tax chargeable for the year of assessment and attributable to the offshore income, assets or activities exceeds "the threshold amount". Reasonable excuse is to be a defence against a charge under new TMA 1970 s 106C but not the lack of intent.

New TMA 1970 s 106D provides for an offence in relation to making an inaccurate return. A person who is required under TMA 1970 s 8 to make and deliver a return for a year of assessment commits an offence if by the end of the amendment period the return contains an inaccuracy to correct which would result in an increase in the amount of income tax and capital gains tax chargeable for the year of assessment and attributable to offshore income, assets or activities and the amount of the increase exceeds "the threshold amount". Reasonable excuse is to be a defence against a charge under new TMA 1970 s 106D but not the lack of intent.

Under new TMA 1970 s 106E a person is not to be guilty of an offence under new TMA 1970 ss 106B, 106C or 106D if he is required to give the notice or make and deliver the return is as a relevant trustee of a settlement or as the executor or administrator of a deceased person.

New TMA 1970 s 106F provides that where a period is extended under TMA 1970 s 118, that extended period is also to apply to the periods referred to in new TMA 1970 ss 106B–106D. The threshold amount is to be set in regulations to be made by HM Treasury but may not be less than £25,000.

New TMA 1970 s 106G provides for the penalties for those found guilty of an offence under new TMA 1970 ss 106B, 106C or 106D. They are to be liable on summary conviction (a) in England and Wales to a fine or imprisonment for a term not exceeding 51 weeks, or to both; (b) in Scotland or Northern Ireland, to a fine not exceeding level 5 on the standard scale or to imprisonment for a term not exceeding six months, or to both. New TMA 1970 s 106H makes provision about regulations under new TMA 1970 ss 106E and 106F.

The amendments made by s 166 are to come into force on a day to be appointed.

PART 11
ADMINISTRATION, ENFORCEMENT AND SUPPLEMENTARY POWERS

Assessment and returns

Section 167 introduces Sch 23, which enables HMRC to make an assessment of an individual's liability to income tax or capital gains tax without a prior requirement on the individual to complete a self-assessment return where HMRC has sufficient information.

Schedule 23 consists of nine paragraphs. Schedule 23 para 1 provides that Sch 23 is to make amendments to TMA 1970. Schedule 23 para 2 amends TMA 1970 s 7 to provide that a person to whom notice is given of a "simple assessment" for the year of assessment is not to be required to give notice of chargeability to tax unless there is any income or gain not included in the simple assessment. Schedule 23 para 3 inserts new TMA 1970 ss 28H–28J.

New TMA 1970 s 28H provides that HMRC may make a simple assessment for a year of assessment on a person unless that person has already delivered a return under TMA 1970 s 8 or is under a requirement to make and deliver a return by virtue of a notice under that section. Such a simple assessment is an assessment of the amounts of income tax and capital gains tax on which the person is chargeable for the particular year of assessment, and of the amount of tax payable taking into account any applicable reliefs and allowances. It must be based on information available to HMRC supplied by the person himself or by a third party.

New TMA 1970 s 28I provides for a simple assessment to be made on trustees and matches new TMA 1970 s 28H with the appropriate modifications.

New TMA 1970 s 28J provides that HMRC may withdraw a simple assessment, which is then to be treated as never having had effect.

Schedule 23 paras 4 and 5 make consequential amendments. Schedule 23 para 6 inserts new TMA 1970 s 31AA, which provides the right to query a simple assessment. A person who has received a simple assessment may query it within 60 days of the issue of the assessment (or later, at HMRC's discretion). HMRC must then consider the query and give a final response, and may postpone the simple assessment in whole or in part to gain more time for consideration. While a simple assessment is postponed, the person concerned is under no obligation to pay the amount charged, unless it relates to a part of the assessment that has not been postponed. HMRC's final response will be to confirm the assessment, make an amended simple assessment or withdraw the simple assessment. Schedule 23 para 7 makes a consequential amendment.

Schedule 23 para 8 inserts new TMA 1970 s 59BA. This provides that the person assessed must pay the difference between the amount of income tax and capital gains tax for the year of assessment shown on the simple assessment and any payments on account the person has made to date and any tax deducted at source. That amount is to be payable on the 31 January immediately following the year of assessment, unless the simple assessment is issued after 31 October immediately following the year of assessment, in which case it is due three months after the date of issue. Schedule 23 para 9 makes a consequential amendment.

With the exception of Sch 23 para 9, the remainder of Sch 23 is to have effect from the tax year 2016/17.

Section 168 seeks to clarify the time limit for making a self-assessment following a notice to make and deliver a return under TMA 1970 ss 8 or 8A. Section 168(2) amends TMA 1970 s 34 to disapply the ordinary four-year time limit under that section to self-assessments, and s 166(3) inserts new TMA 1970 s 34A, which provides that a self-assessment contained in a return under TMA 1970 ss 8 or 8A may be made and delivered at any time not more than four years after the end of the year of assessment to which it relates. Self-assessments for years earlier than 2012/13 may be made and delivered at any time before 6 April 2017.

Section 169 amends TMA 1970 s 8B so that HMRC may withdraw a notice to file a tax return without needing a request to do so from the taxpayer. The amendments made by s 169 have effect in relation to any notice given in relation to tax years beginning with 2014/15.

Judgment debts

Section 170 applies solely in Scotland. It provides that where HMRC is a party to a tax-related judgment debt (in Scots law, where a sum is payable to or by HMRC under a decree or extract issued in court proceedings relating to a taxation matter), the applicable interest rates will be the rates referred to in tax legislation, namely in FA 2009 s 103(1) where the debt is owed to HMRC and in F(No 2)A 2015 s 52 where the debt is owed by HMRC. The equivalent provision for England and Wales was made in F(No 2)A 2015 s 52. Section 170 is to have effect in relation to interest for periods beginning after 14 September 2016.

Section 171 applies solely in Northern Ireland and makes the like provision for judgment debts in Northern Ireland. Section 171 is to have effect in relation to interest for periods beginning after 14 September 2016.

Section 172 applies solely in England and Wales and amends F(No 2)A 2015 s 52 to delete the exclusion of national insurance contributions from the judgment-debts legislation, so that henceforth the rate of interest applicable to tax-related judgments involving national insurance contributions will be that set by tax legislation. Section 172 is to have effect in relation to interest for periods beginning after 14 September 2016.

Enforcement powers

Section 173 amends ITA 2007 s 128 to enable HMRC to make regulations imposing a penalty of no more than £3,000 on intermediaries and charities for failure to comply with obligations relating to gift aid. The amendment is to come into force from a day to be appointed.

Section 174 removes references to HMRC ("the Commissioners") from the definition of the prosecuting authority under CEMA 1979 Pt 11. It also names the Director of Public Prosecutions for Northern Ireland as the prosecuting authority for that territory. The amendments made by s 173 are to apply to proceedings commenced after 14 September 2016.

Section 175 amends CEMA 1979 Schs 2A and 3. Hitherto, CEMA 1979 Sch 2A para 3(2) has exempted HMRC from the duty to take reasonable steps to serve a notice on the owner of any goods to be detained if the detention takes place in the presence of the person whose offence or suspected offence gave rise to the detention or of any servant or agent of the owner. The amendment now made adds a person who has or appears to have possession or control of the thing being detained, and where things are detained from or on a vehicle, the driver, to this class of persons. A similar amendment is made to CEMA 1979 Sch 2A para 4(2), which expands further the class of persons who may give their agreement to the keeping of the thing detained at the place of detention so that it does not have to be removed and to CEMA 1979 Sch 3 para 1(2), which makes the same provisions as to notice in the event of seizure of goods for forfeiture as CEMA 1979 Sch 2A para 3 does for detention of goods. The amendments made by s 175 are to have effect for things detained or seized after 14 September 2016.

Sections 176 and 177 relate to HMRC's bulk-data gathering powers under FA 2011 Sch 23 Pt 2. Section 176 extends those powers to enable HMRC to collect relevant data from providers of electronic stored-value payment services and business intermediaries by the insertion of new FA 2011 Sch 23 paras 13B and 13C. The amendments made by s 176 have effect in relation to relevant data with a bearing on any period. **Section 177** attempts to clarify the position around the daily default penalty imposed under FA 2011 Sch 23 para 31 for continued failure by data-holders to comply with their obligations. The amendments now made to FA 2011 Sch 23 para 38 should make it clear that it is for the tribunal to decide on a new maximum increased daily penalty, which may not be more than £1,000. Consequential amendments are also made.

Payment

Section 178 extends HMRC's rights of set-off under FA 2008 ss 130 and 131, which currently apply only in England, Wales and Northern Ireland, to Scotland. FA 2008 s 130 provides that HMRC may set off credits in relation to a person (sums due by HMRC to that person) against debits (sums due to HMRC by that person). FA 2008 s 131 prohibits HMRC from setting off a post-insolvency credit against a pre-insolvency debit.

Raw tobacco

Section 179 inserts new TPDA 1979 ss 8K-8U and makes consequential amendments. The amendments introduce a new régime for the handling of raw-tobacco products by approved persons. New TPDA 1979 s 8K defines raw tobacco. New TPDA 1979 s 8L requires persons to obtain approval from HMRC before carrying out activities with raw tobacco. New TPDA 1979 s 8M confers regulation-making powers. New TPDA 1979 s 8N provides for exemptions from the requirements for approval. New TPDA 1979 s 8O prescribes penalties for contravention of the new régime. New TPDA 1979 s 8P provides for a special reduction of the penalty in special circumstances. New TPDA 1979 s 8Q provides for the assessment of those penalties. New TPDA 1979 s 8R provides a reasonable-excuse defence. New TPDA 1979 s 8S prevents double jeopardy. New TPDA 1979 s 8T provides for forfeiture in the specified circumstances. New TPDA 1979 s 8U applies provisions of CEMA 1979. The amendments made by s 178 are to come into force from a day or days to be appointed.

State aids granted through provision of tax advantages

Sections 180–182 and Sch 24 introduce new powers for HMRC to collect and publish information on certain state aids in order to comply with EU information obligations. Section 180 and Sch 24 enable HMRC to require that claims made for a tax advantage of the kind listed in Sch 24 Pt 1 are to be accompanied by information of a specified description. In relation to the tax advantages listed in Sch 24 Pt 2, where it appears to HMRC that those advantages have been given or may be given in future, it may require the relevant person to supply specified information.

Schedule 24 has no paragraphs as such but has two Parts, serving the functions described above.

Section 181 enables HMRC to publish any state-aid information where this is necessary to secure compliance with relevant EU obligations. **Section 182** contains definitions and confers regulation-making powers.

Qualifying transformer vehicles

Section 183 confers on HM Treasury the power to make regulations defining "qualifying transformer vehicles" and to provide for special tax treatment for the companies themselves, their investors and transactions involving them. The intention is to enable the creation of a "bespoke" taxation régime for insurance-linked securities business in the UK.

PART 12
OFFICE OF TAX SIMPLIFICATION

Sections 184–189 and Sch 25 provide for the Office of Tax Simplification (OTS) to be put on a permanent statutory footing and for its governance and operation. **Section 184** introduces the OTS and Sch 25. Schedule 25 consists of 15 paragraphs.

Schedule 25 para 1 provides that the OTS may consist of no more than eight members and specifies certain members and their necessary qualifications. Schedule 25 para 2 provides that the term of office of a member may not exceed five years although members may be reappointed. Schedule 25 para 3 provides for initial appointments. Schedule 25 paras 4 and 5 provide for the termination of appointments. Schedule 25 para 6 provides for members to be remunerated. Schedule 25 para 7 provides that the OTS may have staff and facilities provided by HM Treasury. Schedule 25 paras 8 and 9 provide that the OTS may regulate its own procedure. Schedule 25 para 10 provides for supplementary powers. Schedule 25 para 11 provides for financing from the public purse. Schedule 25 paras 12 and 13 disqualify members of parliament and members of the Northern Ireland Assembly from membership of the OTS. Schedule 25 para 14 applies the Freedom of Information Act to the OTS. Schedule 25 para 15 imposes on the OTS public-sector equality duties under the Equality Act 2010 Sch 19 Pt 1.

Section 185 requires the OTS to provide advice to the Chancellor of the Exchequer on the simplification of the tax system. **Section 186** provides that the OTS must conduct reviews as required by the Chancellor of the Exchequer. **Section 187** requires the OTS to produce an annual report. **Section 188** requires HM Treasury to conduct a review of the effectiveness of the OTS before the end of each review period. **Section 189** provides that ss 184–188 and Sch 25 are to come into force on a day to be appointed.

PART 13
FINAL

Section 190 provides a key to interpretation of abbreviations of enactments used in the Act and **s 191** gives the short title.

Zigurds Kronbergs
August 2016

FINANCE ACT 2016

2016 Chapter 24

ARRANGEMENT OF SECTIONS

PART 1

INCOME TAX

PART 2

CORPORATION TAX

Charge and Rates

Research and Development

Loan Relationships

Intangible Fixed Assets

Creative Industry Reliefs

Banking Companies

Oil and Gas

Exploitation of Patents etc

Miscellaneous

PART 3

INCOME TAX AND CORPORATION TAX

Capital Allowances

PART 4

CAPITAL GAINS TAX

PART 5

INHERITANCE TAX ETC

PART 6

APPRENTICESHIP LEVY

PART 7

VAT

PART 8

SDLT AND ATED

Stamp Duty Land Tax

Annual Tax on Enveloped Dwellings

PART 9

OTHER TAXES AND DUTIES

Stamp Duty and Stamp Duty Reserve Tax

An Act to grant certain duties, to alter other duties, and to amend the law relating to the National Debt and the Public Revenue, and to make further provision in connection with finance.

[15th September 2016]

PART 1

INCOME TAX

Charge and Principal Rates etc

1 Income tax charge and rates for 2016–17

(1) Income tax is charged for the tax year 2016–17.

(2) For that tax year

    (a) the basic rate is 20%,
    (b) the higher rate is 40%, and
    (c) the additional rate is 45%.

GENERAL NOTE

Income tax: Charge and principal rates etc

Section 1: Income tax charge and rates for 2016/17

ITA 2007 s 4 provides that income tax is an annual tax.

FA 2016 s 1 imposes the charge for 2016/17, and sub-s (2) sets out the main rates at which income tax for 2016/17 is charged in accordance with ITA 2007 s 6. The basic rate is 20%, the higher rate is 40%, and the additional rate is 45%.

These three rates are subject to the "income tax lock" enacted in F(No 2)A 2015 s 1 which, assuming that the provision is not amended or repealed, will apply from 2016/17 to the tax year beginning before the date of the next general election following the May 2015 election. The effect of the income tax lock is that the basic rate cannot exceed 20%, the higher rate cannot exceed 40% and the additional rate cannot exceed 45%.

There is a growing number of "other" rates at which income tax may be charged, as set out in ITA 2007 s 6(3). For 2016/17 these other rates are as set out in the table:

2016/17 rates	Statutory provisions
Scottish basic, higher and additional rates, which for 2016/17 are identical to the corresponding UK rates ie. 20%, 40% and 45%	ITA 2007 ss 6(3)(za) and ITA 2007 s 6A inserted by FA 2014 s 296, Sch 38 with effect from 2016/17, being the tax year appointed by the Treasury under Scotland Act 2012 s 25(5) (by virtue of SI 2015/2000) as the first year for which a Scottish rate resolution made by the Scottish Parliament under Scotland Act 1998 s 80C (as amended by Scotland Act 2012) was to have effect. ITA 2007 s 6A will be repealed by the Scotland Act 2016 s 14 from a date to be appointed.
Starting rate for savings: 0%	ITA 2007 ss 6(3)(a) and 7
Savings nil-rate: 0%	ITA 2007 ss 6(3)(a) and 7, both amended by FA 2016 s 4
Dividend nil-rate, dividend ordinary rate, dividend upper rate and dividend additional rate: 0%, 7.5%, 32.5% and 38.1% respectively	ITA 2007 ss 6(3)(b) and 8, both amended by FA 2016 s 5
Trust rate and dividend trust rate: 45% and 38.1% respectively	ITA 2007 ss 6(3)(c) and 9, both amended by FA 2016 s 5

In addition, the Wales Act 2014 s 9 will insert with effect from a date to be appointed by Treasury order:
- new ITA 2007 s 6(3)(zb), being a reference to the Welsh basic, higher and additional rates; and
- new ITA 2007 s 6B (Welsh basic, higher and additional rates).

ITA 2007 s 6A, inserted by FA 2014 s 296, Sch 38 with effect from 2016/17, sets out the calculation of the Scottish basic, higher and additional rates. The Scottish Parliament set the Scottish rate at 10% for 2016/17, so that the Scottish basic, higher and additional rates for that year are identical to the corresponding rates for UK taxpayers who are not Scottish taxpayers.

See also FA 2016 s 6 (structure of income tax rates), expected to take effect from 2017/18, which will rename certain rates of income tax in order to distinguish the rates paid by:
- non-UK residents, Scottish taxpayers and Welsh taxpayers; and
- UK residents who are not Scottish or Welsh taxpayers.

2 Basic rate limit for 2017–18

(1) In section 4(1)(b) of FA 2015 (basic rate limit for 2017–18) for "£32,400" substitute "£33,500".

(2) Accordingly, omit section 6(b) of F(No 2)A 2015 (basic rate limit for 2017–18).

GENERAL NOTE

Section 2 amends FA 2015 s 4 to fix the 2017/18 basic rate limit at £33,500. F(No 2)A 2015 s 6, which fixed the limit at £32,400, is repealed.

3 Personal allowance for 2017–18

(1) In section 5(1)(b) of FA 2015 (personal allowance for 2017–18) for "£11,200" substitute "£11,500".

(2) Accordingly, omit section 5(b) of F(No 2)A 2015 (personal allowance for 2017–18).

GENERAL NOTE

Section 3 amends FA 2015 s 5 to fix the 2017/18 personal allowance at £11,500. F(No 2)A 2015 s 5, which fixed the personal allowance at £11,200, is repealed.

Rate Structure

4 Savings allowance, and savings nil rate etc

(1) ITA 2007 is amended in accordance with subsections (2) to (12).

(2) In section 6(3)(a) (other rates: savings), after "starting rate for savings" insert "and savings nil rate".

(3) In section 7 (starting rate for savings)—

  (a) the existing text becomes subsection (1),

  (b) after that subsection insert—

  "(2) The savings nil rate is 0%.", and

  (c) in the heading, after "starting rate for savings" insert "and savings nil rate".

(4) In section 10(4) (provisions displacing charge at basic, higher and additional rates), before the entry relating to section 13 insert—

  "section 12A (savings income charged at the savings nil rate),".

(5) After section 12 insert—

"12A Savings income charged at the savings nil rate

  (1) This section applies in relation to an individual if—

    (a) the amount of the individual's Step 3 income is greater than £L, where £L is the amount of the starting rate limit for savings, and

    (b) when the individual's Step 3 income is split into two parts—

      (i) one ("the individual's income up to the starting rate for savings") consisting of the lowest £L of the individual's Step 3 income, and

      (ii) the other ("the individual's income above the starting rate limit for savings") consisting of the rest of the individual's Step 3 income,

some or all of the individual's income above the starting rate limit for savings consists of savings income (whether or not some or all of the individual's income up to the starting rate limit for savings consists of savings income).

  (2) In this section—

    £A is the amount of the individual's savings allowance (see section 12B),

    "the excess" is so much of the individual's income above the starting rate limit for savings as consists of savings income, and

    £X is the amount of the excess.

  (3) If £X is less than or equal to £A, income tax is charged at the savings nil rate (rather than the basic, higher or additional rate) on the excess.

  (4) If £X is more than £A, income tax is charged at the savings nil rate (rather than the basic, higher or additional rate) on the lowest £A of the excess.

  (5) Subsections (3) and (4) are subject to any provisions of the Income Tax Acts (apart from section 10) which provide for income to be charged at different rates of income tax in some circumstances.

  (6) Section 16 has effect for determining the extent to which the individual's income above the starting rate limit for savings consists of savings income.

(7) For the purposes of this section, an individual's "Step 3 income" is the individual's net income less allowances deducted at Step 3 of the calculation in section 23.

12B Individual's entitlement to a savings allowance

(1) Subsections (2) to (4) determine the amount of an individual's savings allowance for a tax year.

(2) If any of the individual's income for the year is additional-rate income, the individual's savings allowance for the year is nil.

(3) If—

(a) any of the individual's income for the year is higher-rate income, and
(b) none of the individual's income for the year is additional-rate income,

the individual's savings allowance for the year is £500.

(4) If none of the individual's income for the year is higher-rate income, the individual's savings allowance for the year is £1,000.

(5) The Treasury may by regulations substitute a different amount for the amount for the time being specified in subsection (2), (3) or (4); and regulations under this subsection that have effect for a tax year may be made at any time before the end of that tax year.

(6) If regulations under subsection (5) reduce any amount, the regulations may not be made unless a draft of the instrument containing them (whether alone or together with regulations under subsection (5) which increase any amount) has been laid before, and approved by a resolution of, the House of Commons.

(7) Section 1014(4) (negative procedure) does not apply to regulations under subsection (5) which increase any amount if—

(a) the instrument containing them also contains regulations under subsection (5) which reduce any amount, and
(b) a draft of the instrument has been laid before, and approved by a resolution of, the House of Commons.

(8) For the purposes of this section—

(a) each of the following is "additional-rate income"—

(i) income on which income tax is charged at the additional rate or dividend additional rate,
(ii) income on which income tax would be charged at the additional rate but for section 12A (income charged at savings nil rate),
(iii) income on which income tax would be charged at the dividend additional rate but for section 13A (income charged at dividend nil rate), and
(iv) income of an individual who is a Scottish taxpayer or Welsh taxpayer which would, if the individual were not a Scottish taxpayer or Welsh taxpayer (as the case may be), be income on which income tax is charged at the additional rate, and

(b) each of the following is "higher-rate income"—

(i) income on which income tax is charged at the higher rate or dividend upper rate,
(ii) income on which income tax would be charged at the higher rate but for section 12A (income charged at savings nil rate),
(iii) income on which income tax would be charged at the dividend upper rate but for section 13A (income charged at dividend nil rate), and
(iv) income of an individual who is a Scottish taxpayer or Welsh taxpayer which would, if the individual were not a Scottish taxpayer or Welsh taxpayer (as the case may be), be income on which income tax is charged at the higher rate."

(6) In section 16(1) (purposes of rules about highest part of income), before the "and" at the end of paragraph (a) insert—

"(aa) the extent to which a person's income above the starting rate limit for savings consists of savings income,".

(7) In section 17 (repayment where tax paid at basic rate instead of starting rate for savings)—

(a) after subsection (1) insert—

"(1A) This section also applies if income tax at a rate greater than the savings nil rate has been paid on income on which income tax is chargeable at the savings nil rate.", and

(b) in the heading—

(i) for "basic" substitute "greater", and

(ii) after "savings" insert "or savings nil rate".

(8) In sections 55B(2)(b) and 55C(1)(c) (individual liable to tax only at certain rates), after "dividend ordinary rate" insert ", the savings nil rate".

(9) In section 745(1) (transfer of assets abroad: same rate of tax not to be charged twice), after "the starting rate for savings" insert "when that rate is more than 0%,".

(10) In section 828B(5) (individual liable to tax only at certain rates), after "basic rate" insert ", the savings nil rate".

(11) In section 989 (definitions for the purposes of the Income Tax Acts)—
(a) at the appropriate places insert—
""savings allowance" has the meaning given by section 12B,", and
""savings nil rate" means the rate of income tax specified in section 7(2),", and
(b) in the entry for "starting rate of savings", for "has the meaning given by section 7" substitute "means the rate of income tax specified in section 7(1)".

(12) In Schedule 4 (index of defined expressions), at the appropriate places insert—

"savings allowance   section 12B"

"savings nil rate   section 7"

(13) In section 669(3) of ITTOIA 2005 (preventing charge to both income and inheritance tax: meaning of "extra liability"), for paragraphs (a) and (b) substitute—
"(a) income charged at the additional rate or the higher rate were charged at the basic rate, and
(b) income charged at the dividend additional rate or the dividend upper rate were charged at the dividend ordinary rate."

(14) In consequence of the amendment made by subsection (13)—
(a) in Schedule 1 to ITA 2007 omit paragraph 561,
(b) in Schedule 1 to FA 2008 omit paragraph 59, and
(c) in Schedule 2 to FA 2009 omit paragraph 21.

(15) In section 7(6) of TMA 1970 (cases where person not required to give notice of being chargeable to income tax), after "dividend ordinary rate" insert ", the savings nil rate".

(16) In section 91(3)(c) of TMA 1970 (interest adjustments where reliefs given: when to ignore relief from higher rates on income paid subject to deduction of tax) after "basic rate" insert ", the savings nil rate".

(17) Subject to subsection (18), the amendments made by this section have effect for the tax year 2016–17 and subsequent tax years.

(18) The amendments in section 669 of ITTOIA 2005, and the repeals made by subsection (14), have effect where the tax year mentioned in section 669(1)(b) of ITTOIA 2005 is the tax year 2016–17 or a later tax year.

(19) The Treasury may, by regulations made by statutory instrument, make such provision amending, repealing or revoking any provision made by or under the Taxes Acts as the Treasury considers appropriate in consequence of the amendments made by this section; and regulations under this subsection that have effect for the tax year 2016–17 may be made at any time before the end of that tax year.

(20) In subsection (19) "the Taxes Acts" means—
(a) the Tax Acts,
(b) TMA 1970, and
(c) TCGA 1992 and all other enactments relating to capital gains tax.

(21) A statutory instrument containing regulations under subsection (19) is subject to annulment in pursuance of a resolution of the House of Commons.

GENERAL NOTE

Budget 2015 announced a radical reform to the taxation of savings income. A new personal savings allowance, available from 2016/17, provides an exemption for the first £1,000 of savings income for basic rate taxpayers and the first £500 for higher rate taxpayers.

This change, together with abolition of the requirement for banks to deduct income tax from savings interest, means that while some savers are relieved from the task of registering for gross interest or claiming a repayment from HMRC, others will need to pay tax on interest directly to HMRC. Some savers may need to review charitable donations under Gift Aid.

Section 4 amends ITA 2007 from 2016/17 to introduce a savings allowance and a savings nil-rate of income tax. The application of the savings allowance is not straightforward. The allowance is an element in the calculation fixing the amount of savings income chargeable at the savings nil-rate. Savings income is defined in ITA 2007 s 18.

Subsections (2)–(4) amend:

- ITA 2007 s 6(3)(a) to add a reference to the new savings nil-rate;
- ITA 2007 s 7, which fixes the starting rate for savings at 0%, to provide that the new savings nil-rate (which does not replace the starting rate for savings) is 0%;
- ITA 2007 s 10 (income charged at the basic, higher and additional rates) so that the section is now subject to new section 12A (see below).

Section 4 inserts new ITA 2007 s 12A (savings income charged at the savings nil-rate) and new ITA 2007 s 12B (individual's entitlement to a savings allowance) These new provisions are summarised below.

Savings income charged at the savings nil-rate

ITA 2007 s 23 sets out the calculation of an individual's income tax liability.

New ITA 2007 s 12A determines how much of an individual's "step 3 income" (i.e. net income less allowances deducted at step 3 of that calculation) is to be charged at the savings nil-rate where:

- the amount of the step 3 income is greater than £L where £L is the amount of the starting rate limit for savings, currently £5,000; and
- when the step 3 income is split into two parts, being (i) the lowest £L of the step 3 income and (ii) the rest, some or all of the income above the starting rate limit for savings consists, as determined under ITA 2007 s 16 (savings and dividend income to be treated as highest part of total income) as amended, of savings income.

£A below is the amount of the individual's savings allowance (see new ITA 2007 s 12B below), and £X is the amount of the "excess", which is defined as "so much of the individual's income above the starting rate limit for savings as consists of savings income".

Subject to the exceptions mentioned in new ITA 2007 s 12A(5):

- if £X is less than or equal to £A, income tax is charged at the savings nil-rate on the excess; and
- if £X is more than £A, income tax is charged at the savings nil-rate on the lowest £A of the excess.

Individual's entitlement to a savings allowance

New ITA 2007 s 12B provides that an individual's savings allowance is £1,000, £500 or nil as summarised below.

The allowance is £1,000 if none of the individual's income is higher-rate income. Higher-rate income is:

- income charged at the higher rate or dividend upper rate;
- income that would be charged at the higher rate or the dividend upper rate but for new ITA 2007 s 12A and s 13A (income charged at the savings nil-rate and the dividend nil-rate); and
- income of a Scottish taxpayer or Welsh taxpayer which would, but for that tax status, be charged at the higher rate.

The savings allowance is £500 if any of the individual's income is higher-rate income and none of it is additional-rate income.

The savings allowance is nil if any of the income is additional-rate income. Additional-rate income is:

- income charged at the additional rate or the dividend additional rate;
- income that would be charged at the additional rate or the dividend additional rate but for ITA 2007 s 12A and s 13A respectively;
- income of a Scottish taxpayer or Welsh taxpayer which would, but for that tax status, be charged at the additional rate.

The Treasury may amend the amount of the savings allowance by regulations, which may be made at any time before the end of the tax year for which they are to have effect.

There are several consequential amendments to ITA 2007, ITTOIA 2005 and TMA 1970. These include modification of TMA 1970 s 7 (notice of liability to income tax and capital gains tax) to take account of changes to the rate structure.

The effect of new ITA 2007 s 12A is that the new savings nil-rate applies to an individual's savings income that is not covered by other allowances (including the personal allowance) or the 0% starting rate for savings. The table shows the income tax position of taxpayer with pension income of £15,000 and savings income of £2,500 (A) or £3,500 (B).

Example: Savings nil-rate 2016/17	A		B	
Pension		15,000		15,000
Savings income		2,500		3,500
		17,500		18,500
Personal allowance		11,000		11,000
Taxable income		6,500		7,500
Non-savings income 20%	4,000	800.00	4,000	800.00
Starting rate for savings 0% (see note)	1,000	0.00	1,000	0.00
Savings nil-rate 0%	1,000	0.00	1,000	0.00
Savings 20%	500	100.00	1,500	300.00
		900.00		1,100.00
New ITA 1970 s 12A(1)–(4):				
£A: Savings allowance		1,000		1,000
£X: excess		1,500		2,500
Charged at savings nil-rate		1,000		1,000

Note: Income tax is charged at the starting rate for savings, instead of the basic rate, on so much of an individual's taxable income up to the starting rate limit (currently £5,000) as is savings income. The starting rate limit is not available, therefore, where taxable non-savings income exceeds the starting rate limit (see ITA 2007 ss 7, 12 and 16).

5 Rates of tax on dividend income, and abolition of dividend tax credits etc

(1) ITA 2007 is amended in accordance with subsections (2) to (8).

(2) In section 6(3)(b) (other rates: dividends), before "dividend ordinary rate," insert "dividend nil rate,".

(3) In section 8 (dividend ordinary, upper and additional rates)—

(a) in the heading, after "The" insert "dividend nil rate,",

(b) before subsection (1) insert—

"(A1) The dividend nil rate is 0%.",

(c) in subsection (1) (dividend ordinary rate), for "10%" substitute "7.5%", and

(d) in subsection (3) (dividend additional rate), for "37.5%" substitute "38.1%".

(4) In section 9(2) (dividend trust rate), for "37.5%" substitute "38.1%".

(5) After section 13 insert—

"13A Income charged at the dividend nil rate

(1) Subsection (2) applies if, ignoring this section, at least some of an individual's income would be charged to income tax at the dividend ordinary rate, the dividend upper rate or the dividend additional rate.

(2) Income tax is charged at the dividend nil rate (rather than the dividend ordinary rate, dividend upper rate or dividend additional rate) on one or more amounts of the individual's income as follows—

Step 1

Identify the amount ("D") of the individual's income which would, ignoring this section, be charged at the dividend ordinary rate.

Rule 1A: If D is more than £5,000, the first £5,000 of D is charged at the dividend nil rate (rather than the dividend ordinary rate), and is the only amount charged at the dividend nil rate.

Rule 1B: If D is equal to £5,000, D is charged at the dividend nil rate (rather than the dividend ordinary rate), and is the only amount charged at the dividend nil rate.
Rule 1C: If D is less than £5,000 but more than nil, D is charged at the dividend nil rate (rather than the dividend ordinary rate).

Step 2
If D is less than £5,000, identify the amount ("U") of the individual's income which would, ignoring this section, be charged at the dividend upper rate.
Rule 2A: If the total of D and U is more than £5,000—

(a) the first £M of U is charged at the dividend nil rate (rather than the dividend upper rate), where £M is the difference between £5,000 and D, and
(b) the amounts charged under this Rule and Rule 1C are the only amounts charged at the dividend nil rate.

Rule 2B: If the total of D and U is equal to £5,000, U is charged at the dividend nil rate (rather than the dividend upper rate), and the amounts charged under this Rule and Rule 1C are the only amounts charged at the dividend nil rate.
Rule 2C: If the total of D and U is less than £5,000 but more than nil, U is charged at the dividend nil rate (rather than the dividend upper rate).

Step 3
If the total of D and U is less than £5,000, identify the amount ("A") of the individual's income which would, ignoring this section, be charged at the dividend additional rate.
Rule 3A: If the total of D, U and A is more than £5,000, the first £X of A is charged at the dividend nil rate (rather than the dividend additional rate), where £X is the difference between—

£5,000, and
the total of D and U,

and the amounts charged under this Rule, and Rules 1C and 2C, are the amounts charged at the dividend nil rate.
Rule 3B: If the total of D, U and A is less than or equal to £5,000, A is charged at the dividend nil rate (rather than the dividend additional rate), and the amounts charged under this Rule, and Rules 1C and 2C, are the amounts charged at the dividend nil rate."

(6) In section 55B(2) (transferable allowance: conditions for entitlement to tax reduction)—

(a) in paragraph (b) (individual liable to tax only at certain rates), after "the basic rate," insert "the dividend nil rate,", and
(b) after paragraph (b) insert—
"(ba) if for the tax year the individual is liable to tax at the dividend nil rate, the individual would for that year neither be liable to tax at the dividend upper rate, nor be liable to tax at the dividend additional rate, if section 13A (dividend nil rate) were omitted,".

(7) In section 55C(1) (transferable allowance: conditions for entitlement to elect for reduced personal allowance)—

(a) in paragraph (c) (individual would be liable to tax only at certain rates), after "the basic rate," insert "the dividend nil rate,", and
(b) before the "and" at the end of paragraph (c) insert—
"(ca) where on that assumption the individual would for the tax year be liable to tax at the dividend nil rate, the individual on that assumption would for that year neither be liable to tax at the dividend upper rate, nor be liable to tax at the dividend additional rate, if section 13A (dividend nil rate) were omitted,".

(8) In section 989 (definitions for the purposes of the Income Tax Acts), after the entry for "dividend income" insert—

""dividend nil rate" means the rate of income tax specified in section 8(A1),".

(9) In section 7 of TMA 1970 (duty to notify HMRC of liability to tax)—

(a) in subsection (6) (exception for net payments etc)—
(i) after paragraph (a) insert "or",
(ii) at the end of paragraph (b), for "; or" substitute a comma,
(iii) omit paragraph (c), and
(iv) in the words after paragraph (c), after "the basic rate" insert ", the dividend nil rate", and
(b) after subsection (6) insert—

"(6A) A source of income falls within this subsection in relation to any person and any year of assessment if for that year—

    (a) all income from the source is dividend income (see section 19 of ITA 2007), and

    (b) the person—

        (i) is UK-resident,

        (ii) is not liable to tax at the dividend ordinary rate,

        (iii) is not liable to tax at the dividend upper rate,

        (iv) is not liable to tax at the dividend additional rate, and

        (v) is not charged to tax under section 832 of ITTOIA 2005 (relevant foreign income charged on remittance basis) on any dividend income."

(10) The amendments made by the preceding provisions of this section have effect for the tax year 2016–17 and subsequent tax years.

(11) Schedule 1 contains provision for, and connected with, the abolition of dividend tax credits etc.

GENERAL NOTE

Summer Budget 2015 announced that from April 2016 the dividend tax credit would be replaced by a new tax-free "dividend allowance" of £5,000 a year for all taxpayers. "This will ensure that ordinary investors with smaller portfolios and modest dividend income will see no change in their tax liability, and some will pay less tax," the Government said. However, at the same time the rates of tax charged on dividends in excess of the new allowance were to be amended, so that taxpayers receiving more significant dividend income from either a family company or a larger portfolio of shares would pay more tax.

The Government said these changes would "start to reduce the incentive to incorporate and remunerate through dividends rather than through wages to reduce tax liabilities".

Section 5 and Sch 1 amend ITA 2007 to introduce a dividend nil-rate (this is the dividend "allowance") and abolish the dividend tax credit.

Subsections (2)–(4) of s 5 amend ITA 2007 ss 6, 8 and 9 (as indicated in the table to the general note on FA 2016 s 1, see above) in order to:

- Insert references to the new dividend nil-rate in ITA 2007 ss 6 and 8;
- provide in ITA 2007 s 8 that the dividend nil-rate is 0% and the dividend ordinary rate is 7.5% (previously 10%, subject to a tax credit). There is no change to the dividend upper rate of 32.5%; and
- provide in ITA 2007 s 9 that the dividend additional rate and the dividend trust rate are both 38.1% (previously 37.5%, subject to a tax credit).

Income charged at the dividend nil-rate

ITA 2007 ss 10–15 determine the income to be charged at the various income tax rates.

Section 5 inserts a new ITA 2007 s 13A (income charged at the dividend nil-rate). Three steps are prescribed where, in their absence, at least some of an individual's income would be charged at the dividend ordinary rate, the dividend upper rate or the dividend additional rate.

Income tax is charged at the dividend nil-rate on one or more amounts of the individual's income as follows:

Step 1: Identify the amount ("D") of the income that would otherwise be charged at the dividend ordinary rate, following rules 1A to 1C below:

- 1A: if D is more than £5,000, the first £5,000 only of D is charged at the dividend nil-rate;
- 1B: if D is £5,000, D is charged at the dividend nil-rate; and
- 1C: if D is less than £5,000 but more than nil, D is charged at the dividend nil-rate.

Step 2: If D is less than £5,000, identify the amount ("U") of the income that would otherwise be charged at the dividend upper rate, following rules 2A to 2C below:

- 2A: if the total of D and U is more than £5,000, then the first £M of U is charged at the dividend nil-rate, where £M is the difference between £5,000 and D, and the amounts charged under this rule 2A and rule 1C above are the only amounts charged at the dividend nil-rate;
- 2B: if the total of D and U is £5,000, U is charged at the dividend nil-rate, and the amounts charged under this rule 2B and rule 1C are the only amounts charged at the dividend nil-rate; and

- 2C: if the total of D and U is less than £5,000 but more than nil, U is charged at the dividend nil-rate.

Step 3: If the total of D and U is less than £5,000, identify the amount ("A") of the income that would otherwise be charged at the dividend additional rate, following rules 3A and 3B below:

- 3A: If the total of D, U and A is more than £5,000, the first £X of A is charged at the dividend nil-rate, where £X is the difference between (i) £5,000, and (ii) the total of D and U. The amounts charged under this rule 3A, and rules 1C and 2C, are the amounts charged at the dividend nil-rate;
- 3B: if the total of D, U and A is less than or equal to £5,000, A is charged at the dividend nil-rate, and the amounts charged under this rule 3B, and rules 1C and 2C, are the amounts charged at the dividend nil-rate.

The table shows the income tax position of taxpayer with earnings of £12,000 (A) or £40,000 (B) and dividend income of £10,000. Scenario (B) shows that the reference to an allowance is misleading because income charged at the new dividend nil-rate may use up part of the basic rate band, increasing the rate of tax payable on dividend income in excess of £5,000.

Example: Dividend nil-rate 2016/17		A		B
Earnings		12,000		40,000
Dividends		10,000		10,000
		22,000		50,000
Personal allowance		11,000		11,000
Taxable income		11,000		39,000
Non-savings income 20%	1,000	200.00	29,000	5,800.00
Dividend nil-rate 0%	5,000	0.00	5,000	0.00
Dividend ordinary rate 7.5%	5,000	375.00	0	0.00
Dividend upper rate 32.5%	0	0.00	5,000	1,625.00
		575.00		7,425.00

Other amendments

Section 5 also sets out consequential amendments to:
- ITA 2007 s 55B(2) (transferable tax allowance for married couples and civil partners: conditions for entitlement to tax reduction);
- ITA 2007 s 55C(1) (transferable tax allowance: conditions for entitlement to elect for reduced personal allowance);
- ITA 2007 s 989 (inserting a definition of dividend nil-rate);
- TMA 1970 s 7 (notice of liability to income tax and capital gains tax).

6 Structure of income tax rates

(1) ITA 2007 is amended in accordance with subsections (2) to (22).

(2) Before section 10 insert—

"9A Overview of sections 10 to 15

The general effect of sections 10 to 15 is outlined in the following table—

Type of taxpayer	*Rates payable on savings income*	*Rates payable on most dividend income*	*Rates payable on other income*
UK resident individual who is neither a Scottish taxpayer nor a Welsh taxpayer	Savings rates	Dividend rates	Main rates
Scottish taxpayer	Savings rates	Dividend rates	Scottish rates
Welsh taxpayer	Savings rates	Dividend rates	Main rates while section 11B is not in force; Welsh rates if that section is in force
Non-UK resident individual	Savings rates	Dividend rates	Default rates
Non-individual, except that some trustees in some circumstances are subject instead to the trust rate or the dividend trust rate	Default basic rate	Dividend ordinary rate	Default basic rate

Note: the table does not address the effect of some exceptions referred to in sections 10 to 15."

(3) Before section 7 insert—

"6C The default basic, higher and additional rates

The default basic rate, default higher rate and default additional rate for a tax year are the rates determined as such by Parliament for the tax year."

(4) After section 7 insert—

"7A The savings basic, higher and additional rates

The savings basic rate, savings higher rate and savings additional rate for a tax year are the rates determined as such by Parliament for the tax year."

(5) In section 6(3) (other rates)—

(a) before paragraph (a) insert—

"(zc) section 6C (default basic, higher and additional rates),", and

(b) after paragraph (a) insert—

"(aa) section 7A (savings basic, higher and additional rates),".

(6) In section 10(2) (income charged at basic rate) omit the words after "at the basic rate".

(7) In section 10(4) (provisions displacing charge at basic, higher and additional rates), before the entry (inserted by this Act) relating to section 12A insert—

"section 11C (income charged at the default basic, higher and additional rates: non-UK resident individuals),

section 11D (savings income charged at the savings basic, higher and additional rates: individuals),

section 12 (savings income charged at the starting rate for savings),".

(8) In section 11 (income charged at the basic rate: other persons)—

(a) in the heading, for "basic rate: other persons" substitute "default basic rate: non-individuals", and

(b) in subsection (1), before "basic" insert "default".

(9) After section 11B insert—

"11C Income charged at the default basic, higher and additional rates: non-UK resident individuals

(1) Income tax on a non-UK resident individual's income up to the basic rate limit is charged at the default basic rate.

(2) Income tax is charged at the default higher rate on a non-UK resident individual's income above the basic rate limit and up to the higher rate limit.

(3) Income tax is charged at the default additional rate on a non-UK resident individual's income above the higher rate limit.

(4) Subsections (1) to (3) are subject to—

section 11D (savings income charged at the savings basic, higher and additional rates),

section 12 (savings income charged at the starting rate for savings),

section 12A (savings income charged at the savings nil rate),

section 13 (income charged at the dividend ordinary, upper and additional rates: individuals), and

any other provisions of the Income Tax Acts (apart from section 10) which provide for income to be charged at different rates of income tax in some circumstances.

11D Income charged at the savings basic, higher and additional rates

(1) Income tax is charged at the savings basic rate on an individual's income which—

(a) is saving income, and

(b) would otherwise be charged at the basic rate or the default basic rate.

(2) Income tax is charged at the savings higher rate on an individual's income which—

(a) is savings income, and

(b) would otherwise be charged at the higher rate or the default higher rate.

(3) Income tax is charged at the savings additional rate on an individual's income which—

(a) is savings income, and

(b) would otherwise be charged at the additional rate or the default additional rate.

(4) Subsections (1) to (3)—

(a) have effect after sections 12 and 12A have been applied (so that any reference in subsections (1) to (3) to income which would otherwise be charged at a particular rate does not include income charged at the starting rate for savings or at the savings nil rate), and

(b) are subject to any other provisions of the Income Tax Acts (apart from sections 10 and 11C) which provide for income to be charged at different rates of income tax in some circumstances.

(5) Section 16 has effect for determining the extent to which an individual's savings income above the starting rate limit for savings would otherwise be charged at the basic, higher or additional rate or the default basic, default higher or default additional rate.

(6) In relation to an individual who is a Scottish taxpayer, references in this section to income which would otherwise be charged at a particular rate are to be read as references to income that would, if the individual were not a Scottish taxpayer (but were UK resident), be charged at that rate (and subsection (5) is to be read accordingly)."

(10) In section 12(1) (income charged at the starting rate for savings)—

(a) omit "(rather than the basic rate)", and

(b) for "as is savings income" substitute "as—

(a) is savings income, and

(b) would otherwise be charged at the basic rate or the default basic rate".

(11) In section 12A (inserted by this Act)—

(a) in each of subsections (3) and (4), after "rather than the basic, higher or additional rate" insert "or the default basic, default higher or default additional rate", and

(b) in subsection (5), for "section 10" substitute "sections 10 and 11C".

(12) In section 12B (inserted by this Act), in subsection (8) (income charged at savings nil-rate: meaning of "additional-rate income" and "higher-rate income")—

(a) in paragraph (a)(i), after "at the additional rate" insert ", default additional rate",

(b) in paragraph (a)(ii), after "additional rate" insert ", or default additional rate,",

(c) in paragraph (a)(iv), after "additional rate" insert "or default additional rate",

(d) in paragraph (b)(i), after "at the higher rate" insert ", default higher rate",

(e) in paragraph (b)(ii), after "higher rate" insert ", or default higher rate,", and

(f) in paragraph (b)(iv), after "higher rate" insert "or default higher rate".

(13) In section 16(1) (purposes of rules about highest part of income), before the "and" at the end of the paragraph (aa) (inserted by this Act) insert—

"(ab) the rate at which income tax would be charged on a person's savings income above the starting rate limit for savings apart from sections 11D and 12A,".

(14) In section 17(1) (repayment where tax paid at basic rate instead of starting rate for savings), for "at the basic rate" substitute "at a rate greater than the starting rate for savings".

(15) In section 55B (entitlement to transferable tax allowances for married couples and civil partners)—

(a) in subsection (2)(b) as amended by section 5 of this Act, after "other than the basic rate," insert "the default basic rate, the savings basic rate,", and

(b) in subsection (3), after "is the basic rate" insert "or default basic rate".

(16) In section 55C(1)(c) (election to reduce personal allowance conditional on not becoming subject to higher rates) as amended by section 5 of this Act, after "other than the basic rate," insert "the default basic rate, the savings basic rate,".

(17) In section 58(2) ("adjusted net income" includes grossed-up gift aid donations), after "grossed up by reference to the basic rate for the tax year" insert "if for the tax year the individual is UK resident but not a Scottish taxpayer, by reference to the default basic rate for the tax year if for the tax year the individual is non-UK resident".

(18) In section 414(2)(a) (gift aid donation treated as made after deduction of tax at the basic rate or Scottish basic rate), before the "or" at the end of sub-paragraph (i) insert—

"(ia) at the default basic rate if for the tax year the individual is non-UK resident,".

(19) In section 415 (grossing-up rate for gift aid purposes), after "the basic rate for the tax year in which the gift is made" insert "if the gift is made by an individual who for that tax year is UK resident but not a Scottish taxpayer, by reference to the default basic rate for that tax year if the gift is made by an individual who for that tax year is non-UK resident".

(20) In section 828B(5) (exemption for non-domiciled UK residents conditional on not being subject to higher rates) as amended by section 4 of this Act, after "other than the basic rate" insert ", the savings basic rate".

(21) In section 989 (definitions for the purposes of the Income Tax Acts), at the appropriate places insert—

""default additional rate" means the rate of income tax of that name determined pursuant to section 6C,

"default basic rate" means the rate of income tax of that name determined pursuant to section 6C,

"default higher rate" means the rate of income tax of that name determined pursuant to section 6C,"

and—

""savings additional rate" means the rate of income tax of that name determined pursuant to section 7A,"

and—

""savings basic rate" means the rate of income tax of that name determined pursuant to section 7A,

"savings higher rate" means the rate of income tax of that name determined pursuant to section 7A,".

(22) In Schedule 4 (index of defined expressions), at the appropriate places insert—

"default additional rate	section 6C (as applied by section 989)"
"default basic rate	section 6C (as applied by section 989)"
"default higher rate	section 6C (as applied by section 989)"
"savings additional rate	section 7A (as applied by section 989)"
"savings basic rate	section 7A (as applied by section 989)"
"savings higher rate	section 7A (as applied by section 989)"

(23) In sections 4(4) and (5) and 4BA(1) of TCGA 1992 (rate of capital gains tax depends on individual's liability to higher rates of income tax), after "at the higher rate" insert ", the default higher rate, the savings higher rate".

(24) Subject to any provision made by virtue of subsection (25)(b), the amendments made by this section come into force on the day appointed by the Treasury under section 13(14) of the Scotland Act 2016 and have effect—

(a) for the tax year appointed by the Treasury under section 13(15) of the Scotland Act 2016, and

(b) for subsequent tax years.

(25) The Treasury may by regulations make—

(a) such consequential provision as they consider appropriate in connection with any preceding provision of this section;

(b) such transitional or saving provision as they consider appropriate in connection with the coming into force of any provision of the preceding subsections of this section.

(26) Regulations under this section may amend, repeal or revoke an enactment, whenever passed or made (including this Act).

(27) Regulations under this section must be made by statutory instrument.

(28) A statutory instrument containing regulations under this section which includes provision amending or repealing a provision of an Act may not be made unless a draft of the instrument has been laid before and approved by a resolution of the House of Commons.

(29) Any other statutory instrument containing regulations under this section, if made without a draft having been approved by a resolution of the House of Commons, is subject to annulment in pursuance of a resolution of the House of Commons.

(30) In subsection (26) "enactment" includes an enactment contained in subordinate legislation (within the meaning of the Interpretation Act 1978).

GENERAL NOTE

Section 6 introduces more complexity into the income tax system to facilitate votes under the "English votes for English laws" (EVEL) procedure following the devolution of tax rate setting powers to Scotland.

Income tax rates for savings and dividend income are not being devolved and will continue to be set by the UK Parliament. Section 6 renames the income tax rates applicable to savings and dividend income in order to distinguish them from the rates applying other income. It also introduces a "default rate".

These changes are expected to take effect from 2017/18. They are intended to ensure that, when the Scottish Parliament has the power to set rates and thresholds for the non-savings, non-dividends income of Scottish taxpayers, English, Welsh and Northern Irish MPs will be able to vote under the "English votes for English laws" (EVEL) procedure for the UK rates that are not devolved.

Subject to any transitional or saving provisions, the amendments made by s 6 will come into force on the day appointed by the Treasury under Scotland Act 2016 s 13(14) (power of Scottish Parliament to set rates of income tax), with effect for the tax year appointed under Scotland Act 2016 s 13(15) as the first tax year for which the Scottish Parliament will be able to set rates and thresholds for non-savings, non-dividends income.

With effect from the same tax year, Scotland Act 2016 s 14 will make several amendments to ITA 2007 in order to remove the charge to income tax at the "Scottish basic, higher and additional rates" and provide instead that income tax is charged on a Scottish taxpayer's non-savings, non-dividend income at "Scottish rates", i.e. the rates set by a resolution of the Scottish Parliament under Scotland Act 1998 s 80C.

Subsections (1)–(22) of FA 2016 s 6 will amend ITA 2007.

New ITA 2007 s 9A provides in table form an overview of the new rates structure – it does not address certain exceptions. The table shows that a UK-resident individual who is not a Scottish or Welsh taxpayer will pay:

- "savings rates" on savings income;
- "dividend rates" on most dividend income; and
- "main rates" on other income.

A Scottish taxpayer will pay:

- "savings rates" on savings income;
- "dividend rates" on most dividend income; and
- "Scottish rates" on other income.

A Welsh taxpayer will pay:

- "savings rates" on savings income;
- "dividend rates" on most dividend income; and
- either (i) "main rates" on other income while ITA 2007 s 11B (income charged at the Welsh basic, higher and additional rates, which is to be inserted by Wales Act 2014 s 9 with effect from a date to be appointed) is not in force, or (ii) "Welsh rates" if ITA 2007 s 11B is in force.

A non-UK resident individual will pay:

- "savings rates" on savings income;
- "dividend rates" on most dividend income; and
- "default rates" on other income.

Separate rules will apply to trustees.

New TMA 1970 ss 6C and 7A will create the "default" rates and the "savings" rates. The default basic rate, default higher rate and default additional rate for a tax year, and the savings basic rate, savings higher rate and savings additional rate for a tax year, will be the rates that Parliament determines as such for the year.

Subsection (5) will amend ITA 2007 s 6(3) to provide that the "other" rates at which income tax is charged include the new default rates and savings rates, and there are consequential amendments to TMA 1970 ss 10 and 11.

Subsection (9) will insert new ITA 2007 ss 11C and 11D.

New s 11C will provide that income tax on a non-UK resident individual's income is charged at the new "default" basic, higher and additional rates except in relation to savings income, dividend income and any income to which any other provision providing for a different rate, such as the Scottish rates, applies.

New ITA 2007 s 11D (income charged at the savings basic, higher and additional rates) will provide that:

- a new "savings basic rate" is charged on savings income that would otherwise be charged at the basic rate or the default basic rate;
- a new "savings higher rate" is charged on savings income that would otherwise be charged at the higher rate or the default higher rate; and
- a new "savings additional rate" is charged on savings income that would otherwise be charged at the additional rate or the default additional rate.

This rule will have effect only after ITA 2007 s 12 and new ITA 2007 s 12A, which apply the starting rate for savings and the new savings nil-rate, have been applied. It will also be subject to any other provisions of the Income Tax Acts (other than ITA 2007 ss 10 and 11C) which provide for income to be charged at different rates in some circumstances.

ITA 2007 s 16 (savings and dividend income to be treated as highest part of total income) will be applied in determining the extent to which savings income above the starting rate limit for savings would otherwise be charged at the basic, higher or additional rate or the default basic, default higher or default additional rate.

These provisions of new ITA 2007 s 11D will be modified for Scottish taxpayers. References to income that would otherwise be charged at a particular rate are to be read as references to income that would, if the individual were not a Scottish taxpayer (but were UK resident), be charged at that rate.

Subsections (10)–(12) will amend ITA 2007 ss 12(1), 12A and 12B respectively to take account of the introduction of the default rates. There will also be amendments to:

- ITA 2007 ss 16 (savings and dividend income to be treated as higher part of total income), 17 (repayment: tax paid at basic rate instead of starting rate for savings), 55B and 55C(1)(c) (transferable tax allowance for married couples and civil partners), 58(2) ("adjusted net income" includes grossed-up gift aid donations), 414(2)(a) (gift aid donation treated as made after deduction of tax at the basic rate or Scottish basic rate), 415 (grossing-up rate for gift aid purposes), 828B(5) (exemption for non-domiciled UK residents), 989 and Sch 4 (definitions); and
- TCGA 1992 ss 4 and 4BA (rate of capital gains tax depends on individual's liability to higher rates of income tax).

Employment Income: Taxable Benefits

7 Taxable benefits: application of Chapters 5 to 7 of Part 3 of ITEPA 2003

(1) Part 3 of ITEPA 2003 (employment income: earnings and benefits etc treated as earnings) is amended as follows.

(2) In section 97 (living accommodation to which Chapter 5 applies), after subsection (1) insert—

"(1A) Where this Chapter applies to any living accommodation—

(a) the living accommodation is a benefit for the purposes of this Chapter (and accordingly it is immaterial whether the terms on which it is provided to any of those persons constitute a fair bargain), and

(b) sections 102 to 108 provide for the cash equivalent of the benefit of the living accommodation to be treated as earnings."

(3) In section 109 (priority of Chapter 5 over Chapter 1), after subsection (3) insert—

"(4) In a case where the cash equivalent of the benefit of the living accommodation is nil—

(a) subsections (2) and (3) do not apply, and

(b) the full amount mentioned in subsection (1)(b) constitutes earnings from the employment for the year under Chapter 1."

(4) In section 114 (cars, vans and related benefits to which Chapter 6 applies), after subsection (1) insert—

"(1A) Where this Chapter applies to a car or van, the car or van is a benefit for the purposes of this Chapter (and accordingly it is immaterial whether the terms on which it is made available to the employee or member constitute a fair bargain)."

(5) For section 117 substitute—

"117 Meaning of car or van made available by reason of employment

(1) For the purposes of this Chapter a car or van made available by an employer to an employee or member of an employee's family or household is to be regarded as made available by reason of the employment unless subsection (2) or (3) excludes the application of this subsection.

(2) Subsection (1) does not apply where—

(a) the employer is an individual, and

(b) the car or van in question is made available in the normal course of the employer's domestic, family or personal relationships.

(3) Subsection (1) does not apply where—

(a) the employer carries on a vehicle hire business under which cars or vans of the same kind are made available to members of the public for hire,

(b) the car or van in question is hired to the employee or member in the normal course of that business, and

(c) in hiring that car or van the employee or member is acting as an ordinary member of the public."

(6) In section 120 (benefit of car treated as earnings)—

(a) in subsection (2) after "case" insert "(including a case where the cash equivalent of the benefit of the car is nil)", and

(b) after subsection (2) insert—

"(3) Any reference in this Act to a case where the cash equivalent of the benefit of a car is treated as the employee's earnings for a year by virtue of this section includes a case where the cash equivalent is nil."

(7) In section 154 (benefit of van treated as earnings)—

(a) the existing text becomes subsection (1) of that section, and

(b) after that subsection insert—

"(2) In such a case (including a case where the cash equivalent of the benefit of the van is nil) the employee is referred to in this Chapter as being chargeable to tax in respect of the van for that year.

(3) Any reference in this Act to a case where the cash equivalent of the benefit of a van is treated as the employee's earnings for a year by virtue of this section includes a case where the cash equivalent is nil."

(8) In section 173 (loans to which Chapter 7 applies), after subsection (1) insert—

"(1A) Where this Chapter applies to a loan—

(a) the loan is a benefit for the purposes of this Chapter (and accordingly it is immaterial whether the terms of the loan constitute a fair bargain), and

(b) sections 175 to 183 provide for the cash equivalent of the benefit of the loan (where it is a taxable cheap loan) to be treated as earnings in certain circumstances."

(9) The amendments made by this section have effect for the tax year 2016–17 and subsequent tax years.

GENERAL NOTE

FA 2016 s 7 amends and introduces new legislation into ITEPA 2003 Pt 3 (employment income: earnings and benefits etc treated as earnings) in respect of employer-provided living accommodation; cars, vans and related benefits; and beneficial loans. The amendments are effective for the 2016/17 tax year and subsequent tax years.

The changes do not represent a change to government policy but are being made to remove uncertainty about the application of the concept of "fair bargain" to benefits chargeable under ITEPA 2003 Pt 3 Chs 3–9.

The purpose of the changes is to ensure that the concept of "fair bargain" does not apply to certain taxable benefits in kind where there are specific rules to determine the amount of the benefit. In such a circumstance, the benefit in kind is calculated based on the specific charging rules and any employee payments are deducted from the charge. The concept of "fair bargain" is relevant for ITEPA 2003 Pt 3 Ch 10.

The changes also ensure that where a benefit falls into Pt 3 Chs 5 or 6, which is valued at nil, it remains a taxable benefit. This ensures that other charges remain which rely on benefits arising under Chs 5 or 6 being treated as earnings.

FA 2016 s 7(2) introduces new ITEPA 2003 s 97(1A) which relates to living accommodation provided by reason of employment and states that such a provision will be treated as a benefit even where fair bargain applies. New s 97(1A) also includes signposting to other relevant sections of ITEPA.

FA 2016 s 7(3) introduces new ITEPA 2003 s 109(4) which sets out that if the cash equivalent of living accommodation is nil the benefit will not treated as earnings under Pt 3 Ch 5 but will still be treated as earnings (of nil) arising under Pt 3 Ch 1.

FA 2016 s 7(4) introduces new ITEPA 2003 s 114(1A) which relates to cars, vans and related benefits. This makes it clear that for the purposes of s 114(1) it is immaterial whether the terms on which the car or van is made available constitute a fair bargain.

FA 2016 s 7(5) substitutes a new ITEPA 2003 s 117 which provides an extended definition of the meaning of "car or van made available by reason of employment". The new s 117(3) introduces when the hiring of a car or van from an employer whose business is to hire cars and vans is not made available by reason of employment.

FA 2016 s 7(6) amends existing ITEPA 2003 s 120(2) and introduces a new sub-s (3) in respect of cars and FA 2016 s 7(7) introduces new sub-ss (2) and (3) to ITEPA 2003 s 154 in respect of vans. These new subsections provide that where the cash equivalent of the benefit of a car or van is nil the benefit is still to be treated as earnings for other parts of the ITEPA.

FA 2016 s 7(8) introduces new ITEPA 2003 s 173(1A) in respect of employment-related loans and makes it clear that in deciding whether a loan is an employment-related loan, it is immaterial whether the terms of the loan constitute a fair bargain. This new section also includes signposting to other relevant sections of ITEPA 2003.

8 Cars: appropriate percentage for 2019–20 and subsequent tax years

(1) ITEPA 2003 is amended as follows.

(2) Section 139 (car with a CO_2 figure: the appropriate percentage) is amended as set out in subsections (3) and (4).

(3) In subsection (2)—

    (a) in paragraph (a), for "13%" substitute "16%",
    (b) in paragraph (aa), for "16%" substitute "19%", and
    (c) in paragraph (b), for "19%" substitute "22%".

(4) In subsection (3), for "20%" substitute "23%".

(5) Section 140 (car without a CO_2 figure: the appropriate percentage) is amended as set out in subsections (6) and (7).

(6) In subsection (2), in the Table—

    (a) for "20%" substitute "23%", and
    (b) for "31%" substitute "34%".

(7) In subsection (3)(a), for "13%" (as substituted by section 9(3)) substitute "16%".

(8) In section 142(2) (car first registered before 1 January 1998: the appropriate percentage), in the Table—

    (a) for "20%" substitute "23%", and
    (b) for "31%" substitute "34%".

(9) The amendments made by this section have effect for the tax year 2019–20 and subsequent tax years.

GENERAL NOTE

FA 2016 s 8 amends ITEPA 2003 Pt 3 Ch 6 (taxable benefits: cars, vans and related benefits) to insert revised figures for the appropriate percentages in ITEPA 2003 ss 139–142 for the tax year 2019/20. The appropriate percentages determined by those sections are used to calculate the taxable benefit arising when a car is made available by reason of an individual's employment and is available for private use. The appropriate percentage varies according to the car's CO_2 emissions figure or cylinder capacity.

The effect of these changes is to increase the level of chargeable benefit for taxing company cars for employees.

9 Cars which cannot emit CO_2: appropriate percentage for 2017–18 and 2018–19

(1) In section 140(3)(a) of ITEPA 2003 (car which cannot emit CO_2: the appropriate percentage), for "7%" substitute "9%".

(2) The amendment made by subsection (1) has effect for the tax year 2017–18.

(3) In section 140(3)(a) of ITEPA 2003, for "9%" substitute "13%".

(4) The amendment made by subsection (3) has effect for the tax year 2018–19.

GENERAL NOTE

FA 2016 s 9 amends the appropriate percentage in ITEPA 2003 s 140(3)(a) for calculating the cash equivalent of the taxable benefit for cars without a registered CO$_2$ emissions figure and which cannot produce emissions under any circumstances when driven.

For tax year 2017/18 the appropriate percentage increases from 7% to 9% and for the 2018/19 tax year it will increase further from 9% to 13%.

10 Diesel cars: appropriate percentage

(1) In section 24 of FA 2014 (cars: the appropriate percentage), omit the following ("the repealing provisions")—

    (a) subsection (2),
    (b) subsection (6),
    (c) subsection (10),
    (d) subsection (11), and
    (e) subsection (15).

(2) Any provision of ITEPA 2003 amended or omitted by the repealing provisions has effect for the tax year 2016–17 and subsequent tax years as if the repealing provisions had not been enacted.

GENERAL NOTE

FA 2016 s 10 ensures that the diesel supplement of three percentage points applied to calculate the taxable benefit of diesel cars provided by an employer will be retained and not abolished as was previously intended. The government announced the decision to retain the supplement in Autumn Statement 2015 and it will be retained until the new EU-wide testing procedures come into effect for diesel cars.

FA 2016 s 10 repeals certain provisions in FA 2014 which ensures that ITEPA 2003 s 141 is no longer repealed and the diesel supplement continues to apply for tax years 2016/17 onwards.

11 Cash equivalent of benefit of a van

(1) Section 155 of ITEPA 2003 (cash equivalent of the benefit of a van) is amended as follows.

(2) In subsection (1B)(a), for "2019–20" substitute "2021–22".

(3) In subsection (1C), for paragraphs (b) to (e) substitute—

"(b) 20% for the tax year 2016–17;
(c) 20% for the tax year 2017–18;
(d) 40% for the tax year 2018–19;
(e) 60% for the tax year 2019–20;
(f) 80% for the tax year 2020–21;
(g) 90% for the tax year 2021–22."

(4) The amendments made by this section have effect for the tax year 2016–17 and subsequent tax years.

GENERAL NOTE

FA 2016 s 11 amends ITEPA 2003 s155 to change the level of the van benefit charge for company vans which cannot emit CO_2 by being driven (zero emission vans). The rates currently taper up to 100% from 2020/21. The changes extend the tapering until 2021/22 and also retain the current 20% rate for 2016/17 and 2017/18 (where previously it would have tapered up to 60% by then). This is to incentivise the use and production of zero emission vans in the short term. The new rates are set out in the legislation.

12 Tax treatment of payments from sporting testimonials
Schedule 2 contains provision about the tax treatment of payments from sporting testimonials.

GENERAL NOTE
Section 12 introduces Sch 2.

13 Exemption for trivial benefits provided by employers
(1) ITEPA 2003 is amended as follows.
(2) After section 323 insert—

"323A Trivial benefits provided by employers
(1) No liability to income tax arises in respect of a benefit provided by, or on behalf of, an employer to an employee or a member of the employee's family or household if—
    (a) conditions A to D are met, or
    (b) in a case where subsection (2) applies, conditions A to E are met.
(2) This subsection applies where—
    (a) the employer is a close company, and
    (b) the employee is—
        (i) a person who is a director or other office-holder of the employer, or
        (ii) a member of the family or household of such a person.
(3) Condition A is that the benefit is not cash or a cash voucher within the meaning of section 75.
(4) Condition B is that the benefit cost of the benefit does not exceed £50.
(5) In this section "benefit cost", in relation to a benefit, means—
    (a) the cost of providing the benefit, or
    (b) if the benefit is provided to more than one person and the nature of the benefit or the scale of its provision means it is impracticable to calculate the cost of providing it to each person to whom it is provided, the average cost per person of providing the benefit.
(6) For the purposes of subsection (5)(b), the average cost per person of providing a benefit is found by dividing the total cost of providing the benefit by the number of persons to whom the benefit is provided.
(7) Condition C is that the benefit is not provided pursuant to relevant salary sacrifice arrangements or any other contractual obligation
(8) "Relevant salary sacrifice arrangements", in relation to the provision of a benefit to an employee or to a member of an employee's family or household, means arrangements (whenever made, whether before or after the employment began) under

which the employee gives up the right to receive an amount of general earnings or specific employment income in return for the provision of the benefit.

(9) Condition D is that the benefit is not provided in recognition of particular services performed by the employee in the course of the employment or in anticipation of such services.

(10) Condition E is that—

(a) the benefit cost of the benefit provided to the employee, or
(b) in a case where the benefit is provided to a member of the employee's family or household who is not an employee of the employer, the amount of the benefit cost allocated to the employee in accordance with section 323B(4),

does not exceed the employee's available exempt amount (see section 323B).

323B Section 323A: calculation of available exempt amount

(1) The "available exempt amount", in relation to an employee of an employer, is the amount found by deducting from the annual exempt amount the aggregate of—

(a) the benefit cost of eligible benefits provided earlier in the tax year by, or on behalf of, the employer to the employee, and
(b) any amounts allocated to the employee in accordance with subsection (4) in respect of eligible benefits provided earlier in the tax year by, or on behalf of, the employer to a member of the employee's family or household who was not at that time an employee of the employer.

(2) The annual exempt amount is £300.

(3) For the purposes of subsection (1) "eligible benefits" means benefits in respect of which conditions A to D in section 323A are met.

(4) The amount allocated to an employee of an employer in respect of a benefit provided to a person ("P") who—

(a) is a member of the employee's family or household, and
(b) is not an employee of the employer,

is the benefit cost of that benefit divided by the number of persons who meet the condition in subsection (5) and are members of P's family or household.

(5) This condition is met if the person is—

(a) a director or other office-holder of the employer,
(b) an employee of the employer who is a member of the family or household of a person within paragraph (a), or
(c) a former employee of the employer who—

(i) was a director or other office-holder at any time when the employer was a close company, or
(ii) is a member of the family or household of such a person.

(6) In this section "benefit cost" has the same meaning as in section 323A.

323C Power to amend sections 323A and 323B

(1) The Treasury may by regulations amend section 323A so as to alter the conditions which must be met for the exemption conferred by section 323A(1) to apply.

(2) Regulations under subsection (1) may include any amendment of section 323B that is appropriate in consequence of an amendment made under subsection (1).

(3) The Treasury must not make regulations under subsection (1) unless a draft of the regulations has been laid before and approved by a resolution of the House of Commons."

(3) In section 716 (alteration of amounts by Treasury order) in subsection (2), after paragraph (f) insert—

"(fa) section 323A(4) (trivial benefits provided by employers: cost of providing benefit),
(fb) section 323B(2) (trivial benefits provided by employers: annual exempt amount),".

(4) In section 717(4) (negative procedure not to apply to certain statutory instruments) after "other care: meaning of "eligible employee")," insert "section 323C(1) (trivial benefits provided by employers),".

(5) The amendments made by this section have effect for the tax year 2016–17 and subsequent tax years.

GENERAL NOTE

Section 13 inserts new ITEPA 2003 ss 323A, 323B and 323C with effect from 2016/17 to introduce a statutory exemption for certain "trivial" benefits in kind where the cost of providing the benefit is no more than £50. The limit applies to each benefit provided.

There is an annual cap of £300 for benefits provided to a director or office-holder of a close companies and members of such a person's family or household.

The new provisions, which replace concessionary HMRC practice and follow a consultation held in 2014, extend ITEPA 2003 Pt 4 Ch 11 (miscellaneous exemptions). There are corresponding changes to NIC regulations.

New ITEPA 2003 s 323A provides that no liability to income tax arises in respect of a benefit provided by, or on behalf of, an employer to an employee or a member of the employee's family or household if conditions A to D are met. A further condition applies to close companies (see below).

- Condition A is that the benefit is not cash or a cash voucher within ITEPA 2003 s 75.
- Condition B is that the "benefit cost" of the benefit does not exceed £50. The "benefit cost" is:
  - the cost of providing the benefit, or
  - if the benefit is provided to more than one person and the nature or scale of the benefit or provision makes it impracticable to calculate the cost for each person, the average cost of provision per person (found by dividing the total cost by the number of persons).
- Condition C is that the benefit is not provided pursuant to either relevant salary sacrifice arrangements, where the employee gives up the right to receive an amount of income in return for the benefit, or any other contractual obligation.
- Condition D is that the benefit is not provided in recognition of (or in anticipation of) particular services performed by the employee in the course of the employment.

Close companies

If the employer is a close company, and the employee is either a director or other office-holder of the employer, or a member of such a person's family or household, then Condition E also applies:

- Condition E is that the benefit cost of the benefit provided to the employee (or, where the benefit is provided to a member of the employee's family or household who is not an employee of the employer, the benefit cost allocated to the employee) does not exceed the employee's "available exempt amount" (see below).

New ITEPA 2003 s 323B sets out the calculation of the available exempt amount where condition E is met. The "available exempt amount" in relation to an employee is the amount found by deducting from the annual exempt amount, which is set at £300, the aggregate of:

  the benefit cost of eligible benefits (ie. those meeting conditions A to D above) provided earlier in the tax year by, or on behalf of, the employer to the employee; and

- any amounts allocated to the employee (see below) in respect of eligible benefits provided earlier in the tax year by, or on behalf of, the employer to a member of the employee's family or household who was not an employee of the employer.

The amount allocated to an employee of an employer in respect of a benefit provided to a person ("P") who is a member of the employee's family or household but is not an employee of the employer is the benefit cost (as defined above) divided by the number of persons who meet the condition below and are members of P's family or household.

The condition is met if the person:

- is a director or other office-holder of the employer;
- is an employee of the employer who is a member of the family or household of such a person; or
- is a former employee of the employer who either (i) was a director or other office-holder at any time when the employer was a close company, or (ii) is a member of the family or household of such a person.

The Treasury may amend new ITEPA 2003 ss 323A and 323B by means of regulations.

14 Travel expenses of workers providing services through intermediaries

(1) In Chapter 2 of Part 5 of ITEPA 2003 (deductions for employee's expenses), after section 339 insert—

"339A Travel for necessary attendance: employment intermediaries

(1) This section applies where an individual ("the worker")—

(a) personally provides services (which are not excluded services) to another person ("the client"), and

(b) the services are provided not under a contract directly between the client or a person connected with the client and the worker but under arrangements involving an employment intermediary.

This is subject to the following provisions of this section.

(2) Where this section applies, each engagement is for the purposes of sections 338 and 339 to be regarded as a separate employment.

(3) This section does not apply if it is shown that the manner in which the worker provides the services is not subject to (or to the right of) supervision, direction or control by any person.

(4) Subsection (3) does not apply in relation to an engagement if—

(a) Chapter 8 of Part 2 applies in relation to the engagement,

(b) the conditions in section 51, 52 or 53 are met in relation to the employment intermediary, and

(c) the employment intermediary is not a managed service company.

(5) This section does not apply in relation to an engagement if—

(a) Chapter 8 of Part 2 does not apply in relation to the engagement merely because the circumstances in section 49(1)(c) are not met,

(b) assuming those circumstances were met, the conditions in section 51, 52 or 53 would be met in relation to the employment intermediary, and

(c) the employment intermediary is not a managed service company.

(6) In determining for the purposes of subsection (4) or (5) whether the conditions in section 51, 52 or 53 are or would be met in relation to the employment intermediary—

(a) in section 51(1)—

(i) disregard "either" in the opening words, and

(ii) disregard paragraph (b) (and the preceding or), and

(b) read references to the intermediary as references to the employment intermediary.

(7) Subsection (8) applies if—

(a) the client or a relevant person provides the employment intermediary (whether before or after the worker begins to provide the services) with a fraudulent document which is intended to constitute evidence that, by virtue of subsection (3), this section does not or will not apply in relation to the services,

(b) that section is taken not to apply in relation to the services, and

(c) in consequence, the employment intermediary does not under PAYE regulations deduct and account for an amount that would have been deducted and accounted for under those regulations if this section had been taken to apply in relation to the services.

(8) For the purpose of recovering the amount referred to in subsection (7)(c) ("the unpaid tax")—

(a) the worker is to be treated as having an employment with the client or relevant person who provided the document, the duties of which consist of the services, and

(b) the client or relevant person is under PAYE regulations to account for the unpaid tax as if it arose in respect of earnings from that employment.

(9) In subsections (7) and (8) "relevant person" means a person, other than the client, the worker or a person connected with the employment intermediary, who—

(a) is resident, or has a place of business, in the United Kingdom, and

(b) is party to a contract with the employment intermediary or a person connected with the employment intermediary under or in consequence of which—

(i) the services are provided, or

(ii) the employment intermediary, or a person connected with the employment intermediary, makes payments in respect of the services.

(10) In determining whether this section applies, no regard is to be had to any arrangements the main purpose, or one of the main purposes, of which is to secure that this section does not to any extent apply.

(11) In this section—

"arrangements" includes any scheme, transaction or series of transactions, agreement or understanding, whether or not enforceable, and any associated operations;

"employment intermediary" means a person, other than the worker or the client, who carries on a business (whether or not with a view to profit and whether or not in conjunction with any other business) of supplying labour;

"engagement" means any such provision of service as is mentioned in subsection (1)(a);

"excluded services" means services provided wholly in the client's home;

"managed service company" means a company which—

(a) is a managed service company within the meaning given by section 61B, or
(b) would be such a company disregarding subsection (1)(c) of that section."

(2) In section 688A of ITEPA 2003 (managed service companies: recovery from other persons), in subsection (5), in the definition of "managed service company", after "section 61B" insert "but for the purposes of section 339A has the meaning given by subsection (11) of that section".

(3) After section 688A of ITEPA 2003 insert—

"688B Travel expenses of workers providing services through intermediaries: recovery of unpaid tax

(1) PAYE regulations may make provision for, or in connection with, the recovery from a director or officer of a company, in such circumstances as may be specified in the regulations, of amounts within any of subsections (2) to (5).

(2) An amount within this subsection is an amount that the company is to account for in accordance with PAYE regulations by virtue of section 339A(7) to (9) (persons providing fraudulent documents).

(3) An amount within this subsection is an amount which the company is to deduct and pay in accordance with PAYE regulations by virtue of section 339A in circumstances where—

(a) the company is an employment intermediary,
(b) on the basis that section 339A does not apply by virtue of subsection (3) of that section, the company has not deducted and paid the amount, but
(c) the company has not been provided by any other person with evidence from which it would be reasonable in all the circumstances to conclude that subsection (3) of that section applied (and the mere assertion by a person that the manner in which the worker provided the services was not subject to (or to the right of) supervision, direction or control by any person is not such evidence).

(4) An amount within this subsection is an amount that the company is to deduct and pay in accordance with PAYE regulations by virtue of section 339A in a case where subsection (4) of that section applies (services provided under arrangements made by intermediaries).

(5) An amount within this subsection is any interest or penalty in respect of an amount within any of subsections (2) to (4) for which the company is liable.

(6) In this section—

"company" includes a limited liability partnership;
"director" has the meaning given by section 67;
"employment intermediary" has the same meaning as in section 339A;
"officer", in relation to a company, means any manager, secretary or other similar officer of the company, or any person acting or purporting to act as such"

(4) In Part 4 of the Income Tax (Pay As You Earn) Regulations 2003 (SI 2003/2682) (payments, returns and information), after Chapter 3A insert—

"CHAPTER 3B

CERTAIN DEBTS OF COMPANIES UNDER SECTION 339A OF ITEPA (TRAVEL EXPENSES OF WORKERS PROVIDING SERVICES THROUGH EMPLOYMENT INTERMEDIARIES)

97ZG Interpretation of Chapter 3B: "relevant PAYE debt" and "relevant date"

(1) In this Chapter "relevant PAYE debt", in relation to a company means an amount within any of paragraphs (2) to (5).

(2) An amount within this paragraph is an amount that the company is to account for in accordance with these Regulations by virtue of section 339A(7) to (9) of ITEPA (persons providing fraudulent documents).

(3) An amount within this paragraph is an amount which a company is to deduct and pay in accordance with these Regulations by virtue of section 339A of ITEPA in circumstances where—

(a) the company is an employment intermediary,

(b) on the basis that section 339A of ITEPA does not apply by virtue of subsection (3) of that section the company has not deducted and paid the amount, but

(c) the company has not been provided by any other person with evidence from which it would be reasonable in all the circumstances to conclude that subsection (3) of that section applied (and the mere assertion by a person that the manner in which the worker provided the services was not subject to (or to the right of) supervision, direction or control by any person is not such evidence).

(4) An amount within this paragraph is an amount that the company is to deduct and pay in accordance with these Regulations by virtue of section 339A of ITEPA in a case where subsection (4) of that section applies (services provided under arrangements made by intermediaries).

(5) An amount within this paragraph is any interest or penalty in respect of an amount within any of paragraphs (2) to (4) for which the company is liable.

(6) In this Chapter "the relevant date" in relation to a relevant PAYE debt means the date on which the first payment is due on which PAYE is not accounted for.

97ZH Interpretation of Chapter 3B: general

In this Chapter—

"company" includes a limited liability partnership;

"director" has the meaning given by section 67 of ITEPA;

"personal liability notice" has the meaning given by regulation 97ZI(2);

"the specified amount" has the meaning given by regulation 97ZI(2)(a).

97ZI Liability of directors for relevant PAYE debts

(1) This regulation applies in relation to an amount of relevant PAYE debt of a company if the company does not deduct that amount by the time by which the company is required to do so.

(2) HMRC may serve a notice (a "personal liability notice") on any person who was, on the relevant date, a director of the company—

(a) specifying the amount of relevant PAYE debt in relation to which this regulation applies ("the specified amount"), and

(b) requiring the director to pay to HMRC—

(i) the specified amount, and

(ii) specified interest on that amount.

(3) The interest specified in the personal liability notice—

(a) is to be at the rate applicable under section 178 of the Finance Act 1989 for the purposes of section 86 of TMA, and

(b) is to run from the date the notice is served.

(4) A director who is served with a personal liability notice is liable to pay to HMRC the specified amount and the interest specified in the notice within 30 days beginning with the day the notice is served.

(5) If HMRC serve personal liability notices on more than one director of the company in respect of the same amount of relevant PAYE debt, the directors are jointly and severally liable to pay to HMRC the specified amount and the interest specified in the notices.

97ZJ Appeals in relation to personal liability notices

(1) A person who is served with a personal liability notice in relation to an amount of relevant PAYE debt of a company may appeal against the notice.

(2) A notice of appeal must—

(a) be given to HMRC within 30 days beginning with the day the personal liability notice is served, and

(b) specify the grounds of the appeal.

(3) The grounds of appeal are —

(a) that all or part of the specified amount does not represent an amount of relevant PAYE debt, of the company, to which regulation 97ZI applies, or

(b) that the person was not a director of the company on the relevant date.

(4) But a person may not appeal on the ground mentioned in paragraph (3)(a) if it has already been determined, on an appeal by the company, that—
    (a) the specified amount is a relevant PAYE debt of the company, and
    (b) the company did not deduct, account for, or (as the case may be) pay the debt by the time by which the company was required to do so.

(5) Subject to paragraph (6), on an appeal that is notified to the tribunal, the tribunal is to uphold or quash the personal liability notice.

(6) In a case in which the ground of appeal mentioned in paragraph (3)(a) is raised, the tribunal may also reduce or increase the specified amount so that it does represent an amount of relevant PAYE debt, of the company, to which regulation 97ZI applies.

97ZK Withdrawal of personal liability notices

(1) A personal liability notice is withdrawn if the tribunal quashes it.

(2) An officer of Revenue and Customs may withdraw a personal liability notice if the officer considers it appropriate to do so.

(3) If a personal liability notice is withdrawn, HMRC must give notice of that fact to the person upon whom the notice was served.

97ZL Recovery of sums due under personal liability notice: application of Part 6 of TMA

(1) For the purposes of this Chapter, Part 6 of TMA (collection and recovery) applies as if—
    (a) the personal liability notice were an assessment, and
    (b) the specified amount, and any interest on that amount under regulation 97ZI(2)(b)(ii), were income tax charged on the director upon whom the notice is served,

and that Part of that Act applies with the modification in paragraph (2) and any other necessary modifications.

(2) Summary proceedings for the recovery of the specified amount, and any interest on that amount under regulation 97ZI(2)(b)(ii), may be brought in England and Wales or Northern Ireland at any time before the end of the period of 12 months beginning with the day after the day on which the personal liability notice is served.

97ZM Repayment of surplus amounts

(1) This regulation applies if—

    (a) one or more personal liability notices are served in respect of an amount of relevant PAYE debt of a company, and
    (b) the amounts paid to HMRC (whether by directors upon whom notices are served or the company) exceed the aggregate of the specified amount and any interest on it under regulation 97ZI(2)(b)(ii).

(2) HMRC is to repay the difference on a just and equitable basis and without unreasonable delay.

(3) HMRC is to pay interest on any sum repaid.

(4) The interest

    (a) is to be at the rate applicable under section 178 of the Finance Act 1989 for the purposes of section 824 of ICTA, and
    (b) is to be run from the date the amounts paid to HMRC come to exceed the aggregate mentioned in subsection (1)(b)."

(5) The amendment made by subsection (4) is to be treated as having been made by the Commissioners for Her Majesty's Revenue and Customs in exercise of the power conferred by section 688B of ITEPA 2003 (inserted by subsection (3)).

(6) The amendment made by subsection (1) has effect in relation to the tax year 2016–17 and subsequent tax years.

(7) The amendment made by subsection (4) has effect in relation to relevant PAYE debts that are to be deducted, accounted for or paid on or after 6 April 2016.

GENERAL NOTE

FA 2010 s 14 introduces a number of legislative changes by way of implementation of the measures set out in HM Revenue & Customs response of 9 December 2015 to the consultation on Employment Intermediaries and Tax Relief for Travel and Subsistence.

The aim of changes is to prevent workers claiming tax deductible or tax exempt travel and subsistence expenses on travel from home to work where previously such travel could fall to be classified as travel to a temporary workplace and be tax deductible. The changes are particularly targeted at workers supplied through, what are known as, umbrella companies where the company employs workers and then supplies them, via an employment agency, on temporary assignments to end clients. Previously the arrangements were such that the travel to the temporary assignment fell to be treated as travel to a temporary workplace. The changes address the Government's desire to levelling the playing field between employees engaged directly by the entity they work for and those being supplied by a third party. The rules do not seek to define an umbrella company but instead are drafted by reference to a wide definition of "employment intermediary" which will also capture personal service companies. Due to changes to the PAYE regulations (SI 2003/2682) (the repeal of reg 87(1)(a)), where travel and subsistence expenses are reimbursed which are not tax-exempt, they will be subject to PAYE and not reported on P11D.

FA 2016 s 14(1) introduces a new s 339A into ITEPA 2003 ("Travel for necessary attendance: employment intermediaries"). This is operative from tax year 2016/17 onwards.

New ITEPA 2003 s 339A

Subsection (1) provides that s 339A applies where a worker personally provides services to another person ("the client") and the services are provided via arrangements with an employment intermediary and not directly with the client.

Subsection (2) provides that each engagement for the purposes of ITEPA 2003 ss 338 and 339 will be regarded as a separate employment. This will result in any travel expenses which previously fell under ss 338 or 339 no longer being treated as deductible (or exempt under ITEPA 2003 Pt 5 Ch 2).

Subsection (3) restricts the application of ITEPA 2003 s 339A providing that the section does not apply if it is shown that the manner in which the worker provides his services is not subject to, or to the right of, supervision, direction or control by any person. This test is that used in ITEPA 2003 Pt 2 Ch 7 in relation to the taxation of agency workers The application of subsection is restricted by sub-ss (4) and (5).

Subsections (4) and (5) address situations where the employment intermediary is a personal service company. Otherwise than with a managed service company, the supervision, direction and control test does not apply where ITEPA Pt 2 Ch 8 (the IR35 legislation) applies and the conditions in ITEPA 2003 ss51–53 are met. In such a situation the test of whether such a worker falls within s 339A is based on whether the related employment intermediary is taxed under the rules in Pt 2 Ch 8.

Specifically, s 339A does not apply at all where ITEPA Pt 2 Ch 8 would apply but does not because ITEPA 2003 s 49(1)(c) does not apply. This is where, if the services were provided under a contract directly between the client and the worker, the worker would **not** be regarded for income tax purposes as an employee of the client (which is the main test for whether the IR35 rules will apply or not).

Subsection (6) has some consequential amendments needed for sub-ss (4) and (5) to operate correctly.

Subsections (7) and (8) provide that where the client or a 'relevant person' provides fraudulent documents in relation to supervision, direction or control on which the employment intermediary relies to determine if s 339A applies (where the test in s 339A(3) is applicable) and it determines that the travel expenses are not subject to PAYE then the worker is treated as employed by the party providing the fraudulent documents and the PAYE obligation passes to that person. Subsection (9) defines 'relevant person' as the party in the supply chain who contracts with the employment intermediary to supply the worker to the employment intermediary and who is also UK resident or has a UK place of business. Therefore, if the next intermediary down the supply change has no PAYE presence the employment intermediary cannot rely on the fraudulent document defence in relation to that entity. There is no fraudulent document defence in relation to the personal service companies which is logical because the personal service company will normally be owned by the worker that it provides. Subsection (10) provides that when working out if s 339A applies, you look through any arrangements where one of the main purposes is to secure that s 339A does not apply.

Subsection (11) contains the operative definitions for s 339A including 'employment intermediary' and 'managed service company'. It is a key part of the employment intermediary definition that the person carries on a business of 'supplying labour'.

This is designed to ensure s 339A does not capture business that supply services but may, on occasions, second staff to clients The consultation gave the example of professional service firms which second staff to clients

FA 2016 s 14(2) introduces consequential amendments to ITEPA 2003 s 688A in relation to managed service companies

FA 2016 s 14(3) introduces a new s 688A into ITEPA 2003 ('Travel expenses of workers providing services through intermediaries: recovery of unpaid tax'). The new s 688B includes provisions which deal with transfer of the PAYE debt arising from the application of s 339A and are designed to motivate compliance.

New ITEPA 2003 s 688B

Subsection (1) provides the authority for PAYE regulations to be introduced to provide the right to make recovery from a director or officer of a company of PAYE and associated interest and penalties in the circumstances set out in sub-ss (2)–(5).

The circumstances set out by sub-ss (2)–(5) are where PAYE should have been operated as result of the (i) provision of fraudulent documents pursuant to ITEPA 2003 ss 339A(7)–(9); (ii) an employment intermediary not operating PAYE as a result of the application of ITEPA 2003 s 339A on the basis of there being no supervision, direction or control but without holding evidence on which it is reasonable to make such conclusion; or (iii) a personal service company taxed under ITEPA 2003 Pt 2 Ch 8 in relation to the relevant engagement not operating PAYE as a result of the application of ITEPA 2003 s 339A.

Subsection (5) extends the right of recovery to interest and penalties and sub-s (6) contains relevant definitions.

Pursuant to the power provided by the new ITEPA 2003 s 688B, FA 2016 s 14(4) introduces a new Ch 3B (consisting of regs 97ZG–97ZM) into Pt 4 Income Tax (Pay As You Earn) Regulations 2003. It applies to PAYE debts which are to be deducted, accounted for or paid on or after 6 April 2016.

New Income Tax (Pay As You Earn) Regulations 2003 Ch 3B

Paragraph 97ZG replicates the drafting of ITEPA 2003 s 688B and defines the PAYE amount due as the 'relevant PAYE debt' and the 'relevant date' for the relevant PAYE debt as the date on which the first payment is due on which PAYE is not accounted for.

Regulations 97ZH–97J set out that recovery can be from a director at the relevant date via the issue of a personal liability notice, that more than one director can be issued with such a notice and that a director has 30 days to pay or to appeal on the basis that the amount which is the subject of the personal liability notice is not a relevant PAYE debt or the individual was not a director at the relevant time.

Regulation 97ZK set outs when the personal liability notice can be withdrawn.

Regulation 97ZL provides for TMA 1970 Pt 6 to apply in relation to the recovery of sums due under a personal liability notice as if the amounts were income tax assessed on the director and that summary proceedings can brought within 12 months of the issue of the personal liability notice.

Regulation 97ZM deals with repayments of sums where recovery has been made for the same relevant PAYE debt under one or more personal liability notices, with such repayment on a just and equitable basis.

15 Taxable benefits: PAYE

In section 684 of ITEPA 2003 (PAYE regulations), in subsection (2), in item 1ZA(a), for "Chapters 3 and 5 to 10" substitute "Chapters 3 to 10".

GENERAL NOTE

FA 2016 s 15 amends ITEPA 2003 s 684(2) Item 1ZA(a), to extend the scope of the provisions that can be covered by PAYE regulations. The list of specific chapters of ITEPA 2003 Pt 3 is extended to include ITEPA 2003 Pt 3 Ch 4 (vouchers and credit tokens). This amend relates to 'payrolling' of benefits and has the effect of extending the benefits that can be voluntarily payrolled to include vouchers and credit tokens. HMRC stated that it will amend the actual PAYE regulations to give effect to this change in the summer of 2016 to enable employers to voluntarily payroll non-cash vouchers and credit tokens from 6 April 2017.

Employment Income: other Provision

16 Employee share schemes

Schedule 3 contains miscellaneous minor amendments relating to employee share schemes.

GENERAL NOTE

This section introduces Sch 3 which contains a variety of relatively minor amendments to some of the provisions of ITEPA 2003 and TCGA 1992 which deal with employee share schemes.

17 Securities options

(1) In section 418 of ITEPA 2003 (provisions related to Part 7 of ITEPA 2003), in subsection (1), omit "(but not securities options)".

(2) In that section, after subsection (1) insert—

"(1A) But Chapters 1 and 10 of Part 3 do not have effect in relation to—

(a) the acquisition of employment-related securities options (within the meaning of Chapter 5 of Part 7), or

(b) chargeable events (within the meaning given by section 477) occurring in relation to such options."

(3) In section 227 of that Act (scope of Part 4), in subsection (4), before paragraph (a) insert—

"(za) section 418(1A) (acquisition of, and chargeable events occurring in relation to, employment-related securities options);".

(4) The amendments made by this section come into force on 6 April 2016.

GENERAL NOTE

Section 17 applies to employment-related securities that are not acquired under the "tax-advantaged share schemes" (ie. share incentive plans, save as you earn schemes, company share option plans and enterprise management incentives).

It is intended to make it clear that the income tax charge on acquisition of an option, or on a chargeable event, in relation to restricted stock units (RSUs) arises under the rules relating to securities options, rather than the rules relating to earnings.

The words "but not securities options" in ITEPA 2003 s 418(1) are deleted. Instead, a new ITEPA 2003 s 418(1A) provides that ITEPA 2003 Pt 3 Chs 1 (earnings) and 10 (taxable benefits: residual liability to charge) do not have effect in relation to:

- the acquisition of employment-related securities options within the meaning of ITEPA 2003 Part 7 Ch 5 (securities options), or
- chargeable events occurring in relation to such options.

There is a consequential amendment to ITEPA s 227, which sets out the scope of ITEPA 2003 Pt 4 (employment income: exemptions). These amendments come into force on 6 April 2016.

18 Employment income provided through third parties

(1) Part 7A of ITEPA 2003 (employment income provided through third parties) is amended in accordance with subsections (2) and (3).

(2) In section 554Z2 (value of relevant step to count as employment income) after subsection (1) insert—

"(1A) Where the value of a relevant step would (apart from this subsection) count as employment income of more than one person—

(a) the value of the relevant step is to be apportioned between each of those persons on a just and reasonable basis, and

(b) subsection (1) applies as if the reference to the value of the relevant step in relation to A were a reference to so much of the value of the relevant step that is apportioned to A."

(3) In section 554Z8 (cases where consideration given for relevant step) in subsection (5), omit "and" at the end of paragraph (b) and after paragraph (c) insert ", and

(d) there is no connection (direct or indirect) between the payment and a tax avoidance arrangement."

(4) Paragraph 59 of Schedule 2 to FA 2011 (transitional provision relating to Part 7A of ITEPA 2003) is amended in accordance with subsections (5) to (7).

(5) In sub-paragraph (2) for the words from "the earnings" to the end substitute—

"(a) where sub-paragraph (2A) or (2B) applies, the earnings mentioned in sub-paragraph (1)(f)(i) or any return on those earnings mentioned in sub-paragraph (1)(f)(ii), and

(b) in any other case, the earnings mentioned in sub-paragraph (1)(f)(i)."

(6) After sub-paragraph (2) insert—

"(2A) This sub-paragraph applies where—

(a) the agreement mentioned in sub-paragraph (1)(d)(i) is made before 1 April 2017, and

(b) A or B pays, or otherwise accounts for, any tax as mentioned in sub-paragraph (1)(e) in accordance with that agreement.

(2B) This sub-paragraph applies where—

(a) the decision mentioned in sub-paragraph (1)(d)(ii) is made before 1 April 2017, and

(b) A or B pays, or otherwise accounts for, any tax as mentioned in sub-paragraph (1)(e) before 1 April 2017."

(7) At the end insert—

"(5) For the purposes of sub-paragraph (1)(e), a person is not to be regarded as having paid, or otherwise accounted for, any tax by reason only of making—

(a) a payment on account of income tax,

(b) a payment that is treated as a payment on account under section 223(3) of FA 2014 (accelerated payments), or

(c) a payment pending determination of an appeal made in accordance with section 55 of TMA 1970."

(8) In Schedule 2 to FA 2011, omit paragraph 64 (power to make provision dealing with interactions etc).

(9) The amendment made by subsection (3) has effect in relation to payments made on or after 16 March 2016 by way of consideration for a relevant step (as defined in section 554A(2) of ITEPA 2003) taken on or after that date.

(10) The amendment made by subsection (7) has effect in relation to chargeable steps (as defined in paragraph 59(1)(a) of Schedule 2 to FA 2011) taken on or after 16 March 2016.

GENERAL NOTE

Section 18 makes a number of amendments to the rules in ITEPA 2003 Pt 7A in relation to employment income provided through third parties (commonly referred to as the 'disguised remuneration' rules). It also introduces amendments to related transitional rules in FA 2011 Sch 2.

FA 2016 s 18(1) introduces the changes to ITEPA 2003.

A new ITEPA 2003 s 554Z2(1A) (value of relevant step to count as employment income) is introduced by FA 2016 s 18(1). This provides that where the value of a relevant step would count as employment income of more than one person, the value of the relevant step is to be apportioned between each of them on a just and reasonable basis (and ITEPA 2003 s 554Z2(1) shall be interpreted accordingly).

FA 2016 s 18(3) amends s 554Z8 (cases where consideration given for relevant step). It does so by the insertion of new ITEPA 2003 s 554Z8(5)(d), which restricts the availability of the relief in ITEPA 2003 s 554Z8(6). This will prevent the relief where consideration is given from applying if there is any direct or indirect connection between the relevant payment and a tax avoidance arrangement. This targeted anti-avoidance rule has effect in relation to payments made on or after 16 March 2016 as consideration for a relevant step taken on or after that date (FA 2016 s 18(9)).

FA 2016 ss 18(4)–(7) make amendments to FA 2011 Sch 2 para 59 (transitional provision relating to Pt 7A ITEPA).

New FA 2011 Sch 2 paras 59(2A) and (2B) is inserted by FA 2016 ss 18(5) and (6). The effect of the new paragraphs is to restrict the transitional relief provided by para 59 on certain investment returns – broadly, the relief ceases to apply to any return on earnings on certain amounts unless HM Revenue & Customs and the employer and/or employee made an agreement before 1 April 2017that the applicable relevant step was to be treated as giving rise to the relevant employee's earnings (and the tax has been paid or accounted for before 1 April 2017).

FA 2016 s 18(7) inserts new FA 2011 Sch 2 para 59(5). This is intended to clarify and put beyond doubt that the condition in para 59(1)(e) that tax has been paid or otherwise accounted for is not met by making a payment on account of income tax, an accelerated payment or a payment pending determination of an appeal. This amendment has effect in relation to chargeable steps taken on or after 16 March 2016 (FA 2016 s 18(10)).

FA 2011 Sch 2 para 64 (which contains an expired power to make provision dealing with interaction between Pt 7A ITEPA and other tax legislation) is repealed by FA 2016 s 18(8).

Pensions

GENERAL NOTE

A pension from a registered pension scheme cannot normally be reduced when in payment. One exception to this rule is where a bridging pension is paid. This is a pension which is higher at the outset and then reduced when the individual reaches state pension age. As the Department for Work and Pensions introduced a single tier state pension from 6 April 2016, s 20 supports the Government's objective of promoting fairness in the tax system by ensuring pension schemes can continue paying bridging pensions up to a member's state pension age following the introduction of the single tier state pension.

Dependants' scheme pensions may be payable if an individual, who is a member of a registered pension scheme and in receipt of a scheme pension or prospectively entitled to a scheme pension, dies with dependants. If the deceased individual started taking the pension from 6 April 2016 and had reached age 75 at the time of their death, any dependants' scheme pensions must be tested annually against the amount of the member's scheme pension, no matter the size of the member's pension savings or the dependants' scheme pensions. If a part of the dependants' pension exceeds the permitted maximum for that year, the excess is taxed as an unauthorised payment. This ensures excessive amounts from the member's pension savings are not set aside to pay benefits for dependants in order to avoid the member paying a lifetime allowance tax charge. To support the Government's policy to reduce the administrative burden on UK industry, s 21 has been introduced to make the administration of dependants' scheme pensions simpler by providing exceptions from the test of dependants' scheme pensions for low value pensions and where the risk of abuse is low.

The introduction of pension flexibility from 6 April 2015 has meant that individuals are able to access part of their pension savings more easily and leave the remainder to a later date. However, in his Autumn Statement of 25 November 2015 the Chancellor recognised that the changes from 6 April 2015 have not operated as intended in some respects and legislation would be introduced in Finance Bill 2016 to correct this. So s 22 and Sch 5 make various minor changes to FA 2004 Pt 4 effective from the day after Royal Assent to Finance Bill 2016 to ensure that particular payments can be paid and taxed as intended, as well as giving individuals more flexibility in how they want to use their pension funds.

The Netherlands "Wuv" scheme makes payments to individuals who were victims of persecution in Europe or Asia during the Second World War. To benefit from the scheme recipients must either have had Dutch nationality, been a Dutch subject or persecuted on Dutch territory and later acquired Dutch nationality. Payments from the Netherlands' Government via the scheme are currently included in the calculation of an individual's income tax liability. In April 2014 an Appeal on a Housing Benefit claim, where a victim of National Socialist persecution receiving payments from the Netherlands scheme contended that the failure to treat the payments in the same way as pensions and annuities from Germany or Austria, ruled this was unlawful discrimination. So, s 23 contains measures to bring payments to victims of National Socialist and Japanese aggression made through the "Wuv" scheme into line with those made by Germany and Austria by removing the income tax liability of those payments.

19 Standard lifetime allowance from 2016–17

(1) Section 218 of FA 2004 (pension schemes etc: lifetime allowance) is amended in accordance with subsections (2) to (5).

(2) For subsections (2) and (3) (standard lifetime allowance is £1,250,000 but may be increased by Treasury order) substitute—

"(2) The standard lifetime allowance for the tax years 2016–17 and 2017–18 is £1,000,000.

(2A) The standard lifetime allowance for any later tax year ("the subsequent tax year") is the same as the standard lifetime allowance for the tax year immediately preceding the subsequent tax year, unless subsection (2C) provides for it to be higher.

(2B) Subsection (2C) applies if—

(a) the consumer prices index for the month of September in any tax year ("the prior tax year") is higher than it was for the previous September, and
(b) the prior tax year is the tax year 2017–18 or a later tax year.

(2C) The standard lifetime allowance for the tax year following the prior tax year is the standard lifetime allowance for the prior tax year –

(a) increased by the percentage increase in the index, and
(b) if the result is not a multiple of £100, rounded up to the nearest amount which is such a multiple.

(2D) The Treasury must before the tax year 2018–19, and before each subsequent tax year, make regulations specifying the amount given by subsections (2A) to (2C) as the standard lifetime allowance for the tax year concerned."

(3) After subsection (5BB) insert—

"(5BC) Where the operation of a lifetime allowance enhancement factor is provided for by any of sections 220, 222, 223 and 224 and the time mentioned in the definition of SLA in the section concerned fell within the period consisting of the tax year 2014–15 and the tax year 2015–16, subsection (4) has effect as if the amount to be multiplied by LAEF were £1,250,000 if that is greater than SLA.

(5BD) Where more than one lifetime allowance enhancement factor operates, subsection (5BC) does not apply if any of subsections (5A), (5B) and (5BA) applies."

(4) After subsection (5D) insert—

"(5E) Where benefit crystallisation event 7 occurs on or after 6 April 2016 by reason of the payment of a relevant lump sum death benefit in respect of the death of the individual during the period consisting of the tax year 2014–15 and the tax year 2015–16, the standard lifetime allowance at the time of the benefit crystallisation event is £1,250,000."

(5) After subsection (5F) insert—

"(5F) Where—

(a) benefit crystallisation event 5C occurs by reason of the designation on or after 6 April 2015 of sums or assets held for the purposes of an arrangement relating to the individual, and
(b) the individual died before 6 April 2012,

the standard lifetime allowance at the time of the benefit crystallisation event is £1,800,000.

(5G) Where—

(a) benefit crystallisation event 5C occurs by reason of the designation on or after 6 April 2015 of sums or assets held for the purposes of an arrangement relating to the individual, and
(b) the individual died in the period consisting of the tax year 2012–13 and the tax year 2013–14,

the standard lifetime allowance at the time of the benefit crystallisation event is £1,500,000.

(5H) Where—

(a) benefit crystallisation event 5C occurs by reason of the designation on or after 6 April 2016 of sums or assets held for the purposes of an arrangement relating to the individual, and
(b) the individual died in the period consisting of the tax year 2014–15 and the tax year 2015–16,

the standard lifetime allowance at the time of the benefit crystallisation event is £1,250,000.

(5I) Where—

(a) benefit crystallisation event 5D occurs by reason of a person becoming entitled on or after 6 April 2016 to an annuity in respect of the individual, and
(b) the individual died in the period beginning with 3 December 2014 and ending with 5 April 2016,
the standard lifetime allowance at the time of the benefit crystallisation event is £1,250,000."

(6) In section 280 of FA 2004 (abbreviations and general index for Part 4), in the entry for "standard lifetime allowance" for "and (3)" substitute "to (2C)".

(7) In section 282 of FA 2004 (orders and regulations under Part 4), after subsection (2) (negative procedure applies to instruments not approved in draft) insert—

"(3) Subsection (2) does not apply to an instrument containing only regulations under section 218(2D)."

(8) The amendments made by subsections (2) to (4) have effect for the tax year 2016–17 and subsequent tax years.

(9) The amendment made by subsection (5)—
(a) so far as it consists of the insertion of new subsections (5F) and (5G)—
(i) is to be treated as having come into force on 6 April 2015, and
(ii) has effect in relation to benefit crystallisation events occurring on or after that date, and
(b) so far as it consists of the insertion of new subsections (5H) and (5I)—
(i) is to be treated as having come into force on 6 April 2016, and
(ii) has effect in relation to benefit crystallisation events occurring on or after that date.

(10) Schedule 4 contains transitional and connected provision (including provision for "fixed protection 2016" and "individual protection 2016").

GENERAL NOTE

Section 19 reduces the standard lifetime allowance (SLTA) to £1 million for the tax years 2016/17 and 2017/18. HM Treasury must make regulations before the start of tax year 2018/19, and each subsequent tax year, specifying the amount of the SLTA. The SLTA will be increased from 6 April 2018 by the increase in the consumer prices index (CPI) each year, rounded up to the nearest £100. If CPI does not increase in the year, the previous year's SLTA will stand.

The changes were anticipated. They had been announced in the Budget on 18 March 2015, confirmed at the Autumn Statement on 9 December 2015 (accompanied by a Tax Information and Impact Note (TIIN)) and further confirmed in the Budget on 16 March 2016.

Where a lifetime allowance (LTA) enhancement factor applies, and such entitlement occurred between 6 April 2014 and 5 April 2016, the factor is multiplied by £1.25 million if this is greater than the STLA at the time the benefit crystallisation event (BCE) occurred. There is an order of precedence where an individual has more than one such factor. Additionally, the SLTA is replaced by a figure of £1.25 million where certain lump sum death benefits (LSDB) are paid. When uncrystallised funds are designated for dependants' or nominees' flexi-access drawdown, following the death of a member before 6 April 2016, the BCE is tested against the SLTA in force at the time of the member's death. This has effect from 6 April 2015. When the entitlement to a beneficiary's or dependent's annuity arises following the death of a member before 6 April 2016, the BCE is tested against the STLA in force at the time of the member's death. This has effect from 6 April 2016, and has effect in relation to BCEs occurring on or after that date. There are special provisions for deaths before 6 April 2012.

There is no doubt that the reduction in the level of the SLTA further diminishes the attraction of pensions saving for those who can afford it. The reduced level of the annual allowance (to £40,000, and in some cases to £10,000) has exacerbated the problem. Those who have paid off their mortgages, loans, fees and/or inherited money in their later years etc will have to find alternative means of additional saving for their old age. Examples include individual savings accounts (ISA), as described below:

– A fully flexible ISA, whereby investors will be able to take out money and to put it back later without losing their tax-free allowance.
– The ISA limit is being raised from £15,000 to £20,000 per annum from 6 April 2017.

- Regulations will provide that ISAs can retain their tax-advantaged status following the death of the account holder.
- A new "lifetime ISA" (LISA) is being introduced, for those aged from 18 to under 40, from 6 April 2017 under which, for every £4 saved, the Government will put in £1. There will be a limit of £4,000 pa, with a £1,000 Government contribution. Individuals can continue saving until they reach the age of 50. They can use the cash to buy a home, up to a cash limit, any time from 12 months of opening, or access it from age 60 for use in retirement. All withdrawals will be tax-free. The Government has stated that it will discuss the implementation of LISA with the savings and investment industry ahead of April 2017.
- Savers who have already taken out a "Help to Buy ISA" will be able to move their savings into a LISA.
- The Government is looking at savers being allowed to withdraw the money for "other life events" than those envisaged by LISA. However, individuals will not qualify for the bonus. They will also have to pay a 5% charge.
- The Government is considering the USA 401k model, and will consult on plans to allow borrowing against the funds without incurring a charge if the borrowed funds are fully repaid.

20 Pensions bridging between retirement and state pension

(1) In Part 1 of Schedule 28 to FA 2004 (registered pension schemes: the pension rules), paragraph 2 (meaning of "scheme pension") is amended in accordance with subsections (2) to (4).

(2) In sub-paragraph (4) (which specifies circumstances in which amount of scheme pension may go down and gives power to specify additional circumstances) omit paragraph (c) (reduction by reference to state retirement pensions for persons reaching pensionable age before 6 April 2016).

(3) Omit sub-paragraphs (4B), (5) and (5A) (interpretation of sub-paragraph (4)(c)).

(4) In sub-paragraph (8) (regulations under certain sub-paragraphs may make back-dated provision) omit "or (5)".

(5) In consequence of the amendments made by subsections (2) and (3)—
 (a) in FA 2006, in Schedule 23 omit paragraph 20(2) and (3), and
 (b) in FA 2013, omit section 51(2).

(6) Regulations under paragraph 2(4)(h) of Schedule 28 to FA 2004 (power to prescribe permitted reductions of scheme pensions, and to do so with back-dated effect) may provide for the coming into force of the amendments made by subsections (2) to (5), and—
 (a) those amendments have effect in accordance with regulations under paragraph 2(4)(h) of that Schedule, and
 (b) paragraph 2(8) of that Schedule (back-dating) applies for the purposes of regulations bringing the amendments into force only so as to permit the amendments to be given effect in relation to times not earlier than 6 April 2016.

GENERAL NOTE

Subsection (1) provides that FA 2004 (the main pensions tax legislation) at Sch 28 para 2 is amended in accordance with sub-ss (2) to (4). Subsection (2) omits Sch 28 para 4(c) which sets out the current circumstances in which a scheme pension may be reduced when a bridging pension ceases to be paid. Subsections (3) to (5) make consequential amendments as a result of the omission of Sch 28 para 4(c). Subsection (6) provides for the amendments made by sub-ss (2) to (5) to be commenced by regulations made under Sch 28 para 2(4)(h) and that will have effect under Sch 28 para 2(8) from 6 April 2016. HMRC is to consult with pensions industry representatives on the drafting of these regulations and to clarify the exact implications of the single tier state pension on the legislation relating to bridging pensions.

21 Dependants' scheme pensions

(1) Part 2 of Schedule 28 to Part 4 of FA 2004 (pension death benefit rules) is amended as follows.

(2) In paragraph 16A (dependants' scheme pension: when limits in paragraphs 16B and 16C apply), after sub-paragraph (1) insert-

"(1A) Sub-paragraph (1) is subject to paragraphs 16AA and 16AB."

(3) After paragraph 16A insert—

"**16AA** Paragraphs 16B and 16C do not apply if—

(a) each benefit crystallisation event that has occurred in relation to the member by reference to arrangements relating to the member under the scheme is benefit crystallisation event 5B (having unused funds under a money purchase arrangement at age 75), or

(b) paragraph 12 of Schedule 36 (enhanced protection by reference to pre-6 April 2006 rights) applies in the case of the member immediately before the member's death.

16AB (1) Paragraph 16B does not apply if, at all times in the post-death year (as defined in that paragraph), the payable annual rate is less than the limit.

(2) Paragraph 16C does not apply in relation to a period of 12 months within paragraph (a) or (b) of paragraph 16C(1) if, at all times in that period of 12 months, the payable annual rate is less than the limit.

(3) "The payable annual rate", at any time, is arrived at as follows—

(a) identify each dependants' scheme pension payable in respect of the member under the scheme to which a dependant of the member is actually entitled at that time, and

(b) identify the annual rate at which each pension identified at paragraph (a) is payable at that time, and

(c) if only one pension is identified at paragraph (a), the payable annual rate is the annual rate identified at paragraph (b), and

(d) if two or more pensions are identified at paragraph (a), the payable annual rate is the total of the annual rates identified at paragraph (b).

(4) "The limit", at any time, is—

(a) the general limit at that time (see paragraph 16AC), or,

(b) if higher, the personal limit at that time (see paragraph 16AD).

16AC (1) This paragraph applies for the purposes of paragraph 16AB(4).

(2) "The general limit" at a time in the tax year 2016–17 is £25,000.

(3) "The general limit" at a time in a later tax year ("year T")—

(a) is given by—

$$G + (G \times U\%)$$

where G is the general limit at times in the tax year ("year P") that precedes year T, or

(b) if the amount given by paragraph (a) is not a multiple of £100, is that amount rounded up to the nearest amount that is such a multiple.

(4) See paragraph 16AE for the meaning of U%.

16AD (1) This paragraph applies for the purposes of paragraph 16AB(4).

(2) "The personal limit" at a time in the tax year in which the member dies is arrived at as follows—

(a) identify each scheme pension under the scheme to which the member is actually or prospectively entitled immediately before the member's death, and

(b) as regards each pension identified at paragraph (a)—

(i) if it is one to which the member is actually entitled immediately before the member's death, identify the annual rate at which it is payable immediately before the member's death, or

(ii) if it is one to which the member is prospectively entitled immediately before the member's death, identify the annual rate at which it would have been payable immediately before the member's death had the member been actually entitled to it immediately before the member's death, and

(c) if only one pension is identified at paragraph (a), the personal limit is the annual rate identified at paragraph (b), and

(d) if two or more pensions are identified at paragraph (a), the personal limit is the total of the annual rates identified at paragraph (b).

(3) "The personal limit" at a time in a tax year ("year S") later than the tax year in which the member dies—

(a) is given by—

$$L + (L \times U\%)$$

where L is the personal limit at times in the tax year ("year P") that precedes year S, or

(b) if the amount given by paragraph (a) is not a multiple of £100, is that amount rounded up to the nearest amount that is such a multiple.

(4) See paragraph 16AE for the meaning of U%.

(5) If the scheme is a public service pension scheme, ignore any abatement when identifying at sub-paragraph (2)(b) the annual rate of any scheme pension under the scheme.

16AE (1) In paragraphs 16AC(3) and 16AD(3), U% means the highest of—
  (a) 5%,
  (b) CPI% (see sub-paragraph (2)), and
  (c) RPI% (see sub-paragraph (3)).

(2) If the consumer prices index for September in year P is higher than the consumer prices index for September in the tax year preceding year P, CPI% is the percentage increase in the index (but is otherwise 0%).

(3) If the retail prices index for September in year P is higher than the retail prices index for September in the tax year preceding year P, RPI% is the percentage increase in the index (but is otherwise 0%).

(4) In this paragraph "year P" has the same meaning as in paragraph 16AC or (as the case may be) paragraph 16AD."

(4) In paragraph 16B (limit in post-death year)—

(a) in sub-paragraph (3)(c), for "amounts" substitute "uprated amounts (see sub-paragraph (6))", and
(b) after sub-paragraph (5) insert—

"(6) The "uprated amount" of a lump sum is the amount of the lump sum increased by the higher of C% and R%, where—

  (a) if the consumer prices index for the month in which the member dies is higher than it was for the month in which the member became entitled to the lump sum, C% is the percentage increase in the index (but is otherwise 0%), and
  (b) if the retail prices index for the month in which the member dies is higher than it was for the month in which the member became entitled to the lump sum, R% is the percentage increase in the index (but is otherwise 0%)."

(5) In paragraph 16C (limit in subsequent years)—

(a) in sub-paragraph (3)(a), omit "period of",
(b) in sub-paragraph (3)(b), for "subsection" substitute "sub-paragraph",
(c) for sub-paragraphs (4) and (5) substitute—

"(4) The condition is that if the annual rate of a pension payable under the pension scheme to a dependant of the member is increased at any time in the period of 12 months in question

  (a) the dependant is at that time one of a group of at least 20 pensioner members of the pension scheme, and
  (b) all the pensions being paid under the pension scheme to pensioner members of that group are at that time increased at the same rate.",

(d) in sub-paragraph (6)—
  (i) for "month period" substitute "months", and
  (ii) for the words after "increased by" substitute "the permitted margin.",

(e) in sub-paragraph (8)(a), for "end of the post-death year" substitute "member's death",
(f) in sub-paragraph (8)(b), after "first month" insert "ending after the start",
(g) in sub-paragraph (11), for "opening month" substitute "month in which the member died", and
(h) omit sub-paragraphs (13) and (14).

(6) The amendments made by this section are treated as having come into force on 6 April 2016.

(7) The amendments made by subsections (2) to (4), so far as they relate to paragraph 16B of Schedule 28 to FA 2004, have effect where the last day of "the post-death year" (see sub-paragraph (1) of that paragraph) is 6 April 2016 or any later day.

(8) The following amendments—

(a) the amendments made by subsections (2) to (4), so far as they relate to paragraph 16C of Schedule 28 to FA 2004, and
(b) the amendments made by subsection (5),

have effect where the last day of "the 12 months in question" (see sub-paragraph (1) of that paragraph) is 6 April 2016 or any later day.

GENERAL NOTE

Section 21 introduces changes which have effect on or after 6 April 2016 to the anti-avoidance calculations which must otherwise be carried out in respect of annual increases in dependants' scheme pensions where an individual, who was entitled to a scheme pension, dies having reached age 75. Subsection (1) provides that FA 2004 Sch 28 para 16 is amended in accordance with sub-ss (2) to (5).

Subsection (2) provides that application of the limits in FA 2004 Sch 28 paras 16B and 16C operates subject to the provisions of new paras 16AA and 16AB of Sch 28. Subsection (3) inserts new paras 16AA and 16AB in Sch 28. New para 16AA provides when the anti-avoidance calculations in Sch 28 paras 16B and 16C do not apply. New para 16AA(a) provides that the calculations relating to dependants' scheme pensions in Sch 28 paras 16B and 16C do not have to be carried out if the only tests against the member's lifetime allowance were on unused funds in a money purchase arrangement when they reached age 75 (see FA 2004 s 216 benefit crystallisation event 5B). New para 16AA(b) provides that the calculations relating to dependants' scheme pensions in Sch 28 paras 16B and 16C do not have to be carried out where the member had enhanced protection at the time of their death. New para 16AB provides that the calculations relating of dependants' scheme pensions in Sch 28 paras 16B and 16C do not have to be carried out while the total of the amounts payable from a pension scheme as dependants' scheme pensions in respect of a member are less than either the general limit as defined in new para 16AC (see below) or the personal limit as defined in new para 16AD (see below).

New para 16AC sets the general limit for 2016/17 is £25,000 and provides a formula for it to be increased for future years. New para 16AD(1) to (4) defines the personal limit as the total of the annual rate of the member's scheme pensions, both in payment and to which they were entitled, but not yet in payment, in the year in which they died. It too provides a formula for the personal limit to be increased for future years. New para 16AD(5) ignores the amount by which an individual's pension under a public service pension scheme had been reduced in their lifetime thus ensuring the amount of the reduction is added back to determine the maximum rate of the dependants' scheme pension. New para 16AE provides that the rate which the general limit and personal limit in new paras 16AC and 16AD (see above) should be increased is the highest of 5%, the annual increase in the retail prices index or the annual increase in the consumer prices index.

Subsection (4) amends FA 2004 Sch 28 para 16B to allow for the value of tax-free lump sums taken before death to be uprated when calculating the maximum dependants' scheme pension. Subsection 5 amends FA 2004 Sch 28 para 16C by making some minor corrections. Subsection 5(c) amends the "excepted circumstances" in FA 2004 Sch 28 para 16C(4) so that increases to the rate of dependants' scheme pensions are authorised if that rate is the same as that applicable to at least 20 other members of the pension scheme.

Subsection (6) makes it clear that the amendments made by sub-ss (1) to (5) come into force on 6 April 2016. Subsections (7) and (8) also set out that the changes will apply to the calculations in FA 2004 Sch 28 paras 16B and 16C where the last day of the post-death year and the last day of the 12 months in question respectively fall on or after 6 April 2016.

22 Pension flexibility
Schedule 5 makes amendments in connection with pension flexibility.

GENERAL NOTE

Section 22 introduces Sch 5 to make changes to the pensions tax rules removing some unintended consequences that arose following the introduction from 6 April 2015 of pension flexibility in TPA 2014.

23 Netherlands Benefit Act for Victims of Persecution 1940–1945
(1) After section 642 of ITEPA 2003 insert—

"642A Netherlands Benefit Act for Victims of Persecution 1940–1945

No liability to income tax arises on a pension, annuity, allowance or other payment provided in accordance with the provisions of the scheme established under the law of the Netherlands and known as *Wet uitkeringen vervolgingsslachtoffers 1940–1945*."

(2) The amendment made by this section has effect for the tax year 2016–17 and subsequent tax years.

GENERAL NOTE

Section 23(1) amends ITEPA 2003 s 642 to provide that any payments received by individuals under the "Wuv" scheme will be exempt from income tax. Section 23(2) provides that the exemption introduced by s 23(1) applies from 6 April 2016.

Trading and other Income

24 Fixed-rate deductions for use of home for business purposes

(1) In Part 2 of ITTOIA 2005 (trading income), Chapter 5A (trade profits: deductions allowable at a fixed rate) is amended as follows.

(2) Section 94H (use of home for business purposes) is amended as follows.

(3) In subsection (1), for the words from "in respect of" to the end substitute "in respect of—

(a) the use of the person's home for the purposes of the trade, or
(b) where the person is a firm, the use of a partner's home for those purposes."

(4) In subsection (4), for the words from "work done" to the end substitute "qualifying work".

(5) After subsection (4) insert—

"(4A) Qualifying work" means—

(a) work done by the person, or any employee of the person, in the person's home wholly and exclusively for the purposes of the trade, or
(b) where the person is a firm, work done by a partner, or any employee of the firm, in the partner's home wholly and exclusively for those purposes.

(4B) Where more than one person does qualifying work in the same home at the same time, any hour spent wholly and exclusively on that work is to be taken into account only once for the purposes of subsection (4)."

(6) In subsection (5), after "person" insert ", or, where the person is a firm, a partner of the firm,".

(7) After subsection (5) insert—

"(5A) Where a firm makes a deduction for a period under this section in respect of the use of a partner's home for the purposes of a trade, the only deduction which the firm may make for the period in respect of the use of any other partner's home for those purposes is a deduction under this section."

(8) Section 94I (premises used both as a home and as business premises) is amended as follows.

(9) In subsection (1)(b), for "used by the person as a home," substitute "used as a home by—

(i) the person carrying on the trade, or
(ii) where that person is a firm, a partner of the firm,".

(10) After subsection (6) insert—

"(6A) Where a person makes a deduction for a period under this section in respect of expenses incurred in relation to premises falling within subsection (1)(b), the only deduction which the person may make for the period in respect of expenses incurred in relation to any other premises falling within subsection (1)(b) is a deduction under this section."

(11) The amendments made by this section have effect for the tax year 2016–17 and subsequent tax years.

GENERAL NOTE

Section 24 amends from 2016/17 the "simplified expenses" provisions in ITTOIA 2005 Pt 2 Ch 5A (trade profits: deductions allowable at a fixed rate). Amendments to

ITTOIA 2005 ss 94H and 94I are intended to clarify the rules in relation to partnerships and ensure that they are in line with policy objectives.

ITTOIA 2005 s 94H(1) and (5) (use of home for business purposes) are amended to provide that where the taxpayer is a firm, a fixed rate deduction is available in respect of the use of a partner's home for the purposes of the trade.

ITTOIA 2005 s 94H(4) is amended so that the "applicable amount" is calculated by reference to the number of hours spent on "qualifying work". New ITTOIA 2005 s 94H(4A) defines qualifying work to include, where the person is a firm, work done by a partner or any employee of the firm, in the partner's home wholly and exclusively for the purposes of the trade.

New ITTOIA 2005 s 94H(4B) provides that where more than one person does qualifying work in the same home at the same time, any hour spent wholly and exclusively on that work cannot be counted more than once for the purpose of this deduction.

ITTOIA 2005 s 94I(1) (premises used both as a home and as business premises) is amended to provide that where the taxpayer is a firm, a fixed rate deduction is available in respect of a partner's the use of the premises as a home.

There are two new measures to ensure consistency of treatment:

–   new ITTOIA 2005 s 94H(5A) provides that if a firm makes a deduction under ITTOIA 2005 s 94H in respect of the use of a partner's home, the only deduction the firm may make in respect of the use of any other partner's home is a deduction under the same provision; and

–   new ITTOIA 2005 s 94I(6A) provides that where an individual or partnership has more than one premises used for business and as a home, and a deduction is made under ITTOIA 2005 s 94I, then the only deduction the person may make in respect of expenses incurred in relation to any other premises is a deduction under the same provision.

25 Averaging profits of farmers etc

(1) Chapter 16 of Part 2 of ITTOIA 2005 (averaging profits of farmers and creative artists) is amended as specified in subsections (2) to (7).

(2) In section 221 (claim for averaging of fluctuating profits)—

(a) in subsection (2), at the beginning insert "For the purposes of section 222 (two-year averaging)";

(b) after that subsection insert—

"(2A) For the purposes of section 222A (five-year averaging), a trade, profession or vocation is a "qualifying trade, profession or vocation" if it falls within subsection (2)(a) or (b).";

(c) in subsection (3), for "this purpose" substitute "the purpose of subsection (2)".

(3) After section 222 insert—

"222A Circumstances in which claim for five-year averaging may be made

(1) An averaging claim may be made under this section in relation to five consecutive tax years in which a taxpayer is or has been carrying on the qualifying trade, profession or vocation if the volatility condition in subsection (2) is met.

(2) The volatility condition is that—

(a) one of the following is less than 75% of the other—

(i) the average of the relevant profits of the first four tax years to which the claim relates;

(ii) the relevant profits of the last of the tax years to which the claim relates; or

(b) the relevant profits of one or more (but not all) of the five tax years to which the claim relates are nil.

(3) Any of the first four tax years to which an averaging claim under this section relates may be a tax year in relation to which an averaging claim under this section or section 222 has already been made.

(4) An averaging claim ("the subsequent claim") may not be made under this section if an averaging claim in respect of the trade, profession or vocation has already been made under this section or section 222 in relation to a tax year which is later than the last of the tax years to which the subsequent claim relates.

(5) An averaging claim may not be made under this section in relation to the tax year in which the taxpayer starts, or permanently ceases, to carry on the trade, profession or vocation.

(6) An averaging claim under this section must be made on or before the first anniversary of the normal self-assessment filing date for the last of the tax years to which the claim relates.

(7) But see section 225(4) (extended time limit if profits adjusted for some other reason)."

(4) In section 222 (circumstances in which claim may be made)—

(a) in the heading, after "claim" insert "for two-year averaging";
(b) in subsection (1), after "made" insert "under this section";
(c) for subsection (2) substitute—

"(2) The earlier of the two years to which an averaging claim under this section relates may be a tax year in relation to which an averaging claim under this section or section 222A has already been made.";

(d) in subsection (3)—

(i) after "made", in the first place, insert "under this section";
(ii) after "made", in the second place, insert "under this section or section 222A";

(e) in subsection (4), after "made" insert "under this section";
(f) in subsection (5), after "averaging claim" insert "under this section".

(5) In section 223 (adjustment of profits)—

(a) in subsection (2), for "second of the two tax years" substitute "last of the two or five tax years";
(b) for subsection (3) substitute—

"(3) The amount of the adjusted profits of each of the tax years to which the claim relates is the average of the relevant profits of those tax years.";

(c) omit subsection (4).

(6) In section 224 (effect of adjustment)—

(a) in subsection (4), for "either" substitute "any";
(b) in subsection (6), for "second of the two tax years" substitute "last of the two or five tax years".

(7) In section 225 (effect of later adjustment of profits), in subsection (1), for "either or both" substitute "any one or more".

(8) In section 31C of ITTOIA 2005 (excluded provisions), in subsection (6), for "section 221" substitute "Chapter 16".

(9) In section 1025 of ITA 2007 (meaning of "modified net income"), in subsection (2)(d), for "the earlier of the tax years" substitute "any earlier tax year".

(10) In paragraph 3 of Schedule 1B to TMA 1970 (relief for fluctuating profits of farmers etc)

(a) in sub-paragraph (1), for the words from "for two" to the end substitute—
    "(a) in the case of a two-year claim, for two consecutive years of assessment, and
    (b) in the case of a five-year claim, for five consecutive years of assessment.";
(b) in sub-paragraph (2), for "the later year" substitute "the last of the two or five years";
(c) in sub-paragraph (3), for "the earlier year", where it occurs first, substitute "an earlier year";
(d) in sub-paragraph (5)—

(i) for "the earlier year" substitute "an earlier year";
(ii) for "the later year" substitute "the last of the two or five years";

(e) after sub-paragraph (6) insert—

"(7) In this paragraph—

"two-year claim" means a claim under section 222 of ITTOIA 2005;
"five-year claim" means a claim under section 222A of ITTOIA 2005."

(11) In paragraph 4 of Schedule 1B to TMA 1970 (relief claimed by virtue of section 224(4) of ITTOIA 2005)—

(a) in sub-paragraph (1)—

(i) after "for two" insert "or five";
(ii) omit "("the earlier year" and "the later year")",
(iii) for "either" substitute "any";

(b) in sub-paragraph (2), for "the later year" substitute "the last of the two or five years";

(c) in sub-paragraph (3), for "the earlier year", where it occurs first, substitute "an earlier year";

(d) in sub-paragraph (5)—

(i) for "the earlier year" substitute "an earlier year";

(ii) for "the later year" substitute "the last of the two or five years".

(12) The amendments made by this section have effect for the tax year 2016–17 and subsequent tax years.

GENERAL NOTE

Section 25 extends from two to five years the period over which taxpayers carrying on a qualifying trade of farming, or intensive rearing of livestock or fish can average fluctuating profits. ITTOIA 2005 Pt 2 Ch 16 (averaging profits of farmers and creative artists) is amended with effect for 2016/17 onwards.

A claim to average profits may be made if the taxpayer is, or has been, carrying on a qualifying trade, profession or vocation. Averaging is not available where the cash basis is used in calculating profits.

Budget 2015 announced that the averaging period would be extended to five years, but following consultation the Government decided that "the optimum balance between flexibility and simplicity will be achieved by retaining the existing two-year averaging regime and providing an additional option that will give farmers the choice of averaging over a five-year period or a two-year period".

The Government also decided to remove the marginal relief set out in ITTOIA 2005 s 223(4) in order to simplify the regime. The "volatility level" is set at 75%.

ITTOIA 2005 s 221(2) is amended so that, while the activities (a),(b) and (c) below continue to qualify for "two-year averaging", only activities (a) and (b) will qualify for the new "five-year averaging":

— farming or market gardening in the United Kingdom;

— intensive rearing in the United Kingdom of livestock or fish on a commercial basis for the production of food for human consumption;

— creative works.

Five-year averaging

Subsection (3) inserts new ITTOIA 2005 s 222A. A claim for five-year averaging may be made in relation to five consecutive tax years in which the taxpayer is or has been carrying on the qualifying activity if the "volatility condition" is met. That condition is met if:

— one of the following is less than 75% of the other:

— the average of the relevant profits of the first four tax years to which the claim relates, and

— the relevant profits of the last of the tax years to which the claim relates; or

— the relevant profits of one or more, but not all, of the five tax years to which the claim relates are nil.

Any of the first four tax years may be a tax year for which a two-year or five-year averaging claim has already been made. However:

— a five-year averaging claim (the "subsequent claim") may not be made if a two-year or five-year averaging claim has already been made in relation to a tax year later than the last of the tax years to which the subsequent claim relates; and

— a five-year averaging claim may not be made in relation to the tax year in which the taxpayer starts, or permanently ceases, to carry on the trade, profession or vocation.

The claim must be made on or before the first anniversary of the normal self-assessment filing date for the last of the tax years to which it relates, but this time limit may be extended in the event that profits are adjusted for some reason other than an averaging claim.

Two-year averaging

Subsection (4) amends ITTOIA 2005 s 222 which sets out the circumstances in which an two-year averaging claim may be made.

A claim may be made in relation to two consecutive tax years in which the taxpayer is or has been carrying on the qualifying activity if:

- the relevant profits of one of the tax years are less than 75% of the relevant profits of the other tax year, or
- the relevant profits of one (but not both) of the tax years are nil.

The earlier of the two years to which a two-year averaging claim relates may be a tax year in relation to which a two-year or five-year averaging claim has already been made. However:

- a two-year averaging claim may not be made in relation to a tax year if a two-year or five-year averaging claim has already been made in relation to a later tax year in respect of the trade, profession or vocation; and
- a two-year averaging claim may not be made in relation to the tax year in which the taxpayer starts, or permanently ceases, to carry on the trade, profession or vocation (or in the case of a trade, profession or vocation within (c) above the activity begins or ceases to be a qualifying trade, profession or vocation).

The claim must be made on or before the first anniversary of the normal self-assessment filing date for the second of the tax years to which it relates, but this time limit may be extended in the event that profits are adjusted for some reason other than an averaging claim.

Adjustment of profits

Subsection (5) makes consequential changes to ITTOIA 2005 s 223 and repeals the rule in ITTOIA 2005 s 223(4) setting how the adjustment required when the relevant profits of one of the two tax years in a two-year averaging claim are more than 70% but less than 75% of the relevant profits of the other tax year.

Other amendments

There are also consequential amendments to ITTOIA 2005 s 225 (effect of later adjustment of profits), ITTOIA 2005 s 31C (cash basis: excluded persons), and ITA 2007 s 1025 (meaning of "modified net income").

Subsections (10) and (11) amend TMA 1970 Sch 1B paras 3 and 4 respectively to reflect the new five-year averaging claim. Paragraph 3 sets out the effect of an averaging claim. Paragraph 4 sets out the treatment of claims to relief under other provisions that would otherwise be out of time.

26 Relief for finance costs related to residential property businesses

(1) In ITTOIA 2005, for sections 274A and 274B and the preceding italic heading (tax reductions for non-deductible costs of dwelling-related loans: individuals, and accumulated or discretionary trust income) substitute—

"Tax reductions for non-deductible costs of a dwelling-related loan

274A Reduction for individuals: entitlement

(1) If for a tax year an individual has—

(a) a relievable amount in respect of a property business, or

(b) two or more relievable amounts each in respect of a different property business,

the individual is entitled to relief under this section for that year in respect of that relievable amount or (as the case may be) each of those relievable amounts.

(2) An individual has a relievable amount for a tax year in respect of a property business if for that year the individual has any one or more of the following in respect of that business—

(a) a current-year amount;

(b) a current-year estate amount;

(c) a brought-forward amount.

(3) An individual's relievable amount for a tax year in respect of a property business is the total of—

(a) the individual's current-year amount (if any) for that year in respect of that business,

(b) the individual's current-year estate amounts (if any) for that year in respect of that business, and

(c) the individual's brought-forward amount (if any) for that year in respect of that business.

(4) An individual has a current-year amount for a tax year in respect of a property business if—

(a) an amount ("A") would be deductible in calculating the profits for income tax purposes of that business for that year but for section 272A,

(b) the individual is liable for income tax on N% of those profits, where N is a number—

    (i) greater than 0, and

    (ii) less than or equal to 100, and

(c) that liability is not under Chapter 6 of Part 5 (estate income),

in which event the individual's current-year amount for that tax year in respect of that business is equal to N% of A.

(5) An individual has a current-year estate amount for a tax year ("the current year"), in respect of a property business and a particular deceased person's estate, if—

(a) an amount ("A") would, but for section 272A, be deductible in calculating the profits for income tax purposes of that business for a particular tax year ("the profits year"), whether that year is the current year or an earlier tax year,

(b) the personal representatives of the deceased person are liable for income tax on N% of those profits, where N is a number—

    (i) greater than 0, and

    (ii) less than or equal to 100,

(c) the individual is liable for income tax on estate income treated under Chapter 6 of Part 5 as arising in the current year from an interest in the estate, and

(d) the basic amount of that estate income consists of, or includes, an amount representative of E% of the personal representatives' N% of the profits of the business for the profits year, where E is a number—

    (i) greater than 0, and

    (ii) less than or equal to 100,

in which event the individual's current-year estate amount for the current tax year, in respect of that business and estate and the profits year, is equal to E% of N% of A.

(6) As to whether an individual has a brought-forward amount for a tax year in respect of a property business, see section 274AA(4).

(7) In this section and section 274AA—

"estate income", and

"basic amount" in relation to any estate income,

have the same meaning as in Chapter 6 of Part 5 (see sections 649 and 656(4)).

274AA Reduction for individuals: calculation

(1) This section applies if for a tax year an individual is entitled to relief under section 274A in respect of a relievable amount or in respect of each of two or more relievable amounts, and in the following subsections of this section "relievable amount" means that relievable amount or (as the case may be) any of those relievable amounts.

(2) In respect of a relievable amount, the actual amount on which relief for the year is to be given is (subject to subsection (3)) the amount ("L") that is the lower of—

(a) the relievable amount, and

(b) the total of—

    (i) the profits for income tax purposes of the property business concerned for the year after any deduction under section 118 of ITA 2007 ("the adjusted profits") or, if less, the share (if any) of the adjusted profits on which the individual is liable to income tax otherwise than under Chapter 6 of Part 5, and

    (ii) so much (if any) of the relievable amount as consists of current-year estate amounts.

(3) If S is greater than the individual's adjusted total income for the year ("ATI"), the actual amount on which relief for the year is to be given in respect of a relievable amount is given by—

(ATI / S) x L

where—

S is the total obtained by identifying the amount that is L for each relievable amount and then finding the total of the amounts identified, and

L has the same meaning as in subsection (2).

(4) Where—

(a) a relievable amount,

is greater than—

(b) the actual amount on which relief for the year is to be given in respect of the relievable amount,

the difference is the individual's brought-forward amount for the following tax year in respect of the property business concerned.

(5) The amount of the relief for the year in respect of a relievable amount is given by—

AA x BR

     where—

         AA is the actual amount on which relief for the year is to be given in respect of the relievable amount, and

         BR is the basic rate of income tax for the year,

(6) For the purposes of this section, an individual's adjusted total income for a tax year is identified as follows—

Step 1

Identify the individual's net income for the year (see Step 2 of the calculation in section 23 of ITA 2007).

Step 2

Exclude from that net income—

         (a) so much of it as is within section 18(3) or (4) of ITA 2007 (income from savings), and

         (b) so much of it as is dividend income.

Step 3

Reduce what is left after Step 2 of this calculation by the amount of any allowances deducted for the year in the individual's case at Step 3 of the calculation in section 23 of ITA 2007. The result is the individual's adjusted total income for the year.

274B Reduction for accumulated or discretionary trust income: entitlement

(1) If for a tax year the trustees of a settlement have—

         (a) a relievable amount in respect of a property business, or

         (b) two or more relievable amounts each in respect of a different property business,

the trustees of the settlement are entitled to relief under this section for that year in respect of that relievable amount or (as the case may be) each of those relievable amounts.

(2) The trustees of a settlement have a relievable amount for a tax year in respect of a property business if for that year the trustees of the settlement have a current-year amount, or brought-forward amount, in respect of that business (or have both).

(3) In the case of trustees of a settlement, their relievable amount for a tax year in respect of a property business is the total of—

         (a) their current-year amount (if any) for that year in respect of that business, and

         (b) their brought-forward amount (if any) for that year in respect of that business.

(4) The trustees of a settlement have a current-year amount for a tax year in respect of a property business if—

         (a) an amount ("A") would be deductible in calculating the profits for income tax purposes of that business for that year but for section 272A,

         (b) the trustees of the settlement are liable for income tax on N% of those profits, where N is a number—

             (i) greater than 0, and

             (ii) less than or equal to 100, and

         (c) in relation to the trustees of the settlement, that N% of those profits is accumulated or discretionary income,

in which event the current-year amount of the trustees of the settlement for that tax year in respect of that business is equal to N% of A.

(5) As to whether the trustees of a settlement have a brought-forward amount for a tax year in respect of a property business, see section 274C(3).

(6) In this section and section 274C "accumulated or discretionary income" has the meaning given by section 480 of ITA 2007.

274C Reduction for accumulated or discretionary trust income: calculation

(1) This section applies if for a tax year the trustees of a settlement are entitled to relief under section 274B in respect of a relievable amount or in respect of each of

two or more relievable amounts, and in the following subsections of this section "relievable amount" means that relievable amount or (as the case may be) any of those relievable amounts.

(2) The amount of the relief in respect of a relievable amount is given by—

L x BR

   where—

      BR is the basic rate of income tax for the year, and
      L is the lower of—

         (a) the relievable amount, and
         (b) the profits for income tax purposes of the property business concerned for the year after any deduction under section 118 of ITA 2007 ("the adjusted profits") or, if less, the share of the adjusted profits—

            (i) on which the trustees of the settlement are liable for income tax, and
            (ii) which, in relation to the trustees of the settlement, is accumulated or discretionary income.

(3) Where L in the case of a relievable amount is less than the relievable amount, the difference between them is the brought-forward amount of the trustees of the settlement for the following tax year in respect of the property business concerned."

(2) In consequence of the amendment made by subsection (1), in F(No 2)A 2015 omit section 24(5).

GENERAL NOTE

F(No 2)A 2015 radically changed the way in which relief was given for interest and other finance costs incurred in relation to let residential property. Instead of interest, etc being allowed as a deduction in the computation of profits, as had previously been the case, relief would in future instead be given, only at basic rate, as a deduction against a person's total income tax liability. Section 26 does not fundamentally alter the principle of those changes, but makes a number of technical amendments to the legislation to ensure that they operate as intended, particularly in relation to beneficiaries of deceased persons' estates. The new provisions need to read in conjunction with the original F(No 2)A 2015 legislation – they are not a complete code in themselves.

Section 26(1)

This introduces new ITTOIA 2005 ss 274A–274C.

New s 274A: Reduction for individuals: entitlement

New s 274A(1)

This sets out the basic conditions for relief. A person has entitlement to relief if he has a relievable amount in respect of a property business or more than one relievable amount in respect of different property businesses.

New s 274A(2)

This states that a person has a relievable amount for a tax year in respect of a property business if he has one or more of the following: a current year amount, a current year estate amount or a brought-forward amount. All of these terms are defined later in this section.

New s 274A(3)

An individual's total relievable amount for a tax year in respect of a property business is the total of his current year amount, current year estate amount and brought forward amount.

New s 274A(4)

This operates where a person has a current year amount in respect of a property business. Where he has interest of other finance costs which would be deductible against his property profits but for the prohibition in s 272A (i.e. the provision introduced in FA 2015 to disallow such costs in computing profits) the amount of those costs is then restricted by reference to the proportion of the profits of the property business for which he is liable to income tax. A sole trader would be liable to income tax on the whole of the profits and therefore there is no restriction on his current year amount. But a person who carried on a business in an equal share partnership with three other individuals would have a current year amount of 25% of the interest and finance costs. In other words this section ensures that individuals get a tax credit for their share of the total finance costs.

New s 274A(5)

This applies the same principles in new s 274A(4) to current year estate amounts, i.e. income arising as a personal representative of a deceased person's estate.

New s 274A(6)

The test in s 274A(4) applies in determining whether an individual has a brought forward amount for a tax year in respect of a property business.

New s 274A(7)

This imports the definition of estate income and basic amount in relation to any estate income from Pt 5 Ch 6 ITOIA 2005, which is the section defining the way that trust income is taxed.

New s 274AA: Reduction for individuals: calculation

New s 274AA(1)

This introduces the calculation of relief available where a person has a relievable amount or more than one relievable amount under s 274A.

New s 274AA(2)

The amount on which relief is to be given is (subject to the further restriction in sub 3 below) the lower of:
– that relievable amount and
– the total of the adjusted profits for the year (after any deduction under s118 (losses carried forward) or, if less, the share of adjusted profits on which the individual is liable to income tax other than under Chapter 6 part 5 (income of beneficiaries) adding in both cases so much of the relievable amount which consist of current year estate amounts.

This is extremely hard to follow, but what it means is that the amount of interest which will be available for relief will be the actual amount of interest (including amounts brought forward) unless that amount is greater than the sum of the individual's share of the profits of the business plus any estate income from property. In that case it will be restricted to the latter amount.

New s 274AA(3)

This deals with the position where the total relievable amounts for an individual are greater than his total adjusted income. This would be the case, for example where some of the income is covered by the personal allowance. In this case the amount of relief is restricted to the total income after personal allowances, apportioned on a pro rata basis where the individual has more than one property business.

New s 274AA(4)

Where the relievable amount is greater than the amount on which relief is actually given (for example because it exceeds the adjusted profits for the year) the excess becomes that person's brought forward amount for the following year.

New s 274AA(5)

The amount of relief is for the year is the amount on which relief is to be given multiplied by the basic rate of income tax. In other words only basic rate relief is given for interest and other finance costs paid in connection with a property business.

New s 274AA(6)

This sets out the calculation of a person's adjusted total income for a year, which is necessary for the adjustment at sub-s (3) above. The total adjusted income is his net income for the year (i.e. at Step 2 of the calculation in ITA 2007 s 23), less savings and dividend income and less allowances (e.g. the personal allowance).

This and the following section import similar principles to those in ss 274A and 274AA above into the taxation of trust income from property.

New s 274B: Reduction for accumulated or discretionary trust income: entitlement

New s 274B(1)

The section applies where the trustees of a settlement have a relievable amount (or amounts) from one or more property businesses. If this condition applies the trustees are entitlement to relief.

New s 274B(2)

The trustees have a relievable amount if they have a current year amount or a brought forward amount in respect of a property business.

New s 274B(3)

Their relievable amount is the sum of the trustees current year amount and their brought-forward amount.

New s 274B(4)

This defines when trustees have a current year amount. There are three conditions:
– there must be an amount which would be deductible in calculating the profits of a property business apart from s 272A (i.e. finance costs);
– the trustees are liable for income tax on some or all of those profits;
– the profits on which the trustees are liable is accumulated or discretionary income of the trust.

Where these three conditions apply the trustees have a current year amount equal to their percentage of the amount in s 274B(4)(a).

New s 274B(5)

This refers to new s 274C(3) below for a determination of whether the trustees have a brought-forward amount.

New s 274B(6)

This imports the definition of accumulated or discretionary income from ITA 2007 s 480.

New s 274C: Reduction for accumulated or discretionary trust income: calculation

New s 274C(1)

This introduces the section. It applies if the trustees of a settlement are, for a tax year, entitled to one or more relievable amounts under s 274B above.

New s 274C(2)

The amount of relief for a relievable amount is given by the formulate L* BR
BR is the basic rate of income tax for the year
L is the lower of:
– the relievable amount; and
– the adjusted profits for the year of the property business, or -if less – the share of the adjusted profits on which the trustees are liable to income tax and which is accumulated or discretionary income of the settlement.

New s 274C(3)

Where the result of applying the formula in s 274C(2) above results in an amount which is less than the relievable amount the balance is the brought forward amount for the following year.

27 Individual investment plans of deceased investors
(1) In Chapter 3 of Part 6 of ITTOIA 2005 (power to exempt income from individual investment plans from income tax), after section 694 insert—

"694A Deceased investors
    (1) In section 694(1) "income of an individual from investments under a plan" includes—
        (a) income (of any person) from administration-period investments under a plan, and
        (b) income (of any person) from the estate of a deceased person ("D") where the whole or any part of the income of D's personal representatives is income from administration-period investments under a plan.
    (2) For the purposes of sections 694(3)(a) and (4) and 695(1) "individual", in relation to investments that are administration-period investments, includes—
        (a) the personal representatives of the deceased individual concerned, and
        (b) any other person on whose directions plan managers agree to act in relation to the investments.
    (3) In sections 699 and 701 "investor" includes a person entitled to an exemption given by investment plan regulations by virtue of subsection (1) of this section.
    (4) Investments are "administration-period investments" if—
        (a) an individual dies, and
        (b) immediately before the individual's death—
            (i) the investments were held under a plan,
            (ii) the individual was entitled to the income from the investments, and
            (iii) as a result of investment plan regulations, the individual's income from investments under the plan was exempt from income tax (either wholly or to an extent specified in the regulations).
    (5) Investments are also "administration-period investments" if (directly or indirectly) they represent investments that are administration-period investments as a result of subsection (4).
    (6) Investment plan regulations may provide that investments are administration-period investments as a result of subsection (4) or (5) only at times specified in, or ascertained in accordance with, the regulations.
    (7) Provision under subsection (6) may (in particular) be framed by reference to the completion of the administration of a deceased individual's estate.
    (8) In the application of subsection (7) in relation to Scotland, the reference to the completion of the administration is to be read in accordance with section 653(2)."
(2) In section 151(2) of TCGA 1992 (Chapter 3 of Part 6 of ITTOIA 2005 applies with modifications in relation to regulations giving relief from capital gains tax in respect of investments under plans)—
    (a) in the words before paragraph (a), for "section 694(1) to (2)" substitute "sections 694(1) to (2) and 694A(1)", and
    (b) after paragraph (a) insert—
        "(aa) section 694A(2) applies also for the purposes of subsection (1) of this section,
        (ab) the reference in section 694A(3) to section 694A(1) is to be read as a reference to paragraph (aa) of this subsection,
        (ac) the reference in section 694A(4)(b)(iii) to the individual's income from investments under the plan being exempt from income tax is to be read as a reference to the individual being entitled to relief from capital gains tax in respect of the investments,".
(3) In section 62 of TCGA 1992 (death: general provisions), after subsection (4) (acquisition of asset as legatee) insert—
    "(4A) The Treasury may by regulations make provision having effect in place of subsection (4)(b) above in a case where there has been a time when the personal representatives—
        (a) held the asset acquired by the legatee, and
        (b) would, if they had disposed of the asset at that time—
            (i) by way of a bargain at arm's length, and
            (ii) otherwise than to a legatee,
    have been entitled as a result of regulations under section 151 (investments under plans) to relief from capital gains tax in respect of any chargeable gain accruing on the disposal.

(4B) Provision made by regulations under subsection (4A) above may (in particular) treat a person who acquires an asset as legatee as doing so at a time or for a consideration, or at a time and for a consideration, ascertained as specified by the regulations."

(4) In consequence of subsection (2)(a), in FA 2011 omit section 40(6)(a).

GENERAL NOTE

Section 27 amends ITTOIA 2005 Pt 6 Ch 3 (exempt income: income from individual investment plan) so that HM Treasury may provide by regulations that individual savings accounts (ISA) may retain their tax-advantaged status following the account holder's death.

New ITTOIA 2005 s 694A provides that in ITTOIA 2005 s 694(1) "income of an individual under a plan" includes income of any person from:

– administration-period investments (as defined) under a plan;, and
– the estate of a deceased person ("D") where all or part of the income of D's personal representatives is income from administration-period investments under a plan.

"Individual" in relation to such investments includes the deceased individual's personal representatives and any other person on whose directions plan managers agree to act.

TCGA 1992 ss 62 and 151 are amended to providing corresponding relief for capital gains tax.

Reliefs: Enterprise Investment Scheme, Venture Capital Trusts etc

28 EIS, SEIS and VCTs: exclusion of energy generation

(1) In section 192(1) of ITA 2007 (meaning of "excluded activities": EIS and SEIS), for paragraphs (ka) to (kc) substitute—

"(ka) generating or exporting electricity or making electricity generating capacity available,
(kb) generating heat,
(kc) generating any form of energy not within paragraph (ka) or (kb),
(kd) producing gas or fuel, and".

(2) In section 303(1) of ITA 2007 (meaning of "excluded activities": VCTs), for paragraphs (ka) to (kc) substitute—

"(ka) generating or exporting electricity or making electricity generating capacity available,
(kb) generating heat,
(kc) generating any form of energy not within paragraph (ka) or (kb),
(kd) producing gas or fuel, and".

(3) In consequence of subsection (1), ITA 2007 is amended as follows—
  (a) in section 192(2)—
    (i) for paragraph (g) substitute "and
    (g) section 198A (export of electricity).";
    (ii) omit paragraph (h);
  (b) in section 198A—
    (i) in the heading, omit "subsidised generation or";
    (ii) omit subsections (3) to (9);
  (c) omit section 198B.

(4) In consequence of subsection (2), ITA 2007 is amended as follows—
  (a) in section 303(2)—
    (i) for paragraph (g) substitute "and
    (g) section 309A (export of electricity).";
    (ii) omit paragraph (h);
  (b) in section 309A—
    (i) in the heading, omit "subsidised generation or";
    (ii) omit subsections (3) to (9);
  (c) omit section 309B.

(5) The amendments made by subsections (1) and (3) have effect in relation to shares issued on or after 6 April 2016.

(6) The amendments made by subsections (2) and (4) have effect in relation to relevant holdings issued on or after 6 April 2016.

GENERAL NOTE

Over the past few years there has been considerable investment by EIS and VCT investors in companies carrying on a trade of energy production. The Government considers that the nature of these activities no longer requires State aid support, whether the activities are subsidised or not. In addition, recent changes are focussing investment on higher risk activities. There is also a general move to prevent cumulation, i.e. activities benefiting from more than one government subsidy.

Section 28 now excludes all energy generating activities, including the production of gas or other fuel from SEIS, EIS, VCT and SITR for investments made on or after 6 April 2016.

The exclusion of subsidised renewable energy and reserve capacity is now replaced with a new broader exclusion. Any form of energy generating activities, all electricity generating and storage activities including making capacity available, any activities generating heat and those producing gas or fuel, are not qualifying activities for the venture capital tax schemes. The new exclusions apply to both non-renewable and renewable sources of energy generation.

Section 192(1) ITA 2007 is amended for the purposes of EIS and SEIS and paras (ka)–(kc) are replaced to remove exclude all energy generating activities. A new para (kd) excludes the production of gas or fuel. As a consequence of this s 192(2) is further amended, s 192(2)(i)(g) is replaced to exclude the export of electricity and para (h) is removed.

For VCT purposes s 303(1) ITA 2007 is amended and paras (ka)–(kc) are replaced to remove exclude all energy generating activities and a new para (kd) excludes the production of gas or fuel. As a consequence of this s 303(2) is further amended, s 303(2)(i)(g) is replaced to exclude the export of electricity, and para (h) is removed.

29 EIS and VCTs: definition of certain periods

(1) In section 175A of ITA 2007 (EIS: the permitted maximum age requirement)—

(a) in subsection (7) for the words from "five" to the end substitute "relevant five year period.";

(b) after that subsection insert—

"(7A) Subject to subsection (7B), the relevant five year period is the five year period which ends immediately before the beginning of the last accounts filing period.

(7B) If the last accounts filing period ends more than 12 months before the issue date, the relevant five year period is the five year period which ends 12 months before the issue date."

(2) In section 252A of ITA 2007 (EIS: meaning of "knowledge-intensive company")—

(a) in subsection (4), in the definition of "the relevant three preceding years", for the words from "means" to the end substitute "means, subject to subsection (4A), the three consecutive years the last of which ends immediately before the beginning of the last accounts filing period.";

(b) after that subsection insert—

"(4A) If the last accounts filing period ends more than 12 months before the date on which the relevant shares are issued, the relevant three preceding years are the three consecutive years the last of which ends 12 months before the date on which the relevant shares are issued."

(3) In section 280C of ITA 2007 (VCTs: the permitted maximum age condition)—

(a) in subsection (8) for the words from "five" to the end substitute "relevant five year period.";

(b) after that subsection insert—

"(8A) Subject to subsection (8B), the relevant five year period is the five year period which ends immediately before the beginning of the last accounts filing period.

(8B) If the last accounts filing period ends more than 12 months before the investment date, the relevant five year period is the five year period which ends 12 months before the investment date."

(4) In section 294A of ITA 2007 (VCTs: the permitted company age requirement)—

    (a) in subsection (7) for the words from "five" to the end substitute "relevant five year period.";

    (b) after that subsection insert—

"(7A) Subject to subsection (7B), the relevant five year period is the five year period which ends immediately before the beginning of the last accounts filing period.

(7B) If the last accounts filing period ends more than 12 months before the investment date, the relevant five year period is the five year period which ends 12 months before the investment date."

(5) In section 331A of ITA 2007 (VCTs: meaning of "knowledge-intensive company")—

    (a) in subsection (5), in the definition of "the relevant three preceding years", for the words from "means" to the end substitute "means, subject to subsection (5A), the three consecutive years the last of which ends immediately before the beginning of the last accounts filing period.";

    (b) after that subsection insert—

"(5A) If the last accounts filing period ends more than 12 months before the applicable time, the relevant three preceding years are the three consecutive years the last of which ends 12 months before the applicable time."

(6) The amendments made by this section are to be treated as always having had effect; but this is subject to section 30.

GENERAL NOTE

Finance (No 2) Act 2015 introduced radical changes to the venture capital tax schemes. These changes include a permitted maximum age limit for companies receiving finance under the schemes.

For investments made under the EIS and by VCTs, s 29 clarifies the method of determining if a company meets the permitted maximum age limit or if a company is a knowledge-intensive company. The changes apply to all companies that issue shares under the EIS or that receive a relevant investment from a VCT on or after 18 November 2015, and are therefore retrospective in the absence of an election (see Section 30).

The changes are introduced to ensure that the tests at Finance (No 2) Act 2015 Sch 5 paras 12 and 19 (for EIS purposes) and Schedule 6 paras 5, 11 and 20 (for VCT purposes) work as originally intended, and that changing accounting period dates does not provide an advantage.

The average turnover amount in ss 175A(7), 280C(8) and 294A(7) considers a five year period to determine if a company meets Condition B of the permitted maximum age requirement. Sections 252A(4) and 331A(5) consider a three-year period for companies which are "knowledge-intensive".

The changes are designed to clarify the method used to determine the end of the five-year period for average turnover amounts in ss 175A(7), 280C(8) and 294A(7), and the relevant three preceding years for the operating costs conditions in s 252A(4) and s 331A(5).

Subsection (1) amends s 175A ITA 2007 for EIS purposes, sub-s (3) amends s 280A ITA 2007 and sub-s (4) amends s 294A ITA 2007 such that the average turnover amount for the five-year period used to calculate the permitted maximum age requirement becomes one-fifth of the total relevant turnover for the "relevant five year period". That relevant five-year period becomes the five-year period which ends immediately before the beginning of the last account filing period. If the last account filing period ends more than 12 months before the issue date then the relevant five-year period is the five-year period which ends 12 months before the issue date. The measure is introduced to ensure that the most recently filed accounts are used. It means existing accounts can be used negating the need to draw up accounts to a special date.

Subsection (2) amends s 252A ITA 2007 for EIS purposes and sub-s (5) amends s 331A ITA 2007 for VCT purposes so that the definition of the relevant three preceding years becomes the three consecutive years the last of which ends immediately before the beginning of the last accounts filing period. New ss 252A(44) and 331A(5A) are added which applies when the last accounts filing period ends more than 12 months before the date the relevant shares are issued or investment is made, in which case the relevant prior years are the three consecutive years the last of which ends 12 months before the date on which the relevant shares are issued or investment is made.

30 EIS and VCTs: election

(1) If a company ("the relevant company") makes an election for this section to apply, then—

  (a) the amendments made by subsection (1) of section 29 do not apply in relation to shares issued by the relevant company in the material period,

  (b) the amendments made by subsection (2) of that section do not apply for the purposes of determining whether, at the date of issue of any shares issued by the company in the material period, the company is a knowledge-intensive company for the purposes of Part 5 of ITA 2007,

  (c) the amendments made by subsection (3) of that section do not apply in relation to investments made in the relevant company in the material period,

  (d) the amendments made by subsection (4) of that section do not apply for the purposes of determining whether the requirement of section 294A of ITA 2007 is met in relation to any holding of shares or securities issued by the relevant company in the material period, and

  (e) the amendments made by subsection (5) of that section do not apply for the purposes of determining whether, at any time in the material period which is the applicable time within the meaning given by section 331A of ITA 2007, the relevant company is a knowledge-intensive company for the purposes of Part 6 of ITA 2007.

(2) Amendments that by reason of an election under this section do not apply in relation to particular shares or investments or for particular purposes are also to be treated as never having applied in relation to those shares or investments or for those purposes.

(3) Any election under this section must be made in writing and signed by a director of the relevant company.

(4) Where a company has made an election under this section—

  (a) it must include a statement that the election has been made in any compliance statement subsequently provided by it under section 204(2) of ITA 2007 in respect of an issue of shares made by it in the material period, and

  (b) it must provide a copy of the election to each company to which it has issued shares or securities in the material period.

(5) An election under this section is irrevocable.

(6) In this section "the material period" means the period beginning with 18 November 2015 (the date when F(No 2)A 2015 was passed) and ending with 5 April 2016.

GENERAL NOTE

Section 30 permits companies receiving an investment under the EIS or from a VCT to elect for the amendments in s 29 not to apply to investments made before 6 April 2016. The effect is that the five-year period for the average turnover amount and the three year period for the operating cost condition is calculated as set out in Finance (No 2) Act 2015 for shares issued or investments made between 18 November 2015 and 5 April 2016 (inclusive).

Subsection (1) specifies the effect of an election, which is that the rules which determine the applicable five-year period (for the permitted maximum age limit) and the three-year period (for "knowledge-intensive companies) introduced by Schs 5 and 6 Finance (No 2) Act 2015 will apply to all investments made in the company up to and including 5 April 2016.

Subsections (3) and (4) specify the processes. The election must be in writing and a director of the company must sign and date the election. The election will apply to all investments received the company in the period from 18 November 2015 (the date of Royal Assent of Finance (No 2) Act 2015) and 5 April 2016. In addition if any EIS compliance statements are submitted in relation to shares issued before 6 April 2016 the company must state that an election has been made. Further, a copy of the election must be given to every VCT that makes an investment in the company before 6 April 2016.

It should be noted that that election is irrevocable.

31 VCTs: requirements for giving approval

(1) Section 274 of ITA 2007 (requirements for the giving of approval) is amended as follows.

(2) In the table in subsection (2), after the entry beginning "The 70% eligible shares condition" insert—

"The non-qualifying investments condition	The company has not made and will not make, in the relevant period, an investment which is neither of the following— (a)an investment that on the date it is made is included in the company's qualifying holdings; (b)an investment falling within subsection (3A)."

(3) In subsection (3), in each of paragraphs (f), (g) and (h), for "(3A)" substitute "(3ZA)".

(4) After subsection (3) insert—

"(3ZA) In the second column of the table in subsection (2), in the entries for the investment limits condition, the permitted maximum age condition and the no business acquisition condition, any reference to an investment made by the company in a company does not include an investment falling within subsection (3A)."

(5) In subsection (3A)—

(a) for the words from "In the second" to "does not include" substitute "An investment made by a company ("the investor") falls within this subsection if it is";
(b) in paragraph (c) for "the company" substitute "the investor";
(c) after paragraph (c) insert—

"(d) money in the investor's possession;
(e) a sum owed to the investor which—

(i) under section 285(4)(b) (read with section 285(5) and (6)) is to be regarded as an investment of the investor, and
(ii) is such that the investor's right mentioned in section 285(5)(a) may be exercised on 7 days' notice given by the investor."

(6) After subsection (3A) insert—

"(3B) In subsection (3A), any reference to a thing which may be done on 7 days' notice includes a case where that thing may be done—

(a) on less than 7 days' notice, or
(b) without notice."

(7) In subsection (5)—

(a) after paragraph (b) insert—

"(ba) amend or repeal subsection (3B) in consequence of any provision made under paragraph (b),";
(b) in paragraph (c) for the words from "made by" to "(3A)" substitute "falling within subsection (3A) may be held by the company".

(8) The amendments made by this section have effect in relation to investments made on or after 6 April 2016.

GENERAL NOTE

Section 31 amends s 274 ITA 2007 to clarify the non-qualifying investments a VCT is able to make. Finance (No 2) Act 2015 restricted most VCT investments in companies to those which meet the permitted maximum age requirement, the investment limits requirement and the no prohibited acquisitions requirement.

The rationale given for making this additional change is that all funds held by VCTs have all received tax relief, and therefore are regarded as State aided, and further restrictions have been introduced to meet State aid requirements.

A new condition is added to s 274(2) ITA 2007, known as the "non-qualifying investments condition". This is designed to ensure that a VCT may only make investments which are qualifying holdings or a limited selection of investments to be held for liquidity management purposes. Those investments are specifically listed in s 274(3A) ITA 2007. Any other investment made by a VCT could result in the VCT losing its status as a VCT, with consequential withdrawal of tax relief from its investors.

The report stage of the Finance Bill amended s 274(3A) and introduced new s 274(3B) to allow VCTs to hold short term deposits, such as bank accounts. Such deposits must be realisable within 7 days, so longer term bank deposits are not permitted. Bank accounts and similar deposits were overlooked at the first draft of the Bill. HM Revenue & Customs have indicated that VCT status will not be withdrawn if VCTs invested in a longer term deposit after 5 April 2016, but before the amendments were tabled, so long as the VCT withdraws from the arrangements within a reasonable timescale.

The restriction also means that a VCT cannot invest in government gilts, or in corporate bonds with a repayment date of less than five years. Nor can a VCT make a loan of less than five years duration to a company that otherwise would be a qualifying holding. Such short term loans have been made by many VCTs over the 20 years since VCTs were created, so this represents a significant change for VCTs. Together with the changes in Finance (No 2) Act 2015, this restriction means that small companies no longer have access to an important source of finance.

This section applies for investments made by VCTs on or after 6 April 2016.

Reliefs: Peer-to-Peer Lending

32 Income tax relief for irrecoverable peer-to-peer loans

(1) ITA 2007 is amended as follows.

(2) After section 412 insert—

"CHAPTER 1A

IRRECOVERABLE PEER-TO-PEER LOANS

The relief

412A Relief for irrecoverable peer-to-peer loans

(1) A person ("L") is entitled to relief under this section if—

    (a) L has made a peer-to-peer loan ("the relevant loan"),

    (b) the loan was made through an operator,

    (c) L has not assigned the right to recover the principal of the loan, and

    (d) any outstanding amount of the principal of the loan has, on or after 6 April 2015, become irrecoverable.

(2) But if the outstanding amount became irrecoverable before 6 April 2016 L is entitled to relief under this section only on the making of a claim.

(3) The relief is given by deducting the outstanding amount in calculating L's net income for the tax year in which the amount became irrecoverable (see Step 2 of the calculation in section 23).

(4) The deduction under this section is to be made only from income arising from the payment to L of interest on—

    (a) the relevant loan, and

    (b) any other loan within subsection (5) or (6).

(5) A loan is within this subsection if—

    (a) it is a peer-to-peer loan made by L, and

    (b) it was made through the operator through whom the relevant loan was made.

(6) A loan is within this subsection if—

    (a) the loan was made by someone other than L,

    (b) the right to receive interest on the loan has been assigned to L,

    (c) the right was assigned through the operator through whom the relevant loan was made, and

    (d) either—

        (i) L is a person within paragraph (a), (b) or (c) of section 412I(4), or

        (ii) the recipient of the loan is a person within one of those paragraphs and the loan is a personal or small loan.

(7) The amount deducted under this section is limited in accordance with section 25(4) and (5).

(8) In this section "irrecoverable" means irrecoverable other than by legal proceedings or by the exercise of any right granted by way of security for the loan.

412B Claims for additional relief: sideways relief

(1) A person ("L") may make a claim for relief under this section if—

    (a) L is entitled to relief under section 412A in respect of any outstanding amount of the principal of a loan ("the relevant loan"), but

    (b) in the tax year in relation to which L is entitled to that relief ("the relevant year")—

        (i) L has no income of the kind mentioned in section 412A(4) from which to deduct the outstanding amount, or

(ii) L has insufficient income of that kind to enable the outstanding amount to be deducted in full under that section.

(2) The claim is for the outstanding amount or (in a case within subsection (1)(b)(ii)) the part of the outstanding amount not capable of being deducted under section 412A to be deducted under this section in calculating L's net income for the relevant year.

(3) The deduction under this section is to be made only from income arising from the payment to L of interest on loans within subsection (4) or (5).

(4) A loan is within this subsection if—

(a) it is a peer-to-peer loan made by L, and
(b) it was made through an operator who is not the operator through whom the relevant loan was made.

(5) A loan is within this subsection if—

(a) the loan was made by someone other than L,
(b) the right to receive interest on the loan has been assigned to L,
(c) that right was assigned through an operator who is not the operator through whom the relevant loan was made, and
(d) either—

(i) L is a person within paragraph (a), (b) or (c) of section 412I(4), or
(ii) the recipient of the loan is a person within one of those paragraphs and the loan is a personal or small loan.

(6) The amount deducted under this section is limited in accordance with section 25(4) and (5).

412C   Claims for additional relief: carry-forward relief

(1) A person ("L") may make a claim for relief under this section if—

(a) L is entitled to relief under section 412A in respect of any outstanding amount of the principal of a loan ("the relevant loan"), but
(b) in the tax year in relation to which L is entitled to that relief ("the relevant year")—

(i) L has no income of the kind mentioned in section 412A(4) or section 412B(3) from which to deduct the outstanding amount, or
(ii) L has insufficient income of that kind to enable the outstanding amount to be deducted in full under those sections.

(2) The claim is for the outstanding amount or (in a case within subsection (1)(b)(ii)) the part of the outstanding amount not capable of being deducted under sections 412A and 412B to be deducted under this section in calculating L's net income for the four tax years following the relevant year.

(3) The deduction under this section is to be made only from income arising from the payment to L of interest on—

(a) the relevant loan, and
(b) any other loan within subsection (4) or (5).

(4) A loan is within this subsection if—

(a) it is a peer-to-peer loan made by L, and
(b) it was made through an operator (whether or not that operator is the operator through whom the relevant loan was made).

(5) A loan is within this subsection if—

(a) the loan was made by someone other than L,
(b) the right to receive interest on the loan has been assigned to L,
(c) that right was assigned through an operator (whether or not that operator is the operator through whom the relevant loan was made), and
(d) either—

(i) L is a person within paragraph (a), (b) or (c) of section 412I(4), or
(ii) the recipient of the loan is a person within one of those paragraphs and the loan is a personal or small loan.

(6) This section needs to be read with section 412D (how relief works).

412D   How carry-forward relief works

(1) This subsection explains how deductions are to be made under section 412C.

The amount to be deducted at any step is limited in accordance with section 25(4) and (5).

Step 1 Deduct the outstanding amount or (in a case within section 412C(1)(b)(ii)) the part of the outstanding amount not capable of being deducted under sections 412A and 412B from the lending income for the first tax year following the relevant year.

Step 2 Deduct from the lending income for the second tax year following the relevant year any part of the outstanding amount not previously deducted.

Step 3 Apply Step 2 in relation to the lending income for the third and fourth tax years following the relevant year, stopping if all of the outstanding amount is deducted.

(2) In this section—

"lending income" means income of a kind mentioned in section 412C(3);

"relevant year" has the meaning given by section 412C(1)(b).

Supplementary provisions

412E Subsequent recovery of peer-to-peer loans

(1) This section applies where—

(a) any amount of the principal of a loan has been deducted under this Chapter in calculating a person's net income for a tax year, and

(b) the person subsequently recovers that amount or any part of it.

(2) The amount recovered is to be treated for the purposes of this Act as if it were interest on the loan paid to the person at the time it was recovered.

(3) For the purposes of this section, a person is to be treated as recovering an amount if the person (or any other person at his or her direction) receives any money or money's worth—

(a) in satisfaction of the person's right to recover that amount, or

(b) in consideration of the person's assignment of the right to recover it;

and where a person assigns such a right otherwise than by way of a bargain made at arm's length the person shall be treated as receiving money or money's worth equal to the market value of the right at the time of the assignment.

412F Assigned loans treated as made by the assignee etc

(1) This section applies where—

(a) a person ("A") is assigned the right to recover the principal of a loan,

(b) the right is assigned through an operator ("O"),

(c) A makes a payment in consideration of the assignment, and

(d) A does not further assign the right.

(2) The loan is to be treated for the purposes of section 412A(1) as—

(a) having been made by A, and

(b) having been made through O.

(3) The amount (if any) of the principal of the loan which is treated as irrecoverable may not exceed the amount which is arrived at by –

(a) taking the amount of the payment mentioned in subsection (1)(c), and

(b) deducting any amount of the principal of the loan previously recovered by A.

412G Nominees etc

For the purposes of this Chapter—

(a) a loan or a payment made by or to a nominee or bare trustee for a person is treated as made by or to that person, and

(b) a right assigned by or to a nominee or bare trustee for a person is treated as assigned by or to that person.

412H Interaction with other reliefs

(1) Subsection (2) applies in relation to a loan if any person has obtained income tax relief (other than under this Chapter) which is properly attributable to the loan.

(2) The amount (if any) of the principal of the loan which is treated as irrecoverable may not exceed the amount which is arrived at by—

(a) taking the amount of the principal of the loan, and

(b) deducting the amount of the relief mentioned in subsection (1).

Interpretation

412I Meaning of "loan", "peer-to-peer loan" and related terms

(1) This section applies for the purposes of this Chapter.

(2) "Loan" means a loan of money which—

(a) is made on genuine commercial terms, and

(b) is not part of a scheme or arrangement the main purpose or one of the main purposes of which is to obtain a tax advantage (within the meaning given by section 208 of the FA 2013).

(3) A loan is a "peer-to-peer loan" only if it meets—

(a) Condition A or B, and

(b) Condition C.

(4) Condition A is that the person who made the loan is—

(a) an individual,

(b) a partnership which consists of—

(i) two or three persons, and

(ii) at least one person who is not a body corporate, or

(c) an unincorporated body of persons which—

(i) is not a partnership, and

(ii) consists of at least one person who is not a body corporate.

(5) Condition B is that—

(a) the recipient of the loan is a person within paragraph (a), (b) or (c) of subsection (4), and

(b) the loan is a personal or small loan.

(6) Condition C is that, assuming interest were paid on the loan, the person who made the loan would (except for this Chapter) be liable for income tax charged on the interest.

(7) "Personal loan" means a loan which is not used wholly or predominantly for the purposes of a business carried on, or intended to be carried on, by the recipient of the loan.

(8) "Small loan" means a loan of £25,000 or less.

412J Meaning of "operator" and related terms

(1) This section applies for the purposes of this Chapter.

(2) "Operator" means a person who—

(a) has permission under Part 4A of FISMA 2000 to carry on a regulated activity specified in Article 36H of the Financial Services and Markets Act 2000 (Regulated Activities) Order 2001 (SI 2001/544) (operating an electronic system in relation to lending), or

(b) has been granted equivalent permission under the law of a territory outside the United Kingdom that is within the European Economic Area.

(3) A loan is "made through" an operator if the person who makes the loan and the recipient of the loan enter the agreement under which the loan is made at the invitation of the operator.

(4) A right is "assigned through" an operator if the person who assigns the right and the person to whom the right is assigned enter the agreement under which the assignment takes effect at the invitation of the operator.

(5) A person is not to be treated as having entered an agreement at the invitation of an operator if the operator made the invitation otherwise than in the course of carrying on the activity to which the permission mentioned in subsection (2)(a) or (b) relates."

(3) In section 24(1) (list of reliefs deductible at Step 2 of the calculation of income tax liability), in paragraph (b), at the appropriate place insert—

"Chapter 1A of Part 8 (irrecoverable peer-to-peer loans),".

(4) In section 25(3) (list of provisions requiring reliefs to be deducted from particular components of income etc) at the appropriate place insert—

"sections 412A(4), 412B(3) and 412C(3) (relief for irrecoverable peer-to-peer loans only against interest on certain loans),".

GENERAL NOTE

Section 32

Peer-to-Peer lending is a form of lending under which investors lend money via an internet site to individuals or small businesses. These loan arrangements typically involve the individual investor putting money into a fund which is then lent to number of borrowers. This way the investor reduces the risk of default on any one loan. At the moment there is no tax relief available to the investor on any of these "sub loans" which become irrecoverable. Section 32 addresses this problem by introducing a form of relief which will allow such losses to be set against interest received on other parts of the portfolio investment.

Section 32(1)

This introduces a new Ch 1A to ITA 2007.

Section 32(2)

This inserts new ss 412A–412J into ITA 2007.

New s 412A ITA 2007

Section 412A(1)

This sets out the qualification conditions for the new relief. These are:
- a person has made a peer-to-peer loan;
- the loan was made through an operator;
- the person has not assigned the right to recover the principal of the loan; and
- any outstanding amount of the principal of the loan has become irrecoverable on or after 6 April 2015.

Section 412A(2)

If the amount became irrecoverable on or after 6 April 2015 and before 6 April 2016 relief is only available on the making of a claim. This means, as confirmed in the explanatory notes to the finance bill, that if a claim is not made the loss would potentially be available for capital gains tax relief under the loans to traders provisions (TCGA 1992 s 253). From 6 April 2016 relief is available automatically and the ability to claim capital gains tax relief will no longer be available.

Section 412A(3)

The relief is given as a deduction in computing the person's net income for the year in which the loan became irrecoverable.

Section 412A(4)–(6)

These sections restrict the income against which the deduction can be claimed.

Subsection (4)

The first category is income arising from the loan itself – for example if interest income had been received on the loan before it became irrecoverable.

Subsection (5)

The second category is income from other peer-to-peer loans made by that person through the operator through whom the relevant loan was made.

Subsection (6)

The third category is loans made by another person where the right to receive interest on the loan has been assigned to the individual and that right was assigned through the operator through whom the relevant loan was made. There are further restrictions to the relief in this third category. Either the lender must be a person within o 4211(4)(a)–(c) or the recipient of the loan must be within one of those paragraphs and the loan must be a personal or small loan. (Those terms are defined in s 412L.)

Section 412A(7)

The normal rules restricting deductions in ITA ss 25(4) and (5) apply to relief under this section, i.e. relief can only be given if there sufficient income against which to deduct it.

Section 412A(8)

This defines an irrecoverable loan as one which is irrecoverable other than by legal proceedings or by the exercise of any right granted by way of security for the loan. In other words if the loan could be recovered without recourse to legal proceedings or enforcement of security the loan is not irrecoverable for the purposes of this relief. Loans where there may simply be doubt over recoverability are not eligible.

New s 412B ITA 2007

This section allows claims for losses on irrecoverable loans to be made against income from other peer to peer loans made through a different platform. Unlike relief under s 412A this relief is not automatic and is subject to a claim.

Section 412B(1)

A person may make a claim to sideways relief if he is entitled to relief under s 412A for a tax year but has no other income with s 412A(4) against which to set the relief, or the income within s 412A(4) is insufficient to absorb the relief in full.

Section 412B(2)

The relief is to be deducted in computing the person's net income for the year

Section 412B(3)–(6)

These import the further conditions set out in s 412A(4)–(7) above to sideways loss relief under s 412B.

New s 412C ITA 2007

Section 412C(1)

This section applies where a person is entitled to relief under s 412A but in that tax year has no, or insufficient, income of the type specified in s 412A(4) or s 412B(3) to absorb the relief.

Section 412C(2)

The individual may make a claim that the unabsorbed amount of the loss can be deducted in calculating his/her net income for the four tax years following the year of loss.

Section 412C(3)

The relief can only be set against interest received from the relevant loan or from loans with sub-s (4) and (5) below.

Section 412C(4)

A loan is within this subsection if it is a peer-to-peer loan and is made through an operator. It does not matter whether the operator is the same operator through whom the irrecoverable loan was made.

Section 412C(5)

This imports the same test as in s 412A(4)–(6) above, except that there is no requirement that the interest must arise from a loan made through the same operator as the irrecoverable loan was made.

Section 412C(6)

This states that s 412C needs to be read with s 412D.

New s 412D ITA 2007

Section 412D(1)

This explains how carry forward relief deductions are to be calculated. Subject to the overriding restrictions in s 25(4) and (5) the amounts of carried forward relief are to be set against lending income (i.e. income within s 412C(3)) of subsequent years, taking the earliest first. Any amount unrelieved after four years is no longer eligible for relief.

New s 412E ITA 2007

Section 412E(1)

This section applies where the principal of a loan has been deducted under this chapter in computing a person's net income and all or part of that principal is subsequently recovered.

Section 412E(2)

The amount recovered is treated as loan interest paid at the date on which the loan was recovered.

Section 412E(3)

A amount is treated as recovered if the person (or any other person at his or her direction) receives money or money's worth in satisfaction of the right to recover the amount or in consideration of that person's right to recover it. Where the right is assigned otherwise than by way of a bargain at arm's length market value is substituted for the actual value received

New s 412F ITA 2007

Section 412F(1)

The section applies where a person (A) is assigned the right to recover the principal of a loan, the right is assigned through an operator (O), and A makes a payment in consideration of the assignment and does not further assign the right.

Section 412F(2)

Where sub-s (1) above applies the loan is to be treated for the purposes of s 412A(1) as having been made by A and having been made through O. The effect of this is that such loans are brought within the scope of this chapter.

Section 412F(3)

The amount of the principal of the loan which is treated as irrecoverable is not to exceed the amount paid by A for the assignment after deduction of any amount of the principal previously recovered by A.

New s 412G ITA 2007

For the purposes of this chapter a loan or payment made by or to a nominee or bare trustee of a person is treated as made by or to that person, and a right assigned by or to a nominee or bare trustee for a person is treated as assigned buy or to that person.

New s 412H ITA 2007

Section 412H(1)

This restricts relief under this chapter where a person has obtained income tax relief under any other section of the Taxes Acts which is properly attributable to the loan

Section 412H(2)

In these circumstances the amount of the principal of the loan which can be treated as recoverable for the purpose of s 412 relief is reduced by any amount which has been subject to income tax relief under any other section.

New s 412I ITA 2007

Section 412I(1)

This introduces this section, which defines key terms used in this chapter

Section 412I(2)

A Loan is a Loan of money made on genuine commercial terms and which is not part of a scheme or arrangements the main purpose, or one of the main purposes, of which is to obtain a tax advantage. Tax advantage here takes the definition in FA 2013 s208, i.e. the definition used in the General Anti Abuse Rule.

Section 412I(3)

This subsection defines a peer-to-peer loan. The loan has to meet either Condition A or Condition B, and must also meet Condition C

Section 412I(4)

Condition A is that the person who made the loan is either
- an individual;
- a partnership which consists of two or three persons, providing that at least one of those persons is not a body corporate;
- an unincorporated body of persons which is not a partnership and consists of at least one person who is not a corporate.

Section 412I(5)

Condition B is the recipient of the loan is a person within para (a), (b) or (c) of sub-s (4) above and that the loan is a personal or small loan.

Section 412I(6)

Condition C is that on the assumption that interest were paid on the loan the person who made the loan would be liable (except for this chapter) for income tax charged on the interest.

Section 412I(7)

A personal loan is a loan which is not used wholly or predominantly for the purposes of a business carried on (or intended to be carried on) by the recipient of the loan.

Section 412I(8)

A small loan is a loan of £25,000 or less.

Transactions in Securities

33 Transactions in securities: company distributions

(1) Chapter 1 of Part 13 of ITA 2007 (transactions in securities) is amended as follows.

(2) In section 684 (person liable to counteraction), in subsection (1)—

  (a) in the opening words, after "a person" insert "("the party")";
  (b) in paragraph (c), omit "the person in being a party to";
  (c) in paragraph (d), for "the person" substitute "the party or any other person".

(3) In that section, in subsection (2)—

  (a) in paragraph (c), omit the final "and";
  (b) after paragraph (d) insert—
    "(e) a repayment of share capital or share premium, and
    (f) a distribution in respect of securities in a winding up."

(4) In section 685 (receipt of consideration in connection with distribution by or assets of close company)—

  (a) in subsection (2)—
    (i) in the opening words, for "the person" substitute "a relevant person";
    (ii) in the words after paragraph (c), after "and" insert "the relevant person";
  (b) in subsection (3)—
    (i) in paragraph (a), for "the person" substitute "a relevant person";
    (ii) in paragraph (c), for "the person" substitute "the relevant person";

(c) after subsection (3) insert—

"(3A) In subsections (2) and (3) "relevant person" means—

(a) the party, or

(b) any person other than the party in relation to whom the condition in section 684(1)(d) is met."

(d) omit subsection (6);

(e) after subsection (7) insert—

"(7A) The references in subsection (4)(a)(i) and (ii) to assets do not include assets shown to represent return of sums paid by subscribers on the issue of securities merely because the law of the country in which the company is incorporated allows assets of that description to be available for distribution by way of dividend.

(7B) The references in subsections (4)(a)(i) and (5)(a) to assets which are available for distribution by way of dividend by the company include assets which are available for distribution to the company by way of dividend by any other company it controls."

(5) In section 686 (excluded circumstances: fundamental change of ownership)—

(a) in subsection (1)(a), for the words from "the person" to "party")" substitute "the party";

(b) for subsections (2) to (5) substitute—

"(2) There is a fundamental change of ownership of the close company if, as a result of the transaction or transactions in securities, the condition in subsection (3) is met.

(3) The condition in this subsection is that the original shareholder or original shareholders taken together with any associate or associates—

(a) do not directly or indirectly hold more than 25% of the ordinary share capital of the close company,

(b) do not directly or indirectly hold shares in the close company carrying an entitlement to more than 25% of the distributions which may be made by the close company, and

(c) do not directly or indirectly hold shares in the close company carrying more than 25% of the total voting rights in the close company.

(4) In this section "original shareholder" means a person who, immediately before the transaction in securities (or the first of the transactions in securities), held any ordinary share capital of the close company.

(5) For the purposes of this section, shares of or share capital in the close company which are held by a person controlled by an original shareholder, or by two or more original shareholders taken together, count as shares or share capital held by that original shareholder or those original shareholders."

(6) In section 687 (income tax advantage)—

(a) in subsection (1), in the opening words, for "the person" substitute "a person";

(b) in subsection (2)—

(i) after "to the person" insert "or an associate of the person";

(ii) for "the relevant consideration is received" substitute "Condition A or B in section 685 is met".

(7) In section 713 (interpretation), at the appropriate place insert—

""associate" is to be construed in accordance with section 681DL, but as if subsection (4) of that section also included, as persons associated with each other, a person as trustee of a settlement and an individual, where one or more beneficiaries of the settlement are connected or associated with the individual;".

(8) The amendments made by this section have effect in relation to—

(a) a transaction occurring on or after 6 April 2016, or

(b) a series of transactions any one or more of which occurs on or after that date.

(9) Accordingly, Chapter 1 of Part 13 of ITA 2007 has effect without the amendments made by this section in relation to a tax advantage obtained on or after 6 April 2016 in consequence of—

(a) a transaction occurring before that date, or

(b) a series of transactions all of which occur before that date.

(10) Where—

(a) before 6 April 2016 a person provides particulars to the Commissioners for Her Majesty's Revenue and Customs under section 701 of ITA 2007 in respect of a transaction or transactions,

(b) on the basis of Chapter 1 of Part 13 of ITA 2007 as it has effect apart from this section, notification is given under section 701 of that Act that no counteraction notice ought to be served about the transaction or transactions,

(c) the transaction, or any one or more of the transactions, occurs on or after 6 April 2016, and

(d) the person would, but for the notification, be liable for counteraction of an income tax advantage from the transaction or transactions under Chapter 1 of Part 13 of ITA 2007 as amended by this section,

the notification is void and section 702(2) of ITA 2007 does not apply in relation to the transaction or transactions.

GENERAL NOTE

Section 33 amends the conditions for the potential application of the transactions in securities rules at ITA 2007 ss 682–713. The transactions in securities rules are designed to prevent the avoidance of income tax on dividends of company profits by obtaining capital sums, instead, chargeable to capital gains tax. The effect is to permit HMRC to charge income tax on such transactions, as if they were a dividend, instead of capital gains tax. The changes are designed to widen the potential application of these rules.

The changes arise from HMRC's wider concerns about extraction of corporate profits other than by way of dividend, as explained in the consultation document 'Company Distributions' issued in December 2015. The changes at FA 2016 ss 34 and 35 are part of the same project.

Scope

A number of changes to the "gateway" provisions for the transactions in securities rules, in ITA 2007 s 684, are amended by FA 2016, as follows

-   **Purpose test:** Since 24 March 2010, the rules applied where a person was party to one or more transactions in securities and the main purpose, or one of the main purposes, of that person in being party to the transactions in securities was to obtain an income tax advantage. The rules are amended so that it is no longer necessary to consider the purpose of the individual. Instead, what matters is the whole or main purpose of the transaction in securities itself. If the transaction or transactions are designed with a view to obtaining an income tax advantage, that is now sufficient to trigger the operation of these rules.
-   **Person obtaining income tax advantage:** The rules could only be used to counteract an income tax advantage accruing to an individual who was party to one or more transactions in securities, subject to the motive test above. This meant that, if someone else was party to the transactions in securities, not the individual to whom an income tax advantage accrued, then no counteraction was possible. This is now amended so that the new rules will apply if an income tax advantage is obtained by any person.
-   **Transactions in securities:** While the concept of a transaction in securities is widely defined, a number of specific items are listed as to be treated as falling within the scope of this legislation. Following FA 2016, that list now includes the repayment of share capital or share premium and a distribution in respect of securities in a winding up.

    The first of these is considered necessary by HMRC because repayments of share capital and share premium to shareholders have become very common since the change to company law that simplified (and made cheaper) the process for a company to reduce its capital. It is arguable, however, that adding these to the list is otiose, as it seems obvious that a reduction of a company's share capital would be a transaction in securities under any definition, without having to be specified. Nevertheless, this might not be quite so obvious in terms of a reduction of share premium and the addition of both to the list puts the matter beyond any possible doubt.

    The addition of distributions in a winding up is a major change. When the legislation was enacted in FA 1960, it was very clearly stated that neither dividends nor the liquidation of a company were intended to be transaction in securities for the purposes of this legislation. This is now reversed, most likely because of concerns highlighted in the consultation document about funds being retained in a company and realised in capital form at the end of the company's life, by taking distributions in a liquidation. HMRC's view, which very few other people agree with, is that failing to take regular dividends of the majority of a company's profits during its lifetime is a form of tax avoidance! This new provision is clearly intended to counter that problem. We are promised detailed guidance, in due course, which would, in part, be intended to ensure that the transactions in securities legislation would only apply in particularly offensive cases. However, the more likely outcome of this change to the legislation is that HMRC will receive a clearance application in respect of every distribution in the winding up of a company, as the only mechanism for complete certainty over the tax treatment is a pre-transaction clearance from HMRC, not HMRC guidance, which can be changed from time to time without warning.

Amendments to Conditions A and B

The gateway provisions are supplemented by two categories of transaction which will be potentially within the scope of the transactions in securities rules, Conditions A and B, in ITA 2007 s 685. Major changes are also being made to those conditions:

- **Recipient of relevant consideration:** Conditions A and B both require a person to receive "relevant consideration", being consideration on which the person does not bear income tax. This is now extended to ensure that the provisions can still apply if someone else receives the relevant consideration, i.e. someone other than the person who is either party to the original transaction in securities or has obtained the income tax advantage. This ensures that the anti-avoidance rules can apply regardless of who actually receives the proceeds of any transaction or transactions in securities.
- **Return of sums subscribed:** Condition A also included a provision that meant the transactions in securities rules could not apply if the transaction constituted a return of capital subscribed. This is now omitted, which is consistent with the addition of repayments of share capital to the list of potentially counteractable transactions. Nevertheless, it remains something of a mystery why HMRC consider that a reduction of capital is generally offensive.
- **Assets available for distribution:** Relevant consideration also has to represent assets available for distribution by the company, or assets that would have been so available but for something done by the company. This is now modified to exclude the sums subscribed originally for securities, simply because the law of the country of incorporation permits the amounts subscribed to be distributed by way of dividend. This provision is slightly obscure, as it appears almost to mirror the provision omitted from Condition A (described in the previous paragraph). Our suggested interpretation of the intention of this new provision is that it only applies where the company does not actually have any profits to distribute. Thus, although the relevant legal system might permit the capital of the company to be distributed, so that the relevant consideration could represent amounts distributable by way of dividend, the transactions in securities legislation would not be in point, as there is clearly no avoidance of income tax where there is no distribution of profits by the company.
- **Group assets available for distribution:** Another possibly inadvertent restriction to the scope of relevant consideration in the FA 2010 legislation is that, for the measurement of relevant consideration for the purposes of both Conditions A and B, the extent to which it represented profits available for distribution by way of dividend by the company applied only to the company concerned in the transaction in securities. This is now extended to include the distributable reserves of any company under the control of that company. Thus, if a parent company that was involved in a transaction in securities had no distributable reserves, but its subsidiaries had distributable reserves, the relevant consideration is deemed to represent those distributable reserves, as well, not just those of the parent.

Fundamental change of ownership

The fundamental change of ownership test, ITA 2007 s 686, was introduced by FA 2010 to try and make the transactions in securities rules operate more efficiently. HMRC had determined empirically that pre-transaction clearance was always granted if at least 75% of the shares of a company were being sold to a genuine third party. So the fundamental change of ownership test was introduced with the intention of making it clear that all of those cases were outside the scope of the legislation, regardless of the existence of any tax avoidance motives. This would generate increased certainty for taxpayers without the need to apply to HMRC for a clearance and, as a corollary, would reduce HMRC's resource requirements in terms of staffing the clearance and counteraction unit. However, the test as originally enacted was defective in a number of areas and therefore did not have the impact originally hoped for.

The new test looks at who retains shares in the company, rather than who holds the shares that were sold. The test applies to take a transaction or transactions in securities out of the scope of this legislation so long as the original shareholders, together with any associates of theirs, do not directly or indirectly hold more than 25% of the ordinary share capital of the company, shares carrying an entitlement to more than 25% of the distributions that may be made by the company, or shares holding more than 25% of the total voting rights of the company. An original shareholder is a person who immediately before the transaction in securities held any ordinary share capital of the company, and include shares held by a person controlled by an original shareholder (for example, shares in a subsidiary of a company controlled by the individual) or shares held by two or more original shareholders together.

An associate of an original shareholder is to be determined according to the rules of ITA 2007 s 681DL, which, while not previously part of the transactions in securities rules, presumably have the advantage in this situation of being adjacent to them in the Act!

Commencement

The new rules apply in relation to any transaction in securities occurring on or after 6 April 2016. Where there is a series of transactions to which the legislation might be applied, the new rules apply if any of those transactions occurs on or after 6 April 2016. So the old rules apply only if all the transactions in a series were completed before 6 April 2016.

Impact on HMRC clearances

The changes mean that a pre-transaction clearance granted under ITA 2007 s 701, that HMRC would not raise a notice to counteract a tax advantage, might be invalid if it was granted under the old rules but the relevant transactions in securities might be caught under the new rules. A transitional provision, FA 2016 s 33, states that, where any part of the transaction or transactions are carried out on or after 6 April 2016, the previous clearance is void. So it will be necessary to refresh the clearance application, by reference to the new rules, before completing the transaction, if this affects any of your clients.

Technically, in the period between 6 April 2016 and the date that Royal Assent is obtained we are in something of a period of limbo, as the legislation is in force, but might not technically become law if Royal Assent had not been given.

In practical terms, HMRC have considered both of these issues in respect of clearance applications sent in from the date that the draft legislation was originally published, in December 2015. They have worded their clearance letters in a way that first of all makes it clear where they are comfortable that clearance should be granted under both the old and the new rules, or otherwise, and secondly makes it clear that they apply to whichever set of rules is strictly in force between 6 April 2016 and the date of Royal Assent to Finance Act 2016.

34 Transactions in securities: procedure for counteraction of advantage

(1) Chapter 1 of Part 13 of ITA 2007 (transactions in securities) is amended as follows.

(2) For section 695 (preliminary notification) substitute—

"695 Notice of enquiry

(1) An officer of Revenue and Customs may enquire into a transaction or transactions if—

(a) the officer has reason to believe that section 684 (person liable to counteraction of income tax advantage) may apply to a person ("the taxpayer") in respect of the transaction or transactions, and

(b) the officer notifies the taxpayer of his intention to do so.

(2) The notification may be given at any time not more than 6 years after the end of the tax year to which the income tax advantage in question relates."

(3) Omit sections 696 and 697 (opposed notifications).

(4) In section 698 (counteraction notices), for subsection (1) substitute—

"(1) If on an enquiry under section 695 an officer of Revenue and Customs determines that section 684 applies to the taxpayer, the income tax advantage in question is to be counteracted by adjustments, unless the officer is of the opinion that no counteraction is required."

(5) In that section, for subsection (5) substitute—

"(5) An assessment may be made in accordance with a counteraction notice at any time (without regard to any time limit on making the assessment that would otherwise apply)."

(6) After that section insert—

"698A No-counteraction notices

(1) If on an enquiry under section 695 an officer of Revenue and Customs is of the opinion that no counteraction is required, the officer must serve notice on the person (a "no-counteraction notice") stating that no counteraction is required and why.

(2) The taxpayer may apply to the tribunal for a direction requiring an officer of Revenue and Customs to issue one of the following within a specified period—

    (a) a counteraction notice;
    (b) a no-counteraction notice.

(3) Any such application is to be subject to the relevant provisions of Part 5 of TMA 1970 (see, in particular, section 48(2)(b) of that Act).

(4) The tribunal must give the direction applied for unless satisfied that there are reasonable grounds for not serving either a counteraction notice or a no-counteraction notice within a specified period."

(7) In section 684 (person liable to counteraction), for subsection (4) substitute—

"(4) This section is subject to no-counteraction notices issued under section 698A."

(8) The amendments made by this section have effect in relation to—

    (a) a transaction occurring on or after 6 April 2016, or
    (b) a series of transactions any one or more of which occurs on or after that date.

(9) Accordingly, Chapter 1 of Part 13 of ITA 2007 has effect without the amendments made by this section in relation to a tax advantage obtained on or after 6 April 2016 in consequence of—

    (a) a transaction occurring before that date, or
    (b) a series of transactions all of which occur before that date.

GENERAL NOTE

The administrative rules for HMRC to counteract an income tax advantage under the transactions in securities rules were complex. After what were usually lengthy enquiries into a situation, HMRC had to issue a preliminary notification that they intended to counteract a tax advantage. The taxpayers concerned then had to counter that by way of a statutory declaration. HMRC would then submit their preliminary notification, the countering letter from the taxpayer and HMRC's stated position, to the First-tier Tribunal and a Tribunal judge would decide whether HMRC had a *prima facie* case to proceed. Only then could HMRC counteract the tax advantage, usually by the issuing of an assessment, after which the normal procedures for appeals through the tribunal and courts system could take its course.

Not only was this an unwieldy process, and somewhat outdated, as it had not changed since enactment in 1960, there was also some doubt as to the time period during which HMRC had to raise an assessment to counteract a tax advantage. HMRC's view was that they were entitled to raise an assessment within 6 years of the end of the tax year in which the tax advantage arose. Most observers considered that HMRC was limited by the normal four-year restriction.

Simplified counteraction process

The new process is simpler, mirrors as far as possible the self-assessment process, and includes further taxpayer protections. It also removes the uncertainty over timing.

Under the new process HMRC can open an enquiry by notification not more than six years after the end of the tax year to which the income tax advantage relates, if the officer of HMRC has reason to believe that there may be an income tax advantage that should be counteracted. If the officer determines that counteraction is required, an appropriate adjustment can be made. To the extent that the adjustment is made by way of assessment, there is no time limit on making that assessment.

Alternatively, if HMRC come to the view that no adjustment is required, they must formally give notice, called a "No-counteraction Notice", stating that no counteraction will be taken, and also explaining why. This last item might seem a little unusual, but we hope that it will lead to a body of intelligence as to those areas which cause HMRC sufficient concern to open an enquiry under these rules, and should also provide intelligence as to the situations where HMRC will subsequently declare themselves to be satisfied that no counteraction is required.

At any time during the enquiry, taxpayers can apply to the First-tier Tribunal for a direction requiring HMRC to either issue a Counteraction Notice or a No-counteraction Notice. The Tribunal must grant the application unless HMRC are able to explain why they should not do so, much like the process for closure notices under self-assessment. Otherwise the direction will be granted that a notice should be served within a specified period.

Commencement

Once again, the new rules apply to transactions in securities carried out on or after 6 April 2016, or where any part of any transactions in securities in a series of transactions are carried out on or after that date. If a transaction in securities, or a series of transactions in securities, is complete before 6 April 2016, the old process applies.

35 Distributions in a winding up

(1) In Chapter 3 of Part 4 of ITTOIA 2005 (dividends and other distributions from UK resident companies), after section 396A insert—

"396B Distributions in a winding up

(1) For the purposes of this Chapter, a distribution made to an individual in respect of share capital in the winding up of a UK resident company is a distribution of the company if—

    (a) Conditions A to D are met, and
    (b) the distribution is not excluded (see subsection (7)).

(2) Condition A is that, immediately before the winding up, the individual has at least a 5% interest in the company.

(3) Condition B is that the company—

    (a) is a close company when it is wound up, or
    (b) was a close company at any time in the period of two years ending with the start of the winding up.

(4) Condition C is that, at any time within the period of two years beginning with the date on which the distribution is made—

    (a) the individual carries on a trade or activity which is the same as, or similar to, that carried on by the company or an effective 51% subsidiary of the company,
    (b) the individual is a partner in a partnership which carries on such a trade or activity,
    (c) the individual, or a person connected with him or her, is a participator in a company in which he or she has at least a 5% interest and which at that time—

        (i) carries on such a trade or activity, or
        (ii) is connected with a company which carries on such a trade or activity, or

    (d) the individual is involved with the carrying on of such a trade or activity by a person connected with the individual.

(5) Condition D is that it is reasonable to assume, having regard to all the circumstances, that—

    (a) the main purpose or one of the main purposes of the winding up is the avoidance or reduction of a charge to income tax, or
    (b) the winding up forms part of arrangements the main purpose or one of the main purposes of which is the avoidance or reduction of a charge to income tax.

(6) The circumstances referred to in subsection (5) include in particular the fact that Condition C is met.

(7) A distribution to an individual is excluded if or to the extent that—

    (a) the amount of the distribution does not exceed the amount that would result in no gain accruing for the purposes of capital gains tax, or
    (b) the distribution is a distribution of irredeemable shares.

(8) In this section—

"arrangements" includes any agreement, understanding, scheme, transaction or series of transactions, whether or not legally enforceable;
"effective 51% subsidiary" has the meaning given by section 170(7) of TCGA 1992;
"participator" has the meaning given by section 454 of CTA 2010.

(9) For the purposes of this section, an individual has at least a 5% interest in a company if—

(a) at least 5% of the ordinary share capital of the company is held by the individual, and
(b) at least 5% of the voting rights in the company are exercisable by the individual by virtue of that holding.

(10) For the purposes of subsection (9) if an individual holds any shares in a company jointly or in common with one or more other persons, he or she is to be treated as sole holder of so many of them as is proportionate to the value of his or her share (and as able to exercise voting rights by virtue of that holding)."

(2) In Chapter 4 of Part 4 of ITTOIA 2005 (dividends from non-UK resident companies), after section 404 insert—

"404A Distributions in a winding up

(1) For the purposes of this Chapter, a distribution made to an individual in respect of share capital in a winding up of a non-UK resident company is a dividend of the company if—

(a) Conditions A to D are met, and
(b) the distribution is not excluded (see subsection (7)).

(2) Condition A is that, immediately before the winding up, the individual has at least a 5% interest in the company.

(3) Condition B is that the company—

(a) is a close company when it is wound up, or
(b) was a close company at any time in the period of two years ending with the start of the winding up.

(4) Condition C is that, at any time within the period of two years beginning with the date on which the distribution is made—

(a) the individual carries on a trade or activity which is the same as, or similar to, that carried on by the company or an effective 51% subsidiary of the company,
(b) the individual is a partner in a partnership which carries on such a trade or activity,
(c) the individual, or a person connected with him or her, is a participator in a company in which he or she has at least a 5% interest and which at that time—
   (i) carries on such a trade or activity, or
   (ii) is connected with a company which carries on such a trade or activity, or
(d) the individual is involved with the carrying on of such a trade or activity by a person connected with the individual.

(5) Condition D is that it is reasonable to assume, having regard to all the circumstances, that—

(a) the main purpose or one of the main purposes of the winding up is the avoidance or reduction of a charge to income tax, or
(b) the winding up forms part of arrangements the main purpose or one of the main purposes of which is the avoidance or reduction of a charge to income tax.

(6) The circumstances referred to in subsection (5) include in particular the fact that Condition C is met.

(7) A distribution to an individual is excluded if or to the extent that—

(a) the amount of the distribution does not exceed the amount that would result in no gain accruing for the purposes of capital gains tax, or
(b) the distribution is a distribution of irredeemable shares.

(8) In this section—

"arrangements" includes any agreement, understanding, scheme, transaction or series of transactions, whether or not legally enforceable;
"close company" includes a company which would be a close company if it were a UK resident company;
"effective 51% subsidiary" has the meaning given by section 170(7) of TCGA 1992;
"participator" has the meaning given by section 454 of CTA 2010.

(9) For the purposes of this section, a person has at least a 5% interest in a company if—

    (a) at least 5% of the ordinary share capital of the company is held by the individual, and

    (b) at least 5% of the voting rights in the company are exercisable by the individual by virtue of that holding.

(10) For the purposes of subsection (9) if an individual holds any shares in a company jointly or in common with one or more other persons, he or she is to be treated as sole holder of so many of them as is proportionate to the value of his or her share (and as able to exercise voting rights by virtue of that holding)."

(3) The amendments made by this section have effect in relation to distributions made on or after 6 April 2016.

GENERAL NOTE

Section 35 introduces two new targeted anti-avoidance rules to prevent 'phoenixism'. This is the perceived abuse when a company is wound up and its business or trade is continued in another company or in some other form. Essentially, HMRC sees this as being the avoidance of income tax on the distributable reserves of the company which, on a winding-up, are received in capital form. The provisions are, arguably, otiose, as the distributions of assets in the winding-up of a company have also been added to the list of transactions caught by the transactions in securities legislation (see "Section 33"), so HMRC could counteract the tax advantage by charging the proceeds of the winding-up as if they were a dividend, under the transactions in securities rules. Nevertheless, s 35 introduces two identical targeted anti-avoidance rules with this effect, at ITTOIA 2005 ss 396B and 404A, referring to dividends and distributions from UK-resident companies and from non-UK resident companies, respectively.

Scope

The two new rules state that distributions made to an individual in respect of the share capital of the winding-up of a company will be treated as a distribution of the company, i.e. as an income distribution, if four conditions are met.

Condition A is that immediately before the winding-up the individual has at least a 5% interest in the company. This requires the individual to have at least 5% of the ordinary share capital and to be able to exercise at least 5% of the voting rights of the company by virtue of that holding. If any shares are held jointly or in common with another person, the individual is treating his holding shares in appropriate proportion to the value of their holding, and as being able to exercise rights to vote, similarly.

Condition B simply requires that the company be a close company when wound up or at any time in the period of two years prior to the start of the winding-up.

Condition C is the crux of the new rule. This condition is satisfied if any of the following occurs within the period of two years following the date a distribution is made (so that the condition must be considered for two years after every distribution in the winding-up):

- the individual carries on a trade or activity which is the same as, or similar to, the activities carried on by the company or by any 51% subsidiary of the company;
- the individual is a partner in a partnership carrying on such a trade or activity;
- the individual or a person connected with the individual is a participator in a company, and has at least a 5% interest, which carries on such a trade or activity or is connected with a company that carries on such a trade or activity;
- the individual is involved with the carrying on of such a trade or activity by a connected person.

These provisions contain a number of vague terms which are not defined in statute and which are not yet explained in guidance. For example, when we look at a trade or activity which is the same as or similar to one carried on by the company, it is not clear whether this applies only to the trade or activities carried on by the company immediately prior to the winding-up or if it might refer to any trade or activity that the company has ever carried out. Nor is it clear what the word 'similar' means. Does this include a person carrying on elements of the company's trade (for example, continuing a business as a tax advisor although the company was actually a full service accountancy firm)? Finally, since the first three elements of Condition C refer to operating as a sole trader, through a partnership or through a company, the meaning of 'involvement' in the fourth element must mean something different, such as simply employment, although we would assume, given the context of the legislation, that it probably involves some degree higher level involvement rather than simply getting a job in a similar business owned by a relative.

Condition D is the motive test which asks if it is reasonable to assume, having regard to all the circumstances, that the main purpose, or one of the main purposes, of the winding-up is the avoidance or reduction of a charge to income tax, or that the winding-up forms part of arrangements which have that as a main purpose. The circumstances to be taken into account must include the fact that Condition C is met. In other words, HMRC takes the view that Condition D is only satisfied if the elimination or reduction of a charge to income tax arises at least in part through the arrangements whereby the business is carried on in some other form.

More importantly, it is accepted that Condition C is very widely drawn but HMRC's view is that, in many cases, while Condition C might be technically satisfied, Condition D is not because one person winding up their company has no nexus with the fact that, for example, they have a relative that carries on a similar business.

Distributions are excluded to the extent that the distribution would not create a capital gain, so distributions in a winding-up that do not exceed the original base cost of the shares would not be caught.

There is also an exclusion for the distribution of irredeemable shares, which is intended to permit transactions such as schemes of reconstruction involving the liquidation of a company. As currently drafted, however, this does not exclude the distribution of other assets in such a scheme of reconstruction, a point which has been highlighted to HMRC.

As is now usual in anti-avoidance legislation, 'arrangements' includes any agreement, understanding, scheme, transaction or series of transactions, whether or not legally enforceable.

Commencement

These two new anti-avoidance provisions apply to all distributions in a winding-up made on or after 6 April 2016. It does not matter when the winding-up process commenced.

No clearance facility

Despite the obvious overlap with the transactions in securities rules, there is no clearance facility for these provisions. However, clearance under s 701 ITA 2007 that HMRC would not issue a counteraction notice under the transactions in securities rules would, one hopes, be indicative that HMRC would be unlikely to invoke these targeted anti-avoidance rules, either.

Self-Assessment

These targeted anti-avoidance rules are part of self-assessment. Therefore, they will impose a further compliance burden on clients and advisors, alike, in considering whether the rules apply.

Disguised Fees and Carried Interest

36 Disguised investment management fees

(1) Section 809EZA of ITA 2007 (disguised investment management fees: charge to income tax) is amended as specified in subsections (2) and (3).

(2) In subsection (3)—

   (a) in paragraph (a), for "performs" substitute "at any time performs or is to perform";
   (b) omit paragraph (b);
   (c) in paragraph (c), for "the scheme" substitute "an investment scheme".

(3) After subsection (6) insert—

   "(7) The reference in subsection (6)(a) to a collective investment scheme includes—

      (a) arrangements which permit an external investor to participate in investments acquired by the collective investment scheme without participating in the scheme itself, and
      (b) arrangements under which sums arise to an individual performing investment management services in respect of the collective investment scheme without those sums arising from the scheme itself."

(4) In section 809EZE of that Act (interpretation), in subsection (1), in paragraph (a) of the definition of "external investor", for "performs" substitute "at any time performs or is to perform".

(5) The amendments made by this section have effect in relation to sums arising on or after 6 April 2016 (whenever the arrangements under which the sums arise were made).

GENERAL NOTE

Section 36 makes some minor amendment ITA 2007 s 809EZA (Disguised Invest-ment Management fees: Charge to Income Tax) and applies to sums arising on or after 6 April 2016.

Section 36(2) amends ITA 2007 s 809EZA(3) so as to:

– substitute "any time performs or is to perform' for "performs" in para (a) of that section – which simply broadens the circumstance in which an individual investment manager can meet the basic requirement that he or she performs investment management services directly or indirectly in respect of the relevant collective investment scheme;
– delete paragraph (b) of the section – which means that there is no longer a requirement that the relevant collective investment arrangements involve at least one partnership for the disguised investment management fee rules to apply to amounts arising to investment managers; and
– amend para (c) of the section – so that under the arrangement the relevant management fee must arise to the individual from an investment scheme rather than the investment scheme.

Section 36(3) inserts a new sub-s (7) into ITA 2007 s 809EZA which extends the definition of what is an investment scheme for the purposes of the disguised investment management fee rules to include:

– arrangements which permit an external investor to participate in investments required by the collective investment scheme without participating in the scheme itself; and
– arrangements under which sums arise to an individual performing investment management services in respect of the collective investment scheme without those sums arising from the scheme.

This extension will cover certain arrangements whereby amounts arising to individu-als are directly referable to the investments of a collective investment scheme without involving an interest in the scheme. The amendment does not, however, extend the basic definition of "collective investment scheme' for the purposes of the disguised investment management fee rules, so that it is still the case that the rules only apply to collective investment schemes as defined in FSMA 2000 s 235 or investment trusts which meet Conditions A–C of CTA 2010 s 1158.

Section 36(4) amends the definition of 'external investor' in ITA 2007 s 809EZE(1)(a) by substituting "at any time performs or is to perform" for "performs" so that external investor means a participant in the relevant collective investment scheme other than an individual who at any time performs or is to perform investment management services directly or indirectly in respect of the scheme.

These amendments, therefore, make relatively minor extensions to the circum-stances in which the disguised investment management fee rules in ITA 2007 Pt 13 Ch 5E can apply, but do not change those rules significantly.

37 Income-based carried interest

(1) In Chapter 5E of Part 13 of ITA 2007 (tax avoidance: disguised investment management fees), in section 809EZB(1) (meaning of "management fee"), for para-graph (c) substitute—

"(c) carried interest which is not income-based carried interest (see sec-tions 809EZC and 809EZD for carried interest, and Chapter 5F for income-based carried interest)."

(2) After Chapter 5E of Part 13 of ITA 2007 insert—

"CHAPTER 5F
INCOME-BASED CARRIED INTEREST

Income-based carried interest

809FZA Overview

(1) This Chapter determines when carried interest arising to an individual from an investment scheme is "income-based carried interest" for the purposes of Chapter 5E (and, in particular, section 809EZB(1)(c)).

(2) Section 809FZB contains the general rule, under which the extent to which carried interest is income-based carried interest depends on the average holding period of the investment scheme.

(3) Sections 809FZC to 809FZP contain further provision relating to average holding periods.

(4) Sections 809FZQ and 809FZR contain a particular rule for direct lending funds.

(5) Sections 809FZS and 809FZT contain an exception to the general rule for carried interest which is conditionally exempt from income tax.

(6) Sections 809FZU to 809FZZ contain supplementary and interpretative provision.

(7) Nothing in this Chapter affects the liability to any tax of—
    (a) the investment scheme, or
    (b) external investors in the investment scheme.

809FZB Income-based carried interest: general rule

(1) "Income-based carried interest" is the relevant proportion of a sum of carried interest arising to an individual from an investment scheme.

(2) The relevant proportion is determined by reference to the investment scheme's average holding period as follows.

Average holding period	Relevant proportion
Less than 36 months	100%
At least 36 months but less than 37 months	80%
At least 37 months but less than 38 months	60%
At least 38 months but less than 39 months	40%
At least 39 months but less than 40 months	20%
40 months or more	0%

(3) This section is subject to the following provisions of this Chapter.

Average holding period

809FZC Average holding period

(1) The average holding period of an investment scheme, in relation to a sum of carried interest, is the average length of time for which relevant investments have been held for the purposes of the scheme.

(2) In this section, "relevant investments" means investments—
    (a) which are made for the purposes of the scheme, and
    (b) by reference to which the carried interest is calculated.

(3) The average holding period is calculated by reference to the time the carried interest arises.

(4) It is calculated as follows.
Step 1
For each relevant investment, multiply the value invested at the time the investment was made by the length of time for which the investment has been held.
Step 2
Add together the amounts produced under *step 1* in respect of all relevant investments.
Step 3
Divide the amount produced under *step 2* by the total value invested in all relevant investments.

(5) Disregard intermediate holdings or intermediate holding structures (including intermediate investment schemes) by or through which investments are made or held—

(a) when identifying, for the purpose of determining the average holding period of an investment scheme, what relevant investments are held for the purposes of an investment scheme, and

(b) for any other purpose relating to the determination of the average holding period.

This is subject to the following provisions of this Chapter.

(6) In this section, references to the length of time for which a relevant investment has been held are—

(a) in the case of an investment which has been disposed of before the carried interest arises, references to the time for which it was held before being disposed of, and

(b) in any other case, references to the time for which it has been held up to the time the carried interest arises.

(7) For the purposes of this Chapter, carried interest which is deferred carried interest in relation to a person within the meaning of section 103KG of TCGA 1992 is to be treated as arising to that person at the time it would have arisen had it not been deferred as specified in section 103KG(3)(a) or (b) of that Act.

(8) Sections 809FZD to 809FZP apply for the purposes of determining the average holding period of an investment scheme.

Average holding period: disposals

809FZD Disposals

(1) An investment or part of an investment is disposed of where—

(a) there is a disposal of the investment or the part of the investment for the purposes of the investment scheme,

(b) there is a disposal for the purposes of the investment scheme of an intermediate holding or intermediate holding structure (including an intermediate investment scheme) by or through which the investment is held, or

(c) in any other case, there is a deemed disposal under subsection (2).

(2) There is a deemed disposal of an investment or part of an investment under this subsection where—

(a) under any arrangements—

(i) the scheme in substance closes its position on the investment or the part of the investment, or

(ii) the scheme ceases to be exposed to risks and rewards in the respect of the investment or the part of the investment, and

(b) it is reasonable to suppose that the arrangements were designed to secure that result.

(3) In the case of a disposal of part of a holding of securities in a company which are of the same class, suppose for the purposes of determining which investments have been disposed of that the disposal affects the securities in the order in which they were acquired (that is, on a first in first out basis).

(4) The references in subsection (1)(a) and (b) to a disposal are to something which is a disposal for the purposes of TCGA 1992; but for the purposes of subsection (1)(a) disregard section 116 of TCGA 1992 (which disapplies sections 127 to 130 of that Act in relation to qualifying corporate bonds).

809FZE Part disposals

(1) Where there is a disposal of part of an investment, the part disposed of and the part not disposed of are to be treated as two separate investments which were made at the same time.

(2) The value of each of those two separate investments is the appropriate proportion of the value first invested in the whole investment.

(3) The appropriate proportion is the proportion of the value of the part in question to the value of the whole investment at the time of the disposal.

(4) The disposal of part of an asset includes the disposal of an interest in or right over the asset (and "part disposed of" is to be construed accordingly).

809FZF Unwanted short-term investments

(1) The making and disposal of an investment for the purposes of an investment scheme are to be disregarded if—

(a) the investment is an unwanted short-term investment, and

(b) the unwanted short-term investment is excludable.

(2) An investment is an unwanted short-term investment where—

(a) the investment is made as part of a transaction under which one or more other investments are made for the purposes of the scheme,

(b) the value of the investment does not exceed that of the other investments taken together,

(c) it is reasonable to suppose that the investment had to be made in order for the other investments to be made,

(d) at the time the investment is made, managers of the scheme have a firm, settled and evidenced intention to dispose of the investment for the purposes of the scheme within the relevant period,

(e) the investment is disposed of for the purposes of the scheme within the relevant period, and

(f) any profit resulting from the disposal has no bearing on whether a sum of carried interest arises or on the amount of any sum of carried interest which does arise.

(3) An unwanted short-term investment is excludable if it constitutes—

(a) an investment in land,

(b) an investment in securities in an unlisted company,

(c) the making of a direct loan where the other investments specified in subsection (2)(b) are shares or other securities in an unlisted company, or

(d) the making of a direct loan which is a qualifying loan within the meaning given by section 809FZR(2).

(4) In subsection (2)(e) "relevant period" means—

(a) for an investment within subsection (3)(a), 12 months;

(b) for an investment within subsection (3)(b) or (c), 6 months;

(c) for an investment within subsection (3)(d), 120 days.

(5) But if at any time it becomes reasonable to suppose that, when the scheme ceases to invest, 25% or more of the capital of the investment scheme will have been invested in unwanted short-term investments which are excludable, subsection (1) does not apply to any investment made subsequently for the purposes of the scheme.

Average holding period. derivatives and hedging

809FZG Derivatives

(1) A derivative contract entered into for the purposes of an investment scheme is an investment, subject to the following provisions of this section.

(2) The value invested in the derivative contract is

(a) where the contract is an option, the cost of acquiring the option (whether from the grantor or another person),

(b) where the contract is a future, the price specified in the contract for the underlying subject matter, or

(c) where the contract is a contract for differences, the notional principal of the contract.

(3) But where entering into a derivative contract constitutes a deemed disposal of an investment or part of an investment by virtue of section 809FZD(2)(a)(ii)—

(a) the derivative contract is not an investment, and

(b) the subsequent disposal of the derivative contract without a corresponding disposal of the investment or part investment is to be regarded as the making of a new investment to the extent that the scheme becomes materially exposed to risks and rewards in respect of the investment or part investment.

(4) For the purposes of this Chapter, references to disposal, in the case of a derivative contract, include any of the following events (to the extent that the event is not otherwise a disposal under section 809FZD(1) or (2))—

(a) the expiry of the contract,

(b) the termination of the contract (whether or not in accordance with its terms),

(c) the disposal, substantial variation, loss or cancellation of the investment scheme's rights under the contract, and

(d) in the case of a derivative contract which is an option, the exercise of the option,

but do not include the renewal of the contract with the same counterparty on substantially the same terms.

(5) The substantial variation of an investment scheme's rights under a derivative contract constitutes (in addition to the disposal of the contract as originally entered into (see subsection (4)(c)) a new investment consisting of the contract as varied.

809FZH Hedging: exchange gains and losses

(1) This section applies where—

(a) an investment scheme has a hedging relationship between a relevant instrument and a relevant investment, and

(b) the hedging relationship relates to exchange gains or losses.

(2) In this section—

"relevant instrument" means a derivative contract or a liability representing a loan relationship, and

"relevant investment" means—

(a) where the relevant instrument is a derivative contract, an investment made for the purposes of the scheme or a liability representing a loan relationship;

(b) where the relevant instrument is a liability representing a loan relationship, an investment made for the purposes of the scheme.

(3) An investment scheme has a hedging relationship between a relevant instrument and a relevant investment if or to the extent that—

(a) the instrument and the investment are designated by the scheme as a hedge, or

(b) in any other case, the instrument is intended to act as a hedge of exposure to—

(i) changes in fair value of the investment or an identified portion of the investment, or

(ii) variability in cash flows,

where the exposure is attributable to exchange gains or losses and could affect profit or loss of the investment scheme.

(4) Entering into the hedging relationship is not a deemed disposal of the relevant investment under section 809FZD(2).

(5) The relevant instrument is not an investment for the purposes of the investment scheme to the extent that the conditions in subsection (3)(a) and (b) are met.

(6) But the termination of the hedging relationship is the making of an investment constituting the relevant instrument if or to the extent that that instrument continues to subsist.

809FZI Hedging: interest rates

(1) This section applies where an investment scheme has a hedging relationship between—

(a) an interest rate contract, and

(b) a qualifying investment held for the purposes of the fund.

(2) An investment scheme has a hedging relationship between an interest rate contract and a qualifying investment if or to the extent that—

(a) the interest rate contract and the investment are designated by the scheme as a hedge, or

(b) in any other case, the interest rate contract is intended to act as a hedge of exposure to—

(i) changes in fair value of the investment or an identified portion of the investment, or

(ii) variability in cash flows,

where the exposure is attributable to interest rates and could affect profit or loss of the investment scheme.

(3) Entering into the hedging relationship is not a deemed disposal of the relevant investment under section 809FZD(2).

(4) The interest rate contract is not an investment for the purposes of the investment scheme to the extent that the conditions in subsection (2)(a) and (b) are met.

(5) But the termination of the hedging relationship is the making of an investment constituting the interest rate contract if or to the extent that the interest rate contract continues to subsist.

(6) In this section "qualifying investment" means—

(a) money placed at interest,

(b) securities (excluding shares issued by companies),

(c) alternative finance arrangements, and

(d) a liability representing a loan relationship.

Average holding period: aggregation of acquisitions and disposals

809FZJ Significant interests

(1) Where an investment scheme has a controlling interest in a trading company or the holding company of a trading group—

(a) any investment made for the purposes of the scheme in that company after the time when the controlling interest was acquired is to be regarded as having been made at that time, and

(b) any disposal for the purposes of the scheme of an investment in the company after the time the controlling interest was acquired is to be regarded as not being made until a relevant disposal is made.

(2) In subsection (1)(b) "relevant disposal", in relation to a company, means a disposal which (apart from subsection (1)) has the effect that the investment scheme ceases to have a 40% interest in the company.

(3) For the purposes of this section, in determining whether an investment scheme has a controlling interest or a 40% interest in a company, any share capital of the company which is held for the purposes of an associated investment scheme is to be regarded as held for the purposes of the investment scheme.

809FZK Venture capital funds

(1) Where a venture capital fund has a relevant interest in a trading company or the holding company of a trading group—

(a) any venture capital investment made for the purposes of the scheme in the company after the time the relevant interest was acquired (and before a relevant disposal) is to be regarded as having been made at the time the relevant interest was acquired, and

(b) any disposal for the purposes of the scheme of a venture capital investment in the company after that time is to be regarded as not being made until—

(i) a relevant disposal is made, or

(ii) the scheme director condition ceases to be met.

(2) For the purposes of subsection (1) a venture capital fund has a relevant interest in a company if

(a) by virtue of its venture capital investments the fund has at least a 5% interest in the company, or

(b) venture capital investments held for the purposes of the scheme in the company have a value of more than £1 million.

(3) For the purposes of subsection (1) "relevant disposal" means a disposal which (apart from subsection (1)) has the effect that the venture capital fund has disposed of more than 80% of the greatest amount invested at any one time in the company for the purposes of the fund.

(4) In this Chapter, "venture capital fund" means an investment scheme in relation to which the condition in subsection (5) is met.

(5) The condition is that when the scheme starts to invest it is reasonable to suppose that over the investing life of the scheme—

(a) at least two-thirds of the total value invested for the purposes of the scheme will be invested in venture capital investments, and

(b) at least two-thirds of the total value invested for the purposes of the scheme will be invested in investments which are held for 40 months or more.

(6) In determining whether subsection (5)(b) is met in relation to an investment scheme, apply the rule in subsection (1) to the scheme.

(7) In this section, "venture capital investment", in relation to an investment scheme, means an investment in a trading company or the holding company of a trading group where—

(a) at the time the investment is made the company is unlisted and is likely to remain so,

(b) at least 75%of the total value of the investment is invested in—

(i) newly issued shares or

(ii) newly issued securities convertible into shares,

(c) the investment is used in a trade carried on by the trading company or the trading group—

(i) to support its growth, or

(ii) for the development of new products or services,

and is not used directly or indirectly to acquire shares in the company which are not newly issued,

(d) if the investment is the first investment made in the company for the purposes of the scheme, the trading company or group has not carried on that trade for more than 7 years, and

(e) the scheme director condition is met.

(8) In this Chapter, the scheme director condition, in relation to an investment scheme and a company, is that—

(a) the scheme (or the scheme and one or more investment schemes acting together) are entitled to appoint a director ("the scheme director") of—

(i) the company, or

(ii) a company which controls the company, and

(b) the scheme director is entitled to exercise rights within subsection (9).

(9) Those rights are rights which—

(a) are rights conferred under contractual arrangements—

(i) to which some or all of the investors in the company are parties, and

(ii) which it would be reasonable to suppose would not otherwise be capable of being exercised by the scheme director,

(b) relate to the conduct of the business and affairs of the company, and

(c) are at least equivalent to the rights which it is reasonable to suppose a prudent investor would have obtained on making an investment in the company at arm's length of the same size and nature as that held in the company for the purposes of the investment scheme.

(10) In determining whether the condition in subsection (2)(a) or (b) is met in relation to a venture capital fund, any share capital of a company which is held for the purposes of an associated investment scheme is to be regarded as held for the purposes of the venture capital fund.

809FZL Significant equity stake funds

(1) Where a significant equity stake fund has a significant equity stake investment in a trading company or the holding company of a trading group—

(a) any investment made for the purposes of the fund in that company made after the time the significant equity stake investment was acquired is to be regarded as having been made at that time, and

(b) any disposal for the purposes of the fund of an investment in the company after that time is to be regarded as not being made until—

(i) a relevant disposal is made, or

(ii) the scheme director condition ceases to be met.

(2) In subsection (1)(b) "relevant disposal" means a disposal which (apart from subsection (1)) has the effect that the significant equity stake fund ceases to have a 15% interest in the company.

(3) In this Chapter, "significant equity stake fund" means an investment scheme—

(a) which is not a venture capital fund, and

(b) in relation to which the condition in subsection (4) is met.

(4) The condition is that when the scheme starts to invest it is reasonable to suppose that over the investing life of the scheme—

(a) more than 50% of the total value invested for the purposes of the scheme will be invested in investments which are significant equity stake investments, and

(b) more than 50% of that value will be invested in investments which are held for 40 months or more.

(5) In determining whether subsection (4)(b) is met in relation to an investment scheme, apply the rule in subsection (1) to the scheme.

(6) In this section, "significant equity stake investment", in relation to an investment scheme, means an investment in a trading company or the holding company of a trading group where—

(a) at the time the investment is made, the company is unlisted and likely to remain so,

(b) by virtue of the investment (on its own or with other investments) the scheme has a 20% interest in the company, and

(c) the scheme director condition is met.

(7) For the purposes of this section, in determining whether a significant equity stake fund has an interest of a particular percentage in a company, any share capital of the

company which is held for the purposes of an associated investment scheme is to be regarded as held for the purposes of the significant equity stake fund.

809FZM Controlling equity stake funds

(1) Where a controlling equity stake fund has a 25% interest in a trading company or the holding company of a trading group—

(a) any investment made for the purposes of the controlling equity stake fund in the company after the time the 25% interest was acquired is to be regarded as having been made at that time, and

(b) any disposal for the purposes of the controlling equity stake fund of an investment in the company after that time is to be regarded as not being made until a relevant disposal is made.

(2) In subsection (1)(b), "relevant disposal", in relation to a company, means a disposal which (apart from subsection (1)) has the effect that the controlling equity stake fund ceases to have a 25% interest in the company.

(3) In this Chapter, "controlling equity stake fund" means an investment scheme—

(a) which is not a venture capital fund or significant equity stake fund, and

(b) in relation to which the condition in subsection (4) is met.

(4) The condition is that when the scheme starts to invest it is reasonable to suppose that, over the investing life of the scheme—

(a) more than 50% of the total value invested for the purposes of the scheme will be invested in investments which are controlling interests in trading companies or holding companies of trading groups, and

(b) more than 50% of the total value invested for the purposes of the scheme will be invested in investments which are held for 40 months or more.

(5) In determining whether subsection (4)(b) is met in relation to an investment scheme, apply the rule in subsection (1) to the scheme.

(6) For the purposes of this section, in determining whether a controlling equity stake fund has a controlling interest or an interest of a particular percentage in a company, any share capital of the company which is held for the purposes of an associated investment scheme is to be regarded as held for the purposes of the controlling equity stake fund.

809FZN Real estate funds

(1) Where a real estate fund has a major interest in any land—

(a) any investment made for the purposes of the fund in that land after the time the major interest was acquired is to be regarded as having been made at that time, and

(b) any disposal for the purposes of the fund of an investment in the land after that time is to be regarded as not being made until a relevant disposal is made.

(2) In subsection (1)(b) "relevant disposal" means a disposal which (apart from subsection (1)) has the effect that the real estate fund has disposed of more than 50% of the greatest amount invested at any one time in the land for the purposes of the real estate fund.

(3) Where a real estate fund has a major interest in any land ("the original land") and subsequently acquires a major interest in any adjacent land—

(a) the acquisition is an investment in the original land for the purposes of subsection (1)(a), and

(b) after the acquisition, the adjacent land is to be regarded as part of the original land for the purposes of subsections (1) and (2).

(4) In this Chapter, "real estate fund" means an investment scheme—

(a) which is not a venture capital fund, significant equity stake fund or controlling equity stake fund, and

(b) in relation to which the condition in subsection (5) is met.

(5) The condition is that when the scheme starts to invest it is reasonable to suppose that over the investing life of the scheme—

(a) more than 50% of the total value invested for the purposes of the scheme will be invested in land, and

(b) more than 50% of the total value invested for the purposes of the scheme will be invested in investments which are held for 40 months or more.

(6) In determining whether subsection (5)(b) is met in relation to an investment scheme, apply the rule in subsection (1) to the scheme.

809FZO   Funds of funds

(1) Section 809FZC(5) (disregard of intermediate holdings and holding structures) does not apply to an investment made for the purposes of a fund of funds in a collective investment scheme (and, accordingly, such an investment is regarded as an investment in the collective investment scheme itself).

(2) Subsection (1) does not apply in relation to a fund of funds in relation to a collective investment scheme if it is reasonable to suppose that the main purpose or one of the main purposes of the making of any investment in any collective investment scheme for the purposes of the fund of funds is to reduce the proportion of carried interest arising to any person which is income-based carried interest.

(3) Where by virtue of subsection (1) a fund of funds has a significant investment in a collective investment scheme ("the underlying scheme")—

(a) any qualifying investment made for the purposes of the fund in the underlying scheme after the time the significant investment was acquired is to be regarded as having been made at that time, and

(b) any disposal for the purposes of the fund of a qualifying investment in the underlying scheme after that time is to be regarded as not being made until a relevant disposal is made.

(4) In subsection (3)(b) "relevant disposal", in relation to an underlying scheme, means a disposal which (apart from subsection (3)) has the effect that—

(a) the fund of funds has (by virtue of disposals of its interest in the underlying scheme) disposed of at least 50% of the greatest amount invested for its purposes at any one time in the underlying scheme, or

(b) the fund of fund's investment in the underlying scheme is worth less than whichever is the greater of—

(i) £1 million, or

(ii) 5% of the total value of the investments made before the disposal for the purposes of the fund of funds in the underlying scheme.

(5) In this Chapter, "fund of funds" means an investment scheme in relation to which the condition in subsection (6) is met.

(6) The condition is that when the scheme starts to invest it is reasonable to suppose that over the investing life of the scheme—

(a) substantially all of the total value invested for the purposes of the scheme will be invested in collective investment schemes of which the scheme holds less than 50% by value,

(b) more than 50% of the total value invested for the purposes of the scheme will be invested in investments which are held for 40 months or more, and

(c) more than 75% of the total value invested in the scheme will be invested by external investors.

(7) In determining whether subsection (6)(b) is met in relation to an investment scheme, apply the rule in subsection (3) to the scheme.

(8) In this section, "significant investment", in relation to a collective investment scheme, means—

(a) an investment of a least £1 million in the scheme, or

(b) an investment of at least 5% of the total amounts raised or to be raised from external investors in the scheme.

(9) In this section, "qualifying investment" means an investment made for the purposes of an investment scheme in a collective investment scheme ("the underlying scheme") where—

(a) the investment is held on the same terms as other investments made by external investors in the underlying scheme,

(b) the fund of funds, together with any connected funds, does not hold more than 30% by value of the underlying scheme,

(c) the underlying scheme has not made an investment in the fund of funds,

(d) no person providing investment management services to the underlying scheme provides investment management services to the fund of funds, and

(e) it is reasonable to suppose that the investment in the underlying scheme is not part of arrangements the main purpose or one of the main purposes of which is to reward any person involved in providing investment management services to the underlying scheme or a scheme connected with that underlying scheme.

809FZP   Secondary funds

(1) Section 809FZC(5) (disregard of intermediate holdings and holding structures) does not apply to investments acquired for the purposes of a secondary fund in a

collective investment scheme (and, accordingly, such an investment is regarded as an investment in the collective investment scheme itself).

(2) Subsection (1) does not apply in relation to a secondary fund in relation to a collective investment scheme if it is reasonable to suppose that the main purpose or one of the main purposes of the making of any investment in any collective investment scheme for the purposes of the secondary fund is to reduce the proportion of carried interest arising to any person which is income-based carried interest.

(3) Where by virtue of subsection (1) a secondary fund has a significant investment in a collective investment scheme ("the underlying scheme")—

(a) any qualifying investment acquired for the purposes of the fund in the underlying scheme after the time when the significant investment is acquired is to be regarded as having been made at that time, and

(b) any disposal for the purposes of the fund of a qualifying investment in the underlying scheme after that time is to be regarded as not being made until a relevant disposal is made.

(4) In subsection (3)(b) "relevant disposal" means a disposal which (apart from subsection (3)) has the effect that—

(a) the secondary fund has (by virtue of disposals of its interest in the underlying scheme) disposed of at least 50% of the greatest amount invested for its purposes at any one time in the underlying scheme, or

(b) the secondary fund's investment in the underlying scheme is worth less than whichever is the greater of—

(i) £1 million, or

(ii) 5% of the total value of the investments held immediately before the disposal for the purposes of the secondary fund in the underlying scheme.

(5) In this Chapter, "secondary fund" means an investment scheme in relation to which the condition in subsection (6) is met.

(6) The condition is that when the scheme starts to invest it is reasonable to suppose that over the investing life of the scheme—

(a) substantially all of the total value invested for the purposes of the scheme will be in the acquisition of investments in, or the acquisition of portfolios of investments from, unconnected collective investment schemes,

(b) more than 50% of the total value invested for the purposes of the scheme will be invested in investments which are held for 40 months or more, and

(c) more than 75% of the total amount invested in the scheme will be invested by external investors.

(7) In determining whether subsection (6)(b) is met in relation to an investment scheme, apply the rule in subsection (3) to the scheme.

(8) In this section, "significant interest", in relation to a collective investment scheme, means

(a) an investment of at least £1 million in the scheme, or

(b) an investment of at least 5% of the total amounts raised or to be raised from external investors in the scheme.

(9) In this section, "qualifying investment" means an investment in a collective investment scheme ("the underlying scheme") acquired for the purposes of a secondary fund where—

(a) the investment acquired was originally made on the same terms as investments in the underlying scheme made by external investors,

(b) the terms on which the investment was acquired or investments made in the underlying scheme were made by external investors have not significantly changed since the investment was acquired,

(c) the secondary fund, together with any connected funds, does not hold more than 30% by value of the underlying scheme,

(d) no person providing investment management services to the underlying scheme provides investment management services to the secondary fund, and

(e) it is reasonable to suppose that the investment in the underlying scheme is not part of arrangements the main purpose or one of the main purposes of which is to reward any person involved in providing investment management services to the underlying scheme or a scheme connected with that underlying scheme.

Direct lending funds

809FZQ Direct lending funds

(1) Carried interest arising from an investment scheme which is a direct lending fund is income-based carried interest in its entirety.

Subsections (2) to (4) apply for the purposes of this Chapter.

(2) A direct lending fund is an investment scheme—

(a) which is not a venture capital fund, significant equity stake fund, controlling equity stake fund or real estate fund, and

(b) in relation to which it is reasonable to suppose that, when the scheme ceases to invest, a majority of the investments made for the purposes of the scheme (calculated by reference to value invested) will have been direct loans made by the scheme.

(3) An investment scheme makes a direct loan if for the purposes of the scheme money is advanced at interest or for any other return determined by reference to the time value of money.

(4) The acquisition of a direct loan is to be regarded as the making of a direct loan if the loan is acquired within the period of 120 days beginning with the day on which the money is first advanced.

809FZR Direct lending funds: exception

(1) Section 809FZQ does not apply to carried interest arising from a direct lending fund if—

(a) the fund is a limited partnership,

(b) the carried interest is a sum falling within section 809EZD(2) or (3), and

(c) it is reasonable to suppose that, when investments cease to be made for the purposes of the fund, at least 75% of the direct loans made by the fund (calculated by reference to value advanced) will have been qualifying loans.

(2) In this section "qualifying loan" means a direct loan made by an investment scheme where—

(a) the borrower is not connected with the investment scheme,

(b) the money is advanced under a genuine commercial loan agreement negotiated at arm's length,

(c) repayments are fixed and determinable,

(d) maturity is fixed,

(e) the scheme has the positive intention and ability to hold the loan to maturity, and

(f) the relevant term of the loan is at least four years.

(3) In this section "relevant term", in relation to a loan, means the period which—

(a) begins with the time when the money is advanced, and

(b) ends with the time by which, under the terms of the loan, at least 75% of the principal due under the loan must be repaid.

(4) For the purposes of determining the average holding period of a scheme, where—

(a) a qualifying loan made by an investment scheme is repaid by the borrower to any extent before the end of 40 months from the time the loan is made, and

(b) it is reasonable to suppose that the borrower's decision to repay was not affected by considerations relating to the application of this Chapter,

the loan is, to the extent it is repaid by the borrower before the end of 40 months from the time it is made, to be treated as held for 40 months.

(5) In determining for the purposes of subsection (1)(b) whether a sum falls within section 809EZD(2) or (3), read section 809EZD(4)(b) as if the reference to 6% were to 4%.

(6) Section 809FZB applies to carried interest to which, by virtue of subsection (1), section 809FZQ does not apply.

Conditionally exempt carried interest

809FZS Conditionally exempt carried interest

(1) Carried interest which—

(a) arises to an individual from an investment scheme, and

(b) is conditionally exempt from income tax,

is to be treated as if it were not income-based carried interest to any extent.

(2) Carried interest is conditionally exempt from income tax if Conditions A to D are met.

(3) Condition A is that the carried interest arises to the individual in the period of—

(a) four years beginning with the day on which the scheme starts to invest, or

(b) ten years beginning with that day if the carried interest is calculated on the realisation model.

(4) Condition B is that the carried interest would, apart from this section, be income-based carried interest to any extent.

(5) Condition C is that it is reasonable to suppose that, were the carried interest to arise to the individual at the relevant time (but by reference to the same relevant investments), it would not be income-based carried interest to any extent.

(6) The "relevant time" is whichever is the earliest of—

(a) the time when it is reasonable to suppose that the investment scheme will be wound up;

(b) the end of the period of four years beginning with the time when it is reasonable to suppose that the scheme will cease to invest;

(c) the end of the period of—

. (i) four years beginning with the day on which the sum of carried interest arises to the individual, or

(ii) ten years beginning with that day if the carried interest was calculated on the realisation model;

(d) the end of the period of four years beginning with the end of the period by reference to which the amount of the carried interest was determined.

(7) Subsection (5) does not affect what would otherwise be the time at which an investment is disposed of for the purposes of this Chapter.

(8) Condition D is that the individual makes a claim under this section for the carried interest to be conditionally exempt from income tax.

809FZT Carried interest which ceases to be conditionally exempt

(1) Carried interest which is conditionally exempt from income tax ceases to be conditionally exempt from income tax at whichever is the earliest of—

(a) the time when the investment scheme is wound up;

(b) the end of the period of four years beginning with the time the scheme ceases to invest;

(c) the end of the period of—

(i) four years beginning with the day on which the sum of carried interest arises to the individual, or

(ii) ten years beginning with that day if the carried interest was calculated on the realisation model;

(d) the end of the period of four years beginning with the end of the period by reference to which the amount of the carried interest is determined;

(e) the time at which Condition C in section 809FZS(5) ceases to be met.

(2) Carried interest which ceases to be conditionally exempt from income tax is to be treated as having been income-based carried interest at the time it arose to the individual if or to the extent that, had it arisen to the individual at the time it ceased to be conditionally exempt (but in relation to the same relevant investments) it would have been income-based carried interest.

(3) All such assessments and adjustments of assessments are to be made as are necessary to give effect to subsection (2).

(4) Any amount paid by way of capital gains tax in respect of carried interest which is conditionally exempt from income tax is to be treated as if it had been paid in respect of any income tax liability arising under subsection (2).

Supplementary

809FZU Employment-related securities

This Chapter does not apply in relation to carried interest arising to an individual in respect of employment-related securities as defined by section 421B(8) of ITEPA 2003.

809FZV "Loan to own" investments

(1) This section applies where—

(a) an investment scheme acquires a debt,

(b) the debt is to any extent uncollectable or otherwise impaired,

(c) the debt is acquired at a discount with a view to securing direct or indirect ownership of any assets which are—

(i) owned by a company which is the debtor in respect of the debt, or

(ii) subject to a security interest in respect of the debt, and

(d) the fund acquires ownership of the assets within three months of the acquisition of the debt.

(2) For the purposes of this Chapter—

(a) the debt and the assets are to be treated as a single investment, and
(b) the value invested in that single investment is the amount paid for the debt.

(3) In this section "security interest" means an interest or right (other than a rentcharge) held for the purpose of securing the payment of money or the performance of any obligation.

809FZW Anti-avoidance

(1) For the purposes mentioned in subsection (2), no regard is to be had to any arrangements the main purpose of which, or one of the main purposes of which, is to reduce the proportion of carried interest which is income-based carried interest.

(2) The purposes referred to in subsection (1) are—

(a) determining the average holding period, or
(b) determining whether an investment scheme is a venture capital fund, significant equity stake fund, controlling equity stake fund, real estate fund, fund of funds or secondary fund.

(3) In determining to what extent carried interest is income-based carried interest, no regard is to be had to any arrangements the main purpose, or one of the main purposes, of which is to secure that section 809EZA(1) (charge to income tax) does not apply in relation to some or all of the carried interest.

809FZX Treasury regulations

(1) The Treasury may by regulations make—

(a) provision relating to the calculation of the average holding period in some or all cases;
(b) provision repealing, or restricting the application of, section 809FZU (employment-related securities).

(2) The provision referred to in subsection (1)(a) includes in particular—

(a) provision for a method of calculating that period which is different from that in section 809FZC;
(b) provision as to what is and is not to be regarded as an investment;
(c) provision as to when an investment is to be regarded as made or disposed of;
(d) anti-avoidance provision.

(3) Regulations under this section may—

(a) amend this Chapter;
(b) make different provision for different purposes;
(c) contain incidental, supplemental, consequential and transitional provision and savings.

809FZY "Reasonable to suppose"

(1) For the purposes of this Chapter, in determining what it is reasonable to suppose in relation to an investment scheme, regard is to be had to all the circumstances.

(2) Those circumstances include in particular any prospectus or other document which—

(a) is made available to external investors in the investment scheme, and
(b) on which external investors may reasonably be supposed to have relied or been able to rely.

Interpretation

809FZZ Interpretation of Chapter 5F

(1) In this Chapter—

"5% interest", "15% interest", "20% interest", "25% interest" and "40% interest" are to be construed in accordance with subsection (4);

"act together": two or more investment schemes act together in relation to a company if—

(a) they enter into contractual arrangements (with or without other persons) in relation to the conduct of the company's affairs,
(b) the arrangements are negotiated on arm's length terms, and
(c) the investment schemes act together to secure greater control or influence over the company's affairs than they would be able to secure individually;

"alternative finance arrangements" has the same meaning as in Part 6 of CTA 2009 (see section 501(2) of that Act);

"arrangements" has the same meaning as in Chapter 5E (see section 809EZE);

"associated": two (or more) investment schemes are "associated if—

(a) the same or substantially the same individuals provide investment management services to both schemes;

(b) the investment schemes have the same or substantially the same investments, and

(c) the schemes act together in relation to all or substantially all of the investments they acquire;

"carried interest" has the same meaning as in section 809EZB (see sections 809EZC and 809EZD);

"collective investment scheme" has the same meaning as in Chapter 5E (see section 809EZE);

"connected" and "unconnected" are to be construed in accordance with subsections (6) and (7);

"contract for differences" has the same meaning as in Part 7 of CTA 2009 (see section 582 of that Act);

"controlling equity stake fund" has the meaning given in section 809FZM;

"controlling interest" has the meaning given in subsection (3);

"derivative contract" has the same meaning as in Part 7 of CTA 2009 (but see below);

"designated" has the same meaning as for accounting purposes;

"direct lending fund" and "direct loan" have the meanings given in section 809FZQ;

"exchange gain or loss" is to be construed in accordance with section 475 of CTA 2009;

"external investor" has the same meaning as in Chapter 5E (see section 809EZE);

"fund of funds" has the meaning given in section 809FZO;

"future" has the same meaning as in Part 7 of CTA 2009 (see section 581 of that Act);

"interest rate contract" means—

(a) a derivative contract whose underlying subject-matter is, or includes, interest rates, or

(b) a swap contract in which payments fall to be made by reference to a rate of interest;

"investing life" is to be construed in accordance with subsection (2);

"investment" does not include—

(a) cash awaiting investment, or

(b) cash representing the proceeds of the disposal of an investment, where the cash is to be distributed as soon as reasonably practicable to investors in the scheme;

"investment scheme" has the same meaning as in Chapter 5E (see section 809EZA(6));

"limited partnership" means—

(a) a limited partnership registered under the Limited Partnerships Act 1907,

(b) a limited liability partnership formed under the Limited Liability Partnerships Act 2000 or the Limited Liability Partnerships Act (Northern Ireland) 2002 (c 12 (NI)), or

(c) a firm or entity of a similar character to any of those mentioned in paragraph (a) or (b) formed under the law of a country or territory outside the United Kingdom;

"loan relationship" has the meaning given by section 302 of CTA 2009 (but see below);

"major interest", in relation to land, has the meaning given by section 96 of the Value Added Tax Act 1994;

"option" has the same meaning as in Part 7 of CTA 2009, disregarding section 580(2) of that Act;

"real estate fund" has the meaning given by section 809FZN;

"realisation model": a sum of carried interest is calculated on the "realisation model" if it falls within section 809EZD(2) or (3) (disregarding section 809EZD(2)(b) and (3)(b));

"scheme director condition" has the meaning given by section 809FZK(8) and (9);

"secondary fund" has the meaning given by section 809FZP;

"significant equity stake fund" has the meaning given by section 809FZL;

"sum" has the same meaning as in Chapter 5E (see section 809EZB(3));

"trading company" and "trading group" have the meanings given by paragraphs 20 and 21 of Schedule 7AC to TCGA 1992;

"underlying subject matter" has the same meaning as in Part 7 of CTA 2009;

"unlisted": a company is unlisted if—

(a) no shares of any class issued by the company are listed on any stock exchange, and

(b) there are no other trading arrangements in place in respect of shares of any class issued by the company;

"venture capital fund" has the meaning given by section 809FZK.

(2) In this Chapter—

(a) references to when a scheme starts or ceases to invest are to the time when investments start or cease to be made for the purposes of the scheme, and

(b) references to the investing life of the scheme are to the time between when a scheme starts and ceases to invest.

(3) For the purposes of this Chapter, an investment scheme has a controlling interest in a company if share capital of the company is held for the purposes of the scheme which—

(a) amounts to more than 50% of the ordinary share capital of the company, and

(b) carries an entitlement to more than 50% of—

(i) voting rights in the company,

(ii) profits available for distribution to shareholders, and

(iii) assets of the company available for distribution to shareholders in a winding-up.

(4) For the purposes of this Chapter, an investment scheme has an interest of a particular percentage in a company (for example, a 40% interest) if share capital of the company is held for the purposes of the scheme which—

(a) amounts to at least that percentage of the ordinary share capital of the company, and

(b) carries an entitlement to at least that percentage of—

(i) voting rights in the company,

(ii) profits available for distribution to shareholders, and

(iii) assets of the company available for distribution to shareholders in a winding-up.

(5) For the purposes of subsections (3) and (4) any share capital held by a company controlled by an investment scheme is to be regarded as held for the purposes of the investment scheme.

(6) For the purposes of this Chapter, an investment scheme (A) is connected with another investment scheme or person (B) if—

(a) A directly or indirectly has control of B, or

(b) the same person, directly or indirectly, has control of A and B.

(7) For the purposes of subsection (6) "control"—

(a) in the case of control of a company, is to be read in accordance with sections 450 and 451 of CTA 2010;

(b) in the case of control of a partnership, has the meaning given in section 995(3);

(c) in the case of control of an investment scheme which is not a company or partnership, or of any other person which is not a company or partnership, means the ability to secure that the affairs of that scheme or other person are conducted in accordance with one's wishes.

(8) For the purposes of the definition of "derivative contract", read Part 7 of CTA 2009 as if—

(a) references to a company were references to an investment scheme, and

(b) references to a contract of a company were references to a contract for the purposes of an investment scheme.

(9) For the purposes of the definition of "loan relationship", read Part 5 of CTA 2009 as if—

(a) references to a company were references to an investment scheme, and

(b) references to a loan relationship of a company were references to a loan relationship for the purposes of an investment scheme."

(3) In section 2 of ITA 2007 (overview), in subsection (13), after paragraph (hb) insert—

"(hc) income-based carried interest (Chapter 5F),".

(4) The amendments made by this section have effect in relation to sums of carried interest arising on or after 6 April 2016 (whenever the arrangements under which the sums arise were made).

GENERAL NOTE

Section 37 introduces the concept of income-based capital interest ("IBCI") through an amendment to ITA 2007 s 809EZB(1) and the introduction of new ITA 2007 Pt 13 Ch 5F.

By way of explanation, the disguised investment management fee rules in ITA 2007 Pt 13 Ch 5E operate by treating all amounts arising to (or treated as arising to) investment managers from the provision of their services to relevant investment schemes as being management fees and, therefore, taxed as income from a trade unless the amounts constitute the return of capital invested by the investment manager, an "arm's length return" on that amount or "carried interest" (each as defined in the rules).

Section 37(1) amends ITA 2007 s 809EZB(1)(c) so that what is excluded from being treated as a management fee, and so trading income, under the carried interest head is narrowed to being carried interest which is not IBCI. Thus amounts which are treated as IBCI under the new rules in ITA 2007 Pt 13 Ch 5F remain disguised investment management fees and, therefore, taxed as trading income.

New Ch 5F then contains detailed provisions setting out both what is IBCI and how to calculate it.

The rules operate by requiring a determination at each point at which an amount of carried interest arises to an investment manager of the "average holding period" of the "relevant investments' related to the carried interest. The basic rule is that a percentage (between 0% and 100%) of the carried interest is treated as IBCI within the range of average holding period for relevant investments between forty months or more down to less than thirty-six months. The general rule is that the average holding period is calculated on an investment by investment basis, with things like follow on investments, bolt on acquisitions, returns of capital and other transactions related to an existing investment of the scheme being treated as separate investments. There are then a number of provisions that allow for simplified average holding period calculations for certain types of investment schemes that are considered, broadly, to qualify as "long term investment" schemes to the extent that the conditions set out in the relevant individual provisions are satisfied.

The other significant provision in the rules is that whenever an amount of carried interest arises, all existing relevant investments of the scheme are treated as if they are disposed of, thereby allowing an average holding period to be calculated at each time that any amount of carried interest arises. Because this rule will result in an artificial average holding period compared relative to the average holding period that might be determined were the actual disposal events of the investment scheme to be used across the whole life of the investment scheme, the concept of 'conditionally exempt carried interest' is introduced. This allows the time at which carried interest is treated as arising to be deferred for a number of years in certain cases so that the average holding period calculated at the time that the carried interest is treated as arising is more likely to align with the average holding period of the investment scheme over its life.

The specific provisions are discussed in more detailed below.

As stated, s 37(1) amends the carried interest exclusion from disguised investment management fee treatment so that IBCI is treated as if it were a disguised investment management fee and, therefore, taxed as if it were the income from a trade.

Section 37(2) introduces new ITA 2007 Pt 13 Ch 5F which sets out the provisions in respect of IBCI. Chapter 5F comprises ITA 2007 ss 809FZA–809FZZ.

The new IBCI rules will apply to carried interest arising on or after 6 April 2016.

New ITA 2007 s 809FZA

New s 809FZA summarises what is contained in the other provisions in Ch 5F. Section 809FZA(1) states that Ch 5F determines when carried interest arising to an individual from an investment scheme is "income-based carried interest" for the purposes of Ch 5E and, in particular, ITA 2007 s 809EZB(1)(c).

ITA 2007 s 809FZA(7) states that nothing in Ch 5F affects the liability to any tax of the investment scheme or external investors in the investment scheme. This means that the trading income treatment of carried interest which is treated as IBCI is not of any relevance in determining whether the activities of the investment scheme or of the external investors in the investment scheme are trading or investment activities and that the distinction between the two for those purpose remains to be determined under the applicable general law (which was also applied to carried interest returns prior to the introduction of these new rules).

New ITA 2007 s 809FZB

New s 809FZB states in sub-s (1) that IBCI is the relevant proportion of a sum of carried interest arising to an individual from an investment scheme and in sub-section (2) that the "relevant proportion" is determined by reference to the investment scheme's "average holding period" as follows:

- average holding period <36 months – relevant proportion of IBCI 100%;
- average holding period at least 36 months but <37 months – relevant proportion 80%;
- average holding period at least 37 months but <38 months – relevant proportion 60%;
- average holding period at least 38 months but <39 months – relevant proportion 40%;
- average holding period at least 39 months but <40 months – relevant proportion 20%;
- average holding period 40 months or more – relevant proportion 0%.

New ITA 2007 s 809FZC

ITA 2007 s 809FZC sets out the basic rule of determining the average holding period in order to apply the relevant proportions set out in s 809FZB.

Section 809FZC(1) states that the average holding period of an investment scheme in relation to a sum of carried interest is the average length of time for which 'relevant investments" have been held for the purposes of the scheme.

Section 809FZC(2) states that "relevant investments" are investments:

- which are made for the purposes of the scheme; and
- by reference to which the carried interest is calculated.

Section 809FZC(3) states that the average holding period is calculated by reference to the time the carried interest arises.

When determining the average holding period it is necessary, therefore, to determine what are the "relevant investments" in respect of a particular amount of carried interest. Under a normal "fund as a whole" carried interest model, the relevant investments would be all of the investments of the investment scheme. If an investment scheme were to operate a pure 'deal by deal' carried interest model, under which carried interest was calculated by reference to the profits arising on the sale of individual investments with no provisions that might require repayment of such carried interest if a broader range of investments did not generate a stated profit, the relevant investments would be the individual investments by reference to which each amount of carried interest was calculated. What is less clear is what the relevant investments might be in cases where the carried interest is stated to be on a deal by deal basis but included provisions, as is commonly the case, for repayment (or clawback) of carried interest if the investors do not realise a specified return by reference to a wider range (or all) of the investments of the investment scheme. In that case, common sense would imply that the relevant investments would be the broader range, or all, of the investments of the investment scheme as applicable. This is, however, something that will hopefully be clarified when HMRC publishes its guidance on the new rules in due course.

The rest of ITA 2007 s 809FZC sets out how the average holding period of the relevant investments is calculated.

Section 809FZC(4) sets out the basic calculation as involving three steps:

- **Step 1** – for each relevant investment multiply the value invested at the time the investment was made by the length of time for which investment has been held;
- **Step 2** – add together the amounts produced under step 1 in respect of all relevant investments; and
- **Step 3** – divide the amount produced under Step 2 by the total amount invested in all relevant investments.

Section 809FZC(5) states that intermediate holdings or intermediate holding structures (including intermediate investment schemes) by or through with investments are made or held are to be disregarded when identifying for the purpose of determining the average holding period of an investments scheme what relevant investments are held for the purposes of an investment scheme and for any purpose relating to the determination of the average holding period. This means that when calculating investment acquisitions and disposals one must look through intermediate holding structures (such as holding companies established by the investment scheme to hold all of its investments) and, instead, look to what might be considered by investors as the actual "investments' of the scheme. There is no detail in the rules as to when intermediate holdings or intermediate holding structures end and exactly what should be considered to be the relevant investments of the scheme, and one hopes that this might be clarified in HMRC's guidance on the rules. In addition, as discussed below, this disregard provision is specifically excluded in the context of funds of funds and secondary funds, for which the simplified method of calculating the average holding period are included as part of the rules.

Section 809FZC(6) provides that references to the length of time for which relevant investments has been held for the purposes of applying the average holding period calculation in s 809FZC are references to the time for which the investment was held before being disposed of in the case of investments which are disposed of before the carried interest arises and in other cases, to the time for which it has been held up to the time the carried interest arises. This means that in determining the average holding period of relevant investments of the scheme for any specific carried interest receipt, the average holding period calculation operates on the basis that any existing investments of the scheme are disposed of at the time the carried interest arises. As mentioned above, the conditionally exempt carried interest provision discussed below is included in the rules to mitigate the potential consequence of this assumption.

Section 809FZC(7) states that if an amount carried interest would be "deferred carried interest" within the meaning of TCGA 1992 s 103KG, the deferral element of that rule is ignored for the purposes of the IBCI rules. This means that the average holding period calculation is determined at the time that the carried interest arises ignoring the deferral of that arising event under the TCGA 1992 deferred carried interest rule.

Average holding period provisions

Sections 809FZD–809FZR then set out detailed provisions relating to how the average holding period of an investment scheme is calculated in certain circumstances.

Of these, ss 809FZD and 809FZE set out what is a disposal and the consequences of a part disposal, ss 809FZJ–809FZP set out the circumstances in which a simplified average holding period calculation method can be used by certain types of funds characterised, broadly, by certain investment policies, ss 809FZQ and 809FZR contain provisions relating to determining the average holding period for direct lending funds and ss 809FZF–809FZI contain certain other specific provisions. In addition, s 809FZV contains a specific provision relating to "loan to own' investments.

For ease of understanding, it is simpler to consider these provision in this order rather than in the order that they appear in the legislation.

New ss 809FZD and 809FZE

Section 809FZD sets out the circumstances in which there is a disposal of an investment or part of an investment for the purposes of determining the average holding period of the investment scheme.

Section 809FZD(4) states that references to a disposal are to something which is a disposal for the purposes of TCGA 1992, subject to disregarding TCGA 1992 s 116, so that there is no disposal, and the reorganisation rules in TCGA 1992 ss 127–130 apply, in the event that debt which would be a qualifying corporate bond is converted into equity or vice versa (so facilitating debt for equity swaps).

Section 809FZD(1) states that an investment or part of an investment is disposed of where there is an actual disposal of the investment or where there is a disposal from an intermediate holding or intermediate holding structure by through which an investment is held or whether there is a deemed disposal under s 809FZD(2). Where such a deemed disposal of an investment were the scheme in substance closes its position on the investment or part of the investment or the scheme ceases to be exposed to risks and rewards in respect of the investment and its reasonable disposal of the arrangements are designed to secure that result.

Section 809FZD(3) states that if there is a part disposal of securities in a company which are of the same class, a first in first out approach is applied to what is disposed of.

Section 809FZE relates to part disposals and states that whether there is a part disposal of an investment, the part disposed of and the part not disposed of are treated as two separate investments made at the same time, the value of the two separate investments is the appropriate proportion of the value of the first whole investment and the appropriate proportion is the proportion of the value of the part in question to the value of the whole investment at the time of the disposal.

New ss 809FZJ–809FZP

These provisions set out the conditions that need to be satisfied by certain types of investment scheme in order to allow them to determine the average holding period of the relevant investments on a simplified basis. This simplified basis allows all investments to be treated as made at the same time as the relevant reference investment and all disposals to be made at the same time as the relevant reference disposal.

These provisions are intended to apply to types of investments or investment policies that the Government have generally accepted to be in the nature of "long term investment" and so not intended to generate IBCI under the rules, as stated in HMRC's original consultation document on the proposals published in July 2015. It should be noted that the rules do not provide blanket exclusions from the possible generation of IBCI but, rather, apply a simplified average holding period calculation that is less likely to produce IBCI. There is still, however, a requirement for all investment schemes to maintain the relevant records in respect of their investment and disposal activity to be able to operate the required calculations to determine the average holding period of the relevant investments at the time that any carried interest payment arises.

The rules are relatively detailed and complex and will need to be read carefully by any investment scheme wishing to apply the simplified average holding period methodology. A general summary of how the rules operate is discussed below, but this does not cover all of the details of the provisions.

New s 809FZJ – Significant interests

Section 809FZA applies to any investment scheme and permits simplified average holding period methodology in respect of controlling interests held by the investment scheme.

Section 809FZJ(1) states that where an investment scheme has a controlling interest in a trading company or the holding company of a trading group, any investment made for the purposes of the scheme in that company after the time when the controlling interest was acquired is to be regarded as having being made at that time and any disposal for the purposes of the scheme of an investment in the company after the time the controlling interest was acquired is to be regarded as not being made until a relevant disposal is made.

Section 809FZJ(2) states that a relevant disposal in relation to a company is a disposal which has the effect that the investment scheme ceases to have a 40% interest in the company.

Controlling interests is defined in s 809FZZ(3) as an interest comprising share capital amounting to more than 50% of the ordinary share of the company in question and carrying an entitlement to more than 50% of the voting rights in the company, the profits available for distribution to shareholders and the assets of the company available for distribution to shareholders in a winding up.

As is also the case in certain other of the specific fund provisions, s 809FZJ(3) states that any share capital of the company in question which is held for the purposes of an associated investment scheme is treated as held for the purpose of the investment scheme in question in determining whether an investment scheme has a controlling interest or a 40% interest in the company. Associated investment scheme is defined under s 809FZZ(1), is an investment scheme in respect of which the same or substantially the same individuals provide investment management services, which has the same or substantially the same investments and which acts together with the investment scheme in question in relation to all or substantially all of the investments that they acquire. This is, therefore, intended to cover parallel funds in a single investment scheme rather than, for instance, two independent investment schemes acting as co-investors in a particular company.

New ss 809FZK–809FZM

Sections 809FZK to 809FZM contain three provisions applying to what are described as venture capital funds, significant equity stake funds and controlling equity stake funds. These are intended to be, broadly, what might commonly be described as venture capital funds, growth funds and buyout funds.

The provisions work in a broadly consistent manner and on the basis that moving through the three types of funds there is a less restrictive requirement as to how much of a company the fund in question holds but more prescriptive additional conditions that have to be satisfied to meet the definition of the relevant type of fund. For each type of fund the relevant investment must be in a trading company or the holding company of a trading group.

The provisions operate by defining the conditions that need to be satisfied to qualify as each specified type of fund. They then set out what the conditions required for an investment to qualify so that further investments in the company are treated as made at the same time as the first qualifying investment and the point at which a disposal is significant enough that further disposals have to be treated on a standalone basis rather than all being made at the time that the qualifying disposal is made.

New s 809FZK Venture capital funds

Section 809FZK(1) states that where a venture capital fund has a relevant interest in a trading company or the holding company of a trading group, any venture capital investment made for the purposes of the scheme in the company after the time that the relevant interest was acquired and before a relevant disposal is treated as having being made at the time that the relevant interest was acquired and any disposal for the purposes of the scheme of a venture capital investment in the company after that time is to be regarded as not made until the relevant disposal is made or the scheme director conditions ceases to be met.

One must, therefore, determine whether the investment scheme is a venture capital fund, whether any investment that it holds is a venture capital investment and when the relevant interest is acquired and/or the relevant disposal is triggered.

Section 809FZK(4) and (5) set out what qualifies as a venture capital fund. The requirements are that when the investment scheme in question starts to invest it is reasonable to suppose that over the investing life of the scheme:

– at least two-thirds of the total value invested for the purpose of the scheme will be invested in venture capital investments; and
– at least two-thirds of the total value invested for the purpose of the scheme will be invested in investments which are held for 40 months or more.

In applying the 40-month test, the methodology for determining when investments are made and when disposals are made in s 809FZK(1) is to be applied.

Venture capital investment is defined in s 809FZK(7) as an investment in a trading company or the holding company of a trading group where:

– at the time the investment is made the company is unlisted and is likely to remain so;
– at least 75% of the total value of the investment is invested in newly issued shares or newly issued securities convertible into shares;
– the investment is used in a trade carried on by the trading company or the trading group to support its growth or to develop new products or services and is not used directly or indirectly to acquire shares in the company which are not newly issued;
– if the investment is the first investment made in the company by the investment scheme, the trading company or group has not carried on the trade for more than seven years; and
– the scheme director condition is met.

The scheme director condition is significant in the eyes of the Government in differentiating bona fide venture capital funds (and growth funds) from other sorts of funds. It is set out in s 809FZK(8) and requires that the investment scheme or the one or more investment schemes acting together is entitled to appoint a director of the company or a company which controls the company and the scheme director is entitled to exercise the rights set out in s 809FZK(9). Those rights are rights conferred under contractual arrangements to which some or all of the investors in the company are parties and which it would be reasonable to suppose would not otherwise be capable of being exercised by the scheme director, which will relate to the conduct of the business affairs in the company and which are at least equivalent to the rights which is reasonable to suppose a prudent investor would obtain on making invest-ment in the company at arm's length at the same size and nature that is held in the company for the purposes of the investment scheme.

Section 809FZK(2) then sets out that the venture capital fund has a relevant investment in a company if the fund has at least a 5% interest in the company by virtue of its venture capital investments in the company or the venture capital investments held by the scheme when the company have a value of more than £1 million.

Section 809FZK(3) states that a relevant disposal means that a disposal which has the effect that the venture capital fund has disposed of more than 80% of the greatest amount invested at any one time in the company by the investment scheme.

As is the case with the controlling interest referred to above, the 5% or £1 million relevant interest requirement is determined by aggregating investments in the company held by the investment scheme in question and associated investment schemes.

New s 809FZL – Significant equity stake funds

The second type of specified fund is the significant equity stake fund, which broadly equates to what is commonly referred to as a "growth fund". As with the venture capital fund rules in s 809FZK, s 809FZL defines what is a significant equity stake fund, a significant stake investment in a trading company or the holding company of a trading group and a relevant disposal.

Section 809FZL(3) defines a significant equity stake fund as an investments scheme:

– which is not a venture capital fund; and
– in relation to which it is reasonable to suppose when the scheme starts to invest that over the vesting life of the scheme:

  – more than 50% of the total value invested for the purposes of the scheme will be invested in significant equity stake investments; and
  – more than 50% of that value will be invested in investments which are held for 40 months or more.

Section 809FZL(6) defines a significant equity stake investment as an investment in a trading company or the holding company of a trading group where:

– at the time the investment is made, the company is unlisted and is likely to remain so;
– by virtue of the investment (on its own or with other investments) the scheme has a 20% interest in the company; and
– the scheme director conditions is met.

The scheme director condition is the same as that defined in s 809FZK(8) and discussed above.

As for venture capital funds, investments held by associated investment schemes are regarded as held by the investment scheme in question.

A relevant disposal is defined in s 809FZL(2) as being a disposal which has the effect the significant equity stake fund ceases to have a 15% interest in the company.

Section 809FZL(1) states that where a significant increase in stake fund has a significant equity stake investment in the trading company or the holding company of a trading group:

– any investment made for the purposes of the fund in that company made after the time the significant equity stake investment was required is regarded as having been made at that time; and
– any disposal for the purposes of the fund of an investment in the company after that time is regarded as not being made until either a relevant disposal is made or the scheme director conditions ceases to be met in respect of the company.

New s 809FZM – Controlling equity stake funds

Section 809FZN sets out the corresponding simplified average holding period calculation rules for controlling equity stake funds, which are broadly, what might be commonly termed as buyout funds. Under s 809FZM(1) the simplified calculation applies where a controlling equity stake fund has a 25% interest in the trading company or the holding company of a trading group such that any:

– investment made for the purposes of the controlling equity stake fund in the company after the time the 25% interest is required is to be regarded as having been made at that time; and

- disposal of an investment after that time is treated as not made until a relevant disposal is made.

Under s 809FZM(2), a relevant disposal is a disposal which has the effect that the controlling equity stake fund ceases to have a 25% interest in the company.

Under s 809FZM(3), a controlling equity stake fund is an investment scheme:

- which is not a venture capital fund or significant equity stake fund; and
- in relation to which it is reasonable to suppose when the scheme starts to invest that over the investor life of the scheme more than 50% of the total value invested for the purposes of the scheme will be invested in investments which (i) are controlling (i.e. greater than 50%) interest in trading companies or holding companies of trading groups and (ii) are held for 40 months or more.

The same associated investment scheme rule applies as in the previous fund types.

New s 809FZN – Real estate funds

Moving on from archetypal long term equity investment funds, the next three provisions apply the simplified average holding period calculation provisions to real estate funds, funds of funds and secondary funds.

Under s 809FZN(1), where a real estate fund has a major interest in land:

- any investment made for the purposes of the fund in the land after the major interest was acquired is to be regarded as having been made at that time; and
- any disposal for the purposes of the fund of an investment in the land after that time is to be regarded as not being made until a relevant disposal is made.

Under s 809FZZ(1), major interest in land has the meaning in VATA 1994 s 96, being a fee simple or tenancy for a term exceeding 21 years or in Scotland the interest of the owner or the lessee's interest under the lease for a period of not less than 20 years.

Under s 809FZN(2), a relevant disposal is a disposal which has the effect that the real estate fund has disposed of more than 50% of the greatest value invested at any one time in the land for the purposes of the real estate fund.

Under s 809FZN(4), a real estate fund is an investment scheme which is not a venture capital fund, significant equity stake fund or controlling equity stake fund and in relation to which it is reasonable to suppose when the scheme starts to invest that over the investing life of the scheme more than 50% of the total value invested for the purposes of the scheme will be invested in land and invested in investments which are held for 40 months or more.

Under s 809FZN(3), where a real estate fund has a major interest in land and subsequently acquires a major interest in any adjacent land, the acquisition is treated as if it were an investment in the original land for the purposes of determining when it was acquired and after the acquisition the adjacent land is to be regarded as part of the original land for the purposes of determining when a relevant disposal is made.

There is no associated investment scheme provision in s 809FZN.

New s 809FZO – Funds of funds

Funds of funds are treated differently to other types of fund because of the practical difficulty they face in obtaining information about the underlying investments of the funds in which they invest. Accordingly, under s 809FZO(1) the provision in s 809FZC(5) which specifies that intermediate holdings and holding structures should be disregarded when determining what an investment schemes investments are does not apply to an investment made for the purposes of a fund of funds in a collective investment scheme, so that the investment in the collective investment scheme is treated as the fund of funds' investment.

Section 809FZO(2) disapplies s 809FZO(1) in relation to a fund of funds' investment in a collective investment scheme if it is reasonable to suppose that the main purpose or one of the main purposes of the making of any investment in any collective investment scheme for the purposes of the fund of funds is to reduce the proportion of carried interest arising to any person which is income based carried interest. This provision is intended to stop investment schemes using investments in collective investment schemes to artificially extend their average holding period by retaining the investment in the collective investment scheme which itself carries out investment activities in its assets.

Section 809FZO(3) then states that where fund of funds has a significant investment in a collective investment scheme:

- any qualifying investment made for the purposes of the fund in the underlying scheme after the time the significant investment was acquired is to be regarded as having been made at that time; and
- any disposal of a qualifying investment in the collective investment scheme after that time is to be regarded as not being made until a relevant disposal was made. (Actually subpara (b) refers to an investment in a company, but this is clearly a typographical error that one can only expect will be corrected before the legislation is enacted.)

Section 809FZO(5) states that a fund of funds is an investment scheme in relation to which it is reasonable to suppose when the scheme starts to invest that over the investing life of the scheme substantially all of the total value invested for the purposes of the scheme will be invested in collective investment schemes of which the scheme holds less than 50% by value, more than 50% of the total value invested for the purposes of the scheme will be invested in investments which are held for 40 months or more and more than 75% of the total value invested in the scheme will be invested by external investors.

The words "substantially all" are not defined under the legislation, but, in respect of the substantial shareholdings exemption, HMRC treat 80% as substantially all (albeit with the test in the negative in that case).

Under s 809FZO(8), a significant investment in relation to a collective investment scheme is an investment of at least £1 million in the scheme or an investment of at least 5% of the total amounts raised or to be raised from external investors in the scheme.

Under s 809FZO(9), a qualifying investment is an investment made in a collective investment scheme where the investment is held on the same terms as other investments made by external investors in the scheme, the fund of funds (together with any connected funds) does not hold more than 30% by value of the underlying scheme, the underlying scheme has not made an investment in the fund of funds, no person providing investment management services to the underlying scheme provides such services to the fund of funds and it is reasonable to suppose that the investment in the underlying scheme is not part of arrangements a main purpose of which is to reward any person involved in providing investment management services to the underlying scheme or the scheme connected with that underlying scheme.

Connected fund is defined in s 809FZZ(6) as one fund directly or indirectly having control of the other or the same person, directly or indirectly, having control of both of them.

These conditions are again intended to prevent investment schemes taking advantage of the disapplication of the disregard of investment structures provision by investing in collective investment schemes rather than directly in the underlying investments.

New s 809FZP Secondary funds

This provision operates in a similar manner to the fund of funds provision discussed above.

Section 809FZP(1) and (2) state, as with the fund of funds rules, that the disregard of intermediate holdings and intermediate holding structures provision is disapplied except in the case of arrangements with a main purpose of reducing the proportion of carried interest arising to any person which is IBCI.

Section 809FZP(3) states that where a secondary fund has a significant investment in a collective investment scheme:

- any qualifying investment acquired for the purpose of the fund in the underlying scheme after the time when the significant investment is acquired is to be regarded as having been made at that time; and
- any disposal for the purposes of the fund of the qualifying investment in the underlying scheme after that time is to be regarded as not being made until the relevant disposal is made.

Section 809FZP(5) defines the secondary fund as an investment scheme in respect of which it is reasonable to suppose when it starts to invest that over the investing life of the scheme substantially all of the total value invested for the purposes of the scheme will be in the acquisition of investments in, or the acquisition of portfolios of investments from, unconnected collective investment schemes, more than 50% of the total value invested for the purposes of the scheme will be invested in investments which are held for 40 months or more and more than 75% of the total amount invested in the scheme will be invested by external investors.

Under s 809FZP(8) a significant interest is an investment of at least £1 million or of at least 5% of the total amounts raised or to be raised from external investors in the collective investment scheme in question.

Section 809FZP(9) defines a qualifying investment as an investment in a collective investment scheme made by the secondary fund where the investment acquired was originally made on the same terms as investments in the underlying scheme made by external investors, the terms on which the investment was acquired or investments made in the underlying scheme were made by external investors have not significantly changed since the investment was acquired, the secondary fund (together with any connected funds) does not hold more than 30% by value of the underlying scheme, no person providing investment management services to the underlying scheme provides such services to the secondary fund and it is reasonable to suppose that the investment in the underlying scheme is not part of arrangements a main purpose of which is to reward any person involved in providing investment management services to the underlying scheme or a scheme connected with the underlying scheme.

Under s 809FZP(4), the relevant disposal is a disposal which has the effect that the secondary fund has disposed of at least 50% of the greatest value invested in the underlying scheme or the secondary fund's investment in the underlying scheme is worth less than the greater of £1 million or 5% of the total value of the investments In the underlying scheme held immediately before the disposal.

While the original terms of s 809FZP(5) have been extended to permit investment in assets other than interests in collective investment schemes, the simplified acquisition and disposal time calculation in s 809FZP(3) does apply only to investments in collective investment schemes.

New ss 809FZQ and 809FZR – Direct lending funds

Sections 809FZQ and 809FZR apply to what are defined as direct lending funds.

Section 809FZQ broadly defines what is a direct lending fund and states that as a starting point any carried interest arising from a direct lending fund is treated as IBCI in its entirety.

New s 809FZR then provides an exception to this basic total IBCI treatment for direct lending funds meeting the specified conditions.

So, new s 809FZQ(1) states that carried interest arising from a direct lending fund is income based carried interest in its entirety.

Section 809FZQ(2) defines a direct lending fund is being an investment scheme which is not a venture capital fund, significant equity stake fund, controlling equity stake fund or real estate fund and in relation to which it is reasonable to suppose that when the funds ceases to invest the majority of its investments calculated by reference to value invested will have been direct loans made by the scheme. An investment scheme makes a direct loan if it advances money at interest or for any other return determined by reference to the time value of money.

Under s 809FZQ(4), the acquisition of a direct loan is regarded as the making of loan if the loan is acquired within 120 days from the day on which the money was first advanced.

Section 809FZR sets out the circumstances in which all carried interest is not automatically treated as IBCI. This does not itself prevent any of the carried interest arising from the direct lending fund from being IBCI. Rather, it simply means that the general average holding period test needs to be applied to the fund's investments and the average holding period in respect of a particular amount of carried interest needs to be determined.

Section 809FZR(1) states that the presumption of IBCI does not apply to carried interest arising from a direct lending fund if the fund is a limited partnership, the carried interest is an amount falling within ITA 2007 s 809EZD(2) or (3), being carried interest that is payable only after the external investors in the direct lending fund have received back all of their investment and a 'preferred return" on that money, with the 6% per annum preferred return applicable to s 809EZD being replaced by a 4% preferred return (s 809FZR(5)) and it is reasonable to suppose that when investments ceased to be made for the purposes of the direct lending fund at least 75% of the direct loans made by the fund calculated by reference to the value advance would be qualifying loans

Section 809FZR(2) defines the qualifying loan as a direct loan made by the investment scheme where the borrower is not connected with the investment scheme, the money is advanced under a genuine commercial agreement negotiated to arm's length, repayments are fixed and determinable, maturity is fixed, the scheme has the positive intention and the ability to hold the loan to maturity under the relevant term of the loans of at least four years.

Section 809FZR(3) defines the relevant term of a loan as being a period which begins with the time when the money is advanced and ends with the time by which, under the terms of the loan, at last 75% of the principal due under the loan must be repaid.

Section 809FZR(4) then states that in determining the average holding period for the direct lending fund, a loan is treated as held for 40 months if qualifying loan which is made by the fund is repaid to any extent before the end of 40 months from the time the loan is made and it is reasonable to suppose that the borrower's decision to repay was not affected by considerations relating to the application of the IBCI rules. This provision, therefore, makes it more likely that the direct lending fund fall within the scope of s 809FZR will satisfy the 40 months average holding period when any amount of carried interest arises.

It should be noted that if the investment scheme in question is not a direct lending fund and neither the IBCI in its entirety nor the simplified holding period provision applies, the basic principles with no simplification will have to be applied to determine how much, if any, of any carried interest is IBCI.

New s 809FZF – Unwanted short-term investments

New s 809FZF deals with what are commonly referred to as bridging investments made by investment schemes, where they might initially acquire more of an investment than they want to hold with the intention of selling part of it to other third parties reasonably quickly.

New s 809FZF sets out the conditions required to be satisfied for the making and disposal of the relevant unwanted short-term investment to be disregarded. Under s 809FZF(1) the investment is to be disregarded if it is an unwanted short-term investment and it is excludable.

Under s 809FZF(2) an investment is an unwanted short-term investment if it is made as part of a transaction under which one or more other investments are made for the purposes of the investment scheme, the value of the investment does not exceed that of the other investments taken together, it is reasonable to suppose that the investment had to be made in order for the other investment to be made, at the time the investment is made managers of the scheme have a firm, and evidence intention to dispose of the investment within the relevant period, the investment is disposed of within the relevant period and any profits resulting from its disposal has no bearing on whether a sum of carried arises or an amount of any sum of carried interest which does arise.

In respect of the last point, this might require investment schemes to amend their scheme documentation to specifically exclude any profit that might arise on an unwanted short term investment from the calculation of any carried interest.

Under s 809FZF(3) an unwanted short-term investment is excludable if it constitutes:

-   an investment in land;
-   an investment in securities and unlisted company;
-   the making of a direct loan where the other investments acquired at the same time are shares or other securities in an unlisted company; and
-   the making of a direct loan which is a qualifying loan within the meaning given by ITA 2007 s 809FZR(2).

Under s 809FZF(4), the relevant period is 12 months, 6 months or 120 days depending on the type of unwanted short-term investment in question.

Section 809FZF(5) then puts a limit on the disregard treatment for unwanted short term investments and states that if at any time it becomes reasonable to suppose that when the scheme ceases to invest 25% or more of the capital of the investment scheme will have been invested in unwanted short term investments which are excludable then the disregard of acquisition and disposal does not apply to any investment made after that time.

New ss 809FZG to 809FZI – Derivatives

The basic rule under s 809FZG(1) is that a derivative contract entered into for the purposes of an investment scheme is an investment but under s 809FZG(3) where entering into a derivative contract constitutes a deemed disposal of an investment or part of an investment, the derivative contract is not an investment and a subsequent disposal of the derivative contract without a corresponding disposal of the investment or part investment is regarded as making a new investment to the extent that the scheme becomes materially exposed to risks and rewards in respect of the investment or part investment.

This provision, broadly, treats derivatives as investments or disposals by reference to the risks and rewards taken on or given up by the investment scheme.

Sections 809FZH and 809FZI then deal with derivative contracts that are used to hedge exchange gains and losses and interest rates. The two provisions operate in the same way so that, broadly, where the relevant derivative contract is a hedging relationship in respect of a relevant investment and relates to exchange gains and losses or interest rates as applicable, entering into the hedging relationship is not a deemed disposal of the relevant investment and the relevant derivative contract is not an investment for the purposes of the investment scheme to the extent that the derivative contract and the investment designated by the scheme is a hedge or the derivative contract is intended to act as a hedge of exposure to changes in the value of the investment or to variability in cashflows.

Where the hedging relationship is terminated the investment scheme is treated as making an investment constituting the derivative contract if and to the extent that the derivative contract continues to be held by the investment scheme.

New ss 809FZS and 809FZT – Conditionally exempt carried interest

New ss 809FZS and 809FZQ set out the important provisions related to calculating the average holding period in respect of carried interest which qualifies as conditionally exempt carried interest. As stated above, these provisions are required to mitigate the distorted effect that would otherwise occur in respect of carried interest that was paid relatively early in the life of a fund as a result of the requirement to treat the fund as disposing of all of its existing investments at the time that any carried interest arises.

New s 809FZS(1) states that for carried interest to be conditionally exempt carried interest the following conditions must be satisfied:

– the carried interest arises to the individual in the period of four years beginning with the day on which the scheme starts to invest or 10 years beginning with that day if the carried interest is calculated on the realisation model;
– the carried interest would, apart from s 809FZS, be IBCI to some extent;
– it is reasonable to suppose that were the carried interest to arise to the individual at the relevant time it would not be IBCI to any extent; and
– the individual makes a claim for the carried interest to be treated as conditionally exempt carried interest.

The realisation model of carried interest referred to in the first condition above requires the terms of the carried interest to be such that no carried interest is payable unless and until the external investors in the investment scheme have received at least the amount invested by them in the scheme. The relevant time is whichever is the earliest of:

– the time when it is reasonable to suppose that the investment scheme would be wound up;
– the end of the period of four years beginning with the time when it is reasonable to suppose that the scheme will cease investing;
– the end of the period of either four years beginning with the day on which the sum of carried interest arises to the individual or 10 years beginning with that day it carried interest is calculated on the realisation model; or
– the end of the period of four years beginning with the period by reference to which the amount of carried interest was determined.

So, when an amount of carried interest qualifies as conditionally exempt and the relevant claim is made, it will initially be subject to tax at the time it arises under the new carried interest taxation rules in TCGA 1992 Pt 3 Ch 5.

New s 809FZT then specifies what happens when the relevant amount of conditional exempt carried interest ceases to be conditional exempt. Under s 809FZT(1) carried interest ceases to be conditionally exempt at the earliest of the time when the investment scheme is wound up, the end of the period of four years beginning with the time the scheme ceases to invest, the end of the period of four years (or 10 years if the carried interest is calculated on the realisation model) beginning with the day on which the sum of carried interest arises to the individual, the end of the period of four years beginning with the end of the period by reference to which the amount of the carried interest is determined or the time that which it is no longer reasonable to suppose that were the carried interest that arise to the individual at the relevant times specified in s 809FZS it would not IBCI to any extent.

Under s 809FZT(2), the requirement is then to calculate the average holding period applicable to the carried interest as if it had arisen at the time that it ceases to be conditionally exempt. If based on that calculation any amount of the carried interest is IBCI, it is treated as if it was IBCI that arose to the individual at the time that the carried interest actually arose, so that the relevant tax liability in respect of that amount of carried interest would be the additional tax payable on the basis that the carried interest is trading income (with credit for any capital gains tax already paid under s 809FZT(4)) plus interest in respect of that extra tax over the relevant period.

These rules should apply perfectly well to carried interest paid under the prescribed realisation model. Where they are less likely to operate to avoid carried interest being treated as IBCI in the context of funds which would have an average holding period of more than 40 months if the test were applied to the fund's investments over the life of the fund but not if the carried interest is paid relatively early in the life of the fund and the proportion of IBCI has to be calculated on the assumption that all of the assets of the fund a disposed of at the time that the carried arises. This might, for instance, be the case for infrastructure funds, which typically have a long life and hold their investments for a long time but, because it might be a commensurately long time before the external investors have received their investment back, the carried interest model can be based on an increase in net asset value model. Where that resulted in carried interest being payable earlier than four years from the date of the last investment made by the fund, the deemed disposal of all investments requirement might result in an artificially shortened average holding period in respect of that amount of carried interest.

Investment managers will, therefore, have to assess the conditionally exempt carried interest rules against the specific terms of their carried interest arrangements.

New s 809FZU – Employment related securities

Under s 809FZU, the IBCI rules do not apply to any carried interest that arises to an individual in respect of employment related securities for the purposes of ITEPA 2003 Pt 7. This is likely to be the case whenever the relevant manager is an employee rather than a member of the LLP. In conjunction with this general exception from the rules, s 809FZX states that the Treasury may by regulations (that is, through secondary legislation) repeal or restrict the application of this exclusion for employment related securities.

New s 809FZV – "Loan to own" investments

New s 809FZV provides a limited exception to the investment acquisition and disposal provisions where investment schemes acquire debt with a view to converting it into equity.

Under s 809FZV(2) where the loan to own provisions apply, the debt and the assets acquired are treated as a single investment and the value invested in that single investment is the amount paid for the debt.

Under s 809FZV(1), the provision applies where an investment scheme acquires a debt, the debt is to any extent uncollectible or otherwise impaired, the debt is acquired as a discount with a view to securing direct or indirect ownership of any assets which are either owned by the company which is the debtor or subject to a security interest in respect of the debt and the fund acquires ownership of the assets within 3 months of the acquisition of the debt.

While on its face useful for investment schemes with a loan to own policy, commentators have noted that the requirement that the debt is effectively enforced and the relevant assets acquired within 3 months of the acquisition of the debt might make a provision less useful in practice.

New s 809FZW – Anti-avoidance

New s 809FZW introduces the sort of general anti-avoidance provision which has been included in all of the new disguised investment management fee and carried interest tax rules, and states that no regard is to be had to any arrangement the main purpose of which is to reduce the proportion of carried interest which is IBCI. The relevant purposes are determining the average holding period or determining whether an investment scheme and venture capital fund, significant equity stake fund, controlling equity stake fund, real estate fund, fund of funds or secondary fund.

Under s 809FZW(3), determining to what extent carried interest is IBCI, no regard is to be had to any arrangements a main purpose of which is to secure that some or all of the carried interest does not fall within the scope of ITA 2007 s 809EZA(1) as carried interest which is IBCI.

New ss 809FZX–809FZZ

New ss 809FZX–809FZZ cover the power to change the rules by regulations and definitions applicable to the rules.

As well as allowing amendment to the exclusion for employment related securities, s 809FZX permits the Treasury to make provision relating to the calculation of the average holding period of investments by regulations.

New s 809FZZ contains definitions relevant to the operation of the rules and states that the new rules have a effect in relation to sums of carried interest arising on or after 6 April 2016 whenever the relevant arrangements arise were made.

38 Income-based carried interest: persons coming to the UK

(1) In section 809EZA of ITA 2007 (disguised investment management fees: charge to income tax), after subsection (2) insert—

"(2A) Subsection (2B) applies instead of subsections (1) and (2) where—

(a) one or more disguised fees arise to an individual in a tax year ("the relevant tax year") from one or more investment schemes (whether or not by virtue of the same arrangements),

(b) the disguised fees consist of carried interest which is income-based carried interest,

(c) the individual is UK resident in the relevant tax year,

(d) before the relevant tax year, the individual was not UK resident for a period of at least five consecutive tax years ("the period of non-residence"), and

(e) either—

(i) the relevant tax year is the first tax year immediately after the end of the period of non-residence, or

(ii) the relevant tax year is the second, third, or fourth tax year after the end of that period and the individual has been UK resident in all the intervening tax years.

(2B) To the extent that the income-based carried interest arises by virtue of pre-arrival services, the individual is liable for income tax for the relevant tax year in respect of it as if—

(a) in relation to pre-arrival services performed in the United Kingdom—

(i) the individual were carrying on a trade for the relevant year consisting of the performance of those services,

(ii) the income-based carried interest, so far as arising by virtue of those services, were profits of that trade, and

(iii) the individual were the person receiving or entitled to those profits, and

(b) in relation to pre-arrival services performed outside the United Kingdom—

(i) the individual were carrying on a trade for the relevant tax year consisting of the performance of those services,

(ii) the income-based carried interest, so far as arising by virtue of those services, were profits of that trade, and

(iii) the individual were the person receiving or entitled to those profits.

(2C) In subsection (2B) "pre-arrival services" means investment management services performed before the end of the period of non-residence."

(2) The amendment made by this section has effect in relation to sums of carried interest arising on or after 6 April 2016 (whenever the arrangements under which the sums arise were made).

GENERAL NOTE

Section 38 makes amendments to ITA 2007 s 809EZA in respect of the taxation of IBCI relevant for non UK domiciled investment managers who moved to the UK from overseas. This is to apportion the deemed trading income where carried interest is IBCI to periods where the recipient was not resident (or, rather, carrying out their activities) in the UK and periods when he or she was. Without this apportionment, the entirety of an amount of carried interest which was IBCI would be subject to income tax by virtue of being treated as trading income from a UK trade.

The rules introduce new sub-ss (2A), (2B) and (2C) to ITA 2007 s 809EZA.

The new sub-s (2A) applies where one or more disguised fees which are IBCI arise to an individual in a tax year, the individual is UK resident in the relevant tax year, before the relevant tax year the individual was not UK resident for a period of at least five consecutive tax years and either the relevant tax year is the first tax year immediately after the end of the period of non-residence or the relevant tax year is the second, third or fourth tax year after the end of that period and the individual has been UK resident in all of the intervening tax years.

The new sub-s (2B) then states that in relation to the pre-arrival services to which the IBCI relates if:

– the services were performed in the UK, the individual is treated as carrying on the trade in the UK; and
– if the pre-arrival services were performed outside the UK, the individual is treated as carrying on the trade outside the UK.

New sub-s (2C) states that pre-arrival services means investment management services provided before the end of the period of non-residence.

The provision, therefore, requires apportionment of the IBCI to periods before the individual became UK resident and periods after they became UK resident and, within the period before they became UK resident, to activities carried out in the UK and activities carried out outside the UK.

Where the individual is not domiciled in the UK in the tax year in which the IBCI arises, the individual would be able to apply the remittance basis to that proportion of the IBCI with can be allocated to the time before he or she became resident in the UK and to services performed outside the UK.

The amendments made by s 38 have effect in relation to the sums of carried interest arising on or after 6 April 2016 whenever the arrangements under which the sums arising were made.

Deduction at Source

39 Deduction of income tax at source
Schedule 6 contains provisions about deduction of income tax at source.

GENERAL NOTE
Section 39 and Sch 6 amend ITA 2007 Part 15 to remove the obligation for banks, building societies and other deposit-takers to deduct income tax from interest and other returns on certain savings and investments.

Budget 2015 announced that following the introduction of the new personal savings allowance in 2016/17, 95% of taxpayers would be able to "save completely tax free each year". As so many people would no longer be liable to tax on their savings, the deduction of tax by banks and building societies under the tax deduction scheme for interest (TDSI) scheme would no longer be necessary. The change would represent a "major tax simplification", the Government said.

40 Deduction of income tax at source: intellectual property
(1) Part 15 of ITA 2007 (deduction from other payments connected with intellectual property) is amended as specified in subsections (2) and (3).

(2) In section 906 (certain royalties etc where usual place of abode of owner is abroad), for subsections (1) to (3) substitute—

"(1) This section applies to any payment made in a tax year where condition A or condition B is met.

(2) Condition A is that—

(a) the payment is a royalty, or a payment of any other kind, for the use of, or the right to use, intellectual property (see section 907),
(b) the usual place of abode of the owner of the intellectual property is outside the United Kingdom, and
(c) the payment is charged to income tax or corporation tax.

(3) Condition B is that—

(a) the payment is a payment of sums payable periodically in respect of intellectual property,

(b) the person entitled to those sums ("the assignor") assigned the intellectual property to another person,

(c) the usual place of abode of the assignor is outside the United Kingdom, and

(d) the payment is charged to income tax or corporation tax."

(3) For section 907 substitute—

"907 Meaning of "intellectual property"

(1) In section 906 "intellectual property" means—

(a) copyright of literary, artistic or scientific work,

(b) any patent, trade mark, design, model, plan, or secret formula or process,

(c) any information concerning industrial, commercial or scientific experience, or

(d) public lending right in respect of a book.

(2) In this section "copyright of literary, artistic or scientific work" does not include copyright in—

(a) a cinematographic film or video recording, or

(b) the sound-track of a cinematographic film or video recording, except so far as it is separately exploited."

(4) The amendments made by subsections (2) and (3) have effect in respect of payments made on or after 28 June 2016.

(5) In determining whether section 906 of ITA 2007 applies to a payment, no regard is to be had to any arrangements the main purpose of which, or one of the main purposes of which, is to avoid the effect of the amendments made by this section.

(6) Where arrangements are disregarded under subsection (5) in relation to a payment which—

(a) is made before 28 June 2016, and

(b) is due on or after that day,

the payment is to be regarded for the purposes of section 906 of ITA 2007 as made on the date on which it is due.

(7) In determining the date on which a payment is due for the purposes of subsection (6), disregard the arrangements referred to in that subsection.

(8) In this section "arrangements" includes any agreement, understanding, scheme, transaction or series of transactions (whether or not legally enforceable and whether entered into before, or on or after, 28 June 2016).

GENERAL NOTE

Section 40 brings all payments of intellectual property royalties into the scope of withholding tax for payments made on or after 28 June 2016. The previous rules on royalty withholding tax (in Chs 6–8 of Pt 15 of ITA 2007) required, in respect of intellectual property, that income tax at the basic rate be withheld from payments for only specific types of intellectual property in specific circumstances.

The broadening does (arguably) simplify the rules for UK payers of royalties by removing some of the uncertainties as to what is, or is not, within the scope of withholding tax. The changes are not particularly surprising in context, although they had not been consulted on beforehand. It has been clear for a long time, highlighted by the OECD Base Erosion and Profit Shifting ("BEPS") project and EU investigations, that cross-border payments for intellectual property are continuing to increase. Other jurisdictions have also been looking at the range and scope of their withholding taxes on intellectual property royalty payments.

The new rules now cover all payments defined as royalties by the OECD model tax treaty in respect of:

– copyright of literary, artistic or scientific work;

– any patent, trade mark, design, model, plan, or secret formula or process;

– any information concerning industrial, commercial or scientific experience (i.e. know-how); and

– a public lending right in respect of a book.

The effect is that trademarks and know-how, in particular, are now within the scope of UK withholding tax. Film related copyright is still excluded from withholding tax, however.

Any existing licences under which royalties are paid which have not previous had to consider withholding tax should now be reviewed to establish who has the burden of the withholding tax, and double tax treaty claims will need to be considered – particularly where a licence requires payments to be grossed up to ensure that the recipient does not bear the burden.

41 Deduction of income tax at source: intellectual property – tax avoidance
(1) In Part 15 of ITA 2007 (deduction of income tax at source), after section 917 insert—

"Tax avoidance

917A Tax avoidance arrangements
  (1) This section applies if and to the extent that—
    (a) a person ("the payer") makes an intellectual property royalty payment,
    (b) the payment is received by a person ("the payee") who is connected with the payer, and
    (c) the payment is made under DTA tax avoidance arrangements.
  (2) Any duty under Chapter 6 or 7 to deduct a sum representing income tax at any rate applies without regard to any double taxation arrangements.
  (3) Any income tax deducted by virtue of subsection (2) may not be set off under section 967 or 968 of CTA 2010.
  (4) In this section—
    "arrangements" (except in the phrase "double taxation arrangements") includes any agreement, understanding, scheme, transaction or series of transactions, whether or not legally enforceable;
    "DTA tax avoidance arrangements" means arrangements where, having regard to all the circumstances, it is reasonable to conclude that—
      (a) the main purpose, or one of the main purposes, of the arrangements was to obtain a tax advantage by virtue of any provisions of a double taxation arrangement, and
      (b) obtaining that tax advantage is contrary to the object and purpose of those provisions;
    "intellectual property royalty payment" means a payment referred to in section 906(2)(a) or (3)(a);
    "receive" means receive—
      (a) directly or indirectly;
      (b) by one payment or by a series of payments;
    "tax advantage" is to be construed in accordance with section 208 of FA 2013.
  (5) For the purposes of this section the payer is connected with the payee if the participation condition is met as between them.
  (6) Section 148 of TIOPA 2010 (when the participation condition is met) applies for the purposes of subsection (5) as for the purposes of section 147(1)(b) of that Act, but as if references to the actual provision were to the provision made or imposed between the payer and the payee in respect of the arrangements under which the payment is made."

(2) The amendment made by this section has effect in respect of a payment made on or after 17 March 2016 under arrangements entered into at any time (including arrangements entered into before that date).

(3) In relation to payments made (under any such arrangements) on or after 17 March 2016 and on or before the day on which this Act is passed, section 917A of ITA 2007 as inserted by subsection (1) has effect as if the definition of "intellectual property royalty payment" in that section were as follows—
    ""intellectual property royalty payment" means—
      (a) a payment of a royalty or other sum in respect of the use of a patent,
      (b) a payment specified in section 906(1)(a) (as originally enacted), or
      (c) a payment which is a "qualifying annual payment" for the purposes of Chapter 6 by virtue of section 899(3)(a)(ii) (royalties etc from intellectual property);".

(4) In relation to payments made (under any such arrangements) on or after 28 June 2016 and on or before the day on which this Act is passed, section 917A of ITA 2007 as inserted by subsection (1) has effect as if "intellectual property royalty payment" also included (so far as it would not otherwise do so) any payments referred to in section 906(2)(a) or (3)(a) of ITA 2007 as substituted by section 40.

GENERAL NOTE

Section 41 (introduced as clause 40 of the Bill) amends ITA 2007 Pt 15 to introduce anti-avoidance rules intended to prevent abuse of double taxation arrangements to avoid the duty to deduct income tax from royalty payments made to connected persons.

New ITA 2007 s 917A applies where:
- a person ("the payer") makes an "intellectual property royalty payment";
- the payment is received by a person ("the payee") who is connected with the payer;
- and the payment is made under "DTA tax avoidance arrangements".

Subsections (4)–(6) define several terms including "intellectual property royalty payment". "DTA tax avoidance arrangements" are defined as arrangements where, having regard to all the circumstances, it is reasonable to conclude that the main purpose, or one of the main purposes, of the arrangements was to obtain a tax advantage by virtue of any provisions of a double taxation arrangement, and obtaining that tax advantage is contrary to the object and purpose of those provisions.

Where the arrangements are caught by new ITA 2007 s 917A, a duty under ITA 2007 Pt 15 Ch 6 or 7 to deduct a sum representing income tax at any rate applies without regard to any double taxation arrangements, and income tax deducted may not be set off under CTA 2010 ss 967 or 968 (set off of income tax deductions against corporation tax).

The Government introduced a new clause (agreed by the Public Bill Committee on 7 July 2016 and enacted as s 40, see above) amending ITA 2007 ss 906 and 907 (deduction of income tax from payments of royalties to those whose usual place of abode is abroad).

Government amendments to s 41, agreed by the Public Bill Committee on 30 June 2016, are intended to ensure that new ITA 2007 s 917A will apply to all payments of royalties or other sums from which income tax will have to be deducted at source following the amendments made by s 40.

Receipts from Intellectual Property

42 Receipts from intellectual property: territorial scope

(1) In section 577 of ITTOIA 2005 (territorial scope of Part 5 charges), at the end insert—

"(5) See also section 577A (territorial scope of Part 5 charges: receipts from intellectual property)."

(2) After that section insert

"577A Territorial scope of Part 5 charges: receipts from intellectual property

(1) References in section 577 to income which is from a source in the United Kingdom include income arising where—

(a) a royalty or other sum is paid in respect of intellectual property by a person who is non-UK resident, and

(b) the payment is made in connection with a trade carried on by that person through a permanent establishment in the United Kingdom.

(2) Subsection (3) applies where a royalty or other sum is paid in respect of intellectual property by a person who is non-UK resident in connection with a trade carried on by that person only in part through a permanent establishment in the United Kingdom.

(3) The payment referred to in subsection (2) is to be regarded for the purposes of subsection (1)(b) as made in connection with a trade carried on through a permanent establishment in the United Kingdom to such extent as is just and reasonable, having regard to all the circumstances.

(4) In determining for the purposes of section 577 whether income arising is from a source in the United Kingdom, no regard is to be had to arrangements the main purpose of which, or one of the main purposes of which, is to avoid the effect of the rule in subsection (1).

(5) In this section—

"arrangements" includes any agreement, understanding, scheme, transaction or series of transactions (whether or not legally enforceable);

"intellectual property" has the same meaning as in section 579;
"permanent establishment"—

(a) in relation to a company, is to be read (by virtue of section 1007A of ITA 2007) in accordance with Chapter 2 of Part 24 of CTA 2010, and

(b) in relation to any other person, is to be read in accordance with that Chapter but as if references in that Chapter to a company were references to that person."

(3) The amendments made by subsections (1) and (2) have effect in relation to royalties or other sums paid in respect of intellectual property on or after 28 June 2016.

(4) It does not matter for the purposes of subsection (4) of section 577A of ITTOIA 2005 (as inserted by this section) whether the arrangements referred to in that subsection are entered into before, or on or after, 28 June 2016.

(5) Where arrangements are disregarded under subsection (4) of section 577A of ITTOIA 2005 (as inserted by this section) in relation to a payment of a royalty or other sum which—

(a) is made before 28 June 2016, but

(b) is due on or after that day,

the payment is to be regarded for the purposes of subsection (1) of that section as made on the date on which it is due.

(6) In determining the date on which a payment is due for the purposes of subsection (5), disregard the arrangements referred to in that subsection.

(7) Where—

(a) an intellectual property royalty payment within the meaning of section 917A of ITA 2007 is made on or after 28 June 2016,

(b) the payment is made under arrangements (within the meaning of that section) entered into before that day,

(c) the arrangements are not DTA tax avoidance arrangements for the purposes of that section,

(d) it is reasonable to conclude that the main purpose, or one of the main purposes, of the arrangements was to obtain a tax advantage by virtue of any provisions of a foreign double taxation arrangement, and

(e) obtaining that tax advantage is contrary to the object and purpose of those provisions,

the arrangements are to be regarded as DTA tax avoidance arrangements for the purposes of section 917A of ITA 2007 in relation to the payment.

(8) In subsection (7)—

"foreign double taxation arrangement" means an arrangement made by two or more territories outside the United Kingdom with a view to affording relief from double taxation in relation to tax chargeable on income (with or without other tax relief);

"tax advantage" is to be construed in accordance with section 208 of FA 2013 but as if references in that section to "tax" were references to tax chargeable on income under the law of a territory outside the United Kingdom.

(9) Where—

(a) a royalty is paid on or after 28 June 2016,

(b) the right in respect of which the royalty is paid was created or assigned before that day,

(c) section 765(2) of ITTOIA 2005 does not apply in relation to the payment, and

(d) it is reasonable to conclude that the main purpose, or one of the main purposes, of any person connected with the creation or assignment of the right was to take advantage, by means of that creation or assignment, of the law of any territory giving effect to Council Directive 2003/49/EC of 3rd June 2003 on a common system of taxation applicable to interest and royalty payments made between associated companies of different member States,

section 758 of ITTOIA 2005 does not apply in relation to the payment.

GENERAL NOTE

Section 42 is an expansion of withholding tax for the purposes of intellectual property only, which covers the situation where intellectual property is used by a UK permanent establishment ("PE") of an overseas company, where the licence under which the royalties are paid is entered into between the overseas company and a third party overseas entity. The changes apply to payments made on or after 28 June 2016.

The type of scenario envisaged is that where company A makes a royalty payment to company B in respect of intellectual property. Neither A nor B is resident in the UK, but the intellectual property for which the royalty is paid is used by A's UK PE. Because the IP is used by A's UK PE, the payment made by A to B for the use of that IP is treated as having a UK source, and is therefore subject to UK withholding tax under the new provisions.

These changes mean that UK withholding tax is required to be accounted for in the UK (presumably by the UK PE, as that's the only entity with a UK presence and is, equally, likely to be the easiest entity to recover tax from in the case of non-compliance). Where a royalty payment is made in connection with a non-UK resident company's trade, but that trade is only partly carried on in the UK through a UK PE, only the part connected with the UK activities (to be determined on a just and reasonable basis) will be treated as having a UK source (and therefore as subject to UK withholding tax).

43 Receipts from intellectual property: diverted profits tax

(1) Part 3 of FA 2015 (diverted profits tax) is amended as follows.

(2) In section 79 (charge to tax), at the end insert—

"(6) But banking surcharge profits and notional banking surcharge profits, to the extent that they are determined by reference to notional PE profits (or what would have been notional PE profits) for an accounting period, do not include any amount which is (or would have been) included in notional PE profits for that period by virtue of section 88(5)(b)."

(3) In section 88 (which relates to the calculation of taxable diverted profits), for subsection (5) substitute—

"(5) Notional PE profits", in relation to an accounting period, means an amount equal to the sum of—

(a) the amount of profits (if any) which would have been the chargeable profits of the foreign company for that period, attributable (in accordance with sections 20 to 32 of CTA 2009) to the avoided PE, had the avoided PE been a permanent establishment in the United Kingdom through which the foreign company carried on the trade mentioned in section 86(1)(b), and

(b) an amount equal to the total of royalties or other sums which are paid by the foreign company during that period in connection with that trade in circumstances where the payment avoids the application of section 906 of ITA 2007 (duty to deduct tax).

(5A) For the purposes of subsection (5)(b) a payment of a royalty or other sum avoids the application of section 906 of ITA 2007 if—

(a) that section does not apply in relation to the payment, but

(b) that section would have applied in relation to the payment had the avoided PE been a permanent establishment in the United Kingdom through which the foreign company carried on the trade mentioned in section 86(1)(b)."

(4) In section 100 (credit for UK or foreign tax on same profits), for the heading substitute "Credits for tax on the same profits".

(5) In section 100, after subsection (2) insert—

"(2A) Subsection (2)(b) does not allow a credit against a liability to diverted profits tax if or to the extent that the liability arises by virtue of section 88(5)(b) (payments of royalties etc)."

(6) In section 100, after subsection (4) insert—

"(4A) Subsection (4B) applies where—

(a) a company's notional PE profits for an accounting period include an amount under section 88(5)(b) determined by reference to a royalty or other sum,

(b) the company's liability to diverted profits tax for the accounting period is determined by reference to taxable diverted profits calculated under section 91(4) or (5), and

(c) those taxable diverted profits include an amount of relevant taxable income referred to in section 91(4)(b) or (5)(b) determined by reference to the same royalty or other sum.

(4B) A credit equal to the company's liability to diverted profits tax for that accounting period which arises by virtue of section 88(5)(b) in respect of the royalty or other sum, to the extent that it is included in relevant taxable income for the purposes of section 91(4)(b) or (5)(b), is allowed against the company's total liability to diverted profits tax for that period.

(4C) Subsection (4D) applies where—

(a) by reason of the payment of a royalty or other sum a company's liability to diverted profits tax for an accounting period includes liability arising by virtue of section 88(5)(b),

(b) the royalty or other sum is paid to a person who is resident in a country or territory outside the United Kingdom, and

(c) under any relevant provision relief would have been due to that person had the avoided PE been a permanent establishment in the United Kingdom through which the company carried on the trade mentioned in section 86(1)(b).

(4D) Such credit as is just and reasonable having regard to the amount of the relief referred to in subsection (4C)(c) is allowed against the company's liability to diverted profits tax.

(4E) In subsection (4C)(c) "relevant provision" means—

(a) the provision of a double taxation arrangement (as defined by section 2(4) of TIOPA 2010), or

(b) section 758 of ITTOIA 2005 (exemption for certain interest and royalty payments)."

(7) The amendments made by this section have effect in relation to accounting periods ending on or after 28 June 2016.

(8) For the purposes of section 88(5)(b) of FA 2015 as substituted by this section, a royalty or other sum which would not otherwise be regarded as paid during an accounting period ending on or after 28 June 2016 is to be regarded as so paid if—

(a) for the purposes of section 906 of ITA 2007 it is regarded as paid on a date during that period by virtue of section 40(6), or

(b) for the purposes of section 577A(1) of ITTOIA 2005 it is regarded as paid on a date during that period by virtue of section 42(5).

GENERAL NOTE

Section 43 applies a similar principle to that in section 42, but in relation to notional payments by "avoided" permanent establishments ("PEs") under the diverted profits tax ("DPT") rules on or after 28 June 2016.

Since withholding tax does not apply to notional payments, the new rules do this by imposing a 25% DPT charge on an amount equal to the proportion of the royalties in respect of which the withholding tax charge would have applied had the non-resident carried on its trade in the UK through a UK PE.

Supplementary Welfare Payments: Northern Ireland

44 Tax treatment of supplementary welfare payments: Northern Ireland

(1) In this section "supplementary welfare payment" means a payment made under regulations under—

(a) Article 135(1)(a) of the Welfare Reform (Northern Ireland) Order 2015 (SI 2015/2006 (NI 1)) ("the Order") (discretionary support),

(b) Article 137 of the Order (payments to persons suffering financial disadvantage), or

(c) any provision (including future provision) of the Order which enables provision to be made for payments to persons who suffer financial disadvantage as a result of relevant housing benefit changes.

(2) In subsection (1)(c) "relevant housing benefit changes" means changes to social security benefits consisting of or including changes contained in the Housing Benefit (Amendment) Regulations (Northern Ireland) 2016 (SR (NI) 2016 No 258).

(3) The Treasury may by regulations amend any provision of Chapters 1 to 5 of Part 10 of ITEPA 2003 so as to—

(a) provide that no liability to income tax arises on supplementary welfare payments of a specified description;

(b) impose a charge to income tax under Part 10 of ITEPA 2003 on payments of a specified description made under regulations under Article 137 of the Order (payments to persons suffering financial disadvantage).

(4) The regulations may make—

(a) different provision for different cases;
(b) incidental or supplementary provision;
(c) consequential provision (which may include provision amending any provision made by or under the Income Tax Acts).

(5) Regulations made before 6 April 2017 may, so far as relating to the tax year 2016–17, have effect in relation to times before they are made.

(6) Regulations under this section are to be made by statutory instrument.

(7) A statutory instrument containing regulations under this section is subject to annulment in pursuance of a resolution of the House of Commons.

(8) In section 655(2) of ITEPA 2003 (other provisions about the taxation of social security payments) after the entry relating to section 782 of ITTOIA 2005 insert ";

> section 44 of FA 2016 (tax treatment of supplementary welfare payments: Northern Ireland)."

GENERAL NOTE

Section 44 introduces a regulation-making power for the Treasury to make supplementary payments, paid by the Northern Ireland Executive to benefits claimants affected by Welfare Reform, either exempt from income tax or chargeable on a different basis.

The power will apply to supplementary payments funded by the Northern Ireland Executive made on or after 6 April 2016, and allows regulations to be made which are retrospective to that date.

PART 2

CORPORATION TAX

Charge and Rates

45 Charge for financial year 2017

Corporation tax is charged for the financial year 2017.

GENERAL NOTE

This is a very straightforward section, which simply imposes the charge to corporation tax for the financial year 2017, i.e. the year commencing on 1 April 2017. The applicable rate (19%) was set in F(No 2)A 2015 s 7.

46 Rate of corporation tax for financial year 2020

In section 7(2) of F(No 2)A 2015 (main rate of corporation tax for the financial year 2020) for "18%" substitute "17%".

GENERAL NOTE

This gives effect to the then Chancellor's announcement of a further reduction in corporation tax rates. For the financial year 2020 the rate will be 17% rather than the 18% rate set in F(No 2)A 2015.

Research and Development

47 Abolition of vaccine research relief

(1) CTA 2009 is amended in accordance with subsections (2) to (9).

(2) Omit Chapter 7 of Part 13 (vaccine research relief).

(3) In section 1039 (overview of Part 13) omit—

  (a) subsection (6), and
  (b) in subsection (8) "or 7"

(4) In section 1042 (meaning of "relevant research and development") omit subsection (3).

(5) In section 1113 (cap on aid under Chapters 2 and 7)—

(a) in the heading omit "or 7", and
(b) in subsection (4) omit—
   (i) the "or" at the end of paragraph (a), and
   (ii) paragraph (b).

(6) In section 1118(2) (meaning of "qualifying expenditure") omit—
(a) the "or" at the end of paragraph (a), and
(b) paragraph (b).

(7) In section 1133(3) (sub-contractor payments) omit "and section 1102(2)."

(8) In section 1137(1)(b) (accounting periods) omit "or qualifying Chapter 7 expenditure".

(9) In Schedule 4 (index of defined expressions) omit the entries for—
(a) qualifying Chapter 7 expenditure (in Part 13), and
(b) qualifying R&D activity (in Chapter 7 of Part 13).

(10) CTA 2010 is amended in accordance with subsections (11) to (13).

(11) In section 357P (research and development expenditure: introduction and interpretation)—
(a) in subsection (1) omit—
   (i) the "and" at the end of paragraph (b), and
   (ii) paragraph (c), and
(b) omit subsection (2)(d) and (e).

(12) Omit section 357PF (additional deduction under section 1087 CTA 2009).

(13) In Schedule 4 (index of defined expressions) omit the entries for—
(a) Northern Ireland qualifying Chapter 7 expenditure (in Chapter 9 of Part 8B), and
(b) qualifying Chapter 7 expenditure (in Chapter 9 of Part 8B).

(14) In consequence of the amendments made by subsections (1) to (13)—
(a) in Schedule 3 to FA 2012 omit paragraphs 7, 12 to 14, 16(2), 17, 20 to 30, and 31(2), and
(b) in FA 2015 omit section 28(4)(o) and (p).

(15) The amendments made by this section have effect in relation to expenditure incurred on or after 1 April 2017.

GENERAL NOTE

Vaccine Research Relief (VRR) was introduced in FA 2002 with effect from 22 April 2003. Initially it was available to companies of all sizes but FA 2012 withdrew the relief from SMEs for expenditure incurred on or after 1 April 2012.

VRR is an EU State Aid and its approval is due to expire on 31 March 2017. HMRC statistics indicate that fewer than 10 companies claim the relief and the Government has decided that it is not worth seeking to renew the State Aid approval for the relief.

The VRR legislation in CTA 2009 Pt 13 Ch 7 will, therefore, be repealed for expenditure incurred on or after 1 April 2017. VRR can continue to be claimed for expenditure incurred before 1 April 2017 even where the claim is submitted after 31 March 2017.

48 Cap on R&D aid

(1) CTA 2009 is amended as follows.

(2) In section 1114 (calculation of total R&D aid)—
(a) in the formula for "(N x CT)" substitute "N", and
(b) in the definition of "N" for "relief" substitute "R&D expenditure credit".

(3) In section 1118(1) (meaning of "notional relief")—
(a) for "relief" in the first two places it occurs substitute "R&D expenditure credit",
(b) for "Chapter 5 (relief for large companies)" substitute "Chapter 6A of Part 3 (trade profits: R&D expenditure credits)", and
(c) in the heading for "relief" substitute "R&D expenditure credit".

(4) The amendments made by this section have effect in relation to expenditure incurred on or after 1 April 2016.

GENERAL NOTE

FA 2008 introduced legislation, to comply with EU State Aid rules, providing that an SME cannot obtain more than €7.5m in total "Aid" in respect of any one project. The UK legislation has always applied this cap in a rather generous way, essentially defining "Aid" for this purpose as the relief obtained in excess of the notional amount the company could have obtained under the Large Company regime.

Thus, "Aid" is the total benefit that the company receives from SME R&D relief (either as an actual tax reduction due to additional deductions or as payable tax credits) less the value of the notional relief that it could have received had it been a large company entitled to large company relief. The aid is calculated over the life of the project and is defined at CTA 2009 s 1114 as:

$$TC + R + (P \times CT) - (N \times CT)$$

Where:

TC is the total amount of SME R&D tax credit paid in respect of enhanced expenditure attributable to the project;

R is the total reduction in tax liability from setting enhanced expenditure under the SME R&D scheme against tax (whether the liability is that of the company itself or, by way of group relief, of any other company);

P is the potential relief – i.e. any enhanced expenditure under the SME R&D scheme that has been claimed but (at the time the calculation is made) not brought into account;

N is the notional relief. This is the enhanced expenditure that the company would have been able to claim had it been a large company throughout the period in question. Notional relief is calculated by applying the enhancement rate for the large company scheme to the expenditure upon which the company is claiming relief under the SME scheme; and

CT is the main rate of CT when the aid is calculated.

Provided the expenditure is not otherwise excluded, any excess over the project aid cap can be claimed under the Large Company scheme.

For expenditure incurred on or after 1 April 2016, the R&D Expenditure Credit ("RDEC") will be the only form of large company R&D relief available. Accordingly, the aid cap formula above will be amended (from the same date) as follows.

The term "N x CT" is to be replaced by "N". The definition of "N" is amended to be the "notional R&D expenditure credit", which is the amount of RDEC that the claimant could have claimed under CTA 2009 Pt 3 Ch 6A in any accounting period in respect of qualifying R&D expenditure on that project, if the claimant had been a large company throughout that period.

Loan Relationships

49 Loan relationships and derivative contracts

Schedule 7 contains amendments relating to loan relationships and derivative contracts.

50 Loans to participators etc: rate of tax

(1) In section 455 of CTA 2010 (charge to tax in case of loan to participator), in subsection (2), for "25% of the amount of the loan or advance" substitute "such percentage of the amount of the loan or advance as corresponds to the dividend upper rate specified in section 8(2) of ITA 2007 for the tax year in which the loan or advance is made".

(2) The amendment made by subsection (1) has effect in relation to a loan or advance made on or after 6 April 2016.

(3) In section 464A of CTA 2010 (charge to tax: arrangements conferring benefit on participator), in subsection (3), for "25% of the value of the benefit conferred" substitute "such percentage of the value of the benefit conferred as corresponds to the dividend upper rate specified in section 8(2) of ITA 2007 for the tax year in which the benefit is conferred".

(4) The amendment made by subsection (3) has effect in relation to a benefit conferred on or after 6 April 2016.

GENERAL NOTE

Where a close company makes a loan or an advance to a participator, or certain other persons, under CTA 2010 s 455 the close company is required to pay an amount of tax in respect of such loan or advance to HMRC, which is refundable to the extent that the loan or advance is repaid to the company, or is released or written off. Section 50 changes the rate of tax which is payable when such a loan or advance is made from 25% to the rate corresponding to the dividend upper rate for the tax year in which the loan or advance is made. Such amendment takes effect for loans or advances made on or after 6 April 2016. This change is being made in response to the change in the tax treatment of dividends.

Section 50 also makes an amendment to the rate of tax payable under CTA 2010 s 464A, which applies where a close company is at any time a party to tax avoidance arrangements as a result of which benefit is conferred directly or indirectly on an individual who is a participator in the company or is an associate of such a participator. It provides that for a benefit conferred on or after 6 April 2016 tax will be charged at a rate corresponding to the dividend upper rate for the tax year in which the benefit is conferred in place of the current 25%. This amendment is being made in response to the change in the tax treatment of dividends.

51 Loans to participators etc: trustees of charitable trusts

(1) In section 456 of CTA 2010 (exceptions to the charge to tax in case of loan to participator), after subsection (2) insert—

> "(2A) Section 455 does not apply to a loan or advance made to a trustee of a charitable trust if the loan or advance is applied to the purposes of the charitable trust only."

(2) The amendment made by subsection (1) has effect in relation to a loan or advance made on or after 25 November 2015.

GENERAL NOTE

This section introduces a further exception to a charge under CTA 2010 s 455 (loans or advances to participators etc). This exception applies where a loan or advance is made to the trustee of a charitable trust and the loan or advance is applied for the purposes of the charitable trust only. It has effect for those advances made on or after 25 November 2015 and, inter alia, it will permit a trading company owned by a charity to make loans to the charity without a charge arising under CTA 2010 s 455.

Intangible Fixed Assets

52 Intangible fixed assets: pre-FA 2002 assets

(1) Chapter 16 of Part 8 of CTA 2009 (pre-FA 2002 assets) is amended as follows.

(2) In section 882 (application of Part 8 to assets created or acquired on or after 1 April 2002), after subsection (5) insert—

> "(5A) References in this section to one person being (or not being) a related party in relation to another person are to be read as including references to the participation condition being met (or, as the case may be, not met) as between those persons.
>
> (5B) References in subsection (5A) to a person include a firm in a case where, for section 1259 purposes, references in this section to a company are read as references to the firm.
>
> (5C) In subsection (5B) "section 1259 purposes" means the purposes of determining under section 1259 the amount of profits or losses to be allocated to a partner in a firm.
>
> (5D) Section 148 of TIOPA 2010 (when the participation condition is met) applies for the purposes of subsection (5A) as it applies for the purposes of section 147(1)(b) of TIOPA 2010."

(3) In section 894 (preserved status condition etc), after subsection (6) insert—

> "(6A) Section 882(5A) to (5D) applies for the purposes of section 893 and this section."

(4) In section 895 (assets acquired in connection with disposals of pre-FA 2002 assets), at the end insert—

> "(5) Section 882(5A) to (5D) applies for the purposes of this section."

(5) The amendments made by this section have effect in relation to accounting periods beginning on or after 25 November 2015.

(6) For the purposes of subsection (5), an accounting period beginning before and ending on or after 25 November 2015 is to be treated as if so much of the accounting period as falls before that date, and so much of the accounting period as falls on or after that date, were separate accounting periods.

(7) An apportionment for the purposes of subsection (6) must be made—

    (a) in accordance with section 1172 of CTA 2010 (time basis), or

    (b) if that method produces a result that is unjust or unreasonable, on a just and reasonable basis.

GENERAL NOTE

Section 52 is intended to clarify the entry conditions for an intangible fixed asset to be subject to the rules in Pt 8 CTA 2009, the corporate regime for intangible fixed assets. The rules are only intended to apply to assets created or acquired on or after 1 April 2002 and are also intended not to apply to assets acquired on or after that date from connected parties who owned the asset prior to that date. This is to prevent the 'refreshing' of assets into the new regime.

HMRC has identified certain arrangements whereby partnerships or LLPs can bring assets into the new regime without an effective change of economic ownership. Although HMRC also states that they do not believe that these arrangements have the intended effect, nevertheless s 51 is enacted to put the matter beyond doubt.

Section 52 amends CTA 2009 s 882 so that the concept of a related party for the purposes of the corporation tax rules on intangible fixed assets has to take into account the participation condition at TIOPA 2010 s 148. The participation condition is that one of the parties directly or indirectly participates in the management, control or capital of the other or the same person or persons directly or indirectly participates in the management, control or capital of both.

The new rule applies both to companies and to corporate members of partnerships and LLPs.

Commencement

The new rule applies on or after 25 November 2015. Strictly, the legislation applies to accounting periods beginning on or after that date, but accounting periods straddling that date are to be notionally split into two accounting periods, one using the old rules and ending on 24 November 2015, the other staring on 25 November 2015 and to which the new rules will apply.

53 Intangible fixed assets: transfers treated as at market value

(1) In section 845 of CTA 2009 (transfer between company and related party treated as at market value), after subsection (4) insert—

    "(4A) References in subsection (1) to a related party in relation to a company are to be read as including references to a person in circumstances where the participation condition is met as between that person and the company.

    (4B) References in subsection (4A) to a company include a firm in a case where, for section 1259 purposes, references in subsection (1) to a company are read as references to the firm.

    (4C) Section 148 of TIOPA 2010 (when the participation condition is met) applies for the purposes of subsection (4A) as it applies for the purposes of section 147(1)(b) of TIOPA 2010.

    (4D) Subsection (4E) applies where—

        (a) a gain on the disposal of an intangible asset by a firm is a gain to be taken into account for section 1259 purposes, and

        (b) for those purposes, references in subsection (1) to a company are read as references to the firm

    (4E) Where this subsection applies, the gain referred to in subsection (4D)(a) is to be treated for the purposes of this section as if it were a chargeable realisation gain for the purposes of section 741(1) (meaning of "chargeable intangible asset").

(4F) In this section, "section 1259 purposes" means the purposes of determining under section 1259 the amount of profits or losses to be allocated to a partner in a firm."

(2) The amendment made by this section applies in relation to a transfer which takes place on or after 25 November 2015, unless it takes place pursuant to an obligation, under a contract, that was unconditional before that date.

(3) For the purposes of subsection (2), an obligation is "unconditional" if it may not be varied or extinguished by the exercise of a right (whether under the contract or otherwise).

GENERAL NOTE

Section 53 makes a change, similar to s 52, to the rules whereby a transfer of assets between a company and a related party is to be treated as occurring at market value.

Scope

Transfers between a company and a related party are to include transfers between a company and a person in circumstances where the participation condition is met between that person and the company, as detailed in s 52 above.

Once again, this applies both to companies and to corporate members of partnerships and LLPs.

Section 53 also amends CTA 2009 s 845, so that a disposal of intangible fixed assets by a partnership or LLP is brought into the disposal rules of CTA 2009 Pt 8 as a 'chargeable realisable gain' and is therefore subject to the normal market value rule at CTA 2009 s 845.

Commencement

This rule applies to transfers that take place on or after 25 November 2015, unless pursuant to a contractual obligation that was unconditional before that date, i.e. if it may not be varied or extinguished by exercise of a right.

Creative Industry Reliefs

54 Tax relief for production of orchestral concerts

Schedule 8 contains provision about relief in respect of the production of orchestral concerts.

GENERAL NOTE

Orchestra tax relief was originally announced in the 2014 Autumn Statement as an extension to the successful creative sector tax reliefs. There followed a consultation on the design in early 2015. In the March 2015 Budget the rate of relief was disclosed (25% on qualifying expenditure for eligible concerts).

The relief can be claimed by incorporated companies, chargeable to Corporation Tax, which are directly involved in the production of orchestral concerts.

Section 54 introduces Sch 8, which details the new tax relief for qualifying orchestral concerts. The relief will have effect for qualifying expenditure incurred on or after 1 April 2016.

The tax relief has been introduced on the basis of the successful Film Tax Relief; which has generated claims by over 1,200 film projects for a total of £1.3 billion. The aim of the relief is to promote British culture in a sustainable manner by providing support to orchestras in the UK.

55 Television and video games tax relief: consequential amendments

In the following provisions, for "section 1218" substitute "section 1218B"—

   (a) paragraph 8(2)(c) of Schedule 7A to TCGA 1992,
   (b) section 63(1) of CTA 2010, and
   (c) section 729 of CTA 2010.

GENERAL NOTE

The section amends references to Corporation Tax Act 2009 (CTA 2009) ss 1218–1218B in the following three provisions:
- TCGA 1992 Sch 7A para 8(2)(c);
- CTA 2010 s 63(1);
- CTA 2010 s 729.

CTA 2009 s 1218 gives the meaning of "Company with investment business" and "investment business".

Banking Companies

56 Banking companies: excluded entities

(1) Section 133F of CTA 2009 ("excluded company") has effect, and is to be deemed always to have had effect, with the amendments set out in subsections (2) to (4).

(2) After subsection (2) insert—

"(2A) A company is also an "excluded company" at any time (in an accounting period) if—

(a) the company would fall within a relevant relieving provision but for one (and only one) line of business which it carries on,

(b) that line of business does not involve the relevant regulated activity described in the provision mentioned in section 133G(1)(a), and

(c) the company's activities in that line of business would not, on their own, result in it being both a 730k firm and a full scope investment firm.

(2B) For the purposes of subsection (2A) the "relevant relieving provisions" are paragraphs (b), (c), (e), (g) and (h) of subsection (2)."

(3) In subsection (7), before the definition of "authorised corporate director" insert—

""730k firm"—

(a) in relation to any time on or after 1 January 2014, means an IFPRU 730k firm,

(b) in relation to any time before that date, means a BIPRU 730k firm;".

(4) In subsection (7), at the appropriate places insert—

""BIPRU 730k firm" and "full scope BIPRU investment firm" have the same meaning as in subsections (2) to (4) of section 133H;"

""IFPRU 730k firm" and full scope IFPRU investment firm" have the meaning given by the FCA Handbook at the time in question;"

""full scope investment firm"

(a) in relation to any time on or after 1 January 2014, means a full scope IFPRU investment firm,

(b) in relation to any time before that date, means a full scope BIPRU investment firm;".

(5) Section 133M of CTA 2009 has effect, and is to be deemed always to have had effect, with the amendment set out in subsection (6).

(6) For subsection (5)(b)(ii) substitute—

"(ii) the firm would not (if references in section 133F(2) and (3) to companies included firms) be an excluded company for the purposes of section 133E."

(7) Part 7A of CTA 2010 has effect, and is to be deemed always to have had effect, with the amendments set out in subsections (8) and (9).

(8) In section 269BA (excluded entities), after subsection (1) insert—

"(1A) For the purposes of section 269B an entity is also an "excluded entity" if—

(a) the entity would fall within a relevant relieving provision but for one (and only one) line of business which it carries on,

(b) that line of business does not involve the relevant regulated activity described in the provision mentioned in section 269BB(a), and

(c) the entity's activities in that line of business would not, on their own, result in it being both an IFPRU 730k firm and a full scope IFPRU investment firm.

(1B) For the purposes of subsection (1A) the "relevant relieving provisions" are paragraphs (b), (c), (e), (g) and (h) of subsection (1)."

(9) In section 269DO (interpretation)—

(a) after subsection (5) insert—

"(5A) For the purposes of section 269BA(1A) (extension of certain exclusions under subsection (1) of that section) a line of business carried on by a company is not regarded as involving the relevant regulated activity described in the provision mentioned in section 269BB(a) if—

(a) the carrying on of that activity is ancillary to asset management activities the company carries on, and

(b) the company would not carry that activity on but for the fact that it carries on asset management activities.";

(b) in subsection (6) for "subsection (5)" substitute "subsections (5) and (5A)".

(10) In Schedule 19 to FA 2011 (the bank levy), paragraph 73 is amended in accordance with subsections (11) and (12).

(11) In sub-paragraph (1), omit "or" at the end of paragraph (j) and after paragraph (k) insert ", or

(l) an entity falling within sub-paragraph (1A)."

(12) After sub-paragraph (1) insert—

"(1A) An entity falls within this sub-paragraph if—

(a) it would fall within a relevant relieving provision but for one (and only one) line of business which it carries on,

(b) that line of business does not involve the relevant regulated activity described in the provision mentioned in paragraph 79(a), and

(c) the entity's activities in that line of business would not, on their own, result in it being both an IFPRU 730k firm and a full scope IFPRU investment firm.

(1B) For the purposes of sub-paragraph (1A) the "relevant relieving provisions" are paragraphs (b), (c), (e), (g) and (h) of sub-paragraph (1)."

(13) Subsections (10) to (12) have effect in relation to chargeable periods beginning on or after the day on which this Act is passed.

(14) But for the purposes of determining what groups and entities must be listed under subsection (4) of section 285 of FA 2014 (Code of Practice on Taxation for Banks: HMRC reports) in any relevant report under that section—

(a) subsection (13) is to be disregarded, and

(b) Schedule 19 to FA 2011 is to be deemed to have effect, and always to have had effect, with the amendments set out in subsections (10) to (12).

(15) In subsection (14) "relevant report" means a report for the reporting period beginning with 1 April 2015 or any subsequent reporting period.

GENERAL NOTE

Section 56 amends the definition of banking company used in various places in the legislation in order to correct an anomaly in the operation of the exclusions from this definition.

The affected definitions are those in:

— Section 133F CTA 2009 (relevant for the restriction on deducting compensation payments by banks)
— Section 269BA CTA 2010 (relevant for the bank loss restriction rules and bank surcharge)
— FA 2011 Sch 19 para 73 (relevant for the bank levy and the Code of Practice on Taxation for Banks)

As originally enacted these definitions provided for entities carrying on certain regulated activities not to be regarded as banks. For example, an entity which does not carry any relevant regulated activities otherwise than as the manager of a pension scheme should have been excluded from being a "banking company" for surcharge purposes by CTA 2010 s 269BA(1)(c). In each case, however, the exclusion only applied to entities exclusively carrying on the specified regulated activities. This meant that an entity carrying on additional regulated activities was unable to benefit from the exclusions, even in cases where these other activities would not in isolation have been sufficient to bring the entity within the scope of the banking company definition.

In order to address this anomaly FA 2016 s 56 slightly broadens the scope of the existing exclusions to allow these to apply where an entity would fall within the scope of an exclusion but for the fact that it is carrying on another line of business, provided that other line of business would not alone result in it being a 730k firm and full scope investment firm (i.e. in being an investment bank).

This broadened application of the exclusions does not extend to cases where the additional line of business concerned is the regulated activity of deposit taking.

The changes made by s 56 are most cases treated as having always had effect and this will in some cases mean that entities are retrospectively taken out of the scope of the special rules for banking companies.

A key exception to this the change in definition as it applies for the purposes of the bank levy, where the amendment is treated as taking effect only for chargeable periods beginning on or after Royal Assent (i.e. 15 September 2016).

57 Banking companies: restrictions on loss relief etc

(1) Chapter 3 of Part 7A of CTA 2010 (restrictions on banking companies obtaining certain deductions) is amended as follows.

(2) In section 269CA (restriction on deductions for trading losses), in subsection (2), for "50%" substitute "25%".

(3) In section 269CB (restriction on deductions for non-trading deficits from loan relationships), in subsection (2), for "50%" substitute "25%".

(4) In section 269CC (restriction on deductions for management expenses etc), in step 1 in subsection (7), for "50%" substitute "25%".

(5) The amendments made by this section have effect for the purposes of determining the taxable total profits of companies for accounting periods beginning on or after 1 April 2016.

(6) For the purposes of subsection (5), where a company has an accounting period beginning before 1 April 2016 and ending on or after that date ("the straddling period")—

(a) so much of the straddling period as falls before 1 April 2016, and so much of that period as falls on or after that date, are treated as separate accounting periods, and
(b) profits or losses of the company for the straddling period are apportioned to the two separate accounting periods—

(i) in accordance with section 1172 of CTA 2010 (time basis), or
(ii) if that method would produce a result that is unjust or unreasonable, on a just and reasonable basis.

GENERAL NOTE

Section 57 amends the bank loss restriction rules in Chapter 3 of CTA 2010 Pt 7A to reduce the proportion of profits which can be sheltered by restricted losses from 50% to 25%.

The context of this change is the announcement at Budget 2016 of plans to introduce in FA 2017 a general restriction on the use of corporate losses, broadly capping at 50% the proportion of profits which can be sheltered in each period using historic losses. This raised the question of how the new rules should interact with the similar existing restriction applying to banking companies in respect of most losses accruing prior to 1 April 2015. The Government's stated policy continues to be that these bank losses should be subject to more restrictive treatment than general corporate losses, broadly because of the perception that the losses concerned in many cases arose as result of the financial crisis and subsequent misconduct scandals. Accordingly, given the proposal for a general restriction on the use of corporate losses, the decision has been made to lower the cap on the offset of historic losses by banks from 50% of profits to 25%.

Although at the time of writing it is proposed that the general loss restrictions should only come into effect from 1 April 2017, the tightening of the rules relating to banking companies comes into effect from 1 April 2016 (see sub-s (5)). Where, as will often be the case, companies have an accounting period straddling 1 April 2016, then this should be treated as split into two separate accounting periods for the purposes of applying the restriction. Apportionment of profits and losses between the two periods should be on a time basis, unless this would produce an unjust or unreasonable result in which case a just and reasonable apportionment is adopted instead (see sub-s (6)).

Example

A banking company has profits for the year ended 31 December 2016 of £100 million, before offsetting historic losses. It has historic losses brought forward £100 million, all of which are subject to the loss restriction rules. Apportioning the profits on a time basis results in profits of approximately £25 million attributable to the period 1 January 2016 – 31 March 2016 and £75 million attributable to the period 1 April 2016 – 31 December 2016. The offset of the restricted losses is capped at 50% (i.e. £12.5 million) in the first of these periods and 25% (i.e. £18.75 million) in the second period. In total, therefore, the bank should only be able to offset losses of £31.25 million for corporation tax purposes, leaving profits of £68.75 million in charge. The losses which are prevented from being offset as a result of the restriction are carried forward to future periods in the usual way.

The legislative approach to straddling accounting periods is the same as that adopted on the original introduction of the loss restriction rules (see FA 2015 Sch 2 Para 7). It is therefore likely that HMRC will expect banking companies to apply this in the same way, in particular in terms of the criteria used to determine when it is appropriate to move away from the default time basis of apportionment. It is also likely that, as with the original rules, HMRC will reject apportionments which result in a loss being recognised in one notional period and a profit in the other.

The tightened loss restriction only applies to those losses already within the scope of the existing loss restriction rules, broadly those accruing prior to 1 April 2015. Other losses continue to be dealt with in the usual way (and so, in particular, are expected to be subject to the general loss restriction rules if these are enacted as currently proposed).

In practice this results in an increasingly complex picture for how banking companies may use their losses, as the following table illustrates:

Period in which losses arise	Period in which losses are utilised	Cap on utilisation – corporation tax	Cap on utilisation – surcharge
Pre-1 April 2015	Pre-1 April 2015	100%	n/a
	1 April 2015 – 31 December 2015	50%	n/a
	1 January 2016 – 31 March 2016	50%	0%
	Post-1 April 2016	25%	0%
1 April 2015 – 31 December 2015	1 April 2015 – 31 December 2015	100%	n/a
	1 January 2016 – 31 March 2017	100%	0%
	Post-1 April 2017*	50%	0%
Post-31 December 2015	1 January 2016 – 31 March 2017	100%	100%
	Post-1 April 2017*	50%	50%

*   The Government has to announce final proposals for the operation of the loss rules post-1 April 2017 reflecting the outcome of its consultation on the original proposals. The entries in the above table in relation to these periods therefore reflect the published proposals but are liable to change.

Oil and Gas

58 Reduction in rate of supplementary charge

(1) In section 330 of CTA 2010 (supplementary charge in respect of ring fence trades), in subsection (1), for "20%" substitute "10%".

(2) The amendment made by subsection (1) has effect in relation to accounting periods beginning on or after 1 January 2016 (but see also subsection (3)).

(3) Subsections (4) and (5) apply where a company has an accounting period beginning before 1 January 2016 and ending on or after that date ("the straddling period").

(4) For the purpose of calculating the amount of the supplementary charge on the company for the straddling period—

(a) so much of that period as falls before 1 January 2016, and so much of that period as falls on or after that date, are treated as separate accounting periods, and
(b) the company's adjusted ring fence profits for the straddling period are apportioned to the two separate accounting periods in proportion to the number of days in those periods.

(5) The amount of the supplementary charge on the company for the straddling period is the sum of the amounts of supplementary charge that would, in accordance with subsection (4), be chargeable on the company for those separate accounting periods.

(6) In this section—

"adjusted ring fence profits" has the same meaning as in section 330 of CTA 2010;
"supplementary charge" means any sum chargeable under section 330(1) of CTA 2010 as if it were an amount of corporation tax.

GENERAL NOTE

Section 58 provides for the reduction of the rate of the supplementary charge applicable to UK and UK Continental Shelf upstream oil and gas profits from 20% to 10% with effect from 1 January 2016. Most oil and gas companies operating in the UK have December year ends but to the extent that is not the case the profits of the actual accounting period have to be apportioned on a time basis.

59 Investment allowance: disqualifying conditions

(1) Section 332D of CTA 2010 (expenditure on acquisition of asset: disqualifying conditions) is amended as follows.

(2) In subsection (1) after "an asset" insert "("the acquisition concerned")".

(3) In subsection (2)—
(a) for "acquisition," substitute "acquisition concerned," and
(b) after "acquiring," insert "leasing,".

(4) In subsection (3)(b)—
(a) for "acquisition," substitute "acquisition concerned,", and
(b) after "acquiring," insert "leasing,".

(5) After subsection (4) insert—

"(5) In subsection (3)(c) "this Chapter" means the provisions of this Chapter, and of any regulations made under this Chapter, as those provisions have effect at the time when the investment expenditure mentioned in subsection (1) is incurred.

(6) Subsections (7) and (8) apply where investment expenditure mentioned in subsection (1) would, in the absence of this section, be relievable under section 332C by reason of section 332CA (treatment of expenditure incurred before field is determined).

(7) Where this subsection applies—
(a) subsection (2) is to be read as if after "was" there were inserted ", or has become,", and
(b) in determining for the purposes of subsection (2) or (3)(b) whether particular expenditure was incurred "before" the acquisition concerned—
(i) paragraph (b) of section 332CA(3) is to be ignored, and
(ii) accordingly, that expenditure is to be taken (for the purposes of determining whether it was incurred before the acquisition concerned) to have been incurred when it was actually incurred.

(8) Where this subsection applies, in determining whether the second disqualifying condition applies to the asset—
(a) the reference in subsection (3)(a)(i) to a qualifying oil field is to be read as including an area which, at the time of the acquisition concerned, had not been determined to be an oil field but which has subsequently become a qualifying oil field,
(b) the reference in subsection (3)(a)(ii) to a qualifying oil field is to be read as including an area which, at the time of the transfer, had not been determined to be an oil field but which has subsequently become a qualifying oil field,
(c) the reference in subsection (3)(c)(i) to "the qualifying oil field" is to be read accordingly, and
(d) the following sub-paragraph is to be treated as substituted for subsection (3)(c)(ii)—

"(ii) would have been relievable under section 332C if this Chapter had been fully in force and had applied to expenditure incurred at the time when that expenditure was actually incurred and the area in question had been a qualifying oil field at that time."

(9) In subsection (8)(a) and (b) "determined" means determined under Schedule 1 to OTA 1975.

(10) In this section any reference to expenditure which was incurred by a company in "leasing" an asset is to expenditure incurred by the company under an agreement under which the asset was leased to the company."

(6) The amendments made by this section have effect for the purposes of determining whether any expenditure—

(a) incurred by a company on or after 16 March 2016 on the acquisition of an asset, or

(b) treated under section 332CA of CTA 2010 as so incurred,

is relievable expenditure for the purposes of section 332C of CTA 2010.

GENERAL NOTE

Section 59 limits the availability of investment allowance in certain circumstances, broadly where the expenditure represents expenditure which has already qualified for investment allowance. This corrects an anomaly in the original drafting of the investment allowance rules whereby expenditure on the acquisition of licence interests not containing a determined field was not restricted. The rules will also now deny investment allowance where the asset has previously been leased. The changes apply for any expenditure incurred after 16 March 2016.

Subsections (1)–(4) make minor definitional changes to the existing legislation to ensure that expenditure on leasing an asset, in addition to expenditure on acquiring it, is taken into account.

Subsection (5) introduces new sub-ss (5)–(10) in to s 332D CTA 2010

New s 332D(5) provides that any regulations made under the provision of the investment allowance legislation are to apply in determining whether there has been prior qualifying expenditure. This is needed as the rules relating to certain leasing and other opex costs are to be introduced by way of regulation.

New s 332D(6) introduces the new tests in sub-ss 7 and 8 for expenditure incurred in an area of a field before the field has been determined as such. When originally drafted the rules were ineffective for this type of expenditure as until a field is determined the expenditure does not qualify for investment allowance.

New s 332D(7) makes changes to ensure that expenditure on an area where there was no determined field at the time the licence interest was acquired is nevertheless treated as qualifying expenditure (and therefore debars any relief on the licence acquisition cost). For the purpose of determining whether the expenditure was incurred before the licence acquisition costs the deeming rule in s 332CA which deems the expenditure to be incurred at the time the field is determined is ignored.

New s 332D(8) makes various amendments to the second disqualifying test in ss3 to ensure that the fact that a field had not been determined as such at the time any expenditure is incurred does not prevent the disqualifying condition from applying.

New s 332D(9) applies, for the purposes of the section, the normal definition of a determined field contained in the PRT legislation.

New s 332D(10) provides that the references to leasing under the new provisions refer to any costs incurred under an agreement under which an asset is leased. This would therefore catch any up front premium and set up costs under a lease.

Subsection (6) provides that the above changes are effective for expenditure incurred on or after 16 March 2016 and also for any expenditure incurred before that date where a field to which they relate is subsequently determined on or after 16 March 2016. As such the provision is retrospective as relevant expenditure incurred before 16 March 2016 would have qualified prior to these changes being introduced.

60　Investment allowance: power to expand meaning of "relevant income"

(1) Section 332F of CTA 2010 (activation of investment allowance) is amended as follows.

(2) In subsection (2)(b) before "the company's relevant income" insert "the total amount of".

(3) For subsection (3) substitute—

"(3) For the purposes of this Chapter, income is relevant income of a company from a qualifying oil field for an accounting period if it is—

(a) production income of the company from any oil extraction activities carried on in that oil field that is taken into account in calculating the company's adjusted ring fence profits for the accounting period, or

(b) income that—

(i) is income of such description (whether or not relating to the oil field) as may be prescribed by the Treasury by regulations, and

(ii) is taken into account as mentioned in paragraph (a).

(4) The Treasury may by regulations make such amendments of this Chapter as the Treasury consider appropriate in consequence of, or in connection with, any provision contained in regulations under subsection (3)(b).

(5) Regulations under subsection (3)(b) or (4) may provide for any of the provisions of the regulations to have effect in relation to accounting periods ending before (or current when) the regulations are made.

(6) But subsection (5) does not apply to—

(a) any provision of amending or revoking regulations under subsection (3)(b) which has the effect that income of any description is to cease to be treated as relevant income of a company from a qualifying oil field for an accounting period, or

(b) provision made under subsection (4) in consequence of or in connection with provision within paragraph (a).

(7) Regulations under this section may make transitional provision or savings.

(8) Regulations under this section may not be made unless a draft of the instrument containing them has been laid before, and approved by a resolution of, the House of Commons."

GENERAL NOTE

While qualifying expenditure attracts an investment allowance that allowance is only "activated", and thereby becomes available for relief, when there is income from the relevant field in respect of which the expenditure was incurred. As originally enacted the only income that could activate the allowance was production income. This section amends s 332F CTA 2010 with a view to extending the classes of income that can be used to activate the allowance. The income must, however, still be of a type that is brought into account in computing profits subject to the supplementary charge. Any extension must occur by way of Treasury regulations. It is understood that this provision will be used to enable tariff income to activate allowances and that any such extension may be backdated.

New s 332F(3) and (4) facilitate the above change.

New s 332F(4) and (5) provide that the Treasury regulations can effectively back date any changes but only where the scope of income which can be used to activate the allowance is being extended.

61 Onshore allowance: disqualifying conditions

(1) CTA 2010 is amended as follows.

(2) In section 356C after subsection (4) insert—

"(4A) Subsections (1) to (4) are subject to section 356CAA (which prevents expenditure on the acquisition of an asset from being relievable in certain circumstances)."

(3) After section 356CA insert—

"356CAA Expenditure on acquisition of asset: further disqualifying conditions

(1) Capital expenditure incurred by a company ("the acquiring company") on the acquisition of an asset ("the acquisition concerned") is not relievable capital expenditure for the purposes of section 356C if subsection (2), (3) or (8) applies to the asset.

(2) This subsection applies to the asset if capital expenditure incurred before the acquisition concerned, by the acquiring company or another company, in acquiring, bringing into existence or enhancing the value of the asset was relievable under section 356C.

(3) This subsection applies to the asset if—

(a) the asset—

(i) is the whole or part of the equity in a qualifying site, or

(ii) is acquired in connection with a transfer to the acquiring company of the whole or part of the equity in a qualifying site,

(b) capital expenditure was incurred before the acquisition concerned, by the acquiring company or another company, in acquiring, bringing into existence or enhancing the value of the asset, and

(c) any of that expenditure—

(i) related to the qualifying site, and

(ii) would have been relievable under section 356C if this Chapter had been fully in force and had applied to expenditure incurred at that time.

(4) For the purposes of subsection (3)(a)(ii) it does not matter whether the asset is acquired at the time of the transfer.

(5) In subsection (3)(c) "this Chapter" means the provisions of this Chapter as those provisions have effect at the time when the capital expenditure mentioned in subsection (1) is incurred.

(6) The reference in subsection (3)(c)(i) to the qualifying site includes an area that, although not a qualifying site when the expenditure mentioned in subsection (3)(b) was incurred, subsequently became the qualifying site.

(7) Where expenditure mentioned in subsection (3)(b) related to an area which subsequently became the qualifying site, the following sub-paragraph is to be treated as substituted for subsection (3)(c)(ii)—

"(ii) would have been relievable under section 356C if the area in question had been a qualifying site when the expenditure was incurred, or if the area in question had been such a site at that time and this Chapter had been fully in force and had applied to expenditure incurred at that time."

(8) This subsection applies to the asset if—

(a) capital expenditure mentioned in subsection (1) would, in the absence of this section, be relievable under section 356C by reason of an election under section 356CB (treatment of expenditure not related to an established site), and

(b) capital expenditure which was incurred before the acquisition concerned, by the acquiring company or another company, in acquiring, bringing into existence or enhancing the value of the asset, either—

(i) has become relievable under section 356C by reason of an election under section 356CB, or

(ii) would be so relievable if such an election were made in respect of that expenditure.

(9) In determining for the purposes of subsection (8)(b) whether particular expenditure was incurred "before" the acquisition concerned—

(a) paragraph (b) of section 356CB(6) is to be ignored, and

(b) accordingly, that expenditure is to be taken (for the purposes of determining whether it was incurred before the acquistion concerned) to have been incurred when it was actually incurred.

(10) For the purposes of subsection (8)(b)(ii) it does not matter if an election is not in fact capable of being made."

(4) The amendments made by this section have effect for the purposes of determining whether any expenditure—

(a) incurred by a company on or after 16 March 2016 on the acquisition of an asset, or

(b) treated by reason of an election under section 356CB as so incurred,

is relievable expenditure for the purposes of section 356C of CTA 2010.

GENERAL NOTE

This section introduces for Onshore Allowance purposes restrictions similar to those that apply for Investment Allowance purposes as amended in accordance with s 59, to prevent any relief where expenditure on the same asset has previously qualified for onshore allowances. The Onshore Allowance rules previously had no disqualifying rules akin to those in s 332D CTA 2010 (prior to its amendment in this Finance Act). The legislation refers to qualifying sites rather than determined fields as the onshore allowance can apply to both onshore shale gas areas, where no field is typically determined, and also to conventional oil and gas fields (where a field determination will be made). No similar change was needed for the Cluster Allowance rules as they did not contain the same anomaly that existed in the Investment Allowance rules that s 59 relates to.

New s 356CAA(1) provides that expenditure on an asset will not qualify for Onshore Allowances if any of three tests are met.

New s 356CAA(2) the first disqualifying test is where any expenditure on the asset acquired had previously qualified for Onshore Allowance. It is understood that this test is intended to relate to physical assets although arguably it could apply to others.

New s 356CAA(3) the second disqualifying test is where an interest in a qualifying site is acquired (including any physical assets acquired as part of the package) and there has been expenditure prior to the acquisition which has (or would have if the relevant legislation been in place) qualified for Onshore Allowance.

New s 356CAA(4)–(7) provide additional clarification as to how the test in sub-s (3) is to apply.

New s 356CAA(8) the third disqualifying test applies the tests in ss2 and 3 to situations where expenditure has previously not qualified for Onshore Allowance as it did not relate to a qualifying site but an election has been made under s 356CB CTA 2010 for the expenditure to be treated as related to another site.

New s 356CAA(9) and (10) clarify how the test in sub-s (8) is to be applied.

The restrictions introduced by this section apply to expenditure incurred, or deemed to be incurred if an election under s 356CB CTA 2010 is made, on or after 16 March 2016.

62 Cluster area allowance: disqualifying conditions

(1) Section 356JFA of CTA 2010 (expenditure on acquisition of asset: disqualifying conditions) is amended as follows.

(2) In subsection (2) after "acquiring," insert "leasing,".

(3) In subsection (3)(b) after "acquiring," insert "leasing,".

(4) After subsection (4) insert—

"(5) In this section any reference to expenditure which was incurred by a company in "leasing" an asset is to expenditure incurred by the company under an agreement under which the asset was leased to the company."

(5) The amendments made by this section have effect for the purposes of determining whether any expenditure incurred by a company on or after 16 March 2016 on the acquisition of an asset is relievable expenditure for the purposes of section 356JF of CTA 2010.

GENERAL NOTE

This section mirrors to rule in s 59 which applies to Investment Allowance in extending the restriction for cluster allowance purposes for expenditure on an asset where there has previously been leasing expenditure in respect of the asset which has qualified for cluster allowance. There are no additional restricting provisions in connection with asset acquisitions as there are in s 59 (Investment Allowance) and s 61 (Onshore Allowance).

Subsection (5)

The new restriction applies to expenditure incurred on or after 16 March 2016.

63 Cluster area allowance: power to expand meaning of "relevant income"

(1) Section 356JH of CTA 2010 (activation of cluster area allowance) is amended as follows.

(2) In subsection (2)(b) before "the company's relevant income" insert "the total amount of".

(3) For subsection (3) substitute—

"(3) For the purposes of this Chapter, income is relevant income of a company from a cluster area for an accounting period if it is—

(a) production income of the company from any oil extraction activities carried on in that area that is taken into account in calculating the company's adjusted ring fence profits for the accounting period, or

(b) income that—

    (i) is income of such description (whether or not relating to the cluster area) as may be prescribed by the Treasury by regulations, and

    (ii) is taken into account as mentioned in paragraph (a).

(4) The Treasury may by regulations make such amendments of this Chapter as the Treasury consider appropriate in consequence of, or in connection with, any provision contained in regulations under subsection (3)(b).

(5) Regulations under subsection (3)(b) or (4) may provide for any of the provisions of the regulations to have effect in relation to accounting periods ending before (or current when) the regulations are made.

(6) But subsection (5) does not apply to—

(a) any provision of amending or revoking regulations under subsection (3)(b) which has the effect that income of any description is to cease to be treated as relevant income of a company from a cluster area for an accounting period, or

(b) provision made under subsection (4) in consequence of or in connection with provision within paragraph (a).

(7) Regulations under this section may make transitional provision or savings.

(8) Regulations under this section may not be made unless a draft of the instrument containing them has been laid before, and approved by a resolution of, the House of Commons."

GENERAL NOTE

This section mirrors, for Cluster Allowance purposes, the change made for Investment Allowance purposes in s 60, extending the category of income that can activate the allowance. No such similar extension is made for Onshore Allowance, it being assumed that onshore facilities will not be used to generate tariff income from use by other sites.

For an explanation of the new subsections see the commentary on s 60.

Exploitation of Patents etc

64 Profits from the exploitation of patents etc

(1) Part 8A of CTA 2010 (profits arising from the exploitation of patents etc) is amended as follows.

(2) In section 357A (election for special treatment of profits from patents etc)—

  (a) for subsections (6) and (7) substitute—

"(6) Chapter 2A makes provision for determining the relevant IP profits or relevant IP losses of a trade of a company for an accounting period in a case where—

(a) the accounting period begins on or after 1 July 2021, or

(b) the company is a new entrant (see subsection (11)).

(7) Chapters 2B, 3 and 4 make provision for determining the relevant IP profits or relevant IP losses of a trade of a company for an accounting period in various cases where—

(a) the accounting period begins before 1 July 2021, and

(b) the company is not a new entrant.", and

  (b) after subsection (10) insert—

"(11) A company is a "new entrant" for the purposes of this Part if—

(a) the first accounting period for which the company's election (or most recent election) under subsection (1) has effect begins on or after 1 July 2016, or

(b) the company elects to be treated as a new entrant for the purposes of this Part."

(3) After section 357BE insert—

"CHAPTER 2A
RELEVANT IP PROFITS: CASES MENTIONED IN SECTION 357A(6)

Steps for calculating relevant IP profits of a trade

357BF   Relevant IP profits

(1) This section applies for the purposes of determining the relevant IP profits of a trade of a company for an accounting period in a case where—

(a) the accounting period begins on or after 1 July 2021, or
(b) the company is a new entrant (see section 357A(11)).

(2) To determine the relevant IP profits—

Step 1
Take any amounts which are brought into account as credits in calculating the profits of the trade for the accounting period, other than any amounts of finance income (see section 357BG), and divide them into two "streams", amounts of relevant IP income (see sections 357BH to 357BHC) and amounts that are not amounts of relevant IP income.
The stream consisting of relevant IP income is "the relevant IP income stream"; the other stream is the "standard income stream".

Step 2
Divide the relevant IP income stream into "relevant IP income sub-streams" so that each sub-stream is—

(a) a sub-stream consisting of income properly attributable to a particular qualifying IP right (an "individual IP right sub-stream"),
(b) a sub-stream consisting of income properly attributable to a particular kind of IP item (a "product sub-stream"), or
(c) a sub-stream consisting of income properly attributable to a particular kind of IP process (a "process sub-stream").

See subsection (5) for the meaning of "IP item" and "IP process" and see subsections (6) and (7) for further provision in connection with product sub-streams and process sub-streams.

Step 3
Take any amounts which are brought into account as debits in calculating the profits of the trade for the accounting period, other than any excluded debits (see section 357BI), and allocate them on a just and reasonable basis between the standard income stream and each of the relevant IP income sub-streams.

Step 4
Deduct from each relevant IP income sub-stream—

(a) the amounts allocated to the sub-stream at Step 3, and
(b) the routine return figure for the sub-stream (see section 357BJ).

But see section 357BIA (which provides that certain amounts allocated to a relevant IP income sub-stream at Step 3 are not to be deducted from the sub-stream at this Step).

Step 5
Deduct from each relevant IP income sub-stream which is greater than nil following Step 4 the marketing assets return figure for the sub-stream (see section 357BK).

Step 6
Multiply the amount of each relevant IP income sub-stream (following the deductions required at Steps 4 and 5) by the R&D fraction for the sub-stream (see section 357BL).

Step 7
Add together the amounts of the relevant IP income sub-streams (following Step 6).

Step 8
If the company has made an election under section 357BM (which provides in certain circumstances for profits arising before the grant of a right to be treated as relevant IP profits), add to the amount given by Step 7 any amount determined in accordance with subsection (3) of that section.

(3) If the amount given by subsection (2) is greater than nil, that amount is the relevant IP profits of the trade for the accounting period.

(4) If the amount given by subsection (2) is less than nil, that amount is the relevant IP losses of the trade for the accounting period (see Chapter 5).

(5) In this section—
"IP item" means—

(a) an item in respect of which a qualifying IP right held by the company has been granted, or

(b) an item which incorporates one or more items within paragraph (a);

"IP process" means—

(a) a process in respect of which a qualifying IP right held by the company has been granted, or

(b) a process which incorporates one or more processes within paragraph (a).

(6) For the purposes of this section two or more IP items, or two or more IP processes, may be treated as being of a particular kind if they are intended to be, or are capable of being, used for the same or substantially the same purposes.

(7) Income may be allocated at Step 2 of subsection (2) to a product sub-stream or process sub-stream only if—

(a) it would not be reasonably practicable to apportion the income between individual IP right sub-streams, or

(b) it would be reasonably practicable to do that but doing so would result in it not being reasonably practicable to apply any of the remaining steps in subsection (2).

(8) Any reference in this section to a qualifying IP right held by the company includes a reference to a qualifying IP right in respect of which the company holds an exclusive licence.

Finance income

357BG Finance income

(1) For the purposes of this Part "finance income", in relation to a trade of a company, means—

(a) any credits which are treated as receipts of the trade by virtue of—

(i) section 297 of CTA 2009 (credits in respect of loan relationships), or

(ii) section 573 of CTA 2009 (credits in respect of derivative contracts),

(b) any amount which in accordance with generally accepted accounting practice falls to be recognised as arising from a financial asset, and

(c) any return, in relation to an amount, which—

(i) is produced for the company by an arrangement to which it is a party, and

(ii) is economically equivalent to interest.

(2) In subsection (1)—

"economically equivalent to interest" is to be construed in accordance with section 486B(2) and (3) of CTA 2009, and

"financial asset" means a financial asset as defined for the purposes of generally accepted accounting practice.

(3) For the purposes of subsection (1)(c), the amount of a return is the amount which by virtue of the return would, in calculating the company's chargeable profits, be treated under section 486B of CTA 2009 (disguised interest to be regarded as profit from loan relationship) as profit arising to the company from a loan relationship.

But, in calculating that profit for the purposes of this subsection, sections 486B(7) and 486C to 486E of that Act are to be ignored.

Relevant IP income

357BH Relevant IP income

(1) For the purposes of this Part "relevant IP income" means income falling within any of the Heads set out in—

(a) subsection (2) (sales income),

(b) subsection (6) (licence fees),

(c) subsection (7) (proceeds of sale etc),

(d) subsection (8) (damages for infringement), and

(e) subsection (9) (other compensation).

This is subject to section 357BHB (excluded income).

(2) Head 1 is income arising from the sale by the company of any of the following items—

(a) items in respect of which a qualifying IP right held by the company has been granted ("qualifying items");

(b) items incorporating one or more qualifying items;

(c) items that are wholly or mainly designed to be incorporated into items within paragraph (a) or (b).

(3) For the purposes of this Part an item and its packaging are not to be treated as a single item, unless the packaging performs a function that is essential for the use of the item for the purposes for which it is intended to be used.

(4) In subsection (3) "packaging", in relation to an item, means any form of container or other packaging used for the containment, protection, handling, delivery or presentation of the item, including by way of attaching the item to, or winding the item round, some other article.

(5) In a case where a qualifying item and an item that is designed to incorporate that item ("the parent item") are sold together as, or as part of, a single unit for a single price, the reference in subsection (2)(b) to an item incorporating a qualifying item includes a reference to the parent item.

(6) Head 2 is income consisting of any licence fee or royalty which the company receives under an agreement granting another person any of the following rights only—

(a) a right in respect of any qualifying IP right held by the company,
(b) any other right in respect of a qualifying item or process, and
(c) in the case of an agreement granting any right within paragraph (a) or (b), a right granted for the same purposes as those for which that right was granted.

In this subsection "qualifying process" means a process in respect of which a qualifying IP right held by the company has been granted.

(7) Head 3 is any income arising from the sale or other disposal of a qualifying IP right or an exclusive licence in respect of such a right.

(8) Head 4 is any amount received by the company in respect of an infringement, or alleged infringement, of a qualifying IP right held by the company at the time of the infringement or alleged infringement.

(9) Head 5 is any amount of damages, proceeds of insurance or other compensation, other than an amount in respect of an infringement or alleged infringement of a qualifying IP right, which is received by the company in respect of an event and—

(a) is paid in respect of any items that fell within subsection (2) at the time of that event, or
(b) represents a loss of income which would, if received by the company at the time of that event, have been relevant IP income.

(10) But income is not relevant IP income by virtue of subsection (8) or (9) unless the event in respect of which the income is received, or any part of that event, occurred at a time when—

(a) the company was a qualifying company, and
(b) an election under section 357A(1) had effect in relation to it.

(11) In a case where the whole of that event does not occur at such a time, subsection (8) or (9) (as the case may be) applies only to so much of the amount received by the company in respect of the event as on a just and reasonable apportionment is properly attributable to such a time.

(12) Any reference in this section to a qualifying IP right held by the company includes a reference to a qualifying IP right in respect of which the company holds an exclusive licence.

357BHA Notional royalty

(1) This section applies where—

(a) a company holds a qualifying IP right or an exclusive licence in respect of a qualifying IP right,
(b) the qualifying IP right falls within paragraph (a), (b) or (c) of section 357BB(1), and
(c) the income of a trade of the company for an accounting period includes income ("IP-derived income") which—

(i) arises from things done by the company that involve the exploitation by the company of the qualifying IP right, and
(ii) is not relevant IP income, finance income or excluded income.

(2) The company may elect that the appropriate percentage of the IP-derived income is to be treated for the purposes of this Part as if it were relevant IP income.

(3) The "appropriate percentage" is the proportion of the IP-derived income which the company would pay another person ("P") for the right to exploit the qualifying IP right in the accounting period concerned if the company were not otherwise able to exploit it.

(4) For the purposes of determining the appropriate percentage under this section, assume that—

(a) the company and P are dealing at arm's length,

(b) the company, or the company and persons authorised by it, will have the right to exploit the qualifying IP right to the exclusion of any other person (including P),

(c) the company will have the same rights in relation to the qualifying IP right as it actually has,

(d) the right to exploit the qualifying IP right is conferred on the relevant day,

(e) the appropriate percentage is determined at the beginning of the accounting period concerned,

(f) the appropriate percentage will apply for each succeeding accounting period for which the company will have the right to exploit the qualifying IP right, and

(g) no income other than IP-derived income will arise from anything done by the company that involves the exploitation by the company of the qualifying IP right.

(5) In subsection (4)(d) "the relevant day" means—

(a) the first day of the accounting period concerned, or

(b) if later, the day on which the company first began to hold the qualifying IP right or licence.

(6) In determining the appropriate percentage, the company must act in accordance with—

(a) Article 9 of the OECD Model Tax Convention, and

(b) the OECD transfer pricing guidelines.

(7) In this section "excluded income" means any income falling within either of the Heads in section 357BHB.

357BHB Excluded income

(1) For the purposes of this Part income falling within either of the Heads set out in the following subsections is not relevant IP income—

(a) subsection (2) (ring fence income),

(b) subsection (3) (income attributable to non-exclusive licences).

(2) Head 1 is income arising from oil extraction activities or oil rights.

In this subsection "oil extraction activities" and "oil rights" have the same meaning as in Part 8 (see sections 272 and 273).

(3) Head 2 is income which on a just and reasonable apportionment is properly attributable to a licence (a "non-exclusive licence") held by the company which—

(a) is a licence in respect of an item or process, but

(b) is not an exclusive licence in respect of a qualifying IP right.

(4) In a case where—

(a) a company holds an exclusive licence in respect of a qualifying IP right, and

(b) the licence also confers on the company (or on the company and persons authorised by it) any right in respect of the invention otherwise than to the exclusion of all other persons,

the licence is to be treated for the purposes of this Part as if it were two separate licences, one an exclusive licence that does not confer any such rights, and the other a non-exclusive licence conferring those rights.

357BHC Mixed sources of income

(1) This section applies to any income that—

(a) is mixed income, or

(b) is paid under a mixed agreement.

(2) "Mixed income" means the proceeds of sale where an item falling within subsection (2) of section 357BH and an item not falling within that subsection are sold together as, or as part of, a single unit for a single price.

(3) A "mixed agreement" is an agreement providing for—

(a) one or more of the matters in paragraphs (a) to (c) of subsection (4), and

(b) one or more of the matters in paragraphs (d) to (g) of that subsection.

(4) The matters are—

(a) the sale of an item falling within section 357BH(2),

(b) the grant of any right falling within paragraph (a), (b) or (c) of section 357BH(6),

(c) a sale or disposal falling within section 357BH(7),

(d) the sale of any other item,

(e) the grant of any other right,

(f) any other sale or disposal,

(g) the provision of any services.

(5) So much of the income as on a just and reasonable apportionment is properly attributable to—

(a) the sale of an item falling within section 357BH(2),

(b) the grant of any right falling within paragraph (a), (b) or (c) of section 357BH(6), or

(c) a sale or disposal falling within section 357BH(7),

is to be regarded for the purposes of this Part as relevant IP income.

(6) But where the amount of income that on such an apportionment is properly attributable to any of the matters in paragraphs (d) to (g) of subsection (4) is a trivial proportion of the income to which this section applies, all of that income is to be regarded for the purposes of this Part as relevant IP income.

Excluded debits etc

357BI Excluded debits

For the purposes of this Part "excluded debits" means—

(a) the amount of any debits which are treated as expenses of a trade by virtue of—

(i) section 297 of CTA 2009 (debits in respect of loan relationships), or

(ii) section 573 of CTA 2009 (debits in respect of derivative contracts),

(b) the amount of any additional deduction for an accounting period obtained by a company under Part 13 of CTA 2009 for expenditure on research and development in relation to a trade,

(c) the amount of any additional deduction for an accounting period obtained by a company under Part 15A of CTA 2009 in respect of qualifying expenditure on a television programme,

(d) the amount of any additional deduction for an accounting period obtained by a company under Part 15B of CTA 2009 in respect of qualifying expenditure on a video game, and

(e) the amount of any additional deduction for an accounting period obtained by a company under Part 15C of CTA 2009 in respect of qualifying expenditure on a theatrical production.

357BIA Certain amounts not to be deducted from sub-streams at Step 4 of section 357BF

(1) This section applies where a company enters into an arrangement with a person under which—

(a) the person assigns to the company a qualifying IP right or grants or transfers to the company an exclusive licence in respect of a qualifying IP right, and

(b) the company makes to the person an income-related payment.

(2) A payment is an "income-related payment" for the purposes of subsection (1) if—

(a) the obligation to make the payment arises under the arrangement by reason of the amount of income the company has accrued which is properly attributable to the right or licence, or

(b) the amount of the payment is determined under the arrangement by reference to the amount of income the company has accrued which is so attributable.

(3) If the amount of the income-related payment is allocated to a relevant IP income sub-stream at Step 3 of section 357BF(2), the amount is not to be deducted from the sub-stream at Step 4 of section 357BF(2) unless the payment will not affect the R&D fraction for the sub-stream."

Routine return figure

357BJ Routine return figure

(1) This section applies for the purpose of calculating the routine return figure for a relevant IP income sub-stream established at Step 2 in section 357BF(2) in determining the relevant IP profits of a trade of a company for an accounting period.

(2) The routine return figure for the sub-stream is 10% of the aggregate of any routine deductions which—

(a) have been made by the company in calculating the profits of the trade for the accounting period, and

(b) have been allocated to the sub-stream at Step 3 in section 357BF(2).

For the meaning of "routine deductions", see sections 357BJA and 357BJB.

(3) In a case where—

(a) the company ("C") is a member of a group,

(b) another member of the group has incurred expenses on behalf of C,

(c) had they been incurred by C, C would have made a deduction in respect of the expenses in calculating the profits of the trade for the accounting period,

(d) the deduction would have been a routine deduction, and

(e) the deduction would have been allocated to the sub-stream at Step 3 in section 357BF(2),

C is to be treated for the purposes of subsection (2) as having made such a routine deduction and as having allocated the deduction to the sub-stream.

(4) Where expenses have been incurred by any member of the group on behalf of C and any other member of the group, subsection (3) applies in relation to so much of the amount of the expenses as on a just and reasonable apportionment may properly be regarded as incurred on behalf of C.

357BJA Routine deductions

(1) For the purposes of this Part, "routine deductions" means deductions falling within any of the Heads set out in—

(a) subsection (2) (capital allowances),

(b) subsection (3) (costs of premises),

(c) subsection (4) (personnel costs),

(d) subsection (5) (plant and machinery costs),

(e) subsection (6) (professional services), and

(f) subsection (7) (miscellaneous services).

This is subject to section 357BJB (deductions that are not routine deductions).

(2) Head 1 is any allowances under CAA 2001.

(3) Head 2 is any deductions made by the company in respect of any premises occupied by the company.

(4) Head 3 is any deductions made by the company in respect of—

(a) any director or employee of the company, or

(b) any externally provided workers.

(5) Head 4 is any deductions made by the company in respect of any plant or machinery used by the company.

(6) Head 5 is any deductions made by the company in respect of any of the following services—

(a) legal services, other than IP-related services;

(b) financial services, including—

(i) insurance services, and

(ii) valuation or actuarial services;

(c) services provided in connection with the administration or management of the company's directors and employees;

(d) any other consultancy services.

(7) Head 6 is any deductions made by the company in respect of any of the following services—

(a) the supply of water, fuel or power;

(b) telecommunications services;

(c) computing services, including computer software;

(d) postal services;

(e) the transportation of any items;

(f) the collection, removal and disposal of refuse.

(8) In this section—

"externally provided worker" has the same meaning as in Part 13 of CTA 2009 (see section 1128 of that Act),

"IP-related services" means services provided in connection with—

(a) any application for a right to which this Part applies, or

(b) any proceedings relating to the enforcement of any such right,

"premises" includes any land,

"telecommunications service" means any service that consists in the provision of access to, and of facilities for making use of, any telecommunication system (whether or not one provided by the person providing the service), and "telecommunication system" means any system (including the apparatus comprised in it) which exists for the purpose of facilitating the transmission of communications by any means involving the use of electrical or electromagnetic energy.

(9) The Treasury may by regulations amend this section.

357BJB Deductions that are not routine deductions

(1) For the purposes of this Part a deduction is not a "routine deduction" if it falls within any of the Heads set out in—

(a) subsection (2) (loan relationships and derivative contracts),
(b) subsection (3) (R&D expenses),
(c) subsection (4) (capital allowances for R&D or patents),
(d) subsection (5) (R&D-related employee share acquisitions),
(e) subsection (8) (television production expenditure),
(f) subsection (9) (video games development expenditure).

(2) Head 1 is any debits which are treated as expenses of the trade by virtue of—

(a) section 297 of CTA 2009 (debits in respect of loan relationships), or
(b) section 573 of CTA 2009 (debits in respect of derivative contracts).

(3) Head 2 is—

(a) the amount of any expenditure on research and development in relation to the trade—

(i) for which an additional deduction for the accounting period is obtained by the company under Part 13 of CTA 2009, or
(ii) in respect of which the company is entitled to an R&D expenditure credit for the accounting period under Chapter 6A of Part 3 of CTA 2009, and

(b) where the company obtains an additional deduction as mentioned in paragraph (a)(i), the amount of that additional deduction.

(4) Head 3 is any allowances under—

(a) Part 6 of CAA 2001 (research and development allowances), or
(b) Part 8 of CAA 2001 (patent allowances).

(5) Head 4 is the appropriate proportion of any deductions allowed under Part 12 of CTA 2009 (relief for employee share acquisitions) in a case where—

(a) shares are acquired by an employee or another person because of the employee's employment by the company, and
(b) the employee is wholly or partly engaged directly and actively in relevant research and development (within the meaning of section 1042 of CTA 2009).

(6) In subsection (5) "the appropriate proportion", in relation to a deduction allowed in respect of an employee, is the proportion of the staffing costs in respect of the employee which are attributable to relevant research and development for the purposes of Part 13 of CTA 2009 (see section 1124 of that Act).

"Staffing costs" has the same meaning as in that Part (see section 1123 of that Act).

(7) Subsections (5) and (6) of section 1124 of CTA 2009 apply for the purposes of subsection (5)(b) as they apply for the purposes of that section.

(8) Head 5 is—

(a) the amount of any qualifying expenditure on a television programme for which an additional deduction for the accounting period is obtained by the company under Part 15A of CTA 2009, and
(b) the amount of that additional deduction.

(9) Head 6 is—

(a) the amount of any qualifying expenditure on a video game for which an additional deduction for the accounting period is obtained by the company under Part 15B of CTA 2009, and
(b) the amount of that additional deduction.

(10) The Treasury may by regulations amend this section.

Marketing assets return figure

357BK Marketing assets return figure

(1) The marketing assets return figure for a relevant IP income sub-stream is—

$$NMR - AMR$$

where—

NMR is the notional marketing royalty in respect of the sub-stream (see section 357BKA), and

AMR is the actual marketing royalty in respect of the sub-stream (see section 357BKB).

(2) Where—

(a) AMR is greater than NMR, or
(b) the difference between NMR and AMR is less than 10% of the amount of the relevant IP income sub-stream following the deductions required by Step 4 in section 357BF(2),

the marketing assets return figure for the sub-stream is nil.

357BKA Notional marketing royalty

(1) The notional marketing royalty in respect of a relevant IP income sub-stream is the appropriate percentage of the income allocated to that sub-stream at Step 2 in section 357BF(2).

(2) The "appropriate percentage" is the proportion of that income which the company would pay another person ("P") for the right to exploit the relevant marketing assets in the accounting period concerned if the company were not otherwise able to exploit them.

(3) For the purposes of this section a marketing asset is a "relevant marketing asset" in relation to a relevant IP income sub-stream if the sub-stream includes any income arising from things done by the company that involve the exploitation by the company of that marketing asset.

(4) For the purpose of determining the appropriate percentage under this section, assume that—

(a) the company and P are dealing at arm's length,
(b) the company, or the company and persons authorised by it, will have the right to exploit the relevant marketing assets to the exclusion of any other person (including P),
(c) the company will have the same rights in relation to the relevant marketing assets as it actually has,
(d) the right to exploit the relevant marketing assets is conferred on the relevant day,
(e) the appropriate percentage is determined at the beginning of the accounting period concerned,
(f) the appropriate percentage will apply for each succeeding accounting period for which the company will have the right to exploit the relevant marketing assets, and
(g) no income other than income within the relevant IP income sub-stream will arise from anything done by the company that involves the exploitation by the company of the relevant marketing assets.

(5) In subsection (4)(d) "the relevant day", in relation to a relevant marketing asset, means—

(a) the first day of the accounting period concerned, or
(b) if later, the day on which the company first acquired the relevant marketing asset or the right to exploit the asset.

(6) In determining the appropriate percentage, the company must act in accordance with—

(a) Article 9 of the OECD Model Tax Convention, and
(b) the OECD transfer pricing guidelines.

(7) In this section "marketing asset" means any of the following (whether or not capable of being transferred or assigned)—

(a) anything in respect of which proceedings for passing off could be brought, including a registered trade mark (within the meaning of the Trade Marks Act 1994),
(b) anything that corresponds to a marketing asset within paragraph (a) and is recognised under the law of a country or territory outside the United Kingdom,
(c) any signs or indications (so far as not falling within paragraph (a) or (b)) which may serve, in trade, to designate the geographical origin of goods or services, and
(d) any information which relates to customers or potential customers of the company, or any other member of a group of which the company is a member, and is intended to be used for marketing purposes.

357BKB Actual marketing royalty

(1) The actual marketing royalty for a relevant IP income sub-stream is the aggregate of any sums which—

(a) were paid by the company for the purposes of acquiring any relevant marketing assets or the right to exploit any such assets, and

(b) have been allocated to the sub-stream at Step 3 in section 357BF(2).

(2) In this section "relevant marketing asset" has the same meaning as in section 357BKA.

R&D fraction

357BL Introduction

(1) Sections 357BLA to 357BLH apply for the purpose of determining the R&D fraction for a relevant IP income sub-stream established at Step 2 in section 357BF(2) in determining the relevant IP profits of a trade of a company for an accounting period.

(2) In sections 357BLA to 357BLH, references to "the sub-stream", "the trade", "the company" and "the accounting period" are to the relevant IP income sub-stream, the trade, the company and the accounting period referred to in subsection (1).

357BLA The R&D fraction

(1) The R&D fraction for the sub-stream is the lesser of 1 and—

$$((D + S1) \times 1.3) / (D + S1 + S2 + A)$$

where—

D is the company's qualifying expenditure on relevant R&D undertaken in-house (see section 357BLB),

S1 is the company's qualifying expenditure on relevant R&D sub-contracted to unconnected persons (see section 357BLC),

S2 is the company's qualifying expenditure on relevant R&D sub-contracted to connected persons (see section 357BLD), and

A is the company's qualifying expenditure on the acquisition of relevant qualifying IP rights (see section 357BLE).

(2) This section is subject to section 357BLH (R&D fraction: increase for exceptional circumstances).

357BLB Qualifying expenditure on relevant R&D undertaken in-house

(1) In section 357BLA, the company's "qualifying expenditure on relevant R&D undertaken in-house" means the expenditure incurred by the company during the relevant period which meets conditions A and B.

(2) Condition A is that the expenditure is—

(a) incurred on staffing costs,

(b) incurred on software or consumable items,

(c) qualifying expenditure on externally provided workers, or

(d) incurred on relevant payments to the subjects of clinical trials.

(3) Condition B is that the expenditure is attributable to relevant research and development undertaken by the company itself.

(4) If an election made by the company under section 18A of CTA 2009 (election for exemption for profits or losses of company's foreign permanent establishments) applies to the relevant period, expenditure incurred by the company during the period which meets conditions A and B—

(a) is not "qualifying expenditure on relevant R&D undertaken in-house", but

(b) is "qualifying expenditure on relevant R&D sub-contracted to connected persons",

so far as it is expenditure brought into account in calculating a relevant profits amount, or a relevant losses amount, aggregated at section 18A(4)(a) or (b) of CTA 2009 in calculating the company's foreign permanent establishments amount for the period.

(5) In this section and sections 357BLC and 357BLD, "relevant research and development" means research and development (within the meaning of section 1138) which—

(a) in a case where the sub-stream is an individual IP right sub-stream, relates to the qualifying IP right to which the income in the sub-stream is attributable,

(b) in a case where the sub-stream is a product sub-stream, relates to a qualifying IP right granted in respect of any item—

(i) to which income in the sub-stream is attributable, or

(ii) which is incorporated in an item to which income in the sub-stream is attributable, or

(c) in a case where the sub-stream is a process sub-stream, relates to a qualifying IP right granted in respect of any process—

(i) to which income in the sub-stream is attributable, or
(ii) which is incorporated in a process to which income in the sub-stream is attributable.

(6) Research and development "relates" to a qualifying IP right for the purposes of subsection (5) if—

(a) it creates, or contributes to the creation of, the invention,
(b) it is undertaken for the purpose of developing the invention,
(c) it is undertaken for the purpose of developing ways in which the invention may be used or applied, or
(d) it is undertaken for the purpose of developing any item or process incorporating the invention.

(7) The following provisions of CTA 2009 apply for the purposes of this section—

(a) section 1123 (meaning of "staffing costs"),
(b) section 1124 (when staffing costs are attributable to relevant research and development),
(c) section 1125 (meaning of "software or consumable items"),
(d) sections 1126 to 1126B (when software or consumable items are attributable to relevant research and development),
(e) sections 1127 to 1131 (meaning of "qualifying expenditure on externally provided workers"),
(f) section 1132 (when qualifying expenditure on externally provided workers is attributable to relevant research and development), and
(g) section 1140 (meaning of "relevant payments to the subjects of clinical trials"),

and in the application of those provisions for the purposes of this section any reference to "relevant research and development" is to be read as a reference to relevant research and development within the meaning given by subsection (5).

357BLC   Qualifying expenditure on relevant R&D sub-contracted to unconnected persons

(1) In section 357BLA, the company's "qualifying expenditure on relevant R&D sub-contracted to unconnected persons" means the expenditure incurred by the company during the relevant period in making payments within subsection (2).

(2) A payment is within this subsection if—

(a) it is made to a person in respect of relevant research and development contracted out by the company to the person, and
(b) the company and the person are not connected (within the meaning given by section 1122).

(3) If an election made by the company under section 18A of CTA 2009 (election for exemption for profits or losses of company's foreign permanent establishments) applies to the relevant period, expenditure incurred by the company during the period in making payments within subsection (2)—

(a) is not "qualifying expenditure on relevant R&D sub-contracted to unconnected persons", but
(b) is "qualifying expenditure on relevant R&D sub-contracted to connected persons",

so far as it is expenditure brought into account in calculating a relevant profits amount, or a relevant losses amount, aggregated at section 18A(4)(a) or (b) of CTA 2009 in calculating the company's foreign permanent establishments amount for the period.

(4) Where a payment is made to a person in respect of relevant research and development contracted out to the person and in respect of other matters, so much of the payment as is properly attributable to other matters is to be disregarded for the purposes of this section.

357BLD   Qualifying expenditure on relevant R&D sub-contracted to connected persons

(1) In section 357BLA, the company's "qualifying expenditure on relevant R&D sub-contracted to connected persons" means the total of—

(a) any expenditure which is "qualifying expenditure on relevant R&D sub-contracted to connected persons" as a result of section 357BLB(4) or 357BLC(3) (certain expenditure attributed to company's foreign permanent establishments), and

(b) the expenditure incurred by the company during the relevant period in making payments within subsection (2).

(2) A payment is within this subsection if—

(a) it is made to a person in respect of relevant research and development contracted out by the company to the person, and

(b) the company and the person are connected (within the meaning given by section 1122).

(3) Where a payment is made to a person in respect of relevant research and development contracted out to the person and in respect of other matters, so much of the payment as is properly attributable to other matters is to be disregarded for the purposes of this section.

357BLE Qualifying expenditure on acquisition of relevant qualifying IP rights

(1) In section 357BLA, the company's "qualifying expenditure on the acquisition of relevant qualifying IP rights" means the expenditure incurred by the company in making during the relevant period payments within any of subsections (2), (3) and (4).

(2) A payment is within this subsection if it is made to a person in respect of the assignment by that person to the company of a relevant qualifying IP right.

(3) A payment is within this subsection if it is made to a person in respect of the grant or transfer by that person to the company of an exclusive licence in respect of a relevant qualifying IP right.

(4) A payment is within this subsection if—

(a) it is made to a person in respect of the disclosure by that person to the company of any item or process, and

(b) the company applies for and is granted a relevant qualifying IP right in respect of that item or process (or any item or process derived from it).

(5) Where the company has incurred expenditure in making a series of payments to a person in respect of a single assignment, grant, transfer or disclosure, each of the payments in the series is to be treated for the purposes of this section as having been made on the date on which the first payment in the series was made.

(6) "Relevant qualifying IP right" means—

(a) in a case where the sub-stream is an individual IP right sub-stream, the qualifying IP right to which the income in the sub-stream is attributable,

(b) in a case where the sub-stream is a product sub-stream, a qualifying IP right granted in respect of an item—

　(i) to which income in the sub-stream is attributable, or

　(ii) which is incorporated in an item to which income in the sub-stream is attributable, or

(c) in a case where the sub-stream is a process sub-stream, a qualifying IP right granted in respect of a process—

　(i) to which income in the sub-stream is attributable, or

　(ii) which is incorporated in a process to which income in the sub-stream is attributable.

357BLF Meaning of the "relevant period" etc

(1) Subsections (2) to (6) define "the relevant period" for the purposes of sections 357BLB to 357BLE.

(2) The "relevant period" is the period which—

(a) ends with the last day of the accounting period, and

(b) begins on the relevant day or such earlier day as the company may elect.

This is subject to subsection (6).

(3) The "relevant day" is 1 July 2013 in a case where—

(a) the accounting period begins before 1 July 2021, and

(b) the company is a new entrant (see section 357A(11)).

(4) The "relevant day" is 1 July 2016 in any other case.

(5) A day elected under subsection (2)(b) must not be more than 20 years before the last day of the accounting period.

(6) If the last day of the accounting period is, or is after, 1 July 2036 the "relevant period" is the period of 20 years ending with that day.

(7) Expenditure incurred by the company is to be treated for the purposes of sections 357BLB to 357BLD as incurred during the relevant period if (and only if) the expenditure is allowable as a deduction in calculating for corporation tax purposes the profits of the trade for an accounting period which falls, in whole or in part, within the relevant period.

357BLG Cases where the company is a new entrant with insufficient information about pre-enactment expenditure

(1) This section applies if—

(a) the accounting period begins before 1 July 2021 and the company is a new entrant (so that subsection (3) of section 357BLF applies), and

(b) the company has insufficient information about its expenditure in the period which begins with 1 July 2013 and ends with 30 June 2016 to be able to calculate the R&D fraction for the sub-stream.

(2) If the accounting period begins on or after 1 July 2019, the company may elect that, for the purposes of enabling it to determine the R&D fraction for the sub-stream, section 357BLF is to have effect as if in subsection (3) for "1 July 2013" there were substituted "1 July 2016".

(3) If the accounting period begins before 1 July 2019 the company may elect that, for the purposes of enabling it to determine the R&D fraction for the sub-stream, sections 357BL to 357BLE are to have effect as if—

(a) any reference in those sections to the relevant period were to the period of three years ending with the last day of the accounting period,

(b) in section 357BLB, for subsections (5) and (6) there were substituted—

"(5) In this section and sections 357BLC and 357BLD, "relevant research and development" means research and development (within the meaning of section 1138) which relates to the trade.", and

(c) in section 357BLE—

(i) in each of subsections (2), (3) and (4) the word "relevant" were omitted, and

(ii) subsection (6) were omitted.

357BLH R&D fraction: increase for exceptional circumstances

(1) The company may elect to increase the R&D fraction for the sub-stream by the amount mentioned in subsection (2) if (but for the increase)—

(a) it would not be less than 0.325, and

(b) it would, because of exceptional circumstances, be less than the value fraction for the sub-stream (see subsection (3)).

(2) The amount of the increase referred to in subsection (1) is the amount which is equal to the difference between the R&D fraction (before the increase) and the value fraction.

(3) The "value fraction" for the sub-stream is the fraction which, on a just and reasonable assessment, represents the proportion of the value of the relevant qualifying IP rights which is properly attributable to research and development undertaken at any time—

(a) by the company itself, or

(b) on behalf of the company by persons not connected with it.

(4) An election under subsection (1) is made by the company giving notice to an officer of Revenue and Customs.

(5) The notice must be given on or before the last day on which an amendment of the company's tax return for the accounting period could be made under paragraph 15 of Schedule 18 to FA 1998.

(6) In this section—

"relevant qualifying IP rights" has the same meaning as in section 357BLE, and

"research and development" has the meaning given by section 1138.

(7) Section 1122 (meaning of "connected" persons") applies for the purposes of this section.

Profits arising before grant of right

357BM Profits arising before grant of right

(1) This section applies where a company—

(a) holds a right mentioned in paragraph (a), (b) or (c) of section 357BB(1) (rights to which this Part applies) or an exclusive licence in respect of such a right, or

(b) would hold such a right or licence but for the fact that the company disposed of any rights in the invention or (as the case may be) the licence before the right was granted.

(2) The company may elect that, for the purposes of determining the relevant IP profits of a trade of the company for the accounting period in which the right is granted, there is to be added the amount determined in accordance with subsection (3) (the "additional amount").

(3) The additional amount is the difference between—

(a) the aggregate of the relevant IP profits of the trade for each relevant accounting period, and

(b) the aggregate of what the relevant IP profits of the trade for each relevant accounting period would have been if the right had been granted on the relevant day.

(4) For the purposes of determining the additional amount, the amount of any relevant IP profits to which section 357A does not apply by virtue of Chapter 5 (relevant IP losses) is to be disregarded.

(5) In this section "relevant accounting period" means—

(a) the accounting period of the company in which the right is granted, and

(b) any earlier accounting period of the company which meets the conditions in subsection (6).

(6) The conditions mentioned in subsection (5)(b) are—

(a) that it is an accounting period for which an election made by the company under section 357A(1) has effect,

(b) that it is an accounting period for which the company is a qualifying company, and

(c) that it ends on or after the relevant day.

(7) In this section "the relevant day" is the later of—

(a) the first day of the period of 6 years ending with the day on which the right is granted, and

(b) the day on which—

(i) the application for the grant of the right was filed, or

(ii) in the case of a company that holds an exclusive licence in respect of the right, the licence was granted.

(8) Where the company would be a qualifying company for an accounting period but for the fact that the right had not been granted at any time during that accounting period, the company is to be treated for the purposes of this section as if it were a qualifying company for that accounting period.

(9) Where the company would be a qualifying company for the accounting period in which the right was granted but for the fact that the company disposed of the rights or licence mentioned in subsection (1)(b) before the right was granted, the company is to be treated for the purposes of section 357A as if it were a qualifying company for that accounting period.

Small claims treatment

357BN Small claims treatment

(1) This section applies where—

(a) a company carries on only one trade during an accounting period,

(b) section 357BF applies for the purposes of determining the relevant IP profits of the trade for the accounting period, and

(c) the qualifying residual profit of the trade for the accounting period does not exceed whichever is the greater of—

(i) £1,000,000, and

(ii) the relevant maximum for the accounting period.

(2) The company may make any of the following elections for the accounting period—

(a) a notional royalty election (see section 357BNA),

(b) a small claims figure election (see section 357BNB), and

(c) a global streaming election (see section 357BNC).

This is subject to subsections (3) and (4).

(3) The company may not make a notional royalty election, a small claims figure election or a global streaming election for the accounting period if—

(a) the qualifying residual profit of the trade for the accounting period exceeds £1,000,000,

(b) section 357BF applied for the purposes of determining the relevant IP profits of the trade for any previous accounting period beginning within the relevant 4-year period, and

(c) the company did not make a notional royalty election, a small claims figure election or (as the case may be) a global streaming election for that previous accounting period.

(4) The company may not make a small claims figure election for the accounting period if—

(a) the qualifying residual profit of the trade for the accounting period exceeds £1,000,000,

(b) section 357C or 357DA applied for the purposes of determining the relevant IP profits of the trade for any previous accounting period beginning within the relevant 4-year period, and

(c) the company did not make an election under section 357CL for small claims treatment for that previous accounting period.

(5) In subsections (3) and (4) "the relevant 4-year period" means the period of 4 years ending with the beginning of the accounting period mentioned in subsection (1)(a).

(6) For the purposes of this section, the "qualifying residual profit" of a trade of a company for an accounting period is the amount which (assuming the company did not make an election under this section) would be equal to the aggregate of the relevant IP income sub-streams established at Step 2 in section 357BF(2) in determining the relevant IP profits of the trade for the accounting period, following the deductions from those sub-streams required by Step 4 in section 357BF(2) (ignoring the amount of any sub-stream which is not greater than nil following those deductions).

(7) For the purposes of this section, the "relevant maximum" for an accounting period of a company is—

(a) in a case where no company is a related 51% group company of the company in the accounting period, £3,000,000;

(b) in a case where one or more companies are related 51% group companies of the company in the accounting period, the amount given by the formula—

£3,000,000 / (1 + N)

where N is the number of those related 51% group companies in relation to which an election under section 357A(1) has effect for the accounting period.

(8) For an accounting period of less than 12 months, the relevant maximum is proportionally reduced.

357BNA Notional royalty election

(1) Subsection (2) applies where a company has made a notional royalty election for an accounting period under section 357BN(2)(a).

(2) In its application for the purposes of determining the relevant IP profits of the trade of the company for the accounting period, section 357BHA (notional royalty) has effect as if—

(a) in subsection (2) for "the appropriate percentage" there were substituted "75%", and

(b) subsections (3) to (6) were omitted.

357BNB Small claims figure election

(1) Subsection (2) applies where a company has made a small claims figure election for an accounting period under section 357BN(2)(b).

(2) In its application for the purposes of determining the relevant IP profits of the trade of the company for the accounting period, section 357BF(2) (steps for calculating relevant IP profits) has effect as if in Step 5—

(a) for "marketing assets return figure" there was substituted "small claims figure", and

(b) for "(see section 357BK)" there was substituted "(see section 357BNB(3))".

(3) Subsections (4) to (9) apply for the purpose of calculating the small claims figure for a relevant IP income sub-stream established at Step 2 in section 357BF(2) in determining the relevant IP profits of a trade of a company for an accounting period.

(4) If 75% of the qualifying residual profit of the trade for the accounting period is lower than the small claims threshold, the small claims figure for the sub-stream is 25% of the amount of the sub-stream following Step 4 in section 357BF(2).

(5) If 75% of the qualifying residual profit of the trade for the accounting period is higher than the small claims threshold, the small claims figure for the sub-stream is the amount given by—

$$A - ((A / QRP) \times SCT)$$

where—

A is the amount of the sub-stream following the deductions required by Step 4 in section 357BF(2),

QRP is the qualifying residual profit of the trade of the company for the accounting period, and

SCT is the small claims threshold.

(6) If no company is a related 51% group company of the company in the accounting period, the small claims threshold is £1,000,000.

(7) If one or more companies are related 51% group companies of the company in the accounting period, the small claims threshold is—

£1,000,000 / (1 + N)

where N is the number of those related 51% group companies in relation to which an election under section 357A(1) has effect for the accounting period.

(8) For an accounting period of less than 12 months, the small claims threshold is proportionately reduced.

(9) Subsection (6) of section 357BN (meaning of "qualifying residual profit") applies for the purposes of subsection (4) and (5) of this section.

357BNC Global streaming election

(1) Subsection (2) applies where a company has made a global streaming election for an accounting period under section 357BN(2)(c).

(2) In its application for the purpose of determining the relevant IP profits of the trade of the company for the accounting period, this Chapter has effect with the following modifications.

(3) In subsection (2) of section 357BF (relevant IP profits)—

(a) omit Step 2,

(b) in Step 3 for "each of the relevant IP income sub streams" substitute "the relevant IP income stream",

(c) in Step 4—

(i) in the words before paragraph (a), for "each" substitute "the",

(ii) for "sub-stream", in each place it occurs, substitute "stream",

(d) in Step 5

(i) at the beginning insert "If the relevant IP income stream is greater than nil following Step 4,",

(ii) for the words from "each" to "Step 4" substitute "the stream",

(iii) for "sub-stream", in the second place it occurs, substitute "stream",

(e) in Step 6—

(i) for "each relevant IP income sub-stream" substitute "the relevant IP income stream",

(ii) for "sub-stream", in the second place it occurs, substitute "stream",

(f) omit Step 7, and

(g) in Step 8 for "given by Step 7" substitute "of the relevant IP income stream following Step 6".

(4) In subsection (3) of that section for "given by" substitute "of the relevant IP income stream following the Steps in".

(5) In subsection (4) of that section for "given by" substitute "of the relevant IP income stream following the Steps in".

(6) Omit subsections (5) to (7) of that section.

(7) In section 357BIA(3) (certain amounts not to be deducted from sub-streams at Step 4 of section 357BF)—

(a) for "a relevant IP income sub-stream" substitute "the relevant IP income stream";

(b) for "sub-stream", in the second and third places it occurs, substitute "stream".

(8) In section 357BJ (routine return figure)—

(a) for "sub-stream", in each place it occurs, substitute "stream", and

(b) in subsection (1) for "Step 2" substitute "Step 1".

(9) In section 357BK (marketing asset return figure) for "sub-stream", in each place it occurs, substitute "stream".

(10) In section 357BKA (notional marketing royalty)—

    (a) for "sub-stream", in each place it occurs, substitute "stream", and

    (b) in subsection (1) for "Step 2" substitute "Step 1".

(11) In section 357BKB (actual marketing royalty) for "sub-stream", in each place it occurs, substitute "stream".

(12) In section 357BL (R&D fraction: introduction)—

    (a) for "sub-stream" (in each place it occurs) substitute "stream", and

    (b) in subsection (1) for "Step 2" substitute "Step 1".

(13) In section 357BLA(1) (R&D fraction) for "sub-stream" substitute "stream".

(14) In section 357BLB(5) (qualifying expenditure on relevant R&D undertaken in-house) for the words after "1138)" substitute "which relates to a qualifying IP right to which income in the stream is attributable".

(15) In section 357BLE(6) (qualifying expenditure on acquisition of relevant qualifying IP rights) for the words from "means" to the end substitute "means a qualifying IP right to which income in the stream is attributable".

(16) In section 357BLG (cases where the company is a new entrant with insufficient information about pre-enactment expenditure) for "sub-stream", in each place it occurs, substitute "stream".

(17) In section 357BLH (R&D fraction: increase for exceptional circumstances) for "sub-stream", in each place it occurs, substitute "stream".

(18) In section 357BNB (small claims figure election)—

    (a) for "sub-stream", in each place it occurs, substitute "stream", and

    (b) in subsection (3) for "Step 2" substitute "Step 1".

CHAPTER 2B

RELEVANT IP PROFITS: CASES MENTIONED IN SECTION 357A(7): INCOME FROM NEW IP

357BO Relevant IP profits

(1) Section 357BF applies, with the modifications set out in section 357BQ, for the purposes of determining the relevant IP profits of a trade of a company for an accounting period in a case where—

    (a) the accounting period begins before 1 July 2021,

    (b) the company is not a new entrant (see section 357A(11)), and

    (c) any amount of relevant IP income brought into account as a credit in calculating the profits of the trade for the accounting period is properly attributable to a new qualifying IP right (see section 357BP).

(2) Where it is necessary for the purposes of section 357BF, as applied by this section, to determine the R&D fraction for a relevant IP income sub-stream, the company concerned is to be treated for the purposes of sections 357BLF and 357BLG as if it were a new entrant.

(3) Where section 357BF applies by reason of this section for the purposes of determining the relevant IP profits of a trade of a company for an accounting period, the company may not make a global streaming election for the accounting period under section 357BN(2)(c).

357BP Meaning of "new qualifying IP right" and "old qualifying IP right"

(1) This section applies for the purposes of this Part.

(2) "New qualifying IP right", in relation to a company, means a qualifying IP right which meets condition A, B or C.

(3) "Old qualifying IP right", in relation to a company, means a qualifying IP right which does not meet any of those conditions.

(4) Condition A is that the right was granted or issued to the company in response to an application filed on or after the relevant date.

(5) Condition B is that the right was assigned to the company on or after the relevant date.

(6) Condition C is that an exclusive licence in respect of the right was granted to the company on or after the relevant date.

(7) The "relevant date" for the purposes of subsections (4), (5) and (6) is 1 July 2016; but this is subject to subsection (8).

(8) The "relevant date" for the purposes of subsections (5) and (6) is 2 January 2016 if—

(a) the company and the person who assigned the right or granted the licence were connected at the time of the assignment or grant,

(b) the main purpose, or one of the main purposes, of the assignment of the right or the grant of the licence was the avoidance of a foreign tax,

(c) the person who assigned the right or granted the licence was not within the charge to corporation tax at the time of the assignment or grant, and

(d) the person who assigned the right or granted the licence was not liable at the time of the assignment or grant to a foreign tax which is designated for the purposes of this section by regulations made by the Treasury.

(9) Regulations may be made under subsection (8)(d) which designate a foreign tax only if it appears to the Treasury that the tax may be charged at a reduced rate under provisions of the law of the country or territory concerned which correspond to the provisions of this Part.

(10) Regulations may not be made under subsection (8)(d) after 31 December 2016.

(11) In this section "foreign tax" means a tax under the law of a country or territory outside the United Kingdom.

(12) Section 1122 (meaning of "connected" persons) applies for the purposes of this section.

357BQ The modifications

(1) The modifications of section 357BF referred to in section 357BO(1) are as follows.

(2) Omit subsection (1).

(3) In subsection (2)—

(a) in Step 2—

(i) before paragraph (a) insert—

"(aa) a sub-stream consisting of income properly attributable to old qualifying IP rights ("an old IP rights sub-stream"),",

(ii) in paragraph (a) before "qualifying IP right" insert "new",

(iii) in the words after paragraph (c) for "and (7)" substitute "to (7E)",

(b) in Step 6, for "relevant IP income sub-stream" substitute "individual IP right sub-stream, each product sub-stream and each process sub-stream", and

(c) for Step 7 substitute—

"*Step 7*
Add together—

(a) the amount of any old IP rights sub-stream (following Steps 4 and 5), and

(b) the amount of each of the individual IP right sub-streams, each of the product sub-streams and each of the process sub-streams (following Step 6)."

(4) In subsection (7) for paragraph (a) substitute—

"(a) it would not be reasonably practicable to apportion the income between—

(i) individual IP rights sub-streams, or

(ii) individual IP rights sub-streams and an old IP rights sub-stream, or".

(5) After subsection (7) insert—

"(7A) Subsections (7B) to (7E) apply where—

(a) income which is properly attributable to an IP item or IP process may in accordance with subsection (7) be allocated at Step 2 of subsection (2) to a product sub-stream or process sub-stream, and

(b) the IP item or IP process incorporates—

(i) at least one item or process in respect of which an old qualifying IP right held by the company has been granted, and

(ii) at least one item or process in respect of which a new qualifying IP right held by the company has been granted.

(7B) If—

(a) the value of the IP item or IP process is wholly or mainly attributable to the incorporation in it of the items or processes referred to in subsection (7A)(b)(i), or

(b) the old IP percentage for the IP item or IP process is 80% or more,

the income properly attributable to the IP item or IP process may be treated as if it were properly attributable to old qualifying IP rights only; and, accordingly, the income may be allocated at Step 2 of subsection (2) to an old qualifying IP rights sub-stream (rather than to a product sub-stream or process sub-stream).

(7C) If the old IP percentage for the IP item or IP process is less than 80% but not less than 20%, that percentage of the income which is properly attributable to the IP item or IP process may be treated as if it were properly attributable to old qualifying IP rights only; and, accordingly, that percentage of the income may be allocated at Step 2 of subsection (2) to an old IP rights sub-stream (and the remainder is to be allocated to a product sub-stream or process sub-stream).

(7D) Where by reason of subsection (7C) only part of the income properly attributable to the IP item or IP process is allocated to a product sub-stream or process sub-stream, the IP item or IP process is to be treated, in determining the R&D fraction for the sub-stream, as if it did not incorporate the items or processes referred to in subsection (7A)(b)(i).

(7E) For the purposes of subsection (7B) and (7C), the "old IP percentage" for an IP item or IP process is the percentage found by the following calculation—

(O / T) x 100

> where—
>
>> O is the number of items or processes incorporated in the IP item or IP process in respect of which an old qualifying IP right held by the company has been granted, and
>> T is the number of items or processes incorporated in the IP item or IP process in respect of which an old or a new qualifying IP right held by the company has been granted.""

(4) In section 357FB (tax advantage schemes)—

> (a) in subsection (2)(b) (list of ways by which deductions can be inflated)—
>
>> (i) omit "or" at the end of sub-paragraph (ii), and
>> (ii) after sub-paragraph (iii) insert ", or
>>> (iv) an R&D fraction (see subsection (4A)) being greater than it would be but for the scheme.", and
>
> (b) after subsection (4) insert—

"(4A) The reference in subsection (2)(b)(iv) to an R&D fraction is a reference to such a fraction as is mentioned at Step 6 of section 357BF(2)."

(5) After section 357GC insert—

"Transferred trades

357GCA Application of this Part in relation to transferred trades

(1) Where—

> (a) a company ("the transferor") ceases to carry on a trade which involves the exploitation of a qualifying IP right ("the relevant qualifying IP right"),
> (b) the transferor assigns the relevant qualifying IP right, or grants or transfers an exclusive licence in respect of it, to another company ("the transferee"), and
> (c) the transferee begins to carry on the trade,

the following provisions apply in determining under this Part the relevant IP profits of the trade carried on by the transferee.

(2) The transferee is to be treated as not being a new entrant if—

> (a) an election under section 357A(1) has effect in relation to the transferor on the date of the assignment, grant or transfer mentioned in subsection (1)(b) ("the transfer date"), and
> (b) the first accounting period of the transferor for which that election had effect began before 1 July 2016.

(3) The relevant qualifying IP right is to be treated as being an old qualifying IP right in relation to the transferee if by reason of section 357BP it is an old qualifying IP right in relation to the transferor.

(4) Expenditure incurred prior to the transfer date by the transferor which is attributable to relevant research and development undertaken by the transferor is to be treated for the purposes of section 357BLB as if it is expenditure incurred by the transferee which is attributable to relevant research and development undertaken by the transferee.

(5) Expenditure incurred prior to the transfer date by the transferor in making a payment to a person in respect of relevant research and development contracted out by the transferor to that person is to be treated for the purposes of sections 357BLC and 357BLD as if it is expenditure incurred by the transferee in making a payment to that person in respect of relevant research and development contracted out by the transferee to that person.

(6) Expenditure incurred prior to the transfer date by the transferor in making a payment in connection with the relevant qualifying IP right which is within subsection (2), (3) or (4) of section 357BLE is to be treated for the purposes of that section as if it is expenditure incurred by the transferee in making a payment in connection with that right which is within one of those subsections.

(7) Expenditure incurred by the transferee in making a payment to the transferor in respect of the assignment, grant or transfer mentioned in subsection (1)(b) is to be ignored for the purposes of section 357BLE.

(8) In this section—

"trade" includes part of a trade, and

"relevant research and development" means research and development which relates to the relevant qualifying IP right.

(9) For the purposes of this section research and development "relates" to the relevant qualifying IP right if—

(a) it creates, or contributes to the creation of the invention,

(b) it is undertaken for the purpose of developing the invention,

(c) it is undertaken for the purpose of developing ways in which the invention may be used or applied, or

(d) it is undertaken for the purpose of developing any item or process incorporating the invention."

(6) Schedule 9 contains amendments consequential on this section.

(7) The amendments made by this section have effect in relation to accounting periods beginning on or after 1 July 2016.

(8) Subsection (9) applies where a company has an accounting period ("the straddling period") which begins before, and ends on or after, 1 July 2016 or 1 July 2021 ("the relevant date").

(9) For the purposes of this section and Part 8A of CTA 2010—

(a) so much of the straddling period as falls before the relevant date, and so much of that period as falls on or after that date, are treated as separate accounting periods, and

(b) any amounts brought into account for the purposes of calculating for corporation tax purposes the profits of any trade of the company for the straddling period are apportioned to the two separate accounting periods on such basis as is just and reasonable.

(10) Subsection (11) applies if—

(a) an election is made by a company under section 357A(1) of CTA 2010, and

(b) the notice under section 357G of that Act specifies the accounting period of the company which ends on 30 June 2016, or any earlier accounting period, as being the first accounting period for which the election is to have effect.

(11) Nothing in section 357GA(5) prevents the election having effect in relation to the accounting period of the company which ends on 30 June 2016 or any subsequent accounting period.

(12) Subsection (13) applies to an amount of relevant IP income of a company if—

(a) the company is not a new entrant,

(b) the income is properly attributable to a new qualifying IP right which was assigned to the company, or in respect of which an exclusive licence was granted to the company, during the period beginning on 2 January 2016 and ending on 1 July 2016, and

(c) the income accrued to the company during the period beginning on 1 July 2016 and ending on 1 January 2017.

(13) The income is to be treated for the purposes of Part 8A of CTA 2010 as being properly attributable to an old qualifying IP right.

(14) Expressions used in subsections (12) and (13) and in Part 8A of CTA 2010 have the meaning they have in that Part.

GENERAL NOTE

The patent box relief, for UK companies exploiting UK or European patents, will only remain in its current form until 30 June 2021. It will only be available in its current form to companies that have elected into the regime in respect of accounting periods ending on or before 30 June 2016, so an election into the current regime should be made by 30 June 2018, at the latest.

There are therefore two new sets of rules. The first covers accounting periods beginning on or after 1 July 2021 and companies that are "new entrants", i.e. where the first accounting period for which a patent box election is to apply begins on or after 1 July 2016. These rules are at new CTA 2010 Pt 8A Ch 2A. New Chs 2B, 3 and 4 cover the situation where a company is not a new entrant and the accounting period begins before 1 July 2021, but where new intellectual property is brought into the regime. So there are now three sets of rules, including the original rules that apply to companies that have elected in to the current regime and which do not have new intellectual property.

A company can also elect to be a new entrant for patent box purposes (new CTA 2010 s 357A(11)).

The main difference, which is required by the outcome of the Base Erosion and Profit Shifting (BEPS) project, is that there must be a link between the patent on which the relief is claimed and the company carrying on the relevant research and development. The other main change is that the new regime requires streaming of income and expenses, i.e. a direct matching of income with the associated expenses. Under, the current regime, it is possible to apportion a company's turnover between the sale of patented and non-patented items, and apply that fraction to the overall profit figure in calculating the profits eligible for patent box relief. Streaming is only an option under the current regime.

Furthermore, in most cases this streaming must be done on a patent-by-patent or product-by-product basis.

Basic rules unchanged

The basic rules for the patent box remain the same, in terms of the definitions of types of intellectual property, qualifying companies, and the development and management conditions. Similarly, the rules on elections in and out of the regime are largely unchanged.

Transfer of trades

Section 64(5) introduces a new provision, CTA 2010 s 357GCA, which allows the benefit of a patent box claim to be transferred where there is a transfer of a trade from one company to another. In effect, expenditure by the transferor on relevant R&D or IP is treated as expenditure by the transferee company for patent box purposes and the transferee is not treated as a new entrant as long as the transferor was not a new entrant.

Regime for new entrants, and for all companies after 30 June 2021

New CTA 2010 s 357BF gives the steps required to determine the relevant IP profits:

Step 1 – compute the income of the trade, excluding finance income, and divide into two streams; "the relevant IP income stream" and the "standard income stream".

Finance income is defined in new s 357BG and includes credits which are treated as receipts of the trade in respect of loan relationships or in respect of derivative contracts, amounts recognised as arising from a financial asset under generally accepted accounting practice and any return to the company that is economically equivalent to interest.

Step 2 – divide the relevant IP income stream into "relevant IP income sub-streams", with each sub-stream comprising either an individual patent ("an individual IP right sub-stream"), a sub-stream relevant to a specific IP item (a "product sub-stream") or a sub-stream relevant to a specific process (a process sub-stream).

NB This level of computational detail may not be necessary if the company is entitled to make a global streaming election under the small claims treatment.

An IP item is an item in respect of which a qualifying IP right held by the company has been granted or an item incorporating two or more such items. An IP process is a process in respect of which a qualifying IP right held by the company has been granted, or a process which incorporates one or more such processes.

Two or more IP items or IP processes may be treated as being of a particular kind if they are substantially the same as each other bearing in mind the items incorporated in them and the purposes for which they are intended to be used.

A product sub-stream or process sub-stream is permissible, rather than an individual IP right sub-stream, if it would not be reasonably practicable to apportion income between individual IP right sub-streams for a product or it might be reasonably practicable to do so but it would then not be reasonably practicable to apply any of the subsequent steps in determining the relevant IP profits or losses of the period.

Step 3 – take the debits that are brought into account in calculating the trading profits, other than excluded debits, and allocate them on a just and reasonable basis between the standard income stream and each of the relevant IP income sub-streams.

For the purposes of Step 3, excluded debits are defined at s 357BI and include debits treated as expenses of a trade under the loan relationships or derivative contracts rules, the amounts of additional deductions for expenditure on research into development, and the amounts of additional deductions in respect of qualifying expenditure on television programmes, video games and theatrical productions, in Pts 13, 15A, 15B and 15C CTA 2010.

Step 4 – deduct from each relevant IP income sub-stream the amounts allocated against the sub-stream at Step 3. Also deduct the routine return figure for the sub-stream.

The aggregate of the relevant IP income sub-streams at this point is referred to as the "qualifying residual profit" or QRP of the trade (s 357BK(9)).

Step 5 – adjust for the marketing assets return, either under the small claims regime or under the normal regime.

Step 6 – multiply the resultant figure for each sub-stream by the R&D fraction for that sub-stream.

Step 7 – add together the amounts of the relevant IP income sub-streams.

Step 8 – add any amounts relating to relief in respect of profits prior to the granting of the IP right to this amount.

The resultant figure is either the relevant IP profits of the trade for the relevant accounting period or, if negative, it is the relevant IP loss for the accounting period.

Relevant IP Income

Relevant IP income is defined at s 357BH under five sub-headings, and is subject to excluded income, defined at s 357BHB.

Sales Income

Sales income includes income from the sale of a patented item, items incorporating one or more patented items or items which are wholly or mainly designed to be incorporated into either the patented item or an item incorporating the patented item. Packaging is specifically excluded unless the packaging performs an essential function for the use of the item.

Licence Fees

Licence income is any licence fee or royalty which grants another person rights in respect of a qualifying IP right held by the company or any other right in respect of a qualifying item or process. Where there is an agreement granting any such right, this head includes income from any other right granted for the same purposes as those for which that right was granted.

A qualifying process is a process where the company holds a qualifying IP right in respect of it.

Proceeds of Sale

This includes any income arising from the sale or other disposal of a qualifying IP right or of an exclusive licence in respect of such a right.

Damages for Infringement

This includes any amounts received by the company in respect of an infringement or alleged infringement of a qualifying IP right, as long as that right was held by the company at the time of actual or alleged infringement.

Other Compensation

This is any amount of damages, insurance or other compensation, other than infringement payments which is received by the company in respect of an event. It must be paid in respect of any items that fell within the sales income heading and must represent a loss of income which would have been relevant IP income if it had been received by the company at the time of the event.

Damages for infringement or other compensation (the last two categories) is only relevant IP income if the event or any part of it occurred when the company was a qualifying company and that company had elected into the patent box regime. Insofar as only part of an event qualified under this provision, a just and reasonable apportionment of any compensatory amounts received must be made.

Notional Royalty

This provision applies where the company does not actually sell an item which includes or is a patented invention. Instead, the company might have an appropriate right over a process so that it is the results of the process that are sold, whether a manufactured item or a service. In this case, s 357BHA permits the calculation of a notional royalty. This is the proportion of its income which it would have to pay to another person for the right to exploit the qualifying IP right, if the company did not otherwise have rights over that intellectual property. This notional royalty can be treated as if it were relevant IP income, instead. The company must act in accordance with Art 9 of the OECD Model Tax Convention and in accordance with the OECD Transfer Pricing Guidelines in computing this notional royalty.

This only applies to patents under the UK or European patent legislation or the appropriate intellectual property regimes of certain EEA jurisdictions. It does not extend to the supplementary protection certificates, plant breeder's right or plant variety rights detailed at s 357BB, to which the rest of the patent box legislation applies.

Excluded income

Having computed the overall income for patent box purposes, a deduction must be made for anything that is within the category of excluded income, in s 357BHB, being ring-fenced income from oil extraction activities or rights and income properly attributable to a non-exclusive licence, on a just and reasonable apportionment. Where a company holds a licence which confers both exclusive and non-exclusive rights on the company, a further apportionment is required as if there were two separate licences, one exclusive and one non-exclusive.

Mixed sources and mixed agreements

Section 357BHC requires adjustments in respect of mixed sources of income and amounts paid under mixed agreements. Mixed income means the sale proceeds where what is sold partly qualifies as relevant IP income and partly does not, but the items are sold together.

Mixed agreements operate similarly, referring to situations where there are sales, rights granted or disposals which are qualifying IP income as well as the sales of other items or rights or provisions of services within the same agreement which are not qualifying IP income. The general rule is that a just and reasonable apportionment must be made in arriving at the relevant IP income. However, where the amount of non-qualifying income is trivial in proportion to the total, it can be disregarded.

Routine Return

The routine return figure is a proxy for the sales that would have been made had there been no sales of a patented item. So the intention is to reduce the available relief by adjusting for sales that would have happened anyway. The routine return for a given sub-stream is 10% of the aggregate of routine deductions which have been made in calculating the company's trading profits for the accounting period and then allocated specifically to that sub-stream. Where an expense would have been a routine deduction, but was actually incurred by another group company, it is also to be included in the computation of the routine return figure relevant sub-stream. A just and reasonable apportionment will be made where the expense was incurred on behalf of other members of the group, too.

Section 357BJA defines the routine deductions as follows:

Capital allowances: any allowances under CAA 2001.

Costs of premises: any deductions in respect of premises occupied by the company.

Personnel costs: any deduction made by the company in respect of directors, employees or externally provided workers (as defined in s 1128 CTA 2009).

Plant and machinery costs: any deduction in respect of any plant or machinery used by the company. This refers to direct deductions in respect of plant and machinery, separate from any capital allowances claimed, above.

Professional services: this includes legal services, other than IP related legal services, financial services, including insurance, valuation or actuarial services, as well as services provided in connection with the administration or management of the company's directors and employees, and any other consultancy services.

Miscellaneous services: this includes the supply of water, fuel, power, telecommunication services, computing services including software, postal services, transportation of any items, collection, removal and disposal of refuse.

Certain items are specifically determined not to be routine deductions, in s 357BJB. These are:

Loan relationships and derivative contracts: debits treated as expenses of the trade by ss 297 or 573 CTA 2009.

R&D expenses: this is the actual R&D expenses incurred by the company, as long as it can either obtain an additional deduction under Pt 13 CTA 2009 or an R&D expenditure credit under CTA 2009 Pt 3 Ch 6A. Where an additional deduction has also been given, that is also to be excluded from the routine deductions.

Capital Allowances: allowances under CAA 2001 Pt 6 (for R&D) or CAA 2001 Pt 8 (patents).

R&D related employee share acquisitions: deductions allowed under Pt 12 CTA 2009, relief for employee share acquisitions, where the employee is employed by the company and is wholly or partly engaged directly in relevant research and development. If the employee is not wholly employed in research and development work, an appropriate proportion of the deduction must be taken.

Television production expenditure and video games development expenditure: these are the qualifying expenditures and additional deductions under Pts 15A and 15B CTA 2009, respectively. We note, however, that no adjustment is made in respect of qualifying expenditure on a theatrical production.

Notional Marketing Return

The intention here is to adjust for profits of the company that would have arisen simply because of its brand value. The small claims treatment is intended to be a simplified procedure whereby relatively small claims can be dealt with by a straight 25% deduction, while the normal route requires a transfer pricing-like computation of a notional marketing royalty for the brand value.

Where the notional marketing royalty is less than 10% of the amount available for relief after deduction of the routine return figure, no reduction in relief need be made. We understand that HMRC will generally accept, for example, that small companies which simply have a good reputation in their very narrow field are unlikely to require any adjustments under this provision.

Small Claims Treatment

The small claims treatment, in CTA 2010 s 357BN, provides a simplified approach to the notional marketing return for companies making smaller claims. A global streaming election in fact gives a simpler approach to the entire patent box computation.

A company that qualifies for this treatment can elect to make one of three elections:

— a notional royalty election,
— a small claims figure election, or
— a global streaming election.

Qualifying conditions

A company can make one of the elections as long as it carries on only one trade during the accounting period and its qualifying residual profit does not exceed the larger of £1 million in the period, or the relevant maximum for the period. This is £3 million divided by the total number of companies in the 51% group (reduced for short accounting periods). So a singleton company can opt for the small claims treatment with a QRP of £3 million.

A company is excluded from making any of the elections if it was within the new patent box regime in the previous four years, its QRP exceeded £1 million and it had not made one of the elections for that previous accounting period. Similarly, a company is excluded from making such an election if it was within the original regime in the previous 4 years, its QRP exceeded £1 million and it had not made a small claims election for that previous accounting period.

Notional royalty election – s 357BNA

A notional royalty election applies where the company is claiming relief on the basis of using a patented process or items to produce what it sells, whether goods or services. If the election is made, 75% of the company's IP-related income is treated as relevant IP profits for the period.

Small claims figure election – s 357BNB

If a small claims figure election is made, the QRP of the trade is compared to the small claims threshold, which is £1 million divided by the number of 51% group companies, and proportionately reduced for a short accounting period. If the QRP is less than 75% of the small claims threshold, then the routine return small claims figure for the sub-stream is 25% of the sub-stream QRP, following step 4, above.

Otherwise, the small claims figure for the sub-stream is given by A – [(A x SCT)/QRP], where:

A is the amount of the sub-stream following the deductions required by Step 4, above;

QRP is the qualifying residual profit of the trade of the company for the accounting period; and

SCT is the small claims threshold.

Global streaming election – s 357BNC

If a global streaming election is made, the company can claim patent box relief as if it had a single stream of relevant IP profit, rather than having to do separate calculations for each IP sub-stream or product sub-stream.

A company cannot make a global streaming election if it also has patent box assets to which the old regime applies. So this might be a case where a company with mixed 2013 and 2016 regime claims might prefer to elect fully into the 2016 regime.

Marketing Assets Return

Where the small claims treatment is not available or is not claimed, the marketing assets return figure must be computed under s 357BL. This is given by computing a notional marketing royalty in respect of the sub-stream and deducting any actual marketing royalties paid in respect of that sub-stream. If the actual marketing royalty is greater than the notional marketing royalty, or the difference between the two is less than 10% of the amount of the relevant IP income sub-stream following the routine deductions, then no adjustment is to be made.

The notional marketing royalty for a sub-stream is computed by s 357BLA, as the proportion of the income for a given relevant IP income sub-stream that the company would pay a third party for the right to exploit the relevant marketing assets had the company not actually owned them. However, adjustments only need to be made if, for the relevant IP income sub-stream, any income relevant to that sub-stream arises from the exploitation by the company of the marketing asset.

The determination of the appropriate percentage of the marketing asset makes the same assumptions as the calculation of the notional royalty referred to at s 357BHA, above.

Marketing assets are defined as anything in respect of which proceedings for passing off could be brought, including registered trademarks, anything that corresponds to a marketing asset recognised under the law of another country, any signs or indications which may serve, in trade, to designate the geographical origin of goods and services, and any information which relates to customers or potential customers of the company, or any other member of a group of which the company is a member and is intended to be used for marketing purposes.

The actual marketing royalty is the amount paid by the company to acquire any relevant marketing assets or the right to exploit such assets, as allocated to the relevant sub-stream (s 357BLB).

R&D Fraction

Section 357BL onwards explains the computation of the amount of relevant IP income that has been calculated for which relief can be given, calculated by reference to the proportion to the relevant R&D that the company has actually paid for. The R&D fraction is given by s 357BLA and is: $((D + S1) \times 1.3)/(D + S1 + S2 + A)$.

D is the company's qualifying expenditure on relevant R&D undertaken in-house

S1 is the qualifying expenditure on relevant R&D sub-contracted to unconnected persons

S2 is the company's qualifying expenditure on relevant R&D sub-contracted to connected persons

A is the company's qualifying expenditure on the acquisition of relevant qualifying IP rights.

In effect, the letters in the calculation give the proportion of R&D expenditure carried out by the company itself, or sub-contracted to unconnected persons, as a proportion of the overall expenditure on the relevant R&D and intellectual property.

The factor of 1.3 gives an uplift to take into account factors that do not come into the equation but which would dictate that a company should be entitled to a greater proportion of the expenditure for patent box relief. For the vast majority of SMEs, who carry out all of their research in-house, the overall result of this fraction would actually be 1.3, although the R&D fraction cannot exceed 1. In other words, for those companies with in-house R&D and nothing more, no adjustment for this element is required.

As a policy point, it is not obvious why R&D sub-contracted to another group company, for example, is not acceptable as being part of the numerator of the fraction as well as the denominator.

Factor D, in-house R&D, is defined at s 357BLB and requires that Conditions A and B are satisfied. Condition A is the expenditure that is incurred on staffing costs or software or consumable items, or on relevant payments to the subjects of clinical trials, or is qualifying expenditure on externally provided workers. Condition B is that the expenditure is attributable to relevant research and development undertaken by the company itself must relate to the qualifying IP right to which the income in the relevant sub-stream is attributable and relates to a qualifying IP right if it creates or contributes to the creation to the invention, is undertaken for the purposes of developing the invention, is undertaking for the purpose of developing ways in which the invention may be used or applied, or is undertaken for the purposes of developing any new items or process incorporating the invention.

A number of provisions within the R&D rules in CTA 2009 defining allowable costs are specifically applied within section 357BLB.

If the claimant company has made an election under CTA 2009 s 18A, to exclude from its corporation tax liability the results of non-UK permanent establishments, any expenditure by the non-UK PE is treated as expenditure on R&D sub contracted to a connected person, instead, so brought within S2.

S1, qualifying expenditure on relevant R&D sub-contracted to unconnected persons, is covered in s 357BIC. The expenditure must be made to a sub-contractor that is not connected (within the meaning of s 1122 CTA 2010) to the company, and must be for relevant R&D. If a payment is made for mixed purposes, an appropriate apportionment must be made to determine the amount that qualifies for use in the R&D fraction.

If the claimant company has made an election under CTA 2009 s 18A, to exclude from its corporation tax liability the results of non-UK permanent establishments, any expenditure by the non-UK PE is treated as expenditure on R&D sub contracted to a connected person, instead, so brought within S2.

S2, qualifying expenditure on relevant R&D sub-contracted to connected persons, is explained by s 357BLD. This is expenditure incurred in making a payment to a sub-contractor in respect of relevant research and development contracted out by the company to the sub-contractor, where the company and the sub-contractor are connected within the meaning given by s 1122 CTA 2020. Again, an appropriate apportionment needs to be made of any mixed payments.

As already noted, S2 also includes amounts excluded from D and S1 by virtue of the non-UK PE rules.

A, qualifying expenditure on the acquisition of relevant qualifying IP rights, is defined at s 357BLE as the expenditure incurred by the company during the relevant period on the acquisition of a relevant qualifying IP right or of an exclusive licence in respect of such a right. Expenditure also falls into this category where it is made in return for disclosure of an item or process and the company applies for and is granted a relevant qualifying IP right in respect of that item or process.

For the purposes of an individual IP right sub-stream the qualifying IP right must be one to which the income in the sub stream is attributable. Where the sub-stream is a product sub stream the qualifying IP right must be one granted in respect of an item incorporated in a multi-item IP to which income of that sub-stream is attributable.

Each of these relevant factors is taken over a relevant period, defined in s 357BLF. The relevant period ends on the last day of the appropriate accounting period but begins either on the relevant day or such earlier day as the company may elect. The relevant day is 1 July 2013 where the accounting period begins before 1 July 2021 and the company is a new entrant, so this applies to companies that enter the patent box system by election in respect of accounting periods starting on or after 1 July 2016. Otherwise, the relevant day is 1 July 2016, so this will apply to all companies for accounting periods starting on or after 1 July 2021.

A company can elect for an earlier date as long as it is not more than 20 years before the last day of the accounting period.

If the last day of the accounting period is on or after 1 July 2036, the relevant period is the period of 20 years ending with that day.

Expenditure is to be treated as incurred during the relevant period if and only if it is allowable as a deduction in calculating the profits of the trade for corporation tax purposes for an accounting period which falls in whole or in part within the relevant period.

Section 357BLG applies if the accounting period begins before 1 July 2021 and the company is a new entrant, so that the relevant period begins on 2 July 2013 but the company has insufficient information about its expenditure in the period between 1 July 2013 and 30 June 2016 to be able to calculate the R&D fraction for the sub-stream. For accounting periods beginning on or after 1 July 2019, the company can elect for the relevant period to start on 1 July 2016. For earlier accounting periods the company may elect to apply the R&D fraction as if the relevant period were the period of three years ending with the last day of the accounting period. In this case, furthermore, the computation can be based on expenditure on R&D for the company's trade as a whole rather that in respect of specific sub-streams. These provisions recognise the reality that, since the current patent box relief did not require this level of analysis of R&D expenditure, companies might otherwise be excluded from the new regime simply because the new legislation requires more detailed records than the company would have been keeping.

Section 357BLH allows the R&D fraction to be increased in exceptional circumstances. The computation is by reference to the 'value fraction' for the sub-stream, which is the fraction, on a just and reasonable assessment, which represents the proportion of the value of the qualifying IP rights properly attributable to the R&D undertaken by the company itself or on behalf of the company by persons not connected with it. If the R&D fraction for the sub-stream would be at least 0.325 but is less than the value fraction, then the R&D fraction can be increased to the value fraction by election to an officer of HMRC on or before the last day on which an amendment of the company's tax return for the accounting period could be made under FA 1998 Sch 18 para 15.

Profits arising before Grant of Right

Section 357BM allows a company to claim patent box relief in respect of profits arising before a patent is actually granted. It also allows the company to claim relief where the company disposed of the rights in the invention or the licence before the right was granted.

Generally speaking, in the year in which the patent is granted, the company can claim to add to its patent box relief the aggregate of the relevant IP profits of the trade for each relevant accounting period as if the right had been granted on the relevant day. The relevant day is the later of:

— the first day of the period of 6 years ending with the date that the right is granted;
— the date on which an application for the grant of the patent was filed; or
— the date on which a licence was granted, where a company holds an exclusive licence.

This extension only applies to patents under UK or EU legislation or under the specified rules of certain EEA countries.

The relief only applies where the accounting periods concerned are those for which an election made by the company under s 357A has effect and during which the company is a qualifying company, but for the fact that the relevant IP right has not yet been granted or has already been sold. Where the company is not a qualifying company for the accounting period because the appropriate IP right has not yet been granted, the company is to be treated as if it were a qualifying company for that accounting period. Similarly, if the company is not a qualifying company for an accounting period in which the right has been granted, because the company has disposed of the rights or licence before the grant of the right, the company is to be treated as if it were a qualifying company for that accounting period.

Income from New IP

New Ch 2B modifies the rules for new entrants for cases where the accounting period begins before 1 July 2021 and the company is not a new entrant (i.e. it has elected into the patent box regime in respect of accounting periods ending no later than 30 June 2016), but some of the relevant IP income brought into account in calculating the profits of the trader is attributable to a new qualifying IP right (CTA 2010 s 357BO).

Section 357BP distinguishes between "new qualifying IP rights" and "old qualifying IP rights". A new qualifying IP right is one which meets Conditions A, B or C. An old qualifying IP right is one that does not meet any of those conditions.

Condition A is that the right was granted or issued to the company in response to an application filed on or after the relevant date, which is 1 July 2016. Condition B is that the right was assigned to the company on or after the relevant date and Condition C is that an exclusive licence in respect of the right was granted to the company on or after the relevant date.

In each case, the relevant date is 1 July 2016, unless the right was assigned or the licence granted by a person who was not within the charge to corporation tax and not liable to a foreign tax designated by Regulations made by the Treasury in respect of another country's patent box relief. If the person assigning the right or granting the licence was connected with the company at the time of the assignment or grant, and one of the main purposes of the person or the company in being party to the assignment or grant was the avoidance of tax, the relevant date is 2 January 2016. No further assistance is given by the legislation in terms of the meaning of the avoidance of tax, so we must assume that it is given a very wide reading.

Where this provision applies, a global streaming election cannot be made by the company.

The Modifications

Section 357BQ sets out the modifications to be applied in these cases. The main change is that in Step 2 of section 357 BF it is necessary to analyse the company's income into sub-streams consisting of income properly attributable to old qualifying IP rights ("an old IP rights sub-stream") and income attributable to new qualifying IP rights("a new IP rights sub-stream"). In other words, if a product is currently being sold and pattern box under the current regime is being claimed in respect of that product, then a new qualifying IP right is obtained on or after 1 July 2016, and incorporated into that product, it will be necessary to break down the income from that product into sub-streams relating to the old and new IP rights, unless you are able to persuade HMRC that you can continue to claim patent box relief on a product basis.

In determining an R&D fraction, as regards the new IP income sub-stream it will be necessary to treat the company as if it were a new entry.

Step 7 is then applied to individual IP rights sub-streams and each product sub-stream. And Step 8 requires the aggregation of all the various sub-streams.

The rules for multi IP products are amended accordingly to ask whether it would be reasonable practicable to apportion the income between individual IP rights sub-steams or individual IP right sub-streams and an old IP rights sub-stream. There are then detailed rules as to how to compute the relief where there is a multi IP product and the income is allocated to a product sub-stream, and where there are both old and new qualifying IP rights incorporated into the multi IP item. If the value of the multi IP item is wholly or mainly attributable to the old qualifying IP, or if the old IP percentage is 80% or more, all of the income relating to that item can be treated as if it was attributable only to the old qualifying IP rights so that Step 2 can apply to the old qualifying IP rights sub-stream and there is no need for a product sub-stream.

If the old IP percentage is between 20% and less than 80%, the appropriate proportion of the income must be attributed to old and new IP rights sub-streams.

In each case, the old IP percentage is found by dividing the number of items incorporated in the multi IP item in respect of which an old qualifying IP right has been granted by the total number of items in respect of either old or new qualifying IP rights held by the company have been granted. So this is a simple numerical test, rather than requiring an allocation of income according to value between various IP rights.

Commencement

The commencement provisions in relation to this legislation are complex. The amendments have effect in relation to accounting periods beginning on or after 1 July 2016. However, where a company has an accounting period that straddles that date, or which straddles 1 July 2021, for the purposes of the patent box the period falling before the relevant date and the period falling on or after that date are treated as separate accounting periods and amounts brought into account for the purposes of calculating corporation tax profits of any company are apportioned to the separate accounting periods on a just and reasonable basis.

If a company has previously elected out of the patent box regime, under s 357GA(5) CTA 2010, the restriction in that provision as to how long they must wait before they are allowed to re-elect into the patent box regime is disapplied so that companies can return to the patent box regime before 30 June 2016 regardless of that restriction. The election must specify the company's accounting period that ends on 30 June 2016, or earlier, as being the first accounting period for which the election is to have effect.

If a company is not a new entrant but income is attributable to a new qualifying IP right assigned to the company or in respect of which a licence was granted to the company between 2 January 2016 and ending 1 July 2016, and income accrued to the company during the period beginning 1 July 2016 and ending 1 January 2017 that income is to be treated as being attributable to an old qualifying IP right.

Miscellaneous

65 Power to make regulations about the taxation of securitisation companies

(1) Section 624 of CTA 2010 (power to make regulations about the application of the Corporation Tax Acts in relation to securitisation companies) is amended in accordance with subsections (2) to (4).

(2) In subsection (1), for "Corporation Tax Acts" substitute "Taxes Acts".

(3) In subsection (2), for "Corporation Tax Acts" substitute "Taxes Acts".

(4) In subsection (9), after "section" insert "—

the Taxes Acts" has the meaning given by section 118(1) of TMA 1970, and".

(5) In section 625 of CTA 2010 (regulations: supplementary provision) in subsection (3) (power to include retrospective provision) after "may" insert ", insofar as they concern the application of the Corporation Tax Acts in relation to a securitisation company,".

GENERAL NOTE

This section amends the regulation making powers of CTA 2009 ss 624 and 625, which permit regulations to be made to govern the tax treatment of securitisation companies, to enable regulations to be made regarding the application or non-application of the Taxes Acts, as opposed to the Corporation Tax Acts, as is currently the case. The intention behind the amendments introduced by this section is to enable the Taxation of Securitisation Companies Regulations 2006 (SI 2006/3296) to be amended to provide that payments made by a securitisation company on certificates that carry an entitlement on each interest payment date to receive an amount equal to the excess cash in the securitisation company at that date, after all its other expenses have been discharged, will not be treated as being annual payments. HMRC currently consider that this is the generally the case and the intention behind the proposed amendment to the regulations is to avoid clearances having to be sought on this point for tax opinions that are required to be provided to ratings agencies in connection with securitisation transactions.

66 Hybrid and other mismatches

Schedule 10 contains provision that counteracts, for corporation tax purposes, hybrid and other mismatches that would otherwise arise.

67 Insurance companies carrying on long-term business

(1) Part 2 of FA 2012 (insurance companies carrying on long-term business) is amended as follows.

(2) In section 73 (the I-E basis), in step 4—

(a) for "(but not below nil) by the" substitute "by the relievable", and

(b) at the end of the step insert—

"In this step, "the relievable amount" of a non-trading deficit means so much of the deficit as does not exceed the total of—

(a) the amount given by the calculation required by step 1,

(b) the amount given by the calculation required by step 2, and

(c) any amount of an I-E receipt under section 92 brought into account under step 3."

(3) In section 88 (loan relationships, derivative contracts and intangible fixed assets), in subsection (6), for "excess—" and paragraphs (a) and (b), substitute "excess is treated for the purposes of section 76 as a deemed BLAGAB management expense for that period."

(4) In section 126 (restrictions in respect of non-trading deficit), in subsection (2), for "would have under section 388" to the end substitute "has, calculated by reference only to credits and debits—

(a) arising in respect of such of the company's loan relationships as are debtor relationships (see section 302(6) of CTA 2009), and

(b) referable, in accordance with Chapter 4, to the company's basic life assurance and general annuity business."

(5) The amendments made by this section have effect in relation to accounting periods beginning on or after the day on which this Act is passed.

GENERAL NOTE

Section 67 makes three changes to the rules for the corporate taxation of long-term business in FA 2012 Pt 2. The changes will take effect for accounting periods that begin on or after 15 September 2016.

The rules in FA 2012 Pt 2 were a significant change on the previous regime and were the fruit of a long running, positive consultation process between HMRC and the insurance industry. Experience has shown that the rules generally work well in practice but their application over the last three years has identified a number of "snags" where the legislation does not work as intended. Section 67 corrects those defects.

Section 67(2) addresses a drafting error that previously permitted a non-trading deficit from a company's loan relationships to be offset against the minimum profits charge that may arise under FA 2012 s 93. The change ensures that the maximum "relievable amount" against the minimum profits charge is the sum of the company's income, gains and deemed receipts referable to BLAGAB. This amendment prevents the offset of any deficit against the minimum profits charge.

Section 67(3) provides that an excess of debits on intangible fixed assets within the meaning of CTA 2009 Part 8 referable to BLAGAB is to be treated as a deemed BLAGAB management expense of the period in which the excess arises rather than being carried forward and relieved in the next accounting period. This makes the rule for intangible fixed assets consistent with those for loan relationships and derivative contracts. It is unclear why the previous inconsistency existed in the original legislation but it was clearly unintended.

Finally, FA 2012 s 126 provides a restriction on the amount of BLAGAB trade loss available for offset against total profits or surrender as group relief by reference to the amount of any non-trading deficit under the loan relationship or derivative rules, ignoring any credits or debits that arise on the company's creditor relationships. The restriction as originally enacted operated by reference to the company's total non-trading deficits when it should have been by reference to non-trading deficits referable to BLAGAB only since otherwise it was not a like for like restriction.

Section 67(4) now makes it clear that it is only non-trading deficits referable to BLAGAB that are used to restrict the amount of the BLAGAB trade loss.

The policy reason for the restriction remains unchanged; to prevent double relief for the same deficit because it will have been included in the measure of I-E profit.

68 Taking over payment obligations as lessee of plant or machinery

(1) In Part 20 of CTA 2010 (tax avoidance involving leasing plant or machinery), after section 894 insert—

"CHAPTER 3

CONSIDERATION FOR TAKING OVER PAYMENT OBLIGATIONS AS LESSEE TREATED AS INCOME

894A Consideration for taking over payment obligations as lessee treated as income

(1) This section applies where under any arrangements—

(a) a company chargeable to corporation tax (C) agrees to take over obligations of another person (D) as lessee under a lease of plant or machinery,

(b) as a result of that agreement C, or a person connected with C, becomes entitled to income deductions (whether deductions in calculating income or from total profits), and

(c) a payment is payable to C, or a person connected with C, by way of consideration for that agreement.

(2) The payment is treated for the purposes of corporation tax as income received by C in the period of account in which C takes over the obligations mentioned in subsection (1)(a).

(3) Subsection (2) does not apply if and to the extent that the payment is (apart from this section)—

(a) charged to tax on C, or a person connected with C, as an amount of income,

(b) brought into account in calculating for tax purposes any income of C or a person connected with C, or

(c) brought into account for the purposes of any provision of CAA 2001 as a disposal receipt, or proceeds from a balancing event or disposal event, of C or a person connected with C.

(4) It does not matter how C takes over the obligations of D (whether by assignment, novation, variation or replacement of the contract, by operation of law or otherwise).

(5) In this section—

"arrangements" include any scheme, arrangement, understanding, transaction or series of transactions (whether or not legally enforceable);

"lease of plant or machinery" means any kind of agreement or arrangement under which sums are paid for the use of, or otherwise in respect of, plant or machinery;

"payment" includes the provision of any benefit, the assumption of any liability or the transfer of money or money's worth (and "payable" is to be construed accordingly);

"payment by way of consideration" means any payment made, directly or indirectly, in consequence of or otherwise in connection with, the agreement mentioned in subsection (1)(a), where it is reasonable to assume the agreement would not have been made unless the arrangements included provision for the payment.

(6) Any priority rule (other than section 212(1) of FA 2013 (general anti-abuse rule to have priority over other rules)) has effect subject to this section, despite the terms of the priority rule.

(7) For that purpose "priority rule" is a rule (however expressed) to the effect that particular provisions have effect to the exclusion of, or otherwise in priority to, anything else.

(8) Examples of priority rules are section 464 of CTA 2009 (priority of loan relationships rules) and section 6(1) of TIOPA 2010 (effect to be given to double taxation arrangements despite anything in any enactment)."

(2) In Chapter 6 of Part 13 of ITA 2007 (avoidance involving leases of plant or machinery), after section 809ZF insert—

"809ZFA Consideration for taking over payment obligations as lessee treated as income

(1) This section applies where under any arrangements—

(a) a person within the charge to income tax (P) agrees to take over obligations of another person (Q) as lessee under a lease of plant or machinery,

(b) as a result of that agreement P, or a person connected with P, becomes entitled to income deductions (whether deductions in calculating income or from total profits), and

(c) a payment is payable to P, or a person connected with P, by way of consideration for that agreement.

(2) The payment is treated for the purposes of income tax as income received by P in the tax year in which P takes over the obligations mentioned in subsection (1)(a).

(3) Subsection (2) does not apply if and to the extent that the consideration is (apart from this section)—

(a) charged to tax on P, or a person connected with P, as an amount of income,
(b) brought into account in calculating for tax purposes any income of P or a person connected with P, or
(c) brought into account for the purposes of any provision of CAA 2001 as a disposal receipt, or proceeds from a balancing event or disposal event, of P or a person connected with P.

(4) It does not matter how P takes over the obligations of Q (whether by assignment, novation, variation or replacement of the contract, by operation of law or otherwise).

(5) In this section—

"arrangements" include any scheme, arrangement, understanding, transaction or series of transactions (whether or not legally enforceable);
"lease of plant or machinery" means any kind of agreement or arrangement under which sums are paid for the use of, or otherwise in respect of, plant or machinery;
"payment" includes the provision of any benefit, the assumption of any liability or the transfer of money or money's worth (and "payable" is to be construed accordingly),;
"payment by way of consideration" includes a payment made, directly or indirectly, in consequence of or otherwise in connection with, the agreement mentioned in subsection (1)(a), where it is reasonable to assume the agreement would not have been made unless the arrangements included provision for the payment.

(6) Any priority rule (other than section 212(1) of FA 2013 (general anti-abuse rule to have priority over other rules)) has effect subject to this section, despite the terms of the priority rule.

(7) For that purpose "priority rule" is a rule (however expressed) to the effect that particular provisions have effect to the exclusion of, or otherwise in priority to, anything else.

(8) An example of a priority rule is section 6(1) of TIOPA 2010 (effect to be given to double taxation arrangements despite anything in any enactment)."

(3) This section applies to agreements of the kind mentioned in section 894A(1)(a) of CTA 2010 or section 809ZFA of ITA 2007 that are made on or after 25 November 2015.

GENERAL NOTE

Section 68 introduces a new chapter into Pt 20 of the Corporation Tax Act 2010 and a new section in Ch 6 Pt 13 of the Income Tax Act 2007, which ensure that where a taxable person or person connected with them receives payment for taking over existing obligations in relation to plant and machinery leases that will result in tax deductible expenditure, that initial receipt will be treated as taxable income in the period of account in which the company agrees to take over the lease obligations.

The new provisions take effect for relevant transactions taking place on or after 25 November 2015, essentially meaning that they represent retrospective legislation.

The introduction of the new provisions is in response to DOTAS disclosures that HMRC received regarding arrangements that sought to generate non-taxable consideration when taking over a tax deductible lease obligation. Normally this would have arisen when the receipt was capital in nature and not subject to taxation.

The legislation will apply to any situation, and by whatever method, the company or other taxable person takes over the lease obligations. The concept of "consideration" is widely defined and seeks to capture any payment or valuable benefit referable, directly or indirectly, to the agreement.

PART 3

INCOME TAX AND CORPORATION TAX

Capital Allowances

69 Capital allowances: designated assisted areas

In section 45K of CAA 2001 (expenditure on plant and machinery for use in designated assisted area), in subsection (1)(b) (condition that expenditure is incurred in the period of 8 years beginning with 1 April 2012), for "1 April 2012" substitute "the date on which the area is (or is treated as) designated under subsection (2)(a)".

GENERAL NOTE

This section amends s 45K Capital Allowances Act 2001 relating to first-year allowances ("FYAs") for expenditure incurred by a company on plant and machinery for use in designated assisted areas falling within Enterprise Zones.

FYAs at the rate of 100% have been available since 1 April 2012. Initially, expenditure had to be incurred before 1 April 2017, but this was extended to 1 April 2020 by FA 2014 s 64(5)(a) with effect from 17 July 2014.

The existence of a specific end-date meant that the relief was less beneficial in areas which were designated later rather than earlier. Consequently, this section amends the rules so that first-year allowances are available for expenditure incurred in a period of eight years beginning with the date on which the area is (or is treated as) designated.

FYAs are available only for expenditure within designated assisted areas, which are not identical with the Enterprise Zones themselves.

The relief is restricted to UK resident companies liable to corporation tax in respect of a trade or a mining, transport or similar undertaking, and the expenditure must be on new and unused plant. There are sundry exceptions to eligible companies based on European state aid rules. Thus, for example, agricultural firms do not qualify, and nor do vehicles or transport equipment acquired by transport undertakings.

The plant must be acquired for use primarily in a designated assisted area, and anti-avoidance rules exist to ensure this requirement is not abused. Inter alia, there is scope for a claw-back of allowances where the plant begins to be used primarily outside of the designated assisted area within five years. Furthermore, the expenditure must be incurred for the purposes of expanding a business or starting a new type of business not previously carried on by the company.

70 Capital allowances: anti-avoidance relating to disposals

(1) Part 2 of CAA 2001 (plant and machinery allowances) is amended as follows.

(2) Section 213 (relevant transactions: sale, hire purchase etc and assignment) is amended in accordance with subsections (3) and (4).

(3) In subsection (1) for the words from "enters" to "("S")" substitute "and another person ("S") enter into a relevant transaction".

(4) After subsection (3) insert—

"(4) For the purposes of this Chapter, references to the disposal value of the plant or machinery under a relevant transaction are references to the disposal value that is to be brought into account by S as a result of the sale, contract or assignment in question."

(5) Section 215 (transactions to obtain tax advantages) is amended in accordance with subsections (6) to (8).

(6) In subsection (1)—

(a) after "restricted" insert ", and balancing charges are imposed or increased,", and

(b) for the words from "B" to "S" substitute "B and S enter into a relevant transaction".

(7) In subsection (4)—

(a) after "includes" insert "—
    (a) ", and

(b) at end insert ", and
    (b) avoiding liability for the whole or part of a balancing charge to which a person would otherwise be liable."

(8) After subsection (4) insert—

"(4A) If the tax advantage relates to the disposal value of the plant or machinery under the relevant transaction (whether by obtaining a more favourable allowance or by avoiding the whole or part of a balancing charge) then—

(a) the applicable section is section 218ZB, and

(b) the tax advantage is to be disregarded for the purposes of subsection (6) and (8)(b)."

(9) After section 218ZA (restrictions on writing down allowances: section 215) insert—

"218ZB Disposal values: section 215

(1) If—

(a) this section applies as a result of section 215,

(b) a payment is payable to any person under the transaction, scheme or arrangement mentioned in that section,

(c) some or all of the payment would not (apart from this section) be taken into account in determining the disposal value of the plant or machinery under the relevant transaction, and

(d) as a result of the matters mentioned in paragraphs (b) and (c) S would otherwise obtain a tax advantage as mentioned in section 215(3) and (4),

the disposal value of the plant or machinery under the relevant transaction is to be adjusted in a just and reasonable manner so as to include an amount representing so much of the payment as would or would in effect cancel out the tax advantage.

(2) In subsection (1) "payment" includes the provision of any benefit, the assumption of any liability and any other transfer of money or money's worth, and "payable" is to be construed accordingly."

(10) In section 66 (list of provisions outside Chapter 5 about disposal values) insert at the appropriate place—

"section 218ZB　　　disposal of plant or machinery in avoidance cases"

(11) The amendments made by this section have effect in relation to transactions mentioned in section 213(1)(a), (b) or (c) of CAA 2001 that take place on or after 25 November 2015.

GENERAL NOTE

This section amends Capital Allowances Act 2001 in order to counter tax avoidance schemes which seek to reduce disposal values of plant or machinery for capital allowances purposes below the actual full value attributable to the disposal of those assets.

Apparently a number of relevant avoidance schemes had been disclosed to HMRC. Whilst the schemes differed in detail, the common theme was that the amount to be taken into account under the scheme as disposal value for capital allowances purposes was significantly less than the actual value of the plant or machinery being disposed of.

The difference in value was received, directly or indirectly, in such a way as to not form part of the disposal value for capital allowances purposes and did not otherwise attract any actual tax liability. Consequently, by bringing into his pool an artificially low disposal value such the pool balance remained high, the disposer continued to receive capital allowances significantly in excess of the actual economic depreciation of the plant or machinery whilst it was being used for qualifying activities.

The new rules take effect for transactions involving an "avoidance purpose" on or after 25 November 2015. On or after that date, s 215 is amended so that that the term "avoidance purpose" includes not only the obtaining of a more favourable allowance, but also the avoidance of a liability for the whole or part of a balancing charge to which a person would otherwise be liable

Furthermore, where on or after 25 November 2015, all or part of a receipt for the disposal of plant would not otherwise be taken into account in determining the disposal value of that plant, and hence gives rise to a tax advantage, the disposal value of the plant or machinery is adjusted in a just and reasonable manner so as to cancel out the tax advantage.

Trade and Property Business Profits

71 Trade and property business profits: money's worth

(1) ITTOIA 2005 is amended in accordance with subsections (2) and (3).

(2) In Chapter 3 of Part 2 (trade profits: basic rules), after section 28 insert—

"28A Money's worth

(1) Subsection (2) applies—

(a) for the purpose of bringing into account an amount arising in respect of a transaction involving money's worth entered into in the course of a trade, and

(b) if an amount at least equal to the amount that would be brought into account under that subsection is not otherwise brought into account as a receipt in calculating the profits of a trade under a provision of this Part other than a provision mentioned in subsection (3).

(2) For the purpose of calculating the profits of the trade, an amount equal to the value of the money's worth is brought into account as a receipt if, had the transaction involved money, an amount would have been brought into account as a receipt in respect of it.

(3) But where another provision of this Part makes express provision for the bringing into account of an amount in respect of money's worth as a receipt in calculating the profits of a trade (however expressed), that other provision applies instead of subsection (2)."

(3) In Chapter 3 of Part 3 (profits of property businesses), in section 272 (application of trading income rules), in the Table in subsection (2), at the appropriate place insert—

"section 28A   money's worth"

(4) CTA 2009 is amended in accordance with subsections (5) and (6).

(5) In Chapter 3 of Part 3 (trade profits: basic rules), after section 49 insert—

"49A Money's worth
   (1) Subsection (2) applies—
       (a) for the purpose of bringing into account an amount arising in respect of a transaction involving money's worth entered into in the course of a trade, and
       (b) if an amount at least equal to the amount that would be brought into account under that subsection is not otherwise brought into account as a receipt in calculating the profits of a trade under a provision of this Part other than a provision mentioned in subsection (3).

   (2) For the purpose of calculating the profits of the trade, an amount equal to the value of the money's worth is brought into account as a receipt if, had the transaction involved money, an amount would have been brought into account as a receipt in respect of it.

   (3) But where another provision of this Part makes express provision for the bringing into account of an amount in respect of money's worth as a receipt in calculating the profits of a trade (however expressed), that other provision applies instead of subsection (2)."

(6) In Chapter 3 of Part 4 (profits of property businesses), in section 210 (application of trading income rules), in the Table in subsection (2), at the appropriate place insert—

"section 49A   money's worth"

(7) The amendments made by this section have effect in relation to transactions entered into on or after 16 March 2016.

GENERAL NOTE

The courts have held, in a number of cases going back many years, that for tax purposes the receipt in the course of trading of "money's worth" must be taken into account in computing taxable profits. In more recent times this has apparently been challenged, presumably on the basis that the treatment of such items for tax purposes is, following ITTOIA s 25 and CTA 2009, conclusively determined by their treatment under GAAP to which earlier tax case law has no application. Section 71 puts the matter beyond doubt by introducing ITTOIA s 28A and (in identical terms) CTA 2009 s 49A for Income Tax and Corporation Tax purposes respectively.

In each case the provision applies where a transaction is entered into in the course of a trade such that (a) "money's worth" is received; and (b) if the transaction had instead involved the receipt of money, that money would have been brought into account as a receipt of the trade. The section provides in such cases that an amount equal to the value of the money's worth is to be brought into account as a receipt of the trade. The section is extended to apply to the profits of a rental business but does not apply where some other provision already requires such an amount to be brought into account.

The amendments are effective in respect of transactions entered into on or after 16 March 2016. The amendments do not, in the view of HMRC, change the law but merely confirm existing law and practice.

72 Replacement and alteration of tools
(1) Omit the following provisions (replacement and alteration of trade tools)—
   (a) section 68 of ITTOIA 2005 and the italic heading before that section, and

(b) section 68 of CTA 2009 and the italic heading before that section.

(2) In consequence of subsection (1)(a), in ITTOIA 2005—

(a) in subsection (1) of section 56A (cash basis accounting), omit the entry relating to section 68, and

(b) in section 272 (profits of a property business: application of trading income rules), in subsection (2), omit the entry in the table relating to section 68.

(3) In consequence of subsection (1)(b), in section 210 of CTA 2009 (profits of a property business: application of trading income rules), in subsection (2), omit the entry in the table relating to section 68.

(4) The amendments made by this section have effect in relation to expenditure incurred on or after the date in subsection (5).

(5) The date is—

(a) for corporation tax purposes, 1 April 2016, and

(b) for income tax purposes, 6 April 2016.

GENERAL NOTE

ITTOIA s 68 and CTA 2009 s 68 provide for tax relief for capital expenditure on the replacement or alteration of "tools". In HMRC's view the statutory relief was restricted to assets such as cutlery in a café, glasses in a public house and spanners in a garage. But it is understood that the wide definition of "tool" as "any implement, utensil or article" has led to a plethora of claims going far beyond those envisaged by HMRC, especially in the context of part-furnished accommodation for which "Wear and Tear Allowance" is not available. HMRC's response has been to repeal the provisions with effect from 6 April 2016 and 1 April 2016 for Income Tax and Corporation Tax purposes respectively.

HMRC justify the abolition of the relieving provisions by asserting that alternative means of tax relief for capital expenditure of this kind is available to traders through the capital allowance regime and to residential landlords through Replacement Domestic Items Relief introduced by s 73 Finance Act 2016. This is probably true in regard to items provided as part of a property business; it is difficult to think of any "implement, utensil or article" previously qualifying as a "tool" which would not now qualify as a "domestic item". For traders the position is not quite so straightforward. For one thing, there is some possibility hinted at in case law that there may be a category of items whose expected useful life is long enough to render the cost of acquisition or replacement capital expenditure, yet short enough that they fail the test of "permanent employment in the business" required to qualify as plant. It is to be hoped that HMRC would not seek to take such an unmeritorious point and that HMRC will accept that all expenditure by a trader which previously fell within s 68 will rank as expenditure on plant. All the time that Annual Investment Allowance is available in respect of this expenditure, the repeal of s 68 will make no practical difference to a trader. But where AIA is not available (either because it is used up by other expenditure on plant during the period or because expenditure on replacement tools exceeds the AIA limit), the repeal of s 68 will result in increased tax.

Property Business Deductions

73 Property business deductions: replacement of domestic items

(1) In Chapter 5 of Part 3 of ITTOIA 2005 (property income), after section 311 insert—

"Deduction for replacement of domestic items

311A Replacement domestic items relief

(1) This section applies if conditions A to D are met.

(2) Condition A is that a person ("P") carries on a property business in relation to land which consists of or includes a dwelling-house.

(3) Condition B is that—

(a) a domestic item has been provided for use in the dwelling-house ("the old item"),

(b) P incurs expenditure on a domestic item for use in the dwelling-house ("the new item"),

(c) the new item is provided solely for the use of the lessee,

(d) the new item replaces the old item, and

(e) following that replacement, the old item is no longer available for use in the dwelling-house.

(4) Condition C is that a deduction for the expenditure is not prohibited by the wholly and exclusively rule but would otherwise be prohibited by the capital expenditure rule (see subsection (15)).

(5) Condition D is that no allowance under CAA 2001 may be claimed in respect of the expenditure.

(6) In calculating the profits of the business, a deduction for the expenditure is allowed.

But this is subject to subsections (7) and (8).

(7) No deduction is allowed for expenditure in a tax year if—

(a) the business consists of or includes the commercial letting of furnished holiday accommodation (see Chapter 6), and
(b) the dwelling-house constitutes some or all of that accommodation for the tax year.

(8) No deduction is allowed for expenditure in a tax year if—

(a) the person has rent-a-room receipts in respect of the dwelling-house for the tax year, and
(b) section 793 or 797 (rent-a-room relief) applies in relation to those receipts.

(9) The basic amount of the deduction is as follows—

(a) where the new item is the same or substantially the same as the old item, the deduction is equal to the expenditure incurred by P on the new item;
(b) where the new item is not the same or substantially the same as the old item, the deduction is equal to so much of the expenditure incurred by P on the new item as does not exceed the expenditure which P would have incurred on an item which is the same or substantially the same as the old item.

Subsections (10) to (13) make further provision about the calculation of the deduction in certain cases.

(10) If P incurs incidental expenditure of a capital nature in connection with the disposal of the old item or the purchase of the new item, the deduction is increased by the amount of the incidental expenditure.

(11) If the old item is disposed of in part-exchange for the new item—

(a) the expenditure incurred by P on the new item is treated as including an amount equal to the value of the old item, and
(b) the deduction is reduced by that amount.

(12) If the old item is disposed of other than in part-exchange for the new item, the deduction is reduced by the amount or value of any consideration in money or money's worth which P or a person connected with P receives, or is entitled to receive, in respect of the disposal.

(13) For the purposes of subsection (12), where the old item is disposed of together with other consideration, the consideration in respect of the disposal mentioned in that subsection is taken not to include the amount of, or an amount equal to the value of, that other consideration.

(14) In this section, "domestic item" means an item for domestic use (such as furniture, furnishings, household appliances and kitchenware), and does not include anything that is a fixture.

"Fixture"—

(a) means any plant or machinery that is so installed or otherwise fixed in or to a dwelling-house as to become, in law, part of that dwelling-house, and
(b) includes any boiler or water-filled radiator installed in a dwelling-house as part of a space or water heating system.

"Plant or machinery" here has the same meaning as in Part 2 of CAA 2001.

(15) In this section—

"the capital expenditure rule" means the rule in section 33 (capital expenditure), as applied by section 272;
"lessee" means the person who is entitled to the use of the dwelling-house under a lease or other arrangement under which a sum is payable in respect of the use of the dwelling-house;
"the wholly and exclusively rule" means the rule in section 34 (expenses not wholly and exclusively for trade and unconnected losses), as applied by section 272."

(2) In Chapter 5 of Part 4 of CTA 2009 (property income), after section 250 insert—

"Deduction for replacement of domestic items

250A   Replacement domestic items relief

(1) This section applies if conditions A to D are met.

(2) Condition A is that a company ("C") carries on a property business in relation to land which consists of or includes a dwelling-house.

(3) Condition B is that—

(a) a domestic item has been provided for use in the dwelling-house ("the old item"),

(b) C incurs expenditure on a domestic item for use in the dwelling-house ("the new item"),

(c) the new item is provided solely for the use of the lessee,

(d) the new item replaces the old item, and

(e) following that replacement, the old item is no longer available for use in the dwelling-house.

(4) Condition C is that a deduction for the expenditure is not prohibited by the wholly and exclusively rule but would otherwise be prohibited by the capital expenditure rule (see subsection (14)).

(5) Condition D is that no allowance under CAA 2001 may be claimed in respect of the expenditure.

(6) In calculating the profits of the business, a deduction for the expenditure is allowed.

(7) But no deduction is allowed for expenditure in an accounting period if—

(a) the business consists of or includes the commercial letting of furnished holiday accommodation (see Chapter 6), and

(b) the dwelling-house constitutes some or all of that accommodation for the accounting period.

(8) The basic amount of the deduction is as follows—

(a) where the new item is the same or substantially the same as the old item, the deduction is equal to the expenditure incurred by C on the new item;

(b) where the new item is not the same or substantially the same as the old item, the deduction is equal to so much of the expenditure incurred by C on the new item as does not exceed the expenditure which C would have incurred on an item which is the same or substantially the same as the old item.

Subsections (9) to (12) make further provision about the calculation of the deduction in certain cases.

(9) If C incurs incidental expenditure of a capital nature in connection with the disposal of the old item or the purchase of the new item, the deduction is increased by the amount of the incidental expenditure.

(10) If the old item is disposed of in part-exchange for the new item—

(a) the expenditure incurred by C on the new item is treated as including an amount equal to the value of the old item, and

(b) the deduction is reduced by that amount.

(11) If the old item is disposed of other than in part-exchange for the new item, the deduction is reduced by the amount or value of any consideration in money or money's worth which C or a person connected with C receives, or is entitled to receive, in respect of the disposal.

(12) For the purposes of subsection (11), where the old item is disposed of together with other consideration, the consideration in respect of the disposal mentioned in that subsection is taken not to include the amount of, or an amount equal to the value of, that other consideration.

(13) In this section, "domestic item" means an item for domestic use (such as furniture, furnishings, household appliances and kitchenware), and does not include anything that is a fixture.

"Fixture"—

(a) means any plant or machinery that is so installed or otherwise fixed in or to a dwelling-house as to become, in law, part of that dwelling-house, and

(b) includes any boiler or water-filled radiator installed in a dwelling-house as part of a space or water heating system.

"Plant or machinery" here has the same meaning as in Part 2 of CAA 2001.

(14) In this section—

"the capital expenditure rule" means the rule in section 53 (capital expenditure), as applied by section 210;

"lessee" means the person who is entitled to the use of the dwelling-house under a lease or other arrangement under which a sum is payable in respect of the use of the dwelling-house;

"the wholly and exclusively rule" means the rule in section 54 (expenses not wholly and exclusively for trade and unconnected losses), as applied by section 210."

(3) In section 41 of TCGA 1992 (restriction of losses by reference to capital allowances and renewals allowances), in subsection (4), after paragraph (a) insert—

"(aa) any deduction under section 311A of ITTOIA 2005 or section 250A of CTA 2009 (replacement domestic items relief),".

(4) In section 308 of ITTOIA 2005 (furnished lettings), in subsection (1)(b), after "expenses" insert "of a revenue nature".

(5) In section 322 of ITTOIA 2005 (commercial letting of furnished holiday accommodation), after paragraph (za) in subsections (2) and (2A) insert—

"(zb) section 311A (replacement domestic items relief: see subsection (7)),".

(6) In section 248 of CTA 2009 (furnished lettings), in subsection (1)(b), after "expenses" insert "of a revenue nature".

(7) In section 264 of CTA 2009 (commercial letting of furnished holiday accommodation), before paragraph (a) in subsections (2) and (2A) insert—

"(za) section 250A (replacement domestic items relief: see subsection (7)),".

(8) The amendments made by this section have effect in relation to expenditure incurred on or after the date in subsection (9).

(9) The date is—

(a) for corporation tax purposes, 1 April 2016, and

(b) for income tax purposes, 6 April 2016.

74 Property business deductions: wear and tear allowance

(1) In Part 3 of ITTOIA 2005 (property income)—

(a) omit sections 308A to 308C and the italic heading before section 308A (wear and tear allowance), and

(b) in section 327 (capital allowances and loss relief: UK property business), in subsection (2), omit paragraph (c) and the "or" before that paragraph.

(2) The amendments made by subsection (1) have effect for the tax year 2016–17 and subsequent tax years.

(3) In Part 4 of CTA 2009 (property income)—

(a) omit sections 248A to 248C of CTA 2009 and the italic heading before section 248A (wear and tear allowance), and

(b) in section 269 (capital allowances and loss relief: UK property business), in subsection (2), omit paragraph (c) and the "or" before that paragraph.

(4) The amendments made by subsection (3) have effect in relation to accounting periods beginning on or after 1 April 2016.

(5) For the purposes of subsection (3), where a company has an accounting period beginning before 1 April 2016 and ending on or after that date ("the straddling period")—

(a) so much of the straddling period as falls before 1 April 2016, and so much of that period as falls on or after that date, are treated as separate accounting periods, and

(b) any amounts brought into account for the purposes of calculating for corporation tax purposes the profits of a property business for the straddling period are apportioned to the two separate accounting periods in accordance with section 1172 of CTA 2010 (time basis) or, if that method produces a result that is unjust or unreasonable, on a just and reasonable basis.

GENERAL NOTE

Sections 73 and 74

Capital allowances have long been denied for expenditure on plant and machinery provided for use in a dwelling-house except in the case of a commercial letting of furnished holiday accommodation in the UK or the EEA. Until 5 April 2011 (31 March 2011 for companies) extra-statutory concession B47 allowed taxpayers to claim a "wear and tear allowance" (WTA) equal to 10% of gross rental income (after adjusting for the payment by the landlord of any costs more normally borne by the tenant). As an alternative to WTA, a "renewals basis" could be claimed whereby a deduction could be claimed for the net cost of replacing plant and machinery items on a "like for like" basis, though this was seldom advantageous. For Income Tax purposes, WTA was put onto a statutory footing from 6 April 2011 by ITTOIA 2005 s 308A; for Corporation Tax purposes CT 2009 s 248A had the same effect from 1 April 2011. "Renewals basis" continued to be available as an alternative to WTA until 5 April 2013 (Income Tax) or 31 March 2013 (Corporation Tax) since when the statutory WTA has been the only route to relief. WTA has been available only in respect of a letting of a fully furnished property (that is, a dwelling-house "let with sufficient furniture, furnishings and equipment for normal residential use").

In a consultation document issued in July 2015 HMRC identified three main perceived inequities with WTA. First, that WTA should be denied to property businesses letting part-furnished or unfurnished property (which has also sometimes been the cause of dispute as to what provision of furniture is required to be "sufficient for normal residential use"). Second, that WTA is not related to actual expenditure incurred. Third, more specifically that – because relief is linked to rental income – landlords with similar levels of actual expenditure may get very different amounts of relief. The result, after consultation, was to replace WTA with a relief which looks remarkably like the "renewals basis" relief which existed until 2013.

The new rules are implemented for Income Tax purposes by ITTOIA 2005 s 311A and for Corporation Tax purposes by the substantially identical CTA 2009 s 250A.

The relief, styled Replacement Domestic Items Relief (RDIR) is given if four conditions are met: unlike the WTA which it replaces, no claim for RDIR is required.

The first condition is that the taxpayer carries on a property business in relation to land which consists of or includes a dwelling-house. Note that, unlike WTA, there is no requirement that the property be let fully furnished.

The second condition is that expenditure is incurred on the replacement of an existing "domestic item" in the dwelling-house with a new one (new in the sense only of different – there is no requirement that the "new" item be unused) and that the old item ceases to be available for use in the dwelling-house. The new item must be provided solely for the use of the lessee. This would appear to preclude any relief for the introduction to a letting business (as a replacement for an existing item) of any asset previously owned and used by the taxpayer outside the property letting business.

The consultation responses included the suggestion that, if any new relief was to be a proper substitute for capital allowances, it should apply to initial expenditure as well as to the cost of replacements: this was rejected on the questionable grounds that "this would require additional rules to prevent relief being given for personal use of the furniture, based on the market value of the furniture". However, it appears that if a property is purchased together with "domestic items" which are replaced immediately on acquisition, RDIR will be available on the cost of replacement items provided the old items have at some time been "provided" for the use of tenants.

The third condition is that the expenditure is capital expenditure incurred wholly and exclusively for the purposes of the business.

The final condition is that no capital allowance must be available for the expenditure. This would of itself prevent RDIR from being available for the letting of furnished holiday accommodation (for which capital allowances continue to be available), but in addition there is an express denial of relief for such lettings. Relief is also denied for lettings which benefit from rent-a-room relief – effectively RDIR is treated as being already included in the amount of the annual rent-a-room exemption.

"Domestic item" is defined to mean simply an item for domestic use, so includes anything from furniture to crockery but excludes anything that is a fixture (which, for avoidance of doubt, includes boilers and radiators). This exclusion is logical, though perhaps superfluous given the restriction of RDIR to capital expenditure: replacement of fixtures would normally rank as a repair to the dwelling and thus as tax-deductible revenue expenditure. It is not completely clear whether built-in appliances are "domestic items" within RDIR or "fixtures" replacement of which would be a repair, but in most cases it will make no practical difference.

The new rules quantify the amount of the relief as the expenditure incurred on the replacement asset plus the cost (if any) of disposing of the old asset, minus the sale proceeds (if any) of the old asset. Part-exchange of the old for the new is dealt with by treating the part-exchange value as both sale proceeds of the old and as part of the cost of the new, ensuring that only the net replacement cost is deductible. Where the new item is an improvement over the old, relief is restricted to the expenditure which would have been incurred on a "like for like" replacement, as was the case with the former renewals basis.

In summary, therefore, RDIR has some overtones of "back to the future", replicating as it does many of the features of the "renewals basis" which was available until 2012/13. The key difference is that in the past few taxpayers elected for "renewals basis" since it was almost always much more advantageous to claim WTA. Now, however, RDIR is the only game in town and the result will almost always be that the tax payable by landlords will increase.

The new relief applies to expenditure incurred after 5 April 2016 for Income Tax and 31 March 2016 for Corporation Tax and accordingly s 74 repeals the existing WTA rules from the same dates. Where a company accounting period straddles 31 March 2016 it is treated as if it comprised two separate accounting periods, with the old WTA rules applying to the period before 1 April 2016 and the new RDIR rules to the period after 31 March 2016.

Finally, note that TCGA 1992 s 41 is amended so that CGT losses are restricted if and to the extent that they are attributable to expenditure qualifying for RDIR, thus treating RDIR in the same way as capital allowances and renewal allowances. This is logical: the anomaly was that CGT losses were not restricted for WTA.

Transfer Pricing

75 Transfer pricing: application of OECD principles

(1) In section 164(4) of TIOPA 2010 (Part to be interpreted in accordance with OECD principles)—

    (a) in paragraph (a) after "2010" insert "as revised by the report, Aligning Transfer Pricing Outcomes with Value Creation, Actions 8–10 – 2015 Final Reports, published by the OECD on 5 October 2015", and

    (b) in the words after paragraph (b)—

        (i) for "such material" substitute "material which is", and

        (ii) for "as may be so designated" substitute "and which is designated for the time being by order made by the Treasury".

(2) In section 357GE(1) of CTA 2010 (other interpretation), in the definition of "the OECD transfer pricing guidelines", for the words from "means" to the end substitute "has the same meaning as "the transfer pricing guidelines" in section 164 of TIOPA 2010".

(3) The amendments made by subsection (1) have effect (in relation to provision made or imposed at any time)—

    (a) for corporation tax purposes, in relation to accounting periods beginning on or after 1 April 2016, and

    (b) for income tax purposes, in relation to the tax year 2016–17 and subsequent tax years.

(4) The amendment made by subsection (2) has effect in relation to accounting periods beginning on or after 1 April 2016.

GENERAL NOTE

The UK transfer pricing legislation that is contained in Pt 4 TIOPA 2010 has to be interpreted in accordance with OECD principles. This amendment updates the reference to the OECD transfer pricing guidelines to encompass the amendments made as part of the OECD Base Erosion and Profit Shifting Project. This amendment has effect for corporation tax purposes for accounting periods beginning on or after 1 April 2016 and for income tax purposes for the tax year 2016/17 onwards.

The reference to the transfer pricing guidelines as applies for the Patent Box legislation contained in Pt 8A CTA 2010 is also updated. Again this amendment has effect for accounting periods beginning on or after 1 April 2016.

Transactions in UK Land

76 Corporation tax: territorial scope etc

(1) Section 5 of CTA 2009 (territorial scope of charge) is amended in accordance with subsections (2) to (4).

(2) For subsection (2) substitute—

"(2) A non-UK resident company is within the charge to corporation tax only if—
  (a) it carries on a trade of dealing in or developing UK land (see section 5B), or
  (b) it carries on a trade in the United Kingdom (other than a trade of dealing in or developing UK land) through a permanent establishment in the United Kingdom."

(3) After subsection (2) insert—

"(2A) A non-UK resident company which carries on a trade of dealing in or developing UK land is chargeable to corporation tax on all its profits wherever arising that are profits of that trade."

(4) In subsection (4), after "(1)" insert ", (2A)".

(5) After section 5 of CTA 2009 insert—

"5A Arrangements for avoiding tax

(1) Subsection (3) applies if a company has entered into an arrangement the main purpose or one of the main purposes of which is to obtain a relevant tax advantage for the company.

(2) In subsection (1) the reference to obtaining a relevant tax advantage includes obtaining a relevant tax advantage by virtue of any provisions of double taxation arrangements, but only in a case where the relevant tax advantage is contrary to the object and purpose of the provisions of the double taxation arrangements (and subsection (3) has effect accordingly, regardless of section 6(1) of TIOPA 2010).

(3) The relevant tax advantage is to be counteracted by means of adjustments.

(4) For this purpose adjustments may be made (whether by an officer of Revenue and Customs or by the company) by way of an assessment, the modification of an assessment, amendment or disallowance of a claim, or otherwise.

(5) In this section "relevant tax advantage" means a tax advantage in relation to corporation tax to which the company is chargeable (or would without the tax advantage be chargeable) by virtue of section 5(2A).

(6) In this section—

"arrangement" (except in the phrase "double taxation arrangements") includes any agreement, understanding, scheme, transaction or series of transactions, whether or not legally enforceable;
"double taxation arrangements" means arrangements which have effect under section 2(1) of TIOPA 2010 (double taxation relief by agreement with territories outside the United Kingdom);
"tax advantage" has the meaning given by section 1139 of CTA 2010.

5B Trade of dealing in or developing UK land

(1) A non-UK resident company's "trade of dealing in or developing UK land" consists of —
  (a) any activities falling within subsection (2) which it carries on, and
  (b) any activities from which profits, gains or losses arise which are treated under Part 8ZB of CTA 2010 as profits or losses of the company's trade of dealing in or developing UK land.

(2) The activities within this subsection are—
  (a) dealing in UK land;
  (b) developing UK land for the purpose of disposing of it.

(3) In this section "land" includes—
  (a) buildings and structures,
  (b) any estate, interest or right in or over land, and
  (c) land under the sea or otherwise covered by water.

(4) In this section—
  "disposal" is to be interpreted in accordance with section 356OQ of CTA 2010;
  "UK land" means land in the United Kingdom."

(6) In section 3 of CTA 2009 (exclusion of charge to income tax), in subsection (1), for paragraph (b) substitute—

"(b) the company is not UK resident and—
  (i) the income is profits of a trade of dealing in or developing UK land, or
  (ii) the income is within its chargeable profits as defined by section 19."

(7) In section 18A of CTA 2009 (exemption for profits or losses of foreign permanent establishments), after subsection (2) insert—

"(2A) But profits and losses are not to be left out of account as mentioned in subsection (2) so far as they are, or would if the company were non-UK resident be, profits of the company's trade of dealing in or developing UK land (as defined in section 5B)."

(8) In section 19 of CTA 2009 (chargeable profits)—

(a) in subsection (2) for "company's chargeable profits" substitute "company's "chargeable profits"";

(b) after subsection (2) insert—

"(2A) But the company's "chargeable profits" do not include profits of a trade of dealing in or developing UK land (and accordingly such profits are not attributable to any permanent establishment of the company)."

(9) In section 189 of CTA 2009 (post-cessation receipts: extent of charge to tax), in subsection (4), at the end insert "other than a company's trade of dealing in or developing UK land".

(10) In section 107 of CTA 2010 (restrictions on losses etc surrenderable by non-UK resident), in subsection (1), for the words from "non-UK resident" to the end substitute "non-UK resident company—

(a) carrying on a trade of dealing in or developing UK land, or

(b) carrying on a trade in the United Kingdom through a permanent establishment."

(11) In section 1119 of CTA 2010 (definitions for purposes of Corporation Tax Acts), at the appropriate place insert—

""trade of dealing in or developing UK land", in relation to a non-UK resident company, has the meaning given by section 5B of CTA 2009,".

GENERAL NOTE

Sections 76–82

Sections 76–82 radically change the way in which profits from trading and development in UK land are taxed. Essentially the new provisions level the playing field between resident and non-resident companies or individuals by basing the charge on the location of the land rather than the residence of the taxpayer making the disposal. Sections 76 and 77 deal with corporation tax: ss 78 and 79 duplicate, with some necessary modification, those rules for income tax purposes. The intention to legislate was announced in a technical note issue by HMRC on 16 March 2016 but the legislation was only added to the Finance Bill at Report Stage. This means that, subject to some transitional provisions, the new rules take effect from 5 July 2016 rather than from Budget day or Royal Assent.

The rules replace the existing anti avoidance rules for transactions in land, which are repealed.

Section 76

This section expands the territorial scope of the charge to corporation tax to bring dealing and developing in UK land into charge.

Section 76(1)

This introduces amendments to CTA 2009 s 5.

Section 76(2)

This introduces a new s 5(2) to CTA 2009. It widens the scope by defining two types of activity which are within the scope of UK corporation tax. These are:

– the trade of dealing or developing UK land; and
– carrying on a trade in the UK (other than one of dealing in or developing UK land) through a permanent establishment in the UK.

The critical difference here is that a trade of dealing or developing land in the UK no longer requires a permanent establishment for it to be brought within the UK tax charge.

Section 76(3)

This inserts a new s 5(2A). This provided that a non-resident company which carries on a trade of developing or dealing in UK land is chargeable on all of its profits from that trade, wherever they arise.

Section 76(4)

This is a minor drafting amendment.

Section 76(5)

This inserts new CTA 2009 ss 5A and 5B.

New CTA 2009 s 5A – Arrangements for avoiding tax

New CTA 2009 s 5A(1)

This introduces the section and says that sub-s (3) below will apply if a company has entered into an arrangement the main purpose, or one of the main purposes of which, is to obtain a relevant tax advantage for the company.

New CTA 2009 s 5A(2)

This extends the reference to a tax advantage to obtaining a relevant tax advantage by virtue of any provision of a double tax agreement, but only in a case where the tax advantage is contrary to the object and purpose of the provisions of the DTA. Section 5A takes precedence over the normal rules for giving DTR under TIOPA 2010.

New CTA 2009 s 5A(3)

This says that the relevant advantage is to be counteracted by means of adjustments.

New CTA 2009 s 5A(4)

Adjustments may be made either by the company or an officer of HMRC, by way of an assessment, the modification of an assessment, amendment or disallowance of a claim, or otherwise.

New CTA 2009 s 5A(5)

Relevant tax advantage is an advantage in relation to corporation tax to which the company is chargeable (or would without the advantage be chargeable) under the new s 5(2A).

New CTA 2009 s 5A(6)

This defines arrangements to include any agreement, understanding, scheme, transaction or series of transactions, whether or not legally enforceable. The definition does not apply to the phrase "double taxation arrangements" itself.

Double taxation arrangements takes the definition in ITOPA 2010: tax advantage takes the definition in CTA 2010 s 1139.

New CTA 2009 s 5B – Trade of dealing in or developing UK land

New CTA 2009 s 5B(1)

A non-UK resident company's trade of dealing in or developing UK land consists of activities within sub-s (2) below or activities from which profits gains or losses arise which are treated under CTA 2010 Pt 8ZB as profits or losses of the company's trade of dealing in or developing UK Land. Part 8ZB is a new part of CTA 2010 introduced by s 77 below.

New CTA 2009 s 5B(2)

The activities are dealing in UK land or developing UK land for the purpose of disposing of it.

New CTA 2009 s 5B(3)

Land includes buildings and structures; any estate, interest or right in or over land, and land under the sea or otherwise covered by water.

New CTA 2009 s 5B(4)

This takes the definition of disposal from CTA 2010 s 356OQ, which is one of the new sections introduced by s 77. UK land is defined as land in the United Kingdom.

Section 76(6)

This is a drafting amendment to CTA 2009 s 3 which expands the exclusion of the charge to income tax to reflect the revised scope of the corporation tax charge on UK land.

Section 76(7)

CT 2009 s 18A allows a company to make a branch profits election under which profits of foreign branches are left out of account. This is restricted to ensure that a company cannot elect to leave out of account profits from dealing in or developing UK land. Without such a restriction companies would be able to opt out of the new regime for UK land entirely.

Section 76(8)

This introduces a new definition of a company's chargeable profits into CTA 2009 s 19 (chargeable profits of non-UK resident companies). Chargeable profits for this purpose exclude profits of a trade of dealing in or developing UK land. Such profits are thus not treated as being attributable to a permanent establishment.

Section 76(9)–(11)

These are consequential drafting amendments.

77 Corporation tax: transactions in UK land

(1) In CTA 2010, after Part 8ZA insert—

"PART 8ZB
TRANSACTIONS IN UK LAND

Introduction

356OA Overview of Part

This Part contains provision about the corporation tax treatment of certain profits and gains realised from disposals concerned with land in the United Kingdom.

Amounts treated as profits of a trade

356OB Disposals of land in the United Kingdom

(1) Section 356OC(1) applies (subject to subsection (3) of that section) if—

(a) a person within subsection (2)(a), (b) or (c) realises a profit or gain from a disposal of any land in the United Kingdom, and

(b) any of conditions A to D is met in relation to the land.

(2) The persons referred to in subsection (1) are—

(a) the person acquiring, holding or developing the land,

(b) a person who is associated with the person in paragraph (a) at a relevant time, and

(c) a person who is a party to, or concerned in, an arrangement within subsection (3).

(3) An arrangement is within this subsection if—

(a) it is effected with respect to all or part of the land, and

(b) it enables a profit or gain to be realised—

(i) by any indirect method, or

(ii) by any series of transactions.

(4) Condition A is that the main purpose, or one of the main purposes, of acquiring the land was to realise a profit or gain from disposing of the land.

(5) Condition B is that the main purpose, or one of the main purposes, of acquiring any property deriving its value from the land was to realise a profit or gain from disposing of the land.

(6) Condition C is that the land is held as trading stock.

(7) Condition D is that (in a case where the land has been developed) the main purpose, or one of the main purposes, of developing the land was to realise a profit or gain from disposing of the land when developed.

(8) In this section "relevant time" means any time in the period beginning when the activities of the project begin and ending 6 months after the disposal mentioned in subsection (1).

(9) In this section "the project" means all activities carried out for any of the following purposes—

(a) the purposes of dealing in or developing the land, and
(b) any other purposes mentioned in Conditions A to D.

(10) For the purposes of this section a person ("A") is associated with another person ("B") if—

(a) A is connected with B by virtue of any of subsections (5) to (7) of section 1122 (read in accordance with section 1123), or
(b) A is related to B (see section 356OT).

356OC Disposals of land: profits treated as trading profits

(1) The profit or gain is to be treated for corporation tax purposes as profits of a trade carried on by the chargeable company (see section 356OG).

(2) If the chargeable company is non-UK resident, that trade is the company's trade of dealing in or developing UK land (as defined in section 5B of CTA 2009).

(3) But subsection (1) does not apply to a profit or gain so far as it would (apart from this section) be brought into account as income in calculating profits (of any person)—

(a) for corporation tax purposes, or
(b) for income tax purposes.

(4) The profits are treated as arising in the accounting period of the chargeable company in which the profit or gain is realised.

(5) This section applies in relation to gains which are capital in nature as it applies in relation to other gains.

356OD Disposals of property deriving its value from land in the United Kingdom

(1) Section 356OE applies (subject to subsection (3) of that section) if—

(a) a person realises a profit or gain from a disposal of any property which (at the time of the disposal) derives at least 50% of its value from land in the United Kingdom,
(b) the person is a party to, or concerned in, an arrangement concerning some or all of the land mentioned in paragraph (a) ("the project land"), and
(c) the arrangement meets the condition in subsection (2).

(2) The condition is that the main purpose, or one of the main purposes, of the arrangement is to—

(a) deal in or develop the project land, and
(b) realise a profit or gain from a disposal of property deriving the whole or part of its value from that land.

356OE Disposals within section 356OD: profits treated as trading profits

(1) The relevant amount is to be treated for corporation tax purposes as profits of a trade carried on by the chargeable company.

(2) If the chargeable company is non-UK resident, that trade is the company's trade of dealing in or developing UK land.

(3) But subsection (1) does not apply to an amount so far as it would (apart from this section) be brought into account as income in calculating profits (of any person)—

(a) for corporation tax purposes, or
(b) for income tax purposes.

(4) The profits are treated as arising in the accounting period of the chargeable company in which the profit or gain is realised.

(5) In this section the "relevant amount" means so much (if any) of the profit or gain mentioned in section 356OD(1) as is attributable, on a just and reasonable apportionment, to the relevant UK assets.

(6) In this section "the relevant UK assets" means any land in the United Kingdom from which the property mentioned in section 356OD(1) derives any of its value (at the time of the disposal mentioned in that subsection).

(7) This section applies in relation to gains which are capital in nature as it applies in relation to other gains.

356OF Profits and losses

(1) Sections 356OB to 356OE have effect as if they included provision about losses corresponding to the provision they make about profits and gains.

(2) Accordingly, in the following sections of this Part references to a "profit or gain" include a loss.

Person to whom profits attributed

356OG The chargeable company

(1) For the purposes of sections 356OC and 356OE the general rule is that the "chargeable company" is the company ("C") that realises the profit or gain (as mentioned in section 356OB(1) or 356OD(1)).

(2) The general rule in subsection (1) is subject to the special rules in subsections (4) to (6).

(3) But those special rules do not apply in relation to a profit or gain to which section 356OH(3) (fragmented activities) applies.

(4) If all or any part of the profit or gain accruing to C is derived from value provided directly or indirectly by another person ("B") which is a company, B is the "chargeable company".

(5) Subsection (4) applies whether or not the value is put at the disposal of C.

(6) If all or any part of the profit or gain accruing to C is derived from an opportunity of realising a profit or gain provided directly or indirectly by another person ("D") which is a company, D is "the chargeable company" (unless the case falls within subsection (4)).

(7) For the meaning of "another person" see section 356OO.

Anti-fragmentation

356OH Fragmented activities

(1) Subsection (3) applies if—

    (a) a company ("C") disposes of any land in the United Kingdom,
    (b) any of conditions A to D in section 356OB is met in relation to the land, and
    (c) a person ("R") who is associated with C at a relevant time has made a relevant contribution to activities falling within subsection (2).

(2) The following activities fall within this subsection—

    (a) the development of the land,
    (b) any other activities directed towards realising a profit or gain from the disposal of the land.

(3) For the purposes of this Part, the profit or gain (if any) realised by C from the disposal is to be taken to be what that profit or gain would be if R were not a distinct person from C (and, accordingly, as if everything done by or in relation to R had been done by or in relation to C).

(4) Subsection (5) applies to any amount which is paid (directly or indirectly) by R to C for the purposes of meeting or reimbursing the cost of corporation tax which C is liable to pay as a result of the application of subsection (3) in relation to R and C.

(5) The amount—

    (a) is not to be taken into account in calculating profits or losses of either R or C for the purposes of income tax or corporation tax, and
    (b) is not for any purpose of the Corporation Tax Acts to be regarded as a distribution.

(6) In subsection (1) "relevant time" means any time in the period beginning when the activities of the project begin and ending 6 months after the disposal.

(7) For the purposes of this section any contribution made by R to activities falling within subsection (2) is a "relevant contribution" unless the profit made or to be made by R in respect of the contribution is insignificant having regard to the size of the project.

(8) In this section "contribution" means any kind of contribution, including, for example—

(a) the provision of professional or other services, or

(b) a financial contribution (including the assumption of a risk).

(9) For the purposes of this section R is "associated" with C if—

(a) R is connected with C by virtue of any of subsections (5) to (7) of section 1122 (read in accordance with section 1123), or

(b) R is related to C (see section 356OT).

(10) In this section "the project" means all activities carried out for any of the following purposes—

(a) the purposes of dealing in or developing the land, and

(b) any other purposes mentioned in Conditions A to D in section 356OB.

Calculation of profit or gain on disposal

356OI Calculation of profit or gain on disposal

For the purposes of this Part, the profit or gain (if any) from a disposal of any property is to be calculated according to the principles applicable for calculating the profits of a trade under Part 3 of CTA 2009, subject to any modifications that may be appropriate (and for this purpose the same rules are to apply in calculating losses from a disposal as apply in calculating profits).

356OJ Apportionments

Any apportionment (whether of expenditure, consideration or any other amount) that is required to be made for the purposes of this Part is to be made on a just and reasonable basis.

Arrangements for avoiding tax

356OK Arrangements for avoiding tax

(1) Subsection (3) applies if an arrangement has been entered into the main purpose or one of the main purposes of which is to enable a company to obtain a relevant tax advantage.

(2) In subsection (1) the reference to obtaining a relevant tax advantage includes obtaining a relevant tax advantage by virtue of any provisions of double taxation arrangements, but only in a case where the relevant tax advantage is contrary to the object and purpose of the provisions of the double taxation arrangements (and subsection (3) has effect accordingly, regardless of anything in section 6(1) of TIOPA 2010).

(3) The tax advantage is to be counteracted by means of adjustments.

(4) For this purpose adjustments may be made (whether by an officer of Revenue and Customs or by the company) by way of an assessment, the modification of an assessment, amendment or disallowance of a claim, or otherwise.

(5) In this section "relevant tax advantage" means a tax advantage in relation to corporation tax charged (or which would, if the tax advantage were not obtained, be charged) in respect of amounts treated as profits of a trade by virtue of this Part.

(6) In this section—

"double taxation arrangements" means arrangements which have effect under section 2(1) of TIOPA 2010 (double taxation relief by agreement with territories outside the United Kingdom);

"tax advantage" has the meaning given by section 1139.

Exemption

356OL Profits attributable to period before relevant activities etc began

(1) Subsection (2) applies if—

(a) subsection (1) of section 356OC applies because Condition D in section 356OB is met (land developed with purpose of realising a gain from its disposal when developed), and

(b) part of the profit or gain mentioned in that subsection is fairly attributable to a period before the intention to develop was formed.

(2) Section 356OC(1) has effect as if the person mentioned in section 356OB(1) had not realised that part of the profit or gain.

(3) Subsection (4) applies if—

(a) section 356OE(1) applies, and

(b) part of the profit or gain mentioned in section 356OE(5) is fairly attributable to a period before the person mentioned in section 356OD(1) was a party to, or concerned in, the arrangement in question.

(4) Section 356OE has effect as if the person had not realised that part of the profit or gain.

(5) In applying this section account must be taken of the treatment under Part 3 of CTA 2009 (trading income) of a company which appropriates land as trading stock.

Other supplementary provisions

356OM Tracing value

(1) This section applies if it is necessary to determine the extent to which the value of any property or right is derived from any other property or right for the purposes of this Part.

(2) Value may be traced through any number of companies, partnerships, trusts and other entities or arrangements.

(3) The property held by a company, partnership or trust must be attributed to the shareholders, partners, beneficiaries or other participants at each stage in whatever way is appropriate in the circumstances.

(4) In this section—

"partnership" includes an entity established under the law of a country or territory outside the United Kingdom of a similar nature to a partnership; and "partners", in relation to such arrangements, is to be construed accordingly;

"trust" includes arrangements—

(a) which have effect under the law of a country or territory outside the United Kingdom; and

(b) under which persons acting in a fiduciary capacity hold and administer property on behalf of other persons,

and "beneficiaries", in relation to such arrangements, is to be construed accordingly.

356ON Relevance of transactions, arrangements, etc

(1) In determining whether section 356OC(1) or 356OE(1) applies, account is to be taken of any method, however indirect, by which—

(a) any property or right is transferred or transmitted, or

(b) the value of any property or right is enhanced or diminished.

(2) Accordingly—

(a) the occasion of the transfer or transmission of any property or right, however indirect, and

(b) the occasion when the value of any property or right is enhanced,

may be an occasion on which section 356OC(1) or 356OE(1) applies.

(3) Subsections (1) and (2) apply in particular—

(a) to sales, contracts and other transactions made otherwise than for full consideration or for more than full consideration,

(b) to any method by which any property or right, or the control of any property or right, is transferred or transmitted by assigning—

(i) share capital or other rights in a company,

(ii) rights in a partnership, or

(iii) an interest in settled property,

(c) to the creation of an option affecting the disposition of any property or right and the giving of consideration for granting it,

(d) to the creation of a requirement for consent affecting such a disposition and the giving of consideration for granting it,

(e) to the creation of an embargo affecting such a disposition and the giving of consideration for releasing it, and

(f) to the disposal of any property or right on the winding up, dissolution or termination of a company, partnership or trust.

Interpretation

356OO "Another person"

(1) In this Part references to "other" persons are to be interpreted in accordance with subsections (2) to (4).

(2) A partnership or partners in a partnership may be regarded as a person or persons distinct from the individuals or other persons who are for the time being partners.

(3) The trustees of settled property may be regarded as persons distinct from the individuals or other persons who are for the time being the trustees.

(4) Personal representatives may be regarded as persons distinct from the individuals or other persons who are for the time being personal representatives.

356OP "Arrangement"

(1) In this Part "arrangement" (except in the phrase "double taxation arrangements") includes any agreement, understanding, scheme, transaction or series of transactions, whether or not legally enforceable).

(2) For the purposes of this Part any number of transactions may be regarded as constituting a single arrangement if—

(a) a common purpose can be discerned in them, or
(b) there is other sufficient evidence of a common purpose.

356OQ "Disposal"

(1) In this Part references to a "disposal" of any property include any case in which the property is effectively disposed of (whether wholly or in part, as mentioned in subsection (2))—

(a) by one or more transactions, or
(b) by any arrangement.

(2) For the purposes of this Part—

(a) references to a disposal of land or any other property include a part disposal of the property, and
(b) there is a part disposal of property ("the asset") where on a person making a disposal, any form of property derived from the asset remains undisposed of (including in cases where an interest or right in or over the asset is created by the disposal, as well as where it subsists before the disposal).

356OR "Land" and related expressions

(1) In this Part "land" includes—

(a) buildings and structures,
(b) any estate, interest or right in or over land, and
(c) land under the sea or otherwise covered by water.

(2) In this Part references to property deriving its value from land include—

(a) any shareholding in a company deriving its value directly or indirectly from land,
(b) any partnership interest deriving its value directly or indirectly from land,
(c) any interest in settled property deriving its value directly or indirectly from land, and
(d) any option, consent or embargo affecting the disposition of land.

356OS References to realising a gain

(1) For the purposes of sections 356OB(1) and 356OD(1) it does not matter whether the person ("P") realising the profit or gain in question realises it for P or another person.

(2) For the purposes of subsection (1), if, for example by a premature sale, a person ("A") directly or indirectly transmits the opportunity of realising a profit or gain to another person ("B"), A realises B's profit or gain for B.

356OT Related parties

(1) For the purposes of this Part a person ("A") is related to another person ("B")—

(a) throughout any period for which A and B are consolidated for accounting purposes,
(b) on any day on which the participation condition is met in relation to them, or
(c) on any day on which the 25% investment condition is met in relation to them.

(2) A and B are consolidated for accounting purposes for a period if—

(a) their financial results for a period are required to be comprised in group accounts,
(b) their financial results for the period would be required to be comprised in group accounts but for the application of an exemption, or

(c) their financial results for a period are in fact comprised in group accounts.

(3) In subsection (2) "group accounts" means accounts prepared under—

(a) section 399 of the Companies Act 2006, or

(b) any corresponding provision of the law of a territory outside the United Kingdom.

(4) The participation condition is met in relation to A and B ("the relevant parties") on a day if, within the period of 6 months beginning with that day—

(a) one of the relevant parties directly or indirectly participates in the management, control or capital of the other, or

(b) the same person or persons directly or indirectly participate in the management, control or capital of each of the relevant parties.

(5) The 25% investment condition is met in relation to A and B if—

(a) one of them has a 25% investment in the other, or

(b) a third person has a 25% investment in each of them.

(6) Section 259NC of TIOPA 2010 applies for the purposes of determining whether a person has a "25% investment" in another person for the purposes of this section as it applies for the purposes of section 259NB(2) of that Act.

(7) In Chapter 2 of Part 4 of TIOPA 2010, sections 157(2), 158(4), 159(2) and 160(2) (which are about the interpretation of references to direct and indirect participation) apply in relation to subsection (4) as they apply in relation to subsection (4) of section 259NA of that Act."

(2) In section 1 of CTA 2010 (overview), in subsection (4), omit paragraph (e).

(3) In section 481 of CTA 2010 (exemption from charges under provisions to which section 1173 applies), in subsection (2) omit paragraph (a).

(4) In CTA 2010 omit Part 18 (transactions in land).

(5) In section 1173 of CTA 2010 (miscellaneous charges), in Part 2 of the table in subsection (2), omit the entry relating to section 818(1) of CTA 2010.

(6) In section 14B of TCGA 1992 (meaning of "non-resident CGT disposal")—

(a) in subsection (1) for "subsection (5)" substitute "subsections (5) and (6)";

(b) after subsection (5) insert—

"(6) A disposal of a UK residential property interest is not a non-resident CGT disposal if section 356OC(1) of CTA 2010 (gains etc on certain disposals treated as trading profits for corporation tax purposes) or section 517C of ITA 2007 (gains etc on certain disposals treated as trading profits for income tax purposes) applies in relation to it."

(7) In section 37 of TCGA 1992 (consideration chargeable to tax on income), in subsection (5A)(a), for the words from "821(3)" to "not" substitute "356OG(4) or (6) of CTA 2010 (transactions in land: the chargeable company) applies, an amount is charged to corporation tax as profits of a person other than".

(8) In section 39 of TCGA 1992 (exclusion of expenditure by reference to tax on income), in subsection (5)(a), for the words from "821(3)" to "not" substitute "356OG(4) or (6) of CTA 2010 (transactions in land: the chargeable company) applies, an amount is charged to corporation tax as profits of a person other than".

(9) In section 161 of TCGA 1992 (appropriations to and from stock), in subsection (6), for paragraph (a) substitute—

"(a) any person is charged to corporation tax by virtue of sections 356OB and 356OC of CTA 2010 (certain profits or gains on a disposal of land treated as trading profits) on the realisation of a profit or gain because the condition in section 356OB(7) of that Act is met, and".

(10) In section 188A of TCGA 1992 (election for pooling), in subsection (4), at the end insert "or section 14B(6) (gains on certain disposals treated as trading profits)".

GENERAL NOTE

Section 77(1)

This introduces a new Pt 8ZB into CTA 2010 consisting of the following sections.

Section 356OA – Overview of Part

This introduces Pt 8ZB, which deals with the corporation tax treatment of profits and gains on disposals of land in the UK.

Section 356OB – Disposals of land in the United Kingdom

This sets out the basic rule.

Section 356OB(1)

Section 356OC(1) – the new substantive charging provision – applies if a person specified in sub-s (2) below realises a profit or gain from a disposal of any land in the UK and any of Conditions A to D is met.

Section 356OB(2)

The persons specified are:
- the person acquiring, holding or developing the land;
- a person associated with the above at the relevant time; (see sub-s (8) below); or
- a person who is a party to, or concerned in, an arrangement within sub-s (3) below.

Section 356OB(3)

An arrangement is within this subsection if it is effected with respect to all or part of the land and it enables a profit or gain to be realised by any indirect method or by any series of transactions.

Section 356OB(4)

Condition A is that the main purpose, or one of the main purposes, of acquiring the land was to realise a profit or gain from its disposal.

Section 356OB(5)

Condition B is that main purpose of, or one of the main purposes, of acquiring any property deriving its value from the land was to realise a profit or gain from disposing of the land. The most obvious case where this would apply would be in cases where land is held within a company.

Section 356OB(6)

Condition C is that the land is held as trading stock.

Section 356OB(7)

Condition D only applies where the land has been developed. The main purpose, or one of the main purposes, of developing the land was to realise a profit or gain from disposing of the land when developed.

Section 356OB(8)

Relevant time is any time in the period from when the activities of the project begin and ending 6 months after the disposal at sub-s (1) above.

Section 356OB(9)

This defines the project as all activities carried out for the purpose of dealing in or developing the land and any of the purposes in Conditions A to D above.

Section 356OB(10)

A person is associated with another period if they are connected for the purposes of s 1122 (the general definition of connected persons for corporation tax purposes) or they are related to each other (see new s 356OT below).

Section 356OC – Disposals of land: profits to be treated as trading profits

Section 356OC(1)

The profit or gain arising is to be treated as profits of a trade carried on by the chargeable company.

Section 356OC(2)

If the company is non-UK resident the trade is a trade a of dealing in or developing UK land.

Section 356OC(3)

This establishes an order of priority. If the profit or gain would be brought into account by any person in calculating profits for corporation tax or income tax purposes other than under Pt 8ZB (i.e. these new provisions) the existing charge takes priority.

Section 356OC(4)

Profits within this section are treated as arising in the accounting period in which the profit or gain is realised.

Section 356OC(5)

This confirms that the new provisions apply to gains of a capital nature as well as to other gains.

Section 356OD – Disposal of property deriving its value from land in the United Kingdom

Section 356OD(1)

This sets out the scope of s 356OE below. It applies if three conditions are met:
- a person realises a profit or gain on any property which at the time of disposal derives at least 50% of its value from land in the UK;
- That person is a party to (or concerned in) an arrangement concerning some of all of the land above (which is referred to as the project land);
- The condition in sub-s (2) below is met.

Section 356OD(2)

The condition is that the main purpose (or one of the main purposes) of the arrangement is to deal in or develop the project land and realise a profit or gain from a disposal of property deriving the whole or part of its value from that land.

Section 356OE – Disposals with section 356OD: profits treated as trading profits

Section 356OE(1)

The relevant amount (see sub-s (5) below) is treated as profits of a trade carried on by the chargeable company.

Section 356OE(1)

If the company is non-UK resident the trade is a trade of dealing in or developing UK land.

Section 356OE(3) and (4)

These replicate the similar provisions in s 356OC above.

Section 356OE(5)

The relevant amount is so much of the gain in s 356OD(1) which is attributable on a just and reasonable basis to the relevant UK assets.

Section 356OE(6)

The relevant UK assets means any UK land from which the property mentioned in s 356OD(1) above derives its value.

Section 356OE(7)

This replicates s 356OC(7) above.

Section 356F – Profits and losses

The above sections apply to losses in the same way that they apply to profits.

Section 356OG – The chargeable company

This section specifies the person to whom the profits are attributed.

Section 356OG(1)

The general rule is that profit is chargeable on the company which realises the profit or gain.

Section 356OG(2)

The general rule is subject to the special rules in sub-ss (4) to (6) below.

Section 356OG(3)

The special rules do not apply in relation to fragmented activities (see s 356OH).

Section 356OG(4)

If all or any part of the gain arising to the company which makes the gain [C] is derived from value provided directly or indirectly by another company [B], that company [B] is the chargeable person.

Section 356OG(5)

The above rule applies whether not the value is put at the disposal of C.

Section 356OG(6)

If all or any part of the profit or gain accruing to C is derived from an opportunity of realising a gain provided directly or indirectly by another company [D], that company [D] is the chargeable company unless sub-s (4) above applies.

Section 356OG(7)

"Another person" is defined in s 356OO.

Section 356OH – Fragmented activities

Section 356OH(1)

This sets out the three basic conditions which must be met:

- A company [C] disposals of land in the UK;
- Any of the conditions A to D in s 356OB is met in relation to the land;
- A person [R] who is associated (see sub-s (9) below) with C at a relevant time (see sub-s (6) below) has made a relevant contribution (see sub-s (8) below) to activities within sub-s (2) below.

Section 356OH(2)

Activities within this subsection are development of the land and other activities directed towards realising a profit or gain from a disposal of the land.

Section 356OH(3)

This is the substantive provision. In calculating the profit or gain realised by C on the disposal anything done by R is treated as if it were done by C. This means that the entire gain realised by C is charged rather than being split between C and R.

Section 356OH(4)

This introduces sub-s (5) which deals with any amount paid by R to C for the purposes of meeting the cost of corporation tax payable by C under this section.

Section 356OH(5)

Any amount within sub-s (4) above is not to be taken account of in calculating the profits or losses of either R or C for corporation tax purposes and is not to be treated as a distribution.

Section 356OH(6)

This defines relevant time as any time from the beginning of the project and ending six months after the disposal.

Section 356OH(7)

This introduces a de minimis test. Any contribution by R to activities with sub-s (2) above is regarded as a relevant contribution unless the profit to be made by R in respect of the contribution is insignificant having regard to the size of the project.

Section 356OH(8)

Contribution includes provisions of finance (including the assumption of risk) or the provision of professional or other services.

Section 356OH(9)

This defines association for the purposes of sub-s (1) above. It uses the same test as in s 356OB(10) above.

Section 356OH(10)

This uses the same definition of "the project" as that in s 356OB(9) above.

Section 356OI – Calculation of profit or gain on disposal

In calculating the profit or gain arising from the disposal of a property for the purpose of Part 8ZB the principles to be applied are the same as those which apply for the calculating the profits of a trade under CTA 2009 Pt 3 (subject to any necessary modifications). The same principles are also to be applied in calculating losses.

Section 356OJ – Apportionments

Any apportionments required under this part are to be made on a just and reasonable basis.

Section 356OK – Arrangements for avoiding tax

Section 356OK(1)

This introduces sub-s (3) which applies if an arrangement has been entered into whose purpose or one of whose main purposes is enabling a company to obtain a relevant tax advantage.

Section 356OK(2)

A relevant tax advantage includes obtaining relevant tax advantage by virtue of any provisions of double tax arrangements but only where the tax advantage is contrary to the object and purpose of the double tax arrangements. This section takes priority over the general rules for double tax relief in TIPOA 2010 s 6(1).

Section 356OK(3)

The tax advantage is to be counteracted by means of adjustments.

Section 356OK(4)

Adjustments may be made by an officer of HMRC or by the company. They can be made by way of an assessment, modification of an assessment, amendment, disallowance of a claim or otherwise.

Section 356OK(5) and (6)

These repeat the definition of tax advantage etc from new s 5A above.

Section 356OL – Profits attributable to period before relevant activities began, etc

This section allows a limited exemption for profits which accrue before the intention to develop was formed.

Section 356OL(1)

This introduces the section. The starting point is that the condition in s 356OC(1) applies because Condition D of s 356OB is met. In other words the land was developed with the purpose of realising a gain on its disposal after development. The test is then whether part of the profit or gain is fairly attributable to a period before the intention to develop was formed.

Section 356OL(2)

Where the above test is met that part of the gain (i.e. the pre-intention element) is excluded from the amount chargeable under s 356OB(1).

Section 356OL(3) and (4)

These apply similar provisions to cases under s 356OE – ie. cases where a person was party to the arrangement in question.

Section 356OL(5)

Account must be taken of the tax treatment of a company which appropriates land as trading stock.

Section 356OM – Tracing value

Section 356OM(1)

The section applies when it is necessary to determine the extent to which the value of property or rights is derived from any other property or right.

Section 356OM(2)

Value may be traced through any number of companies, partnerships, trusts and other entities or arrangements. Note that there is no requirement that there must be any connection between these entities and the chargeable company.

Section 356OM(3)

This requires property held by a company , partnership or a trust to be attributed to the shareholders, partners, beneficiaries or other participant at each stage in whatever way is appropriate in the circumstances. Again this is a very wide test.

Section 356OM(4)

Partnership included entities established under non-UK law of a similar nature to a partnership and partner is to be construed accordingly.

Trust includes arrangements not under UK law under which persons acting in a fiducial capacity hold and administer property on behalf of other persons. Beneficiaries is to be construed accordingly.

Section 356ON – Relevance of transactions, arrangements, etc

Section 356ON(1)

This extends the scope of the basic charging provisions, s 356OC and s 356OE. In determining whether one or other of those sections apply account is to be taken of any method, however indirect, under which any property or right is transferred or the value of any property or right is enhanced or diminished.

Section 356ON(2)

The occasion of the transfer of any property or right, or of the value being enhanced may be an occasion on which a charge under s 356OC or s 356OE may apply.

Section 356ON(3)

This gives examples of situations to which the extended scope of the above charging provisions may apply. Not that this is a list of examples and not an exhaustive definition.
- sales contracts and other transactions at undervalue or overvalue;
- any method of transferring rights by the assignment of share capital or other rights in a company; partnership rights or interests in settled property;
- the creation of an option over property or rights and giving consideration for the grant of an option;
- the creation of a right of consent and the giving of consideration for it;
- the creation of an embargo and the giving of consideration for releasing it;
- the disposal of any property or right on the winding up etc of a company, partnership or trust.

Section 356OO – "Another person"

Section 356OO(1)

This introduces the section, which defines "other persons".

Section 356OO(2)

Partnership or partners in a partnership may be regarded as distinct from the individuals or other persons who are partners.

Section 356OO(3)

The trustees of settled property may be regarded as distinct from the individuals or other persons who are for the time being the trustees.

Section 356OO(4)

Personal representatives may be regarded as persons distinct from the individual or other persons who are for the time being personal representatives.

Section 356OP – "Arrangement"

Section 356OP(1)

Arrangement includes any agreement, understanding , scheme, transaction or series of transactions, whether or not legally enforceable.

Section 356OP(2)

Any number of transactions may be regarded as a single arrangement if a common purpose can be discerned in them or there is other sufficient evidence of a common purpose.

Section 356OQ – "Disposal"

Section 356OQ(1)

Disposal includes any case where the property is effectively disposed by one or more transactions or by any arrangement

Section 356OQ(2)

Disposal includes part disposal. A part disposal includes any cases where after a disposal the person retains any form of right over property derived from the asset. This extends to cases where the right is created by the disposal.

Section 356OR – "Land" and related expressions

Section 356OR(1)

Land includes building and structures, estates interests or rights over land and land under the sea or otherwise covered by water.

Section 356OR(2)

Property deriving its value from land includes shareholding in a company, partnership interest, or interest in settled property which derives its value directly or indirectly from land. It also includes any option, consent or embargo affecting the disposition of land.

Section 356OS – References to realising a gain

Section 356OS(1)

For the purposes of this part it does not matter whether the person realising the profit of gain does so for himself or for another person.

Section 356OS(2)

Where a person transmits the opportunity of realising a gain to another person – for example by a premature sale – the first person is treated as realising the other person's gain for him.

Section 356OT – Related parties

This sets out the rules for determining which parties are related for the purpose of these provisions.

Section 356OT(1)

There are three tests for determining whether or not a person is related to another person. These are the:
- consolidation test;
- participation test;
- investment condition test.

Section 356OT(2)

Two companies (A and B) meet the consolidation test if their financial results are required to be comprised in group accounts, they would be so comprised but for the application of an exemption, or as a matter of fact are so comprised.

Section 356OT(3)

Group accounts are those prepared under CA 2006 or any corresponding provision under non-UK law.

Section 356OT(4)

Two parties (A and B) meet the participation test on a specific day if, within the period of 6 months beginning with that day) one of the parties directly or indirectly participates in the management , control or capital of the other, or the same person or persons directly or indirectly participate in the management, control or capital of each of the relevant parties.

Section 356OT(5)

A and B meet the investment condition test if one has a 25% investment in the other or a third party as a 25% investment in each of them

Section 356OT(6)

The investment test which applies is that in TIOPA 2010 s 259NC.

Section 356OT(7)

The interpretation sections of TIOPA 2010 Pt 4 Ch 2 (ss 157(2), 159(2) and 160(?) apply for the purposes of sub-s (4) above).

Section 77(2) and (3)
These are minor drafting amendments.

Section 77(4)
This abolishes the whole of CTA 2010 Pt 18, the existing anti-avoidance regime for transactions in land.

Section 77(5)–(10)
These are minor drafting amendments.

78   Income tax: territorial scope etc
(1) In section 6 of ITTOIA 2005 (territorial scope of charge to tax)—
    (a) after subsection (1) insert—
    "(1A) Profits of a trade of dealing in or developing UK land arising to a non-UK resident are chargeable to tax under this Chapter wherever the trade is carried on.";
    (b) in subsection (2), after "Profits of a trade" insert "other than a trade of dealing in or developing UK land".
(2) After section 6 of ITTOIA 2005 insert—

"6A Arrangements for avoiding tax

(1) Subsection (3) applies if a person has entered into an arrangement the main purpose or one of the main purposes of which is to obtain a relevant tax advantage for the person.

(2) In subsection (1) the reference to obtaining a relevant tax advantage includes obtaining a relevant tax advantage by virtue of any provisions of double taxation arrangements, but only in a case where the relevant tax advantage is contrary to the object and purpose of the provisions of the double taxation arrangements (and subsection (3) has effect accordingly, regardless of anything in section 6(1) of TIOPA 2010).

(3) The relevant tax advantage is to be counteracted by means of adjustments.

(4) For this purpose adjustments may be made (whether by an officer of Revenue and Customs or by the person) by way of an assessment, the modification of an assessment, amendment or disallowance of a claim, or otherwise.

(5) In this section "relevant tax advantage" means a tax advantage in relation to income tax to which the person is chargeable (or would without the tax advantage be chargeable) by virtue of section 6(1A).

(6) In this section "tax advantage" includes—

(a) a relief or increased relief from tax,
(b) repayment or increased repayment of tax,
(c) avoidance or reduction of a charge to tax or an assessment to tax,
(d) avoidance of a possible assessment to tax,
(e) deferral of a payment of tax or advancement of a repayment of tax, and
(f) avoidance of an obligation to deduct or account for tax.

(7) In this section—

"arrangement" (except in the phrase "double taxation arrangements") includes any agreement, understanding, scheme, transaction or series of transactions, whether or not legally enforceable;
"double taxation arrangements" means arrangements which have effect under section 2(1) of TIOPA 2010 (double taxation relief by agreement with territories outside the United Kingdom).

6B Trade of dealing in or developing UK land

(1) A non-UK resident person's "trade of dealing in or developing UK land" consists of —

(a) any activities falling within subsection (2) which the person carries on, and
(b) any activities from which profits arise which are treated under Part 9A of ITA 2007 as profits of the person's trade of dealing in or developing UK land.

(2) The activities within this subsection are—

(a) dealing in UK land;
(b) developing UK land for the purpose of disposing of it.

(3) In this section "land" includes—

(a) buildings and structures,
(b) any estate, interest or right in or over land, and
(c) land under the sea or otherwise covered by water.

(4) In this section—

"disposal" is to be interpreted in accordance with section 517R of ITA 2007;
"UK land" means land in the United Kingdom."

(3) In section 3 of ITTOIA 2005 (overview of Part 2), in subsection (4) for "6(2)" substitute "6(1A), (2)".

(4) In section 243 of ITTOIA 2005 (post-cessation receipts: extent of charge to tax), in subsection (4), at the end insert ", other than a person's trade of dealing in or developing UK land".

(5) In section 989 of ITA 2007 (definitions for purposes of Income Tax Acts), at the appropriate place insert—

""trade of dealing in or developing UK land", in relation to a non-UK resident person, has the meaning given by section 6B of ITTOIA 2005,".

GENERAL NOTE

Sections 78 and 79

Sections 78–79 essentially repeat the provisions of ss 76–77 for income tax purposes. This is necessary because the tax law rewrite process resulted in separate acts for income tax and corporation tax purposes. This commentary does not duplicate the commentary for those sections and only points out those areas where there is a substantive difference between the corporation tax and income tax version of the legislation.

Section 78(1)
This inserts new ITTOIA 2005 s 6(IA). Profits or a trade of dealing in or developing UK land arising to a non UK resident are chargeable under this chapter and not under the normal rules for trading.

Section 78(2)
This introduces a new ITTOIA 2005 s 6A "arrangements for avoiding tax".
This mirrors the new CTA 2009 ss 5A and 5B, which were introduced by s 76(5).

Section 78(3)–(5)
These are minor drafting amendments.

79 Income tax: transactions in UK land
(1) In ITA 2007, after Part 9 insert—

"PART 9A
TRANSACTIONS IN UK LAND

Introduction

517A Overview of Part
This Part contains provision about the income tax treatment of certain profits and gains realised from disposals concerned with land in the United Kingdom.

Amounts treated as profits of a trade

517B Disposals of land in the United Kingdom
(1) Section 517C(1) applies (subject to subsection (3) of that section) if—
(a) a person within subsection (2)(a), (b) or (c) realises a profit or gain from a disposal of any land in the United Kingdom, and
(b) any of conditions A to D is met in relation to the land.
(2) The persons referred to in subsection (1) are—
(a) the person acquiring, holding or developing the land,
(b) a person who is associated with the person in paragraph (a) at a relevant time, and
(c) a person who is a party to, or concerned in, an arrangement within subsection (3).
(3) An arrangement is within this subsection if—
(a) it is effected with respect to all or part of the land, and
(b) it enables a profit or gain to be realised—
(i) by any indirect method, or
(ii) by any series of transactions.
(4) Condition A is that the main purpose, or one of the main purposes, of acquiring the land was to realise a profit or gain from disposing of the land.
(5) Condition B is that the main purpose, or one of the main purposes, of acquiring any property deriving its value from the land was to realise a profit or gain from disposing of the land.
(6) Condition C is that the land is held as trading stock.
(7) Condition D is that (in a case where the land has been developed) the main purpose, or one of the main purposes, of developing the land was to realise a profit or gain from disposing of the land when developed.
(8) In this section "relevant time" means any time in the period beginning when the activities of the project begin and ending 6 months after the disposal mentioned in subsection (1).

(9) In this section "the project" means all activities carried out for any of the following purposes—

(a) the purposes of dealing in or developing the land, and

(b) any other purposes mentioned in Conditions A to D.

(10) For the purposes of this section a person ("A") is associated with another person ("B") if—

(a) A is connected with B by virtue of any of subsections (2) to (4) of section 993 (read in accordance with section 994), or

(b) A is related to B (see section 517U).

517C Disposals of land: profits treated as trading profits

(1) The profit or gain is to be treated for income tax purposes as profits of a trade carried on by the chargeable person.

(2) If the chargeable person is non-UK resident, that trade is the person's trade of dealing in or developing UK land (as defined in section 6B of ITTOIA 2005).

(3) But subsection (1) does not apply to a profit or gain so far as it would (apart from this section) be brought into account as income in calculating profits (of any person)—

(a) for income tax purposes, or

(b) for corporation tax purposes.

(4) The profits are treated as arising in the tax year in which the profit or gain is realised.

(5) This section applies in relation to gains which are capital in nature as it applies in relation to other gains.

517D Disposals of property deriving its value from land in the United Kingdom

(1) Section 517E(1) applies (subject to subsection (3) of that section) if—

(a) a person realises a profit or gain from a disposal of any property which (at the time of the disposal) derives at least 50% of its value from land in the United Kingdom,

(b) the person is a party to, or concerned in, an arrangement concerning some or all of the land mentioned in paragraph (a) ("the project land"), and

(c) the arrangement meets the condition in subsection (2).

(2) The condition is that the main purpose, or one of the main purposes, of the arrangement is to—

(a) deal in or develop the project land, and

(b) realise a profit or gain from a disposal of property deriving the whole or part of its value from that land.

517E Disposals within section 517D: profits treated as trading profits

(1) The relevant amount is to be treated for income tax purposes as profits of a trade carried on by the chargeable person.

(2) If the chargeable person is non-UK resident, that trade is the chargeable person's trade of dealing in or developing UK land.

(3) But subsection (1) does not apply to an amount so far as it would (apart from this section) be brought into account as income in calculating profits (of any person)—

(a) for income tax purposes, or

(b) for corporation tax purposes.

(4) The profits are treated as arising in the tax year in which the profit or gain is realised.

(5) In this section the "relevant amount" means so much (if any) of the profit or gain mentioned in section 517D(1) as is attributable, on a just and reasonable apportionment, to the relevant UK assets.

(6) In this section "the relevant UK assets" means any land in the United Kingdom from which the property mentioned in section 517D(1) derives any of its value (at the time of the disposal mentioned in that subsection).

(7) This section applies in relation to gains which are capital in nature as it applies in relation to other gains.

517F Profits and losses

(1) Sections 517B to 517E have effect as if they included provision about losses corresponding to the provision they make about profits and gains.

(2) Accordingly, in the following sections of this Part references to a "profit or gain" include a loss.

Person to whom profits attributed

517G The chargeable person

(1) For the purposes of sections 517C and 517E the general rule is that the "chargeable person" is the person ("P") that realises the profit or gain (as mentioned in section 517B(1) or 517D(1)).

(2) The general rule in subsection (1) is subject to the special rules in subsections (4) to (6).

(3) But those special rules do not apply in relation to a profit or gain to which section 517H(3) (fragmented activities) applies.

(4) If all or any part of the profit or gain accruing to P is derived from value provided directly or indirectly by another person ("B"), B is the "chargeable person".

(5) Subsection (4) applies whether or not the value is put at the disposal of P.

(6) If all or any part of the profit or gain accruing to P is derived from an opportunity of realising a profit or gain provided directly or indirectly by another person ("D"), D is "the chargeable person" (unless the case falls within subsection (4)).

(7) For the meaning of "another person" see section 517P.

Anti-fragmentation

517H Fragmented activities

(1) Subsection (3) applies if—

    (a) a person ("P") disposes of any land in the United Kingdom,
    (b) any of conditions A to D in section 517B is met in relation to the land, and
    (c) a person ("R") who is associated with P at a relevant time has made a relevant contribution to activities falling within subsection (2).

(2) The following activities fall within this subsection —

    (a) the development of the land,
    (b) any other activities directed towards realising a profit or gain from the disposal of the land.

(3) For the purposes of this Part, the profit or gain (if any) realised by P from the disposal is to be taken to be what that profit or gain would be if R were not a distinct person from P (and, accordingly, as if everything done by or in relation to R had been done by or in relation to P).

(4) Subsection (5) applies to any amount which is paid (directly or indirectly) by R to P for the purposes of meeting or reimbursing the cost of income tax which P is liable to pay as a result of the application of subsection (3) in relation to R and P.

(5) The amount—

    (a) is not to be taken into account in calculating profits or losses of either R or P for the purposes of income tax or corporation tax, and
    (b) is not for any purpose of the Corporation Tax Acts to be regarded as a distribution.

(6) In subsection (1) "relevant time" means any time in the period beginning when the activities of the project begin and ending 6 months after the disposal.

(7) For the purposes of this section any contribution made by P to activities falling within subsection (2) is a "relevant contribution" unless the profit made or to be made by P in respect of the contribution is insignificant having regard to the size of the project.

(8) In this section "contribution" means any kind of contribution, including, for example—

    (a) the provision of professional or other services, or
    (b) a financial contribution (including the assumption of a risk).

(9) For the purposes of this section R is "associated" with P if—

    (a) R is connected with P by virtue of any of subsections (2) to (4) of section 993 (read in accordance with section 994), or
    (b) R is related to P (see section 517U).

(10) In this section "the project" means all activities carried out for any of the following purposes—

    (a) the purposes of dealing in or developing the land, and

(b) any other purposes mentioned in Conditions A to D in section 517B.

Calculation of profit or gain on disposal

517I Calculation of surplus on a disposal of land

For the purposes of this Part, the profit or gain (if any) from a disposal of any property is to be calculated according to the principles applicable for calculating the profits of a trade under Part 2 of ITTOIA 2005, subject to any modifications that may be appropriate (and for this purpose the same rules are to apply in calculating losses from a disposal as apply in calculating profits).

517J Apportionments

Any apportionment (whether of expenditure, consideration or any other amount) that is required to be made for the purposes of this Part is to be made on a just and reasonable basis.

Arrangements for avoiding tax

517K Arrangements for avoiding tax

(1) Subsection (3) applies if an arrangement has been entered into the main purpose or one of the main purposes of which is to enable a person to obtain a relevant tax advantage.

(2) In subsection (1) the reference to obtaining a relevant tax advantage includes obtaining a relevant tax advantage by virtue of any provisions of double taxation arrangements, but only in a case where the relevant tax advantage is contrary to the object and purpose of the provisions of the double taxation arrangements (and subsection (3) has effect accordingly, regardless of anything in section 6(1) of TIOPA 2010).

(3) The tax advantage is to be counteracted by means of adjustments.

(4) For this purpose adjustments may be made (whether by an officer of Revenue and Customs or by the person) by way of an assessment, the modification of an assessment, amendment or disallowance of a claim, or otherwise.

(5) In this section "relevant tax advantage" means an advantage in relation to income tax charged (or which would, if the tax advantage were not obtained, be charged) in respect of amounts treated as profits of a trade by virtue of this Part.

(6) In this section "advantage" includes—
    (a) a relief or increased relief from tax,
    (b) repayment or increased repayment of tax,
    (c) avoidance or reduction of a charge to tax or an assessment to tax,
    (d) avoidance of a possible assessment to tax,
    (e) deferral of a payment of tax or advancement of a repayment of tax, and
    (f) avoidance of an obligation to deduct or account for tax.

Exemptions

517L Gain attributable to period before intention to develop formed

(1) Subsection (2) applies if—
    (a) subsection (1) of section 517C applies because Condition D in section 517B is met (land developed with purpose of realising a gain from its disposal when developed), and
    (b) part of the profit or gain mentioned in that subsection is fairly attributable to a period before the intention to develop was formed.

(2) Section 517C(1) has effect as if the person mentioned in section 517B(1) had not realised that part of the profit or gain.

(3) Subsection (4) applies if—
    (a) section 517E(1) applies, and
    (b) part of the profit or gain mentioned in section 517E(5) is fairly attributable to a period before the person mentioned in section 517D(1) was a party to, or concerned in, the arrangement in question.

(4) Section 517E has effect as if the person had not realised that part of the profit or gain.

(5) In applying this section account must be taken of the treatment under Part 2 of ITTOIA 2005 (trading income) of a person who appropriates land as trading stock.

517M Private residences

No liability to income tax arises under this Part in respect of a gain accruing to an individual if—

(a) the gain is exempt from capital gains tax as a result of sections 222 to 226 of TCGA 1992 (private residences), or

(b) it would be so exempt but for section 224(3) of that Act (residences acquired partly with a view to making a gain).

Other supplementary provisions

517N Tracing value

(1) This section applies if it is necessary to determine the extent to which the value of any property or right is derived from any other property or right for the purposes of this Part.

(2) Value may be traced through any number of companies, partnerships, trusts and other entities or arrangements.

(3) The property held by a company, partnership or trust must be attributed to the shareholders, partners, beneficiaries or other participants at each stage in whatever way is appropriate in the circumstances.

(4) In this section—

"partnership" includes an entity established under the law of a country or territory outside the United Kingdom of a similar nature to a partnership; and "partners", in relation to such arrangements, is to be construed accordingly;

"trust" includes arrangements—

(a) which have effect under the law of a country or territory outside the United Kingdom; and

(b) under which persons acting in a fiduciary capacity hold and administer property on behalf of other persons,

and "beneficiaries", in relation to such arrangements, is to be construed accordingly.

517O Relevance of transactions, arrangements, etc

(1) In determining whether section 517C(1) or 517E(1) applies, account is to be taken of any method, however indirect, by which—

(a) any property or right is transferred or transmitted, or

(b) the value of any property or right is enhanced or diminished.

(2) Accordingly—

(a) the occasion of the transfer or transmission of any property or right, however indirect, and

(b) the occasion when the value of any property or right is enhanced,

may be an occasion on which section 517C(1) or 517E(1) applies.

(3) Subsections (1) and (2) apply in particular—

(a) to sales, contracts and other transactions made otherwise than for full consideration or for more than full consideration,

(b) to any method by which any property or right, or the control of any property or right, is transferred or transmitted by assigning—

(i) share capital or other rights in a company,

(ii) rights in a partnership, or

(iii) an interest in settled property,

(c) to the creation of an option affecting the disposition of any property or right and the giving of consideration for granting it,

(d) to the creation of a requirement for consent affecting such a disposition and the giving of consideration for granting it,

(e) to the creation of an embargo affecting such a disposition and the giving of consideration for releasing it, and

(f) to the disposal of any property or right on the winding up, dissolution or termination of a company, partnership or trust.

Interpretation

517P "Another person"

(1) In this Part references to "other" persons are to be interpreted in accordance with subsections (2) to (4).

(2) A partnership or partners in a partnership may be regarded as a person or persons distinct from the individuals or other persons who are for the time being partners.

(3) The trustees of settled property may be regarded as persons distinct from the individuals or other persons who are for the time being the trustees.

(4) Personal representatives may be regarded as persons distinct from the individuals or other persons who are for the time being personal representatives.

517Q "Arrangement"

(1) In this Part "arrangement" (except in the phrase "double taxation arrangements") includes any agreement, understanding, scheme, transaction or series of transactions, whether or not legally enforceable.

(2) For the purposes of this Part any number of transactions may be regarded as constituting a single arrangement if—

(a) a common purpose can be discerned in them, or
(b) there is other sufficient evidence of a common purpose.

517R "Disposal"

(1) In this Part references to a "disposal" of any property include any case in which the property is effectively disposed of (whether wholly or in part, as mentioned in subsection (2))—

(a) by one or more transactions, or
(b) by any arrangement.

(2) For the purposes of this Part—

(a) references to a disposal of land or any other property include a part disposal of the property, and
(b) there is a part disposal of property ("the asset") where on a person making a disposal, any form of property derived from the asset remains undisposed of (including in cases where an interest or right in or over the asset is created by the disposal, as well as where it subsists before the disposal).

517S "Land" and related expressions

(1) In this Part "land" includes—

(a) buildings and structures,
(b) any estate, interest or right in or over land, and
(c) land under the sea or otherwise covered by water.

(2) In this Part references to property deriving its value from land include—

(a) any shareholding in a company deriving its value directly or indirectly from land,
(b) any partnership interest deriving its value directly or indirectly from land,
(c) any interest in settled property deriving its value directly or indirectly from land, and
(d) any option, consent or embargo affecting the disposition of land.

517T References to realising a gain

(1) For the purposes of sections 517B(1) and 517D(1) it does not matter whether the person ("P") realising the profit or gain in question realises it for P or another person.

(2) For the purposes of subsection (1), if, for example by a premature sale, a person ("A") directly or indirectly transmits the opportunity of realising a profit or gain to another person ("B"), A realises B's profit or gain for B.

517U Related parties

(1) For the purposes of this Part a person ("A") is related to another person ("B")—

(a) throughout any period for which A and B are consolidated for accounting purposes,
(b) on any day on which the participation condition is met in relation to them, or
(c) on any day on which the 25% investment condition is met in relation to them.

(2) A and B are consolidated for accounting purposes for a period if—

(a) their financial results for a period are required to be comprised in group accounts,
(b) their financial results for the period would be required to be comprised in group accounts but for the application of an exemption, or
(c) their financial results for a period are in fact comprised in group accounts.

(3) In subsection (2) "group accounts" means accounts prepared under—
(a) section 399 of the Companies Act 2006, or
(b) any corresponding provision of the law of a territory outside the United Kingdom.

(4) The participation condition is met in relation to A and B ("the relevant parties") on a day if, within the period of 6 months beginning with that day—
(a) one of the relevant parties directly or indirectly participates in the management, control or capital of the other, or
(b) the same person or persons directly or indirectly participate in the management, control or capital of each of the relevant parties.

(5) The 25% investment condition is met in relation to A and B if—
(a) one of them has a 25% investment in the other, or
(b) a third person has a 25% investment in each of them.

(6) Section 259NC of TIOPA 2010 applies for the purposes of determining whether a person has a "25% investment" in another person for the purposes of this section as it applies for the purposes of section 259NB(2) of that Act.

(7) In Chapter 2 of Part 4 of TIOPA 2010, sections 157(2), 158(4), 159(2) and 160(2) (which are about the interpretation of references to direct and indirect participation) apply in relation to subsection (4) as they apply in relation to subsection (4) of section 259NA of that Act."

(2) In section 2 of ITA 2007 (overview of Act)—
(a) after subsection (9) insert—

"(9A) Part 9A is about the treatment of certain transactions in UK land.", and

(b) in subsection (13), omit paragraph (c).

(3) In section 482 of ITA 2007 (types of amount to be charged at special rates for trustees), in the words relating to Type 11, for "Chapter 3 of Part 13 of this Act (tax avoidance: transactions in land)" substitute "Part 9A of this Act (transactions in land)".

(4) In section 527 of ITA 2007 (exemption from charges under provisions to which section 1016 applies), in subsection (2)—
(a) insert "and" at the end of paragraph (d), and
(b) omit paragraph (e).

(5) In Part 13 of ITA 2007, omit Chapter 3 (transactions in land).

(6) In section 944 of ITA 2007 (tax avoidance: directions for duty to deduct to apply), in subsection (1)—
(a) omit paragraph (a), and
(b) in paragraph (b) for "that Part" substitute "Part 13".

(7) In section 1016 of ITA 2007 (table of provisions to which that section applies), in Part 2 of the table in subsection (2), omit the entry relating to Chapter 3 of Part 13 of that Act.

(8) In section 37 of TCGA 1992 (consideration chargeable to tax on income), in subsection (5)(a), for the words from "759(4)" to "is" substitute "517G(4) or (6) of ITA 2007 (transactions in land: the chargeable person) applies, an amount is charged to income tax as income of"

(9) In section 39 of TCGA 1992 (exclusion of expenditure by reference to tax on income), in subsection (4)(a), for the words from "759(4)" to "is" substitute "517G(4) or (6) of ITA 2007 (transactions in land: the chargeable person) applies, an amount is charged to income tax as income of".

(10) In section 161 of TCGA 1992 (appropriations to and from stock), in subsection (5), for paragraph (a) substitute—

"(a) any person is charged to income tax by virtue of sections 517B and 517C of CTA 2010 (certain profits or gains on a disposal of land treated as trading profits) on the realisation of a profit or gain because the condition in section 517B(7) of that Act is met, and".

(11) In section 830 of ITTOIA 2005, in subsection (3), for the words from "of" to the end substitute "of—
(a) section 844 (unremittable income: income charged on withdrawal of relief after source ceases), or
(b) section 517C or 517E of ITA 2007 (profits on certain disposals concerned with land in the United Kingdom treated as trading profits)."

GENERAL NOTE

Section 79(1)

This introduces a new ITA 2007 Pt 9A.

New Pt 9A

New s 517A

This mirrors s 356OA above.

New s 517B

This mirrors s 356OB above.

New s 517C

This mirrors s 356OC above.

New s 517D

This mirrors s 356OD above

New s 517E

This mirrors s 356OE above.

New s 517F

This mirrors s 356OF above.

New s 517G

This mirrors s 35OG above.

New s 517H above

This mirrors s 350H above.

New s 517I

This mirrors s 35OI above.

New s 517J

This mirrors s 350J above.

New s 517K

This mirrors s356OK above.

New s 517L

This mirrors s356OL above.

New s 517M

This is section which applies only for income tax purposes.

The new Pt 9A does not apply to a gain which is exempted under the private residence rules in TCGA ss 222–226, or would be exempt but for s 224(3) – residences acquired partly with a view to making a gain.

New s 517N

This mirrors s 356OM above (note from this point the numbering of the new sections moves out of parallel with the equivalent corporation tax provisions because of the insertion of s 517M, which does not have a corporation tax equivalent).

New s 517O

This mirrors s 356ON above.

New s 517P

This mirrors s 356OO above.

New s 517Q

This mirrors s 356OP above.

New s 517R

This mirrors s 356OQ above.

New s 517S

This mirrors s 356OR above.

New s 517T

This mirrors s 356OS above.

New s 517U

This mirrors s 356OT above.

Section 79(2)–(4)

These are minor drafting amendments.

Section 79(5)

This repeals the entirety of the existing rules in ITA 2007 Pt 13 dealing with transactions inland.

Section 79(6)–(11)

These are minor drafting amendments.

80 Pre-trading expenses

(1) Subsection (2) has effect if—

(a) a particular time ("T") is the time when a company ("C") is first within the charge to corporation tax by virtue of subsection (2)(a) of section 5 of CTA 2009 (territorial scope of charge),

(b) immediately before time T, C was within the charge to corporation tax as a result of carrying on the relevant trade in the United Kingdom through a permanent establishment in the United Kingdom, and

(c) expenses which the company has incurred for the purposes of the trade meet the conditions in subsection (3) and (4).

"The relevant trade" means the trade of dealing in or developing UK land mentioned in subsection (2)(a) of section 5 of CTA 2009.

(2) Section 61 of CTA 2009 (pre-trading expenses) has effect in relation to those expenses as if the company had started to carry on the relevant trade at time T.

(3) The condition in this subsection is that—

(a) no deduction would be allowed for the expenses in calculating the profits of the relevant trade for corporation tax purposes (ignoring subsection (2)), but

(b) a deduction would be allowed for them (in accordance with sections 41 and section 61 of CTA 2009) if the company had not been within the charge to corporation tax in respect of the relevant trade immediately before time T.

(4) The condition in this subsection is that no relief has been obtained for the expenses under the law of any country or territory outside the United Kingdom.

GENERAL NOTE

Section 80(1)

This introduces sub-s (2) by setting out the conditions under which it has effect. Subsection (2) applies where immediately before the time at which the company came within the charge under s 5(2)(a) it was carrying on a trade in the UK through a permanent establishment and incurred expenses which meet the conditions in sub-ss (3) and (4) below.

Section 80(2)

Those expenses are treated as pre-trading expenses as if the company had started to carry on the trade at the point at which it came within the s 5(2)(a) charge. The effect of this is that relief is not lost for expenses incurred by a company which was within the charge under the old regime simply because it moves into the new regime as a result of Pt 8ZB.

Section 80(3)

This sets out the first of the conditions referred to in sub-s (1) above. This is that no deduction would be allowed for the expenses in calculating the profits of trade but a deduction would be allowed under ss 41 and 61 – pre trading expenses – if the company had not been within the charge to corporation tax before the company came within the charge under the new rules.

Section 80(4)

The other condition is that no relief has been obtained for the expenses under the law of a country or territory outside the UK.

81 Commencement and transitional provision: sections 76, 77 and 80

(1) The amendments made by sections 76, 77 and 80 have effect in relation to disposals on or after 5 July 2016.

(2) In subsection (1) of section 5A of CTA 2009 (tax avoidance in relation to section 5(2A) of that Act) "arrangement" does not include an arrangement (as defined in section 5A(6) of that Act) entered into before 16 March 2016.

(3) In subsection (1) of section 356OK of CTA 2010 (tax avoidance in relation to Part 8ZB of CTA 2010) "arrangement" does not include an arrangement (as defined in section 356OP of that Act) entered into before 16 March 2016.

(4) Subsection (6) applies if—
(a) a person disposes of a relevant asset to a person who is associated with that person at the relevant time,
(b) the disposal is made on or after 16 March 2016 and before 5 July 2016, and
(c) a company obtains a relevant tax advantage as a result of the disposal.

(5) In subsection (4) the reference to obtaining a relevant tax advantage includes obtaining a relevant tax advantage by virtue of any provisions of double taxation arrangements, but only in a case where the relevant tax advantage is contrary to the object and purpose of the provisions of the double taxation arrangements (and subsection (6) has effect accordingly, regardless of anything in section 6(1) of TIOPA 2010).

(6) The tax advantage is to be counteracted by means of adjustments.

(7) Adjustments for the purposes of subsection (6) may be made (whether by an officer of Revenue and Customs or by the company) by way of an assessment, the modification of an assessment, amendment or disallowance of a claim, or otherwise.

(8) In subsection (4)(c) "relevant tax advantage" means a tax advantage in relation to tax to which the company in question is charged or chargeable (or would, if the tax advantage were not obtained, be charged or chargeable)—
(a) by virtue of section 5(2A) of CTA 2009, or
(b) in respect of amounts treated as profits of a trade by virtue of Part 8ZB of CTA 2010.

(9) For the purposes of this section, where any property is disposed of under a contract, the time at which the disposal is made is the time the contract is made (and not, if different, the time at which the property is conveyed or transferred).

(10) In subsection (9) "contract" includes a conditional contract.

(11) In this section—
"arrangement" includes any scheme, agreement or understanding (whether or not legally enforceable);
"disposal" is to be interpreted in accordance with section 356OQ of CTA 2010;
"relevant asset" means land, or property deriving the whole or part of its value from land;
"tax advantage" has the meaning given by section 1139 of CTA 2010.

(12) For the purposes of this section a person ("A") is "associated" with another person ("B") if—

(a) A is connected with B by virtue of any of subsections (5) to (7) of section 1122 of CTA 2010 (read in accordance with section 1123 of that Act), or

(b) A is related to B.

(13) In subsection (12) "related to" is to be interpreted in accordance with section 356OT of CTA 2010.

(14) In subsection (4) "the relevant time"—

(a) in a case within subsection (8)(a), means the time of the disposal mentioned in subsection (4)(a).

(b) in a case within subsection (8)(b), means any time in the period beginning when the activities of the project began and ending 6 months after the disposal mentioned in section 356OB(1) or 356OD(1) of CTA 2010.

(15) In subsection (14) "the project" means (as the case requires) the project described in section 356OB(9) of CTA 2010 or the activities mentioned in section 356OD(2)(a) of that Act.

GENERAL NOTE

Section 81(1)

Sections 76, 77 and 80, which are the corporation tax version of the legislation, take effect in relation to disposals on or after 5 July 2016. This is the day on which the legislation was introduced at report stage of the bill, for reasons explained in the introductory note to this commentary.

Section 81(2) and (3)

These provide an exemption from the new charge for arrangements entered into before 16 March 2016.

Section 81(4)

This introduces sub-s (6) below which is an anti-forestalling measure. It applies we a porcon dicpococ of a rolevant aooct to a peroon who io aooociatcd with him at the relevant time; the disposal was made between 16 March 2016 and 4 July 2016 inclusive and a company obtains a relevant tax advantage as a result of the disposal.

Section 81(5)

In double tax relief cases there is a tax advantage only when the advantage is contrary to the objects and purposes of the relevant arrangements.

Section 81(6)

Any tax advantage is to be counteracted by means of adjustments.

Section 81(7)

As in the substantive provisions adjustments made be made by an officer of HMRC or the company by way of assessments or modifications of an assessment, amendment or disallowance of a claim or otherwise.

Section 81(8)

This defines relevant tax advantage.

Section 81(9)

This imports the normal rule for the date of a property disposal. Where property is disposed of under a contract the disposal date is the contract date and not the date of conveyance or transfer.

Section 81(10)

Contract for this purpose includes a conditional contract.

Section 81(11)

Arrangements takes its normal wide definition to include any scheme, agreement or understanding, whether or not legally enforceable. Disposal is to be interpreted in accordance with CTA 2010 s 356OQ. Relevant asset means land or property deriving all or part of its value from land. Tax advantage takes the definition in CTA 2010 s 1139.

Section 81(12)
This defines the circumstances in which A is associated with B. They are associated if A is connected to be under any of the tests in CTA 2010 s 1122 or if A is related to B.

Section 81(13)
The test is CTA 2010 s 356OT is to be used to determine if two people are related.

Section 81(14)
The relevant time in a case within s 8(a) above is the time of the disposal. In a case within s 8(b) it is any time beginning with the project began and ending six months after the disposal date

Section 81(15)
For the purposes of sub-s (14) above the project means the project in s 356OB(9) of the activities mentioned in s 356OD(2)(a).

82 Commencement and transitional provision: sections 78 and 79

(1) The amendments made by sections 78 and 79 have effect in relation to disposals on or after 5 July 2016.

(2) In subsection (1) of section 6A of ITA 2007 (tax avoidance arrangements in relation to section 6(1A) of that Act) "arrangement" does not include an arrangement (as defined in section 6A(7) of that Act) entered into before 16 March 2016.

(3) In subsection (1) of section 517K of ITA 2007 (tax avoidance in relation to Part 9A of that Act) "arrangement" does not include an arrangement (as defined in section 517Q of that Act) entered into before 16 March 2016.

(4) Subsection (6) applies if—

(a) a person disposes of a relevant asset to a person who is associated with that person at the relevant time,

(b) the disposal is made on or after 16 March 2016 and before 5 July 2016, and

(c) a person obtains a relevant tax advantage as a result of the disposal.

(5) In subsection (4) the reference to obtaining a relevant tax advantage includes obtaining a relevant tax advantage by virtue of any provisions of double taxation arrangements, but only in a case where the relevant tax advantage is contrary to the object and purpose of the provisions of the double taxation arrangements (and subsection (6) has effect accordingly, regardless of anything in section 6(1) of TIOPA 2010).

(6) The tax advantage is to be counteracted by means of adjustments.

(7) Adjustments for the purposes of subsection (6) may be made (whether by an officer of Revenue and Customs or by the person) by way of an assessment, the modification of an assessment, amendment or disallowance of a claim, or otherwise.

(8) In subsection (4)(c) "relevant tax advantage" means a tax advantage in relation to tax to which the person in question is charged or chargeable (or would, if the tax advantage were not obtained, be charged or chargeable)—

(a) by virtue of section 6(1A) of ITTOIA 2005, or

(b) in respect of amounts treated as profits of a trade by virtue of Part 9A of ITA 2007.

(9) For the purposes of this section, where any property is disposed of under a contract, the time at which the disposal is made is the time the contract is made (and not, if different, the time at which the property is conveyed or transferred).

(10) In subsection (9) "contract" includes a conditional contract.

(11) In this section—

"arrangement" includes any scheme, agreement or understanding (whether or not legally enforceable);

"disposal" is to be interpreted in accordance with section 517R of ITA2007;

"relevant asset" means land, or property deriving the whole or part of its value from land;

"tax advantage" has the same meaning as in section 6A of ITTOIA 2005.

(12) For the purposes of this section a person ("A") is "associated" with another person ("B") if—

(a) A is connected with B by virtue of any of subsections (2) to (4) of section 993 of ITA 2007 (read in accordance with section 994 of that Act), or

(b) A is related to B.

(13) In subsection (12) "related to" is to be interpreted in accordance with section 517U of ITA 2007.

(14) In subsection (4), "the relevant time"—

(a) in a case within subsection (8)(a), means the time when the disposal was made,

(b) in a case within subsection (8)(b), means any time in the period beginning when the activities of the project began and ending 6 months after the disposal mentioned in section 517B(1) or 517D(1) of ITA 2007.

(15) In subsection (14) "the project" means (as the case requires) the project described in section 517B(9) of ITA 2007 or the activities mentioned in section 517D(2)(a) of that Act.

GENERAL NOTE

These provisions replicate for income tax purposes the commencement and transitional provisions in s 81, which apply for corporation tax purposes. The commencement date is, as above, 5 July 2016 and similar anti-forestalling provisions also apply to disposals between 16 March and 5 July 2016.

PART 4

CAPITAL GAINS TAX

Rate

83 Reduction in rate of capital gains tax

(1) Section 4 of TCGA 1992 (rates of capital gains tax) is amended as set out in subsections (2) to (12).

(2) In subsection (1) after "entrepreneurs' relief)" insert "and section 169VC (rate in case of claim for investors' relief)".

(3) In subsection (2)—

(a) after "section" insert "and section 4BA", and

(b) for the words from "in respect" to the end substitute—

"(a) in respect of upper rate gains accruing to a person in a tax year, is 18%, and

(b) in respect of gains accruing to a person in a tax year which are not upper rate gains, is 10%."

(4) After subsection (2) insert—

"(2A) In this section "upper rate gains" means—

(a) residential property gains (see section 4BB),

(b) NRCGT gains (see section 14D), and

(c) carried interest gains (see subsections (12) and (13))."

(5) For subsection (3) substitute—

"(3) The rate of capital gains tax in respect of gains accruing in a tax year to the trustees of a settlement or the personal representatives of a deceased person—

(a) in respect of upper rate gains, is 28%, and

(b) in respect of gains which are not upper rate gains, is 20%."

(6) In subsection (4), for the words from the second "in respect" to the end substitute—

"(a) in respect of upper rate gains accruing to the individual in the tax year, is 28%, and

(b) in respect of gains accruing to the individual in the tax year which are not upper rate gains, is 20%."

(7) In subsection (5) for "28%" substitute "(subject to section 4BA) 20%".

(8) For subsection (6) substitute—

"(6) Subsection (6A) applies for the purposes of subsection (5) where—

(a) there is an excess as mentioned in that subsection ("the higher-rate excess"), and

(b) the amount on which the individual is chargeable to capital gains tax for the tax year includes any special rate gains, that is, gains which are—

    (i) chargeable to capital gains tax at the rate in section 169N(3), or

    (ii) chargeable to capital gains tax at the rate in section 169VC(2).

(6A) Where this subsection applies—

(a) if the total amount of the special rate gains exceeds the unused part of the individual's basic rate band, the higher-rate excess is to be treated as reduced by the amount by which the special rate gains exceed that unused part;

(b) if not, the higher-rate excess is to be treated as consisting of gains other than the special rate gains."

(9) In subsection (7) for "The reference in subsection (5)" substitute "Any reference in this section".

(10) In subsection (9) after "this section" insert "and section 4BA".

(11) In subsection (10) after "and (5)" insert "and section 4BA(1)".

(12) After subsection (11) insert—

"(12) In subsection (2A)(c) "carried interest gains" means—

(a) gains treated as accruing under section 103KA(2) or (3), and

(b) gains accruing to an individual as a result of carried interest arising to the individual where—

    (i) the individual performs investment management services directly or indirectly in respect of an investment scheme under arrangements not involving a partnership,

    (ii) the carried interest arises to the individual under the arrangements, and

    (iii) the carried interest does not constitute a co-investment repayment or return.

(13) For the purposes of subsection (12)(b)—

(a) "carried interest", in relation to any arrangements, has the same meaning as in section 809EZB of ITA 2007 (see sections 809EZC and 809EZD of that Act);

(b) carried interest "arises" to an individual if it arises to him or her for the purposes of Chapter 5E of Part 13 of ITA 2007;

(c) "arrangements", "investment management services" and "investment scheme" have the same meanings as in that Chapter (see sections 809EZA(6) and 809EZE of that Act);

(d) "co-investment repayment or return" has the same meaning as in section 103KA."

(13) In section 4A of TCGA 1992 (special cases), in subsection (5) after "and (5)" insert "and section 4BA(1)".

(14) After section 4B of TCGA 1992 insert—

"4BA Rates, and use of unused basic rate band, in certain cases

(1) This section applies where an individual is chargeable to capital gains tax in respect of gains accruing in a tax year and—

(a) no income tax is chargeable at the higher rate, the Welsh higher rate or the dividend upper rate in respect of the income of the individual for the tax year,

(b) the amount on which the individual is chargeable to capital gains tax for the tax year ("the chargeable gains amount") exceeds the unused part of the individual's basic rate band, and

(c) all or part of the chargeable gains amount consists of upper rate gains.

(2) In the following provisions of this section "the available gains" means the gains on which the individual is chargeable to capital gains tax for the tax year, excluding any special rate gains.

(3) The available gains not used by the individual under subsection (4) are to be charged to capital gains tax—

(a) to the extent that they consist of upper rate gains, at the rate in section 4(4)(a);

(b) to the extent that they consist of gains which are not upper rate gains, at the rate in section 4(5).

(4) The individual may, subject to subsection (5) (which limits the overall amount that can be used under this subsection)—

(a) use any of the available gains that are upper rate gains to be charged at the rate in section 4(2)(a);

(b) use any of the available gains that are not upper rate gains to be charged at the rate in section 4(2)(b).

(5) The total amount of gains used under subsection (4) must equal the qualifying amount.

(6) The "qualifying amount" is the unused part of the individual's basic rate band less the total amount of any special rate gains.

(7) If special rate gains are included in the chargeable gains amount, subsection (4) applies only if the unused part of the individual's basic rate band exceeds the total amount of the special rate gains.

(8) In this section—

"upper rate gains" has the same meaning as in section 4;
"special rate gains" has the same meaning as in section 4(6);
"the unused part of the individual's basic rate band" has the same meaning as in section 4.

4BB Residential property gain or loss

(1) For the purposes of the charge to capital gains tax, a residential property gain or loss is a gain or loss which accrues on the disposal of a residential property interest.

(2) But a residential property gain or loss does not accrue on a non-resident CGT disposal.

(3) In this Act "disposal of a residential property interest" means—

(a) a disposal of a UK residential property interest, or
(b) a disposal of a non-UK residential property interest.

(4) Schedule B1 gives the meaning in this Act of "disposal of a UK residential property interest".

(5) Schedule BA1 gives the meaning in this Act of "disposal of a non-UK residential property interest".

(6) See section 57C and Schedule 4ZZC for how to compute—

(a) the residential property gain or loss accruing on the disposal of a residential property interest, and
(b) the gain or loss accruing on the disposal of a residential property interest which is not a residential property gain or loss."

(15) Schedule 11 inserts Schedule BA1 in TCGA 1992 and makes related amendments.

(16) Schedule 12 inserts section 57C and Schedule 4ZZC in TCGA 1992 and makes related amendments.

(17) The amendments made by this section and Schedules 11 and 12 have effect in relation to gains accruing on or after 6 April 2016.

(18) In relation to a time before the tax year appointed under section 14(3)(b) of the Wales Act 2014 in relation to the provision inserted by section 9(14) of that Act, subsection (1) of section 4BA of TCGA 1992 (inserted by subsection (14) of this section) has effect as if the words ", the Welsh higher rate" were omitted.

(19) In relation to a time before the tax year appointed under section 13(15) of the Scotland Act 2016, subsection (1) of section 4BA of TCGA 1992 (inserted by subsection (14) of this section) has effect as if before "or the dividend upper rate" there were inserted ", the Scottish higher rate".

GENERAL NOTE

This section reduces the general rates of capital gains tax to 10% for basic rate taxpayers and 20% for higher rate taxpayers. It takes effect from 6 April 2016. Whilst this may seem a simple change, it is complicated by the policy decision to retain the former rates of 18% and 28% for residential property and carried interest as set out in TCGA 1992, s 4(2A) – defined as "upper rate gains". Upper rate gains are defined within TCGA 1992 with "residential property gains" requiring a new section – TCGA 1992 s 4BB.

The approach to capital gains tax rates is further complicated by the need to factor in investors' relief gains at 10% which together with entrepreneurs' relief gains are defined as "special rate gains".

The reduction in the rate of capital gains tax was politically controversial and was debated both in the Committee of the Whole House and at Report Stage. A Government Amendment at Report Stage introduced TCGA 1992 s 4(12) and (13) to give a broader and more comprehensive definition of carried interest, in order to avoid carried interest being structured in a way to avoid the higher tax rate.

In the House of Commons Report Stage debate on 6 September 2016, Jane Ellison, The Financial Secretary to the Treasury, said that the reduction in the rate of capital gains tax "provides an incentive for people to invest in companies" and that the 28% and 18% rates for carried interest are "justified by the fact that carried interest is a performance-related award that is hybrid in nature, with characteristics that distinguish it from most other types of capital gain".

The change in rates necessitates computational adjustments. TCGA 1992 s 4(6A) provides that special rate gains use up an individual's unused basic rate band. TCGA 1992 s 4BA is in turn inserted to allow individuals, with both upper rate gains and non-upper rate gains and an unused part of their basic rate band, to choose which gains are treated as falling within their unused basic rate band.

TCGA 1992 s 4BB defines a residential property gain or loss by reference to it being a disposal of a residential property interest. This section makes TCGA 1992 s 14C redundant. Section 4BB(2) excludes non-resident disposals and sub-s (3) further sub-divides a residential property interest into UK and non-UK categories. These are then defined by reference to TCGA 1992 Sch B1 (which was introduced by FA 2015) for UK property interests and TCGA 1992 Sch BA1 which is inserted by FA 2016 Sch 11.

Entrepreneurs' Relief

84 Entrepreneurs' relief: associated disposals

(1) Section 169K of TCGA 1992 (disposal associated with relevant material disposal) is amended as follows.

(2) In subsection (1)—

    (a) in paragraph (a), after "A1," insert "A1A,", and

    (b) in paragraph (b), for "and C" substitute ", C and D".

(3) After subsection (1A) insert—

"(1AA) Condition A1A is that P makes a material disposal of business assets which consists of the disposal of the whole of P's interest in the assets of a partnership, and—

    (a) that interest is an interest of less than 5%,

    (b) P holds at least a 5% interest in the partnership's assets throughout a continuous period of at least 3 years in the 8 years ending with the date of the disposal, and

    (c) at the date of the disposal, no partnership purchase arrangements exist.

(1AB) Subject to subsection (6A), for the purposes of conditions A1 and A1A, in relation to the disposal of an interest in the assets of a partnership, "partnership purchase arrangements" means arrangements (other than the material disposal itself) under which P or a person connected with P is entitled to acquire any interest in, or increase that person's interest in, the partnership (including a share of the profits or assets of the partnership or an interest in such a share)."

(4) In subsection (1E), in the words before paragraph (a)—

    (a) at the beginning insert "Subject to subsection (6A),", and

    (b) after "means arrangements" insert "(other than the material disposal itself)".

(5) After subsection (3A) insert—

"(3AA) Subject to subsection (6A), for the purposes of condition B, in relation to a disposal mentioned in that condition and a partnership, "partnership purchase arrangements" means arrangements under which P or a person connected with P is entitled to acquire any interest in, or increase that person's interest in, the partnership (including a share of the profits or assets of the partnership or an interest in such a share), but does not include any arrangements in connection with a material disposal in relation to which condition A1 or A1A is met."

(6) In subsection (3B), for "arrangements" to the end substitute "share purchase arrangements".

(7) After subsection (3B) insert—

"(3BA) Subject to subsection (6A), for the purposes of condition B, in relation to a disposal mentioned in that condition and company A, "share purchase arrangements" means arrangements under which P or a person connected with P is entitled to acquire shares in or securities of—

    (a) company A, or

(b) a company which is a member of a trading group of which company A is a member,

but does not include any arrangements in connection with a material disposal in relation to which condition A2 or A3 is met."

(8) In subsection (3C), for "(3B)" substitute "(3BA)".

(9) After subsection (4) insert—

"(4A) Condition D is that the disposal mentioned in condition B is of an asset which P owns throughout the period of 3 years ending with the date of that disposal."

(10) Omit subsection (6).

(11) Before subsection (7) insert—

"(6A) For the purposes of this section, in relation to a material disposal of business assets and a disposal mentioned in condition B, arrangements are not partnership purchase arrangements or share purchase arrangements if they were made before both disposals and without regard to either of them."

(12) In subsection (9), after "entitled to share in the" insert "capital".

(13) The amendments made by subsections (2)(a), (3) to (8) and (10) to (12) have effect in relation to disposals made on or after 18 March 2015.

(14) The amendments made by subsections (2)(b) and (9) have effect in relation to disposals of assets which are acquired on or after 13 June 2016.

GENERAL NOTE

Changes made in Finance Act 2015 were intended to restrict the availability of entrepreneurs' relief on associated disposals to situations where the person making the material disposal of business assets was disposing of at least a 5% interest in a partnership or a trading company. There were, however, two main areas of concern as a result of those changes, which are addressed by s 84. Firstly, an individual who was a member of a partnership but did not have a 5% interest in that partnership was nevertheless entitled to entrepreneurs' relief on a disposal of their partnership interests, and would have legitimately expected to be able to claim entrepreneurs' relief on any associated disposals, as well. Clearly, this would not be the case if the associated disposal required a disposal of at least a 5% interest in the partnership. Secondly, in certain industries, particularly farming, it was common for succession to take place down the generations through family partnerships or companies. The anti-avoidance rules, which were designed to prevent somebody selling a 5% interest to satisfy the conditions for an associated disposal, then re-acquiring some or all of that interest at a later date, prevented disposals to relatives because of the connected party test in the anti-avoidance rule.

Scope

A new Condition A1A is inserted into s 169K TCGA 1992, as an alternative to Condition A1 (the requirement that a material disposal of business assets be at least 5% of the partnership interest). This permits an individual to make a material disposal of business assets consisting of the whole of their interest in the assets of a partnership, so long as the individual concerned held at least a 5% interest in the partnership's assets throughout a continuous period of three years in the previous eight years ending with the date of disposal. This additional condition in s 169K means that entrepreneurs' relief may be available on an associated disposal, if the material disposal of business assets comprises the whole of a sub-5% interest.

There is a further requirement that no partnership purchase arrangements exist, both for Conditions A1A and A1 (the requirement that a material disposal of business assets be at least 5% of the partnership interest). Partnership purchase arrangements are arrangements under which the individual or a person connected with the individual is entitled to acquire or increase an interest in the partnership. But the material disposal itself is excluded from being partnership purchase arrangements. So, if an individual sells his residual partnership share, or a 5% partnership share, to his son, for example, this is not a partnership purchase arrangement.

The definition of share purchase arrangements for the purposes of Conditions A2 and A3 (disposals of shares and disposals of securities of a company, respectively), are amended to exclude from share purchase arrangements the material disposal of business assets, itself. Once again, this means that a direct disposal to a relative will not be caught by this anti-avoidance rule, thus permitting family succession.

A further amendment is made so that all of the anti-avoidance rules, i.e. those relating to both share purchase arrangements and partnership purchase arrangements, are subject to a new condition, which excludes any arrangements made before the material disposal of business assets and also before the associated disposal. In effect, this means that longstanding family succession arrangements will not be held to be either partnership purchase arrangements or share purchase arrangements.

The anti-avoidance legislation for Condition B is also amended. Condition B is the requirement for there to be a withdrawal from the business associated with the material disposal of business assets. New s 169K(3AA) defines partnership purchase arrangements as arrangements under which P or a person connected with P is entitled to acquire an interest in, or increase that person's interest in, the partnership, but does not include any arrangements in connection with a material disposal in relation to which Conditions ZA1 or A1 are met. In effect, this overrides the previous definition of partnership purchase arrangements, so that if either of the earlier conditions are met, and are not disapplied by the relevant anti-avoidance provision, then Condition B continues to be satisfied, even if there are partnership purchase arrangements.

New s 169K(3BA) achieves the same result for material disposals of business assets involving shares or securities of a company.

A new Condition D is included which states that, for an associated disposal to qualify for entrepreneurs' relief, the relevant asset must have been held for at least three years continuously, ending with the date of the disposal. However, this only applies to assets acquired on or after 13 June 2016, so that disposals before that date where the asset had not been owned for three years are unaffected.

Commencement

The new rules are effective for disposals on or after 18 March 2015, and are deliberately intended to be retrospective to the date of the original announcement of the FA 2015 changes.

85 Entrepreneurs' relief: disposal of goodwill

(1) Section 169LA of TCGA 1992 (relevant business assets: goodwill transferred to a related party etc) is amended as follows.

(2) In subsection (1)—

   (a) at the beginning insert "Subject to subsection (1A),",
   (b) at the end of paragraph (a) insert "and",
   (c) after paragraph (a) insert—
   "(aa) immediately after the disposal—

      (i) P and any relevant connected person together own 5% or more of the ordinary share capital of C or of any company which is a member of a group of companies of which C is a member, or
      (ii) P and any relevant connected person together hold 5% or more of the voting rights in C or in any company which is a member of a group of companies of which C is a member.", and

   (d) omit paragraphs (b) and (c).

(3) After subsection (1) insert—

   "(1A) Where—

      (a) subsection (1)(aa) applies by virtue of P's ownership, or any relevant connected person's ownership, of C's ordinary share capital, and
      (b) the conditions mentioned in subsection (1B) are met,

   subsection (4) does not apply.

   (1B) The conditions referred to in subsection (1A)(b) are—

      (a) P and any relevant connected person dispose of C's ordinary share capital to another company ("A") such that, immediately before the end of the relevant period, neither P nor any relevant connected person own any of C's ordinary share capital, and
      (b) where A is a close company, immediately before the end of the relevant period—

         (i) P and any relevant connected person together own less than 5% of the ordinary share capital of A or of any company which is a member of a group of companies of which A is a member, and

(ii) P and any relevant connected person together hold less than 5% of the voting rights in A or in any company which is a member of a group of companies of which A is a member.

(1C) In subsection (1B) "the relevant period" means the period of 28 days beginning with the date of the qualifying business disposal, or such longer period as the Commissioners for Her Majesty's Revenue and Customs may by notice allow."

(4) Omit subsections (2) and (3).

(5) In subsection (5), omit the words from "(including" to the end.

(6) In subsection (7), omit paragraph (b) and the "or" at the end of paragraph (a).

(7) In subsection (8)—

(a) after the definition of "arrangements" insert—
""group" is to be construed in accordance with section 170;"
(b) for the definition of "associate", "control", "major interest" and "participator" substitute—
""relevant connected person" means—
(a) a company connected with P, and
(b) trustees connected with P."

(8) In the heading, for "related party etc" substitute "close company".

(9) The amendments made by this section have effect in relation to disposals made on or after 3 December 2014.

GENERAL NOTE

Section 85 amends s 169LA TCGA 1992, which was a new provision introduced by Finance Act 2015 to prevent abuse by partners and sole traders selling their business to companies which they owned and claiming entrepreneurs' relief on the disposal of goodwill to the company when there was no effective change of economic ownership. The legislation was deficient in a number of areas and these amendments are intended to correct the position.

The first concern was that the legislation did not permit a claim for entrepreneurs' relief where an individual sold their trade to a company which was owned or partly owned by somebody who was a relative of theirs, which was a clear barrier to family succession.

Furthermore, the rules prevented a large partnership incorporating immediately before sale to another company. In such cases, the partners would not qualify for entrepreneurs' relief on incorporation, and nor would they qualify for entrepreneurs' relief on disposing of their shares in the new company to the ultimate purchaser, as they would not have held the shares for the required 12 months (and many of them may not have been 5% shareholders, in any case).

The final issue that was identified is that a sole trader or partner might sell their business to someone else's company and be granted a small shareholding as part of the transaction. If that shareholding was less than the requisite 5%, that person would be denied entrepreneurs' relief on a genuine commercial sale to a third party company, under the new anti-avoidance rule, and would again not be entitled to entrepreneurs' relief on disposal of the shares, due to not holding the appropriate percentage.

Scope

The FA 2015 version of s 169LA applied when a person sells their business to a company and they are related persons in relation to the company, as defined in Pt 8 CTA 2009. This rule is now replaced by a rule that says that the entrepreneurs' relief on disposal of goodwill is only denied if the vendor themselves, or a relevant connected person together own 5% or more of the ordinary share capital of the company, or of any company which is a member of the same group of companies, or the vendor and any relevant connected person together hold 5% or more of the voting rights in the company or any member of the companies' group. A relevant connected person in this context means either a company or trustees connected with the vendor individual. Most importantly, relatives and other connected persons are not relevant connected persons.

This amendment means that anyone selling their business to a company where they or a relative is a participator can claim entrepreneurs' relief on the disposal of their goodwill, as long as their shareholding after the transaction is not in excess of the 5% of the ordinary share capital or voting power. So this applies to a retiring person who is simply selling their business, as it does to somebody selling to a company that wishes to issue them a small amount of share capital.

There is an exception to this main rule where the purchaser company is sold to another company within 28 days, or such longer period as HMRC might by notice allow. This applies so long as none of the original business vendors, with any relevant connected persons together own 5% or more of the ordinary share capital of the ultimate purchaser company or of any member of a group of companies of which it is a member, or 5% or more of the voting rights in that company or any group member.

So if a group of partners incorporate their business immediately prior to selling the new trading company to a vendor, which is quite common in the professional services arena, so long as the onward sale occurs within 28 days, or such longer period as HMRC might permit, entrepreneurs' relief can again be claimed on the disposal of goodwill into the original company. It has been suggested that the 28 day period is insufficient in the context of transactions such as a listing (which is becoming more common with professional services firms). However, it may well be that this fall to be one of those cases where HMRC would allow a longer period between the initial incorporation and the actual listing event.

Commencement
These amendments have effect in relation to disposals made on or after 3 December 2014, when the original legislation was first announced.

86 Entrepreneurs' relief: "trading company" and "trading group"
Schedule 13 contains provision about the meaning of "trading company" and "trading group" for the purposes of Chapter 3 of Part 5 of TCGA 1992 (entrepreneurs' relief).

GENERAL NOTE
Section 86 introduces Sch 13, which contains provisions about the meaning of a trading company or a trading group for the purposes of entrepreneurs' relief in the context of joint ventures and partnerships.

Investors' Relief

87 Investors' relief
Schedule 14 contains provision relating to investors' relief.

GENERAL NOTE
Section 87 and Sch 14 introduce Investors' Relief (IR) – described as an extension to Entrepreneurs' Relief (ER) – but legislatively an entirely separate relief. The relief is aimed at encouraging external investment into unquoted trading companies and allows gains arising from the disposal of qualifying shares or interests in such shares to be taxed at a rate of 10%, with a lifetime limit of £10m per individual. Gains in excess of the £10m limit will be taxed at the investor's marginal rate of CGT. The relief applies to subscriptions of newly issued shares made on or after 17 March 2016. To qualify the shares must be held for a continuous period of three years and be disposed of on or after 6 April 2019. An important difference between IR and ER is that IR is not available where an individual, or those connected with him, is an officer or employee of the company or a connected company, although under amendments introduced to the original proposals this restriction will not apply for unremunerated directors and those taking up employment after 180 days of acquiring the shares.

Employee Shareholder Shares

88 Employee shareholder shares: limit on exemption
(1) Section 236B of TCGA 1992 (exemption for employee shareholder shares) is amended in accordance with subsections (2) and (3).
(2) After subsection (1) insert—

"(1A) Where a gain accrues to a person ("P") on the first disposal of a post-16 March 2016 exempt employee shareholder share (the "relevant disposal"), subsection (1) applies only to so much of the gain as, when added to the total amount of previous potentially chargeable gains, does not exceed £100,000.

(1B) For the purposes of subsection (1A), "previous potentially chargeable gain" means a gain accruing to P on the first disposal of a post-16 March 2016 exempt employee shareholder share at any time before the relevant disposal.

(1C) Where a single transaction disposes of more than one post-16 March 2016 exempt employee shareholder share, the reference in subsection (1A) to the first disposal of a share is to be treated as a reference to the disposal of all of the post-16 March 2016 exempt employee shareholder shares first disposed of by that transaction."

(3) After subsection (3) insert—

"(3A) In this section, "post-16 March 2016 exempt employee shareholder share" means an exempt employee shareholder share acquired in consideration of an employee shareholder agreement entered into after 16 March 2016."

(4) Section 236F of TCGA 1992 (reorganisation of share capital involving employee shareholder shares) is amended in accordance with subsections (5) and (6).

(5) After subsection (1) insert—

"(1A) Subsection (1B) applies where—

    (a) an exempt employee shareholder share ("the original EES share") is held by a person ("P") before, and is concerned in, a reorganisation, and
    (b) the original EES share is disposed of on the reorganisation.

(1B) P is to be treated as if the original EES share were disposed of for consideration of an amount determined in accordance with subsections (1D) to (1H) (the "relevant amount").

(1C) In this section "notional gain" means the gain, if any, that would accrue to P if the original EES share were disposed of on the reorganisation for consideration of an amount equal to the market value of the share.

(1D) Subsections (1E) to (1G) apply where a notional gain would accrue to P on the disposal of the original EES share.

(1E) Where the whole of the notional gain would be a chargeable gain by virtue of section 236B(1A), the relevant amount is the amount that would secure that on the disposal neither a gain nor a loss would accrue to P.

(1F) Where part (but not the whole) of the notional gain would be a chargeable gain by virtue of section 236B(1A), the relevant amount is the maximum amount, not exceeding the market value of the share, that would secure that on the disposal no chargeable gain would accrue to P.

(1G) Where no part of the notional gain would be a chargeable gain by virtue of section 236B(1A), the relevant amount is equal to the market value of the original EES share at the time of the disposal.

(1H) Where no notional gain would accrue to P on the disposal of the original EES share, the relevant amount is the amount that would secure that on the disposal neither a gain nor a loss would accrue to P.

(1I) In determining for the purposes of this section whether any part of a notional gain is a chargeable gain by virtue of section 236B(1A), subsection (1B) is to be disregarded.

(1J) Where more than one original EES share is disposed of by P on a reorganisation, references in this section to the disposal of the original EES share are to be treated as references to the disposal of all of the original EES shares disposed of on the reorganisation.

(1K) In this section "reorganisation" has the same meaning as in section 127."

(6) In subsection (2) for "reference in subsection (1) to section 127 includes" substitute "references in this section to section 127 include".

(7) Section 58 of TCGA 1992 (spouses and civil partners) is amended in accordance with subsections (8) and (9).

(8) In subsection (2)(c) after "disposal is" insert "a relevant disposal".

(9) After subsection (2) insert—

"(3) For the purposes of subsection (2) a disposal of exempt employee shareholder shares is a "relevant disposal" if (apart from this section)—

    (a) a gain would accrue on the disposal, and
    (b) no part of the gain would be a chargeable gain.

(4) Subsection (5) applies where the disposal is of exempt employee shareholder shares and (apart from this section)—

(a) a gain would accrue on the disposal, and

(b) part (but not the whole) of the gain would be a chargeable gain by virtue of section 236B(1A).

(5) Where this subsection applies, subsection (1) has effect in relation to the disposal as if—

(a) for "such amount as" there were substituted "the maximum amount, not exceeding the market value of the asset, that", and

(b) for "neither a gain nor a loss" there were substituted "no chargeable gain"."

(10) The amendments made by this section have effect in relation to disposals made after 16 March 2016.

GENERAL NOTE

Section 88 introduces provisions to cap the amount of gains benefitting from the relief from capital gains tax in s 236B TCGA 1992.

The original legislation limited the relief only by reference to the gains arising on shares which, immediately after their acquisition, have a total value not exceeding £50,000. There was no limit on the total amount of gains which might be protected from tax. This created the potential for some shares – typically, growth shares, being shares participating in value above a specified threshold – to result in substantial capital gains being exempt from tax, particularly where the Company issuing the shares had scope for significant share price growth as is often the case where the Company has been subject to a buy-out backed by private equity investors.

The new legislation limits this protection by introducing a lifetime limit of £100,000 of gains. The stated purpose of the legislation is to ensure that "the advantages of Employee Shareholder Status are fair and proportionate and not open to abuse".

Any gains accruing on disposals of shares issued pursuant to employee shareholder agreements made on or before 16 March 2016 will be excluded from the limit, meaning that taxpayers will need to keep a record of exempt gains which count towards the limit.

There are further detailed provisions in sub-ss (3), (4) and (5) to regulate the operation of the limit in relation to transfers between spouses and civil partners.

89 Employee shareholder shares: disguised fees and carried interest

(1) In section 236B of TCGA 1992 (exemption for employee shareholder shares), after subsection (2) insert—

"(2A) Subsection (1) does not apply in relation to a gain accruing on a disposal where the proceeds of the disposal, in relation to any individual, constitute—

(a) a disguised fee for the purposes of Chapter 5E of Part 13 of ITA 2007 (see section 809EZA(3) of that Act), or

(b) carried interest within the meaning given by section 809EZC of that Act."

(2) The amendment made by this section has effect in relation to gains accruing on or after 6 April 2016.

GENERAL NOTE

Section 89 amends TCGA 1992 s 236B (exemption for employee shareholder shares) so as to remove the exemption from capital gains when the relevant capital gain is also a disguised fee or is carried interest.

TCGA 1992 s 236B states that any gain arising on the first disposal of an exempt employee shareholder share is not a chargeable gain.

FA 2016 s 89(1) introduces a new TCGA 1992 s 236B(2A) which states that the capital gains exemption referred to above does not apply is the gain in question constitutes either (a) a disguised fee for the purposes ITA 2007 Pt 13 Ch 5E (for which see ITA 2007 s 809EZA(3)); or (b) carried interest within the meaning given in ITA 2007 s 809EZC.

This then gives clear priority to the tax charging provisions relating to disguised fees and carried interest over the general tax exemption applying to gains on the disposal of employee shareholder shares where the amount derived from the disposal might fall within both a gain on an employee shareholder share and a disguised fee or amount of carried interest.

New TCGA 1992 s 236B(2A) applies to gains on disposals of employee shareholder shares accruing on or after 6 April 2016.

Other Provisions

90 Disposals of UK residential property by non-residents etc

(1) In Schedule 4ZZA to TCGA 1992 (relevant high value disposals: gains and losses), in paragraph 2(1), for "paragraph 6" substitute "paragraph 6A".

(2) In Schedule 4ZZB to TCGA 1992 (non-resident CGT disposals: gains and losses), in paragraph 17—

(a) omit sub-paragraph (2), and
(b) in sub-paragraph (3), omit the words from "If" to "applies".

(3) The amendment made by subsection (1) has effect in relation to disposals made on or after 6 April 2015.

(4) The amendment made by subsection (2) has effect in relation to disposals made on or after 26 November 2015.

GENERAL NOTE

The section corrects errors in the FA 2015 legislation that could potentially occur involving a double charge which from the interaction of the non-resident capital gains tax ("NRCGT") regime with the ATED rules. The change to TCGA 1992 Sch 4ZZA is retro-active to 6 April 2015 and the change to TCGA 1992 Sch 4ZZB is effective from 26 November 2015.

91 NRCGT returns

In TMA 1970, after section 12ZB (NRCGT return) insert—

"12ZBA Elective NRCGT return

(1) A person is not required to make and deliver an NRCGT return under section 12ZB(1), but may do so, in circumstances to which this section applies.

(2) The circumstances to which this section applies are where the disposal referred to in section 12ZB(1) is—

(a) a disposal on or after 6 April 2015 where, by virtue of any of the no gain/no loss provisions, neither a gain nor a loss accrues, or
(b) the grant of a lease on or after 6 April 2015 which is—

(i) for no premium,
(ii) to a person who is not connected with the grantor, and
(iii) under a bargain made at arm's length.

(3) For the purposes of subsection (2)—

"connected" is to be construed in accordance with section 286 of 1992 Act;
"no gain/no loss provisions" has the meaning given by section 288(3A) of the 1992 Act;
"lease" and premium" have the meanings given by paragraph 10 of Schedule 8 to the 1992 Act.

(4) The Treasury may by regulations made by statutory instrument add or remove circumstances to which this section applies.

(5) Regulations under subsection (4) may—

(a) amend this section or any other enactment;
(b) make consequential provision.

(6) A statutory instrument containing regulations under subsection (4) is subject to annulment in pursuance of a resolution of the House of Commons.

(7) Paragraph 1 of Schedule 55 to the Finance Act 2009 (penalty for late returns) does not apply in relation to an NRCGT return which is made and delivered by virtue of this section."

GENERAL NOTE

This section inserts TMA 1970 s 12ZBA to remove the automatic obligation to make a return under TMA 1970 s 12ZB(1) in certain circumstances and to allow for an individual to file a return where one is not required. When NRCGT was introduced, it was necessary to file a return, even where there was no gain to report. NRCGT returns are now optional where a statutory no gain/no loss provision applies or for the grant of a lease for no premium on arm's length terms to an unconnected party. This relaxation will be particularly useful for transfers between spouses who are living together.

The Treasury is empowered to make further changes by statutory instrument and the FA 2009 penalty regime for late returns is not to apply to a voluntary return.

92 Addition of CGT to Provisional Collection of Taxes Act 1968

In section 1 of the Provisional Collection of Taxes Act 1968 (temporary statutory effect of House of Commons resolutions affecting income tax etc), in subsection (1), after "income tax," insert "capital gains tax,".

GENERAL NOTE

This section adds capital gains tax to the taxes that can be adjusted on a provisional basis and is an administrative measure to allow for greater flexibility of tax changes. Non-residents must sometimes pay capital gains tax on account within 30 days of completion of the disposal of an asset and the government proposes to extend this payment on account approach to all residential property disposals from April 2019.

PART 5

INHERITANCE TAX ETC

93 Inheritance tax: increased nil-rate band

Schedule 15 contains provision in connection with the increased nil-rate band provided for by section 8D of IHTA 1984 (extra nil-rate band on death if interest in home goes to descendants etc).

GENERAL NOTE

This introduces and gives effect to Sch 15, which amends the provisions for an IHT residence nil-rate amount which were introduced by F(No 2)A 2015 s 9 so as to extend those provisions to cases where qualifying residences have been downsized or disposed of.

94 Inheritance tax: pension drawdown funds

(1) IHTA 1984 is amended as follows.

(2) In the italic heading before section 10, at the end insert "(and omissions that do not give rise to deemed dispositions)".

(3) In section 12(2G) (interpretation of section 12(2ZA)), in the definition of "entitled", for "166(2)" substitute "167(1A), or section 166(2),".

(4) After section 12 insert—

"12A Pension drawdown fund not used up: no deemed disposition

(1) Where a person has a drawdown fund, section 3(3) above does not apply in relation to any omission that results in the fund not being used up in the person's lifetime.

(2) For the purposes of subsection (1) above, a person has a drawdown fund if the person has—

   (a) a member's drawdown pension fund,
   (b) a member's flexi-access drawdown fund,
   (c) a dependant's drawdown pension fund,
   (d) a dependant's flexi-access drawdown fund,
   (e) a nominee's flexi-access drawdown fund, or

(f) a successor's flexi-access drawdown fund, and

in respect of a money purchase arrangement under a registered pension scheme.

(3) For the purposes of subsection (1) above, a person also has a drawdown fund if sums or assets held for the purposes of a money purchase arrangement under a corresponding scheme would, if that scheme were a registered pension scheme, be the person's—

> (a) member's drawdown pension fund,
> (b) member's flexi-access drawdown fund,
> (c) dependant's drawdown pension fund,
> (d) dependant's flexi-access drawdown fund,
> (e) nominee's flexi-access drawdown fund, or
> (f) successor's flexi-access drawdown fund,

in respect of the arrangement.

(4) In this section—

"corresponding scheme" means—

> (a) a qualifying non-UK pension scheme (see section 271A below), or
> (b) a section 615(3) scheme that is not a registered pension scheme;

"money purchase arrangement" has the same meaning as in Part 4 of the Finance Act 2004 (see section 152 of that Act);

"member's drawdown pension fund", "member's flexi-access drawdown fund", "dependant's drawdown pension fund", "dependant's flexi-access drawdown fund", "nominee's flexi-access drawdown fund" and "successor's flexi-access drawdown fund" have the meaning given, respectively, by paragraphs 8, 8A, 22, 22A, 27E and 27K of Schedule 28 to that Act."

(5) The amendment made by subsection (4)—

(a) so far as relating to a fund within the new section 12A(2)(a) or (c) (drawdown pension funds), or to a fund within the new section 12A(3) that corresponds to a fund within the new section 12A(2)(a) or (c)—

> (i) has effect where the person who has the fund dies on or after 6 April 2011, and
> (ii) is to be treated as having come into force on 6 April 2011, and

(b) so far as relating to a fund mentioned in the new section 12A(2)(b), (d), (e) or (f) (flexi-access drawdown funds), or to a fund within the new section 12A(3) that corresponds to a fund within the new section 12A(2)(b), (d), (e) or (f)—

> (i) has effect where the person who has the fund dies on or after 6 April 2015, and
> (ii) is to be treated as having come into force on 6 April 2015.

(6) Where an amount paid by way of—

(a) inheritance tax, or

(b) interest on inheritance tax,

is repayable as a result of the amendment made by subsection (4), section 241(1) of IHTA 1984 applies as if the last date for making a claim for repayment of the amount were 5 April 2020 if that is later than what would otherwise be the last date for that purpose.

GENERAL NOTE

IHTA 1984 s 3(3) provides that if a person omits to exercise a right, with the consequence that his or her estate is diminished, and there is an increase in the value of another person's estate, or in the value of settled property with no qualifying interest in possession, the omission is a disposition unless it can be shown that it was not deliberate. The time when the disposition occurs is the time or the last time at which the right could be exercised. This provision can thus give rise to a lifetime transfer of value, though one made on the point of death where that was the last time the right could be exercised. This provision was held to apply to failure to exercise rights under pension schemes in two First-tier Tribunal cases, *Fryer v HMRC* [2010] SFTD 632 and *RWJ Parry (Mrs RF Staveley's Personal Representatives) v HMRC* [2014] UKFTT 419. The effect of these was reversed in relation to omission to exercise pension rights under registered pension schemes, qualifying non-UK pension schemes, or schemes falling within TA 1988 s 615(3), by IHTA 1984 s 12(2ZA), inserted by FA 2011 s 65, Sch 16 paras 46 and 47, with effect from 6 April 2011. IHTA 1984 s 12(2ZA) disapplies IHTA 1984 s 3(3) in these circumstances.

Subsection (4) of this section inserts a new IHTA 1984 s 12A, which extends the disapplication of IHTA 1984 s 3(3) to any omission that results in a drawdown fund not being used up in a person's lifetime. What is meant by drawdown fund for this purpose is set out in detail the lists of types of pension fund set out in the new s 12A(2) and (3), with further definitions and cross-references to definitions in FA 2004 Sch 28 in the new s 12A(4).

The section has retroactive effect. It applies to persons dying on or after 6 April 2011 for drawdown pension funds, and to persons dying on or after 6 April 2015 for flexi-access drawdown funds (subs (5)). Anyone who has paid IHT or interest on it which is now repayable as a result of the changes made by this section has until the later of the expiry of four years from the payment or 5 April 2020 to reclaim it (IHTA 1984 new s 12A(6) and s 241).

95 Inheritance tax: victims of persecution during Second World War era

(1) After section 153 of IHTA 1984 insert—

"Payments to victims of persecution during Second World War era

153ZA Qualifying payments

(1) This section applies where a qualifying payment has at any time been received by a person ("P"), or by the personal representatives of P.

(2) The tax chargeable on the value transferred by the transfer made on P's death (the "value transferred") is to be reduced by an amount equal to—

    (a) the relevant percentage of the amount of the qualifying payment, or

    (b) if lower, the amount of tax that would, apart from this section, be chargeable on the value transferred.

(3) In subsection (2) "relevant percentage" means the percentage specified in the last row of the third column of the Table in Schedule 1.

(4) For the purposes of this section, a "qualifying payment" is a payment that meets Condition A, B or C.

(5) Condition A is that the payment—

    (a) is of a kind specified in Part 1 of Schedule 5A, and

    (b) is made to a person, or the personal representatives of a person, who was—

        (i) a victim of National-Socialist persecution, or

        (ii) the spouse or civil partner of a person within sub-paragraph (i).

(6) Condition B is that the payment is of a kind listed in Part 2 of Schedule 5A.

(7) Condition C is that the payment—

    (a) is of a kind specified in regulations made by the Treasury, and

    (b) is made to a person, or the personal representatives of a person, who was—

        (i) held as a prisoner of war, or a civilian internee, during the Second World War, or

        (ii) the spouse or civil partner of a person within sub-paragraph (i).

(8) The Treasury may by regulations add a payment of a specified kind to the list in Part 1 of Schedule 5A.

(9) Regulations under this section are to be made by statutory instrument.

(10) A statutory instrument containing regulations under this section is subject to annulment in pursuance of a resolution of the House of Commons."

(2) After Schedule 5 to IHTA 1984 insert—

"SCHEDULE 5A

QUALIFYING PAYMENTS: VICTIMS OF PERSECUTION DURING SECOND WORLD WAR ERA

Section 153ZA

PART 1

COMPENSATION PAYMENTS

1 A payment of a fixed amount from the German foundation known as "Remembrance, Responsibility and Future" (*Stiftung EVZ*) in respect of a person who was a slave or forced labourer.

2 A payment of a fixed amount in accordance with the arrangements made under the Swiss Bank Settlement (Holocaust Victim Assets Litigation) in respect of the slave or forced labourers qualifying for compensation under the Remembrance, Responsibility and Future scheme.

3 A payment of a fixed amount from the Hardship Fund established by the Government of the Federal Republic of Germany.

4 A payment of a fixed amount from the National Fund of the Republic of Austria for Victims of National-Socialism under the terms of the scheme as at June 1995.

5 A payment of a fixed amount in respect of a slave or forced labourer from the Austrian Reconciliation Fund.

6 A payment of a fixed amount by the Swiss Refugee Programme in accordance with the arrangements made under the Swiss Bank Settlement (Holocaust Victim Assets Litigation) in respect of refugees.

7 A payment of a fixed amount under the foundation established in the Netherlands and known as the Dutch Maror Fund (*Stichting Maror-Gelden Overheid*).

8 A one-off payment of a fixed amount from the scheme established by the Government of the French Republic and known as the French Orphan Scheme.

9 A payment of a fixed amount from the Child Survivor Fund established by the Government of the Federal Republic of Germany.

PART 2
EX-GRATIA PAYMENTS

10 A payment of a fixed amount made from the scheme established by the United Kingdom Government and known as the Far Eastern Prisoners of War Ex Gratia Scheme."

(3) The amendments made by this section have effect in relation to deaths occurring on or after 1 January 2015.

GENERAL NOTE

This section puts on a statutory footing what has until now been Extra-statutory Concession F20, and presumably once this section becomes law the latter concession will be withdrawn. The section will apply in relation to deaths occurring on or after 1 January 2015 (sub-s (3)).

Subsection (1) inserts a new IHTA 1984 s 153ZA which relieves the estate on death of IHT on any payment received by the deceased or his or her personal representatives in any of the three categories of payment specified as Conditions A, B, and C in the new IHTA 1984 s 153ZA(5), (6), or (7).

Condition A in the new IHTA 1984 s 153ZA(5) refers to payments to victims of National-Socialist persecution (or their personal representatives) or to their spouses or civil partners (or their personal representatives) where payment is of the kind listed in Part 1 of the new IHTA 1984 Sch 5A inserted by sub-s (2) of this section. The list in Part 1 of the new Sch 5A is essentially the same as that in Concession F20 with the addition of payments from the Child Survivor Fund established by the German government. The Treasury has power to make regulations adding further categories of payment to Pt 1 of Sch 5A (new IHTA 1984 s 153ZA(8)).

Condition B in the new IHTA 1984 s 153ZA(6) refers to ex gratia payments under the UK government scheme for compensating far eastern prisoners of war. These are also currently relieved under Concession F20.

Condition C in the new IHTA 1984 s 153ZA(7) is payments of a kind specified by regulations made by the Treasury, but limited to payments to a person, or the personal representatives of a person, who was held as a prisoner of war or civilian internee during the Second World War, or to his or her spouse or civil partner (or the latter's personal representatives).

In relation to any given payment, the relief takes the unusual form of a deduction from the tax chargeable on the deceased's death. The deduction is the percentage of the payment which corresponds to the highest marginal rate of IHT, unless the total tax chargeable on the estate is less, in which case it is the latter amount which is deducted (new IHTA 1984 s 153ZA(2) and (3)). In current conditions this means that 40% of the amount of the payment, or if less the total tax payable on the estate, would be deducted from the tax chargeable.

96 Inheritance tax: gifts for national purposes etc
(1) The Schedule 3 IHTA approval function is transferred to the Treasury.

(2) The "Schedule 3 IHTA approval function" is the function of approval conferred by Schedule 3 to IHTA 1984 in the entry beginning "Any other similar national institution" (and which was initially conferred on the Treasury but, along with other functions, transferred to the Commissioners of Inland Revenue under section 95 of FA 1985).

(3) Subsection (1) does not affect any approval given under Schedule 3 to IHTA 1984 before this Act is passed.

(4) In Schedule 3 to IHTA 1984 (gifts for national purposes, etc), in the entry beginning "Any museum", after "and is" insert "or has been".

GENERAL NOTE

IHTA 1984 s 25 provides an exemption for transfers of value where the value transferred is attributable to property which becomes the property of a body listed in IHTA 1984 Sch 3. This is a list of public bodies and national institutions such as museums, libraries, universities the National Trust, government departments, local authorities etc. One of the categories is "any other similar national institution which exists wholly or mainly for the purpose of preserving for the public benefit a collection of scientific, historic or artistic interest and which is approved the purposes of this Schedule by the Treasury". The function of approving further bodies was transferred to the Commissioners of Inland Revenue by FA 1985 s 95. Subsections (1) and (2) transfer this approval function back to the Treasury with effect from the royal assent to this Act (see sub-s (3)).

The other change made by this section is that the category in IHTA 1984 Sch 3 "any museum or art gallery in the UK which exists wholly or mainly for that purpose and is maintained by a local authority or university in the UK" is amended by sub-s (4) to include any museum or art gallery which has been maintained by a local authority or university. This is because many which were formerly maintained by local authorities or universities have become independent charitable trusts. The interest of such museums and art galleries in being included in the IHTA 1984 Sch 3 list is not primarily for the exemption under IHTA 1984 s 25, because a gift to a charity has exemption from IHT under IHTA 1984 s 23. What is important for them is that if they are included in Sch 3 they can be recipients of CGT and IHT exempt disposals of heritage assets (TCGA 1992 s 258(2)(a) and IHTA 1984 s 32(4)).

97 Estate duty: objects of national, scientific, historic or artistic interest
(1) Section 40 of FA 1930 and section 2 of the Finance Act (Northern Ireland) 1931 (exemption from death duties of objects of national etc interest), so far as continuing to have effect, have effect as if after subsection (2) there were inserted—

"(2A) In the event of the loss of any objects to which this section applies, estate duty shall become chargeable on the value of those objects in respect of the last death on which the objects passed at the rate appropriate to the principal value of the estate passing on that death upon which estate duty is leviable, and with which the objects would have been aggregated if they had not been objects to which this section applies.

(2B) Where subsection (2A) applies, any owner of the objects—
   (a) shall be accountable for the estate duty, and
   (b) shall deliver an account for the purposes thereof.

(2C) The account under subsection (2B)(b) must be delivered within the period of one month beginning with—
   (a) in the case of a loss occurring before the coming into force of subsection (2A)—
      (i) the coming into force of subsection (2A), or
      (ii) if later, the date when the owner became aware of the loss;
   (b) in the case of a loss occurring after the coming into force of subsection (2A)—
      (i) the date of the loss, or
      (ii) if later, the date when the owner became aware of the loss.
This is subject to subsection (2E).

(2D) Subsection (2E) applies if—
   (a) no account has been delivered under subsection (2B),

   (b) the Commissioners for Her Majesty's Revenue and Customs have by notice required an owner of the objects to confirm that the objects have not been lost,

   (c) the owner has not so confirmed by the end of—

      (i) the period of three months beginning with the day on which the notice was sent, or

      (ii) such longer period as the Commissioners may allow, and

   (d) the Commissioners are satisfied that the objects are lost.

   (2E) Where this subsection applies—

   (a) the objects are to be treated as lost for the purposes of subsection (2A) on the day on which the Commissioners are satisfied as specified in subsection (2D)(d), and

   (b) the account under subsection (2B)(b) must be delivered within the period of one month beginning with that date.

   (2F) The reference in subsection (2A) to the value of objects is to their value at the time they are lost (or treated as lost).

   (2G) Subsection (2A) does not apply in relation to a loss notified to the Commissioners before the coming into force of that subsection.

   (2H) In this section "owner", in relation to any objects, means a person who, if the objects were sold, would be entitled to receive (whether for their own benefit or not) the proceeds of sale or any income arising therefrom.

   (2I) In this section references to the loss of objects include their theft or destruction; but do not include a loss which the Commissioners are satisfied was outside the owner's control."

(2) Section 48 of FA 1950, so far as continuing to have effect, has effect as if—

   (a) after subsection (3) there were inserted—

"(3A) But where the value of any objects is chargeable with estate duty under subsection (2A) of the said section forty (loss of objects), no estate duty shall be chargeable under this section on that value.";

   (b) after subsection (4) there were inserted—

"(5) Where any objects are lost (within the meaning of the said section forty) after becoming chargeable with estate duty under this section in respect of any death, the value of those objects shall not be chargeable with estate duty under subsection (2A) of the said section forty."

(3) Section 39 of FA 1969, so far as continuing to have effect, has effect as if—

   (a) in subsection (1)—

      (i) after "subsection (2)" there were inserted "or (2A)";

      (ii) after "other disposal" there were inserted "or loss";

   (b) in subsection (2), after "subsection (2)" there were inserted ", (2A)";

   (c) in subsection (3)—

      (i) after "subsection (2)" there were inserted ", (2A)";

      (ii) for the words from "the amount" to the end there were substituted "the amount in respect of which estate duty is chargeable under the said subsection".

(4) Section 6 of the Finance Act (Northern Ireland) 1969, so far as continuing to have effect as originally enacted, has effect as if—

   (a) in subsection (1)—

      (i) after "subsection (2)" there were inserted "or (2A)";

      (ii) after "sale" there were inserted "or loss";

   (b) in subsection (2)—

      (i) for "sale" there were substituted "event";

      (ii) after "subsection (2)" there were inserted "or (2A)";

   (c) in subsection (3)—

      (i) for "sale" there were substituted "event";

      (ii) after "subsection (2)" there were inserted "or (2A)";

      (iii) for "the amount of the proceeds of sale" there were substituted "the amount in respect of which estate duty is chargeable under the said subsection".

(5) Section 6 of the Finance Act (Northern Ireland) 1969, so far as continuing to have effect as amended by Article 7 of the Finance (Northern Ireland) Order 1972 (SI 1972/1100 (NI11)) (deaths occurring after the making of that Order), has effect as if—

   (a) in subsection (1)—

      (i) after "subsection (2)" there were inserted "or (2A)";

(ii) after "sale" there were inserted "or loss";

(b) in subsection (2), after "subsection (2)" there were inserted "or (2A)";

(c) in subsection (3)—

(i) in the opening words, after "subsection (2)" there were inserted "or (2A)";

(ii) in paragraphs (a) and (b), after "otherwise than on sale" there were inserted "or at the time of the loss".

(6) In section 35 of IHTA 1984 (conditional exemption on death before 7th April 1976), in subsection (2), for paragraphs (a) and (b) substitute—

"(a) tax shall be chargeable under section 32 or 32A (as the case may be), or

(b) tax shall be chargeable under Schedule 5,".

(7) In Schedule 6 to IHTA 1984 (transition from estate duty), in paragraph 4 (objects of national etc interest left out of account on death)—

(a) in sub-paragraph (2), for paragraphs (a) and (b) substitute—

"(a) tax shall be chargeable under section 32 or 32A of this Act (as the case may be), or

(b) estate duty shall be chargeable under those provisions,as the Board may elect,", and

(b) in sub-paragraph (4), after "40(2)" insert "or (2A)".

(8) Subsections (6) and (7) have effect in relation to a chargeable event where the conditionally exempt transfer referred to in section 35(2) of or paragraph 4(2) of Schedule 6 to IHTA 1984 occurred after 16 March 2016.

GENERAL NOTE

It seems from this section that HMRC have been conducting cold case reviews of objects which were exempted under FA 1930 s 40 from estate duty as being of national, scientific, historic, or artistic interest. FA 1930 s 40 provides that the estate duty is payable if an exempted chattel is sold, but until FA 1950 s 48 came into force on 28 July 1950 there was no requirement of undertakings, and thus no mechanism for imposing the charge to estate duty in circumstances other than a sale. The amendments made by this section to FA 1930 s 40 impose the estate duty charge where an object exempted from estate duty has been lost (new FA 1930 s 40(2A)), and give HMRC power to treat a chattel as lost for this purpose if they write to the owner enquiring after the chattel and get no reply in three months (new FA 1930 s 40(2D and (2E)). This will only work if they correctly identify the owner, who is defined as the person who would be entitled to receive the proceeds of sale, or any income arising from them, if the object were sold (new FA 1930 s 40(2H)). Where an object is lost or treated as lost the owner has the accounting obligations set out in the new FA 1930 s 40(2B), (2C), and (2E).

The estate duty charge is imposed on the value of the chattel at the time it is lost or treated as lost (new FA 1930 s 40(2F)), and this could be very bad news for the former owner of lost chattels given the combination of modern chattel values and the high marginal rates of estate duty in some periods, particularly between 1946 and 1974 when they could be as much as 80 or 85 per cent. Loss of chattels for this purpose includes their theft or destruction but does not include a loss of which HMRC are satisfied was outside the owner's control (new FA 1930 s 40(2I)). This is a slightly puzzling provision because one would normally expect theft to be outside the owner's control. These provisions come into force at the date of the royal assent to this Act, as there is no specific commencement provision. A provision to note is that the charge does not apply in relation to a loss notified to HMRC before coming into force of the section (new FA 1930 s 40(2H)). This seems to mean that those who own up to loss before that date will be relieved from the estate duty charge under the new FA 1930 s 40(2A), though they could be still liable to pay the duty because of a breach of undertakings imposed by FA 1950 s 48 where the death was on or after 28 July 1950. The amendments to FA 1950 s 48 by sub-s (2) of this section prevent double charging, so that there is either a charge under the new FA 1930 s 40(2A) on loss of a chattel, or a charge in respect of a breach of undertakings given under FA 1950 s 48, but not both.

The further change made by this section, and one which is probably of wider application than the provisions about loss of exempted objects, is in sub-ss (6) and (7). IHTA 1984 Sch 6 para 4 provides for what happens if there has been an item of property exempted from estate duty under FA 1930 s 40, and before any estate duty charge has arisen by reason of a sale or breach of undertaking there has been a conditionally exempt transfer of that property under CTT or IHT. Before the coming into force of this subsection, IHTA 1984 Sch 6 para 4 provides that if there has not been a conditionally exempt transfer on death, on the occurrence of a chargeable event HMRC can elect between charging the estate duty or charging the IHT or CTT, but that if there has been a conditionally exempt transfer on death the charge is to CTT or IHT as the case may be and not to estate duty. The amendment made by sub-s (7) gives HMRC a right to elect between charging estate duty or charging CTT/IHT where there has been a conditionally exempt transfer on death. Subsection (6) makes the same change in relation to cases where there has been exemption for property under FA 1975 ss 31 to 34 in relation to a transfer of value before 7 April 1976, conditional exemption in relation to a transfer of value of the same property on or after that date, and a chargeable event. Again HMRC can opt between the two chargeable event regimes, rather than being obliged to apply the conditional exemption rules under IHTA 1984 ss 32 and 32A where there has been conditional exemption on death. These changes will have effect where the conditionally exempt transfer occurs after 16 March 2016 (sub-s (8)).

PART 6
APPRENTICESHIP LEVY

Basic Provisions

98 Apprenticeship levy

(1) A tax called apprenticeship levy is to be charged in accordance with this Part.

(2) The Commissioners are responsible for the collection and management of apprenticeship levy.

GENERAL NOTE

The apprenticeship levy (the "levy") is a new tax, announced at the Spending Review and Autumn Statement 2015 with the aim of developing the skills base and helping to drive productivity through 3 million apprenticeship starts by 2020.

Section 98 FA 2016 introduces the tax from 6 April 2017, subject to the detailed rules following in ss 99–121 FA 2016.

The Commissioners of Her Majesty's Revenue and Customs (HMRC) will be responsible for collection and management of the levy. A new Institute for Apprenticeships, will advise the Secretary of State for Business, Innovation and Skills (BIS) on the administration of funding raised and will be involved in in designing new apprenticeship standards and maintaining the quality of existing standards.

Note that separate provision was made for a 0% rate of employer's NIC for apprentices under the age of 25 by the National Insurance Contributions Act 2015, which came into effect for the current tax year on 6 April 2016. Legislation relating to drawing down on levy funding is not yet available.

99 Charge to apprenticeship levy

(1) Apprenticeship levy is charged if—

    (a) a person has a pay bill for a tax year, and

    (b) the relevant percentage of that pay bill exceeds the amount of the person's levy allowance (if any) for that tax year.

(2) The amount charged for the tax year is equal to—

$N - A$

    where—

    N is the relevant percentage of the pay bill for the tax year, and
    A is the amount of the levy allowance (if any) to which the person is entitled for the tax year.

(3) The person mentioned in subsection (1) is liable to pay the amount charged.

(4) Except so far as section 103 provides otherwise, a person who has a pay bill for a tax year is entitled to a levy allowance for the tax year.

(5) The amount of the levy allowance is £15,000 (except where section 101 or 102 provides otherwise).

(6) For the purposes of this section the "relevant percentage" is 0.5%.

GENERAL NOTE

The levy will be charged on an employer with a pay bill in a tax year, initially, at a rate of 0.5% (the relevant percentage) of the employer's total pay bill. Subject to the provisions in ss 101–103 relating to connected employers, connected charities, and certain anti-avoidance provisions, an employer will only be liable to the extent the relevant percentage of its total pay bill (N) exceeds the annual levy allowance (A), the latter being set at £15,000 per annum for the time being (see further commentary on the levy allowance). For 2017/18 at least, this means that, subject to the provisions relating to group employers noted above the levy will only be payable by employers with a pay bill in excess of £3m in that year. Liability for the levy must be calculated monthly on a cumulative basis and accounted for through the PAYE Real Time Information ("RTI") regime.

The Government has said it will keep the levy under review, implying the relevant percentage and/or the annual allowance could change in future years.

Further information on the operation of the levy in England can be found in the BIS document responding to the consultation on the levy, which was published alongside the Chancellor's Autumn Statement on 25 November 2015. At the time of writing, no details are yet available as regards Scotland, Wales and Northern Ireland. A Government briefing paper number CBP7523 was published on 1 April 2016. The Scottish government issued a consultation on the operation of the levy in Summer 2016: https://consult.scotland.gov.uk/employability-and-training/apprenticeship-levy.

100 A person's pay bill for a tax year

(1) A person has a pay bill for a tax year if, in the tax year—

    (a) the person is the secondary contributor in relation to payments of earnings to, or for the benefit of, one or more employed earners, and

    (b) in consequence, the person incurs liabilities to pay secondary Class 1 contributions.

(2) The amount of the person's pay bill for the tax year is equal to the total amount of the earnings in respect of which the liabilities mentioned in subsection (1)(b) are incurred.

(3) For the purposes of this section a person is treated as incurring, in respect of any earnings, any liabilities which the person would incur but for the condition in section 6(1)(b) of the Contributions and Benefits Act.

(4) The Treasury may by regulations provide for persons specified in certificates in force under section 120(4) of the Social Security Contributions and Benefits Act 1992 (employment at sea: continental shelf operations) to be treated for the purposes of this section as the secondary contributor in relation to payments of earnings to which the certificate relates and as liable to pay secondary Class 1 contributions to which the certificate relates.

(5) For the purposes of this section—

    (a) references to "payments of earnings" are to be interpreted as they would be interpreted for the purposes of determining liability to pay secondary Class 1 contributions under the Contributions and Benefits Act;

    (b) the amount of any earnings is to be calculated in the same manner and on the same basis as for the purpose of calculating the liabilities mentioned in subsection (1)(b).

(6) In this section references to liability to pay secondary Class 1 contributions are to liability to pay secondary Class 1 contributions under Part 1 of the Contributions and Benefits Act (and are therefore to be interpreted in accordance with sections 9A(6) and 9B(3) of that Act).

GENERAL NOTE

Section 100 provides that someone has a pay bill if they are the secondary contributor in relation to payments of earnings and in consequence, they incur liabilities to secondary (employer's) class 1 NIC. Primary (employee's) class 1 and other classes of NIC are not relevant for this purpose, e.g. class 1A NIC on benefits in kind and class 1B NIC arising on PAYE Settlement Agreements.

The amount of the pay bill subject to secondary class 1 NIC is the start point for determining how much of the pay bill is subject to the levy, but note that these are different amounts. The following adjustments must be made:

First, s 100(3) treats an employer as incurring a secondary class 1 NIC liability as if the secondary threshold (ST) did not exist. So, the pay bill for levy purposes must include earnings up to the secondary threshold, whereas earnings up to the ST will not attract liability for secondary class 1 NIC. The ST in 2016/17 is £8,112 for the year.

Second, s 100(4) deals with workers on the UK Continental Shelf (UKCS). Broadly, employers supplying certain workers to work on the UKCS are liable for NIC if they have a UK associated company, or if they apply for a certificate taking responsibility for NIC in respect of those workers. Otherwise, the oil field licensee is liable. Section 100(4) provides that Regulations may determine that persons specified in certificates are also to be treated as the secondary contributor for the purposes of determining liability for the levy.

Section 100(5) ensures that the calculation of earnings for levy purposes follows the same rules as those which apply for class 1 NIC purposes.

Finally, s 100(6) has the effect that earnings paid to employees under the age of 21 and apprentices under the age of 25, must still be brought into account for levy liability purposes, even where those earnings are subject to the 0% rates of secondary NIC under ss 9A(6) and 9B(3) SSCBA 1992 respectively.

Share schemes

Paragraphs 3A and 3B of Schedule 1 SSCBA 1992 provide for NIC agreements and NIC elections for use in conjunction with share schemes. An NIC election *transfers* an employer's liability for secondary class 1 NIC to an employee. In contrast, under an NIC agreement, the employer retains liability for secondary class 1 NIC, but the employee agrees to settle that liability. It follows that to the extent earnings are subject to an NIC election, they are not included within earnings subject to the levy as the employer is not technically liable for secondary class 1 NIC on earnings subject to such an election; whereas any earnings subject to an NIC agreement should in theory be included on the basis that liability for secondary class 1 NIC remains *prima facie* with the employer. Absent any published guidance on the treatment to be adopted, it is not yet clear whether HMRC will adopt a consistent treatment in practice.

Intermediaries

Where employment agencies are liable for secondary NIC in relation to temporary workers supplied to end clients, they will also be liable for the levy in respect of earnings paid to such workers. This is because the agency is treated as the secondary contributor under the Categorisation of Earners Regulations 1978.

Where a worker provides services through a personal service company (PSC) and IR35 applies, the PSC would potentially be liable for the levy if employment income in the PSC exceeds the annual levy allowance. This is because s 100(1)(a) applies to *secondary contributors* in relation to *payments of earnings* to or for the benefit of *one or more* employed earners. Where IR35 applies, reg 6(3)(b) Social Security (Intermediaries) Regulations 2000 treats the PSC as the secondary contributor and reg 8 of those Regulations aggregates payments of attributable earnings with payments of any other earnings paid to the worker by the PSC in the year concerned.

Public Authorities and PSCs

At the time of writing, the Government is considering proposals to make Public Authorities (as defined in the Freedom of Information Act 2000 and Freedom of Information Act (Scotland) 2002) liable for PAYE and NIC in respect of payments they make to PSCs, where IR35 would apply to such payments. This is proposed to be effective from 6 April 2017, and if adopted, it seems likely that where Public Authorities become liable for secondary Cass 1 NIC on such payments, they will also be liable for the levy in respect of such payments, unless a specific carve out for Public Authority levy liability on PSC payments is introduced at the same time, if considered appropriate to do so.

Connected Companies and Charities

101 Connected companies

(1) Two or more companies which are not charities form a "company unit" for a tax year (and are the "members" of that unit) if—

(a) they are connected with one another at the beginning of the tax year, and

(b) each of them is entitled to a levy allowance for the tax year.

(2) The members of a company unit must determine what amount of levy allowance each of them is to be entitled to for the tax year (and the determination must comply with subsections (3) and (4)).

But see subsections (6) and (11).

(3) A member's levy allowance for a tax year may be zero (but not a negative amount).

(4) The total amount of the levy allowances to which the members of a company unit are entitled for a tax year must equal £15,000.

(5) A determination made under subsection (2) (with respect to a tax year) cannot afterwards be altered by the members concerned (but this does not prevent the correction of a failure to comply with subsection (4)).

(6) If subsection (8) applies—

(a) HMRC must determine in accordance with subsection (7) what amount of levy allowance each of the relevant members (see subsection (8)(a)) of the unit concerned is to be entitled to for the tax year, and

(b) accordingly subsection (2) is treated as never having applied in relation to that company unit and that tax year.

(7) The determination is to be made by multiplying the amount of levy allowance set out in each relevant return (see subsection (8)(a)) by—

$$15,000 \,/\, T$$

where T is the total of the amounts of levy allowance set out in the relevant returns.

The result is, in each case, the amount of the levy allowance to which the relevant member in question is entitled for the tax year (but amounts may be rounded up or down where appropriate provided that subsection (4) is complied with).

(8) This subsection applies if—

(a) HMRC is aware—

(i) that two or more members of a company unit ("the relevant members") have made apprenticeship levy returns ("the relevant returns") on the basis mentioned in subsection (9), and

(ii) that those returns, together, imply that the total mentioned in subsection (4) is greater than £15,000,

(b) HMRC has notified the relevant members in writing that HMRC is considering taking action under subsection (6), and

(c) the remedial action specified in the notice has not been taken within the period specified in the notice.

(9) The basis in question is that the member making the return is entitled to a levy allowance (whether or not of zero) for the tax year concerned.

(10) If any member of the company unit mentioned in subsection (8)(a) is not a relevant member, that member is entitled to a levy allowance of zero for the tax year.

(11) If subsection (13) applies—

(a) HMRC must determine in accordance with subsection (12) what amount of levy allowance each of the members of the unit concerned is to be entitled to for the tax year, and

(b) accordingly subsection (2) is treated as never having applied in relation to that company unit and that tax year.

(12) Each member of the unit is to be entitled to a levy allowance for the tax year equal to—

$$£15,000 \,/\, N$$

where N is the number of the members of the company unit for the tax year.

Amounts determined in accordance with the formula in this subsection may be rounded up or down where appropriate provided that subsection (4) is complied with.

(13) This subsection applies if—

(a) the total amount paid by the members of a company unit in respect of apprenticeship levy for a tax year or any period in a tax year is less than the total of the amounts due and payable by them for the tax year or other period concerned,

(b) either the members of the unit have made no apprenticeship levy returns for any period in the tax year concerned or the returns that have been made do not contain sufficient information to enable HMRC to determine how the whole of the £15,000 mentioned in subsection (4) is to be used by the members of the unit for the tax year,

(c) HMRC has notified all the members of the unit in writing that HMRC is considering taking action under subsection (11), and

(d) the remedial action specified in the notice has not been taken within the period specified in the notice.

(14) Subsection (4) is to be taken into account in calculating the total of the amounts due and payable as mentioned in subsection (13)(a).

(15) The Commissioners may by regulations provide that in circumstances specified in the regulations the members of a company unit may alter a determination made under subsection (2) (despite subsection (5)).

(16) In this section "apprenticeship levy return" means a return under regulations under section 105(4).

(17) Part 1 of Schedule 1 to the National Insurance Contributions Act 2014 (rules for determining whether companies are "connected" with one another) applies for the purposes of subsection (1) as it applies for the purposes of section 3(1) of that Act.

(18) In this Part "company" has the meaning given by section 1121(1) of CTA 2010 and includes a limited liability partnership.

(19) See section 102 for the meaning of "charity".

GENERAL NOTE

Section 101 restricts the availability of the annul levy allowance where companies are 'connected' at the beginning of a tax year. In this case, a single allowance of £15,000 per annum is available between them (***not*** £15,000 each).

Where companies are 'connected' at the beginning of the tax year, they are considered part of a 'company unit' for that tax year. The companies in such a 'unit' will be able to decide how they want to share the allowance between them, and will need to determine the allocation at the start of each tax year. Once the determination is made at the beginning of the tax year, it cannot be altered (except to correct a company unit claiming in excess of £15,000).

Sections 101(6)–(10) apply in situations where two or more companies in a 'company unit' make returns which imply that they have not properly split the £15,000 between them. The legislation provides that HMRC must notify the companies and ask them to take corrective action. If this is not done, then HMRC must make a determination to split the £15,000 proportionately between the companies who have claimed any apprenticeship allowance, proportionate to the amounts they have claimed on returns they have submitted.

Sections 101(11)–(13) apply in situations where the members of a company unit have either not made any returns relating to apprenticeship levy or there is insufficient information on the returns for HMRC to determine whether they have properly divided up the £15,000 apprenticeship allowance between them. Where this is the case, and the total apprenticeship levy paid by the members of the company unit is lower than it should be, HMRC must notify the companies and ask them to take corrective action. If this is not done, then HMRC must make a determination dividing the £15,000 up equally between the members of the company unit.

It is clearly envisaged that apportioning the levy allowance between connected companies in a unit carries a compliance risk. This takes considerable legislation to address for the sake of a £15,000 allowance. For larger units with at least one employer having a pay bill of at £3m or more, it may be simpler and reduce the potential for errors, if the employers in the unit nominate one of them (having a pay bill of at least £3m) to claim the whole allowance. If they wish to reallocate the benefit of this between them, it should be possible to do so through management charges, subject to checks including:

– whether this has any impact on the relative funding that may be claimed for apprenticeships by each employer in the unit;
– the corporation tax treatment of each of the employers concerned, relating to such management charges;

Where no individual company in a unit expects their pay bill to exceed £3m, it is likely to be more beneficial to split the allowance between them at the beginning of the tax year.

Section 101(17) imports the rules relating to the Employment Allowance in Pt 1 of Sch 1 National Insurance Contributions Act 2014, when determining whether companies are connected for levy purposes. The basic rule here is that two companies are "connected" with one another if:

- one of the two has control of the other; or
- both are under the control of the same person or persons;

where "control" has the same meaning as in ss 450, 451 in Pt 10 CTA 2010. Also, a limited liability partnership is to be treated as a company for these purposes.

The basic rule is subject to a number of further provisions, in relation to:

- Companies whose relationship is not one of substantial commercial interdependence;
- When fixed rate preference shares must be ignored when considering control;
- Connection through a loan creditor;
- Connection through a trustee;
- Further connections.

Section 101(18) defines that "company" is to be interpreted as by s 1121(1) CTA 2010. This includes a limited liability partnership.

The rules are adapted for charities in s 102 but give a similar end result.

102 Connected charities

(1) Two or more charities form a "charities unit" for a tax year (and are the "members" of that unit) if—

    (a) they are connected with one another at the beginning of the tax year, and

    (b) each of them is entitled to a levy allowance for the tax year.

(2) The members of a charities unit must determine what amount of levy allowance each of them is to be entitled to for the tax year (and the determination must comply with subsections (3) and (4)).

But see subsections (6) and (11).

(3) A member's levy allowance for a tax year may be zero (but not a negative amount).

(4) The total amount of the levy allowances to which the members of a charities unit are entitled for a tax year must equal £15,000.

(5) A determination made under subsection (2) (with respect to a tax year) cannot afterwards be altered by the members concerned (but this does not prevent the correction of a failure to comply with subsection (4)).

(6) If subsection (8) applies—

    (a) HMRC must determine in accordance with subsection (7) what amount of levy allowance each of the relevant members (see subsection (8)(a)) of the unit concerned is to be entitled to for the tax year, and

    (b) accordingly subsection (2) is treated as never having applied in relation to that charities unit and that tax year.

(7) The determination is to be made by multiplying the amount of levy allowance set out in each relevant return (see subsection (8)(a)) by—

15,000 / T

where T is the total of the amounts of levy allowance set out in the relevant returns.

The result is, in each case, the amount of the levy allowance to which the relevant member in question is entitled for the tax year (but amounts may be rounded up or down where appropriate provided that subsection (4) is complied with).

(8) This subsection applies if—

    (a) HMRC is aware—

        (i) that two or more members of a charities unit ("the relevant members") have made apprenticeship levy returns ("the relevant returns") on the basis mentioned in subsection (9), and

        (ii) that those returns, together, imply that the total mentioned in subsection (4) is greater than £15,000,

    (b) HMRC has notified the relevant members in writing that HMRC is considering taking action under subsection (6), and

    (c) the remedial action specified in the notice has not been taken within the period specified in the notice.

(9) The basis in question is that the member making the return is entitled to a levy allowance (whether or not of zero) for the tax year concerned.

(10) If any member of the charities unit mentioned in subsection (8)(a) is not a relevant member, that member is entitled to a levy allowance of zero for the tax year.

(11) If subsection (13) applies—

(a) HMRC must determine in accordance with subsection (12) what amount of levy allowance each of the members of the unit concerned is to be entitled to for the tax year, and

(b) accordingly subsection (2) is treated as never having applied in relation to that charities unit and that tax year.

(12) Each member of the unit is to be entitled to a levy allowance for the tax year equal to—

£15,000 / N

where N is the number of the members of the charities unit for the tax year.

Amounts determined in accordance with the formula in this subsection may be rounded up or down where appropriate provided that subsection (4) is complied with.

(13) This subsection applies if—

(a) the total amount paid by the members of a charities unit in respect of apprenticeship levy for a tax year or any period in a tax year is less than the total of the amounts due and payable by them for the tax year or other period concerned,

(b) either the members of the unit have made no apprenticeship levy returns for any period in the tax year concerned or the returns that have been made do not contain sufficient information to enable HMRC to determine how the whole of the £15,000 mentioned in subsection (4) is to be used by the members of the unit for the tax year,

(c) HMRC has notified all the members of the unit in writing that HMRC is considering taking action under subsection (11), and

(d) the remedial action specified in the notice has not been taken within the period specified in the notice.

(14) Subsection (4) is to be taken into account in calculating the total of the amounts due and payable as mentioned in subsection (13)(a).

(15) The Commissioners may by regulations provide that in circumstances specified in the regulations the members of a charities unit may alter a determination made under subsection (2) (despite subsection (5)).

(16) In this section "apprenticeship levy return" means a return under regulations under section 105(4).

(17) In this Part "charity" means—

(a) a charity within the meaning of Part 1 of Schedule 6 to FA 2010;

(b) the Trustees of the National Heritage Memorial Fund;

(c) the Historic Buildings and Monuments Commission for England;

(d) a registered club within the meaning of Chapter 9 of Part 13 of CTA 2010 (community amateur sports clubs).

(18) Subsection (17) is subject to section 118(5).

(19) See sections 118 and 119 for provision about the meaning of "connected" in subsection (1).

GENERAL NOTE

Section 102 restricts the availability of the annul levy allowance where charities are 'connected' at the beginning of a tax year, in a very similar way Section 101 does for companies. As with connected companies, a single allowance of £15,000 per annum is available between all connected charities and **not** £15,000 each.

Where charities are 'connected' at the beginning of the tax year, they are considered part of a 'charities unit' for that tax year. The charities in such a 'unit' will be able to decide how they want to share the allowance between them, and will need to determine the allocation at the start of each tax year. Once the determination is made at the beginning of the tax year, it cannot be altered except to correct a charities unit claiming in excess of £15,000). Connected charities will need to ensure they do not claim multiple levy allowances.

Sections 102(6)–(10) apply in situations where two or more charities in a "charities unit" make returns which imply that they have not properly split the £15,000 between them. The legislation provides that HMRC must notify the charities and ask them to take corrective action. If this is not done, then HMRC must make a determination to split the £15,000 proportionately between the charities who have claimed any apprenticeship allowance, proportionate to the amounts they have claimed on returns they have submitted

Sections 102(11)–(13) apply in situations where the members of a charities unit have either not made any returns relating to apprenticeship levy or there is insufficient information on the returns for HMRC to determine whether they have properly divided up the £15,000 apprenticeship allowance between them. Where this is the case, and the total apprenticeship levy paid by the members of the charities unit is lower than it should be, HMRC must notify the companies and ask them to take corrective action. If this is not done, then HMRC must make a determination dividing the £15,000 up equally between the members of the charities unit.

Sections 102(17) contains the definition of 'charity' for this purpose.

Sections 118 and 119 contain the provisions as to whether charities are 'connected' (see below).

Anti-Avoidance

103 Anti-avoidance

(1) For the purposes of this section "avoidance arrangements" are arrangements the main purpose, or one of the main purposes, of which is to secure that a person—

(a) benefits, or further benefits, from an entitlement to a levy allowance for a tax year, or

(b) otherwise obtains an advantage in relation to apprenticeship levy.

(2) Subsection (3) applies where, in consequence of avoidance arrangements within subsection (1)(a) or (b), a person incurs a liability to pay secondary Class 1 contributions in a particular tax year (as opposed to another tax year).

(3) If the person would (apart from this subsection) obtain an advantage in relation to apprenticeship levy as a result of incurring the liability at the time mentioned in subsection (2), section 100 has effect as if the liability had been incurred when it would have been incurred but for the avoidance arrangements.

(4) Subsection (6) applies where (apart from this section) a person ("P")—

(a) would be in a position to use or make greater use of a levy allowance for a tax year, in consequence of avoidance arrangements within subsection (1)(a), or

(b) would otherwise obtain an advantage in relation to apprenticeship levy in consequence of avoidance arrangements within subsection (1)(a).

(5) But subsection (6) only applies so far as the advantage in relation to apprenticeship levy cannot be counteracted under subsection (3).

(6) P is not entitled to a levy allowance for the tax year.

(7) In this section "arrangements" includes any agreement, understanding, scheme, transaction or series of transactions (whether or not legally enforceable).

(8) In this section a reference to "an advantage in relation to apprenticeship levy" includes a reference to—

(a) repayment or increased repayment of apprenticeship levy,

(b) avoidance or reduction of a charge, or an assessment, to the levy,

(c) avoidance of a possible assessment to the levy,

(d) deferral of a payment of, or advancement of a repayment of, the levy, and

(e) avoidance of an obligation to account for the levy.

(9) Sections 101 and 102 are to be ignored for the purpose of determining under subsection (4) what the position would be apart from this section.

(10) In subsection (2) the reference to "a particular tax year" is to be read as including a reference to the period of 12 months beginning with 6 April 2016.

GENERAL NOTE

Section 103 contains anti-avoidance provisions relating to the apprenticeship levy.

Section 103(1) defines "avoidance arrangements" very widely as any arrangements, one of the main purposes of which is to secure either a higher levy allowance entitlement or one of the other advantages mentioned in s 103(8), including a reduction of the charge to the levy, increased repayment or deferment of the levy. Section 103(7) clarifies that an "avoidance arrangement" does not necessarily need to be in the format of a legally enforceable agreement or contract to be captured by the anti-avoidance provisions of s 103.

Section 103(2) and (3) apply to arrangements which attempt to obtain a timing advantage by shifting earnings subject to secondary Class 1 National Insurance into another tax year. This could include attempts to shift earnings into periods before the levy starts (i.e. into 2016/17 – this scenario is included by s 103(10)), or into a tax year in which either the levy allowance is higher or the levy percentage lower than in another tax year. Where such a scheme is in place, s 103(3) has the effect of imposing the levy in the year it would have arisen if the arrangement was not in place. Where the effects of using an "avoidance arrangement" cannot be rectified by s 103(3) (i.e. by applying the levy in the tax year it would have arisen without the arrangement), then s 103(6) will remove secondary contributor's entitlement to the levy allowance for the tax year.

104 Application of other regimes to apprenticeship levy

(1) In section 318(1) of FA 2004 (disclosure of tax avoidance schemes: interpretation), in the definition of "tax", after paragraph (d) insert—

"(da) apprenticeship levy,".

(2) In section 206(3) of FA 2013 (taxes to which the general anti-abuse rule applies), after paragraph (da) insert—

"(db) apprenticeship levy,".

(3) Part 4 of FA 2014 (follower notices and accelerated payments) is amended in accordance with subsections (4) and (5).

(4) In section 200 (meaning of "relevant tax"), after paragraph (c) insert—

"(ca) apprenticeship levy,".

(5) In section 203 (meaning of "tax appeal"), after paragraph (e) insert—

"(ea) an appeal under section 114 of FA 2016 (apprenticeship levy: appeal against an assessment),".

(6) Part 5 of FA 2014 (promoters of tax avoidance schemes) is amended in accordance with subsections (7) and (8).

(7) In section 253(6) (duty to notify the Commissioners: meaning of "tax return"), after paragraph (d) insert—

"(da) a return under regulations made under section 105 of FA 2016 (apprenticeship levy);".

(8) In section 283(1) (interpretation), in the definition of "tax", after paragraph (d) insert—

"(da) apprenticeship levy,".

GENERAL NOTE

As a tax, the apprenticeship levy will be subject to a number of other regimes countering tax avoidance.

Section 104(1) and (2) include the levy in the regimes on the disclosure of tax avoidance schemes (DOTAS) and in the general anti-abuse rule (GAAR).

Section 104(3)–(5) apply the system of accelerated payments in relation to avoidance schemes (APNs) to the apprenticeship levy.

Section 104(6)–(8) apply rules on the promotion of tax avoidance schemes to the levy.

At the time of writing, it is still not absolutely clear whether, as a tax which will be collected under the Income Tax (PAYE) Regulations 2003 (SI 2003/2682), the apprenticeship levy will be subject to the regime on Senior Accounting Officers (SAO) for large corporates. There are no specific provisions within the Finance Act to explicitly confirm this one way or the other. Unless clarified in official guidance on the matter, it would be prudent for employers to agree the position with their Customer Relationship Managers

Finally, it is worth noting that HMRC has indicated in guidance that the levy will be an allowable expense for Corporation Tax purposes (available at https://www.gov.uk/government/publications/apprenticeship-levy-how-it-will-work/apprenticeship-levy-how-it-will-work).

Payment, Collection and Recovery

105 Assessment, payment etc

(1) The Commissioners may by regulations make provision about the assessment, payment, collection and recovery of apprenticeship levy.

(2) Regulations under subsection (1) may include—

(a) provision which applies, with or without modifications, provisions of PAYE regulations;

(b) provision for combining any arrangements under the regulations with arrangements under PAYE regulations.

(3) Regulations under subsection (1) may—

(a) require payments to be made on account of apprenticeship levy;

(b) determine periods ("tax periods") by reference to which payments are to be made;

(c) make provision about the times at which payments are to be made and methods of payment;

(d) require the amounts payable by reference to tax periods to be calculated (and levy allowance to be taken into account) in the manner and on the basis determined by or under the regulations;

(e) make provision for dealing with cases where such calculations lead to overpayment of levy (by repayment or otherwise);

(f) make other provision about the recovery of overpayments of levy.

(4) Regulations under subsection (1) may make provision requiring persons to make returns, including provision about—

(a) the periods by reference to which returns are to be made,

(b) the information to be included in returns,

(c) timing, and

(d) the form of, and method of making, returns.

(5) Regulations under subsection (1) may—

(a) authorise HMRC to assess to the best of their judgement amounts payable by a person in respect of apprenticeship levy;

(b) make provision about the treatment of amounts so assessed, including provision for treating such amounts as apprenticeship levy payable by the person;

(c) make provision about the process of assessments.

(6) Regulations under subsection (1) may make, in relation to amounts of apprenticeship levy which have been repaid to a person and ought not to have been repaid, any provision which may be made in relation to apprenticeship levy payable by a person.

(7) Where—

(a) a repayment of apprenticeship levy has been increased in accordance with section 102 of FA 2009 (repayment interest), and

(b) the whole or part of the repayment has been paid to any person but ought not to have been paid to the person,

any amount by which the repayment paid to the person ought not to have been increased is to be treated for the purposes of regulations made by virtue of subsection (6) as if it were an amount of apprenticeship levy repaid to the person which ought not to have been repaid.

(8) Regulations under subsection (1) may make provision for enabling the repayment or remission of interest under section 101 of FA 2009.

(9) The provision that may be made under subsection (1) includes—

(a) provision for the making of decisions (other than relevant assessments) by HMRC as to any matter required to be decided for the purposes of the regulations and for appeals against such decisions;

(b) provision for appeals with respect to matters arising under the regulations which would otherwise not be the subject of an appeal;

(c) provision for the way in which any matters provided for by the regulations are to be proved.

(10) In subsection (9) "relevant assessment" means an assessment of amounts payable by a person in respect of apprenticeship levy.

(11) Regulations under subsection (1) must not affect any right of appeal to the tribunal which a person would have apart from the regulations.

(12) In this section (except where the context requires otherwise) references to payments are to payments of, or on account of, apprenticeship levy.

GENERAL NOTE

Section 105 sets out HMRC's powers to make regulations on the assessment, payment, collection and recovery of the levy. At the time of writing, the relevant regulations have only been published in draft for consultation, but it is expected that the regulations will apply much of the Real Time Information (RTI) regime which is in place for payments of income tax and National Insurance under PAYE to the apprenticeship levy. Regulations will most likely link to provisions in the Income Tax (PAYE) Regulations 2003 (SI 2003/2682).

Liability for the levy has to be calculated monthly on a cumulative basis and accounted for through RTI. The levy allowance will operate on a monthly basis and will accumulate throughout the year. This means secondary contributors will have an allowance of £1,250 a month in 2017/18. Any unused allowance will be carried from one month to the next.

If the secondary contributor has some unused allowance in a month, but paid the levy previously in the tax year, they can receive a credit which they can use to offset against their other PAYE liabilities.

Connected employers and employers with multiple PAYE schemes will be able to register for payment of the levy on a pooled basis. In contrast, at the time of writing, the Government is considering whether an employer's levy funding can be used by different employers and/or different PAYE schemes. The position is not yet clear but one would hope that a group of connected employers in a unit, would also be able to draw down on their pooled funds as they may agree between them. The position will need to be clarified by BIS/HMRC.

One would hope at least that a single employer with more than one PAYE scheme (say, one for monthly and one for weekly paid employees) would be able to draw down on its pooled funding for employees covered by both of those PAYE schemes as it pleases. The liability and funding requirements under each PAYE scheme may be very different, notwithstanding the employer is the same in each case.

In terms of the levy allowance, where connected employers cannot use the full levy allowance on one PAYE scheme, they will be able to offset the unused amount once the tax year has ended against other PAYE liabilities or claim a refund (see further https://www.gov.uk/government/publications/apprenticeship-levy-how-it-will-work/apprenticeship-levy-how-it-will-work).

106 Recovery from third parties

(1) Regulations under section 105(1) may make corresponding provision for the recovery of amounts in respect of apprenticeship levy from persons other than the person liable to pay the amounts by virtue of section 99(3).

(2) In subsection (1) "corresponding provision" means provision which corresponds to provision made by regulations under the Contributions and Benefits Act for secondary Class 1 contributions in respect of any earnings to be recovered from a person other than the secondary contributor.

GENERAL NOTE

Section 106 gives HMRC the power to provide, by regulations, for the collection of unpaid levy from parties other than the secondary contributor. The regulations have not been made at the time of writing but are expected to mirror those in the National Insurance legislation. This allows, for example, for unpaid debts of managed service companies (MSCs) to be transferred to MSC providers, directors and associates of the MSC or of the MSC provider or to other persons who encouraged the use of an MSC.

As set out above, paras 3A and 3B of Sch 1 SSCBA 1992 provide for NIC agreements and NIC elections for use in conjunction with share schemes. An NIC election *transfers* an employer's liability for secondary Class 1 NIC to an employee. It is not clear what the Government's intention is in regards to a "3B" election to transfer the NIC liability to an employee. Paragraph 3B does not deem the individual to be a secondary contributor and s106 appears not intended for transferring any potentially associated levy debts to the employee in this scenario.

107 Real time information

(1) Regulations under section 105(1) may make provision—

(a) for authorising or requiring relevant service providers to supply to HMRC information about payments of apprenticeship levy with respect to which their service is provided, or any information the Commissioners may request about features of the service provided or to be provided with respect to particular payments of apprenticeship levy;

(b) for requiring clients to provide relevant service providers with information about payments of apprenticeship levy;

(c) for prohibiting or restricting the disclosure, otherwise than to HMRC, of information by a person to whom it was supplied pursuant to a requirement imposed under paragraph (b);

(d) for conferring power on the Commissioners to specify by directions circumstances in which provision made by virtue of paragraph (a) or (b) is not to apply in relation to a payment;

(e) for requiring relevant service providers to take steps for facilitating the meeting by clients of obligations imposed under paragraph (b);

(f) for requiring compliance with any directions the Commissioners may give—

(i) specifying, or further specifying, steps for the purposes of paragraph (e), or

(ii) specifying information that a person making payments of apprenticeship levy must provide about the method by which the payments are made.

(2) Directions made under the regulations may make different provision for different cases or different classes of case.

(3) In this section—

"client", in relation to a relevant service provider, means a person to whom that relevant service provider provides or is to provide a service with respect to a payment of apprenticeship levy;

"payment of apprenticeship levy" includes a payment on account of apprenticeship levy;

"relevant service provider" means a person who provides or is to provide with respect to payments of apprenticeship levy a service that is specified, or of a description specified, by the regulations.

GENERAL NOTE

Section 107 allows HMRC to make regulations to facilitate the flow of information about payments relevant to the apprenticeship levy between clients, service providers (e.g. payroll bureaux) and payers of the levy for situations where the secondary contributor is not dealing with these payroll functions in-house.

This section broadly mirrors HMRC's powers to make regulations for PAYE in provision 4ZA in s 684(2) ITEPA 2003.

108 Time limits for assessment

(1) The general rule is that no assessment under regulations under section 105 may be made more than 4 years after the end of the tax year to which it relates.

(2) An assessment on a person in a case of loss of apprenticeship levy brought about carelessly by the person may be made at any time not more than 6 years after the end of the tax year to which it relates.

(3) An assessment on a person in a case falling within subsection (4) may be made at any time not more than 20 years after the end of the tax year to which it relates.

(4) A case falls within this subsection if it involves a loss of apprenticeship levy—

(a) brought about deliberately by the person,

(b) attributable to arrangements in respect of which the person has failed to comply with an obligation under section 309, 310 or 313 of FA 2004 (obligation of parties to tax avoidance schemes to provide information to HMRC), or

(c) attributable to arrangements which were expected to give rise to a tax advantage in respect of which the person was under an obligation to notify the Commissioners under section 253 of FA 2014 (duty to notify Commissioners of promoter reference number) but failed to do so.

(5) An assessment made by virtue of section 105(6) (amounts of levy repaid which ought not to have been repaid etc) is not out of time as a result of subsection (1) if it is made before the end of the tax year following that in which the amount assessed was repaid or paid (as the case may be).

(6) Subsections (2), (3) and (5) do not limit one another's application.

(7) An objection to the making of an assessment on the ground that the time limit for making it has expired may only be made on an appeal against the assessment.

(8) In subsections (2) and (4) references to a loss brought about by a person include a loss brought about by another person acting on behalf of that person.

GENERAL NOTE

Section 108 sets out the time limits for assessments to be made on an employer's levy payments.

The general rule is that HMRC may make no assessments on an employer's levy payments more than four years after the end of the relevant tax year.

This time limit will be six years rather than four in cases where the loss of the levy has been brought about carelessly by the taxpayer.

The time limit will be extended to 20 years in cases where the loss of the levy was brought about deliberately, or in relation to arrangements where the person has failed to comply with the listed obligations for parties to tax avoidance schemes.

Another exception to the general rule is where a repayment is made in error, the time limit is extended to the end of the tax year after the amount assessed was repaid or paid.

This section broadly mirrors the provisions for Income Tax and Capital Gains Tax contained in ss 34 and 36 TMA 1970.

109 No deduction in respect of levy to be made from earnings

(1) A person ("P") must not—

(a) make from any payment of earnings any deduction in respect of apprenticeship levy for which P (or any other person) is liable,
(b) otherwise recover the cost, or any part of the cost, of P's (or any other person's) liability to apprenticeship levy from any person who is or has been a relevant earner, or
(c) enter into any agreement with any person to do anything prohibited by paragraph (a) or (b).

(2) In this section "relevant earner" means an earner in respect of whom P is or has been liable to pay any secondary Class 1 contributions under Part 1 of the Contributions and Benefits Act.

GENERAL NOTE

Section 109 prevents secondary contributors from deducting or otherwise recovering levy payments from their employees, mirroring similar restrictions of recovery of employer's National Insurance contributions contained in para 3A of Sch 1 SSCBA 1992.

110 Collectors and court proceedings

(1) The following provisions of Part 6 of TMA 1970 apply in relation to apprenticeship levy as they apply in relation to income tax—

(a) section 60 (issue of demand notes and receipts);
(b) section 61 (distraint by collectors: Northern Ireland);
(c) sections 65 to 68 (court proceedings).

(2) See also Chapter 5 of Part 7 of FA 2008 (which makes general provision about payment and enforcement).

GENERAL NOTE

Section 110 sets out that HMRC may recover amounts in respect of the levy which the secondary contributor has not paid, and the relevant process of court proceedings. The procedures will be the same as in relation to Income Tax.

Information and Penalties

111 Records

(1) The Commissioners may by regulations require persons—

(a) to keep for purposes connected with apprenticeship levy records of specified matters, and
(b) to preserve the records for a specified period.

(2) A duty under regulations under this section to preserve records may be discharged—

(a) by preserving them in any form and by any means, or

(b) by preserving the information contained in them in any form and by any means, subject to any conditions or exceptions specified in writing by the Commissioners.

(3) In this section "specified" means specified or described in the regulations.

GENERAL NOTE

Section 111 allows HMRC to make regulations to require employer keep records to support their levy payments for a specified period. Employers will be able preserve the records and the information held within in any form or by any means, as long they comply with conditions set out in the regulations.

At the time of writing HMRC have not yet published details of their record requirements for the levy.

112 Information and inspection powers

In Schedule 36 to FA 2008 (information and inspection powers), in paragraph 63(1), after paragraph (ca) insert—

"(cb) apprenticeship levy,".

GENERAL NOTE

Section 112 applies HMRC's information and inspection powers under Sch 36 Finance Act 2008 to the levy. These are the same powers that currently apply to income tax, capital gains tax, corporation tax and VAT.

113 Penalties

(1) Schedule 24 to FA 2007 (penalties for errors) is amended in accordance with subsections (2) to (4).

(2) In the Table in paragraph 1, after the entry relating to accounts in connection with a partnership return insert—

"Apprenticeship levy	Return under regulations under section 105 of FA 2016."

(3) In paragraph 13—

(a) in sub-paragraph (1ZA), after "CIS returns," insert "or for two or more penalties relating to apprenticeship levy returns,";

(b) in sub-paragraph (1ZD), after the entry relating to "a CIS return" insert—
""an apprenticeship levy return" means a return under regulations under section 105 of FA 2016;".

(4) In paragraph 21C, after "capital gains tax)" insert "and amounts payable on account of apprenticeship levy".

(5) Schedule 55 to FA 2009 (penalty for failure to make returns etc) is amended in accordance with subsections (6) to (8).

(6) In the Table in paragraph 1, after item 4 insert—

"4A	Apprenticeship levy	Return under regulations under section 105 of FA 2016"

(7) In paragraph 6B, after "item 4" insert "or 4A".

(8) In the italic heading before paragraph 6B, at the end insert "and apprenticeship levy".

(9) Schedule 56 to FA 2009 (penalty for failure to make payments on time) is amended in accordance with subsections (10) to (15).

(10) In the Table in paragraph 1, after item 4 insert—

"4A	Apprentice-ship levy	Amount payable under regulations under section 105 of FA 2016	The date determined by or under regulations under section 105 of FA 2016"

(11) In paragraph 3(1)—

(a) in paragraph (b) after "within" insert "item 4A or";

(b) after paragraph (c) insert—

"(ca) an amount in respect of apprenticeship levy falling within item 4A which is payable by virtue of regulations under section 106 of FA 2016 (recovery from third parties)."

(12) In paragraph 5(1), for "or 4" substitute ", 4 or 4A".

(13) In paragraph 5(2), for "or (c)" substitute ", (c) or (ca)."

(14) In paragraph 6(2), after paragraph (b) insert—

"(ba) a payment under regulations under section 105 of FA 2016 of an amount in respect of apprenticeship levy payable in relation to the tax year;".

(15) In the italic heading before paragraph 5, at the end insert "etc".

(16) The amendments made by subsections (1) to (4) of this section come into force in accordance with provision made by the Treasury by regulations.

(17) In subsections (2) and (4) of section 106 of FA 2009 (penalties for failure to make returns: commencement etc) references to Schedule 55 to that Act have effect as references to that Schedule as amended by subsections (5) to (8) of this section.

(18) Schedule 56 to FA 2009, as amended by this section, is taken to come into force for the purposes of apprenticeship levy on the date on which this Act is passed.

GENERAL NOTE

Under s 113, HMRC will be able to charge penalties for errors on returns relating to the levy, or for failure to make such a return, or for late payments in the same manner as they do for income tax, PAYE returns etc. Returns and payments will have to be made under the Real Time Information (RTI) system, in accordance with the PAYE Regulations (SI 2003/2682).

HMRC may charge penalties for errors in any document relating to the apprentice levy under Sch 24 FA 2007.

HMRC may charge penalties for failure to make returns under Sch 55 Finance Act 2009. The changes to Sch 55 for the levy will come into force on a day appointed by the Treasury under the power in s 106 of the Finance Act 2009.

HMRC may charge penalties for failure to make payments on time under Sch 56 FA 2009. This will come into effect on the date this Act is passed.

Logic would suggest that levy payments for employees covered by modified payrolls should be based on the same estimates used to calculate liability for Class 1 NIC payments, with the same true-up at the end of the year. However, at the time of writing, HMRC has yet to confirm this position.

Appeals

114 Appeals

(1) An appeal may be brought against an assessment of apprenticeship levy or other amounts under regulations under section 105.

(2) Notice of appeal must be given—

(a) in writing,

(b) within the period of 30 days beginning with the date on which notice of the assessment was given,

(c) to the officer of Revenue and Customs by whom notice of the assessment was given.

(3) Part 5 of TMA 1970 (appeals and other proceedings) applies in relation to an appeal under this section as it applies in relation to an appeal against an assessment to income tax.

GENERAL NOTE

Section 114 sets out that appeals may be brought against HMRC assessments of the levy made under s 105, within 30 days from the date of assessment.

Part 5 of the Taxes Management Act 1970, which deals with appeals for Income Tax, will apply to appeals in relation to the levy. This brings the apprenticeship levy into the remit of the tax tribunals.

General

115 Tax agents: dishonest conduct

In Schedule 38 to FA 2012 (tax agents: dishonest conduct), in paragraph 37(1), after paragraph (l) insert—

"(la) apprenticeship levy,".

GENERAL NOTE

Section 115 adds the levy to the definition of "tax" for the purposes of HMRCs information and inspection powers under Sch 38 FA 2012, in relation to tax agents (engaging in or who have engaged in dishonest conduct).

116 Provisional collection of apprenticeship levy

In section 1 of the Provisional Collection of Taxes Act 1968 (temporary statutory effect of House of Commons resolutions), in subsection (1), after "diverted profits tax," insert "the apprenticeship levy,".

GENERAL NOTE

Section 116 amends the Provisional Collection of Taxes Act 1968 to facilitate future changes to the levy.

117 Crown application

This Part binds the Crown.

GENERAL NOTE

Section 117 has the effect that the Crown is not excluded from the levy.

118 Charities which are "connected" with one another

(1) Two charities are connected with one another for the purposes of section 102(1) if—

(a) they are connected with one another in accordance with section 993 of ITA 2007 (meaning of "connected persons"), and

(b) their purposes and activities are the same or substantially similar.

(2) In the application of section 993 of ITA 2007 for the purposes of subsection (1)(a)—

(a) a charity which is a trust is to be treated as if it were a company (and accordingly a person), including in this subsection;

(b) a charity which is a trust has "control" of another person if the trustees (in their capacity as trustees of the charity) have, or any of them has, control of the person;

(c) a person (other than a charity regulator) has "control" of a charity which is a trust if—

(i) the person is a trustee of the charity and some or all of the powers of the trustees of the charity could be exercised by the person acting alone or by the person acting together with any other persons who are trustees of the charity and who are connected with the person,

(ii) the person, alone or together with other persons, has power to appoint or remove a trustee of the charity, or

(iii) the person, alone or together with other persons, has any power of approval or direction in relation to the carrying out by the trustees of any of their functions.

(3) For the purposes of section 102(1) a charity which is a trust is also connected with another charity which is a trust if at least half of the trustees of one of the charities are—

(a) trustees of the other charity,

(b) persons who are connected with persons who are trustees of the other charity, or

(c) a combination of both,

and the charities' purposes and activities are the same or substantially similar.

(4) In determining if a person is connected with another person for the purposes of subsection (2)(c)(i) or (3)(b), apply section 993 of ITA 2007 with the omission of subsection (3) of that section (and without the modifications in subsection (2) above).

(5) If a charity ("A") controls a company ("B") which, apart from this subsection, would not be a charity—

    (a) B is to be treated as if it were a charity for the purposes of this Part, and
    (b) A and B are connected with one another for the purposes of section 102(1).

(6) In subsection (5) "control" has the same meaning as in Part 10 of CTA 2010 (see sections 450 and 451 of that Act) (and a limited liability partnership is to be treated as a company for the purposes of that Part as applied by this subsection).

(7) For this purpose, where under section 450 of that Act "C" is a limited liability partnership, subsection (3) of that section has effect as if before (a) there were inserted—

    "(za) rights to a share of more than half the assets, or of more than half the income, of C,".

GENERAL NOTE

Section 102 provides that charities which are connected at the start of a tax year are only entitled to one levy allowance between them (the same applies for connected companies). Section 118 sets out when charities are connected for this purpose.

The basic rule is that two charities are connected with one another if they are connected under the definition of 'connected persons' in s 993 Income Tax Act 2007 (ITA 2007) **and** their purposes and activities are the same or substantially similar.

In applying s 993 ITA 2007, special rules are then set out in s 118(2) and (3) to determine whether a charitable trust controls another person (and vice versa) and whether two charitable trusts are connected through their trustees or persons connected with their trustees. For these purposes, s 118(4) applies s 993 ITA, omitting the provision relating to trustees of settlements.

Where a charity controls a company (for example where a charity carries on a trade through a trading subsidiary), that company is treated as a charity connected to the controlling charity, so that only one levy allowance will be available between them. For this purpose, "control' has the same meaning as in ss 450,451 CTA 2010. Also, limited liability partnerships are treated as companies, as is the case when considering connected companies in s 101.

119 Connection between charities: further provision

(1) This section applies if—

    (a) a charity ("A") is connected with another charity ("B") for the purposes of section 102(1), and
    (b) B is connected with another charity ("C") for the purposes of section 102(1).

(2) A and C are also connected with one another for the purposes of section 102(1) (if that would not otherwise be the case).

(3) In subsection (1)—

    (a) in paragraph (a) the reference to a charity being connected with another charity for the purposes of section 102(1) is to that charity being so connected by virtue of section 118 or this section, and
    (b) in paragraph (b) the reference to a charity being connected with another charity for the purposes of section 102(1) is to that charity being so connected by virtue of section 118.

GENERAL NOTE

Section 119 extends the meaning of connected to a third charity so that, if charity ('A') is connected with another charity ('B') and B is connected with another charity ('C') then A and C are also connected with one another.

The consequence in this example would be that all three charities A, B and C must share one levy allowance between them.

120 General interpretation

(1) In this Part (except where the contrary is indicated, expressly or by implication), expressions which are also used in Part 1 of the Contributions and Benefits Act have the same meaning as in that Part.

(2) In this Part—

"charity" has the meaning given by section 102(17) and (18);

"the Commissioners" means the Commissioners for Her Majesty's Revenue and Customs;

"company" has the meaning given by section 101(18);

"the Contributions and Benefits Act" means the Social Security Contributions and Benefits Act 1992 or (as the case requires) the Social Security Contributions and Benefits (Northern Ireland) Act 1992;

"HMRC" means Her Majesty's Revenue and Customs;

"tax year" means the 12 months beginning with 6 April in 2017 or any subsequent year;

"tribunal" means the First-tier Tribunal or, where determined by or under Tribunal Procedure Rules, the Upper Tribunal.

GENERAL NOTE

Section 120 provides further definitions of the expressions listed in relation to the levy.

121 Regulations

(1) Regulations under this Part—

(a) may make different provision for different purposes;

(b) may include incidental, consequential, supplementary or transitional provision.

(2) Regulations under this Part are to be made by statutory instrument.

(3) A statutory instrument containing regulations under this Part is subject to annulment in pursuance of a resolution of the House of Commons.

(4) Subsection (3) does not apply to a statutory instrument containing only regulations under section 113(16).

GENERAL NOTE

Section 121 provides the authority to make Regulations for various purposes in relation to the levy.

At the time of writing, a consultation on the draft Regulations has been published at https://www.gov.uk/government/publications/draft-legislation-regulations-for-the-calculation-payment-and-recovery-of-the-apprenticehip-levy. These regulations set out the mechanism for the levy to be collected via the PAYE system, as well as the mechanics for connected companies to share a single levy allowance.

PART 7

VAT

122 VAT: power to provide for persons to be eligible for refunds

In Part 2 of VATA 1994 (reliefs, exemptions and repayments), after section 33D insert—

"33E Power to extend refunds of VAT to other persons

(1) This section applies where—

(a) VAT is chargeable on—

(i) the supply of goods or services to a specified person,

(ii) the acquisition of any goods from another member State by a specified person, or

(iii) the importation of any goods from a place outside the member States by a specified person, and

(b) the supply, acquisition or importation is not for the purpose of—

(i) any business carried on by the person, or

(ii) a supply by the person which, by virtue of section 41A, is treated as a supply in the course or furtherance of a business.

(2) If and to the extent that the Treasury so direct, the Commissioners shall, on a claim made by the specified person at such time and in such form and manner as the Commissioners may determine, refund to the person the amount of the VAT so chargeable.

This is subject to subsection (3) below.

(3) A specified person may not make a claim under subsection (2) above unless it has been agreed with the Treasury that, in the circumstances specified in the agreement, the amount of the person's funding is to be reduced by all or part of the amount of the VAT so chargeable.

(4) A claim under subsection (2) above in respect of a supply, acquisition or importation must be made on or before the relevant day.

(5) The "relevant day" is—

(a) in the case of a person who is registered, the last day on which the person may make a return under this Act for the prescribed accounting period containing the last day of the financial year in which the supply is made or the acquisition or importation takes place;
(b) in the case of a person who is not registered, the last day of the period of 3 months beginning immediately after the end of the financial year in which the supply is made or the acquisition or importation takes place.

(6) Subsection (7) applies where goods or services supplied to, or acquired or imported by, a specified person otherwise than for the purpose of—

(a) any business carried on by the person, or
(b) a supply falling within subsection (1)(b)(ii) above,

cannot be conveniently distinguished from goods or services supplied to, or acquired or imported by, the person for such a purpose.

(7) The amount to be refunded under this section is such amount as remains after deducting from the whole of the VAT chargeable on any supply to, or acquisition or importation by, the specified person such proportion of that VAT as appears to the Commissioners to be attributable to the carrying on of the business or (as the case may be) the making of the supply.

(8) In this section, "specified person" means a person specified in an order made by the Treasury.

(9) An order under subsection (8) may make transitional provision or savings.

(10) References in this section to VAT do not include any VAT which, by virtue of an order under section 25(7), is excluded from credit under section 25."

GENERAL NOTE

A new s 33E will be added to VATA 1994, which will refund VAT incurred by named bodies on goods and services purchased or imported for non-business purposes. Before a body can be named, it must have entered into an agreement with HM Treasury to adjust the overall level of its public funding to take into account the VAT that will be recoverable. This is because such funding includes tax liabilities. The aim of the measure is to ensure that public bodies are not deterred from sharing back-office services (which help to create efficiency savings) because of not being able to recover VAT.

123 VAT: representatives and security

(1) Section 48 of VATA 1994 (VAT representatives) is amended in accordance with subsections (2) to (11).

(2) In the heading, at the end insert "and security".

(3) In subsection (1)—

(a) for "Where" substitute "Subsection (1ZA) applies where",
(b) in paragraph (c) after "residence" insert "or permanent address", and
(c) omit the words after paragraph (c).

(4) After subsection (1) insert—

"(1ZA) The Commissioners may direct the person to secure that there is a UK-established person who is—

(a) appointed to act on the person's behalf in relation to VAT, and

(b) registered against the name of the person in accordance with any regulations under subsection (4)."

(5) In subsection (1B) for paragraphs (a) and (b) substitute—

"(a) section 87 of the Finance Act 2011 (mutual assistance for recovery of taxes etc) and Schedule 25 to that Act;

(b) section 173 of the Finance Act 2006 (international tax enforcement arrangements);".

(6) In subsection (2)—

(a) in paragraph (a), for the words from "required" to "VAT" substitute "given a direction under subsection (1ZA)",

(b) in paragraph (b) for "that subsection" substitute "subsection (1)", and

(c) in the words after paragraph (b), for "another" substitute "a UK-established".

(7) In subsection (2A) for "(1)" substitute "(1ZA)".

(8) In subsection (4)—

(a) omit the "and" at the end of paragraph (a), and

(b) after paragraph (b) insert—

"(c) give the Commissioners power to refuse to register a person as a VAT representative, or to cancel a person's registration as a VAT representative, in such circumstances as may be specified in the regulations."

(9) In subsection (7) for the words from the beginning to the first "him" substitute "The Commissioners may require a person in relation to whom the conditions specified in paragraphs (a), (b) and (c) of subsection (1) are satisfied".

(10) After subsection (7A) insert—

"(7B) A direction under subsection (1ZA)—

(a) may specify a time by which it (or any part of it) must be complied with;

(b) may be varied;

(c) continues to have effect (subject to any variation) until it is withdrawn or the conditions specified in subsection (1) are no longer satisfied.

(7C) A requirement under subsection (7)—

(a) may specify a time by which it (or any part of it) must be complied with;

(b) may be varied;

(c) continues to have effect (subject to any variation) until it is withdrawn."

(11) After subsection (8) insert—

"(8A) For the purposes of subsections (1ZA) and (2)—

(a) a person is UK-established if the person is established, or has a fixed establishment, in the United Kingdom, and

(b) an individual is also UK-established if the person's usual place of residence or permanent address is in the United Kingdom."

(12) In paragraph 19 of Schedule 3B to VATA 1994 for "(1)" substitute "(1ZA)".

124 VAT: joint and several liability of operators of online marketplaces

(1) VATA 1994 is amended in accordance with subsections (2) to (4).

(2) After section 77A insert—

"77B Joint and several liability: operators of online marketplaces

(1) This section applies where a person ("P") who is not UK-established—

(a) makes taxable supplies of goods through an online marketplace, and

(b) fails to comply with any requirement imposed on P by or under this Act (whether or not it relates to those supplies).

(2) The Commissioners may give the person who is the operator of the online marketplace ("the operator") a notice—

(a) stating that, unless the operator secures the result mentioned in subsection (3), subsection (5) will apply, and

(b) explaining the effect of subsection (5).

(3) The result referred to in subsection (2)(a) is that P does not offer goods for sale through the online marketplace at any time between—

(a) the end of such period as may be specified in the notice, and

(b) the notice ceasing to have effect.

(4) If the operator does not secure the result mentioned in subsection (3), subsection (5) applies.

(5) The operator is jointly and severally liable to the Commissioners for the amount of VAT payable by P in respect of all taxable supplies of goods made by P through the online marketplace in the period for which the notice has effect.

(6) A notice under subsection (2) ("the liability notice") has effect for the period beginning with the day after the day on which it is given, and ending—

(a) with the day specified in a notice given by the Commissioners under subsection (7), or

(b) in accordance with subsection (8).

(7) The Commissioners may at any time give the operator a notice stating that the period for which the liability notice has effect ends with the day specified in the notice.

(8) If the person to whom the liability notice is given ceases to be the operator of the online marketplace, the liability notice ceases to have effect at the end of—

(a) the day on which the person ceases to be the operator, or

(b) (if later) the day on which the person notifies the Commissioners that the person is no longer the operator.

(9) In this section—

"online marketplace" means a website, or any other means by which information is made available over the internet, through which persons other than the operator are able to offer goods for sale (whether or not the operator also does so);

"operator", in relation to an online marketplace, means the person who controls access to, and the contents of, the online marketplace.

(10) For the purposes of this section a person is "UK-established" if the person is established in the United Kingdom within the meaning of Article 10 of Implementing Regulation (EU) No 282/2011.

(11) The Treasury may by regulations provide that supplies made or goods offered for sale in circumstances specified in the regulations are, or are not, to be treated for the purposes of this section as having been made or offered through an online marketplace.

(12) The Treasury may by regulations amend this section so as to alter the meaning of—

"online marketplace",

"operator", and

"UK-established".

77C Joint and several liability under section 77B: assessments

(1) The Commissioners may assess the amount of VAT due from the operator of an online marketplace by virtue of section 77B to the best of their judgment and notify it to the operator.

(2) Subject to subsections (3) to (6), an assessment may be made for such period or periods as the Commissioners consider appropriate.

(3) An assessment for any month may not be made after the end of—

(a) 2 years after the end of that month, or

(b) (if later) one year after evidence of facts, sufficient in the opinion of the Commissioners to justify the making of an assessment for that month, comes to their knowledge.

(4) Subsection (5) applies if, after the Commissioners have made an assessment for a period, evidence of facts sufficient in the opinion of the Commissioners to justify the making of a further assessment for that period comes to their knowledge.

(5) The Commissioners may, no later than one year after that evidence comes to their knowledge, make a further assessment for that period (subject to subsection (6)).

(6) An assessment or further assessment for a month may not be made more than 4 years after the end of the month.

(7) An amount which has been assessed and notified to a person under this section is deemed to be an amount of VAT due from the person and may be recovered accordingly (unless, or except to the extent that, the assessment is subsequently withdrawn or reduced).

(8) Subsection (7) is subject to the provisions of this Act as to appeals.

(9) Expressions used in this section and in section 77B have the same meaning in this section as in section 77B.

77D Joint and several liability under section 77B: interest

(1) If an amount assessed under section 77C is not paid before the end of the period of 30 days beginning with the day on which notice of the assessment is given, the amount assessed carries interest from the day on which the notice of assessment is given until payment.

(2) Interest under this section is payable at the rate applicable under section 197 of the Finance Act 1996.

(3) Where the operator of an online marketplace is liable for interest under this section the Commissioners may assess the amount due and notify it to the operator.

(4) A notice of assessment under this section must specify a date (not later than the date of the notice) to which the interest is calculated.

(5) A further assessment or assessments may be made under this section in respect of any interest accrued after that date.

(6) An amount of interest assessed and notified to the operator of an online marketplace under this section is recoverable as if it were VAT due from the operator (unless, or except to the extent that, the assessment is withdrawn or reduced).

(7) Interest under this section is to be paid without any deduction of income tax.

(8) Expressions used in this section and in section 77B have the same meaning in this section as in section 77B."

(3) In section 83(1) (appeals) after paragraph (ra) insert—

"(rb) an assessment under section 77C or the amount of such an assessment;".

(4) In section 84 (further provision relating to appeals)—

(a) in subsection (3) after "(ra)" insert ", (rb)", and
(b) in subsection (5) after "83(1)(p)" insert "or (rb)".

GENERAL NOTE

This measure affects overseas businesses selling goods to UK consumers via online marketplaces and businesses that control and support the sale of such goods through their online marketplaces, e.g. Amazon and eBay.

The measure takes effect from 15 September 2016 (the date of Royal Assent to FA 2016) and will hold an online marketplace jointly and severally liable for the unpaid VAT of an overseas business that sells goods in the UK via the online marketplace's website (s 124). It will also provide HMRC with strengthened powers of directing the appointment of a VAT representative based in the UK and greater flexibility in respect of seeking a security (s 123).

This measure should help to prevent the avoidance of VAT by overseas businesses selling their goods in the UK and help to create a more level playing field for UK based businesses, i.e. enabling them to compete in the marketplace.

125 VAT: Isle of Man charities

In Schedule 6 to FA 2010 (charities etc), in paragraph 2(2) (jurisdiction condition: meaning of "a relevant UK court"), after paragraph (c) (and on a new line) insert "(and, for enactments relating to value added tax, includes the High Court of the Isle of Man)."

GENERAL NOTE

This is a tidying up measure with limited practical impact.

126 VAT: women's sanitary products

(1) VATA 1994 is amended as follows.

(2) In Schedule 7A (reduced rate)—

(a) in Part 1 (index), omit the entry relating to women's sanitary products;
(b) in Part 2 (the Groups), omit Group 4 (women's sanitary products).

(3) In Schedule 8 (zero-rating), in Part 1 (index), at the end insert—

"Women's sanitary products | Group 19"

(4) In Schedule 8, in Part 2 (the Groups), after Group 18 insert—

"GROUP 19—WOMEN'S SANITARY PRODUCTS

Item No.

1 The supply of women's sanitary products.

NOTES

(1) In this Group "women's sanitary products" means women's sanitary products of any of the following descriptions—

(a) subject to Note (2), products that are designed, and marketed, as being solely for use for absorbing, or otherwise collecting, lochia or menstrual flow;

(b) panty liners, other than panty liners that are designed as being primarily for use as incontinence products;

(c) sanitary belts.

(2) Note (1)(a) does not include protective briefs or any other form of clothing."

(5) The amendments made by this section have effect in relation to supplies made, and acquisitions and importations taking place, on or after such day as the Treasury may by regulations made by statutory instrument appoint.

(6) The date appointed under subsection (5) must not be after the later of—

(a) 1 April 2017, and

(b) the earliest date that may be appointed consistently with the United Kingdom's EU obligations.

GENERAL NOTE

Sales of women's sanitary products are currently taxed at 5% VAT. The proposed change will enable future sales of these products to be zero-rated. The main products affected will be pads, towels, liners and tampons. The legislation will come into force on a day appointed by Treasury regulations but as soon as possible following Royal Assent. The change is being made by taking the products out of VATA 1994 Sch 7A Group 4 (the reduced rate schedule) and inserting them as a new Group 19 to Sch 8 VATA 1994, i.e. the zero-rate schedule. The measure is expected to cost the Exchequer £15m per annum. It will be interesting to see if retailers pass on the tax savings to consumers in the form of lower prices rather than increased profit margins, which is certainly the intention of the proposed measure.

PART 8

SDLT AND ATED

Stamp Duty Land Tax

127 SDLT: calculating tax on non-residential and mixed transactions

(1) Section 55 of FA 2003 (general rules on calculating the amount of stamp duty land tax chargeable) is amended in accordance with subsections (2) to (7).

(2) In subsection (1) for ", (1C) and (2)" substitute "and (1C)".

(3) In subsection (1B)—

(a) omit the words from "the relevant land" to "and",

(b) in Step 1—

(i) for "Table A" substitute "the appropriate table",

(ii) for "that Table" substitute "the appropriate table",

(iii) at the end insert—

""The "appropriate table" is—

(a) Table A, if the relevant land consists entirely of residential property, and

(b) Table B, if the relevant land consists of or includes land that is not residential property.", and

(c) after Table A insert—

"TABLE B: NON-RESIDENTIAL OR MIXED

Relevant consideration	*Percentage*
So much as does not exceed £150,000	0%
So much as exceeds £150,000 but does not exceed £250,000	2%
The remainder (if any)	5%"

(4) In subsection (1C)—

(a) omit the words from "the relevant land" to "and" (in the first place it occurs),
(b) in Step 1—

    (i) for "Table A" substitute "the appropriate table",
    (ii) for "that Table" substitute "the appropriate table",
    (iii) at the end insert—

""The "appropriate table" is—

    (a) Table A, if the relevant land consists entirely of residential property, and
    (b) Table B, if the relevant land consists of or includes land that is not residential property."

(5) Omit subsection (2).

(6) In subsection (3)—

    (a) in the words before paragraph (a), for "subsections (1B) and (2)" substitute "subsection (1B)", and
    (b) in paragraph (b) omit ", subject as follows".

(7) In subsection (4)—

    (a) in the words before paragraph (a), for the words from "subsections (1C)" to "linked transactions" substitute "subsection (1C)", and
    (b) in paragraph (a) for "those" substitute "the linked".

(8) Schedule 5 to FA 2003 (rules on calculating the amount of stamp duty land tax chargeable in respect of transactions for which the consideration consists of or includes rent) is amended in accordance with subsections (9) to (11).

(9) In paragraph 2(3) (calculation of tax chargeable in respect of rent) in Table B (bands and percentages for non-residential or mixed property) for the final entry substitute—

"Over £150,000 but not over £5 million	1%
Over £5 million	2%"

(10) In paragraph 9 (tax chargeable in respect of consideration other than rent: general), in sub-paragraph (1), omit "(but see paragraph 9A)".

(11) Omit paragraph 9A (calculation of tax chargeable in respect of consideration other than rent: 0% band) and the cross-heading preceding it.

(12) The amendments made by this section have effect in relation to any land transaction of which the effective date is, or is after, 17 March 2016.

(13) But those amendments do not have effect in relation to a transaction if the purchaser so elects and either—

    (a) the transaction is effected in pursuance of a contract entered into and substantially performed before 17 March 2016, or
    (b) the transaction is effected in pursuance of a contract entered into before that date and is not excluded by subsection (15).

(14) An election under subsection (13)—

    (a) must be included in the land transaction return made in respect of the transaction or in an amendment of that return, and
    (b) must comply with any requirements specified by the Commissioners for Her Majesty's Revenue and Customs as to its form or the manner of its inclusion.

(15) A transaction effected in pursuance of a contract entered into before 17 March 2016 is excluded by this subsection if—

    (a) there is any variation of the contract, or assignment of rights under the contract, on or after 17 March 2016,
    (b) the transaction is effected in consequence of the exercise on or after that date of any option, right of pre-emption or similar right, or
    (c) on or after that date there is an assignment, subsale or other transaction relating to the whole or part of the subject-matter of the contract as a result of which a person other than the purchaser under the contract becomes entitled to call for a conveyance.

(16) In this section—

"land transaction return", in relation to a transaction, means the return under section 76 of FA 2003 in respect of that transaction;
"purchaser" has the same meaning as in Part 4 of that Act (see section 43(4) of that Act);
"substantially performed", in relation to a contract, has the same meaning as in that Part (see section 44(5) of that Act).

GENERAL NOTE

Section 127 changes the methodology of calculating Stamp Duty Land Tax ("SDLT") on non-residential property transactions and transactions involving a mixture of residential and non-residential properties. Previously, a "slab" system, whereby the entire consideration for the transaction was charged at the applicable rate depending on the value of the consideration, was in operation. Now, a 'slice' system operates, whereby each marginal rate applies to the portion of the consideration that falls within each band. This change aligns the calculation of SDLT for non-residential and mixed transactions with the way in which SDLT is calculated on residential property transactions. Additionally, the top rate of SDLT on non-residential and mixed transactions has increased from 4% to 5% and the bands have changed. It should be noted that previously, for any lease premium, if the annual rent attributable to non-residential property was more than £1,000, the zero rate band was disapplied. Under s 127, this rule is now abolished.

Section 127(3)(c) inserts updated new and replacement Table B: Non-residential or mixed rates into s 55(1B) FA 2003, removing the old s 55(2). A comparison between the old rates and the new rates is as follows:

Old

Relevant consideration	Percentage on whole consideration
Up to £150,000 – if the annual rent is under £1,000	0%
Up to £150,000 – if the annual rent is £1,000 or more	1%
Over £150,000 to £250,000	1%
Over £250,000 to £500,000	3%
Over £500,000	4%

New

Relevant consideration	Percentage on each tranche
Up to £150,000	0%
Over £150,000 to £250,000	2%
Over £250,000	5%

For example, if the purchase price of a non-residential property was £251,000. Under the old system, the entire consideration would be charged at 3%, resulting in a SDLT charge of £7,530. Under the new system, the SDLT is calculated as follows:

Relevant consideration	Percentage	SDLT charge
Up to £150,000	Zero	£0
Over £150,000 to £250,000	2%	£2,000
Over £250,000	5%	£50
Total		**£2,050**

HM Revenue & Customs have estimated that under the new system, over 90% of non-residential property transactions will pay the same or less in SDLT. In practice, transactions with a purchase price/lease premium or transfer value of more than £1.05 million will result in a higher SDLT charge compared to the old system.

Despite the fact that only 10% of purchasers will seem to have an increased SDLT charge as a result of these changes, HM Revenue & Customs have estimated that approximately £2.6 billion of additional revenue will be raised as a result of the measures up to 2021.

For new leases that require payment of a premium and more than nominal rent, SDLT is due on the premium using the rates aforementioned and the value of rent payable over the term of the lease at present day prices (net present value (NPV) using the rates below which have been inserted by s 127(9). A comparison between the old rates and the new rates is as follows:

Old

NPV of rent	SDLT rate on each tranche
Up to £150,000	Zero
Over £150,000	1%

New

NPV of rent	SDLT rate on each tranche
Up to £150,000	Zero
Over £150,000 to £5,000,000	1%
Over £5,000,000	2%

For example, if the NPV of the rent was £5,500,000, under the old rates, the SDLT due would be £53,500. Under the new system, the SDLT is calculated as follows:

NPV of rent	SDLT rate	SDLT charge
Up to £150,000	Zero	£0
Over £150,000 to £5,000,000	1%	£48,500
Over £5,000,000	2%	£10,000
Total		**£58,500**

If a person purchases six or more dwellings in a single transaction, the non-residential rates apply under the new rules as set out in this section.

Where multiple dwellings are acquired in a single or linked transactions, the purchaser can choose the residential rates of SDLT and make a claim for multiple dwellings relief ("MDR"). The effect of MDR is that the residential rates are applied to the average consideration for each property (the resulting SDLT amount is then multiplied by the number of properties purchased) rather than SDLT being calculated on the entire value.

Transitional rules

These rules apply to land transactions for which the effective date is on or after 17 March 2016 (s 127(12)).

However, s 127(13) provides that where a contract for the purchase of a non-residential property was exchanged before 17 March 2016, but the contract was completed on or after that date, purchasers may make an election to apply the old rates of SDLT rather than the new revised rates.

This election is not available in respect of a contract entered into before 17 March 2016 that is excluded by s 127(15). This includes circumstances where there is an assignment of rights or any variation in the contract on or after 17 March 2016 (s 127(15)(a)), where the transaction completes in consequence of the exercise on or after that date of any option, right of pre-emption or similar right (s 127(15)(b)), or where there is an assignment, sub-sale or other transaction relating to the whole or part of the contract subject matter to another person on or after that date (s 127(15)(c)).

If a purchaser wishes to make an election, it must be made in the land transaction return (s 127(14)(a)).

Further guidance on the operation of the new rules, including transitional issues for leases and linked transactions can be found at https://www.gov.uk/government/publications/stamp-duty-land-tax-reform-of-structure-rates-and-thresholds-for-non-residential-land-transactions.

128 SDLT: higher rates for additional dwellings etc

(1) FA 2003 is amended in accordance with subsections (2) to (4).

(2) In section 55 (amount of tax chargeable: general) after subsection (4) insert—

"(4A) Schedule 4ZA (higher rates for additional dwellings and dwellings purchased by companies) modifies this section as it applies for the purpose of determining the amount of tax chargeable in respect of certain transactions involving major interests in dwellings."

(3) After Schedule 4 insert—

"SCHEDULE 4ZA

STAMP DUTY LAND TAX: HIGHER RATES FOR ADDITIONAL DWELLINGS AND DWELLINGS PURCHASED BY COMPANIES

PART 1

HIGHER RATES

1 (1) In its application for the purpose of determining the amount of tax chargeable in respect of a chargeable transaction which is a higher rates transaction, section 55 (amount of tax chargeable: general) has effect with the modification in sub-paragraph (2).

(2) In subsection (1B) of section 55, for Table A substitute—

"Table A: Residential

Relevant consideration	Percentage
So much as does not exceed £125,000	3%
So much as exceeds £125,000 but does not exceed £250,000	5%
So much as exceeds £250,000 but does not exceed £925,000	8%
So much as exceeds £925,000 but does not exceed £1,500,000	13%
The remainder (if any)	15%"

PART 2

MEANING OF "HIGHER RATES TRANSACTION"

Meaning of "higher rates transaction" etc

2 (1) This paragraph explains how to determine whether a chargeable transaction is a "higher rates transaction" for the purposes of paragraph 1.

(2) In the case of a transaction where there is only one purchaser, determine whether the transaction falls within any of paragraphs 3 to 7; if it does fall within any of those paragraphs it is a "higher rates transaction" (otherwise it is not).

(3) In the case of a transaction where there are two or more purchasers—

(a) take one of the purchasers and determine, having regard to that purchaser only, whether the transaction falls within any of paragraphs 3 to 7, and
(b) do the same with each of the other purchasers.

If the transaction falls within any of those paragraphs when having regard to any one of the purchasers it is a "higher rates transaction" (otherwise it is not).

(4) For the purposes of this Schedule any term of years absolute or leasehold estate is not a "major interest" if its term does not exceed 7 years on the date of its grant.

Single dwelling transactions

3 (1) A chargeable transaction falls within this paragraph if—

(a) the purchaser is an individual,

(b) the main subject-matter of the transaction consists of a major interest in a single dwelling ("the purchased dwelling"), and

(c) Conditions A to D are met.

(2) Condition A is that the chargeable consideration for the transaction is £40,000 or more.

(3) Condition B is that on the effective date of the transaction the purchased dwelling—

(a) is not subject to a lease upon which the main subject-matter of the transaction is reversionary, or

(b) is subject to such a lease but the lease has an unexpired term of no more than 21 years.

(4) Condition C is that at the end of the day that is the effective date of the transaction—

(a) the purchaser has a major interest in a dwelling other than the purchased dwelling,

(b) that interest has a market value of £40,000 or more, and

(c) that interest is not reversionary on a lease which has an unexpired term of more than 21 years.

(5) Condition D is that the purchased dwelling is not a replacement for the purchaser's only or main residence.

(6) For the purposes of sub-paragraph (5) the purchased dwelling is a replacement for the purchaser's only or main residence if—

(a) on the effective date of the transaction ("the transaction concerned") the purchaser intends the purchased dwelling to be the purchaser's only or main residence,

(b) in another land transaction ("the previous transaction") whose effective date was during the period of three years ending with the effective date of the transaction concerned, the purchaser or the purchaser's spouse or civil partner at the time disposed of a major interest in another dwelling ("the sold dwelling"),

(c) at any time during that period of three years the sold dwelling was the purchaser's only or main residence, and

(d) at no time during the period beginning with the effective date of the previous transaction and ending with the effective date of the transaction concerned has the purchaser or the purchaser's spouse or civil partner acquired a major interest in any other dwelling with the intention of it being the purchaser's only or main residence.

(7) For the purposes of sub-paragraph (5) the purchased dwelling may become a replacement for the purchaser's only or main residence if—

(a) on the effective date of the transaction ("the transaction concerned") the purchaser intended the purchased dwelling to be the purchaser's only or main residence,

(b) in another land transaction whose effective date is during the period of three years beginning with the day after the effective date of the transaction concerned, the purchaser or the purchaser's spouse or civil partner disposes of a major interest in another dwelling ("the sold dwelling"), and

(c) at any time during the period of three years ending with the effective date of the transaction concerned the sold dwelling was the purchaser's only or main residence.

4 A chargeable transaction falls within this paragraph if—

(a) the purchaser is not an individual,

(b) the main subject-matter of the transaction consists of a major interest in a single dwelling, and

(c) Conditions A and B in paragraph 3 are met.

Multiple dwelling transactions

5 (1) A chargeable transaction falls within this paragraph if—

(a) the purchaser is an individual,

(b) the main subject-matter of the transaction consists of a major interest in two or more dwellings ("the purchased dwellings"), and

(c) at least two of the purchased dwellings meet conditions A, B and C.

(2) A purchased dwelling meets condition A if the amount of the chargeable consideration for the transaction which is attributable on a just and reasonable basis to the purchased dwelling is £40,000 or more.

(3) A purchased dwelling meets condition B if on the effective date of the transaction the purchased dwelling—

(a) is not subject to a lease upon which the main subject-matter of the transaction is reversionary, or

(b) is subject to such a lease but the lease has an unexpired term of no more than 21 years.

(4) A purchased dwelling meets condition C if it is not subsidiary to any of the other purchased dwellings.

(5) One of the purchased dwellings ("dwelling A") is subsidiary to another of the purchased dwellings ("dwelling B") if—

(a) dwelling A is situated within the grounds of, or within the same building as, dwelling B, and

(b) the amount of the chargeable consideration for the transaction which is attributable on a just and reasonable basis to dwelling B is equal to, or greater than, two thirds of the amount of the chargeable consideration for the transaction which is attributable on a just and reasonable basis to the following combined—

(i) dwelling A,

(ii) dwelling B, and

(iii) each of the other purchased dwellings (if any) which are situated within the grounds of, or within the same building as, dwelling B.

6 (1) A chargeable transaction falls within this paragraph if—

(a) the purchaser is an individual,

(b) the main subject-matter of the transaction consists of a major interest in two or more dwellings ("the purchased dwellings"),

(c) only one of the purchased dwellings meets conditions A, B and C,

(d) the purchased dwelling which meets those conditions is not a replacement for the purchaser's only or main residence, and

(e) at the end of the day that is the effective date of the transaction—

(i) the purchaser has a major interest in a dwelling other than one of the purchased dwellings,

(ii) that interest has a market value of £40,000 or more, and

(iii) that interest is not reversionary on a lease which has an unexpired term of more than 21 years.

(2) Sub-paragraphs (2) to (5) of paragraph 5 apply for the purposes of sub-paragraph (1)(c) of this paragraph as they apply for the purposes of sub-paragraph (1)(c) of that paragraph.

(3) Sub-paragraphs (6) and (7) of paragraph 3 apply for the purposes of sub-paragraph (1)(d) of this paragraph as they apply for the purposes of sub-paragraph (5) of that paragraph.

7 (1) A chargeable transaction falls within this paragraph if—

(a) the purchaser is not an individual,

(b) the main subject-matter of the transaction consists of a major interest in two or more dwellings ("the purchased dwellings"), and

(c) at least one of the purchased dwellings meets conditions A and B.

(2) Sub-paragraphs (2) and (3) of paragraph 5 apply for the purposes of sub-paragraph (1)(c) of this paragraph as they apply for the purposes of sub-paragraph (1)(c) of that paragraph.

PART 3

SUPPLEMENTARY PROVISIONS

Further provision in connection with paragraph 3(6) and (7)

8 (1) This paragraph applies where by reason of paragraph 3(7) a chargeable transaction ("the transaction concerned") ceases to be a higher rates transaction for the purposes of paragraph 1.

(2) The land transaction ("the subsequent transaction") by reference to which the condition in paragraph 3(7)(b) was met may not be taken into account for the purposes of paragraph 3(6)(b) in determining whether any other chargeable transaction is a higher rates transaction.

(3) A land transaction return in respect of the transaction concerned may be amended, to take account of its ceasing to be a higher rates transaction, at any time within whichever of the following periods expires later—

(a) the period of 3 months beginning within the effective date of the subsequent transaction, and

(b) the period of 12 months beginning with the filing date for the return.

(4) Where a land transaction return in respect of the transaction concerned is amended to take account of its ceasing to be a higher rates transaction (and not for any other reason), paragraph 6(2A) of Schedule 10 (notice of amendment of return to be accompanied by the contract for the transaction etc) does not apply in relation to the amendment.

Spouses and civil partners purchasing alone

9 (1) Sub-paragraph (2) applies in relation to a chargeable transaction if—

(a) the purchaser (or one of them) is married or in a civil partnership on the effective date,

(b) the purchaser and the purchaser's spouse or civil partner are living together on that date, and

(c) the purchaser's spouse or civil partner is not a purchaser in relation to the transaction.

(2) The transaction is to be treated as being a higher rates transaction for the purposes of paragraph 1 if it would have been a higher rates transaction had the purchaser's spouse or civil partner been a purchaser.

(3) Persons who are married to, or are civil partners of, each other are treated as living together for the purposes of this paragraph if they are so treated for the purposes of the Income Tax Acts (see section 1011 of the Income Tax Act 2007).

Settlements and bare trusts

10 (1) Sub-paragraph (3) applies in relation to a land transaction if—

(a) the main subject-matter of the transaction consists of a major interest in one or more dwellings,

(b) the purchaser (or one of them) is acting as trustee of a settlement, and

(c) under the terms of the settlement a beneficiary will be entitled to—

(i) occupy the dwelling or dwellings for life, or

(ii) income earned in respect of the dwelling or dwellings.

(2) Sub-paragraph (3) also applies in relation to a land transaction if—

(a) the main subject-matter of the transaction consists of a term of years absolute in a dwelling, and

(b) the purchaser (or one of them) is acting as a trustee of a bare trust.

(3) Where this sub-paragraph applies in relation to a land transaction the beneficiary of the settlement or bare trust (rather than the trustee) is to be treated for the purposes of this Schedule as the purchaser (or as one of them).

(4) Paragraphs 3(3) and 4 of Schedule 16 (trustees to be treated as the purchaser) have effect subject to sub-paragraph (3).

11 (1) Sub-paragraph (3) applies where—

(a) a person is a beneficiary under a settlement,

(b) a major interest in a dwelling forms part of the trust property, and

(c) under the terms of the settlement, the beneficiary is entitled to—

(i) occupy the dwelling for life, or

(ii) income earned in respect of the dwelling.

(2) Sub-paragraph (3) also applies where—

(a) a person is a beneficiary under a bare trust, and

(b) a term of years absolute in a dwelling forms part of the trust property.

(3) Where this sub-paragraph applies—

(a) the beneficiary is to be treated for the purposes of this Schedule as holding the interest in the dwelling, and

(b) if the trustee of the settlement or bare trust disposes of the interest, the beneficiary is to be treated for the purposes of this Schedule as having disposed of it.

12 (1) This paragraph applies where, by reason of paragraph 10 or 11 or paragraph 3(1) of Schedule 16, the child of a person ("P") would (but for this paragraph) be treated for the purposes of this Schedule as—

(a) being the purchaser in relation to a land transaction,

(b) holding an interest in a dwelling, or

(c) having disposed of an interest in a dwelling.

(2) Where this paragraph applies—

(a) P and any spouse or civil partner of P are to be treated for the purposes of this Schedule as being the purchaser, holding the interest or (as the case may be) having disposed of the interest, and

(b) the child is not to be so treated.

(3) But sub-paragraph (2)(a) does not apply in relation to a spouse or civil partner of P if the two of them are not living together.

(4) Sub-paragraph (3) of paragraph 9 applies for the purposes of this paragraph as it applies for the purposes of that paragraph.

(5) "Child" means a person under the age of 18.

13 (1) This paragraph applies in relation to a land transaction if—

(a) the main subject-matter of the transaction consists of a major interest in one or more dwellings,

(b) the purchaser (or one of them) is acting as trustee of a settlement,

(c) that purchaser is an individual, and

(d) under the terms of the settlement a beneficiary is not entitled to—

  (i) occupy the dwelling or dwellings for life, or

  (ii) income earned in respect of the dwelling or dwellings.

(2) In determining whether the transaction falls within paragraph 4 or paragraph 7—

(a) if the purchaser mentioned in sub-paragraph (1) is the only purchaser, ignore paragraph (a) of those paragraphs, and

(b) if that purchaser is not the only purchaser, ignore paragraph (a) of those paragraphs when having regard to that purchaser.

Partnerships

14 (1) Sub-paragraph (2) applies in relation to a chargeable transaction whose subject-matter consists of a major interest in one or more dwellings if—

(a) the purchaser (or one of them) is a partner in a partnership, but

(b) the purchaser does not enter into the transaction for the purposes of the partnership.

(2) For the purposes of determining whether the transaction falls within paragraph 3 or 6 any major interest in any other dwelling that is held by or on behalf of the partnership for the purposes of a trade carried on by the partnership is not to be treated as held by or on behalf of the purchaser.

(3) Paragraph 2(1)(a) of Schedule 15 (chargeable interests held by partnerships treated as held by the partners) has effect subject to sub-paragraph (2).

Alternative finance arrangements

15 (1) This paragraph applies in relation to a chargeable transaction which is the first transaction under an alternative finance arrangement entered into between a person and a financial institution.

(2) The person (rather than the institution) is to be treated for the purposes of this Schedule as the purchaser in relation to the transaction.

(3) In this paragraph—

"alternative finance arrangement" means an arrangement of a kind mentioned in section 71A(1) or 73(1);

"financial institution" has the meaning it has in those sections (see section 73BA);

"first transaction", in relation to an alternative finance arrangement, has the meaning given by section 71A(1)(a) or (as the case may be) section 73(1)(a)(i).

Major interests in dwellings inherited jointly

16 (1) This paragraph applies where by virtue of an inheritance—

(a) a person ("P") becomes jointly entitled with one or more other persons to a major interest in a dwelling, and

(b) P's beneficial share in the interest does not exceed 50% (see sub-paragraph (4)).

(2) P is not to be treated for the purposes of paragraph 3(4)(a) or 6(1)(e) as having the major interest at any time during the period of three years beginning with the date of the inheritance.

(3) But if at any time during that period of three years P becomes the only person beneficially entitled to the whole of the interest or P's beneficial share in the interest exceeds 50% P is, from that time, to be treated as having the major interest for the purposes of paragraph 3(4)(a) and 6(1)(e) (subject to any disposal by P).

(4) P's share in the interest exceeds 50% if—

(a) P is beneficially entitled as a tenant in common or coparcener to more than half the interest,

(b) P and P's spouse or civil partner taken together are beneficially entitled as tenants in common or coparceners to more than half the interest, or

(c) P and P's spouse or civil partner are beneficially entitled as joint tenants to the interest and there is no more than one other joint tenant who is so entitled.

(5) In this section "inheritance" means the acquisition of an interest in or towards satisfaction of an entitlement under or in relation to the will of a deceased person, or on the intestacy of a deceased person.

Dwellings outside England, Wales and Northern Ireland

17 (1) In the provisions of this Schedule specified in sub-paragraph (3), references to a "dwelling" include references to a dwelling situated in a country or territory outside England, Wales and Northern Ireland.

(2) In the application of those provisions in relation to a dwelling situated in a country or territory outside England, Wales and Northern Ireland—

(a) references to a "major interest" in the dwelling are to an equivalent interest in the dwelling under the law of that country or territory,

(b) references to persons being beneficially entitled as joint tenants, tenants in common or coparceners to an interest in the dwelling are to persons having an equivalent entitlement to the interest in the dwelling under the law of that country or territory,

(c) references to a "land transaction" in relation to the dwelling are to the acquisition of an interest in the dwelling under the law of that country or territory,

(d) references to the "effective date" of a land transaction in relation to the dwelling are to the date on which the interest in the dwelling is acquired under the law of that country or territory,

(e) references to "inheritance" are to the acquisition of an interest from a deceased person's estate in accordance with the laws of that country or territory concerning the inheritance of property.

(3) The provisions of this Schedule referred to in sub-paragraphs (1) and (2) are—

(a) paragraph 3(4), (6)(b), (c) and (d) and (7)(b) and (c),

(b) paragraph 6(1)(e),

(c) paragraph 11,

(d) paragraph 14(2), and

(e) paragraph 16.

(4) Where the child of a person ("P") has an interest in a dwelling which is situated in a country or territory outside England, Wales and Northern Ireland, P and any spouse or civil partner of P are to be treated for the purposes of this Schedule as having that interest.

(5) But sub-paragraph (4) does not apply in relation to a spouse or civil partner of P if the two of them are not living together.

(6) Sub-paragraph (3) of paragraph 9 applies for the purposes of sub-paragraph (5) of this paragraph as it applies for the purposes of that paragraph.

What counts as a dwelling

18 (1) This paragraph sets out rules for determining what counts as a dwelling for the purposes of this Schedule.

(2) A building or part of a building counts as a dwelling if—

(a) it is used or suitable for use as a single dwelling, or

(b) it is in the process of being constructed or adapted for such use.

(3) Land that is, or is to be, occupied or enjoyed with a dwelling as a garden or grounds (including any building or structure on that land) is taken to be part of that dwelling.

(4) Land that subsists, or is to subsist, for the benefit of a dwelling is taken to be part of that dwelling.

(5) The main subject-matter of a transaction is also taken to consist of or include an interest in a dwelling if—

(a) substantial performance of a contract constitutes the effective date of that transaction by virtue of a relevant deeming provision,

(b) the main subject-matter of the transaction consists of or includes an interest in a building, or a part of a building, that is to be constructed or adapted under the contract for use as a single dwelling, and

(c) construction or adaptation of the building, or part of a building, has not begun by the time the contract is substantially performed.

(6) In sub-paragraph (5)—

"contract" includes any agreement;

"relevant deeming provision" means any of sections 44 to 45A or paragraph 5(1) or (2) of Schedule 2A or paragraph 12A of Schedule 17A;

"substantially performed" has the same meaning as in section 44.

(7) A building or part of a building used for a purpose specified in section 116(2) or (3) is not used as a dwelling for the purposes of sub-paragraph (2) or (5).

(8) Where a building or part of a building is used for a purpose mentioned in sub-paragraph (7), no account is to be taken for the purposes of sub-paragraph (2) of its suitability for any other use.

Power to modify this Schedule

19 (1) The Treasury may by regulations amend or otherwise modify this Schedule for the purpose of preventing certain chargeable transactions from being higher rates transactions for the purposes of paragraph 1.

(2) The provision which may be included in regulations under this paragraph by reason of section 114(6)(c) includes incidental or consequential provision which may cause a chargeable transaction to be a higher rates transaction for the purposes of paragraph 1."

(4) In paragraph 5 of Schedule 6B (relief for transfers involving multiple dwellings) after sub-paragraph (6) insert—

"(6A) In the application of sub-paragraph (1), account is to be taken of paragraph 1 of Schedule 4ZA if the relevant transaction is a higher rates transaction for the purposes of that paragraph."

(5) The amendments made by this section have effect in relation to any land transaction of which the effective date is, or is after, 1 April 2016.

(6) But those amendments do not have effect in relation to a transaction—

(a) effected in pursuance of a contract entered into and substantially performed before 26 November 2015, or

(b) effected in pursuance of a contract entered into before that date and not excluded by subsection (7).

(7) A transaction effected in pursuance of a contract entered into before 26 November 2015 is excluded by this subsection if—

(a) there is any variation of the contract, or assignment of rights under the contract, on or after 26 November 2015,

(b) the transaction is effected in consequence of the exercise on or after that date of any option, right of pre-emption or similar right, or

(c) on or after that date there is an assignment, subsale or other transaction relating to the whole or part of the subject-matter of the contract as a result of which a person other than the purchaser under the contract becomes entitled to call for a conveyance.

(8) Subsection (9) applies in relation to a land transaction of which the effective date is or is before 26 November 2018.

(9) In its application for the purpose of determining whether a land transaction to which this subsection applies is a higher rates transaction, paragraph 3(6) of Schedule 4ZA to FA 2003 has effect with the following modifications—

(a) in paragraph (b) for "during the period of three years ending with" substitute "the same as or before",

(b) in paragraph (c) for "during that period of three years" substitute "before the effective date of the transaction concerned".

(10) Paragraph 15 of Schedule 4ZA to FA 2003 does not apply in relation to a land transaction of which the effective date is, or is before, the date on which this Act is passed if the effect of its application would be that the transaction is a higher rates transaction for the purposes of paragraph 1 of that Schedule.

GENERAL NOTE

As part of the UK Government's policy towards redressing the balance of power between buyers of homes who need to occupy them and private landlords, new higher rates for the acquisition of residential property have been introduced, and the detailed rules are explained in the following section. Broadly, the new rates apply to individuals who already own another residential property unless they are replacing their only or main residence. They will apply to most acquisitions by non-individuals, and despite expectations at the time of the original consultation, there is no exemption from the higher rates for bulk purchases.

It should be noted that the rules as drafted contain quirks and can give rise to results which are unlikely to be in line with the policy intention – there are pitfalls for the unwary and uncertainties in the meaning of the legislation in some areas.

It should also be noted that although similar changes have been introduced (through the "Additional Dwellings Supplement") for the purposes of Land and Building Transactions Tax (LBTT) in Scotland, those rules operate differently, and importantly include an exemption from the supplement for bulk purchases. [See guidance at https://www.revenue.scot/land-buildings-transaction-tax/guidance/lbtt-legislation-guidance/lbtt10001-lbtt-additional-dwelling]

Section 128 introduces FA 2003 Sch 4ZA which is a new set of higher rates of SDLT for additional dwellings. Broadly, for transactions with an effective date on or after 1 April 2016, the higher rates of SDLT will apply where, at the end of the day of the transaction, an individual owns two or more residential properties and they are not replacing their main residence.

It is important to note that a non-individual purchasing a dwelling or dwellings, even if the property will be that person's only property, may also be subject to the higher rates of SDLT. However, in circumstances where a person is subject to the 15% rate of SDLT (s 55A and Sch 4A) those rules apply in priority.

Section 128(2) inserts sub-s (4A) into s 55 FA 2003 (amount of tax chargeable: general) which modifies s 55 for the purposes of calculating the SDLT chargeable on transactions to which new Sch 4ZA applies (Higher rates for additional dwellings and dwellings purchased by companies).

Section 128(3) inserts Sch 4ZA after Sch 4 in FA 2003.

FA 2003 Sch 4ZA (Higher rates for additional dwellings and dwellings purchased by companies).

Part 1 of Sch 4ZA sets out the amount of tax chargeable if the higher rates of SDLT apply and Pt 2 defines a "higher rates transaction" (i.e. the scope of the new rules). Part 3 contains supplementary rules which include special rules for spouses/civil partners, trusts, partnerships, inherited property and the definition of a "dwelling" for the purposes of "higher rates transactions".

Part 1 – Higher Rates

Paragraph 1

If a land transaction is treated as a "higher rates transaction" in accordance with Sch 4ZA, for the purposes of calculating the amount of SDLT chargeable, s 55(1B) FA 2003 has effect as if Table A was substituted with new *"Table A: Residential"*. The relevant consideration banding in new Table A is the same but the rate of SDLT in each band is increased by 3%.

So, we now have two SDLT rates tables for acquisitions of residential property:
- "normal rates" of SDLT when the acquisition of residential property is *not* treated as a "higher rates transaction" under Sch 4ZA; and
- "Higher rates" of SDLT when the acquisition of residential property *is* treated as a "higher rates transaction" under Sch 4ZA.

The table below compares the "normal rates" against the "higher rates".

Table A: Residential		
Band	*Normal rates*	*Higher rates*
Up to £125,000	Zero	3%
Over £125,000 to £250,000	2%	5%

Over £250,000 to £925,000	5%	8%
Over £925,000 to £1,500,000	10%	13%
Over £1,500,000	12%	15%

Any interest in a dwelling worth less than £40,000 cannot be treated as a "higher rates transaction" (see later) – £40,000 being the normal notifiable transaction threshold for SDLT purposes. However, this does not mean that there is an effective 0% rate on the first £40,000 of chargeable consideration. If an interest in a dwelling is worth more than £40,000 (and it is treated as a "higher rates transaction") then the 3% higher rate applies to the whole of the first £125,000 relevant consideration banding, 5% on the next £125,000, 8% on the next £675,000 and so on.

It is important to understand that the 3% higher rates of SDLT have not been structured as a surcharge to the normal rates of SDLT on residential property. For example, the 15% rate of SDLT which is chargeable under Sch 4A FA 2003 – i.e. acquisitions of higher threshold interests by companies, corporate partnerships or collective investment schemes – is not increased to an 18% rate of SDLT if a land transaction is also treated as a "higher rates transaction" under Sch 4ZA FA 2003.

Mixed transactions

If the purchased property is a mixed transaction – i.e. residential and non-residential – then the acquisition cannot be treated as a higher rates transaction under Sch 4ZA and the non-residential/mixed rates of SDLT would apply. Schedule 4ZA only amends s 55(1B) to insert a new rates table with the 3% higher rates of SDLT for higher rates transactions. There are no other amendments to s 55. Reading s 55(1B) – "*if the relevant land consists entirely of residential property*" – then the residential rates table applies. So, where a property does not consist "entirely of residential property" (including where six or more dwellings are acquired under a single transaction – see further below) then the non-residential/mixed rates of SDLT in Table B apply. There is nothing in Sch 4ZA that would suggest this approach is any way different when the 3% higher rates would otherwise be in question. This is confirmed in para 2.11 of HMRC's Guidance Note [see https://www.gov.uk/government/publications/stamp-duty-land-tax-higher-rates-for-purchases-of-additional-residential-properties].

Part 2 – Meaning of "higher rates transaction"

Paragraph 2

Whether a transaction is treated as a "higher rates transaction" may depend on whether there is only one purchaser or whether there are two or more purchasers (i.e. joint purchasers). It also may depend on whether the purchaser is an individual, a company, a trust or a partnership and whether the purchaser is acquiring only one dwelling or multiple dwellings.

Unless otherwise stated, the following commentary and examples assume that a transaction involves only one purchaser. Specific commentary and examples have been included later to illustrate the difference in the application of the rules for joint purchasers.

Definition of a "major interest"

Paragraph 2(4) defines a "major interest" for the purposes of Sch 4ZA. The definition is important because the additional rates apply only if the main subject matter of the transaction consists of a "major interest "in a dwelling. The core definition is included in s 117 FA 2003. However, for the purposes of Sch 4ZA, a "major interest" does not include any term of years absolute or leasehold estate if its term does not exceed seven years on the date of its grant. So, a leasehold interest is only treated as a "major interest" if it was *originally granted* for a period of more than seven years. For example, a leasehold interest originally granted for 100 years but with only four years left to expiry will be treated as a major interest in land for the purposes of the higher rate rules. However, a leasehold interest originally granted for six years with four years left to run will not

A partnership share is not within the definition of a major interest for this purpose. Therefore, arguably the higher rates of SDLT should not be triggered where the partnership transfer provisions at paras 14 and 17 Sch 15 FA 2003 apply.

Single Dwelling Transactions

Paragraph 3

Under this paragraph, a transaction is treated as a "higher rates transaction" if the purchaser is an individual, the main subject matter of the transaction consists of a major interest in a single dwelling (referred to as "the purchased dwelling") and Conditions A–D are satisfied.

Condition A (Sch 4ZA para 3(2)) is that the chargeable consideration for the transaction must be £40,000 or more. So, if the total price paid for a single dwelling is less than £40,000 it cannot be treated as a "higher rates transaction". It is important to note that this is not an individual's share of the price paid – it is the total price paid for the transaction.

Condition B (Sch 4ZA para 3(3)) is that *on the effective date* of the transaction, the purchased dwelling:

– Is not subject to a reversionary lease; or
– Is subject to a lease with an unexpired term of no more than 21 years

Under the definition of a major interest at para 2(4), a leasehold interest is only treated as a major interest if it was *originally granted* for a period of more than seven years. Under Condition B, the acquisition of a major interest in a single dwelling will not be treated as a "higher rates transaction" if it is subject to a lease with more than 21 years *left to run*. For example, if an individual acquires the freehold interest in a single dwelling which is subject to a lease originally granted for 50 years but with only 15 years left to run, Condition B is satisfied. It is not the length of the lease as originally granted that matters for the purposes of Condition B, it is the length of the lease remaining at the date of acquisition of the freehold interest.

The testing for such a lease "on the effective date" has given rise to questions as to whether if on the same day as acquisition of the major interest in a dwelling either an existing lease is surrendered before or a new lease is granted after acquisition of the major interest, then Condition B may not be met, and the new rates would not apply. It seems doubtful that this would be the intention of the law here.

Condition C (Sch 4ZA para 3(4)) is that *at the end of the effective date* of the transaction:

– the purchaser has (or is treated as having) a major interest in a dwelling other than the purchased dwelling,
– that interest has a market value of £40,000 or more, and
– that interest is not subject to a lease with an unexpired term of more than 21 years.

As with Condition A, if the interest in the other dwelling(s) is worth less than £40,000 the acquisition of the purchased dwelling will not be treated as a "higher rates transaction". The valuation is the market value of that individual's interest in the other dwelling (not the total market value of the other dwelling). So, for example, if an individual has a 25% share in another dwelling valued at £100,000, the market value of that individual's share of the other dwelling is £25,000 and Condition C would not be satisfied.

Condition C is also tested on a dwelling-by-dwelling basis (see para 3.11 HMRC Guidance Note, dated 16 March 2016). So, for example, if an individual has an interest in two other dwellings each with a market value of £30,000, Condition C is determined based on the separate market values of that individual's interests in the other dwellings, not their aggregate market value. In this example, Condition C would, again, not be satisfied.

If the other dwelling(s) is subject to a lease with an unexpired term of more than 21 years, then the purchased dwelling will not be a "higher rates transaction". As with Condition B, this is not the length of the lease as originally granted, it is the length of the lease left to run. See example under Condition B.

It should be noted that partners in partnership will need to take into account dwellings owned by or on behalf of the partnership which are deemed to be held by the partners under para 2 Sch 15. This is subject to specific exception for property held for the purposes of the partnership trade (para 14).

Condition D (Sch 4ZA para 3(5)) is that the purchased dwelling must not be a replacement for the purchaser's only or main residence.

The effect of Condition D is that if a person is replacing a main residence they will not normally be subject to the additional rate. Compare the situations where (a) a person who has a joint interest in a buy to let with a value of, for example, £50,000 and no main residence acquires a main residence and (b) a person who has acquired numerous buy to let properties prior to 25 November 2015 and a very valuable property used as a main residence which they replace. In situation (a), the individual would be subject to the higher rates of SDLT, however there would not be a higher rates charge under scenario (b).

This is a two-step test:

- The disposal test – the purchaser must be disposing of (or have already disposed of) their previous main residence; and
- The acquisition test – the purchaser must be acquiring a dwelling which is intended to be occupied as the purchaser's only or main residence.

What is a main residence?

There is no statutory definition of a main residence. Where an individual resides at only one dwelling – that will be their main residence. However, where an individual resides at more than one dwelling, it is determined as a matter of fact on a case-by-case basis.

In particular, a main residence is not necessarily the residence where that individual spends the majority of their time. HMRC have indicated in their guidance notes a list of points to consider (although not exhaustive) which may be useful in establishing which residence is an individual's main residence (see para 3.34 HMRC Guidance Notes dated 16 March 2016). These include where the individual is registered to vote, the location of their workplace, the address used for correspondence, where the family spends its time etc. HMRC have also identified the case of *Frost v Feltham* [55TC10] which sets out a useful summary of criteria to be applied when considering how to decide which, of two residences, is an individual's main residence.

What is a replacement of a main residence?

There are two situations where the purchase of a dwelling can be a replacement of a main residence:

- where the sale of a previous main residence occurs before the acquisition of the new main residence (Sch 4ZA para 3(6)); and
- where the sale of a previous main residence occurs after the acquisition of the new main residence (Sch 4ZA para 3(7)).

Paragraph 3(6) – Sale of previous main residence before acquisition of new main residence

Under para 3(6), four Conditions need to be satisfied in order for the acquisition of the new main residence (i.e. the purchased dwelling) to be treated as a "replacement for the purchaser's only or main residence".

(1) On the effective date of the transaction, the purchaser intends the purchased dwelling to be the purchaser's only or main residence;

This is the acquisition test – based on assessment criteria (mentioned above) does the purchaser intend the purchased dwelling to be his only or main residence? It is worth noting that it must be the intention of that particular purchaser. The precise application of this Condition to joint purchasers and married couples/civil partners could yield some unusual results (see commentary for joint purchasers and married couples/civil partners, below).

(2) The purchaser (or the purchaser's spouse or civil partner at the time) disposed of a major interest in another dwelling ("the sold dwelling") in the period of three years before the effective date of the acquisition of the purchased dwelling;

There are three key points to consider when determining whether this Condition is satisfied.

Firstly, the disposal of a major interest in the sold dwelling includes not only an outright sale (e.g. the disposal of a freehold interest) but could also include the assignment of a leasehold interest originally granted for a term of more than seven years or the grant of a leasehold interest for more than seven years. It would seem that s 43(3)(a)(ii) makes it clear than the creation of a chargeable interest (which would include the grant of a lease) is a "disposal". Again, it is not clear whether such a wide meaning of disposal for this purpose is the policy intention. (The HMRC guidance at paragraph 3.18 does, however, state that a disposal does not need to be a "sale".)

Secondly, the effective date of disposal of a major interest in the sold dwelling must have occurred in the period of three years before the effective date of acquisition of the purchased dwelling. This test does not apply where the effective date of acquisition of the purchased dwelling occurs prior to the 26 November 2018 (see s 128(8)–(9) FA 2016). This transitional provision is intended not to disadvantage those whose last disposal of a major interest in a previous main residence was before the announcement of the proposed 3% higher rates of SDLT announced in the Autumn Statement on 25 November 2015. In effect, this transitional rule means that a purchaser may be able to rely on the disposal of a major interest in another dwelling, say, 10 years ago in order for the purchased dwelling to be treated as replacement (subject to meeting the third and fourth Conditions of this paragraph).

Thirdly, a purchaser may be able to rely on the disposal of a major interest in another dwelling by his spouse/civil partner in determining whether the acquisition of the purchased dwelling is a replacement of his only or main residence. However, the meaning of the phrase "purchaser's spouse or civil partner *at the time* disposed of a major interest in another dwelling" is not entirely clear. This is discussed in more detail under the commentary for spouses/civil partners (see below).

(3) At any time during that period of three years the sold dwelling was the purchaser's only or main residence; and

This is the disposal test – i.e. based on assessment criteria (mentioned above) did the purchaser use the purchased dwelling as his only or main residence at any time in that three-year period prior to the acquisition of the purchased dwelling. Note that this test applies to the purchaser, even if the second Condition (disposal in the preceding three years) is met by a disposal by that purchaser's spouse. The *purchaser* must have used the property so disposed of as their residence.

As with the second Condition, this test does not apply if the effective date of acquisition of the purchased dwelling occurs before 26 November 2018 (ref. transitional rule at s 128(8)–(9)). This means that, until 26 November 2018, the sold dwelling must simply have been the purchaser's main residence at some point in time (not just at some point in the last three years).

(4) At no time in the period between the effective date of disposal of the sold dwelling and the effective date of acquisition of the purchased dwelling has the purchaser (or the purchaser's spouse or civil partner) acquired a major interest in another dwelling with the intention of it being the purchaser's only or main residence (para 3(6)(d) Sch 4ZA)

This is an anti-avoidance measure designed to prevent purchasers claiming that a purchased dwelling is the replacement of the purchaser's only or main residence by virtue of the disposal of a previous main residence where, in the interim, the purchaser has already replaced that previous main residence with another dwelling (which is not being sold).

Example 1 For example, let's assume that a purchaser sold his previous main residence ("Property 1") on 1 January 2010 and purchased a new main residence ("Property 2") shortly thereafter on the 1 April 2010. The purchaser then acquires a new main residence ("Property 3") on 1 April 2016 and Property 2 is retained and used as a buy-to-let property. In the absence of para 3(6)(d), the purchaser of Property 3 could have claimed that he was replacing his only or main residence by virtue of the disposal of Property 1 on 1 January 2010 (taking advantage of the transitional provisions). However, para 3(6)(d) prevents a purchaser claiming the acquisition of a new main residence (i.e. Property 3) as a "replacement" for previous main residence (i.e. Property 1) if that purchaser has, in the interim, already replaced that previous main residence (i.e. Property 2).

Example 2 Consider the same fact pattern as Example 1. Property 1 is sold on 1 January 2010 and Property 2 is purchased on 1 April 2010. However, in this example, the purchaser occupies rented accommodation and Property 2 is used as a buy-to-let property and has never been the purchaser's only or main residence. Property 3 is then acquired on 1 April 2016 as the purchaser's only or main residence. In this example, Property 3 is not a higher rates transaction because the purchaser would be treated as a replacing his only or main residence and so would not satisfy Condition D. Under the transitional provisions the purchaser can treat his new main residence (i.e. Property 3) as the replacement for his previous main residence (i.e. Property 1) because, at no time in between had he acquired a major interest in another dwelling which he used as his only or main residence (i.e Property 2 was acquired as a buy-to-let property).

As referred to above, the policy objective behind the introduction of higher rates transactions was to level the playing field for first-time buyers by dis-incentivising purchasers from acquiring second homes or buy-to-let properties with higher rates of SDLT. However, it's clear from Example 2 that in certain circumstances purchasers may be able to acquire a buy-to-let property and a main residence without either being treated as a higher rates transaction under Sch 4ZA.

Paragraph 3(7) – Sale of previous main residence after acquisition of new main residence

Under para 3(7), three Conditions need to be satisfied in order for the acquisition of the new main residence (i.e. the purchased dwelling) to be treated as a "replacement for the purchaser's only or main residence".

(1) On the effective date of the transaction, the purchaser intended the purchased dwelling to be the purchaser's only or main residence;

(2) The purchaser (or the purchaser's spouse or civil partner at the time) disposed of a major interest in another dwelling ("the sold dwelling") in the period of three years from the day after the effective date of the acquisition of the purchased dwelling; and

(3) At any time in the period of three years before the effective date of acquisition of the purchased dwelling, the sold dwelling was the purchaser's only or main residence.

The Conditions are broadly the same as the Conditions under para 3(6) with two notable exceptions.

Firstly, the transitional rule for dwellings purchased before 26 November 2018 (s 128(8)–(9) FA 2016) cannot apply where the sold dwelling is disposed of after the acquisition of the purchased dwelling (para 3(7)(b) Sch 4ZA).

Secondly, there is no equivalent anti-avoidance measure to para 3(6)(d).

It should be noted that this three-year window has actually been extended from the 18-month window originally proposed in the consultation document. Ironically, the LBTT legislation has an 18-month window, although it was originally proposed to be a three-year window in the consultation document.

Example 3 A purchaser acquires a dwelling ("Property 1") on 1 January 2010 and uses it as his only or main residence until 1 January 2012 at which date he moves into rented accommodation but retains Property 1 as a buy-to-let property. On 1 April 2016, the purchaser acquires a second property ("Property 2") which he intends to use as his main residence. Property 1 is sold on 1 June 2016. The purchaser had originally intended to use funds from the disposal of Property 1 to finance the deposit on Property 2 but, due to delays in the conveyancing process, he had to obtain a short term loan facility to secure the deposit. Funds from the disposal of Property 1 are then used to repay his short term loan (plus interest).

If Property 1 had been sold prior to the acquisition of Property 2 then the acquisition of Property 2 would not have been treated as a higher rates transaction under para 3(6) Sch 4ZA because (on the application of the transitional rule) at some point prior to the acquisition of Property 2, the purchaser had used Property 1 as his only or main residence. However, because Property 1 is sold after the acquisition of Property 2, the test considers only whether Property 1 was the purchaser's only or main residence in the 3 years prior to the acquisition of Property 2 (the transitional rule doesn't apply). Therefore, on the facts, Property 2 would be treated as a higher rates transaction even though it is a replacement of a previous main residence.

Therefore, Example 3 illustrates how the application of the rules can in some cases arguably create capricious, arbitrary and unfair results.

Example 4 A person acquires a dwelling ("Property 1") on the 1 January 2014 and uses it as his only or main residence. The same person then acquires a second dwelling ("Property 2") on the 1 June 2015 and uses it as his main residence. Property 1 is then used as the purchaser's second home. On the 1 April 2016, the purchaser then acquires a third property ("Property 3") which he intends to use as his main residence. Property 2 is then intended to be used at the purchaser's second home and Property 1 is sold on the 1 June 2016. The purchase of Property 3 may not be treated as a higher rates transaction under Sch4ZA because the purchaser could claim that the acquisition of Property 3 was a replacement of his previous main residence (i.e. Property 1) even though, in the interim, he had purchased another dwelling (i.e. Property 2) as his only or main residence.

Compliance & Administration At this stage it is also worthwhile noting the supplementary provisions at para 8 Sch 4ZA. In practice, where the replacement main residence is acquired prior to the disposal of the previous main residence the purchased dwelling is a higher rates transaction because, at the effective date of acquisition of the purchased dwelling, Conditions A–D in para 3 Sch 4ZA would all be satisfied. So, the purchased dwelling would be subject to the higher rates of SDLT and this would need to be paid to HMRC alongside the land transaction return within 30 days of the acquisition of the purchased dwelling. However, if there is a disposal of a major interest in a previous main residence within the period of three years from the day after the effective date of acquisition of the purchased dwelling (such that it is no longer a higher rates transaction) the purchaser must amend the original land transaction return in order to claim a refund of the overpaid SDLT (Sch 4ZA para 8(3)). This amendment must be made before the later of:

- 12 months after the filing date for the land transaction return; or
- three months after the effective date of disposal of the previous main residence.

The repayment claim is made via a specific SDLT payment request form which is available on the GOV.UK website. The form should be completed online and a printed version submitted to HMRC Birmingham Stamp Office. In future, an online system will be implemented.

The requirement to submit a printed version of the form to HMRC would seem to be very unhelpful in practice, and at odds with the Government's commitments to the digital agenda.

In addition, para 8(2) is an anti-avoidance measure which prevents the disposal of a previous main residence which qualifies the acquisition of a new main residence from being treated as a higher rates transaction under para 3(7)(b) from also qualifying the acquisition of a new main residence from being treated as a higher rates transaction under para 3(6)(b).

Example 5 A purchaser acquires a main residence on 1 April 2014 ("Property 1"). The purchaser then acquires a new main residence on 1 April 2016 ("Property 2"). The purchaser sells Property 1 on 1 June 2017 and acquires a new property ("Property 3") as a main residence on 1 July 2017. Property 2 is retained as a buy-to-let property.

The acquisition of Property 2 is a higher rates transaction because, at the date of acquisition, all of Conditions A–D at para 3 Sch 4ZA would be satisfied. However, because Property 1 is sold within three years after the purchase of Property 2, the acquisition of Property 2 would no longer be treated as a higher rates transaction and the purchaser would be entitled to file an amended land transaction return and claim a refund of overpaid SDLT.

The acquisition of Property 3 would also be a higher rates transaction and because Property 2 was treated as the replacement main residence in respect of Property 1 (under para 3(7)(b)), it cannot also be the replacement main residence in respect of Property 3 (under para 3(6)(b)) by reason of para 8(2).

Paragraph 4

Paragraph 4 Sch 4ZA deals with acquisitions of single dwellings by purchasers who are not individuals, for example companies or partnerships with corporate members (special rules apply to trusts – see paras 10–13). In these circumstances, only Conditions A and B in para 3 need to be satisfied in order for the transaction to be treated as a higher rates transaction.

This means that the acquisition of any dwelling by a company (or a partnership with corporate members) worth £40,000 or more which is not subject to a leasehold interest with more than 21 years left to run is treated as a higher rates transaction and the 3% higher rates of SDLT will apply. It doesn't matter whether it is the first acquisition of a dwelling by a company and there is no "replacement main residence" Condition.

Removal of proposed exemption for large scale investors

The Spending Review and Autumn Statement 2015 indicated that the government would consult on an exemption from the higher rates of SDLT for corporates and funds making significant investments in residential property, given the role of this investment in supporting the government's housing agenda. It was suggested that an exemption might be based on a portfolio test applying to purchasers who had an existing portfolio of 15 or more residential properties. The alternative proposal in the consultation document was an exemption for bulk purchases (e.g. purchasing 15 or more dwellings in one transaction). Neither of these two potential exemptions have been included in the Finance Act 2016. On balance, the government considered that an exemption targeted at large scale investors would not be fair and that the higher rates of SDLT should apply consistently to all purchasers of additional residential property. In particular, the government were apparently not compelled by evidence (presented by several respondents to the consultation document) of the adverse and material effect this measure (without an exemption for large scale investors) would have on the UK housing supply.

It is interesting to note that, in contrast, an exemption has been allowed for LBTT purposes against the Additional Dwellings Supplement for the acquisition of six or more dwellings.

For the avoidance of doubt, there are no business activity reliefs from the 3% higher rates of SDLT such as there are for the 15% rate of SDLT under Sch 4A. So, for example, whereas a company acquiring a residential property for resale in the course of a property development trade would not be subject to the 15% rate of SDLT under Sch 4A, there is no such relief from the 3% higher rates of SDLT under Sch 4ZA.

Multiple Dwelling Transactions

Separate rules apply when an individual purchaser acquires a major interest in two or more dwellings in *the same transaction*. These rules are intended to apply such that the transaction is either wholly subject to the higher rates, or it is not.

In fact, there are two tests to consider when dealing with purchases of multiple dwellings by individuals.

Paragraph 5

The first test (Sch 4ZA para 5) applies if at least two of the purchased dwellings meet Conditions A, B and C:

Condition A

In respect of at least two of the purchased dwellings, the purchase price attributable to each dwelling on a just and reasonable apportionment is £40,000 or more.

Condition B

In respect of at least two of the purchased dwellings, each dwelling is not subject to a leasehold interest with a term of more than 21 years left to run.

Condition C

In respect of at least two of the purchased dwellings, that dwelling is not 'subsidiary' to any of the other purchased dwellings.

According to paragraph 5(5) a purchased dwelling ("dwelling A") is subsidiary to another of the purchased dwellings ("dwelling B") if:

- dwelling A is situated within the grounds of, or within the same building as, dwelling B and
- the amount of the chargeable consideration for the transaction which is attributable on a just and reasonable basis to dwelling B is equal to, or greater than, two thirds of the amount of the chargeable consideration for the transaction which is attributable on a just and reasonable basis to the following combined-
    - dwelling A,
    - dwelling B, and
    - each of the other purchased dwellings (if any) which are situated within the grounds of, or within the same building as, dwelling B.

Condition C and the 'subsidiary dwelling' concept was added to the draft legislation following parliamentary consultation which identified an unfair application of the rules on the purchase of a main dwelling with, say, a granny annex attached. As originally drafted, if both Conditions A and B were satisfied then both the main dwelling and the granny annex would have been subject to the 3% higher rates regardless of whether or not the main dwelling was a replacement of a main residence. Following the introduction of para 5(4) and 5(5) provided the main dwelling is at least two thirds of the value of the property as a whole then para 5 should not apply and the entire transaction should be subject to normal SDLT rates rather than the 3% higher rates of SDLT (assuming the main residence qualifies as a replacement).

Example 0 A person acquires a major interest in five dwellings for a total purchase price of £200,000. A just and reasonable apportionment of the total purchase price valued two of the dwellings at £25,000 each and three of the dwellings at £50,000 each. Even though Condition A is not satisfied in respect of two of the dwellings because both Conditions A and B are satisfied in respect of the other three dwellings (i.e. at least two of them) the whole transaction is treated as a higher rates transaction. It would not be possible to charge SDLT at the normal residential rates on the two dwellings that do not satisfy Conditions A–B and the higher rates on the three dwellings that do. However, a claim for multiple dwellings relief (MDR) may still be possible to limit the rate of SDLT to 3% based on an average price of £40,000.

It is worthwhile mentioning at this stage that the purchase of six or more dwellings in the same transaction may still be treated as not being residential property under s 116(7) FA 2003. There is nothing in Sch 4ZA that overrides this position.

Example 7 A purchaser acquires a major interest in two dwellings under a single transaction – a main dwelling plus a "granny annex" – for a total purchase price of £1,000,000. A just and reasonable apportionment of the purchase price attributes £750,000 to the main dwelling and £250,000 to the granny annex. Condition C at para 5(4) is not satisfied because the granny annex is subsidiary to the main dwelling because it is situated within the grounds of the main dwelling and the value attributable to the main dwelling is at least 2/3rds of the chargeable consideration of the property as a whole. As such, para 5 does not apply and relief from the higher rates is in principle available under para 3(6) or 3(7) if the main residence being acquired is a replacement of another main residence.

It should be noted that under para 5 it is not possible to obtain partial relief from the higher rates (for example if under a single transaction there are two or more dwellings being acquired which meet conditions A to C and one of them is a replacement of a main residence). In principle if the replacement residence is or can be acquired under a separate transaction then relief may be available. This is another example of the unwarranted complexity and difficulties with the new legislation.

Paragraph 6

The second test (Sch 4ZA para 6) applies if two or more dwellings are acquired in a single transaction and Conditions A B and C are only satisfied in respect of one of them.

In these circumstances it is then necessary to determine whether:

(1) the purchased dwelling in respect of which Conditions A to C are satisfied is not a replacement for the purchaser's only or main residence (para 6(d) Sch 4ZA)

(2) at the end of the effective date of the transaction, the purchaser has a major interest in another dwelling (other than the purchased dwellings) which has a market value of £40,000 or more and that interest is not subject to a leasehold interest with an unexpired term of 21 years or more (para 6(e) Sch 4ZA).

Paragraph 3(6) and (7) apply for the purposes of determining whether the purchased dwelling which satisfied Conditions A to C is a replacement for the purchaser's only or main residence (Sch 4ZA para 6(2)). See commentary on para 3(6) and (7) above.

Paragraph 7

Paragraph 7 Sch 4ZA deals with acquisitions of multiple single dwellings by persons other than individuals, e.g. companies or partnerships with corporate members (special rules apply to trusts – see later). In these circumstances, only Conditions A and B in para 5 need to be satisfied in respect of one of the purchased dwellings in order for the transaction to be treated as a higher rates transaction.

This means that if at least one of the dwellings has a purchase price of £40,000 or more on a just and reasonable apportionment of the total purchase price and is not subject to leasehold interests with more than 21 years left to run, the purchased dwellings are treated as a higher rates transaction.

Joint Purchasers

As explained earlier, there are special rules for joint purchasers. Paragraph 2(3) Sch 4ZA explains that, in determining whether or not a land transaction is a higher rates transaction, each joint purchaser needs to be tested separately. If any of the joint purchasers satisfy the Conditions in any of paras 3–7 (as described in detail, above) then the entire transaction is treated as a higher rates transaction (not just that joint purchaser's share of the transaction). This applies whether the purchase is as joint tenants or as tenants in common and it does not matter how small the interest of a particular purchaser is.

Example 8 A young couple (Mr A and Miss B) have been living in rented accommodation for the last few years. They are now looking to jointly purchase their first main residence together ("Property 1") in order to raise a family. However, Miss B already owns a 50% interest in a single dwelling ("Property 2") with another family member which had been used as her main residence prior to moving into rented accommodation with her partner. Property 2 has a total value of £250,000.

Paragraph 2(3) explains that we need to test each joint purchaser separately to determine whether the acquisition of Property 1 would be treated as a higher rates transaction under Sch 4ZA. This is the acquisition of a single dwelling interest by individuals. Therefore, para 3 is the applicable testing provision. Testing Mr A – Condition C at para 3(4) is not satisfied because Mr A does not have a major interest in a dwelling (other than the purchased dwelling) at the end of the effective date of the transaction. However, testing Miss B, all of Conditions A–D at para 3 are satisfied. Miss B satisfies Condition C because she owns a major interest in a dwelling other than the purchased dwelling (i.e. her 50% interest in Property 2) which has a market value of £40,000 or more and is not subject to a leasehold interest of more than 21 years. Miss B also satisfies Condition D because she is not replacing her main residence (i.e. she is not selling her 50% interest in Property 2). Therefore, the acquisition of Property 1 would be treated as a higher rates transaction and the higher rates of SDLT would apply to the whole of the purchase price for Property 1 and not just the share of the purchase price attributable to Miss B (i.e. the joint purchaser satisfying the Conditions for the higher rates to apply).

This example demonstrates the harshness of the application of the rules in some scenarios. In these circumstances, it would not be unreasonable for the couple to assume the normal residential rates of SDLT would apply given that Property 1 is, for all intents and purposes, the couple's first main residence.

If a land transaction is treated as a higher rates transaction under Sch 4ZA by virtue of only one joint purchaser satisfying the Conditions for the higher rates to apply, then it may be worthwhile exploring whether or not the property could be purchased exclusively by the joint purchaser who does not satisfy the higher rates Conditions such that the normal residential rates of SDLT would apply. This may not be a viable option in all circumstances given that one joint purchaser would be surrendering their legal and beneficial interest over the property. However, it is worth noting that whereas this planning may be available for unmarried couples it is not possible in the case of spouses/civil partners.

Spouses and civil partners purchasing alone

Paragraph 9

There are special rules for spouses and civil partners purchasing dwellings alone. Spouses and civil partners are effectively treated as one person (Sch 4ZA para 9(2)). In determining whether or not a transaction is a higher rates transaction both spouses/civil partners need to be tested (even if one of the them isn't acquiring an interest in the purchased dwelling). If either of them satisfy the Condition in any of paras 3–7 (as described in detail, above) then the transaction is treated as a higher rates transaction.

This treatment is slightly odd given that each partner is treated separately for other purposes, i.e. there is no relief from SDLT for transfers between spouses – a common misconception. This can be compared with the position under inheritance tax and capital gains tax, where spousal transfers can be made without a tax charge arising. The effect of the rules is to discriminate against couples who are married, as compared with unmarried co-habitees.

Paragraph 9(2) applies where:

– the purchaser is married or in a civil partnership on the effective date of the transaction;
– the couple are living together on that date; and
– the spouse or civil partner is not a purchaser in the transaction (Sch 4ZA para 9(1)) [otherwise the joint purchaser rules would apply anyway].

Spouses and civil partners must be "living together" in order for para 9(2) to apply. This follows the definition at s 1011 ITA 2007. Therefore, if spouses or civil partners are separated and living in circumstances that are likely to become permanent, or they are separated by a court order or by a deed of separation, they are treated as not living together for the purposes of Sch 4ZA.

The following examples should help to illustrate the apparent unfairness and some of the challenges in the application of the rules in Sch 4ZA to spouses/civil partners.

Example 9 Mr and Mrs A are a recently married couple. They have been living in rented accommodation. However, Mr A has saved enough to secure a deposit on their first main residence ("Property 1"). Mr A and Mrs A have agreed that Mr A will purchase Property 1 in his name only because, a few years ago, Mrs A had used part of her savings to purchase a 50% interest in a single dwelling ("Property 2") with her sister. Mrs A had used Property 2 as her main residence (together with her sister) before she moved into rented accommodation with her husband. Mrs A's sister still uses Property 2 as her main residence.

This is a single dwelling transaction so para 3 is the operative provision in determining whether the acquisition of Property 1 is a higher rates transaction under Sch 4ZA. However, although Mr A is the only purchaser in respect of Property 1, because he is married on the effective date of acquisition of Property 1, both Mr A and Mrs A need to be tested to determine whether or not the purchase of Property 1 is a higher rates transaction (Sch 4ZA para 9(2)).

Mr A does not satisfy Condition C (Sch 4ZA para 3(4)) because he doesn't own a major interest in a dwelling other than the purchased dwelling. However, Mrs A satisfies all of Conditions A–D at para 3. Mrs A satisfies Condition C because she owns a major interest in a dwelling other than the purchased dwelling (i.e. her 50% interest in Property 2) which has a market value of £40,000 or more and is not subject to a leasehold interest of more than 21 years. Mrs A also satisfies Condition D because she is not replacing her main residence (i.e. she is not selling her 50% interest in Property 2). Therefore, the acquisition of Property 1 would be treated as a higher rates transaction and the 3% higher rates of SDLT would apply to the whole of the purchase price for Property 1. This is the case even though Mrs A and not Mr A (i.e. the actual purchaser) is the one satisfying the Conditions for the higher rates to apply.

Example 9 should be compared with Example 8 as an illustration of the difference in approach to joint purchasers and spouses/civil partners in the context of higher rates transactions. Whereas joint purchasers (e.g. unmarried couples) may be able to consider acquiring a dwelling in the name of one person only (so as not to trigger the higher rates of SDLT) – this, rather simple, tax planning is not available to married couples because of the special rule at para 9(2) Sch 4ZA.

Example 10 Mr and Mrs A were married on 1 June 2014. They live together in rented accommodation. The couple want to purchase their first main residence together ("Property 1"). Mr A purchases Property 1 in his name only. Mr A owns a 50% interest in a small buy-to-let property ("Property 2") with his father and, before they were married, Mrs A had owned her own home ("Property 3") which she sold on 1st January 2014.

Paragraph 3 is the operative provision because this is the acquisition of a single dwelling. In this scenario, Mr A satisfies Conditions A–D and the acquisition of Property 1 should be treated as a higher rates transaction. Applying the criteria in para 3(6):

– Mr A intends to use Property 1 as his main residence. Therefore, para 3(6)(a) is satisfied. However, one should note that it must be the intention of that particular spouse for the purchased dwelling to be his main residence and not simply the main residence of his partner. There may be scenarios (for example, on separation) where a new dwelling may be purchased with the intention of it being the main residence for that spouse's partner and children but not necessarily as his own main residence. In which case para 3(6)(a) would not be satisfied.

– Mrs A has disposed of another dwelling (i.e. Property 3) within three years of the effective date of acquisition of Property 1. Strictly, the criterion at para 3(6)(b) is whether "the purchaser's spouse or civil partner *at the time* disposed of a major interest in another dwelling". The phrase *"at the time"* seems to suggest that Mr and Mrs A must have been married at the time of Mrs A's disposal of Property 3 in order for Property 1 to be treated as a replacement main residence. Therefore, on the basis that Mrs A disposed of Property 3 prior to being married to Mr A, para 3(6)(b) does not appear to be satisfied. (It would also appear that a disposal of a dwelling by a spouse from a previous marriage *could* be used as a possible Property 3.)

– Assuming that para 3(6)(b) is satisfied, in any case, Mr A did not use Property 3 as his only or main residence. It doesn't matter that Mrs A used Property 3 as her main residence. For the purposes of para 3(6)(c), it must have been that particular (ie the purchaser) spouse's only or main residence at any time during that period of three years. Therefore, para 3(6)(c) is not satisfied.

Settlements and bare trusts

The treatment of a purchase of one or more dwellings by trustees depends on whether the trust is a bare trust, a life interest trust or a discretionary trust.

Paragraph 10

Where the trustees of either a bare trust or a life interest trust acquire one or more dwellings, then the beneficiary (or beneficiaries) is/are treated as the purchasers in determining whether the higher rates apply. Therefore, whether or not a land transaction entered into by the trustees is a higher rates transaction depends on the circumstances of the beneficiary or beneficiaries.

Paragraph 10(2) and (3) is included to reverse the effect of the rule at Sch 16 para 3(3) which deems a bare trustee to be the purchaser where a lease is granted to them as bare trustee.

Paragraph 11

Where the trustees of either a bare trust or a life interest trust make a disposal of a major interest in a dwelling, then the beneficiary (or beneficiaries) are treated as the person(s) making the disposal. This provision allows a disposal by the trustees of the beneficiaries' main residence to qualify as a replaced main residence for the purposes of para 3(6) and (7).

Paragraph 12

If the beneficiary of a bare trust or a life interest trust is a child of a person ("P") then, by virtue of para 12(2), P is treated as having acquired or disposed of the interest in that dwelling and not the child.

Child is defined as a person under the age of 18. However, P is not defined. Clearly, P can include the biological parents of a child but it is not clear whether or not P can include foster/adoptive parents or legal guardians.

One should also note that, where a child is the beneficiary under a bare trust or life interest trust, the spouse or civil partner of P is also treated as having acquired or disposed of the interest in the dwelling and not the child. Paragraph 12(3) explains that dwellings held for a child on bare trust or under a life interest trust are not attributable to P's spouse or civil partner if they are not living together (e.g. if they are separated). However, this doesn't exempt future spouses/civil partners from being treated as owning dwellings held in bare trust/life interest trusts for the benefit of their partner's child(ren) from a previous marriage/relationship.

Paragraph 13

Where the purchaser is the trustee of a discretionary trust, the trustee is treated as if they were a company (regardless of whether the trustee is an individual). In other words, the land transaction would only need to satisfy Conditions A and B in order for the higher rates of SDLT to apply (see Sch 4ZA paras 4 and 7).

Partnerships

Paragraph 14

Under para 2 Sch 15, a partner is deemed to hold the underlying property held by (or on behalf of) the partnership. However, for the purposes of Sch 4ZA, this principle does not always apply. If a purchaser (who is a partner in a partnership) acquires a major interest in one or more dwellings which are not partnership property, then, in applying the test for pre-existing additional dwellings he would need to consider any dwellings held as partnership property. However, any dwelling which is held by the partnership for the purposes of a trade (e.g. a housebuilding trade or a farmhouse) is not deemed to be owned by the purchaser for the purposes of this test. This principle does not apply if dwellings are owned by the partnership for investment purposes (e.g. property rental business).

If property is acquired by the partnership then, whether or not the partnership is subject to the higher rates of SDLT will depend on the circumstances of each of the partners. In essence, the partners are joint purchasers in relation to a land transaction so, under the normal rules for joint purchasers (see Sch 4ZA para 2(3)) if any of the partners satisfy Conditions A–D then the higher rates will apply to the entire purchase price (not just the pro-rated amount).

A partnership interest is not included within the definition of a major interest (see Sch 4ZA para 2(4)). So it would seem that the transfer of an interest in a property investment partnership (which may be subject to SDLT under paras 14 or 17 of Sch 15 FA 2003) should in principle not be subject to the higher rates of SDLT even if the underlying properties were dwellings.

Example 11 Persons A, B and C carry on a property investment business in partnership. The partnership owns a single freehold dwelling worth £300,000 and each partner has an equal share in the partnership. Person A wants to purchase his first main residence. This will be a higher rates transaction under Sch 4ZA. Although Person A is acquiring his first main residence, Person A satisfies all of Conditions A–D at para 3. Condition C is satisfied because his share in the dwelling owned in partnership is attributed to him, has a market value of £40,000 or more and is not subject to a leasehold interest of more than 21 years.

However, if Persons A, B and C were carrying on a property development trade, the partnership property would not be attributed to any of the partners and Person A would be able to acquire his main residence without the higher rates applying.

Alternative Finance Transactions

Paragraph 15

An amendment was made during the passage of the Bill through Parliament to reflect an oversight in the original draft legislation in the application of the higher rate rules to alternative financing arrangements.

Paragraph 15 has been inserted to ensure that where a financial institution acquires a dwelling under an alternative financing arrangement, the higher rate rules apply as if the person were the purchaser (and not the financial institution). If this amendment had not been made, then the financial institution would always be exposed to the higher rates of SDLT irrespective of whether the person had additional property or was replacing their main residence.

Major interests in dwellings inherited jointly

Paragraph 16

If a person inherited an entire dwelling, this will count as a major interest in another dwelling for Condition C (assuming the market value is £40,000 or more). However, if a person's beneficial interest in an inherited dwelling is 50% or less (i.e. they inherited the dwelling jointly), then they have a three-year "exemption" period (from the date of inheritance) whereby the interest in the inherited dwelling is not treated as a major interest in another dwelling for the purpose of Condition C (para 16(2)).

If at any time during this three-year "exemption" period P becomes entitled to more than 50% of the beneficial interest in the dwelling, from that point, P is to be treated as owning a major interest in another dwelling for the purposes of Condition C (para 16(3)). If P's spouse or civil partner become beneficially entitled to an interest in the dwelling such that the joint beneficial interest in the dwelling between the person and the person's spouse or civil partner exceeds 50%, then both are treated as having a major interest in another dwelling for the purposes of Condition C (para 16(4)).

Example 12 Mr A and Mrs A are a married couple. Mr A currently owns a buy to let property ("Property 1") which he intends to sell in order to fund the deposit on a new property ("Property 2") which will be used by both Mr and Mrs A as their main residence. Mr A will own Property 2 in his name only. Mrs A inherited a 50% interest in a dwelling ("Property 3") from her late mum in January 2016 which has never been their main residence.

Mr A does not satisfy Condition C because, at the end of the effective date of acquisition of Property 2, he does not own an interest in another dwelling. However, under para 9(2), we also need assess whether the transaction would be a higher rates transaction if Mrs A were the purchaser of Property 2. Mrs A does also not satisfy Condition C because her 50% interest in Property 3 does not count as a major interest in anther dwelling for the purposes of Condition C by virtue of para 16(2). However, if Mrs A had inherited greater than 50% of Property 3 or she had inherited Property 3 more than three years before the effective date of acquisition of Property 2 then the purchase of Property 2 would have been a higher rates transaction.

Dwellings outside England, Wales and Northern Ireland

Paragraph 17

There is no territorial restriction in the application of Sch 4ZA. So, references to "dwellings" throughout Sch 4ZA mean any dwelling anywhere in the world and not just dwellings in England, Wales and Northern Ireland. The meaning of the phrases "major interest", beneficial entitlement, "land transaction", effective date" and "inheritance" all take the equivalent meaning under the laws of the relevant territory. Any interest in a dwelling outside of England, Wales and Northern Ireland which is owned by a child is treated as owned by a person ("P") or P's spouse/civil partner. However, for the purposes of para 17, "child" has no definition so it is not clear whether this is a child of less than 18 years or not (although one could reasonably read the definition at para 12(5) – i.e. *"a child is a person under the age of 18"* – into the para 17). The same comments under para 12 apply in relation to the P (see above).

What counts as a dwelling?

Paragraph 18

The definition of a dwelling is clearly important as this will impact on whether or not the transaction is a higher rates transaction. The general definition is imported from s 116 FA 2003 and includes a building that is suitable for use as a single dwelling, or that is in the process of being constructed or adapted for such use (Sch 4ZA para 18(2)). This definition also includes land that is or will be occupied or enjoyed with a dwelling as a garden or grounds (including any building or structure on that land) – Sch 4ZA para 18(3) – and land that subsists or will subsist for the benefit of a dwelling (Sch 4ZA para 18(4)).

So, for example, a property which includes a main dwelling together with a garden/grounds plus a barn and/or stables would be treated, in its entirety, as a single dwelling. However, if the stables had a commercial use and the property was purchased as part of a single transaction then one should consider whether or not the property consists entirely of residential property. If not, then the mixed rates of SDLT should apply regardless of whether the main dwelling would have been treated as a higher rates transaction under Sch 4ZA. As a variation of this example, if the garden/grounds included out-houses (e.g. gardener's cottage) rather than barns/stables then the transaction is a multiple dwelling transaction and para 5 Sch 4ZA would need to be considered including whether the gardener's cottage was "subsidiary" to the main residence. .

Off plan purchases are also treated as a dwelling by virtue of para 18(5) and 18(6) Sch 4ZA (ie under a contract for purchase of a dwelling which is to be constructed or adapted as a dwelling but where construction/adaptation had not commenced on substantial performance of the contract). The Conditions follow the current rules that are used for multiple dwellings relief under para 7 Sch 6B FA 2003.

It should be highlighted that, for the purposes of Sch 4ZA, a building, wholly or partly, used for a purpose specified in s 116(2) and (3) FA 2003 is *not* used as a dwelling (Sch 4ZA para 18(7)) and therefore should continue to be subject to the normal rates of SDLT. Paragraph 18(8) goes on to provide that where a building is used for one of the purposes set out in s 116(2) and (3) FA 2003, no account should be taken of its suitability for any other use.

Section 116(2) FA 2003 lists residential accommodation for school pupils, residential accommodation for students (other than halls or residence for those in higher education), residential accommodation for members of the armed forces or an institution that is the sole or main residence of at least 90% of its residents and does not fall within any of paras (a)–(f) or s 116(3) FA 2003.

Section 116(3) FA 2003 lists homes or institutions providing residential accommodation for children, halls of residence for higher education students, homes or institutions providing residential accommodation with personal care for the elderly, disabled, those with a dependence on alcohol or drugs or past or present mental disorders, a hospital or hospice, a prison or a hotel, inn or similar establishment. It should be noted that property used for such purposes is in any case treated for SDLT purposes as non-residential property.

Power to modify

Paragraph 19

The treasury has the power to amend or modify Sch 4ZA for the purpose of preventing certain chargeable transactions from being subject to the higher rates. The amendments or modifications must be made by regulations..

Miscellaneous/Other

Multiple Dwellings Relief ("MDR")

Section 128(4) of the Finance Act explains that account is to be taken of para 1 Sch 4ZA for MDR purposes if the transaction is a higher rates transaction. This means that if the transaction is a higher rates transaction then the higher rates will apply to the average purchase price per dwelling when calculating the SDLT liability in accordance with Sch 6B FA 2003.

The minimum SDLT liability on a claim for MDR is still 1% of the total chargeable consideration for the transaction (see para 5(2) Sch 6B FA 2003). In reality, if a transaction is a higher rates transaction then the minimum SDLT liability would actually be 3% of the total chargeable consideration for the transaction because the SDLT rate on the average purchase price per dwelling could not be less than 3%. However, the 1% minimum could still be relevant for the acquisition of multiple dwellings which do not satisfy the definition of a "dwelling" for the purposes of para 17 Sch 4ZA, as may be the case for student flats referred to below.

As mentioned earlier, the purchase of six or more dwellings in a single transaction is treated as the acquisition of non-residential property (s 116(7) FA 2003). Indeed, simply treating the purchase of multiple dwellings as non-residential may yield a lower SDLT liability than a claim for multiple dwellings relief (especially if the transaction is treated as a higher rates transaction).

Example 13 Consider the acquisition of 10 dwellings for a total purchase price of £3,500,000 in two different scenarios. In the first scenario, let's assume the dwellings are student accommodation. In the second scenario, let's assume the dwellings are privately rented properties.

Student accommodation Student accommodation is not treated as a "dwelling" for the purposes of Sch 4ZA (Sch 4ZA para 18(7)). Therefore, the normal residential rates of SDLT may apply.

Prima facie, the SDLT liability might be expected to be £333,750 (being 0% on the first £125,000, 2% on the next £125,000, 5% on the next £675,000 and 10% on the next £575,000 and 12% on the next £2,000,000). However, there are two mitigating factors – the purchaser could make a claim for MDR (under Sch6B FA 2003) or as a default the acquisition would be automatically treated as non-residential property (s 116(7) FA 2003).

If MDR were claimed then the SDLT liability would be £75,000. The average purchase price per dwelling is £350,000 on which the SDLT liability would be £7,500 (0% on the first £125,000, 2% on the next £125,000 and 5% on the next £100,000). Multiplied by the total number of dwellings, this results in total SDLT of £75,000.

If a claim for MDR is not made then the property is treated as the acquisition of non-residential property and the SDLT liability would be £164,500 (being 0% on the first £150,000, 2% on the next £100,000 and 5% on the next £3,250,000).

So, where the property is student accommodation, in this case it would be better to make a claim for MDR than applying the non-residential rates SDLT.

Private rented properties Properties that are acquired to be rented privately would be considered a dwelling for the purposes of para 18 Sch 4ZA. The implication of this is that the potential application of the higher rates needs to be considered.

Prima facie, the SDLT liability might be expected to be £438,750 (being 3% on the first £125,000, 5% on the next £125,000, 8% on the next £675,000, 13% on the next £575,000 and 15% on the next £2,000,000). However, as above, the purchaser could claim MDR or the default would be that the non-residential rates should apply.

If MDR were claimed then the SDLT liability would be £180,000. The average purchase price per dwelling is £350,000 and the higher rates would apply.

If the property is treated as the acquisition of non-residential property then the SDLT liability would be £164,500).

So, where the property is not student accommodation, in this case it would be better to adopt the default position of applying the non-residential rates of SDLT rather than making a claim for MDR.

Linked transactions Where two or more property transactions involve the same buyer and seller (or persons connected to the same buyer or seller), they will be "linked" from an SDLT perspective. Neither the guidance nor the legislation currently makes is clear how linked transactions should be dealt with in scenarios where one or more is chargeable at the normal rates of SDLT and one or more is at the higher rates.

For example, there may be scenarios where an individual buys a replacement main home in one transaction and a second dwelling in another from the same seller. The replacement home would be a normal rates transaction, whilst the second dwelling would be a higher rates transaction.

In this scenario, the consideration for both purchases should be aggregated and the relevant SDLT rates applied and apportioned based on the consideration attributable to each transaction in accordance with s 55(1C) FA 2003.

We also understand that MDR will continue to operate in the same way as for usual linked transactions. HMRC are expected to provide worked examples to illustrate the position.

Example 14 A is selling two properties. The first is being sold for £600,000 and the second is being sold for £400,000. B purchases the first property for £600,000 as a replacement for his main residence. C, who is B's sister and therefore connected, purchases the other property for £400,000 to be used as a second home.

Based on the normal residential rates of SDLT, the total SDLT liability on the entire transaction value of £1,000,000 should be £43,750. At the higher rates of SDLT, the total liability would be £73,750.

Applying the linked transactions rules, B might be expected to be required to pay 6/10 of £43,750 (£26,250) and C would be expected to pay 4/10 of £73,750 (£29,500). This result can be contrasted with the potential liabilities that would have arisen if the transactions were not linked (£20,000 for B using normal residential rates and £22,000 for C using the higher SDLT rates).

Transitional rules

The higher rates will only apply to purchases of additional residential property where the effective date (completion or substantial performance if earlier) is on or after 1 April 2016 (s 128 (5)). However, if contracts were exchanged on or before 25 November 2015 (Autumn Statement Day) but not completed until on or after 1 April 2016, the higher rates may not apply (s 128 (6)). It should be noted that if there is, on or after 26 November 2015, an assignment of rights, any variation in the contract or a sub-sale then irrespective of the exchange date, if the contract completes on or after 1 April 2016, it is not grandfathered from the higher rates (s 128(7)).

129 SDLT higher rate: land purchased for commercial use

(1) Schedule 4A to FA 2003 (SDLT: higher rate for certain transactions) is amended in accordance with subsections (2) to (4).

(2) In paragraph 5—

  (a) in sub-paragraph (1)—

    (i) after paragraph (a) insert—

    "(aa) use as business premises for the purposes of a qualifying property rental business (other than one which gives rise to income consisting wholly or mainly of excluded rents);
    (ab) use for the purposes of a relievable trade;";

    (ii) for paragraph (b) substitute—

    "(b) development or redevelopment and—

      (i) resale in the course of a property development trade, or
      (ii) exploitation falling within paragraph (a) or use falling within paragraph (aa) or (ab);";

  (b) in sub-paragraph (2), for "the dwelling" substitute "a dwelling on the land";
  (c) in sub-paragraph (3), at the appropriate place insert—
  ""relievable trade" means a trade that is run on a commercial basis and with a view to profit."

(3) In paragraph 5G, in sub-paragraph (3)(c) for "the dwelling" substitute "any dwelling on the land".

(4) In paragraph 6D(3)(b), for "the dwelling" substitute "any dwelling on the land concerned".

(5) The amendments made by this section have effect in relation to any land transaction of which the effective date is on or after 1 April 2016.

GENERAL NOTE

Section 129 amends Schedule 4A FA 2003, extending the relief from the 15% higher rate of SDLT in circumstances where a non-natural entity acquires an interest in property for consideration in excess of £500,000 in the course of running a trade or property rental business. The relief also applies where the property will be used as business premises, or for conversion or for demolition for use for one or more relievable purposes.

The purpose of this legislation is to ensure that property which is acquired for genuine business reasons is able to benefit from a reduction in the amount of SDLT payable to the standard rate (or in practice now (rather confusingly) likely to be the higher rates under new Sch 4ZA).

Subsection (2)(a) extends the current definition of a relievable purpose so as to include:

- the use of a higher threshold interest as business premises for the purposes of a qualifying property rental business or a "relievable trade", and
- the development or redevelopment of the higher threshold interest for the purposes of a "relievable trade" or qualifying property rental business

Subsection (2)(c) explains that a "relievable trade" must be a trade that is run on a commercial basis with a view to making a profit.

From a practical perspective, this means that high value properties which are acquired with the aim of being redeveloped into (or demolished and replaced by), for example a restaurant, head office or a dental surgery, should now be able to benefit from the relief to the 15% blanket rate of SDLT.

Various consequential amendments are made by s 129(3)–(4) in relation to the withdrawal of the relief.

Commencement date

Section 129 has effect for any land transactions where the effective date is on or after 1 April 2016. There are no transitional rules in place.

130 SDLT higher rate: acquisition under regulated home reversion plan

(1) Schedule 4A to FA 2003 (SDLT: higher rate for certain transactions) is amended as follows.

(2) After paragraph 5C insert—

"Acquisition under a regulated home reversion plan

5CA (1) Paragraph 3 does not apply to a chargeable transaction if (and so far as) the purchaser—

(a) is an authorised plan provider, and

(b) acquires the subject-matter of the chargeable transaction as a plan provider.

(2) For the purposes of this paragraph the purchaser acquires the subject-matter of the chargeable transaction "as a plan provider" so far as the purchaser acquires it under a regulated home reversion plan which the purchaser enters into as plan provider.

(3) In this paragraph—

"authorised plan provider" means a person authorised under the Financial Services and Markets Act 2000 to carry on in the United Kingdom the regulated activity specified in article 63B(1) of the Regulated Activities Order (entering into regulated home reversion plan as plan provider);

"the Regulated Activities Order" means the Financial Services and Markets (Regulated Activities) Order 2001 (SI 2001/544);

"regulated home reversion plan" means an arrangement which is a regulated home reversion plan for the purposes of Chapter 15A of Part 2 of the Regulated Activities Order.

(4) In this section references to entering into a regulated home reversion plan "as plan provider" are to be interpreted as if the references were in the Regulated Activities Order."

(3) After paragraph 5I insert—

"**5IA** (1) This paragraph applies where relief under paragraph 5CA (acquisition under a regulated home reversion plan) has been allowed in respect of a higher threshold interest forming the whole or part of the subject-matter of a chargeable transaction.

(2) The relief is withdrawn if at any time in the period of three years beginning with the effective date of the chargeable transaction the purchaser holds the higher threshold interest otherwise than for the purposes of the regulated home reversion plan (as defined in paragraph 5CA).

(3) But sub-paragraph (2) does not apply if—

(a) after ceasing to hold the higher threshold interest for the purposes of the regulated home reversion plan, the purchaser sells the higher threshold interest without delay (except so far as delay is justified by commercial considerations or cannot be avoided), and

(b) at no time when the higher threshold interest is held by the purchaser as mentioned in sub-paragraph (2) is the dwelling (or any part of the dwelling) occupied by a non-qualifying individual.

(4) In this paragraph—

"the dwelling" means the dwelling to which the relief under paragraph 5CA relates; "non-qualifying individual" is to be interpreted in accordance with paragraph 5A."

(4) The amendments made by this section have effect in relation to any land transaction of which the effective date is on or after 1 April 2016.

GENERAL NOTE

Section 130 introduces a new relief from the 15% blanket rate of SDLT for scenarios where a purchaser acquires the whole or part of a dwelling exclusively for the purposes of entering into a regulated home reversion plan.

A home reversion plan is an equity release scheme whereby an individual sells either all of part of their property to an equity release scheme company for either an annuity or lump sum payment as well as a lifetime tenancy. This allows the individual to continue to live in their property until it is eventually sold on death (or until the individual enters into long term care). Under the previous rules, there was no exemption from the 15% rate of SDLT on the interest acquired by the equity release company.

Section 130(2) inserts a new para 5CA into Sch 4A FA 2003 which provides for the relief for acquisitions under a regulated home reversion plan.

For the relief to apply, the purchaser must be an authorised plan provider under the Financial Services and Markets Act 2000, meaning that it must be a person authorised to carry on in the UK the activity specified in Art 63B(1) of the Regulated Activities Order, i.e. acquiring a property interest under a regulated home reversion plan (para 5CA(1)–(3) Sch 4A FA 2003).

Claw back of relief

Subsection 3 inserts a new para 5IA in to Sch 4A FA 2003 which sets out the circumstances under which the relief could be clawed back.

The new para 5IA(2) sets out that the relief will be withdrawn if at any time during the three-year period beginning from the effective date of the chargeable transaction, the purchaser holds the higher threshold interest for a purpose other than the regulated home reversion plan. This would appear to cover scenarios where the original home owner dies prior to the three-year period elapsing.

There are however important exceptions which are set out at new para 5IA(3). Specifically, relief will continue to apply if, after ceasing to hold the interest in the property for the purposes of the regulated home reversion plan, the purchaser sells the interest without undue delay, except in so far as the delay can be justified by commercial considerations or can't be avoided. The property must also not have been occupied by a non-qualifying individual during the time that it was held by the purchaser.

A non-qualifying individual continues to be given the same definition as already prescribed in para 5A Sch 4A FA 2003, being a person who has an interest in the property, or a person connected to the person who has an interest in the property.

Commencement date

Section 130 has effect for any land transactions with an effective date on or after 1 April 2016.

131 SDLT higher rate: properties occupied by certain employees etc

(1) Schedule 4A to FA 2003 (SDLT: higher rate for certain transactions) is amended as follows.

(2) In paragraph 5D (dwellings for occupation by certain employees etc)—

    (a) in sub-paragraph (1), for "trade" substitute "business";

    (b) in sub-paragraph (2)(b) for "trade" substitute "business";

    (c) for sub-paragraph (4) substitute—

    "(4) Relievable business" means a trade or property rental business that is run on a commercial basis and with a view to profit."

(3) The heading before paragraph 5D becomes "*Dwellings for occupation by certain employees etc of a relievable business*".

(4) After paragraph 5E insert—

"Acquisition by management company of flat for occupation by caretaker

5EA (1) Paragraph 3 does not apply to a chargeable transaction so far as its subject-matter consists of a higher threshold interest in or over a flat which—

    (a) is one of at least three flats contained in the same premises, and

    (b) is acquired by a tenants' management company for the purpose of making the flat available for use as caretaker accommodation.

(2) For the purposes of this paragraph a tenants' management company makes a flat available for use "as caretaker accommodation" if it makes it available to an individual for use as living accommodation in connection with the individual's employment as caretaker of the premises.

(3) In relation to the acquisition of a flat, a company is a "tenants' management company" if—

    (a) the tenants of two or more other flats contained in the premises are members of the company, and

    (b) the company owns, or it is intended that the company will acquire, the freehold of the premises;

but a company which carries on a relievable business is not a tenants' management company.

(4) In this paragraph "premises" means premises constituting the whole or part of a building."

(5) After paragraph 5J insert—

"5JA (1) This paragraph applies where relief under paragraph 5EA (acquisition by management company of flat for occupation by caretaker) has been allowed in respect of a higher threshold interest forming the whole or part of the subject-matter of a chargeable transaction.

(2) The relief is withdrawn if at any time in the period of three years beginning with the effective date of the chargeable transaction the purchaser holds the higher threshold interest otherwise than for the purpose of making the flat available for use as caretaker accommodation.

(3) For the purposes of this paragraph a tenants' management company makes a flat available for use "as caretaker accommodation" if it makes it available to an individual for use as living accommodation in connection with the individual's employment as caretaker of the premises."

(6) In paragraph 5E (meaning of "qualifying partner", "qualifying employee" etc)—

    (a) in sub-paragraph (1) for "trade" substitute "business";

    (b) in sub-paragraph (2) for "qualifying trade" substitute "relievable business";

    (c) in sub-paragraph (4)—

        (i) in the words before paragraph (a), for "trade" substitute "relievable business";

        (ii) in paragraph (a)(i), for "trade" substitute "relievable business".

(7) In paragraph 5J (withdrawal of relief under paragraph 5D), in sub-paragraph (3)—

(a) in paragraph (a), for the words from "trade" to the end substitute "relievable business";

(b) in paragraph (c), for the words from "trade" to the end substitute "relievable business".

(8) In paragraph 6G (withdrawal of relief under paragraph 5D in cases involving alternative finance arrangements), in sub-paragraph (4)—

(a) in paragraph (a), for "qualifying trade" substitute "relievable business";

(b) in paragraph (c) for "trade" substitute "relievable business".

(9) In paragraph 9 (interpretation), at the appropriate place insert—

""relievable business" has the meaning given by paragraph 5D(4)."

(10) The amendments made by this section have effect in relation to any land transaction of which the effective date is on or after 1 April 2016.

GENERAL NOTE

Following similar reliefs introduced for the Annual Tax on Enveloped Dwellings, s 131 introduces new reliefs to the 15% blanket rate of SDLT. Specifically, the section introduces two new reliefs, covering scenarios where a property is purchased to provide living accommodation to an employee of a qualifying property rental business, and scenarios where a caretaker has been permitted to occupy a dwelling in a building owned by a tenants' management company.

Extension of relief to employees of a qualifying property rental business

Section 131(2) amends para 5D Sch 4A FA 2003 so as to extend the definition of a "relievable business" to include a property rental business as well as a trade that is run on a commercial basis and with a view of making a profit. Consequential changes are also made to sub-paras (1) and (2)(b) of para 5D to substitute references to "trades" to "businesses".

Section 131(3) amends the title of para 5D Sch 4A FA 2003 to "Dwellings for occupation by certain employees etc of a relievable business".

Relief for caretakers occupying a dwelling in a building owned by a tenant's management company

Section 131(4) inserts a new para 5EA to Sch 4A FA 2003 to provide for relief to the additional rate of SDLT in scenarios where a tenant management company acquires a property for occupation by a caretaker.

There are two Conditions that need to be satisfied for the relief to apply:

–   the property must be one of at least three flats contained in the same premises, and
–   the property must be acquired by a tenants' management company for the purposes of making the flat available for use as caretaker accommodation.

New para 5EA(2) is clear that to make the flat available for use as caretaker accommodation, the tenants' management company should make it available to an individual for use as living accommodation in connection with their employment as a caretaker of the premises.

New para 5EA(3) provides that a tenants' management company exists if:

–   the tenants of two or more other flats contained in the premises are members of the company and
–   the company owns, or it is intended that the company will acquire, the freehold of the premises

However, if a company carries on a relievable business, then it is not a tenants' management company.

Claw back of relief

Section 131(5) inserts a further new para 5JA which contains the claw back provisions for the relief. New para 5JA(1) and (2) provide that relief cannot be claimed under new para 5EA if at any time during the three years following the effective date of the chargeable transaction, the tenants' management company holds the property interest otherwise than for the purpose of making the flat available for use as caretaker accommodation.

Commencement date

Section 131 has effect for any land transactions with an effective date on or after 1 April 2016.

132 SDLT: minor amendments of section 55 of FA 2003

In section 55 of FA 2003 (general rules on calculating the amount of stamp duty land tax chargeable), in subsection (5)—

(a) for "74(2) and (3)" substitute "74(1B)", and
(b) for "rate" substitute "amount".

GENERAL NOTE

Following the changes introduced regarding the way that SDLT is now required to be calculated, both for non-residential property transactions and transactions involving a mixture of residential and non-residential properties, this clause provides for consequential amendments to FA 2003 s 55(5).

133 SDLT: property authorised investment funds and co-ownership authorised contractual schemes

Schedule 16 contains provision about—

(a) the stamp duty land tax treatment of co-ownership authorised contractual schemes, and
(b) relief from stamp duty land tax for certain acquisitions by such schemes and by property authorised investment funds.

GENERAL NOTE

Section 133 introduces Sch 16.

Schedule 16 inserts new s 102A and new Sch 7A into FA 2003, to make changes to the treatment of Co-ownership Authorised Contractual Schemes (COACSs) and introduce a seeding relief for Property Authorised Investment Funds (PAIFs) and COACSs.

Annual Tax on Enveloped Dwellings

134 ATED: regulated home reversion plans

(1) Part 3 of FA 2013 (annual tax on enveloped dwellings) is amended as follows.

(2) After section 144 insert—

"144A Regulated home reversion plans

(1) A day in a chargeable period is relievable in relation to a single dwelling interest held by a person ("P") who is an authorised plan provider if—

(a) P has, as plan provider, entered into a regulated home reversion plan relating to the single dwelling interest, and
(b) the occupation condition is met on that day.

(2) If no qualifying termination event has occurred, the "occupation condition" is that a person who was originally entitled to occupy the dwelling (or any part of it) under the regulated home reversion plan is still entitled to do so.

(3) If a qualifying termination event has occurred, the "occupation condition" is that—

(a) the single dwelling interest is being held with the intention that it will be sold without delay (except so far as delay is justified by commercial considerations or cannot be avoided), and
(b) no non-qualifying individual is permitted to occupy the dwelling (or any part of it).

(4) In this section—

"authorised plan provider" means a person authorised under the Financial Services and Markets Act 2000 to carry on in the United Kingdom the regulated activity specified in article 63B(1) of the Regulated Activities Order (entering into regulated home reversion plan as plan provider);

"qualifying termination event" is to be interpreted in accordance with article 63B of the Regulated Activities Order;

"the Regulated Activities Order" means the Financial Services and Markets (Regulated Activities) Order 2001 (SI 2001/544);

"regulated home reversion plan" means an arrangement which is a regulated home reversion plan for the purposes of Chapter 15A of Part 2 of the Regulated Activities Order (but see also subsection (6)).

(5) In this section references to entering into a regulated home reversion plan "as plan provider" are to be interpreted as if the references were in the Regulated Activities Order (but see also subsection (6)).

(6) For the purposes of this section—

(a) an arrangement which P entered into before 6 April 2007 is treated for the purposes of this section as a regulated home reversion plan entered into by P as plan provider if that arrangement would have been so treated for the purposes of article 63B(1) of the Regulated Activities Order had P entered into that arrangement on the day mentioned in subsection (1);

(b) an arrangement in relation to which P acquired rights or obligations before 6 April 2007 is treated for the purposes of this section as a regulated home reversion plan entered into by P as plan provider if that arrangement would have been so treated for the purposes of article 63B(1) of the Regulated Activities Order had P acquired those rights or obligations on the day mentioned in subsection (1).

(7) Section 136 (meaning of "non-qualifying individual") applies in relation to this section as in relation to sections 133 and 135."

(3) In section 116 (dwelling in grounds of another dwelling), in the list in subsection (6), at the appropriate place insert—

"section 144A (regulated home reversion plans);".

(4) In section 117 (dwellings in the same building), in the list in subsection (5), at the appropriate place insert—

"section 144A (regulated home reversion plans);".

(5) In section 132 (effect of reliefs under sections 133 to 150), in the list in subsection (3), at the appropriate place insert—

"section 144A (regulated home reversion plans);".

(6) In section 159A (relief declaration returns), in the table in subsection (9), at the appropriate place insert—

"144A (regulated home reversion plans) | 5A"

(7) The amendments made by this section have effect for chargeable periods beginning on or after 1 April 2016.

GENERAL NOTE

Since 1 April 2013 high value residential properties held by companies, partnerships with a corporate partner and collective investment schemes have been subject to an annual charge, the annual tax on enveloped dwellings (ATED). There are various exemptions and reliefs from ATED for example for property rental businesses and properties open to the public.

Section 134 introduces a new relief from the ATED charge for certain types of home equity release plans. Under some types of equity release plans the equity release company will purchase the homeowner's property in return for an annuity or lump sum and a lifetime tenancy. This brings the property within the scope of ATED and a charge is payable if the value of the property exceeds the applicable ATED threshold (£500,000 for 2016/17). The new relief applies for chargeable periods beginning on or after 1 April 2016.

Home reversion plans have been regulated activities for the purposes of the Financial Services and Markets Act 2000 (FSMA) since 6 April 2007. The new relief applies where the plan provider is authorised under FSMA for these purposes.

The relief applies to regulated home reversion plans as defined in the Financial Services and Markets (Regulated Activities) Order 2001 (SI 2001/544). Home reversion plans entered into before 6 April 2007 are treated as regulated under the

Regulated Activities Order if they would have been regulated had they been entered into at the time the ATED relief is claimed. The features of a regulated home reversion plan are:
- the provider purchases all or part of the homeowner's interest in the property;
- the seller (or persons connected with the seller) is entitled to occupy at least 40% of the property in question as a dwelling and intends to do so;
- there are specified events (the termination events) on the occurrence of which the entitlement to occupy ends.

The termination events are:
- the person entitled to occupy the property becoming a resident of a care home;
- the death of the person entitled to occupy the property;
- the expiry of a specified period of at least 20 years from entering into the arrangement.

Where no termination event has occurred, a person originally entitled to occupy the property under the plan must still be entitled to do so. If a qualifying termination event has occurred the company must intend to sell the property without delay, other than delay for commercial reasons and there must be no occupation of the property by a "non-qualifying individual", i.e. an individual with an interest in the property or persons connected with that individual (including connections through membership of partnerships and settlements).

The relief applies by relieving any day on which these conditions are met from the charge. As with other reliefs, this relief must be claimed by means of a relief declaration return.

135 ATED: properties occupied by certain employees etc

(1) Part 3 of FA 2013 (annual tax on enveloped dwellings) is amended as follows.

(2) Section 145 (occupation by certain employees or partners) is amended in accordance with subsections (3) to (5).

(3) In subsection (1)—
(a) in paragraph (b), after "qualifying trade" insert "or qualifying property rental business";
(b) in paragraph (d) for "trade" substitute "qualifying trade or qualifying property rental business".

(4) After subsection (4) insert—
"(5) For the meaning of "qualifying property rental business" see section 133(3)."

(5) The heading of that section becomes "**Occupation by employees or partners of a qualifying trade or property rental business**".

(6) In section 146 (meaning of "qualifying employee" and "qualifying partner" in section 145)—
(a) in subsection (1), after "trade" insert "or property rental business";
(b) in subsection (2)—
(i) in the words before paragraph (a), after "qualifying trade" insert "or qualifying property rental business", and
(ii) in paragraph (a)(i), after "trade" insert "or (as the case may be) property rental business".

(7) After section 147 insert—

"147A Caretaker flat owned by management company

(1) A day in a chargeable period is relievable in relation to a single-dwelling interest if the dwelling in question is a flat in relation to which the conditions in subsection (2) are met.

(2) The conditions are that on that day—
(a) a company ("the management company") holds the single-dwelling interest for the purpose of making the flat available as caretaker accommodation,
(b) the flat is contained in premises which also contain two or more other flats,
(c) the tenants of at least two of the other flats in the premises are members of the management company,
(d) the management company owns the freehold of the premises, and
(e) the management company is not carrying on a trade or property rental business.

(3) For the purposes of subsection (2), the management company makes a flat available "as caretaker accommodation" if it makes it available to an individual for use as living accommodation in connection with the individual's employment as caretaker of the premises.

(4) In this section "premises" means premises constituting the whole or part of a building."

(8) In section 116 (dwelling in grounds of another dwelling), in the list in subsection (6)—

(a) in the entry relating to section 145, for "certain employees or partners" substitute "employees or partners of a qualifying trade or property rental business";

(b) at the appropriate place insert—

"section 147A (caretaker flat owned by management company);".

(9) In section 117 (dwellings in the same building), in the list in subsection (5)—

(a) in the entry relating to section 145, for "certain employees or partners" substitute "employees or partners of a qualifying trade or property rental business";

(b) at the appropriate place insert—

"section 147A (caretaker flat owned by management company);".

(10) In section 132 (effect of reliefs under sections 133 to 150), in the list in subsection (3)—

(a) in the entry relating to section 145, for "certain employees or partners" substitute "employees or partners of a qualifying trade or property rental business";

(b) at the appropriate place insert—

"section 147A (caretaker flat owned by management company);".

(11) In section 159A (relief declaration returns), in the table in subsection (9), in the entry relating to section 145, for "(dwellings used for trade purposes: occupation by certain employees or partners)" substitute "or 147A (occupation by certain employees etc)".

(12) The amendments made by this section have effect for chargeable periods beginning on or after 1 April 2016.

GENERAL NOTE

Relief from the ATED charge can be claimed where the property concerned is occupied for the purposes of a qualifying trade by an employee employed for the purposes of that trade or a partner of a partnership carrying on the trade. Section 135 extends the relief to properties occupied by employees and partners of property rental businesses; and properties occupied by caretakers employed by tenants' management companies. The extended relief applies for chargeable periods beginning on or after 1 April 2016.

Property Rental Businesses

This relief applies where the owner of the property carries on a qualifying property rental business namely a property rental business that is run on a commercial basis with a view to profit: FA 2013 s 133(3).

The property must be made available to a "qualifying partner" or a "qualifying employee" as living accommodation for the purposes of the property rental business.

A qualifying partner is an individual who is a member of the partnership carrying on the property rental business. Partners who are entitled to 10% or more of:

– the income profits of the partnership;
– any company that holds the interest in the property in question;
– the partnership assets;

are not qualifying partners.

A qualifying employee is an individual who is employed in the property rental business. Employees who are entitled to 10% or more of:

– the income profits of the business;
– any company that holds the interest in the property in question;
– the interest in the property itself;

are not qualifying employees

Also excluded are employees whose duties include providing domestic services connected with the actual or intended occupation of the property (or any linked property) by a non-qualifying individual.

Linked properties are defined by reference to FA 2013 s 116(2) (dwellings in grounds of other dwellings) and Finance Act 2013 s 117(1) (dwellings in the same building).

Tenants' Management Companies

Section 135 introduces a new relief for flats occupied by caretakers employed by tenants' management companies. The caretaker must be employed by the company as caretaker of the premises in which the flat is contained. The premises must contain two or more other flats and the tenants of at least two of the other flats must be members of the management company. The management company must own the freehold of the premises and must not be carrying on a trade or a property rental business.

Any day on which these conditions are met will be relieved from the ATED charge. The relief must be claimed by means of a relief declaration return.

136 ATED: alternative property finance – land in Scotland

(1) Part 3 of FA 2013 (annual tax on enveloped dwellings) is amended as follows.

(2) Section 157 (land sold to financial institution and leased to person) is amended in accordance with subsections (3) to (6).

(3) In subsection (1)—

(a) in paragraph (a), omit "or section 72 of that Act (land in Scotland sold to financial institution and leased to person)";
(b) in paragraph (b), after "transaction" insert "is in England, Wales or Northern Ireland and".

(4) In subsection (7)—

(a) in the definition of "the first transaction" omit "or (as the case requires) 72";
(b) in the definition of "the second transaction" omit "or (as the case requires) 72".

(5) Omit subsection (10).

(6) The heading of that section becomes "**Land in England, Wales or Northern Ireland sold to financial institution and leased to person**".

(7) After section 157 insert—

"157A Land in Scotland sold to financial institution and leased to person

(1) This section applies where Conditions A and B are met.

(2) Condition A is that arrangements are entered into between a person ("the lessee") and a financial institution under which the institution—

(a) purchases a major interest in land ("the first transaction"),
(b) grants to the lessee out of that interest a lease (if the interest acquired is the interest of the owner) or a sub-lease (if the interest acquired is the tenant's right over or interest in a property subject to a lease) ("the second transaction"), and
(c) enters into an agreement under which the lessee has a right to require the institution to transfer the major interest purchased by the institution under the first transaction.

(3) Condition B is that the land in which the institution purchases a major interest under the first transaction is in Scotland and consists of or includes one or more dwellings or parts of a dwelling.

(4) If the lessee is a company, this Part has effect in relation to times when the arrangements are in operation (see subsection (5)) as if—

(a) the interest held by the financial institution as mentioned in subsection (5)(b) were held by the lessee (and not by the financial institution), and
(b) the lease or sub-lease granted under the second transaction had not been granted.

(5) The reference in subsection (4) to times when the arrangements are in operation is to times when—

(a) the lessee holds the interest granted to it under the second transaction, and
(b) the interest purchased under the first transaction is held by a financial institution.

(6) A company treated under subsection (4)(a) as holding an interest at a particular time is treated as holding it as a member of a partnership if at the time in question the company holds the interest granted to it under the second transaction as a member of the partnership (and this Part has effect accordingly in relation to the other members of the partnership).

(7) In relation to times when the arrangements operate for the benefit of a collective investment scheme (see subsection (8)), this Part has effect as if—

(a) the interest held by the financial institution as mentioned in subsection (8)(b) were held by the lessee for the purposes of a collective investment scheme (and were not held by the financial institution), and

(b) the lease or sub-lease granted under the second transaction had not been granted.

(8) The reference in subsection (7) to times when the arrangements operate for the benefit of a collective investment scheme is to times when—

(a) the lessee holds the interest granted to it under the second transaction for the purposes of a collective investment scheme, and

(b) the interest purchased under the first transaction is held by a financial institution.

(9) In this section "financial institution" has the same meaning as in section 71A of FA 2003 (see section 73BA of that Act).

(10) References in this section to a "major interest" in land are to—

(a) ownership of land, or

(b) the tenant's right over or interest in land subject to a lease.

(11) Where the lessee is an individual, references in subsections (7) and (8) to the lessee are to be read, in relation to times after the death of the lessee, as references to the lessee's personal representatives."

(8) The amendments made by this section have effect for chargeable periods beginning on or after 1 April 2016.

GENERAL NOTE

Section 136 inserts new s 157A into the ATED provisions of the Finance Act 2013 dealing with alternative property finance arrangements (Islamic finance) in relation to land in Scotland. This mirrors the existing provisions in the ATED legislation for alternative property finance in the rest of the UK and was required because of the Scotland Act 2012. Section 157A applies in relation to chargeable periods beginning on or after 1 April 2016.

In relation to property in Scotland the ATED legislation borrows its definition of alternative property finance from the SDLT legislation (Finance Act 2003 s 72). However, when the taxation of land transactions in Scotland was devolved to the Scottish parliament by the Scotland Act 2012 the SDLT legislation, including s 72, was disapplied in Scotland. Consequently in relation to property in Scotland the ATED legislation relied on a provision that no longer applied for its definition of alternative property finance. Section 157A remedies this.

The alternative property finance arrangements to which s 157A applies are arrangements between a person and a financial institution under which the financial institution purchases or leases a property and leases or sub leases it to the person, with an option for that person to purchase the institution's interest in the property. When the lessee is a company, a partnership with a corporate member or a collective investment scheme, the financial institution is disregarded and the company, partnership or collective investment scheme is regarded as the owner of the property for the purposes of ATED. In effect the alternative finance arrangements are ignored. This is the position in the rest of the UK and s 157A makes it clear it is also the position in Scotland.

PART 9

OTHER TAXES AND DUTIES

Stamp Duty and Stamp Duty Reserve Tax

137 Stamp duty: acquisition of target company's share capital

(1) Section 77 of FA 1986 (acquisition of target company's share capital) is amended as follows.

(2) In subsection (3), omit the "and" at the end of paragraph (g) and after paragraph (h) insert ", and

(i) at the time the instrument mentioned in subsection (1) is executed there are no disqualifying arrangements, within the meaning given by section 77A, in existence."

(3) In subsection (3A) for "(3)" substitute "(3)(b) to (h)".

(4) In subsection (4) after "this section" insert "and section 77A".

(5) After section 77 of FA 1986 insert—

"77A Disqualifying arrangements

(1) This section applies for the purposes of section 77(3)(i).

(2) Arrangements are "disqualifying arrangements" if it is reasonable to assume that the purpose, or one of the purposes, of the arrangements is to secure that—

(a) a particular person obtains control of the acquiring company, or

(b) particular persons together obtain control of that company.

(3) But neither of the following are disqualifying arrangements—

(a) the arrangements for the issue of shares in the acquiring company which is the consideration for the acquisition mentioned in section 77(3);

(b) any relevant merger arrangements.

(4) In subsection (3) "relevant merger arrangements" means arrangements for the issue of shares in the acquiring company to the shareholders of a company ("company B") other than the target company ("company A") in a case where—

(a) that issue of shares to the shareholders of company B would be the only consideration for the acquisition by the acquiring company of the whole of the issued share capital of company B,

(b) the conditions in section 77(3)(c) and (e) would be met in relation to that acquisition (if that acquisition were made in accordance with the arrangements), and

(c) the conditions in paragraphs (f) to (h) of section 77(3) would be met in relation to that acquisition if—

(i) that acquisition were made in accordance with the arrangements, and

(ii) the shares in the acquiring company issued as consideration for the acquisition of the share capital of company A were ignored for the purposes of those paragraphs;

and in section 77(3)(e) to (h) and (3A) as they apply by virtue of this subsection, references to the target company are to be read as references to company B.

(5) Where—

(a) arrangements within any paragraph of subsection (3) are part of a wider scheme or arrangement, and

(b) that scheme or arrangement includes other arrangements which—

(i) fall within subsection (2), and

(ii) do not fall within any paragraph of subsection (3),

those other arrangements are disqualifying arrangements despite anything in subsection (3).

(6) In this section—

"the acquiring company" has the meaning given by section 77(1);

"arrangements" includes any agreement, understanding or scheme (whether or not legally enforceable);

"control" is to be read in accordance with section 1124 of the Corporation Tax Act 2010;

"the target company" has the meaning given by section 77(1)."

(6) The amendments made by this section have effect in relation to any instrument executed on or after 29 June 2016 (and references to arrangements in any provision inserted by this section include arrangements entered into before that date).

GENERAL NOTE

Background

This section amends the existing relief from stamp duty (in s 77 FA 1986) which applies on a share for share exchange.

Section 77 FA 1986 provides relief on the transfer of shares in a UK company (the target company) to another company (the acquiring company) provided that certain conditions are satisfied. These conditions include:

— that the acquiring company must acquire the whole of the issued share capital of the target company;

- that the consideration for the acquisition must consist only of the issue of shares in the acquiring company to the shareholders of the target company; and
- that the shareholding of the target company before the transfer of the shares and the shareholding of the acquiring company after the transfer of the shares "mirror" each other.

These conditions mean that the relief is narrow – it is available for share for share exchanges whose effect is to insert a new holding company between a UK target company and its current shareholders.

Section 77 FA 1986 includes an anti-avoidance rule (at s 77(3)(c) FA 1986) whereby the acquisition must be effected for bona fide commercial reasons and not form part of a scheme or arrangement of which the main purpose or one of the main purposes is avoidance of liability to stamp duty, stamp duty reserve tax, income tax, corporation tax or capital gains tax.

Introduction

Section 137 FA 2016 was announced during the passage of the Finance Bill 2016 at Committee of the Whole House. The policy objective behind the measure is that stamp duty is paid on takeovers of UK companies (including the acquisition of private companies). HMRC state that they have identified transactions whereby share for share relief is claimed on takeovers.

Although not explicit, the transaction which HMRC has presumably identified is the insertion of a non-UK incorporated acquiring company above target company followed by the takeover of that non-UK acquiring company. Section 77 FA 1986 does not require the acquiring company to be a UK company.

Section 137 FA 2016 amends s 77 FA 1986 by inserting a new condition whereby the share for share relief is not available if, at the time of the acquisition by the acquiring company of target company, there are arrangements in place to secure that a particular person or particular persons together, obtain control of the acquiring company.

Details of the clause

FA 2016 s 137

Section 137(1) provides that s 77 FA 1986 is amended and s 137(2) inserts a new condition in section 77 FA 1986 providing that there must be no "disqualifying arrangements" at the time of the acquisition of the shares in the target company by the acquiring company.

Section 137(3) and (4) contain consequential amendments.

Section 137(5) inserts a new s 77A FA 1986 which defines "disqualifying arrangements". New s 77A FA 1986 provides (at sub-s (2)) that arrangements are "disqualifying arrangements" if it is reasonable to assume that the purpose, or one of the purposes, of the arrangements is to secure that a particular person obtains control of the acquiring company or particular persons together obtain control of that company. However s 77A(3) provides that certain arrangements do not constitute "disqualifying arrangements" namely arrangements for the issue of shares in the acquiring company to the shareholders of the target company (i.e. the acquisition itself which can lead to the acquiring company undergoing a 'change of control') and also "relevant merger arrangements".

"Relevant merger arrangements" are defined as arrangements for the issue of shares in the acquiring company (thus potentially leading to a change in control of that company) to shareholders of a third company, known as "company B", in a case where the acquiring company acquires company B, the transfer is affected for bona fide commercial purposes, the only consideration for the transfer is the issue of shares to the shareholders of company B and the shareholding in company B and the acquiring company would be 'mirrored' if the former target shareholders were ignored.

The fact that "relevant merger arrangements" are permitted means that a subsequent share for share exchange by the acquiring company to acquire another company does not preclude relief from being available in respect of the first share for share exchange of target company.

Subsection (5) of new s 77A FA 1986 states that where arrangements fall outside the definition of "disqualifying arrangements" for the reason that they either constitute the issue of the shares in the acquiring company to the shareholders of the target company or they constitute "relevant merger arrangements", and such arrangements are part of a wider scheme or arrangement which falls within the definition of "disqualifying arrangements", then those other arrangements shall constitute "disqualifying arrangements".

Subsection (6) of new s 77A FA 1986 sets out the interpretation of various clauses. In particular "arrangements" is given a wide meaning and "control" is defined by reference to s 1124 CTA 2010.

Section 137(6) FA 2016 is the commencement provision which provides that the amendments have effect in relation to any instrument executed on or after 29 June 2016 (when the amendments were announced) but that references to "arrangements" include arrangements entered into before that date.

138 Stamp duty: transfers to depositaries or providers of clearance services

(1) Part 3 of FA 1986 (stamp duty) is amended as follows.

(2) In section 67 (depositary receipts)—

(a) in subsection (2), for the words from "1.5% of" to the end substitute "1.5% of—
   (a) the amount or value of the consideration for the sale to which the instrument gives effect, or
   (b) where subsection (2A) applies—
      (i) the amount or value of the consideration for the sale to which the instrument gives effect, or
      (ii) if higher, the value of the securities at the date the instrument is executed.",

(b) after subsection (2) insert—

"(2A) This subsection applies where the instrument transferring the securities is executed pursuant to—
   (a) the exercise of an option to buy or to sell the securities, and
   (b) either—
      (i) a term of the option which provides for the securities to be transferred to the person falling within subsection (6), (7) or (8), or
      (ii) a direction, given by or on behalf of the person entitled or bound to acquire the securities pursuant to the exercise of the option, for the securities to be so transferred.", and

(c) in subsection (3), for "In any other case" substitute "If stamp duty is not chargeable on the instrument under Part 1 of Schedule 13 to the Finance Act 1999 (transfer on sale)".

(3) In section 69 (depositary receipts: supplementary), in subsection (4), for "section 67(3)" substitute "section 67(2)(b)(ii) and (3)".

(4) In section 70 (clearance services)—

(a) in subsection (2), for the words from "1.5% of" to the end substitute "1.5% of—
   (a) the amount or value of the consideration for the sale to which the instrument gives effect, or
   (b) where subsection (2A) applies—
      (i) the amount or value of the consideration for the sale to which the instrument gives effect, or
      (ii) if higher, the value of the securities at the date the instrument is executed.",

(b) after subsection (2) insert—

"(2A) This subsection applies where the instrument transferring the securities is executed pursuant to—
   (a) the exercise of an option to buy or to sell the securities, and
   (b) either—
      (i) a term of the option which provides for the securities to be transferred to the person falling within subsection (6), (7) or (8), or
      (ii) a direction, given by or on behalf of the person entitled or bound to acquire the securities pursuant to the exercise of the option, for the securities to be so transferred.", and

(c) in subsection (3), for "In any other case" substitute "If stamp duty is not chargeable on the instrument under Part 1 of Schedule 13 to the Finance Act 1999 (transfer on sale)".

(5) In section 72 (clearance services: supplementary), in subsection (2), for "section 70(3)" substitute "section 70(2)(b)(ii) and (3)".

(6) The amendments made by this section have effect in relation to an instrument which transfers securities pursuant to the exercise of an option where—

(a) the option was granted on or after 25 November 2015, and
(b) the option was exercised on or after 23 March 2016.

139 SDRT: transfers to depositaries or providers of clearance services
(1) Part 4 of FA 1986 (stamp duty reserve tax) is amended as follows.
(2) In section 93 (depositary receipts)—
  (a) in subsection (4)(b), for the words from "worth," to the end substitute "worth—
      (i) the amount or value of the consideration, or
      (ii) where subsection (4A) applies, the amount or value of the consideration or, if higher, the value of the securities;", and
  (b) after subsection (4) insert—
  "(4A) This subsection applies where the transfer of the securities is pursuant to—
    (a) the exercise of an option to buy or to sell the securities, and
    (b) either—
      (i) a term of the option which provides for the securities to be transferred to the person falling within subsection (2) or (3), or
      (ii) a direction, given by or on behalf of the person entitled or bound to acquire the securities pursuant to the exercise of the option, for the securities to be so transferred."
(3) In section 94 (depositary receipts: supplementary), in subsection (4), for "section 93(4)(c)" substitute "section 93(4)(b)(ii) and (c)".
(4) In section 96 (clearance services)—
  (a) in subsection (2)(b), for the words from "worth," to the end substitute "worth—
      (i) the amount or value of the consideration, or
      (ii) where subsection (2A) applies, the amount or value of the consideration or, if higher, the value of the securities;",
  (b) after subsection (2) insert—
  "(2A) This subsection applies where the transfer of the securities is pursuant to—
    (a) the exercise of an option to buy or to sell the securities, and
    (b) either—
      (i) a term of the option which provides for the securities to be transferred to A or (as the case may be) to the person whose business is or includes holding chargeable securities as nominee for A, or
      (ii) a direction, given by or on behalf of the person entitled or bound to acquire the securities pursuant to the exercise of the option, for the securities to be so transferred.", and
  (c) in subsection (10), for "subsection (2)(c)" substitute "subsection (2)(b)(ii) and (c)".
(5) The amendments made by this section have effect in relation to a transfer pursuant to the exercise of an option where—
  (a) the option was granted on or after 25 November 2015, and
  (b) the option was exercised on or after 23 March 2016.

GENERAL NOTE

Introduction
Sections 138 and 139 FA 2016 amend ss 67 (Depositary receipts), 70 (Clearance services), 93 (Depositary receipts) and 96 (Clearance services) FA 1986 to counter avoidance perceived by HMRC of stamp duty and/or SDRT. The "avoidance" in question is the transfer of shares into a clearance service or depositary receipt system pursuant to an option whereby the agreed price for the shares (the "strike price") is significantly lower than their market value and the seller receives a large part of its consideration in the form of a high premium for the option. Given that the 1.5% stamp duty/SDRT charge is under current legislation chargeable by reference to the amount or value of the consideration for the sale, the stamp duty/SDRT charge would, without the amendments introduced in ss 138 and 139 FA 2016, be charged by reference to the low strike price. The amendments in ss 138 and 139 rectify this by introducing new provisions pursuant to which the stamp duty/SDRT charge is by reference to the higher of the consideration or market value of the shares where the shares are transferred to a clearance service or to a depositary receipt issuer pursuant to the exercise of an option.

Detail

FA 2016 s 138

Sections 138(1)–(2) amend s 67 (Depositary receipts) FA 1986 to give effect to the above amendments. Section 138(3) contains a consequential amendment to s 69 FA 1986. Sections 138(4)–(5) amend s 70 (Clearance services) FA 1986 to give effect to the above amendments. Section 138(6) states that the amendments have effect from 23 March 2016 and apply to options which are entered into on or after 25 November 2015 and exercised on or after 23 March 2016.

FA 2016 s 139

Sections 139(1)–(2) amend s 93 (Depositary receipts) FA 1986 to give effect to the above amendments. Section 139(3) contains a consequential amendment to s 94 FA 1986. Section 139(4) amends s 96 (Clearance services) FA 1986 to give effect to the above amendments. Section 139(5) states that the amendments have effect from 23 March 2016 and apply to options which are entered into on or after 25 November 2015 and exercised on or after 23 March 2016.

Petroleum Revenue Tax

140 Petroleum revenue tax: rate

(1) In section 1(2) of OTA 1975 (rate of petroleum revenue tax) for "35" substitute "0".

(2) In paragraph 17 of Schedule 2 to that Act (cap on interest on repayments of tax), in sub-paragraph (5)(b) omit the words from "if that" to the end.

(3) In paragraph 2 of Schedule 19 to FA 1982 (duty to pay instalments based on amount of tax payable in previous chargeable period), after sub-paragraph (4) insert—

"(4A) In sub-paragraph (1) the reference to any chargeable period for an oil field ending on or after 30th June 1983 does not include a chargeable period ending on 31st December 2015."

(4) The amendment made by subsection (1) has effect with respect to chargeable periods ending after 31 December 2015.

GENERAL NOTE

This section provides for a reduction in the rate of petroleum revenue tax (PRT) to zero with effect from 1 January 2016. Although a reduction from the previous 50% to 35% was introduced in Finance Act 2016 this change was also effective from 1 January 2016, so the rate of 35% has never actually applied to any profits.

Where PRT is repaid as a result of loss carry backs the repayment attracts interest (at statutory rates), but this interest is capped relative to the quantum of loss and the rate of PRT applicable for the repayment period. Once the rate of PRT is reduced to zero no repayment can be due so no cap is relevant. Subsection (2) repeals the amendment made by Finance Act 2016 relevant to the 35% rate with the consequence that the cap relevant to a 50% PRT rate will apply from 1 January 2016, but will be of no practical consequence.

The PRT rules required that instalment payments of any chargeable period's liability must be paid from the second month onwards (subject to some reliefs). Subsection (3) introduces new sub-para (4A) to para 2 of Sch 19 FA 1982 which removes the requirement to make instalments for chargeable periods ending after 31 December 2015, when, as set out above, the rate will be nil. It is understood that HMRC will refund any instalment paid, and will not seek collection of further instalments prior to this change in law being enacted, but no interest will be due on any such instalment repaid.

Insurance Premium Tax

141 Insurance premium tax: standard rate

(1) In section 51(2)(b) of FA 1994 (standard rate of insurance premium tax), for "9.5 per cent" substitute "10 per cent".

(2) The amendment made by subsection (1) has effect in relation to a premium falling to be regarded for the purposes of Part 3 of FA 1994 as received under a taxable insurance contract by an insurer on or after 1 October 2016.

(3) The amendment made by subsection (1) does not have effect in relation to a premium which—

(a) is in respect of a contract made before 1 October 2016, and
(b) falls to be regarded for the purposes of Part 3 of FA 1994 as received under the contract by the insurer before 1 February 2017 by virtue of regulations under section 68 of that Act (special accounting schemes).

(4) Subsection (3) does not apply in relation to a premium which—

(a) is an additional premium under a contract,
(b) falls to be regarded for the purposes of Part 3 of FA 1994 as received under the contract by the insurer on or after 1 October 2016 by virtue of regulations under section 68 of that Act, and
(c) is in respect of a risk which was not covered by the contract before that date.

(5) In the application of sections 67A to 67C of FA 1994 (announced increase in rate) in relation to the increase made by this section—

(a) the announcement for the purposes of sections 67A(1) and 67B(1) is to be taken to have been made on 16 March 2016,
(b) the date of the change is 1 October 2016, and
(c) the concessionary date is 1 February 2017.

GENERAL NOTE

Section 141 increases the standard rate of insurance premium tax (IPT) from 9.5% to 10% with effect from 1 October 2016.

The new rate applies to insurance premiums which fall to be received by insurers under taxable insurance contracts incepted on or after 1 October 2016. The rate had risen from 6% to 9.5% on 1 November 2015, but the Chancellor justified the further increase by committing the additional proceeds to spending on flood defences.

Premiums received by insurers using the special accounting scheme benefit from a four-month concessionary transitional period from 1 October 2016 to 31 January 2017, during which the applicable rate is 9.5%. From 1 February 2017 all premiums are to be taxed at the 10% rate, notwithstanding the policy inception date.

The IPT applied to premium refunds will be at the rate originally applied.

Anti-forestalling tax avoidance measures apply to certain premiums received or written during the period 16 March 2016 to 30 September 2016 resulting in the rate of 10% being applied.

Landfill Tax

142 Landfill tax: rates from 1 April 2017

(1) Section 42 of FA 1996 (amount of landfill tax) is amended as follows.

(2) In subsection (1)(a) (standard rate), for "£84.40" substitute "£86.10".

(3) In subsection (2) (reduced rate for certain disposals)—

(a) for "£84.40" substitute "£86.10", and
(b) for "£2.65" substitute "£2.70".

(4) The amendments made by this section have effect in relation to disposals made (or treated as made) on or after 1 April 2017.

GENERAL NOTE

The standard rate and the reduced rate of landfill tax will both increase from £84.40 to £86.10 per whole tonne and from £2.65 to £2.70 per whole tonne respectively. This increase takes effect in relation to disposals of waste material by way of landfill at landfill sites made on or after 1 April 2017.

Following announcements of Budgets 2014 and 2015, the increases to the landfill tax rates are made according to the Retail Prices Index (RPI) rounded to the nearest 5 pence.

143 Landfill tax: rates from 1 April 2018

(1) Section 42 of FA 1996 (amount of landfill tax) (as amended by section 142) is amended as follows.

(2) In subsection (1)(a) (standard rate), for "£86.10" substitute "£88.95".

(3) In subsection (2) (reduced rate for certain disposals)—

   (a) for "£86.10" substitute "£88.95", and
   (b) for "£2.70" substitute "£2.80".

(4) The amendments made by this section have effect in relation to disposals made (or treated as made) on or after 1 April 2018.

GENERAL NOTE

The standard rate and the reduced rate of landfill tax will both increase from £86.10 to £88.95 per whole tonne and from £2.70 to £2.80 per whole tonne respectively. These increases take effect in relation to disposals of waste material by way of landfill at landfill sites made on or after 1 April 2018.

Following announcements of Budgets 2014 and 2015, these increases to the landfill tax rates are made according to the Retail Prices Index (RPI) rounded to the nearest 5 pence.

Climate Change Levy

144 CCL: abolition of exemption for electricity from renewable sources

(1) In Schedule 6 to FA 2000 (climate change levy), in paragraph 19(1) (exemption for electricity from renewable sources)—

   (a) in paragraph (c), omit the final "and";
   (b) after paragraph (d) insert ", and
      (e) the electricity is actually supplied before 1 April 2018."

(2) In that Schedule omit the following—

   (a) in paragraph 5(3), "20(6)(a),";
   (b) paragraphs 19 and 20;
   (c) paragraph 24(2).

(3) The repeals made by subsection (2) come into force on the day appointed by the Treasury by regulations made by statutory instrument.

GENERAL NOTE

Section 144 repeals FA 2000 Sch 6 para 19(1), the exemption from CCL for renewable energy supplied, to businesses and public sector consumers, under renewable source contracts from 1 April 2018.

Renewable electricity has been exempt from the CCL since the introduction of the levy in 2001. The purpose of the exemption was to increase demand for renewable energy from business consumers and so support the UK's climate change and renewable energy targets.

As explained in HM Revenue & Customs Tax Information and Impact Note of 8 July 2015, the exemption was not considered efficient because stimulating demand equally benefits UK and overseas suppliers of renewable energy and since CCL's introduction, the UK Government have put in place other policies to support renewable generation that more directly target UK generators.

The period from 1 August 2015 to 31 March 2018 is a transitional period, agreed following a consultation with various stakeholders and Energy UK discussions. As a result of the Budget announcement on 8 July 2015 that the exemption was to be removed for electricity generated from 1 August 2015, and the resulting amendment to the definition of renewable source electricity for the purpose of the Finance Act 2000, Ofgem ceased to issue Levy Exemption Certificates (LECs) for energy generated from that date. LECs are necessary to evidence entitlement to apply the exemption, so the transitional period allows suppliers that hold LECs in relation to renewable source energy generated before 1 August 2015 to allocate those LECs to supplies they make of that energy up to 31 March 2018.

The High Court dismissed a judicial review challenging the timing of the removal of the exemption.

145 CCL: main rates from 1 April 2017
(1) In paragraph 42(1) of Schedule 6 to FA 2000 (climate change levy: amount payable by way of levy) for the table substitute—

"TABLE

Taxable commodity supplied	Rate at which levy payable if supply is not a reduced-rate supply
Electricity	£0.00568 per kilowatt hour
Gas supplied by a gas utility or any gas supplied in a gaseous state that is of a kind supplied by a gas utility	£0.00198 per kilowatt hour
Any petroleum gas, or other gaseous hydrocarbon, supplied in a liquid state	£0.01272 per kilogram
Any other taxable commodity	£0.01551 per kilogram"

(2) The amendment made by this section has effect in relation to supplies treated as taking place on or after 1 April 2017.

GENERAL NOTE
Sections 145 to 147 set out the main rates of CCL applicable to supplies of taxable commodities (generally, electricity, gas, petroleum gas, coal and coke – but not road fuels) to consumers of those commodities. The rates increase each year in line with Retail Price Index changes.

146 CCL: main rates from 1 April 2018
(1) In paragraph 42(1) of Schedule 6 to FA 2000 (climate change levy: amount payable by way of levy) for the table substitute—

"TABLE

Taxable commodity supplied	Rate at which levy payable if supply is not a reduced-rate supply
Electricity	£0.00583 per kilowatt hour
Gas supplied by a gas utility or any gas supplied in a gaseous state that is of a kind supplied by a gas utility	£0.00203 per kilowatt hour
Any petroleum gas, or other gaseous hydrocarbon, supplied in a liquid state	£0.01304 per kilogram
Any other taxable commodity	£0.01591 per kilogram"

(2) The amendment made by this section has effect in relation to supplies treated as taking place on or after 1 April 2018.

GENERAL NOTE
Sections 145 to 147 set out the main rates of CCL applicable to supplies of taxable commodities (generally, electricity, gas, petroleum gas, coal and coke – but not road fuels) to consumers of those commodities. The rates increase each year in line with Retail Price Index changes.

147 CCL: main rates from 1 April 2019
(1) In paragraph 42(1) of Schedule 6 to FA 2000 (climate change levy: amount payable by way of levy) for the table substitute—

"TABLE

Taxable commodity supplied	Rate at which levy payable if supply is not a reduced-rate supply
Electricity	£0.00847 per kilowatt hour
Gas supplied by a gas utility or any gas supplied in a gaseous state that is of a kind supplied by a gas utility	£0.00339 per kilowatt hour
Any petroleum gas, or other gaseous hydrocarbon, supplied in a liquid state	£0.02175 per kilogram
Any other taxable commodity	£0.02653 per kilogram"

(2) The amendment made by this section has effect in relation to supplies treated as taking place on or after 1 April 2019.

GENERAL NOTE

Sections 145 to 147 set out the main rates of CCL applicable to supplies of taxable commodities (generally, electricity, gas, petroleum gas, coal and coke – but not road fuels) to consumers of those commodities. The rates increase each year in line with Retail Price Index changes.

148 CCL: reduced rates from 1 April 2019

(1) In paragraph 42(1) of Schedule 6 to FA 2000 (climate change levy: amount payable by way of levy)—

(a) in paragraph (ba) (reduced-rate supplies of electricity), for "10" substitute "7";

(b) in paragraph (c) (other reduced-rate supplies), for "35" substitute "22".

(2) The amendments made by this section have effect in relation to supplies treated as taking place on or after 1 April 2019.

GENERAL NOTE

Section 148 lowers the reduced rate of CCL from 1 April 2019, offsetting increases to the main rates of CCL for energy intensive businesses that have entered into climate change agreements with the Environment Agency.

Air Passenger Duty

149 APD: rates from 1 April 2016

(1) In section 30 of FA 1994 (air passenger duty: rates of duty) in subsection (4A) (long haul rates of duty)—

(a) in paragraph (a), for "£71" substitute "£73", and

(b) in paragraph (b), for "£142" substitute "£146".

(2) The amendments made by this section have effect in relation to the carriage of passengers beginning on or after 1 April 2016.

GENERAL NOTE

The standard and reduced rates of Air Passenger Duty (APD) on flights in band B increased from £142 to £146 and from £71 to £73 respectively on 1 April 2016. The new rate applies to the carriage of passengers beginning on or after 1 April 2016.

The rates of APD on band A journeys remain unchanged.

The higher rate of APD likewise remains unchanged.

Note:

Band B journeys are journeys where the destination is in a country or territory, the capital city of which is more than 2,000 miles away from London.

Vehicle Excise Duty

150 VED: rates for light passenger vehicles, light goods vehicles, motorcycles etc

(1) Schedule 1 to VERA 1994 (annual rates of duty) is amended as follows.

(2) In paragraph 1(2) (vehicle not covered elsewhere in Schedule with engine cylinder capacity exceeding 1,549cc), for "£230" substitute "£235".

(3) In paragraph 1B (graduated rates of duty for light passenger vehicles)—

    (a) for the tables substitute—

"Table 1

Rates payable on first vehicle licence for vehicle

CO_2 emissions figure		Rate	
(1)	*(2)*	*(3)*	*(4)*
Exceeding	*Not exceeding*	*Reduced rate*	*Standard rate*
g/km	*g/km*	*£*	*£*
130	140	120	130
140	150	135	145
150	165	175	185
165	175	290	300
175	185	345	355
185	200	490	500
200	225	640	650
225	255	875	885
255	—	1110	1120

Table 2

Rates payable on any other vehicle licence for vehicle

CO_2 emissions figure		Rate	
(1)	*(2)*	*(3)*	*(4)*
Exceeding	*Not exceeding*	*Reduced rate*	*Standard rate*
g/km	*g/km*	*£*	*£*
100	110	10	20
110	120	20	30
120	130	100	110
130	140	120	130
140	150	135	145
150	165	175	185
165	175	200	210
175	185	220	230
185	200	260	270
200	225	285	295
225	255	490	500
255	—	505	515";"

    (b) in the sentence immediately following the tables, for paragraphs (a) and (b) substitute—

        "(a) in column (3), in the last two rows, "285" were substituted for "490" and "505", and

        (b) in column (4), in the last two rows, "295" were substituted for "500" and "515"."

(4) In paragraph 1J (VED rates for light goods vehicles), in paragraph (a), for "£225" substitute "£230".

(5) In paragraph 2(1) (VED rates for motorcycles)—

    (a) in paragraph (b), for "£38" substitute "£39",

    (b) in paragraph (c), for "£59" substitute "£60", and

    (c) in paragraph (d), for "£81" substitute "£82".

(6) The amendments made by this section have effect in relation to licences taken out on or after 1 April 2016.

GENERAL NOTE

The rates of Vehicle Excise Duty (VED) chargeable on vehicles are dependent on the vehicle type, engine size, date of first registration and exhaust pipe emission data. Generally, cars and vans registered prior to 1 March 2001, and all motorcycles, are taxed by reference to the engine size. The rate applying to cars registered on or after 1 March 2001 is generally determined by the vehicle's carbon dioxide emissions. A reduced rate of VED applies when a vehicle uses certain alternative fuels or meets other conditions set out in the Vehicle Excise and Registration Act 1994 (VERA).

Section 150 increases by RPI certain rates of VED by amendment of VERA. Changes to the rates take effect in relation to vehicle licences taken out on or after 1 April 2016. VED rates have increased in line with inflation since 2010.

151   VED: extension of old vehicles exemption from 1 April 2017

(1) Paragraph 1A of Schedule 2 to VERA 1994 (exemption for old vehicles) is amended as follows.

(2) In sub-paragraph (1) for the words from "if" to the end substitute "during the period of 12 months beginning with 1 April in any year if it was constructed more than 40 years before 1 January in that year."

(3) After that sub-paragraph insert—

"(1A) But nothing in sub-paragraph (1) has the effect that a nil licence is required to be in force in respect of a vehicle while a vehicle licence is in force in respect of it."

(4) The amendments made by this section come into force on 1 April 2017.

GENERAL NOTE

Vehicle excise duty (VED) is charged by reference to the annual rate applicable to the relevant description of vehicle (s 2 of the Vehicle Excise and Registration Act 1994 (VERA)). However, no VED is charged in respect of an exempt vehicle (specified in VERA Sch 2 (VERA s 5)).

Paragraph 1A of Sch 2 VERA enacts a VED exemption for old vehicles intended to support classic vehicles and the classic car industry, which the government considers are an important part of the country's historical and cultural heritage.

Section 151 extends the exemption from VED for classic cars from 1 April 2017. This section amends para 1A of Sch 2 VERA.

Subsection (2) provides for the extension of the 40-year rolling exemption for classic vehicles to ensure that the exemption is placed on a permanent basis, so that from 1 April each year vehicles constructed more than 40 years before the 1 January of that year will automatically be exempt from paying VED.

Subsection (3) provides a transitional period so that a nil licence does not need to be in force if there is a vehicle licence already in force. When that existing vehicle licence expires, a nil licence will need to be in force for the vehicle.

Subsection (4) provides that the amendments made by the section come into force on 1 April 2017.

Other Excise Duties

152   Gaming duty: rates

(1) In section 11(2) of FA 1997 (rates of gaming duty), for the table substitute—

"TABLE

Part of gross gaming yield	Rate
The first £2,370,500	15 per cent
The next £1,634,000	20 per cent

The next £2,861,500	30 per cent
The next £6,040,000	40 per cent
The remainder	50 per cent"

(2) The amendment made by this section has effect in relation to accounting periods beginning on or after 1 April 2016.

GENERAL NOTE

Section 152 amends the gross gaming yield bands for Gaming Duty with effect for accounting periods beginning on or after 1 April 2016. The bands have been increased in line with inflation.

Gaming Duty is paid on profits from gaming in land based casinos that takes place in the UK. It is calculated on the gross gaming yield of the premises, which is the total value of stakes and charges made for gaming less winnings paid out. The rate of Gaming Duty depends upon the premise's gross gaming yield.

As stated in the Explanatory Notes, the amendment "ensures that casino operators' profits are not subject to the higher gaming duty bands simply as a result of inflation. There is therefore no duty increase in real terms." The increase in the bands is based on the Retail Price Index for the year ended 31 December 2015, which was calculated at 0.98%.

153 Fuel duties: aqua methanol etc

(1) Schedule 17 contains provision relating to fuel duties.

(2) Part 1 of the Schedule provides for charging excise duty on aqua methanol.

(3) Part 2 of the Schedule contains miscellaneous amendments.

(4) Part 3 of the Schedule makes provision about commencement.

GENERAL NOTE

Section 153 and Sch 17 introduce a reduced excise duty rate of 7.90 pence per litre for aqua methanol used as fuel for any engine, motor or other machinery, with effect from 14 November 2016. Aqua methanol is a fuel that is approximately 95% methanol and 5% water. In Budget 2014, the Government announced that it would apply a reduced rate of fuel duty to aqua methanol, with the intention of encouraging the use of aqua methanol as an alternative fuel to petrol and diesel, in recognition of its environmental benefits.

A lower rate of fuel duty applies to certain alternative fuels, such as compressed natural gas, liquid natural gas and biomethane. In Autumn Statement 2013, the Government announced that the duty differential between alternative fuels and the main fuel duty rate would be maintained until 2024, with a review in Budget 2018. Aqua methanol has now been added to the fuels to which a lower rate applies.

154 Tobacco products duty: rates

(1) For the table in Schedule 1 to TPDA 1979 substitute—

"TABLE

1	Cigarettes	An amount equal to 16.5% of the retail price plus £196.42 per thousand cigarettes
2	Cigars	£245.01 per kilogram
3	Hand-rolling tobacco	£198.10 per kilogram

| 4   Other smoking tobacco and chewing tobacco | £107.71 per kilogram" |

(2) The amendment made by this section is treated as having come into force at 6pm on 16 March 2016.

GENERAL NOTE

Section 154 increases the rates of excise duty on tobacco products (cigarettes, cigars, hand-rolling tobacco, other smoking tobacco and chewing tobacco). The new rates took effect at 6.00pm on 16 March 2016.

It was announced in the 2014 Budget that duty rates on tobacco products would increase by 2 per cent above the Retail Price Index through to the end of the Parliament. Excise duty on hand-rolling tobacco increases by an additional 3 per cent (to 5 per cent above the Retail Price Index), to reduce the difference in the rates applying to hand-rolling tobacco and cigarettes.

155 Alcoholic liquor duties: rates

(1) ALDA 1979 is amended as follows.

(2) In section 62(1A)(a) (rate of duty on sparkling cider of a strength exceeding 5.5%) for "£264.61" substitute "£268.99".

(3) For Part 1 of the table in Schedule 1 substitute—

"PART 1
WINE OR MADE-WINE OF A STRENGTH NOT EXCEEDING 22%

Description of wine or made-wine	Rates of duty per hectolitre £
Wine or made-wine of a strength not exceeding 4%	£85.60
Wine or made-wine of a strength exceeding 4% but not exceeding 5.5%	£117.72
Wine or made-wine of a strength exceeding 5.5% but not exceeding 15% and not being sparkling	£277.84
Sparkling wine or sparkling made-wine of a strength exceeding 5.5% but less than 8.5%	£268.99
Sparkling wine or sparkling made-wine of a strength of at least 8.5% but not exceeding 15%	£355.87
Wine or made-wine of a strength exceeding 15% but not exceeding 22%	£370.41"

(4) The amendments made by this section are treated as having come into force on 21 March 2016.

GENERAL NOTE

Section 155 increases the rates of excise duty, in line with the Retail Price Index, on most wines and higher strength sparkling cider with effect from 21 March 2016. Alcoholic drinks affected include wines with a strength at or below 22% alcohol by volume (abv) and sparkling cider and perry exceeding 5.5% abv but less than 8.5% abv.

Duty rates on beer, spirits and most ciders have been frozen this year.

PART 10
TAX AVOIDANCE AND EVASION

General Anti-Abuse Rule

156 General anti-abuse rule: provisional counteractions

(1) In Part 5 of FA 2013 (general anti-abuse rule), after section 209 insert—

"209A Effect of adjustments specified in a provisional counteraction notice

(1) Adjustments made by an officer of Revenue and Customs which—

(a) are specified in a provisional counteraction notice given to a person by the officer (and have not been cancelled: see sections 209B to 209E),

(b) are made in respect of a tax advantage that would (ignoring this Part) arise from tax arrangements that are abusive, and

(c) but for section 209(6)(a), would have effected a valid counteraction of that tax advantage under section 209,

are treated for all purposes as effecting a valid counteraction of the tax advantage under that section.

(2) A "provisional counteraction notice" is a notice which—

(a) specifies adjustments (the "notified adjustments") which the officer reasonably believes may be required under section 209(1) to counteract a tax advantage that would (ignoring this Part) arise to the person from tax arrangements;

(b) specifies the arrangements and the tax advantage concerned, and

(c) notifies the person of the person's rights of appeal with respect to the notified adjustments (when made) and contains a statement that if an appeal is made against the making of the adjustments—

(i) no steps may be taken in relation to the appeal unless and until the person is given a notice referred to in section 209F(2), and

(ii) the notified adjustments will be cancelled if HMRC fails to take at least one of the actions mentioned in section 209B(4) within the period specified in section 209B(2).

(3) It does not matter whether the notice is given before or at the same time as the making of the adjustments.

(4) In this section "adjustments" includes adjustments made in any way permitted by section 209(5).

209B Notified adjustments: 12 month period for taking action if appeal made

(1) This section applies where a person (the "taxpayer") to whom a provisional counteraction notice has been given appeals against the making of the notified adjustments.

(2) The notified adjustments are to be treated as cancelled with effect from the end of the period of 12 months beginning with the day on which the provisional counteraction notice is given unless an action mentioned in subsection (4) is taken before that time.

(3) For the purposes of subsection (2) it does not matter whether the action mentioned in subsection (4)(c), (d) or (e) is taken before or after the provisional counteraction notice is given (but if that action is taken before the provisional counteraction notice is given subsection (5) does not have effect).

(4) The actions are—

(a) an officer of Revenue and Customs notifying the taxpayer that the notified adjustments are cancelled;

(b) an officer of Revenue and Customs giving the taxpayer written notice of the withdrawal of the provisional counteraction notice (without cancelling the notified adjustments);

(c) a designated HMRC officer giving the taxpayer a notice under paragraph 3 of Schedule 43 which—

(i) specifies the arrangements and the tax advantage which are specified in the provisional counteraction notice, and

(ii) specifies the notified adjustments (or lesser adjustments) as the counteraction that the officer considers ought to be taken (see paragraph 3(2)(c) of that Schedule);

(d) a designated HMRC officer giving the taxpayer a pooling notice or a notice of binding under Schedule 43A which—

(i) specifies the arrangements and the tax advantage which are specified in the provisional counteraction notice, and

(ii) specifies the notified adjustments (or lesser adjustments) as the counteraction that the officer considers ought to be taken;

(e) a designated HMRC officer giving the taxpayer a notice under paragraph 1(2) of Schedule 43B which—

(i) specifies the arrangements and the tax advantage which are specified in the provisional counteraction notice, and

(ii) specifies the notified adjustments (or lesser adjustments) as the counteraction that the officer considers ought to be taken.

(5) In a case within subsection (4)(c), (d) or (e), if—

(a) the notice under paragraph 3 of Schedule 43, or

(b) the pooling notice or notice of binding, or

(c) the notice under paragraph 1(2) of Schedule 43B,

(as the case may be) specifies lesser adjustments the officer must modify the notified adjustments accordingly.

(6) The officer may not take the action in subsection (4)(b) unless the officer was authorised to make the notified adjustments otherwise than under this Part.

(7) In this section "lesser adjustments" means adjustments which assume a smaller tax advantage than was assumed in the provisional counteraction notice.

209C Notified adjustments: case within section 209B(4)(c)

(1) This section applies if the action in section 209B(4)(c) (notice to taxpayer of proposed counteraction of tax advantage) is taken.

(2) If the matter is not referred to the GAAR Advisory Panel, the notified adjustments are to be treated as cancelled with effect from the date of the designated HMRC officer's decision under paragraph 6(2) of Schedule 43 unless the notice under paragraph 6(3) of Schedule 43 states that the adjustments are not to be treated as cancelled under this section.

(3) A notice under paragraph 6(3) of Schedule 43 may not contain the statement referred to in subsection (2) unless HMRC would have been authorised to make the adjustments if the general anti-abuse rule did not have effect.

(4) If the taxpayer is given a notice under paragraph 12 of Schedule 43 which states that the specified tax advantage is not to be counteracted under the general anti-abuse rule, the notified adjustments are to be treated as cancelled unless that notice states that those adjustments are not to be treated as cancelled under this section.

(5) A notice under paragraph 12 of Schedule 43 may not contain the statement referred to in subsection (4) unless HMRC would have been authorised to make the adjustments if the general anti-abuse rule did not have effect.

(6) If the taxpayer is given a notice under paragraph 12 of Schedule 43 stating that the specified tax advantage is to be counteracted—

(a) the notified adjustments are confirmed only so far as they are specified in that notice as adjustments required to give effect to the counteraction, and

(b) so far as they are not confirmed, the notified adjustments are to be treated as cancelled.

209D Notified adjustments: case within section 209B(4)(d)

(1) This section applies if the action in section 209B(4)(d) (pooling notice or notice of binding) is taken.

(2) If the taxpayer is given a notice under paragraph 8(2) or 9(2) of Schedule 43A which states that the specified tax advantage is not to be counteracted under the general anti-abuse rule, the notified adjustments are to be treated as cancelled, unless that notice states that those adjustments are not to be treated as cancelled under this section.

(3) A notice under paragraph 8(2) or 9(2) of Schedule 43A may not contain the statement referred to in subsection (2) unless HMRC would have been authorised to make the adjustments if the general anti-abuse rule did not have effect.

(4) If the taxpayer is given a notice under paragraph 8(2) or 9(2) of Schedule 43A stating that the specified tax advantage is to be counteracted—

(a) the notified adjustments are confirmed only so far as they are specified in that notice as adjustments required to give effect to the counteraction, and

(b) so far as they are not confirmed, the notified adjustments are to be treated as cancelled.

209E Notified adjustments: case within section 209B(4)(e)

(1) This section applies if the action in section 209B(4)(e) (notice of proposal to make generic referral) is taken.

(2) If the notice under paragraph 1(2) of Schedule 43B is withdrawn, the notified adjustments are to be treated as cancelled unless the notice of withdrawal states that the adjustments are not to be treated as cancelled under this section.

(3) The notice of withdrawal may not contain the statement referred to in subsection (2) unless HMRC was authorised to make the notified adjustments otherwise than under this Part.

(4) If the taxpayer is given a notice under paragraph 8(2) of Schedule 43B, which states that the specified tax advantage is not to be counteracted under the general anti-abuse rule, the notified adjustments are to be treated as cancelled, unless that notice states that those adjustments are not to be treated as cancelled under this section.

(5) A notice under paragraph 8(2) of Schedule 43B may not contain the statement referred to in subsection (4) unless HMRC was authorised to make the adjustments otherwise than under this Part.

(6) If the taxpayer is given a notice under paragraph 8(2) of Schedule 43B stating that the specified tax advantage is to be counteracted—

    (a) the notified adjustments are confirmed only so far as they are specified in that notice as adjustments required to give effect to the counteraction, and

    (b) so far as they are not confirmed, the notified adjustments are to be treated as cancelled.

209F Appeals against provisional counteractions: further provision

(1) Subsections (2) to (5) have effect in relation to an appeal by a person ("the taxpayer") against the making of adjustments which are specified in a provisional counteraction notice.

(2) No steps after the initial notice of appeal are to be taken in relation to the appeal unless and until the taxpayer is given—

    (a) a notice under section 209B(4)(b),

    (b) a notice under paragraph 6(3) of Schedule 43 (notice of decision not to refer matter to GAAR advisory panel) containing the statement described in section 209C(2) (statement that adjustments are not to be treated as cancelled),

    (c) a notice under paragraph 12 of Schedule 43,

    (d) a notice under paragraph 8(2) or 9(2) of Schedule 43A, or

    (e) a notice under paragraph 8 of Schedule 43B,

in respect of the tax arrangements concerned.

(3) The taxpayer has until the end of the period mentioned in subsection (4) to comply with any requirement to specify the grounds of appeal.

(4) The period mentioned in subsection (3) is the 30 days beginning with the day on which the taxpayer receives the notice mentioned in subsection (2).

(5) In subsection (2) the reference to "steps" does not include the withdrawal of the appeal."

(2) In section 214(1) of FA 2013 (interpretation of Part 5), at the appropriate place insert—

    ""notified adjustments", in relation to a provisional counteraction notice, has the meaning given by section 209A(2);"

    ""provisional counteraction notice" has the meaning given by section 209A(2);".

(3) The amendments made by this section have effect in relation to tax arrangements (within the meaning of Part 5 of FA 2013) entered into at any time (whether before or on or after the day on which this Act is passed).

GENERAL NOTE

Section 157 introduces provisions to allow a provisional counteraction notice under the general anti-abuse rule. The main rule (at s 209(6)(a) FA 2013) is that counteraction cannot be taken under the GAAR unless the provisions of Sch 43 FA 2013 have been complied with. The new legislation, at FA 2013 s 209A, permits provisional counteractions to be effective, without the provisions of Sch 43 having been complied with.

Scope

By virtue of the new FA 2013 s 209A, an officer of HMRC may specify adjustments in a provisional counteraction notice given to a person in respect of a tax advantage that would otherwise arise from abusive tax arrangements. Such a notice is deemed to be valid as effecting counteraction of the tax advantage, regardless of the failure to comply with Sch 43.

The provisional counteraction notice must specify the adjustments ("notified adjustments") which the officer reasonable believes may be required to counteract a tax advantage that would otherwise arise to the person from the tax arrangements, it must specify the arrangements and the tax advantage concerned and it must notify the taxpayer of their rights of appeal with respect to the notified adjustments.

It must also contain a statement that, if an appeal is made, no steps can be taken in relation to the appeal unless the person has been given a notice under FA 2013 s 209F (see below). The adjustments must be cancelled if HMRC does not take one of the actions specified in FA 2013 s 209B within the relevant period.

The notice can be given before or at the same time as the making of the adjustments but, by implication, not afterwards. "Adjustments" includes adjustments made as permitted by s 209(5) but, again, by implication, suggests that there may be other ways in which adjustments can be made under provisional counteraction notices.

If a person appeals against a provisional counteraction notice (new s 209B FA 2013) the notified adjustments are treated as cancelled twelve months after the provisional counteraction notice is given, unless:

(a) an officer of HMRC notifies the taxpayer that the notified adjustments are cancelled;

(b) an officer of HMRC gives the taxpayer written notice of the withdrawal of the provisional counteraction notice (without cancelling the notified adjustments);

(c) a designated HMRC officers gives the taxpayer a notice under para 3 to FA 2013 Sch 43, specifying the arrangements and the tax advantage specified in the provisional counteraction notice and specifies the notified adjustments as the counteraction that the officer considers should be taken (i.e. makes the counter-action a full counteraction, rather than provisional);

(d) a designated HMRC officer gives the taxpayer a pooling notice or notice of binding under Sch 43A FA 2013 (see "Section 156" below) which specifies the arrangements and the tax advantage specified in the provisional counteraction notice and specifies the notified adjustments or lesser adjustments as the counteraction that the officer considers ought to be taken;

(e) a designated HMRC officer gives the taxpayer a notice under Sch 43B FA 2013 (generic referrals, see "section 145" below), which specifies the arrangements and the tax advantage which are specified in the counteraction notice and specifies the notified adjustments as the counteraction that the officer considers ought to be taken.

The actions under Schs 43, 43A and 43B can be taken before or after the provisional counteraction notice is given. If afterwards, the various actions give the option of imposing lesser adjustments, i.e. counteracting a smaller tax advantage than was originally assumed.

New s 209F FA 2013 applies to appeals against provisional counteractions. Where a person has appealed against the making of adjustments specified in a provisional counteraction notice, no further steps are to be taken until and unless the taxpayer is given appropriate notices in respect of the tax arrangements concerned. The list of arrangements is effectively the list of notices required to be given to a taxpayer when decisions in respect of counteraction have been made.

Where the officer of HMRC gives a formal notice, under (c) above, of proposed counteraction of a tax advantage, under FA 2013 Sch 43 para 3, new s 209C FA 2013 applies. If the matter is not referred to the GAAR Advisory Panel under Sch 43 para 6, the adjustments are to be treated as cancelled with effect from the date of that decision, unless the notice given under new para 6(3) states that the adjustments are not to be treated as cancelled. This can only apply if the adjustments would be valid if the GAAR did not apply.

Similarly, if the taxpayer receives notice under Sch 43 para 12 stating that the tax advantage is not to be counteracted under the GAAR, the notified adjustments are treated as cancelled unless the notice states that they are not to be so treated. Again, this can only apply if HMRC could have made the adjustments in the absence of the GAAR having an effect. In respect of a notification under para 12, if only part of the adjustments are required to give effect to the counteraction, to the extent they are not so confirmed, the notified adjustments are treated as cancelled.

Where a notice of binding is given, under (d), new s 209D FA 2013 applies. The notified adjustments are treated as cancelled if the taxpayer is given notice under Sch 43A that the specified tax advantage is not to be counteracted under the GAAR unless the notice states that the adjustments are not to be treated as cancelled. This can only apply if HMRC could have made those adjustments even though the GAAR does not apply. If the notified adjustments are confirmed only so far as required to give effect to the counteraction, the rest of the notified adjustments are treated as cancelled.

Where there is a notification of proposal to make a generic referral, under (e) above, new s 209E FA 2013 applies. If the notice under Sch 43B is withdrawn, the notional adjustments are treated as cancelled unless the notice states that they should not be. This can only apply if HMRC is authorised to make the notified adjustments otherwise than under the GAAR.

Similarly, if the taxpayer is given notice that the specified tax advantage is not to be counteracted under the GAAR, the adjustments are treated as cancelled unless the notice states that they are not so to be cancelled, which can only apply if HMRC is authorised to make the adjustments otherwise and under the GAAR. And there is similar provision where the adjustments are only partially required to give effect to the counteraction, so that the rest of the adjustments are treated as cancelled.

Commencement

These provisions apply in relation to any tax arrangement entered into at any time, regardless of the date of royal assent to FA 2016.

157 General anti-abuse rule: binding of tax arrangements to lead arrangements

(1) Part 5 of FA 2013 (general anti-abuse rule) is amended in accordance with subsections (2) to (11).

(2) After Schedule 43 insert—

"SCHEDULE 43A

PROCEDURAL REQUIREMENTS: POOLING NOTICES AND NOTICES OF BINDING

Pooling notices

1 (1) This paragraph applies where a person has been given a notice under paragraph 3 of Schedule 43 in relation to any tax arrangements (the "lead arrangements") and the condition in sub-paragraph (2) is met.

(2) The condition is that the period of 45 days mentioned in paragraph 4(1) of Schedule 43 has expired but no notice under paragraph 12 of Schedule 43 or paragraph 8 of Schedule 43B has yet been given in respect of the matter.

(3) If a designated HMRC officer considers—

    (a) that a tax advantage has arisen to another person ("R") from tax arrangements that are abusive,

    (b) that those tax arrangements ("R's arrangements") are equivalent to the lead arrangements, and

    (c) that the advantage ought to be counteracted under section 209,

the officer may give R a notice (a "pooling notice") which places R's arrangements in a pool with the lead arrangements.

(4) There is one pool for any lead arrangements, so all tax arrangements placed in a pool with the lead arrangements (as well as the lead arrangements themselves) are in one and the same pool.

(5) Tax arrangements which have been placed in a pool do not cease to be in the pool except where that is expressly provided for by this Schedule (regardless of whether or not the lead arrangements or any other tax arrangements remain in the pool).

(6) The officer may not give R a pooling notice if R has been given in respect of R's arrangements a notice under paragraph 3 of Schedule 43.

Notice of proposal to bind arrangements to counteracted arrangements

2 (1) This paragraph applies where a counteraction notice has been given to a person in relation to any tax arrangements (the "counteracted arrangements") which are in a pool created under paragraph 1.

(2) If a designated HMRC officer considers—

(a) that a tax advantage has arisen to another person ("R") from tax arrangements that are abusive,

(b) that those tax arrangements ("R's arrangements") are equivalent to the counteracted arrangements, and

(c) that the advantage ought to be counteracted under section 209,

the officer may give R a notice (a "notice of binding") in relation to R's arrangements.

(3) The officer may not give R a notice of binding if R has been given in respect of R's arrangements a notice under—

(a) paragraph 1, or

(b) paragraph 3 of Schedule 43.

(4) In this paragraph "counteraction notice" means a notice such as is mentioned in sub-paragraph (2) of paragraph 12 of Schedule 43 or sub-paragraph (3) of paragraph 8 of Schedule 43B (notice of final decision to counteract).

3 (1) The decision whether or not to give R a pooling notice or notice of binding must be taken, and any notice must be given, as soon as is reasonably practicable after HMRC becomes aware of the relevant facts.

(2) A pooling notice or notice of binding must—

(a) specify the tax arrangements in relation to which the notice is given and the tax advantage,

(b) explain why the officer considers R's arrangements to be equivalent to the lead arrangements or the counteracted arrangements (as the case may be),

(c) explain why the officer considers that a tax advantage has arisen to R from tax arrangements that are abusive,

(d) set out the counteraction that the officer considers ought to be taken, and

(e) explain the effect of—

(i) paragraphs 4 to 10,

(ii) subsection (9) of section 209, and

(iii) section 212A.

(3) A pooling notice or notice of binding may set out steps that R may (subject to subsection (9) of section 209) take to avoid the proposed counteraction.

Corrective action by a notified taxpayer

4 (1) If a person to whom a pooling notice or notice of binding has been given takes the relevant corrective action in relation to the tax arrangements and tax advantage specified in the notice before the beginning of the closed period mentioned in section 209(9), the person is to be treated for the purposes of paragraphs 8 and 9 and Schedule 43B (generic referral of tax arrangements) as not having been given the notice in question (and accordingly the tax arrangements in question are no longer in the pool).

(2) For the purposes of this Schedule the "relevant corrective action" is taken if (and only if) the person takes the steps set out in sub-paragraphs (3) and (4).

(3) The first step is that—

(a) the person amends a return or claim to counteract the tax advantage specified in the pooling notice or notice of binding, or

(b) if the person has made a tax appeal (by notifying HMRC or otherwise) on the basis that the tax advantage specified in the pooling notice or notice of binding arises from the tax arrangements specified in that notice, the person takes all necessary action to enter into an agreement with HMRC (in writing) for the purpose of relinquishing that advantage.

(4) The second step is that the person notifies HMRC—

(a) that the first step has been taken, and

(b) of any additional amount which has or will become due and payable in respect of tax by reason of the first step being taken.

(5) Where a person takes the first step described in sub-paragraph (3)(b), HMRC may proceed as if the person had not taken the relevant corrective action if the person fails to enter into the written agreement.

(6) In determining the additional amount which has or will become due and payable in respect of tax for the purposes of sub-paragraph (4)(b), it is to be assumed that, where the person takes the necessary action as mentioned in sub-paragraph (3)(b), the agreement is then entered into.

(7) No enactment limiting the time during which amendments may be made to returns or claims operates to prevent the person taking the first step mentioned in sub-paragraph (3)(a) before the tax enquiry is closed.

(8) No appeal may be brought, by virtue of a provision mentioned in sub-paragraph (9), against an amendment made by a closure notice in respect of a tax enquiry to the extent that the amendment takes into account an amendment made by the taxpayer to a return or claim in taking the first step mentioned in sub-paragraph (3)(a).

(9) The provisions are—

  (a) paragraph 35(1)(b) of Schedule 33,
  (b) section 31(1)(b) or (c) of TMA 1970,
  (c) paragraph 9 of Schedule 1A to TMA 1970,
  (d) paragraph 34(3) of Schedule 18 to FA 1998, and
  (e) paragraph 35(1)(b) of Schedule 10 to FA 2003.

Corrective action by lead taxpayer

5 If the person mentioned in paragraph 1(1) takes the relevant corrective action (as defined in paragraph 4A of Schedule 43) before the end of the period of 75 days beginning with the day on which the notice mentioned in paragraph 1(1) was given to that person, the lead arrangements are treated as ceasing to be in the pool.

Opinion notices and right to make representations

6 (1) Sub-paragraph (2) applies where—

  (a) a pooling notice is given to a person in relation to any tax arrangements, and
  (b) an opinion notice (or opinion notices) under paragraph 11(2) of Schedule 43 about another set of tax arrangements in the pool ("the referred arrangements") is subsequently given to a designated HMRC officer.

(2) The officer must give the person a pooled arrangements opinion notice.

(3) No more than one pooled arrangements opinion notice may be given to a person in respect of the same tax arrangements.

(4) Where a designated HMRC officer gives a person a notice of binding, the officer must, at the same time, give the person a bound arrangements opinion notice.

7 (1) In relation to a person who is, or has been, given a pooling notice, "pooled arrangements opinion notice" means a written notice which—

  (a) sets out a report prepared by HMRC of any opinion of the GAAR Advisory Panel about the referred arrangements,
  (b) explains the person's right to make representations falling within sub-paragraph (3), and
  (c) sets out the period in which those representations may be made.

(2) In relation to a person who is given a notice of binding "bound arrangements opinion notice" means a written notice which—

  (a) sets out a report prepared by HMRC of any opinion of the GAAR Advisory Panel about the counteracted arrangements (see paragraph 2(1)),
  (b) explains the person's right to make representations falling within sub-paragraph (3), and
  (c) sets out the period in which those representations may be made.

(3) A person who is given a pooled arrangements opinion notice or a bound arrangements opinion notice has 30 days beginning with the day on which the notice is given to make representations in any of the following categories—

  (a) representations that no tax advantage has arisen to the person from the arrangements to which the notice relates;
  (b) representations as to why the arrangements to which the notice relates are or may be materially different from—

      (i) the referred arrangements (in the case of a pooled arrangements opinion notice), or
      (ii) the counteracted arrangements (in the case of a bound arrangements opinion notice).

(4) In sub-paragraph (3)(b) references to "arrangements" include any circumstances which would be relevant in accordance with section 207 to a determination of whether the tax arrangements in question are abusive.

Notice of final decision

8 (1) This paragraph applies where—

(a) any tax arrangements have been placed in a pool by a notice given to a person under paragraph 1, and

(b) a designated HMRC officer has given a notice under paragraph 12 of Schedule 43 in relation to any other arrangements in the pool (the "referred arrangements").

(2) The officer must, having considered any opinion of the GAAR Advisory Panel about the referred arrangements and any representations made under paragraph 7(3) in relation to the arrangements mentioned in sub-paragraph (1)(a), give the person a written notice setting out whether the tax advantage arising from those arrangements is to be counteracted under the general anti-abuse rule.

9 (1) This paragraph applies where—

(a) a person has been given a notice of binding under paragraph 2, and

(b) the period of 30 days for making representations under paragraph 7(3) has expired.

(2) A designated HMRC officer must, having considered any opinion of the GAAR Advisory Panel about the counteracted arrangements and any representations made under paragraph 7(3) in relation to the arrangements specified in the notice of binding, give the person a written notice setting out whether the tax advantage arising from the arrangements specified in the notice of binding is to be counteracted under the general anti-abuse rule.

10 If a notice under paragraph 8(2) or 9(2) states that a tax advantage is to be counteracted, it must also set out—

(a) the adjustments required to give effect to the counteraction, and

(b) if relevant, any steps the person concerned is required to take to give effect to it.

"Equivalent arrangements"

11 (1) For the purposes of paragraph 1, tax arrangements are "equivalent" to one another if they are substantially the same as one another having regard to—

(a) their substantive results,

(b) the means of achieving those results, and

(c) the characteristics on the basis of which it could reasonably be argued, in each case, that the arrangements are abusive tax arrangements under which a tax advantage has arisen to a person.

Notices may be given on assumption that tax advantage does arise

12 (1) A designated HMRC officer may give a notice, or do anything else, under this Schedule where the officer considers that a tax advantage might have arisen to the person concerned.

(2) Accordingly, any notice given by a designated HMRC officer under this Schedule may be expressed to be given on the assumption that a tax advantage does arise (without conceding that it does).

Power to amend

13 (1) The Treasury may by regulations amend this Schedule (apart from this paragraph).

(2) Regulations under sub-paragraph (1) may include—

(a) any amendment of this Part that is appropriate in consequence of an amendment by virtue of sub-paragraph (1);

(b) transitional provision.

(3) Regulations under sub-paragraph (1) are to be made by statutory instrument.

(4) A statutory instrument containing regulations under sub-paragraph (1) is subject to annulment in pursuance of a resolution of the House of Commons."

(3) After Schedule 43A insert—

"SCHEDULE 43B
PROCEDURAL REQUIREMENTS: GENERIC REFERRAL OF TAX ARRANGEMENTS

Notice of proposal to make generic referral of tax arrangements

1 (1) Sub-paragraph (2) applies if—

(a) pooling notices given under paragraph 1 of Schedule 43A have placed one or more sets of tax arrangements in a pool with the lead arrangements,

(b) the lead arrangements (see paragraph 1(1) of Schedule 43A) have ceased to be in the pool, and

(c) no referral under paragraph 5 or 6 of Schedule 43 has been made in respect of any arrangements in the pool.

(2) A designated HMRC officer may determine that, in respect of each of the tax arrangements that are in the pool, there is to be given (to the person to whom the pooling notice in question was given) a written notice of a proposal to make a generic referral to the GAAR Advisory Panel in respect of the arrangements in the pool.

(3) Only one determination under sub-paragraph (2) may be made in relation to any one pool.

(4) The persons to whom those notices are given are "the notified taxpayers".

(5) A notice given to a person ("T") under sub-paragraph (2) must—

(a) specify the arrangements (the "specified arrangements") and the tax advantage (the "specified advantage") to which the notice relates,

(b) inform T of the period under paragraph 2 for making a proposal.

2 (1) T has 30 days beginning with the day on which the notice under paragraph 1 is given to propose to HMRC that it—

(a) should give T a notice under paragraph 3 of Schedule 43 in respect of the arrangements to which the notice under paragraph 1 relates, and

(b) should not proceed with the proposal to make a generic referral to the GAAR Advisory Panel in respect of those arrangements.

(2) If a proposal is made in accordance with sub-paragraph (1) a designated HMRC officer must consider it.

Generic referral

3 (1) This paragraph applies where a designated HMRC officer has given notices to the notified taxpayers in accordance with paragraph 1(2).

(2) If none of the notified taxpayers has made a proposal under paragraph 2 by the end of the 30 day period mentioned in that paragraph, the officer must make a referral to the GAAR Advisory Panel in respect of the notified taxpayers and the arrangements which are specified arrangements in relation to them.

(3) If at least one of the notified taxpayers makes a proposal in accordance with paragraph 2, the designated HMRC officer must, after the end of that 30 day period, decide whether to—

(a) give a notice under paragraph 3 of Schedule 43 in respect of one set of tax arrangements in the relevant pool, or

(b) make a referral to the GAAR Advisory Panel in respect of the tax arrangements in the relevant pool.

(4) A referral under this paragraph is a "generic referral".

4 (1) If a generic referral is made to the GAAR Advisory Panel, the designated HMRC officer must at the same time provide it with—

(a) a general statement of the material characteristics of the specified arrangements, and

(b) a declaration that—

(i) the statement under paragraph (a) is applicable to all the specified arrangements, and

(ii) as far as HMRC is aware, nothing which is material to the GAAR Advisory Panel's consideration of the matter has been omitted.

(2) The general statement under sub-paragraph (1)(a) must—

(a) contain a factual description of the tax arrangements;

(b) set out HMRC's view as to whether the tax arrangements accord with established practice (when the arrangements were entered into);

(c) explain why it is the designated HMRC officer's view that a tax advantage of the nature described in the statement and arising from tax arrangements having the characteristics described in the statement would be a tax advantage arising from arrangements that are abusive;

(d) set out any matters the designated officer is aware of which may suggest that any view of HMRC or the designated HMRC officer expressed in the general statement is not correct;

(e) set out any other matters which the designated officer considers are required for the purposes of the exercise of the GAAR Advisory Panel's functions under paragraph 6.

5 If a generic referral is made the designated HMRC officer must at the same time give each of the notified taxpayers a notice which—

(a) specifies that a generic referral is being made, and

(b) is accompanied by a copy of the statement given to the GAAR Advisory Panel in accordance with paragraph 4(1)(a).

Decision of GAAR Advisory Panel and opinion notices

6 (1) If a generic referral is made to the GAAR Advisory Panel under paragraph 3, the Chair must arrange for a sub-panel consisting of 3 members of the GAAR Advisory Panel (one of whom may be the Chair) to consider it.

(2) The sub-panel must produce—

(a) one opinion notice stating the joint opinion of all the members of the sub-panel, or

(b) two or three opinion notices which taken together state the opinions of all the members.

(3) The sub-panel must give a copy of the opinion notice or notices to the designated HMRC officer.

(4) An opinion notice is a notice which states that in the opinion of the members of the sub-panel, or one or more of those members—

(a) the entering into and carrying out of tax arrangements such as are described in the general statement under paragraph 4(1)(a) is a reasonable course of action in relation to the relevant tax provisions,

(b) the entering into or carrying out of such tax arrangements is not a reasonable course of action in relation to the relevant tax provisions, or

(c) it is not possible, on the information available, to reach a view on that matter,

and the reasons for that opinion.

(5) In forming their opinions for the purposes of sub-paragraph (4) members of the sub-panel must—

(a) have regard to all the matters set out in the statement under paragraph 4(1)(a),

(b) assume (unless the contrary is stated in the statement under paragraph 4(1)(a)) that the tax arrangements do not form part of any other arrangements,

(c) have regard to the matters mentioned in paragraphs (a) to (c) of section 207(2), and

(d) take account of subsections (4) to (6) of section 207.

(6) For the purposes of the giving of an opinion under this paragraph, the arrangements are to be assumed to be tax arrangements.

(7) In this Part, a reference to any opinion of the GAAR Advisory Panel in respect of a generic referral of any tax arrangements is a reference to the contents of any opinion notice given in relation to a generic referral in respect of the arrangements.

Notice of right to make representations

7 (1) Where a designated HMRC officer is given an opinion notice (or opinion notices) under paragraph 6, the officer must give each of the notified taxpayers a copy of the opinion notice (or notices) and a written notice which—

(a) explains the notified taxpayer's right to make representations falling within sub-paragraph (2), and

(b) sets out the period in which those representations may be made.

(2) A notified taxpayer ("T") who is given a notice under sub-paragraph (1) has 30 days beginning with the day on which the notice is given to make representations in any of the following categories—

(a) representations that no tax advantage has arisen from the specified arrangements;

(b) representations that T has already been given a notice under paragraph 6 of Schedule 43A in relation to the specified arrangements;

(c) representations that any matter set out in the statement under paragraph 4(1)(a) is materially inaccurate as regards the specified arrangements (having regard to all circumstances which would be relevant in accordance with section 207 to a determination of whether the tax arrangements in question are abusive).

Notice of final decision after considering opinion of GAAR Advisory Panel

8 (1) A designated HMRC officer who has received a copy of a notice or notices under paragraph 6(3) in respect of a generic referral must consider the case of each notified taxpayer in accordance with sub-paragraph (2).

(2) The officer must, having considered—

(a) any opinion of the GAAR Advisory Panel about the matters referred to it, and

(b) any representations made by the notified taxpayer under paragraph 7,

give to the notified taxpayer a written notice setting out whether the specified advantage is to be counteracted under the general anti-abuse rule.

(3) If the notice states that a tax advantage is to be counteracted, it must also set out—

(a) the adjustments required to give effect to the counteraction, and

(b) if relevant, any steps that the taxpayer is required to take to give effect to it.

Notices may be given on assumption that tax advantage does arise

9 (1) A designated HMRC officer may give a notice, or do anything else, under this Schedule where the officer considers that a tax advantage might have arisen to the person concerned.

(2) Accordingly, any notice given by a designated HMRC officer under this Schedule may be expressed to be given on the assumption that a tax advantage does arise (without conceding that it does).

Power to amend

10 (1) The Treasury may by regulations amend this Schedule (apart from this paragraph).

(2) Regulations under sub-paragraph (1) may include—

(a) any amendment of this Part that is appropriate in consequence of an amendment by virtue of sub-paragraph (1);

(b) transitional provision.

(3) Regulations under sub-paragraph (1) are to be made by statutory instrument.

(4) A statutory instrument containing regulations under sub-paragraph (1) is subject to annulment in pursuance of a resolution of the House of Commons."

(4) In section 209 (counteracting tax advantages), in subsection (6)(a), after "Schedule 43" insert ", 43A or 43B".

(5) In section 210 (consequential relieving adjustments), in subsection (1)(b), after "Schedule 43," insert "paragraph 8 or 9 of Schedule 43A or paragraph 8 of Schedule 43B,".

(6) In section 211 (proceedings before a court or tribunal), in subsection (2)(b), for the words from "Panel" to the end substitute "Panel given—

(i) under paragraph 11 of Schedule 43 about the arrangements or any tax arrangements which are, as a result of a notice under paragraph 1 or 2 of Schedule 43A, the referred or (as the case may be) counteracted arrangements in relation to the arrangements, or

(ii) under paragraph 6 of Schedule 43B in respect of a generic referral of the arrangements."

(7) Section 214 (interpretation of Part 5) is amended in accordance with subsections (8) to (10).

(8) Renumber section 214 as subsection (1) of section 214.

(9) In subsection (1) (as renumbered), at the appropriate places insert—

""designated HMRC officer" has the meaning given by paragraph 2 of Schedule 43;".".

""notice of binding" has the meaning given by paragraph 2(2) of Schedule 43A;"

""pooling notice" has the meaning given by paragraph 1(4) of Schedule 43A;"

""tax appeal" has the meaning given by paragraph 1A of Schedule 43;"

""tax enquiry" has the meaning given by section 202(2) of FA 2014."

(10) After subsection (1) insert—

"(2) In this Part references to any "opinion of the GAAR Advisory Panel" about any tax arrangements are to be interpreted in accordance with paragraph 11(5) of Schedule 43.

(3) In this Part references to tax arrangements which are "equivalent" to one another are to be interpreted in accordance with paragraph 11 of Schedule 43A."

(11) In Schedule 43 (general anti-abuse rule: procedural requirements), in paragraph 6, after sub-paragraph (2) insert—

"(3) The officer must, as soon as reasonably practicable after deciding whether or not the matter is to be referred to the GAAR Advisory Panel, give the taxpayer written notice of the decision."

(12) Section 10 of the National Insurance Contributions Act 2014 (GAAR to apply to national insurance contributions) is amended in accordance with subsections (13) to (16).

(13) In subsection (4), at the end insert ", paragraph 8 or 9 of Schedule 43A to that Act (pooling of tax arrangements: notice of final decision) or paragraph 8 of Schedule 43B to that Act (generic referral of arrangements: notice of final decision)".

(14) After subsection (6) insert—

"(6A) Where, by virtue of this section, a case falls within paragraph 4A of Schedule 43 to the Finance Act 2013 (referrals of single schemes: relevant corrective action) or paragraph 4 of Schedule 43A to that Act (pooled schemes: relevant corrective action)—

(a) the person ("P") mentioned in sub-paragraph (1) of that paragraph takes the "relevant corrective action" for the purposes of that paragraph if (and only if)—

(i) in a case in which the tax advantage in question can be counteracted by making a payment to HMRC, P makes that payment and notifies HMRC that P has done so, or

(ii) in any case, P takes all necessary action to enter into an agreement in writing with HMRC for the purpose of relinquishing the tax advantage, and

(b) accordingly, sub-paragraphs (2) to (8) of that paragraph do not apply."

(15) In subsection (11)—

(a) for "and HMRC" substitute ", "HMRC" and "tax advantage"";

(b) after "2013" insert "(as modified by this section)".

(16) After subsection (11) insert—

"(12) See section 10A for further modifications of Part 5 of the Finance Act 2013."

(17) After section 10 of the National Insurance Contributions Act 2014 insert—

"10A Application of GAAR in relation to penalties

(1) For the purposes of this section a penalty under section 212A of the Finance Act 2013 is a "relevant NICs-related penalty" so far as the penalty relates to a tax advantage in respect of relevant contributions.

(2) A relevant NICs-related penalty may be recovered as if it were an amount of relevant contributions which is due and payable.

(3) Section 117A of the Social Security Administration Act 1992 or (as the case may be) section 111A of the Social Security Administration (Northern Ireland) Act 1992 (issues arising in proceedings: contributions etc) has effect in relation to proceedings before a court for recovery of a relevant NICs-related penalty as if the assessment of the penalty were a NICs decision as to whether the person is liable for the penalty.

(4) Accordingly, paragraph 5(4)(b) of Schedule 43C to the Finance Act 2013 (assessment of penalty to be enforced as if it were an assessment to tax) does not apply in relation to a relevant NICs-related penalty.

(5) In the application of Schedule 43C to the Finance Act 2013 in relation to a relevant NICs-related penalty, paragraph 9(5) has effect as if the reference to an appeal against an assessment to the tax concerned were to an appeal against a NICs decision.

(6) In paragraph 8 of that Schedule (aggregate penalties), references to a "relevant penalty provision" include—

(a) any provision mentioned in sub-paragraph (5) of that paragraph, as applied in relation to any class of national insurance contributions by regulations (whenever made);

(b) section 98A of the Taxes Management Act 1970, as applied in relation to any class of national insurance contributions by regulations (whenever made);

(c) any provision in regulations made by the Treasury under which a penalty can be imposed in respect of any class of national insurance contributions.

(7) The Treasury may by regulations—

(a) disapply, or modify the effect of, subsection (6)(a) or (b);

(b) modify paragraph 8 of Schedule 43C to the Finance Act 2013 as it has effect in relation to a relevant penalty provision by virtue of subsection (6)(b) or (c).

(8) Section 175(3) to (5) of SSCBA 1992 (various supplementary powers) applies to a power to make regulations conferred by subsection (7).

(9) Regulations under subsection (7) must be made by statutory instrument.

(10) A statutory instrument containing regulations under subsection (7) is subject to annulment in pursuance of a resolution of either House of Parliament.

(11) In this section "NICs decision" means a decision under section 8 of the Social Security Contributions (Transfer of Functions, etc) Act 1999 or Article 7 of the Social Security Contributions (Transfer of Functions, etc) (Northern Ireland) Order 1999 (SI 1999/671).

(12) In this section "relevant contributions" means the following contributions under Part 1 of SSCBA 1992 or Part 1 of SSCB(NI)A 1992—

    (a) Class 1 contributions;
    (b) Class 1A contributions;
    (c) Class 1B contributions;
    (d) Class 2 contributions which must be paid but in relation to which section 11A of the Act in question (application of certain provisions of the Income Tax Acts in relation to Class 2 contributions under section 11(2) of that Act) does not apply."

(18) Section 219 of FA 2014 (circumstances in which an accelerated payment notice may be given) is amended in accordance with subsections (19) and (20).

(19) In subsection (4), after paragraph (c) insert—

"(d) a notice has been given under paragraph 8(2) or 9(2) of Schedule 43A to FA 2013 (notice of final decision after considering Panel's opinion about referred or counteracted arrangements) in relation to the asserted advantage or part of it and the chosen arrangements (or is so given at the same time as the accelerated payment notice) in a case where the stated opinion of at least two of the members of the sub-panel of the GAAR Advisory Panel about the other arrangements (see subsection (8)) was as set out in paragraph 11(3)(b) of Schedule 43 to FA 2013;

(e) a notice under paragraph 8(2) of Schedule 43B to FA 2013 (GAAR: generic referral of tax arrangements) has been given in relation to the asserted advantage or part of it and the chosen arrangements (or is so given at the same time as the accelerated payment notice) in a case where the stated opinion of at least two of the members of the sub-panel of the GAAR Advisory Panel which considered the generic referral in respect of those arrangements under paragraph 6 of Schedule 43B to FA 2013 was as set out in paragraph 6(4)(b) of that Schedule."

(20) After subsection (7) insert—

"(8) In subsection (4)(d) "other arrangements" means

    (a) in relation to a notice under paragraph 8(2) of Schedule 43A to FA 2013, the referred arrangements (as defined in that paragraph);
    (b) in relation to a notice under paragraph 9(2) of that Schedule, the counteracted arrangements (as defined in paragraph 2 of that Schedule)."

(21) In section 220 of FA 2014 (content of notice given while a tax enquiry is in progress)—

    (a) in subsection (4)(c), after "219(4)(c)" insert ", (d) or (e)";
    (b) in subsection (5)(c), after "219(4)(c)" insert ", (d) or (e)";
    (c) in subsection (7), for the words from "under" to the end substitute "under—
        (a) paragraph 12 of Schedule 43 to FA 2013,
        (b) paragraph 8 or 9 of Schedule 43A to that Act, or
        (c) paragraph 8 of Schedule 43B to that Act, as the case may be."

(22) Section 287 of FA 2014 (Code of Practice on Taxation for Banks) is amended in accordance with subsections (23) to (25).

(23) In subsection (4), after "(5)" insert "or (5A)".

(24) In subsection (5)(b), after "Schedule" insert "or paragraph 8 or 9 of Schedule 43A to that Act".

(25) After subsection (5) insert—

"(5A) This subsection applies to any conduct—

    (a) in relation to which there has been given—

        (i) an opinion notice under paragraph 6(4)(b) of Schedule 43B to FA 2013 (GAAR advisory panel: opinion that such conduct unreasonable) stating the joint opinion of all the members of a sub-panel arranged under that paragraph, or
        (ii) one or more such notices stating the opinions of at least two members of such a sub-panel, and

    (b) in relation to which there has been given a notice under paragraph 8 of that Schedule (HMRC final decision on tax advantage) stating that a tax advantage is to be counteracted.

(5B) For the purposes of subsection (5), any opinions of members of the GAAR advisory panel which must be considered before a notice is given under paragraph 8 or 9 of Schedule 43A to FA 2013 (opinions about the lead arrangements) are taken to relate to the conduct to which the notice relates."

(26) In Schedule 32 to FA 2014 (accelerated payments and partnerships), paragraph 3 is amended in accordance with subsections (27) and (28).

(27) In sub-paragraph (5), after paragraph (c) insert—

"(d) the relevant partner in question has been given a notice under paragraph 8(2) or 9(2) of Schedule 43A to FA 2013 (notice of final decision after considering Panel's opinion about referred or counteracted arrangements) in respect of any tax advantage resulting from the asserted advantage or part of it and the chosen arrangements (or is given such a notice at the same time as the partner payment notice) in a case where the stated opinion of at least two of the members of the sub-panel of the GAAR Advisory Panel about the other arrangements (see sub-paragraph (7)) was as set out in paragraph 11(3)(b) of Schedule 43 to FA 2013;
(e) the relevant partner in question has been given a notice under paragraph 8(2) of Schedule 43B to FA 2013 (GAAR: generic referral of arrangements) in respect of any tax advantage resulting from the asserted advantage or part of it and the chosen arrangements (or is given such a notice at the same time as the partner payment notice) in a case where the stated opinion of at least two of the members of the sub-panel of the GAAR Advisory Panel which considered the generic referral in respect of those arrangements was as set out in paragraph 6(4)(b) of that Schedule."

(28) After sub-paragraph (6) insert—

"(7) Other arrangements" means—

(a) in relation to a notice under paragraph 8(2) of Schedule 43A to FA 2013, the referred arrangements (as defined in that paragraph);
(b) in relation to a notice under paragraph 9(2) of that Schedule, the counteracted arrangements (as defined in paragraph 2 of that Schedule)."

(29) In Schedule 34 to FA 2014 (promoters of tax avoidance schemes: threshold conditions), in paragraph 7—

(a) in paragraph (a), at the end insert "(referrals of single schemes) or are in a pool in respect of which a referral has been made to that Panel under Schedule 43B to that Act (generic referrals),";
(b) in paragraph (b)—
(i) for "in relation to the arrangements" substitute "in respect of the referral";
(ii) after "11(3)(b)" insert "or (as the case may be) 6(4)(b)";
(c) in paragraph (c)(i) omit "paragraph 10 of".

(30) The amendments made by this section have effect in relation to tax arrangements (within the meaning of Part 5 of FA 2013) entered into at any time (whether before or on or after the day on which this Act is passed).

GENERAL NOTE

Section 156 introduces amendments to the general anti-abuse rule (GAAR) in Pt 5 FA 2013 and introduces new Schs 43A and 43B to that Act. These are intended to permit HMRC to deal with tax avoidance schemes that are the same, or similar, together, rather than having to take separate counteraction in respect of each scheme undertaken by each taxpayer.

New Sch 43A: pooling notices and notices of binding

The main provisions of new Sch 43A require there to have been a notice of proposed counteraction, under para 3 of Sch 43, in respect of any tax arrangements, which are called 'the lead arrangements', and the 45-day period under which the taxpayer can make representations has expired with no notice of an intended counteraction having been issued to the taxpayer under para 12. If a designated HMRC officer then considers that another person has obtained a tax advantage under equivalent tax arrangements, which also ought to be counteracted under FA 2013 s 209, the officer may give the second taxpayer a "pooling notice", so that the arrangements are in a single pool with the lead arrangements, so long as that person has not already had a notice of proposed counteraction under para 3 of Sch 43.

Where a counteraction notice has been issued but a 5-day period under which the taxpayer can make representations has expired with no notice of an intended counteraction having been issued to the taxpayer under para 12. If a designated HMRC officer then considers that another person has obtained a tax advantage under equivalent tax arrangements, which also ought to be counteracted under FA 2013 s 209, the officer may give the second taxpayer a "notice of binding", so long as that person has not already had a notice of proposed counteraction under para 3 of Sch 43 or para 1 of Sch 43A.

The decisions must be made as soon as reasonably practicable after HMRC becomes aware of the relevant facts.

A pooling notice or notice of binding must specify the tax arrangements and the tax advantage, explain why the officer consider the arrangements to be equivalent to the lead arrangements or counteracted arrangements, as appropriate, explain why the officer considers that a tax advantages has arisen to the second taxpayer from tax arrangements that are abusive, set out the counteraction the officer considers appropriate and explain the effects of the appropriate provisions of the GAAR. A condition of binding may include more than one set of lead arrangements, in which case the requirements of a notice of binding must give the appropriate information in respect of each set of lead arrangements.

If a person to whom a pooling notice or notice of binding has been given takes relevant corrective action then they are treated as not having been given the notice, and any pooled arrangements cease to be in the pool. Relevant corrective action means amending the tax return or claim to amend the tax advantage specified, or writing to HMRC to withdraw a tax appeal and relinquish the tax advantage by written agreement with HMRC. Having notified HMRC that these steps have been taken, the taxpayer must also notify HMRC of any additional amount which has or will become due and payable as a result, otherwise the relevant corrective action can be treated as not having been taken. In terms of amending returns or claims, normal time limits are suspended. Once amendments had been made accordingly, no further appeals against any amendment can be made by the taxpayer.

The lead taxpayer can also take relevant corrective action, but must do so within 75 days of the date they received their notice of proposed counteraction in order to have their lead arrangements cease to be within the pool.

Where there is both a pooling notice and an opinion from the GAAR Advisory Panel under Sch 43 about any other arrangements in the pool, HMRC must give a pooled arrangements opinion notice to anyone to whom a pooling notice has been issued in respect of those lead arrangements. This is a written notice setting out a report prepared by HMRC of the GAAR Advisory Panel's opinion, explaining the person's right to make representations and setting out the period in which those might be made. The person who is given a pooled arrangements opinion notice has 30 days to make representations that no tax advantage has arisen to them from the arrange-ments to which the notice relates, that the person has already had a notice in relation to different lead arrangements or an explanation as to why the arrangements to which the notice relates are materially different from the lead arrangements.

Where a notice of binding is issued, a bound arrangements opinion notice must also be issued at the same time (i.e. because the GAAR Advisory Panel must already have given an opinion). This is a written notice which sets out a report prepared by HMRC of any opinion of the GAAR Advisory Panel about the counteracted arrange-ments, explains the person's right to make representations, and sets out the period in which those representations may be made.

A person receiving either type of notice has 30 days to make representations that no tax advantage has arisen to the person from the arrangements to which the notice relates or representations as to why the arrangements to which the notice relates are or may be materially different from the lead arrangements.

Where there is a pool and HMRC has given a final decision in respect of any of the arrangements in the pool, after considering the opinion of the GAAR Advisory Panel, they must then give any person who has a received a pooling notice a written notice setting out whether the tax advantage arising from those lead arrangements is to be counteracted under the GAAR. If an advantage is to be counteracted, the notice must also set out the adjustments required to give effect to the counteraction and if relevant any steps the person concerned is required to take to give effect to it.

Where a notice of binding has been issued, after 30 days HMRC must consider the GAAR Advisory Panel's opinion about the lead arrangements that have been counteracted, as well as the representations that may have been made, and give the taxpayer a written notice as to whether the bound arrangements are to be counter-acted.

For the purposes of this schedule 'equivalent arrangements' means arrangements that are substantially the same as one another in terms of the substantive results, the means of achieving those results and the characteristics by which they could be argued to be abusive tax arrangements under which a tax advantage has arisen to a person.

Notices under Sch 43A can be given where HMRC considers that a tax advantage may have arisen to a person concerned and can be expressed on the assumption that it does, without the necessity for any concession on this point.

New Sch 43B: generic referral of tax arrangements

Where there is a pool under Sch 43A and the lead arrangements have ceased to be within the pool, HMRC can decide to make a generic referral, if none of the arrangements have already been referred to the Advisory Panel. A written notice to this effect must be given to anyone who has had a pooling notice in respect of those arrangements. Only one such decision can be made by HMRC for any pool.

The notice must specify the arrangements and the tax advantage and inform the taxpayers of the period for making proposals under this Schedule.

The taxpayers concerned (referred to as the "notified taxpayers") have 30 days to propose that HMRC, instead, give a notice of proposed counteraction under FA 2013, Sch 43, para 3, and not proceed with the generic referral. HMRC must consider any such proposal.

If no proposals are made, HMRC must refer the arrangements to the GAAR Advisory Panel. If at least one notified taxpayer makes a proposal, HMRC must decide whether to give a notice under FA 2013, Sch 43, para 3 or to refer the pooled arrangements to the Panel under Schedule 43B.

A generic referral to the GAAR Advisory Panel must be accompanied by a general statement of the material characteristics of the arrangements and a declaration that this statement is applicable to all the specified arrangements and that nothing has been omitted which is material to the Advisory Panel's consideration of the matter.

The general statement must contain a factual description of the tax arrangements, set out HMRC's view as to whether they accord with established practice when they were entered into, explain why it is HMRC's view that a tax advantage obtained from tax arrangements with those characteristics would be abusive, set out any matters that the designated officer is aware of which may suggest that any view of HMRC or of the designated officer expressed in the general statement is not correct, and set out other matters that are required for the exercise of the Advisory Panel's functions in this respect. Each of the relevant taxpayers must also be informed that a generic referral is being made and they must each be given a copy of HMRC's statement as to the characteristics of the tax advantages.

The GAAR Advisory Panel must arrange for a three person sub-panel, including the Chair, and must produce one, two or three opinion notices, either stating the joint opinion of all the members of the sub-panel or each of their separate opinions, all of which must be given to the designated HMRC officer. An opinion notice is one that states that in the opinion of the relevant members of the sub-panel, either entering into or carrying out the tax arrangements as described in the general statements is a reasonable course of action in relation to the relevant tax provisions, or it is not a relevant course of action in relation to the relevant tax provisions, or that it is not possible to reach a view on the information available. The sub-panel must have regard to the matters set out in the statement as well as all the other matters they are generally expected to have regard to in respect of an opinion.

HMRC must then give each of the notified taxpayers a copy of the opinion notice along with written notice of their rights to make representations and the periods during which these can be made. The taxpayers can then make representations within 30 days that no tax advantage has arisen from the specified arrangements, that they had already been given a notice under Sch 43A (binding notices) in relation to the arrangements or that some part of the statement made by HMRC to the GAAR Advisory Panel is materially inaccurate as regards the specified arrangements, having regard to all the other circumstances that would be relevant in determining whether the tax arrangements in question are abusive.

HMRC must then consider the opinion of the GAAR Advisory Panel and any representations by the notified taxpayers and give the notified taxpayers a written notice setting out whether the specified advantage is to be counteracted under the GAAR. If it is, the notice must state the adjustments required to give effect to the counteraction and, if relevant, any steps that the taxpayer is required to take to give effect to it.

Notices under Sch 43B can be given where HMRC considers that a tax advantage may have arisen to a person concerned and can be expressed on the assumption that it does, without the necessity for any concession on this point.

Other amendments to GAAR legislation

Paragraph 6 Sch 43 now has a new sub-para (3) stating that, the officer must give the taxpayer written notice of a decision as to whether or not a matter is to be referred to the GAAR Advisory Panel as soon as is reasonably practicable after making that decision.

Notices under Schs 43A (pooling notices of binding) and 43B (generic referrals) are brought within the list of qualifying factors in Condition C of FA 2014 s 219, allowing HMRC to issue accelerated payment notices or partner payment notices.

There are also a number of other consequential amendments to both tax and social security legislation.

Commencement

These amendments have effect in relation to tax arrangements entered into at any time, regardless of when Finance Act 2016 receives Royal Assent.

158 General anti-abuse rule: penalty

(1) Part 5 of FA 2013 (general anti-abuse rule) is amended as follows.

(2) After section 212 insert—

"212A Penalty

(1) A person (P) is liable to pay a penalty if—

(a) P has been given a notice under—

   (i) paragraph 12 of Schedule 43,

   (ii) paragraph 8 or 9 of Schedule 43A, or

   (iii) paragraph 8 of Schedule 43B,

stating that a tax advantage arising from particular tax arrangements is to be counteracted,

(b) a tax document has been given to HMRC on the basis that the tax advantage arises to P from those arrangements,

(c) that document was given to HMRC—

   (i) by P, or

   (ii) by another person in circumstances where P knew, or ought to have known, that the other person gave the document on the basis mentioned in paragraph (c), and

(d) the tax advantage has been counteracted by the making of adjustments under section 209.

(2) The penalty is 60% of the value of the counteracted advantage.

(3) Schedule 43C—

(a) gives the meaning of "the value of the counteracted advantage", and

(b) makes other provision in relation to penalties under this section.

(4) In this section "tax document" means any return, claim or other document submitted in compliance (or purported compliance) with any provision of, or made under, an Act.

(5) In this section the reference to giving a tax document to HMRC is to be interpreted in accordance with paragraph 11(g) and (h) of Schedule 43C."

(3) After Schedule 43B insert—

"SCHEDULE 43C

PENALTY UNDER SECTION 212A: SUPPLEMENTARY PROVISION

Value of the counteracted advantage: introduction

1 Paragraphs 2 to 4 set out how to calculate the "value of the counteracted advantage" for the purposes of section 212A.

Value of the counteracted advantage: basic rule

2 (1) The "value of the counteracted advantage" is the additional amount due or payable in respect of tax as a result of the counteraction mentioned in section 212A(1)(c).

(2) The reference in sub-paragraph (1) to the additional amount due and payable includes a reference to—

(a) an amount payable to HMRC having erroneously been paid by way of repayment of tax, and
(b) an amount which would be repayable by HMRC if the counteraction were not made.

(3) The following are ignored in calculating the value of the counteracted advantage—

(a) group relief, and
(b) any relief under section 458 of CTA 2010 (relief in respect of repayment etc of loan) which is deferred under subsection (5) of that section.

(4) For the purposes of this paragraph consequential adjustments under section 210 are regarded as part of the counteraction in question.

(5) If the counteraction affects the person's liability to two or more taxes, the taxes concerned are to be considered together for the purpose of determining the value of the counteracted advantage.

(6) This paragraph is subject to paragraphs 3 and 4.

Value of counteracted advantage: losses

3 (1) To the extent that the tax advantage mentioned in section 212A(1)(b) ("the tax advantage") resulted in the wrong recording of a loss for the purposes of direct tax and the loss has been wholly used to reduce the amount due or payable in respect of tax, the value of the counteracted advantage is determined in accordance with paragraph 2.

(2) To the extent that the tax advantage resulted in the wrong recording of a loss for purposes of direct tax and the loss has not been wholly used to reduce the amount due or payable in respect of tax, the value of the counteracted advantage is—

(a) the value under paragraph 2 of so much of the tax advantage as results (or would in the absence of the counteraction result) from the part (if any) of the loss which was used to reduce the amount due or payable in respect of tax, plus
(b) 10% of the part of the loss not so used.

(3) Sub-paragraphs (1) and (2) apply both—

(a) to a case where no loss would have been recorded but for the tax advantage, and
(b) to a case where a loss of a different amount would have been recorded (but in that case sub-paragraphs (1) and (2) apply only to the difference between the amount recorded and the true amount).

(4) To the extent that the tax advantage creates or increases (or would in the absence of the counteraction create or increase) an aggregate loss recorded for a group of companies—

(a) the value of the counteracted advantage is calculated in accordance with this paragraph, and
(b) in applying paragraph 2 in accordance with sub-paragraphs (1) and (2), group relief may be taken into account (despite paragraph 2(3)).

(5) To the extent that the tax advantage results (or would in the absence of the counteraction result) in a loss, the value of it is nil where, because of the nature of the loss or the person's circumstances, there was no reasonable prospect of the loss being used to support a claim to reduce a tax liability (of any person).

Value of counteracted advantage: deferred tax

4 (1) To the extent that the tax advantage mentioned in section 212A is a deferral of tax, the value of the counteracted advantage is—

(a) 25% of the amount of the deferred tax for each year of the deferral, or
(b) a percentage of the amount of the deferred tax, for each separate period of deferral of less than a year, equating to 25% per year,

or, if less, 100% of the amount of the deferred tax.

(2) This paragraph does not apply to a case to the extent that paragraph 3 applies.

Assessment of penalty

5 (1) Where a person is liable for a penalty under section 212A, HMRC must assess the penalty.

(2) Where HMRC assess the penalty, HMRC must—

(a) notify the person who is liable for the penalty, and

(b) state in the notice a tax period in respect of which the penalty is assessed.

(3) A penalty under this paragraph must be paid before the end of the period of 30 days beginning with the day on which notification of the penalty is issued.

(4) An assessment—

(a) is to be treated for procedural purposes as if it were an assessment to tax,

(b) may be enforced as if it were an assessment to tax, and

(c) may be combined with an assessment to tax.

(5) An assessment of a penalty under this paragraph must be made before the end of the period of 12 months beginning with—

(a) the end of the appeal period for the assessment which gave effect to the counteraction mentioned in section 212A(1)(b), or

(b) if there is no assessment within paragraph (a), the date (or the latest of the dates) on which that counteraction becomes final.

(6) The reference in sub-paragraph (5)(b) to the counteraction becoming final is to be interpreted in accordance with section 210(8).

Alteration of assessment of penalty

6 (1) After notification of an assessment has been given to a person under paragraph 5(2), the assessment may not be altered except in accordance with this paragraph or paragraph 7, or on appeal.

(2) A supplementary assessment may be made in respect of a penalty if an earlier assessment operated by reference to an underestimate of the value of the counteracted advantage.

(3) An assessment may be revised as necessary if it operated by reference to an overestimate of the value of the counteracted advantage.

Revision of assessment following consequential relieving adjustment

7 (1) Sub-paragraph (2) applies where a person—

(a) is notified under section 210(7) of a consequential adjustment relating to a counteraction under section 209, and

(b) an assessment to a penalty in respect of that counteraction of which the person has been notified under paragraph 5(2) does not take account of that consequential adjustment.

(2) HMRC must make any alterations of the assessment that appear to HMRC to be just and reasonable in connection with the consequential amendment.

(3) Alterations under this paragraph may be made despite any time limit imposed by or under an enactment.

Aggregate penalties

8 (1) Sub-paragraph (3) applies where—

(a) two or more penalties are incurred by the same person and fall to be determined by reference to an amount of tax to which that person is chargeable,

(b) one of those penalties is incurred under section 212A, and

(c) one or more of the other penalties are incurred under a relevant penalty provision.

(2) But sub-paragraph (3) does not apply if section 212(2) of FA 2014 (follower notices: aggregate penalties) applies in relation to the amount of tax in question.

(3) The aggregate of the amounts of the penalties mentioned in subsection (1)(b) and (c), so far as determined by reference to that amount of tax, must not exceed—

(a) the relevant percentage of that amount, or

(b) in a case where at least one of the penalties is under paragraph 5(2)(b) of, or sub-paragraph (3)(b), (4)(b) or (5)(b) of paragraph 6 of, Schedule 55 to FA 2009, £300 (if greater).

(4) In the application of section 97A of TMA 1970 (multiple penalties) no account shall be taken of a penalty under section 212A.

(5) "Relevant penalty provision" means—

(a) Schedule 24 to FA 2007 (penalties for errors),

(b) Schedule 41 to FA 2008 (penalties: failure to notify etc),

(c) Schedule 55 to FA 2009 (penalties for failure to make returns etc), or

(d) Part 5 of Schedule 18 to FA 2016 (penalty under serial tax avoidance regime).

(6) "The relevant percentage" means—

(a) 200% in a case where at least one of the penalties is determined by reference to the percentage in—

(i) paragraph 4(4)(c) of Schedule 24 to FA 2007,

(ii) paragraph 6(4)(a) of Schedule 41 to FA 2008, or

(iii) paragraph 6(3A)(c) of Schedule 55 to FA 2009,

(b) 150% in a case where paragraph (a) does not apply and at least one of the penalties is determined by reference to the percentage in—

(i) paragraph 4(3)(c) of Schedule 24 to FA 2007,

(ii) paragraph 6(3)(a) of Schedule 41 to FA 2008, or

(iii) paragraph 6(3A)(b) of Schedule 55 to FA 2009,

(c) 140% in a case where neither paragraph (a) nor paragraph (b) applies and at least one of the penalties is determined by reference to the percentage in—

(i) paragraph 4(4)(b) of Schedule 24 to FA 2007,

(ii) paragraph 6(4)(b) of Schedule 41 to FA 2008, or

(iii) paragraph 6(4A)(c) of Schedule 55 to FA 2009,

(d) 105% in a case where at none of paragraphs (a), (b) and (c) applies and at least one of the penalties is determined by reference to the percentage in—

(i) paragraph 4(3)(b) of Schedule 24 to FA 2007,

(ii) paragraph 6(3)(b) of Schedule 41 to FA 2008, or

(iii) paragraph 6(4A)(b) of Schedule 55 to FA 2009, and

(e) in any other case, 100%.

Appeal against penalty

9 (1) A person may appeal against—

(a) the imposition of a penalty under section 212A, or

(b) the amount assessed under paragraph 5.

(2) An appeal under sub-paragraph (1)(a) may only be made on the grounds that the arrangements were not abusive or there was no tax advantage to be counteracted.

(3) An appeal under sub-paragraph (1)(b) may only be made on the grounds that the assessment was based on an overestimate of the value of the counteracted advantage (whether because the estimate was made by reference to adjustments which were not just and reasonable or for any other reason).

(4) An appeal under this paragraph must be made within the period of 30 days beginning with the day on which notification of the penalty is given under paragraph 5(2).

(5) An appeal under this paragraph is to be treated in the same way as an appeal against an assessment to the tax concerned (including by the application of any provision about bringing the appeal by notice to HMRC, about HMRC's review of the decision or about determination of the appeal by the First-tier Tribunal or Upper Tribunal).

(6) Sub-paragraph (5) does not apply—

(a) so as to require a person to pay a penalty before an appeal against the assessment of the penalty is determined, or

(b) in respect of any other matter expressly provided for by this Part.

(7) On an appeal against the penalty the tribunal may affirm or cancel HMRC's decision.

(8) On an appeal against the amount of the penalty the tribunal may—

(a) affirm HMRC's decision, or

(b) substitute for HMRC's decision another decision that HMRC has power to make.

(9) In this paragraph "tribunal" means the First-tier Tribunal or Upper Tribunal (as appropriate by virtue of sub-paragraph (5)).

Mitigation of penalties

10 (1) The Commissioners may in their discretion mitigate a penalty under section 212A, or stay or compound any proceedings for such a penalty.

(2) They may also, after judgment, further mitigate or entirely remit the penalty.

Interpretation

11 In this Schedule—

(a) a reference to an "assessment" to tax is to be interpreted, in relation to inheritance tax, as a reference to a determination;

(b) "direct tax" means—

(i) income tax,
(ii) capital gains tax,
(iii) corporation tax (including any amount chargeable as if it were corporation tax or treated as corporation tax),
(iv) petroleum revenue tax, and
(v) diverted profits tax;

(c) a reference to a loss includes a reference to a charge, expense, deficit and any other amount which may be available for, or relied on to claim, a deduction or relief;

(d) a reference to a repayment of tax includes a reference to allowing a credit against tax or to a payment of a corporation tax credit;

(e) "corporation tax credit" means—

(i) an R&D tax credit under Chapter 2 or 7 of Part 13 of CTA 2009,
(ii) an R&D expenditure credit under Chapter 6A of Part 3 of CTA 2009,
(iii) a land remediation tax credit or life assurance company tax credit under Chapter 3 or 4 respectively of Part 14 of CTA 2009,
(iv) a film tax credit under Chapter 3 of Part 15 of CTA 2009,
(v) a television tax credit under Chapter 3 of Part 15A of CTA 2009,
(vi) a video game tax credit under Chapter 3 of Part 15B of CTA 2009,
(vii) a theatre tax credit under section 1217K of CTA 2009,
(viii) an orchestra tax credit under Chapter 3 of Part 15D of CTA 2009, or
(ix) a first-year tax credit under Schedule A1 to CAA 2001;

(f) "tax period" means a tax year, accounting period or other period in respect of which tax is charged;

(g) a reference to giving a document to HMRC includes a reference to communicating information to HMRC in any form and by any method (whether by post, fax, email, telephone or otherwise),

(h) a reference to giving a document to HMRC includes a reference to making a statement or declaration in a document."

(4) In section 209 (counteracting the tax advantages), after subsection (7) insert—

"(8) Where a matter is referred to the GAAR Advisory Panel under paragraph 5 or 6 of Schedule 43, the taxpayer (as defined in paragraph 3 of that Schedule) must not make any GAAR-related adjustments in relation to the taxpayer's tax affairs in the period (the "closed period") which—

(a) begins with the 31st day after the end of the 45 day period mentioned in paragraph 4(1) of that Schedule, and
(b) ends immediately before the day on which the taxpayer is given the notice under paragraph 12 of Schedule 43 (notice of final decision after considering opinion of GAAR Advisory Panel).

(9) Where a person has been given a pooling notice or a notice of binding under Schedule 43A in relation to any tax arrangements, the person must not make any GAAR-related adjustments in the period ("the closed period") that—

(a) begins with the 31st day after that on which that notice is given, and
(b) ends—

(i) in the case of a pooling notice, immediately before the day on which the person is given a notice under paragraph 8(2) or 9(2) of Schedule 43A, or a notice under paragraph 8(2) of Schedule 43B, in relation to the tax arrangements (notice of final decision after considering opinion of GAAR Advisory Panel), or
(ii) in the case of a notice of binding, with the 30th day after the day on which the notice is given.

(10) In this section "GAAR-related adjustments" means—

(a) for the purposes of subsection (8), adjustments which give effect (wholly or in part) to the proposed counteraction set out in the notice under paragraph 3 of Schedule 43;
(b) for the purposes of subsection (9), adjustments which give effect (wholly or partly) to the proposed counteraction set out in the notice of pooling or binding (as the case may be)."

(5) Schedule 43 (general anti-abuse rule: procedural requirements) is amended in accordance with subsections (6) to (9).

(6) After paragraph 1 insert—

"Meaning of "tax appeal"

1A In this Part "tax appeal" means—

(a) an appeal under section 31 of TMA 1970 (income tax: appeals against amendments of self-assessment, amendments made by closure notices under section 28A or 28B of that Act, etc), including an appeal under that section by virtue of regulations under Part 11 of ITEPA 2003 (PAYE),

(b) an appeal under paragraph 9 of Schedule 1A to TMA 1970 (income tax: appeals against amendments made by closure notices under paragraph 7(2) of that Schedule, etc),

(c) an appeal under section 705 of ITA 2007 (income tax: appeals against counteraction notices),

(d) an appeal under paragraph 34(3) or 48 of Schedule 18 to FA 1998 (corporation tax: appeals against amendment of a company's return made by closure notice, assessments other than self-assessments, etc),

(e) an appeal under section 750 of CTA 2010 (corporation tax: appeals against counteraction notices),

(f) an appeal under section 222 of IHTA 1984 (appeals against HMRC determinations) other than an appeal made by a person against a determination in respect of a transfer of value at a time when a tax enquiry is in progress in respect of a return made by that person in respect of that transfer,

(g) an appeal under paragraph 35 of Schedule 10 to FA 2003 (stamp duty land tax: appeals against amendment of self-assessment, discovery assessments, etc),

(h) an appeal under paragraph 35 of Schedule 33 to FA 2013 (annual tax on enveloped dwellings: appeals against amendment of self-assessment, discovery assessments, etc),

(i) an appeal under paragraph 14 of Schedule 2 to the Oil Taxation Act 1975 (petroleum revenue tax: appeal against assessment, determination etc),

(j) an appeal under section 102 of FA 2015 (diverted profits tax: appeal against charging notice etc),

(k) an appeal under section 114 of FA 2016 (apprenticeship levy: appeal against an assessment), or

(l) an appeal against any determination of—

(i) an appeal within paragraphs (a) to (k), or
(ii) an appeal within this paragraph."

(7) In paragraph 3(2)(e), for "of paragraphs 5 and 6" substitute "of—

(i) paragraphs 5 and 6, and
(ii) sections 209(8) and (9) and 212A."

(8) After paragraph 4 insert—

"Corrective action by taxpayer

4A (1) If the taxpayer takes the relevant corrective action before the beginning of the closed period mentioned in section 209(8), the matter is not to be referred to the GAAR Advisory Panel.

(2) For the purposes of this Schedule the "relevant corrective action" is taken if (and only if) the taxpayer takes the steps set out in sub-paragraphs (3) and (4).

(3) The first step is that—

(a) the taxpayer amends a return or claim to counteract the tax advantage specified in the notice under paragraph 3, or

(b) if the taxpayer has made a tax appeal (by notifying HMRC or otherwise) on the basis that the tax advantage specified in the notice under paragraph 3 arises from the tax arrangements specified in that notice, the taxpayer takes all necessary action to enter into an agreement with HMRC (in writing) for the purpose of relinquishing that advantage.

(4) The second step is that the taxpayer notifies HMRC—

(a) that the taxpayer has taken the first step, and

(b) of any additional amount which has or will become due and payable in respect of tax by reason of the first step being taken.

(5) Where the taxpayer takes the first step described in sub-paragraph (3)(b), HMRC may proceed as if the taxpayer had not taken the relevant corrective action if the taxpayer fails to enter into the written agreement.

(6) In determining the additional amount which has or will become due and payable in respect of tax for the purposes of sub-paragraph (4)(b), it is to be assumed that, where the taxpayer takes the necessary action as mentioned in sub-paragraph (3)(b), the agreement is then entered into.

(7) No enactment limiting the time during which amendments may be made to returns or claims operates to prevent the taxpayer taking the first step mentioned in sub-paragraph (3)(a) before the tax enquiry is closed (whether or not before the specified time).

(8) No appeal may be brought, by virtue of a provision mentioned in sub-paragraph (9), against an amendment made by a closure notice in respect of a tax enquiry to the extent that the amendment takes into account an amendment made by the taxpayer to a return or claim in taking the first step mentioned in sub-paragraph (3)(a).

(9) The provisions are

    (a) section 31(1)(b) or (c) of TMA 1970,
    (b) paragraph 9 of Schedule 1A to TMA 1970,
    (c) paragraph 34(3) of Schedule 18 to FA 1998,
    (d) paragraph 35(1)(b) of Schedule 10 to FA 2003, and
    (e) paragraph 35(1)(b) of Schedule 33 to FA 2013."

(9) Before paragraph 5 (but after the heading "Referral to GAAR Advisory Panel") insert

    "**4B** Paragraphs 5 and 6 apply if the taxpayer does not take the relevant corrective action (see paragraph 4A) by the beginning of the closed period mentioned in section 209(8)."

(10) In section 103ZA of TMA 1970 (disapplication of sections 100 to 103 in the case of certain penalties)—

    (a) omit "or" at the end of paragraph (g), and
    (b) after paragraph (g) insert
        "(ga) section 212A of the Finance Act 2013 (general anti-abuse rule), or"

(11) In section 212 of FA 2014 (follower notices: aggregate penalties) (as amended by Schedule 18), in subsection (4)—

    (a) omit "or" at the end of paragraph (c), and
    (b) after paragraph (d) insert ", or
        (e) section 212A of FA 2013 (general anti-abuse rule)."

(12) FA 2015 is amended in accordance with subsections (13) and (14).

(13) In section 120 (penalties in connection with offshore matters and offshore transfers), in subsection (1), omit "and" before paragraph (c) and after paragraph (c) insert—
", and

    (d) Schedule 43C to FA 2013 (as amended by FA 2016)."

(14) In Schedule 20 to that Act, after paragraph 19 insert—

"General anti-abuse rule: aggregate penalties

20 (1) In Schedule 43C to FA 2013 (general anti-abuse rule: supplementary provision about penalty), sub-paragraph (6) of paragraph 8 is amended as follows.

(2) After paragraph (b) insert—

    "(ba) 125% in a case where neither paragraph (a) nor paragraph (b) applies and at least one of the penalties is determined by reference to the percentage in—

        (i) paragraph 4(2)(c) of Schedule 24 to FA 2007,
        (ii) paragraph 6(2)(a) of Schedule 41 to FA 2008,
        (iii) paragraph 6(3A)(a) of Schedule 55 to FA 2009,".

(3) In sub-paragraph (c) for "neither paragraph (a) nor paragraph (b) applies" substitute "none of paragraphs (a) to (ba) applies.

(4) In sub-paragraph (d) for "none of paragraphs (a), (b) and (c) applies" substitute "none of paragraphs (a) to (c) applies".

(15) The amendments made by this section have effect in relation to tax arrangements (within the meaning of Part 5 of FA 2013) entered into on or after the day on which this Act is passed.

GENERAL NOTE

Section 158 introduces provisions for penalties under the general anti-abuse rule (GAAR) regime. It also amends and expands the main GAAR provisions, s 209 and Sch 43 FA 2013. Finally, it makes a number of consequential amendments.

Penalty regime

New s 212A FA 2013 provides that, if a person has been given a notice under FA 2013 Scvh 43 para 12, Sch 43A paras 8 or 9, or Sch 43B para 8 stating that a tax advantage is to be counteracted, a tax document has been given to HMRC in connection with any tax arrangements, and the tax advantage has been counteracted by making of adjustments under s 209, the penalty is 60% of the value of the counteracted advantage.

Tax document means any return, claim or other document submitted in compliance or purported compliance with any provision under the Taxes Act. And it does not matter whether the taxpayer gave it to HMRC or someone else gave it to HMRC on their behalf.

The counteracted advantage is defined in new FA 2013 Sch 43C.

Under Sch 43C, the value of the counteracted advantage is the additional tax payable as a result of the counteraction, which includes amounts payable to HMRC having erroneously been repaid or amounts that would have been repayable by HMRC if there had been no counteraction. The amounts concerned are to be computed ignoring group relief and any relief under CTA 2010 s 458 (repayments of quasi-corporation tax after repayment or release of a loan to a participator).

Consequential adjustments under FA 2013 s 210 are regarded as part of the counteraction. Where more than one tax is involved, they are considered together to determine the quantum of the counteracted advantage.

Where the tax advantage created a loss which was used to reduce an amount due or payable in respect of tax, again, it is that amount of tax to which the penalty applies. If, however, the loss has not been wholly used, the value of the tax advantage is the amount of the loss that is used plus 10% of the part of the loss not used. Where a loss created by a tax advantage gives a group relief advantage, group relief can be taken into account in determining the value of the tax advantage.

Where a tax advantage results in a loss but there is no reasonable prospect of the loss being used to support the reduction of any person's tax liability, the value of the counteracted advantage is nil.

Where the value of the counteractive advantage relates to deferred tax, the value of the advantage is 25% of the deferred tax for each year of the deferral or an appropriate amount for a short accounting period. Alternatively, if it is less, then the value is the whole of the deferred tax.

HMRC must assess the penalties, notify the person liable and state a tax period in which the penalty is assessed. The penalty must then be paid within 30 days of the notification of penalty being issued. For procedural purposes it is to be treated as an assessment of tax, and may be enforced as if it were an assessment of tax and combined with an assessment of tax.

The assessment of a penalty must be made within 12 months of the end of the appeal period for the assessment which gave effect to the counteraction or, if there is no such assessment, the date or latest of the dates on which the counteraction becomes final. There are provisions to increase or reduce an underassessment or overassessment of a penalty. Similarly, there are provisions to revise a penalty following a consequential relieving adjustment under s 210(7) FA 2013.

There is also a general prohibition against penalties exceeding 200% where there are penalties under the GAAR regime and under other provisions by reference to the same amount of tax.

A person may appeal against the penalty but only on the basis that the arrangements were not abusive or that there was no tax advantage to be counteracted. An appeal against an assessment may also be made on the grounds that the assessment was based on an overestimate of the value of the counteracted advantage. The appeals must be made within 30 days of the notification of the penalty having been given and is to be treated in the same way as an appeal against an assessment to the tax concerned, although not so as to require the person to pay a penalty before the appeal against the assessment of penalty is determined.

On appeal, the tribunal may affirm or cancel HMRC's decision where the appeal is against the penalty, but on an appeal against the amount of the penalty the tribunal may affirm HMRC's decision or substitute any other amount that HMRC could have charged. HMRC is also entitled to mitigate the penalties or stay or compound any proceedings for penalties, in their discretion. They may also mitigate or entirely remit a penalty after judgment.

Amendments to main GAAR provisions

Section 209 FA 2013 is amended so that, if a matter is referred to the GAAR advisory panel under paras 5 or 6 of Sch 43, no GAAR-related adjustments in relation to the taxpayer's tax affairs can be made in the closed period, being the period which starts on the 31st day of the 45-day period for representations in response to a notice of proposed counteraction and ending immediately before the date on which the taxpayer is given a final decision under para 12 of Sch 43 as to whether counteraction will be taken, having considered the opinion of the GAAR advisory panel.

Similarly, where a taxpayer has been given a notice of binding under Sch 43A, no GAAR-related adjustments can be made in the period from the 31st day after that on which the notice is given and which ends immediately before the date of final decision under paras 5 or 6 of Sch 43A or para 9 of Sch 43B or, where a notice of binding is given by Condition 2 in Sch 43A, ending with the 30th day after the date on which the notice of binding is given. GAAR-related adjustments are adjustments giving effect to the proposed counteractions set out either in the notice under para 3 of Sch 43 or in the notice of binding.

Schedule 43 FA 2013 is also amended to include a new para 1A, which has a list of proceedings which are defined as being tax appeals for the purposes of the legislation.

There is also a new para 4A about relevant corrective action by taxpayers. Relevant corrective action must be taken before the end of the closed period defined above and now in s 209(8) FA 2013. If such relevant corrective action is taken, no reference is made to the GAAR advisory panel.

Relevant corrective action means amending the tax return or claim to amend the tax advantage specified, or writing to HMRC to withdraw a tax appeal and relinquish the tax advantage by written agreement with HMRC. Having notified HMRC that these steps have been taken, the taxpayer must also notify HMRC of any additional amount which has or will become due and payable as a result. In terms of amending returns or claims, normal time limits are suspended. Once amendments had been made accordingly, no further appeals against any amendment can be made by the taxpayer.

Commencement

These amendments apply in relation to tax arrangements under the GAAR entered into on or after the date on which Finance Act 2016 receives Royal Assent.

Tackling Frequent Avoidance

159 Serial tax avoidance
Schedule 18 contains provision about the issue of warning notices to, and further sanctions for, persons who incur a relevant defeat in relation to arrangements.

GENERAL NOTE

Section 159 and Sch 18 introduce a new regime of warnings and escalating sanctions for those who engage in tax avoidance schemes which HMRC subsequently defeat. New Schedules (43A and 43B) to the FA 2013 concerning with pooling arrangements or similar arrangements for the purposes of GAAR counteraction have broadened the scope from the original draft Bill. The new regime comes into effect from 6 April 2017.

The legislation is drafted to issue a warning notice, which commences a five year clock whereby subsequent defeats within the five-year period result in a penalty based on the understated tax, as well as resetting the clock. The continued use of avoidance schemes which HMRC subsequently defeat results in the rate of penalty being increased to a maximum of 60% of the understated tax.

The taxpayer's details can be published where there are three defeats within the warning or extended warning period.

Where HMRC defeat three avoidance schemes used to exploit reliefs during the warning period, the taxpayer will be denied further benefit of reliefs during the warning period.

160 Promoters of tax avoidance schemes
(1) Part 5 of FA 2014 (promoters of tax avoidance schemes) is amended as follows.
(2) After section 237 insert—

"237A Duty to give conduct notice: defeat of promoted arrangements
(1) If an authorised officer becomes aware at any time ("the relevant time") that a person ("P") who is carrying on a business as a promoter meets any of the conditions in subsections (11) to (13), the officer must determine whether or not P's meeting of that condition should be regarded as significant in view of the purposes of this Part. But see also subsection (14).
(2) An authorised officer must make the determination set out in subsection (3) if the officer becomes aware at any time ("the section 237A(2) relevant time") that—
   (a) a person meets a condition in subsection (11), (12) or (13), and
   (b) at the section 237A(2) relevant time another person ("P"), who is carrying on a business as a promoter, meets that condition by virtue of Part 4 of Schedule 34A (meeting the section 237A conditions: bodies corporate and partnerships).
(3) The authorised officer must determine whether or not—
   (a) the meeting of the condition by the person as mentioned in subsection (2)(a), and
   (b) P's meeting of the condition as mentioned in subsection (2)(b),
should be regarded as significant in view of the purposes of this Part.
(4) Subsections (1) and (2) do not apply if a conduct notice or monitoring notice already has effect in relation to P.
(5) Subsection (1) does not apply if, at the relevant time, an authorised officer is under a duty to make a determination under section 237(5) in relation to P.
(6) Subsection (2) does not apply if, at the section 237A(2) relevant time, an authorised officer is under a duty to make a determination under section 237(5) in relation to P.
(7) But in a case where subsection (1) does not apply because of subsection (5), or subsection (2) does not apply because of subsection (6), subsection (5) of section 237 has effect as if—
   (a) the references in paragraph (a) of that subsection to "subsection (1)", and "subsection (1)(a)" included subsection (1) of this section, and
   (b) in paragraph (b) of that subsection the reference to "subsection (1A)(a)" included a reference to subsection (2)(a) of this section and the reference to subsection (1A)(b) included a reference to subsection (2)(b) of this section.
(8) If the authorised officer determines under subsection (1) that P's meeting of the condition in question should be regarded as significant, the officer must give P a conduct notice, unless subsection (10) applies.
(9) If the authorised officer determines under subsection (3) that—
   (a) the meeting of the condition by the person as mentioned in subsection (2)(a), and
   (b) P's meeting of the condition as mentioned in subsection (2)(b),
should be regarded as significant in view of the purposes of this Part, the officer must give P a conduct notice, unless subsection (10) applies.
(10) This subsection applies if the authorised officer determines that, having regard to the extent of the impact that P's activities as a promoter are likely to have on the collection of tax, it is inappropriate to give P a conduct notice.
(11) The condition in this subsection is that in the period of 3 years ending with the relevant time at least 3 relevant defeats have occurred in relation to P.
(12) The condition in this subsection is that at least two relevant defeats have occurred in relation to P at times when a single defeat notice under section 241A(2) or (6) had effect in relation to P.
(13) The condition in this subsection is that at least one relevant defeat has occurred in relation to P at a time when a double defeat notice under section 241A(3) had effect in relation to P.
(14) A determination that the condition in subsection (12) or (13) is met cannot be made unless—
   (a) the defeat notice in question still has effect when the determination is made, or
   (b) the determination is made on or before the 90th day after the day on which the defeat notice in question ceased to have effect.

(15) Schedule 34A sets out the circumstances in which a "relevant defeat" occurs in relation to a person and includes provision limiting what can amount to a further relevant defeat in relation to a person (see paragraph 6).

237B Duty to give further conduct notice where provisional notice not complied with

(1) An authorised officer must give a conduct notice to a person ("P") who is carrying on a business as a promoter if—

(a) a conduct notice given to P under section 237A(8)—

(i) has ceased to have effect otherwise than as a result of section 237D(2) or 241(3) or (4), and

(ii) was provisional immediately before it ceased to have effect,

(b) the officer determines that P had failed to comply with one or more conditions in the conduct notice,

(c) the conduct notice relied on a Case 3 relevant defeat,

(d) since the time when the conduct notice ceased to have effect, one or more relevant defeats falling within subsection (2) have occurred in relation to—

(i) P, and

(ii) any arrangements to which the Case 3 relevant defeat also relates, and

(e) had that relevant defeat or (as the case may be) those relevant defeats, occurred before the conduct notice ceased to have effect, an authorised officer would have been required to notify the person under section 237C(3) that the notice was no longer provisional.

(2) A relevant defeat falls within this subsection if it occurs by virtue of Case 1 or Case 2 in Schedule 34A.

(3) Subsection (1) does not apply if the authorised officer determines that, having regard to the extent of the impact that the person's activities as a promoter are likely to have on the collection of tax, it is inappropriate to give the person a conduct notice.

(4) Subsection (1) does not apply if a conduct notice or monitoring notice already has effect in relation to the person.

(5) For the purposes of this Part a conduct notice "relies on a Case 3 relevant defeat" if it could not have been given under the following condition.

The condition is that paragraph 9 of Schedule 34A had effect with the substitution of "100% of the tested arrangements" for "75% of the tested arrangements".

237C When a conduct notice given under section 237A(8) is "provisional"

(1) This section applies to a conduct notice which—

(a) is given to a person under section 237A(8), and

(b) relies on a Case 3 relevant defeat.

(2) The notice is "provisional" at all times when it has effect, unless an authorised officer notifies the person that the notice is no longer provisional.

(3) An authorised officer must notify the person that the notice is no longer provisional if subsection (4) or (5) applies.

(4) This subsection applies if—

(a) the condition in subsection (5)(a) is not met, and

(b) a full relevant defeat occurs in relation to P.

(5) This subsection applies if—

(a) two, or all three, of the relevant defeats by reference to which the conduct notice is given would not have been relevant defeats if paragraph 9 of Schedule 34A had effect with the substitution of "100% of the tested arrangements" for "75% of the tested arrangements", and

(b) the same number of full relevant defeats occur in relation to P.

(6) A "full relevant defeat" occurs in relation to P if—

(a) a relevant defeat occurs in relation to P otherwise than by virtue of Case 3 in paragraph 9 of Schedule 34A, or

(b) circumstances arise which would be a relevant defeat in relation to P by virtue of paragraph 9 of Schedule 34A if that paragraph had effect with the substitution of "100% of the tested arrangements" for "75% of the tested arrangements".

(7) In determining under subsection (6) whether a full relevant defeat has occurred in relation to P, assume that in paragraph 6 of Schedule 34A (provision limiting what can amount to a further relevant defeat in relation to a person) the first reference to a "relevant defeat" does not include a relevant defeat by virtue of Case 3 in paragraph 9 of Schedule 34A.

237D Judicial ruling upholding asserted tax advantage: effect on conduct notice which is provisional

(1) Subsection (2) applies if at any time—

(a) a conduct notice which relies on a Case 3 relevant defeat (see section 237B(5)) is provisional, and
(b) a court or tribunal upholds a corresponding tax advantage which has been asserted in connection with any of the related arrangements to which that relevant defeat relates (see paragraph 5(2) of Schedule 34A).

(2) The conduct notice ceases to have effect when that judicial ruling becomes final.

(3) An authorised officer must give the person to whom the conduct notice was given a written notice stating that the conduct notice has ceased to have effect.

(4) For the purposes of this section, a tax advantage is "asserted" in connection with any arrangements if a person makes a return, claim or election on the basis that the tax advantage arises from those arrangements.

In relation to the arrangements mentioned in paragraph (b) of subsection (1) "corresponding tax advantage" means a tax advantage corresponding to any tax advantage the counteraction of which contributed to the relevant defeat mentioned in that paragraph.

(5) For the purposes of this section a court or tribunal "upholds" a tax advantage if—

(a) the court or tribunal makes a ruling to the effect that no part of the tax advantage is to be counteracted, and
(b) that judicial ruling is final.

(6) For the purposes of this Part a judicial ruling is "final" if it is—

(a) a ruling of the Supreme Court, or
(b) a ruling of any other court or tribunal in circumstances where—

  (i) no appeal may be made against the ruling,
  (ii) if an appeal may be made against the ruling with permission, the time limit for applications has expired and either no application has been made or permission has been refused,
  (iii) if such permission to appeal against the ruling has been granted or is not required, no appeal has been made within the time limit for appeals, or
  (iv) if an appeal was made, it was abandoned or otherwise disposed of before it was determined by the court or tribunal to which it was addressed.

(7) In this section references to "counteraction" include anything referred to as a counteraction in any of Conditions A to F in paragraphs 11 to 16 of Schedule 34A."

(3) After section 241 insert—

"Defeat notices

241A Defeat notices

(1) This section applies in relation to a person ("P") only if P is carrying on a business as a promoter.

(2) An authorised officer, or an officer of Revenue and Customs with the approval of an authorised officer, may give P a notice if the officer concerned has become aware of one (and only one) relevant defeat which has occurred in relation to P in the period of 3 years ending with the day on which the notice is given.

(3) An authorised officer, or an officer of Revenue and Customs with the approval of an authorised officer, may give P a notice if the officer concerned has become aware of two (but not more than two) relevant defeats which have occurred in relation to P in the period of 3 years ending with the day on which the notice is given.

(4) A notice under this section must be given by the end of the 90 days beginning with the day on which the matters mentioned in subsection (2) or (as the case may be) (3) come to the attention of HMRC.

(5) Subsection (6) applies if—

(a) a single defeat notice which had been given to P (under subsection (2) or (6)) ceases to have effect as a result of section 241B(1), and
(b) in the period when the defeat notice had effect a relevant defeat ("the further relevant defeat") occurred in relation to P.

(6) An authorised officer or an officer of Revenue and Customs with the approval of an authorised officer may give P a notice in respect of the further relevant defeat (regardless of whether or not it occurred in the period of 3 years ending with the day on which the notice is given).

(7) In this Part—

    (a) "single defeat notice" means a notice under subsection (2) or (6);

    (b) "double defeat notice" means a notice under subsection (3);

    (c) "defeat notice" means a single defeat notice or a double defeat notice.

(8) A defeat notice must—

    (a) set out the dates on which the look-forward period for the notice begins and ends;

    (b) in the case of a single defeat notice, explain the effect of section 237A(12);

    (c) in the case of a double defeat notice, explain the effect of section 237A(13).

(9) HMRC may specify what further information must be included in a defeat notice.

(10) "Look-forward period"—

    (a) in relation to a defeat notice under subsection (2) or (3), means the period of 5 years beginning with the day after the day on which the notice is given;

    (b) in relation to a defeat notice under subsection (6), means the period beginning with the day after the day on which the notice is given and ending at the end of the period of 5 years beginning with the day on which the further relevant defeat mentioned in subsection (6) occurred in relation to P.

(11) A defeat notice has effect throughout its look-forward period unless it ceases to have effect earlier in accordance with section 241B(1) or (4).

241B   Judicial ruling upholding asserted tax advantage: effect on defeat notice

(1) If the relevant defeat to which a single defeat notice relates is overturned (see subsection (5)), the notice has no further effect on and after the day on which it is overturned.

(2) Subsection (3) applies if one (and only one) of the relevant defeats in respect of which a double defeat notice was given is overturned.

(3) The notice is to be treated for the purposes of this Part (including this section) as if it had always been a single defeat notice given (in respect of the other of the two relevant defeats) on the date on which the notice was in fact given.

The look-forward period for the notice is accordingly unchanged.

(4) If both the relevant defeats to which a double defeat notice relates are overturned (on the same date), that notice has no further effect on and after that date.

(5) A relevant defeat specified in a defeat notice is "overturned" if—

    (a) the notice could not have specified that relevant defeat if paragraph 9 of Schedule 34A had effect with the substitution of "100% of the tested arrangements" for "75% of the tested arrangements", and

    (b) at a time when the notice has effect a court or tribunal upholds a corresponding tax advantage which has been asserted in connection with any of the related arrangements to which the relevant defeat relates (see paragraph 5(2) of Schedule 34A).

Accordingly the relevant defeat is overturned on the day on which the judicial ruling mentioned in paragraph (b) becomes final.

(6) If a defeat notice ceases to have effect as a result of subsection (1) or (4) an authorised officer, or an officer of Revenue and Customs with the approval of an authorised officer, must notify the person to whom the notice was given that it has ceased to have effect.

(7) If subsection (3) has effect in relation to a defeat notice, an authorised officer, or an officer of Revenue and Customs with the approval of an authorised officer, must notify the person of the effect of that subsection.

(8) For the purposes of this section, a tax advantage is "asserted" in connection with any arrangements if a person makes a return, claim or election on the basis that the tax advantage arises from those arrangements.

(9) In relation to the arrangements mentioned in paragraph (b) of subsection (5) "corresponding tax advantage" means a tax advantage corresponding to any tax advantage the counteraction of which contributed to the relevant defeat mentioned in that paragraph.

(10) For the purposes of this section a court or tribunal "upholds" a tax advantage if—

    (a) the court or tribunal makes a ruling to the effect that no part of the tax advantage is to be counteracted, and

    (b) that judicial ruling is final.

(11) In this section references to "counteraction" include anything referred to as a counteraction in any of Conditions A to F in paragraphs 11 to 16 of Schedule 34A."

(4) In section 242 (monitoring notices: duty to apply to tribunal), after subsection (5) insert—

"(6) At a time when a notice given under section 237A is provisional, no determination is to be made under subsection (1) in respect of the notice.

(7) If a promoter fails to comply with conditions in a conduct notice at a time when the conduct notice is provisional, nothing in subsection (6) prevents those failures from being taken into account under subsection (1) at any subsequent time when the conduct notice is not provisional."

(5) After Schedule 34 insert—

"SCHEDULE 34A

PROMOTERS OF TAX AVOIDANCE SCHEMES: DEFEATED ARRANGEMENTS

PART 1

INTRODUCTION

1 In this Schedule—

(a) Part 2 is about the meaning of "relevant defeat";
(b) Part 3 contains provision about when a relevant defeat is treated as occurring in relation to a person;
(c) Part 4 contains provision about when a person is treated as meeting a condition in subsection (11), (12) or (13) of section 237A;
(d) Part 5 contains definitions and other supplementary provisions.

PART 2

MEANING OF "RELEVANT DEFEAT"

"Related" arrangements

2 (1) For the purposes of this Part of this Act, separate arrangements which persons have entered into are "related" to one another if (and only if) they are substantially the same.

(2) Sub-paragraphs (3) to (6) set out cases in which arrangements are to be treated as being "substantially the same" (if they would not otherwise be so treated under sub-paragraph (1)).

(3) Arrangements to which the same reference number has been allocated under Part 7 of FA 2004 (disclosure of tax avoidance schemes) are treated as being substantially the same.

For this purpose arrangements in relation to which information relating to a reference number has been provided in compliance with section 312 of FA 2004 are treated as arrangements to which that reference number has been allocated under Part 7 of that Act.

(4) Arrangements to which the same reference number has been allocated under paragraph 9 of Schedule 11A to VATA 1994 (disclosure of avoidance schemes) are treated as being substantially the same.

(5) Any two or more sets of arrangements which are the subject of follower notices given by reference to the same judicial ruling are treated as being substantially the same.

(6) Where a notice of binding has been given in relation to any arrangements ("the bound arrangements") on the basis that they are, for the purposes of Schedule 43A to FA 2013, equivalent arrangements in relation to another set of arrangements (the "lead arrangements")—

(a) the bound arrangements and the lead arrangements are treated as being substantially the same, and
(b) the bound arrangements are treated as being substantially the same as any other arrangements which, as a result of this sub-paragraph, are treated as substantially the same as the lead arrangements.

"Promoted arrangements"

3 (1) For the purposes of this Schedule arrangements are "promoted arrangements" in relation to a person if—

(a) they are relevant arrangements or would be relevant arrangements under the condition stated in sub-paragraph (2), and

(b) the person is carrying on a business as a promoter and—

(i) the person is or has been a promoter in relation to the arrangements, or

(ii) that would be the case if the condition in sub-paragraph (2) were met.

(2) That condition is that the definition of "tax" in section 283 includes, and has always included, value added tax.

Relevant defeat of single arrangements

4 (1) A defeat of arrangements (entered into by any person) which are promoted arrangements in relation to a person ("the promoter") is a "relevant defeat" in relation to the promoter if the condition in sub-paragraph (2) is met.

(2) The condition is that the arrangements are not related to any other arrangements which are promoted arrangements in relation to the promoter.

(3) For the meaning of "defeat" see paragraphs 10 to 16.

Relevant defeat of related arrangements

5 (1) This paragraph applies if arrangements (entered into by any person) ("Set A")—

(a) are promoted arrangements in relation to a person ("P"), and

(b) are related to other arrangements which are promoted arrangements in relation to P.

(2) If Case 1, 2 or 3 applies (see paragraphs 7 to 9) a relevant defeat occurs in relation to P and each of the related arrangements.

(3) "The related arrangements" means Set A and the arrangements mentioned in sub-paragraph (1)(b).

Limit on number of separate relevant defeats in relation to the same, or related, arrangements

6 In relation to a person, if there has been a relevant defeat of arrangements (whether under paragraph 4 or 5) there cannot be a further relevant defeat of

(a) those particular arrangements, or

(b) arrangements which are related to those arrangements.

Case 1: counteraction upheld by judicial ruling

7 (1) Case 1 applies if—

(a) any of Conditions A to E is met in relation to any of the related arrangements, and

(b) in the case of those arrangements the decision to make the relevant counteraction has been upheld by a judicial ruling (which is final).

(2) In sub-paragraph (1) "the relevant counteraction" means the counteraction mentioned in paragraph 11(d), 12(1)(b), 13(1)(d), 14(1)(d) or 15(1)(d) (as the case requires).

Case 2: judicial ruling that avoidance-related rule applies

8 Case 2 applies if Condition F is met in relation to any of the related arrangements.

Case 3: proportion-based relevant defeat

9 (1) Case 3 applies if—

(a) at least 75% of the tested arrangements have been defeated, and

(b) no final judicial ruling in relation to any of the related arrangements has upheld a corresponding tax advantage which has been asserted in connection with any of the related arrangements.

(2) In this paragraph "the tested arrangements" means so many of the related arrangements (as defined in paragraph 5(3)) as meet the condition in sub-paragraph (3) or (4).

(3) Particular arrangements meet this condition if a person has made a return, claim or election on the basis that a tax advantage results from those arrangements and—

(a) there has been an enquiry or investigation by HMRC into the return, claim or election, or

(b) HMRC assesses the person to tax on the basis that the tax advantage (or any part of it) does not arise, or

(c) a GAAR counteraction notice has been given in relation to the tax advantage or part of it and the arrangements.

(4) Particular arrangements meet this condition if HMRC takes other action on the basis that a tax advantage which might be expected to arise from those arrangements, or is asserted in connection with them, does not arise.

(5) For the purposes of this paragraph a tax advantage has been "asserted" in connection with particular arrangements if a person has made a return, claim or election on the basis that the tax advantage arises from those arrangements.

(6) In sub-paragraph (1)(b) "corresponding tax advantage" means a tax advantage corresponding to any tax advantage the counteraction of which is taken into account by HMRC for the purposes of sub-paragraph (1)(a).

(7) For the purposes of this paragraph a court or tribunal "upholds" a tax advantage if—

(a) the court or tribunal makes a ruling to the effect that no part of the tax advantage is to be counteracted, and

(b) that judicial ruling is final.

(8) In this paragraph references to "counteraction" include anything referred to as a counteraction in any of Conditions A to F in paragraphs 11 to 16.

(9) In this paragraph "GAAR counteraction notice" means—

(a) a notice such as is mentioned in sub-paragraph (2) of paragraph 12 of Schedule 43 to FA 2013 (notice of final decision to counteract),

(b) a notice under paragraph 8(2) or 9(2) of Schedule 43A to that Act (pooling or binding of arrangements) stating that the tax advantage is to be counteracted under the general anti-abuse rule, or

(c) a notice under paragraph 8(2) of Schedule 43B to that Act (generic referrals) stating that the tax advantage is to be counteracted under the general anti-abuse rule.

"Defeat" of arrangements

10 For the purposes of this Part of this Act a "defeat" of arrangements occurs if any of Conditions A to F (in paragraphs 11 to 16) is met in relation to the arrangements.

11 Condition A is that—

(a) a person has made a return, claim or election on the basis that a tax advantage arises from the arrangements,

(b) a notice given to the person under paragraph 12 of Schedule 43 to, paragraph 8(2) or 9(2) of Schedule 43A to or paragraph 8(2) of Schedule 43B to FA 2013 stated that the tax advantage was to be counteracted under the general anti-abuse rule,

(c) the tax advantage has been counteracted (in whole or in part) under the general anti-abuse rule, and

(d) the counteraction is final.

12 (1) Condition B is that a follower notice has been given to a person by reference to the arrangements (and not withdrawn) and—

(a) the person has complied with subsection (2) of section 208 of FA 2014 by taking the action specified in subsections (4) to (6) of that section in respect of the denied tax advantage (or part of it), or

(b) the denied tax advantage has been counteracted (in whole or in part) otherwise than as mentioned in paragraph (a) and the counteraction is final.

(2) In this paragraph "the denied tax advantage" is to be interpreted in accordance with section 208(3) of FA 2014.

(3) In this Schedule "follower notice" means a follower notice under Chapter 2 of Part 4 of FA 2014.

13 (1) Condition C is that—

(a) the arrangements are DOTAS arrangements,

(b) a person ("the taxpayer") has made a return, claim or election on the basis that a relevant tax advantage arises,

(c) the relevant tax advantage has been counteracted, and

(d) the counteraction is final.

(2) For the purposes of sub-paragraph (1) "relevant tax advantage" means a tax advantage which the arrangements might be expected to enable the taxpayer to obtain.

(3) For the purposes of this paragraph the relevant tax advantage is "counteracted" if adjustments are made in respect of the taxpayer's tax position on the basis that the whole or part of that tax advantage does not arise.

14 (1) Condition D is that—

(a) the arrangements are disclosable VAT arrangements to which a taxable person is a party,

(b) the taxable person has made a return or claim on the basis that a relevant tax advantage arises,

(c) the relevant tax advantage has been counteracted, and

(d) the counteraction is final.

(2) For the purposes of sub-paragraph (1) "relevant tax advantage" means a tax advantage which the arrangements might be expected to enable the taxable person to obtain.

(3) For the purposes of this paragraph the relevant tax advantage is "counteracted" if adjustments are made in respect of the taxable person's tax position on the basis that the whole or part of that tax advantage does not arise.

15 (1) Condition E is that the arrangements are disclosable VAT arrangements to which a taxable person ("T") is a party and—

(a) the arrangements relate to the position with respect to VAT of a person other than T ("S") who has made supplies of goods or services to T,

(b) the arrangements might be expected to enable T to obtain a tax advantage in connection with those supplies of goods or services,

(c) the arrangements have been counteracted, and

(d) the counteraction is final.

(2) For the purposes of this paragraph the arrangements are "counteracted" if—

(a) HMRC assess S to tax or take any other action on a basis which prevents T from obtaining (or obtaining the whole of) the tax advantage in question, or

(b) adjustments are made on a basis such as is mentioned in paragraph (a).

16 (1) Condition F is that—

(a) a person has made a return, claim or election on the basis that a relevant tax advantage arises,

(b) the tax advantage, or part of the tax advantage would not arise if a particular avoidance-related rule (see paragraph 25) applies in relation to the person's tax affairs,

(c) it is held in a judicial ruling that the relevant avoidance-related rule applies in relation to the person's tax affairs, and

(d) the judicial ruling is final.

(2) For the purposes of sub-paragraph (1) "relevant tax advantage" means a tax advantage which the arrangements might be expected to enable the person to obtain.

PART 3

RELEVANT DEFEATS: ASSOCIATED PERSONS

Attribution of relevant defeats

17 (1) Sub-paragraph (2) applies if—

(a) there is (or has been) a person ("Q"),

(b) arrangements ("the defeated arrangements") have been entered into,

(c) an event occurs such that either—

(i) there is a relevant defeat in relation to Q and the defeated arrangements, or

(ii) the condition in sub-paragraph (i) would be met if Q had not ceased to exist,

(d) at the time of that event a person ("P") is carrying on a business as a promoter (or is carrying on what would be such a business under the condition in paragraph 3(2)), and

(e) Condition 1 or 2 is met in relation to Q and P.

(2) The event is treated for all purposes of this Part of this Act as a relevant defeat in relation to P and the defeated arrangements (whether or not it is also a relevant defeat in relation to Q, and regardless of whether or not P existed at any time when those arrangements were promoted arrangements in relation to Q).

(3) Condition 1 is that—

(a) P is not an individual,

(b) at a time when the defeated arrangements were promoted arrangements in relation to Q—

      (i) P was a relevant body controlled by Q, or

      (ii) Q was a relevant body controlled by P, and

  (c) at the time of the event mentioned in sub-paragraph (1)(c)—

      (i) Q is a relevant body controlled by P,

      (ii) P is a relevant body controlled by Q, or

      (iii) P and Q are relevant bodies controlled by a third person.

(4) Condition 2 is that—

  (a) P and Q are relevant bodies,

  (b) at a time when the defeated arrangements were promoted arrangements in relation to Q, a third person ("C") controlled Q, and

  (c) C controls P at the time of the event mentioned in sub-paragraph (1)(c).

(5) For the purposes of sub-paragraphs (3)(b) and (4)(b), the question whether arrangements are promoted arrangements in relation to Q at any time is to be determined on the assumption that the reference to "design" in paragraph (b) of section 235(3) (definition of "promoter" in relation to relevant arrangements) is omitted.

Deemed defeat notices

18 (1) This paragraph applies if—

  (a) an authorised officer becomes aware at any time ("the relevant time") that a relevant defeat has occurred in relation to a person ("P") who is carrying on a business as a promoter,

  (b) there have occurred, more than 3 years before the relevant time—

      (i) one third party defeat, or

      (ii) two third party defeats, and

  (c) conditions A1 and B1 (in a case within paragraph (b)(i)), or conditions A2 and B2 (in a case within paragraph (b)(ii)), are met.

(2) Where this paragraph applies by virtue of sub-paragraph (1)(b)(i), this Part of this Act has effect as if an authorised officer had (with due authority), at the time of the time of the third party defeat, given P a single defeat notice under section 241A(2) in respect of it.

(3) Where this paragraph applies by virtue of sub-paragraph (1)(b)(ii), this Part of this Act has effect as if an authorised officer had (with due authority), at the time of the second of the two third party defeats, given P a double defeat notice under section 241A(3) in respect of the two third party defeats.

(4) Section 241A(8) has no effect in relation to a notice treated as given as mentioned in sub-paragraph (2) or (3).

(5) Condition A1 is that—

  (a) a conduct notice or a single or double defeat notice has been given to the other person (see sub-paragraph (9)) in respect of the third party defeat,

  (b) at the time of the third party defeat an authorised officer would have had power by virtue of paragraph 17 to give P a defeat notice in respect of the third party defeat, had the officer been aware that it was a relevant defeat in relation to P, and

  (c) so far as the authorised officer mentioned in sub-paragraph (1)(a) is aware, the conditions for giving P a defeat notice in respect of the third party defeat have never been met (ignoring this paragraph).

(6) Condition A2 is that—

  (a) a conduct notice or a single or double defeat notice has been given to the other person (see sub-paragraph (9)) in respect of each, or both, of the third party defeats,

  (b) at the time of the second third party defeat an authorised officer would have had power by virtue of paragraph 17 to give P a double defeat notice in respect of the third party defeats, had the officer been aware that either of the third party defeats was a relevant defeat in relation to P, and

  (c) so far as the authorised officer mentioned in sub-paragraph (1)(a) is aware, the conditions for giving P a defeat notice in respect of those third party defeats (or either of them) have never been met (ignoring this paragraph).

(7) Condition B1 is that, had an authorised officer given P a defeat notice in respect of the third party defeat at the time of that relevant defeat, that defeat notice would still have effect at the relevant time (see sub-paragraph (1)).

(8) Condition B2 is that, had an authorised officer given P a defeat notice in respect of the two third party defeats at the time of the second of those relevant defeats, that defeat notice would still have effect at the relevant time.

(9) In this paragraph "third party defeat" means a relevant defeat which has occurred in relation to a person other than P.

Meaning of "relevant body" and "control"

19 (1) In this Part of this Schedule "relevant body" means—

    (a) a body corporate, or

    (b) a partnership.

(2) For the purposes of this Part of this Schedule a person controls a body corporate if the person has power to secure that the affairs of the body corporate are conducted in accordance with the person's wishes—

    (a) by means of the holding of shares or the possession of voting power in relation to the body corporate or any other relevant body,

    (b) as a result of any powers conferred by the articles of association or other document regulating the body corporate or any other relevant body, or

    (c) by means of controlling a partnership.

(3) For the purposes of this Part of this Schedule a person controls a partnership if the person is a controlling member or the managing partner of the partnership.

(4) In this paragraph "controlling member" has the same meaning as in Schedule 36 (partnerships).

(5) In this paragraph "managing partner", in relation to a partnership, means the member of the partnership who directs, or is on a day-to-day level in control of, the management of the business of the partnership.

PART 4

MEETING SECTION 237A CONDITIONS: BODIES CORPORATE
AND PARTNERSHIPS

Treating persons under another's control as meeting section 237A condition

20 (1) A relevant body ("RB") is treated as meeting a section 237A condition at the section 237A(2) relevant time if—

    (a) that condition was met by a person ("C") at a time when—

        (i) C was carrying on a business as a promoter, or

        (ii) RB was carrying on a business as a promoter and C controlled RB, and

    (b) RB is controlled by C at the section 237A(2) relevant time.

(2) Sub-paragraph (1) does not apply if C is an individual.

(3) For the purposes of determining whether the requirements of sub-paragraph (1) are met by reason of meeting the requirement in sub-paragraph (1)(a)(i), it does not matter whether RB existed at the time when C met the section 237A condition.

Treating persons in control of others as meeting section 237A condition

21 (1) A person other than an individual is treated as meeting a section 237A condition at the section 237A(2) relevant time if—

    (a) a relevant body ("A") met the condition at a time when A was controlled by the person, and

    (b) at the time mentioned in paragraph (a) A, or another relevant body ("B") which was also at that time controlled by the person, carried on a business as a promoter.

(2) For the purposes of determining whether the requirements of sub-paragraph (1) are met it does not matter whether A or B (or neither) exists at the section 237A(2) relevant time.

Treating persons controlled by the same person as meeting section 237A condition

22 (1) A relevant body ("RB") is treated as meeting a section 237A condition at the section 237A(2) relevant time if—

    (a) another relevant body met that condition at a time ("time T") when it was controlled by a person ("C"),

    (b) at time T, there was a relevant body controlled by C which carried on a business as a promoter, and

(c) RB is controlled by C at the section 237A(2) relevant time.

(2) For the purposes of determining whether the requirements of sub-paragraph (1) are met it does not matter whether—

(a) RB existed at time T, or

(b) any relevant body (other than RB) by reason of which the requirements of sub-paragraph (1) are met exists at the section 237A(2) relevant time.

Interpretation

23 (1) In this Part of this Schedule—

"control" has the same meaning as in Part 3 of this Schedule;

"relevant body" has the same meaning as in Part 3 of this Schedule;

"section 237A(2) relevant time" means the time referred to in section 237A(2);

"section 237A condition" means any of the conditions in section 237A(11), (12) and (13).

(2) For the purposes of paragraphs 20(1)(a), 21(1)(a) and 22(1)(a), the condition in section 237A(11) (occurrence of 3 relevant defeats in the 3 years ending with the relevant time) is taken to have been met by a person at any time if at least 3 relevant defeats have occurred in relation to the person in the period of 3 years ending with that time.

PART 5

SUPPLEMENTARY

"Adjustments"

24 In this Schedule "adjustments" means any adjustments, whether by way of an assessment, the modification of an assessment or return, the amendment or disallowance of a claim, the entering into of a contract settlement or otherwise (and references to "making" adjustments accordingly include securing that adjustments are made by entering into a contract settlement).

Meaning of "avoidance-related rule"

25 (1) In this Schedule "avoidance-related rule" means a rule in Category 1 or 2.

(2) A rule is in Category 1 if—

(a) it refers (in whatever terms) to the purpose or main purpose or purposes of a transaction, arrangements or any other action or matter, and

(b) to whether or not the purpose in question is or involves the avoidance of tax or the obtaining of any advantage in relation to tax (however described).

(3) A rule is also in Category 1 if it refers (in whatever terms) to—

(a) expectations as to what are, or may be, the expected benefits of a transaction, arrangements or any other action or matter, and

(b) whether or not the avoidance of tax or the obtaining of any advantage in relation to tax (however described) is such a benefit.

For the purposes of paragraph (b) it does not matter whether the reference is (for instance) to the "sole or main benefit" or "one of the main benefits" or any other reference to a benefit.

(4) A rule falls within Category 2 if as a result of the rule a person may be treated differently for tax purposes depending on whether or not purposes referred to in the rule (for instance the purposes of an actual or contemplated action or enterprise) are (or are shown to be) commercial purposes.

(5) For example, a rule in the following form would fall within Category 1 and within Category 2—

"Example rule

Section X does not apply to a company in respect of a transaction if the company shows that the transaction meets Condition A or B.

Condition A is that the transaction is effected—

(a) for genuine commercial reasons, or

(b) in the ordinary course of managing investments.

Condition B is that the avoidance of tax is not the main object or one of the main objects of the transaction."

"DOTAS arrangements"

26 (1) For the purposes of this Schedule arrangements are "DOTAS arrangements" at any time if at that time a person—

(a) has provided, information in relation to the arrangements under section 308(3), 309 or 310 of FA 2004, or

(b) has failed to comply with any of those provisions in relation to the arrangements.

(2) But for the purposes of this Schedule "DOTAS arrangements" does not include arrangements in respect of which HMRC has given notice under section 312(6) of FA 2004 (notice that promoters not under duty to notify client of reference number).

(3) For the purposes of sub-paragraph (1) a person who would be required to provide information under subsection (3) of section 308 of FA 2004—

(a) but for the fact that the arrangements implement a proposal in respect of which notice has been given under subsection (1) of that section, or

(b) but for subsection (4A), (4C) or (5) of that section,

is treated as providing the information at the end of the period referred to in subsection (3) of that section.

"Disclosable VAT arrangements"

27 For the purposes of this Schedule arrangements are "disclosable VAT arrangements" at any time if at that time—

(a) a person has complied with paragraph 6 of Schedule 11A to VATA 1994 in relation to the arrangements (duty to notify Commissioners),

(b) a person under a duty to comply with that paragraph in relation to the arrangements has failed to do so, or

(c) a reference number has been allocated to the scheme under paragraph 9 of that Schedule (voluntary notification of avoidance scheme which is not a designated scheme).

Paragraphs 26 and 27: supplementary

28 (1) A person "fails to comply" with any provision mentioned in paragraph 26(1)(a) or 27(b) if and only if any of the conditions in sub-paragraphs (2) to (4) is met.

(2) The condition in this sub-paragraph is that—

(a) the tribunal has determined that the person has failed to comply with the provision concerned,

(b) the appeal period has ended, and

(c) the determination has not been overturned on appeal.

(3) The condition in this sub-paragraph is that—

(a) the tribunal has determined for the purposes of section 118(2) of TMA 1970 that the person is to be deemed not to have failed to comply with the provision concerned as the person had a reasonable excuse for not doing the thing required to be done,

(b) the appeal period has ended, and

(c) the determination has not been overturned on appeal.

(4) The condition in this sub-paragraph is that the person admitted in writing to HMRC that the person has failed to comply with the provision concerned.

(5) In this paragraph "the appeal period" means—

(a) the period during which an appeal could be brought against the determination of the tribunal, or

(b) where an appeal mentioned in paragraph (a) has been brought, the period during which that appeal has not been finally determined, withdrawn or otherwise disposed of.

"Final" counteraction

29 For the purposes of this Schedule the counteraction of a tax advantage or of arrangements is "final" when the assessment or adjustments made to effect the counteraction, and any amounts arising as a result of the assessment or adjustments, can no longer be varied, on appeal or otherwise.

Inheritance tax, stamp duty reserve tax, VAT and petroleum revenue tax

30 (1) In this Schedule, in relation to inheritance tax, each of the following is treated as a return—

(a) an account delivered by a person under section 216 or 217 of IHTA 1984 (including an account delivered in accordance with regulations under section 256 of that Act);

(b) a statement or declaration which amends or is otherwise connected with such an account produced by the person who delivered the account;

(c) information or a document provided by a person in accordance with regulations under section 256 of that Act;

and such a return is treated as made by the person in question.

(2) In this Schedule references to an assessment to tax, in relation to inheritance tax, stamp duty reserve tax and petroleum revenue tax, include a determination.

(3) In this Schedule an expression used in relation to VAT has the same meaning as in VATA 1994.

Power to amend

31 (1) The Treasury may by regulations amend this Schedule (apart from this paragraph).

(2) An amendment by virtue of sub-paragraph (1) may, in particular, add, vary or remove conditions or categories (or otherwise vary the meaning of "avoidance-related rule").

(3) Regulations under sub-paragraph (1) may include any amendment of this Part of this Act that is appropriate in consequence of an amendment made by virtue of sub-paragraph (1)."

(6) In section 241 (duration of conduct notice), after subsection (4) insert—

"(5) See also section 237D(2) (provisional conduct notice affected by judicial ruling)."

(7) After section 281 insert—

"281A VAT

(1) In the provisions mentioned in subsection (2)—

(a) "tax" includes value added tax, and

(b) "tax advantage" has the meaning given by section 234(3) and also includes a tax advantage as defined in paragraph 1 of Schedule 11A to VATA 1994.

(2) Those provisions are—

(a) section 237D;

(b) section 241B;

(c) Schedule 34A.

(3) Other references in this Part to "tax" are to be read as including value added tax so far as that is necessary for the purposes of sections 237A to 237D, 241A and 241B and Schedule 34A; but "tax" does not include value added tax in section 237A(10) or 237B(3)."

(8) In section 282 (regulations), in subsection (3), after paragraph (b) insert—

"(ba) paragraph 31 of Schedule 34A,".

(9) In section 283(1) (interpretation of Part 5)—

(a) in the definition of "conduct notice", after paragraph (a) insert—

"(aa) section 237A(8),

(ab) section 237B(1),";

(b) in the definition of "tax", after ""tax"" insert "(except in provisions to which section 281A applies)";

(c) in the definition of ""tax advantage"", after "234(3)" insert "(but see also section 281A)";

(d) at the appropriate places insert—

"""contract settlement" means an agreement in connection with a person's liability to make a payment to the Commissioners under or by virtue of an enactment;"

"""defeat", in relation to arrangements, has the meaning given by paragraph 10 of Schedule 34A;"

"""defeat notice" has the meaning given by section 241A(7);"

"""double defeat notice" has the meaning given by section 241A(7);"

"""final", in relation to a judicial ruling, is to be interpreted in accordance with section 237D(6);"

"""judicial ruling" means a ruling of a court or tribunal on one or more issues;"

"""look-forward period, in relation to a defeat notice, has the meaning given by section 241A(10);"

"""provisional", in relation to a conduct notice given under section 237A(8), is to be interpreted in accordance with section 237C;"

"""relevant defeat", in relation to a person, is to be interpreted in accordance with Schedule 34A;"

""related", in relation to arrangements, is to be interpreted in accordance with paragraph 2 of Schedule 34A;"
""relies on a Case 3 relevant defeat" is to be interpreted in accordance section 237B(5);"
""single defeat notice" has the meaning given by section 241A(7)."

(10) Schedule 36 (promoters of tax avoidance schemes: partnerships) is amended in accordance with subsections (11) to (16).

(11) In Part 2, before paragraph 5 insert—

"Defeat notices

4A A defeat notice that is given to a partnership must state that it is a partnership defeat notice.".

(12) In paragraph 7(1)(b) after "a" insert "defeat notice,".

(13) In paragraph 7(2) after "the" insert "defeat notice,".

(14) After paragraph 7 insert—

"Persons leaving partnership: defeat notices

7A (1) Sub-paragraphs (2) and (3) apply where—

(a) a person ("P") who was a controlling member of a partnership at the time when a defeat notice ("the original notice") was given to the partnership has ceased to be a member of the partnership,

(b) the defeat notice had effect in relation to the partnership at the time of that cessation, and

(c) P is carrying on a business as a promoter.

(2) An authorised officer may give P a defeat notice.

(3) If P is carrying on a business as a promoter in partnership with one or more other persons and is a controlling member of that partnership ("the new partnership"), an authorised officer may give a defeat notice to the new partnership.

(4) A defeat notice given under sub-paragraph (3) ceases to have effect if P ceases to be a member of the new partnership.

(5) A notice under sub-paragraph (2) or (3) may not be given after the original notice has ceased to have effect.

(6) A defeat notice given under sub-paragraph (2) or (3) is given in respect of the relevant defeat or relevant defeats to which the original notice relates."

(15) In paragraph 10—

(a) in sub-paragraph (1)(b) for "conduct notice or a" substitute ", defeat notice, conduct notice or";

(b) in sub-paragraph (3), after "partner—" insert—

"(za) a defeat notice (if the original notice is a defeat notice);".

(c) in sub-paragraph (4), after "("the new partnership")—" insert—

"(za) a defeat notice (if the original notice is a defeat notice);"

(d) after sub-paragraph (5) insert—

"(5A) A notice under sub-paragraph (3)(za) or (4)(za) may not be given after the end of the look-forward period of the original notice."

(16) After paragraph 11 insert—

"11A The look-forward period for a notice under paragraph 7A(2) or (3) or 10(3)(za) or (4)(za)—

(a) begins on the day after the day on which the notice is given, and

(b) continues to the end of the look-forward period for the original notice (as defined in paragraph 7A(1)(a) or 10(2), as the case may be)."

(17) Part 2 of Schedule 2 to the National Insurance Contributions Act 2015 (application of Part 5 of FA 2014 to national insurance contributions) is amended in accordance with subsections (18) and (19).

(18) After paragraph 30 insert—

"Threshold conditions

30A (1) In paragraph 5 of Schedule 34 (non-compliance with Part 7 of FA 2004), in sub-paragraph (4)—

(a) paragraph (a) includes a reference to a decision having been made for corresponding NICs purposes that P is to be deemed not to have failed to comply with the provision concerned as P had a reasonable excuse for not doing the thing required to be done, and

(b) the reference in paragraph (c) to a determination is to be read accordingly.

(2) In this paragraph "corresponding NICs purposes" means the purposes of any provision of regulations under section 132A of SSAA 1992.

Relevant defeats

30B (1) Schedule 34A (promoters of tax avoidance schemes: defeated arrangements) has effect with the following modifications.

(2) References to an assessment (or an assessment to tax) include a NICs decision relating to a person's liability for relevant contributions.

(3) References to adjustments include a payment in respect of a liability to pay relevant contributions (and the definition of "adjustments" in paragraph 24 accordingly has effect as if such payments were included in it).

(4) In paragraph 9(3) the reference to an enquiry into a return includes a relevant contributions dispute (as defined in paragraph 6 of this Schedule).

(5) In paragraph 28(3)—

(a) paragraph (a) includes a reference to a decision having been made for corresponding NICs purposes that the person is to be deemed not to have failed to comply with the provision concerned as the person had a reasonable excuse for not doing the thing required to be done, and

(b) the reference in paragraph (c) to a determination is to be read accordingly.

"Corresponding NICs purposes" means the purposes of any provision of regulations under section 132A of SSAA 1992."

(19) In paragraph 31 (interpretation)—

(a) before paragraph (a) insert—

"(za) NICs decision" means a decision under section 8 of SSC(TF)A 1999 or Article 7 of the Social Security Contributions (Transfer of Functions, etc) (Northern Ireland) Order 1999 (SI 1999/671);"

(b) in paragraph (b), for "are to sections of" substitute "or Schedules are to sections of, or Schedules to".

(20) For the purposes of sections 237A and 241A of FA 2014, a defeat (by virtue of any of Conditions A to F in Schedule 34A to that Act) of arrangements is treated as not having occurred if—

(a) there has been a final judicial ruling on or before the day on which this Act is passed as a result of which the counteraction referred to in paragraph 11(d), 12(1)(b), 13(1)(d), 14(1)(d) or 15(1)(d) (as the case may be) is final for the purposes of Schedule 34A of that Act, or

(b) (in the case of a defeat by virtue of Condition F in Schedule 34A) the judicial ruling mentioned in paragraph 16(1)(d) of that Schedule becomes final on or before the day on which this Act is passed.

(21) Subsection (20) does not apply in relation to a person (who is carrying on a business as a promoter) if at any time after 17 July 2014 that person or an associated person takes action as a result of which the person taking the action—

(a) becomes a promoter in relation to the arrangements, or arrangements related to those arrangements, or

(b) would have become a promoter in relation to arrangements mentioned in paragraph (a) had the person not already been a promoter in relation to those arrangements.

(22) For the purposes of sections 237A and 241A of FA 2014, a defeat of arrangements is treated as not having occurred if it would (ignoring this sub-paragraph) have occurred—

(a) on or before the first anniversary of the day on which this Act is passed, and

(b) by virtue of any of Conditions A to E in Schedule 34A to FA 2014, but otherwise than as a result of a final judicial ruling.

(23) For the purposes of subsection (21) a person ("Q") is an "associated person" in relation to another person ("P") at any time when any of the following conditions is met—

(a) P is a relevant body which is controlled by Q;

(b) Q is a relevant body, P is not an individual and Q is controlled by P;

(c) P and Q are relevant bodies and a third person controls P and Q.

(24) In subsection (23) "relevant body" and "control" are to be interpreted in accordance with paragraph 19 of Schedule 34A to FA 2014.

(25) In subsections (20) to (22) expressions used in Part 5 of FA 2014 (as amended by this section) have the same meaning as in that Part.

GENERAL NOTE

Part 5 and Schs 34–36 FA 2014

Part 5 and Schs 34–36 Finance Act 2014 introduced legislation applying to the Promoters of Tax Avoidance Schemes ("POTAS"). The legislation as introduced provided for a graduated series of sanctions against promoters:

- a conduct notice, which following a decision of an authorised officer may be issued by HMRC where one of the threshold conditions is met; and
- a monitoring notice which HMRC can issue following First Tier Tribunal approval where a promoter breaches a requirement in a conduct notice.

The thresholds conditions include where the promoter:

- is the subject of publication as a deliberate tax defaulter;
- is named in a report for a breach of the Code of Practice on Taxation for Banks;
- receives a conduct notice as a dishonest tax agent;
- failed either to disclose a tax avoidance scheme or to provide details of clients to HMRC;
- has been charged with a specified tax offence;
- has been found guilty of misconduct by a professional body;
- failed to comply with an information notice issued by HMRC;
- requires confidentiality;
- requires a contribution to a fighting fund;
- continues to market or make available a tax avoidance scheme after being given a notice to stop following a judicial ruling.

There is no right of appeal against a decision to give a promoter a conduct notice, which can last for up to two years. Conduct notices impose conditions about how a promoter must behave.

There is a right of appeal against a decision of the First-tier Tribunal to approve the issue of a monitoring notice. If a monitoring notice is issued the monitored promoter is subject to:

- publication by HMRC;
- publication by the promoter of its status on the internet, in publications and correspondence;
- a duty on the promoter to inform clients they are a monitored promoter and to provide them with a promoter reference number;
- a duty on clients to put the PRN on their returns or otherwise to report the PRN to HMRC;
- enhanced information powers for HMRC supported with new penalties;
- preventing the promoter to impose confidentiality on clients in relation to disclosure to HMRC;
- limitations to the defences of reasonable care and reasonable excuse against the imposition of penalties;
- extended time limits for assessment on clients who fail to report a PRN to HMRC;
- a criminal offence of concealing, destroying or disposing of documents.

Finance Act 2016 s 160 makes changes to the POTAS legislation, in particular, it introduces a new threshold condition, which, if met, identifies a person who is a promoter of tax avoidance schemes as a promoter to whom a provisional conduct notice or where there are three defeats within three years a conduct notice may be given.

Broadly, a provisional conduct notice is for promoters of tax avoidance schemes which have fewer than three defeated schemes and further schemes are subject to challenge and those challenges are at least 75% defeated (see further notes). Where a successful challenge results in a defeat a defeat notice is issued and a provisional conduct notice may become a full conduct notice. A full conduct notice may also be issued in circumstances where a provisional conduct notices is not complied with. Where a conduct notice is not complied with, a monitoring notice may be issued.

Section 160(1) and (2)

Introduce new ss 237A–237D into FA 2014.

New s 237A FA 2014

The new s 237A FA 2014 provides that if an authorised officer considers a promoter meets any of the conditions in sub-ss (11)–(13) they must determine if it should it be regarded as significant and whether to issue a conduct notice. Where the authorised officer determines the meeting of the condition is significant, a conduct notice must be issued (s 237A(8)) although under s 237A(10) the authorised officer may determine it is inappropriate to issue a notice having regard to the impact on the collection of taxes. The section does not apply where a conduct or monitoring notice has already been issued to the person.

Subsection (5) provides that sub-s (1) does not apply if at the same time the officer has a duty to decide whether a conduct notice must be given under s 237(5). The authorised officer must however take into account the meeting of a condition within s 237A(11)–(13) when determining under s 237(7) issuing a conduct notice.

The condition at sub-s (11) is that there are three relevant defeats in relation to the promoter in the period of three years. The condition at sub-s (12) is that there are two relevant defeats in relation to the promoter at a time when a single defeat notice under s 241A(2) or (6) had effect. The condition at sub-s (13) is that there is one relevant defeat in relation to the promoter at a time when a single defeat notice under s 241A(3) had effect. Section 241A(2) and (3) require the relevant defeat(s) to have occurred in the period of three years ending with the day on which the notice is given, whereas subsection s 241A(6) does not.

A determination within s 237A(12) or (13) cannot be made unless the defeat notice still has effect when the determination is made and after the 90th day following the expiry of the defeat notice which is in effect.

New s 237B FA 2014

Subsection (1) provides that an officer must give a conduct notice where the officer determines the promoter fails to comply with one or more of the terms of a conduct notice issued under s 237A(1) and that notice was provisional (s 237C). The promoter has not failed to comply where the failure to comply relates to the conduct notice ceases to have effect when a judicial ruling becomes final, is withdrawn by an officer or a monitoring notice takes effect.

Section 237B(1)(c) requires a conduct notice where the conduct notice relied on a Case 3 relevant defeat. Paragraph 9 of Sch 34A defines a relevant defeat within Case 3 as one where at least 75% but less than 100% of any related arrangements have been defeated and there is no final judicial ruling upholding the asserted tax advantage in relation to the arrangements or any of the related arrangements.

An authorised officer is required to issue a conduct notice if there are Case 1 or Case 2 defeats after that time, which had they occurred before the conduct notice ceased, would have resulted in the notice ceasing to be provisional.

Paragraph 7 of Sch 34A defines a relevant defeat within Case 1 as being where the asserted tax advantage has been counteracted under any of Conditions A to E in paras 11–15 of Sch 34A, and that counteraction has been upheld by a judicial ruling which is final. Condition A relates to the General Anti Abuse Rule, Condition B to follower notices, Condition C to DOTAS, and Condition D and E to disclosable VAT arrangements.

Paragraph 8 of Sch 34A defines a relevant defeat within Case 2 as being where the asserted tax advantage has been counteracted under Condition F in para 16 of Sch 34A and that counteraction has been upheld by a judicial ruling which is final. Condition F relates to applicable avoidance related rule (para 18 of Sch 34A).

This requirement is subject to sub-s (3) where if the authorised officer, having regard to the likely impact of the promoter's activities on the collection of tax, determines that a conduct notice is inappropriate.

New s 237C FA 2014

A conduct notice is issued where there are three relevant defeats (s 237A(6), (7) and (8)) within a period of three years.

A conduct notice given under the new s 237A(4) is to be treated as provisional. The notice relies on at least one of the relevant defeats being a Case 3 relevant defeat (para 9 of new Sch 34A). A Case 3 defeat is where HMRC are aware that at least 75% but fewer than 100% of the users of the tested arrangements have been defeated and there is no judicial ruling upholding the purported tax advantage. The condition in sub-s 5(a) requires reading para 9 of Sch 34A and replacing the 75% with 100%, which has the effect of a Case 3 defeat for these purposes being where 100% of the tested arrangements have been defeated and no judicial ruling upholding the purported tax advantage.

Therefore, the provisional notice relies on a Case 3 not becoming a full relevant defeat, which could occur because of a final judicial ruling counteracting all of part of the tax advantage or because all users of the arrangements have been defeated.

Under sub-s (3) an authorised officer must notify the person that the notice is no longer provisional if the condition in subsection 5(a) is *not* met and a full relevant defeat occurs in relation to the promoter.

New s 237D FA 2014

Section 237D provides that a provisional conduct notice relying on a Case 3 relevant defeat will ceases to have effect if a court or tribunal upholds an asserted tax advantage in any of the related arrangements to which the Case 3 relevant defeat relates.

Subsection (6) sets out when a judicial ruling is "final".

Section 160(3)

Subsection (3) introduces new ss 241A and 241B into FA 2014.

New s 241A FA 2014

Where an officer becomes aware of either one or two relevant defeats occurring in relation to a promoter, s 241A provides that an authorised officer or an officer with approval from an authorised officer may issue a defeat notice. The relevant defeat must have been within the period of three years ending with the day on which the notice is given. A notice must be given by the end of 90 days beginning with the day on which matters come to the attention of HMRC.

Subsection 5 sets out the circumstances in which sub-s 6 applies. The circumstances are that a defeat notice ceases to have effect as a result of s 241B(1) and there is a further relevant defeat which occurred to the promoter. An authorised officer or officer with approval from an authorised officer may give a notice in respect of the further relevant defeat regardless of the three-year period set out for the first relevant defeat.

Subsection (8) sets out the information that must be contained in a defeat notice, which includes the dates the look forward begins and ends as well as explaining the effect of the notice. Subsection (9) permits HMRC to specify further information which must be included. It is assumed this further information may detail day and circumstances that matters came to HMRC's attention for the purposes of demonstrating the notice is issued within 90 days.

The look forward period is five years from the day after the day the notice and further relevant defeat notice is given. The defeat notice has effect throughout the look forward period unless s 241B(1) or (4) applies.

New s 241B FA 2014

Section 241B(1) provides for a defeat notice to be disregarded having no further effect on and after the day it is overturned. Subsection (5) specifies when a defeat notice is overturned. It provides that a relevant defeat is overturned if it is reliant on a Case 3 relevant defeat being the relevant defeat could not have effect with the substitution of 100% for 75% within para 9 of Sch 34A, *and* there is a final ruling of a court or tribunal upholding the asserted tax advantage.

Subsections (2)–(3) provides that if one of the defeats to which a double defeat notice relates is overturned, a double defeat notice is treated for all purposes as if it were a single defeat notice. If both relevant defeats to which a double defeat notice relates are overturned on the same day, the notice ceases to have effect from that day.

An authorised officer or an office with approval from an authorised officer must notify the person that there has been a change to a defeat notice or that it has ceased to have effect.

Section 160(4)

Subsection (4) amends FA 2014 s 242 by inserting two new subsections. Subsection (6) provides that an authorised officer cannot apply for a monitoring notice while a conduct notice remains provisional and sub-s (7) provides that where the terms of a provisional conduct notice have been breached, that breach can be taken into account for the purposes of applying for a monitoring notice following a conduct notice ceasing to be provisional.

Section 160(5)

Subsection (5) inserts a new Sch 34A into FA 2014.

New Pt 1 Sch 34A FA 2014

New para 2 Sch 34A FA 2014

Paragraph 2 of Sch 34A defines "related arrangements" for the purposes of the Schedule as arrangements which are substantially the same. Subsections (3)–(6) describe specific circumstances in which the arrangements are always related arrangements, which include those with the same DOTAS reference number, equivalent arrangements for the purposes of GAAR and those in respect of which follower notices have been given by reference to the same judicial ruling.

New para 3 Sch 34A FA 2014

Paragraph 3 of Sch 34A defines the term "promoted arrangements" as relevant arrangements or would be if the definition of tax also included VAT in relation to which a person is carrying on business as a promoter and has been a promoter in relation to the arrangements.

New para 4 Sch 34A FA 2014

Paragraph 4 Sch 34A defines 'relevant defeat' where arrangements are not related to any other arrangements of the promoter.

New para 5 Sch 34A FA 2014

Paragraph 5 of Sch 34A defines relevant defeat where arrangements are related and provides that if the conditions in paras 7, 8 or 9 apply, a relevant defeat occurs in relation to the user of the arrangements and related arrangements.

New para 6 Sch 34A FA 2014

For the purposes of ss 237A and 237B, para 6 Sch 34A prevents multiple relevant defeats of related arrangements counting as more than a single relevant defeat.

New paras 7–9 Sch 34A FA 2014

Paragraph 7 to 9 Sch 34A define a relevant defeats within Cases 1, 2 and 3.

Case 1 applies where the asserted tax advantage has been counteracted under any of Conditions A to E in paras 11–15 Sch 34A, and that counteraction has been upheld by a judicial ruling which is final. Condition A relates to the General Anti Abuse Rule, Condition B to follower notices, Condition C to DOTAS, and Condition D and E to disclosable VAT arrangements.

Case 2 applies where the asserted tax advantage has been counteracted under Condition F in para 16 of Sch 34A and that counteraction has been upheld by a judicial ruling which is final. Condition F relates to applicable avoidance related rule (para 18 Sch 34A).

Case 3 applies where at least 75% but less than 100% of any related arrangements have been defeated and there is no final judicial ruling upholding the asserted tax advantage in relation to the arrangements or any of the related arrangements.

New Pt 3 Sch 34A FA 2014

Part 3 Sch 34A seeks to widen the scope of the originally proposed legislation where either Condition 1 or 2 is met of para 3 – broadly where there are two connected persons and one or both are relevant bodies controlled by a person. The term "controlled" is not defined and it is suspected that the breadth will be applied to situations where in reality what legally appears to be an unconnected arrangement is not so. It is possible that the meaning of controlled will be a subject for legal debate due to the definition at para 19: Meaning of "relevant body" and "control".

New para 18 Sch 34A FA 2014

Paragraph 18 has been inserted since the originally proposed legislation to provide for "Deemed defeat notices" in situations where both conditions A1 and B1 (one third party defeat), and conditions A2 and B2 (two third party defeats) are met. Condition A1 sets out three conditions to be met being that the "other person" has been given a conduct notice or a single or double defeat notice in respect of a third party notice, an authorised officer would have had power to give a double defeat notice subject to being aware that the defeat was a relevant defeat in relation to the person and the authorised officer is aware that the conditions for giving the defeat notice in respect of third party defeats has never been met. Paragraph 7 and 8 set out condition B1 and B2, which result in an authorised officer who could have given a third party defeat notice at the time of a relevant defeat to bring those notices into account. The legislation counters situations where an authorised officer was not aware that notices could have been issued, permitting them to deem a defeat notice exist.

New para 19 Sch 34A FA 2014

Paragraph 19 provides for the meaning of "relevant body" and "control". Its purpose is to ensure the legislation applies to corporates and partnerships as well as situations where those entities conduct their business "in accordance with the persons wishes". However, the legislation refers to the power to secure the affairs are conducted in accordance to the persons wishes either by shareholding or voting power, the articles of association, or means of a controlling partnership. The legislation does not appear to counter arrangements where parties act of their own legal accord although it also appears wide enough to permit challenges in "conduit" situations.

New Pt 4 Sch 34A FA 2014

Part 4 Sch 34A is brought into play by s 160 FA 2016 amending s 237A FA 2014 to include bodies corporate and partnerships. Where a relevant body is another person carrying on a business as a promoter and meets the condition by virtue of Pt 4 of Sch 34A. They are caught within the legislation. Paragraph 1 defines a relevant body as meeting the conditions at s 237A FA 2014 if a person was carrying on a business as a promoter or the person controlled the relevant body that carried on the business as a promoter and the relevant body was controlled by the person at the relevant time. The section does not apply if the person was an individual and is therefore targeted at other relationships. Paragraph 20(3) encapsulates situations where the relevant body did not exist at the same time as the person although para 21 must require them both to exist at some point. The provisions apply similarly to those at para 18 although para 21 looks to connect much wider entities controlled by the same persons and a promoter.

New Pt 5 Sch 34A FA 2014

New para 25 Sch 34A FA 2014

Paragraph 25 of Sch 34A defines 'avoidance-related rule", which encompasses rules more commonly referred to as Targeted Anti-Avoidance Rules (TAAR) and purpose tests.

New para 26 Sch 34A FA 2014

Paragraph 26 of Sch 34A defines 'DOTAS arrangements' for the purposes of the Schedule and includes those arrangements where information has been provided as well as those where information should have but has not been provided, i.e. a DOTAS arrangement that has not been registered as such.

New para 27 Sch 34A FA 2014

Paragraph 27 of Sch 34A defines 'Disclosable VAT arrangements", which includes both arrangements disclosed as well as those that ought to have been disclosed.

New para 28 Sch 34A FA 2014

Paragraph 28 of Sch 34A defines what is meant by failing to comply with any provision mentioned in para 26(1)(a) or 27(b), which broadly includes found by a tribunal or court to have failed or admitted the failure in writing.

New para 30 Sch 34A FA 2014

Paragraph 30 provides a power for the Treasury to make regulations amending Sch 34A to add, vary or remove conditions or categories subject to affirmative resolution procedures in the House of Commons.

161 Large businesses: tax strategies and sanctions for persistently unco-operative behaviour

(1) Schedule 19 contains provisions relating to—

   (a) the publication of tax strategies by bodies which are or are part of a large business,

(b) the imposition of sanctions for such bodies where there has been persistent unco-operative behaviour.

(2) That Schedule, so far as relating to the publication of a tax strategy for a financial year of a relevant body or other entity, has effect only where the financial year begins on or after the day on which this Act is passed.

(3) An officer of HMRC may not give a warning notice under Part 3 of that Schedule to a relevant body or other entity before the beginning of its first financial year beginning on or after the day on which this Act is passed.

(4) In this section and Schedule 19 "HMRC" means Her Majesty's Revenue and Customs.

GENERAL NOTE

Section 161 introduces Sch 19 which contains provisions about publication of tax strategies by bodies which are or are part of a large business. It also imposes sanctions on such bodies where there has been persistently unco-operative behaviour.

Offshore Activities

162 Penalties for enablers of offshore tax evasion or non-compliance

(1) Schedule 20 makes provision for penalties for persons who enable offshore tax evasion or non-compliance by other persons.

(2) Subsection (1) and that Schedule come into force on such day as the Treasury may appoint by regulations made by statutory instrument.

(3) Regulations under this section may—

    (a) commence a provision generally or only for specified purposes,
    (b) appoint different days for different purposes, and
    (c) make supplemental, incidental and transitional provision in connection with the coming into force of any provision of the Schedule.

GENERAL NOTE

The introduction of civil penalties for enablers of offshore tax evasion follows the UK Governments ongoing measures to counter tax evasion. At the time of the consultation, which was issued on 16 July 2015, information exchange agreements had been entered between 94 countries. The UK Government having entered into agreements that will result in more knowledge of offshore structures potentially used to evade or avoid taxes set out what can only be considered a deterrent to those professionals advising on the creation of offshore structures. The clause introduces new civil penalties for deliberate enablers of offshore tax evasion or other non-compliance. The clause also includes a new power to publish information about the enabler. The penalties are applicable in relation to income tax, capital gains tax and inheritance tax.

Subsection (1) introduces Sch 20, which contains the detail of the civil penalties for enablers of offshore tax evasion or non-compliance. Subsections (2) and (3) provide for the day on which the schedule comes into force as well as regulations.

163 Penalties in connection with offshore matters and offshore transfers

(1) Schedule 21 contains provisions amending—

    (a) Schedule 24 to FA 2007 (penalties for errors in tax returns etc),
    (b) Schedule 41 to FA 2008 (penalties for failure to notify etc), and
    (c) Schedule 55 to FA 2009 (penalties for failure to make return etc).

(2) That Schedule comes into force on such day as the Treasury may by regulations made by statutory instrument appoint.

(3) Regulations under this section may—

    (a) commence a provision generally or only for specified purposes,
    (b) appoint different days for different provisions or for different purposes, and
    (c) make supplemental, incidental and transitional provision.

164 Offshore tax errors etc: publishing details of deliberate tax defaulters

(1) Section 94 of FA 2009 (publishing details of deliberate tax defaulters) is amended as follows.

(2) After subsection (4), insert—

"(4A) Subsection (4B) applies where a person who is a body corporate or a partnership has incurred—

(a) a penalty under paragraph 1 of Schedule 24 to FA 2007 in respect of a deliberate inaccuracy which involves an offshore matter or an offshore transfer (within the meaning of paragraph 4A of that Schedule), or

(b) a penalty under paragraph 1 of Schedule 41 to FA 2008 in respect of a deliberate failure which involves an offshore matter or an offshore transfer (within the meaning of paragraph 6A of that Schedule).

(4B) The Commissioners may publish the information mentioned in subsection (4) in respect of any individual who—

(a) controls the body corporate or the partnership (within the meaning of section 1124 of CTA 2010), and

(b) has obtained a tax advantage as a result of the inaccuracy or failure.

(4C) Subsection (4D) applies where one or more trustees of a settlement have incurred—

(a) a penalty under paragraph 1 of Schedule 24 to FA 2007 in respect of a deliberate inaccuracy which involves an offshore matter or an offshore transfer (within the meaning of paragraph 4A of that Schedule), or

(b) a penalty under paragraph 1 of Schedule 41 to FA 2008 in respect of a deliberate failure which involves an offshore matter or an offshore transfer (within the meaning of paragraph 6A of that Schedule).

(4D) The Commissioners may publish the information mentioned in subsection (4) in respect of any trustee who is an individual and who has obtained a tax advantage as a result of the inaccuracy or failure."

(3) In subsection (6), after "information" insert "about a person under subsection (1),".

(4) After subsection (6), insert—

"(6A) Before publishing any information about an individual under subsection (4B) or (4D), the Commissioners—

(a) must inform the individual that they are considering doing so, and

(b) afford the individual reasonable opportunity to make representations about whether it should be published."

(5) In subsection (10)—

(a) omit the word "or" at the end of paragraph (a), and after that paragraph insert—
"(aa) paragraph 10A of that Schedule to the full extent permitted following an unprompted disclosure,";

(b) after paragraph (b) insert ", or

(c) paragraph 13A of that Schedule to the full extent permitted following an unprompted disclosure."

(6) For subsection (16) substitute—

"(16) In this section—

"the Commissioners" means the Commissioners for Her Majesty's Revenue and Customs;

"tax advantage" has the meaning given by section 208 of FA 2013."

(7) The amendments made by this section come into force on such day as the Treasury may by regulations made by statutory instrument appoint.

GENERAL NOTE

This clause strengthens the naming provisions under s 94 Finance Act 2009 ("s 94") by enabling HMRC to name individuals have been charged with a penalty for a deliberate failure to notify or a deliberate inaccuracy to a return and whose affairs are structured through offshore entities, such as companies, partnerships or trusts.

Subsections (1) and (2) insert a new sub-ss (4A), (4B), (4C) and (4D) into s 94. Subsection (4A) stipulates that where, in relation to an offshore matter or transfer, a body corporate or partnership has incurred a penalty in respect of a deliberate failure to notify HMRC of a tax charge; or the submission of a deliberate inaccuracy in a return, and the individual would have obtained a tax advantage had the error not been corrected that sub-s (4B) may apply providing for HMRC to publish the details of the controlling individual. Subsections (4C) and (4D) provide for the same to any trustee of a settlement who, in relation, to an offshore matter or transfer, has incurred a penalty in respect of a deliberate failure to notify HMRC of a tax charge; or the submission of a deliberate inaccuracy in a return, and the trustee as an individual would have obtained a tax advantage had the error not been corrected.

Subsection (4) inserts sub-s (6A) into s 94 and provides that before publishing any information about a person, HMRC must inform the individual that they are considering doing so. The individual must also be given reasonable opportunity to make representations to HMRC about whether their details should be published.

Subsection (5) provides that no information will be published in instances of inaccuracies or failures where the full penalty reduction is given following an unprompted disclosure. The new subsection, therefore, restricts the protection from naming for those who do not come forward to HMRC unprompted.

165 Asset-based penalties for offshore inaccuracies and failures

(1) Schedule 22 contains provision imposing asset-based penalties on certain taxpayers who have been charged a penalty for deliberate offshore inaccuracies and failures.

(2) That Schedule comes into force on such day as the Treasury may by regulations made by statutory instrument appoint.

(3) Regulations under subsection (2) may—

(a) commence a provision generally or only for specified purposes,
(b) appoint different days for different provisions or for different purposes, and
(c) make supplemental, incidental and transitional provision.

GENERAL NOTE

The section gives reference to Sch 22, which details the asset-based penalties that can be applied to taxpayers who have been charged a penalty for deliberate offshore inaccuracies and failures.

166 Offences relating to offshore income, assets and activities

(1) After section 106A of TMA 1970 insert—

"Offshore income, assets and activities

106B Offence of failing to give notice of being chargeable to tax

(1) A person who is required by section 7 to give notice of being chargeable to income tax or capital gains tax (or both) for a year of assessment and who has not given that notice by the end of the notification period commits an offence if—

(a) the tax in question is chargeable (wholly or in part) on or by reference to offshore income, assets or activities, and
(b) the total amount of income tax and capital gains tax that is chargeable for the year of assessment on or by reference to offshore income, assets or activities exceeds the threshold amount.

(2) It is a defence for a person accused of an offence under this section to prove that the person had a reasonable excuse for failing to give the notice required by section 7.

(3) In this section "the notification period" has the same meaning as in section 7 (see subsection (1C) of that section).

106C Offence of failing to deliver return

(1) A person who is required by a notice under section 8 to make and deliver a return for a year of assessment commits an offence if—

(a) the return is not delivered by the end of the withdrawal period,
(b) an accurate return would have disclosed liability to income tax or capital gains tax (or both) that is chargeable for the year of assessment on or by reference to offshore income, assets or activities, and
(c) the total amount of income tax and capital gains tax that is chargeable for the year of assessment on or by reference to offshore income, assets or activities exceeds the threshold amount.

(2) It is a defence for a person accused of an offence under this section to prove that the person had a reasonable excuse for failing to deliver the return.

(3) In this section "the withdrawal period" has the same meaning as in section 8B (see subsection (6) of that section).

106D Offence of making inaccurate return

(1) A person who is required by a notice under section 8 to make and deliver a return for a year of assessment commits an offence if, at the end of the amendment period—

(a) the return contains an inaccuracy the correction of which would result in an increase in the amount of income tax or capital gains tax (or both) that is chargeable for the year of assessment on or by reference to offshore income, assets or activities, and

(b) the amount of that increase exceeds the threshold amount.

(2) It is a defence for a person accused of an offence under this section to prove that the person took reasonable care to ensure that the return was accurate.

(3) In this section "the amendment period" means the period for amending the return under section 9ZA.

106E Exclusions from offences under sections 106B to 106D

(1) A person is not guilty of an offence under section 106B, 106C or 106D if the capacity in which the person is required to give the notice or make and deliver the return is—

(a) as a relevant trustee of a settlement, or

(b) as the executor or administrator of a deceased person.

(2) The Treasury may by regulations provide that a person is not guilty of an offence under section 106B, 106C or 106D if—

(a) conditions specified in the regulations are met, or

(b) circumstances so specified exist.

(3) The conditions may (in particular) include conditions in relation to the income, assets or activities on or by reference to which the tax in question is chargeable.

106F Offences under sections 106B to 106D: supplementary provision

(1) Where a period of time is extended under subsection (2) of section 118 by HMRC, the tribunal or an officer (but not where a period is otherwise extended under that subsection), any reference in section 106B, 106C or 106D to the end of the period is to be read as a reference to the end of the period as so extended.

(2) The Treasury may by regulations specify the amount (which must not be less than £25,000) that is to be the threshold amount for the purposes of sections 106B to 106D.

(3) The Treasury may by regulations make provision as to the calculation for the purposes of sections 106B to 106D of—

(a) the amount of tax that is chargeable on or by reference to offshore income, assets or activities, and

(b) the increase in the amount of tax that is so chargeable as a result of correcting an inaccuracy.

(4) In sections 106B to 106D and this section "offshore income, assets or activities" means—

(a) income arising from a source in a territory outside the United Kingdom,

(b) assets situated or held in a territory outside the United Kingdom, or

(c) activities carried on wholly or mainly in a territory outside the United Kingdom.

(5) In subsection (4), "assets" has the meaning given in section 21(1) of the 1992 Act, but also includes sterling.

106G Penalties for offences under sections 106B to 106D

(1) A person guilty of an offence under section 106B, 106C or 106D is liable on summary conviction—

(a) in England and Wales, to a fine or to imprisonment for a term not exceeding 51 weeks or to both, and

(b) in Scotland or Northern Ireland, to a fine not exceeding level 5 on the standard scale or to imprisonment for a term not exceeding 6 months or to both.

(2) In relation to an offence committed before the coming into force of section 281(5) of the Criminal Justice Act 2003, the reference in subsection (1)(a) to 51 weeks is to be read as a reference to 6 months.

106H Regulations under sections 106E and 106F

(1) This section makes provision about regulations under sections 106E and 106F.

(2) If the regulations contain a reference to a document or any provision of a document and it appears to the Treasury that it is necessary or expedient for the reference to be construed as a reference to that document or that provision as amended from time to time, the regulations may make express provision to that effect.

(3) The regulations—

(a) may make different provision for different cases, and

(b) may include incidental, supplemental, consequential and transitional provision and savings.

(4) The regulations are to be made by statutory instrument.

(5) An instrument containing the regulations is subject to annulment in pursuance of a resolution of the House of Commons."

(2) The amendment made by this section comes into force on such day as the Treasury may by regulations made by statutory instrument appoint.

(3) The regulations—

(a) may appoint different days for different purposes, and

(b) may include incidental, supplemental, consequential and transitional provision and savings.

(4) The amendment made by this section does not have effect in relation to—

(a) a failure to give a notice required by section 7 of TMA 1970,

(b) a failure to make and deliver a return required by section 8 of TMA 1970, or

(c) a return required by section 8 that contains an inaccuracy,

if the notice or return relates to a tax year before that in which the amendment comes into force.

GENERAL NOTE

This clause amends TMA 1970 to introduce new criminal offences which apply for the purposes on income tax and capital gains tax only, where a person has failed to declare offshore income or gains in accordance with TMA (1970) ss 7 and 8. The offence applies to any subsequent loss of tax over a threshold amount, which will be defined in the regulations an annually.

Crucially the offence does not prescribe the need to prove intent for failing to declare taxable offshore income and gains.

Subsection (1) amends TMA 1970 and inserts ss 106B–106H. Sections 106B–106D relate to the new offences.

Section 106B is the offence of failing to give notice to being chargeable to tax. Section 106B(1) establishes a new criminal offence if a person was required and failed to give notice to being chargeable to income tax, capital gains tax or both for a year of assessment and the tax chargeable is wholly or in part on or by reference to offshore income, assets or activities. The section (as is the same for the other offences) specifies a threshold amount of tax below which there is no offence. The amount is currently £25,000 although the Treasury may by regulations specify the amount for the purposes of ss 106B–206D. Section 106B(2) allows a reasonable excuse defence.

Section 106C is the offence of failing to deliver a return. Section 106C(1) establishes the offence where the there is a failing to deliver a tax return following a notice under s 8 TMA 1970 and the returns is not so delivered before the end of the withdrawal period, an accurate return would have disclosed a liability to income tax or capital gain tax or both and the amount of tax is greater than the threshold. A reasonable excuse defence is available.

Section 106D is the offence of making inaccurate return. The offence is where a person who is required by notice under s 8 TMA 1970 to deliver a return and at the end of the amendment period, it contains an inaccuracy and the amendment results in tax greater than the threshold. A reasonable excuse defence is available.

Section 106E sets out exclusions from offences, which include persons responsible for giving notice for making a return by virtue of being a trustee of a settlement or an executor or administrator of a deceased person.

Supplementary provisions under s 106F provide that where HMRC, the Tribunal or an officer extend the time limit for giving notice or delivering a return the period under the new offences is also extended, provide for amending the threshold amount as well as the method of calculating the tax for the purposes of the threshold amount.

Section 106G provides for the penalties for the new offences on summary conviction. Subsections (1)(a) and (2) allow for an unlimited fine in England and Wales and/or a custodial sentence of up to six months for offences committed before s 281(5) of the Criminal Justice Act 2003 comes into force, and 51 weeks thereafter. Subsection 1(b) allows for a fine not exceeding level 5 on the standard scale in Scotland or Northern Ireland and/or a custodial sentence of no more than six months.

PART 11

ADMINISTRATION, ENFORCEMENT AND SUPPLEMENTARY POWERS

Assessment and Returns

167 Simple assessments

(1) Schedule 23 contains provisions about simple assessments by HMRC.

(2) Paragraphs 1 to 8 of that Schedule have effect in relation to the 2016–17 tax year and subsequent years.

(3) Paragraph 9 of that Schedule comes into force on such day as the Treasury may appoint by regulations made by statutory instrument.

(4) Regulations under subsection (3) may—

  (a) commence paragraph 9 generally or only for specified purposes, and
  (b) appoint different days for different purposes.

GENERAL NOTE

Autumn Statement 2015 introduced draft legislation to implement a "new, simpler process" for paying tax. Section 167 and Sch 23 introduce a new power enabling HMRC to assess the income tax or CGT liability of an individual or trust without the taxpayer being required to complete a self-assessment return.

168 Time limit for self assessment tax returns

(1) TMA 1970 is amended as follows.

(2) In section 34 (ordinary time limit of 4 years for assessments), after subsection (2) insert—

  "(3) In this section "assessment" does not include a self-assessment."

(3) After that section insert—

"34A Ordinary time limit for self-assessments

  (1) Subject to subsections (2) and (3), a self-assessment contained in a return under section 8 or 8A may be made and delivered at any time not more than 4 years after the end of the year of assessment to which it relates.

  (2) Nothing in subsection (1) prevents—

    (a) a person who has received a notice under section 8 or 8A within that period of 4 years from delivering a return including a self-assessment within the period of 3 months beginning with the date of the notice,
    (b) a person in respect of whom a determination under section 28C has been made from making a self-assessment in accordance with that section within the period allowed by subsection (5)(a) or (b) of that section.

  (3) Subsection (1) has effect subject to the following provisions of this Act and to any other provisions of the Taxes Acts allowing a longer period in any particular class of case.

  (4) This section has effect in relation to self-assessments for a year of assessment earlier than 2012–13 as if—

    (a) in subsection (1) for the words from "not more" to the end there were substituted "on or before 5 April 2017", and
    (b) in subsection (2)(a) for the words "within that period of 4 years" there were substituted "on or before 5 April 2017.""

GENERAL NOTE

Section 168 amends TMA 1970 s 34 (ordinary time limit of four years) to provide that it does not apply to a self-assessment, and inserts a new TMA 1970 s 34A setting out the time limit for a self-assessment.

The general rule is that a self-assessment contained in a tax return may be made and delivered to HMRC at any time not more than four years after the end of the tax year to which it relates. For example, the last date for delivery of a self-assessment for 2016/17 is 5 April 2021. This is subject to any other provisions of the Taxes Acts allowing a longer period.

New TMA 1970 s 34A(2) provides that the general rule does not prevent a person who has received a notice to deliver a return under TMA 1970 s 8 or s 8A within that four year period from delivering a return, including a self-assessment, within three months from the date of the notice. Nor does it prevent a person for whom a determination under TMA 1970 s 28C (determination of tax where no return delivered) has been made from making a self-assessment within the period allowed in TMA 1970 s 28C(5).

Taxpayers will also have until 5 April 2017 to deliver a self-assessment for years prior to 2012/13.

169 HMRC power to withdraw notice to file a tax return

(1) Section 8B of TMA 1970 (withdrawal of notice under section 8 or 8A) is amended as follows.

(2) In subsection (2) for the words from "the person" to the end substitute "HMRC may withdraw the notice (whether at the request of the person or otherwise)".

(3) In subsection (3) for "no request may be made" substitute "the notice may not be withdrawn".

(4) In subsection (4) omit ", on receiving a request,".

(5) In subsection (6)(b) for "agree with the person" substitute "determine".

(6) In paragraph 17A of Schedule 55 to the Finance Act 2009 (penalty for failure to make returns etc), in sub-paragraph (1)(b) for the words from the beginning to "withdraw" substitute "HMRC decide to give P a notice under section 8B withdrawing".

(7) The amendments made by this section have effect in relation to any notice under section 8 or 8A of TMA 1970 given in relation to the 2014–15 tax year or any subsequent year (and it is immaterial whether the notice was given before or after the passing of this Act).

GENERAL NOTE

Section 169 amends TMA 1970 s 8B (withdrawal of notice to make and deliver a tax return) to enable HMRC to withdraw the notice whether or not the taxpayer has requested withdrawal. There is a consequential amendment to FA 2009 Sch 55 para 17A (penalty for failure to make returns etc: cancellation of penalty). This change applies to notices given for 2014/15 onwards.

Judgment Debts

170 Rate of interest applicable to judgment debts etc: Scotland

(1) This section applies if—

(a) a sum is payable to or by the Commissioners under a decree or extract issued in any court proceedings relating to a taxation matter (a "tax-related judgment debt"), and

(b) interest in relation to the tax-related judgment debt is included in or payable under the decree or extract.

(2) In a case where the rate of interest in relation to the tax-related judgment debt is stated in the decree or extract, the rate stated in relation to that debt may not exceed (and may not be capable of exceeding)—

(a) in the case of a sum payable to the Commissioners, the late payment interest rate, and

(b) in the case of a sum payable by the Commissioners, the special repayment rate.

(3) In a case where the rate of interest in relation to the tax-related judgment debt is not stated in the decree or extract but provided for by an enactment or rule of court

(whenever passed or made), that enactment or rule is to have effect in relation to the debt as if for the rate for which it provides there were substituted—

(a) in the case of a sum payable to the Commissioners, the late payment interest rate, and

(b) in the case of a sum payable by the Commissioners, the special repayment rate.

(4) This section has effect in relation to interest for periods beginning on or after the day on which this Act is passed, regardless of—

(a) the date of the decree or extract in question, and

(b) whether interest begins to run on or after the day on which this Act is passed, or began to run before that date.

(5) In this section—

"the Commissioners" means the Commissioners for Her Majesty's Revenue and Customs;

"enactment" includes an Act of the Scottish Parliament or an instrument made under such an Act;

"late payment interest rate" means the rate provided for in regulations made by the Treasury under section 103(1) of FA 2009;

"special repayment rate" has the same meaning as in section 52 of F(No 2)A 2015 (and subsections (7) to (10) of that section apply for the purposes of this section as they apply for the purposes of that section);

"taxation matter" means anything the collection and management of which is the responsibility of the Commissioners (or was the responsibility of the Commissioners of Inland Revenue or Commissioners of Customs and Excise);

"working day" means any day other than a non-business day as defined in section 92 of the Bills of Exchange Act 1882.

(6) This section extends to Scotland only.

GENERAL NOTE

This section applies to any interest payable to or by HMRC in respect of a tax-related judgment debt under a decree or extract of the court (1) in Scotland only (6).

Subsections (2) and (3) stipulate that the applicable rate of interest may not exceed the late repayment interest rate or special repayment rate under FA 2009 s 103.

Furthermore, the late repayment interest rate and special repayment rate apply regardless of whether a rate of interest is stated in the decree or extract or provided for by an enactment or rule of court.

Subsection (4) provides that the interest rates shall apply from the date of Royal Assent of Finance Act 2016 (15 September 2016). The rates shall apply to all interest payments on or after this date regardless of (a) the date of the decree or extract; or (b) whether interest begins before, on or after that date. The rates will therefore apply to all interest accruing on or after Royal Assent (15 September 2016), but not to interest that has already accrued up to and including the day before Royal Assent (15 September 2016).

Subsection (5) provides various definitions and, notably, states that taxation matter means "anything the collection and management of which is the responsibility of the Commissioners (or was the responsibility of the Commissioners of Inland Revenue or Commissioners of Customs and Excise)" it therefore includes National Insurance Contributions within the scope of tax-related judgments.

It should be noted that, taken together with ss 171 and 172, this subsection harmonises the rates of interest applicable to tax-related debts across the UK.

171 Rate of interest applicable to judgment debts etc: Northern Ireland

(1) This section applies if a sum payable to or by the Commissioners under a judgment or order given or made in any court proceedings relating to a taxation matter (a "tax-related judgment debt") carries interest.

(2) In a case where the rate of interest is specified in the judgment (in the case of the High Court) or directed by the judge (in the case of a county court), the rate specified or directed in relation to that debt may not exceed (and may not be capable of exceeding)

(a) in the case of a sum payable to the Commissioners, the late payment interest rate, and

(b) in the case of a sum payable by the Commissioners, the special repayment rate.

(3) In a case where the rate of interest in relation to the tax-related judgment debt is not specified in the judgment or directed by the judge but provided for by an enactment or rule of court (whenever passed or made), that enactment or rule is to have effect in relation to the debt as if for the rate for which it provides there were substituted—

(a) in the case of a sum payable to the Commissioners, the late payment interest rate, and

(b) in the case of a sum payable by the Commissioners, the special repayment rate.

(4) This section has effect in relation to interest for periods beginning on or after the day on which this Act is passed, regardless of—

(a) the date of the judgment or order in question, and

(b) whether interest begins to run on or after the day on which this Act is passed, or began to run before that date.

(5) In this section—

"the Commissioners" means the Commissioners for Her Majesty's Revenue and Customs;

"enactment" includes Northern Ireland legislation or an instrument made under such legislation;

"late payment interest rate" means the rate provided for in regulations made by the Treasury under section 103(1) of FA 2009;

"special repayment rate" has the same meaning as in section 52 of F(No 2) A 2015 (and subsections (7) to (10) of that section apply for the purposes of this section as they apply for the purposes of that section);

"taxation matter" means anything the collection and management of which is the responsibility of the Commissioners (or was the responsibility of the Commissioners of Inland Revenue or Commissioners of Customs and Excise);

"working day" means any day other than a non-business day as defined in section 92 of the Bills of Exchange Act 1882.

(6) This section extends to Northern Ireland only.

GENERAL NOTE

Subsection (1) provides that, in Northern Ireland, any sum payable to or by HM Revenue & Customs (HMRC) as a result of a tax-related judgment or order of court carries interest.

Subsections (2) and (3) stipulate that the applicable rate of interest may not exceed the late repayment interest rate or special repayment rate under FA (2009) s 103.

Furthermore, the late repayment interest rate and special repayment rate apply regardless of whether a rate of interest is specified in the judgment or order of the court or provided for by an enactment or rule of court.

Subsection (4) provides that the interest rates shall apply from the date of Royal Assent of Finance Act 2016. The rates shall apply to all interest payments on or after this date regardless of (a) the date of the judgment or order; or (b) whether interest begins before, on or after that date. The rates will therefore apply to all interest accruing on or after Royal Assent, but not to interest that has already accrued up to and including the day before Royal Assent.

Subsection (5) provides various definitions and, notably, states that taxation matter means "anything the collection and management of which is the responsibility of the Commissioners (or was the responsibility of the Commissioners of Inland Revenue or Commissioners of Customs and Excise)" it therefore includes National Insurance Contributions within the scope of tax-related judgments.

It should be noted that, taken together with s 170 and 172, this subsection harmonises the rates of interest applicable to tax-related debts across the UK.

172 Rate of interest applicable to judgment debts etc: England and Wales

(1) In section 52 of F(No 2)A 2015 (rates of interest applicable to judgment debts etc in taxation matters: England and Wales), in subsection (15), in the definition of "taxation matter" omit ", other than national insurance contributions,".

(2) This section has effect in relation to interest for periods beginning on or after the day on which this Act is passed, regardless of—

(a) the date of the judgment or order in question, and

(b) whether interest begins to run on or after the day on which this Act is passed, or began to run before that date.

(3) This section extends to England and Wales only.

GENERAL NOTE

The section removes the exclusion of National Insurance Contributions from the definition of "taxation matter" in s 52 F(No 2)A 2015 in England and Wales.

It therefore extends the definition of "taxation matter" and causes any payment or repayment of National Insurance Contributions, which arise under a judgment or order in England and Wales, to carry interest.

Subsection (2) provides that the interest rates shall apply from the date of Royal Assent of Finance Act 2016. The rates apply to all interest payments on or after this date regardless of (a) the date of the judgment or order; or (b) whether interest begins before, on or after that date. The rates will therefore apply to all interest accruing on or after Royal Assent, but not to interest that has already accrued up to and including the day before Royal Assent.

The interest rates applicable to judgment debts in respect of taxation and National Insurance Contributions are therefore to be determined in tax legislation, rather than the Judgments Act or County Courts Act.

It should be noted that, taken together with ss 170 and 171, this subsection harmonises the rates of interest applicable to tax-related debts across the UK.

Enforcement Powers

173 Gift aid: power to impose penalties on charities and intermediaries

(1) At the end of section 428 of ITA 2007 insert—

"(5) The regulations may also make provision—

(a) for the imposition of a penalty of a specified amount (which must not exceed £3000) for a failure to comply with a specified requirement imposed by the regulations,

(h) for the assessment and recovery of the penalty (which may include provision about the reduction of the penalty in specified circumstances), and

(c) conferring a right of appeal against a decision that a penalty is payable."

(2) The amendment made by this section comes into force on such day as the Treasury may by regulations made by statutory instrument appoint.

GENERAL NOTE

Section 173 makes an addition to the FA 2015 prospective technical changes to the meaning of a Gift Aid declaration in ITA 2007 s 428. These permit the making of regulations to allow Gift Aid donations to be made to charities via intermediaries to increase the take up of Gift Aid on eligible donations, including those made by text and other social media. Draft regulations are to be published for consultation in due course.

Section 173(1) inserts a new sub-s (5) into ITA 2007 s 428 allowing the regulations to provide for a penalty of up to £3,000 on charities or intermediaries for failing to comply with specified requirements of the regulations, together with provision for the assessment, recovery and reduction of such a penalty. A right of appeal is also to be included.

Section 173(2) provides that the amendment will come into force from an appointed day to be determined by statutory instrument.

174 Proceedings under customs and excise Acts: prosecuting authority

(1) Part 11 of CEMA 1979 (arrest of persons, forfeiture and legal proceedings) is amended as set out in subsections (2) and (3).

(2) In section 146A(7) (definition of prosecuting authority)—

(a) in the opening words, for "prosecution" substitute "prosecuting";

(b) in paragraph (b), omit "the Commissioners or";

(c) in paragraph (c), for "the Commissioners" substitute "the Director of Public Prosecutions for Northern Ireland".

(3) In section 150(1) (joint and several liability), for the words from "the Director" to "Ireland)" substitute "prosecuting authority (within the meaning of section 146A)".

(4) In consequence of subsection (3), in Schedule 4 to the Commissioners for Revenue and Customs Act 2005, omit paragraph 25.

(5) The amendments made by this section apply in relation to proceedings commenced on or after the day on which this Act is passed.

GENERAL NOTE

Section 174 amends s 146A(7)(b) and (c) of the Customs and Excise Management Act 1979 (CEMA) to remove the reference to "the Commissioners" from the definition of prosecuting authority for Scotland and Northern Ireland. Section 174 also inserts the Director of Public Prosecutions for Northern Ireland as the relevant prosecuting authority for Northern Ireland. The effect of the amendments is to clarify that the time limit for commencing summary proceedings under the customs and excise Acts only starts to run from the date on which the procurator fiscal (for Scotland) or the Director of Public Prosecutions for Northern Ireland, has knowledge of sufficient evidence to justify the proceedings, rather than the Commissioners.

CEMA s 150 is also amended substituting term prosecuting authority in place of the current reference to the Commissioners, to clarify that it is a matter for the procurator fiscal or the Director of Public Prosecutions for Northern Ireland, as appropriate, to decide whether to charge persons jointly or severally with an offence under the customs and excise Acts (defined in CEMA s 1).

Background

Section 146A(3) CEMA provides that proceedings for summary offences under the customs and excise Acts must be commenced within six months from the date on which sufficient evidence came to the knowledge of the prosecuting authority.

Previously the prosecuting authority for Scotland was defined in s 146A(7)(b) as "the Commissioners or the procurator fiscal" and, in s 146A(7)(c) for Northern Ireland, as "the Commissioners", being the Commissioners for HMRC. Section 146A(7)(a), as previously drafted, defines the prosecuting authority for England and Wales as the Director of Public Prosecutions, with no reference to the Commissioners.

However, while offences under the customs and excise Acts are investigated by HMRC, decisions about whether to institute proceedings are made, in Northern Ireland, by the Director of Public Prosecutions for Northern Ireland and in Scotland, by the procurator fiscal.

The amendments ensure that the time limit for summary offences does not start to run before the date at which the procurator fiscal or the Director of Public Prosecutions for Northern Ireland (the independent authorities responsible for determining whether a prosecution should be commenced) has knowledge of sufficient evidence to warrant the proceedings. This removes any possibility that the time limit could be triggered at a date before the matter has been referred to the relevant prosecuting authority. It also aligns the definition of prosecuting authority for Scotland and Northern Ireland with the present drafting of prosecuting authority for England and Wales.

For consistency, the amended definition of prosecuting authority in s 146A(7) is extended to s 150, to replace the current reference to the Commissioners, so that it is for the procurator fiscal or the Director of Public Prosecutions for Northern Ireland to decide whether to proceed against persons jointly or severally for offences under the customs and excise Acts.

175 Detention and seizure under CEMA 1979: notice requirements etc

(1) CEMA 1979 is amended as follows.

(2) Schedule 2A (detention of things as liable to forfeiture) is amended as set out in subsections (3) and (4).

(3) In paragraph 3(2) (exceptions to requirement of notice of detention)—
    (a) omit the "or" at the end of paragraph (b), and after that paragraph insert—
        "(ba) a person who has (or appears to have) possession or control of the thing being detained,";
    (b) in paragraph (c), after "on" insert "or from";
    (c) at the end insert ", or
        (d) in the case of any thing detained on or from a vehicle, the driver of the vehicle."

(4) In paragraph 4(2) (unauthorised removal or disposal of things detained: definition of "responsible person"), for paragraphs (a) and (b) substitute—

"(a) the person whose offence or suspected offence occasioned the detention,
(b) the owner or any of the owners of the thing detained or any servant or agent of such an owner,
(c) a person who has (or appears to have) possession or control of the thing being detained,
(d) in the case of any thing detained on a ship or aircraft, the master or commander,
(e) in the case of any thing detained on a vehicle, the driver of the vehicle, or
(f) a person whom the person who detains the thing reasonably believes to be a person within any of paragraphs (a) to (e)."

(5) In Schedule 3 (seizure and forfeiture), in paragraph 1(2) (exceptions to requirement of notice of seizure)—

(a) after paragraph (b) insert—
"(ba) a person who has (or appears to have) possession or control of the thing being seized; or";
(b) in paragraph (c), for "in" substitute "on or from";
(c) at the end insert "; or
(d) in the case of any thing seized on or from a vehicle, the driver of the vehicle."

(6) The amendments made by this section have effect in relation to things detained or seized on or after the day on which this Act is passed.

GENERAL NOTE

Section 175 amends Schs 2A and 3 to the Customs and Excise Management Act 1979 (CEMA) relating to the detention of things liable to forfeiture and proceeding for condemnation of any thing as being forfeited (see CEMA s 139).

As originally enacted, Sch 3 para 1(1) required the Commissioners to give notice of seizure to the owner of things seized as liable to forfeiture. Paragraph 1(2) provided for an exception to giving notice where the seizure was in the presence of certain persons (offender, owner, servant or agent of owner, master or commander of ship or aircraft). Schedule 2A was inserted by FA 2013 s 226(1) and (7) to make similar provision for notice of detention.

Section 175 amends para 3(2) of Sch 2A and para 1(2) of Sch 3 adding to the list of persons present at seizure that gives rise to the exception. As a result, the owner need not be served where the things are seized in the presence of a person who has, or appears to have, possession or control over any thing being detained or seized or on the driver of any type of vehicle on or from which the goods are detained or seized.

Section 175 is intended to assist HMRC and Border Force officers where it is unclear who is the owner of the goods. The amendment permits officers to treat the driver, or a person in a comparable situation, as if he or she were a representative of the owner.

It was necessary to make consequential amendments to Sch 2A para 4(2). Section 175 also makes other minor drafting amendments to ensure consistency.

The amendments have effect from Royal Assent.

Detail

Subsection 3(a) inserts new sub-para (ba) in Sch 2A para 3(2) (exceptions to requirement of notice of detention) to include a person who has (or appears to have) possession or control of the thing being detained.

Subsection 3(c) inserts new sub-para (d) in Sch 2A para 3(2) to include the driver of the vehicle in the case where any thing is detained on or from any type of vehicle.

Subsection 4 substitutes sub-paras (a) and (b) of Sch 2A para 4(2) with new sub-paras (a) to (f) listing those persons liable for unauthorised removal or disposal. This is to ensure consistency with para 3(2).

Subsection 5(a) inserts new sub-para (ba) in Sch 3 para 1(2) (exceptions to requirement of notice of seizure) to include a person who has (or appears to have) possession or control of the thing being seized.

Subsection 5(c) inserts new sub-para (d) in Sch 3 para 1(2) to include the driver of the vehicle in the case where any thing is seized on or from any type of vehicle.

176 Data-gathering powers: providers of payment or intermediary services

(1) In Part 2 of Schedule 23 to FA 2011 (data-gathering powers: relevant data-holders), after paragraph 13A insert—

   13B

   "Providers of electronic stored-value payment services

   (1) A person who provides electronic stored-value payment services is a relevant data-holder.

   (2) In this paragraph "electronic stored-value payment services" means services by means of which monetary value is stored electronically for the purpose of payments being made in respect of transactions to which the provider of those services is not a party.

   13C

   Business intermediaries

   (1) A person who—

      (a) provides services to enable or facilitate transactions between suppliers and their customers or clients (other than services provided solely to enable payments to be made), and

      (b) receives information about such transactions in the course of doing so,

   is a relevant data-holder.

   (2) In this paragraph "suppliers" means persons supplying goods or services in the course of business.

   (3) For the purposes of this paragraph, information about transactions includes information that is capable of indicating the likely quantity or value of transactions."

(2) This section applies in relation to relevant data with a bearing on any period (whether before, on or after the day on which this Act is passed).

GENERAL NOTE

FA 2013 Sch 13 includes extensive powers for HMRC to gather data. Section 176 extends these powers to data held in digital wallets and other forms of electronic money.

Section 176(1)

This inserts a new para 13B into Sch 13.

New para 13B(1)

This extends the definition of relevant data holder to a person who provides electronic stored value payment services.

New para 13B(2)

This defines electronic stored value payment services as services by which monetary value is stored electronically for the purpose of payment being made in respect of which the provider of those services is not a party. In other words A provides services to allow B to make a purchase from C and pay electronically.

New para 13C(1)

This extends the definition of a relevant data holder to a person who provides services to enable or facilitate transactions (other than actual payment services) between suppliers and the customer or clients and who receives information in the course of so doing.

New para 13C(2)

Suppliers means persons supplying goods or services in the course of business.

New para 13C(3)

Information about transactions includes information which is capable of indicating the likely quantity or value of transactions.

Section 176(2)

The new paras 13B and 13C apply to relevant data with a bearing on any period whether before, on or after the date of Royal Assent. In other words data can be required for a period before the law comes into force. This mirrors the general approach taken in FA 2011 Sch 23 for other bulk data gathering power and is subject to the time limits in that schedule. Broadly speaking Sch 23 allows HMRC to request data for chargeable periods ending in the four years prior to the issue of the notice.

177 Data-gathering powers: daily penalties for extended default
(1) Part 4 of Schedule 23 to FA 2011 (data-gathering powers: penalties) is amended as follows.
(2) In paragraph 38 (increased daily default penalty)—
   (a) in sub-paragraphs (1)(c) and (2), for "imposed" substitute "assessable";
   (b) for sub-paragraphs (3) and (4) substitute—
   "(3) If the tribunal decides that an increased daily penalty should be assessable—
      (a) the tribunal must determine the day from which the increased daily penalty is to apply and the maximum amount of that penalty ("the new maximum amount");
      (b) from that day, paragraph 31 has effect in the data-holder's case as if "the new maximum amount" were substituted for "£60".
    (4) The new maximum amount may not be more than £1,000.";
   (c) in sub-paragraph (5), for "the amount" substitute "the new maximum amount".
(3) In paragraph 39—
   (a) in sub-paragraph (1), for "a data-holder becomes liable to a penalty" substitute "the tribunal makes a determination";
   (b) in sub-paragraph (2), for "the day from which the increased penalty is to apply" substitute "new maximum amount and the day from which it applies";
   (c) omit sub-paragraph (3).
(4) In paragraph 40 (enforcement of penalties), in sub-paragraph (2)(a) omit "or 39".
(5) At the end of paragraph 36 (right to appeal against penalty), the existing text of which becomes sub-paragraph (1), insert—
   "(2) But sub-paragraph (1)(b) does not give a right of appeal against the amount of an increased daily penalty payable by virtue of paragraph 38."

GENERAL NOTE

This section makes changes to the mechanism under which penalties for extended default of the data-gathering rules are administered.

Section 177(1)

This introduces amendments to FA 2011 Sch 23 Pt 4

Section 177(2)(a)

This substitutes the word assessable for the word imposed.

Section 177(2)(b)

This introduces replacement sub-paras (3) and (4) of Sch 23 para 38.

New sub-para (3)

This applies if the tribunal decides that an increased daily penalty should be assessable. If it does so decide the tribunal must determine both the day from which the increased daily penalty is to apply and the maximum amount of that penalty. The new maximum amount replaces the previous fixed amount of £60 from the day determined by the tribunal.

New sub-para (4)

The new maximum amount may not exceed £1,000.

Section 177(3) and (4)

These are consequential drafting amendments.

Section 177(5)

This make it clear that there is no right of appeal against an increased daily penalty payable under para 38.

Payment

178 Extension of provisions about set-off to Scotland

(1) Sections 130 and 131 of FA 2008 (which deal with the availability of set-off in England and Wales and Northern Ireland) extend also to Scotland.

(2) Accordingly, those sections are amended as follows.

(3) In section 130—

    (a) omit subsection (10), and

    (b) in the heading omit ": England and Wales and Northern Ireland".

(4) In section 131—

    (a) in subsection (5), in paragraph (a), after "winding up order" insert "or award of sequestration",

    (b) in that subsection, omit the "or" at the end of paragraph (d) and after paragraph (e) insert ", or

        (f) that person's estate becomes vested in any other person as that person's trustee under a trust deed (within the meaning of the Bankruptcy (Scotland) Act 1985).", and

    (c) omit subsection (9).

GENERAL NOTE

FA 2008 s 130 provides (subject to the exception in FA 2008 s 131 where an insolvency procedure has been applied) that HMRC may set a sum payable to a person against a sum due from the person. This provision applies only to England and Wales, and Northern Ireland. Section 178 extends it to Scotland.

Raw Tobacco

179 Raw tobacco approval scheme

(1) After section 8J of TPDA 1979 insert—

"8K Raw tobacco: definitions

    (1) The following definitions apply for the purposes of sections 8L to 8U.

    (2) "Raw tobacco" means the leaves or any other part of a plant of the genus *Nicotiana* but does not include—

        (a) any part of a living plant, or

        (b) a tobacco product.

    (3) "Controlled activity" means any activity involving raw tobacco.

8L Raw tobacco: requirement for approval

    (1) A person may not carry on a controlled activity otherwise than in accordance with an approval given by the Commissioners under this section.

    (2) The Commissioners may approve a person to carry on a controlled activity only if satisfied that—

        (a) the person is a fit and proper person to carry on the activity, and

        (b) the activity will not be carried on for the purpose of, or with a view to, the fraudulent evasion of the duty of excise charged on tobacco products under section 2(1).

    (3) An approval may—

        (a) specify the period of approval, and

        (b) be subject to conditions or restrictions.

    (4) The Commissioners may at any time for reasonable cause revoke or vary the terms of an approval.

8M Regulations about approval etc

The Commissioners may, by or under regulations, make provision—

(a) regulating the approval of persons under section 8L,

(b) about the form, manner and content of an application for approval,

(c) specifying conditions or restrictions to which an approval is subject,

(d) regulating the variation or revocation of an approval, or of any condition or restriction to which an approval is subject, and

(e) about the surrender or transfer of an approval.

8N Exemptions from requirement for approval

(1) The Commissioners may by regulations provide that section 8L(1) does not apply in relation to a person (an "exempt person") who—

(a) carries on any controlled activity, or a controlled activity of a specified description, and

(b) meets the conditions (if any) specified by or under the regulations.

(2) The regulations may require an exempt person to comply with specified requirements or restrictions relating to the carrying on of a controlled activity.

(3) The regulations may, in particular—

(a) specify the maximum quantity of raw tobacco that may be involved in a controlled activity carried on by an exempt person;

(b) require an exempt person to keep records relating to the activity.

8O Raw tobacco: penalties

(1) A person who contravenes section 8L(1) is liable to a penalty of an amount equal to the amount of duty that would be charged on the relevant quantity of smoking tobacco.

(2) A person who contravenes a requirement or restriction imposed by regulations under section 8N is liable to a penalty of—

(a) £250, or

(b) if less, an amount equal to the amount of duty that would be charged on the relevant quantity of smoking tobacco.

(3) The relevant quantity of smoking tobacco is equal to the quantity by weight of the raw tobacco in respect of which the controlled activity contravening section 8L(1) or (as the case may be) regulations under section 8N has been carried on.

(4) In this section a reference to "smoking tobacco" is a reference to tobacco products within section 1(1)(d) ("other smoking tobacco").

8P Penalties under section 8O: special reduction

(1) If the Commissioners think it right because of special circumstances, they may reduce a penalty under section 8O.

(2) In subsection (1) "special circumstances" does not include ability to pay.

(3) In subsection (1) the reference to reducing a penalty includes a reference to—

(a) staying a penalty, and

(b) agreeing a compromise in relation to proceedings for a penalty.

8Q Penalties under section 8O: assessment of penalty

(1) Where a person becomes liable for a penalty under section 8O—

(a) the Commissioners may assess the penalty, and

(b) if they do so, they must notify the person liable.

(2) A notice under subsection (1)(b) must state the contravention in respect of which the penalty is assessed.

(3) A penalty payable under section 8O must be paid before the end of the period of 30 days beginning with the day on which the notification of the penalty is issued.

(4) An assessment is to be treated as an amount of duty due from the person liable for the penalty and may be recovered accordingly.

(5) An assessment may not be made later than one year after evidence of facts sufficient in the opinion of the Commissioners to indicate the contravention comes to their knowledge.

(6) Two or more contraventions may be treated by the Commissioners as a single contravention for the purposes of assessing a penalty payable under section 8O.

8R Penalties under section 8O: reasonable excuse

(1) A person is not liable to a penalty under section 8O in respect of a contravention if—

(a) the contravention is not deliberate, and
(b) the person satisfies the Commissioners that there is a reasonable excuse for the contravention.

(2) For the purposes of subsection (1)(b)—

(a) where the person relies on another person to do anything, that is not a reasonable excuse unless the first person took reasonable care to avoid the contravention;
(b) where the person had a reasonable excuse for the relevant act or failure but the excuse has ceased, the person is to be treated as having continued to have the excuse if the contravention is remedied without unreasonable delay after the excuse has ceased.

8S Penalties under section 8O: double jeopardy

A person is not liable to a penalty under section 8O in respect of a contravention in respect of which the person has been convicted of an offence.

8T Forfeiture of raw tobacco

Where a person carries on a controlled activity in relation to raw tobacco in contravention of section 8L(1) or a requirement or restriction imposed by regulations under section 8N, the raw tobacco is liable to forfeiture.

8U Raw tobacco: application of Customs and Excise Management Act 1979

The Commissioners may by regulations provide that specified provisions of the Customs and Excise Management Act 1979 apply (with or without modification)—

(a) in relation to persons who carry on controlled activities as they apply in relation to revenue traders whose trade or business relates to tobacco products, and
(b) in relation to raw tobacco as they apply in relation to tobacco products."

(2) In section 9 of TPDA 1979 (regulations)—

(a) in subsection (1), after "statutory instrument and" insert ", subject to subsection (1A),", and
(b) after subsection (1) insert—

"(1A) A statutory instrument containing regulations under section 8M, 8N or 8U is subject to annulment in pursuance of a resolution of the House of Commons."

(3) In section 13A(2) of FA 1994 (customs and excise reviews and appeals: "relevant decisions"), after paragraph (g) insert—

"(gb) any decision by HMRC that a person is liable to a penalty, or as to the amount of the person's liability, under section 8O of the Tobacco Products Duty Act 1979;".

(4) In Schedule 5 to FA 1994 (decisions subject to review and appeal) after paragraph 5 insert—

"**5A** Any decision—

(a) to refuse an approval under section 8L of the Tobacco Products Duty Act 1979 (raw tobacco: approval to carry on a controlled activity);
(b) to impose a condition or restriction on, or to revoke or vary the terms of, an approval under that section."

(5) The amendments made by this section come into force on such day as the Commissioners for Her Majesty's Revenue and Customs may by regulations made by statutory instrument appoint.

(6) Regulations under subsection (5) may appoint different days for different purposes.

GENERAL NOTE

Tobacco products duty (TPD) is charged on certain defined tobacco products (including cigarettes and hand rolling tobacco) imported or manufactured in the UK (Tobacco Products Duty Act 1979 (TPDA) ss 1 and 2). TPD is not charged on raw tobacco which is not yet in a form that may be smoked. The unlawful manufacture of tobacco products from imported raw tobacco has led to the evasion of TPD in the UK. Legally imported raw tobacco has either been processed into tobacco products in unregistered premises or sold to consumers for home processing.

Section 179 amends TPDA to introduce new provisions prohibiting any person from carrying out any activity involving raw tobacco, unless the person holds an approval given by HM Revenue & Customs (HMRC).

Subject to certain exemptions, any individual or business carrying out a controlled activity in relation to raw tobacco, which includes supplying, receiving, storing or using, raw tobacco for smoking or non-smoking purposes will need to be approved. Those persons will be required to show that their involvement with raw tobacco will not result in the fraudulent evasion of TPD.

The scheme will enable HMRC and Border Force (BF) officers to identify and seize raw tobacco when there has been a contravention of the new provisions. HMRC may assess a penalty for carrying on a controlled activity without approval.

HMRC intends to accept applications for approval from October 2016. The scheme is due to have effect from 1 January 2017.

Detail

Section 179 sub-s (1) inserts new ss 8K to 8U after s 8J TPDA.

Section 8K: Raw tobacco: definitions

Section 8K contains the definitions of raw tobacco and controlled activities for the purpose of ss 8L to 8U.

Section 8L: Raw tobacco: requirement for approval

Subsection (1) states that no controlled activity may be carried out by a person otherwise than in accordance with an approval given by the Commissioners.

Subsection (2) specifies that approval will only be given if the applicant is a fit and proper person and the activity is not to be carried on for the purpose of or with a view to the fraudulent evasion of tobacco duty.

Subsection (3) provides that an approval may be time-limited and subject to conditions or restrictions.

Subsection (4) gives the Commissioners power to revoke or vary an approval on the basis of a reasonable cause.

Section 8M: Regulations about approval etc.

Section 8M provides for a power, to be exercised by or under regulations, to regulate applications for and the contents of approvals.

Section 8N: Exemptions from requirement for approval

Subsection (1) allows for the Commissioners by regulations to provide an exemption from the requirement for an approval under s 8L. An exemption may be made subject to compliance with conditions specified by or under regulations.

Subsection (2) states that an exempt person may need to comply with specific requirements or restrictions.

Subsection (3) states that the Commissioners may by regulations provide for a maximum quantity of raw tobacco that can be involved in a controlled activity carried out by an exempt person and that there may be a requirement for an exempt person to keep records.

Section 8O: Raw tobacco: penalties

Subsection (1) states that a person who contravenes the approval requirement will be liable to a penalty that is equal to the amount of duty that would be charged on the "relevant amount" of smoking tobacco.

Subsection (2) provides that a penalty for a person who contravenes a requirement or restriction imposed by or under regulation under s 8N will be either £250 or an amount equal to the duty on smoking tobacco.

Subsection (3) provides that the "relevant amount" of smoking tobacco is an amount equal to the quantity by weight of the raw tobacco which is the subject of the contravention.

Subsection (4) specifies that a reference to smoking tobacco is a reference to smoking tobacco as mentioned within s 1(1)(d) TPDA.

Section 8P: Penalties under section 8O: special reduction

Subsection (1) states that under special circumstances the Commissioners may reduce a penalty under s 8O.

Subsection (2) provides that the ability to pay the penalty does not qualify as a special circumstance.

Subsection (3) provides that reducing a penalty includes staying it, or agreeing to a compromise in relation to proceedings.

Section 8Q: Penalties under section 8O: assessment of penalty

Subsection (1) states that the Commissioners may assess a penalty to a person who is liable. If they do so, they must notify that person.

Subsection (2) specifies that a penalty notice must state the contravention that is being assessed.

Subsection (3) provides that a penalty must be paid before the end of the period of 30 days beginning with the day that the notification of the penalty is issued.

Subsection (4) specifies that an assessment is to be treated as the amount of duty due from the person who is liable.

Subsection (5) specifies that an assessment may not be made later than one year after evidence of facts, which in the opinion of the Commissioners is sufficient to indicate the contravention, comes to their knowledge.

Subsection (6) states that for the purposes of assessing a penalty, two or more contraventions may be treated as one contravention.

Section 8R: Penalties under section 8O: reasonable excuse

Subsection (1) states that a person is not liable to a penalty if the person satisfies the Commissioners that there is a reasonable excuse for the contravention and the contravention is not deliberate.

Subsection (2) details that a reasonable excuse does not include a situation in which the person relies on another person, and that other person did not take reasonable care to avoid the contravention. It also provides that where the reasonable excuse has ceased, it is treated as extant provided that the person remedied the contravention without unreasonable delay.

Section 8S: Penalties under section 8O: double jeopardy

Section 8S states a person is not liable to a penalty if they have been convicted of an offence in relation to the same contravention.

Section 8T: Forfeiture of raw tobacco

Section 8T states that where there is a contravention of either s 8L or a requirement or restriction imposed by or under regulations under s 8N then the raw tobacco will be liable to forfeiture.

Section 8U: Raw tobacco: application of Customs and Excise Management Act 1979

Section 8U provides that the provisions of the Customs and Excise Management Act 1979 may, where provided for by way of regulations, apply to persons who carry on a controlled activity as they apply in relation to revenue traders; and also apply to raw tobacco as they apply in relation to tobacco products.

Subsection (2) provides for an amendment to s 9 TPDA such that a statutory instrument made under ss 8M, 8N or 8U is subject to annulment in pursuance of resolution of the House of Commons.

Subsection (3) provides an amendment to be made to s 13A(2) FA 1994 to include any decision made by HMRC as to the liability or the amount of a penalty under s 8O TPDA.

Subsection (4) amends Sch 5 FA 1994 to include the refusal of an approval request, the imposition of conditions to an approval or the variation or revocation of an approval to be subject to review and appeal.

Subsection (5) allows these amendments to come into force on a day that the Commissioners appoint by way of regulations.

Subsection (6) provides for regulations to come into effect on different days for different purposes.

State Aids Granted Through Provision of Tax Advantages

180 Powers to obtain information about certain tax advantages

(1) The powers conferred by this section are only exercisable for the purpose of complying (or enabling another person to comply) with relevant EU obligations.

(2) The Commissioners may determine that claims made for a tax advantage of a description listed in Part 1 of Schedule 24 must include (or be accompanied by) such information, presented in such form, as the determination may specify.

(3) For the purposes of subsection (2) "information" includes—

(a) information about the claimant (or the claimant's activities),

(b) information about the subject-matter of the claim, and

(c) other information which relates to the grant of state aid through the provision of the tax advantage in question.

(4) A determination under subsection (2)

(a) may make different provision for different descriptions of tax advantages or for different cases or circumstances, and

(b) may be revoked or amended by another determination.

(5) Subsection (6) applies where it appears to the Commissioners that a tax advantage of a description listed in Part 2 of Schedule 24—

(a) has been given, or

(b) may be given in the future.

(6) The Commissioners may give the relevant person a notice requiring the person—

(a) to supply the Commissioners with the information specified in the request, and

(b) if the notice so provides, to present it in the form specified in the request.

(7) The relevant person must comply with those requirements within the period specified in the notice.

(8) In subsections (6) and (7) "the relevant person", in relation to a tax advantage of any description, means the person mentioned in the third column of the entry for that tax advantage in Part 2 of Schedule 24.

(9) For the purposes of subsection (6) "information" includes—

(a) information about

(i) the person to whom the request is given (or their activities),

(ii) any other person who is the beneficiary of the tax advantage,

(b) information about the tax advantage (including the circumstances in which it was obtained), and

(c) any other information which relates to the grant of state aid through the provision of the tax advantage in question.

(10) A determination under subsection (2) may not apply to claims made before 1 July 2016.

(11) A notice under subsection (6) may relate to any information required by the Commissioners for the purpose mentioned in subsection (1) (including information which relates to matters arising before this Act is passed).

GENERAL NOTE

HMRC published a policy paper on 16 March 2016 which relates to the European Commission's programme of modernising state aid. Its stated policy objective is to enable the UK to contribute to the monitoring of state aids and compliance with EU state aid rules. The overall effect of the provisions is to enable HMRC to collect additional information in relation to certain UK tax reliefs and give HMRC a statutory footing to publish that information or disclose it to the European Commission (which may then publish it).

Section 180 enables HMRC to collect additional information. The additional powers may only be exercised for the purpose of complying with EU state aid requirements.

The additional powers apply to a limited range of tax reliefs which are set out in FA 2016 Sch 24. The affected reliefs are relief for small and medium enterprises in respect of research and development costs, the enterprise investment scheme (the "EIS"), the venture capital trust scheme (the "VCT Scheme"), vaccine research relief, reduced rate climate change levy (the "Climate Change Levy"), enhanced capital allowances for enterprise zones, business premises renovation allowances, zero-emission goods vehicle allowances and certain film, television, theatre and orchestra reliefs. Each relief is affected in one of two ways, as summarised below.

First, for the reliefs listed above other than the EIS, the VCT Scheme and the Climate Change Levy, HMRC will be able to issue a determination indicating the scope and form of information required to be provided when such a relief is claimed. The information HMRC may require includes information about the entity making the claim for relief, its activities, the subject matter of the claim and any other information relevant to the granting of state aid through that tax relief. The list is not exhaustive. HMRC will also have the flexibility to require different information for different circumstances and to change their requirements by issuing further determinations. Claims made before 1 July 2016 are grandfathered.

Secondly, for the EIS, the VCT Scheme and the Climate Change Levy reduced rate, HMRC's additional power is to issue a notice to the "relevant person" (for EIS, the company the shares in which are acquired by investors, for the VCT Scheme, the venture capital trust and for the Climate Change Levy, the person receiving the reduced rate supply). That notice will require the relevant person to provide certain information within a period specified in the notice. In such cases, HMRC will be able to require that the relevant person provides information about it or its activities, any other person who has the benefit of the tax relief, information about the relief itself (including the circumstances in which it was obtained) and any other information relevant to the granting of state aid through that tax relief. There is no grandfathering for this aspect of the new rules. Section 180(11) specifically states that information relating to matters arising before the FA 2016 is passed may be required to be provided under the new regime.

181 Power to publish state aid information

(1) The Commissioners may publish any state aid information for the purpose of securing compliance with any relevant EU obligation which requires the publication of that information.

(2) That power includes power to disclose state aid information to another person for the purpose of securing its publication.

(3) In this section "state aid information" means information which relates to the grant of state aid through the provision of a tax advantage and includes (but is not limited to) any information mentioned in section 180(3) or (9).

(4) This section applies to any state aid information (including information which relates to a tax advantage given before the passing of this Act).

GENERAL NOTE

Section 181 gives HMRC the power to publish (or disclose to another person for the purpose of publishing) information for the purpose of complying with EU state aid requirements. This applies to any information that relates to the grant of state aid through the provision of a tax advantage (including the information noted in relation to s 180 above).

There is no grandfathering for this provision. Section 181(4) specifically states that information relating to a tax advantage given before the FA 2016 is passed may be published.

The explanatory note states that information will only be published where the state aid in question is for an amount of €500,000 or more (which is in line with the underlying EU obligations) and that the specific amount of the tax advantage will not be published. Instead, information will be published in ranges.

182 Information powers: supplementary

(1) In sections 180 and 181—

"the Commissioners" means the Commissioners for Her Majesty's Revenue and Customs;

"relevant EU obligations" means—

(a) obligations under the General Block Exemption Regulation that relate to the grant of state aid through the provision of a tax advantage, or

(b) any corresponding obligations under EU law that apply to the grant of a notified state aid through the provision of a tax advantage.

(2) The "General Block Exemption Regulation" is Commission Regulation (EU) No 651/2014 declaring certain categories of aid to be compatible with the internal

market in application of Articles 107 and 108 of the Treaty establishing the European Union (which relate to state aids granted by Member States).

(3) The Treasury may by regulations made by statutory instrument amend Part 1 or Part 2 of Schedule 24 by adding, omitting or varying an entry for any description of tax advantage.

(4) Regulations under subsection (3) may include incidental or supplemental provision.

(5) A statutory instrument containing regulations under subsection (3) is subject to annulment in pursuance of a resolution of the House of Commons.

(6) The powers under sections 180 and 181 are in addition to any other powers of the Commissioners to acquire, disclose or publish information.

GENERAL NOTE

Section 182 clarifies certain aspects of ss 180 and 181. It also gives HM Treasury the power to amend FA 2016 Sch 24 by statutory instrument to change a tax relief listing in that schedule and to add or omit other tax advantages.

Qualifying Transformer Vehicles

183 Qualifying transformer vehicles

(1) In this section "qualifying transformer vehicle" means a transformer vehicle which meets conditions which are specified in regulations made by the Treasury.

(2) The Treasury may by regulations make provision about the treatment for the purposes of any enactment relating to taxation of—

(a) qualifying transformer vehicles;
(b) investors in qualifying transformer vehicles;
(c) transactions involving qualifying transformer vehicles.

(3) Regulations under subsection (2) may, in particular, disapply, apply (with or without modification) or modify the application of any enactment.

(4) Without limiting the generality of subsection (2), regulations under that subsection may in particular include—

(a) provision for profits or other amounts to be calculated with any adjustments, or on any basis, set out in the regulations;
(b) provision conferring, altering or removing an exemption or relief;
(c) provision about the treatment of arrangements the purpose, or one of the main purposes, of which is to secure a tax advantage;
(d) provision about collection and enforcement (including the withholding of tax);
(e) in relation to qualifying transformer vehicles, requirements with regard to the provision of information to investors;
(f) in relation to qualifying transformer vehicles or investors in qualifying transformer vehicles, requirements with regard to—
   (i) the provision of information to Her Majesty's Revenue and Customs,
   (ii) the preparation of accounts,
   (iii) the keeping of records, or
   (iv) other administrative matters.

(5) Regulations under this section—

(a) may provide for Her Majesty's Revenue and Customs to exercise a discretion in dealing with any matter;
(b) may make provision by reference to rules, guidance or other documents issued by any person (as they have effect from time to time).

(6) Regulations under this section may—

(a) make different provision for different cases or different purposes (including different provision in relation to different descriptions of qualifying transformer vehicle or, as the case may be, transformer vehicle);
(b) contain incidental, supplementary, consequential and transitional provision and savings.

(7) Regulations under this section are to be made by statutory instrument.

(8) A statutory instrument containing regulations under subsection (1) is subject to annulment in pursuance of a resolution of the House of Commons.

(9) But the first set of regulations under subsection (1) may not be made unless a draft has been laid before, and approved by a resolution of, the House of Commons.

(10) A statutory instrument containing regulations under subsection (2) may not be made unless a draft has been laid before, and approved by a resolution of, the House of Commons.

(11) In this section—

"enactment" includes subordinate legislation (as defined in section 21 of the Interpretation Act 1978);

"investors" in relation to a qualifying transformer vehicle means holders of investments issued by the qualifying transformer vehicle; and for this purpose "investment" includes any asset, right or interest;

"tax advantage" has the meaning given by section 1139 of CTA 2010;

"transformer vehicle" has the same meaning as in section 284A of the Financial Services and Markets Act 2000.

GENERAL NOTE

In the 2015 Budget the Chancellor announced plans for the government to work with the insurance industry and its regulators on the introduction of a new corporate and tax structure that would allow the UK to compete as a jurisdiction of choice for insurance-linked securitisation vehicles. The Government issued a consultation document on the shape of that regime in February 2016, s 183 being the legislative result of that consultation.

Insurance-linked securities are a means by which insurers can access the capital markets. In essence insurance risk is passed to a special purpose vehicle (referred to in s 183 as a qualifying transformer vehicle) which is financed by capital raised from external investors by the special purpose vehicle itself.

Section 183 lays the foundations for the new tax regime by providing HM Treasury with wide-ranging regulation making powers to determine the tax treatment of qualifying transformer vehicles, the investors in those vehicles and the transactions into which they enter.

PART 12
OFFICE OF TAX SIMPLIFICATION

GENERAL NOTE

Summer Budget 2015 announced that the Office of Tax Simplification (OTS) would be made permanent and put on a statutory footing.

The House of Lords Economic Affairs Committee welcomed the move, but recommended in a March 2016 report on the draft Finance Bill that the OTS's statutory remit be extended to give it "an integral role in tax policy design". The committee noted that the draft legislation did not use the term "independent", adding that in evidence to the committee some experts had questioned "how independent the OTS could be in its operations when it is entirely dependent on HM Treasury for funding".

184 Office of Tax Simplification

(1) There continues to be an Office of Tax Simplification (referred to in this Act as the "OTS").

(2) Schedule 25 contains provision about the OTS.

GENERAL NOTE

Section 184 provides that there continues to be an OTS, and introduces Sch 25.

185 Functions of the OTS: general

(1) The OTS must provide advice to the Chancellor of the Exchequer, on request or as the OTS considers appropriate, on the simplification of the tax system.

(2) For the purposes of this section and section 186—

(a) "the tax system" means the law relating to, and the administration of, relevant taxes,

(b) "relevant taxes" means taxes that the Commissioners for Her Majesty's Revenue and Customs are responsible for collecting and managing, and

(c) a reference to "taxes" includes a reference to duties and national insurance contributions.

(3) References in this section and section 186 (however expressed) to the simplification of the tax system include references to improving the efficiency of the administration of relevant taxes.

GENERAL NOTE

Section 185 requires the OTS to provide advice to the Chancellor of the Exchequer on request or as the OTS considers appropriate, on simplification of the tax system, i.e. the law relating to and the administration of "relevant taxes".

"Relevant taxes" are taxes that HMRC is responsible for collecting and managing, and "taxes" includes duties and national insurance contributions. "Simplification of the tax system" includes references to improving efficiency of the administration of relevant taxes.

186 Functions of the OTS: reviews and reports

(1) At the request of the Chancellor of the Exchequer, the OTS must conduct a review of an aspect of the tax system for the purpose of identifying whether, and if so how, that aspect of the tax system could be simplified.

(2) The OTS must prepare a report—

(a) setting out the results of the review, and

(b) making such recommendations (if any) as the OTS consider appropriate.

(3) The OTS must send a copy of the report to the Chancellor of the Exchequer.

(4) The Chancellor of the Exchequer must—

(a) publish the report, and

(b) lay a copy of the report before Parliament.

(5) The Chancellor of the Exchequer must prepare and publish a response to the report.

GENERAL NOTE

Section 186 provides that at the Chancellor's request the OTS must conduct a review of an aspect of the tax system for the purpose of identifying whether, and if so how, that aspect could be simplified. The OTS must prepare and send to the Chancellor a report setting out the results of its review and making such recommendations as it considers appropriate.

The Chancellor must publish the report, laying a copy before Parliament, and prepare and publish a response.

187 Annual report

(1) The OTS must prepare a report of the performance of its functions in each financial year.

(2) The report relating to a financial year must be prepared as soon as reasonably practicable after the end of the financial year.

(3) The OTS must—

(a) send a copy of the report to the Chancellor of the Exchequer, and

(b) publish the report.

(4) The Chancellor of the Exchequer must lay a copy of the report before Parliament.

(5) For the purposes of this paragraph, each of the following is a "financial year"—

(a) the period beginning with the day on which this section comes into force and ending with the following 31 March, and

(b) each successive period of 12 months.

GENERAL NOTE

Section 187 requires the OTS to prepare, publish and send to the Chancellor reports of the performance of its functions for each financial year, i.e. the year to 31 March.

188 Review of the OTS

(1) The Treasury must, before the end of each review period, conduct a review of the effectiveness of the OTS in performing its functions.

(2) The "review period" means—

(a) in relation to the first review, the period of 5 years beginning with the day on which this section comes into force, and

(b) in relation to subsequent reviews, the period of 5 years beginning with the day on which the previous review was completed.

(3) The Treasury must prepare and publish a report of each review.

GENERAL NOTE

Section 188 requires HM Treasury, before the end of each review period (see below), to conduct and publish a review of the effectiveness of the OTS in performing its functions. The "review period" means:

–   for the first review, the period of five years beginning with the day on which this provision comes into force; and

–   for subsequent reviews, the period of five years beginning with the day on which the previous review was completed.

189 Commencement

Sections 184 to 188 and Schedule 25 come into force on such day as the Treasury may by regulations made by statutory instrument appoint.

GENERAL NOTE

Sections 184–188 and Sch 25 come into force on such day as the Treasury may appoint by means of regulations made by statutory instrument.

PART 13

FINAL

190 Interpretation

In this Act—

"ALDA 1979" means the Alcoholic Liquor Duties Act 1979;

"CAA 2001" means the Capital Allowances Act 2001;

"CEMA 1979" means the Customs and Excise Management Act 1979;

"CTA 2009" means the Corporation Tax Act 2009;

"CTA 2010" means the Corporation Tax Act 2010;

"FA", followed by a year, means the Finance Act of that year;

"F(No 2)A, followed by a year means the Finance (No 2) Act of that year;

"F(No 3)A, followed by a year, means the Finance (No 3) Act of that year;

"HODA 1979" means the Hydrocarbon Oil Duties Act 1979;

"ICTA" means the Income and Corporation Taxes Act 1988;

"IHTA 1984" means the Inheritance Tax Act 1984;

"ITA 2007" means the Income Tax Act 2007;

"ITEPA 2003" means the Income Tax (Earnings and Pensions) Act 2003;

"ITTOIA 2005" means the Income Tax (Trading and Other Income) Act 2005;

"OTA 1975" means the Oil Taxation Act 1975;

"TCGA 1992" means the Taxation of Chargeable Gains Act 1992;

"TIOPA 2010" means the Taxation (International and Other Provisions) Act 2010;

"TMA 1970" means the Taxes Management Act 1970;

"TPDA 1979" means the Tobacco Products Duty Act 1979;

"VATA 1994" means the Value Added Tax Act 1994;

"VERA 1994" means the Vehicle Excise and Registration Act 1994.

191 Short title
This Act may be cited as the Finance Act 2016.

SCHEDULE 1
ABOLITION OF DIVIDEND TAX CREDITS ETC
Section 5

Main repeals

1 (1) In ITTOIA 2005 omit sections 397 to 398, 400, 414 and 421 (distributions: tax credits, and tax treated as paid).

(2) In CTA 2010 omit section 1109 (tax credits for certain distributions).

Further amendments in ITTOIA 2005

2 ITTOIA 2005 is further amended as follows.

3 In the heading of Chapter 3 of Part 4, for "credits etc" substitute "treated as paid".

4 In section 382(2) (other contents of Chapter 3 of Part 4)—
  (a) omit "tax credits,", and
  (b) for "397" substitute "399".

5 Omit section 384(3) (which refers to section 398).

6 Omit section 393(5) (determining entitlement to tax credit).

7 In section 394 (which deems a distribution to be made)—
  (a) omit subsection (5) (determining entitlement to tax credit), and
  (b) in subsection (6), for "But for" substitute "For".

8 In section 395(3) (interpretation of section 395(2)) omit the words from "after" to the end.

9 For section 396A(2)(b) (alternative receipt treated as qualifying distribution for the purposes of sections 397 and 399 and for the purposes of section 1100 of CTA 2010) substitute—
  "(b) for the purposes of sections 1100 to 1103 of CTA 2010 (statements and returns of details of distributions) it is treated as a distribution that—
    (i) is so made, and
    (ii) is one to which section 1100 of CTA 2010 applies."

10 In the italic heading before section 397, omit "Tax credits and".

11 (1) Section 399 (qualifying distribution received by person not entitled to tax credits) is amended as follows.

(2) For subsection (1) substitute—
  "(1) This section applies if—
    (a) a person's income for a tax year includes a distribution of a company, and
    (b) the person is non-UK resident."

(3) In subsection (2) omit "(but see subsection (7))".

(4) Omit subsections (3) to (5) (amount of dividend received by non-UK resident to be treated as its grossed-up amount).

(5) Omit subsection (5A) (amounts treated as qualifying distributions for purposes of the section).

(6) Omit subsection (7) (which provides for subsection (2) to be subject to repealed provisions).

(7) For the heading substitute "Tax treated as paid on distributions received by non-UK resident persons".

12 (1) Section 401 (relief: qualifying distribution after linked non-qualifying distribution) is amended as follows.

(2) For subsections (1) to (6) substitute—
  "(1) Where a person is liable to income tax on a CD distribution, the person's liability to income tax on a subsequent non-CD distribution is reduced in accordance with this section if the non-CD distribution consists of a repayment of—
    (a) the share capital, or
    (b) the principal of the security,
  which constituted the CD distribution.
  (1A) The reduction is—

(a) the amount of income tax to which the person is liable on the CD distribution, or

(b) if lower, the amount of income tax to which the person is liable on the non-CD distribution.

(1B) For the purposes of calculating the amounts mentioned in subsection (1A)(a) and (b) assume—

(a) that the CD distribution is the lowest part of the person's dividend income in the tax year ("year 1") in which it is made,

(b) that the non-CD distribution, if it is made in year 1, is the part of the person's dividend income in year 1 that is next lowest after the CD distribution, and

(c) that the non-CD distribution, if it is made after year 1, is the lowest part of the person's dividend income in the tax year in which it is made."

(3) In subsection (7) (interpretation), for ""security"" substitute "—

"CD distribution" means a distribution which is a distribution for the purposes of the Corporation Tax Acts only because it falls within paragraph C or D in section 1000(1) of CTA 2010 (redeemable share capital or security issued as bonus in respect of shares in, or securities of, the company),

"non-CD distribution" means a distribution which is not a CD distribution, and

"security"".

(4) In the heading, for "qualifying distribution after linked non-qualifying distribution" substitute "distribution repaying shares or security issued in earlier distribution".

13 Omit section 401A (recovery of overpaid tax credit etc).

14 In section 401B (power to obtain information for the purposes of section 397), for "section 397", in each place it occurs, substitute "this Chapter".

15 Omit sections 406(4A) and 407(4A) (determining entitlement to tax credit).

16 In section 408(2A) (interpretation of section 408(2)) omit the words from "after" to the end.

17 In section 411(2) (stock dividends: amount on which tax charged) omit ", grossed up by reference to the dividend ordinary rate for the tax year".

18 In section 416 (released debts: amount on which tax charged)—

(a) in subsection (1) (tax charged on gross amount) omit "gross", and

(b) omit subsection (2) (meaning of "gross amount").

19 In section 418(3) (release of loan: tax only on grossed-up amount of excess where part previously charged) omit ", grossed up by reference to the dividend ordinary rate".

20 In section 651 (meaning of "UK estate" and "foreign estate")—

(a) in subsection (4), for "680(3) or (4) (sums" substitute "664(2)(c) or (d) or 680(4) (sums not liable to tax and sums", and

(b) in subsection (5), for "680(3) or (4)" substitute "664(2)(c) or (d) or 680(4)".

21 In section 657 (tax charged on estate income from foreign estates), for "680(3) or (4)", in both places, substitute "680(4)".

22 In section 663 (applicable rate for purposes of grossing-up under sections 656 and 657), after subsection (4) insert—

"(5) The aggregate income of the estate, so far as it consists of income within section 664(2)(c) or (d), is treated for the purposes of this section as bearing income tax at 0%."

23 In section 670 (applicable rate for purposes of Step 2 in section 665(1)), after subsection (4) insert—

"(4A) The aggregate income of the estate, so far as it consists of income within section 664(2)(c) or (d), is treated for the purposes of this section as bearing income tax at 0%."

24 In section 680 (income of an estate that is treated as bearing income tax)—

(a) in subsection (2) omit "(3) or", and

(b) omit subsection (3) (sums treated as bearing tax at the dividend ordinary rate).

25 In section 680A (estate income treated as dividend income), in each of subsections (1)(a) and (4)(a), after "at the dividend ordinary rate" insert "or as bearing tax at 0% because of section 663(5)".

26 In section 854(6) (carrying on by partner of notional business: meaning of "untaxed income")—

(a) omit the "or" at the end of paragraph (b), and

(b) after paragraph (c) insert—

"(d) income chargeable under Chapter 5 of Part 4 (stock dividends from UK resident companies), or

(e) income chargeable under Chapter 6 of Part 4 (release of loan to participator in closed company)."

27 Omit section 858(3) (partnerships with foreign element: entitlement to tax credit).

Further amendments in CTA 2010

28 CTA 2010 is further amended as follows.

29 (1) Section 279F (ring fence profits: related 51% group company) is amended as follows.

(2) In subsection (7)(c) (conditions to be met by a company's dividend income in order for company to be a passive company), in sub-paragraph (ii) (dividends must be franked investment income) for "franked investment income" substitute "exempt ABGH distributions".

(3) After subsection (9) insert—

"(10) In subsection (7)(c) "exempt ABGH distribution" means a distribution which—

(a) is a distribution for the purposes of the Corporation Tax Acts only because it falls within paragraph A, B, G or H in section 1000(1), and

(b) is exempt for the purposes of Part 9A of CTA 2009 (company distributions)."

30 (1) Section 279G (ring fence profits: meaning of "augmented profits") is amended as follows.

(2) In subsection (1)(b) (franked investment income is part of augmented profits unless excluded)—

(a) for "franked investment income" substitute "exempt ABGH distributions", and

(b) for "is" substitute "are".

(3) In subsection (3) (exclusion of franked investment income received from certain subsidiaries etc), for "franked investment income" substitute "exempt ABGH distribution".

(4) After subsection (4) insert—

"(5) In this section "exempt ABGH distribution" means a distribution which—

(a) is a distribution for the purposes of the Corporation Tax Acts only because it falls within paragraph A, B, G or H in section 1000(1), and

(b) is exempt for the purposes of Part 9A of CTA 2009 (company distributions)."

31 For section 463(7) (loan to trustees of settlement which has ended: amount on which debtor taxed when all or part of loan released or written off) substitute—

"(7) The amount which Y is treated as receiving is equal to the amount released or written off."

32 (1) Section 549 (distributions: supplementary) is amended as follows.

(2) Omit subsection (2) (which excludes entitlement to tax credits).

(3) In subsection (2A) (which disapplies sections 409 to 414 of ITTOIA 2005), for "414" substitute "413A".

33 (1) Section 751 (interpretation of Part 15 (transactions in securities)) is amended as follows.

(2) The existing text becomes subsection (1).

(3) In that subsection, in the definition of "dividends", omit "qualifying".

(4) After that subsection insert—

"(2) In the definition of "dividends" given by subsection (1), "other distributions" does not include a distribution which is a distribution for the purposes of the Corporation Tax Acts only because it falls within paragraph C or D in section 1000(1) (redeemable share capital or security issued as bonus in respect of shares in, or securities of, the company)."

34 Omit section 814D(8) (which excludes entitlement to tax credits).

35 Omit section 997(5) (which introduces sections 1109 to 1111).

36 In sections 1026(1)(b) and 1027(2)(b) (cases where amount paid up in respect of bonus shares does not fall to be treated as a qualifying distribution) omit "qualifying".

37 (1) Section 1070 (distributions by company carrying on mutual business) is amended as follows.

(2) In subsection (2) (provisions about distributions apply to company's distributions only where made out of taxed profits or franked investment income), for paragraph (b) (franked investment income) substitute—

"(b) income of the company consisting of exempt ABGH distributions."

(3) After subsection (5) insert—

"(5A) In subsection (2) "exempt ABGH distribution" means a distribution which—

(a) is a distribution for the purposes of the Corporation Tax Acts only because it falls within paragraph A, B, G or H in section 1000(1), and

(b) is exempt for the purposes of Part 9A of CTA 2009 (company distributions)."

38 (1) Section 1071 (company not carrying on business) is amended as follows.

(2) In subsection (5) (provisions about distributions apply to company's distributions only where made out of taxed profits or franked investment income), for paragraph (b) (franked investment income) substitute—

"(b) income of the company consisting of exempt ABGH distributions."

(3) After subsection (5) insert—

"(5A) In subsection (5) "exempt ABGH distribution" means a distribution which—

(a) is a distribution for the purposes of the Corporation Tax Acts only because it falls within paragraph A, B, G or H in section 1000(1), and

(b) is exempt for the purposes of Part 9A of CTA 2009 (company distributions)."

39 (1) Section 1100 (qualifying distribution: right to request a statement) is amended as follows.

(2) In subsection (1) (requests for statement)—

(a) for "qualifying distribution" substitute "distribution to which this section applies", and

(b) omit paragraph (b) (amount of any tax credit), and the "and" preceding it.

(3) After subsection (4) insert—

"(4A) This section applies to any distribution other than one which is a distribution for the purposes of the Corporation Tax Acts only because it falls within paragraph C or D in section 1000(1) (redeemable share capital or security issued as bonus in respect of shares in, or securities of, the company)."

(4) Omit subsections (2) and (5) (interpretation of subsection (1)(b)).

(5) In subsection (7) (section to be read with section 396A(2) of ITTOIA 2005)—

(a) for "needs" substitute ", and sections 1101 to 1103, need", and

(b) for "as "qualifying distributions" for the purposes of this section" substitute "as distributions to which this section applies".

(6) In the heading, for "Qualifying" substitute "Certain".

40 (1) Section 1101 (non-qualifying distributions etc: returns and information) is amended as follows.

(2) In subsection (1) (duty to make return), for "which is not a qualifying distribution" substitute "to which section 1100 does not apply".

(3) In subsection (4) (duty to make return where not clear whether distribution is non-qualifying), for "which is not a qualifying distribution" substitute "to which section 1100 does not apply".

(4) In the heading, and in the heading of section 1102, for "Non-qualifying" substitute "Other".

41 In section 1103 (regulations about information about non-qualifying distributions)—

(a) in subsection (2) (purpose for which sections 1101 and 1102 may be rewritten), for "which are not qualifying distributions" substitute "to which section 1100 does not apply",

(b) in subsection (4) (special arrangements about matters specified in subsection (5)), for "matters" substitute "matter", and

(c) in subsection (5)—

(i) for "Those matters are" substitute "That matter is", and

(ii) omit paragraph (b) (tax credits), and the "and" preceding it.

42 (1) Section 1106 (interpretation of sections 1104 and 1105) is amended as follows.

(2) In subsection (4) (meaning of "tax certificate")—

(a) after paragraph (a) insert "and", and

(b) omit paragraph (c) (tax credits), and the "and" preceding it.

(3) Omit subsections (5) and (6) (interpretation of subsection (4)(c)).

43 Omit sections 1110 and 1111 (recovery of overpaid tax credits etc).

44 (1) Section 1115 (meaning of "new consideration" in Part 23) is amended as follows.

(2) In subsections (5)(a) and (6)(b) for "qualifying" substitute "non-CD".

(3) After subsection (6) insert—

"(7) In this section "non-CD distribution" means any distribution other than one which is a distribution for the purposes of the Corporation Tax Acts only because it falls within paragraph C or D in section 1000(1) (redeemable share capital or security issued as bonus in respect of shares in, or securities of, the company)."

45 In section 1119 (definitions for the purposes of the Corporation Tax Acts) omit the entries for "franked investment income", "qualifying distribution" and "tax credit".

46 Omit section 1126 (meaning of "franked investment income").

47 Omit section 1136 (meaning of "qualifying distribution").

48 Omit section 1139(4) ("relief" includes tax credit).

49 In Schedule 2 (transitionals and savings etc) omit paragraph 106(1) (operation of sections 1026 and 1027 in relation to share capital issued before 7 April 1973).

50 In Schedule 4 (index of defined expressions) omit the entries for "franked investment income", "qualifying distribution" and "tax credit".

Other amendments

51 (1) TMA 1970 is amended as follows.

(2) In section 8(1AA)(b) (payable income tax is chargeable amount less tax deducted at source and tax credits) omit the words after "source".

(3) In section 8A(1AA)(b) (payable income tax is chargeable amount less tax deducted at source and tax credits) omit the words after "source".

(4) In section 9(1) (self-assessment)—

(a) in paragraph (b) (payable income tax is assessed amount less tax deducted at source and tax credits) omit the words after "source", and
(b) in the words after paragraph (b) omit ", 400(2), 414(1), 421(1)".

(5) In section 12AA(1A)(b) (partner's payable income tax is chargeable amount less tax deducted at source and tax credits) omit the words after "source".

(6) In section 12AB (partnership statement in partnership return)—

(a) in subsection (1)(a)—

(i) after sub-paragraph (ia) insert "and", and
(ii) omit sub-paragraph (iii) (tax credits), and the "and" preceding it,

(b) in subsection (1)(b) for ", tax or credit" substitute "or tax", and
(c) in subsection (5) omit the definition of "tax credit".

(7) In section 12B(4A)(a)(i) (statements themselves must be preserved if of amount of qualifying distribution and tax credit), after "amount" insert "of distribution, formerly amount".

(8) In section 59A(8)(b) (amounts included in annual total of deductions at source) omit "or are tax credits to which section 397(1) or 397A(1) of ITTOIA 2005 applies,".

(9) In section 59B (payment of income tax and capital gains tax)—

(a) in subsection (1) omit ", 400(2), 414(1), 421(1)", and
(b) in subsection (2)(b) omit "or is a tax credit to which section 397(1) or 397A(1) of ITTOIA 2005 applies,".

(10) Omit section 87A(5) (interest on assessments under section 1110 of CTA 2010 on overpaid tax credits etc).

(11) In section 98 (special returns), in the first column of the table omit the entry for section 1109 of CTA 2010.

52 (1) ICTA is amended as follows.

(2) Omit section 231B (arrangements to pass on value of tax credit).

(3) Omit section 824(2) (repayment supplements: tax credits).

(4) In section 824(4A) omit paragraph (b) (repayment supplements: tax credit treated as income tax deducted at source), and the "and" preceding it.

(5) In section 825(1) (repayment supplements: companies) omit paragraph (c) (tax credits comprised in franked investment income), and the "or" preceding it.

(6) In section 826 (interest on tax overpaid by companies)—

(a) in subsection (1) omit paragraph (c) (tax credits), including the "or" at the end, and
(b) in subsection (3)—

(i) omit "or a payment of the whole or part of a tax credit falling within subsection (1)(c) above", and
(ii) omit "or, as the case may be, the franked investment income referred to in subsection (1)(c) above".

53 In FA 1988, in Schedule 13 omit paragraph 7(c) (post-consolidation amendment of section 824(2) of ICTA).

54 In FA 1989—

    (a) omit section 115 (double taxation: tax credits), and

    (b) in section 179(1)(b)(i) (amendments of provisions of TMA 1970 including section 87A(1) and (5)) omit "and (5)".

55 In FA 1993 omit section 171(2B) (which excludes entitlement to tax credits).

56 In FA 1994 omit section 219(4B) (which excludes entitlement to tax credits).

57 (1) F(No 2)A 1997 is amended as follows.

(2) Omit section 22(1) (which inserted section 171(2B) of FA 1993).

(3) Omit section 28 (which inserted section 231B of ICTA).

(4) Omit section 30(9) and (10) (effect of double taxation arrangements in relation to tax credits).

(5) In Schedule 6 (repeal of provisions relating to foreign income dividends), in paragraph 23 (transitional provision for certain foreign income dividends paid before 6 April 1999 but received on or after that date) omit—

    (a) "qualifying", and

    (b) "nine tenths of".

58 (1) FA 1998 is amended as follows.

(2) Omit section 76(3) (regulations about tax credits where non-UK residents have invested in individual savings accounts).

(3) In Schedule 18 (company tax returns etc)—

    (a) omit paragraph 9(3) (certain claims by companies for payment of tax credits),

    (b) in paragraphs 22(3)(a)(i) and 23(3)(a)(i) (which relate to a statement as to amount of qualifying distribution and tax credit), after "amount" insert "of distribution, but formerly amount", and

    (c) in paragraph 52(2)(a) omit "or payment of a tax credit".

59 In the Commonwealth Development Corporation Act 1999, in Schedule 3 omit paragraph 6(2)(b) (provisions about tax credits do not apply in relation to distributions by the Corporation).

60 In the Financial Services and Markets Act 2000 (Consequential Amendments) (Taxes) Order 2001 (SI 2001/3629)—

    (a) omit article 82(a), and

    (b) in article 87(a) omit "and (4B)".

61 (1) ITEPA 2003 is amended as follows.

(2) Omit sections 58(6) and 61H(6) (tax credits to be reduced in line with reductions in distributions).

(3) In Part 2 of Schedule 1 (index of defined expressions) omit the entry for "tax credit".

62 In ITTOIA 2005, in Schedule 1 (minor and consequential amendments) omit paragraphs 116, 331(2), 359, 360, 361(a), 363, 364, 376, 377(3), 464(3), 496, 503 and 510(2).

63 (1) ITA 2007 is amended as follows.

(2) In section 26(1)(b) (list of provisions giving tax reductions), in the entry for section 401 of ITTOIA 2005, for "qualifying distribution after linked non-qualifying distribution" substitute "distribution repaying shares or security issued in earlier distribution".

(3) In section 31 (calculation of total income)—

    (a) omit subsection (3) (dividend etc treated as increased by amount of tax credit), and

    (b) in subsection (4), for "Subsections (2) and (3) apply" substitute "Subsection (2) applies".

(4) In section 425(5) (deductions in calculating total amount of income tax for gift aid purposes)—

    (a) in paragraph (a)—

        (i) in sub-paragraph (i) omit "or 400(2)", and

        (ii) omit sub-paragraphs (ii) and (iii),

    (b) after paragraph (a) insert "and",

    (c) in paragraph (b), for "680(3)(b) or (4)" substitute "680(4)", and

    (d) omit paragraph (c), and the "and" before it.

(5) In section 482 (types of amount charged at special rates for trustees), in the entry for Type 1 amounts, omit "qualifying".

(6) In section 487(6) (non-UK resident trustees: disregarded income which is not included in untaxed income)—

    (a) after paragraph (a) insert "or", and

    (b) omit paragraph (c) (income in respect of which there is a tax credit), and the "or" preceding it.

(7) In section 498 (discretionary payments by trustees: types of tax to be included in trustees' tax pool)—

    (a) in subsection (1)—

        (i) in Type 1 (tax at special rates for trustees on income not attracting tax credits), omit "2, 3 or",

        (ii) omit Types 2 and 3 (tax at dividend trust rate on income attracting dividend tax credits), and

        (iii) in Type 4 (tax charged at basic rate as a result of section 491), omit "at the basic rate", and

    (b) omit subsection (2) (interpretation of Types 2 and 3).

(8) In section 502(3) (non-UK resident beneficiaries: disregarded income which is not included in untaxed income)—

    (a) after paragraph (a) insert "or", and

    (b) omit paragraph (c) (income in respect of which there is a tax credit), and the "or" preceding it.

(9) In section 614ZD (treatment of recipient of manufactured payment)—

    (a) in subsection (3), for "to (6)" substitute "and (5)", and

    (b) omit subsection (6) (which excludes entitlement to tax credits).

(10) In section 687 (transactions in securities: meaning of "income tax advantage")—

    (a) omit "qualifying" in each place, and

    (b) in subsection (4), after "In this section" insert "—

    (a) distribution" does not include a distribution which is a distribution for the purposes of the Corporation Tax Acts only because it falls within paragraph C or D in section 1000(1) of CTA 2010 (redeemable share capital or security issued as bonus in respect of shares in, or securities of, the company), and

    (b) ".

(11) In section 713 (interpretation of Chapter 1 (transactions in securities))—

    (a) the existing text becomes subsection (1),

    (b) in that subsection, in the definition of "dividends", omit "qualifying", and

    (c) after that subsection insert—

"(2) In the definition of "dividends" given by subsection (1), "other distributions" does not include a distribution which is a distribution for the purposes of the Corporation Tax Acts only because it falls within paragraph C or D in section 1000(1) (redeemable share capital or security issued as bonus in respect of shares in, or securities of, the company)."

(12) In section 745(1) (transfer of assets abroad: same rate of tax not to be charged twice)—

    (a) after "at the basic rate," insert "or", and

    (b) omit "or the dividend ordinary rate".

(13) In section 809S(4) (meaning of "income tax advantage") omit the words after paragraph (d).

(14) In section 811(4) (limit on liability to income tax of non-UK residents)—

    (a) after paragraph (a) insert "and", and

    (b) omit paragraph (c) (tax credits), and the "and" preceding it.

(15) In section 815(3) (limit on liability to income tax of non-UK resident companies)—

    (a) after paragraph (a) insert "and", and

    (b) omit paragraph (c) (tax credits), and the "and" preceding it.

(16) In section 989 (definitions for the purposes of the Income Tax Acts) omit the entries for "qualifying distribution" and "tax credit".

(17) In section 1026 ("non-qualifying income" includes income on which tax treated as paid)

    (a) in paragraph (a) (deemed payment under sections 399 and 400 of ITTOIA 2005)—

        (i) omit "or 400(2)", and

(ii) for "from UK resident companies on which there is no tax credit" substitute "to non-UK resident persons", and

(b) omit paragraphs (b) and (c) (deemed payment under sections 414 and 421 of ITTOIA 2005).

(18) In Schedule 1 (minor and consequential amendments) omit paragraphs 26, 245(2)(a) and (3), 446(27), 515(3), 516, 517(2), 520 and 522.

(19) In Schedule 4 (index of defined expressions) omit the entries for "qualifying distribution" and "tax credit".

64 In FA 2008, in Schedule 12 (amendments relating to tax credits) omit paragraphs 3, 5, 6, 8 to 16, 19, 20, 24(b) and 31.

65 (1) CTA 2009 is amended as follows.

(2) In section 1222 (company with investment business: amount deductible for management expenses to be reduced by income from sources not charged to tax)—

(a) in subsection (1) (UK resident company), for paragraph (c) (franked investment income does not reduce deductibles) substitute—

"(c) the income does not consist of exempt ABGH distributions.",

(b) in subsection (2) (non-UK resident company), for paragraph (d) (franked investment income does not reduce deductibles) substitute—

"(d) the income does not consist of exempt ABGH distributions.", and

(c) after subsection (3) insert—

"(4) In this section "exempt ABGH distribution" means a distribution which—

(a) is a distribution for the purposes of the Corporation Tax Acts only because it falls within paragraph A, B, G or H in section 1000(1) of CTA 2010, and

(b) is exempt for the purposes of Part 9A (company distributions)."

(3) Omit section 1266(3) (partnerships with foreign element: entitlement to tax credit).

(4) In Schedule 4 (index of defined expressions) omit the entry for "qualifying distribution".

66 (1) FA 2009 is amended as follows.

(2) In Schedule 19 (amendments relating to tax credits) omit paragraphs 2(2) and (3), 3, 5, 6(2)(a), (3) and (4), 7, 9, 10(a), 11, 12 and 13(c).

(3) In paragraph 14 of Schedule 19 (amendments made by the Schedule have effect in relation to distributions etc arising or paid on or after 22 April 2009), after sub-paragraph (2) insert—

"(3) Section 873(4) of ITTOIA 2005 (inserted by paragraph 8), so far as relating to any order or regulations made after the passing of FA 2016 under any provision of ITTOIA 2005 other than section 397BA of that Act, has effect as if sub-paragraph (1) did not apply in relation to it."

(4) In Schedule 53 (late payment interest) omit—

(a) paragraph 6 (late payment interest start date in relation to assessments of overpaid tax credits etc under section 1110 of CTA 2010), and

(b) the italic heading preceding it.

(5) In paragraph 9B of Schedule 54 (repayment interest start date: companies: income tax and certain tax credits)—

(a) in sub-paragraph (1) omit paragraph (b) (tax credit comprised in franked investment income), and the "and" preceding it, and

(b) in sub-paragraph (2)—

(i) omit "or payment", and

(ii) omit "or the franked investment income mentioned in sub-paragraph (1)(b)".

(6) In paragraph 14 of Schedule 54 (interpretation) omit paragraph (b) (tax deducted at source treated as including tax credits), and the "and" preceding it.

67 In Schedule 1 to CTA 2010 (minor and consequential amendments) omit paragraphs 19, 153, 156(3), 282, 303(2), 456, 562(7), 704(27) and 722.

68 (1) TIOPA 2010 is amended as follows.

(2) In section 6(2) (effect of double taxation arrangements)—

(a) after paragraph (e) insert "or", and

(b) omit paragraph (g) (tax credits), and the "or" preceding it.

(3) In section 187A (excess interest treated as a qualifying distribution), in subsection (2), and the heading, omit "qualifying".

(4) Omit section 234(2) ("relief" includes tax credit).

(5) In Schedule 8 (minor and consequential amendments) omit paragraphs 38, 51, 52, 66 and 67.

69 In FA 2011—

    (a) in Part 6 of Schedule 23 (consequential provisions) omit paragraph 64(3), and
    (b) in Schedule 26 omit paragraph 1(2)(a)(i) (which amended section 231B of ICTA), including the "and" at the end.

70 In FA 2012, in section 169(2) (payments by certain friendly societies treated as qualifying distributions) omit "qualifying".

71 In FA 2013—

    (a) in paragraph 6(2) of Schedule 19 (which amends section 549 of CTA 2010), for "subsections (2) and" substitute "subsection", and
    (b) in Part 3 of Schedule 29 (manufactured dividends: consequential etc amendments) omit paragraphs 13, 14(a) and 44(3).

72 In FA 2015, in section 19—

    (a) in subsection (1), for "credits etc" substitute "treated as paid", and
    (b) omit subsections (5) and (6) (which insert sections 397(5A) and 399(5A) of ITTOIA 2005).

Commencement

73 (1) Subject to the following sub-paragraphs of this paragraph, the amendments made by this Schedule have effect in relation to dividends paid or arising (or treated as paid), and other distributions made (or treated as made), in the tax year 2016–17 or at any later time.

(2) The following have effect for the tax year 2016–17 and subsequent tax years—

    (a) the amendments in sections 8 to 9, 12AA and 59B of TMA 1970,
    (b) the amendments in section 854(6) of ITTOIA 2005,
    (c) the amendments in section 425 except the amendment in section 425(5)(b), and the amendments in sections 498, 745 and 1026, of ITA 2007,
    (d) the repeals of paragraphs 359, 360, 361(a), 363 and 377(3) of Schedule 1 to ITTOIA 2005,
    (e) the repeals of paragraphs 8 to 11 and 14 of Schedule 12 to FA 2008, and
    (f) the repeals of the following provisions of Schedule 19 to FA 2009—

        (i) paragraph 9(a) and (b),
        (ii) paragraph 9(c) so far as relating to section 12AA of TMA 1970, and
        (iii) paragraph 9(d) so far as relating to section 59B of TMA 1970.

(3) The amendment in paragraph 23 of Schedule 6 to F(No 2)A 1997 has effect in relation to foreign income dividends received on or after 6 April 2016.

(4) The amendments in sections 393 and 406 of ITTOIA 2005, and the repeal of paragraph 19 of Schedule 12 to FA 2008, have effect in relation to cash dividends paid over in the tax year 2016–17 or at any later time.

(5) The amendment in section 396A of ITTOIA 2005 has effect in relation to things received on or after 6 April 2016 (even if the choice to receive them was made before that date).

(6) The amendments in section 401 of ITTOIA 2005 have effect where the subsequent distribution is made in the tax year 2016–17 or at any later time, even if the prior distribution is made before 6 April 2016.

(7) The amendments in sections 411 and 414 of ITTOIA 2005, and the repeal of paragraph 520 of Schedule 1 to ITA 2007, have effect in relation to stock dividend income treated as arising in the tax year 2016–17 or at any later time.

(8) The amendments in sections 651 to 680A of ITTOIA 2005 (but not the repeal of section 680(3)(a) of that Act) and the amendment in section 425(5)(b) of ITA 2007—

    (a) so far as they relate to income within section 664(2)(c) of ITTOIA 2005 (stock dividends), have effect in relation to stock dividend income treated as arising in the tax year 2016–17 or at any later time, and
    (b) so far as they relate to income within section 664(2)(d) of ITTOIA 2005 (release of loans), have effect in relation to amounts released or written off in the tax year 2016–17 or at any later time.

(9) The amendments in Chapter 6 of Part 4 of ITTOIA 2005 and in section 463 of CTA 2010, and the repeal of paragraph 522 of Schedule 1 to ITA 2007, have effect in relation to amounts released or written off in the tax year 2016–17 or at any later time.

(10) The amendments in section 614ZD of ITA 2007 have effect in relation to manufactured payments made on or after 6 April 2016.

(11) The amendments in section 687 of ITA 2007 have effect where the relevant consideration is received in the tax year 2016–17 or at any later time.

(12) The amendments in section 1222 of CTA 2009 have effect in relation to income arising in the tax year 2016–17 or at any later time.

(13) The amendment in section 1026(1) of CTA 2010 has effect where the bonus share capital is issued on or after 6 April 2016.

(14) Sub-paragraph (1) does not apply in relation to—

    (a) the amendments in section 401B of ITTOIA 2005;

    (b) the amendment in paragraph 14 of Schedule 19 to FA 2009.

GENERAL NOTE

Abolition of dividend tax credits

Schedule 1 provides for the abolition of dividend tax credits. It repeals ITTOIA 2005 ss 397–398, 400, 414 and 421 (distributions: tax credits, and tax treated as paid) and CTA 2010 s 1109 (tax credits for certain distributions).

There are consequential amendments to TMA 1970 ss 8 (personal return), 8A (trustee's return), 9 (returns to include self-assessment), 12AA and 12AB (partnership returns), 12B (records to be kept for purposes of returns) 59A (payments on account of income tax), 59B (payment of income tax and capital gains tax, 87A (interest on overdue corporation tax etc) and 98 (penalties: special returns etc) and various provisions of CTA 2009, CTA 2010 and ITTOIA 2005.

ITTOIA 2005 s 399 (qualifying distributions received by persons not entitled to tax credits) is rewritten and the heading is changed to read "tax treated as paid on distributions received by non-UK resident persons".

ITTOIA 2005 s 401 (relief: qualifying distribution after linked non-qualifying distribution) is amended and the heading is changed to read "distribution repaying shares or security issued in earlier distribution". The term "CD distribution" replaces "non-qualifying distribution", and "non-CD distribution" replaces "qualifying distribution". A "CD distribution" is a distribution which is a distribution for the purposes of the Corporation Tax Acts only because it falls within paragraph C or D in CTA 2010 s 1000(1).

CTA 2010 ss 279F and 279G (which deal with oil-related activities) are amended to replace the concept of franked investment income with a reference to "exempt ABGH distributions". Similar changes are made to CTA 2010 s 1070 (companies carrying on a mutual business) and CTA 2010 s 1071 (companies not carrying on a business).

CTA 2010 ss 1100–1106, setting out duties to provide information and tax certificates, are also amended. The obligation to provide a tax certificate (CTA 2010 s 1104) is retained, but the obligation in CTA 2010 s 1106(4)(c) to show the amount of the tax credit is removed.

Seven Government amendments to Sch 1, intended to correct technical oversights, were agreed by the Public Bill Committee on 30 June 2016.

A further technical amendment, intended to ensure that Sch 1 operates as intended in relation to discretionary trusts, was agreed at Report stage of the Bill.

SCHEDULE 2

SPORTING TESTIMONIAL PAYMENTS

Section 12

Income tax: sporting testimonial payments treated as earnings

1 After section 226D of ITEPA 2003 (shareholder or connected person having material interest in company) insert—

"Sporting testimonial payments

226E Sporting testimonial payments

    (1) This section applies in relation to an individual who is or has been employed as a professional sportsperson ("S").

    (2) In this section "sporting testimonial" means—

        (a) a series of relevant events or activities which each have the same controller, or

        (b) a single relevant event or activity not forming part of such a series.

    (3) An event or activity is (subject to subsection (4)(b)) a relevant event or activity if—

(a) its purpose (or one of its purposes) is to raise money for or for the benefit of S, and

(b) the only or main reason for doing that is to recognise S's service as a professional sportsperson who is or has been employed as such.

(4) An activity that meets the conditions in subsection (3)(a) and (b) and consists solely of inviting and collecting donations for or for the benefit of S—

(a) is a relevant activity if it is one of a series of relevant events or activities for the purposes of subsection (2)(a), but

(b) is not a relevant activity for the purposes of subsection (2)(b) so long as both conditions in subsection (5) are met while the activity takes place.

(5) The conditions are—

(a) that any person who is responsible (alone or with others) for collecting the donations or who is the controller (or a member of a committee which is the controller) of the activity is not—

(i) S,

(ii) a person who is (or has been) the controller of any other relevant event or activity for or for the benefit of S,

(iii) a person connected with S or a person mentioned in sub-paragraph (ii),

(iv) a person acting for or on behalf of a person mentioned in sub-paragraphs (i) to (iii), and

(b) that the donations collected do not include any sums paid (directly or indirectly) out of money raised by any other relevant event or activity.

(6) A "sporting testimonial payment" is a payment made by (or on behalf of) the controller of a sporting testimonial out of money raised for or for the benefit of S which—

(a) is made to S, to a member of S's family or household, to a prescribed person, to S's order or otherwise for S's benefit, and

(b) does not (apart from this section) constitute earnings from an employment.

(7) A sporting testimonial payment is to be treated as earnings of S from the employment or former employment to which the sporting testimonial is most closely linked.

(8) For the purposes of this section if at any material time S is dead—

(a) anything done for or for the benefit of S's estate is to be regarded as done for or for the benefit of S; and

(b) a payment made to S's personal representatives or to their order is to be treated as a payment to S or to S's order.

(9) In this section—

"controller", in relation to an event or activity which meets the conditions in subsection (3)(a) and (b), means the person who controls the disbursement of any money raised for or for the benefit of S from that event or activity,

"money" includes money's worth and "payment" includes the transfer of money's worth or the provision of any benefit,

"prescribed person" means a person prescribed in regulations made by the Treasury.

(10) Section 993 of ITA 2007 (meaning of "connected" persons) has effect for the purposes of this section."

Income tax: limited exemption for sporting testimonial payments

2 After section 306A of ITEPA 2003 (exemption for carers) insert—

"Professional sportspersons

306B Limited exemption for sporting testimonial payments

(1) This section applies to any sporting testimonial payments which are—

(a) made out of money raised by a sporting testimonial ("the sporting testimonial"), and

(b) treated by virtue of section 226E as earnings of a person ("S").

(2) No liability to income tax arises in respect of sporting testimonial payments to which this section applies.

(3) Subsection (2) has effect subject to and in accordance with the following provisions.

(4) It only applies—

(a) if the controller of the relevant event or activity (or of all the relevant events or activities in a series) constituting the sporting testimonial is an independent person,

(b) if S has not already benefitted from an exemption under this section in relation to one or more sporting testimonial payments made out of money raised by another sporting testimonial, and

(c) where the sporting testimonial consists of a series of relevant events or activities taking place over more than a year, if the sporting testimonial payment is made out of money raised by events or activities taking place within the period of one year beginning with the day on which the first event or activity in the series took place.

(5) It only applies to the first £100,000 of sporting testimonial payments made out of money raised by the sporting testimonial.

(6) If sporting testimonial payments are made (out of money raised by the sporting testimonial) in two or more tax years, any part of the exempt amount that is not used in the first of those years is to be carried forward to the next tax year (and so on).

(7) This section applies to sporting testimonial payments made to or to the order of the personal representatives of S (where S has died) but only if the payments are made within the period of 24 months beginning with the date of death.

(8) In subsection (4)(a) "independent person" means a person who is not (or where the controller is a committee, a committee none of whose members are)—

(a) S or a person connected with S,

(b) an employer or former employer of S or a person connected with an employer or former employer of S, or

(c) a person acting for or on behalf of a person mentioned in paragraph (a) or (b).

(9) If the first relevant event or activity in a series took place before 6 April 2017, subsection (4)(c) has effect as if it referred to the year beginning with 6 April 2017.

(10) Section 993 of ITA 2007 (meaning of "connected" persons) has effect for the purposes of this section.

(11) Terms used in this section and section 226E have the same meaning as in that section."

Corporation tax: deductions from total profits for sporting testimonial payments and associated payments

3 After section 996 of CTA 2010 (miscellaneous provisions: use of different accounting periods within a group of companies) insert—

"Sporting testimonial payments and associated payments

996A Deductions from total profits for sporting testimonial payments and associated payments

(1) This section applies where a company, in any accounting period—

(a) is the controller of a relevant event or activity that constitutes or is part of a sporting testimonial, and

(b) makes a relevant sporting testimonial payment out of money raised by the sporting testimonial.

(2) In this section "relevant sporting testimonial payment" means a sporting testimonial payment that is (or so much of it as is) made out of proceeds of a relevant event or activity which are brought into account in determining the company's total profits or any component of its total profits.

(3) In calculating the amount of corporation tax chargeable for the accounting period, an amount equal to the aggregate of the following amounts is allowed as a deduction from the company's total profits—

(a) so much of the relevant sporting testimonial payment as is paid to or for the benefit of the sportsperson to whom the sporting testimonial relates,

(b) any income tax or employee's national insurance contributions deducted at source from that payment, and

(c) any employer's national insurance contributions relating to that payment.

(4) The amount is deducted—

(a) from the company's total profits for the accounting period in which the relevant sporting testimonial payment is made, and

(b) if a claim by the company for relief so requires, previous accounting periods.

(5) A claim under subsection (4)(b) must be made within 2 years after the end of the accounting period in which the relevant sporting testimonial payment is made.

(6) If for an accounting period deductions under subsection (4) are to be made for relevant sporting testimonial payments made in more than one accounting period, the deductions are to be made in the order in which the payments were made (starting with the earliest of them).

(7) The amount of the deduction to be made under subsection (4) for an accounting period is the amount that cannot be deducted under that subsection for a subsequent accounting period.

(8) The amount of the deduction to be made for any accounting period is limited to the amount that reduces the company's taxable total profits for that period to nil.

(9) The deduction is only available if and to the extent that the amount mentioned in subsection (3) is not otherwise deductible in calculating the company's total profits or any component of its total profits.

(10) Terms used in this section and in section 226E of ITEPA 2003 have the same meaning as in that section."

Application of this Schedule

4 (1) The amendments made by this Schedule have effect in relation to a sporting testimonial payment made out of money raised by a sporting testimonial if—

(a) the sporting testimonial was made public on or after 25 November 2015, and
(b) the payment is made out of money raised by one or more relevant events or activities which take place on or after 6 April 2017.

(2) Terms used in sub-paragraph (1) and section 226E of ITEPA 2003 (as inserted by paragraph 1) have the same meaning as in that section.

GENERAL NOTE

Autumn Statement 2015 announced that, following consultation, the Government would legislate to simplify the tax treatment of income from sporting testimonials. "From 6 April 2017, all income from sporting testimonials and benefit matches for employed sportspersons will be liable to income tax. In addition, an exemption of up to £50,000 will be available for employed sportspersons with income from sporting testimonials that are not contractual or customary," the Government said. The proposed exemption was increased at Budget 2016 to £100,000 in response to representations made during the technical consultation on the Finance Bill.

The £100,000 exemption will ensure that employed sportspersons on modest incomes who are approaching the end of their playing career are protected from the change.

Corresponding legislation will be introduced for national insurance contributions

Sporting testimonial payments

Schedule 2 inserts a new ITEPA 2003 s 226E which applies to an individual who is or has been employed as a professional sportsperson ("S"), and provides that a sporting testimonial payment is to be treated as earnings of S from the employment or former employment to which the sporting testimonial is most closely linked.

Schedule 2 also inserts a new ITEPA 2003 s 306B (limited exemption for sporting testimonial payments) and a new CTA 2010 s 996A (deductions from total profits for sporting testimonial payments and associated payments). Schedule 2 para 4 provides that these amendments have effect in relation to a sporting testimonial payment made out of money raised by a sporting testimonial that was made public on or after 25 November 2015, where the payment is made out of money raised by one or more relevant events or activities taking place on or after 6 April 2017.

New ITEPA 2003 s 226E is an addition to ITEPA 2003 Pt 3 Ch 12 (other amounts treated as earnings). "Sporting testimonial" means:

- a series of relevant events or activities with the same controller, or
- a single relevant event or activity not forming part of such a series.

An event or activity is a relevant event or activity if:

- its purpose, or one of its purposes, is to raise money for or for the benefit of S, and
- the only or main reason for doing that is to recognise S's service as a professional sportsperson who is or has been employed as such.

However, an activity that meets these conditions (a) and (b) and consists solely of inviting and collecting donations for or for the benefit of S:

- is a relevant activity if it is one of a series of relevant events or activities, but
- is not a relevant activity so long as both conditions noted below are met while the activity takes place.

The first condition is that any person who is responsible (alone or with others) for collecting the donations or who is the controller of the activity (or a member of a controlling committee) is not:

- S;
- the controller of any other relevant event or activity for or for the benefit of S;
- a person connected with S or that controller; or
- a person acting for or on behalf of any of the above persons.

The second condition is that the donations collected do not include any sums paid directly or indirectly out of money raised by another relevant event or activity.

A "sporting testimonial payment" is a payment made by or on behalf of the controller of a sporting testimonial out of money raised for or for the benefit of S which:

- is made to S, to a member of S's family or household, to a person prescribed in regulations, to S's order or otherwise for S's benefit, and
- does not, apart from this new provision, constitute employment earnings.

Such a payment is treated as earnings of S from the employment or former employment to which the sporting testimonial is most closely linked. "Controller" and "money" are defined for these purposes, and provision is made for the situation where S has died.

Limited exemption

New ITEPA 2003 s 306B introduces a limited exemption for sporting testimonial payments made out of money raised by a sporting testimonial and treated as earnings of S by virtue of new ITEPA 2003 s 226E.

Where the exemption applies, no income tax liability arises on the first £100,000 of sporting testimonial payments made out of money raised by the sporting testimonial.

The exemption applies only if:

- the controller is an independent person (as defined);
- S has not already benefited from this exemption in relation to one or more sporting testimonial payments made out of money raised by another sporting testimonial; and
- where the sporting testimonial consists of a series of relevant events or activities taking place over more than a year, the sporting testimonial payment is made out of money raised by events or activities taking place within the period of one year beginning with the day on which the first event or activity in the series took place.

If sporting testimonial payments are made in two or more tax years, any part of the exempt amount not used in the first year is to be carried forward to the next year.

Corporation tax deduction

If a company is the controller of a relevant event or activity that constitutes, or is part of, a sporting testimonial and makes a "relevant sporting testimonial payment" out of the money raised, the company entitled to a deduction from total profits for the aggregate of the following sums (but only to the extent that the amount is not otherwise deductible):

- so much of the relevant sporting testimonial payment as is paid to or for the benefit of the sportsperson to whom the sporting testimonial relates;
- any income tax or employee's national insurance contributions deducted at source; and
- any employer's national insurance contributions relating to the payment.

The payment is a "relevant sporting testimonial payment" if, or to the extent that, it is made out of the proceeds of a relevant event or activity that are brought into account in determining the company's profits.

The amount is deducted from the company's total profits:

- for the accounting period in which the relevant sporting testimonial payment is made, and
- if a claim is made within two years after the end of that accounting period, for previous accounting periods.

The deduction is limited to the amount that reduces taxable total profits to nil.

SCHEDULE 3
EMPLOYEE SHARE SCHEMES: MINOR AMENDMENTS
Section 16

Enterprise management incentives and employee ownership trusts

1 (1) In section 534 of ITEPA 2003 (disqualifying events relating to relevant company), at the end insert—

"(7) Subsection (1)(a) and (b) do not apply where the relevant company is subject to an employee-ownership trust (within the meaning of paragraph 27(4) to (6) of Schedule 2)."

(2) The amendment made by this paragraph is treated as having come into force on 1 October 2014.

Share incentive plans

2 (1) Schedule 2 to ITEPA 2003 (share incentive plans) is amended as follows.

(2) In paragraph 1 (introduction), after sub-paragraph (4) insert—

"(5) Sub-paragraph (A1) is also subject to Part 10A of this Schedule (disqualifying events)."

(3) After Part 10 insert—

"PART 10A
DISQUALIFYING EVENTS

85A (1) A SIP ceases to be a Schedule 2 SIP if (and with effect from the time when) a disqualifying event occurs.

(2) The following are disqualifying events—

    (a) an alteration being made in—

        (i) the share capital of a company any of whose shares are subject to the plan trust, or

        (ii) the rights attaching to any shares of such a company,

that materially affects the value of the shares that are subject to the plan trust;

    (b) shares of a class of shares that is subject to the plan trust receiving different treatment in any respect from the other shares of that class.

(3) Sub-paragraph (2)(b) applies in particular to different treatment in respect of—

    (a) the dividend payable,

    (b) repayment, or

    (c) any offer of substituted or additional shares, securities or rights of any description in respect of the shares.

(4) Sub-paragraph (2)(b) does not however apply where the difference in treatment arises from—

    (a) a key feature of the plan, or

    (b) any of the participants' shares being subject to any restriction.

(5) Nor does sub-paragraph (2)(b) apply as a result only of the fact that shares which have been newly issued receive, in respect of dividends payable with respect to a period beginning before the date on which they were issued, treatment less favourable than that accorded to shares issued before that date.

(6) For the purposes of this paragraph a "key feature" of a plan is a provision of it that is necessary to meet the requirements of this Schedule.

(7) This paragraph does not affect the operation of the SIP code in relation to shares awarded to participants in the plan before the disqualifying event occurred."

(4) The amendments made by this paragraph have effect in relation to disqualifying events occurring on or after the day on which this Act is passed.

Notification of plans and schemes to HMRC

3 (1) In Schedule 2 to ITEPA 2003 (share incentive plans), Part 10 (notification of plans etc) is amended as follows.

(2) In paragraph 81A (notice of SIP to be given to HMRC), after sub-paragraph (5) insert—

"(5A) Sub-paragraph (5) does not apply if the company satisfies HMRC (or, on an appeal under paragraph 81K, the tribunal) that there is a reasonable excuse for failing to give notice on or before the initial notification deadline.

(5B) Paragraph 81C(9) (what constitutes a reasonable excuse) applies for the purposes of sub-paragraph (5A).

(5C) Where HMRC are required under sub-paragraph (5A) to consider whether there was a reasonable excuse, HMRC must notify the company of their decision within the period of 45 days beginning with the day on which HMRC received the company's request to consider the excuse.

(5D) Where HMRC are required to notify the company as specified in sub-paragraph (5C) but do not do so—

(a) HMRC are to be treated as having decided that there was no reasonable excuse, and

(b) HMRC must notify the company of the decision which they are treated as having made."

(3) In paragraph 81K (appeals)—

(a) at the beginning insert—

"(A1) The company may appeal against a decision of HMRC under paragraph 81A(5A) that there was no reasonable excuse for its failure to give notice on or before the initial notification deadline.";

(b) in sub-paragraph (6), before paragraph (a) insert—

"(za) in the case of an appeal under sub-paragraph (A1), notice of HMRC's decision is given to the company;";

(c) in sub-paragraph (7), after "sub-paragraph" insert "(A1),".

(4) The amendments made by this paragraph have effect in relation to notices given under paragraph 81A of Schedule 2 to ITEPA 2003 on or after 6 April 2016.

4 (1) In Schedule 3 to ITEPA 2003 (SAYE option schemes), Part 8 (notification of schemes etc) is amended as follows.

(2) In paragraph 40A (notice of scheme to be given to HMRC), after sub-paragraph (5) insert—

"(5A) Sub-paragraph (5) does not apply if the scheme organiser satisfies HMRC (or, on an appeal under paragraph 40K, the tribunal) that there is a reasonable excuse for the failure to give notice on or before the initial notification deadline.

(5B) Paragraph 40C(9) (what constitutes a reasonable excuse) applies for the purposes of sub-paragraph (5A).

(5C) Where HMRC are required under sub-paragraph (5A) to consider whether there was a reasonable excuse, HMRC must notify the scheme organiser of their decision within the period of 45 days beginning with the day on which HMRC received the scheme organiser's request to consider the excuse.

(5D) Where HMRC are required to notify the scheme organiser as specified in sub-paragraph (5C) but do not do so—

(a) HMRC are to be treated as having decided that there was no reasonable excuse, and

(b) HMRC must notify the scheme organiser of the decision which they are treated as having made."

(3) In paragraph 40K (appeals)—

(a) at the beginning insert—

"(A1) The scheme organiser may appeal against a decision of HMRC under paragraph 40A(5A) that there was no reasonable excuse for the failure to give notice on or before the initial notification deadline.";

(b) in sub-paragraph (5), before paragraph (a) insert—

"(za) in the case of an appeal under sub-paragraph (A1), notice of HMRC's decision is given to the scheme organiser;";

(c) in sub-paragraph (6), after "sub-paragraph" insert "(A1),".

(4) The amendments made by this paragraph have effect in relation to notices given under paragraph 40A of Schedule 3 to ITEPA 2003 on or after 6 April 2016.

5 (1) In Schedule 4 to ITEPA 2003 (CSOP schemes), Part 7 (notification of schemes etc) is amended as follows.

(2) In paragraph 28A (notice of scheme to be given to HMRC), after sub-paragraph (5) insert—

"(5A) Sub-paragraph (5) does not apply if the scheme organiser satisfies HMRC (or, on an appeal under paragraph 28K, the tribunal) that there is a reasonable excuse for the failure to give notice on or before the initial notification deadline.

(5B) Paragraph 28C(9) (what constitutes a reasonable excuse) applies for the purposes of sub-paragraph (5A).

(5C) Where HMRC are required under sub-paragraph (5A) to consider whether there was a reasonable excuse, HMRC must notify the scheme organiser of their decision within the period of 45 days beginning with the day on which HMRC received the scheme organiser's request to consider the excuse.

(5D) Where HMRC are required to notify the scheme organiser as specified in sub-paragraph (5C) but do not do so

(a) HMRC are to be treated as having decided that there was no reasonable excuse, and

(b) HMRC must notify the scheme organiser of the decision which they are treated as having made."

(3) In paragraph 28K (appeals)—

(a) at the beginning insert—

"(A1) The scheme organiser may appeal against a decision of HMRC under paragraph 28A(5A) that there was no reasonable excuse for the failure to give notice on or before the initial notification deadline.";

(b) in sub-paragraph (5), before paragraph (a) insert—

"(za) in the case of an appeal under sub-paragraph (A1), notice of HMRC's decision is given to the scheme organiser;";

(c) in sub-paragraph (6), after "sub-paragraph" insert "(A1),".

(4) The amendments made by this paragraph have effect in relation to notices given under paragraph 28A of Schedule 4 to ITEPA 2003 on or after 6 April 2016.

Price for acquisition of shares under share option

6 (1) In Schedule 3 to ITEPA 2003 (SAYE option schemes), paragraph 28 (requirements as to price for acquisition of shares) is amended as follows.

(2) In sub-paragraph (1)—

(a) in paragraph (b), for "at that time" substitute "—

(i) at that time, or

(ii) at such earlier time as may be determined in accordance with guidance issued by the Commissioners for Her Majesty's Revenue and Customs."

(b) for "sub-paragraphs (2) and (3)" substitute "sub-paragraph (3)".

(3) Omit sub-paragraph (2).

7 (1) In Schedule 4 to ITEPA 2003 (CSOP schemes), paragraph 22 (requirements as to price for acquisition of shares) is amended as follows.

(2) In sub-paragraph (1)—

(a) in paragraph (b), for "at the time when the option is granted" substitute "—

(i) at the time when the option is granted, or

(ii) at such earlier time as may be determined in accordance with guidance issued by the Commissioners for Her Majesty's Revenue and Customs.";

(b) for "sub-paragraphs (2) and (3)" substitute "sub-paragraph (3)".

(3) Omit sub-paragraph (2).

Tag-along rights

8 (1) In Schedule 5 to ITEPA 2003 (enterprise management incentives), in paragraph 39 (company reorganisations: introduction), in sub-paragraph (2)(c), after "982" insert "or 983 to 985".

(2) The amendment made by this paragraph is treated as having come into force on 17 July 2013.

Exercise of EMI options

9 (1) In section 238A of TCGA 1992 (share schemes and share incentives), in subsection (2), omit paragraph (d) and the preceding "and".

(2) In Schedule 7D to TCGA 1992 (share schemes and share incentives), omit Part 4.

(3) In section 527 of ITEPA 2003 (enterprise management incentives: qualifying options), in subsection (3)—

(a) after paragraph (a) insert "and";

(b) omit paragraph (c) and the preceding "and".

(4) The amendments made by this paragraph do not affect—

(a) the application of paragraph 14(4) of Schedule 7D to TCGA 1992 in relation to a disqualifying event occurring before 6 April 2016, or

(b) the application of paragraph 16 of that Schedule in relation to an allotment for payment mentioned in section 126(2)(a) of that Act taking place before 6 April 2016.

GENERAL NOTE

This Schedule contains changes which correct some technical points that had previously been overlooked; limit the types of shares that can be used for tax-favoured Share Incentive Plans (SIPs); introduce a "reasonable excuse" defence for late-notification of tax-advantaged share schemes; and simplify the share identification rules for Enterprise Management Incentives (EMIs) on a reorganisation or reduction of share capital.

Paragraph 1

This provision corrects an oversight. EMIs lose their tax advantages if there is a "disqualifying event" and the option is not exercised within 90 days. ITEPA 2003 s 534(1) sets out which changes to the company granting the EMIs count as a disqualifying event: there is a disqualifying event if that company becomes a 51% subsidiary or otherwise comes under the control of another company (s 534(1)(a) and (b)).

Employee Ownership Trusts (EOTs) were introduced by FA 2014 with effect from 1 October 2014. A trust is an EOT if, simplistically, it controls a company and its assets are held for the benefit of all the company's eligible employees (ITEPA 2003 s 312E). Under ITEPA 2003 Sch 5, EMIs cannot normally be granted if the company is not "independent" but, since 1 October 2014, EMIs can be granted by a company controlled by an EOT (Sch 5 para 9(5)). However, the need to amend ITEPA 2003 s 534(1) was overlooked at the time and the amendment to that section by this paragraph is to correct that omission. The purpose of the amendment is to provide that if a company becomes subject to an EOT after granting EMIs that will not be a disqualifying event even though the company loses its independence (though this would be clearer if it read "where the relevant company **becomes** subject to [an EOT]" rather than "**is** subject to" one). As it is to correct an omission in FA 2014, this amendment takes effect from 1 October 2014.

Paragraph 2

ITEPA 2003 Sch 2 sets out the rules that must be satisfied for a plan to qualify as a tax-advantaged SIP (known as a "Schedule 2 SIP"). Prior to 2014 a plan had to be approved by HMRC to obtain those tax advantages and HMRC could withdraw approval of a SIP (with consequent loss of the tax advantages for future awards) if there had been a "disqualifying event" (old paras 83 and 84 of Sch 2). These provisions were repealed when the system of self-certification to become a Schedule 2 SIP (rather than relying on prior HMRC approval) was introduced. Paragraph 2 introduces a new Pt 10A to Sch 2 (consisting only of the new para 85A) which re-introduces the concept of "disqualifying events" into the SIP legislation.

Under new para 85A there will be a disqualifying event if:

– the share capital of the company (or rights attaching to shares in the company) is (are) altered in a way which materially affects the value of the SIP shares; or

– SIP shares receive different treatment in any respect from the other shares of the same class (for instance in relation to the dividend payable) *unless* the difference in treatment results from a "key feature" of the SIP or from the restrictions attaching to the SIP shares.

New para 85A will apply where there is a disqualifying event on or after the date of Royal Assent. If SIP shares have been manipulated so as to cause a disqualifying event, subsequent awards of those type of shares will not obtain the tax advantages available under a Schedule 2 SIP; however, the shares already awarded to employees which benefit from that manipulation will continue to enjoy those tax advantages. This is in line with HMRC's long-standing practice of not penalising employees who have received awards under tax-favoured schemes.

It is not entirely clear at what these changes are aimed. In the Explanatory Notes to Finance (No 2) Bill 2016 (issued on 24 March 2016 and which will eventually be superseded by Notes to the Act), HMRC state: "These disqualifying events enforce the principle that preferential shares in a SIP cannot be issued to select employees". One might suppose from this that HMRC's objection to the share manipulation is that it is not in accord with the "all-employee nature" of a SIP (see para 8 of Sch 2) because it benefits some of the employees holding SIP shares more than others. However, it is an alteration which affects the SIP shares *as a whole* (or where the SIP shares *as a whole* receive different treatment compared to other shares of the same class) that is a disqualifying event, not an alteration affecting some only of the SIP shares. If HMRC's objection is, in fact, based on tax avoidance (i.e. because the SIP shares increase in value, the tax reliefs available to the employee holding them also increase in value), one would have expected Pt 10 to have been amended as well so that a disqualifying event would trigger penalties thereunder.

Paragraph 3

A SIP can only be a Sch 2 SIP (with the consequent tax advantages) if notice is given to HMRC under para 81B of Sch 2. If HMRC is notified before 6 July in the tax year following that in which the first award is made under the SIP (the deadline), it will be a Schedule 2 SIP from (at the latest) the first time an award was made. However, if HMRC is notified after the deadline, it is only a Schedule 2 SIP from the beginning of the tax year in which the notice is given. If the deadline for notification is missed, then inevitably the company will not have made a scheme return for the first tax year the SIP operated (the deadline for which is also 6 July in the next tax year), thereby triggering penalties under para 81C of Sch 2. Further, any awards made to employees will not be tax-advantaged.

Paragraph 3 amends para 81A of Sch 2 ITEPA 2003 so that the tax advantages will not be lost if the company can provide a "reasonable excuse" for not giving notification of the SIP before the deadline. If HMRC do not accept that the excuse is reasonable, there is a right of appeal. This aligns the SIP penalty regime with other penalty provisions in the various Taxes Acts, including in the EMI legislation (para 53 of Sch 5 ITEPA 2003).

Paragraph 4

This introduces a "reasonable excuse" provision into the save-as-you-earn (SAYE) option scheme legislation in the same terms as that for SIPs (see "Paragraph 3" above).

Paragraph 5

This introduces a "reasonable excuse" provision into the Company Share Option Plan (CSOP) legislation in the same terms as that for SIPs (see "Paragraph 3" above).

Paragraph 6

Schedule 3 ITEPA 2003 sets out the requirements that SAYE share option schemes must satisfy to obtain tax advantages (described in the legislation as a "Schedule 3 SAYE option scheme"). One of those requirements is that the price at which the option is granted must not be less than 80% of the market value of shares of that class at the time of option grant (Sch 2 para 28(1)), unless HMRC agrees in writing that an earlier date can be used (para 29(2)). As a practical matter, it is much easier for the company if it can calculate the market value to be used by reference to its value on a day (or the average of specified days) before the actual date of grant.

A large part of the reason for introducing the self-certification regime in 2014 was to reduce HMRC involvement and failing to change para 28(2) at that time was almost certainly an oversight. Paragraph 6 removes the need to get specific HMRC agreement to the market value calculation and to allow a company to do it in accordance with published HMRC guidance (which can be found in the Employee Tax Advantaged Share Scheme Manual). Whilst this may be a practical answer to a practical problem, the desirability of incorporating reliance on guidance (which can be changed at the touch of a keyboard or not updated in a timely fashion) into primary legislation is open to debate.

Paragraph 7

This provision makes the same changes in relation to fixing the market value of a share when a CSOP option is granted as para 6 makes to fixing the market value when an option is granted under an SAYE option scheme (see "Paragraph 6" above).

Paragraph 8

This change is also to correct an oversight and is treated as having come into force on 17 July 2013, the date of Royal Assent to Finance Act 2013.

Paragraph 39 of Sch 5 ITEPA 2003 sets out what counts as "a company reorganisation", a prerequisite to allowing an EMI option to be rolled-over into shares of another company. Paragraph 39(2)(c) currently allows this if the acquiring company become bound or entitled under Companies Act 2006 to buy out minority shareholders holding the same class of shares as those subject to the EMI options. Paragraph 8 amends para 39(2)(c) of Sch 5 so that there is also a "company reorganisation" if the minority shareholders have the right to force the acquiring company to buy their shares under Companies Act 2006.

Paragraph 9

This provision deletes Pt 4 of Sch 7D TCGA 1992 and makes consequential amendments to TCGA 1992 s 238A and ITEPA 2003 s 527.

Part 4 of Sch 7D originally existed to give business asset taper relief when shares acquired on the exercise of EMI options were sold. Since that relief has not been available since the 2007/08 tax year, its only role has been to fix the acquisition date (for share identification purposes) of shares acquired on a rights issue by virtue of a holding of shares originally acquired on the exercise of a qualifying EMI option. It did this by disapplying TCGA 1992 s 127 so that the rights issue shares were treated as acquired at the time of the rights issue for capital gains tax purposes.

Part 4 will no longer apply for that purpose from 6 April 2016. Instead, the shares acquired on the rights issue will be treated for share identification purposes as acquired when the original EMI shares were acquired in the same way as shares acquired on any other rights issue.

SCHEDULE 4

PENSIONS: LIFETIME ALLOWANCE: TRANSITIONAL PROVISION

Section 19

PART 1

"FIXED PROTECTION 2016"

The protection

1 (1) Sub-paragraph (2) applies at any particular time on or after 6 April 2016 in the case of an individual if—

(a) each of the conditions specified in paragraph 2 is met,

(b) there is no protection-cessation event (see paragraph 3) in the period beginning with 6 April 2016 and ending with the particular time,

(c) paragraph 1(2) of Schedule 6 to FA 2014 ("individual protection 2014") does not apply in the individual's case at the particular time, and

(d) at the particular time or any later time, the individual has a reference number (see Part 3 of this Schedule) for the purposes of sub-paragraph (2).

(2) Part 4 of FA 2004 has effect in relation to the individual as if the standard lifetime allowance were the greater of the standard lifetime allowance and £1,250,000.

The initial conditions

2 The conditions mentioned in paragraph 1(1)(a) are—

(a) that, on 6 April 2016, the individual has one or more arrangements under—

(i) a registered pension scheme, or

(ii) a relieved non-UK pension scheme of which the individual is a relieved member,

(b) that paragraph 7 of Schedule 36 to FA 2004 (primary protection) does not make provision for a lifetime allowance enhancement factor in relation to the individual,

(c) that paragraph 12 of that Schedule (enhanced protection) does not apply in the individual's case on 6 April 2016,

(d) that paragraph 14 of Schedule 18 to FA 2011 (transitional provision relating to new standard lifetime allowance for the tax year 2012–13) does not apply in the individual's case on 6 April 2016, and

(e) that paragraph 1 of Schedule 22 to FA 2013 ("fixed protection 2014" relating to new standard lifetime allowance for the tax year 2014–15) does not apply in the individual's case on 6 April 2016.

Protection-cessation events

3 There is a protection-cessation event if—

(a) there is benefit accrual in relation to the individual under an arrangement under a registered pension scheme,

(b) there is an impermissible transfer into any arrangement under a registered pension scheme relating to the individual,

(c) a transfer of sums or assets held for the purposes of, or representing accrued rights under, any such arrangement is made that is not a permitted transfer, or

(d) an arrangement relating to the individual is made under a registered pension scheme otherwise than in permitted circumstances.

Protection-cessation events: interpretation: "benefit accrual"

4 (1) For the purposes of paragraph 3(a) there is benefit accrual in relation to the individual under an arrangement—

(a) in the case of a money purchase arrangement that is not a cash balance arrangement, if a relevant contribution is paid under the arrangement on or after 6 April 2016,

(b) in the case of a cash balance arrangement or defined benefits arrangement, if there is an increase in the value of the individual's rights under the arrangement at any time on or after that date (but subject to sub-paragraph (5)), and

(c) in the case of a hybrid arrangement—

(i) where the benefits that may be provided to or in respect of the individual under the arrangement include money purchase benefits other than cash balance benefits, if a relevant contribution is paid under the arrangement on or after 6 April 2016, and

(ii) in any case, if there is an increase in the value of the individual's rights under the arrangement at any time on or after that date (but subject to sub-paragraph (5)).

(2) For the purposes of sub-paragraphs (1)(b) and (c)(ii) and (5) whether there is an increase in the value of the individual's rights under an arrangement (and its amount if there is) is to be determined—

(a) in the case of a cash balance arrangement (or a hybrid arrangement under which cash balance benefits may be provided to or in respect of the individual under the arrangement), by reference to whether there is an increase in the amount that would, on the valuation assumptions, be available for the provision of benefits to or in respect of the individual (and, if there is, the amount of the increase), and

(b) in the case of a defined benefits arrangement (or a hybrid arrangement under which defined benefits may be provided to or in respect of the individual under the arrangement), by reference to whether there is an increase in the benefits amount.

(3) For the purposes of sub-paragraph (2)(b) "the benefits amount" is—

$(P \times RVF) + LS$

where—

LS is the lump sum to which the individual would, on the valuation assumptions, be entitled under the arrangement (otherwise than by commutation of pension),

P is the annual rate of the pension which would, on the valuation assumptions, be payable to the individual under the arrangement, and

RVF is the relevant valuation factor.

(4) Paragraph 14 of Schedule 36 to FA 2004 (when a relevant contribution is paid under an arrangement) applies for the purposes of sub-paragraph (1)(a) and (c)(i).

(5) Increases in the value of the individual's rights under an arrangement are to be ignored for the purposes of sub-paragraph (1)(b) or (c)(ii) if in no tax year do they exceed the relevant percentage.

(6) The relevant percentage, in relation to a tax year, means—

(a) where the arrangement (or a predecessor arrangement) includes provision for the value of the rights of the individual to increase during the tax year at an annual rate specified in the rules of the pension scheme (or a predecessor registered pension scheme) on 9 December 2015

(i) that percentage (or, where more than one arrangement includes such provision, the higher or highest of the percentages specified), plus

(ii) the relevant statutory increase percentage;

(b) otherwise—

    (i) the percentage by which the consumer prices index for the month of September in the previous tax year is higher than it was for the September before that (or 0% if it is not higher), or

    (ii) if higher, the relevant statutory increase percentage.

(7) In sub-paragraph (6)(a)—

"predecessor arrangement", in relation to an arrangement, means another arrangement (under the same or another registered pension scheme) from which some or all of the sums or assets held for the purposes of the arrangement directly or indirectly derive;

"predecessor registered pension scheme", in relation to a registered pension scheme, means another registered pension scheme from which some or all of the sums or assets held for the purposes of the arrangement under the pension scheme directly or indirectly derive.

(8) In sub-paragraph (6) "the relevant statutory increase percentage", in relation to a tax year, means the percentage increase in the value of the individual's rights under the arrangement during the tax year so far as it is attributable solely to one or more of the following—

    (a) an increase in accordance with section 15 of the Pension Schemes Act 1993 or section 11 of the Pension Schemes (Northern Ireland) Act 1993 (increase of guaranteed minimum where commencement of guaranteed minimum pension postponed);

    (b) a revaluation in accordance with section 16 of the Pension Schemes Act 1993 or section 12 of the Pension Schemes (Northern Ireland) Act 1993 (early leavers: revaluation of earnings factors);

    (c) a revaluation in accordance with Chapter 2 of Part 4 of the Pension Schemes Act 1993 or the Pension Schemes (Northern Ireland) Act 1993 (early leavers: revaluation of accrued benefits);

    (d) a revaluation in accordance with Chapter 3 of Part 4 of the Pension Schemes Act 1993 or the Pension Schemes (Northern Ireland) Act 1993 (early leavers: protection of increases in guaranteed minimum pensions);

    (e) the application of section 67 of the Equality Act 2010 (sex equality rule for occupational pension schemes).

(9) Sub-paragraph (10) applies in relation to a tax year if—

    (a) the arrangement is a defined benefits arrangement which is under an annuity contract treated as a registered pension scheme under section 153(8) of FA 2004,

    (b) the contract provides for the value of the rights of the individual to be increased during the tax year at an annual rate specified in the contract, and

    (c) the contract limits the annual rate to the percentage increase in the retail prices index over a 12 month period specified in the contract.

(10) Sub-paragraph (6)(b)(i) applies as if it referred instead to the annual rate of the increase in the value of the rights during the tax year.

(11) For the purposes of sub-paragraph (9)(c) the 12 month period must end during the 12 month period preceding the month in which the increase in the value of the rights occurs.

Protection-cessation events: interpretation: "impermissible transfer"

5 Paragraph 17A of Schedule 36 to FA 2004 (impermissible transfers) applies for the purposes of paragraph 3(b) but as if—

    (a) the references to a relevant existing arrangement were to the arrangement, and

    (b) the reference in sub-paragraph (2) to 5 April 2006 were to 5 April 2016.

Protection-cessation events: interpretation: "permitted transfer"

6 Sub-paragraphs (7) to (8B) of paragraph 12 of Schedule 36 to FA 2004 (when there is a permitted transfer) apply for the purposes of paragraph 3(c).

Protection-cessation events: interpretation: "permitted circumstances"

7 Sub-paragraphs (2A) to (2C) of paragraph 12 of Schedule 36 to FA 2004 ("permitted circumstances") apply for the purposes of paragraph 3(d).

Protection-cessation events: interpretation: relieved non-UK pension schemes

8 (1) Subject to sub-paragraphs (2) to (4), paragraph 3 applies in relation to an individual who is a relieved member of a relieved non-UK pension scheme as if the relieved non-UK pension scheme were a registered pension scheme; and the other paragraphs of this Part of this Schedule apply accordingly.

(2) Sub-paragraphs (3) and (4) apply for the purposes of paragraph 3(a) (instead of paragraph 4(1)) in determining if there is benefit accrual in relation to an individual under an arrangement under a relieved non-UK pension scheme of which the individual is a relieved member.

(3) There is benefit accrual in relation to the individual under the arrangement if there is a pension input amount under sections 230 to 237 of FA 2004 (as applied by Schedule 34 to that Act) greater than nil in respect of the arrangement for a tax year; and, in such a case, the benefit accrual is treated as occurring at the end of the tax year.

(4) There is also benefit accrual in relation to the individual under the arrangement if—

(a) in a tax year there occurs a benefit crystallisation event in relation to the individual (whether in relation to the arrangement or to any other arrangement under any pension scheme or otherwise), and
(b) had the tax year ended immediately before the benefit crystallisation event, there would have been a pension input amount under sections 230 to 237 of FA 2004 greater than nil in respect of the arrangement for the tax year,

and, in such a case, the benefit accrual is treated as occurring immediately before the benefit crystallisation event.

PART 2

"INDIVIDUAL PROTECTION 2016"

The protection

9 (1) Sub-paragraph (2) applies at any particular time on or after 6 April 2016 in the case of an individual if—

(a) the individual has one or more relevant arrangements (see sub-paragraph (3)) on 5 April 2016,
(b) the individual's relevant amount at the particular time is greater than £1,000,000 (see sub-paragraphs (4) and (7)),
(c) paragraph 7 of Schedule 36 to FA 2004 (primary protection) does not make provision for a lifetime allowance enhancement factor in relation to the individual,
(d) none of the provisions listed in sub-paragraph (5) applies in the individual's case at the particular time, and
(e) at the particular time or any later time, the individual has a reference number (see Part 3 of this Schedule) for the purposes of sub-paragraph (2).

(2) Part 4 of FA 2004 has effect in relation to the individual as if the standard lifetime allowance were—

(a) if the individual's relevant amount at the particular time is greater than £1,250,000, the greater of the standard lifetime allowance and £1,250,000, or
(b) otherwise, the greater of the individual's relevant amount at the particular time and the standard lifetime allowance.

(3) "Relevant arrangement", in relation to an individual, means an arrangement relating to the individual under—

(a) a registered pension scheme of which the individual is a member, or
(b) a relieved non-UK pension scheme of which the individual is a relieved member.

(4) An individual's "relevant amount" is the sum of amounts A, B, C and D (see paragraphs 10 to 13, but see also sub-paragraph (7)).

(5) The provisions mentioned in sub-paragraph (1)(d) are—

(a) paragraph 12 of Schedule 36 to FA 2004 (enhanced protection);
(b) paragraph 14 of Schedule 18 to FA 2011 (fixed protection 2012);
(c) paragraph 1 of Schedule 22 to FA 2013 (fixed protection 2014);
(d) paragraph 1(2) of Schedule 6 to FA 2014 (individual protection 2014);
(e) paragraph 1(2) of this Schedule (fixed protection 2016).

(6) Sub-paragraph (7) applies if rights of an individual under a relevant arrangement become subject to a pension debit where the transfer day falls on or after 6 April 2016.

(7) For the purpose of applying sub-paragraph (2) in the case of the individual on and after the transfer day, the individual's relevant amount is reduced (or further reduced) by the following amount—

X   (Y x Z)

    where—

       X is the appropriate amount,
       Y is 5% of X, and

Z is the number of tax years beginning after 5 April 2016 and ending on or before the transfer day.

(If the formula gives a negative amount, it is to be taken to be nil.)

(8) In sub-paragraphs (6) and (7) "appropriate amount" and "transfer day", in relation to a pension debit, have the same meaning as in section 29 of WRPA 1999 or Article 26 of WRP(NI)O 1999 (as the case may be).

Amount A (pre-6 April 2006 pensions in payment)

10 (1) To determine amount A—

(a) apply sub-paragraph (2) if a benefit crystallisation event has occurred in relation to the individual during the period beginning with 6 April 2006 and ending with 5 April 2016;

(b) otherwise, apply sub-paragraph (6).

(2) If this sub-paragraph is to be applied, amount A is—

25 x ARP x (£1,250,000 / SLT)

where—

ARP is (subject to sub-paragraph (3)) an amount equal to—

(a) the annual rate at which any relevant existing pension was payable to the individual at the time immediately before the benefit crystallisation event occurred, or

(b) if more than one relevant existing pension was payable to the individual at that time, the sum of the annual rates at which each of the relevant existing pensions was so payable, and

SLT is an amount equal to what the standard lifetime allowance was at the time the benefit crystallisation event occurred.

(3) Paragraph 20(4) of Schedule 36 to FA 2004 applies for the purposes of the definition of "ARP" in sub-paragraph (2) (and, for this purpose, in paragraph 20(4) any reference to "the time" is to be read as a reference to the time immediately before the benefit crystallisation event occurred).

(4) If the time immediately before the benefit crystallisation event occurred falls before 6 April 2015, in sub-paragraph (3) references to paragraph 20(4) are to be read as references to that provision as it had effect in relation to benefit crystallisation events occurring at the time immediately before the benefit crystallisation event occurred.

(5) If more than one benefit crystallisation event has occurred, in sub-paragraphs (2) to (4) references to the benefit crystallisation event are to be read as references to the first benefit crystallisation event.

(6) If this sub-paragraph is to be applied, amount A is—

25 x ARP

where ARP is (subject to sub-paragraph (7)) an amount equal to—

(a) the annual rate at which any relevant existing pension is payable to the individual at the end of 5 April 2016, or

(b) if more than one relevant existing pension is payable to the individual at the end of 5 April 2016, the sum of the annual rates at which each of the relevant existing pensions is so payable.

(7) Paragraph 20(4) of Schedule 36 to FA 2004 applies for the purposes of the definition of "ARP" in sub-paragraph (6) (and, for this purpose, in paragraph 20(4) any reference to "the time" is to be read as a reference to 5 April 2016).

(8) In this paragraph "relevant existing pension" means (subject to sub-paragraph (9)) a pension, annuity or right—

(a) which was, at the end of 5 April 2006, a "relevant existing pension" as defined by paragraph 10(2) and (3) of Schedule 36 to FA 2004, and

(b) to the payment of which the individual had, at the end of 5 April 2006, an actual (rather than a prospective) right.

(9) If—

(a) before 6 April 2016, there was a recognised transfer of sums or assets representing a relevant existing pension, and

(b) those sums or assets were, after the transfer, applied towards the provision of a scheme pension ("the new scheme pension"),

the new scheme pension is also to be a "relevant existing pension" (including for the purposes of this sub-paragraph).

Amount B (pre-6 April 2016 benefit crystallisation events)

11 (1) To determine amount B—

(a) identify each benefit crystallisation event that has occurred in relation to the individual during the period beginning with 6 April 2006 and ending with 5 April 2016,

(b) determine the amount that was crystallised by each of those benefit crystallisation events (applying paragraph 14 of Schedule 34 to FA 2004 if relevant), and

(c) multiply each crystallised amount by the following fraction—

1,250,000 / SLT

where SLT is an amount equal to what the standard lifetime allowance was at the time when the benefit crystallisation event in question occurred.

(2) Amount B is the sum of the crystallised amounts determined under sub-paragraph (1)(b) as adjusted under sub-paragraph (1)(c).

Amount C (uncrystallised rights at end of 5 April 2016 under registered pension schemes)

12 Amount C is the total value of the individual's uncrystallised rights at the end of 5 April 2016 under arrangements relating to the individual under registered pension schemes of which the individual is a member as determined in accordance with section 212 of FA 2004.

Amount D (uncrystallised rights at end of 5 April 2016 under relieved non-UK schemes)

13 (1) To determine amount D—

(a) identify each relieved non-UK pension scheme of which the individual is a relieved member at the end of 5 April 2016, and

(b) in relation to each such scheme—

(i) assume that a benefit crystallisation event occurs in relation to the individual at the end of 5 April 2016, and

(ii) in accordance with paragraph 14 of Schedule 34 to FA 2004, determine what the untested portion of the relevant relieved amount would be immediately before the assumed benefit crystallisation event.

(2) Amount D is the sum of the untested portions determined under sub-paragraph (1)(b)(ii).

PART 3

REFERENCE NUMBERS ETC

Issuing of reference numbers for fixed or individual protection 2016

14 (1) An individual has a reference number for the purposes of paragraph 1(2), or for the purposes of paragraph 9(2), if a reference number—

(a) has been issued by or on behalf of the Commissioners in respect of the individual for the purposes concerned, and

(b) has not been withdrawn.

(2) Such a reference number—

(a) may include, or consist of, characters other than figures, and

(b) may be issued only if a valid application for its issue is received by or on behalf of the Commissioners.

(3) A valid application is an application—

(a) made by or on behalf of the individual concerned,

(b) made on or after 6 April 2016,

(c) made by means of a digital service provided for the purpose by or on behalf of the Commissioners, or by other means authorised in a particular case by an officer of Revenue and Customs,

(d) containing—

(i) the following details for the individual and, where the individual is not the applicant, also for the applicant: title, full name, full postal address and e-mail address,

(ii) the individual's date of birth,

(iii) the individual's national insurance number, or the reason why the individual does not qualify for a national insurance number, and

(iv) a declaration that everything stated in the application is true and complete to the best of the applicant's knowledge and belief,

(e) containing also in the case of an application for a reference number for the purposes of paragraph 1(2)—

  (i) a declaration that the conditions specified in paragraph 2 are met in the individual's case, and

  (ii) a declaration that there has been no protection-cessation event (see paragraph 3) in the individual's case in the period beginning with 6 April 2016 and ending with the making of the application, and

(f) containing also in the case of an application for a reference number for the purposes of paragraph 9(2)—

  (i) the individual's relevant amount (see paragraph 9(4) and (7)),

  (ii) amounts A, B, C and D for the individual (see paragraphs 10 to 13),

  (iii) if rights of the individual under a relevant arrangement have become subject to a relevant pension debit, the appropriate amount and transfer day for each such pension debit,

  (iv) a declaration that the condition in paragraph 9(1)(c) is met in the individual's case, and

  (v) a declaration that paragraph 1(2) of Schedule 6 to FA 2014 ("individual protection 2014") does not apply in the individual's case.

(4) Where an application for a reference number for the purposes of paragraph 1(2) or 9(2) is unsuccessful, or is successful on a dormant basis, that must be notified to the applicant by or on behalf of the Commissioners.

(5) In sub-paragraph (3)(f)(iii) and this sub-paragraph—

"relevant arrangement" has the meaning given by paragraph 9(3);

"relevant pension debit", in relation to an application for a reference number, means a pension debit where—

  (a) the transfer day falls on or after 6 April 2016 and before the day on which the application is made, and

  (b) the individual has, before the day on which the application is made, received notice under regulation 8(2) or (3) of the Pensions on Divorce etc (Provision of Information) Regulations 2000 (SI 2000/1048) relating to discharge of liability in respect of the pension credit corresponding to the pension debit;

"appropriate amount" and "transfer day", in relation to a pension debit, have the same meaning as in paragraph 9(6) and (7) (see paragraph 9(8)).

(6) Sub-paragraph (3)(c) is not to be read as requiring a digital service to be provided and available for the purpose referred to.

(7) For the purposes of this Part of this Schedule, an application for a reference number for the purposes of paragraph 1(2) is successful on a dormant basis if the decision on the application is that—

  (a) the application would have been unconditionally successful but for the fact that paragraph 1(2) of Schedule 6 to FA 2014 ("individual protection 2014") applies in the case of the individual concerned, and

  (b) a reference number for the purposes of paragraph 1(2) will be issued in response to the application but only when paragraph 1(2) of Schedule 6 to FA 2014 does not apply in the individual's case.

(8) For the purposes of this Part of this Schedule, an application for a reference number for the purposes of paragraph 9(2) is successful on a dormant basis if the decision on the application is that—

  (a) the application would have been unconditionally successful but for the fact that a prior provision applies in the case of the individual concerned, and

  (b) a reference number for the purposes of paragraph 9(2) will be issued in response to the application but only when no prior provision applies in the individual's case.

(9) For the purposes of sub-paragraph (8), the prior provisions are—

  (a) paragraph 12 of Schedule 36 to FA 2004 (enhanced protection),

  (b) paragraph 14 of Schedule 18 to FA 2011 (fixed protection 2012),

  (c) paragraph 1 of Schedule 22 to FA 2013 (fixed protection 2014), and

  (d) paragraph 1(2) of this Schedule (fixed protection 2016).

Withdrawal of reference numbers

15 (1) This paragraph applies where a reference number for the purposes of paragraph 1(2) or 9(2) has been issued by or on behalf of the Commissioners in respect of an individual.

(2) The number may be withdrawn by an officer of Revenue and Customs.

(3) The number may be withdrawn only if—

(a) something contained in the application for the number was incorrect, or

(b) where the number was for the purposes of paragraph 1(2)—

    (i) there has been a protection-cessation event (see paragraph 3) in the individual's case since the making of the application, or

    (ii) paragraph 1(2) of Schedule 6 to FA 2014 has come to apply in the individual's case, or

(c) where the number was for the purposes of paragraph 9(2)—

    (i) a provision listed in paragraph 9(5) has come to apply in the individual's case, or

    (ii) paragraph 9(2) has ceased to apply in the individual's case as a result of the operation of paragraph 9(7), or

(d) the individual—

    (i) has been given a notice under paragraph 1 of Schedule 36 to FA 2008 (information and inspection powers: taxpayer notice) in connection with (as the case may be) Part 1 or 2 of this Schedule, and

    (ii) fails to comply with the notice within the period specified in the notice.

(4) Where the number is withdrawn—

(a) notice of the withdrawal, and

(b) reasons for the withdrawal,

are to be given by an officer of Revenue and Customs to the individual.

(5) Where the number is withdrawn, the effect of the withdrawal is as follows—

(a) in the case of withdrawal in reliance on sub-paragraph (3)(a), the number is treated as never having been issued,

(b) in the case of withdrawal in reliance on paragraph (b) or (c) of sub-paragraph (3), the number is treated as having been withdrawn at the time of the event mentioned in sub-paragraph (i) or (ii) of that paragraph, and

(c) in the case of withdrawal in reliance on sub-paragraph (3)(d), the number is treated as having been withdrawn at the time specified in the notice of the withdrawal as the effective time of the withdrawal, which may be any time not earlier than the time of issue of the number.

Appeals against non-issue or withdrawal of reference numbers

16 (1) Where—

(a) an application is made for a reference number for the purposes of paragraph 1(2) or 9(2) in respect of an individual, and

(b) the application is unsuccessful (see sub-paragraph (9)),

the individual may appeal against the decision on the application.

(2) Where a reference number issued in respect of an individual for the purposes of paragraph 1(2) or 9(2) is withdrawn, the individual may appeal against the withdrawal.

(3) Where a reference number issued in respect of an individual for the purposes of paragraph 1(2) or 9(2) is withdrawn in reliance on paragraph 15(3)(d), the individual may appeal against the time specified (in the notice of the withdrawal) as the effective time of the withdrawal.

(4) Where an appeal under sub-paragraph (1) is notified to the tribunal, the tribunal—

(a) must allow the appeal if satisfied—

    (i) that the application was a valid application,

    (ii) that everything in the application was correct, and

    (iii) that, at the time of deciding the appeal, paragraph 15(3)(b), (c) or (d) does not authorise withdrawal of the requested number (assuming it had been issued), and

(b) must otherwise dismiss the appeal.

(5) Where an appeal under sub-paragraph (2) is notified to the tribunal, the tribunal—

(a) must allow the appeal if satisfied that the withdrawal was not authorised by paragraph 15(3), and

(b) must otherwise dismiss the appeal.

(6) Where an appeal under sub-paragraph (3) is notified to the tribunal, the tribunal must decide whether it was just and reasonable to specify the particular time specified and—

(a) if the tribunal decides that it was, the tribunal must dismiss the appeal, and

(b) otherwise—

    (i) the tribunal must decide what time it would have been just and reasonable to specify, and

(ii) the withdrawal has effect as if the notice of the withdrawal had specified the time decided by the tribunal.

(7) Notice of an appeal under this paragraph must be given to Her Majesty's Revenue and Customs before the end of 30 days beginning with the date on which notice under paragraph 14(4) or 15(4) (as the case may be) is given.

(8) In this paragraph "the tribunal" means the First-tier Tribunal or, where determined by or under Tribunal Procedure Rules, the Upper Tribunal.

(9) The references in sub-paragraph (1) and paragraph 17(3)(b)(ii) to an application being unsuccessful do not include a case where an application for a reference number for the purposes of paragraph 1(2) or 9(2) is successful on a dormant basis (see paragraph 14(7) and (8)).

Notification of subsequent protection-cessation events

17 (1) Sub-paragraph (2) applies if, in the case of an individual, there is a protection-cessation event (see paragraphs 3 to 8) at a time when—

(a) the individual has a reference number for the purposes of paragraph 1(2),
(b) there is a pending application for a reference number for those purposes in respect of the individual, or
(c) an appeal under paragraph 16(2) or (3) is in progress in connection with withdrawal of a reference number issued for those purposes in respect of the individual.

(2) The individual—

(a) must notify the Commissioners of the event, and
(b) must do so—

(i) before the end of 90 days beginning with the day on which the individual could first reasonably be expected to have known that the event had occurred, and
(ii) by means of a digital service provided for the purpose by or on behalf of the Commissioners, or by other means authorised in a particular case by an officer of Revenue and Customs.

(3) For the purposes of this paragraph—

(a) an application is pending if—

(i) it has been made,
(ii) no reference number has been issued in response to the application, and
(iii) the applicant has not been notified that the application has been unsuccessful;

(b) an application is also pending if—

(i) it has been made,
(ii) it has been unsuccessful, and
(iii) an appeal under paragraph 16(1) is in progress against the decision on the application;

(c) an appeal under paragraph 16(1), (2) or (3) is in progress until one of the following happens—

(i) it, or any further appeal, is withdrawn, or
(ii) it and any further appeal brought have been determined, and there is no prospect of further appeal.

Notification of subsequent pension debits

18 (1) Sub-paragraph (2) applies if an individual receives a discharge notice related to a pension debit at a time when—

(a) the individual has a reference number for the purposes of paragraph 9(2),
(b) there is a pending application for a reference number for those purposes in respect of the individual, or
(c) an appeal under paragraph 16(2) or (3) is in progress in connection with withdrawal of a reference number issued for those purposes in respect of the individual.

(2) The individual—

(a) must notify the Commissioners of the appropriate amount and transfer day for the pension debit, and
(b) must do so—

(i) before the end of 60 days beginning with the date of the discharge notice related to the pension debit, and
(ii) by means of a digital service provided for the purpose by or on behalf of the Commissioners, or by other means authorised in a particular case by an officer of Revenue and Customs.

(3) For the purposes of this paragraph—

(a) a notice is a discharge notice related to a pension debit if it is notice under regulation 8(2) or (3) of the Pensions on Divorce etc (Provision of Information) Regulations 2000 (SI 2000/1048) relating to discharge of liability in respect of the pension credit corresponding to the pension debit;

(b) an application is pending if—

   (i) it has been made,
   (ii) no reference number has been issued in response to the application,
   (iii) the applicant has not been notified that the application has been unsuccessful, and
   (iv) the applicant has not been notified that the application has been successful on a dormant basis (see paragraph 14(8));

(c) an application is also pending if—

   (i) it has been made,
   (ii) it has been unsuccessful, and
   (iii) an appeal under paragraph 16(1) is in progress against the decision on the application;

(d) an appeal under paragraph 16(1), (2) or (3) is in progress until one of the following happens—

   (i) it, or any further appeal, is withdrawn, or
   (ii) it and any further appeal brought have been determined, and there is no prospect of further appeal.

Personal representatives

19 If an individual dies—

(a) anything which could have been done under or by virtue of this Part of this Schedule by the individual may be done by the individual's personal representatives,

(b) paragraph 14(3)(d)(ii) has effect in relation to an application made in respect of the individual after the individual's death as if it also required a valid application to contain the individual's date of death, and

(c) any notice or reasons given under paragraph 15(4) after the individual's death are to be given to the individual's personal representatives.

Penalties for non-supply, or fraudulent etc supply, of information under paragraph 17 or 18

20 In column 2 of the Table in section 98 of TMA 1970 (provisions about information where non-compliance etc attracts penalties), at the appropriate place insert—

> "paragraph 17 or 18 of Schedule 4 to FA 2016;"

PART 4

INFORMATION

Preservation of records in connection with individual protection 2016

21 If an individual is issued with a reference number for the purposes of paragraph 9(2), the individual must preserve, for the period of 6 years beginning with the date the application for the reference number was made, all such records as were required for the purpose of enabling the individual's relevant amount (see paragraph 9), and amounts A, B, C and D for the individual (see paragraphs 10 to 13), to be correctly calculated.

Amendments of regulations

22 (1) The Registered Pension Schemes (Provision of Information) Regulations 2006 (SI 2006/567) are amended in accordance with paragraphs 23 to 26.

(2) The amendments made by those paragraphs are to be treated as having been made by the Commissioners under such of the powers cited in the instrument containing the Regulations as are applicable.

23 In regulation 2(1) (interpretation)—

(a) after the entry for "fixed protection 2014" insert—
   ""fixed protection 2016" means protection under paragraph 1(2) of Schedule 4 to FA 2016;", and

(b) after the entry for "individual protection 2014" insert—
   ""individual protection 2016" means protection under paragraph 9(2) of Schedule 4 to FA 2016,".

24 (1) In the table in regulation 3(1) (provision of event reports by scheme administrators to HM Revenue and Customs), the entry for reportable event 6 (report where benefit crystallisation event occurs in relation to member of scheme) is amended as follows.

(2) In column 1 of the entry, in paragraph (b)—

(a) omit the "or" at the end of sub-paragraph (iv), and
(b) after sub-paragraph (v) insert ", or

(vi) fixed protection 2016 or individual protection 2016."

(3) In column 2 of the entry—

(a) in the words before paragraph (a), before "the Commissioners" insert "or on behalf of",
(b) omit the "or" at the end of paragraph (c), and
(c) after paragraph (d) insert ", or

(e) Schedule 4 to the Finance Act 2016 (where the member relies on fixed protection 2016 or individual protection 2016)."

(4) In the heading of the entry, for the words after "Benefit crystallisation events and" substitute "non-standard lifetime allowances".

25 (1) Regulation 11 (information provided to scheme administrator by member intending to rely on transitional protection in connection with lifetime allowance) is amended as follows.

(2) In paragraph (1)—

(a) omit the "or" at the end of sub-paragraph (b),
(b) after sub-paragraph (c) (but before the closing words of paragraph (1)) insert ", or

(d) fixed protection 2016 by virtue of Part 1 of Schedule 4 to the Finance Act 2016,", and
(c) in those closing words—

(i) before "the Commissioners" insert "or on behalf of", and
(ii) before "in respect of that entitlement" insert "or Schedule 4 to the Finance Act 2016".

(3) After paragraph (2) insert—

"(3) If the member of a registered pension scheme intends to rely on individual protection 2016 by virtue of Part 2 of Schedule 4 to the Finance Act 2016, the member must notify the scheme administrator of—

(a) the reference number in respect of the member issued by or on behalf of the Commissioners for the purposes of paragraph 9(2) of that Schedule, and
(b) the member's relevant amount calculated in accordance with Part 2 of that Schedule."

(4) In the heading—

(a) for the "or" substitute a comma, and
(b) at the end insert ", fixed protection 2016 or individual protection 2016".

26 After regulation 14B insert—

"14C Individual protection 2016: provision of information by scheme administrator to member on request

(1) Where—

(a) an individual is a member of a registered pension scheme on 5 April 2016,
(b) the individual makes a written request to the scheme administrator for the information mentioned in paragraph (2), and
(c) the request is received by the scheme administrator before 6 April 2020,

the scheme administrator must provide the individual with the information within 3 months following receipt of the request.

(2) The information is such information relating to the member's rights under the scheme as is necessary for calculating, in accordance with Part 2 of Schedule 4 to the Finance Act 2016 (individual protection 2016), the member's relevant amount for the purposes of paragraph 9(2) of that Schedule."

27 In consequence of paragraph 24(4), in each of—

(a) the Registered Pension Schemes (Provision of Information) (Amendment) Regulations 2013 (SI 2013/1742), and
(b) the Registered Pension Schemes (Provision of Information) (Amendment) Regulations 2014 (SI 2014/1843),

omit regulation 4(2)(a).

PART 5

AMENDMENTS IN CONNECTION WITH PROTECTION OF PRE-6 APRIL 2006 RIGHTS

28 (1) In Part 1 of Schedule 29 to FA 2004 (pension schemes: interpretation of the lump sum rule), in paragraph 2 (permitted maximum amount of pension commencement lump sums, calculated in certain cases by deducting adjusted value of previously crystallised amounts from current standard lifetime allowance), in sub-paragraph (10) (modified adjustments where member has protection under paragraph 7 or 12 of Schedule 36 by reference to pre-6 April 2006 rights), after "have effect" insert "—

    (a) where the member becomes entitled to the lump sum on or after 6 April 2014, as if PSLA in the case of any previous benefit crystallisation event which occurs on or after 6 April 2014 were £1,500,000 if that is greater than PSLA in that case, and

    (b) ".

(2) In paragraph 28(3) of Schedule 36 to FA 2004 (transitional provision for pre-6 April 2006 rights: modified version of paragraph 2 of Schedule 29 that applies in certain cases), in the sub-paragraph (7) treated as substituted in paragraph 2 of Schedule 29 to FA 2004, in the definition of "PSLA", after "became entitled to the lump sum" insert "if that occurred before 6 April 2012 but, if that occurred on or after 6 April 2012, PSLA is the greater of £1,800,000 and the standard lifetime allowance at the time the individual became entitled to the lump sum".

(3) The amendment made by sub-paragraph (1) is treated as having come into force on 6 April 2014.

(4) The amendment made by sub-paragraph (2) is treated as having come into force on 6 April 2012.

PART 6

INTERPRETATION AND REGULATIONS

Interpretation of Parts 1, 2 and 3

29 (1) Expressions used in Part 1, 2 or 3 of this Schedule, and in Part 4 of FA 2004 (pension schemes), have the same meaning in that Part of this Schedule as in that Part of that Act.

(2) In particular, references to a relieved non-UK pension scheme or a relieved member of such a scheme are to be read in accordance with paragraphs 13(3) and (4) and 18 of Schedule 34 to FA 2004 (application of lifetime allowance charge provisions to members of overseas pension schemes).

Interpretation of Parts 3 and 4 and this Part

30 In Parts 3 and 4, and this Part, of this Schedule "the Commissioners" means the Commissioners for Her Majesty's Revenue and Customs.

Regulations

31 (1) The Commissioners may by regulations amend Part 1, 2 or 3 of this Schedule.

(2) Regulations under this paragraph may (for example)—

    (a) add to the cases in which paragraph 1(2) is to apply or is to cease to apply;
    (b) add to the cases in which paragraph 9(2) is to apply.

(3) Regulations under this paragraph may include provision having effect in relation to a time before the regulations are made, but—

    (a) the time must not be earlier than 6 April 2016, and
    (b) the provision must not increase any person's liability to tax.

(4) Regulations under this paragraph may include—

    (a) supplementary or incidental provision;
    (b) consequential amendments of the Table in section 98 of TMA 1970 (information requirements: penalties).

(5) Power to make regulations under this paragraph is exercisable by statutory instrument.

(6) A statutory instrument containing regulations under this paragraph is subject to annulment in pursuance of a resolution of the House of Commons.

GENERAL NOTE

Part 1 "Fixed Protection 2016"

Part 1 of Schedule 4 introduces transitional provisions to protect pension savers affected by the reduction to the standard lifetime allowance (SLTA). The protection is referred to as "fixed protection 2016" (FP 2016) and it applies from 6 April 2016. Personal representatives of deceased individuals may also apply for FP 2016.

The protection was announced in the Budget on 18 March 2015, confirmed at the Autumn Statement on 9 December 2015 (accompanied by a Tax Information and Impact Note (TIIN)) and further confirmed in the Budget on 16 March 2016.

HMRC published a Pension Schemes Newsletter (PSN 77) on 27 March 2016 and PSN 78 on 17 May 2016 with Appendices containing information and the relevant application form for scheme members seeking FP 2016 and describing the interim application process for FP 2016.

On 18 February 2016 HMRC published PSN 76. It addressed members planning on taking benefits between 6 April 2016 and July 2016, and stated that they can apply to HMRC for FP 2016 using the interim application process. To help members with this HMRC produced pro forma letter text, which is appended to the PSN. This will be AJ followed by four digits – for example AJ1234.

The reference numbers provided by the online application process will be very different from the temporary reference numbers provided through the interim process. This makes it easy for HMRC, scheme administrators and members to identify whether protection is temporary and needs to be followed up with an online application.

As well as basic information (name, date of birth and national insurance number), the member must confirm that as at 5 April 2016 they did not hold any of the following protections:

- primary protection (PP);
- enhanced protection (EP);
- fixed protection 2012 (FP 2012); and
- fixed protection 2014 (FP 2014).

PSN 75 had previously drawn attention to the interim process for applying for FP 2016 which was contained in PSN 74. It stated that some members could not apply for FP 2016 before 6 April 2016 because as part of the application members had to declare that they did not hold other protections (EP, PP, FP 2012 or FP 2014) before 6 April 2016.

HMRC stated that it was unable to process any interim applications for protection that are received before the above dates, and that any requests received would not be retained. Therefore, the scheme member has to resubmit their application for protection on or after 6 April 2016.

Interim applications received on or after 6 April 2016 are dealt with in date order and HMRC will write to scheme members with a temporary reference number. The temporary reference number is only valid until 31 July 2016, meaning that members must make a full online application and receive a permanent reference number to ensure their pension savings continue to be protected from the lifetime allowance (LTA) charge.

If a pension scheme member is not planning to take benefits between 6 April 2016 and July 2016, they should wait and apply for protection using the online digital service which was to be made available in July 2016.

The protection

Paragraphs 1 and 2 describe FP 2016 as a protected lifetime allowance (LTA) of £1.25 million. Individuals with fixed protection 2012 (FP 2012); fixed protection 2014 (FP 2014); primary protection (PP); or enhanced protection (EP) at any date on or after 6 April 2016 are already protected with a higher LTA and so FP 2016 does not apply.

Protection-cessation events

Paragraph 3 explains that protection will be lost where any of the listed events occur on or after 6 April 2016. The events are described in paras 4, 5, 6 and 7.

Protection-cessation events: interpretation: "benefit accrual"

Paragraph 4:

- Defines (relevant) benefit accrual (RBA) for all types of scheme or arrangement.
- States that RBA occurs in the case of a money purchase (DC) arrangement that is not a cash balance arrangement, if a relevant contribution is paid under the arrangement on or after 6 April 2016.
- States that RBA occurs in the case of a hybrid arrangement in circumstances described above if the arrangement includes DC benefits other than cash balance benefits; and, in any case, if there is an increase in the value of the individual's rights under the arrangement on or after 6 April 2016.
- Explains how to determine the increase in the value of the individual's rights under a cash balance or defined benefit (DB) arrangement.
- Provides a formula for determining an increase in the value of an individual's rights.
- Defines when a relevant contribution is paid.
- States that increases in an individual's rights under an arrangement are to be ignored for the purposes of determining whether RBA has occurred if they don't exceed the "relevant percentage" in a tax year. This applies for DBs and cash balance arrangements as well as hybrid arrangements where the benefits to be provided may be DBs or cash balance benefits.
- Describes the relevant percentage as generally being an annual rate of increase specified in the scheme rules as at 9 December 2015, plus any relevant statutory increase percentage (there is an exception for "predecessor arrangements"). Where no rate of increase is specified in the scheme rules, the relevant percentage is either the annual percentage increase in the consumer price index (CPI), or if it is higher, the relevant statutory increase percentage.
- States that, under a deferred annuity contract which limits increases in rights to annual increases in the retail prices index (RPI), the CPI increase described above is replaced by the annual rate of increase in the value of the individual's rights during the tax year.

Protection-cessation events: interpretation: "impermissible transfer"

Paragraph 5 defines impermissible transfers, in keeping with existing legislation, but with effect from 6 April 2016.

Protection-cessation events: interpretation: "permitted transfer"

Paragraph 6 defines permitted transfers, in keeping with existing legislation.

Protection-cessation events: interpretation: "permitted circumstances"

Paragraph 7 defines permitted circumstances, in keeping with existing legislation.

Protection-cessation events: interpretation: relieved non-UK pension schemes

Paragraph 8 applies similar interpretation for relieved non-UK pension schemes as for UK registered pension schemes, but explains the meaning of relevant benefit accrual (RBA) within the context.

Part 2 "Individual Protection 2016"

Part 2 of Sch 4 introduces "individual protection 2016" (IP 2016). Under para 9 it applies from 6 April 2016.

The protection was announced in the Budget on 18 March 2015, confirmed at the Autumn Statement on 9 December 2015 (accompanied by a Tax Information and Impact Note (TIIN)) and further confirmed in the Budget on 16 March 2016. Personal representatives of deceased individuals may also apply for IP 2016.

HMRC published Pension Schemes Newsletter (PSN 77) on 27 March 2016 and PSN 78 on 17 May 2016 with Appendices containing information and the relevant application form for scheme members seeking IP 2016 and describing the interim application process for IP 2016.

On 18 February 2016 HMRC published PSN 76. It addressed members planning on taking benefits between 6 April 2010 and July 2010, and stated that they can apply to HMRC for IP 2016 using the interim application process. To help members with this HMRC has produced pro forma letter text, which is appended to the PSN. For IP 2016 this will be four digits followed by AJ — for example 1234AJ.

The reference numbers provided by the online application process will be very different from the temporary reference numbers provided through the interim process. This makes it easy for HMRC, scheme administrators and members to identify whether protection is temporary and needs to be followed up with an online application.

As well as basic information (name, date of birth and national insurance number) and confirmation that the member did not hold primary protection (PP) or IP 2014 at 5 April 2016, the scheme member will need to provide HMRC with amounts A to D and their total relevant amount. The total relevant amount is the sum of amounts A to D (A+B+C+D). These are shown in Sch 4 Pt 2 paras 10–13.

PSN 75 had previously drawn attention to the interim process for applying for IP2016 which was contained in PSN 74. It stated that some members could not apply for IP 2016 before 6 April 2016 because as part of the application members they had to provide certain values as at 5 April 2016 relating to their pension savings.

HMRC stated that it was unable to process any interim applications for protection that are received before these dates, and that any requests received would not be retained. Therefore, the scheme member has to resubmit their application for protection on or after 6 April 2016.

Interim applications received on or after 6 April 2016 are dealt with in date order and HMRC will write to scheme members with a temporary reference number. The temporary reference number is only be valid until 31 July 2016, meaning that members must make a full online application and receive a permanent reference number to ensure their pension savings continue to be protected from the lifetime allowance (LTA) charge.

If a pension scheme member is not planning to take benefits between 6 April 2016 and July 2016, they should wait and apply for protection using the online digital service which would be made available in July 2016.

The protection

Paragraph 9 applies from 6 April 2016. The paragraph:

- States that individual protection 2016 (IP 2016) can be sought if an individual has pension rights (the "relevant amount"), greater than £1 million on 5 April 2016 and they do not have:
  - primary protection (PP) which makes provision for a lifetime allowance enhancement factor in relation to the individual;
  - enhanced protection (EP);
  - fixed protection 2012 (FP 2012);
  - fixed protection 2014 (FP 2014);
  - individual protection 2014 (IP 2014);
  - fixed protection 2014 (FP 2014)

  and they have a reference number issued by HMRC (see the GENERAL NOTE to PART 3 of Sch 4).
- Defines the relevant amount as the value on 5 April 2016 of the individual's pensions in payment plus their pension savings, not yet taken, that have benefited from UK tax relief. Paragraphs 10–13 describe amounts A–D, the sum of which are the relevant amount.
- States that an application on a dormant basis applies will be successful where an application would have been unconditionally successful but for the fact that IP 2014 applies. IP 2016 does not apply for individuals with one of the existing protections below for so long as the existing protection continues to apply:
  - EP;
  - FP 2012;
  - FP 2014; and
  - fixed protection 2016 (FP 2016).
- Explains that, following a divorce on or after 6 April 2016, where a pension debit is incurred, the relevant amount is reduced by the amount of the debit in keeping with existing legislation.

Amount A (pre-6 April 2006 pensions in payment)

Paragraph 10 explains how amount A is calculated. It is the value of the pension that the individual was receiving on 6 April 2006.

Where a benefit crystallisation event (BCE) occurred on or before 5 April 2016, amount A is 25 times the annual rate of the pre A-day pension immediately before the

BCE, multiplied by a factor of £1.25 million over the standard lifetime allowance (SLTA). Where no BCE has occurred in respect of the individual since 6 April 2006, amount A is 25 times the annual rate at which the pre A-day pension is payable on 5 April 2016.

In other words, the percentage of the SLTA used up by the pre A-day pension is the same on 5 April 2016 as it was on the date of the BCE.

Amount B (pre-6 April 2016 benefit crystallisation events)

Paragraph 11 explains how amount B is calculated. The required steps are:
- to identify each benefit crystallisation event (BCE) from 6 April 2006 to 5 April 2016;
- to determine the amount of each such BCE; and
- to multiply each crystallised amount by the fraction provided.

Amount C (uncrystallised rights at end of 5 April 2016 under registered pension schemes)

Paragraph 12 explains that amount C is the value of any uncrystallised pension rights under a UK pension scheme on 5 April 2016.

Amount D (uncrystallised rights at end of 5 April 2016 under relieved non-UK schemes)

Paragraph 13 explains that amount D is the value of any uncrystallised pension rights under a non-UK pension scheme on 5 April 2016.

Part 3 Reference Numbers etc

Part 3 of Sch 4 describes application and reference numbers for fixed protection 2016 or individual protection 2016 (FP 2016 or IP 2016) effective from 6 April 2016.

Issuing of reference numbers for fixed or individual protection 2016

Paragraph 14 concerns applications for fixed protection 2016 or individual protection 2016 (FP 2016 or IP 2016), and the issue by HMRC of a reference number to evidence that the individual is entitled to such protection. It explains the form of the reference number, when it will be issued and what information is required by HMRC.

HMRC must notify the individual if their application is unsuccessful or, in the case of IP 2016, the application was successful but a reference number is not being issued because the protection is dormant. A "dormant basis" means that the application would have been successful but for the fact that the individual held another form of transitional protection at the time of the application.

Withdrawal of reference numbers

Paragraph 15 sets out the circumstances in which HMRC may withdraw a reference number, and requires HMRC to tell the individual the reasons for doing so.

Appeals against non-issue or withdrawal of reference numbers

Paragraph 16 provides for an appeal to the First-tier Tribunal or, where determined by or under Tribunal Procedure Rules, the Upper Tribunal, against the non-issue or the withdrawal of a reference number.

Notification of subsequent protection-cessation events

Paragraph 17 requires individuals who have a reference number, or a pending application for a reference number, for the purposes of individual protection 2016 (IP 2016), to notify HMRC within 90 days if a "protection-cessation event" described in Sch 4 Pt 2 paras 3–8 occurs.

Notification of subsequent pension debits

Paragraph 18 requires individuals who have a reference number, or a pending application for a reference number, for the purposes of individual protection 2016 (IP 2016), to notify HMRC within 60 days if they receive a discharge notice related to a pension debit. A discharge notice is a notice under reg 8(2) or (3) of the Pensions on Divorce etc (Provision of Information) Regulations 2000 (SI 2000/1048).

Personal representatives

Paragraph 19 provides for personal representatives of deceased individuals to be able to apply for fixed or individual protection 2016 (FP 2016 and IP 2016).

Penalties for non-supply, or fraudulent etc supply, of information under paragraph 17 or 18

Paragraph 20 amends TMA 1970 s 98 so that where an individual fails to comply with the requirements in either Sch 4 Pt 3 para 17 or 18, then the penalties as set out in TMA 1970 s 98(1)(b) and (2) apply, This includes a penalty of up to £300 where required information is not provided.

Part 4 Information

Part 4 of Sch 4 sets out the information requirements in connection with fixed protection 2016 and individual protection 2016 (FP 2016 and IP 2016) through changes to existing secondary legislation.

Preservation of records in connection with individual protection 2016

Paragraph 21 requires individuals who have a reference number for individual protection 2016 (IP 2016) to preserve the documents that have been used in the calculation of their relevant amount, for six years from the date of application for the reference number.

Amendments of regulations

Paragraphs 22 to 25 amend the Registered Pension Schemes (Provision of Information) Regulations 2006 (SI 2006/567) to include references to fixed protection 2016 and individual protection 2016 (FP 2016 and IP 2016). The information required to be provided by the member to the scheme administrator and from the scheme administrator to HMRC is similar to the lifetime allowance (LTA) protection regimes.

Paragraph 26 amends the Registered Pension Schemes (Provision of Information) Regulations 2006 so that, if the member requests it and as long as the request is received by the scheme administrator before 6 April 2020, scheme administrators must provide information, to enable a member to calculate their relevant amount. Scheme administrators may also, if they so choose, provide this information for requests received after this date. In view of the foregoing, for purposes of certainty, individuals may wish to seek confirmation of their relevant amount within the stated timescale.

Paragraph 27 makes the necessary changes to the information regulations.

Part 5 Amendments in Connection with Protection of Pre-6 April 2006 Rights

Part 5 of Sch 4 revises FA 2004 in respect of primary protection and enhanced protection (PP and EP) so that certain individuals are able to receive the right amount of tax free pension commencement lump sum (PCLS) intended by legislation. Paragraph 28 makes the necessary changes:

– For a member who becomes entitled to the lump sum on or after 6 April 2014, the lump sum in respect of any previous benefit crystallisation event (BCE) which occurs on or after 6 April 2014 is treated as £1.5 million if that is greater than the standard lifetime allowance (SLTA). The amendment is treated as having come into force on 6 April 2014.

– For a member who becomes entitled to the lump sum on or after 6 April 2012, the lump sum is the greater of £1,800,000 and the SLTA at the time the individual became entitled to the lump sum. The amendment is treated as having come into force on 6 April 2012.

The revisions were announced in the Budget on 18 March 2015, confirmed at the Autumn Statement on 9 December 2015 (accompanied by a Tax Information and Impact Note (TIIN)) and further confirmed in the Budget on 16 March 2016.

Part 6 Interpretation and Regulations

Part 6 of Sch 4 sets out the interpretation of expressions used in the Schedule and provides a power to make regulations amending Pts 1, 2 and 3 of the Schedule. It contains a power to make changes to Pts 1, 2 and 3 of the Schedule by regulations.

Such regulations may be retrospective providing they do not increase any person's liability to tax and do not have effect before 6 April 2016.

SCHEDULE 5
PENSION FLEXIBILITY
Section 22

Serious ill-health lump sums

1 (1) Part 4 of FA 2004 (registered pension schemes etc) is amended as follows.

(2) Omit section 205A (serious ill-health lump sum charge on payment to member who has reached 75).

(3) In Part 1 of Schedule 29 (interpretation of lump sum rule), paragraph 4 (serious ill-health lump sums) is amended in accordance with sub-paragraphs (4) and (5).

(4) In sub-paragraph (1) (meaning of "serious ill-heath lump sum")—

  (a) at the end of paragraph (b) insert "and", and
  (b) for paragraphs (c) and (d) substitute—
    "(ca) either—
      (i) it is paid in respect of an uncrystallised arrangement, and it extinguishes the member's entitlement to benefits under the arrangement, or
      (ii) it is paid in respect of uncrystallised rights of the member under an arrangement other than an uncrystallised arrangement, and it extinguishes the member's uncrystallised rights under the arrangement."

(5) After sub-paragraph (2) insert—

  "(2A) In subsection (1)(ca)(ii) "uncrystallised rights", in relation to the member, means rights of the member that are uncrystallised rights as defined by section 212(1) and (2)."

2 (1) Section 636A of ITEPA 2003 (exemption for certain lump sums under registered pension schemes) is amended as follows.

(2) In the heading, for "Exemption" substitute "Exemptions and liabilities".

(3) For subsection (3A) (serious ill-health lump sum paid to member who has reached 75 is taxed only under section 205A of FA 2004) substitute—

  "(3A) Section 579A applies in relation to a serious ill-health lump sum which is paid under a registered pension scheme to a member who has reached the age of 75 as it applies to any pension under a registered pension scheme."

3 (1) In consequence of the amendment made by paragraph 1(2), in Part 4 of FA 2004—

  (a) in section 164(2)(b) omit ", the serious ill-health lump sum charge",
  (b) omit section 272A(7)(a)(ii),
  (c) in section 280(2) omit the entry for "serious ill-health lump sum charge", and
  (d) in Schedule 34—

    (i) omit paragraph 1(3)(ca), and
    (ii) in paragraph 5 omit ", serious ill-health lump sum charge".

(2) In consequence of the amendment made by paragraph 1(2), in section 30(1) of ITA 2007 omit the entry for section 205A of FA 2004.

(3) In consequence of the amendments made by paragraphs 1 and 2 and sub-paragraphs (1) and (2)—

  (a) in Schedule 16 to FA 2011, omit paragraphs 28(2)(a), 40, 42(3), 63, 77(4), 81(2) and (4)(b) and 83, and
  (b) omit section 2(4) of the Taxation of Pensions Act 2014.

4 The amendments made by paragraphs 1 to 3 have effect in relation to lump sums paid after the day on which this Act is passed.

Charity lump sum death benefits

5 (1) In paragraph 18(1A) of Schedule 29 to FA 2004 (when lump sum paid out of uncrystallised funds is charity lump sum death benefit), omit paragraph (a) (member must have died after reaching 75).

(2) The amendment made by sub-paragraph (1) has effect in relation to lump sums paid after the day on which this Act is passed.

Dependants' flexi-access drawdown funds

6 (1) Part 2 of Schedule 28 to FA 2004 (interpretation of pension death benefit rules) is amended as follows.

(2) In paragraph 15 (meaning of "dependant"), after sub-paragraph (2) insert—

"(2A) A child of the member is a dependant of the member if the child—

(a) has reached the age of 23, and
(b) is not within sub-paragraph (2)(b).

(2B) But this paragraph, so far as it has effect for the purpose of determining the meaning of "dependant"—

(a) in paragraphs 16 to 17 and 27A, and
(b) in paragraph 18 of Schedule 29,

has effect with the omission of sub-paragraph (2A)."

(3) In paragraph 22 (meaning of "dependant's drawdown pension fund")—

(a) in sub-paragraph (2)(a) and (aa) omit "to the dependant", and
(b) in sub-paragraph (3), after "representing a" insert "person's".

(4) The amendments made by this paragraph come into force on the day after the day on which this Act is passed.

(5) The sub-paragraphs inserted by sub-paragraph (2)—

(a) apply for the purpose of determining whether a payment of an annuity is a payment of a dependants' short-term annuity only if the annuity is purchased after the day on which this Act is passed, and
(b) apply for the purpose of determining whether a payment to a person is a payment of dependants' income withdrawal if, but only if, the person reaches the age of 23 after the day on which this Act is passed.

(6) In sub-paragraph (5) "dependants' short-term annuity" and "dependants' income withdrawal" have the same meaning as in Part 4 of FA 2004.

Trivial commutation lump sum

7 (1) Paragraph 7 of Schedule 29 to FA 2004 (interpretation of lump sum rule: meaning of "trivial commutation lump sum") is amended as follows.

(2) In sub-paragraph (1)(aa) (sum must be paid in respect of a defined benefits arrangement), after "arrangement," insert "or in respect of a scheme pension payable by the scheme administrator to which the member has become entitled under a money purchase arrangement (an "in-payment money-purchase in-house scheme pension"), or partly in respect of the former and partly in respect of the latter,".

(3) In sub-paragraph (1)(d) (sum must extinguish member's entitlement to defined benefits under the scheme), after "defined benefits" insert ", and any entitlement to payments of in-payment money-purchase in-house scheme pensions,".

8 (1) Section 636B of ITEPA 2003 (taxation of trivial commutation, and winding-up, lump sums) is amended as follows.

(2) In subsection (3) (taxation of lump sum where member has uncrystallised rights under the pension scheme)—

(a) in the words before paragraph (a) omit "(within the meaning of section 212 of FA 2004)", and
(b) in paragraph (b), for "the uncrystallised rights calculated in accordance with that section" substitute "any uncrystallised rights extinguished by the lump sum".

(3) After subsection (4) insert—

"(5) In this section "uncrystallised rights" has the same meaning as in section 212 of FA 2004; and the value for the purposes of this section of any uncrystallised rights is to be calculated in accordance with that section."

9 The amendments made by paragraphs 7 and 8 have effect in relation to lump sums paid after the day on which this Act is passed.

Top-up of dependants' death benefits

10 (1) In paragraph 15 of Schedule 29 to FA 2004 (uncrystallised funds lump sum death benefits), after sub-paragraph (2) insert—

"(2A) Where—

(a) the arrangement is a cash balance arrangement,
(b) under the arrangement, a dependant of the member is entitled to be paid after the member's death an amount by way of a lump sum,

(c) the dependant's entitlement to a lump sum of that amount under the arrangement comes into being at a time no later than the member's death,
(d) such of the sums and assets held for the purposes of the arrangement immediately after the member's death as are held for the purpose of meeting the liability to pay the lump sum are insufficient for that purpose (including where that is because none are held for that purpose), and
(e) a person who was an employer in relation to the member pays a contribution to the scheme—
  (i) for or towards making good that insufficiency, and
  (ii) of no more than is needed for making good the insufficiency,
the sums and assets held for the purposes of the arrangement that represent the contribution are to be treated as "relevant uncrystallised funds" for the purposes of this paragraph."
(2) The amendment made by sub-paragraph (1) has effect in relation to contributions paid after the day on which this Act is passed.

Inheritance tax as respects cash alternatives to annuities for dependants etc

11 (1) In section 152 of the Inheritance Tax Act 1984 (where annuity payable on person' death to dependant etc, person treated as not beneficially entitled to sum that could have been paid to personal representatives instead of being used for annuity), for "or dependant" substitute ", dependant or nominee".
(2) The amendment made by sub-paragraph (1)—
  (a) is to be treated as having come into force on 6 April 2015, and
  (b) has effect where the person on whose death an annuity is payable dies on or after that date.

GENERAL NOTE

Schedule 5 makes various minor changes to FA 2004 Pt 4 to ensure greater pension flexibility regarding serious ill-health lump sums, charity lump sum death benefits, dependants with drawdown pension funds and flexi-access drawdown funds where the dependant reaches age 23, trivial commutation lump sums and dependants' death benefits under cash balance arrangements.

Serious ill-health lump sums

Paragraphs 1 to 4 amend various legislation regarding the payment of serious ill-health lump sums from registered pension schemes to remove the 45% tax charge and replace it with a tax charge at the recipient's marginal rate where the recipient is over 75.

Paragraph 1(2) deletes FA 2004 s 205A which had applied a 45% tax charge on serious ill-health lump sums. Paragraph 1(3) to (5) amends FA 2004 Sch 29 para 4 regarding the definition of a serious ill-health lump sum to allow a lump sum to be paid out of unused funds in a drawdown fund. Paragraph 2 amends ITEPA 2003 s 636A so that a taxable serious ill-health lump sum is taxed as a pension paid under a registered pension scheme and thus subject to the recipient's marginal rate of tax. As a result of the amendment made by para 1(2) (see above), para 3 makes consequential amendments to FA 2004 ss 164(2)(b), 205A, 272A(7)(a)(ii) and 280(2), and Sch 34 para 1(3)(ca) and 5, to FA 2011 Sch 16 and to TPA 2014 s 2(4). Paragraph 4 provides that the changes made by paras 1 to 3 above apply to any serious ill-health lump sum paid from the day after Finance Bill 2016 receives Royal Assent.

Charity lump sum death benefits

Paragraph 5 amends FA 2004 Sch 29 para 18(1A) allowing payment of a charity lump sum death benefit from uncrystallised funds in respect of a member who had not reached age 75 at the time of their death. Once again the change made by this para applies to any charity lump sum death benefit paid from the day after Finance Bill 2016 receives Royal Assent.

Dependants' flexi-access drawdown funds

Paragraph 6 amends FA 2004 Sch 28 Part 2 regarding the conditions that must be met for a drawdown fund to be a dependants' flexi-access drawdown fund or a dependants' drawdown fund to enable dependants with these types of funds, who would currently have to use all of this fund before age 23, to be able to continue accessing these funds as they wish after their 23rd birthday.

Paragraph 6(2) amends FA 2004 Sch 28 para 15 to extend the meaning of dependant in certain circumstances to include a child who has reached age 23. Paragraph 6(3) amends the meaning of dependants' drawdown pension fund in FA 2004 Sch 28 para 22 so that the recipient may be a dependant under the extended meaning. Paragraph 6(4) provides that the changes made by para 6(2) and (3) apply to any dependants' flexi-access drawdown funds from the day after Finance Bill 2016 received Royal Assent (which was 15 September 2016). Paragraph 6(5) provides further clarification of the amendments contained in para 6(2) above. Paragraph 6(6) ensures that the terms "dependants' short-term annuity" and "dependants' income withdrawal" in para 6(5) above have the same meaning as in FA 2004 Pt 4.

Trivial commutation lump sum

Paragraphs 7 to 9 amend various legislation regarding the trivial commutation of lump sums. Paragraph 7(1) to (3) amends FA 2004 Sch 29 para 7 to allow a scheme pension to be paid as an authorised payment where it is commuted to be a trivial commutation lump sum. Paragraph 8(1) to (3) amends ITEPA 2003 s 636B in respect of a trivial lump sum or winding-up lump sum paid out of uncrystallised rights. The amendments ensure that only 75% of rights which have not been accessed (uncrystallised rights) are taxed, even when they are paid together with crystallised rights. This aligns the tax treatment with lump sums that are paid entirely out of uncrystallised rights. Paragraph 9 provides that the changes made by paras 7 and 8 apply to lump sums paid from the day after Finance Bill 2016 receives Royal Assent.

Top-up of dependants' death benefits

Paragraph 10(1) amends FA 2004 Sch 29 para 15 allowing employers to top up the amount of any shortfall in funds in a promised uncrystallised fund lump sum death benefit in a cash balance arrangement at the time of the member's death. The top-up can only be made in respect of a shortfall at the time of death. Paragraph 10(2) provides that the change made by para 10(1) applies to contributions paid from the day after Finance Bill 2016 receives Royal Assent.

Inheritance tax as respects cash alternatives to annuities for dependants etc

Paragraph 11(1) amends ITA 1984 s 152 to provide that, where an annuity is payable on death to a nominee and some or all of the cost of the annuity could instead have been paid to a personal representative, those funds shall not form part of that person's chargeable estate for IHT purposes. Paragraph 10(2)(a) provides that the change made by para 11(1) applies from 6 April 2015.

SCHEDULE 6

DEDUCTION OF INCOME TAX AT SOURCE

Section 39

PART 1

ABOLITION OF DUTY TO DEDUCT TAX FROM INTEREST ON CERTAIN INVESTMENTS

1 In Chapter 2 of Part 15 of ITA 2007 (deduction of income tax at source by deposit-takers and building societies) omit—

(a) section 851 (duty to deduct when making payment of interest on relevant investment), and

(b) the italic heading preceding it.

PART 2

DEDUCTION OF TAX FROM YEARLY INTEREST: EXCEPTION FOR DEPOSIT-TAKERS

2 In section 876 of ITA 2007 (interest paid by deposit-takers), for subsections (1) and (2) substitute—

"(1) The duty to deduct a sum representing income tax under section 874 does not apply to a payment of interest on an investment if—

(a) the payment is made by a deposit-taker, and

(b) when the payment is made, the investment is a relevant investment.

(1A) In this section "deposit-taker", "investment" and "relevant investment" have the meaning given by Chapter 2."

PART 3

AMENDMENTS OF OR RELATING TO CHAPTER 2 OF PART 15 OF ITA 2007

Amendments of Chapter 2 of Part 15 of ITA 2007

3 Chapter 2 of Part 15 of ITA 2007 (deduction of income tax at source by deposit-takers and building societies) is amended in accordance with paragraphs 4 to 18.

4 For the Chapter heading substitute "Meaning of "relevant investment" for purposes of section 876".

5 (1) Section 850 (overview of Chapter) is amended as follows.

(2) For subsection (1) substitute—

"(1) This Chapter has effect for the purposes of section 876 (duty under section 874 to deduct tax from payments of yearly interest: exception for deposit-takers)."

(3) Omit subsection (2) (which introduces sections 851 and 852).

(4) In subsection (4)(b) (which introduces sections 858 to 870), for "858" substitute "863".

(5) In subsection (5) (which introduces sections 871 to 873), for "871 to" substitute "872 and".

(6) In subsection (6) (interpretation), for the words from "Chapter—" to "crediting" substitute "Chapter, crediting".

6 Omit section 852 (power to disapply section 851).

7 In section 853(1) (meaning of "deposit-taker"), after "In this Chapter" insert "and section 876".

8 In section 854(3) (meaning of "relevant investment" in section 851(1)(b)), for "851(1)(b)" substitute "876(1)(b)".

9 For section 855(1) (meaning of "investment") substitute—

"(1) In this Chapter, and section 876, "investment" means a deposit with a deposit-taker."

10 (1) Section 856 (meaning of "relevant investment") is amended as follows.

(2) In subsection (1), for "this Chapter" substitute "section 876".

(3) In subsection (2) (exceptions), for "858" substitute "863".

11 In section 857 (treating investments as being or not being relevant investments) omit "or building society" in each place.

12 Omit—

(a) sections 858 to 861 (investments which are not relevant investments and in relation to which duty under section 874 does not apply), and

(b) the italic heading preceding section 858.

13 In the italic heading preceding section 863, for "Other investments" substitute "Investments".

14 In sections 863, 864, 865 and 868(4) (investments with deposit-takers or building societies) omit "or building society" in each place.

15 Omit sections 868(3), 869 and 870(2) (investments with building societies).

16 Omit section 871 (power to make regulations to give effect to Chapter).

17 In section 872 (power to amend Chapter)—

(a) in subsection (2) (different provision for different deposit-takers)—

(i) for "which amends this Chapter in its application to deposit-takers may do so" substitute "may amend this Chapter", and

(ii) in each of paragraphs (a) and (b), for "relation" substitute "its application", and

(b) omit subsections (4) and (5) (which refer to provisions repealed by this Act).

18 Omit section 873(3) to (6) (interpretation of section 861).

Amendments relating to Chapter 2 of Part 15 of ITA 2007

19 In Schedule 12 to FA 1988 (transfer of building society's business to a company), in paragraph 6(1) (treatment for tax purposes of benefits conferred in connection with a transfer) omit—

(a) "either", and

(b) paragraph (b) (benefit not to be subject to deduction of tax under Chapter 2 of Part 15 of ITA 2007), and the "or" preceding it.

20 (1) In section 564Q(1) of ITA 2007 (alternative finance return: deduction of income tax at source under Chapter 2 of Part 15)—

(a) after "Chapter 2 of Part 15" insert "and section 876",

(b) for "deduction by deposit-takers and building societies" substitute "exception for deposit-takers", and

(c) after "Chapter 2 of that Part" insert "and section 876".

(2) In section 564Q(5) of ITA 2007 (alternative finance return: deduction of income tax at source under Chapters 3 to 5 of Part 15)—

(a) after "of Part 15" insert "except section 876", and

(b) for "those Chapters" substitute "those provisions".

21 In section 847 of ITA 2007 (overview of Part 15)—

(a) in subsection (2) omit paragraph (a) (which introduces Chapter 2), and

(b) in subsection (5) (which introduces Chapters containing provision connected with the duties to deduct), before paragraph (a) insert—

"(za) Chapter 2 (interpretation of section 876 in Chapter 3: exception for deposit-takers),".

22 In section 946 of ITA 2007 (collection of tax deducted at source: payments to which Chapter applies) omit paragraph (a) (payments from which deductions required to be made under section 851).

23 In Schedule 2 to ITA 2007 omit paragraphs 154 to 156 (transitional provisions related to Chapter 2 of Part 15 of ITA 2007).

24 In Schedule 4 to ITA 2007 (index of defined expressions)—

(a) omit the entry for "beneficiary under a discretionary or accumulation settlement (in Chapter 2 of Part 15)",

(b) in the entry for "deposit-taker (in Chapter 2 of Part 15)", after "Part 15" insert "and section 876",

(c) omit the entry for "dividend (in Chapter 2 of Part 15)",

(d) in the entry for "investment (in Chapter 2 of Part 15)", after "Part 15" insert "and section 876", and

(e) omit the entry for "relevant investment (in Chapter 2 of Part 15)".

25 In consequence of the amendments made by Part 1 of this Schedule and the preceding provisions of this Part of this Schedule—

(a) in Schedule 1 to ITA 2007 omit paragraph 277,

(b) in Schedule 1 to FA 2008 omit paragraph 25,

(c) in Schedule 46 to FA 2013—

(i) in paragraph 68(1) omit paragraph (a) including the "and" at the end,

(ii) in paragraph 69(1) omit paragraph (a) including the "and" at the end,

(iii) omit paragraph 70(1), and

(iv) in paragraph 71(3) omit paragraph (b) and the "and" preceding it, and

(d) in FA 2014 omit section 3(4).

PART 4

DEDUCTION OF TAX FROM UK PUBLIC REVENUE DIVIDENDS

26 In section 877 of ITA 2007 (duty to deduct under section 874: exception relating to UK public revenue dividends)—

(a) for "in respect of" substitute "that is", and

(b) after "dividend" insert "(as defined by section 891)".

27 (1) Chapter 5 of Part 15 of ITA 2007 (deduction from payments of UK public revenue dividends) is amended as follows.

(2) In section 893(2) (securities which are gross-paying government securities)—

    (a) before the "or" at the end of paragraph (a) insert—

        "(aa) securities, so far as they are not gilt-edged securities, issued or treated as issued under—

            (i) the National Loans Act 1939, or
            (ii) the National Loans Act 1968,", and

    (b) in paragraph (b), for "894(1) or (3)" substitute "894(3)".

(3) In section 894 (power to direct that securities are gross-paying government securities)—

    (a) omit subsections (1) and (2) (power in relation to securities within the new section 893(2)(aa)), and
    (b) in subsection (5) omit "(1) or".

PART 5
COMMENCEMENT

28 (1) The amendments made by Parts 1 and 3 of this Schedule have effect in relation to—

    (a) interest paid or credited on or after 6 April 2016, and
    (b) dividends or other distributions paid by a building society on or after that date.

(2) Sub-paragraph (1) does not apply to—

    (a) the repeals in Schedule 12 to FA 1988;
    (b) the amendments in section 564Q of ITA 2007;
    (c) the repeal of paragraph 277 of Schedule 1 to ITA 2007.

(3) The repeals mentioned in sub-paragraph (2)(a) and (c) have effect in relation to benefits conferred on or after 6 April 2016.

(4) The amendments mentioned in sub-paragraph (2)(b) have effect in relation to alternative finance return paid on or after 6 April 2016.

(5) The amendments made by Part 2 of this Schedule, and the amendments made by this Schedule in sections 893 and 894 of ITA 2007, have effect in relation to interest paid on or after 6 April 2016.

GENERAL NOTE

Section 39 and Sch 6 amend ITA 2007 Part 15 to remove the obligation for banks, building societies and other deposit-takers to deduct income tax from interest and other returns on certain savings and investments.

Budget 2015 announced that following the introduction of the new personal savings allowance in 2016/17, 95% of taxpayers would be able to "save completely tax free each year". As so many people would no longer be liable to tax on their savings, the deduction of tax by banks and building societies under the tax deduction scheme for interest (TDSI) scheme would no longer be necessary. The change would represent a "major tax simplification", the Government said.

Schedule 6 Pt 1 repeals ITA 2007 s 851 (duty to deduct sums representing income tax).

Schedule 6 Pt 2 amends ITA 2007 s 876 so that the duty to deduct a sum representing income tax under ITA 2007 s 874 (duty to deduct from certain payments of yearly interest) does not apply to a payment of interest on an investment if the payment is made by a deposit-taker and, when the payment is made, the investment is a "relevant investment" as defined in ITA 2007 Pt 15 Ch 2.

Schedule 6 Pt 3 makes several consequential amendments to ITA 2007 Pt 15 Ch 2.

Schedule 6 Pt 4 amends ITA 2007 s 877 and Pt 15 Ch 5 in relation to deduction of tax from UK public revenue dividends

The amendments made by Sch 6 Pts 1 and 3 apply to interest paid or credited on or after 6 April 2016, and dividends or other distributions paid by a building society on or after that date.

SCHEDULE 7

LOAN RELATIONSHIPS AND DERIVATIVE CONTRACTS

Section 49

Introductory

1 CTA 2009 is amended as follows.

Non-market loans

2 In Chapter 15 of Part 5 (loan relationships: tax avoidance), after section 446 insert—

"Non-market loans

446A Non-market loans

(1) This section applies as respects any accounting period if—

(a) a company has a debtor relationship in the period,

(b) the amount recognised in the company's accounts in respect of the debt at the time the company became party to the debtor relationship was less than the transaction price,

(c) credits in respect of the whole or part of the discount were not brought into account for the purposes of this Part, and

(d) in a case where the creditor is a company, the non-qualifying territory condition is met.

(2) The debits which are to be brought into account for the accounting period for the purposes of this Part by the debtor company in respect of the loan relationship are not to include debits relating to the relevant discount amount, to the extent that that amount is referable to the accounting period.

(3) In this section "relevant discount amount" means—

(a) in a case where credits in respect of the whole of the discount were not brought into account for the purposes of this Part, an amount equal to the whole discount, and

(b) in a case where credits in respect of part of the discount were not brought into account for the purposes of this Part, an amount equal to that part of the discount.

(4) The non-qualifying territory condition referred to in subsection (1)(d) is that the creditor company is—

(a) resident for tax purposes in a non-qualifying territory at any time in the accounting period, or

(b) effectively managed in a non-taxing non-qualifying territory at any such time.

(5) In this section—

"discount" means the difference between the two amounts referred to in subsection (1)(b);

"non-qualifying territory" has the meaning given in section 173 of TIOPA 2010;

"non-taxing non-qualifying territory" means a non-qualifying territory under whose law companies are not liable to tax by reason of domicile, residence or place of management;

"resident for tax purposes" means liable, under the law of the non-qualifying territory, to tax there by reason of domicile, residence or place of management."

Transfer pricing

3 In section 446 (loan relationships: bringing transfer-pricing adjustments into account), after subsection (7) insert—

"(8) No credit is to be brought into account for the purposes of this Part to the extent that it corresponds to an amount which, as a result of the preceding provisions of this section, has not previously been brought into account as a debit."

4 In section 693 (derivative contracts: bringing transfer-pricing adjustments into account), after subsection (5) insert—

"(6) No credit is to be brought into account for the purposes of this Part to the extent that it corresponds to an amount which, as a result of the preceding provisions of this section, has not previously been brought into account as a debit."

Exchange gains and losses

5 In section 447 (exchange gains and losses on debtor relationships: loans disregarded under Part 4 of TIOPA 2010), after subsection (4) insert—

"(4A) If the debtor relationship is to any extent matched, subsections (2) and (3) apply to leave out of account only the lesser of—

(a) the amount of the exchange gain or loss (in the case of subsection (2)) or the proportion of the exchange gain or loss (in the case of subsection (3)) which would be left out of account apart from this subsection, and

(b) the amount of the exchange gain or loss arising in respect of a liability representing the debtor relationship to the extent that the debtor relationship is unmatched (an amount which may be nil)."

6 In section 448 (exchange gains and losses on debtor relationships: equity notes where holder associated with issuer), after subsection (2) insert—

"(3) If the debtor relationship is to any extent matched, subsection (2) applies to leave out of account only the amount of the exchange gain or loss arising in respect of a liability representing the debtor relationship to the extent that the debtor relationship is unmatched (an amount which may be nil)."

7 In section 449 (exchange gains and losses on creditor relationships: no corresponding debtor relationship), after subsection (4) insert—

"(4A) If the creditor relationship is to any extent matched, subsection (2) applies to leave out of account only the amount of the exchange gain or loss arising in respect of an asset representing the creditor relationship to the extent that the creditor relationship is unmatched (an amount which may be nil)."

8 In section 451 (exception to section 449 where loan exceeds arm's length amount), after subsection (4) insert—

"(4A) If the creditor relationship is to any extent matched, subsections (3) and (4) apply to leave out of account only the lesser of—

(a) the proportion of the exchange gain or loss which would be left out of account apart from this subsection, and

(b) the amount of the exchange gain or loss arising in respect of an asset representing the creditor relationship to the extent that the creditor relationship is unmatched (an amount which may be nil)."

9 (1) Section 452 (exchange gains and losses where loan not on arm's length terms) is amended as follows.

(2) For subsection (3) substitute—

"(3) Subsections (4) and (5) apply if, because of a claim made under section 192(1) of TIOPA 2010, or because of the claim that is assumed to be made under subsection (2)—

(a) one company is treated for any purpose as having a debtor relationship, or

(b) more than one company is treated for any purpose as having a debtor relationship represented by the same liability."

(3) In subsection (4)—

(a) after "exchange gains" insert "from that debtor relationship (in a subsection (3)(a) case) or";

(b) after "those debtor relationships" insert "(in a subsection (3)(b) case)";

(c) for the words from "debits" to the end substitute "exchange gains or the proportion of the exchange gains to be left out of account under section 447 by the issuing company in respect of the loan relationship".

(4) In subsection (5)—

(a) after "exchange losses" insert "from that debtor relationship (in a subsection (3)(a) case) or";

(b) after "those debtor relationships" insert "(in a subsection (3)(b) case)";

(c) for the words from "credits" to the end substitute "exchange losses or the proportion of the exchange losses to be left out of account under section 447 by the issuing company in respect of the loan relationship".

(5) After subsection (5) insert—

"(5A) In this section "issuing company" is to be construed in accordance with section 191(1)(a) of TIOPA 2010."

10 After section 475A insert—

"Meaning of "matched"

475B Meaning of "matched"

(1) This section applies for the purposes of this Part.

(2) A loan relationship of a company is matched if and to the extent that

(a) it is in a matching relationship with another loan relationship or a derivative contract of the company, or

(b) exchange gains or losses arising in relation to an asset or liability representing the loan relationship are excluded from being brought into account under regulations under section 328(4),

and "unmatched" is to be construed accordingly.

(3) A loan relationship is in a matching relationship with another loan relationship or derivative contract if one is intended by the company to act to eliminate or substantially reduce the economic risk of the other.

(4) In this section "economic risk" means a risk which can be attributed to fluctuations in exchange rates between currencies over a period of time.

(5) In this section "derivative contract" has the same meaning as in Part 7 (see section 576)."

11 (1) Section 694 (derivative contracts: exchange gains and losses) is amended as follows.

(2) After subsection (3) insert—

"(3A) If the contract is to any extent matched, subsection (3) applies to leave out of account only the amount of the exchange gains or losses arising to the company in relation to the contract to the extent that the contract is unmatched (an amount which may be nil)."

(3) After subsection (7) insert—

"(7A) Subsections (5) to (7) apply only to the extent that the contract is unmatched."

(4) After subsection (10) insert—

"(11) For the purposes of this section a derivative contract of a company is matched if and to the extent that—

(a) it is in a matching relationship with another derivative contract or loan relationship of the company, or

(b) exchange gains or losses arising in relation to the derivative contract are excluded from being brought into account under regulations under section 606(4)(b),

and "unmatched" is to be construed accordingly.

(12) A derivative contract is in a matching relationship with another derivative contract or loan relationship if one is intended by the company to act to eliminate or substantially reduce the economic risk of the other.

(13) In this section "economic risk" means a risk which can be attributed to fluctuations in exchange rates between currencies over a period of time.

(14) In this section "loan relationship" has the same meaning as in Part 5 (see section 302)."

Commencement

12 (1) The amendments made by this Schedule have effect in relation to accounting periods beginning on or after 1 April 2016.

(2) For the purposes of sub-paragraph (1), where the accounting period of a company begins before 1 April 2016 and ends on or after that date (the "straddling period"), so much of the straddling period as falls before that date, and so much of the straddling period as falls on or after that date, are to be treated as separate accounting periods.

GENERAL NOTE

Schedule 7 makes a number of changes to the loan relationships and derivative contracts legislation. All the changes introduced by this Schedule take effect for accounting periods beginning on or after 1 April 2016. Where an accounting period straddles this date the amendments have effect for such part of the accounting period as falls on or after 1 April 2016 (see para 12).

Paragraph 2 makes changes in respect of non-market loans. Following changes introduced by the Finance (No 2) Act 2015 profits and losses arising on a loan relationship are generally recognised for tax purposes on the basis that amounts are recognised as items of profit or loss in a company's accounts in accordance with generally accepted accounting practice. Under FRS 102 and IAS 39 where a company enters into a debtor relationship and the loan is either interest-free or the interest rate payable on the loan is less than a market rate of interest, unless the loan is repayable on demand, the company is required to discount the cash flows arising on the loan using a market rate of interest. This means that in such cases the loan would be reflected in the debtor company's accounts at a discount to its nominal value and the loan would be accreted up to its redemption amount over its remaining life, with the annual accretion being recognised as an interest expense in profit or loss. Generally, such interest expense is recognised in computing a company's loan relationship profits on the basis that it is recognised in its accounts as an item of profit or loss in accordance with generally accepted accounting practice. Before the new CTA 2009 s 446A introduced by para 2 took effect there were three exceptions to this rule, which continue to apply. First where the debtor relationship is a connected companies relationship and the debtor company was a party to the debtor relationship before the start of its first accounting period beginning on or after 1 January 2016. In such cases the former definition of an amortised cost basis of accounting contained in s 313(4) CTA 2009 continues to apply with the result that the debtor company is treated as if it had become a party to the loan relationship for an amount equal to the amount borrowed, such that any accounting discount is disregarded. Secondly the discount and linked interest expense that a company recognises in its accounts will generally be disregarded where an arm's length rate of interest is imputed on the corresponding creditor relationship under the transfer pricing legislation contained in TIOPA 2010 Pt 4 and the borrower makes a claim for a compensating adjustment under TIOPA 2010 s 174. Finally where the borrower would not have been able to borrow the amount in question on interest or discount-bearing terms were it dealing at arm's length and a restriction arises under TIOPA 2010 Pt 4 on the amount of the discount/ interest expense for which the borrower can claim tax relief.

Paragraph 2 inserts a new CTA 2009 s 446A, which introduces a further exception to this rule. This exception applies to deny the debtor tax relief for the discount that it recognises in its accounts as an interest expense for an accounting period where either the creditor is not a company, or in the case of a company creditor where at any time during that accounting period the creditor is resident for tax purposes, or is effectively managed, in (broadly) a tax haven and is not acting through a UK permanent establishment.

Paragraph 3 amends CTA 2009 s 446 (loan relationships) and para 4 amends CTA 2009 s 693 (derivative contracts). The intention of these amendments is to provide that, where a debit has been denied in respect of a loan relationship or a derivative contract under the transfer pricing legislation that is contained in TIOPA 2010 Pt 4, a credit will not be brought into account for the purposes of the loan relationships legislation or the derivative contracts legislation respectively to the extent that it represents the subsequent reversal of all or part of that debit.

Paragraphs 5 to 9 amend the provisions of the loan relationships legislation that deal with exchange gains and losses on non-arm's-length loans.

First an amendment is made to CTA 2009 s 447, which applies where an adjustment under TIOPA 2010 s 147(3) or (5) is made to the profit or loss that is recognised for tax purposes in respect of a debtor relationship. Under CTA 2009 s 447, where for transfer pricing purposes the debtor relationship is disregarded, no exchange movements arising in respect of that relationship are recognised in computing the debtor company's loan relationship profits. Where the amount of the loan is adjusted to an arm's-length amount, only exchange movements arising on the arm's-length amount of the loan are taken into account in computing the company's loan relationship profits. As a result of the amendment made by para 5, CTA 2009 s 447 will not apply to disregard an exchange movement arising on the debtor relationship on or after 1 April 2016 to the extent that the debtor relationship is treated as matched (see para 10).

CTA 2009 s 448 provides that any exchange movements arising on a debtor relationship are to be disregarded in computing a company's loan relationship profits where interest payable on the loan relationship is treated as a distribution under the equity note provisions of CTA 2010 1015(6). Paragraph 6 amends CTA 2009 s 448 so that it will only apply to disregard exchange movements to the extent that the debtor relationship is not treated as matched (see para 10).

Paragraphs 7 and 8 amend CTA 2009 ss 449 and 451 respectively. These sections deal with exchange movements arising on non-arm's-length creditor relationships. In each case as a result of the amendments the relevant section will only apply to the extent that the creditor relationship is not treated as matched (see para 10).

Paragraph 9 amends CTA 2009 s 452. This section covers cases where a company is a guarantor of a debtor relationship and is connected with the creditor. In such cases where a transfer pricing adjustment arises in respect of the debtor relationship, for the purposes of the determining the exchange gains or losses to be brought into account in respect of the debtor loan relationship the guarantor is deemed to make a claim under TIOPA 2010 s 192 to be treated as if it and not the debtor were the debtor in respect of the non-arm's-length element of the loan. In such cases the exchange movements arising on the debtor relationship are treated as arising to the guarantor. CTA 2009 s 452 is amended to provide that the exchange movements that are brought into account by a guarantor as a result of a claim or deemed claim under TIOPA 2010 s 192 will be limited to the exchange movements that are disregarded as a result of the application of CTA 2009 s 447 to the debtor relationship (i.e. exchange movements arising on the unmatched portion of the debtor relationship).

Paragraph 10 defines "matched". The definition covers cases where a loan relationship is matched by another loan relationship or a derivative contract, as well as cases where a debtor or creditor relationship is treated as matched under reg 3 of the Loan Relationships and Derivative Contracts (Disregard and Bringing into Account of Profits and Losses) Regulations 2004 (SI 2004/3256). A loan relationship will be treated as matched by another loan relationship or derivative contract if one is intended by the company to eliminate or substantially reduce the economic risk arising on the other in respect of exchange rate fluctuations.

Paragraph 11 amends CTA 2009 s 694 (exchange gains and losses arising on a derivative contract entered into on a non-arm's-length terms) to provide that an adjustment will not arise under this section to the extent that a derivative contract is treated as matched. A derivative contract is treated as matched for these purposes where it is in a matching relationship with another derivative contract or loan relationship, or the derivative contract is treated as matched under reg 4 of the Loan Relationships and Derivative Contracts (Disregard and Bringing into Account of Profits and Losses) Regulations 2004 (SI 2004/3256). A derivative contract is treated as being in a matching relationship with another derivative contract or loan relationship where that other derivative contract or loan relationship is intended by the company to eliminate or substantially reduce the economic risk arising on the derivative contract in respect of exchange rate fluctuations.

SCHEDULE 8
TAX RELIEF FOR PRODUCTION OF ORCHESTRAL CONCERTS
Section 54

PART 1
AMENDMENT OF CTA 2009

1 After Part 15C of CTA 2009 insert—

"PART 15D
ORCHESTRA TAX RELIEF

CHAPTER 1
INTRODUCTION

Overview

1217P Overview

(1) This Part is about the production of orchestral concerts, and applies for corporation tax purposes.

(2) This Chapter explains what is meant by "orchestral concert" and how a company comes to be treated as the production company in relation to a concert.

(3) Chapter 2 is about the taxation of the activities of a production company and includes—

(a) provision for the company's activities in relation to its concert, or its concert series, to be treated as a separate trade, and

(b) provision about the calculation of the profits and losses of that trade.

(4) Chapter 3 is about relief (called "orchestra tax relief") which may be given to a production company in relation to its concert or concert series—

(a) by way of additional deductions to be made in calculating the profits or losses of the company's separate trade, or

(b) by way of a payment (an "orchestra tax credit") to be made on the company's surrender of losses from that trade,

and describes the conditions a company must meet to qualify for orchestra tax relief.

(5) Chapter 4 contains provision about the use of losses of the separate trade (including provision about relief for terminal losses).

(6) Chapter 5 provides—

(a) for relief under Chapters 3 and 4 to be given on a provisional basis, and

(b) for such relief to be withdrawn if it turns out that conditions that must be met for such relief to be given are not actually met.

Interpretation

1217PA "Orchestral concert"

(1) In this Part "orchestral concert" means a concert by an orchestra, ensemble, group or band consisting wholly or mainly of instrumentalists who are the primary focus of the concert.

(2) But a concert is not an orchestral concert if—

(a) the main purpose, or one of the main purposes, of the concert is to advertise or promote any goods or services,

(b) the concert is to consist of or include a competition or contest, or

(c) the making of a relevant recording is the main object of the production company's activities in relation to the concert.

(3) A recording of a concert is a "relevant recording" if the recording is made for the purpose of using it (or an edited version of it) in any of the following ways—

(a) broadcast, at the time of the concert or later, to the general public;

(b) release, at the time of the concert or later, to the paying public (by digital or other means);

(c) use as a soundtrack (or part of a soundtrack) to a television, radio, theatre, video game or similar production for broadcast, exhibition or release to the general public;

(d) use in a film (or part of a film) for exhibition to the paying public at the commercial cinema.

(4) In this section—

"broadcast" means broadcast by any means (including television, radio or the internet);

"film" has the same meaning as in Part 15 (see section 1181).

1217PB Production company

(1) A company is the production company in relation to a concert if the company (acting otherwise than in partnership)—

(a) is responsible for putting on the concert from the start of the production process to the finish, including employing or engaging the performers,

(b) is actively engaged in decision-making in relation to the concert,

(c) makes an effective creative, technical and artistic contribution to the concert, and

(d) directly negotiates for, contracts for and pays for rights, goods and services in relation to the concert.

(2) No more than one company can be the production company in relation to a concert.

(3) If more than one company meets the conditions in subsection (1) in relation to a concert, the company that is most directly engaged in the activities mentioned in that subsection is the production company.

(4) If no company meets the conditions in subsection (1), there is no production company in relation to the concert.

CHAPTER 2

TAXATION OF ACTIVITIES OF PRODUCTION COMPANY

Separate orchestral trade

1217Q Separate orchestral trade

(1) Subsection (2) applies to a company in relation to a concert if—

(a) the company qualifies for orchestra tax relief in relation to the production of the concert (see section 1217RA(2)), and

(b) the concert is not included in a concert series in relation to which the company has made an election under subsection (4).

(2) The company's activities in relation to the production of the concert are treated as a trade separate from any other activities of the company (including activities in relation to the production of any other concert).

(3) Subsections (4) and (5) apply to a company in relation to concerts in a series if the conditions in section 1217RA(4)(a), (b), (c) and (d) are met in relation to the company and the concert series.

(4) The company may, for the purposes of this Part, make an election in relation to the concert series.

See section 1217QA for provision about making an election.

(5) Where the company makes an election in relation to a concert series (and accordingly qualifies for orchestra tax relief in relation to the production of the series), the company's activities in relation to the production of the concert series are treated as a trade separate from any other activities of the company (including activities in relation to the production of any other concert).

(6) In this Part the separate trade mentioned in subsection (2) or (5) is called the "separate orchestral trade".

(7) If the separate orchestral trade relates to a single concert, the company is treated as beginning to carry on that trade—

(a) at the beginning of the pre-performance stage of the concert, or

(b) if earlier, at the time of the first receipt by the company of any income from the production of the concert.

1217QA Election for concert series

(1) An election under section 1217Q(4) must be made by the company by notice in writing to an officer of Her Majesty's Revenue and Customs before the date of the first concert in the series.

(2) An election has effect in relation to the orchestral concerts specified in it, and must also specify which of those concerts (if any) are not to be qualifying orchestral concerts (see section 1217RA(3)).

(3) An election—

(a) may have effect in relation to concerts in two or more accounting periods, and

(b) is irrevocable.

(4) If the separate orchestral trade relates to a concert series, the company is treated as beginning to carry on that trade—

(a) at the beginning of the pre-performance stage of the first concert in the series, or

(b) if earlier, at the time of the first receipt by the company of any income from the production of the concert series.

Profits and losses of separate orchestral trade

1217QB Calculation of profits or losses of separate orchestral trade

(1) This section applies for the purpose of calculating the profits or losses of the separate orchestral trade.

(2) For the first period of account during which the separate orchestral trade is carried on, the following are brought into account—

(a) as a debit, the costs of the production of the concert or concert series incurred to date;

(b) as a credit, the proportion of the estimated total income from that production treated as earned at the end of that period.

(3) For subsequent periods of account the following are brought into account—

(a) as a debit, the difference between the amount ("C") of the costs of the production of the concert or concert series incurred to date and the amount corresponding to C for the previous period, and

(b) as a credit, the difference between the proportion ("PI") of the estimated total income from that production treated as earned at the end of that period and the amount corresponding to PI for the previous period.

(4) The proportion of the estimated total income treated as earned at the end of a period of account is—

$(C / T) \times I$

where—

C is the total to date of costs incurred;
T is the estimated total cost of the production of the concert or concert series;
I is the estimated total income from the production of the concert or concert series.

1217QC Income from the production

(1) References in this Chapter to income from a production of a concert or concert series are to any receipts by the company in connection with the production or exploitation of the concert or concert series.

(2) This includes—

(a) receipts from the sale of tickets or of rights in the concert or concert series;
(b) royalties or other payments for use of the concert or concert series;
(c) payments for rights to produce merchandise;
(d) receipts by the company by way of a profit share agreement.

(3) Receipts that (apart from this subsection) would be regarded as being of a capital nature are treated as being of a revenue nature.

1217QD Costs of the production

(1) References in this Chapter to the costs of a production of a concert or concert series are to expenditure incurred by the company on—

(a) activities involved in developing and putting on the concert or concert series, or
(b) activities with a view to exploiting the concert or concert series.

(2) This is subject to any provision of the Corporation Tax Acts prohibiting the making of a deduction, or restricting the extent to which a deduction is allowed, in calculating the profits of a trade.

(3) Expenditure which, apart from this subsection, would be regarded as being of a capital nature only because it is incurred on the creation of an asset (the concert or concert series) is treated as being of a revenue nature.

1217QE When costs are taken to be incurred

(1) For the purposes of this Chapter, the costs that have been incurred on a production of a concert or concert series at a given time do not include any amount that has not been paid unless it is the subject of an unconditional obligation to pay.

(2) Where an obligation to pay an amount is linked to income being earned from the production of the concert or concert series, the obligation is not treated as having become unconditional unless an appropriate amount of income is or has been brought into account under section 1217QB.

1217QF Pre-trading expenditure

(1) This section applies if, before the company begins to carry on the separate orchestral trade, it incurs expenditure on activities falling within section 1217QD(1)(a).

(2) The expenditure may be treated as expenditure of the separate orchestral trade and as if incurred immediately after the company begins to carry on that trade.

(3) If expenditure so treated has previously been taken into account for other tax purposes, the company must amend any relevant company tax return accordingly.

(4) Any amendment or assessment necessary to give effect to subsection (3) may be made despite any limitation on the time within which an amendment or assessment may normally be made.

1217QG Estimates

Estimates for the purposes of section 1217QB must be made as at the balance sheet date for each period of account, on a just and reasonable basis taking into consideration all relevant circumstances.

CHAPTER 3
ORCHESTRA TAX RELIEF

Introduction

1217R Overview of orchestra tax relief

(1) Relief under this Chapter ("orchestra tax relief") is given by way of—

(a) additional deductions (see sections 1217RD to 1217RF), and

(b) orchestra tax credits (see sections 1217RG to 1217RJ).

(2) See Schedule 18 to FA 1998 (in particular, Part 9D) for provision about the procedure for making claims for orchestra tax relief.

Companies qualifying for orchestra tax relief

1217RA Companies qualifying for orchestra tax relief

(1) Subsection (2) applies in the case of an orchestral concert which is not included in a concert series in relation to which an election has been made under section 1217Q(4).

(2) A company qualifies for orchestra tax relief in relation to the production of a concert if—

(a) the concert is a qualifying orchestral concert,

(b) the company is the production company in relation to the concert,

(c) the company intends that the concert should be performed live—

(i) before the paying public, or

(ii) for educational purposes, and

(d) the EEA expenditure condition is met in relation to the concert (see section 1217RB).

(3) In this Part "qualifying orchestral concert" means an orchestral concert—

(a) in which the instrumentalists number at least 12, and

(b) in which none of the musical instruments to be played, or a minority of those instruments, is electronically or directly amplified.

(4) A company qualifies for orchestra tax relief in relation to the production of a concert series if—

(a) the concert series is a qualifying orchestral concert series,

(b) the company is the production company in relation to every concert in the series,

(c) the company intends that all or a high proportion of the concerts in the series should be performed live—

(i) before the paying public, or

(ii) for educational purposes,

(d) the EEA expenditure condition is met in relation to the series, and

(e) the company has made an election under section 1217Q(4) in relation to the series.

(5) In this section "qualifying orchestral concert series" means two or more orchestral concerts, all or a high proportion of which are qualifying orchestral concerts.

(6) For the purposes of this section a concert is "live" if it is to an audience before whom the musicians are actually present.

(7) A concert is not regarded as performed for educational purposes if the production company is, or is associated with, a person who—

(a) has responsibility for the beneficiaries, or

(b) is otherwise connected with the beneficiaries (for instance, by being their employer).

(8) For the purposes of subsection (7), a production company is associated with a person ("P") if—

(a) P controls the production company, or

(b) P is a company which is controlled by the production company or by a person who also controls the production company.

(9) In this section—

"the beneficiaries" means persons for whose benefit the concert will or may be performed;

"control" has the same meaning as in Part 10 of CTA 2010 (see section 450 of that Act).

(10) There is further related provision in section 1217RL (tax avoidance arrangements).

1217RB The EEA expenditure condition

(1) The "EEA expenditure condition" is that at least 25% of the core expenditure on the production of the concert or concert series incurred by the company is EEA expenditure.

(2) In this Part "EEA expenditure" means expenditure on goods or services that are provided from within the European Economic Area.

(3) Any apportionment of expenditure as between EEA and non-EEA expenditure for the purposes of this Part is to be made on a just and reasonable basis.

(4) The Treasury may by regulations—

(a) amend the percentage specified in subsection (1);
(b) amend subsection (2).

(5) See also sections 1217T and 1217TA (which are about the giving of relief provisionally on the basis that the EEA expenditure condition will be met).

1217RC "Core expenditure"

(1) In this Part "core expenditure", in relation to the production of a concert or concert series, means expenditure on the activities involved in producing the concert or concert series.

(2) The reference in subsection (1) to "expenditure on the activities involved in producing the concert or concert series" includes expenditure on travel to and from a venue which is not a usual venue for concerts produced by the company.

(3) But that reference does not include—

(a) expenditure on any matters not directly involved with putting on the concert or concerts (for instance, financing, marketing, legal services or storage),
(b) speculative expenditure on activities not involved with putting on the concert or concerts, and
(c) expenditure on the actual performance or performances (for instance, payments to musicians for their performances in the concert or concert series).

Additional deduction

1217RD Claim for additional deduction

(1) A company which qualifies for orchestra tax relief in relation to the production of a concert or concert series may claim an additional deduction in relation to the production.

(2) A claim under subsection (1) is made with respect to an accounting period.

(3) Where a company has made a claim, the company is entitled to make an additional deduction, in accordance with section 1217RE, in calculating the profit or loss of the separate orchestral trade for the accounting period concerned.

(4) Where the company tax return in which a claim is made is for an accounting period later than that in which the company begins to carry on the separate orchestral trade, the company must make any amendments of company tax returns for earlier periods that may be necessary.

(5) Any amendment or assessment necessary to give effect to subsection (4) may be made despite any limitation on the time within which an amendment or assessment may normally be made.

1217RE Amount of additional deduction

(1) The amount of an additional deduction to which a company is entitled as a result of a claim under section 1217RD is calculated as follows.

(2) For the first period of account during which the separate orchestral trade is carried on, the amount of the additional deduction is E, where E is—

(a) so much of the qualifying expenditure incurred to date as is EEA expenditure, or
(b) if less, 80% of the total amount of qualifying expenditure incurred to date.

(3) For any period of account after the first, the amount of the additional deduction is—

$$E - P$$

where E is—

(a) so much of the qualifying expenditure incurred to date as is EEA expenditure, or

(b) if less, 80% of the total amount of qualifying expenditure incurred to date, and

P is the total amount of the additional deductions given for previous periods.

(4) The Treasury may by regulations amend the percentage specified in subsection (2) or (3).

1217RF "Qualifying expenditure"

(1) In this Chapter "qualifying expenditure", in relation to the production of a concert or concert series, means core expenditure (see section 1217RC) on the production that—

(a) falls to be taken into account under sections 1217QB to 1217QG in calculating the profit or loss of the separate orchestral trade for tax purposes, and

(b) is not expenditure which is otherwise relievable.

(2) For the purposes of this section expenditure is otherwise relievable if it is expenditure in respect of which (assuming a claim were made) the company would be entitled to—

(a) film tax relief under Chapter 3 of Part 15,

(b) television tax relief under Chapter 3 of Part 15A,

(c) video games tax relief under Chapter 3 of Part 15B,

(d) an additional deduction under Part 15C (theatrical productions), or

(e) a theatre tax credit under Part 15C.

Orchestra tax credits

1217RG Orchestra tax credit claimable if company has surrenderable loss

(1) A company which qualifies for orchestra tax relief in relation to the production of a concert or concert series may claim an orchestra tax credit in relation to the production for an accounting period in which the company has a surrenderable loss.

(2) Section 1217RH sets out how to calculate the amount of any surrenderable loss that the company has in the accounting period.

(3) A company making a claim may surrender the whole or part of its surrenderable loss in the accounting period.

(4) The amount of the orchestra tax credit to which a company making a claim is entitled for the accounting period is 25% of the amount of the loss surrendered.

(5) The company's available loss for the accounting period (see section 1217RH(2)) is reduced by the amount surrendered.

1217RH Amount of surrenderable loss

(1) The company's surrenderable loss in the accounting period is—

(a) the company's available loss for the period in the separate orchestral trade (see subsections (2) and (3)), or

(b) if less, the available qualifying expenditure for the period (see subsections (4) and (5)).

(2) The company's available loss for an accounting period is—

$L + RUL$

where—

L is the amount of the company's loss for the period in the separate orchestral trade, and

RUL is the amount of any relevant unused loss of the company (see subsection (3)).

(3) The "relevant unused loss" of a company is so much of any available loss of the company for the previous accounting period as has not been—

(a) surrendered under section 1217RG, or

(b) carried forward under section 45 of CTA 2010 and set against profits of the separate orchestral trade.

(4) For the first period of account during which the separate orchestral trade is carried on, the available qualifying expenditure is the amount that is E for that period for the purposes of section 1217RE(2).

(5) For any period of account after the first, the available qualifying expenditure is—

$E - S$

where—
E is the amount that is E for that period for the purposes of section 1217RE(3), and
S is the total amount previously surrendered under section 1217RG.

(6) If a period of account of the separate orchestral trade does not coincide with an accounting period, any necessary apportionments are to be made by reference to the number of days in the periods concerned.

1217RI Payment in respect of orchestra tax credit

(1) If a company—
(a) is entitled to an orchestra tax credit for an accounting period, and
(b) makes a claim,
the Commissioners for Her Majesty's Revenue and Customs ("the Commissioners") must pay the amount of the credit to the company.

(2) An amount payable in respect of—
(a) an orchestra tax credit, or
(b) interest on an orchestra tax credit under section 826 of ICTA,
may be applied in discharging any liability of the company to pay corporation tax.
To the extent that it is so applied the Commissioners' liability under subsection (1) is discharged.

(3) If the company's company tax return for the accounting period is enquired into by the Commissioners, no payment in respect of an orchestra tax credit for that period need be made before the Commissioners' enquiries are completed (see paragraph 32 of Schedule 18 to FA 1998).
In those circumstances the Commissioners may make a payment on a provisional basis of such amount as they consider appropriate.

(4) No payment need be made in respect of an orchestra tax credit for an accounting period before the company has paid to the Commissioners any amount that it is required to pay for payment periods ending in that accounting period—
(a) under PAYE regulations,
(b) under section 966 of ITA 2007 (visiting performers), or
(c) in respect of Class 1 national insurance contributions under Part 1 of the Social Security Contributions and Benefits Act 1992 or Part 1 of the Social Security Contributions and Benefits (Northern Ireland) Act 1992.

(5) A payment in respect of an orchestra tax credit is not income of the company for any tax purpose.

1217RJ Limit on State aid

In accordance with Commission Regulation (EU) No 651/2014 of 17 June 2014 declaring certain categories of aid compatible with the internal market, the total amount of orchestra tax credits payable under section 1217RI in the case of any undertaking is not to exceed 50 million euros per year.

1217RK No account to be taken of amount if unpaid

(1) In determining for the purposes of this Chapter the amount of costs incurred on a production of a concert or concert series at the end of a period of account, ignore any amount that has not been paid 4 months after the end of that period.

(2) This is without prejudice to the operation of section 1217QE (when costs are taken to be incurred).

Anti-avoidance etc

1217RL Tax avoidance arrangements

(1) A company does not qualify for orchestra tax relief in relation to the production of a concert or concert series if there are any tax avoidance arrangements relating to the production.

(2) Arrangements are "tax avoidance arrangements" if their main purpose, or one of their main purposes, is the obtaining of a tax advantage.

(3) In this section
"arrangements" includes any scheme, agreement or understanding, whether or not legally enforceable;
"tax advantage" has the meaning given by section 1139 of CTA 2010.

1217RM Transactions not entered into for genuine commercial reasons

(1) A transaction is to be ignored for the purpose of determining orchestra tax relief so far as the transaction is attributable to arrangements (other than tax avoidance arrangements) entered into otherwise than for genuine commercial reasons.

(2) In this section "arrangements" and "tax avoidance arrangements" have the same meaning as in section 1217RL.

CHAPTER 4

LOSSES OF SEPARATE ORCHESTRAL TRADE

1217S Application of sections 1217SA to 1217SC

(1) Sections 1217SA to 1217SC apply to a company which is treated under section 1217Q(2) or (5) as carrying on a separate trade in relation to the production of a concert or concert series.

(2) In those sections—

(a) "the completion period" means the accounting period in which the company ceases to carry on the separate orchestral trade;
(b) "loss relief" includes any means by which a loss might be used to reduce the amount in respect of which a company, or any other person, is chargeable to tax.

1217SA Restriction on use of losses before completion period

(1) Subsection (2) applies if a loss is made by the company in the separate orchestral trade in an accounting period preceding the completion period.

(2) The loss is not available for loss relief, except to the extent that the loss may be carried forward under section 45 of CTA 2010 to be set against profits of the separate orchestral trade in a subsequent period.

1217SB Use of losses in the completion period

(1) Subsection (2) applies if a loss made in the separate orchestral trade is carried forward under section 45 of CTA 2010 to the completion period.

(2) So much (if any) of the loss as is not attributable to orchestra tax relief (see subsection (4)) may be treated for the purposes of loss relief as if it were a loss made in the completion period.

(3) If a loss is made in the separate orchestral trade in the completion period, the amount of the loss that may be—

(a) deducted from total profits of the same or an earlier period under section 37 of CTA 2010, or
(b) surrendered as group relief under Part 5 of that Act,

is restricted to the amount (if any) that is not attributable to orchestra tax relief (see subsection (4)).

(4) The amount of a loss in any period that is attributable to orchestra tax relief is found by—

(a) calculating what the amount of the loss would have been if there had been no additional deduction under Chapter 3 in that or any earlier period, and
(b) deducting that amount from the total amount of the loss.

(5) This section does not apply to loss surrendered, or treated as carried forward, under section 1217SC (terminal losses).

1217SC Terminal losses

(1) This section applies if—

(a) the company ceases to carry on the separate orchestral trade, and
(b) if the company had not ceased to carry on that trade, it could have carried forward an amount under section 45 of CTA 2010 to be set against profits of that trade in a later period ("the terminal loss").

Below in this section the company is referred to as "company A" and the separate orchestral trade is referred to as "trade 1".

(2) If company A—

(a) is treated under section 1217Q(2) or (5) as carrying on a separate trade in relation to the production of another concert or concert series ("trade 2"), and
(b) is carrying on trade 2 when it ceases to carry on trade 1,

company A may (on making a claim) make an election under subsection (3).

(3) The election is to have the terminal loss (or a part of it) treated as if it were a loss brought forward under section 45 of CTA 2010 to be set against the profits of trade 2 of the first accounting period beginning after the cessation and so on.

(4) Subsection (5) applies if—

(a) another company ("company B") is treated under section 1217Q(2) or (5) as carrying on a separate trade ("company B's trade") in relation to the production of another concert or concert series,

(b) company B is carrying on that trade when company A ceases to carry on trade 1, and

(c) company B is in the same group as company A for the purposes of Part 5 of CTA 2010 (group relief).

(5) Company A may surrender the loss (or a part of it) to company B.

(6) On the making of a claim by company B the amount surrendered is treated as if it were a loss brought forward by company B under section 45 of CTA 2010 to be set against the profits of company B's trade of the first accounting period beginning after the cessation and so on.

(7) The Treasury may by regulations make administrative provision in relation to the surrender of a loss under subsection (5) and the resulting claim under subsection (6).

(8) "Administrative provision" means provision corresponding, subject to such adaptations or other modifications as appear to the Treasury to be appropriate, to that made by Part 8 of Schedule 18 to FA 1998 (company tax returns: claims for group relief).

CHAPTER 5
PROVISIONAL ENTITLEMENT TO RELIEF

1217T Provisional entitlement to relief

(1) In relation to a company and the production of a concert or concert series, "interim accounting period" means any accounting period that—

(a) is one in which the company carries on a separate orchestral trade, and

(b) precedes the accounting period in which it ceases to do so.

(2) A company is not entitled to orchestra tax relief for an interim accounting period unless—

(a) its company tax return for the period states the amount of planned core expenditure on the production of the concert or concert series that is EEA expenditure (see section 1217RB(2)), and

(b) that amount is such as to indicate that the EEA expenditure condition (see section 1217RB) will be met in relation to the production.

If those requirements are met, the company is provisionally treated in relation to that period as if the EEA expenditure condition were met.

1217TA Clawback of provisional relief

(1) If a statement is made under section 1217T(2) but it subsequently appears that the EEA expenditure condition will not be met on the company's ceasing to carry on the separate orchestral trade, the company—

(a) is not entitled to orchestra tax relief for any period for which its entitlement depended on such a statement, and

(b) must amend accordingly its company tax return for any such period.

(2) When a company ceases to carry on the separate orchestral trade, the company's company tax return for the period in which that cessation occurs must—

(a) state that the company has ceased to carry on the separate orchestral trade, and

(b) be accompanied by a final statement of the amount of the core expenditure on the production of the concert or concert series that is EEA expenditure.

(3) If that statement shows that the EEA expenditure condition is not met—

(a) the company is not entitled to orchestra tax relief or to relief under section 1217SC (transfer of terminal losses) for any period, and

(b) must amend accordingly its company tax return for any period for which such relief was claimed.

(4) Any amendment or assessment necessary to give effect to this section may be made despite any limitation on the time within which an amendment or assessment may normally be made.

CHAPTER 6
INTERPRETATION

1217U Interpretation

In this Part—

"company tax return" has the same meaning as in Schedule 18 to FA 1998 (see paragraph 3(1) of that Schedule);

"core expenditure" has the meaning given by section 1217RC;

"costs", in relation to a concert or concert series, has the meaning given by section 1217QD;

"EEA expenditure" has the meaning given by section 1217RB(2);

"EEA expenditure condition" has the meaning given by section 1217RB;

"income", in relation to a concert or concert series, has the meaning given by section 1217QC;

"orchestra tax relief" is to be read in accordance with Chapter 3 (see in particular section 1217R(1));

"orchestral concert" has the meaning given by section 1217PA;

"production company" has the meaning given by section 1217PB;

"qualifying expenditure" has the meaning given by section 1217RF;

"qualifying orchestral concert" has the meaning given by section 1217RA(3);

"qualifying orchestral concert series" has the meaning given by section 1217RA(5);

the "separate orchestral trade" is to be read in accordance with section 1217Q."

PART 2
CONSEQUENTIAL AMENDMENTS

ICTA

2 (1) Section 826 of ICTA (interest on tax overpaid) is amended as follows.

(2) In subsection (1), after paragraph (fc) insert—

"(fd) a payment of orchestra tax credit falls to be made to a company; or".

(3) In subsection (3C), for "or theatre tax credit" substitute ", theatre tax credit or orchestra tax credit".

(4) In subsection (8A)—

(a) in paragraph (a), for "or (fc)" substitute ", (fc) or (fd)", and
(b) in paragraph (b)(ii), after "theatre tax credit" insert "or orchestra tax credit".

(5) In subsection (8BA), after "theatre tax credit" (in both places) insert "or orchestra tax credit".

FA 1998

3 Schedule 18 to FA 1998 (company tax returns, assessments and related matters) is amended as follows.

4 In paragraph 10 (other claims and elections to be included in return), in sub-paragraph (4), for "or 15C" substitute ", 15C or 15D".

5 (1) Paragraph 52 (recovery of excessive repayments etc) is amended as follows.

(2) In sub-paragraph (2), after paragraph (bg) insert—

"(bh) orchestra tax credit under Part 15D of that Act,".

(3) In sub-paragraph (5)—

(a) after paragraph (ai) insert—
"(aj) an amount of orchestra tax credit paid to a company for an accounting period,", and
(b) in the words after paragraph (b), after "(ai)" insert ", (aj)".

6 In Part 9D (certain claims for tax relief)—

(a) in the heading, for "or 15C" substitute ", 15C or 15D", and
(b) in paragraph 83S (introduction), after sub-paragraph (e) insert—
"(f) orchestra tax relief."

CAA 2001

7 In Schedule A1 to CAA 2001 (first-year tax credits), in paragraph 11(4), omit the "and" at the end of paragraph (e) and after paragraph (f) insert ", and

(g) Chapter 3 of Part 15D of that Act (orchestra tax credits)."

FA 2007

8 In Schedule 24 to FA 2007 (penalties for errors), in paragraph 28(fa) (meaning of "corporation tax credit"), omit the "or" at the end of paragraph (ivc) and after that paragraph insert—

"(ivd) an orchestra tax credit under Chapter 3 of Part 15D of that Act, or".

CTA 2009

9 In Part 8 of CTA 2009 (intangible fixed assets), in Chapter 10 (excluded assets), after section 808C insert—

"808D Assets representing expenditure incurred in course of separate orchestral trade

(1) This Part does not apply to an intangible fixed asset held by an orchestral concert production company so far as the asset represents expenditure on an orchestral concert or orchestral concert series that is treated under Part 15D as expenditure of a separate trade (see particularly sections 1217Q and 1217QF).

(2) In this section—

"orchestral concert" has the same meaning as in Part 15D (see section 1217PA);
"orchestral concert production company" means a company which, for the purposes of that Part, is the production company in relation to a concert (see section 1217PB)."

10 In section 1310 of CTA 2009 (orders and regulations), in subsection (4), after paragraph (em) insert—

"(cn) section 1217RB (EEA expenditure condition),
(eo) section 1217RE (amount of additional deduction),".

11 In Schedule 4 to CTA 2009 (index of defined expressions), insert at the appropriate places—

"company tax return (in Part 15D)	section 1217U"
"core expenditure (in Part 15D)	section 1217RC"
"costs, in relation to a concert or concert series (in Part 15D)	section 1217QD"
"EEA expenditure (in Part 15D)	section 1217RB(2)"
"EEA expenditure condition (in Part 15D)	section 1217RB"
"income, in relation to a concert or concert series (in Part 15D)	section 1217QC"
"orchestra tax relief (in Part 15D)	section 1217R(1)"
"orchestral concert (in Part 15D)	section 1217PA"
"production company (in Part 15D)	section 1217PB"
"qualifying expenditure (in Part 15D)	section 1217RF"
"qualifying orchestral concert (in Part 15D)	section 1217RA(3)"
"qualifying orchestral concert series (in Part 15D)	section 1217RA(5)"
"separate orchestral trade (in Part 15D)	section 1217Q"

FA 2009

12 In Schedule 54A to FA 2009 (which is prospectively inserted by F(No 3)A 2010 and contains provision about the recovery of certain amounts of interest paid by HMRC), in paragraph 2—

(a) in sub-paragraph (2), omit the "or" at the end of paragraph (g) and after paragraph (h) insert ", or
(i) a payment of orchestra tax credit under Chapter 3 of Part 15D of CTA 2009 for an accounting period.";
(b) in sub-paragraph (4), for "(h)" substitute "(i)".

CTA 2010

13 In Part 8B of CTA 2010 (trading profits taxable at Northern Ireland rate), in section 357H(7) (introduction), after "Chapter 14 for provision about theatrical productions;" insert "Chapter 14A for provision about orchestra tax relief;".

14 In Part 8B of CTA 2010, after section 357UI insert—

"CHAPTER 14A
ORCHESTRA TAX RELIEF

Introductory

357UJ Introduction and interpretation

(1) This Chapter makes provision about the operation of Part 15D of CTA 2009 (orchestra tax relief) in relation to expenditure incurred by a company in an accounting period in which it is a Northern Ireland company.

(2) In this Chapter—

(a) "Northern Ireland expenditure" means expenditure incurred in a trade to the extent that the expenditure forms part of the Northern Ireland profits or Northern Ireland losses of the trade;

(b) the "separate orchestral trade" has the same meaning as in Part 15D of CTA 2009 (see section 1217Q(6) of that Act);

(c) "qualifying expenditure" has the same meaning as in Chapter 3 of that Part (see section 1217RF of that Act).

(3) References in Part 15D of CTA 2009 to "orchestra tax relief" include relief under this Chapter.

Orchestra tax relief

357UK Northern Ireland additional deduction

(1) In this Chapter "a Northern Ireland additional deduction" means so much of a deduction under section 1217RD of CTA 2009 (claim for additional deduction) as is calculated by reference to qualifying expenditure that is Northern Ireland expenditure.

(2) A Northern Ireland additional deduction forms part of the Northern Ireland profits or Northern Ireland losses of the separate orchestral trade.

357UL Northern Ireland supplementary deduction

(1) This section applies where—

(a) a company is entitled under section 1217RD of CTA 2009 to an additional deduction in calculating the profit or loss of the separate orchestral trade in an accounting period,

(b) the company is a Northern Ireland company in the period,

(c) the additional deduction is wholly or partly a Northern Ireland additional deduction, and

(d) any of the following conditions is met—

(i) the company does not have a surrenderable loss in the accounting period;

(ii) the company has a surrenderable loss in the accounting period, but does not make a claim under section 1217RG of CTA 2009 (orchestra tax credit claimable if company has surrenderable loss) for the period;

(iii) the company has a surrenderable loss in the accounting period and makes a claim under that section for the period, but the amount of Northern Ireland losses surrendered on the claim is less than the Northern Ireland additional deduction.

(2) The company is entitled to make another deduction ("a Northern Ireland supplementary deduction") in respect of qualifying expenditure.

(3) See section 357UM for provision about the amount of the Northern Ireland supplementary deduction.

(4) The Northern Ireland supplementary deduction—

(a) is made in calculating the profit or loss of the separate orchestral trade, and

(b) forms part of the Northern Ireland profits or Northern Ireland losses of the separate orchestral trade.

(5) In this section "surrenderable loss" has the meaning given by section 1217RH of CTA 2009.

357UM Northern Ireland supplementary deduction: amount

(1) This section contains provision for the purposes of section 357UL(2) about the amount of the Northern Ireland supplementary deduction.

(2) If the accounting period falls within only one financial year, the amount of the Northern Ireland supplementary deduction is—

$(A - B) \times ((MR - NIR) / NIR)$

where—
A is the amount of the Northern Ireland additional deduction brought into account in the accounting period;
B is the amount of Northern Ireland losses surrendered in any claim under section 1217RG of CTA 2009 for the accounting period;
MR is the main rate for the financial year;
NIR is the Northern Ireland rate for the financial year.

(3) If the accounting period falls within more than one financial year, the amount of the Northern Ireland supplementary deduction is determined by taking the following steps.

Step 1
Calculate, for each financial year, the amount that would be the Northern Ireland supplementary deduction for the accounting period if it fell within only that financial year (see subsection (2)).

Step 2
Multiply each amount calculated under step 1 by the proportion of the accounting period that falls within the financial year for which it is calculated.

Step 3
Add together each amount found under step 2.

357UN   Orchestra tax credit: Northern Ireland supplementary deduction ignored

For the purpose of determining the available loss of a company under section 1217RH of CTA 2009 (amount of surrenderable loss) for any accounting period, any Northern Ireland supplementary deduction made by the company in the period (and any Northern Ireland supplementary deduction made in any previous accounting period) is to be ignored.

Losses of separate orchestral trade

357UO   Restriction on use of losses before completion period

(1) Section 1217SA of CTA 2009 (restriction on use of losses before completion period) has effect subject as follows.

(2) The reference in subsection (1) of that section to a loss made in the separate orchestral trade in an accounting period preceding the completion period is, if the company is a Northern Ireland company in that period, a reference to—

(a) any Northern Ireland losses of the trade of the period, or
(b) any mainstream losses of the trade of the period;

and references to losses in subsection (2) of that section are to be read accordingly.

(3) Subsection (4) applies if a Northern Ireland company has, in an accounting period preceding the completion period—

(a) both Northern Ireland losses of the trade and mainstream profits of the trade, or
(b) both mainstream losses of the trade and Northern Ireland profits of the trade.

(4) The company may make a claim under section 37 (relief for trade losses against total profits) for relief for the losses mentioned in subsection (3)(a) or (b).

(5) But relief on such a claim is available only—

(a) in the case of a claim for relief for Northern Ireland losses, against mainstream profits of the trade of the same period;
(b) in the case of a claim for relief for mainstream losses, against Northern Ireland profits of the trade of the same period.

(6) In this section "the completion period" has the same meaning as in section 1217SA of CTA 2009 (see section 1217S(2) of that Act).

357UP   Use of losses in the completion period

(1) Section 1217SB of CTA 2009 (use of losses in the completion period) has effect subject as follows.

(2) The reference in subsection (1) of that section to a loss made in the separate orchestral trade is, in relation to a loss made in a period in which the company is a Northern Ireland company, a reference to—

(a) any Northern Ireland losses of the trade of the period, or
(b) any mainstream losses of the trade of the period;

and references to losses in subsections (2) and (4) of that section are to be read accordingly.

(3) The references in subsection (3) of that section to a loss made in the separate orchestral trade in the completion period are, where the company is a Northern Ireland company in the period, references to—

(a) any Northern Ireland losses of the trade of the period, or
(b) any mainstream losses of the trade of the period;

and references to losses in subsection (4) of that section are to be read accordingly.

(4) Subsection (4) of that section has effect, in relation to Northern Ireland losses, as if the reference to an additional deduction under Chapter 3 of Part 15D of CTA 2009 included a reference to a Northern Ireland supplementary deduction under this Chapter.

357UQ Terminal losses

(1) Section 1217SC of CTA 2009 (terminal losses) has effect subject as follows.

(2) Where—

(a) a company makes an election under subsection (3) of that section (election to treat terminal loss as loss brought forward of different trade) in relation to all or part of a terminal loss, and
(b) the terminal loss is a Northern Ireland loss,

that subsection has effect as if the reference in it to a loss brought forward were to a Northern Ireland loss brought forward.

(3) Where—

(a) a company makes a claim under subsection (6) of that section (claim to treat terminal loss as loss brought forward by different company) in relation to part or all of a terminal loss, and
(b) the terminal loss is a Northern Ireland loss,

that subsection has effect as if the reference in it to a loss brought forward were to a Northern Ireland loss brought forward."

15 (1) Schedule 4 to CTA 2010 (index of defined expressions) is amended as follows.

(2) In the entry for "Northern Ireland expenditure"—

(a) for "14" substitute "14A", and
(b) for "and 357U(2)" substitute ", 357U(2) and 357UJ(2)".

(3) Insert at the appropriate places—

"qualifying expenditure (in Chapter 14A of Part 8B)	section 357UJ(2)"
"the separate orchestral trade (in Chapter 14A of Part 8B)	section 357UJ(2)"

PART 3

COMMENCEMENT

16 Any power to make regulations conferred on the Treasury by virtue of this Schedule comes into force on the day on which this Act is passed.

17 (1) The amendments made by the following provisions of this Schedule have effect in relation to accounting periods beginning on or after 1 April 2016—

(a) Part 1, and
(b) in Part 2, paragraphs 2 to 12.

(2) Sub-paragraph (3) applies where a company has an accounting period beginning before 1 April 2016 and ending on or after that date ("the straddling period").

(3) For the purposes of Part 15D of CTA 2009—

(a) so much of the straddling period as falls before 1 April 2016, and so much of that period as falls on or after that date, are separate accounting periods, and
(b) any amounts brought into account for the purposes of calculating for corporation tax purposes the profits of a trade for the straddling period are apportioned to the two separate accounting periods on such basis as is just and reasonable.

18 (1) The amendments made by paragraphs 13 to 15 of this Schedule have effect in relation to accounting periods beginning on or after the first day of the financial year appointed by the Treasury by regulations under section 5(3) of the Corporation Tax (Northern Ireland) Act 2015 ("the commencement day").

(2) Sub-paragraph (3) applies where a company has an accounting period beginning before the commencement day and ending on or after that day ("the straddling period").

(3) For the purposes of Chapter 14A of Part 8B of CTA 2010—

(a) so much of the straddling period as falls before the commencement day, and so much of that period as falls on or after that day, are separate accounting periods, and

(b) any amounts brought into account for the purposes of calculating for corporation tax purposes the profits of a trade for the straddling period are apportioned to the two separate accounting periods on such basis as is just and reasonable.

GENERAL NOTE

Part 1 Amendment of CTA 2009

Orchestra tax relief is introduced to CTA 2009 after Pt 15C as Pt 15D.

Chapter 1

Chapter 1 provides an overview of the relief and defines the terms "orchestral concert" and "production company" in relation to a concert.

"Orchestral concert" is defined in s 1217PA as a concert by an orchestra, ensemble, group or band consisting wholly or mainly of instrumentalists who are the primary focus of the concert. The explanatory notes show as an example that instrumentalists should not be just a backing band for a singer.

There are three criteria laid out where the concert will not be treated as an orchestral concert, these are:

- advertising or promoting goods or services as the main purpose, or one of the main purposes;
- the concert consists of, or includes, a competition or contest;
- primary purpose is to make a relevant recording.

A relevant recording is defined as a recording made for the purpose of using it (or an edited version) in any of the following ways:

- broadcast (including television, radio or the internet) live, or at a later point, to the general public;
- release live, or at a later point, to the paying public (including digital or other means);
- use as a soundtrack (or part of) to a television, radio, theatre, video game or similar production for broadcast, exhibition or release to the general public;
- use in a film (or part of) for exhibition to the paying public at the commercial cinema.

"Production company" is defined in s 1217PB(1) as a company that:

- is responsible for putting on the concert from the start of the production process to the finish;
- actively engages in the decision-making for the concert;
- directly negotiates for and pays for rights, goods and services in relation to the concert;
- employs and engages the performers.

There can only be on production company for the concert; the company can not act in partnership and co-productions are disallowed.

In the scenario where there is more than one company that meets the criteria of a production company, the company that is most directly engaged in the activities in s 1217PB(1) is deemed to be the production company.

If no company meets the conditions in s 1217PB(1), then there is no production company for the concert.

Chapter 2 – Taxation of activities of production company

Section 1217Q explains how the company should treat each qualifying concert as a separate trade. The separate trade is treated as beginning on the earlier of:

- the start date of the prep-performance stage of the concert; or
- first receipt by the company of any income for the production of the concert.

The company can elect for concerts in a series to be treated as a separate trade as a whole. The election is made in writing to HMRC before the first concert in the series. In the election, you can include concerts that won't be qualifying. You should note that the election is irrevocable once made.

Section 1217QB explains how to initially recognise the income and expenses and so calculate the profits or losses from the separate orchestra trade in the first accounting period. There is also guidance on subsequent periods and the formula used to calculate further profits or losses.

Income from the production is detailed in s 1217QC, including:

- sale of tickets or rights in the concert (or series);
- royalties or other payments for the concert (or series);
- payments for rights to produce merchandise;
- profit share agreement receipts.

Costs of production are defined in s 1217QD as direct costs:

- to develop and put on the concert (or series);
- with a view to exploit the concert (or series).

It is worth noting here that for both income and expenses (incurred on production), items that would be regarded as capital in nature are treated as revenue.

The costs are recognised when they have been paid, or when there is an unconditional obligation to pay.

Qualifying expenses incurred before the separate orchestra trade commenced can be treated as occurring immediately after the start of the separate trade.

Chapter 3 – Orchestra tax relief

To qualify for orchestra tax relief for the production of a concert, the company must show that the:

- concert is a qualifying orchestral concert;
- company qualifies as the production company;
- concert should be performed live to the paying public or to be for educational purposes;
- EEA expenditure condition is met for the concert.

A qualifying orchestral concert needs to have a minimum of 12 instrumentalists and the majority of the instruments are not electronically or directly amplified.

To meet the EEA expenditure condition, at least 25% of the core expenditure of the production of the concert are goods or services that are provided from within the European Economic Area.

Core expenditure includes any expenses directly involved in producing the concert (or series). Allowable costs include:

- rehearsals;
- commissioning new music specifically for the concert (or series).

Any expenses that are not directly involved in producing the concert (or series) will not be allowed. Examples include:

- marketing;
- financing;
- legal and accountancy fees;
- storage of instruments.

A key point to note, is that the costs of the actual performance of the concert are not eligible as core expenditure. These costs would include payments to the musicians for their performances at the concert.

It should also be noted that there is no difference in relief available depending on whether the production company is touring or not (unlike theatre tax relief).

The production company can either claim (i) an additional deduction; or (ii) a tax credit.

(i) The additional deduction is the lesser of:

- total amount of EEA qualifying expenses;
- 80% of the qualifying expenses.

Qualifying expenses are defined in s 1217RF. An adjustment will need to be made for expenses that have already been used to claim other creative tax reliefs (film, television, video games and theatre).

(ii) The tax credit can be claimed if the production company has a surrenderable loss for the period.

The company's surrenderable loss can be calculated using the formula in s 1217RH.

The tax credit is 25% of the eligible loss surrendered. The tax credit is payable by HMRC once the corporation tax return (including the tax credit claim) has been submitted for the period. Where there are any other taxes outstanding (corporation tax, VAT or PAYE) then the credit is used to cover those liabilities first.

The orchestra tax credits are limited to €50 million per year for each undertaking.

If there are any tax arrangements in place, where their main purpose (or one of their main purposes) is to obtain a tax advantage, the company will not qualify for orchestra tax relief.

Any transactions, which are not entered into for genuine commercial reasons, will be ignored for orchestra tax relief.

Chapter 4 – Losses of separate orchestral trade

Losses from the separate orchestra trade are only available to be set against the future profits of the separate orchestra trade.

Section 1217SC details how losses are treated in the final accounting period of the separate orchestra trade and the use of the terminal losses.

Chapter 5 – Provisional entitlement to relief

The company can include a claim for provisional relief in an interim accounting period as long as there is a statement of the planned amount of qualifying expenditure (as defined by s 1217RB).

The provisional relief can be clawed back if it appears at a later date that the expenses are not qualifying expenses (as defined by s 1217RB).

When the company ceases to carry on the separate orchestra trade, a disclosure is required in the company's corporation tax return for the period.

Chapter 6 – Interpretation

Interprets the meanings of various words and phrases used within CTA 2009 Pt 15D.

Part 2 Consequential Amendments

Amendments have been made to the following acts to accommodate orchestra tax relief:

- ICTA;
- FA 1998;
- CAA 2001;
- FA 2007;
- CTA 2009;
- FA 2009;
- CTA 2010 (Northern Ireland).

Part 3 Commencement

The relief will apply to qualifying expenditure incurred on or after 1 April 2016.

Where an accounting period begins before the 1 April 2016 and ends after this date, for this relief there are deemed to be two accounting periods; the first ends on 31 March 2016 and the second begins on 1 April 2016. Only the qualifying expenditure in the second deemed accounting period (from 1 April 2016) will be eligible for the relief.

There are separate commencement provisions under the Corporation Tax (Northern Ireland) Act 2015.

SCHEDULE 9

PROFITS FROM THE EXPLOITATION OF PATENTS ETC: CONSEQUENTIAL

Section 64

1 CTA 2010 is amended in accordance with this Schedule.

2 In section 357B (meaning of "qualifying company"), in subsection (3)(b)(ii), for "section 357A" substitute "section 357A(1)".

3 In the heading of Chapter 3 of Part 8A, after "profits" insert ": cases mentioned in section 357A(7): no income from new IP".

4 (1) Section 357C (relevant IP profits) is amended as follows.

(2) Before subsection (1) insert—

"(A1) This section applies for the purposes of determining the relevant IP profits of a trade of a company for an accounting period in a case where—

(a) the accounting period began before 1 July 2021,

(b) the company is not a new entrant (see section 357A(11)), and

(c) none of the amounts of relevant IP income brought into account as credits in calculating the profits of the trade for the accounting period is properly attributable to a new qualifying IP right (see section 357BP).

But see also section 357D (alternative method of calculating relevant IP profits in such a case)."

(3) In subsection (1)—

(a) in the words before Step 1, omit "of a trade of a company for an accounting period",

(b) in Step 2, for "357CC and 357CD" substitute "357BH to 357BHC",

(c) in Step 4, after "routine return figure" insert "in relation to the trade for the accounting period",

(d) in Step 5, for "elected" substitute "made an election under section 357CL", and

(e) in Step 6, after "marketing assets return figure" insert "in relation to the trade for the accounting period".

5 In section 357CA (total gross income of a trade), in subsection (2), for "section 357CB" substitute "section 357BG".

6 Omit sections 357CB to 357CF.

7 (1) Section 357CG (adjustments in calculating profits of trade) is amended as follows.

(2) In subsection (1) after "determining" insert "under section 357C".

(3) In subsection (4), in the words after paragraph (b), for "section 357CB" substitute "section 357BG".

(4) In subsection (6), in paragraph (a)(ii) of the definition of "relevant accounting period", for "section 357A" substitute "section 357A(1)".

8 In section 357CI (routine return figure), in Step 1 in subsection (1), for "sections 357CJ and 357CK" substitute "sections 357BJA and 357BJB".

9 Omit sections 357CJ and 357CK.

10 (1) Section 357CL (companies eligible to elect for small claims treatment) is amended as follows.

(2) In subsection (1) for "elect" substitute "make an election under this section".

(3) In subsection (6) for "section 357A" substitute "section 357A(1)".

11 In section 357CM (small claims amount), in subsection (1), for "elects" substitute "makes an election under section 357CL".

12 (1) Section 357D (alternative method of calculating relevant IP profits: "streaming") is amended as follows.

(2) In subsection (1) at the end insert "in a case where—

(a) the accounting period began before 1 July 2021,

(b) the company is not a new entrant (see section 357A(11)), and

(c) none of the amounts of relevant IP income brought into account as credits in calculating the profits of the trade for the accounting period is properly attributable to a new qualifying IP right (see section 357BP)."

(3) For subsection (4) substitute—

"(4) A company must apply section 357DA (instead of section 357C) for the purposes of determining the relevant IP profits of a trade of the company for an accounting period in a case mentioned in subsection (1) if any of the mandatory streaming conditions in section 357DC is met in relation to the trade for the period."

13 (1) Section 357DA (relevant IP profits) is amended as follows.

(2) In subsection (1)—

(a) in Step 1—

(i) for "section 357CB" substitute "section 357BG", and

(ii) for "sections 357CC and 357CD" substitute "sections 357BH to 357BHC",

(b) in Step 4, after "routine return figure" insert "in relation to the trade for the accounting period",

(c) in Step 5, for "elected" substitute "made an election under section 357CL", and

(d) in Step 6, after "marketing assets return figure" insert "in relation to the trade for the accounting period".

(3) In subsection (4), in the words after paragraph (b), for "sections 357CJ and 357CK" substitute "sections 357BJA and 357BJB".

14 (1) Section 357DC (the mandatory streaming conditions) is amended as follows.

(2) In subsection (8)(a) for "section 357CC" substitute "section 357BH".

(3) In subsection (9)(a) for "section 357CC(6)" substitute "section 357BH(6)".

15 In section 357EB (allocation of set-off amount within a group) in subsection (3)(a) for "section 357A" substitute "section 357A(1)".

16 In section 357ED (company ceasing to carry on trade etc) in subsection (2)(c) for "section 357A" substitute "section 357A(1)".

17 In section 357FA (incorporation of qualifying items), in subsection (2), for "357CC(2)" substitute "357BH(2)".

18 In section 357FB (tax advantage schemes) in subsection (4)(b) for "section 357A" substitute "section 357A(1)".

19 (1) Section 357G (making an election under section 357A) is amended as follows.

(2) In the heading, for "section 357A" substitute "section 357A(1) or (11)(b)".

(3) In subsection (1) for "section 357A" substitute "section 357A(1) or (11)(b)".

20 (1) Section 357GA (revocation of election made under section 357A) is amended as follows.

(2) In the heading, for "section 357A" substitute "section 357A(1)".

(3) In subsection (1) for "section 357A" substitute "section 357A(1)".

(4) In subsection (5) for "section 357A" substitute "section 357A(1)".

21 (1) Section 357GB (application of Part 8A in relation to partnerships) is amended as follows.

(2) In subsection (11)—

    (a) in the words before paragraph (a), after "Sections" insert "357BK, 357BKA", and

    (b) in paragraph (a) after "section" insert "357BK or".

(3) In subsection (12) for "section 357CB(1)(c)" substitute "section 357BG(1)(c)".

22 In section 357GC (application of Part 8A in relation to cost-sharing arrangements), in subsection (3), for "section 357CB(1)(c)" substitute "section 357BG(1)(c)".

23 (1) Section 357GE (other interpretation) is amended as follows.

(2) In subsection (1)—

    (a) at the appropriate place insert—

    ""payment" includes payment in money's worth.", and

    (b) omit the definition of "qualifying residual profit".

(3) After subsection (1) insert—

    "(1A) In Chapters 3 and 4 of this Part "qualifying residual profit" of a trade, in relation to any accounting period, is the amount obtained by the application of Steps 1 to 4 in section 357C or (as the case may be) section 357DA in relation to the trade for the accounting period."

24 In Schedule 4 (index of defined expressions)—

    (a) for the entry for "finance income (in Part 8A)" substitute—

"finance income (in Part 8A)	| section 357BG"

    (b) after the entry for "new consideration (in Part 23)" insert—

"new entrant (in Part 8A)	| section 357A(11)"

    (c) in the entry for "qualifying residual profit of a trade (in Part 8A)", in the left hand column, after "in" insert "Chapters 3 and 4 of", and

    (d) for the entry for "relevant IP income (in Part 8A)" substitute—

"relevant IP income (in Part 8A)	| section 357BH"

GENERAL NOTE

Schedule 9 is a supplementary schedule to the new patent box legislation, making mainly consequential amendments to existing legislation. Most of this is uncontroversial, such as stating that the current rules only apply when the accounting period ends before 30 June 2021 and the company is not a new entrant and is not claiming patent box in respect of any new qualifying IP rights. However, there appear to be some substantive changes, as follows:

- In Step 2, the provisions relating to the measurement of relevant IP income and of the notional royalty, at section 357CC and 357CD, respectively, are replaced by the more detailed rules (described above) at ss 357BH to 357BHC.
- In determining the total gross income of a trade, the reference to finance income in s 357CB is replaced by a reference to the new definition at s 357BG.
- Similarly, in s 357CG, adjustments in calculating profits of a trade, the legislation now refers to the meaning of finance income under new s 357BG, rather than to the old reference definition in s 357CB.

- In s 357CI, the routine return calculation, the reference is to ss 357CJ and 357CK are replaced by references to new ss 357BJA and 357BJB.
- In s 357DA, the provisions for determining relevant IP profits by streaming, the various references are replaced by references to the new definitions of, for example, finance income and relevant IP income.

It does, therefore, appear as though even when we are applying the old legislation to a scenario, it is important to consider the application of the new rules as many of the new definitions or some of the concepts appear to be used instead.

Commencement

The commencement provisions for Sch 9 are the same as for the substantive legislation introduced by s 60 above.

SCHEDULE 10

HYBRID AND OTHER MISMATCHES

Section 66

PART 1

MAIN PROVISIONS

1 In TIOPA 2010, after Part 6 insert—

"PART 6A

HYBRID AND OTHER MISMATCHES

CHAPTER 1

INTRODUCTION

259A Overview of Part

(1) This Part has effect for the purposes of counteracting certain cases that it is reasonable to suppose would otherwise give rise to—

(a) a deduction/non-inclusion mismatch, or

(b) a double deduction mismatch.

(2) A deduction/non-inclusion mismatch arises where an amount is deductible from a person's income—

(a) without a corresponding amount of ordinary income arising to another person, or

(b) where an amount of ordinary income does arise to a person but is under taxed.

(3) A double deduction mismatch arises where—

(a) an amount is deductible from more than one person's income, or

(b) an amount is deductible from a person's income for the purposes of more than one tax.

(4) The cases with which this Part is concerned involve—

(a) payments or quasi-payments under or in connection with financial instruments or repos, stock lending arrangements or other transfers of financial instruments,

(b) hybrid entities,

(c) companies with permanent establishments, or

(d) dual resident companies.

(5) This Part counteracts mismatches that would otherwise arise by making certain adjustments to a person's treatment for corporation tax purposes.

(6) Chapter 2 contains some key definitions for the purposes of this Part, see in particular—

(a) section 259B which provides that "tax" means income tax, corporation tax on income, the diverted profits tax, the CFC charge, foreign tax or a foreign CFC charge,

(b) section 259BB which defines "payment", "quasi-payment", "payment period", "relevant deduction", "payer", "payee", and "payee jurisdiction",

(c) section 259BC which defines "ordinary income" and "taxable profits", in relation to taxes other than the CFC charge and foreign CFC charges,

(d) section 259BD which contains corresponding provision for the CFC charge and foreign CFC charges,

(e) section 259BE which defines "hybrid entity" and other related terms, and

(f) section 259BF which defines "permanent establishment".

(7) Chapter 3 contains provision for the counteraction of certain deduction/non-inclusion mismatches arising from payments or quasi-payments under, or in connection with, financial instruments.

(8) Chapter 4 contains provision for the counteraction of certain deduction/non-inclusion mismatches arising from payments or quasi-payments and involving certain repos, stock lending arrangements or other arrangements for, or relating to, transfers of financial instruments.

(9) Chapter 5 contains provision for the counteraction of certain deduction/non-inclusion mismatches arising from payments or quasi-payments in relation to which the payer is a hybrid entity.

(10) Chapter 6 contains provision for the counteraction of certain deduction/non-inclusion mismatches arising in relation to internal transfers of money or money's worth made, or treated as made, by a multinational company's permanent establishment in the United Kingdom to the territory in which the company is resident for tax purposes.

(11) Chapter 7 contains provision for the counteraction of certain deduction/non-inclusion mismatches arising from payments or quasi-payments in relation to which a payee is a hybrid entity.

(12) Chapter 8 contains provision for the counteraction of certain deduction/non-inclusion mismatches arising from payments or quasi-payments in relation to which a payee is a multinational company.

(13) Chapter 9 contains provision for the counteraction of certain double deduction mismatches arising from a company being a hybrid entity.

(14) Chapter 10 contains provision for the counteraction of certain double deduction mismatches involving dual resident companies or relevant multinational companies.

(15) Chapter 11 contains provision about imported mismatches.

(16) Chapter 12 contains provision—

(a) for adjustments to be made where a reasonable supposition made for the purposes of this Part turns out to be mistaken or otherwise ceases to be reasonable, and

(b) for deductions from taxable total profits to be made where a relevant deduction has been denied under certain provisions of this Part and amounts of ordinary income arise later than is permitted.

(17) Chapter 13 contains anti-avoidance provision.

(18) Chapter 14 contains definitions and other provision about the interpretation of this Part.

(19) Each of Chapters 3 to 10 contains provision specifying that some or all of this Part (and any corresponding provision under the law of a territory outside the United Kingdom) is to be disregarded when determining whether a mismatch arises for the purposes of that Chapter and, if so, in what amount, see—

(a) section 259CA(4) and (5),

(b) section 259DA(5),

(c) section 259EA(5) and (6),

(d) section 259FA(4), (5) and (6),

(e) section 259GA(5) and (6),

(f) section 259HA(6) and (7),

(g) section 259IA(2) and (3), and

(h) section 259JA(5).

(20) The effect of the provisions mentioned in subsection (19) is that Chapters 3 to 10 (or any corresponding provision under the law of a territory outside the United Kingdom) have effect in the following sequence—

(a) Chapter 4,

(b) Chapter 3,

(c) Chapter 5,

(d) Chapter 6,

(e) Chapter 7,

(f) Chapter 8,

(g) Chapter 9, and

(h) Chapter 10.

CHAPTER 2
KEY DEFINITIONS

Meaning of "tax"

259B "Tax" means certain taxes on income and includes foreign tax etc

(1) In this Part "tax" means—

(a) income tax,
(b) the charge to corporation tax on income,
(c) diverted profits tax,
(d) the CFC charge,
(e) foreign tax, or
(f) a foreign CFC charge.

(2) In subsection (1) "foreign tax" means a tax chargeable under the law of a territory outside the United Kingdom so far as it—

(a) is charged on income and corresponds to United Kingdom income tax, or
(b) is charged on income and corresponds to the United Kingdom charge to corporation tax on income.

(3) A tax is not outside the scope of subsection (2) by reason only that it—

(a) is chargeable under the law of a province, state or other part of a country, or
(b) is levied by or on behalf of a municipality or other local body.

(4) In this Part—

"CFC" and "the CFC charge" have the same meaning as in Part 9A (see section 371VA);
"foreign CFC charge" means a charge (by whatever name known) under the law of a territory outside the United Kingdom which is similar to the CFC charge (and reference to a "foreign CFC" is to be read accordingly).

Equivalent provision to this Part under foreign law

259BA References to equivalent provision to this Part under the law of a territory outside the United Kingdom

(1) A reference in this Part to provision under the law of a territory outside the United Kingdom that is equivalent to—

(a) this Part, or
(b) a provision of this Part,

is to be read in accordance with subsection (2).

(2) The reference is to provision under the law of a territory outside the United Kingdom that it is reasonable to suppose—

(a) is based on the Final Report on Neutralising the Effects of Hybrid Mismatch Arrangements published by the Organisation for Economic Cooperation and Development ("OECD") on 5 October 2015 or any replacement or supplementary publication, and
(b) has effect for the same, or similar, purposes to this Part or (as the case may be) the provision of this Part.

(3) In paragraph (a) of subsection (2) "replacement or supplementary publication" means any document that is approved and published by the OECD in place of, or to update or supplement, the report mentioned in that paragraph (or any replacement of, or supplement to, it).

Payments and quasi-payments etc

259BB Meaning of "payment", "quasi-payment", "payer", "payee" etc

(1) In this Part "payment" means any transfer—

(a) of money or money's worth directly or indirectly from one person ("the payer") to one or more other persons, and
(b) in relation to which (disregarding this Part and any equivalent provision under the law of a territory outside the United Kingdom) an amount (a "relevant deduction") may be deducted from the payer's income for a taxable period (the "payment period") for the purposes of calculating the payer's taxable profits.

(2) For the purposes of this Part, there is a "quasi-payment", in relation to a taxable period (the "payment period") of a person ("the payer"), if (disregarding this Part and any equivalent provision under the law of a territory outside the United Kingdom)—

(a) an amount (a "relevant deduction") may be deducted from the payer's income for that period for the purposes of calculating the payer's taxable profits, and

(b) making the assumptions in subsection (4), it would be reasonable to expect an amount of ordinary income to arise to one or more other persons as a result of the circumstances giving rise to the relevant deduction.

(3) But a quasi-payment does not arise under subsection (2) if—

(a) the relevant deduction is an amount that is deemed, under the law of the payer jurisdiction, to arise for tax purposes, and

(b) the circumstances giving rise to the relevant deduction do not include any economic rights, in substance, existing between the payer and a person mentioned in subsection (2)(b).

(4) The assumptions are that (so far as would not otherwise be the case)—

(a) any question as to whether an entity is a distinct and separate person from the payer is determined in accordance with the law of the payer jurisdiction,

(b) any persons to whom amounts arise, or potentially arise, as a result of the circumstances giving rise to the relevant deduction adopt the same approach to accounting for those circumstances as the payer, and

(c) any persons to whom amounts arise, or potentially arise, as a result of those circumstances—

(i) are, under the law of the payer jurisdiction, resident in that jurisdiction for tax purposes, and

(ii) carry on a business, in connection with which those circumstances arise, in the payer jurisdiction.

(5) In this Part—

(a) references to a quasi-payment include all the circumstances giving rise to the relevant deduction mentioned in subsection (2)(a), and

(b) references to a quasi-payment being made are to those circumstances arising.

(6) In this Part "payee" means—

(a) in the case of a payment, any person—

(i) to whom the transfer is made as mentioned in subsection (1)(a), or

(ii) to whom an amount of ordinary income arises as a result of the payment, and

(b) in the case of a quasi-payment, any person—

(i) to whom it would be reasonable to expect an amount of ordinary income to arise as mentioned in subsection (2)(b), or

(ii) to whom an amount of ordinary income arises as a result of the quasi-payment.

(7) For the purposes of this Part, in the case of a quasi-payment, the payer is "also a payee" if—

(a) an entity is not a distinct and separate person from the payer for the purposes of a tax charged under the law of the United Kingdom,

(b) that entity is a distinct and separate person from the payer for the purposes of a tax charged under the law of the payer jurisdiction, and

(c) it would be reasonable to expect an amount of ordinary income to arise to that entity as mentioned in subsection (2)(b).

(8) In this section "payer jurisdiction" means the jurisdiction under the law of which the relevant deduction may (disregarding this Part and any equivalent provision under the law of a territory outside the United Kingdom) be deducted.

(9) In this Part "payee jurisdiction", in relation to a payee, means a territory in which—

(a) the payee is resident for tax purposes under the law of that territory, or

(b) the payee has a permanent establishment.

Ordinary income

259BC The basic rules

(1) This section has effect for the purposes of this Part.

(2) "Ordinary income" means income that is brought into account, before any deductions, for the purposes of calculating the income or profits on which a relevant tax is charged ("taxable profits")

(3) But an amount of income is not brought into account for those purposes to the extent that it is excluded, reduced or offset by any exemption, exclusion, relief or credit—

(a) that applies specifically to all or part of the amount of income (as opposed to ordinary income generally), or

(b) that arises as a result of, or otherwise in connection with, a payment or quasi-payment that gives rise to the amount of income.

(4) If all the relevant tax charged on taxable profits is, or falls to be, refunded, none of the income brought into account in calculating those taxable profits is "ordinary income".

(5) If a proportion of the relevant tax charged on taxable profits is, or falls to be, refunded, the amount of any income brought into account in calculating those taxable profits that is "ordinary income" is proportionally reduced.

(6) For the purposes of subsections (4) and (5) an amount of relevant tax is refunded if and to the extent that—

(a) any repayment of relevant tax, or any payment in respect of a credit for relevant tax, is made to any person, and

(b) that repayment or payment is directly or indirectly in respect of the whole or part of the amount of relevant tax,

but an amount refunded is to be ignored if and to the extent that it results from qualifying loss relief.

(7) In subsection (6) "qualifying loss relief" means—

(a) any means by which a loss might be used for corporation tax or income tax purposes to reduce the amount in respect of which a person is liable to tax, or

(b) any corresponding means by which a loss corresponding to a relevant tax loss might be used for the purposes of a relevant tax other than corporation tax or income tax to reduce the amount in respect of which a person is liable to tax,

(and in paragraph (b) "relevant tax loss" means a loss that might be used as mentioned in paragraph (a)).

(8) References to an amount of ordinary income being "included in" taxable profits are to that amount being brought into account for the purposes of calculating those profits.

(9) In this section "relevant tax" means a tax other than the CFC charge or a foreign CFC charge.

(10) Section 259BD contains provision for ordinary income to arise to chargeable companies by virtue of the CFC charge or a foreign CFC charge.

259BD Chargeable companies in respect of CFCs and foreign CFCs

(1) This section has effect for the purposes of this Part.

(2) Subsections (3) to (7) apply where an amount of income arises to an entity ("C") that is a CFC, a foreign CFC or both and all or part of that amount (the "relevant income")—

(a) is not ordinary income of C under section 259BC, or

(b) arises as a result of a payment or quasi-payment under, or in connection with, a financial instrument or hybrid transfer arrangement and—

(i) is (disregarding subsection (4)) ordinary income of C under section 259BC for a taxable period, but

(ii) under taxed.

(3) The following steps determine whether, and to what extent, the relevant income is "ordinary income" of a chargeable company in relation to the CFC charge or a foreign CFC charge.

Step 1
Determine—

(a) whether any of the relevant income is brought into account in calculating C's chargeable profits for the purposes of the CFC charge or a foreign CFC charge, and

(b) if so, the amount of the relevant income that is so brought into account for the purposes of each relevant charge.

If none of the relevant income is so brought into account, then none of it is "ordinary income" of a chargeable company and no further steps are to be taken. See subsections (10) to (12) for further provision about how this step is to be taken.

For the purposes of this section—

"relevant chargeable profits" are chargeable profits in relation to the calculation of which, for the purposes of the CFC charge or a foreign CFC charge, any of the relevant income is brought into account;

"relevant charge" means a charge in relation to which any of the relevant income is brought into account in calculating chargeable profits.

Step 2

In relation to each relevant charge, determine the proportion of C's relevant chargeable profits, for the purposes of that charge, that is apportioned to each chargeable company.

For the purposes of this section, each chargeable company to which 25% or more of C's relevant chargeable profits for the purposes of a relevant charge are apportioned is a "relevant chargeable company".

If there are no relevant chargeable companies in relation to any relevant charges, then none of the relevant income is "ordinary income" of a chargeable company and no further steps are to be taken.

Step 3

In relation to each relevant chargeable company, determine what is the appropriate proportion of the relevant income brought into account in calculating relevant chargeable profits, for the purposes of the relevant charge concerned.

That proportion of that income is "ordinary income" of that company for the taxable period for which that charge is charged on it by reference to those profits.

For the purposes of this step, the "appropriate proportion", in relation to a relevant chargeable company, is the same as the proportion of the relevant chargeable profits that is apportioned to it for the purposes of the relevant charge.

(4) An amount of relevant income that is ordinary income of a relevant chargeable company in accordance with subsection (3) is not ordinary income of C (so far as it otherwise would be).

(5) Relevant chargeable profits apportioned to a relevant chargeable company for the purposes of a relevant charge are "taxable profits" of that company for the taxable period for which the charge is charged on it by reference to those profits.

(6) The amount of the relevant income that is ordinary income of that relevant chargeable company under subsection (3), by virtue of being brought into account in calculating those relevant chargeable profits, is "included in" those taxable profits.

(7) References to tax charged on taxable profits include a relevant charge charged by reference to relevant chargeable profits that are taxable profits under subsection (5).

(8) For the purposes of subsection (2)(b), an amount of ordinary income is "under taxed" if the highest rate at which tax is charged, for C's taxable period, on the taxable profits in which the amount is included, taking into account on a just and reasonable basis any credit for underlying tax, is less than C's full marginal rate for that period.

(9) In subsection (8)—

(a) C's "full marginal rate" means the highest rate at which the tax that is chargeable on those taxable profits could be charged on taxable profits, of C for the taxable period, which include ordinary income that arises from, or in connection with, a financial instrument, and

(b) "credit for underlying tax" means a credit or relief given to reflect tax charged on profits that are wholly or partly used to fund (directly or indirectly) the payment or quasi-payment mentioned in subsection (2)(b).

(10) For the purposes of step 1 in subsection (3), section 259BC(3) applies for the purposes of determining the extent to which an amount of relevant income is brought into account in calculating chargeable profits as it applies for the purposes of determining the extent to which an amount of income is brought into account for the purposes of calculating taxable profits.

(11) Subsection (12) applies for the purposes of step 1 in subsection (3), if—

(a) the amount of income arising to C mentioned in subsection (2)—

(i) is not all relevant income, and

(ii) is only partly brought into account in calculating chargeable profits for the purposes of the CFC charge or a foreign CFC charge, and

(b) accordingly, it falls to be determined whether, and to what extent, the relevant income is brought into account in calculating those profits for the purposes of the charge concerned.

(12) The relevant income is to be taken to be brought into account (if at all) only to the extent that the total amount of income mentioned in subsection (2) that is brought into account exceeds the amount of income mentioned in that subsection that is not relevant income.

(13) In this section—

"chargeable company"—

(a) in relation to the CFC charge, has the same meaning as in Part 9A (see section 371VA), and

(b) in relation to a foreign CFC charge, means an entity (by whatever name known) corresponding to a chargeable company within the meaning of that Part;

"chargeable profits"—

(a) in relation to the CFC charge, has the same meaning as in that Part (see that section), and

(b) in relation to a foreign CFC charge, means the concept (by whatever name known) corresponding to chargeable profits within the meaning of that Part;

"hybrid transfer arrangement" has the meaning given by section 259DB.

Hybrid entity etc

259BE Meaning of "hybrid entity", "investor" and "investor jurisdiction"

(1) For the purposes of this Part, an entity is "hybrid" if it meets conditions A and B.

(2) Condition A is that the entity is regarded as being a person for tax purposes under the law of any territory.

(3) Condition B is that—

(a) some or all of the entity's income or profits are treated (or would be if there were any) for the purposes of a tax charged under the law of any territory, as the income or profits of a person or persons other than the person mentioned in subsection (2), or

(b) under the law of a territory other than the one mentioned in subsection (2), the entity is not regarded as a distinct and separate person to an entity or entities that are distinct and separate persons under the law of the territory mentioned in that subsection.

(4) For the purposes of this Part—

(a) where subsection (3)(a) applies, a person who is treated as having the income or profits of the hybrid entity is an "investor" in it,

(b) where subsection (3)(b) applies, an entity that—

(i) is regarded as a distinct and separate person to the hybrid entity under the law of the territory mentioned in subsection (2), but

(ii) is not regarded as a distinct and separate person to the hybrid entity under the law of another territory,

is an "investor" in the hybrid entity, and

(c) any territory under the law of which an investor is within the charge to a tax is an "investor jurisdiction" in relation to that investor.

Permanent establishments

259BF Meaning of "permanent establishment"

(1) In this Part "permanent establishment" means anything that is—

(a) a permanent establishment of a company within the meaning of the Corporation Tax Acts (see section 1119 of CTA 2010), or

(b) within any similar concept under the law of a territory outside the United Kingdom.

(2) A concept is not outside the scope of subsection (1)(b) by reason only that it is not based on Article 5 of a Model Tax Convention on Income and Capital published by the Organisation for Economic Cooperation and Development.

CHAPTER 3
HYBRID AND OTHER MISMATCHES FROM FINANCIAL INSTRUMENTS

Introduction

259C Overview of Chapter

(1) This Chapter contains provision that counteracts hybrid or otherwise impermissible deduction/non-inclusion mismatches that it is reasonable to suppose would otherwise arise from payments or quasi-payments under, or in connection with, financial instruments.

(2) The Chapter counteracts mismatches where the payer or a payee is within the charge to corporation tax and does so by altering the corporation tax treatment of the payer or a payee.

(3) Section 259CA contains the conditions that must be met for this Chapter to apply.

(4) Section 259CB defines "hybrid or otherwise impermissible deduction/non-inclusion mismatch" and provides how the amount of the mismatch is to be calculated.

(5) Section 259CC contains definitions of certain terms used in section 259CB.

(6) Section 259CD contains provision that counteracts the mismatch where the payer is within the charge to corporation tax for the payment period.

(7) Section 259CE contains provision that counteracts the mismatch where a payee is within the charge to corporation tax and neither section 259CD nor any equivalent provision under the law of a territory outside the United Kingdom fully counteracts the mismatch.

(8) See also—

(a) section 259BB for the meaning of "payment", "quasi-payment", "payment period", "relevant deduction", "payer" and "payee", and
(b) section 259N for the meaning of "financial instrument".

Application of Chapter

259CA Circumstances in which the Chapter applies

(1) This Chapter applies if conditions A to D are met.

(2) Condition A is that a payment or quasi-payment is made under, or in connection with, a financial instrument.

(3) Condition B is that—

(a) the payer is within the charge to corporation tax for the payment period, or
(b) a payee is within the charge to corporation tax for an accounting period some or all of which falls within the payment period.

(4) Condition C is that it is reasonable to suppose that, disregarding the provisions mentioned in subsection (5), there would be a hybrid or otherwise impermissible deduction/non-inclusion mismatch in relation to the payment or quasi-payment (see section 259CB).

(5) The provisions are—

(a) this Chapter and Chapters 5 to 10, and
(b) any equivalent provision under the law of a territory outside the United Kingdom.

(6) Condition D is that—

(a) it is a quasi-payment that is made as mentioned in subsection (2) and the payer is also a payee (see section 259BB(7)),
(b) the payer and a payee are related (see section 259NC) at any time in the period—

(i) beginning with the day on which any arrangement is made by the payer or a payee in connection with the financial instrument, and
(ii) ending with the last day of the payment period, or

(c) the financial instrument, or any arrangement connected with it, is a structured arrangement.

(7) The financial instrument, or an arrangement connected with it, is a "structured arrangement" if it is reasonable to suppose that—

(a) the financial instrument, or arrangement, is designed to secure a hybrid or otherwise impermissible deduction/non-inclusion mismatch, or
(b) the terms of the financial instrument or arrangement share the economic benefit of the mismatch between the parties to the instrument or arrangement or otherwise reflect the fact that the mismatch is expected to arise.

(8) The financial instrument or arrangement may be designed to secure a hybrid or otherwise impermissible deduction/non-inclusion mismatch despite also being designed to secure any commercial or other objective.

(9) Sections 259CD (cases where the payer is within the charge to corporation tax for the payment period) and 259CE (cases where a payee is within the charge to corporation tax) contain provision for the counteraction of the hybrid or otherwise impermissible deduction/non-inclusion mismatch.

259CB Hybrid or otherwise impermissible deduction/non-inclusion mismatches and their extent

(1) There is a "hybrid or otherwise impermissible deduction/non-inclusion mismatch", in relation to a payment or quasi-payment, if either or both of case 1 or 2 applies.

(2) Case 1 applies where—

(a) the relevant deduction exceeds the sum of the amounts of ordinary income that, by reason of the payment or quasi-payment, arise to each payee for a permitted taxable period, and

(b) all or part of that excess arises by reason of the terms, or any other feature, of the financial instrument.

(3) So far as the excess arises by reason of a relevant debt relief provision, it is to be taken not to arise by reason of the terms, or any other feature, of the financial instrument (whether or not it would have arisen by reason of the terms, or any other feature, of the financial instrument regardless of the relevant debt relief provision).

(4) Subject to that and subsection (9), for the purposes of subsection (2)(b)—

(a) it does not matter whether the excess or part arises for another reason as well as the terms, or any other feature, of the financial instrument (even if it would have arisen for that other reason regardless of the terms, or any other feature, of the financial instrument), and

(b) an excess or part of an excess is to be taken to arise by reason of the terms, or any other feature, of the financial instrument (so far as would not otherwise be the case) if, on making such of the relevant assumptions in relation to each payee as apply in relation to that payee (see subsections (5) and (6)), it could arise by reason of the terms, or any other feature, of the financial instrument.

(5) These are the "relevant assumptions"—

(a) where a payee is not within the charge to a tax under the law of a payee jurisdiction because the payee benefits from an exclusion, immunity, exemption or relief (however described) under that law, assume that the exclusion, immunity, exemption or relief does not apply;

(b) where an amount of income is not included in the ordinary income of a payee for the purposes of a tax charged under the law of a payee jurisdiction because the payment or quasi-payment is not made in connection with a business carried on by the payee in that jurisdiction, assume that the payment or quasi-payment is made in connection with such a business;

(c) where a payee is not within the charge to a tax under the law of any territory because there is no territory where the payee is—

(i) resident for the purposes of a tax charged under the law of that territory, or

(ii) within the charge to a tax under the law of that territory as a result of having a permanent establishment in that territory,

assume that the payee is a company that is resident for tax purposes, and carries on a business in connection with which the payment or quasi-payment is made, in the United Kingdom.

(6) Where the relevant assumption in subsection (5)(c) applies in relation to a payee the following provisions are to be disregarded in relation to that payee for the purposes of subsection (4)(b)—

(a) section 441 of CTA 2009 (loan relationships for unallowable purposes);

(b) section 690 of that Act (derivative contracts for unallowable purposes);

(c) Part 4 (transfer pricing);

(d) this Part;

(e) Part 7 (tax treatment of financing costs and income).

(7) Case 2 applies where there are one or more amounts of ordinary income ("under-taxed amounts") that—

(a) arise, by reason of the payment or quasi-payment, to a payee for a permitted taxable period, and

(b) are under taxed by reason of the terms, or any other feature, of the financial instrument.

(8) Subject to subsection (9), for the purposes of subsection (7)(b) it does not matter whether an amount of ordinary income is under taxed for another reason as well as the terms, or any other feature, of the financial instrument (even if it would have been under taxed for that other reason regardless of the terms, or any other feature, of the financial instrument).

(9) For the purposes of this section disregard—

(a) any excess or part of an excess mentioned in subsection (2), and

(b) any under-taxed amount,

that arises as a result of a payee being a relevant investment fund (see section 259NA).

(10) Where case 1 applies, the amount of the hybrid or otherwise impermissible deduction/non-inclusion mismatch is equal to the excess that arises as mentioned in subsection (2)(b).

(11) Where case 2 applies, the amount of the hybrid or otherwise impermissible deduction/non-inclusion mismatch is equal to the sum of the amounts given in respect of each under-taxed amount by—

(UTA x (FMR – R)) / FMR

where—

"UTA" is the under-taxed amount;

"FMR" is the payee's full marginal rate (expressed as a percentage) for the permitted taxable period for which the under-taxed amount arises;

"R" is the highest rate (expressed as a percentage) at which tax is charged on the taxable profits in which the under-taxed amount is included, taking into account on a just and reasonable basis the effect of any credit for underlying tax.

(12) Where cases 1 and 2 both apply, the amount of the hybrid or otherwise impermissible deduction/non-inclusion mismatch is the sum of the amounts given by subsections (10) and (11).

(13) See section 259CC for the meaning of "permitted taxable period", "relevant debt relief provision" and "under taxed".

259CC Interpretation of section 259CB

(1) This section has effect for the purposes of section 259CB.

(2) A taxable period of a payee is "permitted" in relation to an amount of ordinary income that arises as a result of the payment or quasi-payment if—

(a) the period begins before the end of 12 months after the end of the payment period, or

(b) where the period begins after that—

(i) a claim has been made for the period to be a permitted period in relation to the amount of ordinary income, and

(ii) it is just and reasonable for the amount of ordinary income to arise for that taxable period rather than an earlier period.

(3) Each of these is a "relevant debt relief provision"—

(a) section 322 of CTA 2009 (release of debts: cases where credits not required to be brought into account),

(b) section 357 of that Act (insolvent creditors),

(c) section 358 of that Act (exclusion of credits on release of connected companies' debts: general),

(d) section 359 of that Act (exclusion of credits on release of connected companies' debts during creditor's insolvency),

(e) section 361C of that Act (the equity-for-debt exception),

(f) section 361D of that Act (corporate rescue: debt released shortly after acquisition), and

(g) section 362A of that Act (corporate rescue: debt released shortly after connection arises).

(4) An amount of ordinary income of a payee, for a permitted taxable period, is "under taxed" if the highest rate at which tax is charged on the taxable profits of the payee in which the amount is included, taking into account on a just and reasonable basis the effect of any credit for underlying tax, is less than the payee's full marginal rate for that period.

(5) The payee's "full marginal rate" means the highest rate at which the tax that is chargeable on the taxable profits mentioned in subsection (4) could be charged on taxable profits, of the payee for the permitted taxable period, which include ordinary income that arises from, or in connection with, a financial instrument.

(6) A "credit for underlying tax" means a credit or relief given to reflect tax charged on profits that are wholly or partly used to fund (directly or indirectly) the payment or quasi-payment.

Counteraction

259CD Counteraction where the payer is within the charge to corporation tax for the payment period

(1) This section applies where the payer is within the charge to corporation tax for the payment period.

(2) For corporation tax purposes, the relevant deduction that may be deducted from the payer's income for the payment period is reduced by an amount equal to the hybrid or otherwise impermissible deduction/non-inclusion mismatch mentioned in section 259CA(4).

259CE Counteraction where a payee is within the charge to corporation tax

(1) This section applies in relation to a payee where—

(a) the payee is within the charge to corporation tax for an accounting period some or all of which falls within the payment period, and

(b) it is reasonable to suppose that—

(i) neither section 259CD nor any equivalent provision under the law of a territory outside the United Kingdom applies, or

(ii) a provision of the law of a territory outside the United Kingdom that is equivalent to section 259CD applies, but does not fully counteract the hybrid or otherwise impermissible deduction/non-inclusion mismatch mentioned in section 259CA(4).

(2) A provision of the law of a territory outside the United Kingdom that is equivalent to section 259CD does not fully counteract that mismatch if (and only if)—

(a) it does not reduce the relevant deduction by the full amount of the mismatch, and

(b) the payer is still able to deduct some of the relevant deduction from income in calculating taxable profits.

(3) In this section "the relevant amount" is—

(a) in a case where subsection (1)(b)(i) applies, an amount equal to the hybrid or otherwise impermissible deduction/non-inclusion mismatch mentioned in section 259CA(4), or

(b) in a case where subsection (1)(b)(ii) applies, the lesser of—

(i) the amount by which that mismatch exceeds the amount by which it is reasonable to suppose the relevant deduction is reduced by a provision under the law of a territory outside the United Kingdom that is equivalent to section 259CD, and

(ii) the amount of the relevant deduction that may still be deducted as mentioned in subsection (2)(b).

(4) If the payee is the only payee, the relevant amount is to be treated as income arising to the payee for the counteraction period.

(5) If there is more than one payee, an amount equal to the payee's share of the relevant amount is to be treated as income arising to the payee for the counteraction period.

(6) The payee's share of the relevant amount is to be determined by apportioning that amount between all the payees on a just and reasonable basis, having regard (in particular)—

(a) to any arrangements as to profit sharing that may exist between some or all of the payees,

(b) to whom any under-taxed amounts (within the meaning given by section 259CB(7)) arise, and

(c) to whom any amounts of ordinary income that it would be reasonable to expect to arise as a result of the payment or quasi-payment, but that do not arise, would have arisen.

(7) An amount of income that is treated as arising under subsection (4) or (5) is chargeable under Chapter 8 of Part 10 of CTA 2009 (income not otherwise charged) (despite section 979(2) of that Act).

(8) The "counteraction period" means—

(a) if an accounting period of the payee coincides with the payment period, that accounting period, or

(b) otherwise, the first accounting period of the payee that is wholly or partly within the payment period.

CHAPTER 4

HYBRID TRANSFER DEDUCTION/NON-INCLUSION MISMATCHES

Introduction

259D   Overview of Chapter

(1) This Chapter contains provision that counteracts deduction/non-inclusion mismatches that it is reasonable to suppose would otherwise arise from payments or quasi-payments as a consequence of hybrid transfer arrangements.

(2) The Chapter counteracts mismatches where the payer or a payee is within the charge to corporation tax and does so by altering the corporation tax treatment of the payer or a payee.

(3) Section 259DA contains the conditions that must be met for this Chapter to apply.

(4) Section 259DB defines "hybrid transfer arrangement".

(5) Section 259DC defines "hybrid transfer deduction/non-inclusion mismatch" and provides how the amount of the mismatch is to be calculated.

(6) Section 259DD contains definitions of certain terms used in section 259DC.

(7) Section 259DE contains provision in connection with excluding mismatches from counteraction by the Chapter where they arise as a consequence of the tax treatment of a financial trader.

(8) Section 259DF contains provision that counteracts the mismatch where the payer is within the charge to corporation tax for the payment period.

(9) Section 259DG contains provision that counteracts the mismatch where a payee is within the charge to corporation tax and neither section 259DF nor any equivalent provision under the law of a territory outside the United Kingdom fully counteracts the mismatch.

(10) See also section 259BB for the meaning of "payment", "quasi-payment", "payment period", "relevant deduction", "payer" and "payee".

Application of Chapter

259DA   Circumstances in which the Chapter applies

(1) This Chapter applies if conditions A to E are met.

(2) Condition A is that there is a hybrid transfer arrangement in relation to an underlying instrument (see section 259DB).

(3) Condition B is that a payment or quasi-payment is made under or in connection with—

    (a) the hybrid transfer arrangement, or
    (b) the underlying instrument.

(4) Condition C is that—

    (a) the payer is within the charge to corporation tax for the payment period, or
    (b) a payee is within the charge to corporation tax for an accounting period some or all of which falls within the payment period.

(5) Condition D is that it is reasonable to suppose that, disregarding this Part and any equivalent provision under the law of a territory outside the United Kingdom, there would be a hybrid transfer deduction/non-inclusion mismatch in relation to the payment or quasi-payment (see section 259DC).

(6) Condition E is that—

    (a) it is a quasi-payment that is made as mentioned in subsection (3) and the payer is also a payee (see section 259BB(7)),
    (b) the payer and a payee are related (see section 259NC) at any time in the period—

        (i) beginning with the day on which the hybrid transfer arrangement is made, and
        (ii) ending with the last day of the payment period, or

    (c) the hybrid transfer arrangement is a structured arrangement.

(7) The hybrid transfer arrangement is a "structured arrangement" if it is reasonable to suppose that—

    (a) the hybrid transfer arrangement is designed to secure a hybrid transfer deduction/non-inclusion mismatch, or

(b) the terms of the hybrid transfer arrangement share the economic benefit of the mismatch between the parties to the arrangement or otherwise reflect the fact that the mismatch is expected to arise.

(8) The hybrid transfer arrangement may be designed to secure a hybrid transfer deduction/non-inclusion mismatch despite also being designed to secure any commercial or other objective.

(9) Sections 259DF (cases where the payer is within the charge to corporation tax for the payment period) and 259DG (cases where a payee is within the charge to corporation tax) make provision for the counteraction of the hybrid transfer deduction/non-inclusion mismatch.

259DB Meaning of "hybrid transfer arrangement", "underlying instrument" etc

(1) This section has effect for the purposes of this Chapter.

(2) A "hybrid transfer arrangement" means—

(a) a repo,

(b) a stock lending arrangement, or

(c) any other arrangement,

that is an arrangement within subsection (3).

(3) An arrangement is within this subsection if it provides for, or relates to, the transfer of a financial instrument ("the underlying instrument") and—

(a) the dual treatment condition is met in relation to the arrangement, or

(b) a substitute payment could be made under the arrangement.

(4) The dual treatment condition is met in relation to the arrangement if—

(a) in relation to a person, for the purposes of a tax—

(i) the arrangement is regarded as equivalent, in substance, to a transaction for the lending of money at interest, and

(ii) a payment or quasi-payment made under, or in connection with, the arrangement or the underlying instrument could be treated so as to reflect the fact the arrangement is so regarded, and

(b) in relation to another person, for the purposes of a tax (whether or not the same one), such a payment or quasi-payment would not be treated so as to reflect the arrangement being regarded as equivalent, in substance, to a transaction for the lending of money at interest.

(5) A payment or quasi-payment is a "substitute payment" if—

(a) it consists of or involves—

(i) an amount being paid, or

(ii) a benefit being given (including the release of the whole or part of any liability to pay an amount),

(b) that amount, or the value of that benefit, is representative of a return of any kind ("the underlying return") that arises on, or in connection with, the underlying instrument, and

(c) the amount is paid, or the benefit is given, to someone other than the person to whom the underlying return arises.

(6) For the purposes of subsection (3) where there is an arrangement, to which a person ("P") and another person ("Q") are party, under which—

(a) a financial instrument ("the first instrument") ceases to be owned by P (whether or not because it ceases to exist), and

(b) Q comes to own a financial instrument ("the second instrument") under which Q has the same, or substantially the same, rights and liabilities as P had under the first instrument,

the second instrument is to be treated as being transferred from P to Q.

259DC Hybrid transfer deduction/non-inclusion mismatches and their extent

(1) There is a "hybrid transfer deduction/non-inclusion mismatch", in relation to a payment or quasi-payment, if either or both of case 1 or 2 applies.

(2) Case 1 applies where—

(a) the relevant deduction exceeds the sum of the amounts of ordinary income that, by reason of the payment or quasi-payment, arise to each payee for a permitted taxable period, and

(b) all or part of that excess arises for a reason mentioned in subsection (8).

(3) Subject to subsection (9), for the purposes of subsection (2)(b)—

(a) it does not matter whether the excess or part arises for another reason as well (even if it would have arisen for that other reason regardless of any reasons mentioned in subsection (8)), and

(b) an excess or part of an excess is to be taken to arise for a reason mentioned in subsection (8) (so far as would not otherwise be the case) if, on making such of the relevant assumptions in relation to each payee as apply in relation to that payee (see subsections (4) and (5))), it could arise for a reason mentioned in subsection (8).

(4) These are the "relevant assumptions"—

(a) where a payee is not within the charge to a tax under the law of a payee jurisdiction because the payee benefits from an exclusion, immunity, exemption or relief (however described) under that law, assume that the exclusion, immunity, exemption or relief does not apply;

(b) where an amount of income is not included in the ordinary income of a payee for the purposes of a tax charged under the law of a payee jurisdiction because the payment or quasi-payment is not made in connection with a business carried on by the payee in that jurisdiction, assume that the payment or quasi-payment is made in connection with such a business;

(c) where a payee is not within the charge to a tax under the law of any territory because there is no territory where the payee is—

   (i) resident for the purposes of a tax charged under the law of that territory, or
   (ii) within the charge to a tax under the law of that territory as a result of having a permanent establishment in that territory,

assume that the payee is a company that is resident for tax purposes, and carries on a business in connection with which the payment or quasi-payment is made, in the United Kingdom.

(5) Where the relevant assumption in subsection (4)(c) applies in relation to a payee the following provisions are to be disregarded in relation to that payee for the purposes of subsection (3)(b)—

(a) section 441 of CTA 2009 (loan relationships for unallowable purposes);
(b) Part 4 (transfer pricing);
(c) this Part;
(d) Part 7 (tax treatment of financing costs and income).

(6) Case 2 applies where there are one or more amounts of ordinary income ("under-taxed amounts") that—

(a) arise, by reason of the payment or quasi-payment, to a payee for a permitted taxable period, and
(b) are under taxed for a reason mentioned in subsection (8).

(7) Subject to subsection (9), for the purposes of subsection (6)(b) it does not matter whether an amount of ordinary income is under taxed for another reason as well (even if it would have been under taxed for that other reason regardless of any reason mentioned in subsection (8)).

(8) The reasons are—

(a) the dual treatment condition being met in relation to a hybrid transfer arrangement under, or in connection with, which the payment or quasi-payment is made (see section 259DB(4));
(b) the payment or quasi-payment being a substitute payment.

(9) For the purposes of this section, disregard—

(a) any excess or part of an excess mentioned in subsection (2), and
(b) any under-taxed amount,

in relation to which the financial trader exclusion applies (see section 259DE) or that arises as a result of a payee being a relevant investment fund (see section 259NA).

(10) Where case 1 applies, the amount of the hybrid transfer deduction/non-inclusion mismatch is equal to the excess that arises as mentioned in subsection (2)(b).

(11) Where case 2 applies, the amount of the hybrid transfer deduction/non-inclusion mismatch is equal to the sum of the amounts given in respect of each under-taxed amount by—

$$(UTA \times (FMR - R)) / FMR$$
where

"UTA" is the under-taxed amount;
"FMR" is the payee's full marginal rate (expressed as a percentage) for the permitted taxable period for which the under-taxed amount arises;

"R" is the highest rate (expressed as a percentage) at which tax is charged on the taxable profits in which the under-taxed amount is included, taking into account on a just and reasonable basis the effect of any credit for underlying tax.

(12) Where cases 1 and 2 both apply, the amount of the hybrid transfer deduction/non-inclusion mismatch is the sum of the amounts given by subsections (10) and (11).

(13) See section 259DD for the meaning of "permitted taxable period" and "under taxed".

259DD Interpretation of section 259DC

(1) This section has effect for the purposes of section 259DC.

(2) A taxable period of a payee is "permitted" in relation to an amount of ordinary income that arises as a result of the payment or quasi-payment if—

(a) the period begins before the end of 12 months after the end of the payment period, or
(b) where the period begins after that—

(i) a claim has been made for the period to be a permitted period in relation to the amount of ordinary income, and
(ii) it is just and reasonable for the amount of ordinary income to arise for that taxable period rather than an earlier period.

(3) An amount of ordinary income of a payee, for a permitted taxable period, is "under taxed" if the highest rate at which tax is charged on the taxable profits of the payee in which the amount is included, taking into account on a just and reasonable basis the effect of any credit for underlying tax, is less than the payee's full marginal rate for that period.

(4) The payee's "full marginal rate" means the highest rate at which the tax that is chargeable on the taxable profits mentioned in subsection (3) could be charged on taxable profits, of the payee for the permitted taxable period, which include ordinary income that arises from, or in connection with, a financial instrument.

(5) A "credit for underlying tax" means a credit or relief given to reflect tax charged on profits that are wholly or partly used to fund (directly or indirectly) the payment or quasi-payment.

259DE The financial trader exclusion

(1) This section has effect for the purposes of section 259DC(9).

(2) The financial trader exclusion applies, in relation to an excess or part of an excess mentioned in section 259DC(2) or an under-taxed amount, where conditions A to C are met.

(3) Condition A is that the excess or part arises, or the under-taxed amount is under taxed, because the payment or quasi-payment—

(a) is a substitute payment,
(b) is treated, for the purposes of tax charged on a person, so as to reflect the fact that it is representative of the underlying return, and
(c) is brought into account by another person ("the financial trader") in calculating the profits of a trade under—

(i) Part 3 of CTA 2009 (trading income), or
(ii) an equivalent provision of the law of a territory outside the United Kingdom.

(4) Condition B is that the financial trader also brings any associated payments into account as mentioned in subsection (3)(c).

(5) In subsection (4) "associated payment" means a payment or quasi-payment—

(a) in relation to which the financial trader is the payer or a payee, and
(b) that is made under, or in connection with, the underlying instrument or an arrangement that relates to the underlying instrument.

(6) Condition C is that—

(a) if the underlying return were to arise, and be paid directly, to the payee or payees in relation to the substitute payment, neither Chapter 3 (hybrid and other mismatches from financial instruments) nor any equivalent provision under the law of a territory outside the United Kingdom would apply, and
(b) the hybrid transfer arrangement under, or in connection with, which the substitute payment is made is not a structured arrangement (within the meaning given by section 259DA(7) and (8)).

Counteraction

259DF Counteraction where the payer is within the charge to corporation tax for the payment period

(1) This section applies where the payer is within the charge to corporation tax for the payment period.

(2) For corporation tax purposes, the relevant deduction that may be deducted from the payer's income for the payment period is reduced by an amount equal to the hybrid transfer deduction/non-inclusion mismatch mentioned in section 259DA(5).

259DG Counteraction where a payee is within the charge to corporation tax

(1) This section applies in relation to a payee where—

(a) the payee is within the charge to corporation tax for an accounting period some or all of which falls within the payment period, and
(b) it is reasonable to suppose that—

(i) neither section 259DF nor any equivalent provision under the law of a territory outside the United Kingdom applies, or
(ii) a provision of the law of a territory outside the United Kingdom that is equivalent to section 259DF applies, but does not fully counteract the hybrid transfer deduction/non-inclusion mismatch mentioned in section 259DA(5).

(2) A provision of the law of a territory outside the United Kingdom that is equivalent to section 259DF does not fully counteract that mismatch if (and only if)—

(a) it does not reduce the relevant deduction by the full amount of the mismatch, and
(b) the payer is still able to deduct some of the relevant deduction from income in calculating taxable profits.

(3) In this section "the relevant amount" is—

(a) in a case where subsection (1)(b)(i) applies, an amount equal to the hybrid transfer deduction/non-inclusion mismatch mentioned in section 259DA(5), or
(b) in a case where subsection (1)(b)(ii) applies, the lesser of—

(i) the amount by which that mismatch exceeds the amount by which it is reasonable to suppose the relevant deduction is reduced by a provision under the law of a territory outside the United Kingdom that is equivalent to section 259DF, and
(ii) the amount of the relevant deduction that may still be deducted as mentioned in subsection (2)(b).

(4) If the payee is the only payee, the relevant amount is to be treated as income arising to the payee for the counteraction period.

(5) If there is more than one payee, an amount equal to the payee's share of the relevant amount is to be treated as income arising to the payee for the counteraction period.

(6) The payee's share of the relevant amount is to be determined by apportioning that amount between all the payees on a just and reasonable basis, having regard (in particular)—

(a) to any arrangements as to profit sharing that may exist between some or all of the payees,
(b) to whom any under-taxed amounts (within the meaning given by section 259DC(6)) arise, and
(c) to whom any amounts of ordinary income that it would be reasonable to expect to arise as a result of the payment or quasi-payment, but that do not arise, would have arisen.

(7) An amount of income that is treated as arising under subsection (4) or (5) is chargeable under Chapter 8 of Part 10 of CTA 2009 (income not otherwise charged) (despite section 979(2) of that Act).

(8) The "counteraction period" means—

(a) if an accounting period of the payee coincides with the payment period, that accounting period, or
(b) otherwise, the first accounting period of the payee that is wholly or partly within the payment period.

CHAPTER 5

HYBRID PAYER DEDUCTION/NON-INCLUSION MISMATCHES

Introduction

259E Overview of Chapter

(1) This Chapter contains provision that counteracts deduction/non-inclusion mismatches that it is reasonable to suppose would otherwise arise from payments or quasi-payments because the payer is a hybrid entity.

(2) The Chapter counteracts mismatches where the payer or a payee is within the charge to corporation tax and does so by altering the corporation tax treatment of the payer or a payee.

(3) Section 259EA contains the conditions that must be met for this Chapter to apply.

(4) Section 259EB defines "hybrid payer deduction/non-inclusion mismatch" and provides how the amount of the mismatch is to be calculated.

(5) Section 259EC contains provision that counteracts the mismatch where the payer is within the charge to corporation tax for the payment period.

(6) Section 259ED contains provision that counteracts the mismatch where a payee is within the charge to corporation tax and the mismatch is not fully counteracted by provision under the law of a territory outside the United Kingdom that is equivalent to section 259EC.

(7) See also—

(a) section 259BB for the meaning of "payment", "quasi-payment", "payment period", "relevant deduction", "payer" and "payee", and
(b) section 259BE for the meaning of "hybrid entity", "investor" and "investor jurisdiction".

Application of Chapter

259EA Circumstances in which the Chapter applies

(1) This Chapter applies if conditions A to E are met.

(2) Condition A is that a payment or quasi-payment is made under, or in connection with, an arrangement.

(3) Condition B is that the payer is a hybrid entity ("the hybrid payer").

(4) Condition C is that—

(a) the hybrid payer is within the charge to corporation tax for the payment period, or
(b) a payee is within the charge to corporation tax for an accounting period some or all of which falls within the payment period.

(5) Condition D is that it is reasonable to suppose that, disregarding the provisions mentioned in subsection (6), there would be a hybrid payer deduction/non-inclusion mismatch in relation to the payment or quasi-payment (see section 259EB).

(6) The provisions are—

(a) this Chapter and Chapters 6 to 10, and
(b) any equivalent provision under the law of a territory outside the United Kingdom.

(7) Condition E is that—

(a) it is a quasi-payment that is made as mentioned in subsection (2) and the hybrid payer is also a payee (see section 259BB(7)),
(b) the hybrid payer and a payee are in the same control group (see section 259NB) at any time in the period—

(i) beginning with the day on which the arrangement mentioned in subsection (2) is made, and
(ii) ending with the last day of the payment period, or
(c) that arrangement is a structured arrangement.

(8) The arrangement is "structured" if it is reasonable to suppose that—

(a) the arrangement is designed to secure a hybrid payer deduction/non-inclusion mismatch, or
(b) the terms of the arrangement share the economic benefit of the mismatch between the parties to the arrangement or otherwise reflect the fact that the mismatch is expected to arise.

(9) The arrangement may be designed to secure a hybrid payer deduction/non-inclusion mismatch despite also being designed to secure any commercial or other objective.

(10) Sections 259EC (cases where the hybrid payer is within the charge to corporation tax for the payment period) and 259ED (cases where a payee is within the charge to corporation tax) contain provision for the counteraction of the hybrid payer deduction/non-inclusion mismatch.

259EB Hybrid payer deduction/non-inclusion mismatches and their extent

(1) There is a "hybrid payer deduction/non-inclusion mismatch", in relation to a payment or quasi-payment, if—

(a) the relevant deduction exceeds the sum of the amounts of ordinary income that, by reason of the payment or quasi-payment, arise to each payee for a permitted taxable period, and

(b) all or part of that excess arises by reason of the hybrid payer being a hybrid entity.

(2) The amount of the hybrid payer deduction/non-inclusion mismatch is equal to the excess that arises as mentioned in subsection (1)(b).

(3) For the purposes of subsection (1)(b)—

(a) it does not matter whether the excess or part arises for another reason as well (even if it would have arisen for that other reason regardless of whether the hybrid payer is a hybrid entity), and

(b) an excess or part of an excess is to be taken to arise by reason of the hybrid payer being a hybrid entity (so far as would not otherwise be the case) if, on making such of the relevant assumptions in relation to each payee as apply in relation to that payee (see subsection (4)), it could arise by reason of the hybrid payer being a hybrid entity.

(4) These are the "relevant assumptions"—

(a) where a payee is not within the charge to a tax under the law of a payee jurisdiction because the payee benefits from an exclusion, immunity, exemption or relief (however described) under that law, assume that the exclusion, immunity, exemption or relief does not apply;

(b) where an amount of income is not included in the ordinary income of a payee for the purposes of a tax charged under the law of a payee jurisdiction because the payment or quasi-payment is not made in connection with a business carried on by the payee in that jurisdiction, assume that the payment or quasi-payment is made in connection with such a business.

(5) A taxable period of a payee is "permitted" in relation to an amount of ordinary income that arises as a result of the payment or quasi-payment if—

(a) the period begins before the end of 12 months after the end of the payment period, or

(b) where the period begins after that—

(i) a claim has been made for the period to be a permitted period in relation to the amount of ordinary income, and

(ii) it is just and reasonable for the amount of ordinary income to arise for that taxable period rather than an earlier period.

Counteraction

259EC Counteraction where the hybrid payer is within the charge to corporation tax for the payment period

(1) This section applies where the hybrid payer is within the charge to corporation tax for the payment period.

(2) For corporation tax purposes, the relevant deduction so far as it does not exceed the hybrid payer deduction/non-inclusion mismatch mentioned in section 259EA(5) ("the restricted deduction") may not be deducted from the hybrid payer's income for the payment period unless it is deducted from dual inclusion income for that period.

(3) So much of the restricted deduction (if any) as, by virtue of subsection (2), cannot be deducted from the payer's income for the payment period—

(a) is carried forward to subsequent accounting periods of the payer, and

(b) for corporation tax purposes, may be deducted from dual inclusion income for any such period (and not from any other income), so far as it cannot be deducted under this paragraph for an earlier period.

(4) In this section "dual inclusion income" of the payer for an accounting period means an amount that arises in connection with the arrangement mentioned in section 259EA(2) and is both—

(a) ordinary income of the payer for that period for corporation tax purposes, and
(b) ordinary income of an investor in the payer for a permitted taxable period for the purposes of any tax charged under the law of an investor jurisdiction.

(5) A taxable period of an investor is "permitted" for the purposes of paragraph (b) of subsection (4) if—

(a) the period begins before the end of 12 months after the end of the accounting period mentioned in paragraph (a) of that subsection, or
(b) where the period begins after that—

(i) a claim has been made for the period to be a permitted period in relation to the amount of ordinary income, and
(ii) it is just and reasonable for the amount of ordinary income to arise for that taxable period rather than an earlier period.

259ED Counteraction where a payee is within the charge to corporation tax

(1) This section applies in relation to a payee where—

(a) the payee is within the charge to corporation tax for an accounting period some or all of which falls within the payment period, and
(b) it is reasonable to suppose that—

(i) no provision under the law of a territory outside the United Kingdom that is equivalent to section 259EC applies, or
(ii) such a provision does apply, but does not fully counteract the hybrid payer deduction/non-inclusion mismatch mentioned in section 259EA(5).

(2) A provision of the law of a territory outside the United Kingdom that is equivalent to section 259EC does not fully counteract that mismatch if (and only if)—

(a) the amount of the relevant deduction that the provision prevents from being deducted from income of the hybrid payer, for the payment period, other than dual inclusion income, is less than the amount of the mismatch, and
(b) the hybrid payer is still able to deduct some of the relevant deduction from income, for the payment period, that is not dual inclusion income.

(3) In this section "the relevant amount" is—

(a) in a case where subsection (1)(b)(i) applies, an amount equal to the hybrid payer deduction/non-inclusion mismatch mentioned in section 259EA(5), or
(b) in a case where subsection (1)(b)(ii) applies, the lesser of—

(i) the amount by which that mismatch exceeds the amount of the relevant deduction that it is reasonable to suppose is prevented, by a provision of the law of a territory outside the United Kingdom that is equivalent to section 259EC, from being deducted from income of the hybrid payer, for the payment period, other than dual inclusion income, and
(ii) the amount of the relevant deduction that may still be deducted as mentioned in subsection (2)(b).

(4) If the payee is the only payee, an amount equal to—

(a) the relevant amount, less
(b) any dual inclusion income,

is to be treated as income arising to the payee for the counteraction period.

(5) If there is more than one payee, an amount equal to—

(a) the payee's share of the relevant amount, less
(b) the relevant proportion of any dual inclusion income,

is to be treated as income arising to the payee for the counteraction period.

(6) The payee's share of the relevant amount is to be determined by apportioning that amount between all the payees on a just and reasonable basis, having regard (in particular)—

(a) to any arrangements as to profit sharing that may exist between some or all of the payees, and
(b) to whom any amounts of ordinary income that it would be reasonable to expect to arise as a result of the payment or quasi-payment, but that do not arise, would have arisen.

(7) The "relevant" proportion of any dual inclusion income for the payment period is the same as the proportion of the relevant amount apportioned to the payee in accordance with subsection (6).

(8) An amount of income that is treated as arising under subsection (4) or (5) is chargeable under Chapter 8 of Part 10 of CTA 2009 (income not otherwise charged) (despite section 979(2) of that Act).

(9) In this section—

"counteraction period" means—

(a) if an accounting period of the payee coincides with the payment period, that accounting period, or

(b) otherwise, the first accounting period of the payee that is wholly or partly within the payment period;

"dual inclusion income" means an amount that arises in connection with the arrangement mentioned in section 259EA(2) and is both—

(a) ordinary income of the payer for the payment period, and

(b) ordinary income of an investor in the payer for a permitted taxable period for the purposes of a tax charged under the law of an investor jurisdiction.

(10) A taxable period of an investor is "permitted" for the purposes of subsection (9) if—

(a) the period begins before the end of 12 months after the end of the payment period, or

(b) where the period begins after that—

(i) a claim has been made for the period to be a permitted period in relation to the amount of ordinary income, and

(ii) it is just and reasonable for the amount of ordinary income to arise for that taxable period rather than an earlier period.

CHAPTER 6
DEDUCTION/NON-INCLUSION MISMATCHES RELATING TO TRANSFERS BY PERMANENT ESTABLISHMENTS

Introduction

259F Overview of Chapter

(1) This Chapter contains provision that counteracts certain excessive deductions that arise in relation to transfers of money or money's worth made, or taken to be made, by a multinational company's permanent establishment in the United Kingdom to the company in the parent jurisdiction.

(2) The Chapter counteracts such deductions by altering the corporation tax treatment of the company.

(3) Section 259FA contains the conditions that must be met for this Chapter to apply.

(4) Subsection (3) of that section defines "multinational company" and "the parent jurisdiction".

(5) Subsection (8) of that section defines "the excessive PE deduction".

(6) Section 259FB contains provision for the counteraction of the excessive PE deduction.

(7) See also section 259BF for the meaning of "permanent establishment".

Application of Chapter

259FA Circumstances in which the Chapter applies

(1) This Chapter applies if conditions A to C are met.

(2) Condition A is that a company is a multinational company.

(3) For the purposes of this Chapter, a company is a multinational company if—

(a) it is resident in a territory outside the United Kingdom ("the parent jurisdiction") for the purposes of a tax charged under the law of that territory, and

(b) it is within the charge to corporation tax because it carries on a business in the United Kingdom through a permanent establishment in the United Kingdom.

(4) Condition B is that, disregarding the provisions mentioned in subsection (5), there is an amount ("the PE deduction") that—

(a) may (in substance) be deducted from the company's income for the purposes of calculating the company's taxable profits for an accounting period ("the relevant PE period") for corporation tax purposes, and

(b) is in respect of a transfer of money or money's worth from the company in the United Kingdom to the company in the parent jurisdiction that—

(i) is actually made, or

(ii) is (in substance) treated as being made for corporation tax purposes.

(5) The provisions are—

(a) this Chapter and Chapters 7 to 10, and

(b) any equivalent provision under the law of a territory outside the United Kingdom.

(6) Condition C is that it is reasonable to suppose that, disregarding the provisions mentioned in subsection (5)—

(a) the circumstances giving rise to the PE deduction will not result in—

(i) an increase in the taxable profits of the company for any permitted taxable period, or

(ii) a reduction of a loss made by the company for any permitted taxable period,

for the purposes of a tax charged under the law of the parent jurisdiction, or

(b) those circumstances will result in such an increase or reduction for one or more permitted taxable periods, but the PE deduction exceeds the aggregate effect on taxable profits.

(7) "The aggregate effect on taxable profits" is the sum of—

(a) any increases, resulting from the circumstances giving rise to the PE deduction, in the taxable profits of the company, for a permitted taxable period, for the purposes of a tax charged under the law of the parent jurisdiction, and

(b) any amounts by which a loss made by the company, for a permitted taxable period, for the purposes of a tax charged under the law of the parent jurisdiction, is reduced as a result of the circumstances giving rise to the PE deduction.

(8) In this Chapter "the excessive PE deduction" means—

(a) where paragraph (a) of subsection (6) applies, the PE deduction, or

(b) where paragraph (b) of subsection (6) applies, the PE deduction so far as it is reasonable to suppose that it exceeds the aggregate effect on taxable profits.

(9) For the purposes of subsections (6) and (7) a taxable period of the company, for the purposes of a tax charged under the law of the parent jurisdiction, is "permitted" if—

(a) the period begins before the end of 12 months after the end of the relevant PE period, or

(b) where the period begins after that—

(i) a claim has been made for the period to be a permitted period for the purposes of subsections (6) and (7), and

(ii) it is just and reasonable for the circumstances giving rise to the PE deduction to affect the profits or loss made for that period rather than an earlier period.

(10) Section 259FB contains provision for counteracting the excessive PE deduction.

Counteraction

259FB Counteraction of the excessive PE deduction

(1) For corporation tax purposes, the excessive PE deduction may not be deducted from the company's income for the relevant PE period unless it is deducted from dual inclusion income for that period.

(2) So much of the excessive PE deduction (if any) as, by virtue of subsection (1), cannot be deducted from the company's income for the relevant PE period—

(a) is carried forward to subsequent accounting periods of the company, and

(b) for corporation tax purposes, may be deducted from dual inclusion income of the company for any such period (and not from any other income), so far as it cannot be deducted under this paragraph for an earlier period.

(3) In this section "dual inclusion income" of the company for an accounting period means an amount that is both—

(a) ordinary income of the company for that period for corporation tax purposes, and

(b) ordinary income of the company for a permitted taxable period for the purposes of a tax charged under the law of the parent jurisdiction.

(4) A taxable period of the company is "permitted" for the purposes of paragraph (b) of subsection (3) if—

(a) the period begins before the end of 12 months after the end of the accounting period mentioned in paragraph (a) of that subsection, or

(b) where the period begins after that—

(i) a claim has been made for the period to be a permitted period in relation to the amount of ordinary income, and

(ii) it is just and reasonable for the amount of ordinary income to arise for that taxable period rather than an earlier period.

CHAPTER 7

HYBRID PAYEE DEDUCTION/NON-INCLUSION MISMATCHES

Introduction

259G Overview of Chapter

(1) This Chapter contains provision that counteracts deduction/non-inclusion mismatches that it is reasonable to suppose would otherwise arise from payments or quasi-payments because a payee is a hybrid entity.

(2) The Chapter counteracts mismatches by—

(a) altering the corporation tax treatment of the payer for the payment period,

(b) treating income chargeable to corporation tax as arising to an investor who is within the charge to corporation tax, or

(c) treating income chargeable to corporation tax as arising to a payee that is a hybrid entity and a limited liability partnership.

(3) Section 259GA contains the conditions that must be met for this Chapter to apply.

(4) Section 259GB defines "hybrid payee deduction/non-inclusion mismatch" and provides how the amount of the mismatch is to be calculated.

(5) Section 259GC contains provision that counteracts the mismatch where the payer is within the charge to corporation tax for the payment period.

(6) Section 259GD contains provision that counteracts the mismatch where an investor in the payee is within the charge to corporation tax and the mismatch is not fully counteracted by section 259GC or an equivalent provision under the law of a territory outside the United Kingdom.

(7) Section 259GE contains provision that counteracts the mismatch where a payee is a hybrid entity and limited liability partnership and the mismatch is not otherwise fully counteracted.

(8) See also—

(a) section 259BB for the meaning of "payment", "quasi-payment", "payment period", "relevant deduction", "payer" and "payee";

(b) section 259BE for the meaning of "hybrid entity", "investor" and "investor jurisdiction".

Application of Chapter

259GA Circumstances in which the Chapter applies

(1) This Chapter applies if conditions A to E are met.

(2) Condition A is that a payment or quasi-payment is made under, or in connection with, an arrangement.

(3) Condition B is that a payee is a hybrid entity (a "hybrid payee").

(4) Condition C is that—

(a) the payer is within the charge to corporation tax for the payment period,

(b) an investor in a hybrid payee is within the charge to corporation tax for an accounting period some or all of which falls within the payment period, or

(c) a hybrid payee is a limited liability partnership.

(5) Condition D is that it is reasonable to suppose that, disregarding the provisions mentioned in subsection (6), there would be a hybrid payee deduction/non-inclusion mismatch in relation to the payment or quasi-payment (see section 259GB).

(6) The provisions are—

(a) this Chapter and Chapters 8 to 10, and

(b) any equivalent provision under the law of a territory outside the United Kingdom.

(7) Condition E is that—

(a) it is a quasi-payment that is made as mentioned in subsection (2) and the payer is also a hybrid payee (see section 259BB(7)),

(b) the payer and a hybrid payee or an investor in a hybrid payee are in the same control group (see section 259NB) at any time in the period—

(i) beginning with the day on which the arrangement mentioned in subsection (2) is made, and

(ii) ending with the last day of the payment period, or

(c) that arrangement is a structured arrangement.

(8) The arrangement is "structured" if it is reasonable to suppose that—

(a) the arrangement is designed to secure a hybrid payee deduction/non-inclusion mismatch, or

(b) the terms of the arrangement share the economic benefit of the mismatch between the parties to the arrangement or otherwise reflect the fact that the mismatch is expected to arise.

(9) The arrangement may be designed to secure a hybrid payee deduction/non-inclusion mismatch despite also being designed to secure any commercial or other objective.

(10) The following provisions contain provision for the counteraction of the hybrid payee deduction/non-inclusion mismatch—

(a) section 259GC (cases where the payer is within the charge to corporation tax for the payment period),

(b) section 259GD (cases where an investor in a hybrid payee is within the charge to corporation tax), and

(c) section 259GE (cases where a hybrid payee is a limited liability partnership).

259GB Hybrid payee deduction/non-inclusion mismatches and their extent

(1) There is a "hybrid payee deduction/non-inclusion mismatch", in relation to a payment or quasi-payment, if—

(a) the relevant deduction exceeds the sum of the amounts of ordinary income that, by reason of the payment or quasi-payment, arise to each payee for a permitted taxable period, and

(b) all or part of that excess arises by reason of one or more payees being hybrid entities.

(2) The extent of the hybrid payee deduction/non-inclusion mismatch is equal to the excess that arises as mentioned in subsection (1)(b).

(3) A relevant amount of the excess is to be taken (so far as would not otherwise be the case) to arise as mentioned in subsection (1)(b) where—

(a) a payee is a hybrid entity,

(b) there is no territory—

(i) where that payee is resident for the purposes of a tax charged under the law of that territory, or

(ii) under the law of which ordinary income arises to that payee, by reason of the payment or quasi-payment, for the purposes of a tax that is charged on that payee by virtue of that payee having a permanent establishment in that territory, and

(c) no income arising to that payee, by reason of the payment or quasi-payment, is brought into account in calculating chargeable profits for the purposes of the CFC charge or a foreign CFC charge.

(4) For the purposes of subsection (3), the "relevant amount" of the excess is the lesser of—

(a) the amount of the excess, and

(b) an amount equal to the amount of ordinary income that it is reasonable to suppose would, by reason of the payment or quasi-payment, arise to the payee for corporation tax purposes, if—

(i) the payee were a company, and

(ii) the payment or quasi-payment were made in connection with a trade carried on by the payee in the United Kingdom through a permanent establishment in the United Kingdom.

(5) In subsection (3)(c) "chargeable profits"—

(a) in relation to the CFC charge, has the same meaning as in Part 9A (see section 371VA), and

(b) in relation to a foreign CFC charge, means the concept (by whatever name known) corresponding to chargeable profits within the meaning of that Part.

(6) A taxable period of a payee is "permitted" in relation to an amount of ordinary income that arises as a result of the payment or quasi-payment if—

(a) the period begins before the end of 12 months after the end of the payment period, or

(b) where the period begins after that—

    (i) a claim has been made for the period to be a permitted period in relation to the amount of ordinary income, and

    (ii) it is just and reasonable for the amount of ordinary income to arise for that taxable period rather than an earlier period.

Counteraction

259GC Counteraction where the payer is within the charge to corporation tax for the payment period

(1) This section applies where the payer is within the charge to corporation tax for the payment period.

(2) For corporation tax purposes, the relevant deduction that may be deducted from the payer's income for the payment period is reduced by an amount equal to the hybrid payee deduction/non-inclusion mismatch mentioned in section 259GA(5).

259GD Counteraction where the investor is within the charge to corporation tax

(1) This section applies in relation to an investor in a hybrid payee where—

(a) the investor is within the charge to corporation tax for an accounting period some or all of which falls within the payment period, and

(b) it is reasonable to suppose that—

    (i) neither section 259GC nor any equivalent provision under the law of a territory outside the United Kingdom applies, or

    (ii) a provision of the law of a territory outside the United Kingdom that is equivalent to section 259GC applies, but does not fully counteract the hybrid payee deduction/non-inclusion mismatch mentioned in section 259GA(5).

(2) A provision of the law of a territory outside the United Kingdom that is equivalent to section 259GC does not fully counteract that mismatch if (and only if)—

(a) it does not reduce the relevant deduction by the full amount of the mismatch, and

(b) the payer is still able to deduct some of the relevant deduction from income in calculating taxable profits.

(3) In this section "the relevant amount" is—

(a) in a case where subsection (1)(b)(i) applies, an amount equal to the hybrid payee deduction/non-inclusion mismatch, or

(b) in a case where subsection (1)(b)(ii) applies, the lesser of—

    (i) the amount by which that mismatch exceeds the amount by which it is reasonable to suppose the relevant deduction is reduced by a provision of the law of a territory outside the United Kingdom that is equivalent to section 259GC, and

    (ii) the amount of the relevant deduction that may still be deducted as mentioned in subsection (2)(b).

(4) If the investor is the only investor in the hybrid payee, the appropriate proportion of the relevant amount is to be treated as income arising to the investor for the counteraction period.

(5) If there is more than one investor in the hybrid payee, an amount equal to the investor's share of the appropriate proportion of the relevant amount is to be treated as income arising to the investor for the counteraction period.

(6) For the purposes of subsections (4) and (5) the "appropriate proportion of the relevant amount"—

(a) if the hybrid payee is the only hybrid payee, is all of the relevant amount, or

(b) if there is more than one hybrid payee, is the proportion of the relevant amount apportioned to the hybrid payee upon an apportionment of that amount between all the hybrid payees on a just and reasonable basis having regard (in particular) to—

    (i) any arrangements as to profit sharing that may exist between some or all of the payees, and

    (ii) the extent to which it is reasonable to suppose that the hybrid payee deduction/non-inclusion mismatch mentioned in section 259GA(5) arises by reason of each hybrid payee being a hybrid entity.

(7) The investor's share of the appropriate proportion of the relevant amount is to be determined by apportioning that proportion of that amount between all the investors in the hybrid payee on a just and reasonable basis, having regard (in particular) to any arrangements as to profit sharing that may exist between some or all of those investors.

(8) An amount of income that is treated as arising under subsection (4) or (5) is chargeable under Chapter 8 of Part 10 of CTA 2009 (income not otherwise charged) (despite section 979(23) of that Act).

(9) The "counteraction period" means—

(a) if an accounting period of the investor coincides with the payment period, that accounting period, or

(b) otherwise, the first accounting period of the investor that is wholly or partly within the payment period.

259GE Counteraction where a hybrid payee is an LLP

(1) This section applies in relation to a hybrid payee where the hybrid payee is a limited liability partnership and it is reasonable to suppose that—

(a) none of the following provisions applies—

(i) section 259GC;

(ii) section 259GD;

(iii) any provision under the law of a territory outside the United Kingdom that is equivalent to either of those sections, or

(b) one or more of those provisions apply, but the hybrid payee deduction/non-inclusion mismatch mentioned in section 259GA(5) is not fully counteracted.

(2) The mismatch is not fully counteracted if (and only if), after the application of such of those provisions as apply—

(a) the relevant deduction is not reduced by the full amount of the mismatch,

(b) the payer is still able to deduct some of the relevant deduction from income in calculating taxable profits, and

(c) the lesser of—

(i) the difference between the amount of the mismatch and the amount by which it is reasonable to suppose the relevant deduction is reduced, and

(ii) the amount of the relevant deduction that may still be deducted,

exceeds the sum of any amounts of income treated as arising under section 259GD or any equivalent provision under the law of a territory outside the United Kingdom.

(3) In this section "the relevant amount" is—

(a) in a case where subsection (1)(a) applies, an amount equal to the hybrid payee deduction/non-inclusion mismatch mentioned in section 259GA(5), or

(b) in a case where subsection (1)(b) applies, an amount equal to the excess mentioned in subsection (2)(c).

(4) If the hybrid payee is the only hybrid payee, an amount equal to the relevant amount is to be treated as income arising to the hybrid payee on the last day of the payment period.

(5) If there is more than one hybrid payee, an amount equal to the hybrid payee's share of the relevant amount is to be treated as income arising to the hybrid payee on the last day of the payment period.

(6) The hybrid payee's share of the relevant amount is to be determined by apportioning that amount between all the hybrid payees on a just and reasonable basis, having regard (in particular) to—

(a) any arrangements as to profit sharing that may exist between some or all of the payees, and

(b) the extent to which it is reasonable to suppose that the hybrid payee deduction/non-inclusion mismatch mentioned in section 259GA(5) arises by reason of each hybrid payee being a hybrid entity.

(7) An amount of income that is treated as arising under subsection (4) or (5) is chargeable to corporation tax on the hybrid payee (as opposed to being chargeable to tax on any of its members) under Chapter 8 of Part 10 of CTA 2009 (income not otherwise charged) (despite section 979(2) of that Act).

(8) Section 863 of ITTOIA 2005 (treatment of certain limited liability partnerships for income tax purposes) and section 1273 of CTA 2009 (treatment of certain limited liability partnerships for corporation tax purposes) are disapplied in relation to the hybrid payee to the extent necessary for the purposes of subsection (7).

(9) This section is to be disregarded for the purposes of determining whether the hybrid payee is within the charge to corporation tax for the purposes of any other provision of this Part, except section 259M (anti-avoidance).

CHAPTER 8
MULTINATIONAL PAYEE DEDUCTION/NON-INCLUSION MISMATCHES

Introduction

259H Overview of Chapter

(1) This Chapter contains provision that counteracts deduction/non-inclusion mismatches that it is reasonable to suppose would otherwise arise from payments or quasi-payments, where the payer is within the charge to corporation tax, because a payee is multinational company.

(2) The Chapter counteracts mismatches by altering the corporation tax treatment of the payer.

(3) Section 259HA contains the conditions that must be met for this Chapter to apply.

(4) Subsection (4) of that section defines "multinational company", "parent jurisdiction" and "PE jurisdiction".

(5) Section 259HB defines "multinational payee deduction/non-inclusion mismatch" and provides how the amount of the mismatch is to be calculated.

(6) Section 259HC contains provision that counteracts the mismatch.

(7) See also—

(a) section 259BB for the meaning of "payment", "quasi-payment", "payment period", "relevant deduction", "payer" and "payee";
(b) section 259BF for the meaning of "permanent establishment".

Application of Chapter

259HA Circumstances in which the Chapter applies

(1) This Chapter applies if conditions A to E are met.

(2) Condition A is that a payment or quasi-payment is made under, or in connection with, an arrangement.

(3) Condition B is that a payee is a multinational company.

(4) For the purposes of this Chapter, a company is a "multinational company" if—

(a) it is resident in a territory ("the parent jurisdiction") for tax purposes under the law of that territory, and
(b) it is regarded as carrying on a business in another territory ("the PE jurisdiction") through a permanent establishment in that territory (whether it is so regarded under the law of the parent jurisdiction, the PE jurisdiction or any other territory).

(5) Condition C is that the payer is within the charge to corporation tax for the payment period.

(6) Condition D is that it is reasonable to suppose that, disregarding the provisions mentioned in subsection (7), there would be a multinational payee deduction/non-inclusion mismatch in relation to the payment or quasi-payment (see section 259HB).

(7) The provisions are—

(a) this Chapter and Chapters 9 and 10, and
(b) any equivalent provision under the law of a territory outside the United Kingdom.

(8) Condition E is that—

(a) it is a quasi-payment that is made as mentioned in subsection (2) and the payer is also a payee (see section 259BB(7)),
(b) the payer and the multinational company are in the same control group (see section 259NB) at any time in the period—

(i) beginning with the day on which the arrangement mentioned in subsection (2) is made, and
(ii) ending with the last day of the payment period, or

(c) that arrangement is a structured arrangement.

(9) The arrangement is "structured" if it is reasonable to suppose that—

(a) the arrangement is designed to secure a multinational company deduction/non-inclusion mismatch, or

(b) the terms of the arrangement share the economic benefit of the mismatch between the parties to the arrangement or otherwise reflect the fact that the mismatch is expected to arise.

(10) The arrangement may be designed to secure a multinational payee deduction/non-inclusion mismatch despite also being designed to secure any commercial or other objective.

(11) Section 259HC contains provision for the counteraction of the multinational payee deduction/non-inclusion mismatch.

259HB Multinational payee deduction/non-inclusion mismatches and their extent

(1) There is a "multinational payee deduction/non-inclusion mismatch", in relation to a payment or quasi-payment, if—

(a) the relevant deduction exceeds the sum of the amounts of ordinary income that, by reason of the payment or quasi-payment, arise to each payee for a permitted taxable period, and

(b) all or part of that excess arises by reason of one or more payees being multinational companies.

(2) The extent of the multinational payee deduction/non-inclusion mismatch is equal to the excess that arises as mentioned in subsection (1)(b).

(3) For the purposes of subsection (1)(b)—

(a) where the law of a PE jurisdiction in relation to a payee that is a multinational company makes no provision for charging tax on any companies, so much of the excess as arises as a result is to be taken not to arise by reason of that payee being a multinational company, but

(b) subject to that, it does not matter whether the excess or part arises for another reason as well as one or more payees being multinational companies (even if it would have arisen for that other reason regardless of whether any payees are multinational companies).

(4) A taxable period of a payee is "permitted" in relation to an amount of ordinary income that arises as a result of the payment or quasi-payment if—

(a) the period begins before the end of 12 months after the end of the payment period, or

(b) where the period begins after that—

(i) a claim has been made for the period to be a permitted period in relation to the amount of ordinary income, and

(ii) it is just and reasonable for the amount of ordinary income to arise for that taxable period rather than an earlier period.

Counteraction

259HC Counteraction of the multinational payee deduction/non-inclusion mismatch

For corporation tax purposes, the relevant deduction that may be deducted from the payer's income for the payment period is reduced by an amount equal to the multinational payee deduction/non-inclusion mismatch mentioned in section 259HA(6).

CHAPTER 9
HYBRID ENTITY DOUBLE DEDUCTION MISMATCHES

Introduction

259I Overview of Chapter

(1) This Chapter contains provision that counteracts double deduction mismatches that it is reasonable to suppose would otherwise arise by reason of a person being a hybrid entity.

(2) The Chapter counteracts mismatches where the hybrid entity, or an investor in the hybrid entity, is within the charge to corporation tax and does so by altering the corporation tax treatment of the entity or investor.

(3) Section 259IA contains the conditions that must be met for this Chapter to apply.

(4) Subsection (4) of that section defines "hybrid entity double deduction amount".

(5) Section 259IB contains provision that counteracts the mismatch where an investor in the hybrid entity is within the charge to corporation tax.

(6) Section 259IC contains provision that, in certain circumstances, counteracts the mismatch where the hybrid entity is within the charge to corporation tax and the mismatch is not fully counteracted by provision under the law of a territory outside the United Kingdom that is equivalent to section 259IB.

(7) See also section 259BE for the meaning of "hybrid entity", "investor" and "investor jurisdiction".

Application of Chapter

259IA Circumstances in which the Chapter applies

(1) This Chapter applies if conditions A to C are met.

(2) Condition A is that there is an amount or part of an amount that, disregarding the provisions mentioned in subsection (3), it is reasonable to suppose—

(a) could be deducted from the income of a hybrid entity for the purposes of calculating the taxable profits of that entity for a taxable period ("the hybrid entity deduction period"), and
(b) could also be deducted, under the law of the investor jurisdiction, from the income of an investor in the hybrid entity for the purposes of calculating the taxable profits of that investor for a taxable period ("the investor deduction period").

(3) The provisions are—

(a) this Chapter and Chapter 10, and
(b) any equivalent provision under the law of a territory outside the United Kingdom.

(4) In this Chapter the amount or part of an amount mentioned in subsection (2) is referred to as "the hybrid entity double deduction amount".

(5) Condition B is that—

(a) the investor is within the charge to corporation tax for the investor deduction period, or
(b) the hybrid entity is within the charge to corporation tax for the hybrid entity deduction period.

(6) Condition C is that—

(a) the hybrid entity and any investor in it are related (see section 259NC) at any time
(i) in the hybrid entity deduction period, or
(ii) in the investor deduction period, or
(b) an arrangement, to which the hybrid entity or any investor in it is party, is a structured arrangement.

(7) An arrangement is "structured" if it is reasonable to suppose that—

(a) the arrangement is designed to secure the hybrid entity double deduction amount, or
(b) the terms of the arrangement share the economic benefit of that amount being deductible by both the hybrid entity and the investor between the parties to the arrangement or otherwise reflect the fact that the amount is expected to arise.

(8) The arrangement may be designed to secure the hybrid entity double deduction amount despite also being designed to secure any commercial or other objective.

(9) Sections 259IB (cases where the investor is within the charge to corporation tax for the investor deduction period) and 259IC (cases where the hybrid entity is within the charge to corporation tax for the hybrid entity deduction period) contain provision for the counteraction of the hybrid entity double deduction amount.

Counteraction

259IB Counteraction where the investor is within the charge to corporation tax

(1) This section applies in relation to the investor in the hybrid entity where the investor is within the charge to corporation tax for the investor deduction period.

(2) For corporation tax purposes, the hybrid entity double deduction amount may not be deducted from the investor's income for the investor deduction period unless it is deducted from dual inclusion income of the investor for that period.

(3) So much of the hybrid entity double deduction amount (if any) as, by virtue of subsection (2), cannot be deducted from the investor's income for the investor deduction period—

(a) is carried forward to subsequent accounting periods of the investor, and

(b) for corporation tax purposes, may be deducted from dual inclusion income of the investor for any such period (and not from any other income), so far as it cannot be deducted under this paragraph for an earlier period.

(4) If the Commissioners are satisfied that the investor will have no dual inclusion income—

(a) for an accounting period after the investor deduction period ("the relevant period"), nor

(b) for any accounting period after the relevant period,

any of the hybrid entity double deduction amount that has not been deducted from dual inclusion income for an accounting period before the relevant period in accordance with subsection (2) or (3) ("the stranded deduction") may be deducted at step 2 in section 4(2) of CTA 2010 in calculating the investor's taxable total profits of the relevant period.

(5) So much of the stranded deduction (if any) as cannot be deducted, in accordance with subsection (4), at step 2 in section 4(2) of CTA 2010 in calculating the investor's taxable total profits of the relevant period—

(a) is carried forward to subsequent accounting periods of the investor, and

(b) may be so deducted for any such period, so far as it cannot be deducted under this paragraph for an earlier period.

(6) Subsection (7) applies if it is reasonable to suppose that all or part of the hybrid entity double deduction amount is (in substance) deducted ("the illegitimate overseas deduction"), under the law of a territory outside the United Kingdom, from income of any person, for a taxable period, that is not dual inclusion income of the investor for an accounting period.

(7) For the purposes of determining how much of the hybrid entity double deduction amount may be deducted (if any) for the accounting period of the investor in which the taxable period mentioned in subsection (6) ends, and any subsequent accounting periods of the investor, an amount of it equal to the illegitimate overseas deduction is to be taken to have already been deducted for a previous accounting period of the investor.

(8) In this section "dual inclusion income" of the investor for an accounting period means an amount that is both—

(a) ordinary income of the investor for that period for corporation tax purposes, and

(b) ordinary income of the hybrid entity for a permitted taxable period for the purposes of any tax under the law of a territory outside the United Kingdom.

(9) A taxable period of the hybrid entity is "permitted" for the purposes of paragraph (b) of subsection (8) if—

(a) the period begins before the end of 12 months after the end of the accounting period of the investor mentioned in paragraph (a) of that subsection, or

(b) where the period begins after that—

(i) a claim has been made for the period to be a permitted period in relation to the amount of ordinary income, and

(ii) it is just and reasonable for the amount of ordinary income to arise for that taxable period rather than an earlier period.

259IC Counteraction where the hybrid entity is within the charge to corporation tax

(1) This section applies where—

(a) the hybrid entity is within the charge to corporation tax for the hybrid entity deduction period,

(b) it is reasonable to suppose that—

(i) no provision under the law of an investor jurisdiction that is equivalent to section 259IB applies, or

(ii) such a provision does apply, but the hybrid entity double deduction amount exceeds the amount that, under that provision, cannot be deducted from income, for the investor deduction period, other than dual inclusion income of the hybrid entity for the hybrid entity deduction period, and

(c) the secondary counteraction condition is met.

(2) The secondary counteraction condition is met if—

(a) the hybrid entity and any investor in it are in the same control group (see section 259NB) at any time in—

(i) the hybrid entity deduction period, or

(ii) the investor deduction period, or

(b) there is an arrangement, to which the hybrid entity or any investor in it is party, that is a structured arrangement (within the meaning given by section 259IA(7) and (8)).

(3) In this section "the restricted deduction" means—

(a) in a case where subsection (1)(b)(i) applies, the hybrid entity double deduction amount, or

(b) in a case where subsection (1)(b)(ii) applies, the hybrid entity double deduction amount so far as it exceeds the amount that it is reasonable to suppose, under a provision of the law of a territory outside the United Kingdom that is equivalent to section 259IB, cannot be deducted from income, for the investor deduction period, other than dual inclusion income of the hybrid entity for the hybrid entity deduction period.

(4) For corporation tax purposes, the restricted deduction may not be deducted from the hybrid entity's income for the hybrid entity deduction period unless it is deducted from dual inclusion income for that period.

(5) So much of the restricted deduction (if any) as, by virtue of subsection (4), cannot be deducted from the hybrid entity's income for the hybrid entity deduction period—

(a) is carried forward to subsequent accounting periods of the hybrid entity, and

(b) for corporation tax purposes, may be deducted from dual inclusion income of the hybrid entity for any such period (and not from any other income), so far as it cannot be deducted under this paragraph for an earlier period.

(6) If the Commissioners are satisfied that the hybrid entity will have no dual inclusion income –

(a) for an accounting period after the hybrid entity deduction period ("the relevant period"), nor

(b) for any accounting period after the relevant period,

any of the restricted deduction that has not been deducted from dual inclusion income for an accounting period before the relevant period in accordance with subsection (4) or (5) ("the stranded deduction") may be deducted at step 2 in section 4(2) of CTA 2010 in calculating the hybrid entity's taxable total profits of the relevant period.

(7) So much of the stranded deduction (if any) as cannot be deducted, in accordance with subsection (6), at step 2 in section 4(2) of CTA 2010 in calculating the hybrid entity's taxable total profits of the relevant period—

(a) is carried forward to subsequent accounting periods of the hybrid entity, and

(b) may be so deducted for any such period, so far as it cannot be deducted under this paragraph for an earlier period.

(8) Subsection (9) applies if it is reasonable to suppose that all or part of the hybrid entity double deduction amount is (in substance) deducted ("the illegitimate overseas deduction"), under the law of a territory outside the United Kingdom, from income of any person, for a taxable period, that is not dual inclusion income of the hybrid entity for an accounting period.

(9) For the purposes of determining how much of the hybrid entity double deduction amount may be deducted (if any) for the accounting period of the hybrid entity in which the taxable period mentioned in subsection (8) ends, and any subsequent accounting periods of the hybrid entity, an amount of it equal to the illegitimate overseas deduction is to be taken to have already been deducted for a previous accounting period of the hybrid entity.

(10) In this section "dual inclusion income" of the hybrid entity for an accounting period means an amount that is both—

(a) ordinary income of the hybrid entity for that period for corporation tax purposes, and

(b) ordinary income of an investor in the hybrid entity for a permitted taxable period for the purposes of any tax charged under the law of an investor jurisdiction.

(11) A taxable period of an investor is "permitted" for the purposes of paragraph (b) of subsection (10) if—

(a) the period begins before the end of 12 months after the end of the accounting period mentioned in paragraph (a) of that subsection, or

(b) where the period begins after that—

(i) a claim has been made for the period to be a permitted period in relation to the amount of ordinary income, and

(ii) it is just and reasonable for the amount of ordinary income to arise for that taxable period rather than an earlier period.

CHAPTER 10
DUAL TERRITORY DOUBLE DEDUCTION CASES

Introduction

259J Overview of Chapter

(1) This Chapter contains provision that counteracts double deduction mismatches that it is reasonable to suppose would otherwise arise as a result of a company—

(a) being a dual resident company, or

(b) being a relevant multinational company.

(2) The counteraction operates by altering the corporation tax treatment of the company.

(3) Section 259JA contains the conditions that must be met for this Chapter to apply.

(4) Subsection (3) of that section defines "dual resident company".

(5) Subsection (4) of that section defines "relevant multinational company", "parent jurisdiction" and "PE jurisdiction".

(6) Subsection (5) of that section defines "dual territory double deduction amount".

(7) Section 259JB contains provision that counteracts the mismatch where the company is a dual resident company.

(8) Section 259JC contains provision that counteracts the mismatch where the company is a multinational company and the United Kingdom is the parent jurisdiction.

(9) Section 259JD contains provision that counteracts the mismatch where the company is a relevant multinational company, the United Kingdom is the PE jurisdiction and the mismatch is not counteracted under a provision of the law of a territory outside the United Kingdom that is equivalent to section 259JC.

(10) See also section 259BF for the meaning of "permanent establishment".

Application of Chapter

259JA Circumstances in which the Chapter applies

(1) This Chapter applies if conditions A and B are met.

(2) Condition A is that a company is a—

(a) dual resident company, or

(b) relevant multinational company.

(3) For the purposes of this Chapter a company is a "dual resident company" if—

(a) it is UK resident, and

(b) it is also within the charge to a tax under the law of a territory outside the United Kingdom because—

(i) it derives its status as a company from that law,

(ii) its place of management is in that territory, or

(iii) it is for some other reason treated under that law as resident in that territory for the purposes of that tax.

(4) For the purposes of this Chapter a company is a "relevant multinational company" if—

(a) it is within the charge to a tax, under the law of a territory ("the PE jurisdiction") in which it is not resident for tax purposes, because it carries on business in that territory through a permanent establishment in that territory, and

(b) either—

(i) the PE jurisdiction is the United Kingdom, or

(ii) the territory in which the company is resident for tax purposes ("the parent jurisdiction") is the United Kingdom.

(5) Condition B is that there is an amount ("the dual territory double deduction amount") that, disregarding this Chapter and any equivalent provision under the law of a territory outside the United Kingdom, it is reasonable to suppose could, by reason of the company being a dual resident company or a relevant multinational company—

(a) be deducted from the company's income for an accounting period ("the deduction period") for corporation tax purposes, and

(b) also be deducted from the company's income for a taxable period ("the foreign deduction period") for the purposes of a tax charged under the law of a territory outside the United Kingdom.

(6) The following provisions provide for the counteraction of the dual territory double deduction amount—

(a) section 259JB (cases where a company is dual resident),

(b) section 259JC (cases where a company is a relevant multinational and the United Kingdom is the parent jurisdiction), and

(c) section 259JD (cases where a company is a relevant multinational, the United Kingdom is the PE jurisdiction and the amount is not counteracted in the parent jurisdiction).

Counteraction

259JB Counteraction where mismatch arises because of a dual resident company

(1) This section applies where the dual territory double deduction amount arises by reason of the company being a dual resident company.

(2) For corporation tax purposes, the dual territory double deduction amount may not be deducted from the company's income for the deduction period unless it is deducted from dual inclusion income of the company for that period.

(3) So much of the dual territory double deduction amount (if any) as, by virtue of subsection (2), cannot be deducted from the company's income for the deduction period—

(a) is carried forward to subsequent accounting periods of the company, and

(b) for corporation tax purposes, may be deducted from dual inclusion income of the company for any such period (and not from any other income), so far as it cannot be deducted under this paragraph for an earlier period.

(4) If the Commissioners are satisfied that the company has ceased to be a dual resident company, any of the dual territory double deduction amount that has not been deducted from dual inclusion income in accordance with subsection (2) or (3) ("the stranded deduction") may be deducted at step 2 in section 4(2) of CTA 2010 in calculating the company's taxable total profits of the accounting period in which it ceased to be a dual resident company.

(5) So much of the stranded deduction (if any) as cannot be deducted, in accordance with subsection (4), at step 2 in section 4(2) of CTA 2010 in calculating the company's taxable total profits of the accounting period in which the company ceased to be a dual resident company—

(a) is carried forward to subsequent accounting periods of the company, and

(b) may be so deducted for any such period, so far as it cannot be deducted under this paragraph for an earlier period.

(6) Subsection (7) applies if it is reasonable to suppose that all or part of the dual territory double deduction amount is (in substance) deducted ("the illegitimate overseas deduction"), under the law of a territory outside the United Kingdom, from income of any person, for a taxable period, that is not dual inclusion income of the company for an accounting period.

(7) For the purposes of determining how much of the dual territory double deduction amount may be deducted (if any) for the accounting period of the company in which the taxable period mentioned in subsection (6) ends, and any subsequent accounting periods of the company, an amount of it equal to the illegitimate overseas deduction is to be taken to have already been deducted for a previous accounting period of the company.

(8) In this section "dual inclusion income" of the company for an accounting period means an amount that is both—

(a) ordinary income of the company for that period for corporation tax purposes, and

(b) ordinary income of the company for a permitted taxable period for the purposes of a tax charged under the law of a territory outside the United Kingdom.

(9) A taxable period of the company is "permitted" for the purposes of paragraph (b) of subsection (8) if—

(a) the period begins before the end of 12 months after the end of the accounting period mentioned in paragraph (a) of that subsection, or

(b) where the period begins after that—

(i) a claim has been made for the period to be a permitted period in relation to the amount of ordinary income, and

(ii) it is just and reasonable for the amount of ordinary income to arise for that taxable period rather than an earlier period.

259JC Counteraction where mismatch arises because of a relevant multinational and the UK is the parent jurisdiction

(1) This section applies where—

(a) the dual territory double deduction amount arises by reason of the company being a relevant multinational company, and

(b) the United Kingdom is the parent jurisdiction.

(2) If some or all of the dual territory double deduction amount is (in substance) deducted ("the impermissible overseas deduction"), for the purposes of a tax under the law of a territory outside the United Kingdom, from the income of any person, that is not dual inclusion income of the company—

(a) the dual territory double deduction amount that may be deducted, for corporation tax purposes, from the company's income for the deduction period is reduced by the amount of the impermissible overseas deduction, and

(b) such just and reasonable adjustments (if any) as are required to give effect to that reduction, for corporation tax purposes, are to be made.

(3) Any adjustment required to be made under subsection (2) may be made (whether or not by an officer of Revenue and Customs)—

(a) by way of an assessment, the modification of an assessment, amendment or disallowance of a claim, or otherwise, and

(b) despite any time limit imposed by or under any enactment.

(4) In this section "dual inclusion income" of the company means an amount that is both—

(a) ordinary income of the company for an accounting period for corporation tax purposes, and

(b) ordinary income of the company for a permitted taxable period for the purposes of a tax charged under the law of a territory outside the United Kingdom.

(5) A taxable period is "permitted" for the purposes of paragraph (b) of subsection (4) if—

(a) the period begins before the end of 12 months after the end of the accounting period of the company mentioned in paragraph (a) of that subsection, or

(b) where the period begins after that—

(i) a claim has been made for the period to be a permitted period in relation to the amount of ordinary income, and

(ii) it is just and reasonable for the amount of ordinary income to arise for that taxable period rather than an earlier period.

259JD Counteraction where mismatch arises because of a relevant multinational and is not counteracted in the parent jurisdiction

(1) This section applies where—

(a) the dual territory double deduction amount arises as a result of the company being a relevant multinational company,

(b) the United Kingdom is the PE jurisdiction, and

(c) it is reasonable to suppose that no provision of the law of the parent jurisdiction that is equivalent to section 259JC applies.

(2) For corporation tax purposes, the dual territory double deduction amount may not be deducted from the company's income for the deduction period unless it is deducted from dual inclusion income of the company for that period.

(3) So much of the dual territory double deduction amount (if any) as, by virtue of subsection (2), cannot be deducted from the company's income for the deduction period—

(a) is carried forward to subsequent accounting periods of the company, and

(b) for corporation tax purposes, may be deducted from dual inclusion income of the company for any such period (and not from any other income), so far as it cannot be deducted under this paragraph for an earlier period.

(4) If the Commissioners are satisfied that the company has ceased to be a relevant multinational company, any of the dual territory double deduction amount that has not been deducted from dual inclusion income in accordance with subsection (2) or

(3) ("the stranded deduction") may be deducted at step 2 in section 4(2) of CTA 2010 in calculating the company's taxable total profits of the accounting period in which it ceased to be a relevant multinational company.

(5) So much of the stranded deduction (if any) as cannot be deducted, in accordance with subsection (4), at step 2 in section 4(2) of CTA 2010 in calculating the company's taxable total profits of the accounting period in which the company ceased to be a relevant multinational company—

(a) is carried forward to subsequent accounting periods of the company, and
(b) may be so deducted for any such period, so far as it cannot be deducted under this paragraph for an earlier period.

(6) Subsection (7) applies if it is reasonable to suppose that all or part of the dual territory double deduction amount is (in substance) deducted ("the illegitimate overseas deduction"), under the law of a territory outside the United Kingdom, from income of any person, for a taxable period, that is not dual inclusion income of the company for an accounting period.

(7) For the purposes of determining how much of the dual territory double deduction amount may be deducted (if any) for the accounting period of the company in which the taxable period mentioned in subsection (6) ends, and any subsequent accounting periods of the company, an amount of it equal to the illegitimate overseas deduction is to be taken to have already been deducted for a previous accounting period of the company.

(8) In this section "dual inclusion income" of the company for an accounting period means an amount that is both –

(a) ordinary income of the company for that period for corporation tax purposes, and
(b) ordinary income of the company for a permitted taxable period for the purposes of a tax charged under the law of a territory outside the United Kingdom.

(9) A taxable period of the company is "permitted" for the purposes of paragraph (b) of subsection (8) if—

(a) the period begins before the end of 12 months after the end of the accounting period mentioned in paragraph (a) of that subsection, or
(b) where the period begins after that—

(i) a claim has been made for the period to be a permitted period in relation to the amount of ordinary income, and
(ii) it is just and reasonable for the amount of ordinary income to arise for that taxable period rather than an earlier period.

CHAPTER 11
IMPORTED MISMATCHES

Introduction

259K Overview of Chapter

(1) This Chapter contains provision denying deductions in connection with payments or quasi-payments that are made under, or in connection with, imported mismatch arrangements where the payer is within the charge to corporation tax for the payment period.

(2) Section 259KA contains the conditions that must be met for this Chapter to apply and defines "imported mismatch payment" and "imported mismatch arrangement".

(3) Section 259KB defines "dual territory double deduction", "excessive PE deduction" and "PE jurisdiction".

(4) Section 259KC contains provision for denying some or all of a relevant deduction in relation to an imported mismatch payment.

(5) See also section 259BB for the meaning of "payment", "quasi-payment", "relevant deduction", "payment period" and "payer".

Application of Chapter

259KA Circumstances in which the Chapter applies

(1) This Chapter applies if conditions A to G are met.

(2) Condition A is that a payment or quasi-payment ("the imported mismatch payment") is made under, or in connection with, an arrangement ("the imported mismatch arrangement").

(3) Condition B is that, in relation to the imported mismatch payment, the payer ("P") is within the charge to corporation tax for the payment period.

(4) Condition C is that the imported mismatch arrangement is one of a series of arrangements.

(5) A "series of arrangements" means a number of arrangements that are each entered into (whether or not one after the other) in pursuance of, or in relation to, another arrangement ("the over-arching arrangement").

(6) Condition D is that—

(a) under an arrangement in the series other than the imported mismatch arrangement, there is a payment or quasi-payment ("the mismatch payment") in relation to which it is reasonable to suppose that there is or will be—

(i) a hybrid or otherwise impermissible deduction/non-inclusion mismatch (see section 259CB),
(ii) a hybrid transfer deduction/non-inclusion mismatch (see section 259DC),
(iii) a hybrid payer deduction/non-inclusion mismatch (see section 259EB),
(iv) a hybrid payee deduction/non-inclusion mismatch (see section 259GB),
(v) a multinational payee deduction/non-inclusion mismatch (see section 259HB),
(vi) a hybrid entity double deduction amount (see section 259IA(4)), or
(vii) a dual territory double deduction (see section 259KB), or

(b) as a consequence of an arrangement in the series other than the imported mismatch arrangement, there is or will be an excessive PE deduction (see section 259KB),

and in this Chapter "the relevant mismatch" means the mismatch, amount or deduction concerned.

(7) Condition E is that it is reasonable to suppose—

(a) where subsection (6)(a) applies, that no provision of any of Chapters 3 to 5 or 7 to 10 nor any equivalent provision under the law of a territory outside the United Kingdom applies, or will apply, in relation to the tax treatment of any person in respect of the mismatch payment, or
(b) where subsection (6)(b) applies, that no provision of Chapter 6 nor any equivalent provision under the law of a territory outside the United Kingdom applies, or will apply, in relation to the tax treatment of the company in relation to which the excessive PE deduction arises.

(8) Condition F is that—

(a) subsection (6)(a) applies and it is reasonable to suppose that a provision of any of Chapters 3 to 5 or 7 to 10, or an equivalent provision under the law of a territory outside the United Kingdom, would apply in relation to the tax treatment of P if—

(i) P were the payer in relation to the mismatch payment,
(ii) P were a payee in relation to the mismatch payment, or
(iii) where the relevant mismatch is a hybrid payee deduction/non-inclusion mismatch or a hybrid entity double deduction amount, P were an investor in the hybrid entity concerned, or

(b) the relevant mismatch is an excessive PE deduction.

(9) Condition G is that—

(a) subsection (6)(a) applies and P is in the same control group (see section 259NB) as the payer, or a payee, in relation to the mismatch payment, at any time in the period—

(i) beginning with the day the over-arching arrangement is made, and
(ii) ending with the last day of the payment period in relation to the imported mismatch payment,

(b) subsection (6)(b) applies and P is in the same control group as the company in relation to whom the excessive PE deduction arises at any time in that period, or
(c) the imported mismatch arrangement, or the over-arching arrangement, is a structured arrangement.

(10) The imported mismatch arrangement, or the over-arching arrangement, is a "structured arrangement" if it is reasonable to suppose that—

(a) the arrangement concerned is designed to secure the relevant mismatch, or
(b) the terms of the arrangement concerned share the economic benefit of the relevant mismatch between the parties to that arrangement or otherwise reflect the fact that the relevant mismatch is expected to arise.

(11) An arrangement may be designed to secure the relevant mismatch despite also being designed to secure any commercial or other objective.

(12) Section 259KC contains provision for denying all or part of the relevant deduction in relation to the imported mismatch payment by reference to the relevant mismatch.

259KB Meaning of "dual territory double deduction", "excessive PE deduction" and "PE jurisdiction"

(1) This section has effect for the purposes of this Chapter.

(2) A "dual territory double deduction" means an amount that can be deducted by a company both—

(a) from income for the purposes of a tax charged under the law of one territory, and

(b) from income for the purposes of a tax charged under the law of another territory.

(3) A "PE deduction" is an amount that—

(a) may (in substance) be deducted from a company's income for the purposes of calculating the company's taxable profits, for a taxable period, for the purposes of a tax that is charged on the company, under the law of a territory ("the PE jurisdiction"), by virtue of the company having a permanent establishment in that territory, and

(b) is in respect of a transfer of money or money's worth, from the company in the PE jurisdiction to the company in another territory ("the parent jurisdiction") in which it is resident for the purposes of a tax, that—

(i) is actually made, or

(ii) is (in substance) treated as being made for tax purposes.

(4) A PE deduction is "excessive" so far as it exceeds the sum of—

(a) any increases, resulting from the circumstances giving rise to the PE deduction, in the taxable profits of the company, for a permitted taxable period, for the purposes of a tax charged under the law of the parent jurisdiction, and

(b) any amounts by which a loss made by the company, for a permitted taxable period, for the purposes of a tax charged under the law of the parent jurisdiction, is reduced as a result of the circumstances giving rise to the PE deduction.

(5) A taxable period of the company is "permitted" for the purposes of subsection (4) if—

(a) the period begins before the end of 12 months after the end of the taxable period mentioned in subsection (3)(a), or

(b) where the period begins after that—

(i) a claim has been made for the period to be a permitted period for the purposes of subsection (4), and

(ii) it is just and reasonable for the circumstances giving rise to the PE deduction to affect the profits or loss made for that period rather than an earlier period.

Counteraction

259KC Denial of the relevant deduction in relation to the imported mismatch payment

(1) If, in addition to the imported mismatch payment, there are, or will be, one or more relevant payments in relation to the relevant mismatch, subsection (3) applies.

(2) Otherwise, for corporation tax purposes, in relation to the imported mismatch payment, the relevant deduction that may be deducted from P's income for the payment period is to be reduced by the amount of the relevant mismatch.

(3) For corporation tax purposes, where this subsection applies, in relation to the imported mismatch payment, the relevant deduction that may be deducted from P's income for the payment period is to be reduced by P's share of the relevant mismatch.

(4) P's share of the relevant mismatch is to be determined by apportioning the relevant mismatch between P and every payer in relation to a relevant payment on a just and reasonable basis—

(a) where subsection (6)(a) applies, having regard (in particular) to the extent to which the imported mismatch payment and each relevant payment funds (directly or indirectly) the mismatch payment, or

(b) where the relevant mismatch is an excessive PE deduction, having regard (in particular) to—

(i) if the transfer of money or money's worth mentioned in section 259KB(3)(b) is actually made, the extent to which the imported mismatch payment and each relevant payment funds (directly or indirectly) the transfer, or

(ii) if the transfer of money or money's worth mentioned in section 259KB(3)(b) is (in substance) treated as being made, the extent to which the imported mismatch payment and each relevant payment would have funded (directly or indirectly) the transfer if it had actually been made.

(5) For the purposes of subsection (4)(a) and (b)(i), the imported mismatch payment is to be taken to fund the mismatch payment or transfer to the extent that the mismatch payment or transfer cannot be shown instead to be funded (directly or indirectly) by one or more relevant payments.

(6) For the purposes of subsection (4)(b)(ii), it is to be assumed that the imported mismatch payment would have funded the transfer if it had actually been made to the extent that it cannot be shown by P that, if it had been made, the transfer would have instead been funded (directly or indirectly) by one or more relevant payments.

(7) For the purposes of this section, a payment or quasi-payment, other than the imported mismatch payment or any mismatch payment, is a "relevant payment" in relation to the relevant mismatch if it is made under an arrangement in the series of arrangements mentioned in section 259KA(4) and—

(a) where subsection (6)(a) applies, it funds (directly or indirectly) the mismatch payment,

(b) where the relevant mismatch is an excessive PE deduction and the transfer of money or money's worth mentioned in section 259KB(3)(b) is actually made, it funds (directly or indirectly) that transfer, or

(c) where the relevant mismatch is an excessive PE deduction and the transfer of money or money's worth mentioned in section 259KB(3)(b) is (in substance) treated as being made, it would have funded (directly or indirectly) that transfer had that transfer actually been made.

(8) In proceedings before a court or tribunal in connection with this section—

(a) in relation to subsection (1), it is for P to show that, in addition to the imported mismatch payment, there are one or more relevant payments in relation to the relevant mismatch, and

(b) in relation to subsection (5), it is for P to show that the mismatch payment or transfer is funded (directly or indirectly) by one or more relevant payments instead of by the imported mismatch payment.

CHAPTER 12

ADJUSTMENTS IN LIGHT OF SUBSEQUENT EVENTS ETC

259L Adjustments where suppositions cease to be reasonable

(1) Where—

(a) a reasonable supposition is made for the purposes of any provision of this Part, and

(b) the supposition turns out to be mistaken or otherwise ceases to be reasonable,

such consequential adjustments as are just and reasonable may be made.

(2) The adjustments may be made (whether or not by an officer of Revenue and Customs) by way of an assessment, the modification of an assessment, amendment or disallowance of a claim, or otherwise.

(3) But the power to make adjustments by virtue of this section is subject to any time limit imposed by or under any enactment other than this Part.

(4) No adjustment is to be made under this section on the basis that an amount of ordinary income arises, as a result of a payment or quasi-payment, to a payee after that payee's last permitted taxable period in relation to the payment or quasi-payment (see section 259LA, which makes provision about certain such cases).

259LA Deduction from taxable total profits where an amount of ordinary income arises late

(1) This section applies where—

(a) a relevant deduction in respect of a payment or quasi-payment is reduced by section 259CD, 259DF, 259GC or 259HC or by more than one of those sections,

(b) no other provision of this Part, or any equivalent provision of the law of a territory outside the United Kingdom, applies or will apply to the tax treatment of any person in respect of the payment or quasi-payment,

(c) the section or sections had effect because it was reasonable to suppose that the relevant deduction exceeded, or would exceed, the sum of the amounts of ordinary income arising, by reason of the payment or quasi-payment, to each payee for a permitted taxable period, and

(d) an amount of ordinary income ("the late income") arises—

(i) by reason of the payment or quasi-payment, but

(ii) not as a consequence of any provision of this Part or any equivalent provision of the law of a territory outside the United Kingdom,

to a payee for a taxable period ("the late period") that is not a permitted taxable period.

(2) An amount equal to the late income may be deducted at step 2 in section 4(2) of CTA 2010 in calculating the payer's taxable total profits of the accounting period in which the late period ends.

(3) So much of that amount (if any) as cannot be deducted, in accordance with subsection (2), at step 2 in section 4(2) of CTA 2010 in calculating the taxable total profits of the accounting period in which the late period ends—

(a) is carried forward to subsequent accounting periods of the payer, and

(b) may be so deducted for any such period, so far as it cannot be deducted under this paragraph for an earlier period.

(4) But the total amount deducted from taxable total profits under this section, in relation to a payment or quasi-payment, may not exceed the total amount by which the relevant deduction is reduced as mentioned in (1)(a).

(5) In this section "permitted taxable period"—

(a) where the relevant deduction was reduced under section 259CD, has the meaning given by section 259CC(2),

(b) where the relevant deduction was reduced under section 259DF, has the meaning given by section 259DD(2),

(c) where the relevant deduction was reduced under section 259GC, has the meaning given by section 259GB(6),

(d) where the relevant deduction was reduced under section 259HC, has the meaning given by section 259HB(4), or

(e) where the relevant deduction was reduced under two or more of the sections mentioned in the preceding paragraphs of this subsection, includes any taxable period that is a permitted period under a provision mentioned in the paragraphs concerned.

CHAPTER 13

ANTI-AVOIDANCE

259M Countering the effect of avoidance arrangements

(1) This section applies where—

(a) relevant avoidance arrangements exist,

(b) as a result of those arrangements, any person (whether party to the arrangements or not) would, apart from this section, obtain a relevant tax advantage, and

(c) that person is—

(i) within the charge to corporation tax at the time the person would obtain the relevant tax advantage, or

(ii) would be within the charge to corporation tax at that time but for the relevant avoidance arrangements.

(2) The relevant tax advantage is to be counteracted by making such adjustments to the person's treatment for corporation tax purposes as are just and reasonable.

(3) Any adjustments required to be made under this section (whether or not by an officer of Revenue and Customs) may be made by way of an assessment, the modification of an assessment, amendment or disallowance of a claim, or otherwise.

(4) A person obtains a "relevant tax advantage" if—

(a) the person avoids, to any extent, any provision of this Part, or any equivalent provision of the law of a territory outside the United Kingdom, restricting whether or how that person may make a deduction from income for the purposes of calculating taxable profits, or

(b) the person avoids, to any extent, an amount being treated as income of that person under any provision of this Part or any equivalent provision of the law of a territory outside the United Kingdom.

(5) "Relevant avoidance arrangements" means arrangements the main purpose, or one of the main purposes, of which is to enable any person to obtain a relevant tax advantage.

(6) But arrangements are not "relevant avoidance arrangements" if the obtaining of the relevant tax advantage can reasonably be regarded as consistent with the

principles on which the provisions of this Part, or the equivalent provisions under the law of a territory outside the United Kingdom, that are relevant to the arrangements are based (whether express or implied) and the policy objectives of those provisions.

(7) For the purposes of determining the principles and policy objectives mentioned in subsection (6), regard may, where appropriate, be had to the Final Report on Neutralising the Effects of Hybrid Mismatch Arrangements published by the Organisation for Economic Cooperation and Development ("OECD") on 5 October 2015 or any replacement or supplementary publication.

(8) In subsection (7) "replacement or supplementary publication" means any document that is approved and published by the OECD in place of, or to update or supplement, the report mentioned in that subsection (or any replacement of, or supplement to, it).

CHAPTER 14

INTERPRETATION

Financial instruments

259N Meaning of "financial instrument"

(1) A "financial instrument" means—

(a) an arrangement profits or deficits arising from which would, on the assumption that the person to whom they arise is within the charge to corporation tax, fall to be brought into account for corporation tax purposes in accordance with Part 5 or 6 of CTA 2009 (loan relationships and relationships treated as loan relationships),

(b) a contract profits or losses arising from which would, on the assumption that the person to whom they arise is within the charge to corporation tax, fall to be brought into account for corporation tax purposes in accordance with Part 7 of CTA 2009 (derivative contracts),

(c) a type 1, type 2 or type 3 finance arrangement for the purposes of Chapter 2 of Part 16 of CTA 2010 (factoring of income etc: finance arrangements),

(d) a share forming part of a company's issued share capital or any arrangement that provides a person with economic rights corresponding to those provided by holding such a share, or

(e) anything else that is a financial instrument.

(2) In subsection (1)(e) "financial instrument" has the meaning that it has for the purposes of UK generally accepted accounting practice.

(3) But "financial instrument" does not include—

(a) a hybrid transfer arrangement (within the meaning given by section 259DB), or

(b) anything that is a regulatory capital security for the purposes of the Taxation of Regulatory Capital Securities Regulations 2013 (SI 2013/3209) (as amended from time to time).

(4) Subsection (3)(b) is subject to any provision to the contrary that may be made by regulations under section 221 of FA 2012 (tax consequences of financial sector regulation).

Relevant investment funds

259NA Meaning of "relevant investment fund"

(1) "Relevant investment fund" means—

(a) an open-ended investment company within the meaning of section 613 of CTA 2010,

(b) an authorised unit trust within the meaning of section 616 of that Act, or

(c) an offshore fund within the meaning of section 354 of this Act (see section 355),

which meets the genuine diversity of ownership condition (whether or not a clearance has been given to that effect).

(2) "The genuine diversity of ownership condition" means—

(a) in the case of an offshore fund, the genuine diversity of ownership condition in regulation 75 of the Offshore Funds (Tax) Regulations 2009 (SI 2009/3001), and

(b) in the case of an open-ended investment company or an authorised unit trust, the genuine diversity of ownership condition in regulation 9A of the Authorised Investment Funds (Tax) Regulations 2006 (SI 2006/964).

Control groups and related persons

259NB Control groups

(1) A person ("A") is in the same control group as another person ("B")—

(a) throughout any period for which they are consolidated for accounting purposes,

(b) on any day on which the participation condition is met in relation to them, or

(c) on any day on which the 50% investment condition is met in relation to them.

(2) A and B are consolidated for accounting purposes for a period if—

(a) their financial results for the period are required to be comprised in group accounts,

(b) their financial results for the period would be required to be comprised in group accounts but for the application of an exemption, or

(c) their financial results for the period are in fact comprised in group accounts.

(3) In subsection (2), "group accounts" means accounts prepared under—

(a) section 399 of the Companies Act 2006, or

(b) any corresponding provision of the law of a territory outside the United Kingdom.

(4) The participation condition is met in relation to A and B ("the relevant parties") on a day if, within the period of 6 months beginning with the day –

(a) one of the relevant parties directly or indirectly participates in the management, control or capital of the other, or

(b) the same person or persons directly or indirectly participate in the management, control or capital of each of the relevant parties.

(5) For the interpretation of subsection (4), see sections 157(1), 158(4), 159(1) and 160(1) (which have the effect that references in subsection (4) to direct or indirect participation are to be read in accordance with provisions of Chapter 2 of Part 4).

(6) The 50% investment condition is met in relation to A and B if—

(a) A has a 50% investment in B, or

(b) a third person has a 50% investment in each of A and B.

(7) Section 259ND applies for the purposes of determining whether a person has a "50% investment" in another person.

259NC Related persons

(1) Two persons are "related" on any day that—

(a) they are in the same control group (see section 259NB), or

(b) the 25% investment condition is met in relation to them.

(2) The 25% investment condition is met in relation to a person ("A") and another person ("B") if—

(a) A has a 25% investment in B, or

(b) a third person has a 25% investment in each of A and B.

(3) Section 259ND applies for the purposes of determining whether a person has a "25% investment" in another person.

259ND Meaning of "50% investment" and "25% investment"

(1) Where this section applies for the purposes of determining whether a person has a "50% investment" in another person for the purposes of section 259NB(6), references in this section to X% are to be read as references to 50%.

(2) Where this section applies for the purposes of determining whether a person has a "25% investment" in another person for the purposes of section 259NC(2), references in this section to X% are to be read as references to 25%.

(3) A person ("P") has an X% investment in a company ("C") if it is reasonable to suppose that—

(a) P possesses or is entitled to acquire X% or more of the share capital or issued share capital of C,

(b) P possesses or is entitled to acquire X% or more of the voting power in C, or

(c) if the whole of C's share capital were disposed of, P would receive (directly or indirectly and whether at the time of disposal or later) X% or more of the proceeds of the disposal.

(4) A person ("P") has an X% investment in another person ("Q") if it is reasonable to suppose that—

(a) if the whole of Q's income were distributed, P would receive (directly or indirectly and whether at the time of the distribution or later) X% or more of the distributed amount, or

(b) in the event of a winding-up of Q or in any other circumstances, P would receive (directly or indirectly and whether or not at the time of the winding-up or other circumstances or later) X% or more of Q's assets which would then be available for distribution.

(5) In this section, references to a person receiving any proceeds, amount or assets include references to the proceeds, amount or assets being applied (directly or indirectly) for that person's benefit.

(6) For the purposes of subsections (3) and (4), in determining what percentage investment a person ("P") has in another person ("U"), where P acts together with a third person ("T") in relation to U, P is to be taken to have all of T's rights and interests in relation to U.

(7) P is to be taken to "act together" with T in relation to U if (and only if)—

(a) P and T are connected (within the meaning given by section 163),

(b) for the purposes of influencing the conduct of U's affairs—

(i) P is able to secure that T acts in accordance with P's wishes,

(ii) T can reasonably be expected to act, or typically acts, in accordance with P's wishes,

(iii) T is able to secure that P acts in accordance with T's wishes, or

(iv) P can reasonably be expected to act, or typically acts, in accordance with T's wishes,

(c) P and T are party to any arrangement that—

(i) it is reasonable to suppose is designed to affect the value of any of T's rights or interests in relation to U, or

(ii) relates to the exercise of any of T's rights in relation to U, or

(d) the same person manages—

(i) some or all of P's rights or interests in relation to U, and

(ii) some or all of T's rights or interests in relation to U.

(8) But P does not "act together" with T in relation to U under paragraph (d) of subsection (7) where—

(a) the person who manages the rights or interests of P mentioned in sub-paragraph (i) of that paragraph, does so as the operator of a collective investment scheme,

(b) that person manages the rights or interests of T mentioned in sub-paragraph (ii) of that paragraph as the operator of a different collective investment scheme, and

(c) the Commissioners are satisfied that the management of the schemes is not coordinated for the purpose of influencing the conduct of U 's affairs.

(9) In subsection (8) "collective investment scheme" and "operator" have the same meaning as in Part · 17 of the Financial Services and Markets Act 2000 (see sections 235 and 237 of that Act).

Partnerships

259NE Treatment of a person who is a member of a partnership

(1) This section applies where a person is a member of a partnership.

(2) Any reference in this Part to income, profits or an amount of the person includes a reference to the person's share of (as the case may be) income, profits or an amount of the partnership.

(3) For this purpose "the person's share" of income, profits or an amount is determined by apportioning the income, profits or amount between the partners on a just and reasonable basis.

(4) In this section—

(a) "partnership" includes an entity established under the law of a territory outside the United Kingdom of a similar character to a partnership, and

(b) "member" of a partnership is to be read accordingly.

Definitions

259NF Definitions

In this Part—

"arrangement" includes any agreement, understanding, scheme, transaction or series of transactions (whether or not legally enforceable);

"CFC" and "CFC charge" have the meaning given by section 259B(4);

"the Commissioners" means the Commissioners for Her Majesty's Revenue and Customs;

"control group" has the meaning given by section 259NB;

"financial instrument" has the meaning given by section 259N;

"foreign CFC" and "foreign CFC charge" have the meaning given by section 259B(4);

"hybrid entity" has the meaning given by section 259BE;

"investor", in relation to a hybrid entity, has the meaning given by section 259BE(4);

"investor jurisdiction" has the meaning given by section 259BE(4);

"ordinary income" is to be read in accordance with sections 259BC and 259BD;

"payee"—

(a) in relation to a payment, has the meaning given by section 259BB(6)(a), and

(b) in relation to a quasi-payment, has the meaning given by section 259BB(6)(b);

"payee jurisdiction" has the meaning given by 259BB(9);

"payer"—

(a) in relation to a payment, has the meaning given by section 259BB(1)(a), and

(b) in relation to a quasi-payment, has the meaning given by section 259BB(2);

"payment" has the meaning given by section 259BB(1);

"payment period"—

(a) in relation to a payment, has the meaning given by section 259BB(1)(b), and

(b) in relation to a quasi-payment, has the meaning given by section 259BB(2);

"permanent establishment" has the meaning given by section 259BF;

"quasi-payment" has the meaning given by section 259BB(2) to (5);

"related" has the meaning given by section 259NC;

"relevant deduction"—

(a) in relation to a payment, has the meaning given by section 259BB(1)(b), and

(b) in relation to a quasi-payment, has the meaning given by section 259BB(2)(a);

"relevant investment fund" has the meaning given by section 259NA;

"tax" has the meaning given by section 259B;

"taxable period" means—

(a) in relation to corporation tax, an accounting period,

(b) in relation to income tax, a tax year,

(c) in relation to the CFC charge, a relevant corporation tax accounting period (within the meaning given by section 371BC(3)),

(d) in relation to a foreign CFC charge, a period (by whatever name known) that corresponds to a relevant corporation tax accounting period, and

(e) in relation to any other tax, a period for which the tax is charged;

"taxable profits" is to be read in accordance with sections 259BC(2) and 259BD(5)."

PART 2

CONSEQUENTIAL AMENDMENTS

FA 1998

2 Schedule 18 to FA 1998 (company tax returns) is amended as follows.

3 In paragraph 25(3)—

(a) insert "or" at the end of paragraph (b), and

(b) omit paragraph (d) and the "or" preceding it.

4 In paragraph 42(4)—

(a) insert "or" at the end of paragraph (a), and

(b) omit paragraph (c) and the "or" preceding it.

CTA 2009

5 In section A1 of CTA 2009 (overview of the Corporation Tax Acts), in subsection (2)—

(a) omit paragraph (h), and

(b) after that paragraph insert—
"(ha) Part 6A of that Act (hybrid and other mismatches),".

CTA 2010

6 CTA 2010 is amended as follows.

7 In section 938N (group mismatch schemes: priority)—
(a) omit paragraph (d), and
(b) after that paragraph insert—
"(da) Part 6A of that Act (hybrid and other mismatches);".

8 In section 938V (tax mismatch schemes: priority)—
(a) omit paragraph (c), and
(b) after that paragraph insert—
"(ca) Part 6A of TIOPA 2010 (hybrid and other mismatches);".

TIOPA 2010

9 TIOPA 2010 is amended as follows.

10 In section 1 (overview of Act), in subsection (1)—
(a) omit paragraph (c), and
(b) after that paragraph insert—
"(ca) Part 6A (hybrid and other mismatches),".

11 In section 157 (direct participation), in subsection (1)—
(a) omit the "and" at the end of paragraph (b), and
(b) after paragraph (c) insert ", and
(d) in Part 6A, section 259NB(4)."

12 In section 158 (indirect participation: defined by sections 159 to 162), in subsection (4)—
(a) omit the "and" at the end of paragraph (b), and
(b) after paragraph (c) insert ", and
(d) in Part 6A, section 259NB(4),".

13 In section 159 (indirect participation: potential direct participant), in subsection (1)—
(a) omit the "and" at the end of paragraph (b), and
(b) after paragraph (c) insert ", and
(d) in Part 6A, section 259NB(4)."

14 In section 160 (indirect participation: one of several major participants), in subsection (1)—
(a) omit the "and" at the end of paragraph (b), and
(b) after paragraph (c) insert ", and
(d) in Part 6A, section 259NB(4)."

15 Omit Part 6 (tax arbitrage).

16 Omit Part 4 of Schedule 11 (tax arbitrage: index of defined expressions used in Part 6).

17 After that Part of that Schedule insert—

"PART 4A

HYBRID AND OTHER MISMATCHES: INDEX OF DEFINED EXPRESSIONS USED IN PART 6A

arrangement (in Part 6A)	section 259NF
CFC and CFC charge (in Part 6A)	section 259B(4)
the Commissioners (in Part 6A)	section 259NF
control group (in Part 6A)	section 259NB
deduction period (in Chapter 10 of Part 6A)	section 259JA(5)(a)
dual resident company (in Chapter 10 of Part 6A)	section 259JA(3)
dual territory double deduction amount (in Chapter 10 of Part 6A)	section 259JA(5)
dual territory double deduction (in Chapter 11 of Part 6A)	section 259KB
excessive PE deduction (in Chapter 6 of Part 6A)	section 259FA(8)
excessive PE deduction (in Chapter 11 of Part 6A)	section 259KB
financial instrument (in Part 6A)	section 259N
foreign CFC and foreign CFC charge (in Part 6A)	section 259B(4)

foreign deduction period (in Chapter 10 of Part 6A)	section 259JA(5)(b)
hybrid entity (in Part 6A)	section 259BE
hybrid entity deduction period (in Chapter 9 of Part 6A)	section 259IA(2)(a)
hybrid entity double deduction amount (in Chapter 9 of Part 6A)	section 259IA(4)
hybrid or otherwise impermissible deduction/non-inclusion mismatch (in Chapter 3 of Part 6A)	section 259CB
hybrid payee (in Chapter 7 of Part 6A)	section 259GA(3)
hybrid payee deduction/non-inclusion mismatch (in Chapter 7 of Part 6A)	section 259GB
hybrid payer (in Chapter 5 of Part 6A)	section 259EA(3)
hybrid payer deduction/non-inclusion mismatch (in Chapter 5 of Part 6A)	section 259EB
hybrid transfer arrangement (in Chapter 4 of Part 6A)	section 259DB
hybrid transfer deduction/non-inclusion mismatch (in Chapter 4 of Part 6A)	section 259DC
imported mismatch payment (in Chapter 11 of Part 6A)	section 259KA(2)
imported mismatch arrangement (in Chapter 11 of Part 6A)	section 259KA(2)
investor (in Part 6A)	section 259BE(4)
investor deduction period (in Chapter 9 of Part 6A)	section 259IA(2)(b)
investor jurisdiction (in Part 6A)	section 259BE(4)
mismatch payment (in Chapter 11 of Part 6A)	section 259KA(6)
multinational company (in Chapter 6 of Part 6A)	section 259FA(3)
multinational company (in Chapter 8 of Part 6A)	section 259HA(4)
multinational payee deduction/non-inclusion mismatch (in Chapter 8 of Part 6A)	section 259HB
ordinary income (in Part 6A)	sections 259BC and 259BD
over arching arrangement (in Chapter 11 of Part 6A)	section 259KA(5)
P (in Chapter 11 of Part 6A)	section 259KA(3)
parent jurisdiction (in Chapter 6 of Part 6A)	section 259FA(3)(a)
parent jurisdiction (in Chapter 8 of Part 6A)	section 259HA(4)(a)
parent jurisdiction (in Chapter 10 of Part 6A)	section 259JA(4)(b)(ii)
payee (in Part 6A)	section 259BB(6)
payee jurisdiction (in Part 6A)	section 259BB(9)
payer (in Part 6A)	section 259BB(1)(a) or (2)
payment (in Part 6A)	section 259BB(1)
payment period (in Part 6A)	section 259BB(1)(b) or (2)
PE jurisdiction (in Chapter 8 of Part 6A)	section 259HA(4)(b)
PE jurisdiction (in Chapter 10 of Part 6A)	section 259JA(4)(a)
PE jurisdiction (in Chapter 11 of Part 6A)	section 259KB(3)(a)
permanent establishment (in Part 6A)	section 259BF
quasi-payment (in Part 6A)	section 259BB(2) to (5)
related (in Part 6A)	section 259NC
relevant deduction (in Part 6A)	section 259BB(1)(b) or (2)(a)
relevant investment fund (in Part 6A)	section 259NA
relevant mismatch (in Chapter 11 of Part 6A)	section 259KA(6)
relevant multinational company (in Chapter 10 of Part 6A)	section 259JA(4)
relevant PE period (in Chapter 6 of Part 6A)	section 259FA(4)
series of arrangements (in Chapter 11 of Part 6A)	section 259KA(5)
substitute payment (in Chapter 4 of Part 6A)	section 259DB(5)
tax (in Part 6A)	section 259B
taxable period (in Part 6A)	section 259NF
taxable profits (in Part 6A)	sections 259BC(2) and 259BD(3)
underlying instrument (in Chapter 4 of Part 6A)	section 259DB(3)
underlying return (in Chapter 4 of Part 6A)	section 259DB(5)(b)"

PART 3

COMMENCEMENT

18 Chapters 3 to 5 and 7 and 8 of Part 6A of TIOPA 2010 (counteraction of deduction/non-inclusion mismatches arising from payments and quasi-payments) have effect in relation to—

(a) payments made on or after the commencement date, and
(b) quasi-payments in relation to which the payment period begins on or after the commencement date.

19 Chapter 6 of Part 6A of TIOPA 2010 (counteraction of deduction/non-inclusion mismatches relating to intra-company transfers from permanent establishments) has effect in relation to excessive PE deductions in relation to which the relevant PE period begins on or after the commencement date.

20 Chapters 9 and 10 of Part 6A of TIOPA 2010 (counteraction of double deduction mismatches) have effect for accounting periods beginning on or after the commencement date.

21 Chapter 11 of Part 6A of TIOPA 2010 (imported mismatch payments) has effect in relation to imported mismatch payments that are—

(a) payments made on or after the commencement date, or
(b) quasi-payments in relation to which the payment period begins on or after the commencement date.

22 The following provisions of this Schedule have effect in relation to accounting periods beginning on or after the commencement date—

(a) paragraphs 2 to 4, and
(b) paragraphs 5(a), 7(a), 8(a), 10(a), 15 and 16.

23 For the purposes of paragraph 18 and 21, where a payment period begins before the commencement date and ends on or after that date ("the straddling period")—

(a) so much of the straddling period as falls before the commencement date, and so much of that period as falls on or after that date, are to be treated as separate taxable periods, and
(b) where it is necessary to apportion an amount for the straddling period to the two separate taxable periods, it is to be apportioned—

(i) on a time basis according to the respective length of the separate taxable periods, or
(ii) if that method would produce a result that is unjust or unreasonable, on a just and reasonable basis.

24 For the purposes of paragraphs 19, 20 and 22(b), where a company has an accounting period beginning before the commencement date and ending on or after that date ("the straddling period")—

(a) so much of the straddling period as falls before the commencement date, and so much of the straddling period as falls on or after that date, are to be treated as separate accounting periods, and
(b) where it is necessary to apportion an amount for the straddling period to the two separate accounting periods, it is to be apportioned—

(i) in accordance with section 1172 of CTA 2010 (time basis), or
(ii) if that method would produce a result that is unjust or unreasonable, on a just and reasonable basis.

25 In this Part of this Schedule "the commencement date" means 1 January 2017.

GENERAL NOTE

Schedule 10 inserts new Pt 6A TIOPA 2010 ("Hybrid and other mismatches"), which is a significant 14-chapter new piece of law. The origin of this law is the OECD/G20's Base Erosion and Profit Shifting ("BEPS") Project, which commenced in earnest in 2013. The BEPS Project was ordered into a number of separate working parties, each working on a common Action Plan. "Action 2" of the BEPS Project was focussed on neutralising the effects of "hybrid mismatch" arrangements. Hybrid mismatch arrangements, as contemplated by Working Party 11, are broadly those where the tax treatment of a transaction differs between jurisdictions, and the difference arises due to a hybrid element of the transaction (typically, either a transacting party or an instrument/arrangement between two transacting parties, is treated differently for tax purposes in two or more jurisdictions, giving rise to an asymmetric tax treatment).

The Final OECD/G20 BEPS Action 2 Report, containing recommendations for jurisdictions as to the detailed design of such rules, was issued in October 2015.

The UK Government originally made clear their intention to introduce legislation aligned with the recommendations of Action 2, and consulted on the proposed design of the UK law on hybrid mismatches in December 2014. Following the publication of the BEPS Action 2 Report in October 2015, draft legislation was included in the draft Finance Bill clauses published in December 2015, which broadly reflected the proposed approach in the BEPS Action 2 Report. However, there are differences – for example, the UK rules could apply to UK-UK as well as cross-border arrangements. This was substantially amended/added to in the draft Finance Bill then published in March 2016. The final enacted version then included further amendments which arose as the Finance Bill passed through the legislative process. This iterative nature of the drafting reflects the complexity of the technical issues and continuing engagement between HMRC, taxpayers and advisors in respect of the application of the rules over the period in question.

Part 1 Main Provisions

Part 1 inserts new Pt 6A TIOPA 2010 ("Hybrid and other mismatches"), with provisions as follows:

New TIOPA 2010 Pt 6A Ch 1 s 259A

Chapter 1 is an overview of Pt 6A, setting out the two broad heads of mismatch that are targeted by the rules – "deduction/non-inclusion" and "double deduction", and the cases involving such mismatches which are targeted:

- Payments or quasi-payments under financial instruments and repos/stock lending/etc;
- Hybrid entities;
- Companies with permanent establishments; and
- Dual resident companies.

Also described in Chapter is the content of each subsequent Chapter. In brief:

- Chapter 2 contains pivotal definitions of terms which are used throughout the Part;
- each of Chs 3 to 10 contains provision regarding the identification and counter-action of a particular type of mismatch arrangement;
- Chapter 11 covers "imported mismatches" – i.e. broadly where an offshore mismatch is linked to some extent to a payment of a company within the charge to corporation tax;
- Chapter 12 covers adjustments to deal with subsequent events which might impact the original treatment of an arrangement (for example, where an expectation about an overseas tax treatment proves to be mistaken, which changes the analysis as to whether a mismatch arises);
- Chapter 13 contains anti-avoidance provisions;
- Chapter 14 contains further interpretational provisions and definitions (in addition to those contained in Ch 2).

New TIOPA 2010 Pt 6A Ch 2 ss 259B–259BF

Chapter 2 contains the key definitions which are crucial to understand in interpreting the main Chs 3–11 and establishing whether a relevant mismatch arrangement exists. The definitions are summarised as follows:

"tax" in general means UK and foreign taxes on income, including diverted profits tax and CFC charges. For foreign taxes to meet the definition, they must "correspond" to UK income tax or corporation tax on income – a broadly similar test to that for double tax relief creditability in s 9 TIOPA 2010. It is explicitly stated that state/provincial/municipal taxes can meet the definition.

"equivalent provision to Pt 6A TIOPA 2010 under the law of a territory outside the UK" is essentially defined as any provision which it is reasonable to suppose is based upon the October 2015 BEPS Action 2 Report (mentioned above), or any OECD publication which supplements or supersedes it and has a similar purpose to the UK rules. At the time of enactment of Finance Act 2016, it is not thought that there are any other territories which have already enacted provisions which would fall within this definition.

"payment" means a transfer of money or money's worth directly or indirectly from one person (**"the payer"**) to one or more persons, in relation to which the payer would obtain a 'relevant' (i.e. tax) deduction, absent hybrid mismatch rules.

"quasi-payment" does not require a transfer of money or money's worth – merely that a relevant deduction arises to a person (**"the payer"**) (absent hybrid mismatch rules), and where certain assumptions are made as to equivalence of accounting/residence with the payer, "ordinary income" (as defined later in the Chapter) would arise to another person. A simple example of a quasi-payment would be the unwind of discount that accrues to a borrower on a discount note. There is a specific carve out from this definition for deductions that are pure tax-deemed deductions in the payer jurisdiction and the circumstances giving rise to that deduction do not involve any economic rights in substance existing between the (quasi) payer and the person to whom ordinary income would arise under the above assumptions. It is generally understood that this carve out is applicable to interest-free loans where the borrower jurisdiction grants a deemed deduction for interest (this carve out would also be in line with the principles of the October 2015 BEPS Action 2 Report, as illustrated in Example 1.14 from that report).

"payee" in relation to a payment is either the transferee of the money/money's worth, or any person to whom "ordinary income" arises as a result of the payment. "Payee" in relation to a quasi-payment is similarly defined by reference to the person who does or would reasonably expected under the relevant quasi-payment assumptions to recognise ordinary income. It is set out that a payer is "also a payee" in relation to a quasi-payment where the entity to whom ordinary income would arise when making the relevant quasi-payment assumptions is not seen as a distinct and separate person from the payer under UK law.

"payer jurisdiction" is the territory which grants the tax deductions mentioned above as arising from a payment or quasi-payment.

"payee jurisdiction" is a territory in which a payee is resident or has a permanent establishment.

"ordinary income" is defined in new s 259BC. Broadly, it is income that is brought into account, before any deductions, for the purposes of calculating income or profits upon which a "tax" (excluding CFC type taxes) is charged. It will not meet the definition however to the extent of any exemption, exclusion, relief or credit applying specifically to the piece of income under consideration or arising from a payment/quasi-payment giving rise to the income. Also, any tax which is refunded will prevent the income upon which it originally arose from being ordinary income, except where that refund arises from normal tax loss relief. Section 259BD then deals with a situation where a company does not have ordinary income under the law of its territory of residence, but where a parent jurisdiction may impose a CFC charge (either UK CFC or foreign CFC regime) upon a controlling company (or companies), and broadly provides that the CFC profits subject to charge in the controlling company jurisdiction is then ordinary income of the controlling company.

"hybrid entity" is defined in similar terms to the provision at s 236 in the UK "tax arbitrage" rules of Pt 6 TIOPA 2010 (to be repealed at the same time that the hybrid mismatch rules begin to have effect), i.e. broadly that one territory regards an entity as a person for tax purposes, whereas another territory regards any income or profits of the entity as belonging to a different person (or persons) for tax purposes. There is an alternative second leg of this test here, which is that another territory does not regard the entity as a distinct and separate person to an entity which is a distinct and separate person under the law of the first-mentioned territory.

An **"investor"** in a hybrid entity is, essentially, the person to whom profits (or losses) of the hybrid entity would arise under the law of the "other" territory (i.e. not the first-mentioned territory in the hybrid entity definition above). That territory is defined as an **"investor jurisdiction"**.

"permanent establishment" is defined in line with the definition at s 1119 CTA 2010, albeit extended to include any "similar concept" under the law of any other territory. Explicit mention is made that such a concept does not have to be based on the approach of Art 5 of the OECD Model Tax Convention in order to be considered similar.

New TIOPA 2010 Pt 6A Chs 3–11

Chapters 3 to 11 in general follow the same basic structure and contain a section (or sections) covering each of the following:
–   Overview of Chapter;
–   Circumstances in which the Chapter applies;
–   Identification of the relevant deduction/non-inclusion mismatch and its extent;
–   Counteraction provisions as appropriate to circumstances;

Chapters 6, 9, 10 and 11 however have no need for a detailed separate mismatch identification section by virtue of the type of mismatch they deal with.

New TIOPA 2010 Pt 6A Ch 3 ss 259C–259CD

Chapter 3 addresses "hybrid and other mismatches from financial instruments" ("financial instruments" are defined later in Ch 14). Section 259C is the overview of the Chapter.

Section 259CA contains the four Conditions (A–D) which must all be met for the chapter to apply. These are summarised as:

- Condition A – a payment or quasi-payment is made under, or in connection with, a financial instrument;
- Condition B – either the payer or the payee is within the charge to corporation tax (with reference to the "payment period" in which the payment or quasi-payment is made);
- Condition C – it is reasonable to suppose that a "hybrid or otherwise impermissible deduction/non-inclusion mismatch" (as defined in s 259CB) arises in relation to the payment/quasi-payment, ignoring Ch 3, Chs 5–10, and any overseas equivalent provision to Pt 6A TIOPA 2010;
- Condition D – any of the following three circumstances exist:
  - it is a quasi-payment where the payer is "also a payee" (i.e. the payer and payee are not seen as distinct and separate persons under UK law),
  - the payer and payee are related (as defined in Ch 14, but broadly requiring a 25%+ investment test to be met) during a relevant timeframe which includes the payment/quasi-payment,
  - the financial instrument is (or is connected to) a "structured arrangement". For these purposes an arrangement is, broadly, "structured" if it is reasonable to suppose that either it is designed to secure a hybrid mismatch as defined in s 259CB, or the terms of the financial instrument/arrangement share the benefit of the mismatch between the parties (or otherwise reflect the fact that it is expected to arise). For these purposes, an arrangement can be so designed even if it is designed to secure any other objectives.

In summary, Ch 3 could broadly be expected to be potentially applicable to financial instruments in related party situations (or situations where the terms of a financial instrument are suitably structured) and either the payer or payee are subject to UK corporation tax.

The main operative part of the Chapter however, contained in s 259CB, is whether or not a hybrid or otherwise impermissible deduction/non-inclusion mismatch arises. Such a mismatch arises in either of two "cases", as follows:

Case 1

This case is where the relevant deduction (i.e. that available to the payer by reason of the payment or quasi-payment) exceeds the sum of the amounts of ordinary income that, by reason of the payment or quasi-payment, arise to each payee for a "permitted taxable period" *and* all or part of that excess arises by reason of the terms, or any other feature, of the financial instrument.

A simple example of an arrangement intended to be caught by Case 1 is an instrument which by reason of its terms is considered as debt by the payer jurisdiction (thus the payer obtains a relevant deduction for the payment), but as equity by the payee jurisdiction (and as a result the payee recognises no ordinary income, or reduced ordinary income because of a participation exemption or credit relief being available).

For the purposes of the above, a "permitted taxable period" broadly is any that begins no later than 12 months after the end of the payment period (i.e. the payer's accounting period) – with additional provision for this potentially to be later if that is "just and reasonable" (and a claim is made), i.e. the concept of the permitted taxable period is to establish a cut-off point for the period of time over which one can look to decide whether or not a deduction has been matched by ordinary income.

It is explicitly stated here that the "reason for the excess being the terms or other feature of the instrument" test will not be met in circumstances where it arises by reason of one of the following 'relevant debt relief' provisions: ss 322, 357, 358, 359, 361C, 301D, 302A CTA 2009; each of these being a provision which permits loan relationship credits not to be brought into account in respect of releases (or otherwise deemed releases), without the debit side being affected – thereby giving rise to a prima facie "excess". This provision may apply so that debts which are contractually released upon a 'trigger' clause and whose treatment is determined by one of these provisions (therefore potentially could be said to have a term or feature which gives rise to an excess) should not be captured by Case 1. There is also a carve-out for any excess that arises because a payee is a 'relevant investment fund' as defined later in s 259NZA.

Subject to these particular carve-outs, it is then provided that the "reason for the excess being the terms or other feature of the instrument" test will be met whether or not the excess arises for any other reason as well. Also, as far as it is not already clear whether the test is met, if it *could* arise by reason of the terms/any feature of the financial instrument upon making certain "relevant assumptions", then the test is considered met. There are three potential "relevant assumptions":

- If a payee is not within the charge to tax due to an exclusion, immunity, exemption or relief (however described), assume that such exclusion, etc does not apply.
- If a payee excludes a payment/quasi-payment from ordinary income because it is not considered as made in connection with a business carried on in the payee jurisdiction, assume that the payment/quasi-payment is so made.
- If a payee has no taxable presence anywhere (either through residence or permanent establishment), assume that it is UK resident and the payment/quasi-payment is made in connection with a business carried on in the UK (but ignoring the UK transfer pricing, unallowable purpose, worldwide debt cap, and hybrid mismatch rules in determining whether/how an excess could arise in this counter-factual situation).

It is anticipated that the "relevant assumptions" provision may give rise to significant complexity and uncertainty when analysing many financing arrangements in practice, due to the counter-factual assumptions which need to be made in undertaking the analysis, and the extent to which this counter-factual deeming applies (the same general approach is also adopted by a number of the other deduction/non-inclusion mismatch Chapters).

However, for very simple circumstances, it can be seen that the effect of the "relevant assumptions" approach would be to confirm that the "reason for the excess being the terms or other feature of the financial instrument" test is not met where the financial instrument itself is "vanilla" but the payee has no (or lower) ordinary income, solely because the payee is in any of the three circumstances contemplated by the "relevant assumptions". For example, where a UK resident borrowing company makes a tax-deductible (absent the hybrid mismatch rules) payment under a plain loan note to a related lending company which is resident in a territory which levies no corporate tax on extra-territorial income, then there would clearly be an "excess". However, the initial analysis would be that this doesn't arise from the terms or any other feature of the financial instrument. This would then be confirmed when one makes the appropriate counterfactual "relevant assumption", i.e. that extra-territorial income is instead not exempt in the payee, and one concludes that in that case, the excess would no longer arise (or, put differently, "*could not* arise by reason of the terms/any other feature of the financial instrument").

Under Case 1, the amount of the "hybrid or otherwise impermissible deduction/non-inclusion mismatch" is equal to the excess which meets the "reason for the excess" test described above.

Case 2

This case is where ordinary income arising to any payee for a permitted taxable period is "under taxed" by reason of the terms, or any other feature, of the financial instrument. As with Case 1, there is a carve-out here from the rule for under taxed amounts that arise as a result of a payee being a 'relevant investment fund'.

For the purposes of the above an amount is broadly considered as "under taxed" in circumstances where the payee obtains a credit for underlying tax in respect of tax paid by the payer on profits which are used directly or indirectly to fund the payment/quasi-payment, and as a result the highest tax rate the payee suffers on its taxable profits (taking into account a just and reasonable proportion of the credit for underlying tax) are lower than its "full marginal rate".

Under Case 2, the amount of the "hybrid or otherwise impermissible deduction/non-inclusion mismatch" is given by an apportioning formula. A numerical example would be as follows: a payment of 100 under a financial instrument which (by reason of its terms) qualified it for an underlying tax credit in the payee of 10. The payee has taxable profits of 100, which are subject to tax at the payee territory "full marginal rate" of 20%, giving an initial tax charge of 20, which it can then reduce to 10 via credit for the 10 of underlying tax. If it is "just and reasonable" to include the impact of the whole credit for underlying tax in determining the effective tax rate in the payee, this would then be $10/100 = 10\%$. The variables for the formula in s 259CB(11) are then UTA = 100, FMR = 20%, R = 10%. As a result, the "hybrid or otherwise impermissible deduction/non-inclusion mismatch" is $(100 \times (20\%-10\%))/(20\%) = 50$.

Finally, where Cases 1 and 2 both apply, the amount of the "hybrid or otherwise impermissible deduction/non-inclusion mismatch" is given by adding together the sums determined by each of the processes.

Sections 259CD and 259CE provide how the situations which meet all four Conditions (A–D) of s 259CA are counteracted. Where the payer is within the charge to corporation tax, s 259CD provides that its relevant deduction is to be reduced by the amount of the "hybrid or otherwise impermissible deduction/non-inclusion mismatch".

Where the payee is within the charge to corporation tax, under s 259CE it is treated as having income arising to it under Ch 8 of Pt 10 CTA 2009 (Income not Otherwise Charged), however this is subject to the following:

- This counteraction only applies to the extent that the payer has not already had its relevant deduction counteracted by either s 259CD or an equivalent overseas provision. This gives effect to the principle, set out in the October 2015 BEPS Action 2 Report, that counteracting the payer is the "primary rule" and counteracting the payee is the "defensive rule" for this type of mismatch.
- Where there are multiple payees (e.g. corporate partners in a partnership which receives a payment) there is an apportioning provision which requires a just and reasonable approach, having regard to any profit-sharing agreement and to whom ordinary income/under-taxed amounts would have arisen (but in fact, do not).

New TIOPA 2010 Pt 6A Ch 4 ss 259C–259CD

Chapter 4 addresses "hybrid transfer deduction/non-inclusion mismatches". Section 259D is the overview of the Chapter.

Section 259DA contains the five Conditions (A–E) which must all be met for the chapter to apply. These are summarised as:

- Condition A – there is a hybrid transfer arrangement in relation to an underlying instrument.
- Condition B – a payment or quasi-payment is made in connection with either the hybrid transfer arrangement or the underlying instrument.
- Condition C – either the payer or a payee is within the charge to corporation tax (with reference to the "payment period" in which the payment or quasi-payment is made)
- Condition D – it is reasonable to suppose that a "hybrid transfer deduction/non-inclusion mismatch" (as defined in s 259DC) arises in relation to the payment/quasi-payment, ignoring Pt 6A TIOPA 2010 and any overseas equivalent provision.
- Condition E – any of the following three circumstances exist:
  - it is a quasi-payment where the payer is "also a payee" (i.e. the payer and payee are not seen as distinct and separate persons under UK law),
  - the payer and payee are related (as defined in Ch 14) during a relevant timeframe which includes the payment/quasi-payment,
  - the hybrid transfer arrangement is a "structured arrangement". Similarly to Ch 3, for these purposes an arrangement is, broadly, "structured" if it is reasonable to suppose that either it is designed to secure a hybrid mismatch as defined in s 259DC, or the terms of the hybrid transfer arrangement share the benefit of the mismatch between the parties (or otherwise reflect the fact that it is expected to arise).

Section 259DB defines "hybrid transfer arrangement". A "hybrid transfer arrangement" includes repos, stock lending arrangements and any other arrangement involving the transfer of an underlying instrument which meets one of two comprehensively-framed conditions which capture the broad principles of such transactions. Broadly, this is that either:

- one person treats the arrangement as equivalent in substance to a transaction for the lending of money at interest, but another person does not treat it in this way ("dual treatment condition"); or
- an amount could be paid (or benefit given), which is representative of any underlying return on the underlying instrument, and the amount is paid (or benefit given) to a person other than the person to whom the return on the underlying instrument arises ("a substitute payment").

Section 259DC contains provisions determining the extent to which a "hybrid transfer deduction/non-inclusion mismatch" arises. The form of this section is substantively similar to that of s 259CB which determines the extent of a "hybrid or otherwise impermissible deduction/non-inclusion mismatch". That is, a "hybrid transfer deduction/non-inclusion" mismatch arises in two "cases", as follows:

Case 1

This case is where the relevant deduction (i.e. that available to the payer by reason of the payment or quasi-payment) exceeds the sum of the amounts of ordinary income that, by reason of the payment or quasi-payment, arise to each payee for a "permitted taxable period" **and** all or part of that excess arises by reason of the "dual treatment condition" being met, or the payment/quasi-payment being a "substitute payment" (both being terms defined in s 259DB).

An example of an arrangement intended to be caught by Case 1 is a "repo" arrangement over some underlying shares whereby one person (A, the payer) agrees to sell the underlying shares to another person (B, the payee) and buy the shares back at a later date for a fixed or determinable price. The payer jurisdiction treats A as entering into a borrowing transaction and it obtains a relevant deduction, whereas the payee jurisdiction treats B as simply buying an equity instrument and, later selling it back to A (with tax consequences being that reduced or zero ordinary income arises to the payee). This would meet the dual treatment condition.

The concept of the "permitted taxable period" is the same as in Ch 3.

Also equivalent to Ch 3, it is provided here that the "reason for the excess being the dual treatment/substitute payment reason" test will be met whether or not the excess arises for any other reason as well. The "relevant assumptions" counterfactual test to confirm whether or not an excess arises for one of these reasons is almost identical to the "relevant assumptions" included in Ch 3, and so in practice the same complexities may arise under these assumptions in any Ch 4 analysis.

Under Case 1, the amount of the "hybrid transfer deduction/non-inclusion mismatch" is equal to the excess which meets the "reason for the excess" test described above.

Case 2

This case is where ordinary income arising to any payee for a permitted taxable period is "under taxed" by reason of the dual treatment/substitute payment test being met.

The concept of an amount being "under-taxed", and the determination of the extent of the mismatch, is identical to Case 2 situations as contemplated in Ch 3, i.e. intended to capture arrangements where the mismatch benefit is obtained by reason of an underlying tax credit giving rise to overall lower effective taxation in the payee than would otherwise be the case.

Similarly to Ch 3, there is an exclusion from both Case 1 (for any excess or part thereof) and Case 2 (for any under taxed amount) to the extent it arises as a result of a payee being a "relevant investment fund". However, additionally for Ch 4, s 259DE contains an exclusion from an amount being within Case 1 or Case 2 where three conditions are met. The broad aim of the exclusion is not to impose the rules of Ch 4 on certain amounts which are treated as profits of a trade of a financial trader (either in accordance with Pt 3 CTA 2009, or an equivalent provision under the law of another territory).

Sections 259DF and 259DG provide how the situations which meet all five Conditions (A–E) of s 259DA are counteracted.

Under s 259DF, where the payer is within the charge to corporation tax, its relevant deduction is to be reduced by the amount of the "hybrid transfer deduction/non-inclusion mismatch".

Under s 259DG, where the payee is within the charge to corporation tax, it is treated as having income arising to it under Ch 8 of Pt 10 CTA 2009 (Income Not Otherwise Charged), however this is subject to the following:

– This counteraction only applies to the extent that the payer has not already had its relevant deduction counteracted by either s 259DF or an equivalent overseas provision. This gives effect to the principle, set out in the October 2015 BEPS Action 2 report that counteracting the payer is the "primary rule" and counteracting the payee is the "defensive rule" for this type of mismatch.
– Where there are multiple payees (e.g. corporate partners in a partnership which receives a payment) there is an apportioning provision which requires a just and

reasonable approach, having regard to any profit-sharing agreement and to whom ordinary income/under-taxed amounts would have (but in fact, do not) arisen.

New TIOPA 2010 Pt 6A Ch 5 ss 259E–259ED

Chapter 5 addresses "hybrid payer deduction/non-inclusion mismatches". Section 259E is the overview of the Chapter.

Section 259EA contains the five Conditions (A–E) which must all be met for the chapter to apply. These are summarised as:

– Condition A – a payment or quasi-payment is made under, or in connection with, an arrangement;
– Condition B – the payer is a hybrid entity ("the hybrid payer");
– Condition C – either the hybrid payer or a payee is within the charge to corporation tax (with reference to the "payment period" in which the payment or quasi-payment is made);
– Condition D – it is reasonable to suppose that a "hybrid payer deduction/non-inclusion mismatch" (as defined in s 259EB) arises in relation to the payment/quasi-payment, ignoring Chs 5–10 Pt 6A TIOPA 2010 and any overseas equivalent provision,
– Condition E – any of the following three circumstances exist:
– it is a quasi-payment where the hybrid payer is "also a payee" (i.e. the hybrid payer and payee are not seen as distinct and separate persons under UK law),
– the hybrid payer and payee are in the same control group (as defined in Ch 14) during a relevant timeframe which includes the payment/quasi-payment. Note that this is a different, narrower, test to the equivalent condition in Chs 3 and 4, where the test is whether or not the payer and payee are "related",
– the arrangement is a "structured arrangement". For these purposes an arrangement is, broadly, "structured" if it is reasonable to suppose that either it is designed to secure a hybrid mismatch as defined in s 259EB, or the terms of the arrangement share the benefit of the mismatch between the parties (or otherwise reflect the fact that it is expected to arise).

Section 259EB determines the extent to which a "hybrid payer deduction/non-inclusion" mismatch arises. This is the case where the relevant deduction in relation to a payment or quasi-payment exceeds the sum of the amounts of ordinary income that arise to each payee for a permitted taxable period, **and** all or part of that excess arises by reason of the hybrid payer being a hybrid entity.

An example of an arrangement intended to be caught by Ch 5 is one whereby an entity (A) has a loan payable to its parent entity (B), and A is a person for tax purposes under the law of its territory of residence, but the income or profits (and by extension, expenses or losses) of A are treated as those of B under the law of B's territory of residence. As a result, A will be a hybrid entity (as defined in s 259BE), and will be a hybrid payer in respect of payments/quasi-payments made under the loan. Absent Ch 5, A would obtain a relevant deduction in respect of the payment/quasi-payment, but B may not have any corresponding ordinary income, and if so that would clearly be by reason of A being a hybrid entity.

It is provided here that the "reason for the excess being the hybrid entity nature of the payer" test will be met whether or not the excess arises for any other reason as well. Also, as far as it is not already clear whether the test is met, if it *could* arise by reason of the payer being a hybrid entity upon making certain "relevant assumptions", then the test is considered met. These "relevant assumptions" are similar to those contemplated in Chs 3 and 4 in the equivalent test, however in Ch 5 they do not include the relevant assumption that a payee that is not resident anywhere must be assumed to be a UK resident company, carrying on a business in the UK in connection with the payment or quasi-payment.

As noted in relation to those earlier Chapters, this test may give rise to significant complexity and uncertainty when analysing many arrangements in practice, due to the counter-factual assumptions which need to be made in undertaking the analysis, and the extent to which this counter-factual deeming applies and the impacts that it has upon the broader analysis (e.g. in the counter-factual situation, whether the identity of payers/payees stays the same).

The amount of the "hybrid payer deduction/non-inclusion mismatch" is equal to the excess which meets the "reason for the excess" test described above.

Sections 259EC and 259ED contain the counteraction provisions for Ch 5. Where the hybrid payer is within the charge to corporation tax, s 259EC provides that the part of the payer's relevant deduction which corresponds to the "hybrid payer deduction/non-inclusion mismatch" may not be deducted from the hybrid payer's income for the payment period unless it is deducted from "dual inclusion income". "Dual inclusion income" is any income arising in connection with the arrangement which is ordinary income of both the hybrid payer for corporation tax purposes and an investor in the hybrid payer for the purposes of the law of the investor jurisdiction (the latter as long as it arises in a "permitted period", defined similarly to elsewhere in the Part). This provision therefore ensures that two lots of relief are not prevented for a payment to the extent that the relief is being set against income which is subject to tax in the two relevant jurisdictions. There is also a provision permitting carry-forward of a restricted deduction arising in a period, for potential offset against dual inclusion income arising in future.

Where the payee is within the charge to corporation tax, s 259ED sets out that it is treated as having income arising to it under Ch 8 of Pt 10 CTA 2009 (income not otherwise chargeable), however this is subject to the following:

- This counteraction only applies to the extent that the payer has not already had its relevant deduction counteracted by either s 259EC or an equivalent overseas provision. This gives effect to the principle, set out in the October 2015 BEPS Action 2 report that counteracting the payer is the "primary rule" and counteracting the payee is the "defensive rule" for this type of mismatch.
- This counteraction only applies to the extent that it exceeds dual inclusion income.

Where there are multiple payees, there is an apportioning provision which requires a just and reasonable approach, having regard to any profit-sharing agreement and to whom ordinary income would have arisen (but in fact, does not). This apportioning provision is for the purposes of determining both the amount of the "hybrid payer deduction/non-inclusion mismatch" which is allocable to each payee, and also the amount of dual inclusion income so allocable.

New TIOPA 2010 Pt 6A Ch 6 ss 259F–259FC

Chapter 6 addresses "deduction/non-inclusion mismatches relating to transfers by permanent establishments". Section 259F is the overview of the Chapter. Note that whilst such situations were not covered by the scope of the October 2015 BEPS Action 2 report, the principle outlined by Ch 6 appears to be broadly in line with the content of the OECD BEPS Action 2 Discussion Draft paper on 'Branch Mismatch Structures', published in August 2016 (the OECD having chosen to consider 'branch mismatches' separately to 'hybrid mismatches').

Section 259FA contains the three Conditions (A–C) which must all be met for the Chapter to apply. These are summarised as:

- Condition A – a company is a "multinational company". A "multinational company" for these purposes is a company which is resident in a territory outside the UK (the "parent jurisdiction") but is within the charge to corporation tax in the UK by reason of carrying on a business through a permanent establishment in the UK.
- Condition B – disregarding Chs 6–10 Pt 6A TIOPA 2010 and any equivalent overseas provision, a deduction arises to the PE that may (in substance) may be deductible against taxable income of the PE for an accounting period ("the relevant PE period") in the UK, **and** it is in respect of a transfer of money or money's worth from the UK to the parent jurisdiction that is either actually made, or is (in substance) treated as being made for corporation tax purposes. This condition may give rise to some uncertainty in practice, as it is not clear, as a technical matter, whether any deductions in general are available to UK PEs for corporation tax purposes under the relevant provisions of CTA 2009 "in respect of a transfer to the parent jurisdiction".
- Condition C – the circumstances giving rise to the PE deduction will not result in an increase in the taxable profits (or a reduction to the losses) of the company in the parent jurisdiction for any "permitted taxable period". Alternatively, if there is some impact on the taxable profits, but its 'aggregate effect on taxable profits' is lower than the PE deduction, then this condition will also be met.

Where all these conditions are met, there is an "excessive PE deduction", which is either the whole amount of the PE deduction where there is no corresponding impact at all on the parent company position under Condition C, or the excess of the PE deduction over the aggregate effect on taxable profits where there is some effect under Condition C.

Section 259FB contains the counteraction provisions for Ch 6, providing that the excessive PE deduction may not be deducted from the company's income for the PE period unless it is deducted from "dual inclusion income" for that period. "Dual inclusion income" for an accounting period is any income which is ordinary income for the purposes of both corporation tax in the accounting period and also ordinary income under the parent jurisdiction law for a "permitted taxable period". A permitted taxable period is defined similarly to the other Chapters, i.e. it must begin no later than 12 months after the end of the PE period in question, or if 'just and reasonable' (and a claim is made), some time later.

The "permitted taxable period" impact on both the PE deduction and dual inclusion income may allow some practical flexibility where there are timing mismatches in respect of deductions/taxable income between the tax systems of the UK and the parent jurisdiction.

There is a carry-forward provision, similar to that in Ch 5, for denied excessive PE deductions, which can then potentially be offset against dual inclusion income of a later period.

New TIOPA 2010 Pt 6A Ch 7 ss 259G–259GE

Chapter 7 addresses "hybrid payee deduction/non-inclusion mismatches". Section 259G is the overview of the Chapter.

Section 259GA contains the five Conditions (A–E) which must all be met for the Chapter to apply. These are summarised as:

–   Condition A – a payment or quasi-payment is made under, or in connection with, an arrangement.
–   Condition B – a payee is a hybrid entity ("the hybrid payee").
–   Condition C – one of the following is the case:
    –   the payer is within the charge to corporation tax for the "payment period";
    –   an investor in a hybrid payee is within the charge to corporation tax for an accounting period which is at least partly overlapping with the payment period; or
    –   a hybrid payee is a limited liability partnership. For these purposes, a "limited liability partnership" is taken to mean one which is constituted under the law of the UK in accordance with previous onactments, although this term is not expressly defined elsewhere in Pt 6A.
–   Condition D – it is reasonable to suppose that a "hybrid payee deduction/non-inclusion mismatch" (as defined in s 259GB) arises in relation to the payment/quasi-payment, ignoring Chs 7–10 Pt 6A TIOPA 2010 and any equivalent overseas provision.
–   Condition E – any of the following three circumstances exist:
    –   it is a quasi-payment where the payer is "also a hybrid payee" (i.e. the payer and hybrid payee are not seen as distinct and separate persons under UK law);
    –   the payer and a hybrid payee or an investor in a hybrid payee are in the same control group (as defined in Ch 14) during a relevant timeframe which includes the payment/quasi-payment. Again, note that this is the same test to the equivalent condition in Ch 5, but different to those in Chs 3 and 4, where the test is whether or not the payer and payee are "related";
    –   the arrangement is a "structured arrangement". For these purposes an arrangement is, broadly, "structured" if it is reasonable to suppose that either it is designed to secure a hybrid mismatch as defined in s 259GB, or the terms of the arrangement share the benefit of the mismatch between the parties (or otherwise reflect the fact that it is expected to arise).

Section 259GB determines the extent to which a "hybrid payee deduction/non-inclusion" mismatch arises. This is the case where the relevant deduction in relation to a payment or quasi-payment exceeds the sum of the amounts of ordinary income that arise to each payee for a permitted taxable period, **and** all or part of that excess arises by reason of one or more hybrid payees being hybrid entities.

An example of an arrangement intended to be caught by Ch 7 is one whereby an entity (A) is transparent for tax purposes under the law of its territory of establishment (e.g. it is a UK LLP), but its majority partner (B) treats it as a person for tax purposes (e.g. it is a US company which has "reverse checked" the LLP for US federal tax purposes). As a result, A is a hybrid entity as defined in s 259BF, A has a plain loan receivable from an intragroup borrower (C), and will thus be a hybrid payee in respect of payments/quasi-payments made under the loan. Absent Ch 7, C would obtain a relevant deduction for the payment/quasi-payment, but it may not give rise to ordinary income in either the UK or the US. The absence of ordinary income, and thus the existence of the "excess", would arise by reason of A being a hybrid entity.

Ch 7 does not adopt the "relevant assumptions" approach of earlier Chapters in determining certain situations in which an "excess" should be considered to arise by reason of the hybrid status of the payee. Instead, where a payee meets each of the following three conditions, some or all of the excess is automatically taken to arise by reason of its hybrid status:

- A payee is a hybrid entity;
- That payee is not resident for tax purposes in any territory, nor does it have a taxable PE anywhere which causes ordinary income to arise in respect of the payment/quasi-payment;
- No income arising from the payment/quasi-payment is brought into account in calculating chargeable profits for the purposes of either a UK or foreign CFC charge.

In such a case, the proportion of the excess captured by the rule is the amount of ordinary income that would arise to the payee for corporation tax purposes if it were a company and the payment/quasi-payment were made to it in connection with a trade carried on by it through a UK PE (capped at the amount of the excess in total).

Sections 259GC, 259GD and 259GE contain the counteraction provisions for Ch 7. There are three separate provisions for Ch 7 because there are three alternative scenarios in which Condition C of s 259GA can apply:

- Where the payer is within the charge to corporation tax, s 259GC provides that its relevant deduction is reduced by the amount of the "hybrid payee deduction/non-inclusion mismatch".
- Where the investor in a hybrid payee is within the charge to corporation tax, s 259GD sets out that it is treated as having income arising to it under Ch 8 of Pt 10 CTA 2009 (income not otherwise chargeable) equivalent to the "hybrid payee deduction/non-inclusion mismatch", however this is subject to the following:
  - this counteraction only applies to the extent that the payer has not already had its relevant deduction counteracted by either s 259GC or an equivalent overseas provision. It is worth noting that the October 2015 BEPS Action 2 Report does not recommend any counteraction for an investor in a "reverse hybrid" (i.e. a hybrid payee), only a payer jurisdiction disallowance;
  - where there are multiple investors in a hybrid payee, there is an apportioning provision which requires a just and reasonable approach, having regard to any profit-sharing agreement and to whom ordinary income would have arisen (but in fact, does not).
- Where the hybrid payee is an LLP (as entity A is in the example above), s 259GE provides that the LLP is treated as having income arising to it under Ch 8 Pt 10 CTA 2009 (income not otherwise chargeable) equivalent to the "hybrid payee deduction/non-inclusion mismatch", however this is subject to the following:
  - this counteraction only applies to the extent that the payer or an investor in the hybrid payee have not already had their position counteracted by any of s 259GC, s 259GD or an equivalent overseas provision. Again, this particular counteraction arguably goes beyond the principles drawn out in the October 2015 BEPS Action 2 report, since the latter only mentions payer counteraction in these circumstances.
  - where there are multiple hybrid payees, there is an apportioning provision which requires a just and reasonable approach, having regard to any profit-sharing agreement and to whom ordinary income would have arisen (but in fact, does not).

This counteraction provision is notable in that it subjects a UK LLP directly to a corporation tax charge, in contrast with the general tax transparency principles established by s 863 ITTOIA 2005 and s 1273 CTA 2009 – it is for this reason that s 259GE(8) specifically disapplies these sections in relation to the hybrid payee "to the extent necessary" for these purposes.

New TIOPA 2010 Pt 6A Ch 8 ss 259H–259HD

Chapter 8 addresses "multinational payee deduction/non-inclusion mismatches". Section 259H is the overview of the Chapter. Note that, similarly to Ch 6, the principle outlined by Ch 8 appears to be broadly in line with circumstances covered by the OECD BEPS Action 2 Discussion Draft paper on 'Branch Mismatch Structures', published in August 2016.

Section 259HA contains the five Conditions (A–E) which must all be met for the Chapter to apply. These are summarised as:

- Condition A – a payment or quasi-payment is made under, or in connection with, an arrangement.
- Condition B – a payee is a "multinational company". In Ch 8, a multinational company is a company that is resident in one territory ("the parent jurisdiction"), and is regarded as carrying on a business in another territory ("the PE jurisdiction") through a permanent establishment in that territory (whether it is so regarded under the law of the parent jurisdiction, the PE jurisdiction or any other territory). Note, this definition of "multinational company" is wider than the definition used for Ch 6.
- Condition C – the payer is within the charge to corporation tax (with reference to the "payment period" in which the payment or quasi-payment is made).
- Condition D – it is reasonable to suppose that a "multinational payee deduction/ non-inclusion mismatch" (as defined in s 259HB) arises in relation to the payment/quasi-payment, ignoring Chs 8–10 Pt 6A TIOPA 2010 and any equivalent overseas provision.
- Condition E – any of the following three circumstances exist:
  - it is a quasi-payment where the payer is "also a payee" (i.e. the payer and payee are not seen as distinct and separate persons under UK law);
  - the payer and the multinational company are in the same control group (as defined in Ch 14) during a relevant timeframe which includes the payment/ quasi-payment;
  - the arrangement is a "structured arrangement". For these purposes an arrangement is, broadly, "structured" if it is reasonable to suppose that either it is designed to secure a "multinational payee deduction/non-inclusion mismatch" as defined in s 259HB, or the terms of the arrangement share the benefit of this mismatch between the parties (or otherwise reflect the fact that it is expected to arise).

Section 259HB determines the extent to which a "multinational payee deduction/non-inclusion" mismatch arises. This is the case where the relevant deduction in relation to a payment or quasi-payment exceeds the sum of the amounts of ordinary income that arise to each payee for a permitted taxable period, *and* all or part of that excess arises by reason of one or more payees being multinational companies.

An example of an arrangement intended to be caught by Ch 8 is one whereby a company (X) is resident in territory A and under the law of territory A the company is considered to be carrying on a business through a PE in territory B. The results of the PE are exempt from tax in territory A. Territory B does not seek to tax any income of the company, perhaps because under the law of territory B, the company is not considered to have established a taxable presence there through carrying on a business. Another company (Y) in the same control group and resident in the UK, makes a payment under a plain loan note to the PE of company X. Company X is the payee in this arrangement, and neither territory A nor territory B seek to tax the income – thus no ordinary income arises to company X.

It is provided here that the "reason for the excess being the multinational company nature of the payee" test will be met whether or not the excess arises for any other reason as well, although for Ch 8 there is a specific carve out: where the law of a PE jurisdiction "makes no provision for charging tax on any companies", the amount of any resulting excess is automatically taken not to arise by reason of the payee being a multinational company.

As with Ch 7, there is no "relevant assumptions" test equivalent to Chs 3, 4 or 5 in Ch 8. The amount of the "multinational payee deduction/non-inclusion mismatch" is equal to the excess which meets the "reason for the excess" test described above.

Section 259HC contains the simple counteraction provision for Ch 8, which is that the payer's relevant deduction is to be reduced by the amount of the "multinational payee deduction/non-inclusion mismatch".

New TIOPA 2010 Pt 6A Ch 9 ss 259I–259IC

Chapter 9 addresses "hybrid entity double deduction mismatches". Section 259I is the overview of the Chapter.

Section 259IA contains the three Conditions (A–C) which must all be met for the Chapter to apply. These are summarised as:

- Condition A – there is an amount (or part thereof) which, ignoring Chs 9 and 10 Pt 6A TIOPA 2010 and any equivalent overseas provision, it is reasonable to suppose could both:

    – be deducted from the income of a hybrid entity for a taxable period; and
    – be deducted from the income of an investor in the hybrid entity for a taxable period.

The amount is the "hybrid entity double deduction amount".

– Condition B – either the hybrid entity or the investor in it is within the charge to corporation tax.
– Condition C – the hybrid entity and any investor in it are related during a relevant timeframe involving the double deduction amount, or the arrangement is a 'structured arrangement'.

Sections 259IB and 259IC contain the counteraction provisions. Where the investor is within the charge to corporation tax, s 259IB provides that the hybrid entity double deduction amount may not be deducted from the investor's income for corporation tax purposes unless it is deducted from dual inclusion income of the investor. Any denied deduction on these grounds can be carried forward by the investor and potentially deducted from dual inclusion income in future periods.

There is an additional set of provisions at s 259IB(4)–(7) which may, in limited cases, permit the investor to deduct an otherwise denied "hybrid entity double deduction amount" directly from its profits generally chargeable to corporation tax. However, broadly this would only apply in cases where both:

– HMRC are satisfied there will never be any dual inclusion income of the investor in any period after the accounting period of the investor in which the hybrid entity double deduction amount arises; and
– It is not reasonable to suppose that the hybrid entity double deduction amount has already been deducted from the income of any person which is not dual inclusion income of the investor for the purposes of an overseas tax.

This would essentially seem to permit UK tax relief for the investor in respect of the hybrid entity double deduction amount, provided it has not relieved non-dual inclusion income of the investor overseas.

Where the hybrid entity is within the charge to corporation tax, under s 259IC, the hybrid entity double deduction amount may not be deducted from the hybrid entity's income for corporation tax purposes unless it is deducted from dual inclusion income of the hybrid entity. However this is subject to the following:

– This counteraction only applies to the extent that the investor has not already had its position counteracted by s 259IB or an equivalent overseas provision.
– This counteraction also only applies if the hybrid entity is in the same control group as any investor in it, or the hybrid entity/any investor are party to a "structured arrangement". So whilst Ch 9 may in general be applicable where a hybrid entity is *related* to any investor (or there is a structured arrangement) through Condition C of s 259IA, the counteraction can only apply to a hybrid entity which is in the same *control group* as any investor in it (or there is a structured arrangement).

There are equivalent provisions at s 259IC(6)–(9) for the hybrid entity as described above at s259IB(4)–(7) for the investor. That is, in some circumstances it may be possible for a hybrid entity to deduct a "hybrid entity double deduction amount" from non-dual inclusion income, however that would only be possible where no overseas person has deducted the corresponding amount from non-dual inclusion income of the hybrid entity.

By way of example (assuming one of the following territories were the UK), Ch 9 may be considered as applying to counteract a situation where a partnership (A) established in territory X has a plain loan payable to a third party. The partnership receives no income. Partnership A is considered as a person for tax purposes in territory X and is a member of a fiscal consolidation there. The relief for interest expense on the loan is used to relieve other income of fiscal unity members in territory X. The majority partner in partnership A is company B, resident in territory Y. Territory Y considers partnership A as transparent for tax purposes, and therefore company B obtains relief for part of partnership A's interest expense in territory Y. Partnership A would be considered as a hybrid entity, and the amount of the interest expense would be considered as a hybrid entity double deduction amount. Neither partnership A nor company B are offsetting the deduction against dual inclusion income, so it would be counteracted in full (depending upon which territory were the UK, and potentially whether it had already been counteracted in the other territory).

New TIOPA 2010 Pt 6A Ch 10 ss 259J–259JC

Chapter 10 addresses "dual territory double deduction cases". Section 259J is the overview of the Chapter.

Section 259JA contains the two conditions A and B which must both be met for the Chapter to apply. These are summarised as:

– Condition A – a company is either a dual resident company, or a relevant multinational company. For these purposes, a dual resident company is one which is both resident in the UK and another territory. A relevant multinational company is:

   – one which is subject to tax under the law of a territory outside its territory of residence, by reason of carrying on a business through a PE there ("the PE jurisdiction"); and

   – the UK is either the PE jurisdiction or the territory of residence ("the parent jurisdiction").

– Condition B – there is an amount which, ignoring Ch 10 Pt 6A TIOPA 2010 and any equivalent overseas provision, it is reasonable to suppose could, by reason of the company being a dual resident company or relevant multinational company, both:

   – be deducted from the income of the company for an accounting period for corporation tax purposes; and

   – be deducted from the income of the company for a taxable period for the purposes of an overseas tax.

The amount is the "dual territory double deduction amount".

Sections 259JB, 259JC and 259JD contain the counteraction provisions. Where the company is a dual resident company, s 259JB provides that the dual territory double deduction amount may not be deducted from the company's income for corporation tax purposes unless it is deducted from dual inclusion income of the company.

Any denied deduction on these grounds can be carried forward by the company and potentially deducted from dual inclusion income in future periods.

Similarly to Ch 9, there is an additional set of provisions at s 259JB(4)–(7) which may, in limited cases, permit the company to deduct an otherwise denied "dual territory double deduction amount" directly from its regular profits chargeable to corporation tax. However, broadly this would only apply in cases where both:

– HMRC are satisfied that the company has ceased to be a dual resident company; and

– It is not reasonable to suppose that the dual territory double deduction amount has already been deducted by a person from non-dual inclusion income of the company for the purposes of an overseas tax.

Where the company is a relevant multinational company and the UK is the parent jurisdiction, under s 259JC any portion of the dual territory double deduction which is (in substance) deducted for overseas tax purposes from non-dual inclusion income of the company is considered the "impermissible overseas deduction" This is then not permitted as deductible by the company for corporation tax purposes in the deduction period, subject to any "just and reasonable" adjustments that should be made to the amount. Any such adjustment can be made by "assessment, the modification of an assessment, amendment or disallowance of a claim, or otherwise" and the timing for doing so is not impacted by any time limit imposed by any other enactment.

Where the company is a relevant multinational company where the UK is the PE jurisdiction, under s 259JD, the dual territory double deduction amount may not be deducted from the company's income for corporation tax purposes unless it is deducted from dual inclusion income of the company. However this counteraction only applies to the extent that the company has not already had its position counteracted by an overseas provision equivalent to s 259JC.

There are equivalent provisions at s 259JD(4)–(7) for this circumstance (i.e. relevant multinational company with the UK as PE jurisdiction) as described above at s 259JB(4)–(7) for the circumstance in which the company is a dual resident company. That is, in some cases it may be possible for a company to deduct a dual territory double deduction amount from non-dual inclusion income, however that would only be possible where no overseas person has deducted the corresponding amount from non-dual inclusion income of the company.

New TIOPA 2010 Pt 6A Ch 11 ss 259K–259KB

Chapter 11 addresses "imported mismatches" Section 259K is the overview of the Chapter.

Section 259KA contains the seven Conditions (A–G) which must all be met for the Chapter to apply. These are summarised as:

- Conditions A, B and C – a payment or quasi-payment ("the imported mismatch payment") is made under/in connection with an arrangement ("the imported mismatch arrangement") by a payer ("P") who is within the charge to corporation tax. The imported mismatch arrangement is one of a series of arrangements entered into in pursuance of, or in relation to, an "over-arching arrangement".
- Condition D – under a different arrangement in the series, there is a payment or quasi-payment which it is reasonable to suppose gives rise to any of the mismatches defined in any of Chs 3–10 (or, in the case of Ch 6, not a payment/quasi-payment, but simply an arrangement (since no payment/quasi-payment is relevant to the operation of Ch 6). Where the UK is integral to any definition of mismatch arrangements in the earlier Chapters (e.g. UK PEs in Ch 6, UK being one of the deduction territories in the definition of "dual territory double deduction amount" in Ch 10), these definitions are broadened for the purposes of the Ch 11 test in s 259KB. This mismatch is the "relevant mismatch".
- Condition E – it is reasonable to suppose that no provision of Chs 3–10 Pt 6A TIOPA 2010 nor any equivalent overseas provision applies to the tax treatment of any person who is party to the "relevant mismatch" contemplated in Condition D.
- Condition F – it is reasonable to suppose that a provision of Chs 3–10 Pt 6A TIOPA 2010 or an equivalent overseas provision *would* apply to the tax treatment of P *if* P were the payer/payee/investor/etc as appropriate in respect of the relevant mismatch.
- Condition G – P is in the same control group as any party to the relevant mismatch, or the imported mismatch arrangement/over-arching arrangement is a structured arrangement (as generally defined and used across all other Chapters).

Thus it can be seen that the basic intention of Ch 11 is to apply to situations in which a mismatch arrangement between parties who are not themselves subject to the rules of Pt 6A TIOPA 2010 is linked in some way to a regular (non-mismatch) payment by a UK payer which would otherwise be deductible for UK purposes.

Section 259KC covers the counteraction of imported mismatches. Where no "linkage" can be shown between the relevant mismatch and any payments other than P's imported mismatch payment, the whole of P's relevant deduction for the imported mismatch payment is denied. In other cases, to the extent that such linkage can be shown, an exercise is carried out to apportion on a just and reasonable basis the relevant mismatch amongst all the payments which can be linked to it (including P's imported mismatch payment). The proportion which is attributable to P's imported mismatch payment is the proportion of P's relevant deduction which is denied. It is worth noting that in s 259KC(8) it is explicitly provided that in proceedings before a court or tribunal in connection with an imported mismatch, the burden of proof is on P to show any such "linkage" which would reduce the quantum of its disallowance (i.e. that payment(s) other than P's imported mismatch payment fund the relevant mismatch arrangement).

New TIOPA 2010 Pt 6A Ch 12 ss 259L–259LA

Chapter 12 covers adjustments to deal with subsequent events which might impact the original treatment of an arrangement (for example, where something ceases to be a mismatch). The main overarching provision of Ch 12 broadly provides that where a reasonable supposition is made for the purposes of any provision in Pt 6A TIOPA 2010, and that supposition turns out to be mistaken or otherwise ceases to be reasonable, such consequential amendments as are just and reasonable may be made. For example, many "reasonable supposition" provisions of Pt 6A are in relation to how one side of a mismatch arrangement might be treated for the purposes of an overseas tax, in relation to which the UK resident party in practice may have limited information. Therefore a reasonable supposition must be made for the purposes of the relevant Pt 6A analysis which may lead one to conclude that there is a mismatch to be counteracted. If, however, the UK resident party later receives additional information about the overseas tax treatment, and discovers that there is no mismatch arising after all, one might expect that a "just and reasonable" consequential amendment is to amend the counteraction originally imposed under Pt 6A.

Notwithstanding the above, the time limit to make any amendments arising is to be governed by any time limits imposed by any other enactment.

Chapter 12 contains one other broad rule, concerning a mismatch situation under any of Chs 3, 4, 7 or 8. Where income arises to a payee later than the end of the "permitted taxable period", it would be considered as a mismatch under those Chapters. It may, however, under Ch 12 be treated as deductible against the payer's profits generally chargeable to corporation tax in the period in which the late income arises to the payee, or it may be carried forward to a later period of the payer if necessary.

New TIOPA 2010 Pt 6A Ch 13 s 259M

Chapter 13 contains provision countering the effect of avoidance arrangements, and applies as follows:

Any person who is within the charge to corporation tax (or who would be but for the avoidance) and obtains a "relevant tax advantage" as a result of "relevant avoidance arrangements" will have the relevant tax advantage counteracted by the making of just and reasonable adjustments to their corporation tax treatment.

The two key concepts are:

- A "relevant tax advantage" is obtained if a person avoids the restriction of a deduction or the imposition of income under Pt 6A or an equivalent overseas provision.
- "Relevant avoidance arrangements" are arrangements the main purpose, or one of the main purposes, of which is to enable any person to obtain a relevant tax advantage.

However, where the obtaining of a relevant tax advantage is considered as consistent with the principles (whether express or implied) and policy objectives of Pt 6A or equivalent overseas provision (as appropriate), this will not give rise to relevant avoidance arrangements. In order to determine such principles and policy objectives, regard may be had where appropriate to the October 2015 BEPS Action 2 report (or any replacement or supplementary publication).

Therefore, in summary, any arrangements to "structure away" from Pt 6A applying may *prima facie* be considered as having no effect (or some different effect, determined "justly and reasonably") by reason of Ch 13. However if the method of such structuring away can be shown to be in line with the principles/policy objectives of Pt 6A, then it may not be counteracted under Ch 13. In practice, analysing transactions in many cases is expected to be complex and uncertain unless it can be easily and clearly understood what the particular relevant principles of Pt 6A are in connection with the transaction(s).

New TIOPA 2010 Pt 6A Ch 14 ss 259N–259NF

Chapter 14 contains further definitions/interpretational points not already covered in Ch 2. The main definitions/interpretational points are summarised as:

> **"financial instrument"** (relevant in particular for Ch 3) broadly includes:
> - anything which would fall to be taxed in accordance with Pts 5, 6 or 7 CTA 2009 if UK corporation tax principles were relevant to it (i.e. loan relationships, certain matters treated as loan relationships, and derivative contracts);
> - any finance arrangement defined in Ch 2 Pt 16 CTA 2010;
> - a share or instrument giving economic rights equivalent to a share; or
> - anything accounted for under UK GAAP as a financial instrument.
>
> This definition however excludes a hybrid transfer arrangement (since that is dealt with separately by Ch 4) and any regulatory capital security (as defined in SI 2013/3209).

- **"relevant investment fund"** (relevant for certain exceptions to the application of Chs 3 and 4) is any open-ended investment company (under s 613 CTA 2010), authorised unit trust (under s 616 CTA 2010) or offshore fund (under s 354 CTA 2010) which meets the "genuine diversity of ownership" test from relevant regulations.

- Persons A and B are in the same **"control group"** if any of three tests is met:
  - they are consolidated for accounting purposes;
  - the participation condition is met (this is an equivalent condition to that included in the transfer pricing rules of Part 4 TIOPA 2010); or
  - either A has a 50% investment in B, or vice versa, or a third person has a 50% investment in both A and B.

  The 50% investment test is defined by reference to any of: share capital ownership, voting power, economic interest in shares, income distribution entitlement and liquidation distribution entitlement. Furthermore, there is an investment proportion pooling provision for persons "acting together" in relation to an investee.

- Persons A and B are **"related"** to each other if they are in the same control

group, or the investment test noted above is met, but with a 25% threshold instead of 50%. Therefore it can be seen that all persons within the same control group will be related, but not all related persons will be within the same control group.
– Some points around the treatment of partnerships in Pt 6A are confirmed. In particular, a reference to income, profits or an amount of a person include a reference to the person's share of such income, profits or an amount of a partnership in which it is a member. The person's share should be determined on a just and reasonable basis.

Part 2 Consequential Amendments

Part 2 contains consequential provisions. These are all routine in nature, except to note that Pt 6 TIOPA 2010 ("tax arbitrage") is repealed in its entirety. This is aligned with the intention that new Pt 6A deals comprehensively (and, broadly, without purpose-driven tests) with mismatch arrangements.

Part 3 Commencement

Part 3 contains the commencement provisions. "The commencement date" is 1 January 2017 and, broadly:
– For provisions in Pt 6A which operate by reference to payments, commencement will be for payments made on or after the commencement date.
– For provisions in Pt 6A which operate by reference to periods (e.g. double deductions, quasi-payments, etc), any period which straddles the commencement date will be treated as two separate periods and Pt 6A will apply to the later straddling period.
– The repeal of Pt 6 will be transitioned under the same straddling period approach.
As a result of the above, 1 January 2017 should be the date upon which all provisions of Pt 6A effectively begin to have effect on relevant arrangements (and Pt 6 correspondingly ceases to have effect).

SCHEDULE 11

DISPOSALS OF NON-UK RESIDENTIAL PROPERTY INTERESTS

Section 83

1 TCGA 1992 is amended in accordance with this Schedule.

2 In section 14B(1) (meaning of "non-resident CGT disposal"), in paragraph (a) after "disposal of a UK residential property interest" insert "(within the meaning given by Schedule B1)".

3 Omit section 14C (which introduces Schedule B1 and is superseded by the section 4BB inserted by section 83 of this Act).

4 In Schedule B1 (disposals of UK residential property interests), in paragraph 1—
  (a) in sub-paragraph (4) for "6 April 2015" substitute "the relevant date";
  (b) after that sub-paragraph insert—
  "(4A) In sub-paragraph (4) "the relevant date" means—
    (a) for the purpose of determining whether a disposal is a non-resident CGT disposal, 6 April 2015;
    (b) for any other purpose, 31 March 1982."

5 After Schedule B1 insert—

"SCHEDULE BA1

DISPOSALS OF NON-UK RESIDENTIAL PROPERTY INTERESTS

Section 4BB.

Meaning of "disposal of a non-UK residential property interest"

1 (1) For the purposes of this Act, the disposal by a person ("P") of an interest in non-UK land (whether made before or after this Schedule comes into force) is a "disposal of a non-UK residential property interest" if the first or second condition is met.

(2) The first condition is that—

(a) the land has at any time in the relevant ownership period consisted of or included a dwelling, or

(b) the interest in non-UK land subsists for the benefit of land that has at any time in the relevant ownership period consisted of or included a dwelling.

(3) The second condition is that the interest in non-UK land subsists under a contract for an off-plan purchase.

(4) In sub-paragraph (2) "relevant ownership period" means the period—

(a) beginning with the day on which P acquired the interest in non-UK land or 31 March 1982 (whichever is later), and

(b) ending with the day before the day on which the disposal occurs.

(5) If the interest in non-UK land disposed of by P as mentioned in sub-paragraph (1) results from interests in non-UK land which P has acquired at different times ("the acquired interests"), P is regarded for the purposes of sub-paragraph (4)(a) as having acquired the interest when P first acquired any of the acquired in-terests.

(6) In this paragraph—

"contract for an off-plan purchase" means a contract for the acquisition of land consisting of, or including, a building or part of a building that is to be constructed or adapted for use as a dwelling;

"dwelling" is to be read in accordance with paragraph 4.

(7) Paragraphs 6 and 20 of Schedule 4ZZC contain further provision about interests under contracts for off-plan purchases.

"Interest in non-UK land"

2 (1) In this Schedule "interest in non-UK land" means—

(a) an estate, interest, right or power in or over land outside the United Kingdom, or

(b) the benefit of an obligation, restriction or condition affecting the value of any such estate, interest, right or power,

other than an excluded interest.

(2) The following are excluded interests—

(a) any security interest;

(b) a licence to use or occupy land.

(3) In sub-paragraph (2) "security interest" means an interest or right held for the purpose of securing the payment of money or the performance of any other obligation.

(4) The Treasury may by regulations—

(a) provide that any other description of interest or right in relation to land outside the United Kingdom is an excluded interest;

(b) exclude from sub-paragraph (2) such interests or rights as may be prescribed in the regulations.

(5) Regulations under sub-paragraph (4) may make incidental, consequential, supplementary or transitional provision or savings.

Grants of options

3 (1) Sub-paragraph (2) applies where—

(a) a person ("P") grants at any time an option binding P to sell an interest in non-UK land, and

(b) a disposal by P of that interest in non-UK land at that time would be a disposal of a non-UK residential property interest by virtue of paragraph 1.

(2) The grant of the option is regarded for the purposes of this Schedule as the disposal of an interest in the land in question (if it would not be so regarded apart from this paragraph).

(3) Nothing in this paragraph affects the operation of section 144 in relation to the grant of the option (or otherwise).

(4) Subsection (6) of section 144 (interpretation of references to "sale" etc) applies for the purposes of this paragraph as it applies for the purposes of that section.

Meaning of "dwelling"

4 (1) Paragraph 4 of Schedule B1 (meaning of "dwelling"), read with paragraphs 6 to 10 of that Schedule, applies for the purposes of this Schedule as it applies for the purposes of Schedule B1, but as if—

(a) in paragraph 4, sub-paragraphs (5) and (6) were omitted,

(b) in paragraphs 6 and 8—

(i) any reference to an interest in UK land were to an interest in non-UK land within the meaning of this Schedule, and

(ii) any reference to paragraph 1(4) of that Schedule were a reference to paragraph 1(4) of this Schedule, and

(c) in paragraphs 7 to 9 any reference to planning permission or development consent were to any permission or consent corresponding to planning permission or development consent within the meaning of that Schedule.

(2) In paragraph 5 of Schedule B1 (power to amend), the reference to paragraph 4 includes paragraph 4 as applied by this paragraph.

(3) The Treasury may by regulations under this sub-paragraph make provision changing or clarifying the cases where a building outside the United Kingdom counts as a dwelling for the purposes of this Schedule (and sub-paragraph (1) has effect subject to any such regulations).

(4) Provision made under sub-paragraph (3) may include provision corresponding to paragraph 4(5) of Schedule B1.

Interpretation

5 In this Schedule "land" includes a building."

GENERAL NOTE

Schedule 11 makes various amendments to the TCGA 1992 and inserts a new TCGA 1992 Sch BA1. A new sub-para (4A) is inserted into TCGA 1992 Sch B1. This changes the date on which the 'relevant ownership period' starts for the purposes of identifying a disposal of a UK residential property interest by UK residents so that it is the later of the date of acquisition or 31 March 1982.

Paragraph 1 of Sch BA1 defines a 'disposal of a non-UK residential property interest' as, broadly, the disposal of either an interest in non-UK land that has consisted of or included a dwelling at any time during the relevant ownership period or a disposal of a contract for an off-plan purchase. Paragraph 2 defines an 'interest in non-UK land' and para 3 provides that the grant of an option is treated as the disposal of an interest in the land.

Paragraph 4 defines a 'dwelling' for the purposes of the schedule. It imports the definition in TCGA 1992 Sch B1, subject to certain modifications. The definitions in Schs B1 and BA1 are close – but not identical. Great care continues to be required on the differing definitions of residential property and dwellings throughout the UK tax legislation and even the differing definitions within different parts of the same statute.

SCHEDULE 12

DISPOSALS OF RESIDENTIAL PROPERTY INTERESTS: GAINS AND LOSSES

Section 83

1 TCGA 1992 is amended in accordance with this Schedule.

2 In section 57A(3) (gains and losses on relevant high value disposals: interaction with other provisions)—

(a) the words from "Part 4" to the end become paragraph (a), and

(b) after that paragraph insert "or,

(b) Part 3 of Schedule 4ZZC applies (other disposals of residential property interests which are or involve relevant high value disposals)."

3 After section 57B insert—

"CHAPTER 7

COMPUTATION OF GAINS AND LOSSES: DISPOSALS OF RESIDENTIAL PROPERTY INTERESTS

57C Gains and losses on disposals of residential property interests

Schedule 4ZZC makes provision about the computation of—

(a) residential property gains or losses, and

(b) other gains or losses,

on disposals of residential property interests which are not non-resident CGT disposals."

4 In Schedule B1 (disposals of UK residential property interests), in paragraph 1(7) after "Schedule 4ZZB" insert "and paragraphs 6 and 20 of Schedule 4ZZC".

5 After Schedule 4ZZB insert—

"SCHEDULE 4ZZC

DISPOSALS OF RESIDENTIAL PROPERTY INTERESTS: GAINS AND LOSSES

Section 57C

PART 1

INTRODUCTION AND INTERPRETATION

Introduction

1 (1) In this Schedule "RPI disposal" means a disposal of a residential property interest which is not a non-resident CGT disposal.

(2) This Schedule applies for the purpose of determining, in relation to an RPI disposal—

(a) whether a residential property gain or loss accrues on the disposal, and the amount of any such gain or loss, and

(b) whether a gain or loss other than a residential property gain or loss accrues on the disposal, and the amount of any such gain or loss.

(3) In this Schedule—

(a) Part 2 contains the main rules for computing the gains and losses;

(b) Part 3 contains the rules for computing the gains and losses in a case where the RPI disposal is, or involves, a relevant high value disposal (as defined in section 2C).

Interpretation

2 (1) For the purposes of this Schedule, a relevant high value disposal is "comprised in" an RPI disposal if—

(a) the RPI disposal is treated for the purposes of section 2C and Schedule 4ZZA as two or more disposals, and

(b) the relevant high value disposal is one of those.

(2) In this Schedule—

"chargeable interest" has the same meaning as in Part 3 of the Finance Act 2013 (annual tax on enveloped dwellings) (see section 107 of that Act);

"dwelling" has the meaning given by —

(a) paragraph 4 of Schedule B1, in relation to a disposal of a UK residential property interest;

(b) paragraph 4 of Schedule BA1, in relation to a disposal of a non-UK residential property interest;

"subject-matter", in relation to an interest in land (or a chargeable interest) means the land to which the interest relates.

PART 2

RPI DISPOSALS NOT INVOLVING RELEVANT HIGH VALUE DISPOSALS

Application of Part

3 (1) This Part of this Schedule applies where a person ("P") makes an RPI disposal of (or of part of) an interest in land.

(2) But this Part of this Schedule does not apply if the disposal is—

(a) a relevant high value disposal, or

(b) a disposal in which a relevant high value disposal is comprised.

(3) In this Part of this Schedule "the disposed of interest" means—

(a) the interest in land, or

(b) if the disposal is of part of that interest, the part disposed of.

Computation of residential property gains and losses

4 (1) The residential property gain or loss accruing on the disposal is computed as follows.

Step 1

Determine the amount of the gain or loss that accrues to P.

Step 2

The residential property gain or loss accruing on the disposal is an amount equal to the relevant fraction of that gain or loss (but see Step 3).

Step 3

If there has been mixed use of the subject matter of the disposed of interest on one or more days in the relevant ownership period, the residential property gain or loss accruing on the disposal is equal to the appropriate fraction of the amount given by Step 2.

(2) In Step 2 "the relevant fraction" means—

RD / TD

where—

"RD" is the number of days in the relevant ownership period on which the subject matter of the disposed of interest consists wholly or partly of a dwelling;
"TD" is the total number of days in the relevant ownership period.

(3) For the purposes of Step 3 there is "mixed use" of land on any day on which the land consists partly, but not exclusively, of one or more dwellings.

(4) In Step 3 "the appropriate fraction" means the fraction that is, on a just and reasonable apportionment, attributable to the dwelling or dwellings.

(5) In this paragraph the "relevant ownership period" means the period—

(a) beginning with the day on which P acquired the disposed of interest or, if later, 31 March 1982, and

(b) ending with the day before the day on which the disposal occurs.

Computation of balancing gains and loses

5 The gain or loss accruing on the disposal which is not a residential property gain or loss is computed as follows.

Step 1

In a case where there is a gain under Step 1 of paragraph 4(1), determine the amount of that gain remaining after the deduction of the residential property gain determined under that paragraph.

That remaining gain is the gain accruing on the disposal which is not a residential property gain.

Step 2

In a case where there is a loss under Step 1 of paragraph 4(1), determine the amount of that loss remaining after the deduction of the residential property loss determined under that paragraph.

That remaining loss is the loss accruing on the disposal which is not a residential property loss.

Interest subsisting under contract for off-plan purchase

6 (1) This paragraph applies where the disposal referred to in paragraph 3(1) is a disposal of a residential property interest only because of—

(a) the second condition in paragraph 1 of Schedule B1, or

(b) the second condition in paragraph 1 of Schedule BA1,

(interest subsisting under a contract for the acquisition of land that consists of, or includes, a building that is to be constructed for use as a dwelling).

(2) The land that is the subject of the contract concerned is treated for the purposes of this Part of this Schedule as consisting of (or, as the case requires, including) a dwelling throughout P's period of ownership of the disposed of interest.

PART 3

RPI DISPOSALS INVOLVING RELEVANT HIGH VALUE DISPOSALS

Application of Part

7 (1) This Part of this Schedule applies where—

(a) a person (other than an excluded person) ("P") makes an RPI disposal of (or of part of) an interest in land, and

(b) that disposal ("the disposal of land") is a relevant high value disposal or a relevant high value disposal is comprised in it.

(2) "Excluded person" has the meaning given by section 2B(2).

Interpretation of Part

8 (1) This paragraph applies for the interpretation of this Part of this Schedule.

(2) "The asset", in relation to a relevant high value disposal, means the chargeable interest which (or a part of which) is the subject of that disposal.

(3) "The disposed of interest", in relation to a relevant high value disposal, means the asset or, if only part of the asset is the subject of the relevant high value disposal, that part of the asset.

(4) A day is a "residential property chargeable day" in relation to a relevant high value disposal if—

(a) it is a day on which the subject matter of the disposed of interest consists wholly or partly of a dwelling, but
(b) it is not an ATED chargeable day (as defined in paragraph 3 of Schedule 4ZZA).

Computation of residential property gains or losses on the RPI disposal

9 (1) The residential property gain or loss accruing on the disposal of land is computed as follows.

Step 1
Determine in accordance with paragraphs 10 to 15 the amount of the residential property gain or loss accruing on each relevant high value disposal.
Step 2
Add together the amounts of any gains or losses determined under Step 1 (treating any amount which is a loss as a negative amount).

(2) If the result is a positive amount, that amount is the residential property gain on the disposal of land.

(3) If the result is a negative amount, that amount (expressed as a positive number) is the residential property loss on the disposal of land.

Computation of residential property gains or losses on relevant high value disposal not within Case 1, 2 or 3 (or where an election is made)

10 (1) This paragraph applies to a relevant high value disposal where—

(a) the disposal does not fall within any of Cases 1, 2 or 3 in paragraph 2 of Schedule 4ZZA, or
(b) P has made an election under paragraph 5 of that Schedule in respect of the asset.

(2) The residential property gain or loss accruing on the relevant high value disposal is computed as follows—

Step 1
Determine the amount of gain or loss which accrues to P.
(For the purpose of determining the amount of that gain or loss, no account is taken of section 57C or this Schedule.)
Step 2
The residential property gain or loss accruing on the relevant high value disposal is equal to the special fraction of that gain or loss.

(3) The "special fraction" is—

SD / TD
where—

"SD" is the number of residential property chargeable days in the relevant ownership period;
"TD" is the total number of days in the relevant ownership period.

(4) "Relevant ownership period" means the period—

(a) beginning with the day on which P acquired the disposed of interest or, if later, 31 March 1982, and
(b) ending with the day before the day on which the relevant high value disposal occurs.

Computation of residential property gains and losses on relevant high value disposal within Case 1, 2 or 3 (and no election made)

11 (1) This paragraph applies to a relevant high value disposal where—

(a) the disposal falls within Case 1, 2 or 3 in paragraph 2 of Schedule 4ZZA, and

(b) P has not made an election under paragraph 5 of that Schedule in respect of the asset.

(2) The residential property gain or loss accruing on the relevant high value disposal is computed in accordance with paragraphs 12 to 15.

(3) In those paragraphs "the relevant year" means—

(a) where the relevant high value disposal falls within Case 1 in paragraph 2 of Schedule 4ZZA, 2013,

(b) where it falls within Case 2 in that paragraph, 2015, and

(c) where it falls within Case 3 in that paragraph, 2016.

12 (1) Take the following steps—

Step 1

Determine the amount equal to the special fraction of the notional pre-ATED gain or loss (as the case may be) (see paragraph 13).

Step 2

Determine the amount equal to the special fraction of the notional post-ATED gain or loss (as the case may be) (see paragraph 14).

Step 3

Add (treating any amount which is a loss as a negative amount)—

(a) the amount of any gain or loss determined under Step 1, and

(b) the amount of any gain or loss determined under Step 2.

(2) If the result is a positive amount, that amount is the residential property gain on the relevant high value disposal.

(3) If the result is a negative amount, that amount (expressed as a positive number) is the residential property loss on the relevant high value disposal.

13 (1) This paragraph applies for the purposes of Step 1 in paragraph 12.

(2) "Notional pre-ATED gain or loss" means the gain or loss which would have accrued on 5 April of the relevant year had the disposed of interest been disposed of for a consideration equal to the market value of the interest on that date.

(3) The "special fraction" is—

SD / TD

where—

"SD" is the number of residential property chargeable days in the relevant ownership period;

"TD" is the total number of days in the relevant ownership period.

(4) The "relevant ownership period" is the period—

(a) beginning with the day on which P acquired the disposed of interest or, if later, 31 March 1982, and

(b) ending with 5 April of the relevant year.

14 (1) This paragraph applies for the purposes of Step 2 in paragraph 12.

(2) "Notional post-ATED gain or loss" means the gain or loss which would have accrued on the relevant high value disposal had P acquired the disposed of interest on 5 April of the relevant year for a consideration equal to its market value on that date (and see paragraph 15).

(3) The "special fraction" is—

SD / TD

where—

"SD" is the number of residential property chargeable days in the relevant ownership period;

"TD" is the total number of days in the relevant ownership period.

(4) The "relevant ownership period" is the period beginning with 6 April of the relevant year and ending with the day before the day on which the relevant high value disposal occurs.

15 (1) This paragraph applies for the purposes of computing the notional post-ATED gain or loss for the purposes of Step 2 in paragraph 12.

(2) In determining whether the asset which is the subject of the relevant high value disposal is a wasting asset (as defined for the purposes of Chapter 2 of Part 2), ignore the assumption that the asset was acquired on 5 April of the relevant year.

(3) Sections 41 (restriction of losses by reference to capital allowances and renewals allowances) and 47 (wasting assets subject to capital allowances) apply in relation to any capital allowance or renewals allowance made in respect of the expenditure actually incurred by P in acquiring or providing the asset as if that allowance were made in respect of the expenditure treated as incurred by P on 5 April of the relevant year.

Computation of balancing gains or losses on the RPI disposal

16 (1) The gain or loss on the disposal of land which is neither ATED-related nor a residential property gain or loss ("the balancing gain or loss") is computed as follows.

Step 1
Determine in accordance with paragraphs 17 and 18 the amount of the gain or loss accruing on each relevant high value disposal which is neither ATED-related nor a residential property gain or loss.
This is the "balancing" gain or loss for each disposal.

Step 2
Add together the amounts of any balancing gains or losses determined under Step 1 (treating any amount which is a loss as a negative amount).

(2) If the result is a positive amount, that amount is the balancing gain on the disposal of land.

(3) If the result is a negative amount, that amount (expressed as a positive number) is the balancing loss on the disposal of land.

Computation of balancing gains or losses on relevant high value disposal not within Case 1, 2 or 3 (or where an election is made)

17 (1) In the case of a relevant high value disposal to which paragraph 10 applies, the amount of the balancing gain or loss is determined as follows.

(2) Determine the number of balancing days in the relevant ownership period.

(3) "Balancing day" means a day which is neither—

(a) a residential property chargeable day, nor
(b) an ATED chargeable day (as defined in paragraph 3 of Schedule 4ZZA).

(4) The balancing gain or loss on the disposal is equal to the balancing fraction of the amount of the gain or (as the case may be) loss determined under Step 1 of paragraph 10(2).

(5) The "balancing fraction" is—

BD / TD

where

"BD" is the number of balancing days in the relevant ownership period;
"TD" is the total number of days in the relevant ownership period.

(6) In this paragraph "relevant ownership period" has the same meaning as in paragraph 10.

Computation of balancing gains or losses on relevant high value disposal within Case 1, 2 or 3 (and no election made)

18 (1) The amount of the balancing gain or loss on a relevant high value disposal to which paragraph 11 applies is found by adding—

(a) the amount of the balancing gain or loss belonging to the notional pre-ATED gain or loss, and
(b) the amount of the balancing gain or loss belonging to the notional post-ATED gain or loss,

(treating any amount which is a loss as a negative amount).

(2) If the result is a positive amount, that amount is the balancing gain on the relevant high value disposal.

(3) If the result is a negative amount, that amount (expressed as a positive number) is the balancing loss on the relevant high value disposal.

(4) The balancing gain or loss belonging to the notional pre-ATED gain or loss is equal to the balancing fraction of the notional pre-ATED gain or loss.

(5) The balancing gain or loss belonging to the notional post-ATED gain or loss is equal to the balancing fraction of the notional post-ATED gain or loss.

(6) The balancing fraction is—

BD / TD

where—

"BD" is the number of balancing days in the appropriate ownership period;
"TD" is the total number of days in the appropriate ownership period.

(7) "Balancing day" means a day which is neither—

(a) a residential property chargeable day, nor

(b) an ATED chargeable day (as defined in paragraph 3 of Schedule 4ZZA).

(8) The appropriate ownership period is—

(a) for the purpose of computing the balancing gain or loss belonging to the notional pre-ATED gain or loss, the relevant ownership period mentioned in paragraph 13(4);

(b) for the purpose of computing the balancing gain or loss belonging to the notional post-ATED gain or loss, the relevant ownership period mentioned in paragraph 14(4).

(9) In this paragraph—

"notional pre-ATED gain or loss" means the same as in paragraph 13(2);
"notional post-ATED gain or loss" means the same as in paragraph 14(2).

Relevant high value disposal and "other" disposal are comprised in the disposal of land

19 (1) This paragraph applies where the disposals comprised in the disposal of land include a disposal (the "non-ATED related disposal") which is not a relevant high value disposal.

(2) This Part of this Schedule (apart from this paragraph) applies in relation to the non-ATED related disposal as if it were a relevant high value disposal.

(3) Sub-paragraph (4) applies if there has, at any time in the relevant ownership period, been mixed use of the subject matter of the disposed of interest.

(4) The amount of any residential property gain or loss on the non-ATED related disposal computed under this Part of this Schedule is taken to be the appropriate fraction of the amount that it would otherwise be.

(5) In sub-paragraph (4) "the appropriate fraction" means the fraction that is, on a just and reasonable apportionment, attributable to the dwelling or dwellings.

(6) In this paragraph the "relevant ownership period" means—

(a) where paragraph 10 applies, the relevant ownership period as defined in paragraph 10(4), or

(b) where paragraph 11 applies, the relevant ownership period as defined in paragraphs 13(4) and 14(4).

Interest subsisting under contract for off-plan purchase

20 (1) This paragraph applies where the RPI disposal made by P is a disposal of a residential property interest only because of—

(a) the second condition in paragraph 1 of Schedule B1, or

(b) the second condition in paragraph 1 of Schedule BA1,

(interest subsisting under a contract for the acquisition of land that consists of, or includes, a building that is to be constructed for use as a dwelling).

(2) The land that is the subject of the contract concerned is treated for the purposes of this Part of this Schedule as consisting of (or, as the case requires, including) a dwelling throughout P's period of ownership of the interest in land."

GENERAL NOTE

The need to deal with computational complications arising from the reduction of the capital gains tax rate necessitates the insertion of TCGA 1992 s 57C and TCGA 1992 Sch 4ZZC which are both introduced by FA 2016 Sch 12. Section 57A is amended to provide that where there is no ATED-related gain or loss accruing on a disposal, TCGA 1992 Sch 4ZZA continues to apply if Pt 3 of the new Sch 4ZZC applies.

TCGA 1992 Sch 4ZZC Pt 2 contains the rules for computing the amount of residential property interest (RPI) gain or loss in a case where the disposal does not involve a disposal that is chargeable to ATED-related capital gains tax. This includes computational complications arising from mixed use and differences in usage of a property over time since 1982. The definition of an RPI disposal includes the off-plan purchase of a dwelling. The adoption of the term "RPI disposal" for the disposal of a residential property interest is somewhat unhelpful given the history of the retail prices index within capital gains tax.

TCGA 1992 Sch 4ZZC para 4 provides that the RPI gain or loss is that proportion of the gain or loss over the period of ownership (since 31 March 1982) that reflects the amount of days in which the asset is used as a dwelling. Any mixed use on the same day is apportioned on a just and reasonable basis.

The distinction between residential and non-residential property gains necessitates the need to consider changes in the usage of an asset over time and different usage of the same asset at the same time (mixed use). Mixed use has typically been an issue in the capital gains tax legislation as between business and non-business usage – such as for roll-over, hold-over and taper reliefs. The computation in para 4 is entirely independent of main residence relief under TCGA 1992 s 222.

TCGA 1992 Sch 4ZZC Pt 3 contains the rules for computing the amount of RPI gain or loss in a case where the disposal either is, or involves, a disposal that is chargeable to ATED-related capital gains tax.

TCGA 1992 Sch 4ZZC para 10 provides that in a case where there is no rebasing for the purposes of ATED-related capital gains tax, the amount of RPI gain or loss is that proportion of the gain or loss over the period of ownership (since 31 March 1982) that reflects the amount of days in which the asset is used as a dwelling and the days are not ATED chargeable days.

TCGA 1992 Sch 4ZZC paras 11–14 provide that in a case where there is rebasing for the purposes of ATED-related capital gains tax, the rebasing also applies for the purposes of the computation. The amount of RPI gain or loss is the sum of the RPI gain or loss that relates to the period up to the rebasing date and the RPI gain or loss from the rebasing date. The amount of RPI gain or loss in each case is that proportion of the gain or loss over the period of ownership or from the rebasing date that reflects the amount of days in which the asset is used as a dwelling and the days are not ATED chargeable days.

TCGA 1992 Sch 4ZZC para 15 explains how rules relating to wasting assets and capital allowances should be taken into account when computing the RPI gain or loss that relates to the period from the rebasing date.

TCGA 1992 Sch 4ZZC paras 16–18 provide the computational rules for the amount of the gain or loss that is neither ATED-related nor a RPI gain or loss. Paragraph 17 contains provisions for when para 10 applies and para 18 contains provisions for when para 11 applies.

TCGA 1992 Sch 4ZZC para 19 provides that where part only of the land disposed of is a relevant high value disposal such that the gains that accrue on its disposal is wholly or in part chargeable to ATED-related capital gains tax, the remaining part of the land is treated in the same way as if it formed part of the relevant high value disposal. Any mixed use on the same day is apportioned on a just and reasonable basis.

SCHEDULE 13

ENTREPRENEURS' RELIEF: "TRADING COMPANY" AND "TRADING GROUP"

Section 86

1 TCGA 1992 is amended as follows.

2 In section 169H(7) (introduction), for "Section 169S contains" substitute "Sections 169S and 169SA contain".

3 In section 169S (interpretation of Chapter), subsection (4A) is treated as never having had effect, and is omitted accordingly.

4 After section 169S insert—

"169SA   Meaning of "trading company" and "trading group"

   Schedule 7ZA gives the meaning in this Chapter of "trading company" and "trading group"."

5 After Schedule 7 insert—

"SCHEDULE 7ZA

ENTREPRENEURS' RELIEF: "TRADING COMPANY" AND "TRADING GROUP"

Section 169SA

PART 1

MEANING OF "TRADING COMPANY" AND "TRADING GROUP"

1 (1) This paragraph gives the meaning of "trading company" and "trading group" where used in the following provisions of Chapter 3 of Part 5 (entrepreneurs' relief)—

(a) in section 169I (material disposal of business assets)—

(i) paragraphs (a) and (b) of subsection (6) (which apply for the purposes of conditions A and B in that section), and
(ii) sub-paragraphs (i) and (ii) of subsection (7A)(c) (which apply for the purposes of conditions C and D in that section), and

(b) section 169J(4) (disposal of trust business assets).

(2) "Trading company" and "trading group" have the same meaning as in section 165 (see section 165A), but as modified by Part 2 of this Schedule.

(3) "Trading activities" (see section 165A(4) and (9)) is to be read in accordance with Part 3 of this Schedule.

2 In provisions of Chapter 3 of Part 5 not mentioned in paragraph 1(1), "trading company" and "trading group" have the same meaning as in section 165 (see section 165A), except that subsections (7) and (12) of section 165A are to be disregarded.

PART 2

JOINT VENTURE COMPANIES

Attribution of activities of a joint venture company

3 In relation to a disposal of assets consisting of (or of interests in) shares in or securities of a company ("company A"), activities of a joint venture company are to be attributed to a company under subsections (7) and (12) of section 165A only if P—

(a) passes the shareholding test in relation to the joint venture company (see paragraphs 5 to 8), and
(b) passes the voting rights test in relation to the joint venture company (see paragraphs 9 to 12).

Meaning of "investing company"

4 (1) For the purposes of this Part, a company is an "investing company" in relation to P and a joint venture company if it meets conditions 1 and 2.

(2) Condition 1 is that—

(a) the company is company A (see paragraph 3), or
(b) P directly owns some portion of the ordinary share capital of the company.

(3) Condition 2 is that the company owns some portion of the ordinary share capital of the joint venture company (whether it is owned directly, indirectly, or partly directly and partly indirectly).

(4) In sub-paragraph (3) the reference to a company owning share capital indirectly is to be read in accordance with section 1155 of CTA 2010.

Shareholding test

5 P passes the shareholding test in relation to a joint venture company if, throughout the relevant period, the sum of the percentages given by paragraphs (a) and (b) is at least 5%—

(a) the percentage of the ordinary share capital of the joint venture company that is owned directly by P, and
(b) P's indirect shareholding percentage (see paragraph 6).

6 P's "indirect shareholding percentage" is found by—

(a) calculating the percentage of the ordinary share capital of the joint venture company that is owned indirectly by P through a particular investing company (see paragraph 7), and

(b) where there are two or more investing companies, adding those percentages together.

7 The percentage of the ordinary share capital of a joint venture company that is owned indirectly by P through a particular investing company ("company IC") at a particular time is given by—

R x S x 100

where—

R is the fraction of company IC's ordinary share capital that is owned by P at that time, and
S is the fraction of the joint venture company's ordinary share capital that is owned by company IC at that time (whether it is owned directly, indirectly, or partly directly and partly indirectly) (see paragraph 8).

8 (1) The fraction of the joint venture company's ordinary share capital that is owned indirectly by company IC is calculated—

(a) by applying sections 1156 and 1157 of CTA 2010, as read with section 1155 of that Act, and
(b) on the assumptions specified in sub-paragraph (2).

(2) The assumptions are—

(a) where company IC directly owns more than 50% of the ordinary share capital of a company, company IC is taken to own the whole of the ordinary share capital of that company;
(b) where a company other than company IC ("company B") directly owns more than 50% of the ordinary share capital of another company ("company C") which is a member of a group of companies of which company IC is a member, company B is taken to own the whole of the ordinary share capital of company C.

Voting rights test

9 P passes the voting rights test in relation to a joint venture company if, throughout the relevant period, the sum of the percentages given by paragraphs (a) and (b) is at least 5%—

(a) the percentage of the voting rights that P holds directly in the joint venture company, and
(b) P's indirect voting rights percentage (see paragraph 10).

10 P's "indirect voting rights percentage" is found by—

(a) calculating the percentage of the voting rights in the joint venture company that P holds indirectly through a particular investing company (see paragraph 11), and
(b) where there are two or more investing companies, adding those percentages together.

11 The percentage of the voting rights in a joint venture company that P holds indirectly through a particular investing company ("company IC") at a particular time is given by—

T x U x 100

where—

T is the fraction of the voting rights in company IC that is held by P at that time, and
U is the fraction of the voting rights in the joint venture company that is held by company IC at that time (whether the voting rights are held directly, indirectly, or partly directly and partly indirectly) (see paragraph 12).

12 (1) The fraction of the voting rights in the joint venture company that is held indirectly by company IC is calculated—

(a) by applying sections 1156 and 1157 of CTA 2010, as read with section 1155 of that Act, as if references in those sections to owning the ordinary share capital of a company were references to holding voting rights in a company, and
(b) on the assumptions specified in sub-paragraph (2).

(2) The assumptions are—

(a) where company IC directly holds more than 50% of the voting rights in a company, company IC is taken to hold all the voting rights in that company;
(b) where a company other than company IC ("company B") directly holds more than 50% of the voting rights in another company ("company C") which is a member of a group of companies of which company IC is a member, company B is taken to hold all the voting rights in company C.

PART 3

PARTNERSHIPS

Activities of a company as a member of a partnership

13 (1) In relation to a disposal of assets consisting of (or of interests in) shares in or securities of a company ("company A"), activities carried on by a company as a member of a partnership are to be treated as not being trading activities of the company (see section 165A(4) and (9)) if P fails either or both of the following—

(a) the profits and assets test in relation to the partnership (see paragraphs 15 to 20);

(b) the voting rights test in relation to the partnership (see paragraphs 21 to 23).

(2) In relation to such a disposal, activities carried on by a company as a member of a partnership are also to be treated as not being trading activities of the company if the company is not a member of the partnership throughout the relevant period.

Meaning of "direct interest company" and "relevant corporate partner"

14 (1) This paragraph applies for the purposes of this Part.

(2) A company is a "direct interest company" in relation to P if—

(a) it is company A (see paragraph 13(1)), or

(b) P directly owns some portion of the ordinary share capital of the company.

(3) A company is a "relevant corporate partner" in relation to P and a partnership if—

(a) a direct interest company in relation to P ("company DIC") owns some portion of the ordinary share capital of the company (whether it is owned directly, indirectly or partly directly and partly indirectly),

(b) the company is a member of a group of companies of which company DIC is a member, and

(c) the company is a member of the partnership.

(4) In sub-paragraph (3) the reference to a company owning share capital indirectly is to be read in accordance with section 1155 of CTA 2010.

Profits and assets test

15 P passes the profits and assets test in relation to a partnership if, throughout the relevant period, the sum of the percentages given by paragraphs (a), (b) and (c) is at least 5%—

(a) the percentage which is P's direct interest in the assets of the partnership,

(b) the percentage which is P's share of the partnership through direct interest companies that are members of the partnership (see paragraph 16), and

(c) the percentage which is P's share of the partnership through direct interest companies and relevant corporate partners in the partnership (see paragraph 18).

16 P's "share of the partnership through direct interest companies that are members of the partnership" is found by—

(a) calculating the percentage which is P's indirect share of the partnership through each direct interest company that is a member of the partnership (see paragraph 17), and

(b) where there are two or more direct interest companies that are members of the partnership, adding those percentages together.

17 The percentage which is P's indirect share of the partnership through a particular direct interest company that is a member of the partnership ("company DICP") at a particular time is given by—

R x V x 100

where—

R is the fraction of company DICP's ordinary share capital that is owned by P at that time, and

V is the lower of—

(a) the fraction of the profits of the partnership in which company DICP has an interest at that time, and

(b) the fraction of the assets of the partnership in which company DICP has an interest at that time.

18 P's "share of the partnership through direct interest companies and relevant corporate partners in the partnership" is found by—

(a) calculating the percentage which is P's indirect share of the partnership through each direct interest company and each relevant corporate partner in the partnership (see paragraph 19), and

(b) where there are two or more direct interest companies or two or more relevant corporate partners, or both, adding those percentages together.

19 The percentage which is P's indirect share of the partnership through a particular direct interest company ("company DIC") and a particular relevant corporate partner in the partnership ("company CP") at a particular time is given by—

$R \times V \times W \times 100$

where—

R is the fraction of company DIC's ordinary share capital that is owned by P at that time,

V is the lower of—

(a) the fraction of the profits of the partnership in which company CP has an interest at that time, and

(b) the fraction of the assets of the partnership in which company CP has an interest at that time, and

W is the fraction of company CP's ordinary share capital that is owned by company DIC at that time (whether it is owned directly, indirectly, or partly directly and partly indirectly) (see paragraph 20).

20 (1) The fraction of a company's ordinary share capital that is owned indirectly by company DIC is calculated—

(a) by applying sections 1156 and 1157 of CTA 2010, as read with section 1155 of that Act, and

(b) on the assumptions specified in sub-paragraph (2).

(2) The assumptions are—

(a) where company DIC directly owns more than 50% of the ordinary share capital of a company, company DIC is taken to own the whole of the ordinary share capital of that company;

(b) where a company other than company DIC ("company B") directly owns more than 50% of the ordinary share capital of another company ("company C") which is a member of a group of companies of which company DIC is a member, company B is taken to own the whole of the ordinary share capital of company C.

Voting rights test

21 (1) P passes the voting rights test in relation to a partnership if, throughout the relevant period, the sum of P's direct voting rights percentage and P's indirect voting rights percentage is at least 5%.

(2) P's "direct voting rights percentage" is found by—

(a) taking the percentage of the voting rights that P holds directly in each direct interest company that is a member of the partnership, and

(b) where P directly holds voting rights in two or more direct interest companies that are members of the partnership, adding those percentages together.

(3) P's "indirect voting rights percentage" is found by—

(a) calculating the percentage which is P's indirect holding of voting rights in each relevant corporate partner in the partnership through each direct interest company (see paragraph 22), and

(b) where there are two or more relevant corporate partners or two or more direct interest companies, or both, adding those percentages together.

22 The percentage which is P's indirect holding of voting rights in a particular relevant corporate partner in the partnership ("company CP") through a particular direct interest company ("company DIC") at a particular time is given by—

$T \times X \times 100$

where—

T is the fraction of the voting rights in company DIC that is held by P at that time, and

X is the fraction of the voting rights in company CP that is held by company DIC at that time (whether the voting rights are held directly, indirectly, or partly directly and partly indirectly) (see paragraph 23).

23 (1) The fraction of the voting rights in a company that is held indirectly by company DIC is calculated—

(a) by applying sections 1156 and 1157 of CTA 2010, as read with section 1155 of that Act, as if references in those sections to owning the ordinary share capital of a company were references to holding voting rights in a company, and

(b) on the assumptions specified in sub-paragraph (2).

(2) The assumptions are—

(a) where company DIC directly holds more than 50% of the voting rights in a company, company DIC is taken to hold all the voting rights in that company;

(b) where a company other than company DIC ("company B") directly holds more than 50% of the voting rights in another company ("company C") which is a member of a group of companies of which company DIC is a member, company B is taken to hold all the voting rights in company C.

PART 4

INTERPRETATION OF THIS SCHEDULE

Meaning of "P"

24 (1) In the case of a material disposal of business assets, "P" means the individual making the disposal.

(2) In the case of a disposal of trust business assets—

(a) "P" means any relevant beneficiary, but

(b) in any reference to P passing or failing the tests mentioned in paragraphs 3 and 13(1), P is to be read as being a single body consisting of all the relevant beneficiaries (so that, for the purposes of determining if those tests are met, percentages are to be calculated in respect of each relevant beneficiary and then aggregated).

(3) The following are "relevant beneficiaries"—

(a) the qualifying beneficiary in relation to the disposal (see section 169J(3)), and

(b) any other beneficiary who is, in relation to the disposal, a beneficiary mentioned in section 169O(1).

Meaning of "relevant period"

25 "The relevant period" means—

(a) for the purposes of conditions A and C in section 169I, the period of 1 year ending with the date of the disposal,

(b) for the purposes of conditions B and D in section 169I, the period of 1 year ending with the date mentioned in subsection (7)(a) or (b) or (7O)(a) or (b) of that section, and

(c) for the purposes of section 169J(4), a period of 1 year ending not earlier than 3 years before the date of the disposal.

Other interpretation provisions

26 (1) Terms used in this Schedule which are defined in subsection (14) of section 165A have the same meaning as they have in that subsection.

(2) References to a person holding voting rights include references to a person who has the ability to control the exercise of voting rights by another person.

(3) For the purposes of Part 3 of this Schedule, the assets of—

(a) a Scottish partnership, or

(b) a partnership under the law of any other country or territory under which assets of a partnership are regarded as held by or on behalf of the partnership as such,

are to be treated as held by the members of the partnership in the proportions in which they are entitled to share in the capital profits of the partnership.

References in Part 3 to a person's interest in the assets of a partnership are to be construed accordingly."

6 (1) The amendments made by this Schedule (except paragraph 3) have effect in relation to disposals made on or after 18 March 2015, but only for the purposes of determining what is a trading company or trading group at times on or after that date.

(2) In conditions B and D in section 169I of TCGA 1992 (material disposal of business assets)—

(a) a reference to a company ceasing to be a trading company does not include a case where, as a result of the coming into force of the amendments made by this Schedule,

a company which was a trading company immediately before 18 March 2015 is treated as ceasing on that day to be a trading company, and
(b) a reference to a company ceasing to be a member of a trading group does not include a case where, as a result of the coming into force of the amendments made by this Schedule, a company which was a member of a trading group immediately before 18 March 2015 is treated as ceasing on that day to be a member of a trading group.
(3) Sub-paragraph (2) is without prejudice to the operation of section 43(4) of FA 2015.

GENERAL NOTE

Schedule 13 introduces new Sch 7ZA into TCGA 1992. This schedule is designed to define the meaning of a trading company or a trading group in the context of joint ventures and corporate partnerships. The schedule represents a retroactive change to the definitions which were changed by the Finance Act 2015 in a way which denied entrepreneurs' relief to shareholders in any company that was a member of a joint venture structure and any company that was a partner in a corporate partnership. The purpose of the schedule is to allow relief where the interest of a shareholder in the underlying business of a joint venture or partnership is at least 5%.

Schedule 7ZA applies to the definitions of trading company and trading group in the context of Conditions (a), (b), (c) and (d) of s 169I TCGA 1992. It also applies in respect of the disposal of trust business assets in s 169J(4) TZGA 1992.

The definitions of trading company and trading group continue to take the same meaning as in s 165A TCGA 1992, subject to Pt 2 of the schedule. The concept of trading activities in s 165A(4) and (9) TCGA 1992 is now to be read in accordance with Pt 3 of the schedule.

Part 2 Joint Venture Companies

The rules relating to joint venture companies are that the shareholding in the company is ignored and, instead, an appropriate proportion of the company's activities are treated as being carried on by the shareholder company. However, this is only done if the shareholder, referred to throughout as "P", passes both the shareholding and voting rights tests in relation to the joint venture company. The tests are in relation to the disposal of shares or securities of a company, referred to as Company A.

For the purposes of these tests, we have a definition of an "investing company" in relation to P, which is that the company satisfies two conditions. Condition 1 is that it must be either Company A (i.e. the company whose shares are being sold) or a company of which P owns some portion of the ordinary share capital. Condition 2 is that the company owns some portion of the ordinary share capital, must own some portion of the ordinary share capital of the joint venture company, directly or indirectly. This is to be read in accordance with s 1155 CTA 2010.

P passes the shareholding test in relation to a joint venture company if the aggregate of his direct and indirect shareholdings in that company is at least 5%. The indirect holdings are found by multiplying P's holding in the investing company ("Company IC") by Company IC's holding in the joint venture company. Indirect holdings by Company IC in the joint venture company are calculated according to the rules in ss 1156 and 1156 CTA 2010, except that a holding that exceeds 50% is to be treated as a holding of 100% of the appropriate company. Where there is more than one investing company in which P has a direct or indirect shareholding, the overall proportions are aggregated in arriving at the total interest that P has in the underlying joint venture company.

The voting rights percentages are found by exactly the same mechanism, multiplying the relevant direct and indirect voting rights, rather than holdings of ordinary share capital. Once again, the rules at ss 1155 to 1157 CTA 2010 are applied, taking voting rights in excess of 50% as being full voting rights in the relevant company.

Part 3 Partnership Rights

Where P is selling shares in company A, and company A is a member of a partnership, P must satisfy both the profits and assets test and the voting rights test in relation to the partnership in order to be entitled to entrepreneurs' relief on the disposal of shares. Once again, the intention is to arrive at an overall figure of at least 5% interest.

In relation to P, a company is a "direct interest company", also referred to as "company DIC", if it is company A, or another company of which P directly owns some portion of the ordinary share capital. A company is a "relevant corporate partner" in relation to P or a partnership if it is a member of the partnership, it is a member of a group of companies of which company DIC is a member and some portion of its ordinary share capital is owned directly or indirectly by company DIC. These shareholding tests are to be read in accordance with s 1155 CTA 2010.

The profits and assets test requires us to find P's overall interest in the profits and assets of the partnership. This comprises three elements:

- P's direct interest in the partnership, taking the lower of his interests in the profits or the assets.
- P's percentage interest in the partnership through direct interest companies that are members of the partnership.
- P's share of the partnership through direct interest companies and relevant corporate partners.

P's share of the partnership through direct interest companies that are members of the partnership is found by multiplying's P's interest in a direct interest company that is a member of the partnership ("company DICP") by the lower of that company's interest in the profits or assets of the partnership. If there are more than one company DICP, the figures are aggregated.

P's share of the partnership through direct interest companies and relevant corporate partners in the partnership is found by multiplying P's interest in company DIC by company DIC's interest in the corporate partner ("company CP") and by the lower of the interest that company CP has in the profits or the assets of the partnership.

Once again, the rules at ss 1156 and 1157 CTA 2010 are applied, except that where a company holds more than 50% of the ordinary share capital of another company, it is deemed to hold the whole of it.

The voting rights test in respect of a partnership is similarly checked by aggregating P's direct voting rights in the partnership along with those of all the direct interest companies and any relevant corporate partners, calculated according to the same mechanism above, applied to voting rights, rather than to profits and assets.

Part 4 Interpretation

As already noted, P is generally speaking the individual making the disposal. However, P is the relevant beneficiary in the case of a disposal of trust business assets.

Activities carried on by a company as a member of a partnership are not treated as trading activities if the company is not a member of the partnership throughout the relevant period.

In all cases, the relevant period is the qualifying period for entrepreneurs' relief to be available in the main provisions, being usually twelve months to the date of disposal or twelve months to the date of the cessation of the trade.

References to a person having voting rights include references to their ability to control the exercise of such rights by another person.

Commencement

Schedule 13 has effect from 18 March 2015.

SCHEDULE 14

INVESTORS' RELIEF

Section 87

1 (1) In the heading to Part 5 of TGCA 1992, after "ASSETS" insert ", ENTREPRE-NEURS' RELIEF AND INVESTORS' RELIEF".

(2) In the heading to Chapter 1 of that Part, before "GENERAL PROVISIONS" insert "TRANSFER OF BUSINESS ASSETS:"

2 In Part 5 of TCGA 1992, after section 169V insert—

"CHAPTER 5
INVESTORS' RELIEF

Overview

169VA Overview of Chapter

(1) This Chapter provides for a relief, in the form of a lower rate of capital gains tax, in respect of disposals of (and disposals of interests in) certain ordinary shares in unlisted companies.

(2) Section 169VB defines "qualifying shares", "potentially qualifying shares" and "excluded shares".

(3) Section 169VC creates the relief, and relief under that section is to be known as "investors' relief".

(4) Section 169VD makes provision about disposals from holdings consisting partly of qualifying shares.

(5) Sections 169VE to 169VG contain rules for cases where there have been previous disposals from a holding, to determine which shares remain in the holding.

(6) Sections 169VH and 169VI make provision about disposals by trustees of a settlement.

(7) Section 169VJ makes provision about disposals of interests in shares.

(8) Sections 169VK and 169VL provide for a cap on the amount of investors' relief that can be claimed.

(9) Section 169VM makes provision about claims for investors' relief.

(10) Sections 169VN to 169VT make provision about how investors' relief applies following a company's reorganisation of its share capital, an exchange of shares or securities or a scheme of reconstruction.

(11) Sections 169VU to 169VY contain definitions for the purposes of this Chapter.

Qualifying shares

169VB Qualifying shares, potentially qualifying shares and excluded shares

(1) Where there is a disposal of all or part of (or of an interest in) a holding of shares in a company, this section applies to determine whether a share which is in the holding at the time immediately before the disposal ("the relevant time") is for the purposes of this Chapter—

(a) a qualifying share,
(b) a potentially qualifying share, or
(c) an excluded share.

(2) The share is a "qualifying share" at the relevant time if—

(a) the share was subscribed for, within the meaning given by section 169VU, by the person making the disposal ("the investor"),
(b) the investor has held the share continuously for the period beginning with the issue of the share and ending with the relevant time ("the share-holding period"),
(c) the share was issued on or after 17 March 2016,
(d) at the time the share was issued, none of the shares or securities of the company that issued it were listed on a recognised stock exchange,
(e) the share was an ordinary share when issued and is an ordinary share at the relevant time,
(f) the company that issued the share—

   (i) was a trading company or the holding company of a trading group (as defined by section 169VV) when the share was issued, and
   (ii) has been so throughout the share-holding period,

(g) at no time in the share-holding period was the investor or a person connected with the investor a relevant employee in respect of that company (within the meaning given by section 169VW), and
(h) the period beginning with the date the share was issued and ending with the date of the disposal is at least 3 years.

(3) The share is a "potentially qualifying share" at the relevant time if—

(a) the conditions in subsection (2)(a) to (g) are met, but
(b) the period beginning with the date the share was issued and ending with the date of the disposal is less than 3 years.

(4) The share is an "excluded share" at the relevant time if it is, at that time—

(a) not a qualifying share, and

(b) not a potentially qualifying share.

(5) This section is subject to Schedule 7ZB (disqualification of share where value received by investor).

(6) In relation to a share issued on or after 17 March 2016 but before 6 April 2016, any reference in subsection (2)(h) or (3) to "3 years" is to be read as a reference to the minimum period.

(7) In subsection (6) "the minimum period" means the period of 3 years extended by a period equal in length to the period beginning with the date the share was issued and ending with 5 April 2016.

The relief

169VC Investors' relief

(1) This section applies where—

(a) a qualifying person disposes of a holding, or part of a holding, of shares in a company, and
(b) immediately before that disposal some or all of the shares in the holding are qualifying shares.

(2) If—

(a) a chargeable gain accrues to the qualifying person on the disposal, and
(b) a claim for relief under this section is made,

the rate of capital gains tax in respect of the relevant gain is 10 per cent.

(3) In subsection (2) "the relevant gain" means—

(a) where immediately before the disposal all the shares in the holding are qualifying shares, the chargeable gain on the disposal;
(b) where at that time only some of the shares in the holding are qualifying shares, the appropriate part of that chargeable gain (defined by section 169VD).

(4) In this section—

(a) subsection (1) is subject to section 169VH (disposals by trustees of a settlement: further conditions for relief), and
(b) subsection (2) is subject to—

section 169VI (reduction of relief for certain disposals by trustees of a settlement), and
sections 169VK and 169VL (cap on investors' relief).

(5) A reference in subsection (3) to the chargeable gain on the disposal, or to the appropriate part of that gain, is a reference to that chargeable gain, or (as the case may be) that part, after any deduction of allowable losses which is made in accordance with this Act from that chargeable gain or from that part.

(6) For the application of this section to disposals of interests in shares, see section 169VJ.

(7) In this Chapter a "qualifying person" means—

(a) an individual, or
(b) the trustees of a settlement.

169VD Disposal where holding consists partly of qualifying shares

(1) This section applies where—

(a) a disposal ("the disposal concerned") is made as mentioned in section 169VC(1), and
(b) at the time immediately before the disposal, only some of the shares in the holding are qualifying shares.

(2) Where this section applies, for the purposes of section 169VC(3) "the appropriate part" of the chargeable gain on the disposal is so much of that chargeable gain as is found by multiplying it by the appropriate fraction.

(3) The appropriate fraction is—

Q / T
where—

Q is the number of qualifying shares found under subsection (4), and
T is the total number of shares disposed of in the disposal concerned.

(4) The number of qualifying shares found under this subsection is—

(a) all the qualifying shares in the holding at the time immediately before the disposal concerned, or

(b) if less, such number of those qualifying shares as equals the number of shares disposed of in that disposal.

169VE Which shares are in holding immediately before disposal

(1) This section applies where—

(a) a particular disposal is made as mentioned in section 169VC(1)(a) ("the current disposal"),

(b) there have been one or more previous disposals of shares from the holding mentioned in section 169VC(1) before the current disposal, and

(c) it is necessary to determine for the purposes of this Chapter which shares are to be treated as in the holding immediately before the current disposal (and, accordingly, which shares are to be treated as having been disposed of in those previous disposals).

(2) In the case of a previous disposal as regards which investors' relief has been claimed or is being claimed, the shares to be treated as disposed of in that previous disposal are to be determined in accordance with the rules in section 169VF.

(3) In the case of a previous disposal not falling within subsection (2), the shares to be treated as disposed of in that previous disposal are to be determined in accordance with the rules in section 169VG.

169VF Shares treated as disposed of in previous disposal where claim made

(1) The rules referred to in section 169VE(2) are as follows; and in this section "the disposal concerned" means the previous disposal mentioned in section 169VE(2).

(2) There are to be treated as having been disposed of in the disposal concerned—

(a) all the qualifying shares in the holding at the time immediately before that disposal ("the material time"), or

(b) if less, such number of those qualifying shares as equals the number of shares disposed of in that disposal.

(3) If—

(a) the number of qualifying shares in the holding at the material time was less than the total number of shares disposed of, and

(b) excluded shares were in the holding at the material time,

the available excluded shares are also to be treated as having been disposed of.

(4) "The available excluded shares" means—

(a) all the excluded shares in the holding at the material time, or

(b) if less, such number of those excluded shares as is equal to the difference between—

(i) the total number of shares disposed of, and

(ii) the number of qualifying shares in the holding at the material time.

(5) If the number of shares treated under subsections (2) to (4) as disposed of in the disposal concerned is less than the total number of shares disposed of, such number of the potentially qualifying shares in the holding at the material time as is equal to the difference are also to be treated as having been disposed of.

(6) Where the number of potentially qualifying shares in the holding at the material time exceeds the difference mentioned in subsection (5), under that subsection potentially qualifying shares acquired later are to be treated as disposed of in preference to ones acquired earlier.

(7) In this section "disposed of" (without more) means disposed of in the disposal concerned.

169VG Shares treated as disposed of in previous disposal: no claim made

(1) The rules referred to in section 169VE(3) are as follows; and in this section "the disposal concerned" means the previous disposal mentioned in section 169VE(3).

(2) If any excluded shares were in the holding at the time immediately before the disposal concerned ("the material time"), the maximum number of excluded shares are to be treated as having been disposed of in the disposal concerned.

(3) "The maximum number of excluded shares" means—

(a) all the excluded shares in the holding at the material time, or

(b) if less, such number of those excluded shares as is equal to the number of shares disposed of.

(4) If—

(a) there were no excluded shares in the holding at the material time, or the number of such shares was less than the total number of shares disposed of, and

(b) potentially qualifying shares were in the holding at the material time,

the available potentially qualifying shares are to be treated as having been disposed of.

(5) "The available potentially qualifying shares" means—

(a) all the potentially qualifying shares in the holding at the material time, or

(b) if less, such number of those potentially qualifying shares as is equal to the difference between—

(i) the total number of shares disposed of, and

(ii) the number of excluded shares in the holding at the material time.

(6) Where the number of potentially qualifying shares in the holding at the material time exceeds the difference mentioned in subsection (5), potentially qualifying shares acquired later are to be treated as disposed of in preference to ones acquired earlier.

(7) If the number of shares treated under subsections (2) to (5) as disposed of in the disposal concerned is less than the total number of shares disposed of, such number of the qualifying shares in the holding at the material time as is equal to the difference are to be treated as having been disposed of.

(8) In this section "disposed of" (without more) means disposed of in the disposal concerned.

Trustees of a settlement: special provision

169VH Disposals by trustees: further conditions for relief

(1) Where a disposal falling within section 169VC(1)(a) and (b) is made by the trustees of a settlement, section 169VC does not apply to the disposal unless there is at least one individual who is an eligible beneficiary in respect of the disposal.

(2) For the purposes of this section, an individual is an "eligible beneficiary" in respect of the disposal if—

(a) at the time immediately before the disposal, the individual has under the settlement an interest in possession in settled property that includes or consists of the holding of shares mentioned in section 169VC(1),

(b) the individual has had such an interest in possession under the settlement throughout the period of 3 years ending with the date of the disposal,

(c) at no time in that period has the individual been a relevant employee in respect of the company that issued the shares (within the meaning given by section 169VW), and

(d) the individual has (by the time of the claim under section 169VC in respect of the disposal) elected to be treated as an eligible beneficiary in respect of the disposal.

(3) For the purposes of subsection (2)(d), an individual elects to be treated as an eligible beneficiary in respect of a disposal if the individual tells the trustees (by whatever means) that he or she wishes to be so treated; and an election under subsection (2)(d) may be withdrawn by the individual at any time until the claim is made.

(4) In this section "interest in possession" does not include an interest in possession for a fixed term.

(5) In relation to a disposal made by the trustees of a settlement, any reference in section 169VB(2)(g) to the investor is to be read as a reference to any trustee of the settlement.

169VI Disposals by trustees: relief reduced in certain cases

(1) Subsection (2) applies where—

(a) a disposal falling within section 169VC(1)(a) and (b) is made by the trustees of a settlement,

(b) section 169VC applies to the disposal by reason of there being at least one individual who is an eligible beneficiary in respect of the disposal (see section 169VH), and

(c) at the time immediately before the disposal, there are two or more persons each of whom has under the settlement an interest in possession in the settled property.

(2) In such a case the reference in section 169VC(2) to the relevant gain is to be read as a reference—

(a) to the eligible beneficiary's share of the relevant gain (see subsections (3) to (6)), or

(b) if there is more than one individual who is an eligible beneficiary in respect of the disposal, to so much of the relevant gain as is equal to the aggregate of the eligible beneficiaries' shares of that gain.

(3) In this section—

"eligible beneficiary" has the meaning given by section 169VH(2);

"relevant gain" has the meaning given by section 169VC(3);

"the settled property" means settled property that includes or consists of the holding of shares mentioned in section 169VC(1).

(4) Subsection (5) applies to determine for the purposes of this Chapter, in relation to any individual who is an eligible beneficiary in respect of a disposal within section 169VC(1) made by the trustees of a settlement, that individual's share of the relevant gain.

(5) That individual's share of the relevant gain on the disposal is so much of the relevant gain on the disposal as bears to the whole of that gain the same proportion as X bears to Y, where—

X is the interest in possession (other than for a fixed term) which, at the time immediately before the disposal, that individual has under the settlement in the income from the holding of shares mentioned in section 169VC(1), and

Y is all the interests in that income that persons (including that individual) with interests in possession in that holding have under the settlement at that time.

Disposals of interests in shares

169VJ Disposals of interests in shares: joint holdings etc

(1) In section 169VC(1)(a), the reference to the case where a qualifying person disposes of a holding, or part of a holding, of shares in a company includes the case where a qualifying person disposes of an interest in a relevant holding.

(2) In this section a "relevant holding" means either—

(a) a number of shares in a company which are of the same class and were acquired in the same capacity jointly by the same two or more persons including the qualifying person, or

(b) a number of shares in a company which are of the same class and were acquired in the same capacity by the qualifying person solely.

(3) In this section—

(a) "an interest" in a relevant holding means any interests of the qualifying person, in any of the shares in the relevant holding, which are by virtue of section 104 to be regarded as a single asset, and

(b) references to an interest include part of an interest.

(4) Where section 169VC(1) applies by reason of this section, section 169VD(3) and (4) have effect as if any reference to the number of shares disposed of were a reference to the number of shares an interest in which is disposed of.

(5) In relation to a disposal by the trustees of a settlement of an interest in a relevant holding falling within subsection (2)(a), sections 169VH(2) and 169VI(3) and (5) have effect as if any reference to the holding of shares mentioned in section 169VC(1) were to the interest disposed of.

(6) In accordance with subsection (1)—

(a) in sections 169VN(1)(d), 169VP(1)(d) and 169VS(1)(d) (reorganisations), any reference to a disposal of all or part of a holding includes a disposal by the qualifying person of an interest in the holding, and

(b) the reference in section 169VT(2) to a disposal of the original shares is to be read, in relation to a case where the original shares fall within subsection (2)(a) above, as a reference to a disposal of the qualifying person's interest in those shares.

Cap on relief

169VK Cap on relief for disposal by an individual

(1) This section applies if, on a disposal within section 169VC(1) made by an individual ("the individual concerned"), the aggregate of—

(a) the amount of the relevant gain on the disposal ("the gain in question"),

(b) the total amount of any gains that, in relation to earlier disposals by the individual concerned, were charged at the rate in section 169VC(2), and

(c) the total amount of any reckonable trust gains that, on any previous trust disposals in respect of which the individual concerned was an eligible beneficiary, were charged at the rate in section 169VC(2), exceeds £10 million.

(2) The rate in section 169VC(2) applies only to so much (if any) of the gain in question as, when added to the aggregate of the total amounts mentioned in subsection (1)(b) and (c), does not exceed £10 million.

(3) Section 4 (rates of capital gains tax) applies to so much of the gain in question as is not subject to the rate in section 169VC(2).

(4) In this section—

"eligible beneficiary", in relation to a disposal, is to be read in accordance with section 169VH(2);
"reckonable trust gain", in relation to a trust disposal in respect of which the individual concerned was an eligible beneficiary, means—

(a) if section 169VI(1)(c) applied in relation to the disposal, that individual's share of the relevant gain on that disposal, within the meaning given by section 169VI(4) and (5);
(b) otherwise, the relevant gain on that disposal;

"the relevant gain", in relation to a disposal, has the meaning given by section 169VC(3);
"trust disposal" means a disposal by the trustees of a settlement.

169VL Cap on relief for disposal by trustees of a settlement

(1) This section applies where—

(a) a disposal ("the disposal in question") is made by the trustees of a settlement,
(b) that disposal is within section 169VC(1), and
(c) there is an excess amount in relation to an individual who is an eligible beneficiary in respect of the disposal in question ("the individual concerned").

(2) For the purposes of this section there is an "excess amount" in relation to the individual concerned if the aggregate of—

(a) the amount of the current gain,
(b) the total amount of any gains that, in relation to earlier disposals made by the individual concerned, were charged at the rate in section 169VC(2), and
(c) the total amount of any reckonable trust gains that, on any previous trust disposals in respect of which the individual concerned was an eligible beneficiary, were charged at the rate in section 169VC(2),

exceeds £10 million.

(3) The rate in section 169VC(2) applies to the current gain only to the extent (if any) that the current gain when added to the aggregate of the total amounts mentioned in subsection (2)(b) and (c) does not exceed £10 million.

(4) Section 4 (rates of capital gains tax) applies to so much of the current gain as is not subject to the rate in section 169VC(2).

(5) In this section—

"the current gain" means the reckonable trust gain on the disposal in question;
"eligible beneficiary", in relation to a disposal, is to be read in accordance with section 169VH(2);
"reckonable trust gain", in relation to any trust disposal in respect of which the individual concerned is an eligible beneficiary, means—

(a) if section 169VI(1)(c) applies in relation to the disposal, that individual's share of the relevant gain on that disposal, within the meaning given by section 169VI(4) and (5);
(b) otherwise, the relevant gain on that disposal;

"the relevant gain", in relation to a disposal, has the meaning given by section 169VC(3);
"trust disposal" means a disposal by the trustees of a settlement.

Claims for relief

169VM Claims for relief

(1) Any claim for investors' relief must be made—

(a) in the case of a disposal by an individual, by that individual;
(b) in the case of a disposal by the trustees of a settlement, jointly by—

(i) the trustees, and
(ii) the eligible beneficiary in respect of the disposal, within the meaning given by section 169VH(2) (or, if more than one, all those eligible beneficiaries).

(2) Any claim for investors' relief in respect of a disposal must be made on or before the first anniversary of the 31 January following the tax year in which the disposal is made.

Reorganisations

169VN Reorganisations where no consideration given

(1) This section applies where—

(a) there is a reorganisation within the meaning of section 126,

(b) immediately before the reorganisation, a qualifying person holds ordinary shares which, in relation to that reorganisation, are original shares within the meaning of section 126,

(c) on the reorganisation that person does not give or become liable to give any consideration for, or for any part of, a new holding, and

(d) at a time after the reorganisation, there is a disposal of all or part of a new holding.

(2) In this section a "new holding" means—

(a) the holding that immediately after the reorganisation is (in relation to the original shares) the new holding within the meaning of section 126, or

(b) where the new holding within the meaning of section 126 consists of two or more actual holdings, any of those actual holdings.

(3) Subsections (4) and (5) apply for the purposes of determining (for any purpose of this Chapter) the status of shares that immediately before the disposal mentioned in subsection (1)(d) are in the new holding mentioned there ("the new holding concerned").

(4) Where a number of the original shares were—

(a) subscribed for by the qualifying person,

(b) issued on a particular date ("the relevant issue date"), and

(c) held continuously by that person for a particular period ending immediately before the reorganisation ("the period concerned"),

the following assumption is to be made.

(5) That assumption is that an appropriate number of the new shares were—

(a) subscribed for by the qualifying person,

(b) issued on the relevant issue date, and

(c) had by the time immediately after the reorganisation already been held continuously by that person for the period concerned.

(6) In subsections (4) and (5)—

"the appropriate number" has the meaning given by section 169VO;

"the original shares" means the shares held by the qualifying person immediately before the reorganisation that were original shares in relation to the reorganisation;

"the new shares" means the shares that immediately after the reorganisation were in the new holding concerned (including such, if any, of the original shares as remained after the reorganisation and were in that holding).

(7) In this section a reference to the "status" of a share is to whether it is qualifying, potentially qualifying or excluded.

(8) Section 169VE applies to determine, for the purposes of this Chapter, which shares are included in a holding immediately before a reorganisation as it applies for the purposes of determining which shares are included in a holding immediately before a particular disposal.

(9) References in this section to consideration are to be read in accordance with section 128(2).

169VO The appropriate number

(1) The "appropriate number" for the purposes of section 169VN(5) is the number found by multiplying the number of shares that are in the new holding concerned immediately after the reorganisation by the fraction—

A / B

where—

A is the number of the original shares that were—

(a) subscribed for by the qualifying person,

(b) issued on the relevant issue date, and

(c) continuously held by that person for the period concerned, and

B is the total number of the original shares.

(2) In this section—

"the new holding concerned" has the meaning given by section 169VN(3);
"the original shares" has the meaning given by section 169VN(6);
"the relevant issue date" has the meaning given by section 169VN(4);
"the period concerned" has the meaning given by section 169VN(4).

169VP Reorganisations where consideration given

(1) This section applies where—

(a) there is a reorganisation within the meaning of section 126,
(b) immediately before the reorganisation, a qualifying person holds ordinary shares which, in relation to that reorganisation, are original shares within the meaning of section 126,
(c) on the reorganisation that person gives or becomes liable to give consideration for shares ("shares issued for consideration") which—

(i) are issued to that person on the reorganisation, and
(ii) immediately after the reorganisation are in a new holding, and

(d) at a time after the reorganisation, there is a disposal of all or part of that new holding.

(2) In this section a "new holding" means—

(a) the holding that immediately after the reorganisation is (in relation to the original shares) the new holding within the meaning of section 126, or
(b) where the new holding within the meaning of section 126 consists of two or more actual holdings, any of those actual holdings.

(3) In determining, for any purpose of this Chapter, the status of shares that immediately before the disposal mentioned in subsection (1)(d) are in the new holding mentioned there—

(a) the date of issue of the shares issued for consideration is to be taken to be their actual date of issue (rather than the date of issue of any of the original shares), and
(b) in relation to any part of the new holding for which consideration was not given, sections 169VN(3) to (6) and 169VO apply but as if any reference to the new holding concerned were to that part of the new holding.

(4) Section 169VN(3) to (6) and 169VO also apply in relation to any other holding which is a new holding in relation to the reorganisation and as respects which the person did not, on the reorganisation, give or become liable to give any consideration.

(5) In this section a reference to the "status" of a share is to whether it is qualifying, potentially qualifying or excluded.

(6) References in this section to consideration are to be read in accordance with section 128(2).

169VQ Exchange of shares for those in another company

(1) This section applies where section 135 applies in relation to an issue of shares in a company ("company B") in exchange for shares in another company ("company A").

(2) For the purposes of sections 169VN to 169VP—

(a) companies A and B are to be treated as if they were the same company, and
(b) the exchange of shares is to be treated as if it were a reorganisation of that company's share capital.

169VR New shares issued on scheme of reconstruction

(1) This section applies where—

(a) section 136 applies in relation to an arrangement between a company ("company A") and the persons holding shares, or any class of shares, in company A, under which another company ("company B") issues shares to those persons, and
(b) under section 136(2)(a) those persons are treated as exchanging shares in company A for the shares held by them in consequence of the arrangement.

(2) For the purposes of sections 169VN to 169VP—

(a) companies A and B are to be treated as if they were the same company, and
(b) the exchange of shares is to be treated as if it were a reorganisation of that company's share capital.

(3) In the following provisions of this Chapter, any reference to an exchange of shares includes anything that section 136(2)(a) treats as an exchange of shares.

169VS Modification of conditions for being a qualifying share

(1) This section applies where—

(a) an ordinary share ("the original share") is subscribed for by a qualifying person ("the investor");

(b) the conditions in section 169VB(2)(c) and (d) are met in relation to the original share,

(c) the share is involved in an exchange of shares treated under section 169VQ or 169VR as a reorganisation of share capital, and accordingly is included in the original shares within the meaning of section 169VN(6), and

(d) subsequently there is a disposal of all or part of a holding of shares that in relation to that exchange is a new holding within the meaning given by section 169VN(2).

(2) As respects a share which is in that holding immediately before that disposal, the conditions in section 169VB(2)(f) and (g) are to be regarded as met if (and only if)—

(a) in relation to the period beginning with the issue of the original share and ending with the exchange of shares, those conditions were met by the original share, and

(b) in relation to the period beginning with the exchange of shares and ending with the disposal, those conditions were met by a share representing the original share.

(3) Accordingly—

(a) in section 169VB(2)(f) and (g) as they apply to the original share, any reference to the share-holding period is to be read as to the period mentioned in subsection (2)(a) above, and

(b) in section 169VB(2)(f) and (g) as they apply to a share representing the original share, any reference to the share-holding period is to be read as to the period mentioned in subsection (2)(b) above.

(4) In subsection (1)(c) "the share" includes a share that, following a reorganisation or following an exchange of shares in relation to which section 169VQ or 169VR applies, represents the original share, and subsections (2) and (3) apply in such a case with the necessary modifications.

169VT Election to disapply section 127

(1) This section applies where—

(a) there is—

(i) a reorganisation (within the meaning of section 126), or

(ii) an exchange of shares which is treated as such a reorganisation by virtue of section 135 or 136, and

(b) the original shares and the new holding would fall to be treated by virtue of section 127 as the same asset.

(2) If an election is made under this section, a claim for investors' relief may be made as if the reorganisation or exchange of shares involved a disposal of the original shares; and if such a claim is made section 127 and sections 169VN to 169VS do not apply.

(3) Any election under this section must be made—

(a) if the reorganisation or exchange of shares would (apart from section 127) involve a disposal by the trustees of a settlement, jointly by—

(i) the trustees, and

(ii) the person who if the disposal were made would be the eligible beneficiary in respect of the disposal, within the meaning given by section 169VH(2) (or, if more than one, all the persons who would be such eligible beneficiaries);

(b) otherwise, by the individual concerned.

(4) Any election under this section must be made on or before the first anniversary of the 31 January following the tax year in which the reorganisation or exchange of shares takes place.

(5) In this section "the original shares" and "the new holding" have the meaning given by section 126.

Supplemental

169VU "Subscribe" etc

(1) For the purposes of this Chapter (other than this subsection) a person "subscribes for" a share in a company if—

(a) that person subscribes for the share,

(b) the share is issued to that person by the company for consideration consisting wholly of cash,

(c) the share is fully paid up at the time it is issued,

(d) the share is subscribed for, and issued, for genuine commercial reasons and not as part of arrangements the main purpose, or one of the main purposes, of which is to secure a tax advantage to any person, and

(e) the share is subscribed for, and issued, by way of a bargain at arm's length.

(2) In subsection (1) "arrangements" and "tax advantage" have the same meaning as in section 16A.

(3) If—

(a) an individual ("A") subscribed for, or is treated under this subsection as having subscribed for, any shares,

(b) A transferred the shares to another individual ("B") during their lives, and

(c) A was living together with B as B's spouse or civil partner at the time of the transfer,

B is to be treated for the purposes of this Chapter as having subscribed for the shares.

(4) Accordingly, for the purposes of this Chapter any period for which A held the shares continuously is to be added to, and treated as part of, the period for which B held the shares continuously.

(5) In this Chapter, apart from subsections (3) and (4), references to a person's having subscribed for a share include the person's having subscribed for the share jointly with any other person (and references to a person's holding a share or to a share being issued to a person are to be read accordingly).

169VV "Trading company" etc

(1) In this Chapter "trading company" and "the holding company of a trading group" have the same meaning as in section 165 (see section 165A).

(2) For the purposes of this Chapter a company is not to be regarded as ceasing to be a trading company, or the holding company of a trading group, merely because of anything done in consequence of—

(a) the company, or any of its subsidiaries, being in administration or receivership, or

(b) a resolution having been passed, or an order made, for the winding up of the company or any of its subsidiaries.

(3) But subsection (2) applies only if—

(a) the entry into administration or receivership, or the resolution or order for winding up, and

(b) everything done as a result of the company concerned being in administration or receivership, or as a result of that resolution or order,

is for genuine commercial reasons and is not part of a scheme or arrangement the main purpose or one of the main purposes of which is the avoidance of tax.

169VW "Relevant employee"

(1) This section applies to determine for the purposes of—

(a) section 169VB(2)(g), or

(b) section 169VH(2)(c),

whether a particular person has at any time in the relevant period been a "relevant employee" in respect of the issuing company.

(2) A person who has at any time in the relevant period been an officer or employee of—

(a) the issuing company, or

(b) a connected company,

is to be regarded as having at that time been a relevant employee in respect of the issuing company, but this is subject to subsections (3) and (5).

(3) If—

(a) a person is an unremunerated director of the issuing company or a connected company at any time in the relevant period, and

(b) the condition in subsection (4) is met,

the fact that the person holds that directorship at that time does not make the person a relevant employee in respect of the issuing company at that time.

(4) The condition referred to in subsection (3) is that at no time before the relevant period had the person mentioned in that subsection, or a person connected with that person, been—

(a) connected with the issuing company, or

(b) involved in carrying on (whether on the person's own account or as a partner, director or employee) the whole or any part of the trade, business or profession carried on by the issuing company or a company connected with that company.

(5) If—

(a) a person becomes an employee of the issuing company or a connected company at a time which is—

(i) within the relevant period, but

(ii) not within the first 180 days of that period,

(b) at the beginning of the relevant period, there was no reasonable prospect that the person would become such an employee within the relevant period, and

(c) the person is not at any time in the relevant period a director of the issuing company or a connected company,

that employment of the person does not make the person a relevant employee in respect of the issuing company at any time in the relevant period.

(6) For the purposes of subsection (5) there is a "reasonable prospect" of a thing if it is more likely than not.

(7) In this section—

"director" is to be read in accordance with section 452 of CTA 2010,

"connected company" means a company which at any time in the relevant period is connected with the issuing company (and it does not matter for this purpose whether that time is a time when the person in question is an officer or employee of either company);

"the issuing company" means the company mentioned in (as the case may be) section 169VB(2)(g) or section 169VH(2)(c);

"the relevant period" means the period mentioned in (as the case may be) section 169VB(2)(g) or section 169VH(2)(c);

"unremunerated director" has the meaning given by section 169VX.

169VX "Unremunerated director"

(1) For the purposes of section 169VW a person ("the person concerned") is an "unremunerated director" of the issuing company or a connected company at a particular time in the relevant period if that person is a director of that company at that time and—

(a) does not receive in the relevant period any disqualifying payment from the issuing company or a related person, and

(b) is not entitled to receive any such payment in respect of that period or any part of it.

(2) In this section "disqualifying payment" means any payment other than—

(a) a payment or reimbursement of travelling or other expenses wholly, exclusively and necessarily incurred by the person concerned in the performance of his or her duties as a director,

(b) any interest which represents no more than a reasonable commercial return on money lent to the issuing company or a related person,

(c) any dividend or other distribution which does not exceed a normal return on the investment to which the dividend or distribution relates,

(d) any payment for the supply of goods which does not exceed their market value,

(e) any payment of rent for any property occupied by the issuing company or a related person which does not exceed a reasonable and commercial rent for the property, or

(f) any necessary and reasonable remuneration which is—

(i) paid for qualifying services that are provided to the issuing company or a related person in the course of a trade or profession carried on wholly or partly in the United Kingdom, and

(ii) taken into account in calculating for tax purposes the profits of that trade or profession.

(3) In this section a "related person" means—

(a) a connected company of which the person concerned is a director, or

(b) any person connected with the issuing company or with a company within paragraph (a).

(4) In this section any reference to a payment to the person concerned includes a payment made to that person indirectly or to that person's order or for that person's benefit.

(5) In this section "qualifying services" means services which are—

(a) not secretarial or managerial services, and

(b) not services of a kind provided by the person to whom they are provided.

(6) In this section the following expressions have the same meaning as in section 169VW—

"connected company";

"director";

"issuing company";

"relevant period".

169VY General definitions

In this Chapter—

"employee" (except in the expression "relevant employee", which is to be read in accordance with section 169VW) has the meaning given by section 4 of ITEPA 2003;

"employment" has the meaning given by section 4 of ITEPA 2003;

"exchange of shares" is to be read in accordance with section 169VR(3);

"excluded share" has the meaning given by section 169VB;

a "holding" of shares in a company means a holding of such shares which by virtue of section 104(1) is to be regarded as a single asset;

"investors' relief" has the meaning given by section 169VA(3);

"office" has the meaning given by section 5(3) of ITEPA 2003;

"ordinary shares", in relation to a company, means any shares forming part of the company's ordinary share capital (within the meaning given by section 989 of ITA 2007);

"potentially qualifying share" has the meaning given by section 169VB;

"qualifying person" has the meaning given by section 169VC(7);

"qualifying share" has the meaning given by section 169VB;

"subscribe" is to be read in accordance with section 169VU;

"trading company" and "the holding company of a trading group" are to be read in accordance with section 169VV."

3 After Schedule 7ZA of TCGA 1992 (inserted by Schedule 13) insert—

"SCHEDULE 7ZB

INVESTORS' RELIEF: DISQUALIFICATION OF SHARES

Section 169VB

Disqualification of shares where value received in period of restriction

1 (1) Sub-paragraph (2) applies where—

(a) shares in a company are issued to a qualifying person ("the investor") on a particular date,

(b) any of those shares would, apart from this Schedule, be or be treated as being qualifying shares or potentially qualifying shares at a particular time ("the relevant time"), and

(c) the investor receives any value, other than insignificant value, from the company at any time in the period of restriction.

(2) The shares in question are to be treated for the purposes of this Chapter as being excluded shares at the relevant time.

(3) Where—

(a) the investor receives value ("the relevant receipt") from the company during the period of restriction,

(b) the investor has received from the company one or more receipts of insignificant value at a time or times—

(i) during that period, but

(ii) not later than the time of the relevant receipt, and

(c) the aggregate amount of the value of the receipts within paragraphs (a) and (b) is not an amount of insignificant value,

the investor is to be treated for the purposes of this Schedule as if the relevant receipt had been a receipt of an amount equal to that aggregate amount.

For this purpose a receipt does not fall within paragraph (b) in relation to the shares if it has previously been aggregated under this sub-paragraph in relation to them.

(4) In this Schedule "the period of restriction" means the period—

(a) beginning one year before the date the shares are issued, and

(b) ending immediately before the third anniversary of the date the shares are issued.

(5) In sub-paragraphs (3) and (4) and in the following provisions of this Schedule references to "the shares" are to the shares referred to in sub-paragraph (1)(a).

(6) This paragraph is subject to paragraph 4.

"Receives value"

2 (1) For the purposes of this Schedule the investor receives value from the company if the company—

(a) repays, redeems or repurchases any of its share capital or securities which belong to the investor or makes any payment to the investor for giving up a right to any of the company's share capital or any security on its cancellation or extinguishment,

(b) repays, in pursuance of any arrangements for or in connection with the acquisition of the shares, any debt owed to the investor other than a debt which was incurred by the company—

(i) on or after the date of issue of the shares, and

(ii) otherwise than in consideration of the extinguishment of a debt incurred before that date,

(c) makes to the investor any payment for giving up the investor's right to any debt on its extinguishment,

(d) releases or waives any liability of the investor to the company or discharges, or undertakes to discharge, any liability of the investor to a third person,

(e) makes a loan or advance to the investor which has not been repaid in full before the issue of the shares,

(f) provides a benefit or facility for the investor,

(g) disposes of an asset to the investor for no consideration or for a consideration which is or the value of which is less than the market value of the asset,

(h) acquires an asset from the investor for a consideration which is or the value of which is more than the market value of the asset, or

(i) makes any payment to the investor other than a qualifying payment.

(2) For the purposes of sub-paragraph (1)(e) there is to be treated as if it were a loan made by the company to the investor—

(a) the amount of any debt (other than an ordinary trade debt) incurred by the investor to the company, and

(b) the amount of any debt due from the investor to a third person which has been assigned to the company.

(3) For the purposes of this paragraph the investor also receives value from the company if any person connected with the company—

(a) purchases any of its share capital or securities which belong to the investor, or

(b) makes any payment to the investor for giving up any right in relation to any of the company's share capital or securities.

(4) In this paragraph "qualifying payment" means—

(a) the payment by any company of such remuneration for service as an officer or employee of that company as may be reasonable in relation to the duties of that office or employment,

(b) any payment or reimbursement by any company of travelling or other expenses wholly, exclusively and necessarily incurred by the investor to whom the payment is made in the performance of duties as an officer or employee of that company,

(c) the payment by any company of any interest which represents no more than a reasonable commercial return on money lent to that company,

(d) the payment by any company of any dividend or other distribution which does not exceed a normal return on any investment in shares in or other securities of that company,

(e) any payment for the supply of goods which does not exceed their market value,

(f) any payment for the acquisition of an asset which does not exceed its market value,

(g) the payment by any company, as rent for any property occupied by the company, of an amount not exceeding a reasonable and commercial rent for the property,

(h) any reasonable and necessary remuneration which—

    (i) is paid by any company for services rendered to that company in the course of a trade or profession carried on wholly or partly in the United Kingdom; and
    (ii) is taken into account in calculating for tax purposes the profits of that trade or profession, or

(i) a payment in discharge of an ordinary trade debt.

(5) For the purposes of this paragraph a company is to be treated as having released or waived a liability if the liability is not discharged within 12 months of the time when it ought to have been discharged.

(6) In this paragraph—

(a) references to a debt or liability do not, in relation to a company, include references to any debt or liability which would be discharged by the making by that company of a qualifying payment, and
(b) references to a benefit or facility do not include references to any benefit or facility provided in circumstances such that, if a payment had been made of an amount equal to its value, that payment would be a qualifying payment.

(7) In this paragraph and paragraph 3—

(a) any reference to a payment or disposal to the investor includes a reference to a payment or disposal made to the investor indirectly or to the investor's order or for the investor's benefit;
(b) any reference to the investor includes an associate of the investor;
(c) any reference to a company includes a person who at any time in the period of restriction is connected with the company, whether or not that person is connected at the material time.

(8) In this paragraph "ordinary trade debt" means any debt for goods or services supplied in the ordinary course of a trade or business where any credit given—

(a) does not exceed six months, and
(b) is not longer than that normally given to customers of the person carrying on the trade or business.

Amount of value

3 (1) For the purposes of paragraph 1, the value received by the investor is—

(a) in a case within paragraph 2(1)(a), (b) or (c), the amount received by the investor or, if greater, the market value of the share capital, securities or debt in question;
(b) in a case within paragraph 2(1)(d), the amount of the liability;
(c) in a case within paragraph 2(1)(e), the amount of the loan or advance reduced by the amount of any repayment made before the issue of the shares;
(d) in a case within paragraph 2(1)(f), the cost to the company of providing the benefit or facility less any consideration given for it by the investor;
(e) in a case within paragraph 2(1)(g) or (h), the difference between the market value of the asset and the consideration (if any) given for it;
(f) in a case within paragraph 2(1)(i), the amount of the payment;
(g) in a case within paragraph 2(3), the amount received by the investor or, if greater, the market value of the share capital or securities in question.

(2) In this Schedule references to a receipt of insignificant value (however expressed) are references to a receipt of an amount of insignificant value.

This is subject to sub-paragraph (4).

(3) For the purposes of this Schedule "an amount of insignificant value" means an amount of value which does not exceed £1,000.

(4) For the purposes of this Schedule, if at any time in the period—

(a) beginning one year before the shares are issued, and
(b) expiring at the end of the issue date,

arrangements are in existence which provide for the investor to receive or to be entitled to receive, at any time in the period of restriction, any value from the company that issued the shares, no amount of value received by the investor is to be treated as a receipt of insignificant value.

(5) In sub-paragraph (4)—

(a) any reference to the investor includes a reference to any person who, at any time in the period of restriction, is an associate of the investor (whether or not that person is such an associate at the material time), and

(b) the reference to the company includes a reference to any person who, at any time in the period of restriction, is connected with the company (whether or not that person is so connected at the material time).

Receipt of replacement value

4 (1) Where—

(a) by reason of a receipt of value within sub-paragraph (1) (other than paragraph (b)) or sub-paragraph (3) of paragraph 2 ("the original value"), any shares would, in the absence of this paragraph, be treated under this Schedule as excluded shares at a particular time,

(b) at or before that time the original supplier receives value ("the replacement value") from the original recipient by reason of a qualifying receipt, and

(c) the amount of the replacement value is not less than the amount of the original value,

the receipt of the original value is to be disregarded for the purposes of this Schedule.

(2) This paragraph is subject to paragraph 5.

(3) For the purposes of this paragraph and paragraph 5—

(a) "the original recipient" means the person who receives the original value, and

(b) "the original supplier" means the person from whom that value was received.

(4) A receipt of the replacement value is a qualifying receipt for the purposes of sub-paragraph (1) if it arises—

(a) by reason of the original recipient doing one or more of the following—

(i) making a payment to the original supplier, other than a payment which falls within paragraph (c) or to which sub-paragraph (5) applies,

(ii) acquiring any asset from the original supplier for a consideration the amount or value of which is more than the market value of the asset,

(iii) disposing of any asset to the original supplier for no consideration or for a consideration the amount or value of which is less than the market value of the asset,

(b) where the receipt of the original value was within paragraph 2(1)(d), by reason of an event the effect of which is to reverse the event which constituted the receipt of the original value, or

(c) where the receipt of the original value was within paragraph 2(3), by reason of the original recipient repurchasing the share capital or securities in question, or (as the case may be) reacquiring the right in question, for a consideration the amount or value of which is not less than the amount of the original value.

(5) This sub-paragraph applies to—

(a) any payment for any goods, services or facilities, provided (whether in the course of a trade or otherwise) by —

(i) the original supplier, or

(ii) any other person who, at any time in the period of restriction, is an associate of, or connected with, that supplier (whether or not that person is such an associate, or so connected, at the material time),

which is reasonable in relation to the market value of those goods, services or facilities,

(b) any payment of any interest which represents no more than a reasonable commercial return on money lent to—

(i) the original recipient, or

(ii) any person who, at any time in the period of restriction, is an associate of the original recipient (whether or not such an associate at the material time),

(c) any payment for the acquisition of an asset which does not exceed its market value,

(d) any payment, as rent for any property occupied by—

(i) the original recipient, or

(ii) any person who, at any time in the period of restriction, is an associate of the original recipient (whether or not such an associate at the material time),

of an amount not exceeding a reasonable and commercial rent for the property,

(e) any payment in discharge of an ordinary trade debt (within the meaning of paragraph 2(8)), and

(f) any payment for shares in or securities of any company in circumstances that do not fall within sub-paragraph (4)(a)(ii).

(6) For the purposes of this paragraph, the amount of the replacement value is—

(a) in a case within paragraph (a) of sub-paragraph (4), the aggregate of—

(i) the amount of any payment within sub-paragraph (i) of that paragraph, and
(ii) the difference between the market value of any asset within sub-paragraph (ii) or (iii) of that paragraph and the amount or value of the consideration
(if any) received for it,

(b) in a case within sub-paragraph (4)(b), the same as the amount of the original
value, and

(c) in a case within sub-paragraph (4)(c), the amount or value of the consideration
received by the original supplier,

and paragraph 3(1) applies for the purposes of determining the amount of the
original value.

(7) In this paragraph any reference to a payment to a person (however expressed)
includes a reference to a payment made to the person indirectly or to the person's
order or for the person's benefit.

5 (1) The receipt of the replacement value by the original supplier is to be disregarded
for the purposes of paragraph 4, as it applies in relation to the shares, to the extent to
which that receipt has previously been set (under that paragraph) against any receipts
of value which are, in consequence, disregarded for the purposes of paragraph 4 as
that paragraph applies in relation to those shares or any other shares subscribed for
by the investor.

(2) The receipt of the replacement value by the original supplier ("the event") is also
be disregarded for the purposes of paragraph 4 if—

(a) the event occurs before the start of the period of restriction, or
(b) in a case where the event occurs after the time the original recipient receives the
original value, it does not occur as soon after that time as is reasonably practicable
in the circumstances.

But nothing in paragraph 4 or this paragraph requires the replacement value to be
received after the original value.

(3) In this paragraph "the original value" and "the replacement value" are to be
construed in accordance with paragraph 4.

Interpretation

6 In this Schedule—

"arrangements" includes any scheme, agreement, understanding, transaction or
series of transactions (whether or not legally enforceable);
"associate" has the meaning that would be given by section 448 of CTA 2010 if in
that section "relative" did not include a brother or sister;
"period of restriction" has the meaning given by paragraph 1(4);
"the shares" has the meaning given by paragraph 1(5)."

GENERAL NOTE

Section 87 and Sch 14 introduce Investors' Relief (IR) – described as an extension to
Entrepreneurs' Relief (ER) – but legislatively an entirely separate relief. The relief is
aimed at encouraging external investment into unquoted trading companies and
allows gains arising from the disposal of qualifying shares or interests in such shares
to be taxed at a rate of 10%, with a lifetime limit of £10m per individual. Gains in
excess of the £10m limit will be taxed at the investor's marginal rate of CGT. The relief
applies to subscriptions of newly issued shares made on or after 17 March 2016. To
qualify the shares must be held for a continuous period of three years and be
disposed of on or after 6 April 2019. An important difference between IR and ER is
that IR is not available where an individual, or those connected with him, is an officer
or employee of the company or a connected company, although under amendments
introduced to the original proposals this restriction will not apply for unremunerated
directors and those taking up employment after 180 days of acquiring the shares.

The Finance Bill introduced to Pt V of TCGA 1992 a new Ch 5 and Sch 7ZB to
accommodate the relief, with the main legislation being contained in s 169VA et seq
of Ch 5 of TCGA 1992.

Section 169VB governs which shares are qualifying, potentially qualifying and
excluded shares.

In summary a share is a qualifying share if:

– the investor (or their spouse or civil partner) subscribes in cash for the share on
or after 17 March 2016;

- the share is held continuously from the issue date, and for a minimum period of at least three years;
- it is disposed of on or after 6 April 2019;
- at the time of subscription none of the company's securities were listed on a recognised stock exchange – however there is no ongoing requirement for the company to remain unlisted;
- the issuing company must be a trading company (or holding company of a trading group) for the entire duration of the share holding period;
- in addition, the shares need to be ordinary shares (as defined by ITA 2007 s 989) at the date of subscription and at disposal; and
- neither the investor, nor anyone connected with them may be an officer or employee of the company – at any point in time in the ownership of the shares. In the original Finance Bill no guidance was given in relation to the definition of 'officer or employee' for these circumstances. However, on 13 June 2016 s 169VQA was introduced (discussed below) which goes some way to dealing with this point.

Crucially, there is no minimum shareholding required to benefit from IR, in contrast to the 5% requirement for ER.

A potentially qualifying share is one that meets the above conditions, but has yet to be held for three years. Any shares that are not qualifying or potentially qualifying are defined as excluded shares.

Section 169VF sets out the timeline for claiming the relief which is the first anniversary of 31 January following the end of the tax year of disposal.

Section 169VC sets out that for the relief to apply a "qualifying person" must dispose of "qualifying shares" or an interest in "qualifying shares". It should be noted that originally this relief was only intended to be available to individuals who were the sole holders of shares. However on 13 June 2016 the Committee of the Whole House extended the relief to trustees and to joint shareholders, in certain circumstances.

The relief must also be claimed, and where a claim is made the capital gains tax rate on the relevant gain is 10%.

Sections 169VD to 169VG sets out which shares are to be treated as disposed of where an investor owns a mixture of qualifying, potentially qualifying and excluded shares, with the ordering different depending on whether a claim for IR is made or not.

Where a claim for IR is made in relation to a disposal, the rules provide for qualifying shares to be treated as disposed of first, then excluded shares, and finally potentially qualifying shares.

Where no claim for IR is made on a disposal (because for example none of the shares are currently qualifying shares as they have not been held for three years), the rules provide for excluded shares to be treated as disposed of first, then potentially qualifying shares and finally qualifying shares.

These provisions are aimed at allowing shareholders to maximise their ability to benefit from IR.

Surprisingly as the gains on shares of the same class are pooled in the normal way, inherent gains on excluded shares will be taken into account when calculating the gain that qualifies for IR on qualifying shares.

Section 169VH (introduced on 13 June 2016) describes the conditions which disposals made by trustees need to meet in order to benefit from the relief. In essence the relief is only available if there is an "eligible beneficiary" – which is a beneficiary with an interest in possession (for a non-fixed term) in a trust fund holding the shares. Interestingly whilst there needs to have been an eligible beneficiary for three years prior to the date of disposal, there is no requirement for there to have been an eligible beneficiary for the whole period the trust held the shares. This is in contrast to the position for individual shareholders who need to have held qualifying shares continuously since the issue of the share to the date of disposal.

In order for trustees to claim the relief the life tenant has first to make an election to the trustees to be treated as an "eligible beneficiary". The legislation is widely drafted as to how the beneficiary makes this election – it is 'by whatever means' before the claim is made and could therefore include verbal methods – which may well cause evidential problems down the line.

Section 169VI (also introduced on 13 June 2016) provides for pro rata calculations of the gains where there is more than one life tenant (but only one "eligible beneficiary") in order to determine the amount of gain for which trustees can claim relief.

Sections 169VK and VL contain rules that ensure an individual cannot benefit from more than the lifetime allowance of £10 million, by ensuring personal gains and gains realised by trusts where the individual is a qualifying beneficiary are aggregated. This will require close monitoring, particularly by trustees who make disposals to ensure the appropriate claims are made.

Section 169VJ (introduced on 13 June 2016) extends the relief to joint holdings and other forms of interest in shares. The original draft legislation expressly referred to a sole shareholder, which caused some adverse comments, so this extension is welcomed. The relief is extended to a qualifying person disposing of an interest in a relevant holding. The definition for relevant holding is fairly narrowly drafted and comprises same class shares which were acquired in the same capacity by the same two or more persons (including the qualifying person) or a number of shares of the same class acquired in the same capacity by the qualifying person alone.

Sections 169VN to 169VS provide details as to how the relief works where a reorganisation of share capital is undertaken. For cases where no new consideration is given for the share reorganisation, such as a bonus issue, the new shares stand in the shoes of the old shares.

Where the situation involves a reorganisation with new consideration being given by the shareholder, such as a rights issue, the date of issue of the shares that relate to the new consideration given is taken to be the actual date of issue rather than the date of issue of any original shares. Shares that do not relate to new consideration being given stand in the shoes of the old shares.

Similarly to ER, s 169VT provides the option to elect to disapply the s 127 "paper for paper" rules allowing taxpayers to treat a tax free reorganisation as a taxable disposal if a claim for IR is made. In practice this is likely to be of benefit to shareholders who expect shares held after a reorganisation not to qualify for IR, when the shares held prior to the reorganisation do. If trusts wish to disapply s 127, both the trustees and the 'eligible beneficiary' need to jointly make this election.

Sections 169VU to 169VY provide further clarification as to the definitions used.

Section 169VU provides detail as to what is meant by subscribed for – in essence issued as a bargain at arm's length and fully paid up (in cash) at the issue date. Interestingly it appears that the crucial date for "subscribed" purposes is the date upon which the company's share register first reflects their existence, rather than the date of application – so shares applied for before Budget Day but issued on or after 17 March 2016 will have the potential to be qualifying shares.

It also contains the overarching anti abuse provision that the shares must be subscribed for, and issued, for genuine commercial reasons and not as part of a scheme or arrangement the main purpose or one of the main purposes is to secure a tax advantage to any person (using the definitions set out in s 16A). The original wording was narrower than this and referred to tax avoidance. HMRC is clearly signalling with this broader wording that the benefit of this relief will be withdrawn should investors attempt to contrive situations whereby they use the relief against the spirit of the legislation.

Section 169VU also provides for inter spouse/civil partner transfers, with the transferee being treated as having subscribed for the shares originally. Whilst the spouse/civil partner needs to be living with the original subscriber at the time of the transfer there is no requirement for them to have been so doing at the time of subscription. In addition, here, the transferee spouse is to be treated as having subscribed for the shares and any period for which the transferor spouse held the shares is to be added to, and treated as part of, the period for which the transferee spouse held them, ending with a disposal to a third party, in contrast to the position under ER.

Section 169VV aligns the definition of trading company to that in s 165A. This is the definition that was originally used for ER purposes, which includes the ability for companies to be treated as trading by virtue of the joint venture provisions.

Section 169VW (introduced on 13 June 2016) provides welcome guidance as to the definition of officer or employee with the inclusion of the definition "relevant employee". It includes any individual who has during the relevant time been an officer/employee of either the issuing company or a connected company. Connected company here is defined in s 286, and includes companies under common control and so the restriction is relatively wide reaching.

An exclusion from the definition of relevant employee applies for "unremunerated directors" to ensure "business angels" are not precluded from benefiting from the relief if they decide to take an active role in the business as a director, as long as they are not remunerated for this. However, this exclusion is restricted by s169 VW (4), which says an individual who is an unremunerated director will still be a relevant employee if they, or anyone connected with them, has ever been connected with the company or involved in carrying on the business of the company or a connected company.

A further exclusion from the definition of relevant employee applies if an individual becomes an employee of the issuing company/connected company more than 180 days after the commencement of the relevant period, and, at the beginning of the relevant period there was no "reasonable prospect" that this would happen. Whilst "reasonable prospect" is defined as "if it is more likely than not" this looks highly likely to cause great debate in the absence of further guidance.

Section 169VX defines "unremunerated directors" as a director who is both not entitled to receive any disqualifying payment for the relevant period and does not receive any such disqualifying payment from the issuing company or a related payment.

Disqualifying payment for these purposes is any payment other than (i) reimbursement of expenses incurred wholly, exclusively and necessarily in the fulfilment of duties; (ii) any interest in excess of reasonable commercial return on monies lent; (iii) dividends representing normal returns on investments; (iv) market value payments for goods; (v) commercial value rent for property; and (vi) any reasonable and necessary remuneration for qualifying services to the issuing company/related person as part of a trade/profession carried out wholly or partly in the UK and included in that trade's/profession's tax calculations. The legislation is widely drawn with "related persons" consisting of connected companies (of which the individual is a director) and any person connected with the issuing company or with the aforementioned connected company.

Schedule 7ZB introduces overriding counter avoidance measures in relation to return of value – with shares which would otherwise qualify becoming disqualified if the investor (or an associate) receives value from the company during the period of restriction – such period beginning one year prior to subscription and ending three years after the share issue. This is in contrast to the requirements for shares to meet the definition of qualifying shares which need to be met for the entire period of ownership. A de minimis of £1,000 is applied, although this de minimis exclusion is removed if at any time in the restricted period there are arrangements to facilitate the return of value – although investors will be relieved that payments such as commercial return on lent money, market value payment for goods and the payment of dividends are not caught by this or the disqualifying payments provisions.

SCHEDULE 15

INHERITANCE TAX: INCREASED NIL-RATE BAND

Section 93

1 IHTA 1984 is amended as follows.

2 (1) Section 8D (extra nil-rate band on death if interest in home goes to descendants etc) is amended as follows.

(2) In subsection (4), after "8G" insert "(and see also section 8M)".

(3) In subsection (9), before the definition of "tax year" insert—

""consumer prices index" means the all items consumer prices index published by the Statistics Board,".

3 (1) Section 8E (residence nil-rate amount: interest in home goes to descendants etc) is amended as follows.

(2) In subsection (6), after "(7)" insert "and sections 8FC and 8M(2B) to (2E)".

(3) In subsection (7), for paragraphs (a) and (b) substitute—

"(a) the person's residence nil-rate amount is equal to VT,
(b) where E is less than or equal to TT, an amount, equal to the difference between VT and the person's default allowance, is available for carry-forward, and
(c) where E is greater than TT, an amount, equal to the difference between VT and the person's adjusted allowance, is available for carry-forward."

(4) In subsection (8)—

(a) before the entry for section 8H insert—

"section 8FC (modifications of this section where there is entitlement to a downsizing addition),", and

(b) in the entry for section 8H, after ""qualifying residential interest"" insert ", "qualifying former residential interest" and "residential property interest"".

4 In section 8F(4) (list of other relevant sections)—

(a) before the entry for section 8H insert—

"section 8FD (which applies instead of this section where there is entitlement to a downsizing addition),", and

(b) in the entry for section 8H, after ""qualifying residential interest"" insert ", "qualifying former residential interest" and "residential property interest"".

5 After section 8F insert—

"8FA Downsizing addition: entitlement: low-value death interest in home

(1) There is entitlement to a downsizing addition in calculating the person's residence nil-rate amount if each of conditions A to F is met (see subsection (8) for the amount of the addition).

(2) Condition A is that—

(a) the person's residence nil-rate amount is given by section 8E(2) or (4), or
(b) the person's estate immediately before the person's death includes a qualifying residential interest but none of the interest is closely inherited, and—

(i) where E is less than or equal to TT, so much of VT as is attributable to the person's qualifying residential interest is less than the person's default allowance, or
(ii) where E is greater than TT, so much of VT as is attributable to the person's qualifying residential interest is less than the person's adjusted allowance.

Section 8E(6) and (7) do not apply, and any entitlement to a downsizing addition is to be ignored, when deciding whether paragraph (a) of condition A is met.

(3) Condition B is that not all of VT is attributable to the person's qualifying residential interest.

(4) Condition C is that there is a qualifying former residential interest in relation to the person (see sections 8H(4A) to (4F) and 8HA).

(5) Condition D is that the value of the qualifying former residential interest exceeds so much of VT as is attributable to the person's qualifying residential interest.

Section 8FE(2) explains what is meant by the value of the qualifying former residential interest.

(6) Condition E is that at least some of the remainder is closely inherited, where "the remainder" means everything included in the person's estate immediately before the person's death other than the person's qualifying residential interest.

(7) Condition F is that a claim is made for the addition in accordance with section 8L(1) to (3).

(8) Where there is entitlement as a result of this section, the addition—

(a) is equal to the lost relievable amount (see section 8FE) if that amount is less than so much of VT as is attributable to so much of the remainder as is closely inherited, and
(b) otherwise is equal to so much of VT as is attributable to so much of the remainder as is closely inherited.

(9) Subsection (8) has effect subject to section 8M(2G) (reduction of downsizing addition in certain cases involving conditional exemption).

(10) See also—

section 8FC (effect of an addition: section 8E case),
section 8FD (effect of an addition: section 8F case),
section 8H (meaning of "qualifying residential interest", "qualifying former residential interest" and "residential property interest"),
section 8J (meaning of "inherit"),
section 8K (meaning of "closely inherited"), and
section 8M (cases involving conditional exemption).

8FB Downsizing addition: entitlement: no residential interest at death

(1) There is also entitlement to a downsizing addition in calculating the person's residence nil-rate amount if each of conditions G to K is met (see subsection (7) for the amount of the addition).

(2) Condition G is that the person's estate immediately before the person's death ("the estate") does not include a residential property interest.

(3) Condition H is that VT is greater than nil.

(4) Condition I is that there is a qualifying former residential interest in relation to the person (see sections 8H(4A) to (4F) and 8HA).

(5) Condition J is that at least some of the estate is closely inherited.

(6) Condition K is that a claim is made for the addition in accordance with section 8L(1) to (3).

(7) Where there is entitlement as a result of this section, the addition—

(a) is equal to the lost relievable amount (see section 8FE) if that amount is less than so much of VT as is attributable to so much of the estate as is closely inherited, and

(b) otherwise is equal to so much of VT as is attributable to so much of the estate as is closely inherited.

(8) Subsection (7) has effect subject to section 8M(2G) (reduction of downsizing addition in certain cases involving conditional exemption).

(9) See also—

section 8FD (effect of an addition: section 8F case),

section 8H (meaning of "qualifying residential interest", "qualifying former residential interest" and "residential property interest"),

section 8J (meaning of "inherit"),

section 8K (meaning of "closely inherited"), and

section 8M (cases involving conditional exemption).

8FC Downsizing addition: effect: section 8E case

(1) Subsection (2) applies if—

(a) as a result of section 8FA, there is entitlement to a downsizing addition in calculating the person's residence nil-rate amount, and

(b) the person's residence nil-rate amount is given by section 8E.

(2) Section 8E has effect as if, in subsections (2) to (5) of that section, each reference to NV/100 were a reference to the total of—

(a) NV/100, and

(b) the downsizing addition.

8FD Downsizing addition: effect: section 8F case

(1) This section applies if—

(a) as a result of section 8FA or 8FB, there is entitlement to a downsizing addition in calculating the person's residence nil-rate amount, and

(b) apart from this section, the person's residence nil-rate amount is given by section 8F.

(2) Subsections (3) to (6) apply instead of section 8F.

(3) The person's residence nil-rate amount is equal to the downsizing addition.

(4) Where—

(a) E is less than or equal to TT, and the downsizing addition is equal to the person's default allowance, or

(b) E is greater than TT, and the downsizing addition is equal to the person's adjusted allowance,

no amount is available for carry-forward.

(5) Where—

(a) E is less than or equal to TT, and

(b) the downsizing addition is less than the person's default allowance,

an amount, equal to the difference between the downsizing addition and the person's default allowance, is available for carry-forward.

(6) Where—

(a) E is greater than TT, and

(b) the downsizing addition is less than the person's adjusted allowance,

an amount, equal to the difference between the downsizing addition and the person's adjusted allowance, is available for carry-forward.

8FE Calculation of lost relievable amount

(1) This section is about how to calculate the person's lost relievable amount for the purposes of sections 8FA(8) and 8FB(7).

(2) For the purposes of this section and section 8FA(5), the value of the person's qualifying former residential interest is the value of the interest at the time of completion of the disposal of the interest.

(3) In this section, the person's "former allowance" is the total of—

(a) the residential enhancement at the time of completion of the disposal of the qualifying former residential interest,

(b) any brought-forward allowance that the person would have had if the person had died at that time, having regard to the circumstances of the person at that time (see section 8G as applied by subsection (4)), and

(c) if the person's allowance on death includes an amount of brought-forward allowance which is greater than the amount of brought-forward allowance given by paragraph (b), the difference between those two amounts.

(4) For the purposes of calculating any brought-forward allowance that the person ("P") would have had as mentioned in subsection (3)(b)—

(a) section 8G (brought-forward allowance) applies, but as if references to the residential enhancement at P's death were references to the residential enhancement at the time of completion of the disposal of the qualifying former residential interest, and

(b) assume that a claim for brought-forward allowance was made in relation to an amount available for carry-forward from a related person's death if, on P's death, a claim was in fact made in relation to the amount.

(5) For the purposes of subsection (3)(c), where the person's allowance on death is equal to the person's adjusted allowance, the amount of brought-forward allowance included in the person's allowance on death is calculated as follows.

Step 1
Express the person's brought-forward allowance as a percentage of the person's default allowance.
Step 2
Multiply—
$(E - TT) / 2$
by the percentage given by step 1.
Step 3
Reduce the person's brought-forward allowance by the amount given by step 2.
The result is the amount of brought-forward allowance included in the person's allowance on death.

(6) If completion of the disposal of the qualifying former residential interest occurs before 6 April 2017—

(a) for the purposes of subsection (3)(a), the residential enhancement at the time of completion of the disposal is treated as being £100,000, and

(b) for the purposes of subsection (3)(b), the amount of brought-forward allowance that the person would have had at that time is treated as being nil.

(7) In this section, the person's "allowance on death" means—

(a) where E is less than or equal to TT, the person's default allowance, or

(b) where E is greater than TT, the person's adjusted allowance.

(8) For the purposes of this section, "completion" of the disposal of a residential property interest occurs at the time of the disposal or, if the disposal is under a contract which is completed by a conveyance, at the time when the interest is conveyed.

(9) Where, as a result of section 8FA, there is entitlement to a downsizing addition in calculating the person's residence nil-rate amount, take the following steps to calculate the person's lost relievable amount.

Step 1
Express the value of the person's qualifying former residential interest as a percentage of the person's former allowance, but take that percentage to be 100% if it would otherwise be higher.
Step 2
Express QRI as a percentage of the person's allowance on death, where QRI is so much of VT as is attributable to the person's qualifying residential interest, but take that percentage to be 100% if it would otherwise be higher.
Step 3
Subtract the percentage given by step 2 from the percentage given by step 1, but take the result to be 0% if it would otherwise be negative.
The result is P%.

Step 4

The person's lost relievable amount is equal to P% of the person's allowance on death.

(10) Where, as a result of section 8FB, there is entitlement to a downsizing addition in calculating the person's residence nil-rate amount, take the following steps to calculate the person's lost relievable amount.

Step 1

Express the value of the person's qualifying former residential interest as a percentage of the person's former allowance, but take that percentage to be 100% if it would otherwise be higher.

Step 2

Calculate that percentage of the person's allowance on death.

The result is the person's lost relievable amount."

6 In section 8G (meaning of "brought-forward allowance"), in subsection (3)(a), for "and 8F" substitute ", 8F and 8FD".

7 (1) Section 8H (meaning of "qualifying residential interest") is amended as follows.

(2) In the heading, at the end insert ", "qualifying former residential interest" and "residential property interest"".

(3) In subsection (1), for "and 8F" substitute "to 8FE and section 8M".

(4) In subsection (2), for "In this section" substitute "A".

(5) After subsection (4) insert—

"(4A) Subsection (4B) or (4C) applies where—

(a) a person disposes of a residential property interest in a dwelling-house on or after 8 July 2015 (and before the person dies), and

(b) the person's personal representatives nominate—

(i) where there is only one such dwelling-house, that dwelling-house, or

(ii) where there are two or more such dwelling-houses, one (and only one) of those dwelling-houses.

(4B) Where—

(a) the person—

(i) disposes of a residential property interest in the nominated dwelling-house at a post-occupation time, or

(ii) disposes of two or more residential property interests in the nominated dwelling-house at the same post-occupation time or at post-occupation times on the same day, and

(b) the person does not otherwise dispose of residential property interests in the nominated dwelling-house at post-occupation times,

the interest disposed of is, or the interests disposed of are, a qualifying former residential interest in relation to the person.

(4C) Where—

(a) the person disposes of residential property interests in the nominated dwelling-house at post-occupation times on two or more days, and

(b) the person's personal representatives nominate one (and only one) of those days,

the interest or interests disposed of at post-occupation times on the nominated day is or are a qualifying former residential interest in relation to the person.

(4D) For the purposes of subsections (4A) to (4C)—

(a) a person is to be treated as not disposing of a residential property interest in a dwelling-house where the person disposes of an interest in the dwelling-house by way of gift and the interest is, in relation to the gift and the donor, property subject to a reservation within the meaning of section 102 of the Finance Act 1986 (gifts with reservation), and

(b) a person is to be treated as disposing of a residential property interest in a dwelling-house if the person is treated as making a potentially exempt transfer of the interest as a result of the operation of section 102(4) of that Act (property ceasing to be subject to a reservation).

(4E) Where—

(a) a transfer of value by a person is a conditionally exempt transfer of a residential property interest, and

(b) at the time of the person's death, no chargeable event has occurred with respect to that interest, that interest may not be, or be included in, a qualifying former residential interest in relation to the person.

(4F) In subsections (4B) and (4C) "post-occupation time" means a time—

(a) on or after 8 July 2015,

(b) after the nominated dwelling-house first became the person's residence, and

(c) before the person dies.

(4G) For the purposes of subsections (4A) to (4C), if the disposal is under a contract which is completed by a conveyance, the disposal occurs at the time when the interest is conveyed."

8 After section 8H insert—

"8HA Qualifying former residential interest": interests in possession

(1) This section applies for the purposes of determining whether certain interests may be, or be included in, a qualifying former residential interest in relation to a person (see section 8H(4A) to (4C)).

(2) This section applies where—

(a) a person ("P") is beneficially entitled to an interest in possession in settled property, and

(b) the settled property consists of, or includes, an interest in a dwelling-house.

(3) Subsection (4) applies where—

(a) the trustees of the settlement dispose of the interest in the dwelling-house to a person other than P,

(b) P's interest in possession in the settled property subsists immediately before the disposal, and

(c) P's interest in possession—

(i) falls within subsection (7) throughout the period beginning with P becoming beneficially entitled to it and ending with the disposal, or

(ii) falls within subsection (8).

(4) The disposal is to be treated as a disposal by P of the interest in the dwelling-house to which P is beneficially entitled as a result of the operation of section 49(1).

(5) Subsection (6) applies where—

(a) P disposes of the interest in possession in the settled property, or P's interest in possession in the settled property comes to an end in P's lifetime,

(b) the interest in the dwelling-house is, or is part of, the settled property immediately before the time when that happens, and

(c) P's interest in possession—

(i) falls within subsection (7) throughout the period beginning with P becoming beneficially entitled to it and ending with the time mentioned in paragraph (b), or

(ii) falls within subsection (8).

(6) The disposal, or (as the case may be) the coming to an end of P's interest in possession, is to be treated as a disposal by P of the interest in the dwelling-house to which P is beneficially entitled as a result of the operation of section 49(1).

(7) An interest in possession falls within this subsection if—

(a) P became beneficially entitled to it before 22 March 2006 and section 71A does not apply to the settled property; or

(b) P becomes beneficially entitled to it on or after 22 March 2006 and the interest is—

(i) an immediate post-death interest,

(ii) a disabled person's interest, or

(iii) a transitional serial interest.

(8) An interest in possession falls within this subsection if P becomes beneficially entitled to it on or after 22 March 2006 and it falls within section 5(1B)."

9 In section 8J (meaning of "inherited"), in subsection (1), for "and 8F" substitute ", 8F, 8FA, 8FB and 8M".

10 In section 8K (meaning of "closely inherited"), in subsection (1), for "and 8F" substitute ", 8F, 8FA, 8FB and 8M".

11 In section 8L (claims for brought-forward allowance)—

(a) in the heading, at the end insert "and downsizing addition", and

(b) in subsection (1), after "(see section 8G)" insert "or for a downsizing addition for a person (see sections 8FA to 8FD)".

12 (1) Section 8M (residence nil-rate amount: cases involving conditional exemption) is amended as follows.

(2) For subsections (1) and (2) substitute—

"(1) This section applies where—

(a) a person ("D") dies on or after 6 April 2017,

(b) ignoring the application of this section, D's residence nil-rate amount is greater than nil, and

(c) some or all of the transfer of value under section 4 on D's death is a conditionally exempt transfer of property consisting of, or including, any of the following—

(i) some or all of a qualifying residential interest;

(ii) some or all of a residential property interest, at least some portion of which is closely inherited, and which is not, and is not included in, a qualifying residential interest;

(iii) one or more closely inherited assets that are not residential property interests.

(2) Subsections (2B) to (2E) apply for the purposes of sections 8E to 8FD if—

(a) ignoring the application of this section, D's residence nil-rate amount is given by section 8E, and

(b) some or all of the transfer of value under section 4 is a conditionally exempt transfer of property mentioned in subsection (1)(c)(i).

(2A) In subsections (2B) to (2E), but subject to subsection (3)(a), "the exempt percentage of the QRI" is given by—

(X / QRI) x 100

where—

X is the attributable portion of the value transferred by the conditionally exempt transfer,

QRI is the attributable portion of the value transferred by the transfer of value under section 4, and

"the attributable portion" means the portion (which may be the whole) attributable to the qualifying residential interest.

(2B) If—

(a) the exempt percentage of the QRI is 100%, and

(b) D has no entitlement to a downsizing addition,

D's residence nil-rate amount and amount available for carry-forward are given by section 8F(2) and (3) (instead of section 8E).

(2C) If—

(a) the exempt percentage of the QRI is 100%, and

(b) D has an entitlement to a downsizing addition,

D's residence nil-rate amount and amount available for carry-forward are given by section 8FD(3) to (6) (instead of section 8E as modified by section 8FC(2)).

See also subsection (2G).

(2D) If—

(a) the exempt percentage of the QRI is less than 100%, and

(b) D has no entitlement to a downsizing addition,

D's residence nil-rate amount and amount available for carry-forward are given by section 8E but as if, in subsections (2) to (5) of that section, each reference to NV/100 were a reference to NV/100 multiplied by the percentage that is the difference between 100% and the exempt percentage of the QRI.

(2E) If—

(a) the exempt percentage of the QRI is less than 100%, and

(b) D has an entitlement to a downsizing addition,

D's residence nil-rate amount and amount available for carry-forward are given by section 8E as modified by section 8FC(2), but as if the reference to NV/100 in section 8FC(2)(a) were a reference to NV/100 multiplied by the percentage that is the difference between 100% and the exempt percentage of the QRI.

See also subsection (2G).

(2F) Subsection (2G) applies for the purposes of sections 8FA to 8FD if—

(a) some or all of the transfer of value under section 4 is a conditionally exempt transfer of property mentioned in subsection (1)(c)(ii) or (iii) (or both),

(b) D has an entitlement to a downsizing addition, and

(c) DA exceeds Y (see subsection (2H)).

(2G) Subject to subsection (3)(aa) and (ab), the amount of the downsizing addition is treated as reduced by whichever is the smaller of—

(a) the difference between DA and Y, and
(b) Z.

(2H) In subsections (2F) and (2G)—

DA is the amount of the downsizing addition to which D has an entitlement (ignoring the application of subsection (2G));
Y is so much (if any) of the value transferred by the transfer of value under section 4 as—

(a) is not transferred by a conditionally exempt transfer, and
(b) is attributable to—

(i) the closely inherited portion (which may be the whole) of any residential property interests that are not, and are not included in, a qualifying residential interest, or
(ii) closely inherited assets that are not residential property interests;

Z is the total of—

(a) the closely inherited conditionally exempt values of all residential property interests mentioned in subsection (1)(c)(ii), and
(b) so much of the value transferred by the conditionally exempt transfer as is attributable to property mentioned in subsection (1)(c)(iii).

(2I) For the purposes of the definition of "Z", "the closely inherited conditionally exempt value" of a residential property interest means—

(a) so much of the value transferred by the conditionally exempt transfer as is attributable to the interest, multiplied by
(b) the percentage of the interest which is closely inherited."

(3) In subsection (3), for the words before paragraph (b) substitute—

"(3) For the purposes of calculating tax chargeable under section 32 or 32A by reference to a chargeable event related to property forming the subject-matter of the conditionally exempt transfer where D is the relevant person for the purposes of section 33—

(a) where subsections (2B) to (2E) apply and the chargeable event relates to property mentioned in subsection (1)(c)(i), in calculating the exempt percentage of the QRI, X is calculated as if the attributable portion of the value transferred by the conditionally exempt transfer had not included the portion (which may be the whole) of the qualifying residential interest on which the tax is chargeable,
(aa) where subsection (2G) applies and the chargeable event relates to property mentioned in subsection (1)(c)(ii), Z is calculated as if it had not included the portion (which may be the whole) of the closely inherited conditionally exempt value of the residential property interest on which the tax is chargeable,
(ab) where subsection (2G) applies and the chargeable event relates to an asset mentioned in subsection (1)(c)(iii) ("the taxable asset"), Z is calculated as if it had not included so much of the value transferred by the conditionally exempt transfer as is attributable to the taxable asset,".

(4) In subsection (3)—

(a) at the beginning of paragraph (b) insert "in the cases mentioned in paragraphs (a), (aa) and (ab),",
(b) at the end of paragraph (b) omit "and",
(c) in paragraph (c), for "less" substitute "reduced (but not below nil) by", and
(d) after paragraph (c) insert ", and

(d) where the chargeable event relates to property mentioned in subsection (1)(c)(i) and subsections (2B) to (2E) do not apply, section 33 has effect as if in subsection (1)(b)(ii) after "in accordance with" there were inserted "section 8D(2) and (3) above and"."

(5) In subsection (5), for "the qualifying residential interest which" substitute "property which forms the subject-matter of the conditionally exempt transfer where the chargeable event".

(6) In subsection (6), for "the qualifying residential interest which" substitute "property which forms the subject-matter of the conditionally exempt transfer and the chargeable event".

(7) In subsection (7), for "the qualifying residential interest" substitute "property which forms the subject-matter of the conditionally exempt transfer".

GENERAL NOTE

IHTA 1984 ss 8D–8M, inserted by F(No 2)A 2015 s 9, provide for a "residence nil-rate amount" in relation to the IHT charge on the death of a person who dies on or after 6 April 2017. This is an amount of the person's estate which is charged to IHT at a nil rate in addition to the generally applicable nil-rate band (currently £325,000). The additional nil-rate amount is limited to the value of any interest in a dwelling-house which had been the person's residence, which was possessed by that person at death, and which devolves on his or her direct descendants, subject to two further limiting factors. One is that each person's additional nil-rate amount is limited to a cash maximum, which is £100,000 for deaths in the tax year 2017/18, and is increased in amounts of £25,000 for deaths in each succeeding tax year until it is £175,000 in 2020/21 and subsequent years, but with the possible addition of carry-forward of additional nil-rate amount not used by a deceased spouse or civil partner (including carry-forward from a spouse or civil partner who died before 6 April 2017). The other limiting factor is that such additional nil-rate amount is subject to a tapered reduction by £1 for every £2 of the value of the estate in excess of £2million. The £175,000 maximum and the £2 million threshold of the tapered reduction are subject to an annual indexation increase from 6 April 2021 in the same manner as the general nil-rate band, but for simplicity of exposition this commentary is in terms of the current figures.

Further legislation was promised to extend the benefit of the residence nil-rate amount to cases where a person downsizes or ceases to own a home on or after 8 July 2015 and assets of an equivalent value are passed on death to direct descendants. This Schedule is that promised further legislation. It is something of a drafting masterpiece, but it is a difficult read, and too complicated for ease of use by the ageing members of the middle classes for whom it is intended. That is the fault not of the draftsman, but of the policy of having such a specifically targeted tax break as the residence nil-rate amount.

Some definitions already in place in IHTA 1984 ss 8D–8M need to be borne in mind:

- The "residential enhancement" is the cash limit on the residence nil-rate amount, depending on the year of death: £100,000 in the tax year 2017/18, £125,000 in 2018/19, £150,000 in 2019/20, £175,000 in 2020/21 and subsequently, subject to possible upwards indexation after 2020/21 (IHTA 1984 s 8D(5)(a), (6), and (7)).
- "Closely inherited" means inherited by lineal descendants, and the latter have an extended meaning so as to include stepchildren and their descendants, and descendants who have been adopted and their descendants, certain spouses of descendants, and foster children (IHTA 1984 s 8K).
- A "qualifying residential interest" is an interest in a residence which the deceased lived in at some point while owning an interest in it; if he had more than one the executors must elect between them (IHTA 1984 s 8H).
- The "default allowance" is the residential enhancement for the relevant tax year but increased by any available brought-forward allowance (for which see below): IHTA 1984 s 8D(5)(f).
- An "adjusted allowance" is where the deceased's estate exceeds £2 million, and is the default allowance subject to reduction (possibly to nil) by half the excess of the estate over £2 million (IHTA 1984 s 8D(5)(g)).
- A "brought-forward allowance" (IHTA 1984 s 8G) is that of unused residence nil-rate amount from a predeceased person of whom the deceased was the surviving spouse or civil partner. It is similar to nil-rate band transfer under IHTA 1984 ss 8A–8C and adopts in essence the same procedure. It is a percentage uplift to the residential enhancement corresponding to the percentage of the allowance unused on the previous death, but limited to 100%.
- A "residence nil-rate amount" is the additional amount of a deceased person's estate charged to IHT at the nil rate, corresponding to the value of a closely inherited whole or part of a qualifying residential interest, so far as it does not exceed the default or adjusted allowance (as the case may be), and determined as provided in IHTA 1984 ss 8D, 8E, 8F, and 8G–8M inserted by F(No 2)A 2015 s 9.

The amendments made to IHTA 1984 by this Schedule apply where a deceased person's estate's entitlement to a residence nil-rate amount is zero or less than the available maximum, and there has been a "qualifying former residential interest". This can give rise to an entitlement in some circumstances to a "downsizing addition" to the residence nil-rate amount. It comes in two alternative kinds: "low value death interest in home", and "no residential interest at death".

Definition of "qualifying former residential interest"

This is defined in the new IHTA 1984 8H(4A)–(4G) inserted by para 7. It is an interest in a residential property which the deceased had lived in at some point while owning an interest in it, and where the deceased made a lifetime disposal of the interest after he had lived in the property and on or after 8 July 2015. The disposal could have been a gift or a sale, and if it is under a contract which is completed by conveyance or transfer, the date of it for these purposes is that of the conveyance or transfer, not the contract. For the interest to qualify, if there is only one such property there must be nomination of the property by the personal representatives, and if there are more than one such property the personal representatives must nominate one of them. If there was just one interest disposed of by the deceased in the nominated property, or two or more interests disposed of on the same day, that or those are the qualifying former residential interest. If there were more than one interest in the nominated property which were the subject of lifetime disposals on different days, the personal representatives must nominate one of the days, with the consequence that the interest or interests disposed of on that day is or are the qualifying former residential interest, though they can only nominate in relation to interests disposed of on or after 8 July 2015 and after the deceased had lived in the property. However, an interest cannot qualify if it has been the subject of conditional exemption and there has been no chargeable event.

There are special rules for two types of disposal, of property subject to a reservation and settled property subject to an interest in possession.

A gift with reservation within FA 1986 s 102 of an interest in a qualifying dwelling is not treated as a disposal, but if the reservation comes to an end in the donor's lifetime that is treated as a disposal of the property which was subject to a reservation (new IHTA 1984 s 8H(4D)).

New IHTA 1984 s 8HA (inserted by para 8) provides for what constitutes a lifetime disposal of a qualifying former residential interest, where what the deceased had was an interest in possession under a settlement in an interest in a dwelling-house. New s 8HA only applies where the deceased had an interest in possession which commenced before 22 March 2006, or which was an immediate post-death interest, a disabled person's interest, a transitional serial interest, or an interest falling within IHTA 1984, s. 5(1B), in other words one of the types of interest in possession which are treated for IHT purposes as if the beneficiary entitled to the interest was entitled to the underlying property. If such an interest came to an end during the deceased's lifetime, or was assigned or surrendered by him or her, or if the trustees disposed of (other than to the deceased) the underlying interest in the dwelling-house, that is treated as having been a disposal of the interest in the dwelling-house by the deceased for the purposes of the definition of qualifying former residential interest. New IHTA 1984 s 8HA, combined with new s 8H(4B) and (4C) mentioned above which enable the disposal of two interests in the same dwelling-house on the same day to be aggregated to form a qualifying former residential interest, is important for the common arrangement where spouses or civil partners own their principal residence as tenants in common in equal shares, and the will of the first of them to die gives a life interest in the latter's half share to the survivor. It is thus possible for the entire property to be a qualifying former residential interest of the surviving spouse or civil partner, for the purposes of the downsizing addition, by means of disposals of the absolutely-owned half share and the settled half share on the same day.

Low value death interest in home: the preconditions

The new IHTA 1984 s 8FA(2)–(7), inserted by para 5, sets out the six pre-conditions for there to be an entitlement to a downsizing addition in the category of "low value death interest in home". These conditions, and the subsequent stages in the calculation of the downsizing addition, are illustrated by the following Example.

Example

Janet and John are a married couple who have owned Upsize House as tenants in common in equal shares and lived for many years there. Neither has been in a previous marriage or civil partnership. John's health declines and he cannot manage the stairs any longer, and so in November 2015 they sell Upsize House for £400,000 and purchase Downsize Bungalow to which they move. John dies on 3 June 2016. His will leaves all his property to Janet, and his estate is less than £2 million in value. Janet dies on 15 August 2020. Her estate on death consists of Downsize Bungalow, valued at £150,000, and chattels, cash and investments worth £1,200,000. Her will leaves Downsize Bungalow to her and John's children David and Mary, and leaves residue as to a quarter to charity and as to three quarters to David's and Mary's children.

Condition A (new s 8FA(2)) is either of two alternatives:

- The first alternative is that the residence nil-rate amount is given by IHTA 1984 s 8E(2) or (4), namely that there is a closely-inherited qualifying residential interest in the estate, but the value transferred by the transfer of value on the deceased's death which is attributable to it is less than the default allowance (see above) where the estate is £2 million or less, or is less than the adjusted allowance (see above) where the estate exceeds £2 million. This can be, for example, because the whole of the residential interest is closely inherited but is of too low a value or because not all of the residential interest is closely inherited. In assessing whether this condition is fulfilled, the value transferred by the chargeable transfer on death is not treated as an upper limit on the value of the closely-inherited qualifying residential interest taken into account (see the final sentence of the new s 8FA(2) which disapplies s 8E(6) and (7)).

- The second alternative is that there is a qualifying residential interest in the estate of which none is closely inherited, but the value transferred by the chargeable transfer on the deceased's death which is attributable to the qualifying residential interest is either less than the default allowance (see above), where the estate is £2 million or less, or is less than the adjusted allowance (see above), where the estate exceeds £2 million.

In the Example Janet's estate's default allowance is her £175,000 and a brought-forward allowance from John also of £175,000 (IHTA 1984 ss 8F and 8G), a total of £350,000. Downsize Bungalow is a closely-inherited qualifying residential interest worth only £150,000, and so alternative (a) is applicable.

Condition B (new s 8FA(3)) is that not all of the value transferred by the chargeable transfer on the deceased's death is attributable to the deceased's qualifying residential interest. This condition is clearly fulfilled in the Example.

Condition C (new s 8FA(4)) is that there is a qualifying former residential interest in relation to the deceased. In the Example this condition is satisfied in relation to Janet's estate by her former share of Upsize House.

Condition D (new s 8FA(5)) is that the value of the qualifying former residential interest at the time when the deceased disposed of it exceeds so much of the chargeable transfer on death as is attributable to the deceased's qualifying residential Interest. The comparison in the Example is between the former interest in Upsize House of a value of £200,000 (ignoring for the purposes of exposition the possibility that a half share is worth less than half the whole) and the chargeable value of Downsize Bungalow of £150,000. This condition is fulfilled in the Example.

Condition E (new s 8FA(6)) is that at least some of the deceased's estate other than the qualifying residential interest is closely inherited. In the Example this is satisfied by the three-quarters of residue left to Janet's grandchildren.

Condition F (new s 8FA(7)) is that a claim is made for the downsizing addition in accordance with IHTA 1984 s 8L. This is primarily a matter for the personal representatives, who have two years from the death in which to do it. If they do not, other persons liable for the IHT may be able to. Assume that Janet's executors claim the maximum and also nominate Upsize House under new s 8H(4A)(b).

If all these conditions are fulfilled, there is a downsizing addition to the residence nil-rate amount which is determined by reference to the "lost relievable amount".

Low value death interest in home: calculation of the lost relievable amount

This is determined under the new IHTA 1984 s 8FE. The steps in the calculation continue to be illustrated by the Example set out above.

- The value of the qualifying former residential interest is its value at the time of completion of the disposal of it (new s 8FE(2)). In the Example this is £200,000.

- The next step is to establish the "former allowance" (new s 8FE(3)). There are a number of different elements to this. The first element is what would have been the residential enhancement at the time of the disposal of the qualifying former residential interest. In the Example this is treated as being £100,000 because the disposal was before 6 April 2017 (new s 8FE(6)(a)).

- There is then added, as part of the former allowance, any brought-forward allowance the deceased would have been entitled to if he or she had died at the time of the disposal (new s 8FE(3)(b) and (4)). In the Example Janet did not at the time of the disposal have any entitlement to brought-forward allowance, and even if she had, it would have been treated as nil because the disposal was before 6 April 2017 (new s 8FE(6)(b)).

– There is then added, as a further part of the former allowance, if the deceased had an entitlement to brought-forward allowance at death greater than the amount of brought-forward allowance already taken into account as set out above, the difference between the two brought-forward allowances. However, if the deceased's estate on death is more than £2million there is a proportional reduction of the brought-forward allowance on death under new s 8FE(5) before this difference is calculated. In the Example Janet's estate has a brought-forward allowance from the death of John equal to the residential enhancement at her death, ie £175,000 (IHTA 1984 ss 8F and 8G). Her estate is less than £2million and so her former allowance is £100,000 + £175,000 = £275,000.

– The value of the qualifying former residential interest is then expressed as a percentage of the former allowance, taking the percentage to be 100% if it would otherwise be higher (new s 8FE(9) Step 1). In the Example the value of the qualifying former residential interest of £200,000 is 72.73% of the former allowance of £275,000.

– The value transferred by the chargeable transfer on the deceased's death which is attributable to the qualifying residential interest owned by the deceased at his or her death is then expressed as a percentage of the default allowance or adjusted allowance as case may be, according to whether or not the deceased's estate exceeds £2 million (new s 8FE(9) Step 2). In the Example the value of the qualifying residential interest, ie Downsize Bungalow, is £150,000, and Janet's default allowance is £350,000. This percentage is therefore 42.86%.

– The Step 2 percentage (under new s 8FE(9)—see above) is deducted from the Step 1 percentage (under new s 8FE(9)see above), taking the result as 0% if it would otherwise be negative (new s 8FE(9) Step 3). In the Example Step 3 produces 72.73% – 42.86% = 29.87%.

– The lost relievable amount is the Step 3 percentage (under new s 8FE(9)—see above) of the default allowance or adjusted allowance (as the case may be) on the deceased's death (new s 8FE(9) Step 4). Janet's default allowance on death is £350,000 and 29.87% of it is £104,545.

Low value death interest in home: calculation of the residence nil-rate amount and downsizing addition

The downsizing addition to the residence nil-rate amount is the lost relievable amount, or the amount of the chargeable transfer on the deceased's death which is attributable to property in the estate, other than the qualifying residential interest owned by the deceased at his or her death, which is closely-inherited (new s 8FA(1) and (8)). Where the qualifying residential interest is wholly or partly closely inherited, the residence nil-rate amount is increased by the downsizing addition up to the upper limit represented by the default allowance or the adjusted allowance (see the new IHTA 1984 s 8FC and also s 8E). Where none of the qualifying residential interest is closely inherited, the downsizing addition is the deceased's residence nil-rate amount (new s 8FD).

In the Example, the downsizing addition is the whole of the lost relievable amount of £104,545, because the amount of residue which is closely inherited is of greater value. The downsizing addition is then added to what would be Janet's estate's residence nil-rate amount, apart from any downsizing addition, of £150,000 (the value of Downsize Bungalow), to produce a residence nil-rate amount of £254,545. It would be limited to £350,000 if the sum of these two items exceeded that amount. Accordingly, combining this with nil-rate band transfer under IHTA 1984 s 8A ff, there is a nil-rate band of £904,545 on Janet's death. The chargeable transfer is £1,050,000. IHT is charged at more than the nil-rate on £145,455, and at the reduced rate of 36% in view of the relative size of the gift to charity (see IHTA 1984 Sch 1A).

The purpose of this category of downsizing addition is to deal with cases where a more valuable qualifying residential property has been sold and replaced by a less valuable one. The downsizing addition relates to the difference in the two values, so far as property other than the qualifying residential interest which the deceased owned at his or her death is closely inherited. The qualifying residential interest in the deceased's estate at death will only qualify for additional nil-rate band to the extent that it itself is closely inherited.

Something which emerges from the above Example is that although there can be carry forward of John's unused allowance, there is no carry forward to Janet of his qualifying former residential interest. If Upsize House had been sold by Janet after John's death once she owned the whole of it she would have been entitled to the full £350,000 residence nil-rate amount. In appropriate cases where a married couple downsize from a residence in shared ownership they may wish to change their wills so that the first to die leaves property to lineal descendants, though this would need to be weighed against the other consequences for the utilisation of nil-rate bands. In circumstances such as these the residence nil-rate amount rules will still discourage downsizing despite the creation of the downsizing addition.

No residential interest at death: the preconditions

The new IHTA 1984 s 8FB(2)–(6), inserted by para 5, sets out the five pre-conditions for there to be an entitlement to a downsizing addition in the category of "no residential interest at death". By way of Example, the facts are as above, but in December 2019 Downsize Bungalow is sold for £150,000 and Janet moves into a nursing home. Janet's estate on death consists of chattels, cash and investments worth £1,350,000. Janet's will leaves £300,000 to charity and residue is divided between her children and grandchildren.

–   Condition G is that the deceased's estate does not include any interest in a residential property in which the deceased had lived at a time when he or she owned an interest in it. In the Example this is satisfied.
–   Condition H is that the circumstances of the deceased's estate are such that there is a value transferred by the chargeable transfer on the deceased's death of an amount greater than zero. This is also satisfied in the Example.
–   Condition I is that there is a qualifying former residential interest (see above) in relation to the deceased. There are potentially two, between which Janet's executors must elect. They nominate her interest in Downsize House.
–   Condition J is that at least some of the deceased's estate is closely inherited. This is also satisfied in the Example.
–   Condition K is that is that a claim is made for the downsizing addition in accordance with IHTA 1984 s 8L. This is primarily a matter for the personal representatives, who have two years from the death in which to do it. If they do not, other persons liable for the IHT may be able to. Assume in the Example that they make a claim.

If all these conditions are fulfilled, there is a downsizing addition to the residence nil-rate amount based on the lost relievable amount.

No residential interest at death: calculation of the lost relievable amount

The value of the qualifying former residential interest and former allowance are calculated in the same way as described above for low value death interest in home cases. In the Example, as described above, the value of the qualifying former residential interest is £200,000 and the former allowance is £275,000. The remaining steps in the calculations are:

–   The value of the qualifying former residential interest is then expressed as a percentage of the former allowance, taking the percentage to be 100% if it would otherwise be higher (new s 8FE(10) Step 1). In the Example the value of the qualifying former residential interest (£200,000) is 72.73% of the former allowance of £275,000.
–   Apply that percentage to the deceased's default allowance or adjusted allowance (as the case may be) and the result is his or her lost relievable amount (new s 8FE(10) Step 2). In the Example Janet's estate's default allowance is £350,000 and so her lost relievable amount is £350,000 X 72.73% = £254,555.

No residential interest at death: calculation of the residence nil-rate amount and downsizing addition

The downsizing addition is the residence nil-rate amount, and is equal to whichever is the less of: the lost relievable amount; or the amount of the chargeable transfer on death which is attributable to closely-inherited property in the estate (new s 8FB(1) and (7) and s 8FD). In the Example enough of Janet's estate is closely inherited for the lost relievable amount of £254,555 to be available in full as the downsizing addition. Accordingly, combining this with nill-rate band transfer under IHTA 1984 s 8A ff, there is a nil-rate band of £904,555 on Janet's death. The chargeable transfer is

£1,050,000. IHT is charged at more than the nil rate on £145,445, and at the reduced rate of 36% in view of the relative size of the gift to charity (see IHTA 1984 Sch 1A). Interestingly the result is much the same as if Downsize Bungalow had been retained by Janet until her death. It remains the case that the full residence nil-rate amount of £350,000 would have applied if Janet had sold Upsize House after John's death.

Where there is conditional exemption

Conditional exemption under IHTA 1984 s 31, which can be obtained for buildings of outstanding historic or architectural interest, is the one kind of exemption which could apply to closely-inherited property which qualifies for a residence nil-rate amount, or a downsizing addition. F(No 2)A 2015 s 9 inserted IHTA 1984 s 8M to provide for where conditional exemption is obtained for a qualifying residential interest which is inherited by lineal descendants. Paragraph 12 of this Schedule amends s 8M to take account of the downsizing addition rules. The general scheme is that conditionally exempt property is excluded from qualifying for the residence nil-rate amount or downsizing addition, but if subsequently there is a chargeable event under IHTA 1984 s 32 or s 32A in relation to the conditionally exempt property, the rate of charge takes into account the residence nil-rate amount or downsizing addition not used on the deceased's death because of the conditional exemption, and not used up in the intervening period by a spouse or civil partner.

The new IHTA 1984 s 8M(2)–(2E) inserted by para 12(2) deal with cases where apart from s 8M a deceased person's estate has an entitlement to a residence nil-rate amount, and where the estate includes a qualifying residential interest which is conditionally exempt. The value of the qualifying residential interest which is conditionally exempt is expressed as a percentage of the value of that qualifying residential interest, as provided by the formula in the new s 8M(2A). If that percentage is 100%, and there is no downsizing addition, there is no residence nil-rate amount for the deceased's estate (new s 8M(2B)). If that percentage is 100% and there is a downsizing addition, the latter constitutes the residence nil-rate amount (new s 8M(2C)). If the conditionally exempt part is a percentage of the value of the qualifying residential interest less than 100%, then the residence nil-rate amount is calculated as if the percentage of the qualifying residential interest which is closely inherited were multiplied by the percentage which is the difference between 100 % and the percentage represented by the conditionally exempt part (new s 8M(2D) and (2E)). Thus if 70% of a qualifying residential interest worth £800,000 is conditionally exempt, and 60% of it is closely inherited, the residence nil-rate amount (to which any downsizing addition would be added) is £800,000 x (60% x (100%-70%)) = £144,000.

The new IHTA 1984 s 8M(2F) to (2I) inserted by para 12(2) deal with cases where a deceased person's estate contains closely inherited conditionally exempt property other than a qualifying residential interest, and there is entitlement to a downsizing addition. If the downsizing addition apart from these provisions is greater than the value of the closely inherited parts of the estate which are not conditionally exempt, the downsizing addition is reduced by the smaller of two values: either the difference between the downsizing addition apart from these provisions and the value of the closely inherited parts of the estate which are not conditionally exempt, or the value of the closely inherited parts of the estate which are conditionally exempt.

IHTA 1984 s 8M(3)–(7) as amended by para 12(3)–(7) govern the calculation of the IHT on a chargeable event (such as a sale or breach of undertakings) on conditionally exempt property which was closely inherited and which qualified (apart from the conditional exemption) for a residence nil-rate amount or downsizing addition on a deceased person's death. Where the charge (see IHTA 1984 s 33) is as if the property formed part of the deceased's estate, the IHT is recalculated and residence nil-rate amount or downsizing addition given effect to as if the conditionally exempt property now subject to the IHT charge was not conditionally exempt. However, in these circumstances the available residence nil-rate amount and downsizing addition are subject to a reduction to the extent that they have already been used in the form of brought-forward allowance on the death of a surviving spouse or civil partner of the deceased, or on the death of a surviving spouse or civil partner of a surviving spouse or civil partner of the deceased). If the chargeable event takes place before the deceased's surviving spouse's or civil partner's death, the latter's brought-forward allowance is adjusted downwards to take account of the using up of the deceased's residence nil-rate amount in determining the IHT charge on the chargeable event.

SCHEDULE 16

PROPERTY AUTHORISED INVESTMENT FUNDS AND CO-OWNERSHIP AUTHORISED CONTRACTUAL SCHEMES

Section 133

PART 1

CO-OWNERSHIP AUTHORISED CONTRACTUAL SCHEMES

1 In FA 2003, after section 102 insert—

"102A Co-ownership authorised contractual schemes

(1) This section has effect for the purposes of this Part.

(2) This Part, with the exception of Schedule 7 (see subsection (10)), applies in relation to a co-ownership authorised contractual scheme as if—

  (a) the scheme were a company, and

  (b) the rights of the participants were shares in the company.

(3) An "umbrella COACS" means a co-ownership authorised contractual scheme—

  (a) whose arrangements provide for separate pooling of the contributions of the participants and the profits or income out of which payments are made to them ("pooling arrangements"), and

  (b) under which the participants are entitled to exchange rights in one pool for rights in another.

(4) A "sub-scheme", in relation to an umbrella COACS, means such of the pooling arrangements as relate to a separate pool.

(5) Each of the sub-schemes of an umbrella COACS is regarded as a separate co-ownership authorised contractual scheme, and the umbrella COACS as a whole is not so regarded.

(6) In relation to a sub-scheme of an umbrella COACS—

  (a) references to chargeable interests are references to such of the chargeable interests as under the pooling arrangements form part of the separate pool to which the sub-scheme relates, and

  (b) references to the scheme documents are references to such parts of the documents as apply to the sub-scheme.

(7) References to a co-ownership authorised contractual scheme are treated as including a collective investment scheme which- -

  (a) is constituted under the law of an EEA State other than the United Kingdom by a contract,

  (b) is managed by a body corporate incorporated under the law of an EEA State, and

  (c) is authorised under the law of the EEA State mentioned in paragraph (a) in a way which makes it, under that law, the equivalent of a co-ownership authorised contractual scheme as defined in subsection (8),

provided that, apart from this section, no charge to tax is capable of arising to the scheme under this Part.

(8) Subject to any regulations under subsection (9)—

  "co-ownership authorised contractual scheme" means a co-ownership scheme which is authorised for the purposes of FSMA 2000 by an authorisation order in force under section 261D(1) of that Act;

  "co-ownership scheme" has the same meaning as in FSMA 2000 (see section 235A of that Act).

(9) The Treasury may by regulations provide that a scheme of a description specified in the regulations is to be treated as not being a co-ownership authorised contractual scheme for the purposes of this Part.

Any such regulations may contain such supplementary and transitional provisions as appear to the Treasury to be necessary or expedient.

(10) A co-ownership authorised contractual scheme is not to be treated as a company for the purposes of Schedule 7 (group relief, reconstruction relief or acquisition relief).

(11) In relation to a land transaction in respect of which a co-ownership authorised contractual scheme is treated as the purchaser by virtue of this section, references to the purchaser in the following provisions are to be read as references to the operator of the scheme—

(a) sections 76, 80, 81, 81A and 108(2) and Schedule 10 (provisions about land transaction returns and further returns, enquiries, assessments and related matters),

(b) section 85 (liability for tax), and

(c) section 90 (application to defer payment in case of contingent or unascertained consideration).

(12) In this section—

"collective investment scheme" has the meaning given by section 235 of FSMA 2000;

"FSMA 2000" means the Financial Services and Markets Act 2000;

"operator"—

(a) in relation to a co-ownership authorised contractual scheme constituted under the law of the United Kingdom, has the meaning given by section 237(2) of FSMA 2000, and

(b) in relation to a collective investment scheme treated as a co-ownership authorised contractual scheme by virtue of subsection (7) (equivalent EEA schemes), means the corporate body responsible for the management of the scheme (however described);

"participant" is to be read in accordance with section 235 of FSMA 2000."

PART 2

SEEDING RELIEF FOR PROPERTY AUTHORISED INVESTMENT FUNDS

AND CO-OWNERSHIP AUTHORISED CONTRACTUAL SCHEMES

2 FA 2003 is amended in accordance with this Part.

3 After section 65 insert—

"65A PAIF seeding relief and COACS seeding relief

(1) Schedule 7A provides for relief from stamp duty land tax.

(2) In that Schedule—

(a) Part 1 makes provision for relief for property authorised investment funds (PAIF seeding relief), and

(b) Part 2 makes provision for relief for co-ownership authorised contractual schemes (COACS seeding relief).

(3) Any relief under that Schedule must be claimed in a land transaction return or an amendment of such a return, and must be accompanied by a notice to HMRC referring to the claim.

(4) In the case of a claim for PAIF seeding relief, the notice must confirm that the purchaser is—

(a) a property AIF as defined in paragraph 2(2) of Schedule 7A, or

(b) a company treated as a property AIF by virtue of paragraph 2(5) of Schedule 7A (equivalent EEA funds).

(5) In the case of a claim for COACS seeding relief, the notice must confirm that the purchaser is—

(a) a co-ownership authorised contractual scheme as defined in section 102A(8), or

(b) an entity treated as a co-ownership authorised contractual scheme by virtue of section 102A(7) (equivalent EEA schemes).

(6) The notice must be in such form, and contain such further information, as HMRC may require."

4 After Schedule 7 insert—

"SCHEDULE 7A

PAIF SEEDING RELIEF AND COACS SEEDING RELIEF

Section 65A

PART 1

PROPERTY AUTHORISED INVESTMENT FUNDS

PAIF seeding relief

1 (1) A land transaction is exempt from charge if conditions A to D are met.

Relief under this paragraph is referred to in this Part of this Act as "PAIF seeding relief".

(2) Condition A is that the purchaser is a property AIF (see paragraph 2).

(3) Condition B is that the main subject-matter of the transaction consists of a major interest in land.

(4) Condition C is that the only consideration for the transaction is the issue of units in the property AIF to a person who is the vendor.

(5) Condition D is that the effective date of the transaction is a day within the seeding period (see paragraph 3).

(6) This paragraph is subject to paragraph 4 (restrictions on availability of relief) and paragraphs 5 to 8 (withdrawal of relief).

Meaning of "property AIF"

2 (1) This paragraph has effect for the purposes of this Schedule.

(2) A "property AIF" is an open-ended investment company to which Part 4A of the AIF (Tax) Regulations applies.

(3) In sub-paragraph (2) "open-ended investment company" is to be read in accordance with regulation 7(1) and (2) of those Regulations (part of an umbrella company is regarded as an open-ended investment company).

(4) Regulation 7(3)(a) of those Regulations applies for the purposes of this Schedule as it applies for the purposes of those Regulations but as if references to investments and scheme property were a reference to chargeable interests.

(5) References to a property AIF are treated as including a collective investment scheme which—

(a) is a company incorporated under the law of an EEA State other than the United Kingdom, and
(b) is authorised under the law of that EEA State in a way which makes it, under that law, the equivalent of a property AIF as defined in sub-paragraph (2).

(6) In sub-paragraph (5) "collective investment scheme" has the meaning given by section 235 of FSMA 2000.

Meaning of "seeding period"

3 (1) In this Part of this Schedule, subject to sub-paragraph (2), the "seeding period" means—

(a) the period beginning with the first property seeding date and ending with the date of the first external investment into the property AIF, or
(b) if shorter, the period of 18 months beginning with the first property seeding date.

(2) The property AIF may elect to bring the seeding period to an end sooner than it would otherwise end under sub-paragraph (1).

Where an election is made, the seeding period is the period beginning with the first property seeding date and ending with the date specified in the election.

(3) An election under sub-paragraph (2) may be made—

(a) by being included in a notice accompanying a claim for PAIF seeding relief (see section 65A), or
(b) by separate notice in writing to HMRC.

(4) In sub-paragraphs (1) and (2), "the first property seeding date" means the earliest effective date of a transaction in respect of which conditions A to C in paragraph 1 are met.

(5) In this paragraph—

"external investment" means a non-land transaction in which the vendor is an external investor;
"external investor" means a person other than a person who has been a vendor in a transaction—

(a) the effective date of which is on or before the date of the non-land transaction, and
(b) in respect of which conditions A to C in paragraph 1 are met;

"non-land transaction" means a transaction by which the property AIF acquires assets which do not consist of or include a chargeable interest.

Restrictions on availability of relief

4 (1) This paragraph restricts the availability of PAIF seeding relief for a transaction in respect of which conditions A to D in paragraph 1 are met.

(2) PAIF seeding relief is not available unless, at the effective date of the transaction, the property AIF has arrangements in place requiring a person who is the vendor to notify the authorised corporate director of the property AIF of the following matters—

(a) the identity of the beneficial owner of the units in the property AIF received in consideration of the transaction, and

(b) any disposal of units in the property AIF on or after the effective date of that transaction by that owner (or, where that person is a company, by a group company) which is or could be a relevant disposal (see paragraph 7).

In paragraph (b) "group company" means a company which is a member of the same group of companies as the person mentioned in paragraph (a) for the purposes mentioned in paragraph 1(2) of Schedule 7 (group relief).

(3) PAIF seeding relief is not available if at the effective date of the transaction there are arrangements in existence by virtue of which, at that or some later time, a person who is the vendor makes or could make a disposal of units in the property AIF which is or could be a relevant disposal (see paragraph 7).

(4) PAIF seeding relief is not available if the transaction—

(a) is not effected for bona fide commercial reasons, or

(b) forms part of arrangements of which the main purpose, or one of the main purposes, is the avoidance of liability to tax.

"Tax" here means stamp duty, income tax, corporation tax, capital gains tax or tax under this Part.

Withdrawal of relief: ceasing to be property AIF

5 (1) Where PAIF seeding relief has been allowed in respect of a transaction ("the relevant transaction"), and the purchaser ceases to be a property AIF—

(a) at any time after the effective date of that transaction but within the seeding period,

(b) at any time in the control period (see paragraph 21), or

(c) in pursuance of, or in connection with, arrangements made before the end of the control period,

then, subject to sub-paragraph (2), the relief, or an appropriate proportion of it, is withdrawn, and tax is chargeable in accordance with this paragraph.

(2) Relief is withdrawn only if, at the time when the purchaser ceases to be a property AIF, the purchaser holds—

(a) the chargeable interest that was acquired by the purchaser under the relevant transaction, or

(b) a chargeable interest that is derived from that interest.

(3) The amount chargeable is the amount that would have been chargeable in respect of the relevant transaction but for PAIF seeding relief or, as the case may be, an appropriate proportion of the tax that would have been so chargeable.

(4) In sub-paragraphs (1) and (3) an "appropriate proportion" means an appropriate proportion having regard to the subject-matter of the relevant transaction and what is held by the purchaser at the time it ceases to be a property AIF.

Withdrawal of relief: portfolio test not met

6 (1) Where PAIF seeding relief has been allowed in respect of a transaction, and the portfolio test is not met immediately before the end of the seeding period, the relief is withdrawn and tax is chargeable in accordance with sub-paragraph (2).

See sub-paragraph (7) for the meaning of "portfolio test".

(2) The amount chargeable is the amount that would have been chargeable in respect of the transaction but for PAIF seeding relief.

(3) Where PAIF seeding relief has been allowed in respect of a transaction ("the relevant transaction"), and the portfolio test is met immediately before the end of the seeding period, but is not met—

(a) at a time in the control period, or

(b) at a time after the end of the control period, where the failure is pursuant to or in connection with arrangements made before the end of that period, then, subject to sub-paragraph (4), the relief, or an appropriate proportion of it, is withdrawn, and tax is chargeable in accordance with sub-paragraph (5).

(4) The requirement to meet the portfolio test at a time mentioned in sub-paragraph (3)(a) or (b) applies only to times when the property AIF holds—

(a) the chargeable interest that was acquired by the property AIF under the relevant transaction, or

(b) a chargeable interest that is derived from that interest.

(5) The amount chargeable is the amount that would have been chargeable in respect of the relevant transaction but for PAIF seeding relief or, as the case may be, an appropriate proportion of the tax that would have been so chargeable.

(6) In sub-paragraphs (3) and (5) an "appropriate proportion" means an appropriate proportion having regard to the subject-matter of the relevant transaction and what is held by the property AIF at the time when the portfolio test is not met.

(7) The portfolio test is a requirement that the property AIF meets—

(a) the non-residential portfolio test (see sub-paragraph (8)), or

(b) the residential portfolio test (see sub-paragraph (9)).

(8) The "non-residential portfolio test" is met at any time if—

(a) the property AIF holds at least 10 seeded interests at that time,

(b) so much of the total chargeable consideration as is attributable to all the seeded interests held by the property AIF at that time ("the seeded portfolio") is at least £100 million, and

(c) so much of the total chargeable consideration as is attributable to so many of those seeded interests as are interests in or over residential property (if any) does not exceed 10% of the seeded portfolio.

(9) The "residential portfolio test" is met at any time if—

(a) so much of the total chargeable consideration as is attributable to all the seeded interests held by the property AIF at that time is at least £100 million, and

(b) at least 100 of the seeded interests held by the property AIF at that time are interests in or over residential property.

(10) In sub-paragraphs (8) and (9)—

"seeded interest" means a chargeable interest acquired by the property AIF in a transaction for which PAIF seeding relief is allowed (whether or not relief is subsequently withdrawn to any extent) (a "seeding transaction"), and

"total chargeable consideration" means the total of the chargeable consideration for all seeding transactions.

(11) For the purposes of this paragraph, section 116(7) does not apply (modification of what counts as residential property).

Withdrawal of relief: units disposed of

7 (1) This paragraph applies where—

(a) a person ("V") makes a relevant disposal of one or more units in a property AIF—

(i) at any time in the seeding period,

(ii) at any time in the control period, or

(iii) in pursuance of, or in connection with, arrangements made before the end of the control period, and

(b) there is, in relation to that disposal, a relevant seeding transaction (see sub-paragraph (6)).

(2) In respect of a transaction which is, in relation to the relevant disposal, a relevant seeding transaction—

(a) PAIF seeding relief is withdrawn to the extent set out in this paragraph, and

(b) tax is chargeable in accordance with this paragraph.

(3) V's disposal of units in a property AIF is a "relevant disposal" for the purposes of this paragraph if, in relation to the disposal, A exceeds B.

(4) In this paragraph—

"A" means—

(a) where the value of V's investment in the property AIF immediately before the disposal is equal to or greater than the total of the chargeable consideration for all relevant seeding transactions, the total of the chargeable consideration for all relevant seeding transactions, or

(b) where the value of V's investment in the property AIF immediately before the disposal is less than the total of the chargeable consideration for all relevant seeding transactions, the value of V's investment in the property AIF immediately before the disposal, and

"B" means the value of V's investment in the property AIF immediately after the disposal.

(5) The amount chargeable in respect of a relevant seeding transaction ("RST") is—

(C / CCRST) x SDLT

where—

"C" means the difference between A and B;

"CCRST" means the total of the chargeable consideration for all relevant seeding transactions;

"SDLT" means the amount of tax that would have been chargeable in respect of RST but for PAIF seeding relief, ignoring any amount of tax that has been charged under this paragraph in respect of RST in relation to an earlier disposal of units by V.

(6) In this paragraph—

"group company" means (where V is a company) a company which is a member of the same group of companies as V for the purposes mentioned in paragraph 1(2) of Schedule 7 (group relief);

"relevant seeding transaction", in relation to a disposal of units by V in a property AIF, means a seeding transaction—

(a) the effective date of which is, or is before, the date of the disposal,

(b) in which that property AIF is the purchaser, and

(c) in which a vendor is—

(i) V, or

(ii) (where V is a company) a company which is a group company at the time of the disposal;

"seeding transaction" means a transaction in respect of which PAIF seeding relief is allowed (whether or not relief is subsequently withdrawn to any extent);

"the value of V's investment in the property AIF" at a particular time means the market value of all units in the property AIF held at that time by—

(a) V, and

(b) (where V is a company) a company which—

(i) is a group company at that time, and

(ii) before that time, has been a vendor in one or more seeding transactions in which the property AIF was the purchaser.

(7) For the purposes of this paragraph, the "market value" on a particular date of units in the property AIF is an amount equal to the buying price (that is, the lower price) published by the authorised corporate director on that date (or, if no such price is published on that date, on the latest date before).

Withdrawal of relief: dwelling occupied by non-qualifying individual

8 (1) This paragraph applies to a transaction ("the relevant transaction") if—

(a) PAIF seeding relief has been allowed in respect of the transaction,

(b) the main subject-matter of the transaction consists of a chargeable interest in or over land which is or includes a dwelling, and

(c) a non-qualifying individual (see paragraph 9) is permitted to occupy the dwelling at any time on or after the effective date of the transaction.

The dwelling which a non-qualifying individual is permitted to occupy is referred to as "the disqualifying dwelling".

(2) The relief, or an appropriate proportion of it, is withdrawn, and tax is chargeable in accordance with this paragraph.

This is subject to sub-paragraphs (3) and (4).

(3) Relief is withdrawn only if, at the time a non-qualifying individual is permitted to occupy the disqualifying dwelling, the property AIF holds a chargeable interest in or over that dwelling—

(a) that was acquired by the property AIF under the relevant transaction, or

(b) that is derived from an interest so acquired.

(4) Where a non-qualifying individual is first permitted to occupy the disqualifying dwelling at a time after the end of the control period, relief is withdrawn only if, at

that time, the purchaser in the relevant transaction fails to meet the genuine diversity of ownership condition set out in regulation 9A of the AIF (Tax) Regulations.

For the purposes of this sub-paragraph, regulation 9A(2)(a) of those Regulations is to be read as if the words "throughout the accounting period" were omitted.

(5) The amount chargeable is the amount that would have been chargeable in respect of the relevant transaction but for PAIF seeding relief or, as the case may be, an appropriate proportion of the tax that would have been so chargeable.

(6) In sub-paragraphs (2) and (5), an "appropriate proportion" means an appropriate proportion having regard to the extent to which the subject-matter of the relevant transaction was an interest in or over land other than the disqualifying dwelling.

9 (1) In paragraph 8 "non-qualifying individual", in relation to a land transaction and a property AIF, means any of the following—

(a) an individual who is a major participant in the property AIF;
(b) an individual who is connected with a major participant in the property AIF;
(c) an individual who is connected with the property AIF;
(d) a relevant settlor;
(e) the spouse or civil partner of an individual falling within paragraph (b), (c) or (d);
(f) a relative of an individual falling within paragraph (b), (c) or (d), or the spouse or civil partner of a relative of an individual falling within paragraph (b), (c) or (d);
(g) a relative of the spouse or civil partner of an individual falling within paragraph (b), (c) or (d);
(h) the spouse or civil partner of an individual falling within paragraph (g).

(2) An individual who participates in a property AIF is a "major participant" in it if the individual—

(a) is entitled to a share of at least 50% either of all the profits or income arising from the property AIF or of any profits or income arising from it that may be distributed to participants, or
(b) would in the event of the winding up of the property AIF be entitled to 50% or more of the assets of the property AIF that would then be available for distribution among the participants.

(3) The reference in sub-paragraph (2)(a) to profits or income arising from the property AIF is to profits or income arising from the acquisition, holding, management or disposal of the property subject to the property AIF.

(4) In this paragraph—

"relative" means brother, sister, ancestor or lineal descendant;
"relevant settlor", in relation to a land transaction, means an individual who is a settlor in relation to a relevant settlement (as defined in sub-paragraph (5));
"settlement" has the same meaning as in Chapter 5 of Part 5 of ITTOIA 2005 (see section 620 of that Act).

(5) Where a person, in the capacity of trustee of a settlement, is connected with a person who is the purchaser under a land transaction, that settlement is a "relevant settlement" in relation to the transaction.

(6) In sub-paragraph (5) "trustee" is to be read in accordance with section 1123(3) of CTA 2010 ("connected" persons: supplementary).

(7) Section 1122 of CTA 2010 (connected persons) has effect for the purposes of this paragraph, but for those purposes, subsections (7) and (8) of that section (application of rules about connected persons to partnerships) are to be disregarded.

PART 2
CO-OWNERSHIP AUTHORISED CONTRACTUAL SCHEMES

COACS seeding relief

10 (1) A land transaction is exempt from charge if conditions A to D are met.

Relief under this paragraph is referred to in this Part of this Act as "COACS seeding relief".

(2) Condition A is that the purchaser is a co-ownership authorised contractual scheme (see section 102A).

(3) Condition B is that the main subject-matter of the transaction consists of a major interest in land.

(4) Condition C is that the only consideration for the transaction is the issue of units in the co-ownership authorised contractual scheme to a person who is the vendor.

(5) Condition D is that the effective date of the transaction is a day within the seeding period (see paragraph 11).

(6) This paragraph is subject to paragraph 12 (restrictions on availability of relief) and paragraphs 13, 14, 16, 17 and 18 (withdrawal of relief).

Meaning of "seeding period"

11 (1) In this Part of this Schedule, subject to sub-paragraph (2), the "seeding period" means—

(a) the period beginning with the first property seeding date and ending with the date of the first external investment into the co-ownership authorised contractual scheme, or

(b) if shorter, the period of 18 months beginning with the first property seeding date.

(2) The co-ownership authorised contractual scheme may elect to bring the seeding period to an end sooner than it would otherwise end under sub-paragraph (1).

Where an election is made, the seeding period is the period beginning with the first property seeding date and ending with the date specified in the election.

(3) An election under sub-paragraph (2) may be made—

(a) by being included in a notice accompanying a claim for COACS seeding relief (see section 65A), or

(b) by separate notice in writing to HMRC.

(4) In sub-paragraphs (1) and (2), "the first property seeding date" means the earliest effective date of a transaction in respect of which conditions A to C in paragraph 10 are met.

(5) In this paragraph—

"external investment" means a non-land transaction in which the vendor is an external investor;

"external investor" means a person other than a person who has been a vendor in a transaction—

(a) the effective date of which is on or before the date of the non-land transaction, and

(b) in respect of which conditions A to C in paragraph 10 are met;

"non-land transaction" means a transaction by which the scheme acquires assets which do not consist of or include a chargeable interest.

Restrictions on availability of relief

12 (1) This paragraph restricts the availability of COACS seeding relief for a transaction in respect of which conditions A to D in paragraph 10 are met.

(2) COACS seeding relief is not available unless, at the effective date of the transaction, the arrangements constituting the co-ownership authorised contractual scheme require a person who is the vendor to notify the operator of the scheme of the following matters—

(a) the identity of the beneficial owner of the units in the scheme received in consideration of the transaction, and

(b) any disposal of units in the scheme on or after the effective date of that transaction by that owner (or, where that person is a company, by a group company) which is or could be a relevant disposal (see paragraph 17).

In paragraph (b) "group company" means a company which is a member of the same group of companies as the person mentioned in paragraph (a) for the purposes mentioned in paragraph 1(2) of Schedule 7 (group relief).

(3) COACS seeding relief is not available if at the effective date of the transaction there are arrangements in existence by virtue of which, at that or some later time, a person who is the vendor makes or could make a disposal of units in the co-ownership authorised contractual scheme which is or could be a relevant disposal (see paragraph 17).

(4) COACS seeding relief is not available if the transaction—

(a) is not effected for bona fide commercial reasons, or

(b) forms part of arrangements of which the main purpose, or one of the main purposes, is the avoidance of liability to tax.

"Tax" here means stamp duty, income tax, corporation tax, capital gains tax or tax under this Part.

Withdrawal of relief: ceasing to be co-ownership authorised contractual scheme

13 (1) Where COACS seeding relief has been allowed in respect of a transaction ("the relevant transaction"), and the purchaser ceases to be a co-ownership authorised contractual scheme—

(a) at any time after the effective date of that transaction but within the seeding period,

(b) at any time in the control period (see paragraph 21), or

(c) in pursuance of, or in connection with, arrangements made before the end of the control period,

then, subject to sub-paragraph (2), the relief, or an appropriate proportion of it, is withdrawn, and tax is chargeable in accordance with this paragraph.

(2) Relief is withdrawn only if, at the time when the purchaser ceases to be a co-ownership authorised contractual scheme, the purchaser holds—

(a) the chargeable interest that was acquired by the purchaser under the relevant transaction, or

(b) a chargeable interest that is derived from that interest.

(3) The amount chargeable is the amount that would have been chargeable in respect of the relevant transaction but for COACS seeding relief or, as the case may be, an appropriate proportion of the tax that would have been so chargeable.

(4) In sub-paragraphs (1) and (3) an "appropriate proportion" means an appropriate proportion having regard to the subject-matter of the relevant transaction and what is held by the purchaser at the time it ceases to be a co-ownership authorised contractual scheme.

Withdrawal of relief: genuine diversity of ownership condition not met

14 (1) Where COACS seeding relief has been allowed in respect of a transaction ("the relevant transaction"), and the genuine diversity of ownership condition (see paragraph 15) is not met—

(a) immediately before the end of the seeding period,

(b) at a time in the control period, or

(c) at a time after the end of the control period, where the failure is pursuant to or in connection with arrangements made before the end of that period,

then, subject to sub-paragraph (2), the relief, or an appropriate proportion of it, is withdrawn, and tax is chargeable in accordance with this paragraph.

(2) The requirement to meet the genuine diversity of ownership condition at a time mentioned in sub-paragraph (1) applies only to times when the co-ownership authorised contractual scheme holds—

(a) the chargeable interest that was acquired by the scheme under the relevant transaction, or

(b) a chargeable interest that is derived from that interest.

(3) The amount chargeable is the amount that would have been chargeable in respect of the relevant transaction but for COACS seeding relief or, as the case may be, an appropriate proportion of the tax that would have been so chargeable.

(4) In sub-paragraphs (1) and (3) an "appropriate proportion" means an appropriate proportion having regard to the subject-matter of the relevant transaction and what is held by the scheme at the time when the genuine diversity of ownership condition is not met.

(5) For the purposes of this paragraph, the operator of a co-ownership authorised contractual scheme may apply to HMRC in writing for clearance that the scheme meets the genuine diversity of ownership condition, and where an application is made, HMRC must notify the scheme of its decision within 28 days of the receipt of all the information that is needed to make the decision.

(6) Any such clearance has effect only for so long as the information on which HMRC relies in granting clearance is materially unchanged and the scheme is operated in accordance with it (including, in particular, continuing to operate in accordance with condition C of the genuine diversity of ownership condition).

Genuine diversity of ownership condition

15 (1) This paragraph has effect for the purposes of paragraphs 14 and 18(4).

(2) A co-ownership authorised contractual scheme meets the genuine diversity of ownership condition at any time when it meets conditions A to C.

(3) Condition A is that the scheme documents, which are available to investors and to HMRC, contain—

(a) a statement specifying the intended categories of investor,

(b) an undertaking that units in the scheme will be widely available, and

(c) an undertaking that units in the scheme will be marketed and made available in accordance with the requirements of sub-paragraph (6)(a).

(4) Condition B is that—

(a) the specification of the intended categories of investor does not have a limiting or deterrent effect, and

(b) any other terms or conditions governing participation in the scheme do not have a limiting or deterrent effect.

(5) In sub-paragraph (4) "limiting or deterrent effect" means an effect which—

(a) limits investors to a limited number of specific persons or specific groups of connected persons, or

(b) deters a reasonable investor falling within one of (what are specified as) the intended categories of investor from investing in the scheme.

(6) Condition C is that—

(a) units in the scheme are marketed and made available—

(i) sufficiently widely to reach the intended categories of investors, and

(ii) in a manner appropriate to attract those categories of investors, and

(b) a person who falls within one of the intended categories of investors can, upon request to the operator of the scheme, obtain information about the scheme and acquire units in it.

(7) A scheme is not regarded as failing to meet condition C at any time by reason of the scheme's having, at that time, no capacity to receive additional investments, unless—

(a) the capacity of the scheme to receive investments in it is fixed by the scheme documents (or otherwise), and

(b) a pre-determined number of specific persons or specific groups of connected persons make investments in the scheme which collectively exhaust all, or substantially all, of that capacity.

(8) A co-ownership authorised contractual scheme also meets the genuine diversity of ownership condition at any time when—

(a) there is a feeder fund in relation to the scheme (see paragraph 20), and

(b) conditions A to C are met in relation to the scheme after taking into account—

(i) the scheme documents relating to the feeder fund, and

(ii) the intended investors in the feeder fund.

(9) Section 1122 of CTA 2010 (connected persons) has effect for the purposes of this paragraph.

Withdrawal of relief: portfolio test not met

16 (1) Where COACS seeding relief has been allowed in respect of a transaction, and the portfolio test is not met immediately before the end of the seeding period, the relief is withdrawn and tax is chargeable in accordance with sub-paragraph (2).

See sub-paragraph (7) for the meaning of "portfolio test".

(2) The amount chargeable is the amount that would have been chargeable in respect of the transaction but for COACS seeding relief.

(3) Where COACS seeding relief has been allowed in respect of a transaction ("the relevant transaction"), and the portfolio test is met immediately before the end of the seeding period, but is not met—

(a) at a time in the control period, or

(b) at a time after the end of the control period, where the failure is pursuant to or in connection with arrangements made before the end of that period,

then, subject to sub-paragraph (4), the relief, or an appropriate proportion of it, is withdrawn, and tax is chargeable in accordance with sub-paragraph (5).

(4) The requirement to meet the portfolio test at a time mentioned in sub-paragraph (3)(a) or (b) applies only to times when the co-ownership authorised contractual scheme holds—

(a) the chargeable interest that was acquired by the scheme under the relevant transaction, or

(b) a chargeable interest that is derived from that interest.

(5) The amount chargeable is the amount that would have been chargeable in respect of the relevant transaction but for COACS seeding relief or, as the case may be, an appropriate proportion of the tax that would have been so chargeable.

(6) In sub-paragraphs (3) and (5) an "appropriate proportion" means an appropriate proportion having regard to the subject-matter of the relevant transaction and what is held by the scheme at the time when the portfolio test is not met.

(7) The portfolio test is a requirement that the scheme meets—

    (a) the non-residential portfolio test (see sub-paragraph (8)), or
    (b) the residential portfolio test (see sub-paragraph (9)).

(8) The "non-residential portfolio test" is met at any time if—

    (a) the scheme holds at least 10 seeded interests at that time,
    (b) so much of the total chargeable consideration as is attributable to all the seeded interests held by the scheme at that time ("the seeded portfolio") is at least £100 million, and
    (c) so much of the total chargeable consideration as is attributable to so many of those seeded interests as are interests in or over residential property (if any) does not exceed 10% of the seeded portfolio.

(9) The "residential portfolio test" is met at any time if—

    (a) so much of the total chargeable consideration as is attributable to all the seeded interests held by the scheme at that time is at least £100 million, and
    (b) at least 100 of the seeded interests held by the scheme at that time are interests in or over residential property.

(10) In sub-paragraphs (8) and (9)—

"seeded interest" means a chargeable interest acquired by the scheme in a transaction for which COACS seeding relief is allowed (whether or not relief is subsequently withdrawn to any extent) (a "seeding transaction"), and
"total chargeable consideration" means the total of the chargeable consideration for all seeding transactions.

(11) For the purposes of this paragraph, section 116(7) does not apply (modification of what counts as residential property).

Withdrawal of relief: units disposed of

17 (1) This paragraph applies where—

    (a) a person ("V") makes a relevant disposal of one or more units in a co-ownership authorised contractual scheme—

        (i) at any time in the seeding period,
        (ii) at any time in the control period, or
        (iii) in pursuance of, or in connection with, arrangements made before the end of the control period, and

    (b) there is, in relation to that disposal, a relevant seeding transaction (see sub-paragraph (6)).

(2) In respect of a transaction which is, in relation to the relevant disposal, a relevant seeding transaction—

    (a) COACS seeding relief is withdrawn to the extent set out in this paragraph, and
    (b) tax is chargeable in accordance with this paragraph.

(3) V's disposal of units in a scheme is a "relevant disposal" for the purposes of this paragraph if, in relation to the disposal, A exceeds B.

(4) In this paragraph—

"A" means—

    (a) where the value of V's investment in the scheme immediately before the disposal is equal to or greater than the total of the chargeable consideration for all relevant seeding transactions, the total of the chargeable consideration for all relevant seeding transactions, or
    (b) where the value of V's investment in the scheme immediately before the disposal is less than the total of the chargeable consideration for all relevant seeding transactions, the value of V's investment in the scheme immediately before the disposal, and

"B" means the value of V's investment in the scheme immediately after the disposal.

(5) The amount chargeable in respect of a relevant seeding transaction ("RST") is—

(C / CCRST) x SDLT

where—

    "C" means the difference between A and B;
    "CCRST" means the total of the chargeable consideration for all relevant seeding transactions;

"SDLT" means the amount of tax that would have been chargeable in respect of RST but for COACS seeding relief, ignoring any amount of tax that has been charged under this paragraph in respect of RST in relation to an earlier disposal of units by V.

(6) In this paragraph—

"group company" means (where V is a company) a company which is a member of the same group of companies as V for the purposes mentioned in paragraph 1(2) of Schedule 7 (group relief);

"relevant seeding transaction", in relation to a disposal of units by V in a co-ownership authorised contractual scheme, means a seeding transaction—

(a) the effective date of which is, or is before, the date of the disposal,

(b) in which that scheme is the purchaser, and

(c) in which a vendor is—

(i) V, or

(ii) (where V is a company) a company which is a group company at the time of the disposal;

"seeding transaction" means a transaction in respect of which COACS seeding relief is allowed (whether or not relief is subsequently withdrawn to any extent);

"the value of V's investment in the scheme" at a particular time means the market value of all units in the co-ownership authorised contractual scheme held at that time by—

(a) V, and

(b) (where V is a company) a company which—

(i) is a group company at that time, and

(ii) before that time, has been a vendor in one or more seeding transactions in which the scheme was the purchaser.

(7) For the purposes of this paragraph, the "market value" on a particular date of units in the scheme is an amount equal to the buying price (that is, the lower price) published by the operator on that date (or, if no such price is published on that date, on the latest date before).

Withdrawal of relief: dwelling occupied by non-qualifying individual

18 (1) This paragraph applies to a transaction ("the relevant transaction") if—

(a) COACS seeding relief has been allowed in respect of the transaction,

(b) the main subject-matter of the transaction consists of a chargeable interest in or over land which is or includes a dwelling, and

(c) a non-qualifying individual (see paragraph 19) is permitted to occupy the dwelling at any time on or after the effective date of the transaction.

The dwelling which a non-qualifying individual is permitted to occupy is referred to as "the disqualifying dwelling".

(2) The relief, or an appropriate proportion of it, is withdrawn, and tax is chargeable in accordance with this paragraph.

This is subject to sub-paragraphs (3) and (4).

(3) Relief is withdrawn only if, at the time a non-qualifying individual is permitted to occupy the disqualifying dwelling, the co-ownership authorised contractual scheme holds a chargeable interest in or over that dwelling—

(a) that was acquired by the scheme under the relevant transaction, or

(b) that is derived from an interest so acquired.

(4) Where a non-qualifying individual is first permitted to occupy the disqualifying dwelling at a time after the end of the control period, relief is withdrawn only if, at that time, the scheme fails to meet the genuine diversity of ownership condition (see paragraph 15).

(5) The amount chargeable is the amount that would have been chargeable in respect of the relevant transaction but for COACS seeding relief or, as the case may be, an appropriate proportion of the tax that would have been so chargeable.

(6) In sub-paragraphs (2) and (5), an "appropriate proportion" means an appropriate proportion having regard to the extent to which the subject-matter of the relevant transaction was an interest in or over land other than the disqualifying dwelling.

19 (1) In paragraph 18 "non-qualifying individual", in relation to a land transaction and a co-ownership authorised contractual scheme, means any of the following—

(a) an individual who is a major participant in the scheme;

(b) an individual who is connected with a major participant in the scheme;

(c) an individual who is connected with the operator of the scheme (see section 102A) or the depositary of the scheme;

(d) a relevant settlor;

(e) the spouse or civil partner of an individual falling within paragraph (b), (c) or (d);

(f) a relative of an individual falling within paragraph (b), (c) or (d), or the spouse or civil partner of a relative of an individual falling within paragraph (b), (c) or (d);

(g) a relative of the spouse or civil partner of an individual falling within paragraph (b), (c) or (d);

(h) the spouse or civil partner of an individual falling within paragraph (g).

(2) An individual who participates in a scheme is a "major participant" in it if the individual—

(a) is entitled to a share of at least 50% either of all the profits or income arising from the scheme or of any profits or income arising from it that may be distributed to participants, or

(b) would in the event of the winding up of the scheme be entitled to 50% or more of the assets of the scheme that would then be available for distribution among the participants.

(3) The reference in sub-paragraph (2)(a) to profits or income arising from the scheme is to profits or income arising from the acquisition, holding, management or disposal of the property subject to the scheme.

(4) In this paragraph—

"depositary", in relation to a co-ownership authorised contractual scheme, means the person to whom the property subject to the scheme is entrusted for safekeeping;

"relative" means brother, sister, ancestor or lineal descendant;

"relevant settlor", in relation to a land transaction, means an individual who is a settlor in relation to a relevant settlement (as defined in sub-paragraph (5));

"settlement" has the same meaning as in Chapter 5 of Part 5 of ITTOIA 2005 (see section 620 of that Act).

(5) Where a person, in the capacity of trustee of a settlement, is connected with a person who is the purchaser under a land transaction, that settlement is a "relevant settlement" in relation to the transaction.

(6) In sub-paragraph (5) "trustee" is to be read in accordance with section 1123(3) of CTA 2010 ("connected" persons: supplementary).

(7) Section 1122 of CTA 2010 (connected persons) has effect for the purposes of this paragraph, but for those purposes, subsections (7) and (8) of that section (application of rules about connected persons to partnerships) are to be disregarded.

PART 3

INTERPRETATION

"Feeder fund" and "units"

20 In this Schedule—

a "feeder fund" of a property AIF means a unit trust scheme—

(a) one of the main objects of which is investment in the property AIF, and

(b) which is managed by the same person as the property AIF;

a "feeder fund" of a co-ownership authorised contractual scheme means an open-ended investment company, an offshore fund or a unit trust scheme—

(a) one of the main objects of which is investment in the co-ownership authorised contractual scheme, and

(b) which is managed by the same person as the scheme;

"units in the property AIF" means—

(a) units in the property AIF (and, where the property AIF is a part of an umbrella company as mentioned in regulation 7(1) and (2) of the AIF (Tax) Regulations, this means units in the separate pool to which that part of the umbrella company relates), and

(b) units in a feeder fund of the property AIF;

"units in the co-ownership authorised contractual scheme" means—

(a) units in the co-ownership authorised contractual scheme (and, where the co-ownership authorised contractual scheme is a sub-scheme of an umbrella COACS (see section 102A(3) and (4)), this means units in the separate pool to which that sub-scheme relates), and

(b) units in a feeder fund of the scheme;

"units" means the rights or interests (however described) of the participants in the property AIF or the co-ownership authorised contractual scheme.

Interpretation of other terms

21 In this Schedule—

the "AIF (Tax) Regulations" means the Authorised Investment Funds (Tax) Regulations 2006 (SI 2006/964);

"arrangements" includes any scheme, agreement or understanding, whether or not legally enforceable;

"attributable" means attributable on a just and reasonable basis;

"authorised corporate director", in relation to a property AIF, has the same meaning as in regulation 8 of the AIF (Tax) Regulations;

"COACS seeding relief" means relief under paragraph 10;

"control period" means the period of 3 years beginning with the day following the last day of the seeding period;

"co-ownership authorised contractual scheme" is to be construed in accordance with section 102A (see in particular subsections (2), (5), (7) and (8) of that section);

"CTA 2010" means the Corporation Tax Act 2010;

"FSMA 2000" means the Financial Services and Markets Act 2000;

the "genuine diversity of ownership condition", in relation to a co-ownership authorised contractual scheme, has the meaning given by paragraph 15;

"ITTOIA 2005" means the Income Tax (Trading and Other Income) Act 2005;

"non-qualifying individual" has the meaning given by paragraph 9 (in relation to a property AIF) and paragraph 19 (in relation to a co-ownership authorised contractual scheme);

"offshore fund" has the meaning given by section 355 of the Taxation (International and Other Provisions) Act 2010;

"open-ended investment company" has the meaning given by section 236 of FSMA 2000;

"operator", in relation to a co-ownership authorised contractual scheme, has the same meaning as in section 102A;

"PAIF seeding relief" means relief under paragraph 1;

"participant" is to be read in accordance with section 235 of FSMA 2000;

"portfolio test" has the meaning given by paragraph 6(7) (in relation to a property AIF) and paragraph 16(7) (in relation to a co-ownership authorised contractual scheme);

"property AIF" is to be construed in accordance with paragraph 2 (see in particular sub-paragraphs (2), (3) and (5) of that paragraph);

"relevant disposal" has the meaning given by paragraph 7(3) (in relation to a property AIF) and paragraph 17(3) (in relation to a co-ownership authorised contractual scheme);

"seeding period" has the meaning given by paragraph 3 (in relation to a property AIF) and paragraph 11 (in relation to a co-ownership authorised contractual scheme);

"unit trust scheme" has the meaning given by section 237(1) of FSMA 2000."

PART 3

CONSEQUENTIAL AMENDMENTS

5 FA 2003 is amended in accordance with this Part.

6 In section 75C (anti-avoidance: supplemental), in subsection (4), after "Schedule 6A" insert ", 7A".

7 (1) Section 81 (further return where relief withdrawn) is amended as follows.

(2) In subsection (1)—

(a) omit "or" at the end of paragraph (b), and

(b) after paragraph (b) insert—

"(ba) paragraph 5, 7 or 8 of Schedule 7A (PAIF seeding relief),

(bb) paragraph 13, 17 or 18 of Schedule 7A (COACS seeding relief), or".

(3) In subsection (1A), after "transactions)" insert ", or under paragraph 6 of Schedule 7A (PAIF seeding relief) or paragraph 14 or 16 of Schedule 7A (COACS seeding relief),".

(4) In subsection (1B), after paragraph (e) insert—

"(f) in the case of relief under paragraph 6 of Schedule 7A (PAIF seeding relief: portfolio test)—

    (i) where relief is withdrawn under paragraph 6(1), the last day of the seeding period (see paragraph 3 of that Schedule), or

    (ii) where relief is withdrawn under paragraph 6(3), the first time mentioned in paragraph 6(3)(a) or (b) at which the portfolio test was not met;

(g) in the case of relief under paragraph 14 of Schedule 7A (COACS seeding relief: genuine diversity of ownership condition), the first time mentioned in paragraph 14(1) at which the genuine diversity of ownership condition was not met;

(h) in the case of relief under paragraph 16 of Schedule 7A (COACS seeding relief: portfolio test)—

    (i) where relief is withdrawn under paragraph 16(1), the last day of the seeding period (see paragraph 11 of that Schedule), or

    (ii) where relief is withdrawn under paragraph 16(3), the first time mentioned in paragraph 16(3)(a) or (b) at which the portfolio test was not met."

(5) In subsection (4), after paragraph (b) insert—

"(ba) in relation to the withdrawal of PAIF seeding relief—

    (i) the purchaser ceasing to be a property AIF as mentioned in paragraph 5 of Schedule 7A,

    (ii) a person making a relevant disposal of units as mentioned in paragraph 7 of that Schedule, or

    (iii) the grant of permission to a non-qualifying individual to occupy a dwelling as mentioned in paragraph 8 of that Schedule;

(bb) in relation to the withdrawal of COACS seeding relief—

    (i) the purchaser ceasing to be a co-ownership authorised contractual scheme as mentioned in paragraph 13 of Schedule 7A,

    (ii) a person making a relevant disposal of units as mentioned in paragraph 17 of that Schedule, or

    (iii) the grant of permission to a non-qualifying individual to occupy a dwelling as mentioned in paragraph 18 of that Schedule;".

8 In section 86 (payment of tax), in subsection (2)—

(a) omit "or" at the end of paragraph (b), and

(b) after paragraph (b) insert—

"(ba) Part 1 of Schedule 7A (PAIF seeding relief),

(bb) Part 2 of Schedule 7A (COACS seeding relief), or".

9 (1) Section 87 (interest on unpaid tax) is amended as follows.

(2) In subsection (3)—

(a) in paragraph (a)—

    (i) omit "or" at the end of sub-paragraph (ii), and

    (ii) after sub-paragraph (ii) insert—

    "(iia) paragraph 5, 7 or 8 of Schedule 7A (PAIF seeding relief),

    (iib) paragraph 13, 17 or 18 of Schedule 7A (COACS seeding relief), or";

(b) after paragraph (aza) insert—

"(azb) in the case of an amount payable under paragraph 6(3) of Schedule 7A (PAIF seeding relief: portfolio test), the first time mentioned in paragraph 6(3)(a) or (b) at which the portfolio test was not met;

(azc) in the case of an amount payable under paragraph 14(1) of Schedule 7A (COACS seeding relief: genuine diversity of ownership condition) because the genuine diversity of ownership condition was not met at a time mentioned in paragraph 14(1)(b) or (c), the first time mentioned in paragraph 14(1)(b) or (c) at which that condition was not met;

(azd) in the case of an amount payable under paragraph 16(3) of Schedule 7A (COACS seeding relief: portfolio test), the first time mentioned in paragraph 16(3)(a) or (b) at which the portfolio test was not met;".

(3) In subsection (4), for "means—" to the end substitute "has the same meaning as in section 81(4)."

10 In section 118 (market value)—

(a) the existing text becomes subsection (1), and

(b) after subsection (1) insert—

"(2) This is subject to paragraphs 7(7) and 17(7) of Schedule 7A (which define "market value" for certain purposes of PAIF seeding relief and COACS seeding relief)."

11 In section 122 (index of defined expressions), at the appropriate place insert—

"COACS seeding relief	Schedule 7A, paragraph 10(1)"
"co-ownership authorised contractual scheme	section 102A"
"operator (in relation to a co-ownership authorised contractual scheme)	section 102A"
"PAIF seeding relief	Schedule 7A, paragraph 1(1)"

12 In Schedule 4A (SDLT: higher rate for certain transactions), in paragraph 2(6)—

(a) omit "and" at the end of paragraph (d),

(b) after paragraph (d) insert—

"(da) Schedule 7A (PAIF seeding relief and COACS seeding relief), and", and

(c) in paragraph (e), for "(d)" substitute "(da)".

13 In Schedule 6B (transfers involving multiple dwellings), in paragraph 2(4)(b), after "Schedule 7" insert ", Schedule 7A".

14 (1) In Schedule 17A (further provisions relating to leases), paragraph 11 (cases where assignment of lease treated as grant of lease) is amended as follows.

(2) In sub-paragraph (3), after paragraph (b) insert—

"(ba) Part 1 or 2 of Schedule 7A (PAIF seeding relief and COACS seeding relief);".

(3) In sub-paragraph (4), after "acquisition relief" insert ", PAIF seeding relief, COACS seeding relief".

(4) In sub-paragraph (5), after paragraph (b) insert—

"(ba) in relation to the withdrawal of PAIF seeding relief—

(i) the purchaser ceasing to be a property AIF as mentioned in paragraph 5 of Schedule 7A,

(ii) a person making a relevant disposal of units as mentioned in paragraph 7 of that Schedule, or

(iii) the grant of permission to a non-qualifying individual to occupy a dwelling as mentioned in paragraph 8 of that Schedule;

(bb) in relation to the withdrawal of COACS seeding relief—

(i) the purchaser ceasing to be a co-ownership authorised contractual scheme as mentioned in paragraph 13 of Schedule 7A,

(ii) a person making a relevant disposal of units as mentioned in paragraph 17 of that Schedule, or

(iii) the grant of permission to a non-qualifying individual to occupy a dwelling as mentioned in paragraph 18 of that Schedule;".

(5) After sub-paragraph (5) insert—

"(6) This paragraph also does not apply where the relief in question is PAIF seeding relief or COACS seeding relief and is withdrawn as a result of a requirement not being met at a time which is before the effective date of the assignment of the lease.

(7) For the purposes of sub-paragraph (6), the reference to a requirement not being met is a reference to—

(a) in relation to the withdrawal of PAIF seeding relief under paragraph 6 of Schedule 7A, the portfolio test not being met (see paragraph 6(7));

(b) in relation to the withdrawal of COACS seeding relief under paragraph 14 of Schedule 7A, the genuine diversity of ownership condition not being met (see paragraph 15);

(c) in relation to the withdrawal of COACS seeding relief under paragraph 16 of Schedule 7A, the portfolio test not being met (see paragraph 16(7))."

PART 4

COMMENCEMENT

15 (1) The amendments made by Parts 2 and 3 of this Schedule have effect in relation to any land transaction of which the effective date is, or is after, the date on which this Act is passed.

(2) But those amendments do not have effect in relation to a transaction if—

(a) the transaction is effected in pursuance of a contract entered into and substantially performed before the date on which this Act is passed, or

(b) the transaction is effected in pursuance of a contract entered into before that date and is not excluded by sub-paragraph (3).

(3) A transaction effected in pursuance of a contract entered into before the date on which this Act is passed is excluded by this sub-paragraph if—

(a) there is any variation of the contract, or assignment of rights under the contract, on or after that date,

(b) the transaction is effected in consequence of the exercise on or after that date of any option, right of pre-emption or similar right, or

(c) on or after that date there is an assignment, subsale or other transaction relating to the whole or part of the subject-matter of the contract as a result of which a person other than the purchaser under the contract becomes entitled to call for a conveyance.

(4) In this paragraph—

"purchaser" has the same meaning as in Part 4 of FA 2003 (see section 43(4) of that Act);

"substantially performed", in relation to a contract, has the same meaning as in that Part (see section 44(5) of that Act).

GENERAL NOTE

Section 102A and Sch 7A make changes to the treatment of COACSs and introduce a seeding relief for Property Authorised Investment Funds (PAIFs) and Co-ownership Authorised Contractual Schemes (COACSs).

PAIFs were introduced in 2008 essentially as a tax-efficient, regulated property fund structure established as an open-ended investment company.

Authorised Contractual Schemes (ACSs) also known as "tax-transparent funds" were introduced in the UK by the Collective Investment in Transferable Securities (Contractual Scheme) Regulations 2013 and the Financial Conduct Authority's rules for the authorisation of ACSs. There are two types of ACS: a Partnership ACS and a COACS. These changes relate to the latter.

ACSs were introduced as part of the Government's "Investment Management Strategy" also launched in 2013. The aim of the strategy is to reinforce the UK's position as a global centre of fund management and to develop the UK's position as a centre of fund domicile, improving its competitive offering.

It is expected that the changes to the treatment of COACSs and seeding relief will encourage more property funds to set up in the UK and facilitate greater collective investment in property situated in England, Wales and Northern Ireland (rUK). Although the government expects that the main application will be to life companies and pension funds, the benefit of the changes is not restricted to these entities.

The rules are meant to be shaped by the Government's objective of making the tax system fairer, ensuring there is no SDLT charge when the underlying economic ownership of property is unchanged and ensuring consistent treatment of PAIFs and COACSs. To this end there was a period of consultation which ran from 18 July 2014 to 12 September 2014, to gather views on the potential market impact absent a seeding relief. There has been little change from what was originally proposed in the consultation document with one of the Government's main aims being to balance its objectives with countering the potential for SDLT avoidance.

Commencement

The amendments generally have effect for transactions with an effective date on or after Royal Assent.

Section 102A is essentially a deeming provision which introduces opaque treatment for COACSs: deeming a COACS to be a company (except in relation to Sch 7, i.e. group, reconstruction and acquisition relief) and deeming an investor's units in a COACS to be shares in the company for SDLT purposes. These provisions coupled with the exemptions from stamp duty and stamp duty reserve tax in FA 1999 Sch 13 para 25A and FA 1986 s 90(7B) mean that trading in COACS units will not generally be subject to stamp duty, SDRT or SDLT (subject to the withdrawal of any SDLT seeding relief claimed under Sch 7A). In contrast, acquisitions of real property by a PAIF are subject to SDLT and a market value charge will apply to acquisitions from connected parties.

Section 102A(8) extends for SDLT purposes the definition of a COACS contained in the Financial Services and Markets Act 2000 s 261D(1) to include certain other contractual schemes constituted, managed and authorised under the law of an EEA State other than the UK.

Where land transactions are entered into, these provisions have the effect of treating a COACS as the purchaser and s 102A(11) deems the "purchaser" in relation to certain provisions including land transaction returns, enquires, assessment, liability for SDLT and deferment applications to be the operator of the COACS.

Section 65A introduces Sch 7A to the Finance Act 2003 which provides an SDLT seeding relief for PAIFs and COACSs. Both reliefs must be claimed in a land transaction return, or an amendment to such a return, and accompanied by a notice confirming that the purchaser is a PAIF or COACS, or in either case an EEA equivalent.

Schedule 7A Pt 1 provides a seeding relief during the seeding period which runs from the date that the PAIF is first seeded (provided it is not yet opened up to investors) until the date that a person who was not a seed investor transfers non-property assets to the PAIF or if sooner, a period of 18 months. Following consultation, seed investors can also now elect to end the seeding period within which the seeding conditions must be met and consequently accelerate the start of the period during which the seeding relief can be withdrawn.

The relief is restricted to major interests in land, i.e. freehold and leasehold interests so despite representations and lobbying, other land interests including interests in property investment partnerships will not qualify.

Paragraph 4 further restricts the relief by introducing a two-part motive test and a requirement that there are no arrangements in place which would or could give rise to a subsequent withdrawal of seeding relief on disposal of the units.

Paragraph 5 provides for a withdrawal of seeding relief if the purchaser ceases to be a PAIF within the seeding period or within three years following the end of the seeding period ("the control period") or pursuant to arrangements made within either of those periods.

Paragraph 6 provides that seeding relief is withdrawn if, immediately before the end of the seeding period or within the control period or following arrangements made within either period the PAIF does not hold the minimum number or value of properties. In respect of the control period the relief will only be withdrawn to the extent that the PAIF holds the seed property or an interest deriving from it.

For non-residential property the PAIF must hold at least 10 seeded interests and the chargeable consideration attributable to all the seed interests must be at least £100m with a maximum of 10% attributable to residential property. In relation to residential property, the PAIF must hold at least 100 seeded interests with a chargeable consideration attributable to all the seeded interests of at least £100m.

Residential property is defined in s 116 but s 116(7) is disapplied such that where six or more properties are acquired in a single transaction they continue to be treated as residential property for the purpose of applying the portfolio tests.

Paragraph 7 provides that seeding relief is withdrawn where there is a disposal of certain units by a vendor which relate to a seeding transaction. This operates on a "first in" but "last out" basis such that where the vendor has made investment in the fund other than seed properties, the units received by a vendor for non-seed properties are deemed to be the first to be disposed of. A withdrawal is only triggered where the disposal of the units means that the value of the units held by the vendor after the disposal is below the total consideration for the seeding transactions by that vendor. Following representations made as part of the consultation on the seeding relief, para 7(6) provides where the vendor is a company, any seeding units held by companies that are grouped with the vendor at the time of the disposal are also taken into account in calculating the value of the vendor's investment.

Paragraph 8 provides that seeding relief is withdrawn in respect of a dwelling which a non-qualifying individual is permitted to occupy.

Paragraph 9 defines a non-qualifying individual to include major participants in the PAIF or connected individuals, persons connected with the PAIF, relevant settlors in relation to the transaction or those who have a connection to such a person as a spouse, civil partner or relative.

Schedule 7A Pt 2 provides a seeding relief during the seeding period which runs from the date that a COACS is first seeded (provided it is not yet opened up to investors) until the date that a person who was not a seed investor transfers non-property assets to the COACS or if sooner, a period of 18 months. Following consultation, seed investors can also now elect to end the seeding period within which the seeding conditions must be met and consequently accelerate the start of the period during which the seeding relief can be withdrawn.

The relief is restricted to major interests in land, i.e. freehold and leasehold interests so despite representations and lobbying, other land interests including interests in property investment partnerships will not qualify.

Paragraph 12 further restricts the relief by introducing a two-part motive test and a requirement that there are no arrangements in place which would or could give rise to a subsequent withdrawal of seeding relief on disposal of the units.

Paragraph 13 provides for a withdrawal of seeding relief if the purchaser ceases to be a COACS within the seeding period or within three years following the end of the seeding period ("the control period") or pursuant to arrangements made within either of those periods.

Paragraphs 14 and 15 these provide for a genuine diversity of ownership (GDO) test (a test that is implicit for a PAIF and does not need to be restated in Sch 7A) and that the seeding relief can be withdrawn where this is not met at any time during the seeding period or the control period or pursuant to arrangements made within either period. Following consultation and lobbying a statutory GDO clearance process is now also included in para 14(5).

Paragraph 16 provides that seeding relief is withdrawn if, immediately before the end of the seeding period or within the control period or following arrangements made within either period the PAIF does not hold the minimum number or value of properties. In respect of the control period the relief will only be withdrawn to the extent that the PAIF holds the seed property or an interest deriving from it.

For non-residential property the PAIF must hold at least 10 seeded interests and the chargeable consideration attributable to all the seed interests must be at least £100m with a maximum of 10% attributable to residential property. In relation to residential property, the PAIF must hold at least 100 seeded interests with a chargeable consideration attributable to all the seeded interests of at least £100m.

Residential property is defined in s 116 but the s 116(7) is disapplied such that where six or more properties are acquired in a single transaction they continue to be treated as residential property.

Paragraph 17 provides that seeding relief is withdrawn where there is a disposal of certain units by a vendor which relate to a seeding transaction. This operates on a "first in" but "last out" basis such that where the vendor has made investment in the fund other than seed properties, the units received by a vendor for non-seed properties are deemed to be the first to be disposed of. A withdrawal is only triggered where the disposal of the units means that the value of the units held by the vendor after the disposal is below the total consideration for the seeding transactions by that vendor. Following representations made as part of the consultation on the seeding relief, para 7(6) provides where the vendor is a company, any seeding units held by companies that are grouped with the vendor at the time of the disposal are also taken into account in calculating the value of the vendor's investment.

Paragraph 18 provides that seeding relief is withdrawn in respect of a dwelling which a non-qualifying individual is permitted to occupy.

Paragraph 19 defines a non-qualifying individual to include major participants in the PAIF or connected individuals, persons connected with the PAIF, relevant settlors in relation to the transaction or those who have a connection to such a person as a spouse, civil partner or relative.

SCHEDULE 17
AQUA METHANOL ETC
Section 153

PART 1
AQUA METHANOL

Introductory

1 HODA 1979 is amended as follows.

Definition

2 After section 2AB insert—

"2AC Aqua methanol

In this Act "aqua methanol" means a liquid fuel which meets each of the following conditions—

(a) the amount of water it contains is not less than 4.7 per cent and not more than 5.3 per cent by volume,

(b) the amount of methanol it contains is not less than 96 per cent by volume of the remainder of the substance, and

(c) at a temperature of 15°C and under a pressure of 1013.25 millibars, it has a density of not less than 0.81 g/ml and not more than 0.82 g/ml."

3 In section 2A (power to amend definitions), in subsection (1), after paragraph (b) insert—

"(ba) aqua methanol;".

Charging of excise duty

4 After section 6AF insert—

"6AG Excise duty on aqua methanol

(1) A duty of excise shall be charged on the setting aside for a chargeable use by any person, or (where it has not already been charged under this section) on the chargeable use by any person, of aqua methanol.

(2) In subsection (1) "chargeable use" means use—

(a) as fuel for any engine, motor or other machinery, or

(b) as an additive or extender in any substance so used.

(3) The rate of duty under this section is—

(a) in the case of a chargeable use within subsection (2)(a), £0.079 a litre;

(b) in the case of a chargeable use within subsection (2)(b), the rate prescribed by order made by the Treasury.

(4) In exercising their power under subsection (3)(b), the Treasury shall so far as practicable secure that aqua methanol set aside for use or used as an additive or extender in any substance is charged with duty at the same rate as the substance in which it is an additive or extender.

(5) The power of the Treasury to make an order under this section shall be exercisable by statutory instrument subject to annulment in pursuance of a resolution of the House of Commons.

(6) An order under this section—

(a) may make different provision for different cases, and

(b) may prescribe the rate of duty under subsection (3)(b) by reference to the rate of duty under this Act in respect of any other substance.

6AH Application to aqua methanol of provisions relating to hydrocarbon oil

(1) The Commissioners may by regulations provide for—

(a) references in this Act, or specified references in this Act, to hydrocarbon oil to be construed as including references to aqua methanol;

(b) references in this Act, or specified references in this Act, to duty on hydrocarbon oil to be construed as including references to duty under section 6AG above;

(c) aqua methanol to be treated for the purposes of such of the following provisions of this Act as may be specified as if it fell within a specified description of hydrocarbon oil.

(2) Where the effect of provision made under subsection (1) above is to extend any power to make regulations, provision made in exercise of the power as extended may be contained in the same statutory instrument as the provision extending the power.

(3) In this section "specified" means specified by regulations under this section.

(4) Regulations under this section may make different provision for different cases.

(5) Paragraph (b) of subsection (1) above shall not be taken as prejudicing the generality of paragraph (a) of that subsection."

5 In section 6A (fuel substitutes), in subsection (1)—

(a) omit the "or" after paragraph (d), and

(b) after paragraph (e) insert ", or

(f) aqua methanol."

Mixing of aqua methanol

6 (1) For the italic heading before section 20A substitute "Mixing".

(2) After section 20AAB insert—

"20AAC Prohibition on mixing of aqua methanol

(1) Aqua methanol on which duty under section 6AG(3)(a) of this Act has been charged must not be mixed with any relevant substance.

(2) In subsection (1) "relevant substance" means biodiesel, bioethanol, bioblend, bioethanol blend or hydrocarbon oil.

(3) A person commits an offence under this subsection if—

(a) the person intentionally uses aqua methanol in contravention of subsection (1) above, or

(b) the person supplies aqua methanol, intending that it will be used in contravention of subsection (1) above.

(4) A person guilty of an offence under subsection (3) above shall be liable—

(a) on summary conviction in England and Wales—

(i) to imprisonment for a term not exceeding 12 months (or 6 months, if the offence was committed before the commencement of section 154(1) of the Criminal Justice Act 2003), or

(ii) to a fine not exceeding £20,000 or (if greater) 3 times the value of the aqua methanol in question,

or both;

(b) on summary conviction in Scotland—

(i) to imprisonment for a term not exceeding 12 months, or

(ii) to a fine not exceeding the statutory maximum or (if greater) 3 times the value of the aqua methanol in question,

or both;

(c) on summary conviction in Northern Ireland—

(i) to imprisonment for a term not exceeding 6 months, or

(ii) to a fine not exceeding the statutory maximum or (if greater) 3 times the value of the aqua methanol in question,

or both;

(d) on conviction on indictment, to imprisonment for a term not exceeding 7 years or a fine, or both.

(5) Any aqua methanol, or any mixture containing aqua methanol, in respect of which an offence under subsection (3) above has been committed shall be liable to forfeiture.

20AAD Mixing of aqua methanol in contravention of prohibition: adjustment of duty

(1) A duty of excise shall be charged on a mixture which is produced by mixing aqua methanol on which duty under section 6AG(3)(a) of this Act has been charged with a relevant substance.

(2) In subsection (1) "relevant substance" means biodiesel, bioethanol, bioblend, bioethanol blend or hydrocarbon oil.

(3) The rate of duty on a mixture under subsection (1) shall be the rate of duty specified in section 6(1A)(c) (general rate for heavy oil).

(4) The person liable to pay duty charged under this section on production of a mixture is the person producing the mixture.

(5) Where it appears to the Commissioners—

(a) that a person ("P") has produced a mixture on which duty is charged under this section, and

(b) that P is the person liable to pay the duty,

they may assess the amount of duty due from P to the best of their judgment and notify that amount to P or P's representative.

(6) An assessment under subsection (5) above shall be treated as if it were an assessment under section 12(1) of the Finance Act 1994.

(7) Where duty under a provision of this Act has been paid on an ingredient of a mixture, the duty charged under this section shall be reduced by the amount of any duty which the Commissioners are satisfied has been paid on the ingredient (but not to a negative amount).

(8) The Commissioners may exempt a person from liability to pay duty under this section in respect of production of a mixture of a kind described in subsection (1) if satisfied that—

(a) the liability was incurred accidentally, and

(b) in the circumstances the person should be exempted.*Powers to allow reliefs".*

Enforcement

7 (1) Section 22 (prohibition on use of petrol substitutes on which duty has not been paid) is amended as follows.

(2) After subsection (1AB) insert—

"(1AC) Where any person—

(a) puts any aqua methanol to a chargeable use (within the meaning of section 6AG above), and

(b) knows or has reasonable cause to believe that there is duty charged under section 6AG above on that aqua methanol which has not been paid and is not lawfully deferred,

his putting the aqua methanol to that use shall attract a penalty under section 9 of the Finance Act 1994 (civil penalties), and any goods in respect of which a person contravenes this section shall be liable to forfeiture."

(3) In subsection (1A), for "or (1AB)" substitute ", (1AB) or (1AC)".

(4) For the heading substitute "Prohibition on use of fuel substitutes on which duty has not been paid".

Consequential amendments

8 In section 23C (warehousing), in subsection (4), after paragraph (d) insert—

"(da) aqua methanol,".

9 In section 27(1) (interpretation), before the definition of "aviation gasoline" insert—

""aqua methanol" has the meaning given by section 2AC above;".

10 In section 16 of FA 1994 (appeals to a tribunal), in subsection (6)(c), before "section 23(1)" insert "or (1AC)".

11 In paragraph 3 of Schedule 41 to FA 2008 (penalties for putting product to use that attracts higher duty), in the Table in sub-paragraph (1), at the appropriate place insert—

"HODA 1979 section 20AAD(5) | Mixtures containing aqua methanol."

PART 2

HYDROCARBON OILS: MISCELLANEOUS AMENDMENTS

HODA 1979

12 In section 20AAA of HODA 1979 (mixing of rebated oil), in subsection (4)(a), for "section 6A(1A)(c)" substitute "section 6(1A)(c)".

FA 1994

13 In section 16 of FA 1994 (appeals to a tribunal), in subsection (6)(c), after "section 22(1)" insert "(1AA), (1AB)".

PART 3

COMMENCEMENT

14 The amendments made by this Schedule come into force—

(a) so far as they confer a power to make regulations or an order, on the day on which this Act is passed, and

(b) for all other purposes, on 14 November 2016.

GENERAL NOTE

Section 153 and Sch 17 introduce a reduced excise duty rate of 7.90 pence per litre for aqua methanol used as fuel for any engine, motor or other machinery, with effect from 14 November 2016. Aqua methanol is a fuel that is approximately 95% methanol and 5% water. In Budget 2014, the Government announced that it would apply a reduced rate of fuel duty to aqua methanol, with the intention of encouraging the use of aqua methanol as an alternative fuel to petrol and diesel, in recognition of its environmental benefits.

A lower rate of fuel duty applies to certain alternative fuels, such as compressed natural gas, liquid natural gas and biomethane. In Autumn Statement 2013, the Government announced that the duty differential between alternative fuels and the main fuel duty rate would be maintained until 2024, with a review in Budget 2018. Aqua methanol has now been added to the fuels to which a lower rate applies.

SCHEDULE 18
SERIAL TAX AVOIDANCE
Section 159

PART 1
CONTENTS OF SCHEDULE

1 In this Schedule—

(a) Part 2 provides for HMRC to give warning notices to persons who incur relevant defeats and includes—

(i) provision about the duration of warning periods under warning notices (see paragraph 3), and

(ii) definitions of "relevant defeat" and other key terms;

(b) Part 3 contains provisions about persons to whom a warning notice has been given, and in particular—

(i) imposes a duty to give information notices, and

(ii) allows the Commissioners to publish information about such persons in certain cases involving repeated relevant defeats;

(c) Part 4 contains provision about the restriction of reliefs;

(d) Part 5 imposes liability to penalties on persons who incur relevant defeats in relation to arrangements used in warning periods;

(e) Part 6 contains provisions about corporate groups, associated persons and partnerships;

(f) Part 7 contains definitions and other supplementary provisions.

PART 2
ENTRY INTO THE REGIME AND BASIC CONCEPTS

Duty to give warning notice

2 (1) This paragraph applies where a person incurs a relevant defeat in relation to any arrangements.

(2) HMRC must give the person a written notice (a "warning notice").

(3) The notice must be given within the period of 90 days beginning with the day on which the relevant defeat is incurred.

(4) The notice must—

(a) set out when the warning period begins and ends (see paragraph 3),

(b) specify the relevant defeat to which the notice relates, and

(c) explain the effect of paragraphs 3 and 17 to 46.

(5) A warning notice given by virtue of paragraph 49 must also explain the effect of paragraph 51 (information in certain cases involving partnerships).

(6) In this Schedule "arrangements" includes any agreement, understanding, scheme, transaction or series of transactions (whether or not legally enforceable).

(7) For the meaning of "relevant defeat" and provision about when a relevant defeat is incurred see paragraph 11.

Warning period

3 (1) If a person is given a warning notice with respect to a relevant defeat (and sub-paragraph (2) does not apply) the period of 5 years beginning with the day after the day on which the notice is given is a "warning period" in relation to that person.

(2) If a person incurs a relevant defeat in relation to arrangements during a period which is a warning period in relation to that person, the warning period is extended to the end of the 5 years beginning with the day after the day on which the relevant defeat occurs.

(3) In relation to a warning period which has been extended under this Schedule, references in this Schedule (including this paragraph) to the warning period are to be read as references to the warning period as extended.

Meaning of "tax"

4 In this Schedule "tax" includes any of the following taxes—

(a) income tax,

(b) corporation tax, including any amount chargeable as if it were corporation tax or treated as if it were corporation tax,

(c) capital gains tax,

(d) petroleum revenue tax,

(e) diverted profits tax,

(f) apprenticeship levy,

(g) inheritance tax,

(h) stamp duty land tax,

(i) annual tax on enveloped dwellings,

(j) VAT, and

(k) national insurance contributions.

Meaning of "tax advantage" in relation to VAT

5 (1) In this Schedule "tax advantage", in relation to VAT, is to be read in accordance with sub-paragraphs (2) to (4).

(2) A taxable person obtains a tax advantage if—

(a) in any prescribed accounting period, the amount by which the output tax accounted for by the person exceeds the input tax deducted by the person is less than it would otherwise be,

(b) the person obtains a VAT credit when the person would not otherwise do so, or obtains a larger VAT credit or obtains a VAT credit earlier than would otherwise be the case,

(c) in a case where the person recovers input tax as a recipient of a supply before the supplier accounts for the output tax, the period between the time when the input tax is recovered and the time when the output tax is accounted for is greater than would otherwise be the case, or

(d) in any prescribed accounting period, the amount of the person's non-deductible tax is less than it would otherwise be.

(3) A person who is not a taxable person obtains a tax advantage if the person's non-refundable tax is less than it otherwise would be.

(4) In sub-paragraph (3) "non-refundable tax", in relation to a person who is not a taxable person, means—

(a) VAT on the supply to the person of any goods or services,

(b) VAT on the acquisition by the person from another member State of any goods, and

(c) VAT paid or payable by the person on the importation of any goods from a place outside the member States,

but excluding (in each case) any VAT in respect of which the person is entitled to a refund from the Commissioners by virtue of any provision of VATA 1994.

Meaning of "non-deductible tax"

6 (1) In this Schedule "non-deductible tax", in relation to a taxable person, means—

(a) input tax for which the person is not entitled to credit under section 25 of VATA 1994, and

(b) any VAT incurred by the person which is not input tax and in respect of which the person is not entitled to a refund from the Commissioners by virtue of any provision of VATA 1994.

(2) For the purposes of sub-paragraph (1)(b), the VAT "incurred" by a taxable person is—

(a) VAT on the supply to the person of any goods or services,

(b) VAT on the acquisition by the person from another member State of any goods, and

(c) VAT paid or payable by the person on the importation of any goods from a place outside the member States.

"Tax advantage": other taxes

7 In relation to taxes other than VAT, "tax advantage" includes—

(a) relief or increased relief from tax,

(b) repayment or increased repayment of tax,

(c) receipt, or advancement of a receipt, of a tax credit,

(d) avoidance or reduction of a charge to tax, an assessment of tax or a liability to pay tax,

(e) avoidance of a possible assessment to tax or liability to pay tax,

(f) deferral of a payment of tax or advancement of a repayment of tax, and

(g) avoidance of an obligation to deduct or account for tax.

"DOTAS arrangements"

8 (1) For the purposes of this Schedule arrangements are "DOTAS arrangements" at any time if they are notifiable arrangements at the time in question and a person—

(a) has provided information in relation to the arrangements under section 308(3), 309 or 310 of FA 2004, or

(b) has failed to comply with any of those provisions in relation to the arrangements.

(2) But for the purposes of this Schedule "DOTAS arrangements" does not include arrangements in respect of which HMRC has given notice under section 312(6) of FA 2004 (notice that promoters not under duty to notify client of reference number).

(3) For the purposes of sub-paragraph (1) a person who would be required to provide information under subsection (3) of section 308 of FA 2004—

(a) but for the fact that the arrangements implement a proposal in respect of which notice has been given under subsection (1) of that section, or

(b) but for subsection (4A), (4C) or (5) of that section,

is treated as providing the information at the end of the period referred to in subsection (3) of that section.

(4) In this paragraph "notifiable arrangements" has the same meaning as in Part 7 of FA 2004.

"Disclosable VAT arrangements"

9 For the purposes of this Schedule arrangements are "disclosable VAT arrangements" at any time if at that time —

(a) a person has complied with paragraph 6 of Schedule 11A to VATA 1994 in relation to the arrangements (duty to notify Commissioners),

(b) a person under a duty to comply with that paragraph in relation to the arrangements has failed to do so, or

(c) a reference number has been allocated to the scheme under paragraph 9 of that Schedule (voluntary notification of avoidance scheme which is not a designated scheme).

Paragraphs 8 and 9: "failure to comply"

10 (1) A person "fails to comply" with any provision mentioned in paragraph 8(1) or 9(a) if and only if any of the conditions in sub-paragraphs (2) to (4) is met.

(2) The condition in this sub-paragraph is that—

(a) the tribunal has determined that the person has failed to comply with the provision concerned,

(b) the appeal period has ended, and

(c) the determination has not been overturned on appeal.

(3) The condition in this sub-paragraph is that—

(a) the tribunal has determined for the purposes of section 118(2) of TMA 1970 that the person is to be deemed not to have failed to comply with the provision concerned as the person had a reasonable excuse for not doing the thing required to be done,

(b) the appeal period has ended, and

(c) the determination has not been overturned on appeal.

(4) The condition in this sub-paragraph is that the person admitted in writing to HMRC that the person has failed to comply with the provision concerned.

(5) In this paragraph "the appeal period" means—

(a) the period during which an appeal could be brought against the determination of the tribunal, or

(b) where an appeal mentioned in paragraph (a) has been brought, the period during which that appeal has not been finally determined, withdrawn or otherwise disposed of.

(6) In this paragraph "the tribunal" means the First-tier tribunal or, where determined by or under Tribunal Procedure Rules, the Upper Tribunal.

11 (1) A person ("P") incurs a "relevant defeat" in relation to arrangements if any of Conditions A to E is met in relation to P and the arrangements.

(2) The relevant defeat is incurred when the condition in question is first met.

Condition A

12 (1) Condition A is that—

(a) P has been given a notice under paragraph 12 of Schedule 43 to FA 2013 (general anti-abuse rule: notice of final decision), paragraph 8 or 9 of Schedule 43A to that Act (pooling and binding of arrangements: notice of final decision) or paragraph 8 of Schedule 43B to that Act (generic referrals: notice of final decision) stating that a tax advantage arising from the arrangements is to be counteracted,

(b) that tax advantage has been counteracted under section 209 of FA 2013, and

(c) the counteraction is final.

(2) For the purposes of this paragraph the counteraction of a tax advantage is "final" when the adjustments made to effect the counteraction, and any amounts arising as a result of those adjustments, can no longer be varied, on appeal or otherwise.

Condition B

13 (1) Condition B is that (in a case not falling within Condition A above) a follower notice has been given to P by reference to the arrangements (and not withdrawn) and—

(a) the necessary corrective action for the purposes of section 208 of FA 2014 has been taken in respect of the denied advantage, or

(b) the denied advantage has been counteracted otherwise than as mentioned in paragraph (a) and the counteraction of the denied advantage is final.

(2) In sub-paragraph (1) the reference to giving a follower notice to P includes a reference to giving a partnership follower notice in respect of a partnership return in relation to which P is a relevant partner (as defined in paragraph 2(5) of Schedule 31 to FA 2014).

(3) For the purposes of this paragraph it does not matter whether the denied advantage has been dealt with—

(a) wholly as mentioned in one or other of paragraphs (a) and (b) of sub-paragraph (1), or

(b) partly as mentioned in one and partly as mentioned in the other of those paragraphs.

(4) In this paragraph "the denied advantage" has the same meaning as in Chapter 2 of Part 4 of FA 2014 (see section 208(3) of and paragraph 4(3) of Schedule 31 to that Act).

(5) For the purposes of this paragraph the counteraction of a tax advantage is "final" when the adjustments made to effect the counteraction, and any amounts arising as a result of those adjustments, can no longer be varied, on appeal or otherwise.

(6) In this Schedule "follower notice" means a follower notice under Chapter 2 of Part 4 of FA 2014.

(7) For the purposes of this paragraph a partnership follower notice is given "in respect of" the partnership return mentioned in paragraph (a) or (b) of paragraph 2(2) of Schedule 31 to FA 2014.

Condition C

14 (1) Condition C is that (in a case not falling within Condition A or B)—

(a) the arrangements are DOTAS arrangements,

(b) P has relied on the arrangements (see sub-paragraph (2))—

(c) the arrangements have been counteracted, and

(d) the counteraction is final.

(2) For the purposes of sub-paragraph (1), P "relies on the arrangements" if—

(a) P makes a return, claim or election, or a partnership return is made, on the basis that a relevant tax advantage arises, or

(b) P fails to discharge a relevant obligation ("the disputed obligation") and there is reason to believe that P's failure to discharge that obligation is connected with the arrangements.

(3) For the purposes of sub-paragraph (2) "relevant tax advantage" means a tax advantage which the arrangements might be expected to enable P to obtain.

(4) For the purposes of sub-paragraph (2) an obligation is a "relevant obligation" if the arrangements might be expected to have the result that the obligation does not arise.

(5) For the purposes of this paragraph the arrangements are "counteracted" if—

(a) adjustments, other than taxpayer emendations, are made in respect of P's tax position—

(i) on the basis that the whole or part of the relevant tax advantage mentioned in sub-paragraph (2)(a) does not arise, or

(ii) on the basis that the disputed obligation does (or did) arise, or

(b) an assessment to tax other than a self-assessment is made, or any other action is taken by HMRC, on the basis mentioned in paragraph (a)(i) or (ii) (otherwise than by way of an adjustment).

(6) For the purposes of this paragraph a counteraction is "final" when the assessment, adjustments or action in question, and any amounts arising from the assessment, adjustments or action, can no longer be varied, on appeal or otherwise.

(7) For the purposes of sub-paragraph (1) the time at which it falls to be determined whether or not the arrangements are DOTAS arrangements is when the counteraction becomes final.

(8) The following are "taxpayer emendations" for the purposes of sub-paragraph (5)—

(a) an adjustment made by P at a time when P had no reason to believe that HMRC had begun or were about to begin enquiries into P's affairs relating to the tax in question;

(b) an adjustment (by way of an assessment or otherwise) made by HMRC with respect to P's tax position as a result of a disclosure made by P which meets the conditions in sub-paragraph (9).

For the purposes of paragraph (a) a payment in respect of a liability to pay national insurance contributions is not an adjustment unless it is a payment in full.

(9) The conditions are that the disclosure—

(a) is a full and explicit disclosure of an inaccuracy in a return or other document or of a failure to comply with an obligation, and

(b) was made at a time when P had no reason to believe that HMRC were about to begin enquiries into P's affairs relating to the tax in question.

(10) For the purposes of this paragraph a contract settlement which HMRC enters into with P is treated as an assessment to tax (other than a self-assessment); and in relation to contract settlements references in sub-paragraph (5) to the basis an which any assessment or adjustments are made, or any other action is taken, are to be read with any necessary modifications.

Condition D

15 (1) Condition D is that—

(a) P is a taxable person;

(b) the arrangements are disclosable VAT arrangements to which P is a party;

(c) P has relied on the arrangements (see sub-paragraph (2));

(d) the arrangements have been counteracted, and

(e) the counteraction is final.

(2) For the purposes of sub-paragraph (1) P "relies on the arrangements" if—

(a) P makes a return or claim on the basis that a relevant tax advantage arises, or

(b) P fails to discharge a relevant obligation ("the disputed obligation") and there is reason to believe that P's failure to discharge that obligation is connected with those arrangements.

(3) For the purposes of sub-paragraph (2) "relevant tax advantage" means a tax advantage which the arrangements might be expected to enable P to obtain.

(4) For the purposes of sub-paragraph (2) an obligation is a "relevant obligation" if the arrangements might be expected to have the result that the obligation does not arise.

(5) For the purposes of this paragraph the arrangements are "counteracted" if—

(a) adjustments, other than taxpayer emendations, are made in respect of P's tax position—

(i) on the basis that the whole or part of the relevant tax advantage mentioned in sub-paragraph (2)(a) does not arise, or

(ii) on the basis that the disputed obligation does (or did) arise, or

(b) an assessment to tax is made, or any other action is taken by HMRC, on the basis mentioned in paragraph (a)(i) or (ii) (otherwise than by way of an adjustment).

(6) For the purposes of this paragraph a counteraction is "final" when the assessment, adjustments or action in question, and any amounts arising from the assessment, adjustments or action, can no longer be varied, on appeal or otherwise.

(7) For the purposes of sub-paragraph (1) the time at which it falls to be determined whether or not the arrangements are disclosable VAT arrangements is when the counteraction becomes final.

(8) The following are "taxpayer emendations" for the purposes of sub-paragraph (5)—

(a) an adjustment made by P at a time when P had no reason to believe that HMRC had begun or were about to begin enquiries into P's affairs relating to VAT;

(b) an adjustment made by HMRC with respect to P's tax position (by way of an assessment or otherwise) as a result of a disclosure made by P which meets the conditions in sub-paragraph (9).

(9) The conditions are that the disclosure—

(a) is a full and explicit disclosure of an inaccuracy in a return or other document or of a failure to comply with an obligation, and

(b) was made at a time when P had no reason to believe that HMRC were about to begin enquiries into P's affairs relating to VAT.

Condition E

16 (1) Condition E is that the arrangements are disclosable VAT arrangements to which P is a party and—

(a) the arrangements relate to the position with respect to VAT of a person other than P ("S") who has made supplies of goods or services to P,

(b) the arrangements might be expected to enable P to obtain a tax advantage in connection with those supplies of goods or services,

(c) the arrangements have been counteracted, and

(d) the counteraction is final.

(2) For the purposes of this paragraph the arrangements are "counteracted" if—

(a) HMRC assess S to tax or take any other action on a basis which prevents P from obtaining (or obtaining the whole of) the tax advantage in question, or

(b) adjustments, other than taxpayer emendations, are made in relation to S's VAT affairs on a basis such as is mentioned in paragraph (a).

(3) For the purposes of this paragraph a counteraction is "final" when the assessment, adjustments or action in question, and any amounts arising from the assessment, adjustments or action, can no longer be varied, on appeal or otherwise.

(4) For the purposes of sub-paragraph (1) the time when it falls to be determined whether or not the arrangements are disclosable VAT arrangements is when the counteraction becomes final.

(5) The following are "taxpayer emendations" for the purposes of sub-paragraph (2)—

(a) an adjustment made by S at a time when neither P nor S had reason to believe that HMRC had begun or were about to begin enquiries into the affairs of S or P relating to VAT;

(b) an adjustment (by way of an assessment or otherwise) made by HMRC with respect to S's tax position as a result of a disclosure made by S which meets the conditions in sub-paragraph (6).

(6) The conditions are that the disclosure—

(a) is a full and explicit disclosure of an inaccuracy in a return or other document or of a failure to comply with an obligation, and

(b) was made at a time when neither S nor P had reason to believe that HMRC were about to begin enquiries into the affairs of S or P relating to VAT.

PART 3

ANNUAL INFORMATION NOTICES AND NAMING

Annual information notices

17 (1) A person ("P") who has been given a warning notice under this Schedule must give HMRC a written notice (an "information notice") in respect of each reporting period in the warning period (see sub-paragraph (11)).

(2) An information notice must be given not later than the 30th day after the end of the reporting period to which it relates.

(3) An information notice must state whether or not P—

(a) has in the reporting period delivered a return, or made a claim or election, on the basis that a relevant tax advantage arises, or has since the end of the reporting period delivered on that basis a return which P was required to deliver before the end of that period,

(b) has in the reporting period failed to take action which P would be required to take under or by virtue of an enactment relating to tax but for particular DOTAS arrangements or disclosable VAT arrangements to which P is a party,

(c) has in the reporting period become a party to arrangements which—

    (i) relate to the position with respect to VAT of another person ("S") who has made supplies of goods or services to P, and

    (ii) might be expected to enable P to obtain a relevant tax advantage ("the expected tax advantage") in connection with those supplies of goods or services,

(d) has failed to deliver a return which P was required to deliver by a date falling in the reporting period.

(4) In this paragraph "relevant tax advantage" means a tax advantage which particular DOTAS arrangements or disclosable VAT arrangements enable, or might be expected to enable, P to obtain.

(5) If P has, in the reporting period concerned, made a return, claim or election on the basis mentioned in sub-paragraph (3)(a) or failed to take action as mentioned in sub-paragraph (3)(b) the information notice must—

    (a) explain (on the assumptions made by P in so acting or failing to act) how the DOTAS arrangements or disclosable VAT arrangements enable P to obtain the tax advantage, or (as the case may be) have the result that P is not required to take the action in question, and

    (b) state (on the same assumptions) the amount of the relevant tax advantage mentioned in sub-paragraph (3)(a) or (as the case may be) the amount of any tax advantage which arises in connection with the absence of a requirement to take the action mentioned in sub-paragraph (3)(b).

(6) If P has, in the reporting period, become a party to arrangements such as are mentioned in sub-paragraph (3)(c), the information notice—

    (a) must state whether or not it is P's view that the expected tax advantage arises to P, and

    (b) if that is P's view, must explain how the arrangements enable P to obtain the tax advantage and state the amount of the tax advantage.

(7) If the time by which P must deliver a return falls within a reporting period and P fails to deliver the return by that time, HMRC may require P to give HMRC a written notice (a "supplementary information notice") setting out any matters which P would have been required to set out in an information notice had P delivered the return in that reporting period.

(8) A requirement under sub-paragraph (7) must be made by a written notice which states the period within which P must comply with the notice.

(9) If P fails to comply with a requirement of (or imposed under) this paragraph HMRC may by written notice extend the warning period to the end of the period of 5 years beginning with—

    (a) the day by which the information notice or supplementary information notice should have been given (see sub-paragraphs (2) and (8)) or, as the case requires,

    (b) the day on which P gave the defective information notice or supplementary information notice to HMRC,

or, if earlier, the time when the warning period would have expired but for the extension.

(10) HMRC may permit information notices given by members of the same group of companies (as defined in paragraph 46(9)) to be combined.

(11) For the purposes of this paragraph—

    (a) the first reporting period in any warning period begins with the first day of the warning period and ends with a day specified by HMRC ("the specified day"),

    (b) the remainder of the warning period is divided into further reporting periods each of which begins immediately after the end of the preceding reporting period and is twelve months long or (if that would be shorter) ends at the end of the warning period.

Naming

18 (1) The Commissioners may publish information about a person if the person—

    (a) incurs a relevant defeat in relation to arrangements which the person has used in a warning period, and

(b) has been given at least two warning notices in respect of other defeats of arrangements which were used in the same warning period.

(2) Information published for the first time under sub-paragraph (1) must be published within the 12 months beginning with the day on which the most recent of the warning notices falling within that sub-paragraph has been given to the person.

(3) No information may be published (or continue to be published) after the end of the period of 12 months beginning with the day on which it is first published.

(4) The information that may be published is—

(a) the person's name (including any trading name, previous name or pseudonym),
(b) the person's address (or registered office),
(c) the nature of any business carried on by the person,
(d) information about the fiscal effect of the defeated arrangements (had they not been defeated), for instance information about total amounts of tax understated or total amounts by which claims, or statements of losses, have been adjusted,
(e) the amount of any penalty to which the person is liable under paragraph 30 in respect of the relevant defeat of any defeated arrangements,
(f) the periods in which or times when the defeated arrangements were used, and
(g) any other information the Commissioners may consider it appropriate to publish in order to make clear the person's identity.

(5) If the person mentioned in sub-paragraph (1) is a member of a group of companies (as defined in paragraph 46(9)), the information which may be published also includes—

(a) any trading name of the group, and
(b) information about other members of the group of the kind described in sub-paragraph (4)(a), (b) or (c).

(6) If the person mentioned in sub-paragraph (1) is a person carrying on a trade or business in partnership, the information which may be published also includes—

(a) any trading name of the partnership, and
(b) information about other members of the partnership of the kind described in sub-paragraph (4)(a) or (b).

(7) The information may be published in any manner the Commissioners may consider appropriate.

(8) Before publishing any information the Commissioners—

(a) must inform the person that they are considering doing so, and
(b) afford the person reasonable opportunity to make representations about whether or not it should be published.

(9) Arrangements are "defeated arrangements" for the purposes of sub-paragraph (4) if the person used them in the warning period mentioned in sub-paragraph (1) and a warning notice specifying the defeat of those arrangements has been given to the person before the information is published.

(10) If a person has been given a single warning notice in relation to two or more relevant defeats, the person is treated for the purposes of this paragraph as having been given a separate warning notice in relation to each of those relevant defeats.

(11) Nothing in this paragraph prevents the power under sub-paragraph (1) from being exercised on a subsequent occasion in relation to arrangements used by the person in a different warning period.

PART 4

RESTRICTION OF RELIEFS

Duty to give a restriction relief notice

19 (1) HMRC must give a person a written notice (a "restriction of relief notice") if—

(a) the person incurs a relevant defeat in relation to arrangements which the person has used in a warning period,
(b) the person has been given at least two warning notices in respect of other relevant defeats of arrangements which were used in that same warning period, and
(c) the defeats mentioned in paragraphs (a) and (b) meet the conditions in sub-paragraph (2).

(2) The conditions are—

(a) that each of the relevant defeats is by virtue of Condition A, B or C,
(b) that each of the relevant defeats relates to the misuse of a relief (see sub-paragraph (5)), and
(c) in the case of each of the relevant defeats, either—

(i) that the relevant counteraction (see sub-paragraph (7)) was made on the basis that a particular avoidance-related rule applies in relation to a person's affairs, or

(ii) that the misused relief is a loss relief.

(3) In sub-paragraph (2)(c)—

(a) the "misused relief" means the relief mentioned in sub-paragraph (5), and

(b) "loss relief" means any relief under Part 4 of ITA 2007 or Part 4 or 5 of CTA 2010.

(4) A restriction of relief notice must—

(a) explain the effect of paragraphs 20, 21 and 22, and

(b) set out when the restricted period is to begin and end.

(5) For the purposes of this Part of this Schedule, a relevant defeat by virtue of Condition A, B or C "relates to the misuse of a relief" if—

(a) the tax advantage in question, or part of the tax advantage in question, is or results from (or would but for the counteraction be or result from) a relief or increased relief from tax, or

(b) it is reasonable to conclude that the making of a particular claim for relief, or the use of a particular relief, is a significant component of the arrangements in question.

(6) In sub-paragraph (5) "the tax advantage in question" means—

(a) in relation to a defeat by virtue of Condition A, the tax advantage mentioned in paragraph 12(1)(a),

(b) in relation to a defeat by virtue of Condition B, the denied advantage (as defined in paragraph 13(4)), or

(c) in relation to a defeat by virtue of Condition C—

(i) the tax advantage mentioned in paragraph 14(2)(a), or, as the case requires,

(ii) the absence of the relevant obligation (as defined in paragraph 14(4)).

(7) In this paragraph "the relevant counteraction", in relation to a relevant defeat means—

(a) in the case of a defeat by virtue of Condition A, the counteraction referred to in paragraph 12(1)(c);

(b) in the case of a defeat by virtue of Condition B, the action referred to in paragraph 13(1);

(c) in the case of a defeat by virtue of Condition C, the counteraction referred to in paragraph 14(1)(d).

(8) If a person has been given a single warning notice in relation to two or more relevant defeats, the person is treated for the purposes of this paragraph as having been given a separate warning notice in relation to each of those relevant defeats.

Restriction of relief

20 (1) Sub-paragraphs (2) to (15) have effect in relation to a person to whom a relief restriction notice has been given.

(2) The person may not, in the restricted period, make any claim for relief.

(3) Sub-paragraph (2) does not have effect in relation to—

(a) a claim for relief under Schedule 8 to FA 2003 (stamp duty land tax: charities relief);

(b) a claim for relief under Chapter 3 of Part 8 of ITA 2007 (gifts of shares, securities and real property to charities etc);

(c) a claim for relief under Part 10 of ITA 2007 (special rules about charitable trusts etc);

(d) a claim for relief under double taxation arrangements;

(e) an election under section 426 of ITA 2007 (gift aid: election to treat gift as made in previous year).

(4) Claims under the following provisions in Part 4 of FA 2004 (registered pension schemes: tax reliefs etc) do not count as claims for relief for the purposes of this paragraph—

section 192(4) (increase of basic rate limit and higher rate limit);

section 193(4) (net pay arrangements: excess relief);

section 194(1) (relief on making of a claim).

(5) The person may not, in the restricted period, surrender group relief under Part 5 of CTA 2010.

(6) No deduction is to be made under section 83 of ITA 2007 (carry forward against subsequent trade profits) in calculating the person's net income for a relevant tax year.

(7) No deduction is to be made under section 118 of ITA 2007 (carry-forward property loss relief) in calculating the person's net income for a relevant tax year.

(8) The person is not entitled to relief under section 448 (annual payments: relief for individuals) or 449 (annual payments: relief for other persons) of ITA 2007 for any payment made in the restricted period.

(9) No deduction of expenses referable to a relevant accounting period is to be made under section 1219(1) of CTA 2009 (expenses of management of a company's investment business).

(10) No reduction is to be made under section 45(4) of CTA 2010 (carry-forward of trade loss relief) in calculating the profits for a relevant accounting period of a trade carried on by the person.

(11) In calculating the total amount of chargeable gains accruing to a person in a relevant tax year (or part of a relevant tax year), no losses are to be deducted under subsections (2) to (2B) of section 2 of TCGA 1992 (persons and gains chargeable to capital gains tax, and allowable losses).

(12) In calculating the total amount of ATED-related chargeable gains accruing to a person in a relevant tax year, no losses are to be deducted under subsection (3) of section 2B of TCGA 1992 (persons chargeable to capital gains tax on ATED-related gains).

(13) In calculating the total amount of chargeable NRCGT gains accruing to a person in a relevant tax year on relevant high value disposals, no losses are to be deducted under subsection (2) of section 14D of TCGA 1992 (persons chargeable to capital gains tax on NRCGT gains).

(14) If the person is a company, no deduction is to be made under section 62 of CTA 2010 (relief for losses made in UK property business) from the company's total profits of a relevant accounting period.

(15) No deduction is to be made under regulation 18 of the Unauthorised Unit Trusts (Tax) Regulations 2013 (SI 2013/2819) (relief for deemed payments by trustees of an exempt unauthorised unit trust) in calculating the person's net income for a relevant tax year.

(16) In this paragraph "relevant tax year" means any tax year the first day of which is in the restricted period.

(17) In this paragraph "relevant accounting period" means an accounting period the first day of which is in the restricted period.

(18) In this paragraph "double taxation arrangements" means arrangements which have effect under section 2(1) of TIOPA 2010 (double taxation relief by agreement with territories outside the UK).

The restricted period

21 (1) In paragraphs 19 and 20 (and this paragraph) "the restricted period" means the period of 3 years beginning with the day on which the relief restriction notice is given.

(2) If during the restricted period (or the restricted period as extended under this sub-paragraph) the person to whom a relief restriction notice has been given incurs a further relevant defeat meeting the conditions in sub-paragraph (4), HMRC must give the person a written notice (a "restricted period extension notice").

(3) A restricted period extension notice extends the restricted period to the end of the period of 3 years beginning with the day on which the further relevant defeat occurs.

(4) The conditions mentioned in sub-paragraph (2) are that—

(a) the relevant defeat is incurred by virtue of Condition A, B or C in relation to arrangements which the person used in the warning period mentioned in paragraph 19(1)(a), and
(b) the warning notice given to the person in respect of the relevant defeat relates to the misuse of a relief.

(5) If the person to whom a relief restriction notice has been given incurs a relevant defeat which meets the conditions in sub-paragraph (4) after the restricted period has expired but before the end of a concurrent warning period, HMRC must give the person a restriction of relief notice.

(6) In sub-paragraph (5) "concurrent warning period" means a warning period which at some time ran concurrently with the restricted period.

Reasonable excuse

22 (1) If a person who has incurred a relevant defeat satisfies HMRC or, on an appeal under paragraph 24, the First-tier Tribunal or Upper Tribunal that the person had a reasonable excuse for the matters to which that relevant defeat relates, then—

(a) for the purposes of paragraph 19(1)(a) and 21(2) and (5), the person is treated as not having incurred that relevant defeat, and

(b) for the purposes of paragraph 19(1)(b) and (c) any warning notice given to the person which relates to that relevant defeat is treated as not having been given to the person.

(2) For the purposes of this paragraph, in the case of a person ("P")—

(a) an insufficiency of funds is not a reasonable excuse unless attributable to events outside P's control,

(b) where P relies on another person to do anything, that is not a reasonable excuse unless P took reasonable care to avoid the relevant failure, and

(c) where P had reasonable excuse for the relevant failure but the excuse had ceased, P is to be treated as having continued to have the excuse if the failure is remedied without unreasonable delay after the excuse ceased.

(3) In determining for the purposes of this paragraph whether or not a person ("P") had a reasonable excuse for any action, failure or inaccuracy, reliance on advice is to be taken automatically not to constitute a reasonable excuse if the advice is addressed to, or was given to, a person other than P or takes no account of P's individual circumstances.

(4) In this paragraph "relevant failure", in relation to a relevant defeat, is to be interpreted in accordance with sub-paragraphs (2) to (7) of paragraph 43.

Mitigation of restriction of relief

23 (1) The Commissioners may mitigate the effects of paragraph 20 in relation to a person ("P") so far as it appears to them that there are exceptional circumstances such that the operation of that paragraph would otherwise have an unduly serious impact with respect to the tax affairs of P or another person.

(2) For the purposes of sub-paragraph (1) the Commissioners may modify the effects of paragraph 20 in any way they think appropriate, including by allowing P access to the whole or part of a relief to which P would otherwise not be entitled as a result of paragraph 20.

Appeal

24 (1) A person may appeal against—

(a) a relief restriction notice, or

(b) a restricted period extension notice.

(2) An appeal under this paragraph must be made within the period of 30 days beginning with the day on which the notice is given.

(3) An appeal under this paragraph is to be treated in the same way as an appeal against an assessment to income tax (including by the application of any provision about bringing the appeal by notice to HMRC, about HMRC's review of the decision or about determination of the appeal by the First-tier Tribunal or Upper Tribunal).

(4) On an appeal the tribunal may—

(a) cancel HMRC's decision, or

(b) affirm that decision with or without any modifications in accordance with sub-paragraph (5).

(5) On an appeal the tribunal may rely on paragraph 23 (mitigation of restriction of relief)—

(a) to the same extent as HMRC (which may mean applying the same mitigation as HMRC to a different starting point), or

(b) to a different extent, but only if the tribunal thinks that HMRC's decision in respect of the application of paragraph 23 was flawed.

(6) In this paragraph "tribunal" means the First-tier Tribunal or Upper Tribunal (as appropriate by virtue of sub-paragraph (3)).

Meaning of "avoidance-related rule"

25 (1) In this Part of this Schedule "avoidance-related rule" means a rule in Category 1 or 2.

(2) A rule is in Category 1 if it refers (in whatever terms)—

(a) to the purpose or main purpose or purposes of a transaction, arrangements or any other action or matter, and

(b) to whether or not the purpose in question is or involves the avoidance of tax or the obtaining of any advantage in relation to tax (however described).

(3) A rule is also in Category 1 if it refers (in whatever terms) to—

(a) expectations as to what are, or may be, the expected benefits of a transaction, arrangements or any other action or matter, and

(b) whether or not the avoidance of tax or the obtaining of any advantage in relation to tax (however described) is such a benefit.

For the purposes of paragraph (b) it does not matter whether the reference is (for instance) to the "sole or main benefit" or "one of the main benefits" or any other reference to a benefit.

(4) A rule falls within Category 2 if as a result of the rule a person may be treated differently for tax purposes depending on whether or not purposes referred to in the rule (for instance the purposes of an actual or contemplated action or enterprise) are (or are shown to be) commercial purposes.

(5) For example, a rule in the following form would fall within Category 1 and within Category 2—

"Example rule

Section X does not apply to a company in respect of a transaction if the company shows that the transaction meets Condition A or B.

Condition A is that the transaction is effected—

(a) for genuine commercial reasons, or

(b) in the ordinary course of managing investments."

Meaning of "relief"

26 The following are "reliefs" for the purposes of this Part of this Schedule—

(a) any relief from tax (however described) which must be claimed, or which is not available without making an election,

(b) relief under section 1219 of CTA 2009 (expenses of management of a company's investment business),

(c) any relief (not falling within paragraph (a)) under Part 4 of ITA 2007 (loss relief) or Part 4 or 5 of CTA 2010 (loss relief and group relief), and

(d) any relief (not falling within paragraph (a) or (b)) under a provision listed in section 24 of ITA 2007 (reliefs deductible at Step 2 of the calculation of income tax liability).

"Claim" for relief

27 In this Part of this Schedule "claim for relief" includes any election or other similar action which is in substance a claim for relief.

VAT

28 In this Part of this Schedule "tax" does not include VAT.

Power to amend

29 (1) The Treasury may by regulations—

(a) amend paragraph 20;

(b) amend paragraph 26.

(2) Regulations under sub-paragraph (1)(a) may, in particular, alter the application of paragraph 20 in relation to any relief, exclude any relief from its application or extend its application to further reliefs.

(3) Regulations under sub-paragraph (1)(b) may amend the meaning of "relief" in any way (including by extending or limiting the meaning).

(4) Regulations under this paragraph may—

(a) make supplementary, incidental and consequential provision;

(b) make transitional provision.

(5) Regulations under this paragraph are to be made by statutory instrument.

(6) A statutory instrument containing regulations under this paragraph may not be made unless a draft of the instrument has been laid before and approved by a resolution of the House of Commons.

PART 5
PENALTY

Penalty

30 (1) A person is liable to pay a penalty if the person incurs a relevant defeat in relation to any arrangements which the person has used in a warning period.

(2) The penalty is 20% of the value of the counteracted advantage if neither sub-paragraph (3) nor sub-paragraph (4) applies.

(3) The penalty is 40% of the value of the counteracted advantage if before the relevant defeat is incurred the person has been given, or become liable to be given, one (but not more than one) relevant prior warning notice.

(4) The penalty is 60% of the value of the counteracted advantage if before the current defeat is incurred the person has been given, or become liable to be given, two or more relevant prior warning notices.

(5) In this paragraph "relevant prior warning notice" means a warning notice in relation to the defeat of arrangements which the person has used in the warning period mentioned in sub-paragraph (1).

(6) For the meaning of "the value of the counteracted advantage" see paragraphs 32 to 37.

Simultaneous defeats etc

31 (1) If a person incurs simultaneously two or more relevant defeats in relation to different arrangements, sub-paragraphs (2) to (4) of paragraph 30 have effect as if the relevant defeat with the lowest value was incurred last, the relevant defeat with the next lowest value immediately before it, and so on.

(2) For this purpose the "value" of a relevant defeat is taken to be equal to the value of the counteracted advantage.

(3) If a person has been given a single warning notice in relation to two or more relevant defeats, the person is treated for the purposes of paragraph 30 as having been given a separate warning notice in relation to each of those relevant defeats.

Value of the counteracted advantage: basic rule for taxes other than VAT

32 (1) In relation to a relevant defeat incurred by virtue of Condition A, B or C, the "value of the counteracted advantage" is—

(a) in the case of a relevant defeat incurred by virtue of Condition A, the additional amount due or payable in respect of tax as a result of the counteraction mentioned in paragraph 12(1)(c);
(b) in the case of a relevant defeat incurred by virtue of Condition B, the additional amount due or payable in respect of tax as a result of the action mentioned in paragraph 13(1);
(c) in the case of a relevant defeat incurred by virtue of Condition C, the additional amount due or payable in respect of tax as a result of the counteraction mentioned in paragraph 14(1)(d).

(2) The reference in sub-paragraph (1) to the additional amount due and payable includes a reference to—

(a) an amount payable to HMRC having erroneously been paid by way of repayment of tax, and
(b) an amount which would be repayable by HMRC if the counteraction mentioned in paragraph (a) or (c) of sub-paragraph (1) were not made or the action mentioned in paragraph (b) of that sub-paragraph were not taken (as the case may be).

(3) The following are ignored in calculating the value of the counteracted advantage—

(a) group relief, and
(b) any relief under section 458 of CTA 2010 (relief in respect of repayment etc of loan) which is deferred under subsection (5) of that section.

(4) This paragraph is subject to paragraphs 33 and 34.

Value of counteracted advantage: losses for purposes of direct tax

33 (1) This paragraph has effect in relation to relevant defeats incurred by virtue of Condition A, B or C.

(2) To the extent that the counteracted advantage (see paragraph 35) has the result that a loss is wrongly recorded for the purposes of direct tax and the loss has been wholly used

to reduce the amount due or payable in respect of tax, the value of the counteracted advantage is determined in accordance with paragraph 32.

(3) To the extent that the counteracted advantage has the result that a loss is wrongly recorded for purposes of direct tax and the loss has not been wholly used to reduce the amount due or payable in respect of tax, the value of the counteracted advantage is—

(a) the value under paragraph 32 of so much of the counteracted advantage as results from the part (if any) of the loss which is used to reduce the amount due or payable in respect of tax, plus
(b) 10% of the part of the loss not so used.

(4) Sub-paragraphs (2) and (3) apply both—

(a) to a case where no loss would have been recorded but for the counteracted advantage, and
(b) to a case where a loss of a different amount would have been recorded (but in that case sub-paragraphs (2) and (3) apply only to the difference between the amount recorded and the true amount).

(5) To the extent that a counteracted advantage creates or increases an aggregate loss recorded for a group of companies—

(a) the value of the counteracted advantage is calculated in accordance with this paragraph, and
(b) in applying paragraph 32 in accordance with sub-paragraphs (2) and (3), group relief may be taken into account (despite paragraph 32(3)).

(6) To the extent that the counteracted advantage results in a loss, the value of it is nil where, because of the nature of the loss or the person's circumstances, there is no reasonable prospect of the loss being used to support a claim to reduce a tax liability (of any person).

Value of counteracted advantage: deferred tax

34 (1) To the extent that the counteracted advantage (see paragraph 35) is a deferral of tax (other than VAT), the value of that advantage is—

(a) 25% of the amount of the deferred tax for each year of the deferral, or
(b) a percentage of the amount of the deferred tax, for each separate period of deferral of less than a year, equating to 25% per year,

or, if less, 100% of the amount of the deferred tax.

(2) This paragraph does not apply to a case to the extent that paragraph 33 applies.

Meaning of "the counteracted advantage" in paragraphs 33 and 34

35 (1) In paragraphs 33 and 34 "the counteracted advantage" means—

(a) in relation to a relevant defeat incurred by virtue of Condition A, the tax advantage mentioned in paragraph 12(1)(b);
(b) in relation to a relevant defeat incurred by virtue of Condition B, the denied advantage in relation to which the action mentioned in paragraph 13(1) is taken;
(c) in relation to a relevant defeat incurred by virtue of Condition C, means any tax advantage in respect of which the counteraction mentioned in paragraph 14(1)(c) is made.

(2) In sub-paragraph (1)(c) "counteraction" is to be interpreted in accordance with paragraph 14(5).

Value of the counteracted advantage: Conditions D and E

36 (1) In relation to a relevant defeat incurred by a person by virtue of Condition D or E, the "value of the counteracted advantage" is equal to the sum of any counteracted tax advantages determined under sub-paragraphs (3) to (6).

(2) In this paragraph "the counteraction" means the counteraction mentioned in paragraph 15(1) or 16(1) (as the case may be).

(3) If the amount of VAT due or payable by the person in respect of any prescribed accounting period (X) exceeds the amount (Y) that would have been so payable but for the counteraction, the amount by which X exceeds Y is a counteracted tax advantage.

(4) If the person obtains no VAT credit for a particular prescribed accounting period, the amount of any VAT credit which the person would have obtained for that period but for the counteraction is a counteracted tax advantage.

(5) If for a prescribed accounting period the person obtains a VAT credit of an amount (Y) which is less than the amount (X) of the VAT credit which the person would have obtained but for the counteraction, the amount by which X exceeds Y is a counteracted tax advantage.

(6) If the amount (X) of the person's non-deductible tax for any prescribed accounting period is greater than Y, where Y is what would be the amount of the person's non-deductible tax for that period but for the counteraction, then the amount by which X exceeds Y is a counteracted tax advantage, but only to the extent that amount is not represented by a corresponding amount which is the whole or part of a counteracted tax advantage by virtue of sub-paragraphs (3) to(5).

(7) In this paragraph "non-deductible tax", in relation to the person who incurred the relevant defeat, means—

(a) input tax for which the person is not entitled to credit under section 25 of VATA 1994, and

(b) any VAT incurred by the person which is not input tax and in respect of which the person is not entitled to a refund from the Commissioners by virtue of any provision of VATA 1994.

(8) For the purposes of sub-paragraph (7)(b) the VAT "incurred" by a taxable person is—

(a) VAT on the supply to the person of any goods or services,

(b) VAT on the acquisition by the person from another member State of any goods;

(c) VAT on the importation of any goods from a place outside the member States.

(9) References in sub-paragraph (3) to amounts due and payable by the person in respect of a prescribed accounting period include references to—

(a) amounts payable to HMRC having erroneously been paid by way of repayment of tax, and

(b) amounts which would be repayable by HMRC if the counteraction mentioned in sub-paragraph (3) were not made.

Value of counteracted advantage: delayed VAT

37 (1) Sub-paragraph (3) of paragraph 36 has effect as follows so far as the tax advantage which is counteracted as mentioned in that sub-paragraph is in the nature of a delay in relation to the person's obligations with respect to VAT.

(2) That sub-paragraph has effect as if for "the amount by which X exceeds Y is a counteracted tax advantage" there were substituted, "there is a counteracted tax advantage of—

"(d) 25% of the amount of the delayed VAT for each year of the delay, or

(e) a percentage of the amount of the delayed VAT, for each separate period of delay of less than a year, equating to 25% per year,or, if less, 100% of the amount of the delayed VAT"".

Assessment of penalty

38 (1) Where a person is liable for a penalty under paragraph 30, HMRC must assess the penalty.

(2) Where HMRC assess the penalty, HMRC must—

(a) notify the person who is liable for the penalty, and

(b) state in the notice a tax period in respect of which the penalty is assessed.

(3) A penalty under this paragraph must be paid before the end of the period of 30 days beginning with the day on which the person is notified of the penalty under sub-paragraph (2).

(4) An assessment—

(a) is to be treated for procedural purposes as if it were an assessment to tax,

(b) may be enforced as if it were an assessment to tax, and

(c) may be combined with an assessment to tax.

(5) An assessment of a penalty under this paragraph must be made before the end of the period of 12 months beginning with the date of the defeat mentioned in paragraph 30(1).

Alteration of assessment of penalty

39 (1) After notification of an assessment has been given to a person under paragraph 38(2), the assessment may not be altered except in accordance with this paragraph or on appeal.

(2) A supplementary assessment may be made in respect of a penalty if an earlier assessment operated by reference to an underestimate of the value of the counteracted advantage.

(3) An assessment may be revised as necessary if operated by reference to an overestimate of the value of the counteracted advantage.

Aggregate penalties

40 (1) The amount of a penalty for which a person is liable under paragraph 30 is to be reduced by the amount of any other penalty incurred by the person, or any surcharge for late payment of tax imposed on the person, if the amount of the penalty or surcharge is determined by reference to the same tax liability.

(2) In sub-paragraph (1) "any other penalty" does not include a penalty under section 212A of FA 2013 (GAAR penalty) or Part 4 of FA 2014 (penalty where corrective action not taken after follower notice etc).

(3) In the application of section 97A of TMA 1970 (multiple penalties) no account shall be taken of a penalty under paragraph 30.

Appeal against penalty

41 (1) A person may appeal against a decision of HMRC that a penalty is payable under paragraph 30.

(2) A person may appeal against a decision of HMRC as to the amount of a penalty payable by P under paragraph 30.

(3) An appeal under this paragraph must be made within the period of 30 days beginning with the day on which notification of the penalty is given under paragraph 38.

(4) An appeal under this paragraph is to be treated in the same way as an appeal against an assessment to the tax concerned (including by the application of any provision about bringing the appeal by notice to HMRC, about HMRC's review of the decision or about determination of the appeal by the First-tier Tribunal or Upper Tribunal).

(5) Sub-paragraph (4) does not apply—

(a) so as to require a person to pay a penalty before an appeal against the assessment of the penalty is determined, or

(b) in respect of any other matter expressly provided for by this Part of this Schedule.

(6) On an appeal under sub-paragraph (1) or (2) the tribunal may—

(a) affirm HMRC's decision, or

(b) substitute for HMRC's decision another decision that HMRC has power to make.

(7) In this paragraph "tribunal" means the First-tier Tribunal or Upper Tribunal (as appropriate by virtue of sub-paragraph (4)).

Penalties: reasonable excuse

42 (1) A person is not liable to a penalty under paragraph 30 in respect of a relevant defeat if the person satisfies HMRC or (on appeal) the First-tier Tribunal or Upper Tribunal that the person had a reasonable excuse for the relevant failure to which that relevant defeat relates (see paragraph 43).

(2) Sub-paragraph (3) applies if—

(a) a person has incurred a relevant defeat in respect of which the person is liable to a penalty under paragraph 30, and

(b) before incurring that defeat the person had been given, or become liable to be given, an excepted warning notice.

(3) The person is treated for the purposes of sub-paragraphs (2) to (4) of paragraph 30 (rate of penalty) as not having been given, and not having become liable to be given, the excepted notice (so far as it relates to the relevant defeat in respect of which the person had a reasonable excuse).

(4) A warning notice is "excepted" for the purposes of this paragraph if the person was not liable to a penalty in respect of the defeat specified in it because the person had a reasonable excuse for the relevant failure in question.

(5) For the purposes of this paragraph, in the case of a person ("P")—

(a) an insufficiency of funds is not a reasonable excuse unless attributable to events outside P's control,

(b) where P relies on another person to do anything, that is not a reasonable excuse unless P took reasonable care to avoid the relevant failure, and

(c) where P had a reasonable excuse for the relevant failure but the excuse had ceased, P is to be treated as having continued to have the excuse if the failure is remedied without unreasonable delay after the excuse ceased.

(6) In determining for the purposes of this paragraph whether or not a person ("P") had a reasonable excuse for any action, failure or inaccuracy, reliance on advice is to be taken automatically not to constitute a reasonable excuse if the advice is addressed to, or was given to, a person other than P or takes no account of P's individual circumstances.

Paragraph 42: meaning of "the relevant failure"

43 (1) In paragraph 42 "the relevant failure", in relation to a relevant defeat, is to be interpreted in accordance with sub-paragraphs (2) to (7).

(2) In relation to a relevant defeat incurred by virtue of Condition A, "the relevant failure" means the failures or inaccuracies as a result of which the counteraction under section 209 of FA 2013 was necessary

(3) In relation to a relevant defeat incurred by virtue of Condition B, "the relevant failure" means the failures or inaccuracies in respect of which the action mentioned in paragraph 13(1) was taken.

(4) In relation to a relevant defeat incurred by virtue of Condition C, "the relevant failure" means the failures of inaccuracies as a result of which the adjustments, assessments, or other action mentioned in paragraph 14(5) are required.

(5) In relation to a relevant defeat incurred by virtue of Condition D, "the relevant failure" means the failures or inaccuracies as a result of which the adjustments, assessments or other action mentioned in paragraph 15(5) are required.

(6) In relation to a relevant defeat incurred by virtue of Condition E, "the relevant failure" means P's actions (and failures to act), so far as they are connected with matters in respect of which the counteraction mentioned in paragraph 16(1) is required.

(7) In sub-paragraph (6) "counteraction" is to be interpreted in accordance with paragraph 16(2).

Mitigation of penalties

44 (1) The Commissioners may in their discretion mitigate a penalty under paragraph 30, or stay or compound any proceedings for such a penalty.

(2) They may also, after judgment, further mitigate or entirely remit the penalty.

PART 6
CORPORATE GROUPS, ASSOCIATED PERSONS AND PARTNERSHIPS

Representative member of a VAT group

45 (1) Where a body corporate ("R") is the representative member of a group (and accordingly is treated for the purposes of this Schedule as mentioned in section 43(1) of VATA 1994), anything which has been done by or in relation to another body corporate ("B") in B's capacity as representative member of that group is treated for the purposes of this Schedule as having been done by or in relation to R in R's capacity as representative member of the group.

Accordingly paragraph 3 (warning period) operates as if the successive representative members of a group were a single person.

(2) This Schedule has effect as if the representative member of a group, so far as acting in its capacity as such, were a different person from that body corporate so far as acting in any other capacity.

(3) In this paragraph the reference to a "group" is to be interpreted in accordance with sections 43A to 43D of VATA 1994.

Corporate groups

46 (1) Sub-paragraphs (2) and (3) apply if HMRC has a duty under paragraph 2 to give a warning notice to a company ("C") which is a member of a group.

(2) That duty has effect as a duty to give a warning notice to each current group member (see sub-paragraph (8)).

(3) Any warning notice which has been given (or is treated as having been given) previously to any current group member is treated as having been given to each current group member (and any provision in this Schedule which refers to a "warning period" in relation to a person is to be interpreted accordingly).

(4) In relation to a company which incurs a relevant defeat, paragraph 19(1) (duty to give relief restriction notice) does not have effect unless the warning period mentioned in that sub-paragraph would be a warning period in relation to the company regardless of sub-paragraph (3).

(5) A company which incurs a relevant defeat is not liable to pay a penalty under paragraph 30 unless the warning period mentioned in sub-paragraph (1) of that paragraph would be a warning period in relation to the company regardless of sub-paragraph (3).

(6) HMRC may discharge any duty to give a warning notice to a current group member in accordance with sub-paragraph (2) by delivering the notice to C (and if it does so may combine one or more warning notices in a single notice).

(7) If a company ceases to be a member of a group, and—

(a) immediately before it ceases to be a member of the group, a warning period has effect in relation to the company, but

(b) no warning period would have effect in relation to the company at that time but for sub-paragraph (2) or (3),

that warning period ceases to have effect in relation to the company when it ceases to be a member of that group.

(8) In this paragraph "current group member" means a company which is a member of the group concerned at the time when the warning notice mentioned in sub-paragraph (1) is given.

(9) For the purposes of this paragraph two companies are members of the same group of companies if—

(a) one is a 75% subsidiary of the other, or

(b) both are 75% subsidiaries of a third company.

(10) In this paragraph "75% subsidiary" has the meaning given by section 1154 of CTA 2010.

(11) In this paragraph "company" has the same meaning as in the Corporation Tax Acts (see section 1121 of CTA 2010).

Associated persons treated as incurring relevant defeats

47 (1) Sub-paragraph (2) applies if a person ("P") incurs a relevant defeat in relation to any arrangements (otherwise than by virtue of this paragraph).

(2) Any person ("S") who is associated with P at the relevant time is also treated for the purposes of paragraphs 2 (duty to give warning notice) and 3(2) (warning period) as having incurred that relevant defeat in relation to those arrangements (but see sub-paragraph (3)).

For the meaning of "associated" see paragraph 48.

(3) Sub-paragraph (2) does not apply if P and S are members of the same group of companies (as defined in paragraph 46(9)).

(4) In relation to a warning notice given to S by virtue of sub-paragraph (2), paragraph 2(4)(c) (certain information to be included in warning notice) is to be read as referring only to paragraphs 3, 17 and 18.

(5) A warning notice which is given to a person by virtue of sub-paragraph (2) is treated for the purposes of paragraphs 19(1) (duty to give relief restriction notice) and 30 (penalty) as not having been given to that person.

(6) In sub-paragraph (2) "the relevant time" means the time when P is given a warning notice in respect of the relevant defeat.

Meaning of "associated"

48 (1) For the purposes of paragraph 47 two persons are associated with one another if—

(a) one of them is a body corporate which is controlled by the other, or

(b) they are bodies corporate under common control.

(2) Two bodies corporate are under common control if both are controlled—

(a) by one person,

(b) by two or more, but fewer than six, individuals, or

(c) by any number of individuals carrying on business in partnership.

(3) For the purposes of this section a body corporate ("H") is taken to control another body corporate ("B") if—

(a) H is empowered by statute to control B's activities, or

(b) H is B's holding company within the meaning of section 1159 of and Schedule 6 to the Companies Act 2006.

(4) For the purposes of this section an individual or individuals are taken to control a body corporate ("B") if the individual or individuals, were they a body corporate, would be B's holding company within the meaning of those provisions.

Partners treated as incurring relevant defeats

49 (1) Where paragraph 50 applies in relation to a partnership return, each relevant partner is treated for the purposes of this Schedule as having incurred the relevant defeat mentioned in paragraph 50(1)(b), (2) or (3)(b) (as the case may be).

(2) In this paragraph "relevant partner" means any person who was a partner in the partnership at any time during the relevant reporting period (but see sub-paragraph (3)).

(3) The "relevant partners" do not include—

(a) the person mentioned in sub-paragraph (1)(b), (2) or (3)(b) (as the case may be) of paragraph 50, or
(b) any other person who would, apart from this paragraph, incur a relevant defeat in connection with the subject matter of the partnership return mentioned in sub-paragraph (1).

(4) In this paragraph the "relevant reporting period" means the period in respect of which the partnership return mentioned in sub-paragraph (1), (2) or (3) of paragraph 50 was required.

Partnership returns to which this paragraph applies

50 (1) This paragraph applies in relation to a partnership return if—

(a) that return has been made on the basis that a tax advantage arises to a partner from any arrangements, and
(b) that person has incurred, in relation to that tax advantage and those arrangements, a relevant defeat by virtue of Condition A (final counteraction of tax advantage under general anti-abuse rule).

(2) Where a person has incurred a relevant defeat by virtue of sub-paragraph (2) of paragraph 13 (Condition B: case involving partnership follower notice) this paragraph applies in relation to the partnership return mentioned in that sub-paragraph.

(3) This paragraph applies in relation to a partnership return if—

(a) that return has been made on the basis that a tax advantage arises to a partner from any arrangements, and
(b) that person has incurred, in relation to that tax advantage and those arrangements, a relevant defeat by virtue of Condition C (return, claim or election made in reliance on DOTAS arrangements).

(4) The references in this paragraph to a relevant defeat do not include a relevant defeat incurred by virtue of paragraph 47(2).

Partnerships: information

51 (1) If paragraph 50 applies in relation to a partnership return, the appropriate partner must give HMRC a written notice (a "partnership information notice") in respect of each sub-period in the information period.

(2) The "information period" is the period of 5 years beginning with the day after the day of the relevant defeat mentioned in paragraph 50.

(3) If, in the case of a partnership, a new information period (relating to another partnership return) begins during an existing information period, those periods are treated for the purposes of this paragraph as a single period (which includes all times that would otherwise fall within either period).

(4) An information period under this paragraph ends if the partnership ceases.

(5) A partnership information notice must be given not later than the 30th day after the end of the sub-period to which it relates.

(6) A partnership information notice must state—

(a) whether or not any relevant partnership return which was, or was required to be, delivered in the sub-period has been made on the basis that a relevant tax advantage arises, and
(b) whether or not there has been a failure to deliver a relevant partnership return in the sub-period.

(7) In this paragraph—

(a) "relevant partnership return" means a partnership return in respect of the partnership's trade, profession or business;
(b) "relevant tax advantage" means a tax advantage which particular DOTAS arrangements enable, or might be expected to enable, a person who is or has been a partner in the partnership to obtain.

(8) If a partnership information notice states that a relevant partnership return has been made on the basis mentioned in sub-paragraph (6)(a) the notice must—

(a) explain (on the assumptions made for the purposes of the return) how the DOTAS arrangements enable the tax advantage concerned to be obtained, and

(b) describe any variation in the amounts required to be stated in the return under section 12AB(1) of TMA 1970 which results from those arrangements.

(9) HMRC may require the appropriate partner to give HMRC a notice (a "supplementary information notice") setting out further information in relation to a partnership information notice.

In relation to a partnership information notice "further information" means information which would have been required to be set out in the notice by virtue of sub-paragraph (6)(a) or (8) had there not been a failure to deliver a relevant partnership return.

(10) A requirement under sub-paragraph (9) must be made by a written notice and the notice must state the period within which the notice must be complied with.

(11) If a person fails to comply with a requirement of (or imposed under) this paragraph, HMRC may by written notice extend the information period concerned to the end of the period of 5 years beginning with—

(a) the day by which the partnership information notice or supplementary information notice was required to be given to HMRC or, as the case requires,

(b) the day on which the person gave the defective notice to HMRC,

or, if earlier, the time when the information period would have expired but for the extension.

(12) For the purposes of this paragraph—

(a) the first sub-period in an information period begins with the first day of the information period and ends with a day specified by HMRC,

(b) the remainder of the information period is divided into further sub-periods each of which begins immediately after the end of the preceding sub-period and is twelve months long or (if that would be shorter) ends at the end of the information period.

(13) In this paragraph "the appropriate partner" means the partner in the partnership who is for the time being nominated by HMRC for the purposes of this paragraph.

Partnerships: special provision about taxpayer emendations

52 (1) Sub-paragraph (2) applies if a partnership return is amended at any time under section 12ABA of TMA 1970 (amendment of partnership return by representative partner etc) on a basis that—

(a) results in an increase or decrease in, or

(b) otherwise affects the calculation of,

any amount stated under subsection (1)(b) of section 12AB of that Act (partnership statement) as a partner's share of any income, loss, consideration, tax or credit for any period.

(2) For the purposes of paragraph 14 (Condition C: counteraction of DOTAS arrangements), the partner is treated as having at that time amended—

(a) the partner's return under section 8 or 8A of TMA 1970, or

(b) the partner's company tax return,

so as to give effect to the amendments of the partnership return.

(3) Sub-paragraph (4) applies if a partnership return is amended at any time by HMRC as a result of a disclosure made by the representative partner or that person's successor on a basis that—

(a) results in an increase or decrease in, or

(b) otherwise affects the calculation of,

any amount stated under subsection (1)(b) of section 12AB of TMA 1970 (partnership statement) as the share of a particular partner (P) of any income, loss, consideration, tax or credit for any period.

(4) If the conditions in sub-paragraph (5) are met, P is treated for the purposes of paragraph 14 as having at that time amended—

(a) P's return under section 8 or 8A of TMA 1970, or

(b) P's company tax return,

so as to give effect to the amendments of the partnership return.

(5) The conditions are that the disclosure—

(a) is a full and explicit disclosure of an inaccuracy in the partnership return, and

(b) was made at a time when neither the person making the disclosure nor P had reason to believe that HMRC was about to begin enquiries into the partnership return.

Supplementary provision relating to partnerships

53 (1) In paragraphs 49 to 52 and this paragraph—

"partnership" is to be interpreted in accordance with section 12AA of TMA 1970 (and includes a limited liability partnership);

"the representative partner", in relation to a partnership return, means the person who was required by a notice served under or for the purposes of section 12AA(2) or (3) of TMA 1970 to deliver the return;

"successor", in relation to a person who is the representative partner in the case of a partnership return, has the same meaning as in TMA 1970 (see section 118(1) of that Act).

(2) For the purposes of this Part of this Schedule a partnership is treated as the same partnership notwithstanding a change in membership if any person who was a member before the change remains a member after the change.

PART 7

SUPPLEMENTAL

Meaning of "adjustments"

54 (1) In this Schedule "adjustments" means any adjustments, whether by way of an assessment, the modification of an assessment or return, amendment or disallowance of a claim, a payment, the entering into of a contract settlement, or otherwise (and references to "making" adjustments accordingly include securing that adjustments are made by entering into a contract settlement).

(2) "Adjustments" also includes a payment in respect of a liability to pay national insurance contributions.

Time of "use" of defeated arrangements

55 (1) With reference to a particular relevant defeat incurred by a person in relation to arrangements, the person is treated as having "used" the arrangements on the dates set out in this paragraph.

(2) If the person incurs the relevant defeat by virtue of Condition A, the person is treated as having "used" the arrangements on the following dates

(a) the filing date of any return made by the person on the basis that the tax advantage mentioned in paragraph 12(1)(a) arises from the arrangements;

(b) the date on which the person makes any claim or election on that basis;

(c) the date of any relevant failure by the person to comply with an obligation.

(3) For the purposes of sub-paragraph (2) a failure to comply with an obligation is a "relevant failure" if the whole or part of the tax advantage mentioned in paragraph 12(1)(b) arose as a result of, or in connection with, that failure.

(4) If the person incurs the relevant defeat by virtue of Condition B, the person is treated as having "used" the arrangements on the following dates—

(a) the filing date of any return made by the person on the basis that the asserted advantage (see section 204(3) of FA 2014) results from the arrangements,

(b) the date on which any claim is made by the person on that basis,

(c) the date of any failure by the person to comply with a relevant obligation.

In this sub-paragraph "relevant obligation" means an obligation which would not have fallen on the person (or might have been expected not to do so), had the denied advantage arisen (see section 208(3) of FA 2014).

(5) If the person incurs the relevant defeat by virtue of Condition C, the person is treated as having "used" the arrangements on the following dates—

(a) the filing date of any return made by the person on the basis mentioned in paragraph 14(2)(a);

(b) the date on which the person makes any claim or election on that basis;

(c) the date of any failure by the person to comply with a relevant obligation (as defined in paragraph 14(4)).

(6) If the person incurs the relevant defeat by virtue of Condition D, the person is treated as having "used" the arrangements on the following dates—

(a) the filing date of any return made by the person on the basis mentioned in paragraph 15(2)(a);

(b) the date on which the person makes any claim on that basis;

(c) the date of any failure by the person to comply with a relevant obligation (as defined in paragraph 15(4)).

(7) If the person incurs the relevant defeat by virtue of Condition E, the person is treated as having "used" the arrangements on the following dates—

(a) the filing date of any return made by S to which the counteraction mentioned in paragraph 16(1)(c) relates;

(b) the date on which S made any claim to which that counteraction relates;

(c) the date of any relevant failure by S to which that counteraction relates.

(8) In sub-paragraph (7) "relevant failure" means a failure to comply with an obligation relating to VAT.

(9) In this paragraph "filing date", in relation to a return, means the earlier of—

(a) the day on which the return is delivered, or

(b) the last day of the period within which the return must be delivered.

(10) References in this paragraph to the date on which a person fails to comply with an obligation are to the date on which the person is first in breach of the obligation.

Inheritance tax

56 (1) In the case of inheritance tax, each of the following is treated as a return for the purposes of this Schedule—

(a) an account delivered by a person under section 216 or 217 of IHTA 1984 (including an account delivered in accordance with regulations under section 256 of that Act);

(b) a statement or declaration which amends or is otherwise connected with such an account produced by the person who delivered the account;

(c) information or a document provided by a person in accordance with regulations under section 256 of that Act;

and such a return is treated as made by the person in question.

(2) In this Schedule (except where the context requires otherwise) "assessment", in relation to inheritance tax, includes a determination.

National insurance contributions

57 (1) In this Schedule references to an assessment to tax include a NICs decision relating to a person's liability for relevant contributions.

(2) In this Schedule a reference to a provision of Part 7 of FA 2004 (disclosure of tax avoidance schemes) (a "DOTAS provision") includes a reference to—

(a) that DOTAS provision as applied by regulations under section 132A of the Social Security Administration Act 1992 (disclosure of contributions avoidance arrangements);

(b) any provision of regulations under that section that corresponds to that DOTAS provision,

whenever the regulations are made.

(3) Regulations under section 132A of that Act may disapply, or modify the effect of, sub-paragraph (2).

(4) In this paragraph "NICs decision" means a decision under section 8 of the Social Security Contributions (Transfer of Functions, etc) Act 1999 or Article 7 of the Social Security Contributions (Transfer of Functions, etc) (Northern Ireland) Order 1999 (SI 1999/671).

General interpretation

58 (1) In this Schedule—

"arrangements" has the meaning given by paragraph 2(6);

"the Commissioners" means the Commissioners for Her Majesty's Revenue and Customs;

"contract settlement" means an agreement in connection with a person's liability to make a payment to the Commissioners under or by virtue of an enactment;

"disclosable VAT arrangements" is to be interpreted in accordance with paragraph 9;

"DOTAS arrangements" is to be interpreted in accordance with paragraph 8 (and see also paragraph 57(2));

"follower notice" has the meaning given by paragraph 13(6);

"HMRC" means Her Majesty's Revenue and Customs;

"national insurance contributions" means contributions under Part 1 of the Social Security Contributions and Benefits Act 1992 or Part 1 of the Social Security Contributions and Benefits (Northern Ireland) Act 1992;

"net income" has the meaning given by section 23 of ITA 2007 (see Step 2 of that section);

"partnership follower notice" has the meaning given by paragraph 2(2) of Schedule 31 to FA 2014;

"partnership return" means a return under section 12AA of TMA 1970;

"relevant contributions" means the following contributions under Part 1 of the Social Security Contributions and Benefits Act 1992 or Part 1 of the Social Security Contributions and Benefits (Northern Ireland) Act 1992—

(a) Class 1 contributions;
(b) Class 1A contributions;
(c) Class 1B contributions;
(d) Class 2 contributions which must be paid but in relation to which section 11A of the Act in question (application of certain provisions of the Income Tax Acts in relation to Class 2 contributions under section 11(2) of that Act) does not apply;

"relevant defeat" is to be interpreted in accordance with paragraph 11;

"tax" has the meaning given by paragraph 4;

"tax advantage" has the meaning given by paragraph 7;

"warning notice" has the meaning given by paragraph 2.

(2) In this Schedule an expression used in relation to VAT has the same meaning as in VATA 1994.

(3) In this Schedule (except where the context requires otherwise) references, however expressed, to a person's affairs in relation to tax include the person's position as regards deductions or repayments of, or of sums representing, tax that the person is required to make by or under an enactment.

(4) For the purposes of this Schedule a partnership return is regarded as made on the basis that a particular tax advantage arises to a person from particular arrangements if—

(a) it is made on the basis that an increase or reduction in one or more of the amounts mentioned in section 12AB(1) of TMA 1970 (amounts in the partnership statement in a partnership return) results from those arrangements, and
(b) that increase or reduction results in that tax advantage for the person.

Consequential amendments

59 In section 103ZA of TMA 1970 (disapplication of sections 100 to 103 in the case of certain penalties)—

(a) omit "or" at the end of paragraph (ga), and
(b) after paragraph (h) insert "or
  (i) Part 5 of Schedule 18 to the Finance Act 2016 (serial tax avoidance)."

60 In section 212 of FA 2014 (follower notices: aggregate penalties), in subsection (4)—

(a) omit "or" at the end of paragraph (b), and
(b) after paragraph (c) insert ", or
  (d) Part 5 of Schedule 18 to FA 2016 (serial tax avoidance) "

61 (1) The Social Security Contributions and Benefits Act 1992 is amended as follows.

(2) In section 11A (application of certain provisions of the Income Tax Acts in relation to Class 2 contributions under section 11(2)), in subsection (1), at the end of paragraph (e) insert—

"(ea) the provisions of Schedule 18 to the Finance Act 2016 (serial tax avoidance);".

(3) In section 16 (application of Income Tax Acts and destination of Class 4 contributions), in subsection (1), at the end of paragraph (d) insert "and

(e) the provisions of Schedule 18 to the Finance Act 2016 (serial tax avoidance),".

62 In the Social Security Contributions and Benefits (Northern Ireland) Act 1992, in section 11A (application of certain provisions of the Income Tax Acts in relation to Class 2 contributions under section 11(2)), in subsection (1), at the end of paragraph (e) insert—

"(ea) the provisions of Schedule 18 to the Finance Act 2016 (serial tax avoidance);".

Commencement

63 Subject to paragraphs 64 and 65, paragraphs 1 to 62 of this Schedule have effect in relation to relevant defeats incurred after the day on which this Act is passed.

64 (1) A relevant defeat is to be disregarded for the purposes of this Schedule if it is incurred before 6 April 2017 in relation to arrangements which the person has entered into before the day on which this Act is passed.

(2) A relevant defeat incurred on or after 6 April 2017 is to be disregarded for the purposes of this Schedule if—

(a) the person entered into the arrangements concerned before the day on which this Act is passed, and

(b) before 6 April 2017—

(i) the person incurring the defeat fully discloses to HMRC the matters to which the relevant counteraction relates, or

(ii) that person gives HMRC notice of a firm intention to make a full disclosure of those matters and makes such a full disclosure within any time limit set by HMRC.

(3) In sub-paragraph (2) "the relevant counteraction" means—

(a) in a case within Condition A, the counteraction mentioned in paragraph 12(1)(c);

(b) in a case within Condition B, the action mentioned in paragraph 13(1);

(c) in a case within Condition C, the counteraction mentioned in paragraph 14(1)(c);

(d) in a case within Condition D, the counteraction mentioned in paragraph 15(1)(d);

(e) in a case within Condition E, the counteraction mentioned in paragraph 16(1)(c).

(4) In sub-paragraph (3)—

(a) in paragraph (c) "counteraction" is to be interpreted in accordance with paragraph 14(5);

(b) in paragraph (d) "counteraction" is to be interpreted in accordance with paragraph 15(5);

(c) in paragraph (e) "counteraction" is to be interpreted in accordance with paragraph 16(2).

(5) See paragraph 11(2) for provision about when a relevant defeat is incurred.

65 (1) A warning notice given to a person is to be disregarded for the purposes of—

(a) paragraph 18 (naming), and

(b) Part 4 of this Schedule (restriction of reliefs),

if the relevant defeat specified in the notice relates to arrangements which the person has entered into before the day on which this Act is passed.

(2) Where a person has entered into any arrangements before the day on which this Act is passed—

(a) a relevant defeat incurred by a person in relation to the arrangements, and

(b) any warning notice specifying such a relevant defeat,

is to be disregarded for the purposes of paragraph 30 (penalty).

GENERAL NOTE

Section 159 and Sch 18 introduce a new regime of warnings and escalating sanctions for those who engage in tax avoidance schemes which HMRC subsequently defeat. New Scheduless (43A and 43B) to the FA 2013 concerning with pooling arrangements or similar arrangements for the purposes of GAAR counteraction have broadened the scope from the original draft Bill. The new regime comes into effect from 6 April 2017.

The legislation is drafted to issue a warning notice, which commences a five year clock whereby subsequent defeats within the five-year period result in a penalty based on the understated tax, as well as resetting the clock. The continued use of avoidance schemes which HMRC subsequently defeat results in the rate of penalty being increased to a maximum of 60% of the understated tax.

The taxpayer's details can be published where there are three defeats within the warning or extended warning period.

Where HMRC defeat three avoidance schemes used to exploit reliefs during the warning period, the taxpayer will be denied further benefit of reliefs during the warning period.

Part 2 Entry into the Regime and Basic Concepts

Part 2 is mainly concerned with identifying when a user of an arrangement that is subject to a relevant defeat enters the regime. Entering the regime results in HMRC issuing the person a written notice under para 2(2). It also results a number of sanctions on the person and starts a clock (the "warning period") for considering other relevant defeats, thereby permitting more penal sanctions where there are subsequent defeats within the warning period.

A warning notice must only be issued where a person ("P") incurs a relevant defeat in relation to any arrangements. A relevant defeat is defined at paragraph 11 as occurring in relation to arrangements if any of conditions A to E is met in relation to P and the arrangements.

The warning notice must be given within 90 days from the day of the relevant defeat. If a notice is given after 90 days, it will not be valid.

The warning notice *must* specify the warning period, relevant defeat as well as explain the effect of paras 3 (the "warning period") and 17 to 46 (Pts 3, 4, 5 and 6). Given that a warning notice must specify certain information, it must follow that if it does not it is not valid. It is anticipated that HMRC will have to ensure that the explanation for paras 17 to 46 will need to be comprehensive.

The warning period begins the day after the day on which the notice is given for a period of five years – the first warning period. The clock is reset where there is a subsequent relevant defeat within the first warning period being replaced by a new warning period of five years beginning the day after the day on which the relevant defeat occurs.

It appears that a second relevant defeat would still require HMRC to provide written notice given that the person incurs a relevant defeat in relation to any arrangements and where that occurs HMRC must give the person a written notice. The duty to give warning notice requires the notice to be given within 90 days and to specify the warning period. HMRC should therefore provide the person with a written notice revising the warning period within 90 days of the defeat.

Paragraph 4 defines the meaning of tax,

Paragraph 5 defines the meaning of "tax advantage" in relation to VAT by applying the definition in para 2 of Sch 11A VATA 1994. Schedule 11A made provisions for the disclosure of VAT avoidance schemes. The definition is wide and includes the reduction in output tax; obtaining a VAT credit; and reduction of non-refundable VAT that would "otherwise be the case".

Paragraph 7 defines "tax advantage" for all other taxes and includes the relief or repayment of tax, an increase in relief or repayment; receiving a tax credit; avoidance or reduction of an assessment; deferral of tax; or the avoidance of a tax obligation.

Paragraph 8 defines "DOTAS arrangements" which includes arrangements are "notifiable" to HMRC. The scope therefore includes arrangements that were notifiable and not notified and were not given a notice by HMRC under s 312(6) Finance Act 2004 (notice not under a duty to notify). The legislation has purposely been drafted to catch the circumstances where it is established that the arrangements used were notifiable. Furthermore, the definition of "DOTAS arrangements" for the purposes of the schedule includes arrangements that were properly notified as proposed arrangements or are substantially the same as arrangements already notified to HMRC. Paragraph 9 defines "Disclosable VAT arrangements" similarly as those notified or that should have been notified. Paragraph 10 clarifies the situation where a person fails to comply with a DOTAS or VADR requirement to notify. The failure requires the decision of a Tribunal admittance by the person in writing.

Paragraph 11 requires that, for there to be a "relevant defeat", any of the conditions A to E (paras 12 to 16) is met in relation to the person ("P") and the arrangements.

Condition A is where a notice under the General Anti-Abuse Rule (under Finance Act 2013 Sch 43 para 12 or the new schedules: Sch 43A para 8 or 9, Sch 43B para 8) is given to P and the counteraction is final. The counteraction under Sch 43 para 12 is final where the tax advantage has been successfully counteracted.

Schedule 43A FA 2013 provides that a designated HMRC officer may issue a notice (a "pooling notice") where there is a "lead arrangement" under para 3 of Sch 43 and considers arrangements are equivalent and the advantage ought to be counteracted under s 209 FA 2013. Pursuant to a pooling notice a designated officer may issue a "notice of binding" under para 2 Sch 43A FA 2013. Where the notified person takes corrective action in relation to the tax arrangements within the period prior to the arrangements being referred to the GAAR panel, the person is to be treated as if the notice had not been issued. A person has thirty days with which they can make representations. Schedule 43A para 8 and 9 make provisions for the notice of final decision for the tax advantage is to be counteracted.

Paragraph 1(2) Sch 43B FA 2013 applies if a pooling notice has been given, the lead arrangements cease to be in the pool and no referral for representations is made under para 5 or 6 Sch 43 FA 2013. Paragraph 1(2) provides for a designated HMRC officer to give a written notice of a proposal to make a generic referral to the GAAR Advisory Panel in respect of the arrangements in the pool. The notice must specify the arrangements and the advantage and inform the recipient they have 30 days from the day of the notice to propose they are given a notice under para 3 Sch 43 and should not proceed to make a generic referral to the GAAR Advisory Panel. If such a proposal is made under para 2(1) a designated office must consider it. Paragraph 3 Sch 43B provides that in the absence of a proposal, the officer must make a referral to the GAAR Advisory Panel. If at least one notified person makes a proposal, the designated officer mush at the end of the 30 day period decide whether to give notice under para 3 Sch 43 or make a referral to the GAAR Advisory Panel. A referral will be a "generic referral" although must under para 4 Sch 43B provide a general statement of material characteristics of the arrangements and declare that it applies to all specified arrangements and HMRC is not aware of any material information for the GAAR Advisory Panel to consider the matter. A specific format is set out at para 6 Sch 43B for a sub-panel of the GAAR Advisory Panel to meet, have regard to certain matters, produce an opinion, provide the opinion to the designated officer. A designated officer in receipt of an opinion must under para 7 Sch 43B provide a copy to the recipients of the notice explaining the right to make representations within the period of 30 days of the day on which the notice to make representation is given. Representations are limited to that of no tax advantage, a notice has alredy been issued under para 6 Sch 43A and that the general statement the officer made to the GAAR Advisory Panel contains material inaccuracies which would be relevant in accordance with section 207 FA 2013 to determine whether the arrangements are abusive. Paragraph 8 Sch 43B makes provisions for the notice of final decision for the tax advantage is to be counteracted.

Condition B is where a person or partnership has been issued with a Follower Notice and either has taken the necessary corrective action or HMRC have taken action to recover the understated tax. The denied advantage must be final. The counteraction of a tax advantage is final when adjustments are made and the tax arising cannot be subject to variation on appeal or otherwise.

Condition C applies where P uses and relies on arrangements which are notified or notifiable to HMRC under the DOTAS regime, the arrangements are counteracted and that counteraction is final. Effectively, P would have relied on the arrangements where the relevant tax advantage was sought by making a return, claim or election. Paragraph 14(5) defines when arrangements are counteracted and specifically excludes "taxpayer emendations", which is set out para 14(8) as an adjustment made by P where there was no knowledge or reason to believe that HMRC had begun or were about to begin enquiries relating to the tax in question. Guidance will be required to ascertain the circumstances to establish "reason to believe" or "were about to begin". The legislation is drafted to consider what is in P's mind. This could result in a dispute where HMRC have, say, undertaken a compliance check in a seemingly unrelated area and P also amends the position through adjustment or disclosure.

Condition D is the equivalent of Condition C for VAT.

Condition E applies where a person receives supplies of goods or services and there are VAT arrangements which purport to provide a tax advantage and HMRC counteract that advantage. The denied advantage must be final. The counteraction of a tax advantage is final when adjustments are made and the tax arising cannot be subject to variation on appeal or otherwise.

Part 3 Annual Information Notices and Naming

Part 3 contains provision to require a person issued with a warning notice to provide certain information (an information notice) no later than the 30th day after the end of a reporting period as well as a right for the commissioners to name the person where there are continues defeats within the warning period.

Paragraph 17 provides that a person who has been given a warning notice must send HMRC a written notice for each reporting period. The written notice must state whether or not the person has used any arrangements to gain a tax advantage or avoid a tax obligation. Paragraph 17(4) defines a relevant tax advantage as one which particular DOTAS arrangements or disclosable VAT arrangements enable or might be expected to enable P to obtain.

Where there is a relevant tax advantage, the written notice must include an explanation of how the arrangements enable P to obtain the tax advantage along with quantifying the advantage.

Where there is a failure to provide a written notice, HMRC may require P to complete a supplementary information notice as well as extend the warning period under para 17(9) by five years from the relevant day.

Paragraph 18 provides that HMRC may publish the details of P where they are subject to three warning notices within the same warning period. Details to be published include the person's or partnership's name, address or registered office, nature of business carried on, Details of the avoidance, amount of penalty. The commissioners also have an ability to publish any other information they may consider appropriate to make clear the persons identity. Information published for the first time must be done so within 12 months beginning with the day on which the most recent of the warning notices has been given.

Part 4 Restriction of Reliefs

Paragraph 19 sets out that HMRC must give a restriction relief notice where there is a relevant defeat in relation to arrangements used within a warning period; there have been two warning notices within the same warning period; and certain conditions are met.

Paragraph 19(2) sets out the conditions the first of which requires *each* of the relevant defeats to be by virtue of condition A, B or C. The conditions A, B and C are set out at Pt 2 of the Schedule and relate to the issue and finality of a counteraction notice (pooling notice or notice of generic referral of tax arrangements) under the General Anti Abuse Rule; Follower Notice; or finality of counteraction on arrangements notified or notifiable to HMRC under the DOTAS regime.

The second condition is that the relevant counteraction was made on the basis that a particular avoidance related rule applies in relation to a person's affairs. Paragraph 25 defines an "avoidance related rule" relief for the purposes of the Schedule as a rule in category 1 or 2. Category 1 refers instance where the main purpose or purposes of a transaction, arrangements or other action or matter involves the avoidance of tax or obtaining of any advantage in relation to tax however described. Subsection (3) clarifies how wide the meaning is by ensuring expected benefits are caught and not limiting the rule to "sole or main" or "one of the main" benefits.

The third condition is that each of the relevant defeats relates to misused relief as set out on para 19(5) and loss relief under Pt 4 ITA 2007 or Pt 4 or 5 CTA 2010.

The relevant arrangements must relate to the misuse of relief and para 19(5) defines this as the tax advantage (or part of the advantage) results from a relief or increased relief or it is reasonable to conclude the claim or use of a relief is a significant component of the arrangements.

The restriction relief notice must explain the restriction of relief, the period it applies and the right to appeal where there is a reasonable excuse.

Where a restriction relief notice has been issued the person may not in the restricted period make any claim for relief. Certain reliefs relating to charities, international double taxation agreements and registered pension schemes are excluded.

The restrictions that apply are for either a relevant tax year or relevant accounting period falling within the restriction period and include the surrender of group relief, carry forward of trading losses for income tax and corporation tax purposes, relief for annual payments, management expenses of a company's investment business, CGT loss relief including those against annual tax on enveloped dwellings and non-resident capital gains tax gains, company losses made in a UK property business and deemed payments by trustees of an exempt unauthorised unit trust. A relevant tax year or relevant accounting period means a period the first day of which is in the restricted period.

Paragraph 21 sets out the restricted period to be three years beginning with the day on which the restriction notice is given. HMRC must give the person a restriction period extension notice where there is a further relevant defeat incurred by virtue of condition A, B or C and the warning notice relates to a misuse of a relief.

Furthermore, under para 21(5), HMRC must give a person a restriction of relief notice where there is a relevant defeat after the restriction period (three years) has expired but a concurrent warning period has not expired (five years). The definition of "concurrent warning period" at para 21(6) means a warning period which at some time ran concurrently with the restricted period.

Where person satisfies HMRC or, on an appeal, the First Tier Tribunal or Upper Tribunal that he has a reasonable excuse for the defeat, para 22 provides that a relevant defeat is disregarded for a restriction of relief notice.

Reasonable excuse for the purposes of the paragraph is further defined by sub-s (?), which excludes insufficiency of funds unless attributable to events outside of control. It also excludes reliance on another person unless the person took reasonable care to avoid the relevant failure. However, where there is a reasonable excuse but the excuse had ceased, the reasonable excuse will only by valid where the failure is remedied without unreasonable delay. Interestingly, sub-s (3) prevents the reasonable excuse where advice was provided and that advice was given to another person or takes no account of the person's circumstances. This appears to place the onus on the person to make sure the advice they receive is tailored to them, which is an attack on how promoters of schematic planning have historically provided blanket advice.

Paragraph 24 provides a right to appeal against a relief restriction notice or restricted period extension notice within 30 days on which the notice is given. An appeal under para 24 is to be treated in the same way as an appeal against an assessment to income tax.

Paragraph 26 sets out the meaning of relief, which includes any relief that must be claimed or an election made as well as those set out above.

Paragraph 27 defines what a claim for relief.

Paragraph 29 gives power to the Treasury to make regulations amending paras 20 and 26 to effectively change application, widen or limit the applicability to reliefs. Regulations must be made by Statutory Instrument and a draft must be laid and approved by the House of Commons.

Part 5 Penalty

Paragraph 30 sets out the liability to a penalty where a person incurs a relevant defeat in relation to any arrangements the person used in a warning period. The penalty is 20% of the counteracted advantage although increases to 40% where there is one relevant prior warning notice and 60% where there are two or more relevant warning notices.

Paragraph 31 sets out the treatment where a person incurs simultaneous defeats in relation to different arrangements. The defeat with the lowest value of counteracted value is treated as being incurred last. Where a single warning notice is issued for two or more relevant defeats, each defeat is treated for para 30 purposes as a separate notice.

Paragraph 32 defines the value of the counteracted advantage for direct taxes as the additional amount due or payable as a result of the counteraction. Adjustment may be made in calculating the counteracted advantage of group relief and relief in respect of repayment etc of loan (CTA 2010 s 458).

Paragraph 33 makes provisions where the counteracted advantage includes wrongly recorded losses. It provides that 10% of any part of a loss not used to reduce the amount of tax due and payable shall be included in the value of the denied advantage. Paragraph 33(5) provides that where a group of companies has an aggregate loss for Corporation Tax, group relief is not disregarded when calculating the denied advantage.

Paragraph 34 quantifies the tax advantage (other than VAT) where the counteracted advantage is a deferral of tax. The value is 25% of the deferred tax for each year or equating to 25% per year where the period of deferral is less than a year, or if less, 100% of the deferred tax. Paragraph 37 has the effect of replicating the position for VAT.

Paragraphs 35 and 36 define counteracted advantage for direct taxes and VAT respectively. Paragraph 35 refers to condition A, B and C whereas para 36, condition D and E. Paragraph 36 sets out a method for ascertaining the counteracted tax advantage being broadly the difference between the VAT due or payable and that so payable but for the counteraction. The same principle is applied with regard to a VAT credit position and non-deductible expenses.

Under para 38, HMRC must assess the penalty and notify the person so liable and state in the notice the tax period in which the penalty is assessed. The assessment must be made before the end of 12 months from the date of the defeat. The penalty must be paid at the end of 30 days on which the person is notified of the penalty and is to be treated as if it were an assessment to tax and enforced as such.

Paragraph 40 deals with situations where more than one penalty may arise in respect of the same tax liability thereby reducing the penalty under para 30 by the amount of other penalties.

A right to appeal the penalty is set out in para 41. The appeal must be made within 30 days beginning with the day of notification was given. The penalty does not have to be paid in order to make an appeal. The appeal is to be treated in the same way as an appeal against an assessment to tax.

Where person satisfies HMRC or, following a successful appeal, the First Tier Tribunal or Upper Tribunal, that he has a reasonable excuse for the relevant failure, para 42 allows that there will be no liability to the penalty.

Reasonable excuse for the purposes of para 42 excludes an insufficiency of funds unless attributable to events outside of the person's control. Reliance on another person, unless the person took reasonable care to avoid the relevant failure, is similarly excluded.

Where there is a reasonable excuse but the excuse had ceased, the reasonable excuse will only by valid where the failure is remedied without unreasonable delay. Reasonable excuse is prevented where advice was given to another person or takes no account of the person's circumstances.

Paragraph 44 permits the commissioners to mitigate a para 30 penalty.

Part 6 Corporate Groups, Associated Persons and Partnerships

HMRC has a duty to give a warning notice to a company which is a member of a group and is notice treated as being given to each current group member.

HMRC must issue a warning notice to each member of a corporate group when any one member of the group incurs a relevant defeat. Furthermore, para 46(3) provides that a warning notice issued to a company before it becomes a member of a corporate group is treated as issued to each group member although para 46(4) provides that no account is taken of this notice in relation to a relief restriction notice or penalties (para 46(5)).

Paragraph 46(7) deals with companies leaving a group where if it were not for another member they would not have been given a warning notice, the warning period ceases at the time they cease to be a member.

Paragraphs 47 widens the scope of the legislation to catch "associated persons" which is clearly defined by paragraph 48.

Paragraph 50 sets out when para 49 applies to a partnership return. Broadly where a tax advantage arises to a partner in relation to the partnership return and there is a relevant defeat of Condition A, B or C, each relevant partner is treated as incurring a relevant defeat. Paragraph 51 introduces the partnership information notice (PIN) where para 50 applies. A reporting obligation over a five-year period begins for the purposes of HMRC obtaining information in relation to partnership returns. The information period is split into sub-periods of 12 months or to the end of the information period if shorter. The information notice requires notification whether a return contains a relevant tax advantage and whether there has been a failure to deliver a relevant partnership return. A relevant tax advantage is defined as one arising or being capable of arising from DOTAS arrangements for a partner or a previous partner. It is noted that a tax advantage does not actually have to be obtained to be a relevant tax advantage. The notice can require the arrangements to be explained and variations in the return arising from those arrangements, which is likely to assist issuing, where appropriate, accurate accelerated payment notices or assessments. A partner (the appropriate partner, who is nominated by HMRC) may also be issued with a supplementary information notice requiring further information than the PIN. Failure to respond to notices can result in an extension to the information period.

Part 7 Supplemental

Part 7 includes various definitions, clarifications and provisions giving effect to the Schedule.

Paragraph 48 defines the time of use of defeated arrangements.

Paragraph 56 details the commencement of the regime from the day after the Act is passed. Paragraph 57 provides that any arrangements a person enters into which is defeated on or after 6 April 2017 will qualify as defeated arrangement. Where, before 6 April 2017, a person makes a full disclosure of the arrangements or notifies their intention to do so to HMRC, a relevant defeat will be disregarded.

Arrangements entered into and defeated between the day the Act is passed and 6 April 2017 will qualify as defeated arrangements. Paragraph 58 provides that defeated arrangements entered into before the Act is passed will be disregarded for the purposes of penalties, naming and restricting reliefs.

SCHEDULE 19

LARGE BUSINESSES: TAX STRATEGIES AND SANCTIONS

Section 161

PART 1

INTERPRETATION

Purpose of Part 1

1 This Part defines terms for the purposes of this Schedule.

"Relevant body"

2 (1) "Relevant body" means a UK company or any other body corporate (wherever incorporated), but does not include a limited liability partnership.

(2) A relevant body is a "foreign" relevant body (or member of a group or sub-group) if it is incorporated outside the United Kingdom.

"UK company"

3 (1) "UK company" means a company which is (or is treated as if it is) formed and registered under the Companies Act 2006, unless it falls within sub-paragraph (2).

(2) The term "UK company" does not include a company which is—

(a) an open-ended investment company within the meaning of section 613 of CTA 2010, or

(b) an investment trust within the meaning of section 1158 of CTA 2010.

"UK permanent establishment"

4 (1) "UK permanent establishment" means a permanent establishment in the United Kingdom of a foreign relevant body.

(2) In sub-paragraph (1) "permanent establishment" has the same meaning as it has for the purposes of the Corporation Tax Acts (see section 1141 to 1144 of CTA 2010).

"Qualifying company"

5 (1) A UK company is a "qualifying company" in any financial year (subject to any regulations under sub-paragraph (5)) if sub-paragraph (2) or (3) applies to it.

(2) This sub-paragraph applies to the company if, at the end of the previous financial year—

(a) it satisfied the qualification test for a UK company, and

(b) was not a member of a UK group or a UK sub-group.

(3) This sub-paragraph applies to the company if, at the end of the previous financial year—

(a) it was a member of a foreign group,

(b) the group met the qualification test for a group, and

(c) it was not a member of a UK sub-group of that foreign group.

(4) The qualification test for a UK company is that the company satisfied either or both of the following conditions (by reference to the previous financial year)—

1 The company's turnover	More than £200 million
2 The company's balance sheet total	More than £2 billion.

(5) The Treasury may by regulations provide that a company of a description specified in the regulations is not a qualifying company for the purposes of this Schedule (or any such purpose specified in the regulations).

(6) For the purposes of this paragraph a UK permanent establishment of a foreign relevant body is to be treated as if it were—

(a) a UK company, and

(b) if the foreign relevant body is a member of a UK group or a UK sub-group, a member of that group or sub-group.

"Group" and related expressions

6 (1) "Group" means two or more relevant bodies which together constitute—

(a) an MNE Group (see paragraph 7), or

(b) a group other than an MNE group (see paragraph 8).

(2) "UK group" means a group whose head is a relevant body incorporated in the United Kingdom.

(3) "Foreign group" means a group whose head is a foreign relevant body.

(4) For the purposes of sub-paragraphs (2) and (3) it is immaterial where other members of the group are incorporated.

7 (1) "MNE Group" has the same meaning (subject to sub-paragraph (2) below) as in the OECD Model Legislation in the OECD Country-by-Country Reporting Implementation Package as contained in the OECD's Guidance on Transfer Pricing Documentation and Country-by-Country Reporting published in 2014.

(2) Paragraph (ii) (excluded MNE Group) of the Implementation Package is not part of the definition applied by sub-paragraph (1) above for the purposes of this Schedule.

(3) In sub-paragraph (1) "OECD" means the Organisation for Economic Co-operation and Development.

8 (1) A "group other than an MNE group" means a group consisting of two or more relevant bodies—

    (a) each of which is a member of the group by virtue of sub-paragraph (3) or (4),

    (b) at least two of which are UK companies,

which is not an MNE Group.

(2) For the purposes of the condition in sub-paragraph (1)(b) a UK permanent establishment of a foreign member of a group is to be treated as if it were a UK company and a member of the group.

(3) A relevant body is a member of a group if—

    (a) another relevant body is its 51% subsidiary, or

    (b) it is a 51% subsidiary of another relevant body.

(4) Two relevant bodies are members of the same group if—

    (a) one is a 51% subsidiary of the other, or

    (b) both are 51% subsidiaries of another relevant body.

(5) Chapter 3 of Part 24 of CTA 2010 (meaning of 51% subsidiary) applies for the purposes of this Schedule as it applies for the purposes of the Corporation Tax Acts (but with the modification in sub-paragraph (6)).

(6) It applies as if references to a body corporate were references to a relevant body.

9 A group is headed by whichever relevant body within the group is not a 51% subsidiary of another relevant body within the group (and "head", in relation to the group, means that body).

"Qualifying group"

10 (1) A group is a "qualifying group" in any financial year if, at the end of the previous financial year—

    (a) in the case of a group other than an MNE Group, the group satisfied the qualification test for such a group (subject to any regulations under sub-paragraph (6)), or

    (b) in the case of an MNE Group—

        (i) there was a mandatory reporting requirement in respect of the group under regulations made under section 122 of FA 2015 (country-by-country reporting), or

        (ii) there would have been such a requirement if the head of the group were resident in the United Kingdom for tax purposes.

(2) The qualification test for a group other than an MNE Group is that the group satisfied either or both of the following conditions (by reference to the previous financial year)—

1 Group turnover	More than £200 million
2 Group balance sheet total	More than £2 billion.

(3) In sub-paragraph (2)—

    (a) "group turnover" means the aggregate turnover of the UK companies that are members of the group at the end of the previous financial year, and

    (b) "group balance sheet total", means the aggregate balance sheet totals for all those UK companies.

(4) Where the financial year of a UK company within in the group does not end on the same day as the previous financial year of the head of the group, the figures from the company that are to be included in the aggregate figures are those for the company's financial year ending last before the end of the previous financial year of the head of the group.

(5) For the purposes of assessing the turnover or balance sheet total of the group, sub-paragraphs (3) and (4) apply as if a UK permanent establishment of a foreign member of the group were a UK company and a member of the group.

(6) The Treasury may by regulations provide—

(a) that a group other than an MNE Group which is of a specified description is not a qualifying group for the purposes, or any specified purpose, of this Schedule, or

(b) that a relevant body, or a UK permanent establishment, of a specified description is to be disregarded in determining whether the qualification test is satisfied by a group other than an MNE Group;

and in this sub-paragraph "specified" means specified in the regulations.

(7) In this paragraph "financial year", in relation to a group, means a financial year of the head of the group.

"UK sub-group" and "head" (in relation to a UK sub-group)

11 (1) A "UK sub-group" consists of two or more relevant bodies that would be a UK group, but for the fact that they are members of a larger group headed by a relevant body incorporated outside the United Kingdom.

(2) A UK sub-group is headed by the company or other relevant body incorporated in the United Kingdom that is not a 51% subsidiary of another member of the UK sub-group (and "head", in relation to the sub-group, means that company or body).

"UK partnership", "qualifying partnership" and "representative partner"

12 (1) "UK partnership" means a body of any of the following descriptions which is carrying on a trade, business or profession with a view to profit—

(a) a partnership within the meaning of the Partnership Act 1890,

(b) a limited partnership registered under the Limited Partnerships Act 1907, or

(c) a limited liability partnership incorporated in the United Kingdom.

(2) A UK partnership is a "qualifying partnership" in a financial year, if it satisfied the qualification test for a UK partnership at the end of the previous financial year (subject to any regulations under sub-paragraph (4)).

(3) The qualification test for a UK partnership is that the partnership satisfied either or both of the following conditions (by reference to the previous financial year)—

1 The partnership's turnover	More than £200 million
2 The partnership's balance sheet total	More than £2 billion.

(4) The Treasury may by regulations provide that a UK partnership of a description specified in the regulations is not a qualifying partnership for the purposes of this Schedule (or any such purpose specified in the regulations).

(5) "Representative partner", in relation to a UK partnership, means the partner who is required by a notice served under or by virtue of section 12AA(2) or (3) of TMA 1970 to make and deliver returns to an officer of HMRC.

"Financial year"

13 "Financial year"—

(a) in relation to a UK company, has the meaning given by the Companies Act 2006 (see section 390 of that Act),

(b) in relation to any other relevant body, means any period in respect of which a profit and loss account for the body's undertaking is required to be made up (whether by its constitution or by the law under which it is established), whether that period is a year or not,

(c) in relation to a UK partnership, means any period of account for which its representative partner has provided or is required to provide a partnership statement under a return issued under section 12AB TMA 1970.

"Turnover" and "balance sheet total"

14 (1) "Turnover"—

(a) in relation to a UK company, has the same meaning as in Part 15 of the Companies Act 2006 (see section 474 of that Act), and

(b) in relation to a UK partnership or a UK permanent establishment, has a corresponding meaning.

(2) "Balance sheet total", in relation to a UK company, UK partnership or UK permanent establishment and a financial year, means the aggregate of the amounts shown as assets in its balance sheet at the end of the financial year.

"UK taxation"

15 (1) "UK taxation" means —

(a) income tax,

(b) corporation tax, including any amount assessable or chargeable as if it were corporation tax or treated as if it were corporation tax,

(c) value added tax,

(d) amounts for which the company is accountable under PAYE regulations,

(e) diverted profits tax,

(f) insurance premium tax,

(g) annual tax on enveloped dwellings,

(h) stamp duty land tax,

(i) stamp duty reserve tax,

(j) petroleum revenue tax;

(k) customs duties,

(l) excise duties,

(m) national insurance contributions.

(2) In relation to a tax strategy required to be published by Part 2, "UK taxation" refers to the taxes or duties mentioned above so far as relating to or affecting the bodies or body to which the required tax strategy relates.

PART 2

PUBLICATION OF TAX STRATEGIES

Qualifying UK groups: duty to publish a group tax strategy

16 (1) This paragraph applies in relation to a UK group which is a qualifying group in any financial year ("the current financial year").

(2) The head of the group must ensure that a group tax strategy for the group, containing the information required by paragraph 17, is prepared and published on behalf of the group in accordance with this paragraph.

(3) The group tax strategy—

(a) must be published before the end of the current financial year, and

(b) if the group was a qualifying group in the previous financial year, must not be published more than 15 months after the day on which its previous group tax strategy was published.

(4) The group tax strategy—

(a) must be published on the internet by any of the UK companies that are members of the group so as to be accessible to the public free of charge (whether or not it is also published in any other way), and

(b) may be published as a separate document or as a self-contained part of a wider document

(5) The head of the group must ensure that the group tax strategy published on the internet remains accessible to the public free of charge—

(a) if a group tax strategy for the group's next financial year is required by this paragraph to be published, until that tax strategy is published, or

(b) if paragraph (a) does not apply, for at least one year.

(6) For the purposes of this paragraph—

(a) a group tax strategy is published when it is first published on the internet as mentioned in paragraph (4)(a),

(b) the identity of the group is not to be regarded as altered by any change in its membership during the current financial year resulting from a relevant body—

(i) becoming a 51% subsidiary of a member of the group, or

(ii) ceasing to be a 51% subsidiary of another member of the group; and

(c) if the group becomes a UK sub-group of a foreign group during the current financial year, it is to be treated for the rest of that year as if it were still a UK group.

(7) In this paragraph and paragraph 17 "financial year", in relation to a UK group, means a financial year of the head of the group.

Content of group tax strategy

17 (1) A group tax strategy required to be published on behalf of a UK group by paragraph 16 must set out—

(a) the approach of the group to risk management and governance arrangements in relation to UK taxation,

(b) the attitude of the group towards tax planning (so far as affecting UK taxation),
(c) the level of risk in relation to UK taxation that the group is prepared to accept, and
(d) the approach of the group towards its dealings with HMRC.

(2) The group tax strategy may—

(a) include other information relating to taxation (whether UK taxation or otherwise), and
(b) deal with a matter mentioned in sub-paragraph (1) by reference to the group as a whole or to individual members of the group (or to both).

(3) The information required by sub-paragraph (1) to be included in the group tax strategy does not include any information about activities of any member of the group that consists of the provision of tax advice or related professional services to persons who are not members of the group.

(4) The publication of information as the group tax strategy does not constitute publication of the strategy for the purposes of paragraph 16 unless the UK company publishing it makes clear (in a way that will be readily apparent to anyone accessing the information online) that the company regards its publication as complying with the duty under paragraph 16(2) in the current financial year.

(5) For the purposes of this paragraph a UK permanent establishment of a foreign member of the group is to be treated as if it were a member of the group.

(6) The Treasury may by regulations require the group tax strategy to include a country-by-country report.

(7) In this paragraph "country-by-country report" has the meaning given by the Taxes (Base Erosion and Profit Shifting) (Country-by-Country Reporting) Regulations 2016.

Penalty for non-compliance with paragraph 16

18 (1) This paragraph applies where paragraph 16 requires a group tax strategy to be published for a UK group in any financial year of the head of the UK group.

(2) The head of the group is liable to a penalty of £7,500 if—

(a) there is a failure to publish a group tax strategy for the group that complies with paragraph 16(2), or
(b) where a group tax strategy has been published, there is a failure to comply with paragraph 16(5).

(3) Subject to sub-paragraph (5) the head of the group is only liable to one penalty by virtue of sub-paragraph (2) in respect of a group tax strategy required for the financial year in question.

(4) Sub-paragraph (5) applies where—

(a) the head of the group is liable to a penalty under this paragraph in respect of a failure mentioned in sub-paragraph (2)(a), and
(b) no group tax strategy for the group that complies with paragraph 16(2) (disregarding paragraph 16(3)) is published within the period of 6 months after the last day on which the duty under paragraph 16(2) could have been complied with.

(5) At the end of that period, the head of the group—

(a) is liable to a further penalty of £7,500, and
(b) where the failure mentioned in sub-paragraph (4)(b) continues, is liable to a further penalty of £7,500 at the end of each subsequent month in which no such group tax strategy is published.

UK sub-groups: duty to publish a sub-group tax strategy

19 (1) This paragraph applies to a UK sub-group of a foreign group if in any financial year ("the current financial year") the foreign group is a qualifying group.

(2) The head of the sub-group must ensure that a sub-group tax strategy for the sub-group, giving the information required by paragraph 20, is prepared and published in accordance with this paragraph.

(3) The sub-group tax strategy—

(a) must be published before the end of the current financial year, and
(b) if the group of which the sub-group is part was a qualifying group in the previous financial year, must not be published more than 15 months after the day on which its sub-group tax strategy for that year was published;

(4) The sub-group tax strategy—

(a) must be published on the internet by any of the UK companies that are members of the foreign group so as to be accessible to the public free of charge (whether or not it is also published in any other way), and

(b) may be published as a separate document or as a self-contained part of a wider document.

(5) The head of the sub-group must ensure that the sub-group tax strategy published on the internet remains accessible to the public free of charge—

(a) if a sub-group tax strategy for the sub-group's next financial year is required by this paragraph to be published, until that tax strategy is published, or

(b) if paragraph (a) does not apply, for at least one year.

(6) For the purposes of this paragraph—

(a) a sub-group tax strategy is published when it is first published on the internet as mentioned in sub-paragraph (4)(a),

(b) the identity of the sub-group is not affected by any change in its membership in the current financial year resulting from a relevant body becoming or ceasing to be a 51% subsidiary of a member of the sub-group, and

(c) if the sub-group becomes a UK sub-group of another foreign group during the current financial year, for the rest of that year it is to be treated as if it were still a UK sub-group of the original foreign group (but only a UK company within the sub-group may publish a sub-group tax strategy for the sub-group after that change).

(7) In this paragraph "financial year", in relation to a UK sub-group, means a financial year of the head of the group of which it is a sub-group.

Content of a sub-group tax strategy

20 (1) Paragraph 17 applies in relation to a sub-group tax strategy required to be published on behalf of a UK sub-group by paragraph 19 as it applies to a group tax strategy required to be published by a qualifying UK group.

(2) In the application of paragraph 17 to a sub-group tax strategy, references to the group or members of the group are to be read as references to the UK sub-group or members of the UK sub-group.

(3) In the application of paragraph 17 as modified by this paragraph to a sub-group tax strategy, a UK permanent establishment of a foreign member of the UK sub-group is to be treated as if it were a member of the sub-group.

Penalty for non-compliance with requirements of paragraph 19

21 (1) This paragraph applies where paragraph 19 requires a sub-group tax strategy to be published for a UK sub-group in any financial year of the head of the sub-group.

(2) The head of the sub-group is liable to a penalty of £7,500 if—

(a) there is a failure to publish a sub-group tax strategy for the sub-group that complies with paragraph 19(2), or

(b) where a sub-group tax strategy has been published, there is a failure to comply with paragraph 19(5).

(3) Subject to sub-paragraph (5), the head of the sub-group is only liable to one penalty by virtue of sub-paragraph (2) in respect of a sub-group tax strategy required for the financial year in question.

(4) Sub-paragraph (5) applies where—

(a) the head of the sub-group is liable to a penalty under this paragraph in respect of a failure mentioned in sub-paragraph (2)(a), and

(b) no sub-group tax strategy for the sub-group that complies with paragraph 19(2) (disregarding paragraph 19(3)) is published within the period of 6 months after the last day on which the duty under paragraph 19(2) could have been complied with.

(5) At the end of that period, the head of the sub-group is liable—

(a) to a further penalty of £7,500, and

(b) where the failure mentioned in sub-paragraph (4)(b) continues, to a further penalty of £7,500 at the end of each subsequent month in which no such sub-group tax strategy is published.

Qualifying companies: duty to publish a company tax strategy

22 (1) This paragraph applies in relation to a UK company which in any financial year ("the current financial year") is a qualifying company.

(2) The company must prepare and publish a company tax strategy, containing the information required by paragraph 23, in accordance with this paragraph.

(3) The duty under sub-paragraph (2) applies even if the company becomes a member of a UK group or a UK sub-group during the current financial year.

(4) The company tax strategy—

(a) must be published by the company before the end of the current financial year, and

(b) if the company was a qualifying company in the previous financial year, must not be published more than 15 months after the day on which its company tax strategy was published in the previous financial year.

(5) The company tax strategy—

(a) must be published on the internet so as to be accessible to the public free of charge (whether or not published in any other way), and

(b) may be published as a separate document or a self- contained part of a wider document.

(6) The company must ensure that the company tax strategy published on the internet remains accessible to the public free of charge—

(a) if a company tax strategy for the next financial year is required by this paragraph to be published, until that tax strategy is published, or

(b) if paragraph (a) does not apply, for at least one year.

(7) For the purposes of this paragraph a company tax strategy is published when it is first published as mentioned in sub-paragraph (5)(a).

(8) A UK permanent establishment which in any financial year is by virtue of paragraph 5(6) to be treated as a qualifying company is to be treated for the purposes of this paragraph and paragraphs 23 and 24 as if it were a UK company which in that financial year is a qualifying company.

Content of a company tax strategy

23 (1) The company tax strategy must set out—

(a) the company's approach to risk management and governance arrangements in relation to UK taxation,

(b) the company's attitude towards tax planning (so far as affecting UK taxation),

(c) the level of risk in relation to UK taxation that the company is prepared to accept,

(d) the company's approach towards its dealings with HMRC.

(2) The company tax strategy may include other information relating to taxation (whether UK taxation or otherwise).

(3) The information required by sub-paragraph (1) to be included in a company tax strategy does not include any information about activities of the company that consist of the provision of tax advice or related professional services to other persons.

(4) The publication of information as a company tax strategy does not constitute publication of the strategy for the purposes of paragraph 22 unless the company makes clear (in a way that will be readily apparent to anyone accessing the information online) that the company regards its publication as complying with the duty under paragraph 22(2) in the current financial year.

Penalty for non-compliance with paragraph 22

24 (1) This paragraph applies where paragraph 22 requires a company tax strategy to be published for a UK company in any financial year.

(2) The company is liable to a penalty of £7,500 if—

(a) there is a failure to publish a company tax strategy for the company that complies with paragraph 22(2), or

(b) where a company tax strategy has been published, there is a failure to comply with paragraph 22(6).

(3) Subject to sub-paragraph (5), the company is only liable to one penalty by virtue of sub-paragraph (2) in respect of a company tax strategy required for the financial year in question.

(4) Sub-paragraph (5) applies where—

(a) a penalty is imposed under this paragraph in respect of a failure mentioned in sub-paragraph (2)(a), and

(b) no company tax strategy that complies with paragraph 22(2) (disregarding paragraph 22(4)) is published within the period of 6 months after the last day on which the duty under paragraph 22(2) could have been complied with.

(5) At the end of that period, the company is liable—

(a) to a further penalty of £7,500, and

(b) where the failure mentioned in sub-paragraph (4)(b) continues, to a further penalty of £7,500 at the end of each subsequent month in which no such company tax strategy is published.

Qualifying partnerships: duty to publish a partnership tax strategy

25 (1) Paragraphs 22 to 24 apply in relation to a UK partnership which is (in any financial year of the partnership) a qualifying partnership as they apply to a UK company which is (in any financial year of the company) a qualifying company.

(2) Those paragraphs have effect in their application to a qualifying partnership—

(a) with the omission of paragraph 22(3) and (8),

(b) as if for "company tax strategy" (in each place) there were substituted "partnership tax strategy", and

(c) as if for "company" and "company's" (in each place) there were substituted respectively "partnership" and "partnership's".

Penalties under this Part: general provisions

26 (1) Paragraphs 27 to 33 apply in relation to the liability of any person to a penalty under this Part and, accordingly, in those paragraphs—

"failure", in relation to a liability for a penalty, means a failure which could give rise to that liability,

"liability to a penalty" means a liability under paragraph 18, 21 or 24 (including paragraph 24 as applied to a qualifying UK partnership), and

"penalty" means a penalty under any of those paragraphs.

(2) In those paragraphs "tribunal" means the First-tier Tribunal or, where determined by or under the Tribunal Procedure Rules, the Upper Tribunal.

Failure to comply with a time limit

27 A failure to do anything required by this Part to be done within a limited period of time does not give rise to liability to a penalty if it is done within such further time (if any) as an officer of Revenue and Customs may have allowed.

Reasonable excuse

28 (1) Liability to a penalty for a failure does not arise if the person who would otherwise be liable to that penalty satisfies HMRC or (on an appeal notified to the tribunal) the tribunal that the person had a reasonable excuse for that failure.

(2) For the purposes of this paragraph—

(a) an insufficiency of funds is not a reasonable excuse unless attributable to events outside the person's control,

(b) where the person relies on another person to do anything, that cannot be a reasonable excuse—

(i) unless the first person took reasonable care to avoid the failure, or

(ii) if the first person is a UK group or UK sub-group, where the person relied on is another member of the group or sub-group,

(c) where the person had a reasonable excuse but the excuse has ceased, the person is to be treated as having continued to have the excuse if the failure is remedied without unreasonable delay after the excuse ceased.

Assessment of penalties

29 (1) Where a person becomes liable to a penalty—

(a) HMRC may assess the penalty, and

(b) if they do so, HMRC must notify the person of the assessment.

(2) An assessment of a penalty may not be made—

(a) more than 6 months after the failure first comes to the attention of an officer of Revenue and Customs, or

(b) more than 6 years after the end of the financial year in which the tax strategy to which the failure relates was (or was originally) required to be published.

Appeal

30 (1) A person may appeal against a decision of HMRC that a penalty is payable by that person.

(2) Notice of an appeal must be given—

(a) in writing,

(b) before the end of the period of 30 days beginning with the date on which the notification under paragraph 29(1)(b) was issued,

(3) Notice of an appeal must state the grounds of appeal.

(4) On an appeal that is notified to the tribunal, the tribunal may confirm or cancel the decision.

(5) Subject to this paragraph and paragraph 31, the provisions of Part 5 of TMA 1970 relating to appeals have effect in relation to appeals under this Schedule as they have effect in relation to an appeal against an assessment to income tax.

Enforcement

31 (1) A penalty must be paid—

(a) before the end of the period of 30 days beginning with the date on which the notification under paragraph 29(1)(b) was issued, or

(b) if a notice of appeal is given, before the end of 30 days beginning with the day on which the appeal is determined or withdrawn.

(2) A penalty may be enforced as if it were corporation tax charged in an assessment and due and payable.

Power to change amount of penalties

32 (1) If it appears to the Treasury that there has been a change in the value of money since the last relevant date, they may by regulations substitute for any sums for the time being specified in paragraph 18, 21 or 24 such other sum as appear to them to be justified by the change.

(2) In sub-paragraph (1) "relevant date" means—

(a) the date on which this Act is passed, and

(b) each date on which the power conferred by that sub-paragraph has been exercised.

(3) Regulations under this paragraph do not apply to a failure that occurs in respect of a financial year (of the body or partnership responsible for the failure) that begins before the date on which they come into force.

Application of provisions of TMA 1970

33 Subject to the provisions of this Part, the following provisions of TMA 1970 apply for the purposes of this Part as they apply for the purposes of the Taxes Acts—

(a) section 108 (responsibility of company officers),

(b) section 114 (want of form), and

(c) section 115 (delivery and service of documents).

Meaning of "tax strategy"

34 In this Part "tax strategy" means—

(a) a group tax strategy (see paragraphs 16 to 18),

(b) a sub-group tax strategy (see paragraphs 19 to 21),

(c) a company tax strategy (see paragraphs 22 to 24), or

(d) a partnership tax strategy (see paragraph 25).

PART 3
SANCTIONS FOR PERSISTENTLY UNCO-OPERATIVE LARGE BUSINESSES

Large groups falling within Part 3

35 A UK group falls within this Part of this Schedule ("this Part") if—

(a) the group has persistently engaged in unco-operative behaviour (see paragraphs 36 to 38),

(b) some or all of the unco-operative behaviour has caused there to be, or contributed to there being, two or more significant tax issues in respect of the group or members of the group which are unresolved (see paragraph 39), and

(c) there is a reasonable likelihood of further instances of the group engaging in unco-operative behaviour in a manner which causes there to be, or contributes to there being, significant tax issues in respect of the group or members of the group.

36 (1) A UK group has "engaged in unco-operative behaviour" if—

(a) a member of the group has satisfied either or both of the conditions listed in sub-paragraph (2), or

(b) two or more of the members of the group, taken together, have satisfied either or both of those conditions.

(2) Those conditions are—

    (a) the behaviour condition (see paragraph 37);

    (b) the arrangements condition (see paragraph 38).

(3) A UK group has engaged in unco-operative behaviour "persistently" if—

    (a) a member of the group has done so persistently, or

    (b) two or more members of the group, taken together, have done so persistently.

(4) References in this Part to doing something "persistently" include doing it on a sufficient number of occasions for it to be clear that it represents a pattern of behaviour.

37 (1) A member of a UK group has, or two or more members of a UK group (taken together) have, "satisfied the behaviour condition" if it has, or they have, behaved in a manner which has delayed or otherwise hindered HMRC in the exercise of their functions in connection with determining the liability to UK taxation of the group or a member of the group.

(2) Factors which may indicate that a member of a UK group has behaved as described in sub-paragraph (1) include—

    (a) the extent to which HMRC have used statutory powers to obtain information relating to the UK group or members of the group;

    (b) the reasons why those powers have been used;

    (c) the number and seriousness of inaccuracies in, and omissions from, documents given to HMRC by or on behalf of the UK group or members of the group;

    (d) the extent to which, in dealings with HMRC, members of the group (or people acting on their behalf) have relied on interpretations of legislation relating to UK taxation which, at the time, are speculative.

(3) An interpretation of legislation relating to UK taxation is "speculative" if it is likely that a court or tribunal would disagree with it.

38 (1) A member of a UK group has "satisfied the arrangements condition" if it is a party to a tax avoidance scheme.

(2) "Tax avoidance scheme" means—

    (a) arrangements in respect of which a notice of final decision has been given under—

        (i) paragraph 12 of Schedule 43 to FA 2013,

        (ii) paragraph 5 or 6 of Schedule 43A to FA 2013, or

        (iii) paragraph 9 of Schedule 43B to FA 2013,

stating that a tax advantage arising from the arrangements is to be counteracted;

    (b) arrangements which are notifiable arrangements for the purposes of Part 7 of FA 2004 (disclosure of tax avoidance schemes), other than arrangements in relation to which HMRC have given notice under section 312(6) of FA 2004 (notice that promoters not under duty to provide clients with prescribed information);

    (c) a scheme which is a notifiable scheme for the purposes of Schedule 11A to VATA 1994 (disclosure of avoidance schemes).

39 (1) There is a significant tax issue in respect of a UK group or a member of a UK group where—

    (a) there is a disagreement between HMRC and a member of the group about an issue affecting the amount of the liability of the group or a member of the group to UK taxation,

    (b) the issue has been, or could be, referred to a court or tribunal to determine, and

    (c) as regards the amount of the liability, the difference between HMRC's view and the view of the member is, or is likely to be, not less than £2 million.

(2) The reference in sub-paragraph (1)(a) to circumstances in which there is a disagreement include circumstances in which there is a reasonable likelihood of a disagreement.

(3) The Treasury may by regulations substitute a higher amount for the amount for the time being specified in sub-paragraph (1)(c).

40 The references in paragraphs 36 to 39 to things done by a member of a UK group ("the group in question")—

    (a) include acts and omissions of a relevant body that is not a member of the group in question if they took place at a time when the relevant body was a member of a group headed by the body that is the head of the group in question;

    (b) do not include acts or omissions of a relevant body that is a member of the group in question if they took place at a time when the relevant body was not a member of a group headed by the body that is the head of the group in question.

Warning notices

41 (1) A designated HMRC officer may give the head of a UK group a notice under this paragraph (a "warning notice") if the officer considers that the group is a qualifying group that falls within this Part.

(2) The notice must set out the reasons why the officer considers that the group falls within this Part.

(3) The notice—

(a) may be withdrawn by a designated HMRC officer at any time by giving a further notice to the head of the group, and

(b) expires (if not previously withdrawn) at the end of the period of 15 months beginning with the day on which it was given.

(4) Once a warning notice has been given —

(a) it is immaterial for the purposes of this Part whether the group remains a qualifying group,

(b) the identity of the group is not to be regarded as altered by any change in its membership resulting from a relevant body—

(i) becoming a 51% subsidiary of a member of the group, or

(ii) ceasing to be a 51% subsidiary of another member of the group; and

(c) if the group becomes a UK sub-group of a foreign group it is to be treated as if it were still a UK group.

(5) Sub-paragraph (4) applies while the group is subject to—

(a) the warning notice, or

(b) any other notice under this Part issued as a result of the group having been given the warning notice.

Special measures notices

42 (1) This paragraph applies to a UK group if—

(a) the head of the group has been given a warning notice in relation to the group that has not been withdrawn,

(b) the period of 12 months beginning with the day on which the warning notice was given has elapsed, and

(c) the period of 15 months beginning with that day has not elapsed.

(2) If a designated HMRC officer considers that the group falls within this Part, the officer may give the head of the group a notice under this paragraph (a "special measures notice").

(3) When considering whether the group falls within this Part, the officer may take into account any relevant behaviour, whether or not it is mentioned in the warning notice.

(4) When deciding whether to give a special measures notice, the designated HMRC officer must consider any representations made by a member of the group before the end of the period of 12 months beginning with the day on which the warning notice was given.

(5) The special measures notice must set out the reasons why the officer considers that the group falls within this Part.

(6) Paragraph 45 deals with other circumstances in which a UK group may be given a special measures notice.

43 (1) A special measures notice—

(a) may be withdrawn by a designated HMRC officer at any time by giving a further notice to the head of the UK group, and

(b) expires, if not previously withdrawn, at the end of the period of 27 months beginning with the relevant day.

(2) "The relevant day" means the later of—

(a) the day on which the special measures notice was given, and

(b) the day on which it was last confirmed under paragraph 44.

44 (1) This paragraph applies to a UK group if—

(a) the head of the group has been given a special measures notice in relation to the group which has not been withdrawn,

(b) the period of 24 months beginning with the relevant day has elapsed, and

(c) the period of 27 months beginning with that day has not elapsed.

(2) If a designated HMRC officer considers that the group falls within this Part, the officer may give the head of the group a notice under this paragraph (a "confirmation notice") confirming the special measures notice given in relation to the group.

(3) When considering whether the group falls within this Part, the officer may take into account any relevant behaviour, whether or not it is mentioned in the special measures notice which is to be confirmed, in any previous confirmation notice or in the warning notice.

(4) "The relevant day" has the same meaning as in paragraph 43(2).

(5) The confirmation notice must set out the reasons why the officer considers that the group falls within this Part.

(6) When deciding whether to give a confirmation notice, a designated HMRC officer must consider any representations made by a member of the group before the end of the period of 24 months beginning with the relevant day.

(7) A confirmation notice—

(a) may be withdrawn by a designated HMRC officer at any time by giving a further notice to the head of the group, and

(b) expires, if not previously withdrawn, at the end of the period of 27 months beginning with the day on which it is given.

45 (1) This paragraph applies in relation to a UK group where—

(a) the head of the group has been given a warning notice or a special measures notice in relation to the group, and

(b) that notice has expired.

(2) A designated HMRC officer may give the head of a UK group a special measures notice if—

(a) it appears to the officer that—

(i) during the period of 6 months beginning with the day on which the notice mentioned in sub-paragraph (1)(a) expired ("the expiry day"), the group has engaged in unco-operative behaviour (see paragraphs 36 to 38), and

(ii) there is a reasonable likelihood that, if it had engaged in the behaviour before the notice expired, a designated HMRC officer would have considered that the group fell within this Part (so that a special measures notice or confirmation notice could have been given to the head of the group),

(b) during the period of 7 months beginning with the expiry day, a designated HMRC officer has notified the head of the group that the power under this paragraph may be exercised in relation to the group, and

(c) the period of 9 months beginning with that day has not elapsed.

(3) When deciding whether to give a special measures notice under this paragraph, the officer must consider any representations made by a member of the group before the end of the period of 8 months beginning with the expiry day.

Circumstances in which warning and special measures notices are treated as having been given

46 (1) Sub-paragraphs (2) and (3) apply where

(a) a relevant body ("B1") is given a warning notice, and

(b) before the notice ceases to have effect, B1 becomes a member of a group headed by another relevant body ("H1").

(2) H1 is to be treated as having been given a warning notice on the day on which the warning notice was given to B1.

(3) A warning notice treated as given under sub-paragraph (2) is valid whether or not, on the day mentioned in that sub-paragraph, H1 was the head of a qualifying UK group that fell within this Part.

(4) Sub-paragraphs (5) to (7) apply where—

(a) a relevant body ("B2") is given a special measures notice, and

(b) before the notice ceases to have effect, B2 becomes a member of a group headed by another relevant body ("H2").

(5) H2 is to be treated as having been given a special measures notice on the day on which the special measures notice was given to B2.

(6) A special measures notice treated as given under sub-paragraph (5) is valid whether or not, on the day mentioned in that sub-paragraph, H2 was the head of a qualifying UK group that fell within this Part.

(7) Paragraph 47(1) does not by virtue of sub-paragraphs (5) and (6) of this paragraph apply to an inaccuracy in a document given to HMRC by or on behalf of a person—

(a) at a time when the person was a member of a group headed by H2, but

(b) before the day B2 becomes a member of H2.

(8) Sub-paragraphs (9) and (10) apply where—

(a) a relevant body ("B3") is given a confirmation notice, and

(b) before the notice ceases to have effect, B3 becomes a member of a group headed by another relevant body ("H3").

(9) H3 is to be treated as having been given a confirmation notice on the day on which the confirmation notice was given to B3.

(10) A confirmation notice treated as given under sub-paragraph (9) is valid whether or not, on the day mentioned in that sub-paragraph, H3 was the head of a qualifying UK group that fell within this Part.

(11) The Treasury may by regulations make provision for warning notices, special measures notices and confirmation notices to be treated as having been given to relevant bodies in other circumstances described in the regulations.

(12) Regulations under this paragraph may, in particular—

(a) make provision about the validity of notices treated as given by virtue of the regulations;

(b) make provision about the effect of paragraph 47(1) in cases involving such notices.

Sanctions: liability for penalties for errors in documents given to HMRC

47 (1) For the purposes of Schedule 24 to FA 2007 (penalties for errors), an inaccuracy in a document given to HMRC by or on behalf of a person is to be treated as being due to failure by the person to take reasonable care if—

(a) the document was given to HMRC at a time when the person was a member of a group subject to a special measures notice, and

(b) the inaccuracy—

(i) relates to a tax avoidance scheme (as defined in paragraph 38) entered into by the person at a time when the person was a member of a group subject to a special measures notice, or

(ii) is, entirely or partly, attributable to an interpretation of legislation relating to UK taxation which, at the time the document was given to HMRC, was speculative.

(2) A group is "subject to a special measures notice" if a special measures notice—

(a) has been given to the head of the group in relation to the group, and

(b) is in force.

(3) An interpretation of legislation relating to UK taxation is "speculative" if it is likely that a court or tribunal would disagree with it.

(4) Sub-paragraph (1) does not apply to an inaccuracy if—

(a) it is deliberate on the part of the person or someone acting on the person's behalf,

(b) it is in fact due to a failure by the person or someone acting on the person's behalf to take reasonable care, or

(c) it is treated as due to such a failure by virtue of another enactment.

48 In Schedule 24 to FA 2007 (penalties for errors), at the end of paragraph 3 (meaning of "careless" etc) insert—

"(3) Paragraph 47 of Schedule 19 to FA 2016 (special measures for persistently unco-operative large businesses) provides for certain inaccuracies to be treated, for the purposes of this Schedule, as being due to a failure by P to take reasonable care."

Sanctions: Commissioners publishing information

49 (1) If a group is subject to a confirmed special measures notice, the Commissioners for Her Majesty's Revenue and Customs ("the Commissioners") may publish the following information—

(a) the name of the group, including any previous name;

(b) the address or registered office of the head of the group;

(c) any other information that the Commissioners consider it appropriate to publish in order to identify the group;

(d) the fact that the group is subject to a confirmed special measures notice.

(2) A group is "subject to a confirmed special measures notice" if sub-paragraph (3) or (4) is satisfied.

(3) This sub-paragraph is satisfied if—

(a) a special measures notice has been given to the head of the group and confirmed under paragraph 44, and

(b) the special measures notice is in force.

(4) This sub-paragraph is satisfied if—

(a) a special measures notice has been given to the head of the group and confirmed under paragraph 44,

(b) that notice has ceased to have effect,

(c) a further special measures notice has been given to the head of the group under paragraph 45 in the period of 9 months beginning with the day on which the special measures notice mentioned in paragraph (a) ceased to have effect, and

(d) that notice is in force.

(5) Before publishing the information, the Commissioners must—

(a) inform the head of the group that they are considering doing so, and

(b) allow the head of the group a reasonable opportunity to make representations about whether the information should be published.

(6) If, after information about a group is published under this paragraph, the group ceases to be subject to a confirmed special measures notice, the Commissioners must publish a notice stating that the group is no longer subject to a confirmed special measures notice.

(7) A notice under sub-paragraph (6) must be published before the end of the period of 30 days beginning with the day on which the special measures notice is withdrawn or has expired.

(8) The Commissioners may publish information and notices under this paragraph in any manner they consider appropriate.

Application of Part 3 to large UK sub-groups

50 (1) A UK sub-group of a foreign group falls within this Part if—

(a) the sub-group has persistently engaged in unco-operative behaviour (see paragraphs 36 to 38),

(b) some or all of the unco-operative behaviour has caused there to be, or contributed to there being, two or more significant tax issues in respect of the sub-group or members of the sub-group which are unresolved (see paragraph 39), and

(c) there is a reasonable likelihood of further instances of the sub-group engaging in unco-operative behaviour in a manner which causes there to be, or contributes to there being, significant tax issues in respect of the sub-group or members of the sub-group.

(2) Paragraphs 36 to 40 apply in relation to a UK sub-group as they apply in relation to a UK group.

(3) Paragraphs 41 to 45 apply in relation to the head of a UK sub-group of a foreign group that is a qualifying group at the material time as they apply in relation to the head of a UK group.

(4) In the application of paragraph 41 in the case of a UK sub-group, sub-paragraph (4) has effect in relation to a UK sub-group as if for paragraphs (b) and (c) there were substituted—

"(b) the identity of the sub-group is not to be regarded as altered by any change in its membership resulting from a relevant body—

(i) becoming a 51% subsidiary of a member of the sub-group, or

(ii) ceasing to be a 51% subsidiary of another member of the sub- group; and

(c) if the sub-group becomes a UK sub-group of another foreign group, it is to be treated as if it were still a UK sub-group of the original foreign group."

(5) As applied by this paragraph, paragraphs 36 to 45 have effect as if references to a UK group (including in references to the head of a UK group or members of a UK group) were references to a UK sub-group.

(6) In paragraphs 40, 41, 46, 47 and 49, references to a group (including in references to the head of a group or members of a group) include a UK sub-group.

(7) In paragraph 46, references to the head of a UK group include the head of a UK sub-group.

Application of Part 3 to large companies

51 (1) A UK company falls within this Part if—

(a) the company has persistently engaged in unco-operative behaviour (see paragraphs 36 to 38),

(b) some or all of the unco-operative behaviour has caused there to be, or contributed to there being, two or more significant tax issues in respect of the company which are unresolved (see paragraph 39), and

(c) there is a reasonable likelihood of further instances of the company engaging in unco-operative behaviour in a manner which causes there to be, or contributes to there being, significant tax issues in respect of the company,

(2) Paragraphs 36 to 39 apply in relation to a company as they apply in relation to a UK group.

(3) Paragraphs 41 to 45 apply in relation to a company as they apply in relation to the head of a UK group.

(4) As applied by this paragraph, paragraphs 36 to 39 and 41 to 45 have effect as if references to a UK group, the head of a UK group or a member of a UK group were references to a company.

(5) Paragraph 47 applies in relation to a company as it applies in relation to a member of a group.

(6) Paragraph 49 applies in relation to a company as it applies in relation to a group.

(7) As applied by this paragraph, paragraphs 47 and 49 have effect as if references to a group, the head of a group or a member of a group were references to a company.

Application of Part 3 to large partnerships

52 (1) A UK partnership falls within this Part if—

(a) the partnership has persistently engaged in unco-operative behaviour (see paragraphs 36 to 38),
(b) some or all of the unco-operative behaviour has caused there to be, or contributed to there being, two or more significant tax issues in respect of the partnership which are unresolved (see paragraph 39), and
(c) there is a reasonable likelihood of further instances of the partnership engaging in unco-operative behaviour in a manner which causes there to be, or contributes to there being, significant tax issues in respect of the partnership.

(2) Paragraphs 36 to 39 of this Schedule apply in relation to a UK partnership as they apply in relation to a UK group.

(3) Paragraphs 41 to 45 of this Schedule apply in relation to the representative partner of a UK partnership as they apply in relation to the head of a UK group.

(4) As applied by this paragraph, paragraphs 36 to 39 and 41 to 45 have effect as if—

(a) references to a UK group were references to a UK partnership;
(b) references to the head of a UK group were references to the representative partner of a UK partnership;
(c) references to a member of a UK group were references to a partner of a UK partnership, acting in the person's capacity as such.

(5) The Treasury may by regulations make provision for warning notices, special measures notices and confirmation notices to be treated as having been given to the representative partner of a UK partnership in circumstances described in the regulations.

(6) Paragraph 46(12) applies to regulations under this paragraph.

(7) Paragraph 47 applies in relation to an inaccuracy in a document given to HMRC by a partner of a UK partnership, acting in the person's capacity as such, as if—

(a) references to a group were references to a partnership;
(b) references to the head of a group were references to the representative partner of a partnership;
(c) references to a member of a group were references to a partner of a partnership.

(8) Paragraph 47 applies in relation to an inaccuracy in any other document given to HMRC on behalf of a UK partnership as if—

(a) references to a person included a UK partnership;
(b) references to a group, or a member of a group, were references to a UK partnership;
(c) references to the head of a group were references to the representative partner of a UK partnership.

(9) Paragraph 49 applies in relation to a UK partnership as it applies in relation to a group.

(10) As applied by this paragraph, paragraph 49 has effect as if—

(a) references to a group were references to a UK partnership;
(b) references to the head of a group were references to the representative partner of a UK partnership.

Meaning of "designated HMRC officer"

53 In this Part "designated HMRC officer" means an officer of Revenue and Customs who has been designated by the Commissioners for Her Majesty's Revenue and Customs for the purposes of this Part.

PART 4

SUPPLEMENTARY

Amendment of power under section 122 of FA 2015

54 The power to make regulations under section 122(6)(c) of FA 2015 (country-by-country reporting: incidental etc provision that may be included in regulations) includes power to amend paragraph 7 above.

Regulations

55 (1) Regulations under this Schedule are to be made by statutory instrument.

(2) A statutory instrument containing regulations under this Schedule is subject to annulment in pursuance of a resolution of the House of Commons.

Terms defined for purposes of more than one paragraph of this Schedule

Term	Paragraph
balance sheet total	paragraph 14(2)
confirmation notice (in Part 3)	paragraph 44
designated HMRC officer (in Part 3)	paragraph 53
engaged in unco-operative behaviour (in Part 3)	paragraph 36
failure (in paragraphs 27 to 33)	paragraph 26(1)
financial year (in relation to a UK group) (in paragraphs 16 and 17)	paragraph 16(7)
foreign (in relation to a relevant body)	paragraph 2(2)
foreign (in relation to a group)	paragraph 6(3)
group	paragraph 6(1)
group other than an MNE Group	paragraph 8
head (in relation to a group)	paragraph 9
head (in relation to a UK sub-group)	paragraph 11(2)
"liability to a penalty" (in paragraphs 27 to 33)	paragraph 26(1)
MNE Group	paragraph 7(1)
member (in relation to a group)	paragraph 8(2) and (3)
penalty (in paragraphs 27 to 33)	paragraph 26(1)
qualifying company	paragraph 5
qualifying group	paragraph 10
qualifying UK partnership	paragraph 12(2)
relevant body	paragraph 2(1)
representative partner	paragraph 12(5)
satisfied the arrangements condition (in Part 3)	paragraph 38
satisfied the behaviour condition (in Part 3)	paragraph 37
special measures notice	paragraphs 42 and 45
tax strategy (in Part 2)	paragraph 34
tribunal (in paragraphs 27 to 33)	paragraph 26(2)

turnover	paragraph 14(1)
UK company	paragraph 3
UK group	paragraph 6(2)
UK partnership	paragraph 12(1)
UK permanent establishment	paragraph 4(1)
UK sub-group	paragraph 11(1)
UK taxation	paragraph 15
warning notice	paragraph 41.

BACKGROUND NOTE

The provisions have two separate components: a requirement that large business publish their tax strategy on the internet; and increased penalties for those who have engaged in what is termed unco-operative behaviour. The application of the latter component depends in part upon the application of the disclosure of tax avoidance schemes (DOTAS) in Pt 7 FA 2004.

These have provisions in relation to a financial year beginning on or after the date of Royal Assent (FA 2016 s 161(2) and (3)).

GENERAL NOTE

The provisions apply to what are termed bodies which are or are part of large business. This includes companies, permanent establishments and partnerships. There are two components to the provisions: publication of tax strategies and penalties for unco-operative behaviour.

Bodies to which the provisions apply

Qualification test

The provisions apply where the relevant body (being a company, a group, or a partnership), in the previous financial year, had a turnover of more than £200 million or a balance sheet of more than £2 billion (paras 5(4), 10(2) and 12(3)).

For these purposes turnover for a UK company (defined one which is formed and registered under the Companies Act 2006 and is neither an open ended investment company nor an investment (para 3)) has the meaning in Pt 15 Companies Act 2006 (para 14(1)) and balance sheet means the amounts shown as assets on the balance sheet at the end of the financial year (para 14(2)).

The financial year has the Companies Act 2006 meaning for a UK company (para 13(a)). For other relevant bodies (meaning any body corporate other than a limited liability partnership (para 2(1)) it means any period in respect of which a profit and loss account is required to be made up (para 13(b)). For a partnership it is any period of account for which its representative partner has provided or is required to provide a partnership statement under a return issued under s 12AB TMA 1970 (para 13(c)).

Qualifying groups

There are two relevant definitions of groups: MNE Groups and groups other than MNE Groups (para 6(1)).

A group is headed by whichever relevant body is not 51% subsidiary of another relevant body (para 9). A UK group is one whose head is a relevant body incorporated in the UK and a foreign group is one whose head is foreign relevant body (paras 6(2) and (3)). A foreign relevant body is a body corporate other than an LLP incorporated outside the UK (para 2(2)).

A group will be a qualifying group if, in the case of an MNE Group it is subject to a mandatory reporting requirement under FA 2015 s122 or would be if the head of the group was resident in the UK. Any other group will be a qualifying group if, in the previous financial year that group meets the qualification test.

MNE Group

An MNE Group has the same meaning as in the OECD Model Legislation in the OECD Country-by-Country Reporting Implementation Package (para 7(1)). This is a group (being a collection of enterprises required to prepare consolidated financial statements or which would be so required if traded on a public securities exchange) which includes bodies resident in different jurisdiction or a permanent establishment subject to tax in a different jurisdiction (Art 1(1) and (2) Model Legislation Related to Country-by-Country Reporting). The exclusion in the Model Legislation for groups with a total consolidated group revenue of less than 750 million euros does not apply for Sch 19 (para 7(2)).

Groups other than MNE Groups

Paragraph 8 defines a group other than an MNE group. This is one which is not an MNE group. There must be two or more relevant bodies where one is the 51% subsidiary of the other of the other or both are 51% subsidiaries of a third body (para 8(3) and (4). For these purposes 51% subsidiary has the same meaning in CTA 2010 Pt 24 Ch 3 (more than 50% of share capital is owned directly or indirectly) (para 8(5) and CTA 2010 s1154). Finally, at least two of the members of the group must be UK companies or are treated as a UK company. A UK permanent establishment of a foreign member of the group will be treated as a UK company for these purposes.

UK sub-groups

A UK sub-group consists of two or more relevant bodies that would be a UK group but for the fact that they are members of larger group headed by a foreign relevant body. The head of the UK sub-group is the UK relevant body that is not a 51% subsidiary of another member of the UK sub-group.

Qualifying company

A company will be a qualifying company if it is a UK company, it satisfies the qualification test and it is not a member of a UK group or a UK sub-group (para 5(2)). Alternatively, it will be a qualifying company if It is a member of a foreign group which met the qualification test and is not a member of a UK sub-group (para 5(3)).

For these purposes a UK permanent establishment of a foreign relevant body is to be treated as a UK company or where the foreign relevant body is a member of a UK group or UK sub-group, a member of that group.

UK partnership

A UK partnership is any body carrying on a trade, business or profession with a view to profit which Is a partnership within the Partnership Act 1890, a limited partnership within the Limited Partnerships Act 1907 or an LLP incorporated in the UK.

It is a qualifying partnership if it meets the qualification test.

Publication of tax strategies

The obligation to publish a tax strategy applies in similar terms to: qualifying UK groups (para 16); UK sub-groups of qualifying foreign groups (para 19); qualifying UK companies (para 22); UK permanent establishments treated as qualifying UK companies (para 22(8) and qualifying partnerships (para 25).

Content of tax strategy

The publication must make clear that it is intended to meet the obligation to publish a tax strategy for a given financial year (paras 17(4), 20, 23(4) and 25(1)).

The tax strategy must include information setting out: (a) the approach to risk management and governance arrangements in relation to UK taxation; (b) the attitude towards tax planning (so far as affecting UK taxation); (c) the level of risk in relation to UK taxation that will be accepted; and (d) the approach towards dealings with HMRC (paras 17(1), 20, 23(1) and 25(1)). It may include other information relating to taxation (paras 17(2), 20, 23(2) and 25(1)) and for groups and sub groups this may be by reference to the group as a whole or by reference to individual companies (paras 17(2)(2)(b) and 20).

Information about activities consisting of the provision of tax advice or related professional services to other persons is not required to be included (paras 17(3), 20(1), 23(3) and 25(1)).

Provision is included for the Treasury to make regulations requiring a group strategy to include country by country report (para 17(6) and (7)).

Date of publication

The obligation applies where the qualification test is met in a financial year (which for groups and sub-groups means the financial year of the head of that group or sub group. The tax strategy must be published before the end of that financial year and not later than 15 months from the date on which the previous tax strategy was published (paras 16(3), 19(3), 22(4) and 25(1)).

Manner of publication

The tax strategy must be published on the internet so as to be accessible by the public free of charge (paras 16(4)(a), 19(4)(a), 22(5)(a) and 25(1)), It may be published as a separate document or as a self-contained part of a wider document (paras 16(4)(b), 19(4)(b), 22(5)(b) and 25(1)). It must remain accessible to the public free of charge until a subsequent tax strategy is published or for at least a year (paras 16(5), 19(5), 22(6) and 25(1)).

For groups and sub-groups, the obligation to ensure that the tax strategy is prepared and published the falls on the head of that group or sub-group (paras 16(2) and 19(2)) but it must be published by all UK companies in the group (para 16(4)(a).

Penalty for non-compliance

A failure to meet an obligation to publish a tax strategy and/or a failure to ensure that it remains published and accessible for the requisite period will result in liability to a penalty of £7,500 with a further £7,500 penalty if the obligation is not met within a subsequent six-month period (paras 18, 21, 24 and 26). There is, however, provision allowing for extension of time limits with the agreement of an officer of HMRC (para 27). The penalty must be assessed within six months of HMRC becoming aware of the failure (para 29) or six years of the financial year giving rise to the obligation to publish. There is a defence of reasonable excuse (para 28) and a right of appeal (para 30).

Sanctions for persistently unco-operative large businesses

Large businesses

Although the legislation refers to "large" businesses this term is undefined. The sanctions are drafted by reference to to UK groups (paras 35 to 49) and are extended in their application to UK sub-groups (para 50), UK companies (para 51) and UK partnerships (para 52). Notices may only be given to those entities meeting the qualification test (para 41) and require two or more tax issues relating to a dispute over liabilities of not less than £2 million.

Where a company in receipt of a notice becomes a member of another group, notices previously given to that company are treated as having given to the head of the new group (para 46).

Application of provisions

The provisions apply where (i) an entity (being the group, sub-group, partnership or company) has engaged in persistently unco-operative behaviour; (ii) some or all of which has led to there being two or more significant tax issues; and (iii) there is a reasonable likelihood of further unco-operative behaviour causing or contributing to significant tax issues (para 35).

Persistently engaging in unco-operative behaviour

Engaging in unco-operative behaviour is either (i) being a party to a tax avoidance scheme (para 38); or (ii) acting in in a manner which delays or otherwise hinders HMRC in the exercise of their functions in connection with determining liability to UK taxation (para 37).

For these purposes delaying or hindering HMRC may be indicated by HMRC having to use statutory powers and/or persons relying on legislative interpretations which it is likely a court or tribunal would disagree with (para 37(2) and (3)).

A tax avoidance scheme is widely defined to cover anything counteracted by the GAAR and anything notifiable under DOTAS, unless HMRC have given notice that there is no duty on promoters to provide clients with prescribed information (para 38).

Persistent behaviour is behaviour which has been engaged in on sufficient number of occasions for it to be clear that it represents a pattern (para 36(4).

For groups this can apply to the group generally, a member of the group or by reference to two or more members, and taken together (para 36(1) and (3)).

Significant tax issue

There is a significant tax issue if there is (i) a disagreement or reasonable likelihood of disagreement with HMRC; (ii) the issue has been or could be referred to a court or tribunal; and (iii) the amount of liability at stake is likely to be not less than £2 million (para 39).

Warning notice

Where an officer of HMRC considers that an entity which meets the qualifying test falls within the provisions for persistently unco-operative large business an officer he can issue a warning notice setting out the reasons for considering the provisions apply. That notice expires after 15 months if not withdrawn before then (para 41).

Special measures notice

If 12 months have passed from the issue of the warning notice and it has not been withdrawn or expired, then of the conditions for application of the provisions continue to be met a special measures notice may be issued. The officer must take into account representations made within 12 months of the warning notice and set out the officer's reasons for considering the provisions apply (para 42).

A special measures notice may be withdrawn but otherwise expires within 27 months of the day on which it was given or of a confirmation notice (para 43). A confirmation notice is one given between 24 and 27 months of the special measures notice confirming that the provisions still apply to the entity (para 44).

If there is unco-operative behaviour within six months of a notice expiring and that behaviour would likely have led to a special measures notice or a confirmation notice, a special measures notice may be issued within nine months of the previous notice expiring (para 45).

Consequences of a special measures notice

Where there is an inaccuracy in a document given to HMRC by a person who is subject to a special measures notice, then penalties will be assessed on the basis that at the very least there has been a failure to take reasonable care if either (i) it relates to a tax avoidance scheme; or (ii) it is attributable to an interpretation of legislation which it is likely that a court or tribunal would disagree with (para 47).

HMRC are also empowered to publish details of a person or group which has been subject of a special measures notice, including whether that notice has been subject of a confirmation notice. A decision to publish can only be made after informing the relevant persons and offering an opportunity for representations. There is an obligation to notify within 30 days if a confirmation notice ceases to apply (para 49).

SCHEDULE 20

PENALTIES FOR ENABLERS OF OFFSHORE TAX EVASION OR NON-COMPLIANCE

Section 162

PART 1

LIABILITY FOR PENALTY

Liability for penalty

1 (1) A penalty is payable by a person (P) who has enabled another person (Q) to carry out offshore tax evasion or non-compliance, where conditions A and B are met.

(2) For the purposes of this Schedule—

(a) Q carries out "offshore tax evasion or non-compliance" by—

(i) committing a relevant offence, or
(ii) engaging in conduct that makes Q liable (if the applicable conditions are met) to a relevant civil penalty,

where the tax at stake is income tax, capital gains tax or inheritance tax, and

(b) P "has enabled" Q to carry out offshore tax evasion or non-compliance if P has encouraged, assisted or otherwise facilitated conduct by Q that constitutes offshore tax evasion or non-compliance.

(3) The relevant offences are-

(a) an offence of cheating the public revenue involving offshore activity, or
(b) an offence under section 106A of TMA 1970 (fraudulent evasion of income tax) involving offshore activity,
(c) an offence under section 106B, 106C or 106D of TMA 1970 (offences relating to certain failures to comply with section 7 or 8 by a taxpayer chargeable to income tax or capital gains tax on or by reference to offshore income, assets or liabilities).

(4) The relevant civil penalties are—

(a) a penalty under paragraph 1 of Schedule 24 to FA 2007 (errors in taxpayer's document) involving an offshore matter or an offshore transfer (within the meaning of that Schedule),
(b) a penalty under paragraph 1 of Schedule 41 to FA 2008 (failure to notify etc) in relation to a failure to comply with section 7(1) of TMA 1970 involving offshore activity,
(c) a penalty under paragraph 6 of Schedule 55 to FA 2009 (failure to make return for 12 months) involving offshore activity,
(d) a penalty under paragraph 1 of Schedule 21 to FA 2015 (penalties in connection with relevant offshore asset moves).

(5) Condition A is that P knew when P's actions were carried out that they enabled, or were likely to enable, Q to carry out offshore tax evasion or non-compliance.

(6) Condition B is that—

(a) in the case of offshore tax evasion or non-compliance consisting of the commission of a relevant offence, Q has been convicted of the offence and the conviction is final, or
(b) in the case of offshore tax evasion or non-compliance consisting of conduct that makes Q liable to a relevant penalty—

(i) Q has been found to be liable to such a penalty, assessed and notified, and the penalty is final, or
(ii) a contract has been made between the Commissioners for Her Majesty's Revenue and Customs and Q under which the Commissioners undertake not to assess the penalty or (if it has been assessed) not to take proceedings to recover it.

(7) For the purposes of sub-paragraph (6)(a)—

(a) "convicted of the offence" means convicted of the full offence (and not for example of an attempt), and
(b) a conviction becomes final when the time allowed for bringing an appeal against it expires or, if later, when any appeal against conviction has been determined.

(8) For the purposes of sub-paragraph (6)(b)(i) a penalty becomes final when the time allowed for any appeal or further appeal relating to it expires or, if later, any appeal or final appeal relating to it is determined.

(9) It is immaterial for the purposes of condition B that—

(a) any offence of which Q was convicted, or
(b) any penalty for which Q was found to be liable,

relates also to other tax evasion or non-compliance by Q.

(10) In this Schedule "other tax evasion or non-compliance by Q" means conduct by Q that—

(a) constitutes an offence of cheating the public revenue or an offence of fraudulent evasion of tax, or
(b) makes Q liable to a penalty under any provision of the Taxes Acts,

but does not constitute offshore tax evasion or non-compliance.

(11) Nothing in condition B affects the law of evidence as to the relevance if any of a conviction, assessment of a penalty or contract mentioned in sub-paragraph (6) for the purpose of proving that condition A is met in relation to P.

(12) In this Schedule "conduct" includes a failure to act.

Meaning of "involving offshore activity" and related expressions

2 (1) This paragraph has effect for the purposes of this Schedule.

(2) Conduct involves offshore activity if it involves—

(a) an offshore matter,

(b) an offshore transfer, or

(c) a relevant offshore asset move.

(3) Conduct involves an offshore matter if it results in a potential loss of revenue that is charged on or by reference to—

(a) income arising from a source in a territory outside the United Kingdom,

(b) assets situated or held in a territory outside the United Kingdom,

(c) activities carried on wholly or mainly in a territory outside the United Kingdom, or

(d) anything having effect as if it were income, assets or activities of the kind described above.

(4) Where the tax at stake is inheritance tax, assets are treated for the purposes of sub-paragraph (3) as situated or held in a territory outside the United Kingdom if they are so held or situated immediately after the transfer of value by reason of which inheritance tax becomes chargeable.

(5) Conduct involves an offshore transfer if—

(a) it does not involve an offshore matter,

(b) it is deliberate (whether or not concealed) and results in a potential loss of revenue,

(c) the condition set out in paragraph 4AA of Schedule 24 to FA 2007 is satisfied.

(6) Conduct involves a relevant offshore asset move if at a time when Q is the beneficial owner of an asset ("the qualifying time")—

(a) the asset ceases to be situated or held in a specified territory and becomes situated or held in a non-specified territory,

(b) the person who holds the asset ceases to be resident in a specified territory and becomes resident in a non-specified territory, or

(c) there is a change in the arrangements for the ownership of the asset,

and Q remains the beneficial owner of the asset, or any part of it, immediately after the qualifying time.

(7) Paragraphs 4(2) to (4) of Schedule 21 to FA 2015 apply for the purposes of sub-paragraph (6) above as they apply for purposes of paragraph 4 of that Schedule.

(8) In sub-paragraph (6) above, "specified territory" has the same meaning as in paragraph 4(5) of Schedule 21 to FA 2015.

Amount of penalty

3 (1) The penalty payable under paragraph 1 is (except in a case mentioned in sub-paragraph (2)) the higher of—

(a) 100% of the potential lost revenue, or

(b) £3,000.

(2) In a case where P has enabled Q to engage in conduct which makes Q liable to a penalty under paragraph 1 of Schedule 21 to FA 2015, the penalty payable under paragraph 1 is the higher of—

(a) 50% of the potential lost revenue in respect of the original tax non-compliance, and

(b) £3,000.

(3) In sub-paragraph (2)(a) "the original tax non-compliance" means the conduct that incurred the original penalty and "the potential lost revenue" (in respect of that non-compliance) is—

(a) the potential lost revenue under Schedule 24 to FA 2007,

(b) the potential lost revenue under Schedule 41 to FA 2008, or

(c) the liability to tax which would have been shown on the return (within the meaning of Schedule 55 to FA 2009),

according to whether the original penalty was incurred under paragraph 1 of Schedule 24, paragraph 1 of Schedule 41 or paragraph 6 of Schedule 55.

Potential lost revenue: enabling Q to commit relevant offence

4 (1) The potential lost revenue in a case where P is liable to a penalty under paragraph 1 for enabling Q to commit a relevant offence is the same amount as the potential lost revenue applicable for the purposes of the corresponding relevant civil penalty (determined in accordance with the relevant sub-paragraph of paragraph 5).

(2) Where Q's offending conduct is—

    (a) an offence of cheating the public revenue involving offshore activity, or

    (b) an offence under section 106A of TMA 1970 involving offshore activity,

the corresponding relevant civil penalty is the penalty which Q is liable for as a result of that offending conduct.

(3) Where Q's offending conduct is an offence under section 106B, 106C or 106D of TMA 1970, the corresponding relevant civil penalty is—

    (a) for an offence under section 106B of TMA 1970, a penalty under paragraph 1 of Schedule 41 to FA 2008,

    (b) for an offence under section 106C of TMA 1970, a penalty under paragraph 6 of Schedule 55 to FA 2009, and

    (c) for an offence under section 106D of TMA 1970, a penalty under paragraph 1 of Schedule 24 to FA 2007.

(4) In determining any amount of potential lost revenue for the purposes of this paragraph, the fact Q has been prosecuted for the offending conduct is to be disregarded.

Potential lost revenue: enabling Q to engage in conduct incurring relevant civil penalty

5 (1) The potential lost revenue in a case where P is liable to a penalty under paragraph 1 for enabling Q to engage in conduct that makes Q liable (if the applicable conditions are met) to a relevant civil penalty is to be determined as follows.

(2) In the case of a penalty under paragraph 1 of Schedule 24 to FA 2007 involving an offshore matter or an offshore transfer, the potential lost revenue is the amount that under that Schedule is the potential lost revenue in respect of Q's conduct.

(3) In the case of a penalty under paragraph 1 of Schedule 41 to FA 2008 in relation to a failure to comply with section 7(1) of TMA 1970 involving offshore activity, the potential lost revenue is the amount that under that Schedule is the potential lost revenue in respect of Q's conduct.

(4) In the case of a penalty under paragraph 6 of Schedule 55 to FA 2009 involving offshore activity, the potential lost revenue is the liability to tax which would have been shown in the return in question (within the meaning of that Schedule).

Treatment of potential lost revenue attributable to both offshore tax evasion or non-compliance and other tax evasion or non-compliance

6 (1) This paragraph applies where any amount of potential lost revenue in a case falling within paragraph 4 or 5 is attributable not only to Q's offshore tax evasion or non-compliance but also to any other tax evasion or non-compliance by Q.

(2) In that case the potential lost revenue in respect of Q's offshore tax evasion or non-compliance is to be taken for the purposes of assessing the penalty to which P is liable as being or (as the case may be) including such share as is just and reasonable of the amount mentioned in sub-paragraph (1).

Reduction of penalty for disclosure etc by P

7 (1) If P (who would otherwise be liable to a penalty under paragraph 1)—

    (a) makes a disclosure to HMRC of—

        (i) a matter relating to an inaccuracy in a document, a supply of false information or a failure to disclose an under-assessment,

        (ii) P's enabling of actions by Q that constituted (or might constitute) a relevant offence or that made (or might make) Q liable to a relevant penalty, or

        (iii) any other matter HMRC regard as assisting them in relation to the assessment of P's liability to a penalty under paragraph 1, or

    (b) assists HMRC in any investigation leading to Q being charged with a relevant offence or found liable to a relevant penalty,

HMRC must reduce the penalty to one that reflects the quality of the disclosure or assistance.

(2) But the penalty may not be reduced—

    (a) in the case of unprompted disclosure or assistance, below whichever is the higher of—

        (i) 10% of the potential lost revenue, or

        (ii) £1,000, or

    (b) in the case of prompted disclosure or assistance, below whichever is the higher of—

        (i) 30% of the potential lost revenue, or

(ii) £3,000.

8 (1) This paragraph applies for the purposes of paragraph 7.

(2) P discloses a matter by—

(a) telling HMRC about it,

(b) giving HMRC reasonable help in relation to the matter (for example by quantifying an inaccuracy in a document, an inaccuracy attributable to the supply of false information or withholding of information or an under-assessment), and

(c) allowing HMRC access to records for any reasonable purpose connected with resolving the matter (for example for the purpose of ensuring that an inaccuracy in a document, an inaccuracy attributable to the supply of false information or withholding of information or an under-assessment is fully corrected).

(3) P assists HMRC in relation to an investigation leading to Q being charged with a relevant offence or found liable to a relevant penalty by—

(a) assisting or encouraging Q to disclose all relevant facts to HMRC,

(b) allowing HMRC access to records, or

(c) any other conduct which HMRC considers assisted them in investigating or assessing Q's liability to such a penalty.

(4) Disclosure or assistance by P—

(a) is "unprompted" if made at a time when P has no reason to believe that HMRC have discovered or are about to discover Q's offshore tax evasion or non-compliance (including any inaccuracy in a document, supply of false information or withholding of information, or under-assessment), and

(b) otherwise is "prompted".

(5) In relation to disclosure or assistance, "quality" includes timing, nature and extent.

9 (1) If they think it right because of special circumstances, HMRC may reduce a penalty under paragraph 1.

(2) In sub-paragraph 1 "special circumstances" does not include—

(a) ability to pay, or

(b) the fact that a potential loss of revenue from one taxpayer is balanced by a potential overpayment by another.

(3) In sub-paragraph (1) the reference to reducing a penalty includes a reference to

(a) staying a penalty, or

(b) agreeing a compromise in relation to proceedings for a penalty.

Procedure for assessing penalty, etc

10 (1) Where a person is found liable for a penalty under paragraph 1 HMRC must—

(a) assess the penalty,

(b) notify the person, and

(c) state in the notice the period in respect of which the penalty is assessed.

(2) A penalty must be paid before the end of the period of 30 days beginning with the day on which notification of the penalty is issued.

(3) An assessment of a penalty—

(a) is to be treated for procedural purposes in the same way as an assessment to tax (except in respect of a matter expressly provided for by this Schedule), and

(b) may be enforced as if it were an assessment to tax.

(4) A supplementary assessment may be made in respect of a penalty if an earlier assessment operated by reference to an underestimate of the liability to tax that would have been shown in a return.

(5) Sub-paragraph (6) applies if—

(a) an assessment in respect of a penalty is based on a liability to tax that would have been shown on a return, and

(b) that liability is found by HMRC to have been excessive.

(6) HMRC may amend the assessment so that it is based upon the correct amount.

(7) But an amendment under sub-paragraph (6)—

(a) does not affect when the penalty must be paid, and

(b) may be made after the last day on which the assessment in question could have been made under paragraph 11.

11 An assessment of a person as liable to a penalty under paragraph 1 may not take place more than 2 years after the fulfilment of the conditions mentioned in paragraph 1(1) (in relation to that person) first came to the attention of an officer of Revenue and Customs.

Appeals

12 A person may appeal against—

(a) a decision of HMRC that a penalty under paragraph 1 is payable by that person, or

(b) a decision of HMRC as to the amount of a penalty under paragraph 1 payable by the person.

13 (1) An appeal under paragraph 12 is to be treated in the same way as an appeal against an assessment to the tax at stake (including by the application of any provision about bringing the appeal by notice to HMRC, about HMRC review of the decision or about determination of the appeal by the First-tier Tribunal or Upper Tribunal).

(2) Sub-paragraph (1) does not apply—

(a) so as to require the person bringing the appeal to pay a penalty before an appeal against the assessment of the penalty is determined,

(b) in respect of any other matter expressly provided for by this Schedule.

14 (1) On an appeal under paragraph 12(a) that is notified to the tribunal, the tribunal may affirm or cancel HMRC's decision.

(2) On an appeal under paragraph 12(b) that is notified to the tribunal, the tribunal may—

(a) affirm HMRC's decision, or

(b) substitute for that decision another decision that HMRC had power to make.

(3) If the tribunal substitutes its own decision for HMRC's, the tribunal may rely on paragraph 7 or 9 (or both)—

(a) to the same extent as HMRC (which may mean applying the same percentage reduction as HMRC to a different starting point),

(b) to a different extent, but only if the tribunal thinks that HMRC's decision in respect of the application of that paragraph was flawed.

(4) In sub-paragraph (3)(b) "flawed" means flawed when considered in the light of the principles applicable in proceedings for judicial review.

(5) In this paragraph "tribunal" means the First-tier Tribunal or Upper Tribunal (as appropriate by virtue of paragraph 13(1).

Double jeopardy

15 A person is not liable to a penalty under paragraph 1 in respect of conduct for which the person—

(a) has been convicted of an offence, or

(b) has been assessed to a penalty under any provision other than paragraph 1.

Application of provisions of TMA 1970

16 Subject to the provisions of this Part of this Schedule, the following provisions of TMA 1970 apply for the purposes of this Part of this Schedule as they apply for the purposes of the Taxes Acts—

(a) section 108 (responsibility of company officers),

(b) section 114 (want of form), and

(c) section 114 (delivery and service of documents).

Interpretation of Part 1

17 (1) This paragraph applies for the purposes of this Schedule.

(2) References to an assessment to tax, in relation to inheritance tax, are to a determination.

PART 2

APPLICATION OF SCHEDULE 36 TO FA 2008: INFORMATION POWERS

General application of information and inspection powers to suspected enablers

18 (1) Schedule 36 to FA 2008 (information and inspection powers) applies for the purpose of checking a relevant person's position as regards liability for a penalty under paragraph 1 as it applies for checking a person's tax position, subject to the modifications in paragraphs 19 to 21.

(2) In this Part of this Schedule "relevant person" means a person an officer of Revenue and Customs has reason to suspect has or may have enabled offshore tax evasion or non-compliance by another person so as to be liable to a penalty under paragraph 1.

General modifications

19 In its application for the purpose mentioned in paragraph 18(1) Schedule 36 to FA 2008 has effect as if—

(a) any provisions which can have no application for that purpose, or are specifically excluded by paragraph 20, were omitted,

(b) references to "the taxpayer" were references to the relevant person whose position as regards liability for a penalty under paragraph 1 is to be checked, and references to "a taxpayer" were references to a relevant person,

(c) references to a person's "tax position" are to the relevant person's position as regards liability for a penalty under paragraph 1,

(d) references to prejudice to the assessment or collection of tax included a reference to prejudice to the investigation of the relevant person's position as regards liability for a penalty under paragraph 1,

(e) references to information relating to the conduct of a pending appeal relating to tax were references to information relating to the conduct of a pending appeal relating to an assessment of liability for a penalty under paragraph 1.

Specific modifications

20 The following provisions are excluded from the application of Schedule 36 to FA 2008 for the purpose mentioned in paragraph 18(1)—

(a) paragraph 24 (exception for auditors),

(b) paragraph 25 (exception for tax advisers),

(c) paragraphs 26 and 27 (provisions supplementary to paragraphs 24 and 25),

(d) paragraphs 50 and 51 (tax-related penalty).

21 In the application of Schedule 36 to FA 2008 for the purpose mentioned in paragraph 18(1), paragraph 10A (power to inspect business premises of involved third parties) has effect as if the reference in sub-paragraph (1) to the position of any person or class of persons as regards a relevant tax were a reference to the position of a relevant person as regards liability for a penalty under paragraph 1.

PART 3

PUBLISHING DETAILS OF PERSONS FOUND LIABLE TO PENALTIES

Naming etc of persons assessed to penalty or penalties under paragraph 1

22 (1) The Commissioners for Her Majesty's Revenue and Customs ("the Commissioners") may publish information about a person if—

(a) in consequence of an investigation the person has been found to have incurred one or more penalties under paragraph 1 (and has been assessed or is the subject of a contract settlement), and

(b) the potential lost revenue in relation to the penalty (or the aggregate of the potential lost revenue in relation to each of the penalties) exceeds £25,000.

(2) The Commissioners may also publish information about a person if the person has been found to have incurred 5 or more penalties under paragraph 1 in any 5 year period.

(3) The information that may be published is—

(a) the person's name (including any trading name, previous name or pseudonym),

(b) the person's address (or registered office),

(c) the nature of any business carried on by the person,

(d) the amount of the penalty or penalties in question,

(e) the periods or times to which the actions giving rise to the penalty or penalties relate,

(f) any other information that the Commissioners consider it appropriate to publish in order to make clear the person's identity.

(4) The information may be published in any manner that the Commissioners consider appropriate.

(5) Before publishing any information the Commissioners must—

(a) inform the person that they are considering doing so, and

(b) afford the person the opportunity to make representations about whether it should be published.

(6) No information may be published before the day on which the penalty becomes final or, where more than one penalty is involved, the latest day on which any of the penalties becomes final.

(7) No information may be published for the first time after the end of the period of one year beginning with that day.

(8) No information may be published if the amount of the penalty—

(a) is reduced under paragraph 7 to—

(i) 10% of the potential lost revenue (in a case of unprompted disclosure or assistance), or

(ii) 30% of potential lost revenue (in a case of prompted disclosure or assistance),

(b) would have been reduced to 10% or 30% of potential lost revenue but for the imposition of the minimum penalty,

(c) is reduced under paragraph 9 to nil or stayed.

(9) For the purposes of this paragraph a penalty becomes final—

(a) if it has been assessed, when the time for any appeal or further appeal relating to it expires or, if later, any appeal or final appeal relating to it is finally determined, and

(b) if a contract settlement has been made, at the time when the contract is made.

(10) In this paragraph "contract settlement", in relation to a penalty, means a contract between the Commissioners and the person under which the Commissioners undertake not to assess the penalty or (if it has been assessed) not to take proceedings to recover it.

23 (1) The Treasury may by regulations amend paragraph 22(1) to vary the amount for the time being specified in paragraph (b).

(2) Regulations under this paragraph are to be made by statutory instrument.

(3) A statutory instrument under this paragraph is subject to annulment in pursuance of a resolution of the House of Commons.

GENERAL NOTE

Part 1 Liability for Penalty

Paragraph 1(1) of Sch 20 provides that a penalty is payable by a person who has enabled another person to carry out offshore tax evasion or non-compliance, where conditions A *and* B are met. Condition A is set out at para 1(5) and Condition B at 1(6). An assessment to a penalty under para 1 may not take place more than two years after the fulfilment of Condition A and B first came to the attention of an officer of Revenue and Customs (para 11). Therefore, the penalty may arise in relation to historic transactions when they come to light of an officer. Understanding what is offshore tax evasion or non-compliance for these purposes is important.

A person has enabled another if they encourage, assist or otherwise facilitate conduct that constitutes offshore tax evasion or non-compliance and a person carries out 'offshore tax evasion or noncompliance' where they commit a relevant offence or have been liable to a relevant civil penalty in relation to income tax, capital gain tax of inheritance tax. A "Relevant Offence" is defined at para 1(3) and brings this legislation together with the legislation introduced to create strict offshore criminal offence. The offences relating to offshore income, assets and activities that are applicable for the purposes of Sch 20 are ss 106A–106D. These offences are for failing to give notice of being chargeable to tax or deliver a return and for delivering an inaccurate return. A relevant offence also includes cheating the public revenue involving offshore activity. A "Relevant Civil Penalty" is set out at para 1(4) and relates to the existing penalties that may arise as a result of involving an offshore matter, activity or assets.

Both Condition A and B need to be met. Condition A is that the person knew, when carrying out their actions, that those actions enabled or were likely to enable offshore tax evasion or non-compliance. A likely area that may be tested is where those who have historically "encouraged, assisted or otherwise facilitated" offshore tax planning held the view that they have not known when carrying out their actions that they would enable or would likely to enable offshore tax evasion or non-compliance. This may be a particular concern where a person who was enabled is charged with a relevant offence or becomes liable to a relevant civil penalty. Contentious circumstances could involve failed offshore tax planning or avoidance schemes.

Condition B can be met in three ways based on the whether the enabled person has (i) been convicted of a relevant offence and the time allowed for appeal has expired, (ii) is liable to a relevant penalty, and the time allowed for appeal or further appeal has expired, (iii) entered a contract under which the Commissioners undertake not to assess and/or recover the penalty.

The potential scope of the legislation is made clear through para 1(12) which defines 'conduct' as including a failure to act. Considering para 1(2) (a)(ii) the term "engaging in conduct" includes failing to act, which for example could include not taking advice or acting on advice, and under para 1(6)(b) the person enabling would have simply encouraged, assisted or otherwise facilitated. In this situation, reliance may fall back to not knowing those actions enable or were likely to enable tax evasion or non-compliance under Condition A.

Paragraph 2(2) sets out conduct involving offshore activity, which is drafted widely to involve an offshore activity if it involves an offshore matter or transfer, or a relevant offshore asset move. Paragraph 2(3)–(8) expands the definition and broadly covers income, assets or activities in a territory other than the UK. For inheritance tax purposes para 2(4) considers where assets are held following a transfer of value.

The quantum of penalty is set by para 3(1) or 3(2). Paragraph 3(1) relates to a penalty payable under para 1. Paragraph 3(2) relates to a penalty under para 1 of Sch 21 FA 2015: Penalties in connection with offshore asset moves. The Sch 21 penalty applies to income tax, capital gains tax and inheritance tax relating where assets are moved from a "specified territory" to a "non-specified territory". Territories that qualify as specified include those committed to the automatic exchange of information under the common reporting standard. The penalty is aimed at those who move the assets with the intention of avoiding HMRC identifying them.

In the case of para 3(1) the penalty payable is the higher of 100% of the potential lost revenue or £3,000 and in the case of para 3(2) 50% of the potential lost revenue of the original tax non-compliance or £3,000 respectively.

Paragraphs 4 to 5 set out what is meant by 'potential lost revenue' which broadly takes the amount of lost revenue that arising for the purposes of penalties to the person who was enabled to carry out offshore tax evasion or non-compliance. Paragraph 5 sets out what the potential lost revenue is for each relevant penalty and para 6 permits a just and reasonable apportionment in the case where the potential lost revenue relates to both offshore tax evasion or non-compliance and other evasion or non-compliance for the purposes of calculating the enabler's penalty.

The penalty may be mitigated. Paragraph 7 sets out a number of reductions where the enabler makes a disclosures or assist HMRC with any investigation leading to the person who was enabled being charged with a relevant offence or found liable to a relevant penalty. The mitigation appears to create a number of problems given that the factors to mitigate a penalty take place potentially before a liability has been established because it is dependent on either disclosures or HMRC's investigation. A number of other potential issues arise including the potential breach of confidentiality as well as money laundering responsibilities may have to be considered by the professional adviser. Paragraph 7(2) restricts the mitigation in the case of unprompted and prompted disclosure or assistance. Paragraph 8(4) defines unprompted being where there is no reason to believe that HMRC have discovered or are about to discover the offshore tax evasion or non compliance. Anything else is prompted.

Paragraphs 8(1)–(5) sets out what constitutes disclosure which includes telling, giving reasonable help and allowing access to records. For the purposes of assisting HMRC in relation to an investigation leading to the enabled person being charged to a relevant offence or found liable to a relevant penalty the term assistance includes assisting or encouraging the enabled person to disclose, access to records and any other conduct which assists HMRC. Often for those holding professional qualifications, a professional body recommends an independent adviser is appointed to assist with a disclosure in such circumstances although assisting with this should still constitute assisting or encouraging the enabled person to disclose.

HMRC may reduce the penalty because of special circumstances – para 9.

The procedure for assessing the penalty is set out a paras 10(1)–(7). The penalty must be paid within 30 days beginning on the day notification is issued. An assessment to a penalty under paragraph 1 may not take place more than two years after the fulfilment of Condition A and B first came to the attention of an officer of Revenue and Customs (para 11).

There is a right of appeal at para 11 against the decision to assess a penalty under paragraph 1 as well as the amount of penalty. An appeal against a penalty is subject to the same appeal rights and procedure, as an appeal against an assessment to tax. There is no requirement for the appellant to pay a penalty before an appeal is determined.

Part 2 Application of Schedule 36 to FA 2008: Information Powers

In order to check a relevant person's liability to a penalty under para 1 of Sch 20, information powers have been adapted by Pt 2 which under para 18(1) applies Sch FA 2008 as subject to the modifications at paras 19–21.

The definition of a 'relevant person' is one an officer of Revenue and Customs has reason to **suspect** has or may have enabled offshore tax evasion or non-compliance by another person so as to be liable to a penalty under para 1. It therefore brings into play the information powers to assist an officer to determine whether there is a potential liability to the penalty under para 1.

Paragraph 19 sets out general modifications that apply to Sch 36 although most of these are simply enabling the operation of the information powers in the context of Sch 20. Paragraph 20 sets out provisions in Sch 36 do not apply for the purpose of checking a person's liability to a penalty under para 1, which broadly permit the powers to be applied to relevant professionals. Schedule 36 denies a "tax adviser" as a person appointed to give advice about the tax affairs of another person (whether appointed directly by that person or by another tax adviser of that person). The wide meaning of tax adviser could therefore apply to any person holding themselves in a position of authority as to the tax treatment of a particular transaction to another person.

Paragraph 21 sets out that the power to inspect business premises of involved third parties where it is reasonably required by the officer for the purpose of checking the position of any person or class of persons as regards a liability for a penalty under para 1.

Part 3 Publishing Details of Persons Found Liable to Penalties

Part 3 provides HMRC with the power to publish details of persons found have been liable to penalties and assessed or has entered into a contract settlement. The potential lost revenue must be at least £25,000. Where a person incurs five or more penalties in five years (or less), HMRC may also publish information about the person regardless of the amount of lost revenue.

The details that may be published are set out at para 22(3) and broadly permit the identity to be established by including trading names and pseudonyms. The Commissioners may also publish any details so as to permit the identity to be established which would potentially allow them to publish subsequent trading names or entity names connected with the relevant person. The amount of penalties and period to which they relate can also be published.

No information may be published where the penalty is reduced by the maximum amounts allowed under para 5, or is reduced to nil or stayed under the special circumstances provision at para 7.

SCHEDULE 21

PENALTIES RELATING TO OFFSHORE MATTERS AND OFFSHORE TRANSFERS

Section 163

Amendments to Schedule 24 to the Finance Act 2007 (c 11)

1 Schedule 24 to FA 2007 (penalties for errors) is amended as follows.

2 (1) Paragraph 9 (reductions for disclosure) is amended as follows.

(2) For sub-paragraph (A1) substitute—

"(A1) Paragraph 10 provides for reductions in penalties—

(a) under paragraph 1 where a person discloses an inaccuracy that involves a domestic matter,

(b) under paragraph 1A where a person discloses a supply of false information or withholding of information, and

(c) under paragraph 2 where a person discloses a failure to disclose an under-assessment.

(A2) Paragraph 10A provides for reductions in penalties under paragraph 1 where a person discloses an inaccuracy that involves an offshore matter or an offshore transfer.

(A3) Sub-paragraph (1) applies where a person discloses—

(a) an inaccuracy that involves a domestic matter,

(b) a careless inaccuracy that involves an offshore matter,

(c) a supply of false information or withholding of information, or

(d) a failure to disclose an under-assessment."

(3) In sub-paragraph (1), in the words before paragraph (a), for the words from "an inaccuracy" to "under-assessment" substitute "the matter".

(4) After sub-paragraph (1) insert—

"(1A) Sub-paragraph (1B) applies where a person discloses –

(a) a deliberate inaccuracy (whether concealed or not) that involves an offshore matter, or

(b) an inaccuracy that involves an offshore transfer.

(1B) A person discloses the inaccuracy by—

(a) telling HMRC about it,

(b) giving HMRC reasonable help in quantifying the inaccuracy,

(c) allowing HMRC access to records for the purpose of ensuring that the inaccuracy is fully corrected, and

(d) providing HMRC with additional information.

(1C) The Treasury must make regulations setting out what is meant by "additional information" for the purposes of sub-paragraph (1B)(d).

(1D) Regulations under sub-paragraph (1C) are to be made by statutory instrument.

(1E) An instrument containing regulations under sub-paragraph (1C) is subject to annulment in pursuance of a resolution of the House of Commons."

(5) At the end insert—

"(4) Paragraph 4A(4) to (5) applies to determine whether an inaccuracy involves an offshore matter, an offshore transfer or a domestic matter for the purposes of this paragraph."

3 In paragraph 10 (amount of reduction for disclosure), for the Table in sub-paragraph (2) substitute—

"Standard %	Minimum % for prompted disclosure	Minimum % for unprompted disclosure
30%	15%	0%
70%	35%	20%
100%	50%	30%"

4 After paragraph 10 insert—

"**10A** (1) If a person who would otherwise be liable to a penalty of a percentage shown in column 1 of the Table (a "standard percentage") has made a disclosure, HMRC must reduce the standard percentage to one that reflects the quality of the disclosure.

(2) But the standard percentage may not be reduced to a percentage that is below the minimum shown for it—

(a) in the case of a prompted disclosure, in column 2 of the Table, and

(b) in the case of an unprompted disclosure, in column 3 of the Table.

Standard %	Minimum % for prompted disclosure	Minimum % for unprompted disclosure
30%	15%	0%
37.5%	18.75%	0%
45%	22.5%	0%
60%	30%	0%
70%	45%	30%
87.5%	53.75%	35%
100%	60%	40%
105%	62.5%	40%
125%	72.5%	50%
140%	80%	50%
150%	85%	55%
200%	110%	70%"

Amendments to Schedule 41 to the Finance Act 2008 (c 9)

5 Schedule 41 to FA 2008 (penalties: failure to notify etc) is amended as follows.

6 (1) Paragraph 12 (reductions for disclosure) is amended as follows.

(2) For sub-paragraph (1) substitute—

"(1) Paragraph 13 provides for reductions in penalties—

(a) under paragraph 1 where P discloses a relevant failure that involves a domestic matter, and

(b) under paragraphs 2 to 4 where P discloses a relevant act or failure.

(1A) Paragraph 13A provides for reductions in penalties under paragraph 1 where P discloses a relevant failure that involves an offshore matter or an offshore transfer.

(1B) Sub-paragraph (2) applies where P discloses—

(a) a relevant failure that involves a domestic matter,

(b) a non-deliberate relevant failure that involves an offshore matter, or

(c) a relevant act or failure giving rise to a penalty under any of paragraphs 2 to 4."

(3) In sub-paragraph (2), for "a" substitute "the".

(4) After sub-paragraph (2) insert—

"(2A) Sub-paragraph (2B) applies where P discloses—

(a) a deliberate relevant failure (whether concealed or not) that involves an offshore matter, or

(b) a relevant failure that involves an offshore transfer.

(2B) P discloses the failure by—

(a) telling HMRC about it,

(b) giving HMRC reasonable help in quantifying the tax unpaid by reason of it,

(c) allowing HMRC access to records for the purpose of checking how much tax is so unpaid, and

(d) providing HMRC with additional information.

(2C) The Treasury must make regulations setting out what is meant by "additional information" for the purposes of sub-paragraph (2B)(d).

(2D) Regulations under sub-paragraph (2C) are to be made by statutory instrument.

(2E) An instrument containing regulations under sub-paragraph (2C) is subject to annulment in pursuance of a resolution of the House of Commons."

(5) At the end insert—

"(5) Paragraph 6A(4) to (5) applies to determine whether a failure involves an offshore matter, an offshore transfer or a domestic matter for the purposes of this paragraph.

(6) In this paragraph "relevant failure" means a failure to comply with a relevant obligation."

7 In paragraph 13 (amount of reduction for disclosure), for the Table in sub-paragraph (3) substitute—

"Standard %	Minimum % for prompted disclosure	Minimum % for unprompted disclosure
30%	case A: 10% case B: 20%	case A: 0% case B: 10%
70%	35%	20%
100%	50%	30%"

8 After paragraph 13 insert—

"**13A** (1) If a person who would otherwise be liable to a penalty of a percentage shown in column 1 of the Table (a "standard percentage") has made a disclosure, HMRC must reduce the standard percentage to one that reflects the quality of the disclosure.

(2) But the standard percentage may not be reduced to a percentage that is below the minimum shown for it—

(a) for a prompted disclosure, in column 2 of the Table, and

(b) for an unprompted disclosure, in column 3 of the Table.

(3) Where the Table shows a different minimum for case A and case B—

(a) the case A minimum applies if HMRC becomes aware of the failure less than 12 months after the time when the tax first becomes unpaid by reason of the failure;

(b) otherwise, the case B minimum applies.

Standard %	Minimum % for prompted disclosure	Minimum % for unprompted disclosure
30%	case A: 10% case B: 20%	case A: 0% case B: 10%

37.5%	case A: 12.5% case B: 25%	case A: 0% case B: 12.5%
45%	case A: 15% case B: 30%	case A: 0% case B:15%
60%	case A: 20% case B: 40%	case A: 0% case B: 20%
70%	45%	30%
87.5%	53.75%	35%
100%	60%	40%
105%	62.5%	40%
125%	72.5%	50%
140%	80%	50%
150%	85%	55%
200%	110%	70%

Amendments to Schedule 55 to the Finance Act 2009 (c 10)

9 Schedule 55 to FA 2009 (penalty for failure to make returns etc) is amended as follows

10 (1) Paragraph 14 (reductions for disclosure) is amended as follows.

(2) At the beginning insert—

"(A1) In this paragraph, "relevant information" means information which has been withheld by a failure to make a return."

(3) In sub-paragraph (1)—

(a) after "6(3) or (4)" insert "where P discloses relevant information that involves a domestic matter";

(b) for the words from "information which" to the end substitute "relevant information".

(4) After sub-paragraph (1) insert—

"(1A) Paragraph 15A provides for reductions in the penalty under paragraph 6(3) or (4) where P discloses relevant information that involves an offshore matter or an offshore transfer.

(1B) Sub-paragraph (2) applies where—

(a) P is liable to a penalty under paragraph 6(3) or (4) and P discloses relevant information that involves a domestic matter, or

(b) P is liable to a penalty under any of the other provisions mentioned in sub-paragraph (1) and P discloses relevant information."

(5) After sub-paragraph (2) insert—

"(2A) Sub-paragraph (2B) applies where P is liable to a penalty under paragraph 6(3) or (4) and P discloses relevant information that involves an offshore matter or an offshore transfer.

(2B) P discloses relevant information by—

(a) telling HMRC about it,

(b) giving HMRC reasonable help in quantifying any tax unpaid by reason of its having been withheld,

(c) allowing HMRC access to records for the purpose of checking how much tax is so unpaid, and

(d) providing HMRC with additional information.

(2C) The Treasury must make regulations setting out what is meant by "additional information" for the purposes of sub-paragraph (2B)(d).

(2D) Regulations under sub-paragraph (2C) are to be made by statutory instrument.

(2E) An instrument containing regulations under sub-paragraph (2C) is subject to annulment in pursuance of a resolution of the House of Commons."

(6) At the end insert—

"(5) Paragraph 6A(4) to (5) applies to determine whether relevant information involves an offshore matter, an offshore transfer or a domestic matter for the purposes of this paragraph."

11 In paragraph 15 (amount of reduction for disclosure), for the Table in sub-paragraph (2) substitute—

"Standard %	Minimum % for prompted disclosure	Minimum % for unprompted disclosure
70%	35%	20%
100%	50%	30%"

12 After paragraph 15 insert—

"**15A** (1) If a person who would otherwise be liable to a penalty of a percentage shown in column 1 of the Table (a "standard percentage") has made a disclosure, HMRC must reduce the standard percentage to one that reflects the quality of the disclosure.

(2) But the standard percentage may not be reduced to a percentage that is below the minimum shown for it—

   (a) in the case of a prompted disclosure, in column 2 of the Table, and
   (b) in the case of an unprompted disclosure, in column 3 of the Table.

Standard %	Minimum % for prompted disclosure	Minimum % for unprompted disclosure
70%	45%	30%
87.5%	53.75%	35%
100%	60%	40%
105%	62.5%	40%
125%	72.5%	50%
140%	80%	50%
150%	85%	55%
200%	110%	70%

(3) But HMRC must not under this paragraph reduce a penalty below £300."

GENERAL NOTE

Section 163 and Sch 21 increase the minimum penalties for inaccuracies, failure to notify a charge to tax or failure to deliver a return, where the penalty relates to an offshore matter or transfer where the behaviour that led to the penalty was deliberate or deliberate and concealed. The amendments also require that additional details of any offshore inaccuracies or failures are disclosed in order to receive the maximum penalty reductions.

The amendments to FA 2007 Sch 24 (penalties for errors in tax returns etc) differentiate between the penalty regimes applying to domestic and offshore matters. The regime in respect of domestic matters remains as before. Paragraph 10 of Sch 24 will apply to penalty reductions following disclosures in connection to domestic matters and the newly inserted para 10A following disclosures in connection with offshore matters or transfers.

Paragraph 2(4) of Sch 21 tightens the provisions reducing penalties for deliberate offshore inaccuracies by requiring the provision of additional information above and beyond what would be required to resolve a domestic disclosure. The Treasury may stipulate what constitutes additional information by statutory instrument.

The amendments to FA 2008 Sch 41 (penalties for failure to notify etc) differentiate between the penalty regimes applying to domestic and offshore matters and offshore matters with deliberate behaviour and offshore transfers. The existing rules under para 6A(4)–(5) of Sch 41 determine whether the inaccuracy involves an offshore matter, an offshore transfer or a domestic matter. Paragraph 13 of Sch 41 will apply to penalty reductions following disclosures in connection to domestic matters and non-deliberate offshore matters and the newly inserted para 13A will apply to penalty reductions following disclosures in connection with offshore matters with deliberate behaviour and offshore transfers.

Paragraph 6(4) of Sch 21 tightens the provisions for reducing penalties for deliberate offshore inaccuracies by requiring the provision of additional information. The Treasury may stipulate what constitutes additional information by statutory instrument.

The amendments to FA 2009 Sch 55 (penalties for failure to make a return etc) differentiate between the penalty regimes applying to domestic and offshore matters and offshore transfers. The existing rules under para 6A(4)–(5) of Sch 55 determine whether the inaccuracy involves an offshore matter, an offshore transfer or a domestic matter. Schedule 55 para 15 will apply to penalty reductions following disclosures in connection to domestic matters and the newly inserted para 15A will apply to penalty reductions following disclosures in connection with offshore matters or transfers.

Paragraph 10(5) of Sch 21 tightens the provisions for reducing penalties for deliberate offshore inaccuracies by requiring the taxpayer to provide additional information. The Treasury may stipulate what constitutes additional information by statutory instrument.

SCHEDULE 22
ASSET-BASED PENALTY FOR OFFSHORE INACCURACIES AND FAILURES

Section 165

PART 1
LIABILITY FOR PENALTY

Circumstances in which asset-based penalty is payable

1 (1) An asset-based penalty is payable by a person (P) where—

(a) one or more standard offshore tax penalties have been imposed on P in relation to a tax year (see paragraphs 2 and 3), and

(b) the potential lost revenue threshold is met in relation to that tax year (see paragraph 4).

(2) But this is subject to paragraph 6 (restriction on imposition of multiple asset-based penalties in relation to the same asset).

Meaning of standard offshore tax penalty

2 (1) A standard offshore tax penalty is a penalty that falls within sub-paragraph (2), (3) or (4).

(2) A penalty falls within this sub-paragraph if—

(a) it is imposed under paragraph 1 of Schedule 24 to FA 2007 (inaccuracy in taxpayer's document),

(b) the inaccuracy for which the penalty is imposed involves an offshore matter or an offshore transfer,

(c) it is imposed for deliberate action (whether concealed or not), and

(d) the tax at stake is (or includes) capital gains tax, inheritance tax or asset-based income tax.

(3) A penalty falls within this sub-paragraph if—

(a) it is imposed under paragraph 1 of Schedule 41 to FA 2008 (penalty for failure to notify),

(b) the failure for which the penalty is imposed involves an offshore matter or an offshore transfer,

(c) it is imposed for a deliberate failure (whether concealed or not), and

(d) the tax at stake is (or includes) capital gains tax or asset-based income tax.

(4) A penalty falls within this sub-paragraph if—

(a) it is imposed under paragraph 6 of Schedule 55 to FA 2009 (penalty for failure to make return more than 12 months after filing date),

(b) it is imposed for the withholding of information involving an offshore matter or an offshore transfer,

(c) it is imposed for a deliberate withholding of information (whether concealed or not), and

(d) the tax at stake is (or includes) capital gains tax, inheritance tax or asset-based income tax.

(5) In a case where the inaccuracy, failure or withholding of information for which a penalty is imposed involves both an offshore matter or an offshore transfer and a domestic matter, the standard offshore tax penalty is only that part of the penalty that involves the offshore matter or offshore transfer.

(6) In a case where the tax at stake in relation to a penalty includes a tax other than capital gains tax, inheritance tax or asset-based income tax, the standard offshore tax penalty is only that part of the penalty which relates to capital gains tax, inheritance tax or asset-based income tax.

(7) "Asset-based income tax" means income tax that is charged under any of the provisions mentioned in column 1 of the table in paragraph 13(2).

Tax year to which standard offshore tax penalty relates

3 (1) Where a standard offshore tax penalty is imposed under paragraph 1 of Schedule 24 to FA 2007, the tax year to which that penalty relates is—

(a) if the tax at stake as a result of the inaccuracy is income tax or capital gains tax, the tax year to which the document containing the inaccuracy relates;

(b) if the tax at stake as a result of the inaccuracy is inheritance tax, the year, beginning on 6 April and ending on the following 5 April, in which the liability to tax first arose.

(2) Where a standard offshore tax penalty is imposed under paragraph 1 of Schedule 41 to FA 2008 for a failure to comply with an obligation specified in the table in that paragraph, the tax year to which that penalty relates is the tax year to which the obligation relates.

(3) Where a standard offshore tax penalty is imposed under paragraph 6 of Schedule 55 to FA 2009 for a failure to make a return or deliver a document specified in the table of paragraph 1 of that Schedule, the tax year to which that penalty relates is—

(a) if the tax at stake is income tax or capital gains tax, the tax year to which the return or document relates;

(b) if the tax at stake is inheritance tax, the year, beginning on 6 April and ending on the following 5 April, in which the liability to tax first arose.

Potential lost revenue threshold

4 (1) The potential lost revenue threshold is reached where the offshore PLR in relation to a tax year exceeds £25,000.

(2) The Treasury may by regulations change the figure for the time being specified in sub-paragraph (1).

(3) Regulations under sub-paragraph (2) are to be made by statutory instrument.

(4) A statutory instrument containing regulations under sub-paragraph (2) is subject to annulment in pursuance of a resolution of the House of Commons.

(5) Regulations under sub-paragraph (2)—

(a) may make different provision for different purposes;

(b) may contain supplemental, incidental, consequential, transitional and transitory provision.

Offshore PLR

5 (1) The offshore PLR, in relation to a tax year, is the total of—

(a) the potential lost revenue (in the case of a standard offshore tax penalty imposed under Schedule 24 to FA 2007 or Schedule 41 to FA 2008), and

(b) the liability to tax (in the case of a standard offshore tax penalty imposed under Schedule 55 to FA 2009),

by reference to which all of the standard offshore tax penalties imposed on P in relation to the tax year are assessed.

(2) Sub-paragraphs (3) to (5) apply where—

(a) a penalty is imposed on P under paragraph 1 of Schedule 24 to FA 2007, paragraph 1 of Schedule 41 to FA 2008 or paragraph 6 of Schedule 55 to FA 2009, and

(b) the potential lost revenue or liability to tax by reference to which the penalty is assessed relates to a standard offshore tax penalty and one or more other penalties.

In this paragraph, such a penalty is referred to as a "combined penalty".

(3) Only the potential lost revenue or liability to tax relating to the standard offshore tax penalty is to be taken into account in calculating the offshore PLR.

(4) Where the calculation of the potential lost revenue or liability to tax by reference to which a combined penalty is assessed depends on the order in which income or gains are treated as having been taxed, for the purposes of calculating the offshore PLR—

(a) income and gains relating to domestic matters are to be taken to have been taxed before income and gains relating to offshore matters and offshore transfers;

(b) income and gains relating to taxes that are not capital gains tax, inheritance tax or asset-based income tax are to be taken to have been taxed before income and gains relating to capital gains tax, inheritance tax and asset-based income tax.

(5) In a case where it cannot be determined—

(a) whether income or gains relate to an offshore matter or offshore transfer or to a domestic matter, or

(b) whether income or gains relate to capital gains tax, asset-based income tax or inheritance tax or not,

for the purposes of calculating the offshore PLR, the potential lost revenue or liability to tax relating to the standard offshore tax penalty is to be taken to be such share of the total potential lost revenue or liability to tax by reference to which the combined penalty was calculated as is just and reasonable.

(6) Sub-paragraph (7) applies where—

(a) a standard offshore tax penalty or a combined penalty is imposed on P, and

(b) there are two or more taxes at stake, including capital gains tax and asset-based income tax.

(7) Where the calculation of the potential lost revenue or liability to tax by reference to which the penalty is assessed depends on the order in which income or gains are treated as having been taxed, for the purposes of calculating the offshore PLR, income and gains relating to asset-based income tax are to be taken to have been taxed before income and gains relating to capital gains tax.

Restriction on imposition of multiple asset-based penalties in relation to the same asset

6 (1) Sub-paragraphs (2) and (3) apply where—

(a) a standard offshore tax penalty has been imposed on P, and

(b) the potential lost revenue threshold is met,

in relation to more than one tax year falling within the same investigation period.

(2) Only one asset-based penalty is payable by P in the investigation period in relation to any given asset.

(3) The asset-based penalty is to be charged by reference to the tax year in the investigation period with the highest offshore PLR.

(4) An "investigation period" is—

(a) the period starting with the day on which this Schedule comes into force and ending with the last day of the last tax year before P was notified of an asset-based penalty in respect of an asset, and

(b) subsequent periods beginning with the day after the previous period ended and ending with the last day of the last tax year before P is notified of a subsequent asset-based penalty in respect of the asset,

and different investigation periods may apply in relation to different assets.

PART 2

AMOUNT OF PENALTY

Standard amount of asset-based penalty

7 (1) The standard amount of the asset-based penalty is the lower of—

(a) 10% of the value of the asset, and

(b) offshore PLR x 10.

(2) See also—

(a) paragraphs 8 and 9, which provide for reductions in the standard amount, and

(b) Part 3, which makes provision about the identification and valuation of the asset.

Reductions for disclosure and co-operation

8 (1) HMRC must reduce the standard amount of the asset-based penalty where P does all of the following things—

(a) makes a disclosure of the inaccuracy or failure relating to the standard offshore tax penalty;

(b) provides HMRC with a reasonable valuation of the asset;

(c) provides HMRC with information or access to records that HMRC requires from P for the purposes of valuing the asset.

(2) A reduction under sub-paragraph (1) must reflect the quality of the disclosure, valuation and information provided (and for these purposes "quality" includes timing, nature and extent).

(3) The Treasury must make regulations setting out the maximum amount of the penalty reduction under sub-paragraph (1).

(4) The maximum amount may differ according to whether the case involves only unprompted disclosures or involves prompted disclosures.

(5) A case involves only unprompted disclosures where—

(a) in a case where the asset-based penalty relates to only one standard offshore tax penalty, that standard offshore tax penalty was reduced on the basis of an unprompted disclosure, or

(b) in a case where the asset-based penalty relates to more than one standard offshore tax penalty, all of those standard offshore tax penalties were reduced on the basis of unprompted disclosures.

(6) A case involves prompted disclosures where any of the standard offshore tax penalties to which the asset-based penalty relates was reduced on the basis of a prompted disclosure.

(7) Regulations under sub-paragraph (3) are to be made by statutory instrument.

(8) A statutory instrument containing regulations under sub-paragraph (3) is subject to annulment in pursuance of a resolution of the House of Commons.

(9) Regulations under sub-paragraph (3)—

(a) may make different provision for different purposes;

(b) may contain supplemental, incidental, consequential, transitional and transitory provision.

Special reduction

9 (1) If HMRC think it right because of special circumstances, they may reduce the standard amount of the asset-based penalty.

(2) In sub-paragraph (1) "special circumstances" does not include—

(a) ability to pay, or

(b) the fact that a potential loss of revenue from one taxpayer is balanced by a potential over-payment by another.

(3) In sub-paragraph (1) the reference to reducing a penalty includes a reference to—

(a) staying a penalty, and

(b) agreeing a compromise in relation to proceedings for a penalty.

PART 3

IDENTIFICATION AND VALUATION OF ASSETS

Introduction

10 (1) This Part makes provision about the identification and valuation of the asset for the purposes of calculating the amount of the asset-based penalty.

(2) An asset-based penalty may relate to more than one asset.

(3) The identification and valuation of the asset is to be determined—

(a) under paragraph 11 where the principal tax at stake is capital gains tax,

(b) under paragraph 12 where the principal tax at stake is inheritance tax, and

(c) under paragraph 13 where the principal tax at stake is asset-based income tax.

See also paragraph 14 (jointly held assets).

(4) The principal tax at stake—

(a) in a case where the standard offshore tax penalty (or penalties) relates to only one type of tax, is the tax to which that standard offshore tax penalty (or penalties) relates;

(b) in a case where the standard offshore tax penalty (or penalties) relate to more than one type of tax, is the tax which gives rise to the highest offshore PLR value.

(5) The offshore PLR value, in relation to a type of tax, is the potential lost revenue or liability to tax by reference to which the part of the penalty relating to that type of tax was assessed.

(6) The rules in paragraph 5(2) to (7) apply for the purposes of calculating the offshore PLR value, in relation to a type of tax, as they apply for the purposes of calculating the offshore PLR.

Capital gains tax

11 (1) This paragraph applies where the principal tax at stake is capital gains tax.

(2) The asset is the asset that is the subject of the disposal (or deemed disposal) on or by reference to which the capital gains tax to which the standard offshore penalty relates is charged.

(3) For the purposes of calculating the amount of the asset-based penalty, the value of the asset is to be taken to be the consideration for the disposal of the asset that would be used in the computation of the gain under TCGA 1992 (other than in a case where sub-paragraph (4) applies).

(4) In a case where the disposal on or by reference to which the capital gains tax is charged is a part disposal of an asset, the asset-based penalty is to be calculated by reference to the full market value of the asset immediately before the part disposal took place.

(5) Terms used in this paragraph have the same meaning as in TCGA 1992.

Inheritance tax

12 (1) This paragraph applies where the principal tax at stake is inheritance tax.

(2) The asset is the property the disposition of which gave rise to the transfer of value by reason of which the inheritance tax to which the standard offshore penalty relates became chargeable.

(3) For the purposes of calculating the amount of the asset-based penalty, the value of the property is to be the value of the property used by HMRC in assessing the liability to inheritance tax.

(4) Terms used in this paragraph have the same meaning as in IHTA 1984.

Asset-based income tax

13 (1) This paragraph applies where the principal tax at stake is asset-based income tax.

(2) Where the standard offshore tax penalty relates to income tax charged under a provision shown in column 1 of the Table, the asset is the asset mentioned in column 2 of the Table.

Provision under which income tax is charged	Asset
Chapters 3, 7 and 10 of Part 3 of ITTOIA 2005 (property businesses)	The estate, interest or right in or over the land that generates the income for the business (see sections 264 to 266 of ITTOIA 2005)
Chapter 8 of Part 3 of ITTOIA 2005 (rent receivable in connection with a s12(4) concern)	The estate, interest or right in or over the land that generates the rent receivable in connection with a UK section 12(4) concern (see sections 335 and 336 of ITTOIA 2005)
Chapters 2 and 2A of Part 4 of ITTOIA 2005 (interest and disguised interest)	The asset that generates the interest
Chapters 3 to 5 of Part 4 of ITTOIA 2005 (dividends etc)	The shares or other securities in relation to which the dividend or distribution is paid
Chapter 7 of Part 4 of ITTOIA 2005 (purchased life annuity payments)	The annuity that gives rise to the payments
Chapter 8 of Part 4 of ITTOIA 2005 (profits from deeply discounted securities)	The deeply discounted securities that are disposed of (see sections 427 to 430 of ITTOIA 2005)
Chapter 9 of Part 4 of ITTOIA 2005 (gains from contracts for life insurance etc)	The policy or contract from which the gain is treated as arising
Chapter 11 of Part 4 of ITTOIA 2005 (transactions in deposits)	The deposit right which is disposed of (see sections 551 and 552 of ITTOIA 2005)
Chapter 2 of Part 5 of ITTOIA 2005 (receipts from intellectual property)	The intellectual property, know-how or patent rights which generate the income (see sections 579, 583 and 587 of ITTOIA 2005)
Chapter 4 of Part 5 of ITTOIA 2005 (certain telecommunication rights: non-trading income)	The relevant telecommunication right from which the income derives (see section 614 of ITTOIA 2005)
Chapter 5 of Part 5 of ITTOIA 2005 (settlements: amounts treated as income of settlor)	The settlement which gives rise to the income or capital sums treated as income of a settlor

(3) For the purposes of calculating the amount of the asset-based penalty, the asset is to be valued as follows.

(4) In a case where the charge to income tax was triggered by a disposal of the asset, the value of the asset is to be taken as its market value on the date of disposal (and in the case of a part disposal, the value of the asset is to be taken as its full market value immediately before the part disposal took place).

(5) In any other case—

(a) where P still owns the asset on the last day of the tax year to which the standard offshore tax penalty relates, the value of the asset is to be taken as its market value on that day;

(b) where P disposed of the asset during the course of the tax year to which the standard offshore tax penalty relates, the value of the asset is to be taken as its market value on the date of disposal;

(c) where P disposed of part of the asset during the course of the tax year to which the standard offshore tax penalty relates, the value of the asset is to be taken as the market value of the part disposed on the date (or dates) of disposal plus the market value of the part still owned by the person on the last day of that tax year.

(6) But if the value of the asset, as determined in accordance with sub-paragraphs (4) and (5), does not appear to HMRC to be a fair and reasonable value, then HMRC may value the asset for the purposes of this Schedule in any other way which appears to them to be fair and reasonable.

(7) For the purposes of sub-paragraph (5)—

(a) P owns an asset if P is liable to asset-based income tax in relation to that asset;

(b) references to a disposal (and related expressions) have the same meaning as in TCGA 1992.

(8) In this paragraph "market value" has the same meaning as in TCGA 1992 (see section 272 of that Act).

(9) Other terms used in this paragraph have the same meaning as in ITTOIA 2005.

Jointly held assets

14 (1) This paragraph applies where an asset-based penalty is chargeable in relation to an asset that is jointly held by P and another person (A).

(2) The value of the asset is to be taken to be the value of P's share of the asset.

(3) In a case where P and A—

(a) are married to, or are civil partners of, each other, and

(b) live together,

the asset is to be taken to be jointly owned by P and A in equal shares, unless it appears to HMRC that this is not the case.

PART 4
PROCEDURE

Assessment

15 (1) Where a person (P) becomes liable for an asset-based penalty under paragraph 1, HMRC must—

(a) assess the penalty,

(b) notify P, and

(c) state in the notice—

(i) the tax year to which the penalty relates, and

(ii) the investigation period within which that tax year falls (see paragraph 6).

(2) A penalty under paragraph 1 must be paid before the end of the period of 30 days beginning with the day on which notification of the penalty is issued.

(3) An assessment—

(a) is to be treated for procedural purposes in the same way as an assessment to tax (except in respect of a matter expressly provided for by this Schedule),

(b) may be enforced as if it were an assessment to tax, and

(c) may be combined with an assessment to tax.

(4) An assessment of an asset-based penalty under paragraph 1 must be made within the period allowed for making an assessment of the standard offshore tax penalty to which the asset-based penalty relates (and where an asset-based penalty relates to more than one standard offshore tax penalty, the assessment must be made within the latest of those periods).

(5) In this Part of this Schedule references to an assessment to tax, in relation to inheritance tax, are to a determination.

Appeal

16 (1) P may appeal against a decision of HMRC that a penalty is payable by P.

(2) P may appeal against a decision of HMRC as to the amount of a penalty payable by P.

17 (1) An appeal is to be treated in the same way as an appeal against an assessment to the tax concerned (including by the application of any provision about bringing the appeal by notice to HMRC, about HMRC review of the decision or about determination of the appeal by the First-tier Tribunal or the Upper Tribunal).

(2) Sub-paragraph (1) does not apply—

(a) so as to require P to pay a penalty before an appeal against the assessment of the penalty is determined, or

(b) in respect of any other matter expressly provided for by this Schedule.

18 (1) On an appeal under paragraph 16(1), the tribunal may affirm or cancel HMRC's decision.

(2) On an appeal under paragraph 16(2), the tribunal may—

(a) affirm HMRC's decision, or

(b) substitute for HMRC's decision another decision that HMRC had power to make.

(3) If the tribunal substitutes its decision for HMRC's, the tribunal may rely on paragraph 9—

(a) to the same extent as HMRC (which may mean applying the same percentage reduction as HMRC to a different starting point), or

(b) to a different extent, but only if the tribunal thinks that HMRC's decision in respect of the application of paragraph 9 was flawed.

(4) In sub-paragraph (3), "flawed" means flawed when considered in the light of the principles applied in proceedings for judicial review.

(5) In this paragraph "tribunal" means the First-tier Tribunal or the Upper Tribunal (as appropriate by virtue of paragraph 17(1)).

PART 5

GENERAL

Interpretation

19 (1) In this Schedule—

"asset" has the same meaning as in TCGA 1992 (but also includes currency in sterling);

"asset-based income tax" has the meaning given in paragraph 2(7);

"HMRC" means Her Majesty's Revenue and Customs;

"investigation period" has the meaning given in paragraph 6(4);

"offshore PLR" has the meaning given in paragraph 5;

"standard amount of the asset-based penalty" has the meaning given in paragraph 7;

"standard offshore tax penalty" has the meaning given in paragraph 2.

(2) Terms used in relation to a penalty imposed under Schedule 24 to FA 2007, Schedule 41 to FA 2008 or Schedule 55 to FA 2009 have the same meaning as in the Schedule under which the penalty was imposed.

(3) References in this Schedule to capital gains tax do not include capital gains tax payable by companies in respect of chargeable gains accruing to them to the extent that those gains are NRCGT gains in respect of which the companies are chargeable to capital gains tax under section 14D or 188D of TCGA 1992 (see section 1(2A)(b) of that Act).

Consequential amendments etc

20 (1) In section 103ZA to TMA 1970 (disapplication of sections 100 to 103 in case of certain penalties), omit the "or" at the end of paragraph (h), and at the end insert ", or

(j) Schedule 22 to the Finance Act 2016 (asset-based penalty)".

(2) In section 107A of that Act (relevant trustees)—

(a) in subsection (2)(a), after "Schedule 55 to the Finance Act 2009" insert "or Schedule 22 to the Finance Act 2016";

(b) after subsection (3)(a) insert—

"(aa) in relation to a penalty under Schedule 22 to the Finance Act 2016, or to interest under section 101 of the Finance Act 2009 on such a penalty, the time when the relevant act or omission occurred;";

(c) in the words after paragraph (c), after "paragraph" insert "(aa) and".

(3) In Schedule 24 to FA 2007 (penalties for errors), in paragraph 12 (interaction with other penalties etc), in sub-paragraph (2A) at the end insert "or Schedule 22 to FA 2016 (asset-based penalty)".

(4) In Schedule 41 to FA 2008 (penalties for failure to notify), in paragraph 15 (interaction with other penalties etc), in sub-paragraph (1A) at the end insert "or Schedule 22 to FA 2016 (asset-based penalty)."

(5) In Schedule 55 to FA 2009 (penalty for failure to make return etc), in paragraph 17 (interaction with other penalties etc), in sub-paragraph (2), at the end insert ", or

(d) a penalty under Schedule 22 to FA 2016 (asset-based penalty)."

21 Section 97A of TMA 1970 (two or more tax-geared penalties in respect of same tax) does not apply in relation to an asset-based penalty imposed under this Schedule.

GENERAL NOTE

Schedule 22 is one of several provisions included in FA 2016 dealing with penalties. Schedule 22 introduces new asset-based penalties for deliberate offshore errors.

The schedule is split into five parts:

- Part 1 – Liability for penalty;
- Part 2 – Amount of penalty;
- Part 3 – Identification and valuation of assets;
- Part 4 – Procedure; and
- Part 5 – General.

Part 1 Liability for penalty

The asset-based penalty can only be applied if both conditions below are met:

- one or more standard offshore tax penalties have been imposed on the individual for the tax year in question; and
- the offshore potential lost revenue for the tax year exceeds £25,000.

"Standard offshore penalties" include:

- inaccuracy in the taxpayer's document (FA 2007 Sch 24 para 1);
- penalty for failure to notify (FA 2008 Sch 41 para 1); and
- penalty for failure to make return more than 12 months after the filing date (FA 2009 Sch 55 para 6).

For each of the penalties, the criteria are:

- involves an offshore matter or offshore transfer;
- inaccuracy is deliberate.

Tax at stake (wholly or in part) is capital gains tax, inheritance tax or asset-based income tax.

The asset-based penalty has an overriding restriction where more than one tax year is under investigation. Only one asset-based penalty can be applied to any given asset – the asset-based penalty is charged using the tax year under investigation with the highest offshore potential lost revenue.

Part 2 Amount of penalty

The asset-based penalty is the lower of:

- 10% of the asset's value; and
- the offshore potential lost revenue multiplied by 10.

HMRC will reduce the asset-based penalty if the individual complies with all the following:

- makes a disclosure of the inaccuracy or failure that led to the offshore penalty;
- provides HMRC with a reasonable valuation of the asset;
- provides HMRC with information or access to allow HMRC to value the asset.

The reduction of the asset-based penalty will depend on the timing, nature and extent of the disclosure, valuation and information provided by the individual.

A further allowance for reduction of the standard amount of the asset-based penalty has been included for special circumstances.

"Special circumstances" specifically do not include the individual's ability to pay, or if the loss of revenue from one taxpayer is met by a potential over-payment by another taxpayer.

Part 3 Identification and valuation of assets

The asset-based penalty can relate to more than one asset.

The asset(s) will depend on the type of tax that the standard offshore penalty relates to. Where there are a mix of taxes, the tax which gives rise to the highest offshore potential lost revenue is used.

Capital gains tax
– the asset is the asset which has been disposed (or deemed to have been disposed) and where the standard offshore penalty has been charged;
– the value of the asset is the one that would have been used in the computation of the gain (using TCGA 1992);
– for part disposals, the value is the full market value of the asset immediately before the part disposal.

Inheritance tax
– the asset is the property where there has been a transfer of value and the standard offshore penalty has been charged;
– the value of the property is the one used by HMRC to calculate the inheritance tax charge.

Asset-based income tax
– the assets are detailed in column 2 of para 13 of Pt 3 of Sch 22;
– the value of assets that have been disposed of are their market value on the date of disposal;
– the value of assets still held on the last day of the tax year are their market value on that day;
– HMRC have the right to revalue the asset if they believe that it is not a fair and reasonable value.

Where assets are held jointly, the value is the individual's share of the acoct. If the asset is held jointly by a married couple (or civil partners) and they live together, the asset is taken to be owned in equal shares (unless it is apparent to HMRC that this is not the case).

Part 4 Procedure

When the asset-based penalty has been applied, HMRC are required to notify the individual of the amount of the penalty, the tax year that it relates to and the investigation period.

Once the penalty has been applied, the penalty must be paid within 30 days from the date of the notification of the penalty.

The asset-based penalty is treated the same way as an assessment to tax – it can be enforced as if it was an assessment to tax and can be combined with an assessment to tax.

Appealing

The asset-based penalty can be appealed, with the appeal treated in the same way as an appeal against an assessment to tax.

Part 5 General

Interprets the meanings of various words and phrases used within Sch 22 and details the consequential amendments.

SCHEDULE 23

SIMPLE ASSESSMENTS

Section 167

1 TMA 1970 is amended in accordance with paragraphs 2 to 8 of this Schedule.

2 In section 7 (notice of liability to income tax and capital gains tax), after subsection (2) insert—

"(2A) A person who—

(a) falls within subsection (1A) or (1B), and

(b) is notified of a simple assessment for the year of assessment,

is not required to give notice under subsection (1) for that year unless the person is chargeable to income tax or capital gains tax for the year of assessment on any income or gain that is not included in the assessment."

3 After section 28G (determination of amount notionally chargeable where no NRCGT return delivered) insert—

"28H Simple assessments by HMRC: personal assessments

(1) HMRC may make a simple assessment for a year of assessment in respect of a person (other than a person to whom section 28I applies) if, when the assessment is made, the person is not excluded by subsection (2) in relation to that year.

(2) Subsection (1) does not apply to a person at any time in relation to that year of assessment if—

(a) the person has delivered a return under section 8 for that year, or

(b) the person is at that time subject to a requirement to make and deliver such a return by virtue of a notice under section 8.

but nothing in this subsection prevents HMRC from giving the person notice of a simple assessment at the same time as a notice withdrawing a notice under section 8.

(3) A simple assessment is—

(a) an assessment of the amounts in which the person is chargeable to income tax and capital gains tax for the year of assessment to which it relates, and

(b) an assessment of the amount payable by the person by way of income tax for that year, that is to say, the difference between the amount in which the person is assessed to income tax under paragraph (a) and the aggregate amount of any income tax deducted at source;

but nothing in this subsection enables an assessment to show as repayable any income tax which any provision of the Income Tax Acts provides is not repayable.

(4) The amounts in which a person is chargeable to income tax and capital gains are net amounts, taking into account any relief or allowance that is applicable.

(5) A simple assessment must be based on information relating to the person that is held by HMRC (whether or not supplied by the person to whom the assessment relates).

(6) The notice of a simple assessment required to be sent to the person by section 30A(3) must (among other things)—

(a) include particulars of the income and gains, and any relief or allowance, taken into account in the assessment, and

(b) state any amount payable by the person by virtue of section 59BA (with particulars of how it may be paid and the date by which it is payable).

(7) The tax to be assessed on a person by a simple assessment does not include any tax which—

(a) is chargeable on the scheme administrator of a registered pension scheme under Part 4 of Finance Act 2004,

(b) is chargeable on the sub-scheme administrator of a sub-scheme under Part 4 of the Finance Act 2004 as modified by the Registered Pension Schemes (Splitting of Schemes) Regulations 2006, or

(c) is chargeable on the person who is (or persons who are) the responsible person in relation to an employer-financed retirement benefits scheme under section 394(2) of ITEPA 2003.

(8) Nothing in this section prevents HMRC issuing more than one simple assessment to the same person in respect of the same year of assessment (whether or not any earlier simple assessment for that year is withdrawn).

(9) In this section references to a simple assessment are to an assessment under this section.

28I Simple assessments by HMRC: trustees

(1) HMRC may make a simple assessment for a year of assessment in respect of a settlement if, when the assessment is made, the relevant trustees of the settlement are not excluded by subsection (2) in relation to that year.

(2) Subsection (1) does not apply at any time in relation to that year of assessment if—

(a) a return under section 8A has been delivered for that year by the relevant trustees or any of them, or

(b) there is at that time a subsisting requirement to make and deliver such a return by virtue of a notice under section 8A;

but nothing in this subsection prevents HMRC from giving notice of a simple assessment at the same time as a notice withdrawing a notice under section 8A.

(3) A simple assessment is—

(a) an assessment of the amounts in which the relevant trustees are chargeable to income tax and capital gains tax for the year of assessment to which it relates, and

(b) an assessment of the amount payable by them by way of income tax for that year, that is to say, the difference between the amount in which they are assessed to income tax under paragraph (a) and the aggregate amount of any income tax deducted at source;

but nothing in this subsection enables an assessment to show as repayable any income tax which any provision of the Income Tax Acts provides is not repayable.

(4) The amounts in which the relevant trustees are chargeable to income tax and capital gains are net amounts, taking into account any relief or allowance that is applicable.

(5) A simple assessment must be based only on information relating to the settlement that is held by HMRC (whether or not supplied by the relevant trustees).

(6) The notice of a simple assessment required by section 30A(3) may be given to any one or more of the relevant trustees.

(7) That notice must (among other things)—

(a) include particulars of the income and gains, and any relief or allowance, taken into account in the assessment, and

(b) state any amount payable by the relevant trustees by virtue of section 59BA (with particulars of how it may be paid and the date by which it is payable).

(8) The tax to be assessed by a simple assessment does not include any tax which—

(a) is chargeable on the scheme administrator of a registered pension scheme under Part 4 of Finance Act 2004,

(b) is chargeable on the sub-scheme administrator of a sub-scheme under Part 4 of the Finance Act 2004 as modified by the Registered Pension Schemes (Splitting of Schemes) Regulations 2006, or

(c) is chargeable on the person who is (or persons who are) the responsible person in relation to an employer-financed retirement benefits scheme under section 394(2) of ITEPA 2003.

(9) Nothing in this section prevents HMRC issuing more than one simple assessment in respect of the same settlement and the same year of assessment (whether or not any earlier simple assessment for that year is withdrawn).

(10) In this section references to a "simple assessment" are to an assessment under this section.

(11) In this Act references to the person to whom a simple assessment relates are, in relation to one made under this section, to the relevant trustees of the settlement to which it relates.

28J Power to withdraw a simple assessment

(1) HMRC may withdraw a simple assessment by notice to the person to which it relates.

(2) An assessment that has been withdrawn ceases to have effect (and is to be taken as never having had any effect)."

4 In section 31 (appeals: right to appeal), before subsection (4) insert—

"(3A) In the case of a simple assessment, the right to appeal under subsection (1)(d) does not apply unless and until the person concerned has—

(a) raised a query about the assessment under section 31AA, and

(b) been given a final response to that query."

5 (1) Section 31A (appeals: notice of appeal) is amended as follows.

(2) In subsection (4), after "this Act" insert "(other than an appeal against a simple assessment)".

(3) After subsection (4) insert

"(4A) In relation to an appeal under section 31(1)(d) against a simple assessment—

(a) the specified date is the date on which the person concerned is given notice under section 31AA of the final response to the query the person is required by section 31(3A) to make, and
(b) the relevant officer of the Board is the officer by whom the notice of assessment was given."

6 After section 31A (notice of appeal) insert—

"31AA Taxpayer's right to query simple assessment

(1) This section applies where a person has been given notice of a simple assessment.

(2) The person may query the simple assessment by notifying HMRC of—

(a) a belief that the assessment is or may be incorrect, and
(b) the reasons for that belief.

(3) The person may exercise the power to query the simple assessment at any time within—

(a) the period of 60 days after the date on which the notice of assessment was issued, or
(b) such longer period as HMRC may allow.

(4) If the simple assessment is queried, HMRC must—

(a) consider the query and the matters raised by it, and
(b) give a final response to the query.

(5) The person may at any time withdraw a query (which terminates HMRC's duties under subsection (4)).

(6) If it appears to HMRC that—

(a) they need time to consider the matters raised by the query, or
(b) further information (whether from the person or anyone else) is required,

HMRC may postpone the simple assessment in whole or part (according to how much of it is being queried by the person).

(7) If the simple assessment is postponed in whole or part, HMRC must notify the person in writing—

(a) whether the assessment is postponed in whole or part, and
(b) if it is postponed in part, of the amount that remains payable under the assessment.

(8) While the simple assessment is postponed the person is under no obligation to pay—

(a) the payable amount specified in the notice of assessment (if the whole assessment is postponed), or
(b) the postponed part of the payable amount so specified (if the assessment is postponed in part).

(9) After considering the query the final response must be to—

(a) confirm the simple assessment,
(b) give the person an amended simple assessment (which supersedes the original assessment), or
(c) withdraw the simple assessment (without replacing it).

(10) HMRC must notify the person in writing of their final response.

(11) This section does not apply to an amended simple assessment given as a final response to the query.

(12) Nothing in this section affects—

(a) a person's right to request an explanation from HMRC of a simple assessment or the information on which it is based, or
(b) HMRC's power to give a person such explanation or information as they consider appropriate,

whether as part of the querying process under this section or otherwise.

(13) In subsection (12) "person" means a person who has been given notice of a simple assessment".

7 (1) Section 59B (payment of income tax and capital gains tax) is amended as follows.

(2) In the heading, at end insert "**: assessments other than simple assessments**".

(3) In subsection (6), after "9" insert ", 28H or 28I".

8 After section 59B insert—

"59BA Payment of income tax and capital gains tax: simple assessments

(1) This section applies where a person has been given a simple assessment in relation to a year of assessment.

(2) Subject to subsection (3), the difference between—

(a) the amount of income tax and capital gains tax for that year contained in the simple assessment, and

(b) the aggregate of any payments on account made by the person in respect of that year (whether under section 59A or 59AA or otherwise) and any income tax which in respect of that year has been deducted at source,

is payable by that person as mentioned in subsection (4) or (5).

(3) Nothing in subsection (2) is to be read as requiring the repayment of any income tax which any provision of the Income Tax Acts provides is not repayable.

(4) In a case where the person is given notice of the simple assessment after the 31st October next after the year of assessment, the difference is payable at the end of the period of 3 months after the day on which that notice was given.

(5) In any other case the difference is payable on or before the 31st January next after the end of the year of assessment.

(6) Section 59B(7) (which explains references to income tax deducted at source) applies for the purposes of this section.

(7) PAYE regulations may provide that, for the purpose of determining the amount of the difference mentioned in subsection (2), any necessary adjustments in respect of matters prescribed in the regulations shall be made to the amount of tax deducted at source under PAYE regulations."

9 (1) Schedule 56 to FA 2009 (penalty for failure to make payments on time) is amended as follows.

(2) In the Table in paragraph 1, after item 1 insert—

"1A	Income tax or capital gains tax	Amount payable under section 59BA(4) or (5) of TMA 1970	The date falling 30 days after the date specified in section 59BA(4) or (5) of TMA 1970 as the date by which the amount must be paid."

(3) In paragraph 3(1)(a), after "items 1," insert "1A,".

GENERAL NOTE

Autumn Statement 2015 introduced draft legislation to implement a "new, simpler process" for paying tax. Section 167 and Sch 23 introduce a new power enabling HMRC to assess the income tax or CGT liability of an individual or trust without the taxpayer being required to complete a self-assessment return.

With effect from 2016/17, HMRC will issue "simple assessments" to taxpayers with relatively straightforward affairs where the department holds sufficient information to calculate the tax position without a completed return. The reform is part of the Government's initiative to "abolish" the tax return, HMRC said in a tax information and impact note.

The March 2015 Budget had announced that the Government will "transform" the tax system by introducing digital tax accounts. Although the Making Tax Digital strategy has been promoted as facilitating the end of the tax return, HMRC's December 2015 "roadmap" said that "for the vast majority" there would be no need to fill in an annual return.

HMRC said the new power will eventually benefit up to two million individuals, most of whom are likely to be unpresented taxpayers in receipt of a low income. The power will be used, for example, where it is not possible to collect the whole of a person's annual income tax liability through PAYE.

Initially simple assessment have to be introduced as a paper process, HMRC said, but when taken in conjunction with wider changes to modernise the tax system the measure will lead to "significant operational cost savings". The introduction of a new assessment with a right of appeal may result in a "small increase" in the number of appeals going to tribunal.

Schedule 23 paras 1–8 amend TMA 1970 with effect for 2016/17 onwards. Schedule 23 para 2 amends TMA 1970 s 7 (notice of liability to income tax and capital gains tax) so that a person who:

- is chargeable to income tax or CGT for a tax year and has not received a notice requiring a tax return for that year (or has had such a notice withdrawn); and
- is notified of a simple assessment for the tax year

is not required to give notice of liability unless the person is chargeable to income tax or CGT on any income or gain that is not included in the simple assessment.

Schedule 23 para 3 inserts new TMA 1970 sections:

- 28H (simple assessments by HMRC: personal assessments);
- 28I (simple assessments by HMRC: trustees); and
- 28J (power to withdraw a simple assessment).

New TMA 1970 s 28H provides that HMRC may issue a simple assessment in respect of a person (who is not a relevant trustee, see below) other than a person who either (a) has delivered a tax return; or (b) is subject to a requirement to make a return by virtue of a notice under TMA 1970 s 8.

A simple assessment is an assessment of:

- the amounts in which the person is chargeable to income tax and CGT for the tax year, taking account of any applicable relief or allowance; and
- the amount payable by the person by way of income tax for that year, ie. the difference between the amount in which the person is assessed to income tax and the aggregate amount of any income tax deducted at source.

The assessment must be based on information held by HMRC relating to the person, whether or not it was the person who supplied the information.

TMA 1970 s 30A already sets out the assessing procedure to be followed for assessments that are not self-assessments. New TMA 1970 s 28H provides that a notice of a simple assessment must include particulars of the income and gains, and any relief or allowance, taken into account in the assessment. It must also state any amount payable by the person under new TMA 1970 s 59BA (see below) and it must set out the due date and how the tax may be paid.

HMRC may issue more than one simple assessment for a tax year, whether or not an earlier simple assessment is withdrawn.

New TMA 1970 s 28I introduces corresponding rules for the relevant trustees of a settlement (as defined in TMA 1970 s 7(9)). Notice of a simple assessment may be given to any one or more of the relevant trustees.

New TMA 1970 s 28J allows HMRC to withdraw a simple assessment, by notice to the person to whom it relates. Once withdrawn, the simple assessment ceases to have effect and is taken as never having had any effect.

New rules will allow the taxpayer to query a simple assessment outside the traditional appeals process. "The aim is that the majority of queries will be agreed at the query stage and the individual will not need to make a formal appeal," HMRC said in an explanatory note.

Schedule 23 para 6 inserts new TMA 1970 s 31AA (taxpayer's right to query simple assessment). The taxpayer may query the simple assessment by notifying HMRC of a belief that the assessment is or may be incorrect and the reasons for that belief. The taxpayer may exercise this right at any time within 60 days after the date on which the notice of the simple assessment was issued, or such longer period as HMRC may allow.

(Schedule 23 para 4 amends TMA 1970 s 31 (appeals: right of appeal) so that a person who receives a simple assessment must exercise the "right to query" the simple assessment, and receive a final response to that query, before the person can exercise the existing right (provided by TMA 1970 s 31(1)(d) for an assessment that is not a self-assessment) of formal appeal to a tribunal. Any such formal appeal must be made within 30 days of the "specified date", ie. the date when the final response to the query is given (TMA 1970 s 31A(4A) inserted by Sch 23 para 5(3)).)

HMRC must consider a query made under new TMA 1970 s 31AA and the matters raised by it, and give a final response to it. The person may at any time withdraw a query, in which case HMRC is no longer obliged to consider it.

If it appears to HMRC that it needs time to consider the matters raised by the query, or that it needs further information from the person or from someone else, HMRC may postpone the simple assessment in whole or part according to how much of it is being queried.

In the event of postponement, HMRC must notify the person in writing whether the assessment is postponed in whole or part, and the amount (if any) that remains payable. The person is under no obligation to pay the amount postponed.

HMRC must notify the person in writing of its final response, which must:

- confirm the simple assessment,
- give the person an amended simple assessment, or
- withdraw the simple assessment without replacing it.

This "right to query" a simple assessment does not affect a person's right to ask HMRC to explain it or provide the information on which it is based, nor does it affect HMRC's power to give a person such explanation or information as it considers appropriate.

The legislation does not provide the taxpayer with the right to query an amended simple assessment that has been issued as a final response to the query.

Schedule 23 para 7 amends TMA 1970 s 59B (payment of income tax and capital gains tax) so that it does not apply to simple assessments.

Schedule 23 para 8 inserts a new TMA 1970 s 59BA (payment of income tax and capital gains tax: simple assessments) after s 59B. It provides that the difference between (a) the amount of income tax and capital gains tax contained in a simple assessment for a tax year and (b) the aggregate of any payments on account made and any income tax deducted at source is payable as set out below:

- where the person is given notice of the simple assessment after 31 October following the end of the tax year, at the end of the period of three months after the day when the notice was given; or
- in any other case, on or before 31 January following the end of the tax year.

Schedule 23 para 9 inserts, with effect from such day (or days) as the Treasury may appoint by regulations, a new item in the table in FA 2009 Sch 56 para 1 (penalty for failure to pay tax) so that an amount payable under new TMA 1970 s 59BA will be subject to the late payment penalty.

SCHEDULE 24

TAX ADVANTAGES CONSTITUTING THE GRANT OF STATE AID

Section 180(2) and (5)

PART 1

TAX ADVANTAGES TO WHICH SECTION 180(2)APPLIES

Enhanced capital allowances

Tax advantage	Provision under which tax advantage is given
Business premises renovation allowances	Part 3A of CAA 2001
Zero-emission goods vehicle allowances	Section 45DA, 45DB and 212T of CAA 2001
Expenditure on plant and machinery for use in designated assisted areas (enhanced capital allowances for enterprise zones)	Sections 45K to 45N and 212U of CAA 2001

Creative tax reliefs

Tax advantage	Provision under which tax advantage is given
Film tax relief	Part 15 of CTA 2009
Television tax reliefs	Part 15A of CTA 2009
Theatre relief	Part 15C of CTA 2009
Orchestra tax relief	Part 15D of CTA 2009

Research and development reliefs

Tax advantage	Provision under which tax advantage is given
Relief for SMEs: cost of research and development incurred by SME	Chapter 2 of Part 13 of CTA 2009
Vaccine research relief	Chapter 7 of Part 13 of CTA 2009

PART 2
TAX ADVANTAGES TO WHICH SECTION 180(5) APPLIES

Tax advantage	Provision under which tax advantage is given to beneficiary	Person liable to receive request under section 180(5)
Reduced rate of climate change levy payable in respect of a reduced rate supply (for supplies covered by climate change agreement)	Paragraphs 42 and 44 of Schedule 6 to FA 2000	The person to whom the reduced rate taxable supply is supplied
Relief granted to investors in a company under the enterprise investment scheme	Part 5 of ITA 2007	The company whose shares are acquired by investors
Relief granted to investors in a venture capital trust under the venture capital trust scheme	Part 6 of ITA 2007	The venture capital trust

GENERAL NOTE

HMRC published a policy paper on 16 March 2016 which relates to the European Commission's programme of modernising state aid. Its stated policy objective is to enable the UK to contribute to the monitoring of state aids and compliance with EU state aid rules. The overall effect of the provisions is to enable HMRC to collect additional information in relation to certain UK tax reliefs and give HMRC a statutory footing to publish that information or disclose it to the European Commission (which may then publish it).

Section 180 enables HMRC to collect additional information. The additional powers may only be exercised for the purpose of complying with EU state aid requirements.

The additional powers apply to a limited range of tax reliefs which are set out in FA 2016 Sch 24. The affected reliefs are relief for small and medium enterprises in respect of research and development costs, the enterprise investment scheme (the "EIS"), the venture capital trust scheme (the "VCT Scheme"), vaccine research relief, reduced rate climate change levy (the "Climate Change Levy"), enhanced capital allowances for enterprise zones, business premises renovation allowances, zero-emission goods vehicle allowances and certain film, television, theatre and orchestra reliefs. Each relief is affected in one of two ways, as summarised below.

First, for the reliefs listed above other than the EIS, the VCT Scheme and the Climate Change Levy, HMRC will be able to issue a determination indicating the scope and form of information required to be provided when such a relief is claimed. The information HMRC may require includes information about the entity making the claim for relief, its activities, the subject matter of the claim and any other information relevant to the granting of state aid through that tax relief. The list is not exhaustive. HMRC will also have the flexibility to require different information for different circumstances and to change their requirements by issuing further determinations. Claims made before 1 July 2016 are grandfathered.

Secondly, for the EIS, the VCT Scheme and the Climate Change Levy reduced rate, HMRC's additional power is to issue a notice to the "relevant person" (for EIS, the company the shares in which are acquired by investors, for the VCT Scheme, the venture capital trust and for the Climate Change Levy, the person receiving the reduced rate supply). That notice will require the relevant person to provide certain information within a period specified in the notice. In such cases, HMRC will be able to require that the relevant person provides information about it or its activities, any other person who has the benefit of the tax relief, information about the relief itself (including the circumstances in which it was obtained) and any other information relevant to the granting of state aid through that tax relief. There is no grandfathering for this aspect of the new rules. Section 180(11) specifically states that information relating to matters arising before the FA 2016 is passed may be required to be provided under the new regime.

SCHEDULE 25
OFFICE OF TAX SIMPLIFICATION
Section 184

Membership
1 (1) The OTS is to consist of not more than eight members.

(2) The members of the OTS must include—

(a) a chair,
(b) a tax director (see sub-paragraph (5)),
(c) a representative of Her Majesty's Revenue and Customs, and
(d) a representative of the Treasury.

(3) The additional members, if any, are to be nominated by the chair.

(4) The members of the OTS are to be appointed by the Chancellor of the Exchequer.

(5) A person may be appointed as a tax director of the OTS only if the Chancellor of the Exchequer is satisfied that the person has the necessary qualifications and experience to direct the manner in which the OTS discharges its functions.

(6) The Chancellor of the Exchequer must consult the chair of the OTS before appointing a person as a tax director (subject to paragraph 3(3)).

Term of office
2 (1) A person holds and vacates office as a member of the OTS in accordance with the terms of the appointment, subject to the following provisions.

(2) A period of appointment may not exceed 5 years.

(3) A person who ceases to be a member of the OTS is eligible for re-appointment.

Appointment of initial members
3 (1) Sub-paragraphs (2) and (3) apply where a person ("P") appointed under paragraph 1(2)(a) or (b) was, immediately before the appointment, the chair or tax director (as the case may be) of the non-statutory Office of Tax Simplification.

(2) P's period of appointment is to be taken to have begun with the appointment of P as the chair or tax director (as the case may be) of the non-statutory Office of Tax Simplification.

(3) The requirement in paragraph 1(6) does not apply where P was, immediately before P's appointment under paragraph 1(2)(b), the tax director of the non-statutory Office of Tax Simplification.

Termination of appointments
4 A member of the OTS may at any time resign by giving written notice to the Chancellor of the Exchequer.

5 (1) The Chancellor of the Exchequer may terminate the appointment of a member of the OTS by giving the member written notice.

(2) In the case of a member appointed for the purposes of paragraph 1(2)(a) or (b) or (3), the Chancellor of the Exchequer may only terminate the appointment if—

(a) the member has been absent from meetings of the OTS without the OTS's permission for a period of more than 3 months,
(b) the member becomes bankrupt (see sub-paragraph (3)),
(c) the member has failed to comply with the terms of the appointment, or
(d) the member is, in the opinion of the Chancellor of the Exchequer, unable, unfit or unwilling to carry out the member's functions.

(3) A member becomes bankrupt if—

(a) in England and Wales or Northern Ireland, a bankruptcy order is made in relation to the member;
(b) in Scotland, the member's estate is sequestrated.

Remuneration
6 The Treasury may pay a member of the OTS such remuneration and allowances as the Treasury may determine.

Provision of staff and facilities etc

7 The Treasury may provide the OTS with such staff, accommodation, services and other facilities as appear to the Treasury to be necessary or expedient for the proper performance by the OTS of its functions.

Validity of proceedings

8 The OTS may regulate its own procedure.

9 The validity of anything done by the OTS is not affected by—

(a) any vacancy in the membership of the OTS, or

(b) any defect in the appointment of a member of the OTS.

Supplementary powers

10 The OTS may do anything that appears to it to be necessary or appropriate for the purpose of, or in connection with, the performance of its functions.

Finance

11 (1) The Treasury may make to the OTS such payments out of money provided by Parliament as the Treasury considers appropriate for the purpose of enabling the Office to meet its expenses.

(2) Payments are to be made at such times, and subject to such conditions, as the Treasury may determine.

Disqualification

12 In Part 2 of Schedule 1 to the House of Commons Disqualification Act 1975 (bodies of which all members are disqualified) insert at the appropriate place—

"The Office of Tax Simplification."

13 In Part 2 of Schedule 1 to the Northern Ireland Assembly Disqualification Act 1975 (bodies of which all members are disqualified) insert at the appropriate place—

"The Office of Tax Simplification."

Freedom of information

14 In Part 6 of Schedule 1 to the Freedom of Information Act 2000 (public authorities to which the Act applies) insert at the appropriate place—

"The Office of Tax Simplification."

Public sector equality duty

15 In Part 1 of Schedule 19 to the Equality Act 2010 (authorities subject to the public sector equality duty) under the heading "Industry, business, finance etc" insert at the appropriate place—

"The Office of Tax Simplification."

GENERAL NOTE

Summer Budget 2015 announced that the Office of Tax Simplification (OTS) would be made permanent and put on a statutory footing.

The House of Lords Economic Affairs Committee welcomed the move, but recommended in a March 2016 report on the draft Finance Bill that the OTS's statutory remit be extended to give it "an integral role in tax policy design". The committee noted that the draft legislation did not use the term "independent", adding that in evidence to the committee some experts had questioned "how independent the OTS could be in its operations when it is entirely dependent on HM Treasury for funding".

Schedule 25 sets out the OTS's constitutional framework, and provides that the OTS is to consist of not more than eight members.

The members must include a chair, a tax director and representatives of HMRC and the Treasury. Any additional members are to be nominated by the chair.

The members are to be appointed by the Chancellor, who must appoint a person as a tax director:

– only after consulting with the chair (except in relation to an appointment as tax director of a person who was, immediately before that appointment, the tax director of the non-statutory OTS); and

– only if the Chancellor is satisfied that the person has the necessary qualifications and experience to direct how the OTS discharges its functions.

A period of appointment may not exceed five years but a person who ceases to be a member may be re-appointed. Where a person appointed as chair or tax director was, immediately before the appointment, chair or tax director of the non-statutory OTS, his period of appointment is taken to have begun with his appointment as the chair or tax director of the non-statutory OTS.

A member may resign at any time, and the Chancellor may terminate a member's appointment at any time. However, the Chancellor may only terminate the appointment of the chair, the tax director, or an additional member nominated by the chair in any of the circumstances – including bankruptcy and absence from meetings – specified in Sch 23 para 5 (absence from meetings, bankruptcy etc).

The Treasury may pay members of the OTS remuneration and allowances and provide the OTS with staff, accommodation, services and facilities. The OTS may regulate its own procedure and may do anything that appears to it to be necessary or appropriate for the purpose of the proper performance of its functions.

Sections 184–188 and Sch 25 come into force on such day as the Treasury may appoint by means of regulations made by statutory instrument.

The OTS published on 12 May 2016 a strategy document for "stakeholder consultation". OTS chair Angela Knight said that having had some early discussions with business stakeholders, the tax profession and Government, the OTS was now bringing questions to a broader audience. Specific areas of work would include engaging with HMRC on its Making Tax Digital programme. The OTS held a stakeholder conference in July 2016, and *Taxation* reported (28 July 2016, page 8) a consensus that the OTS's priorities should be "the interface between employment, self-employment and incorporation; the interaction between the tax and benefits system; and the operation of reliefs".

FINANCE BILL DEBATES

Publisher's note

The Finance Bill was published on 24 March 2016.

Please note that the Bill was renumbered during its passage through Parliament. Section and Schedule *headings* below are numbered as they appear in the Finance Act 2016. Section and Schedule numbers referred to in the *text* below are as set out in the Hansard Debates.

Extracts from the debates

Section/Schedule	*Extracts from House of Commons Hansard Debates*
Section 5, Sch 1 – Abolition of dividend tax credits etc	Public Bill Committee: 30 June 2016
Section 22, Sch 5 – Pension flexibility	Public Bill Committee: 30 June 2016
Sections 36–38 – Disguised fees and carried interest	Public Bill Committee: 30 June 2016
Section 41 – Deduction of income tax at source: intellectual property	Public Bill Committee: 30 June 2016
Section 64, Sch 9 – Profits from the exploitation of patents etc	Public Bill Committee: 5 July 2016
Section 64, Sch 9 – Profits from the exploitation of patents etc	Report Stage, House of Commons: 5 Sept 2016
Sections 76–82 – Transactions in UK land	Public Bill Committee: 7 July 2016
Section 84 – Entrepreneurs' relief: associated disposals	Committee of Whole House: 28 June 2016
Section 87, Sch 14 – Investors' relief	Committee of Whole House: 28 June 2016
Section 88 – Employee shareholder shares: limit on exemption	Committee of Whole House: 28 June 2016
Section 93, Sch 15 – Inheritance tax: increased nil-rate band	Public Bill Committee: 5 July 2016
Section 97 – Estate duty: objects of national, scientific, historic or artistic interest	Public Bill Committee: 5 July 2016
Sections 98–120 – Apprenticeship levy	Public Bill Committee: 5 July 2016
Section 128 – SDLT: higher rates for additional dwellings etc	Public Bill Committee: 7 July 2016
Section 137 – Stamp duty: acquisition of target company's share capital	Public Bill Committee: 7 July 2016
Section 156 – General anti-abuse rule: provisional counteractions	Report Stage, House of Commons: 5 Sept 2016
Section 159, Sch 18 – Serial tax avoidance	Committee of Whole House: 28 June 2016

Section 160 – Promoters of tax
avoidance schemes

Committee of Whole House:
28 June 2016

Section 161, Sch 19 – Large businesses:
tax strategies and sanctions for
persistently unco-operative behaviour

Committee of Whole House:
28 June 2016

Section 161 – Large businesses: tax
strategies and sanctions for persistently
unco-operative behaviour

Report Stage, House of Commons:
5 Sept 2016

Section 5, Sch 1
Abolition of dividend tax credits etc

Public Bill Committee: 30 June 2016

(Col 18)

David Gauke: The Government have tabled seven amendments to schedule 1. The amendments result from technical oversights during the drafting process and will not materially affect the measure. Amendment 127 will stop tax being treated as paid on certain types of income received on shares held in an estate. That will align the taxation of that income with other taxpayers and other types of income received by the estate. Beneficiaries will be given a credit for the tax relief paid on their income. Overall, the change will not increase the tax that is due.

Amendment 128 will ensure that all company distributions received by members of partnerships will continue to be taxed on the tax year basis, rather than by reference to the partnership's accounting period. That will provide consistency of treatment for all partnerships receiving that type of income, and remove the need for more complicated transitional rules.

Amendment 130 will ensure that the beneficiary of a trust receives full credit for all the tax already paid by the trustee. That will prevent income being taxed twice. Amendments 129, 131 and 133 are consequential amendments following those first three changes.

...

Section 22, Sch 5
Pension flexibility

Public Bill Committee: 30 June 2016

(Col 32)

David Gauke: Government amendment 134 to schedule 5 clarifies that the sums or assets available to fund a lump sum death benefit are valued immediately after the member's death. The change is a minor, technical one to provide clarity and to ensure that the legislation works.

To conclude, the Government introduced pension flexibility because we believe that individuals who have worked and saved responsibly throughout their life should be trusted to make their own decisions about their pension savings. The changes made in the clause will help to ensure that the flexibilities work for everyone. I hope that it may stand part of the Bill.

Rob Marris (Wolverhampton South West) (Lab): It is a pleasure to appear before you again, Mr Howarth.

The Labour party supports clause 22, schedule 5 and the amendment, which will come as no surprise. Pension flexibility was in the manifesto on which you and I got elected, Mr Howarth, and we support it. I have a few technical questions that the Minister may wish to write to me about, or not. As ever, I was helped by the Chartered Institute of Taxation briefing, which, in reference to paragraph 6(3) of schedule 5, on page 297 of the latest print edition of the Bill, states: "This is complicated, although we agree that it achieves the stated aim. However, it is not clear to us what exactly paragraph 6(3) is trying to do, and it is unclear whether the 'person' is the dependant or the original member." Perhaps the Minister will clarify that.

More importantly, the CIOT goes on to state: "It will be very complicated in future to determine who might be a dependant for various legislative purposes." Thirdly, it said that it contacted Her Majesty's Revenue and Customs about various typographical errors. Perhaps the Minister will reassure the Committee about that, or look into it to ensure that any of the errors CIOT discovered have been tidied up, or will be on Report, if necessary. Notwithstanding all that, we welcome the five small changes to which the Minister referred.

Mr Gauke: I thank the hon. Gentleman for his support for pension flexibility, which I debated with some of his colleagues and predecessors over many months in the previous Parliament. Inevitably, when a fundamental change is undertaken in how we address these matters, there will be areas that require refinement and correction, and that is what we are doing.

The hon. Gentleman asked about the definition of "dependant". Hopefully I can reassure him by saying that that will be clarified in the guidance that will be produced.

I can also assure him that any typographical errors are being dealt with, with regard to the guidance and so on. We welcome engagement from the CIOT in these matters, as with other matters.

As for paragraph 6(3), I will be—

Rob Marris: Sometimes it is helpful to sort this out in Committee, because it goes on the record in Hansard. However, if the Minister is unable immediately to bring the answer to mind, I appreciate that he might clarify later the contents of paragraph 6(3).

Mr Gauke: For paragraph 6(3), guidance will be produced dealing specifically with that point. I hope that is helpful and that the clause will be accepted by the Committee.

...

Sections 36–38
Disguised fees and carried interest

Public Bill Committee: 30 June 2016

(Col 41)

David Gauke: With your permission, Mr Howarth, my remarks will cover clauses 36, 37 and 38, amendments 43 to 49.

...

These clauses introduce a test to limit the circumstances in which performance-based rewards paid to asset managers will be taxed as chargeable gains. The main test will be introduced by clause 37. Clause 36 will change some related definitions in the disguised investment management fees rules. Clause 38 sets out how the rules will work with regard to individuals coming to the UK. Taken together, these clauses will ensure that only fund managers engaging in long-term investment activity pay capital gains tax on their performance-related reward or carried interest; otherwise, that form of remuneration will be fully charged to income tax.

In 2015, we legislated to ensure management fees are always subject to income tax. Where carried interest is taxable as a chargeable gain, the full amount will be taxable without reduction through arrangements such as base cost shift. These clauses build on the previous legislation. They will ensure that capital gains treatment for carried interest is reserved only for those managing funds that are genuinely long-term investments. Treating carried interest as a capital gain rather than an income is the right approach and keeps the UK in step with other countries. It is also the approach that has been adopted consistently by previous Governments in this country over a long period. However, to ensure the regime is fair and not open to abuse, these changes limit capital gains tax treatment to those managers who can demonstrate long-term investment activity by the fund they manage.

Clauses 37 and 38 will insert a test that applies to all payments of carried interest. On receipt of carried interest, asset managers will be required to calculate the average holding period of the investments in the fund. If the average holding period is less than 36 months, the payment will be subject to income tax. If the period is more than 40 months, the payment will be subject to capital gains tax. There is a taper in between those two time limits, and targeted anti-avoidance rules to ensure that the rules cannot be exploited. The rule is slightly different for managers of debt funds, turnaround funds or venture capital funds, reflecting the specific investment strategies of those kinds of funds.

Clause 38 specifically sets out how individuals who move to the UK will be taxed in certain situations. It will apply in the first five years after an individual moves to the UK when he or she receives a reward that is taxable to income under the time held test, which I referred to earlier. Where the reward relates to services performed outside the UK, before they were resident in the UK, it will be charged to UK tax only when it is remitted to the UK. That reflects the fact that the reward relates to work done before the individual lived in this country, and it will help to ensure these rules do not make it harder for UK asset managers to attract the best talent in the global labour market.

Clause 36 will amend definitions in the disguised investment management fees rules to ensure the rules introduced by clauses 37 and 38 work as intended, especially in relation to more complicated investment fund structures.

The Government tabled seven amendments to clause 37. They are technical changes to ensure the provisions operate as intended. Amendments 43, 46 and 48 make the same technical change in three of the specialised rules we have included in clause 37. Each rule will apply a targeted calculation rule to a particular type of fund investment strategy—for example, a fund that invests in real estate or provides venture capital—thus ensuring that the average investment holding test accurately captures a fund's underlying activity.

A fundamental concept in all these rules is that of a relevant disposal. A relevant disposal is, in effect, a disposal that is taken into account when calculating a fund's average holding period. These changes will ensure that the legislation uses a consistent definition throughout the various specialised regimes that is clear and understood by industry and their advisers.

Amendments 44, 45 and 47 will correct a technical error that would have prevented the relevant provisions from working in practice.

Amendment 49 will expand the definition of a secondary fund to include the acquisition of investment portfolios from unconnected investment schemes. Stakeholders have informed us that many secondary funds undertake that type of activity, and that amendment is necessary to ensure that the relevant rules still apply to those funds.

...

Clauses 36 to 38 will ensure that only those managers engaged in genuinely long-term investment activity pay capital gains tax on their performance-related rewards, and I therefore hope that those clauses stand part of the Bill and amendments 43 to 49 are made.

...

Section 41 (originally clause 40)
Deduction of income tax at source: intellectual property

Public Bill Committee: 30 June 2016

(Col 47)

David Gauke: Before I conclude, I will speak briefly to amendments 20 and 21, also tabled by the Government. The amendments are being introduced to ensure that royalty payments subject to the anti-abuse rule include those payments brought within the scope of withholding tax by new clause 8. Together, the proposed new clauses will protect the UK from arrangements that seek to avoid UK tax through the use of royalty payments.

I hope that my explanation helps the Committee to understand the issues set out both on the odd-numbered pages and on the even-numbered pages.

...

Section 64 (originally clause 60), Sch 9
Profits from the exploitation of patents etc

Public Bill Committee: 5 July 2016

(Col 72)

David Gauke: The Government amendments to clause 60 introduce features that ensure that the benefit of the patent box is protected for claimant taxpayers and respond to specific issues raised by interested parties during formal consultation. If some of these amendments were not introduced, a number of interested parties would see their claims significantly reduced under the new patent box rules. The new rules could also potentially be open to manipulation and abuse. These amendments do not cover provisions addressing the issue of how the revised rules will apply in the context of more complex, collaborative R and D arrangements, such as cost share agreements. It is the Government's intention to include such provisions in Finance Bill 2017, to provide an opportunity for consultation with interested parties.

Amendment 50 allows taxpayers to forgo the right to use the transitional provisions, should they prefer to opt straight into the new patent box. Amendments 51 to 56, 60 to 63, 69 to 70, 78 to 79 and 88 to 112 give companies greater flexibility to track IP income and R and D expenditure at product or product family level, by removing the requirement that a product must contain more than one IP asset. We have created rules to account for the implementation of the international framework, which, incidentally, has a double impact on a taxpayer's patent box claims where an acquisition of IP involves staged payments made to the seller, allowing for sharing in the success of further development. We are also extending the definition of an acquisition of IP to cover expenditure on such an acquisition from which the relevant qualifying IP is derived, evolved or enhanced. These features are introduced by amendments 57, 66, 77, 80 and 81, and 121.

Amendments 58 and 59, 64, 67, 82 to 84 and 116 to 120 introduce simplification rules for taxpayers with smaller claims, so that they are not discouraged from claiming the patent box. Amendment 65 addresses the fact that legislation does not currently exclude finance income from the overall income that can benefit from the patent box; the measures would otherwise result in unintentional widening of the patent box.

Amendments 68, 73 and 74 ensure that any relevant R and D expenditure incurred by a foreign branch of a UK claimant company that has opted out of UK taxation under foreign branch exemption rules is treated as related party subcontract expenditure of the UK company for the purposes of calculating the R and D fraction. Under the Bill, only 65% of subcontracted R and D costs are used in the R and D fraction. Amendments 71, 72, 75 and 76 remove the treatment on subcontracted R and D costs, so that the entire amount is counted towards qualifying expenditure amounts.

The safeguard in the transitional provisions requires a determination as to whether an IP asset has been acquired from a country with or without a preferential IP regime in place. Amendments 85 to 87 clarify that the power to designate foreign tax regimes operates properly when it is used after Royal Assent. Amendment 113 widens the existing anti-avoidance provisions to take into account potential abuses of the changing rules. Finally, amendments 114 and 115 ensure that where one company takes over a trade from another, the transferee will be able to step into the shoes of the transferrer, inheriting both the IP and the expenditure history on that IP.

...

To conclude, the changes made by clause 60 will ensure that the patent box complies with the new internationally agreed framework, while the amendments ensure that the benefit of the patent box is protected for claimant taxpayers. I therefore commend clause 60, schedule 9 and amendments 50 to121.

...

Section 64 (after PBC stage: clause 63), Sch 9
Profits from the exploitation of patents etc

Report Stage, House of Commons: 5 September 2016

(Col 107)

Jane Ellison: On Government amendments 152 and 153, clause 63 and schedule 9 make changes to ensure that the patent box operates in line with the newly agreed international framework resulting from the OECD's base erosion and profit shifting action plan. As currently drafted, the changes in the Bill could result in different definitions of the term "qualifying residual profit" applying to the same parts of the patent box legislation. The amendments address that problem by providing a coherent and consistent definition for that phrase.

...

Sections 76–82 (introduced as New Clauses 11–17)
Transactions in UK land

Report Stage, House of Commons: 5 September 2016

(Col 204)

Mr Gauke: New clauses 11 to 17 will introduce the legislation announced in the 2016 Budget for a specific charge to income tax or corporation tax on profits from the disposal of land in the UK. The new clauses will ensure that offshore structures cannot be used to avoid UK tax on profits generated from dealing in or developing land in the UK.

New clauses 11, 12 and 15 will introduce new rules to ensure that profits generated by a company from dealing in or developing land in the UK will be chargeable to UK corporation tax. Those rules will apply regardless of the residence of the person carrying on the trade and regardless of whether the developer has a permanent establishment in the UK.

New clauses 13 and 14 will ensure that the profits generated by an individual from dealing in or developing land will always be chargeable to UK income tax. To prevent avoidance, the new charge will also apply where, instead of dealing in land, a developer sells shares in a company that carries on such developments. It will also apply where arrangements are put in place to split profits from development activity between the developer and related entities that could otherwise reduce chargeable allowance. In addition, the Government have strengthened long-standing rules on transactions in land to ensure that they can effectively counter abuse of the new rules.

To support those new rules, the Government are introducing an anti-avoidance rule to prevent manipulation between the policy announcement on Budget day 2016 and the introduction of the new clauses. The anti-avoidance rule is in new clause 16 for corporation tax and new clause 17 for income tax, along with other commencement and transitional rules. We have taken steps to amend our double taxation treaties; I am grateful to our partners in Guernsey, the Isle of Man and Jersey for agreeing to make changes to those treaties, taking effect from Budget day 2016. These measures will raise £2.2 billion over the scorecard period and take effect from 5 July 2016; they will affect developers of UK property who choose to operate from somewhere other than the UK to reduce their tax bills. There will be no effect on companies, based in the UK or elsewhere, whose profits are already fully taxed in the UK.

The changes made by new clauses 11 to 17 will continue the Government's fight against aggressive tax planning and profit shifting. They will bring the UK in line with other major economies and ensure fair treatment between UK and overseas developers.

Rebecca Long Bailey: The measures appear to be closing a tax loophole. On that basis, we do not oppose them, especially as they are estimated to bring in £130 million in this financial year, rising to a peak of £640 million in 2019–20. I must say, however, that this important addition to the Bill was tabled rather late in the day, even if the outline of the measure itself was announced for consultation at the Budget. I could be argued that the Opposition and stakeholders have been given insufficient time to go through the detail of the legislation.

None the less, the Chartered Institute of Taxation has identified two areas of concern on which it would like some clarification. First, will the Minister confirm that the Government do not intend pure investment structures to be affected by the new measures? Secondly, will he confirm that new clause 16 is simply a timing rule dealing with the opposition of pre-trading expenditure that would not be deductible under normal principles and where reliance needs to be placed on section 61 of the Corporation Tax Act 2009? The concern is that the clause seeks to restrict normal trading expenses incurred prior to the company's falling within the new charge. Some clarification from the Minister on those points would be appreciated.

Mr Gauke: I will of course address the questions that the hon. Lady has raised, but it might be helpful if I first provide a bit of background. Stamp duty is usually payable at 0.5% on instruments that transfer shares—no, I do not want to give that background. [Interruption.]

Yes, let us turn to this new clause. To give a bit of background, it is worth pointing out that this measure has two key principles. First, UK land is a national resource and profits from dealing in or developing land should be fully taxed in the UK. This is an internationally accepted principle. However, some companies based offshore have organised their operations to reduce their UK tax on these profits. The new specific charge on these profits will put an end to such arrangements.

Secondly, this measure is about fairness. It will level the playing field between UK and offshore developers by preventing arrangements that are designed to avoid UK tax. This will ensure that UK and overseas businesses are put on the same tax footing when carrying out the same activities. This measure was announced at Budget 2016 alongside an anti-avoidance rule that had immediate effect. HMRC has also created a taskforce to ensure that tax on these profits is effectively collected by identifying and investigating offshore businesses that try to avoid paying tax.

This measure is targeted at those who have a property building trade; it does not impact the tax profile for investors in UK property. On the timing, I understand why the hon. Member for Salford and Eccles raised the fact that we have done this through new clauses. It is important that we get this legislation right. In these particular circumstances, it was not possible to bring the legislation forward at the time the Finance Bill was published. None the less, I think these new clauses deliver what the Government are seeking to do. I therefore hope that they will stand part of the Bill.

...

Section 84 (originally clause 73)
Entrepreneurs' relief: associated disposals

Committee of Whole House: 28 June 2016

(Col 235)

David Gauke: Clauses 73 to 75 make changes to ensure that entrepreneurs' relief on capital gains tax rewards business owners and entrepreneurial investors while safeguarding the effect of measures introduced last year to prevent abuse of the relief. The Government are committed to supporting enterprise and entrepreneurship, but they are equally committed to fairness in the tax system. Entrepreneurs' relief allows certain capital gains to be taxed at 10%, rather than the normal rates, and plays an important role in supporting the enterprise culture of this country, but, as with all tax reliefs, we need to make sure that it is not being claimed in circumstances where it does not achieve its intended purpose.

These changes will improve the targeting of the anti-abuse rules introduced in 2015. The changes in clause 73 will allow relief for gains on disposal of a private asset used in a business in cases of genuine retirement or where members of the claimant's family succeed to the claimant's business. These changes will level the playing field for family-run businesses and allow them to be passed to the next generation without an unfair tax charge.

The changes in clause 74 will allow someone selling their business to a limited company to claim relief on the goodwill of that business, providing they have only a small stake in the company. The relief will still be denied where the former proprietor or partner could continue running the business through the company and benefit directly from future profits and business growth. Entrepreneurs' relief on gains on shares is due only where those shares are in trading companies or the holding companies of trading groups. Clause 75 amends the definition of a trading company to ensure that relief is available for shares in a company that has no trade of its own but which holds shares in a trading joint venture company where the investor effectively holds 5% or more of the joint venture company. The further changes made by these clauses will be backdated to the date on which the 2015 changes came into effect, meaning that no one who has made a genuine disposal for commercial reasons should be disadvantaged by the new rules.

The Government have tabled several minor amendments to the clauses. Amendments 30 to 33 simply move one of the new conditions introduced by clause 73 to a different place in the relevant statute. Amendments 34 and 35 correct two unintended retrospective effects of clause 73. Without the amendments, someone who made a disposal after Budget day 2015 and was eligible for entrepreneurs' relief could find themselves deprived of that relief by changes announced at Budget 2016. Amendments 36 to 38 clarify the commencement provisions for the new rules introduced by clause 75 and ensure that the new definition of a trading company supersedes the definition used by the Finance Act 2015. These amendments do not reflect any change in policy and will have no impact on the costings of the measures.

...

Section 87 (originally clause 76), Sch 14
Investors' relief

Committee of Whole House: 28 June 2016

(Col 236)

David Gauke: Clause 76 and schedule 14 introduce investors' relief and apply a 10% rate of capital gains tax to gains accruing on the disposal of qualifying shares held by an external investor in an unlimited trading company for at least three years. Many companies struggle to attract the long-term external investment they need to grow and expand, and this can be particularly difficult for unlisted companies, which is why, on top of cutting the capital gains tax rates, the Government are introducing this additional financial incentive to invest in these companies over the longer term. Investors relief has been designed to help unlisted companies attract inward equity investment from external investors. This clause and schedule apply a 10% rate of capital gains tax to gains accruing on the disposal of qualifying shares held by an investor in an unlisted trading company or trading group. The investor must not be an employee or officer of the company at the time of subscription. In addition, the shares must have been newly issued after 17 March 2016 and held for a period of at least three years starting from 6 April 2016. The amount of relief is capped, with individuals subject to a lifetime cap of £10 million on qualifying gains.

We are today making a number of amendments to this clause to ensure that the rules surrounding the relief are fair and clear, and to extend the scope of the relief to prevent market distortions and unlock further sources of capital. Amendments 39 to 41, 43, 44, 50 and 61 will ensure that trustees of a settlement as well individuals who choose jointly to subscribe with other individuals are able to subscribe for investor relief qualifying shares. In the case of trusts, amendment 51 includes rules that prevent individuals from creating multiple trusts, each with a £10 million lifetime limit.

Amendments 45 to 49 clarify how to determine the number of shares that qualify for investors relief when a disposal is made that consists of a mixture of qualifying and non-qualifying shares. Amendments 52 to 60 and amendments 65 to 68 clarify the provisions that deal with share disposals, share exchanges, elections, subscriptions and the distribution of value to existing shareholders.

Finally, some investors may wish to monitor and protect their investment through a seat on a company's board. Amendments 42 and 62 to 64 allow such an investor to become a director after their investment has been made as long as they are not remunerated in that capacity. They also allow an individual who becomes an employee of the company to access relief in most situations after 180 days of the share issue. Investors' relief is designed to attract new capital into unlisted companies, enabling them to grow their business. It will help to advance this Government's aims for a growing economy driven by investment and supporting businesses to grow.

...

Section 88 (originally clause 77)
Employee shareholder shares: limit on exemption

Committee of Whole House: 28 June 2016

(Col 237)

David Gauke: Clause 77 relates to shares given to employees who accept employee shareholder status. It places a lifetime limit of £100,000 on the capital gains tax exempt gains that a person can make on disposal of those shares. The limit will apply to shares received under arrangements entered into after 16 March 2016. The change will enable employee shareholders to realise the significant growth in the value of their shares without paying any capital gains tax, while helping to ensure that the status is not misused. The clause provides for fair and consistent treatment of transfers of shares to a spouse or partner. The change will benefit the Exchequer by £10 million in 2019–20 and £35 million in 2020–21.

It is also an appropriate point to address amendment 182, which was tabled by Opposition Members. It proposes that the lifetime limit be £50,000 rather than Government's proposed £100,000. This is not a change that the Government would welcome. The introduction of a cap of £100,000 where there was none before is, we believe, a significant change. The level of the cap is a matter of weighing up two policy objectives—ensuring that employee shareholder status is not misused, and encouraging and rewarding entrepreneurship. The Government believe that setting the cap at £100,000 strikes the right balance. It encourages entrepreneurship by allowing an exemption from capital gains tax which is still generous while reducing the likelihood of abuse by ensuring that the benefits for individuals are proportionate and fair. I therefore invite hon. Members to reject amendment 182.

On Government amendment 29, the normal CGT rule is that when a share is involved in certain paper-for-paper transactions, such as a bonus issue or a share-for-share takeover, a tax charge is prevented from arising at that time because the shareholder receives no cash from which to pay that tax. The new lifetime cap in clause 77 means we need a rule to ensure fair and consistent treatment when an exempt employee shareholder share is involved in these types of transactions. This amendment ensures that an employee shareholder will not have to pay CGT at the time of those transactions. Without the amendment, an employee shareholder who has used the whole of his or her lifetime limit may suffer a tax charge owing to events beyond their control although they receive no cash from which to pay that tax. That would plainly be unfair and inconsistent with the treatment of other shareholders in similar circumstances.

...

Section 93 (originally clause 82), Sch 15
Inheritance tax: increased nil-rate band

Public Bill Committee: 5 July 2016

(Col 100)

David Gauke: Clause 82 and schedule 15 ensure that the residence nil-rate band for inheritance tax will continue to be available when an individual downsizes or ceases to own a home. The clause builds on the provisions in the Finance Act 2015, which introduced a new residence nil-rate band, by creating an effective inheritance tax threshold of up to £1 million for many married couples and civil partners by the end of the Parliament, making it easier for most families to pass on the family home to their children and grandchildren without the burden of inheritance tax.

The combined effect of this package will almost halve the number of estates expected to face an inheritance tax bill in future. The Office for Budget Responsibility now forecasts that 33,000 estates will be liable for inheritance tax in 2020–21. As a result of this package, 26,000 estates will be taken out of inheritance tax altogether and 18,000 will pay less.

We recognise that people's circumstances change as they get older and that they may want to downsize or may have to sell their property. We do not want the residence nil-rate band to act as a disincentive for people thinking about making such changes. That is why we announced in the summer Budget that anyone who downsizes or ceases to own a home on or after 8 July 2015 will still be able to benefit from the new residence allowance. Clause 82 and schedule 15 allow an estate to qualify for all or part of the residence nil-rate band that would otherwise be lost as a result of the downsizing move or disposal of the residence.

The extra residence nil-rate band or downsizing edition will only be available for one former residence that the deceased lived in. Where more than one property might qualify, executors of an estate will be able to nominate which former residence should qualify. The approach reduces complexity and ensures flexibility in the system.

The Government have tabled seven amendments to schedule 15 to ensure that the legislation works as intended in certain situations that are not currently covered by the downsizing provisions. Amendment 15 caters for situations in which an individual had more than one interest in a former residence, to ensure that they are not disadvantaged compared with those who owned the entire former residence outright. Amendment 16 clarifies the meaning of disposal in situations where an individual gave away a former residence but continued to live in it. Amendment 19 ensure that where an estate is held in a trust for the benefit of a person during their lifetime, a disposal of that former residence by the trustees would also qualify for the residence nil-rate band.

Amendments 13, 14, 17 and 18 make minor consequential changes to take into account the other amendments. Clause 82 and schedule 15 will help to deliver the Government's commitment to take the ordinary family home out of inheritance tax by ensuring that people are not disadvantaged if they move into smaller homes or into care. That commitment was made in our manifesto and I am pleased to deliver it fully with this clause.

...

Rebecca Long Bailey: I will touch briefly on Government amendments 13 to 19, which according to the Minister's helpful letter of 30 June make a number of technical amendments to ensure that the legislation operates as intended in a limited number of specific circumstances that are not currently covered by the downsizing provisions. I am glad that the Government are taking steps to improve the legislation, but I cannot see how the amendments address the concerns outlined by the Chartered Institute of Taxation.

The Opposition do not feel that these measures, which expand the number of situations in which inheritance tax is not due, are a priority, given the apparent funding constraints we often hear about from the Government. We will therefore oppose clause 82 and schedule 15.

...

David Gauke: Some technical points were made by Opposition Members. I was asked whether the downsizing rules will apply when the former house was held in a trust. Amendment 19 caters for such situations. The measure will apply only where the former home was held in a type of trust that was set up for the benefit of a person during their lifetime and that person had a right to the trust assets. It does not apply to former homes held in discretionary trusts because they would not qualify for the resident's nil-rate band in those circumstances.

...

Section 97 (originally clause 86)
Estate duty: objects of national, scientific, historic or artistic interest

Public Bill Committee: 5 July 2016

(Col 109)

David Gauke: Clause 86 amends existing legislation on estate duty to stop individuals from using the provisions to pay inheritance tax at a lower rate than estate duty would be payable. That will ensure that the exemption is used as intended: to preserve objects of national heritage rather than as a tax-planning tool. The change will also bring legislation in line with provisions for lifetime transfers, where HMRC can elect for either an inheritance tax or estate duty charge. The second change will bring in a charge on objects that were exempted from estate duty but have subsequently been lost. The definition of loss will include theft and destruction by fire, although HMRC will have the discretion not to impose a charge when such a loss is not attributable to the negligence of the owner.

I turn now to the five amendments that the Government have tabled to clause 86. They are being made in response to comments we received following publication of the Finance Bill in 2016 and will ensure that the legislation works as intended. Amendment 122 clarifies that when an item is lost, HMRC will raise only a single charge for duty on the loss of the item, rather than a dual charge for the loss and breach of the conditions under which the item was originally exempt from duty.

Amendment 123 provides that clause 86 will apply to objects granted exemptions under the terms of the Finance Act 1975. That is necessary because the subsequent Finance Act 1976 failed to bring a discrete subset of material granted conditional exemption between March 1975 and April 1976 within the auspices of the new Act. If the legislation is not amended, such objects will be treated inconsistently with those exempted under the post-Finance Act 1976 regime. There are no good reasons to treat these exempted objects differently.

Amendment 124 ensures that in identifying the last death on which an object was passed, any death on or after 6 April 1976 is to be disregarded. That will ensure that the appropriate rate of estate duty is used. Amendments 125 and 126 make minor consequential changes to take into account the other amendments.

It goes without saying that the value of our culture and heritage to society is immeasurable. The changes that I have outlined will mean that our museums and galleries can continue to benefit from tax exemptions that will allow them to purchase more works of art for the enjoyment of the British public. The changes will also provide much needed consistency in the way that conditionally exempt objects are treated. I therefore hope that the clauses can stand part of the Bill.

Rebecca Long Bailey: The Minister has given us an articulate and detailed summary of how the clauses work in practice, so I will not go over too much of that again. I briefly note that the provisions make technical changes to the tax treatment of gifts or sales of property to public museums and galleries and objects of national scientific, historic or artistic interest respectively.

Clause 85 makes technical changes to support the exemption from inheritance tax of gifts or sales of property to public museums and galleries. It is necessary, as the Minister said, because recent changes in local authorities have led museum collections to be placed in charitable trusts. Those trusts do not presently fall within schedule 3 to the Inheritance Tax Act 1984, which describes the bodies that attract inheritance tax and capital gains tax relief. The clause simply rectifies that and moves the power to designate schedule 3 bodies from HMRC to HM Treasury. We have no issue with this technical clause, but I am interested to know what the justification was for moving the power to add bodies to schedule 3 from HMRC to HM Treasury. As a general question, what assessment was made in the long term of the efficacy of local authorities in managing museums and galleries? The Minister might want to refer that question to another Department and get back to me in writing.

Clause 86 puts a stop to using existing law to pay inheritance tax at a lower rate than estate duty. Estate duty was replaced in 1975 by capital transfer tax, which was replaced by inheritance tax in 1984. However, legacy estate duty legislative provisions still remain in force in relation to exemptions given pre-March 1975. Estate duty can be levied at up to 80%, whereas inheritance tax is currently at 40%. The clause stops individuals using a gap in legislation to claim conditional exemption solely to facilitate a later sale of 40% instead of up to 80%.

There is also provision for HMRC to be able to raise a charge when the owner loses an estate duty exempt object. That leads me nicely on to Government amendments 122 to 126, which make technical changes to ensure that the legislation operates as intended. Amendment 122 clarifies the rules around HMRC's ability to raise a charge for duty on the loss of an item, so that it will raise only a single charge rather than a dual one. Amendments 123 and 124 ensure that the legislation works in specific circumstances, as intended, and amendments 125 and 126 simply make minor consequential changes. We are more than happy to support these clauses and Government amendments.

...

Sections 98–120 (previously clauses 88 to 109)
Apprenticeship levy

Public Bill Committee: 5 July 2016

(Col 116)

David Gauke: I now turn to the apprenticeship levy amendments. Amendments 22 to 25 and amendment 27 all concern the rules relating to connected companies and charities and the levy allowance of £15,000. As I mentioned earlier when outlining clauses 88, 90 and 91, the Government have tabled amendments to enable groups of connected companies or charities to share the £15,000 levy allowance. The original proposal was that, if a group of companies or charities were connected, any one of them could apply the allowance. That followed the approach of the employment allowance, which has worked well. However, in response to representations, we have considered the matter further and have concluded that that would lead to a significant increase in the employer population subject to the levy, which was never the intention.

The amendments to clauses 90 and 91 and the consequential amendment to clause 88 will, therefore, allow a group of connected employers to decide what proportion of the levy allowance each of them will apply. The group must decide the allowance split at the beginning of the tax year and it will be fixed for that year unless a correction is necessary because the total amount of the levy allowance exceeds £15,000. Connected employers must notify HMRC of the amount of allowance to be applied for their PAYE schemes, and where that does not occur, or where the total notified does not equal £15,000, the amendments allow for the levy allowance to be determined by HMRC if the employer fails to take corrective action. Employers and their representatives have welcomed our decision to bring forward the amendments and I hope that Committee members will join in supporting the change.

Amendments 26 and 28 are technical amendments that seek to clarify the definition of "company" in clauses 90 and 109 to avoid any uncertainty and to ensure that the provisions are clear. I will also address new clause 2, tabled by SNP Members. The new clause seeks to delay the implementation of the apprenticeship levy until a report has been laid before Parliament on how different parts of the UK are equitably treated when the levy is eventually implemented.

...

Col 121

Rebecca Long Bailey: I turn now to Government amendments 22 to 28, which relate to clauses 88, 90, 91 and 109. Clause 90, as drafted, states that where the aggregate pay bill of a group of connected companies that will qualify to pay the apprenticeship levy and would each be entitled to a levy allowance, only one will in fact be entitled to the allowance. The connected companies must nominate which company will qualify. Similarly, clause 91 sets out that at the beginning of the tax year, where two or more qualified charities are connected with one another, only one will be entitled to the levy allowance to be offset against the apprenticeship levy.

Government amendments to those two clauses allow companies and charities that are connected for the purposes of the apprenticeship levy to share their annual levy allowance of £15,000 between them, instead of only one company or charity being entitled to the allowance. There is also a consequential amendment to clause 88, which, according to the Minister's letter,

"allows for the levy allowance not being the full £15,000, if a group of connected employers choose to split it under sections 90 or 91."

The Government have stated that these changes are in response to representations they have received, and the Opposition are also aware of concerns from stakeholders about the legislation as currently drafted. We therefore fully support these amendments.

Amendments 26 and 28 are technical amendments that clarify that the definition of a company in clause 90 applies to the whole of part 6 of the Bill relating to the apprenticeship levy. Again, we are happy to support these Government amendments.

...

Section 128 (originally clause 117)
SDLT: higher rates for additional dwellings etc

Public Bill Committee: 7 July 2016

(Col 150)

David Gauke: The Government have tabled three groups of amendments to rectify certain technical issues that have become apparent since the introduction of the higher rates. The first set, amendments 29 to 39, will ensure that so-called granny annexes will be exempt from higher SDLT when purchased with a main residence in the same transaction. We have decided that it would be unfair to change the higher rate when someone buys a main house that includes self-contained living space for an elderly relative. The Bill as drafted would usually but not always exclude that, so we are amending it to put this beyond doubt. An annex will be defined by objective criteria. It must be on the same site as the main home and worth no more than one third of the total transaction value to ensure that the regime remains robust against avoidance. I again thank my right hon. Friend the Member for Brentwood and Ongar (Sir Eric Pickles) for bringing this issue to my attention.

The second correction, in amendment 40, will allow the Government to ensure that those who use Islamic finance to purchase their main residence will not be unfairly caught by the higher rate. This will ensure that the Islamic finance provisions are consistent with those that already exist within SDLT legislation.

Finally, we are introducing a power to make wholly relieving changes by regulation in amendments 41 and 42. Those will allow us to react quickly if another unintended consequence, such as the treatment of annexes, comes to light, and they will ensure that taxpayers are not disadvantaged unnecessarily while waiting for the changes to come into force.

In summary, clause 117 seeks to redress the balance between investment and home ownership and supports owner-occupation and first-time buyers. I hope that it has the Committee's support.

...

Section 137 (introduced as New Clause 10)
Stamp duty: acquisition of target company's share capital

Public Bill Committee: 7 July 2016

(Col 202)

David Gauke: I will speak briefly about new clause 10, unless there are questions. The new clause stops an unfair stamp duty advantage where takeovers are brought about through share-for-share exchanges with no stamp duty becoming due. It will ensure that the tax system operates fairly by preventing share-for-share relief from being claimed in situations for which it was not intended. The change made by the clause will catch the insertion of a new company above another by way of a share-for-share exchange as part of a wider transaction involving transfer of a controlling stake in the new company. The change will mean that no share-for-share relief will be available where arrangements are in place, at the time of the share-for-share exchange, for a change of control of the new company. The measure will apply to any instrument exercised on or after 29 June 2016.

New clause 10 will stop share-for-share relief being claimed inappropriately on takeovers. The Government have acted quickly to prevent an unfair tax advantage and to protect significant tax revenue.

...

Section 156 (after PBC: clause 155)
General anti-abuse rule: provisional counteractions

Report Stage, House of Commons: 5 September 2016

(Col 146)

Jane Ellison: Clause 155 makes an administrative change to strengthen the procedural efficiency of the GAAR. Amendments 136 and 137 make small technical changes to the clause, which incorporate the new terms introduced by clause 156. The new terms provide a new way of counteracting under the GAAR procedure to enable the same advisory panel opinion to apply to multiple users of marketed tax avoidance schemes. We believe that the changes will streamline the procedure without altering the fundamental test to which taxpayers are subject under the GAAR. They will ensure that a provisional GAAR counteraction will apply equally to all counteraction procedures, and enable tax to be protected for the cases that we intend to address.

...

Section 159 (originally clause 147), Sch 18
Serial tax avoidance

Committee of Whole House: 28 June 2016

(Col 156)

David Gauke: Clause 147 and schedule 18 introduce the new serial avoidance regime and a new threshold condition for the existing POTAS—promoters of tax avoidance schemes— regime introduced by clause 148. The new serial avoidance regime will tackle those tax avoiders who use multiple tax avoidance schemes. It will work by putting avoiders on notice when HMRC defeats a scheme they have used. If they use further schemes and HMRC defeats them, they will face serious and escalating sanctions, including a penalty starting at 20% of tax understated and reaching 60% for a third scheme defeat while under notice. Clause 148 introduces a new threshold condition for the promoters of tax avoidance schemes regime so that promoters who have promoted three schemes that have been defeated by HMRC over an eight-year period risk entering the POTAS regime.

The Government have tabled 27 amendments to clause 148 and schedule 18. The amendments to schedule 18 provide for those who try to avoid tax through companies they own or partnerships to be brought within the scope of the new regime. Amendments to clause 148 provide for POTAS to cover circumstances where tax avoidance is promoted through associated persons. The remaining amendments make minor changes to ensure the schemes work as intended.

...

Section 160 (originally clause 148)
Promoters of tax avoidance schemes

Committee of Whole House: 28 June 2016

(Col 156)

David Gauke: Clause 148 introduces a new threshold condition for the promoters of tax avoidance schemes regime so that promoters who have promoted three schemes that have been defeated by HMRC over an eight-year period risk entering the POTAS regime.

The Government have tabled 27 amendments to clause 148 and schedule 18. The amendments to schedule 18 provide for those who try to avoid tax through companies they own or partnerships to be brought within the scope of the new regime. Amendments to clause 148 provide for POTAS to cover circumstances where tax avoidance is promoted through associated persons. The remaining amendments make minor changes to ensure the schemes work as intended.

...

Section 161 (originally clause 149), Sch 19
Large businesses: tax strategies and sanctions for persistently unco-operative behaviour

Committee of Whole House: 28 June 2016

(Col 157)

David Gauke: The amendment to clause 149, tabled by the right hon. Member for Don Valley (Caroline Flint), seeks to require large multinational enterprises to publish a country-by-country report on their activities within their published tax strategy. As I have set out, this Government fully share her aims of increasing transparency and clamping down on avoidance and evasion wherever it occurs. Indeed, this Government have led the way in calling at an international level for public country-by-country reports. However, I do not believe that her amendment would help to achieve the objectives that we all share. It is technically flawed, and hence would not achieve the stated transparency or pro-business objectives that we all espouse.

The right hon. Lady has said that multinational businesses such as Google would be forced to publish headline information about where they do business, the money that they make and the tax that they pay, but that is not the case. According to Government legal advice, the amendment would, in practice, place such a requirement only on UK-headquartered multinationals. Foreign-headquartered multinationals such as Google would not be caught at all, and that undermines the transparency objective of the amendment.

The amendment also risks putting UK multinationals at a competitive disadvantage by imposing a reporting requirement that does not apply to foreign competitors operating in the same market. For example, a company headquartered in the UK, whether on the mainland or in Northern Ireland, would have to file public reports, but a company headquartered in the Republic of Ireland—or, indeed, pretty well anywhere else—would not. That, I think, contradicts the level playing field objective whose importance the right hon. Lady has emphasised. At a time of increased uncertainty, we should be particularly cautious about disadvantaging UK-based businesses and imposing on them a further commitment that does not apply to their foreign competitors.

Dame Margaret Hodge (Barking) (Lab): I am grateful to the Minister for giving way, especially as he is in pain. He said earlier that the amendment was "technically flawed", but that is not the advice that my right hon. Friend has received. It seems to me that, in reality, the Government are more driven by their ideas about tax competition. Will the Minister confirm that that is the case? If it is, I suggest to him that transparency is more important for the British people in particular, and that if any global company chooses to leave the UK simply because of demands for transparency and demands that it pay fair tax, which will be a rare occurrence, it may well be that it is not the sort of company that we want to be headquartered here.

Mr Gauke: There are some issues of timing, but I must emphasise that the only companies that would fall within the scope of the amendment would be UK-headquartered companies. The Googles of this world would be unaffected. We believe that all this should be done on a multilateral basis, and—although my timing may be slightly unfortunate—I should point out that considerable progress has been made at European Union level. Indeed, the relevant commissioner has said that we are on the cusp of a deal and that he hopes that it will be concluded during the course of the Slovakian presidency, in the second half of this year. The UK has been leading the way in that debate, and, indeed, we have been calling for the Commission to toughen up its rules.

Several hon. Members rose—

Mr Gauke: I will just finish what I am saying before I give way. I am being bombarded by distinguished right hon. Members.

We know that the debate on corporation tax tends to focus on companies' sales, but corporation tax is not based on sales; it is based on activity. If a company takes part in a lot of activity in the UK but makes a lot of sales in another jurisdiction, it is likely to pay a lot of tax in the UK, but not a lot of tax in other jurisdictions where there is little or no activity but a great many sales. If the UK is the only jurisdiction that is putting out this information, or requiring its companies to put it out, there will be many examples of UK companies that are acting completely properly in foreign jurisdictions and not paying a lot of tax in those jurisdictions, but are vulnerable to criticism. It would be very much easier for all businesses to be able to point to an Italian, German, French or Swedish company that is in the same position, with a lot of activity in its own jurisdiction and a lot of sales in another jurisdiction, and is paying its tax where the activity is, not where the sales are. If the UK is acting unilaterally, I worry about unfair reputational criticism of our companies. As the right hon. Member for Barking (Dame Margaret Hodge) knows very well, reputational damage to a business can damage its commercial interests,.

Caroline Flint (Don Valley) (Lab): Surely the problem is that so much of what we are finding out about companies—about where they do their business, where their profits are, and where they pay their taxes—is emerging through leaks. Massive reputational damage is being done to those companies. The amendment gives us a chance to put things on a much better footing by providing not all the information about companies, but the baseline headlines about where they do business, where they trade and where their profits are. Surely that is something on which we can lead.

Mr Gauke: I think that the principle and the destination are pretty clear. We are moving in the direction of companies' publishing this information, and I believe that the UK should be leading the way in working out a multilateral deal in which a number of countries impose essentially the same requirements. That, I think, would help to improve transparency and would provide a level playing field.

I do not think that the UK should be the last mover in this respect by any means. The United States seems to be some way away from moving in this direction, and I do not think that we should wait for the United States; I think we should be there before it. We should be able to deliver, especially given that such good progress is being made at European Union level. We remain members of the European Union, and there is appetite for this in other EU states. I have no doubt that, if no progress has been made in a year or two, the right hon. Member for Don Valley will come back and ask, "Why has this not happened?", and in that event her case would be strengthened. However, I think that until we have given the deal a fair wind, it would be premature to act unilaterally.

Mr Andrew Mitchell (Sutton Coldfield) (Con): The Minister has a perfectly justified and extremely good reputation for being sympathetic in driving this agenda forward. He will recall our discussions, both in opposition and back in 2010, about precisely the point that is addressed in the amendment. We all agree that companies should pay tax where their profits are earned.

The Minister knows as well as I do that some of the poorest people in the world live on top of some of the richest real estate, and that extraction taxes should be paid where those profits are earned. May I ask him to respond fully to the point that is being made by the right hon. Member for Don Valley (Caroline Flint)? If he thinks that her amendment is defective in some way, will he commit the Government to looking at those defects and considering whether they can frame a clause that would address the first part of what she said, with which I understood him to say he agreed?

Mr Gauke: The Finance Bill is not the ideal way in which to address this issue fully. I make no criticism whatsoever of the right hon. Member for Don Valley, who has shown much ingenuity in managing to ensure that her amendment was in order, but this is essentially an issue for company law.

We are keen to implement public country-by-country reporting, and we want to do it on a multilateral basis. As I have said, if there was a lack of progress the Government would obviously want to return to the issue, given the concerns that I think are felt by Members in all parts of the House. However, I think that we are in a position to aim for what I am sure we all agree would be the best result: achieving our aims on a multilateral basis.

Meg Hillier (Hackney South and Shoreditch) (Lab/Co-op): Will the Minister give way?

Mr Gauke: I will certainly give way to the Chairman of the Public Accounts Committee.

Meg Hillier: It is clear that the Minister has some sympathy with the amendment tabled by my right hon. Friend the Member for Don Valley (Caroline Flint) and most of the Public Accounts Committee, along with many other Members in many parties. Rather than requiring my right hon. Friend to come back to the House, will he therefore commit the Government to looking at this matter unilaterally if multilateral agreement is not achieved? Or will he go even further today and agree to a sunrise clause to add to the proposals that my right hon. Friend and I, and others, have put forward, so that this can come into action if the multilateral agreement that he is hoping for does not come to fruition?

Mr Gauke: We are in quite a fast-moving area, and the progress that has been made in recent months has been considerable. Just at the beginning of this year, it looked unlikely that a deal would be possible, but now it looks as though the EU is heading in that direction. As I have said, the EU Commissioner has said that something is likely to happen by the end of this year. I must add the slight caveat that we will have a new Prime Minister by then, but it is certainly my view that if we have not made progress by this time next year on reaching a multilateral agreement, we will need to look carefully at the issue once again. I do not want to make a full commitment on this because—I am standing here desperately with the Dispatch Box as a source of support—I might no longer be in this position by then. I make that caveat, but I believe that there is every chance of an agreement. I would be disappointed if we did not make progress, but in the event of that happening—I hope it is unlikely—we would need to look at this again. I suspect that there is agreement between us here that it would be better for us to get a multilateral agreement than for us to go off alone.

David Mowat (Warrington South) (Con): I think I have heard the Minister say that there will not be a multilateral agreement that includes the United States. So is it the Government's position that we do not want to act unilaterally for the UK, but we will act unilaterally within the EU—even if we are not in it—even though the EU itself contains only 20% of the world's multi- nationals? Is he saying that this does not need to be multilateral, and that it just needs to be EU-lateral?

Mr Gauke: I do not think that this has to be universal, but there would be disadvantages for the UK if we were the only country to do it. There is a sense that UK companies would be criticised for failing to pay very much tax in jurisdictions where they did not have a lot of activities but had a lot of sales. This comes back to the point about educating the public about how corporation tax works. I think it would be an awful lot easier if there were just a few examples of other countries doing this. I do not think it needs to involve every other country, but if, for example, Germany, France and Italy had the same type of system, every time a UK company was criticised we could say, "What about that French company? What about that Italian company? The same principles apply to them."

We do not have to move at the pace of the slowest, but if we adopt an isolated position on this, there would be a reputational risk for UK businesses. We do not need to run that risk, particularly as good progress is being made, and I urge the House not to accept this amendment. Instead, I hope that we will be able to implement a measure over the next few months.

David Mowat: I suppose it depends which multinationals are in which segment of competition, but is the Minister saying that as long as, say, two or three other countries were to do this, the UK would join in?

Mr Gauke: I do not want to put a precise number on this. There is a threshold, and it depends on which those countries might be, but if I thought that three or four significant economies were going in the same direction, the case for doing this would be much stronger. Or, to put the reverse argument, if I were standing here next year and two or three other countries had gone down this route, the concerns that I am expressing from the Dispatch Box today would clearly carry less weight than I think they do today.

Meg Hillier: Perhaps I can help the Minister. On behalf of the Public Accounts Committee, I sent an open letter to the chairs of European finance and public accounts committees or their equivalents. The Minister might have picked up the fact that, to date, the letter has been signed by the chairs of parliamentary finance committees in Germany, Hungary, Finland, Norway and Slovakia, as well as by senior MPs in the Netherlands, the Czech Republic and Bulgaria. We also know that the French Finance Minister, Michel Sapin, is doing some interesting work in this area, as are many others. Does that help to push the Minister in the right direction and enable him to make us more of an offer today?

Mr Gauke: Well, it supports my optimism that we are on the cusp of a multilateral deal, and that will enable us to work out the legislation in the most comprehensive and effective way. As I have said, our preference would be to do this through company law rather than through a Finance Bill, but the hon. Lady's intervention supports what I was saying earlier about the comments of the relevant EU Commissioner at the last ECOFIN meeting in Luxembourg, which I attended 11 days ago. He was optimistic that we would reach agreement by the end of this calendar year. If that is the case, it is hugely encouraging, and the point that the hon. Lady has just made supports that proposition.

Nigel Mills (Amber Valley) (Con): I hope that the Minister will be willing to channel the leadership and enthusiasm that the UK showed in relation to the diverted profits tax, when we chose to go out alone and not wait for international agreements on base erosion and profit shifting. We introduced a whole new tax, with compliance burdens and penalties, and I suspect that that was a far bigger deal than requiring companies simply to disclose what they are already disclosing but in a slightly different format. I think that that was the right way to go.

Mr Gauke: My hon. Friend is right to mention the fact that we went ahead with the diverted profits tax, although doing so was clearly consistent with the direction of the base erosion and profit shifting process. That tax also brought in significant revenue to the UK, which has been very helpful.

If we want to achieve greater transparency, as I believe we all do, it is right that we should focus on driving forward international efforts on public country-by-country reporting. In order to get full information on foreign multinational entities' global activities, multilateral agreement will be required to enable countries to introduce comprehensive rules with the widest possible scope. This will allow for a comprehensive multilateral approach that applies consistently across UK and foreign multinational entities. We must get this right so that, when it is introduced into UK law, it is effective and enforceable. We will continue to support and drive this multilateral change forward following the result of the referendum, and I share the determination of the Members supporting this amendment not to move at the pace of the slowest.

...

Mr Mitchell: The Minister is being extremely generous in giving way. I am sure we all agree with him that this should be done multilaterally—there is nothing between us on that—and I am sure that it will be helpful to his aim of being able to demonstrate strong support for this across the House of Commons when he is dealing with his international partners. I should like to make a suggestion, and I hope that it will be helpful. Would he consider asking his officials to draft a clause for public discussion that is not defective and that he could put to his colleagues multilaterally as a measure that they might wish to include in their parliamentary legislation?

Mr Gauke: I am grateful to my right hon. Friend for that suggestion. Let me take it away, because there are a number of ways in which this could be done, and we would want to consider it. I believe that this debate will be helpful to our parliamentary and governmental colleagues in other jurisdictions in that it demonstrates our cross-party determination to make progress on this matter. We are committed to acting swiftly to implement international agreements, as we have done with the OECD BEPS recommendations on country-by-country reporting. We are committed to improving the transparency of multinational tax affairs, but we support an effective multilateral approach. At this time of increased uncertainty, a domestic measure of the sort being discussed today would, I fear, disadvantage UK business for the reason that I outlined. I look forward to hearing the contribution of the right hon. Member for Don Valley, but I hope she is satisfied with the assurances that I have provided today.

...

Section 161 (originally clause 149), Sch 19
Large businesses: tax strategies and sanctions for persistently unco-operative behaviour

Report Stage, House of Commons: 5 September 2016

(Col 132)

Roger Mullin: It is certainly a very important issue, but I think it would be better if we could get the Government to carry out the kind of detailed scrutiny that would enable them to enact the necessary legislation. Their voice would be far more powerful than mine in this regard.

I should also like to pass comment on amendment 145, tabled in the name of the right hon. Member for Don Valley (Caroline Flint), which we will certainly be supporting. I am sure that she will have much more to say about it in a moment. It is a modest amendment to encourage much-needed country-by-country reporting for corporations, and I look forward to hearing her remarks. She can be assured that her actions have the full support of Members on these Benches. Similarly, we hope that the Opposition will press new clause 13 to a vote. We also intend to support that proposal.

This whole section dealing with tax evasion is very important, and it is vital that the UK as a whole lives up to its responsibility to ensure that we do not get a name for encouraging tax dodgers. I want to mention the remarkable and brave journalist Roberto Saviano, who has been admired for exposing the murderous criminal underworld of the Italian mafia. In a recent article in The Daily Telegraph, he warned that the UK financial world was effectively allowing what he called "criminal capitalism" to thrive. Surely we must take steps today to ensure that that is not the case.

Caroline Flint (Don Valley) (Lab): In speaking to amendment 145 today, I am grateful for the chance once again to put the case that large multinationals should co-operate with public country-by-country reporting in the UK so that we can all gain greater insight into the trading activities that determine the amount of corporation tax being paid.

As a new member of the Public Accounts Committee in February, I heard first hand Google and Her Majesty's Revenue and Customs try to explain how £130 million represented a good deal after a decade's-worth of unpaid taxes and reasons to justify non-payment. This cross-party Committee of the House felt that the way in which global multinationals play the system denies a fair take for HMRC, having an impact on our public services, and is unfair to British taxpayers and businesses, for whom such a complicated organisation of tax affairs is not an option.

Stephen Phillips (Sleaford and North Hykeham) (Con): Does the issue not go further than that? Our constituents' money generates the revenues and therefore the profits of such companies. It is not just unfair to them because they pay their taxes; their money funds the profits that generates the taxation that ought to be paid to the Revenue.

Caroline Flint: I congratulate the hon. and learned Gentleman, who is a former colleague on the PAC, on his promotion.

Meg Hillier (Hackney South and Shoreditch) (Lab/Co-op): He's still on it.

Caroline Flint: The Chair of the PAC has corrected me. The hon. and learned Gentleman is absolutely right; it is almost a double whammy. Customers of such companies pay for their services in good faith and expect, as both taxpayers and consumers, big companies to play fair by them and by the country in which they operate.

The PAC is not alone in worrying about how such companies organise themselves. Around the world, people and their Governments are questioning the loopholes and convoluted legal arrangements that create inaccurate descriptions of multinationals' trading activities in individual countries. The problem is not confined to tech firms such as Google, but their massive global presence has exposed the fault lines of an old-fashioned tax structure that has not kept up with today's online business world. Many of today's high-tech household names were not always so big or so profitable. The investigation into Google began under the previous Labour Government, and the coalition Government continued the work to get on top of these relatively new business models, both nationally and internationally. Tax policy is not easy. Once one tax loophole is closed, another one opens up.

Wes Streeting (Ilford North) (Lab): I commend my right hon. Friend's work on this issue over a long period of time. Does she share my concern that even when the Government have tried to take the initiative, such as through the diverted profits tax—the so-called Google tax—that has not delivered the expected revenues? Indeed, Google does not pay a great deal through that tax. A measure such as that proposed by my right hon. Friend would clearly help to make companies do the right thing.

Caroline Flint: I hope so, because transparency is an important ingredient in ensuring that the rules we apply have some bite. It sometimes seems as though we are trying to catch jelly.

The whole debate has brought into question the legal and moral difference between tax evasion and tax avoidance. Companies often rightly defend themselves on grounds of working within the rules, but politicians and civil servants are often caught out by clever manipulation of those rules. That is not illegal but cannot be said to be in the spirit of what was expected.

I have no illusions about having a perfect tax system. Keeping one step ahead is a never-ending task for modern tax authorities. I welcome the Government's introduction at HMRC of country-by-country tax reporting, which is now up and running, and I agree with the Minister's summer announcement that those who advise individuals and companies on their tax affairs will be subject to greater accountability for their actions when wrongdoing is exposed.

However, public transparency can make a real difference in ensuring fair taxation and fair play. That is why, with the support of PAC colleagues and cross-party support from across the House, I introduced my ten-minute rule Bill in March to legislate for public country-by-country reporting. The backing I received spurred me on to try to amend the Finance Bill in June, gaining the support of eight parliamentary parties: Labour—I thank Front-Bench spokespeople past and present, including my hon. Friend the Member for Wolverhampton South West (Rob Marris), for their support— the SNP, the Liberal Democrats, Plaid Cymru, the Social Democratic and Labour party, the Ulster Unionist party, the United Kingdom Independence party, the Green party, the independent hon. Member for North Down (Lady Hermon), and a number of Conservative MPs, too. Oxfam, Christian Aid, Save the Children, ActionAid, the

ONE campaign and the Catholic Agency for Overseas Development joined our efforts, adding an important and necessary dimension to the argument for public country-by-country reporting.

Meg Hillier: I, too, congratulate my right hon. Friend on her sterling work in raising this issue up the agenda. Does she agree that if the Government were to adopt this amendment, they would be setting a tone for other parts of the world? We have had a lot of interest from around Europe and elsewhere about the work being done in Parliament and by our Government, and adopting this would really set the example.

Caroline Flint: I agree with my hon. Friend on that. I commend her work as the Chair of our Committee and the work she has done with other public accounts committees in other countries, because there is an appetite for doing more in this area and we are leading the way. We can do that from our House of Commons Committees, but we hope today that we can give some added muscle to the Government to lead the way in this important area, too.

I talked about the charities and organisations working in the development sphere, because I am seeking tax justice not only here, but for those developing countries that lose out too. I have said it before but it is worth saying again: if developing countries got their fair share of tax, it would vastly outstrip what is currently available through aid. The lack of tax transparency is one of the major stumbling blocks to their self-sufficiency. My thanks also go to the Tax Justice Network, Global Witness and the business-led Fair Tax Mark, as well as to tax experts Richard Murphy and Jolyon Maugham, QC, who have helped me to make the case and to get the wording right to amend legislation. This proposal demonstrates the widespread view that bolder measures to hold multinationals to account are necessary.

John Redwood: Is not the bigger issue: where should the profit be fairly struck? Where was the value added? Where did the work take place? Where is the intellectual property residing? Getting transparency is one thing, but we could still get transparency for an answer that we do not like.

Caroline Flint: There is a debate about where best to recoup the money from those who trade and the profits they make. Different options are available, but perhaps that is a wider debate for another day. The BEPS—Base Erosion and Profit Shifting—debate was partly about addressing that, but transparency has to be at the heart of all this, whatever system we set up to identify what is a fair contribution for business. I hope that my amendment will be supported and will be one small step forward.

Mr Barry Sheerman (Huddersfield) (Lab/Co-op): My right hon. Friend knows that I support this amendment and the wonderful work she does. Does she remember all the difficulties we had with the banking sector and the people who were supposed to be the auditors—these great companies that are specialising in obscurity, hiding ownership and moving ownership? Surely this must go in tandem with taking on those big people who did not audit the banks properly. They are the same people who allow these big companies to evade taxation.

Caroline Flint: My hon. friend is right about that. As the Parliament that represents the people of this country, we have a duty not to allow markets to be unfettered, but to provide a framework in which they should operate, work, be successful and do the right thing. I must say that there are companies doing the right thing. Increasingly, companies are volunteering to do the right thing by publishing the sort of information that I am asking to be made more public today.

Rob Marris: Will my right hon. Friend give way?

Caroline Flint: I will give way once more, but I am conscious that other people wish to speak.

Rob Marris: Can my right hon. Friend confirm my understanding, or correct me if I am wrong, that what she is seeking in this amendment would not cause any burden to business because the information is already being gathered and reported but is not then being published? Her amendment seeks merely to get that which is already gathered and reported to be published.

Caroline Flint: That is correct.

I was hopeful for my June amendment, because since the 2015 general election, the Government had, on a number of occasions indicated their support for public country-by-country reporting, and I welcome that. I am grateful to the former Financial Secretary, now Chief Secretary to the Treasury, as his approach was always constructive as we sought the best way to proceed.

At the debate in June, four days after the EU referendum, the Minister and others were concerned that introducing my amendment at that time might put UK multinationals at a competitive disadvantage for reputational reasons. I have no doubt that a number of the businesses to which my amendment would apply have already suffered reputational damage and more transparency could actually enhance their standing. To the Government's credit, the UK was the first to introduce public registers of beneficial ownership, and others followed. Backing public country-by-country reporting is an opportunity to show leadership again. Indeed, it is a pro-business measure. This kind of reporting already exists within the extractive sector and in financial services. Some companies are ahead of the curve and have started to publish this information. I am talking about companies such as SSE, the energy supplier, and the cosmetics retailer Lush, which operates in 49 different countries. The Government also said that, although they supported the principle, they would prefer to move ahead with others rather than alone.

As the Government make plans to leave the European Union, which may not be all smooth sailing, I do appreciate Ministers' caution. I am grateful to the new Financial Secretary, the hon. Member for Battersea (Jane Ellison), for the constructive dialogue that we have had over the past two months. I am grateful, too, to my colleagues from the Public Accounts Committee—my hon. Friend the Member for Hackney South and Shoreditch (Meg Hillier), and the hon. Members for Berwick-upon-Tweed (Mrs Trevelyan), and for Amber Valley (Nigel Mills)— for their advice and support during the recess, and I thank all those who have signed Amendment 145.

I hope that the Government will regard this amendment as a friendly proposal. If it is passed today, the Commons will enshrine in law support for the principle of public country-by-country reporting with the power for the Government to introduce when the time is most appropriate. That sends a very powerful message, confirming the UK's leading role in addressing tax evasion and avoidance and providing the Government with the tools to move quickly, when the time is right, without the need for primary legislation.

Last week, the European Commission served a €13 billion tax bill on tech giant Apple. Although the rate of corporation tax in Ireland is low at 12.5%, the Commission concluded that Apple had, in effect, paid 1% corporation tax from 2003 and a tiny 0.005% in corporation tax since 2014. I am afraid that that implies that even low corporation tax rates are no guarantee that a country will collect its rightful share. In this case, €13 billion is equivalent to paying £50 of tax on every £1 million of profits. Apple is entitled to defend its position, but the case highlights the need for more transparency in multinational business affairs.

Finally, having listened to the Government's concerns and shared with them my arguments for today's amendment, I hope that the House can come together and make UK public country-by-country reporting a matter not of if, but when.

Charlie Elphicke (Dover) (Con): I do not intend to detain the House for an unduly lengthy period of time, because I know that everyone wants to get to bed before midnight. I want to set out why country-by-country reporting is so very important, and why the whole culture of tax avoidance by big business and multinationals is something that we cannot condone or tolerate.

People ask what is wrong with an organisation such as Apple organising its tax affairs to its best possible advantage. After all, is that not the principle of taxation— that there is no equity in taxation and that only the literal taxation rules should apply? However, my concern is that the conduct of Apple is unacceptable for three key reasons. If a big business organises its tax affairs so that it basically pays no tax whatsoever, then it is inevitably warping the free market, because it is getting an unfair tax advantage, or a tax advantage that gives it a competitive advantage over other enterprises that are paying tax on their profit. For me, that is a really serious issue.

The other issue with Apple in Ireland is that to have a special deal for one business that does not apply to everyone else is counter to the fundamental principle of the rule of law, which is that everyone should be treated the same—be they a cleaner at Apple or Apple itself. What is offensive is if a cleaner in the office is paying more in tax than the massive, profitable enterprise whose offices they are cleaning.

Let me continue with the case of Apple. My right hon. Friend the Member for Wokingham (John Redwood) made a powerful point. If it has created all this intellectual property, he asked what was wrong with its not being caught in the UK tax net. My answer is that that intellectual property was in fact created in Silicon Valley, but is the organisation paying tax in Silicon Valley? Is it paying tax in America? No, it is not. It has set up a clever structure. Early in its evolution as a business—some 10 or 20 years ago—it sold its outside American intellectual property rights for $1, or some other small sum, to a Bermuda company, which would then have a conduit through Ireland to invest across the rest of Europe.

The company then checks the box for US tax purposes in respect of everything below Bermuda so that, from the Internal Revenue Service's point of view, it looks as though the Bermuda company is the trading company, and because it is a trading company and the only enterprise that there is for US tax purposes, it is not caught by subpart F of the controlled foreign companies regulations, meaning that no tax can be deemed to have to be repatriated to the United States. As a result, the Bermuda enterprise becomes a cash box for reinvestment across the European theatre. Therein lies the unfair competitive advantage.

John Redwood: I remind my hon. Friend that I did not mention the word "Apple" and I expressed no view on Apple's tax affairs, one way or the other. I asked a question about how we as legislators globally can produce a system that is fair and sensible so that people know what companies should be paying. I have not studied Apple's tax affairs in detail so I would not presume to lecture either for or against what that company does.

Charlie Elphicke: I stand corrected by my right hon. Friend. It is not a question of Apple; it is a question of general US outbound tax planning. That is why country-by-country reporting matters.

Stephen Timms (East Ham) (Lab): I agree with the points that the hon. Gentleman makes, but can he confirm my understanding that if the amendment tabled by my right hon. Friend the Member for Don Valley (Caroline Flint) had applied in Ireland in the case of Apple, we would have known that very, very large profits were being made by the company, which seems to have existed only on paper, and we would also have known that it was paying a tiny amount of tax? Would not that have been a valuable step forward in understanding what was going on?

Charlie Elphicke: The key issue is that we did know. As I recall, Apple had to report the situation in some investigation by the Senate in the United States. The Senate was wondering why very little tax had been paid by Apple in the United States. If my recollection is not correct, I am sure a fellow Member of this House will correct me. The issue is one of transparency. These things come to light because the US Senate holds an investigation, or some other enterprise or organisation, such as the Public Accounts Committee, carries out an investigation and starts asking questions.

In the previous Parliament, I myself went through the accounts of Google, Amazon and Starbucks and looked at what they were paying as a proportion of profits. That is why I think country-by-country reporting ought to be considered, and on an international basis. It is important that countries act together to make sure that the international tax system is suitably robust for the internet age.

The reason that that matters is that when large enterprises, big businesses and the elites do not pay tax, it affects small businesses. It is the small business rooted in our soil which employs our neighbours and pays its dues that suffers when the competitive advantage, the level playing field and the rule of law are warped in that way. That is my prime concern. Small businesses in my constituency in Dover and Deal are the lifeblood of my local economy and I want them to have a fair crack. I want the towns and regions of this great nation, England, that I represent, and Wales and Scotland to have a fair crack and to be able to come to the fore. Particularly in Brexit Britain, it is important that they are able to come to the fore, to be galvanised and to be part of the leadership of this nation. That is why we need a Britain that works for the 90%, which is the towns and regions of our nations, rather than for big business and the elite 10%. That is important and it is why we need a tax system that works for everyone.

I have been deeply concerned recently when looking at accounts in the car rental industry. Colleagues may recall that Avis was accused of imposing a Brexit tax on people renting its cars. I looked at its accounts and saw that Avis had paid no tax itself. It taxed its British customers but did not seem to pay any British corporation tax on its profits.

Ian Murray (Edinburgh South) (Lab): The hon. Gentleman is making an incredibly powerful speech about the reasons for tax transparency, but in the case of companies such as Avis, which he mentions, should we not have transparency for one simple reason only—so that consumers can vote with their feet? If they believe that they are purchasing products from companies that are not paying tax in this country or in other countries, they can go and buy those products from other companies that are paying tax.

Charlie Elphicke: That is a very powerful point. This is why transparency matters. If people know that they are being taken for a ride, they do not have to use an organisation that uses a Luxembourg structure, which is a common kind of intermediate structure for pan-European tax planning to organise things so that no tax need be paid.

This is not just about Avis. I had a look at the accounts of Hertz, another large US car rental company that also does not seem to have paid any tax in the past few years. It is hard to tell how it is doing that, and I had to look at the accounts in very great detail. It has some let-out whereby the company does not have to report related-party transactions. One would think that it may well be renting its car fleets through the Luxembourg company or the Netherlands BV that it uses. Hertz uses a Netherlands BV and Avis uses a Luxembourg company to get money out of the UK tax net so that it is not subject to tax on any profit. However, I cannot tell, because we do not have that level of reporting. That is why country-by-country reporting is important, not just as a tax concept but as an accounting concept, so that one can see where the money has gone. Similarly, inter-company loans and borrowings are often at the much higher rate. That is certainly the case with Avis, which was paying more in its inter-company loans than in its borrowings to the bank. That, too, caused me a level of concern. There seemed perhaps to be some trademark royalties in there, or some royalties to do with its internal IT and computer systems, but it was hard to tell because we do not have that granularity in the accounts.

We ought to have a greater level of knowledge, a greater level of reporting, and a greater level of understanding of how money is being paid, the taxes that are due, and the nature of the planning that is being undertaken so that our laws are more robust and we can make sure that everyone in this nation pays a fair share of tax, be they the cleaner or the largest enterprise that is trading. It matters for the rule of law, for a fair and open market, and for a level competitive playing field that all businesses and enterprises are treated the same.

Mike Wood (Dudley South) (Con): As a Conservative, I believe that taxes, whether direct or indirect, need to be kept as low as possible, consistent with the need to raise finances for our vital public services and for our national security. Unnecessarily high taxation not only strangles growth and development but means Government taking from those who have earned money, whether through labour, innovation, or capital.

However, the flipside of keeping tax levels low is that everybody must pay their fair share. Aggressive tax avoidance, bending the rules of the tax system to gain an advantage that Parliament never intended, means that a heavier burden falls on others, who are able to keep less of the money that they have earned. This Government are rightly committed to supporting businesses through low taxes—that is why corporation tax is being cut again to 17%—but those taxes do have to be paid.

This Bill therefore addresses many of the ways that companies use to avoid paying their fair level of tax. That includes the amendments that we are debating, tabled by the Government, to reform hybrid mismatches. The amendments will reduce aggressive tax planning, typically involving a multinational group. The introduction of these rules will, in essence, remove the tax advantage arising from the use of hybrid entities and instruments, and ought to encourage more businesses to adopt less complicated, more transparent cross-border investment structures. I look forward to similar rules being introduced by other jurisdictions. However, in line with OECD regulations, the Bill contains provisions for counteraction in the UK where the other country does not counteract the mismatch within its own hybrid mismatch rules. The Bill introduces the new penalty of 60% of tax due that was announced in the Budget, to be charged in all cases successfully tackled by the general anti-avoidance rule.

Government amendments 136 and 137 help to ensure that the changes announced in the Budget work as intended, cracking down further on unscrupulous and aggressive tax avoidance. I agree with the comments made by my hon. Friend the Member for Dover (Charlie Elphicke) on country-by-country reporting, as well as those raised so regularly by the right hon. Member for Don Valley (Caroline Flint). There is widespread and growing agreement that there is a need to move to country-by-country reporting so that the information is out there and available both to national tax authorities and to the wider public. That brings us back to the question of whether the best way to achieve that is for individual countries to act unilaterally or for the UK to move in partnership with our international allies and through a range of international organisations both within and beyond Europe.

Rob Marris: Of course, the Opposition want international action, we want international co-operation and we want our international friends to copy the amendment tabled by my right hon. Friend the Member for Don Valley (Caroline Flint), which we hope will be successful tonight. However, we also need to bear it in mind that half the tax havens in the world are British overseas territories. We have a particular responsibility in this regard worldwide. It is not about some sort of moral responsibility—to use the old-fashioned phrase, the white man's burden—or any of that nonsense. It is to do with the fact that British overseas territories are responsible for half of these shenanigans.

Mike Wood: The hon. Gentleman makes a valid point, but we should also recognise, as I am sure he will, the progress that has been made in recent years to insist on those overseas territories moving into the 21st century so that their tax arrangements comply with what we would expect for international standards. In a globalised world, we must be clear that concerted international effort is needed to stop continued cross-border tax avoidance, evasion or plain old-fashioned aggressive but unscrupulous planning.

The UK Government have done more than any previous Government and more than most of our international allies and competitors to eradicate these practices, and they continue to do so, but of course more must be done and I welcome the reassurances we have heard from the Government that this remains a priority. I am pleased that the Government are now pursuing country-by-country reporting and that it will be discussed at the forthcoming G20 Finance Ministers meeting. This measure will by itself help to increase transparency across multinationals, supporting not only our tax authorities but, perhaps more importantly, those of the developing countries of which we have heard, which are almost literally being robbed of vital sources of income.

In conclusion, the Finance Bill and the amendments tabled to it include both pioneering and bold measures. It will ensure that taxes are paid and that everybody pays their fair share, and I look forward to supporting it this evening.

John Redwood: I remind the House that I have declared in the register of interests that I am a registered investment adviser, but obviously I am not speaking on their behalf in this debate.

It seems to me that there is common ground among all parties in this House that we need to collect a decent amount of tax revenue and that we want to ensure that those who are rich, particularly companies that seem to generate a lot of turnover and possibly profit, pay their fair share. We recognise, I think, that we have to operate in a global market. We are talking about what are usually large corporations that genuinely make different levels of profit and generate different amounts of turnover in different jurisdictions, and that have genuinely complicated arrangements when they switch components, technology, ideas and work between different centres. Even in a service business that does that through electronic communication and digital activity, there may be different people in different centres around the world who contribute to servicing the client and to dealing with the particular product. There are, therefore, genuine issues for the honest company in trying to define and measure precisely where work is done, where added value is greatest and what is a fair attribution.

We as legislators have to understand that complexity and try to come up with a good judgment, collectively and globally between the main jurisdictions, on what is a fair way to instruct those global companies to report in our different jurisdictions so that sensible amounts of tax are captured.

We also need to remember that we as legislators often help create the very problem that offends quite a lot of MPs, because we speak with forked tongue when it comes to tax matters. When discussing tax, this House often wants to offer tax breaks. The House will say, "We would like companies to do more R and D or invest more in plant and equipment," or, "We would like individuals to save for their retirement, save generally or be entrepreneurial, set up a business and then sell it in few years at a good profit." We collectively decide that we should encourage more of that conduct by letting people off income tax, capital gains tax, corporation tax or a combination of general taxes as an incentive for them to behave in the way we would like. We must, therefore, take some responsibility for tax avoidance—obviously not for law-breaking—by those who use the tax breaks we provide.

We are now trying to define something that is not strictly law-breaking, which we all condemn and is an enforcement matter, or a friendly tax incentive, which we probably still agree on. I suspect that every MP in this House thinks that something should be encouraged by tax incentive, but we are trying to define something in the middle, which has come to be called aggressive avoidance, where there are elements of doubt. That is where legislators need to do a better job, because we need to be able to say to people and companies, "This is illegal conduct and you will be prosecuted for it, and everything else is legal conduct and meets your obligations." If we find that we are not collecting enough tax, perhaps the problem lies with us and perhaps we have to review the whole range of incentives and tax breaks that we offer, because that may be the origin of the problem of our not collecting as much tax as we need or would like to meet the requirements of our public services and other needs.

I will keep my remarks suitably brief. We need a certain amount of humility as legislators. It is very easy to get on a high horse about rich individuals and rich companies. Some of them do break the law—a minority, I trust—and they need to be pursued and prosecuted. Many others are honestly trying to report their tax affairs, complicated as they are, in multiple jurisdictions. This evening we are debating a 644-page addition to our tax code. Given that we are just one medium-sized country and that a multinational company may have to report to 30, 40 or 50 different countries, all of which are generating tax codes on that monumental scale, we should pause a little and ask ourselves whether we are getting in the way of levying fair tax by the very complexity of the rules we are establishing.

Rebecca Long Bailey: I will speak to a number of amendments in my name and those of my hon. Friends. New clause 12 would require the Government to report within one year on the impact of the criminal offences relating to offshore income assets and activities created by clause 165. Amendments 167 and 168 would make it compulsory, rather than just possible, for HMRC to publish the names of those who hide behind entities such as companies and trusts when committing offshore tax evasion. Amendments 171 to 173 would expand the definition of "reasonable" referred to in clause 165 to include

"an honest belief that all of the information included was true and accurate",

because the Opposition are concerned that the category of reasonableness is, on its own, far too subjective. Amendments 163 and 164 would strengthen the penalty for enablers of offshore tax evasion to include 100% of the fees received by the enabler of the service—for the lawyers in the Chamber, the principle of just enrichment, as it were. The aim of that is to neutralise somewhat the commercial aspect of the tax avoidance industry.

Amendments 165 and 166 would increase the minimum penalties for inaccuracy, failure to notify a charge to tax or failure to deliver a return, in relation to offshore matters and transfers, by 15% rather than the Government's suggested 10%. In their consultation "Strengthening civil deterrents for offshore evaders" the Government considered increasing the minimum penalties by 15% rather than 10%. These are probing amendments to find out why the Government opted for a smaller increase than the one that they initially considered.

Up next we have amendment 170, which would increase from 10% to 15% the asset-based penalty introduced by schedule 22. The Government's consultation on this penalty cited different rates for such asset-based penalties across the world, including in Italy where the penalty is up to 15%. As I will expand on in a moment, the Opposition think that we must be world leaders on stamping out tax avoidance, so I think our penalty should be, at the very least, on a par with precedents across the world. Those penalties are a start, but I would add that in the light of the latest Government consultation on tackling offshore tax evasion, which would introduce a separate offence not covered by the Bill, there appears to be a clear move by stakeholders to suggest that even higher penalties are required. I urge the Government to consider those suggestions carefully.

I confirm Labour's support of cross-party amendment 145 on public country-by-country reporting, which was tabled by my right hon. Friend the Member for Don Valley (Caroline Flint). I place on record my thanks to her for the hard work that she has put into pursuing this important issue. It is testimony to that hard work that many Members across the House—including members of the Public Accounts Committee and more than 60 MPs from eight political parties, as my right hon. Friend illustrated—and organisations outside this House have supported this amendment. I will not go over the ground that she has covered, because she has put her case articulately. The enabling power contained in the amendment would give the UK scope to strengthen its influence on international tax transparency negotiations, and it would build greater consensus.

Finally, new clause 13 would require a comprehensive report into the UK tax gap, which is defined as the difference in any financial year between the amount of tax HMRC should be entitled to collect and the tax that it collects. Such difference derives from tax avoidance and evasion. The contents of the report would be as set out in the new clause, and it would have to be carried out in consultation with stakeholders. It would examine a number of areas relating to tax avoidance in the hope that the Government might review their policy and tailor it to deal adequately with such issues.

Chris Stephens (Glasgow South West) (SNP): Does not new clause 13 expose the idiocy of closing HMRC offices, as the Government are planning to do to 90% of them? Would it not also allow Members to look at the number of staff in HMRC dealing with tax avoidance and set that against the 3,765 staff in the Department for Work and Pensions who deal with £1.2 billion of so-called social security fraud?

Rebecca Long Bailey: The hon. Gentleman makes a very good point. The report is intended to highlight any deficiencies that might be found in HMRC's resources or structures that affect its ability to tackle tax avoidance.

As Members who read new clause 13 will see, the part relating to HMRC goes into a lot of detail. Briefly, however, the report would be required to cover figures for the UK tax gap for the past five financial years; details of the model used by HMRC for estimating the UK tax gap; an assessment of HMRC's efficacy in dealing with the UK tax gap; details of the tax revenue benefits for companies engaged in public procurement that are registered in the UK only for tax purposes; an assessment of the efficacy of the general anti-abuse rule in discouraging tax avoidance; consideration of the benefits for tax revenue of introducing a set of minimum standards in tax transparency for all British Crown dependencies and overseas territories; and, finally, an assessment of the impact on tax revenues of establishing a public register of all trusts located within the UK, British Crown dependencies and overseas territories.

The new clauses and amendments we have tabled are necessary now more than ever. I appreciate that we have limited time today, so we will push to a vote only new clause 13. As I have said, we will support my right hon. Friend the Member for Don Valley should she wish to press her amendment 145. We also support new clause 7, which has been articulately outlined by the hon. Member for Kirkcaldy and Cowdenbeath (Roger Mullin).

On the other amendments, I hope that the Minister will listen very carefully to the comments throughout my speech. The Government have ample opportunity outside the scope of the Bill—if, indeed, there is the will—to implement many of my requests. I will explain the rationale behind our various amendment.

The law on tax avoidance has been greatly influenced by the words of Lord Tomlin in the case of the Inland Revenue Commissioners v. the Duke of Westminster in 1935. Lord Tomlin decided that it was the right of every Englishman to organise his affairs so as to minimise his liability for tax. Sadly, that idea fuels the tax avoidance industry even today. In this age of so-called austerity, with pressure on the NHS, the armed forces, our teachers and our young people—the list goes on—quite frankly it is not acceptable for people to seek to avoid their taxes.

Hon. Members on both sides of the House have come to agree that tax avoidance should be fought. The trouble is that this Government have failed to tackle the problem head-on, but simply tinkered here and there with piecemeal bits of legislation, and this Finance Bill is no different. We need a real commitment from this Government to an overarching strategy that provides genuine legal teeth to tackle the millionaire tax dodgers and the advisers surrounding them.

To take hon. Members on a little historical, magical mystery tour, in the 1980s judges, not Parliament, developed a principle that put a dent in the tax avoidance industry— the Ramsay doctrine. The principle provided that artificial tax avoidance schemes should be analysed as a whole, not analysed by each piece separately. That meant that clever tax schemes could be dismantled by taking out all the artificial elements, with what was left being taxed as though the artificial elements had never existed. The effect on tackling tax avoidance schemes was huge.

Unfortunately, case law has moved on over the years, and we have now returned to a world in which tax law is considered to be entirely a matter of statutory interpretation. There are no general principles at work that can be used when interpreting legislation to combat tax avoidance in practice. In addition, our tax statutes are extraordinarily long and very detailed. That is meat and drink to tax specialists. Any Member of the House my age or above may remember the "Peanuts" cartoons. In one episode, Linus says, "Now I know the rules, I know how to get round them." Linus could have been a tax lawyer.

Tax lawyers love playing with the rules, and we should not underestimate the expertise and determination of the tax avoidance community. In fact, one tax law specialist recently told me something really harrowing about a firm of accountants in the 1990s. A specific piece of legislation had been drafted to tax any trust that shifted offshore. An exception to that rule arose if one of the trustees died and the trust shifted offshore as a consequence. Those accountants canvassed a cancer ward to see whether the relatives of people dying of cancer would be prepared to have their dying family member signed up to act as a trustee of their clients' trusts. They sought reassurances that the patient would die soon and promised to pay a small fee. That is an extreme case, but is an example of the depths to which people will sink to avoid paying their taxes and of how loopholes can be found in the depths of legislation.

A complete reorganisation of our tax avoidance laws is therefore needed. We need a general anti-avoidance principle that is broadly drawn, so that it empowers courts to interpret all tax laws purposefully. That is something that many of us on the Opposition Benches have been calling for, as has the TUC, but Government attempts thus far have been piecemeal at best.

To continue my history tour of a general anti-avoidance principle, we first had the narrow rule, in the Finance Act 2013, that focused only on abusive arrangements. Those arrangements had to be considered to be unreasonable by a panel of industry tax experts before HMRC could act. That is an obvious example of poachers, in the form of a panel of industry tax experts, being established to advise on how to catch poachers, essentially; alternatively, we might think of them as turkeys being asked to advise about the menu for Christmas lunch.

Secondly in the Government's timid tax avoidance legislation, there was a slight broadening out of the rule to impose penalties on avoiders. Thirdly, we gained the power to name evaders. Fourthly, we had provisions to catch those who enable tax evaders. Now there is a consultation on whether those who enable tax avoiders should be treated similarly. It is all far too slow, and far too little. As the Minister will be able to note from the number of amendments we have tabled today and on previous occasions in this House, the legislation does not have the strength or clarity it deserves. We can continue to tinker about in successive Finance Bills, trying to stick plasters over our deficient tax legislation, or we can develop a comprehensive tax avoidance strategy with heavyweight legislation to match.

As I mentioned earlier, the Labour party has tabled new clause 13 to encourage the Government to carry out a wide-ranging report on the UK tax gap. It is hoped that that report will help the Government to assess carefully the pressure points and areas of weakness in their current tax avoidance policy. We are limited by the scope of the Bill to calling for a report specifically; but Labour is committed to a full public inquiry on the matter, and I would welcome the Minister's support for that.

This whole sorry mess—from the exposure of offshore tax havens with the Panama papers through to the largest corporations in the world paying next to nothing in tax, investment banks using financial instruments to avoid tax and clever tax advisers designing off-the-peg avoidance schemes—needs to be exposed to the disinfectant properties of daylight. It needs disinfectant because quite frankly it stinks. We need transparency in our tax system, and a full inquiry to help us design a system that will really challenge the tax avoidance industry. We need to change fundamentally the way in which we organise our tax laws so that they are based on broad principles that make it difficult to avoid them. We must then fund and equip HMRC so that it can actually take the fight to the tax dodgers, by arming it with better tax statutes and staffing it with more highly qualified staff. We must provide it with real support in combating tax avoidance.

The Panama papers are a symptom of another well known disease. Many of the world's most appalling tax havens are British overseas territories or protectorates We have to recognise that we have allowed that to happen. Essentially, new clause 13 asks the Government to explore the creation of a set of minimum standards on tax transparency for all British Crown dependencies and overseas territories. Further to that, it is imperative for the Foreign and Commonwealth Office to work seriously with Crown dependencies and the British overseas territories to establish genuine information sharing, so that they are transparent about the ownership of trusts and companies in their territories, and stop enabling the tax avoidance industry to flourish on their shores.

By allowing the super-wealthy tax dodgers of the world to moor their superyachts and their money in such places, we ensure that billions of pounds, dollars and euros are lost to the public finances of the world. As a result, hospitals are not built, schools are not refurbished and jobs are lost. Misery and deprivation in our communities here in the UK is caused by tax avoidance, so it is time to stop taking piecemeal action in fighting it. It is time the Government dealt with the problem head-on. If the Government wanted to do anything about the tax avoidance industry, they would lift their heads up from fiddling about with the detail of successive Finance Bills and agree to the proposals the Opposition have tabled.

The Labour party is calling for the new Britain, which will soon be making its way out of the EU, to take a central role in the OECD initiative to fight corporate tax avoidance such as the base expansion scheme to fight transfer pricing and other corporation tax dodges. We are calling for support for the EU's recent initiative to confront the fact that billions of dollars in tax are being avoided by the world's largest corporations.

We must stop the game that the tax dodgers and their well paid advisers play with HMRC. We must stop the warped and dysfunctional dance between them, in which sweetheart deals are done with companies such as Vodafone, Google and Goldman

Sachs. We must invest in HMRC, simplify our tax codes and build our laws on the simple principle that being a part of our society means paying a fair share towards its upkeep.

If Members of the House agree with those basic principles, I urge them to support the Opposition proposals as a small step towards that goal. Ultimately, however, I hope the Minister has listened carefully, because we deserve much more than the few tax avoidance provisions in the Bill. I should like to press new clause 13 to a Division.

Jane Ellison: It has been a wide-ranging and at times passionate debate. I shall address the Government amendments before addressing the amendments and new clauses tabled by the Opposition.

…

Amendment 145, to which the right hon. Member for Don Valley (Caroline Flint) spoke, would give the Treasury the power to require groups to publish a country-by-country report showing their profits, taxes paid and other financial information for the countries in which they operate. As she and others acknowledged in the debate, the UK has led international efforts, although the hon. Member for Salford and Eccles (Rebecca Long Bailey), who spoke for the Opposition, was, to say the least, miserable about the leadership that the UK has shown. I did not recognise the description she applied, but others were more generous, noting the fact that the UK has rightly led those international efforts to tackle tax avoidance by multinational enterprises, for all the reasons so brilliantly articulated by colleagues such as my hon. Friend the Member for Dover (Charlie Elphicke). We all support what he said. The Government have been a firm supporter of greater tax transparency and greater public disclosure of the tax affairs of large businesses. For those reasons, we fully support the intentions of amendment 145 and will support its inclusion in the Bill.

The Government have consistently pushed for a multilateral solution for country-by-country reporting. For example, the Chancellor made the case for looking at this at the G20 in July. Amendment 145 is very much in keeping with that aim and provides the Government with the power to implement when appropriate. It is none the less important that the power is used to deliver a comprehensive and effective model—as was acknowledged by the right hon. Lady—of public country-by-country reporting that is agreed on a multilateral basis. I am sure we will return to this issue and the basis on which we can go forward. It means a model that requires all groups, both UK headquartered and non-UK headquartered, to report accessible information for the full range of countries in which they operate. It is vital for ensuring that the policy intention of greater transparency is delivered. It is also important for ensuring that UK headquartered groups are not put at a competitive disadvantage. Again, I pay tribute to the right hon. Lady for recognising that concern, as expressed earlier in the year in a previous stage of the Bill, and that disclosure requirements cannot be avoided through group restructuring—another issue that we want to ensure we are on top of.

The Government remain focused on getting international agreement for such a model, as part of their continued efforts to ensure that taxes are paid and paid in jurisdictions where economic activities take place. The right hon. Lady and the House have my assurance that the Government will continue to take every opportunity to champion this agenda at an international level. It is increasingly clear that we move forward with a welcome degree of agreement across this House.

Caroline Flint: I thank the Minister for the Treasury's decision to support my amendment. I hope we can work together to consider how we can make the journey to introducing this in this country, with others, a real possibility in the future.

INDEX